Encyclopedia of

AFRICAN AMERICAN HISTORY

Volume 3

**Leslie M. Alexander and
Walter C. Rucker, Editors**

ABC-CLIO

Santa Barbara, California • Denver, Colorado • Oxford, England

Library of Congress Cataloging-in-Publication Data

Encyclopedia of African American history / Leslie M. Alexander and Walter C. Rucker, editors.
    p. cm.
    Includes bibliographical references and index.
    ISBN 978-1-85109-769-2 (alk. paper) — ISBN 978-1-85109-774-6 (ebook)
  1. African Americans—History—Encyclopedias.   2. African Americans—Biography—Encyclopedias.
I. Alexander, Leslie M.   II. Rucker, Walter C., 1970–
    E185.E544   2010
    973'.0496073—dc22   2009051262

14   13   12   11   10   1 2 3 4 5

This book is also available on the World Wide Web as an eBook.
Visit www.abc-clio.com for details.

ABC-CLIO, LLC
130 Cremona Drive, P.O. Box 1911
Santa Barbara, California 93116–1911

This book is printed on acid-free paper ∞

Printed in the United States of America

Contents

List of Entries

Culture, Identity, and Community: From Slavery to the Present

Political Activity and Resistance to Oppression: From the American Revolution to the Civil War

Political Activity, Migration, and Urbanization: Reconstruction, Civil Rights, and Modern African America

Political Activity, Migration, and Urbanization: Reconstruction, Civil Rights, and Modern African America

With the passage of the Thirteenth Amendment on January 31, 1865, came a new era in African American life in the United States. The promise of freedom finally realized, the post-Civil War and Reconstruction Era was a time of simultaneous hope and despair. The chains of bondage forever shattered, many African Americans used their new freedom as an opportunity to reconnect with lost family, gain the rudiments of education, and carve out a space for themselves in American society. Reconstruction was a watershed in the sense that the era represented a complete break from the central paradox in American life—slavery in the land of freedom and savage inequity in a country premised on the equality of all. Reconstruction also paved the way to the African American future as progressive legislation—the Civil Rights Acts of 1866 and 1875, the Fourteenth Amendment, and the Fifteenth Amendment—set important precedents that laid the foundation for the Civil Rights movement of the mid-20th century.

In the period between 1865 and 1877, African Americans in the South enjoyed a brief experiment with democracy, justice, and the protections normally afforded all citizens. With the Reconstruction Act of 1867, which serves as the beginning of Congressional or Radical Reconstruction, the federal government became even more of an active agent in guaranteeing and protecting African American rights. Under martial law, Southern states had to rewrite their constitutions, and through the principle of universal male suffrage, African American men would play an integral role in this process. Creating public schools, eliminating property qualifications for voting and holding political office, and rebuilding the infrastructure of the South were just a few of the many achievements of these new governments and the many Reconstruction-era black politicians who participated in them.[1]

Ultimately, Reconstruction would be a failure because of the reluctance of Congress to support land redistribution. As W. E. B. Du Bois recounts in his 1935 masterpiece, *Black Reconstruction in America*, Radical Republican Thaddeus Stevens

recognized [the need to distribute land] and sought to transform the emancipated freedmen into peasant proprietors. If he had succeeded, he would have changed the economic history of the United States...But to furnish 50,000,000 acres of good land to the Negroes would have cost more money than the North was willing to pay....The whole attempt to furnish land and capital for the freedmen fell through, and no comprehensive economic plan was advanced until the advent of Booker T. Washington.[2]

In the end, freedmen were betrayed and their high hopes in the era immediately after emancipation were dashed. By 1876, the Republican Party had lost interest in waving the "Bloody Shirt" of race and slavery, and with the

Compromise of 1877 came the official end of Reconstruction with the withdrawal of federal troops from the South. Between 1877 and 1896, African Americans witnessed a steady erosion of their rights as white redemption and "home rule"—euphemisms for white Southern supremacy—became the counter to the more progressive elements of the postemancipation period.

The 1896, *Plessy v. Ferguson* Supreme Court ruling gave federally sanctioned form to the substance of Jim Crow segregation and the nearly insurmountable color line that had long been a major component of American society. By establishing the "separate but equal" doctrine, this pivotal decision rendered two previous civil rights acts (1866, 1875) and the Fourteenth Amendment essentially null and void. Southern blacks would be forced to suffer through what Rayford Logan refers to as the "Black Nadir," as they would have to face the five-headed hydra of sharecropping, political disfranchisement, social segregation, antiblack propaganda, and racial violence during the century after the Civil War. In 1903, when Du Bois prophetically announced that "the problem of the Twentieth Century is the problem of the color line," he, like many of his contemporaries, saw the 1896 ruling as the pinnacle of the movement by state and federal government officials to make white supremacy the official law of the land.[3]

Undeniably, the most heinous expression of white supremacy in late 19th and early 20th century America was the act of lynching. Defined as the extralegal murder of an individual accused or convicted of a crime or otherwise violating social mores, lynching and other forms of sadistic torture went unchecked by the federal government. Not one American president had the courage to support antilynching legislation before the 1960s and three antilynching bills were defeated in Congress in the early half of the century. In the 1890s alone, lynching claimed the lives of 104 black men, women, and children each year. As historian Leon Litwack notes: "Between 1882 and 1968, an estimated 4,742 blacks met their deaths at the hands of lynch mobs. As many if not more blacks were victims of legal lynchings (speedy trials and executions), private white violence, and *"nigger hunts,"* murdered by a variety of means in isolated rural sections and dumped into rivers and creeks."[4] Lacking the ability to serve on juries, to hold political office, or even to vote, African Americans throughout the South were virtually powerless in the face of violent antiblack repression of this sort.

African Americans in the South responded to these multiple layers of oppression through a variety of means. They left the South, particularly during the 1879 Kansas Exodus and the Great Migration (1910–1940). At first tens of thousands and then millions left for better lives in the North, the Midwest, the Great Plains, and the West. In their eyes, anything had to be better than the constant assaults against their very presence and existence in the South. Although their new hosts were not always accommodating (e.g., Red Summer Race Riots of 1919), the new economic opportunities in urban regions throughout the country meant an end to back-breaking agricultural life and the ability to accumulate wealth and property for the first time for entire African American families.

In addition to leaving the South, African Americans used any means at their disposal to eke out an existence. Resistance to the various forms of oppression; accommodation with Southern whites; back-to-Africa movements; religious conversion to Islam; the creation of positive images of blackness through literary, visual, and expressive art; and embracing radical ideologies (e.g., socialism and communism) as means of breaking the cycle of capitalist exploitation were among the many activities African Americans engaged in during the early- to mid-20th century. Indeed, tracking African American history in the period between 1896 and 1968 is akin to tracking the myriad movements they developed to ameliorate their condition and achieve rights granted to them during the Reconstruction era. The capstone of this would be, of course, the modern Civil Rights movement that gained momentum after the landmark *Board v. Brown* decision in 1954.

The tumultuous decades encompassing the Civil Rights movement can be described as perhaps one of the most significant movements for social change in the history of the Western Hemisphere. Literally tens of thousands of dedicated individuals sought to create an American reality that truly reflected certain American ideals concerning justice, democracy, and equality, reflecting a continuity of aspirations existing at least since Reconstruction. The successes of the Civil Rights movement were not due entirely to the work of activists; the context of the Cold War provided both a significant hurdle and a facilitating environment in which fundamental change in America could occur.

The Cold War hindered activism because, at least during the 1950s, McCarthyism and red baiting shaped the contours of "acceptable" protest and ensured that radical ideologies would not typify the views held by most pre-1965 civil rights activists. The examples of Paul Robeson and W. E. B. Du Bois are instructive in this regard. Both men, avowed socialists, were sent before the House Un-American Affairs Committee (HUAC), had their passports and ability to travel abroad stripped away, and were, in effect, silenced by the U.S. government. In addition, because of a keen fear of being labeled communists, many civil rights organizations between 1947 and 1955 avoided direct action protest methods.

More important, the reality of racial strife and segregation in the United States meant to the nonwhite world that America was not the standard bearer of liberty and justice, and this reality undermined American efforts to sway third world countries in Latin America, Asia, and Africa away from the orbit of the Soviet Union. Thus one could argue that in the absence of the external pressures exerted from abroad during the Cold War, perhaps the movement would not have been as successful as it eventually was. From Harry Truman through Richard Nixon, every American President—Democratic or Republican—was keenly aware that every time a civil rights worker was murdered or beaten, every time dogs and water hoses were used to assault black children, and every time another American city was set ablaze in the aftermath of a race riot the entire world was watching.

The tremendous impact that the Civil Rights movement had on the course of history in the Western Hemisphere and the world begs a significant question: how did the movement begin? Scholars from a variety of disciplines have dealt with this question of origins, and that will be the dominant theme of the first half of this essay. One of the more popular perspectives on origins deals with the movement as the "second Reconstruction." This notion has recently been popularized by Manning Marable's *Race, Reform, and Rebellion: The Second Reconstruction in Black America, 1945–1990* (1991); however, one can find this theme resonating in the works of Du Bois, C. Vann Woodward, and Eric Foner among others.

For Du Bois, the first Reconstruction was an idealistic attempt to create an egalitarian, democratic, and interracial society that was thwarted by a counterrevolution in which property triumphed over labor.[5] In 1956, C. Vann Woodward wrote an influential article in which he compared the 1950s with Reconstruction.[6] The idea developed by Du Bois that Reconstruction was a promise unfulfilled can also be

found in Eric Foner's *Reconstruction: America's Unfinished Revolution, 1863–1877*. To Foner, property also triumphed over labor, but the main failure of Reconstruction was that land was not distributed to ex-slaves. Land ownership was prerequisite to the self-sufficiency and autonomy that black families sought after abolition, but this would have threatened the goals of Northern capitalists who feared a severe labor shortage and a drop in cash crop production. The point implicitly made by both Du Bois and Foner is that if the first Reconstruction had truly been revolutionary, then there would have been no need for a 20th-century Civil Rights movement and, therefore, a second Reconstruction.

Another work that emphasizes this theme is Jack Bloom's *Class, Race, and the Civil Rights Movement* (1987). In his analysis of Reconstruction, Bloom states that the Reconstruction governments "set aside some of the Black Codes, tried to enact a free labor market, established the conditions and to some degree regulated the contracts for labor, and tried to protect black civil rights."[7] White planters inspired by visions of home rule, however, consolidated their efforts to drive Northern whites out of the South and blacks from both government positions and the political franchise.

For Bloom, Southern Redemption meant the end of democracy in the South and created the need for the second Reconstruction beginning even before the 1954 *Brown* decision. He concludes by stating:

> the term *Second Reconstruction* [as] applied to the civil rights movement is apt: the first Reconstruction attempted but failed to do away with the power of the Southern landed elite. The Second Reconstruction succeeded where the first failed; it accomplished this change by carrying out what was, in effect, a social revolution.[8]

Referring to the Civil Rights movement as a "social revolution" is problematic at best, but one can generally agree that the societal position of African Americans was relatively better in the post-1960s era compared to the post-1870s era.

The last work of the "second Reconstruction" genre, Manny Marable's *Race, Reform, and Rebellion* (1991), contends that "[t]he failure of the federal government to recognize the necessity for massive land redistribution, along the lines of what blacks themselves called 'forty acres and a mule,' would be the principal reason for the failure of the First Reconstruction."[9] White planter intransigence and entrenchment along with Republican acquiescence to

Southern Democratic demands of home rule led to the establishment of Jim Crowism and the context against which 20th century activists fought.

Quite obviously there is a certain amount of continuity between the first and second Reconstruction; the failures of one created the problems that made necessary the second. The major flaw in many of these perceptions is the notion that the Civil Rights movement was less a product of human endeavor than of an almost deterministic cycle of history. In fact, one could argue that the "second Reconstruction" notion does not explain the origin of the Civil Rights movement; instead it shows how unresolved problems from one era created problems in a later period. Simply put, the mere existence of major problems does not begin to explain why thousands of activists worked for social change after the 1950s. In sum, the "second Reconstruction" school is ultimately a subtle denial of human agency.

Aldon Morris, in *The Origins of the Civil Rights Movement: Black Communities Organizing for Change* (1984), promotes the idea that even if the starting point of the movement was the 1953 Baton Rouge boycott, the "modern" movement was related to previous civil rights activities and protest movements. Morris discusses a "protest tradition" that included slave uprisings, the Underground Railroad, protest organizations, the Garvey movement, and A. Philip Randolph's March on Washington Movement (MOWM).[10] Thus important precedents in activism were being set by African Americans even before the Civil War era, and important lines of continuity exist between protest movements of the past and present.

One can extrapolate from Morris's views that essentially the Civil Rights movement actually began in 1619, the year when the first enslaved Africans reached North America. This is an overly broad conceptualization, and Morris is careful to avoid this type of conflation. He distinguishes what he refers to as the "modern" Civil Rights movement from other protest movements of the past. To him, "the modern movement was directly linked to the activism of the 1940s via civil rights organizations and activists who played important roles in both periods."[11]

There is still a major flaw in Morris's analysis of continuities. Placing protest movements, past and present, under the rubric of "Civil Rights movements" misstates the purpose and goal of certain types of organizational efforts of the past. One of the underlying principles of civil rights advocates is their goal to bring about the inclusion of a formerly marginalized group into mainstream society as citizens whose rights are guaranteed and protected by the federal Constitution. Civil rights advocates of the 1960s sought black political enfranchisement, social equality, justice, and rights within the context of the American system. Slave rebels and Universal Negro Improvement Association (UNIA) members were not seeking further inclusion into American society, but rather and escape from it. The term "civil rights" therefore does not reflect the goals of those individuals in any shape or form. Instead, perhaps, the nascent and embryonic origins of black power can be found within the writings of David Walker, the actions of Nat Turner, and the organization apparatus created by Marcus Garvey.

In terms of Morris's explanation of the causes of the modern movement, he takes a grass roots approach and identifies the black church (not organizations like the NAACP) as providing the necessary impetus to facilitate change. The church played a decided role in organizing and sustaining the Montgomery bus boycott in 1955–1956.[12] The black church also played a profound role in the event that sparked the activist stage of the modern movement, the Baton Rouge bus boycott of 1953. In this boycott, the church provided the grass roots leadership (Rev. T. J. Jemison), the numerical support for the protest (Mt. Zion Baptist was the largest church in the city with about 3,000 supporters), the experience in organization, the financial backing, and the moral fervor to facilitate a successful protest.

The black church in general also created an organization, the Southern Christian Leadership Conference (SCLC), which replaced the NAACP as the main cog in civil rights activism and which also gave birth to one of the most important protest organizations in the 1960s, the Student Nonviolent Coordinating Committee (SNCC). The success of the Baton Rouge movement encouraged similar protests in Montgomery, Tallahassee, and New Orleans in subsequent years.[13]

Morris's essential argument that African Americans led and created the Civil Rights movement is generally accepted now, but there are other scholarly opinions predating his work that offer different interpretations. A work that epitomizes this is Anthony Oberschall's 1973 work entitled *Social Conflict and Social Movements*. Oberschall contends that Southern rural blacks lacked the ability to make massive changes themselves. Although he recognizes human agency on a certain level, Oberschall's perspective is skewed because of a lack of appreciation of grass roots leadership and organizations. He instead sees the movement as the product of an emerging black middle class and also points to the significance of college students as key leaders in the movement.[14]

Also important to his analysis were white allies and the major national level organizations like the NAACP and the Congress of Racial Equality (CORE). In essence, these variegated forces converged to help uplift the basically passive black rural masses who lacked the ability to help themselves. This demonstrates a surprising lack of understanding, especially as his model cannot explain the Baton Rouge boycott, the Montgomery boycott, and the thousands of other grass roots movements throughout the South.

In terms of the issue of the origins of the Civil Rights movement, monocausal explanations are obviously useless. Several factors played a part in stimulating African Americans to initiate this massive movement for social justice and citizenship rights: the pre-World War II northern migration and subsequent urbanization of blacks, the returning World War II veterans who fought the evil of racism abroad, the pre-McCarthy era influence of Communist organizers among rural blacks,[15] the powerful role of the black church, the existence of a continuity of struggle in the urban North and rural South, and the inertia created by local movements and community organizers.[16]

The Civil Rights movement has had lasting impacts and became a shaping influence on other types of movements and organizations, namely black power (and other empowerment movements), the New Left, the free speech movement, and the women's liberation movement. Specifically, both Sara Evans and Clayborne Carson have offered interpretations about the role of SNCC in the Civil Rights movement and how the organization impacted Students for a Democratic Society (SDS), the Economic Research and Action Projects (ERAP), and the New Left in general, as well as the resurgence of feminism in the second half of the 20th century. Sara Evans, a white southern activist/feminist turned scholar, analyzes the reemergence of feminism in the mid-20th century in *Personal Politics: The Roots of Women's Liberation in the Civil Rights Movement and the New Left* (1979). Feminism itself, according to Evans, had a life of its own. The latest incarnation of the ideology was given birth in the reaction against dominant themes of domesticity during the relatively apolitical 1950s. Important

aspects of both feminism and the women's liberation movement, however, were given impetus and shape by the Civil Rights movement.[17]

It is no surprise that according to Evans, SNCC was to be the organization that exerted the most influence on the women's movement; it was the only organization that involved young southern white women; both SCLC and CORE members and leadership tended to be older and male. During the freedom summer campaign in 1964, SNCC enlisted the help of hundreds of white northern students, and once again many of these students were women. Problems soon mounted as Evans states, "self-assertion generated new forms of anxiety; new expectations existed alongside traditional ideas about roles; and ideas like 'freedom' and 'equality' were often subordinated to assumptions about women as mere houseworkers and sexual objects."[18]

Evans notes clearly, however, that SNCC would not have been created nor would it have sustained itself without the tireless and continuous efforts of women. Ella Baker first came up with the idea of an independent student and youth oriented movement organization. She was the one who urged students to maintain an independent existence from SCLC and single handedly fought off attempts by SNCC's parent organization to exert influence and control. Diane Nash was clearly the most charismatic member of the "Nashville group," which gave SNCC its original numerical impetus and moral foundation; in fact, Nash was a popular choice for the first chairperson of SNCC, although she turned down the offer. It must also be remembered that Fannie Lou Hamer's impassioned televised testimony at the Atlantic City Democratic convention gave the Mississippi Freedom Democratic Party (SNCC's political arm) and SNCC national legitimacy. But the women described here were all black women, and the roles inhabited by white women in the movement were much more circumscribed in comparison.

The marginalization that white women experienced in the movement was best expressed by Casey Hayden and Mary King's SNCC position paper presented at the Waveland Retreat in 1965. Some of the grievances included being referred to as "girls" and the automatic assignment of clerical and secretarial work to women.[19] Despite the validity of these problems, Stokely Carmichael responded derisively to the question of women's positions in SNCC by stating they should be "prone."[20] In spite of this, the sexism white women would face within SNCC ranks would not compare, according to Evans, to what they would face in New Left organizations.

In sum, Evans concludes that feminism grew within the contradiction that an increase in sexism occurred in the same places (e.g., SNCC, SDS, Economic Research and Action Projects, ERAP) where women found new strength, potential, and self-confidence. In response to this contradiction, Hayden and King collaborated again in 1965 to draft a feminist manifesto. Also at the annual national conference for SDS in 1967, a "Women's Liberation Workshop" was organized to sensitize men in the organization to sexism and sexual oppression. The women were met with the same type of derisiveness that was strikingly reminiscent of Carmichael's 1965 comment.

The experience of women like Hayden and King in SNCC provided both negative and positive stimulus for feminism and women's liberation. The black power phase, which is usually seen as the beginning of the end for SNCC, served also as a positive model on which feminism would build. As Evans contends, the type of sexism faced by women in both SNCC and SDS proved that women needed a women's organization to fight against sexism and for women's liberation. Taking cues from black power advocates, drafters of the paper titled "To the Women of the Left" presented at the 1967 National Conference for New Politics made the following statement:

> Women must not make the same mistake the blacks did at first of allowing others (whites in their case, men in ours) to define our issues, methods and goals. Only we can and must define the terms of our struggle.... it is incumbent on us, as women, to organize a movement for women's liberation.[21]

This statement demonstrated quite explicitly that the move toward racial separation and black power within SNCC ranks had broader implications.

One major problem with Evans's analysis of the Waveland paper written by Hayden and King emerges with the complaint made by Mary King that Evans simply misinterpreted the meaning of the "Women's Position" paper. In her massive work entitled *Freedom Song: A Personal Story of the 1960s Civil Rights Movement* (New York, 1987), King states:

> One damaging notion implanted in the literature, even by such pathfinding authors as history professor Sara M. Evans...was that in the years after 1965 the movement

became increasingly alienating for women. This was true for me, but *not* for the reasons given. As this story goes, women in the movement were relegated to typing, running mimeograph machines, preparing and serving coffee, washing dishes, and being available for sex. This is not correct and is not an explanation of Casey's and my protests.[22]

Essentially King goes on to argue that the contentions she and Hayden were writing about had more to do with the "freedom high" versus the "hierarchical structuralist" debate that, according to both Evans and Carson, convulsed SNCC during the postfreedom summer era.[23] Hayden and King were advocates of the democratic, antihierarchical, and pro-decentralization "freedom high" sect. King states clearly that with centralized hierarchy, the problems she and Hayden wrote about in the women's position paper would persist. Evans took King's testimony and twisted it until it fit within the confines of her ideological critique of SNCC and the positive and negative stimulus it provided both feminism and the women's liberation movement.

Carson's work entitled *In Struggle: SNCC and the Black Awakening of the 1960s* demonstrates the impact SNCC had on other organizations of the civil rights era. More specifically, he devotes an entire chapter to SNCC's role as the model by which New Left groups found a sense of direction and purpose. As Sara Evans also points out, before 1965, SDS was primarily known as an enclave of radical white intellects that were initially both hierarchically structured and not involved in active protest. After the summer of 1964 when many northern whites returned home after the freedom summer voter registration drive in Mississippi, SDS and other New Left groups were invigorated by the new energy derived from students who gained invaluable experience working with SNCC.

On the most obvious level, Casey Hayden was married to Tom Hayden who was the chair of SDS in 1964. Also individuals such as Betty Garman, Jim Monsonis, Bob Zellner, and Maria Varela played significant roles in both SNCC and SDS. But direct influences, demonstrated by both Evans and Carson, appear in other forms. Carson notes that "[s]ome observers attributed SNCC's radicalism to the presence of white leftist in the southern struggle; yet SNCC is more accurately seen as a source of insights and inspiration for the New Left."[24]

The SNCC-derived notion of participatory democracy and the debate between freedom highs and structuralists prefigured the anarchists factions of SDS.[25] Also, the launching of SDS's ERAP demonstrates to Carson that SDS was "attempting to apply many of SNCC's techniques developed in the deep South to the problems of the northern urban poor."[26] ERAP ushered in a new era of SDS and New Left activities that went far beyond the relatively passive intellectualism of their pre-1965 past. The open infatuation that SDS leaders showed for SNCC efforts are reflected in the "Port Huron Statement" of 1962, which, according to Carson, applauded the political emphasis of the southern student movement.[27]

The view that SNCC inspired SDS and the New Left in a variety of ways is mirrored in the works of Aldon Morris and Todd Gitlin. And although Carson notes that some "observers" have tended to attribute SNCC's radicalism to the influence of white leftists, these observers remain unnamed and no major historical monograph makes that argument. Hence the consensus is aptly summed up by Morris's comment that "the activist stage of the modern white student movement was generated by the 1960 sit-ins, because they provided these students with a protest model with both a tactical and an organizational blueprint."[28]

The Civil Rights movement was a product of both impersonal and personal forces. The Cold War provided the political backdrop, the failures of the Reconstruction era provided the enemy, while rural and urban southern churches produced the means to bring about momentous changes. Southern churches began the movement in Baton Rouge, and soon boycotts appeared throughout the Jim Crow South. Southern churches (in the guise of the SCLC), and more specifically Ella Baker, helped coalesce the student sit-in movement into an organization (SNCC) that fought for much more than hamburgers and Cokes. SNCC was to eventually fight for voter registration and rights, for black power, against the Vietnam War, and against imperialism. In turn, SNCC affected both the New Left and the women's liberation movement in significant ways, as mentioned earlier. In a very tangible sense, SNCC was also the bridge between Civil Rights and Black Power, especially beginning after 1965.

Looking back from the vantage of the events of November 4, 2008—with the historic election of President Barack Obama—it would be impossible to track a linear historical trajectory from Reconstruction to that date without using words like "miraculous," "surprising," or "extraordinary." In a very real sense African Americans stood at the edge of Armageddon in the 1890s and bore witness to a conscious and concerted campaign to eliminate their rights and to rid the country of their presence. Their survival and, later, their ingenuity in facilitating a Civil Rights movement that overturned centuries of racist legislation, executive orders and actions, and judicial rulings were as monumental an undertaking as any other in human history. Combined, the Civil Rights and Black Power movements created a foundation (e.g., the Civil Rights Act of 1964, the Voting Rights Act of 1965, the creation of the Congressional Black Caucus) from which the election of President Barack Obama was even possible. Perhaps then, when viewed from this particular perspective, the first Reconstruction should be considered a success.

Walter C. Rucker

Notes

1. W. E. B. Du Bois, *Black Reconstruction: An Essay Toward a History of the Part Which Black Folk Played in the Attempt to Reconstruct Democracy in America, 1860–1880* (New York: Harcourt, Brace, 1935), passim.

2. W. E. B. Du Bois, "A Negro Nation within a Nation," *Current History and Forum* 42 (June 1935):266–67.

3. W. E. B. Du Bois, *The Souls of Black Folk* (New York: New American Library, 1982: originally published in 1903), xi.

4. James Allen, Hilton Als, Leon Litwack, et al., *Without Sanctuary: Lynching Photography in America* (Santa Fe, NM: Twin Palms Publishers, 2000), 12.

5. C. Vann Woodward, "The 'New Reconstruction' in the South: Desegregation in Historical Perspective," *Commentary* 21 (June 1956): 503–7.

6. Jack Bloom, *Class, Race, and the Civil Rights Movement* (Bloomington: Indiana University Press, 1987), 30.

7. Ibid., 214.

8. Manning Marable, *Race, Reform, and Rebellion: The Second Reconstruction in Black America, 1945–1990* (Jackson: University of Mississippi Press, 1991), 6.

9. Aldon Morris, *The Origins of the Civil Rights Movement* (New York: Free Press, 1984), x.

10. Ibid.

11. This is in definite evidence in Martin Luther King Jr.'s *Stride Toward Freedom: The Montgomery Story* (San Francisco: Harper & Row, 1958). Although the back-of-the-book blurb states that King "led the first successful large-scale application of non-violent resistance in America," King states on page 9 that the boycott is instead "the chronicle of 50,000 Negroes who took to heart the principles of nonviolence, who learned to fight for their rights...." It should also be noted that the boycott began before King became involved, deriving much of its energy from grass roots leaders like Jo Ann Gibson Robinson, the Women's Political Council, E. D. Nixon and the tireless efforts of thousands of black maids and servants who walked miles to work for more than a year. See Robinson, Jo Ann Gibson, and David J. Garrow, *The Montgomery Bus Boycott and the Women Who Started It: The Memoir*

of Jo Ann Gibson Robinson (Knoxville: University of Tennessee Press, 1987).

12. Morris, *Origins of the Civil Rights Movement*, 17–26.

13. Anthony Oberschall, *Social Conflict and Social Movements* (Englewood Cliffs, NJ: Prentice-Hall, 1973), 187–211.

14. See Robin D. G. Kelley, *Hammer and Hoe: Alabama Communists During the Great Depression* (Chapel Hill: University of North Carolina Press, 1990).

15. In terms of the continuity of struggle, August Meier and Elliot Rudwick make the argument that despite a long black protest tradition "the use of [nonviolent] direct-action tactics has been episodic and characterized by sharp discontinuities." See Meier and Rudwick, "The Origins of Nonviolent Direct Action in Afro-American Protest: A Note on Historical Discontinuities," in David Garrow, *We Shall Overcome: The Civil Rights Movement in the United States in the 1950s and 1960s* (Brooklyn, NY: Carlson Publishing, 1989), 3: 908. It should be noted that nonviolent direct action did not start with King; this concept resonates in the moral suasionism of the mid-19th century championed by both Frederick Douglass and Sojourner Truth, as well as the tactics espoused by A. Philip Randolph and the 1941 March on Washington Movement. Even if direct lines of continuity cannot be demonstrated, what is important is that the tactic of nonviolent direct action has a history that precedes King by at least a century.

16. Clayborne Carson, *In Struggle: SNCC and the Black Awakening of the 1960s* (Cambridge, MA: Harvard University Press, 1981); Sara Evans, *Personal Politics: The Roots of Women's Liberation in the Civil Rights Movement and the New Left* (New York: Random House, 1979).

17. Evans, *Personal Politics*, 76.

18. Ibid., 233–34.

19. Ibid., 87. Evans tries to explain this statement by assuming Carmichael was referring to the fact that many white women spent Freedom Summer on their backs. Despite efforts to recuperate Carmichael's image, the comment remains as a glaring example of insensitivity.

20. Ibid., 200.

21. Mary King, *Freedom Song: A Personal Story of the 1960s Civil Rights Movement* (New York: Morrow, 1987), 459.

22. Ibid., 460. In her words, King notes "[a]utonomous local movements as opposed to a centralized hierarchy would have supported diversity and variation."

23. Carson, *In Struggle*, 175.

24. Evans, *Personal Politics*, 95.

25. Carson, *In Struggle*, 175.

26. Ibid., 176.

27. Morris, *Origins of the Civil Rights Movement*, 223.

28. Leon F. Litwack, "'Fight the Power!' The Legacy of the Civil Rights Movement," *Journal of Southern History* 75 (February 2009): 3–28.

1936 Summer Olympics, Berlin

The 1936 Olympics took place during a politically tense period in which growing disapproval over Nazi aggression and racism prompted many countries to consider boycotting the games altogether. For Germany, the games became an arena to trumpet Aryan supremacy while pacifying the anxieties of the world community. For many Black and Jewish athletes—including African Americans like Jesse Owens and Ralph Metcalf—successful participation in the 1936 Olympics damaged Nazi racial ideology and helped to codify antifascist sentiment in America.

When the International Olympic Committee (IOC) awarded Berlin the games in 1931, few anticipated Adolf Hitler becoming chancellor in 1933 and the subsequent rise of the Nazi party. IOC organizers respected German sports leaders and viewed the Berlin games as a way to reintroduce Germany to the world sports community. The IOC felt that German participation was necessary to revitalize the fledgling Olympic movement. World War I had already forced the cancellation of the 1916 Berlin games, and German teams were not invited to Antwerp in 1920 or Paris in 1924. Furthermore, worldwide economic depression severely limited participation in the 1932 games, as many European teams could not afford the trip to Los Angeles. In awarding Berlin the 1936 games, the IOC was anxious to create a strong Olympic field by centering the games in Europe and drawing participants from Germany.

On seizing power in 1933, Hitler was intent on building a "New Germany." In public speeches and political pamphlets, the Nazis stressed the importance of Aryan racial purity and the superiority of the "Germanic race." Hitler launched a widespread campaign of fear and intimidation aimed at Jews, blacks, political dissenters, homosexuals, Gypsies, and even the mentally and physically handicapped. Foreign journalists revealed to the entire world the rapid expansion of Nazi racial policies. In July 1933, a Nazi law sought to cleanse the Aryan gene pool by mandating the sterilization of individuals with certain physical and mental conditions such as epilepsy, blindness, or schizophrenia. In September 1935, the "Nuremberg Laws" prohibited sexual relations between Aryan Germans and those of "alien blood." Germany's small black population also faced the brunt of Nazi white supremacy. Most blacks in Germany were the teenage descendents of French-African soldiers and German mothers, settled mainly in the Rhineland after World War I. Referred to as the "Rhineland bastards" in Nazi propaganda, these African Germans were also subject to forced sterilization.

Nazi propaganda stressed physical prowess and athletic achievement as hallmarks of Aryan supremacy. Hitler saw the Olympics as an international forum to showcase German athletic achievement and reinforce the racial ideology of social Darwinism. The Nazis, however, also recognized the need to pacify foreign nations and address the concerns of the world community surrounding Nazi atrocities. Hitler and Minister of Propaganda Joseph Goebbels launched a campaign to deceive foreign journalists, athletes, and visitors by showing only the positive aspects of life in "New Germany." Immediately before the games, the Nazis censored German newspapers and periodicals from publishing offensive, racial rhetoric. In addition, Hitler ordered that the streets be cleared of anti-Jewish posters and the city of Berlin thoroughly cleaned. While the new and massive Reich Sports Field remained draped with Nazi banners and symbols, police cleared 800 Gypsies from Berlin's streets and imprisoned them outside the city for the duration of the festivities. The regime even removed anti-Jewish newspapers, such as *Der Stürmer,* from newsstands. For many foreign visitors to Berlin in 1936, the city's façade of hospitality successfully shielded the world from the oppression and atrocity of Nazi rule.

Many officials in America, however, remained unconvinced that U.S. athletes should participate in the Berlin games. Spurred by the Nuremberg Laws and reports of Jewish oppression, the president of the Amateur Athletic Foundation (AAU), Jeremiah Mahoney, called for a complete American boycott of the games. Some former Olympians supported such a move, as did a wide spectrum of American society including liberal Catholics, evangelical Protestants, trade union leaders, and a coalition of university presidents. Avery Brundage, head of the American Olympic Committee (AOC), became the leading voice of support for U.S. involvement and helped defeat the boycott movement. Many on the AOC board called for Congress and President Franklin D. Roosevelt to intervene on behalf of a boycott, but Roosevelt remained silent on the issue throughout the entire ordeal. The president even denied requests from the AOC to speak with U.S. athletes upon their departure and did not invite the team to the White House after its return.

Most African American newspapers, such as the *Chicago Defender* and the *Philadelphia Tribune,* supported participation in the games and trumpeted the opportunity for America's black athletes. Sportswriters and editorials agreed that athletic achievement on such a high-profile stage would strike a powerful blow to Nazi racial ideology. Yet many reporters placed even more importance on the

opportunity to make significant statements about discrimination and civil rights at home in America. Throughout the 1930s, Jim Crow segregation barred African Americans from numerous jobs and public areas while the country wallowed in economic depression. Segregation remained entrenched on many playing fields as well. At the college and professional level, discrimination limited the opportunities for black participation in nearly every sport. Professional boxing was one of the few exceptions, and beginning in 1935, many African Americans had come to support black fighters like Joe Louis. Louis had even garnered national support from both white and black Americans when he fought a series of bouts against foreign fighters including the Italian Primo Carnera in 1935 and the German Max Schmeling in 1936 and 1938. Louis, however, had suffered a bitter defeat at the hands of Schmeling in June 1936, just months before the Berlin games in August. While Germany's ministry of propaganda had lauded Schmeling's victory as an affirmation of Aryan supremacy, many African Americans immediately turned their attention to a group of young, amateur Olympians whom they hoped could defeat Nazi ideology on its home turf.

A large number of African Americans contended for the 1936 team, most of them from northern universities. In all, 19 athletes—17 men and 2 women—eventually went to Berlin. Although this was the largest group of African American athletes ever to compete, they were not the first African Americans to make headlines in the Olympics. In Paris, University of Michigan track star William DeHart Hubbard became the first black athlete to win an individual gold medal in track and field, setting a world record in the long jump in 1924. Nevertheless, three times more African American athletes went to Berlin in 1936 than had participated in the 1932 Los Angles games.

A total of 49 nations chose to attend the Berlin games, sending nearly 4,000 athletes to compete in 148 events. The Americans dominated the popular track and field competition, led by Ohio State track star Jesse Owens. Owens took home four gold medals, equaling the world record in the 100-meter sprint with a time of 10.3 seconds. Owens also broke the world record in the 200-meter run (20.7 seconds) and the running broad jump (26.4 feet). In addition, Owens ran the final segment for the U.S. team in the 4 × 100-meter relay, helping to set another world record (39.8 seconds). On hearing of the Nuremberg Laws in 1935, Owens had publicly declared his intention to withdraw from the competition. Some African American sportswriters supported a black boycott of the games and applauded the star athlete, but Owens's coach Larry Snydor eventually convinced the young star to compete.

Owens was the biggest American star in Berlin, yet many other black athletes contributed to the team's success. Marquette University sprinter Ralph Metcalf finished right behind Owens in the 100-meters, taking the silver medal. As an Olympic veteran, Metcalf took a role as team leader, urging his African American teammates to avoid political confrontations in Europe and make their statements instead on the field of play. Another black athlete, Matthew "Mack" Robinson of the University of Oregon, finished second to Owens in the 200-meters. Robinson's younger brother Jackie became the first African American major league baseball player in 1947. Cornelius Johnson of California and Ohio State graduate David Albritton finished first and second in the high jump competition; two other African Americans—University of California, Berkeley star Archie Williams and James LuValle from UCLA—took gold and bronze, respectively, in the 400-meter run. University of Pittsburgh freshman John Woodruff took gold in the 800-meter run, and Frederick "Fritz" Pollard, from the University of North Dakota, finished third in the 110-meter hurdles. In addition, African American fighter Jack Wilson won the silver medal in bantamweight boxing. Two African American women—Louise Stokes and Tidye Pickett—also competed for the U.S. track squad in Berlin.

The German public treated America's black athletes with approval, inviting African American athletes into their homes and cheering Owens every time he entered the Olympic stadium. The mainstream press in America reported widely on the developing friendship between Owens and the German Carl Ludwig Long, his competitor in the long jump. Germans routinely besieged Owens for his autograph outside the stadium and quickly made him the most popular athlete in the city.

Nazi leaders, however, reacted more tepidly, censoring the German press from demeaning the athletes' race yet criticizing America's "black auxiliaries" in private. Many American newspapers reported that Hitler refused to shake Owens's hand or speak to African American participants, yet the Führer had decided before the competition not to receive any athletes. Nevertheless, Hitler had appeared publicly with athletes throughout the smaller Winter Games, held also in Germany (Garmisch-Partenkirchen)

in February 1936. There Hitler frequently spent time with white athletes, such as Norwegian figure skater Sonja Henie, and many Americans viewed Hitler's policy during the Berlin games as a sign of his disdain toward America's black participants.

Many black commentators charged the American public with hypocrisy for echoing concerns over Nazi discrimination abroad while maintaining indifference toward African American struggles at home. Upon the athletes' return, the black press celebrated the success of Owens, Metcalf, and the other African American participants yet lamented the continued social and economic discrimination that existed in the United States. Unlike other Berlin athletes, Owens did not receive the endorsements or Hollywood contracts that many expected. Owens even struggled to make money in the wake of his success, performing as a nightclub entertainer and political campaigner, and participating in athletic exhibitions including races against horses. Some African American stars from Berlin joined heavyweight boxer Joe Louis and served in the armed forces during World War II, including Archie Williams and John Woodruff.

Although many Americans trumpeted the success of black athletes—specifically in track and field—as a blow to Nazi ideology and global fascism, the Berlin Olympics were nevertheless a success for Hitler. The German team dominated many events and captured the most medals of any nation. In addition, foreign journalists and athletes praised the city of Berlin and the reception they received from its citizens. In a calculated plan, Hitler and the ministry of propaganda had temporarily stopped its brutal harassment of Jews and foreign aliens and convinced many observers that a "New Germany" had emerged from the ruins of Versailles, once again ready to join the world stage. The success of African American athletes, however, complicated Nazi ideology and confronted many Americans with a choice between supporting racial discrimination at home and exhibiting antifascist patriotism abroad.

See also: Black Athletes; Owens, Jesse

Lane Demas

Bibliography

Bachrach, Susan. *The Nazi Olympics: Berlin 1936.* New York: Little, Brown, 2000.

Guttmann, Allen. "The 'Nazi Olympics' and the American Boycott Controversy." In *Sport and International Politics: The Impact of Fascism and Communism on Sport*, Pierre Arnaud and James Riordan, eds., 47–62. New York: E & FN Spon, 1998.

Hart-Davis, Duff. *Hitler's Games: The 1936 Olympics.* New York: Harper & Row, 1986.

Holmes, Judith. *Olympiad 1936: Blaze of Glory for Hitler's Reich.* New York: Ballantine, 1971.

Mandell, Richard. *The Nazi Olympics.* Chicago: University of Illinois Press, 1987.

1968 Summer Olympics, Mexico City

On the morning of October 16, 1968, the Black Power movement found expression at the XIX Olympiad in Mexico City. In the aftermath of the assassination of Martin Luther King Jr. and the rise of the Black Panther Party for Self-Defense, Tommie Smith and John Carlos of the U.S. track and field team provided a lasting, if controversial, image for the world stage after the 200-meter race. Teammates at San Jose State University, both men were initially influenced by calls for African American athletes to boycott the 1968 Summer Olympics as a means of bringing attention and focus to the Civil Rights movement in the United States and the movement against South African apartheid. Organized by sociologist Harry Edwards, a professor at San Jose State, this initial call for a boycott led to the establishment of an organization called the Olympic Project for Human Rights (OPHR). Although the call for a boycott was not successful, the OPHR did gain the support of several prominent athletes, intellectuals, and civil rights leaders, including Smith and Carlos.

Influenced by the goal of OPHR and the leadership of Dr. Harry Edwards, Smith and Carlos staged a silent protest to occur during the awards ceremony after the 200-meter race. Although the most discussed aspect of their protest were their black-gloved raised fists and bowed heads during the playing of the national anthem, the men were adorned with symbols of protest. Smith, who won the race in world-record time, wore a black scarf to represent African American pride. Carlos, who placed third, unzipped the top of his track suit to symbolize solidarity with blue collar workers in the United States and wore beads around his neck in protest of the violence of the Middle Passage,

At the Summer Olympic games in Mexico City, Mexico, in October 1968, runners Tommie Smith and John Carlos gave black power salutes during the medal ceremony to show their solidarity with radical black activists in the United States. (Bettmann/Corbis)

slavery, and Jim Crow-era lynchings and race riots. Both men received their medals shoeless, wearing only black socks, to symbolize African American poverty. In solidarity with Smith and Carlos, Australia's Peter Norman, who placed second in the race, wore an OPHR badge and even suggested that Carlos don Smith's left-handed black glove and wear it as a symbol of unity among African Americans. During the course of the protest, the crowd booed the two athletes, and this would only be the beginning of the backlash.

Avery Brundage, president of the International Olympic Committee, responded almost immediately to the protest. Brundage, who had served as the U.S. Olympic Committee president in 1936, raised no objections to the Nazi salutes and symbols, including swastikas, adorned by German athletes during the XI Olympiad, but he was openly appalled by the actions of Smith and Carlos. Because the Nazi salute was considered as the national salute of Germany at the time, it was not seen in the same light as the black power salutes of Smith and Carlos, which indeed were meant as protests against their sponsoring country. Noting that the Olympic Games were to be apolitical and generally devoid of overt political statements, Brundage ordered the two athletes suspended from the U.S. team and prohibited them from entering the Olympic Village. When the U.S. Olympic Committee initially balked, Brundage began maneuvering to ban the entire U.S. track team. With this threat and its implications, Smith and Carlos were formally expelled from the XIX Olympiad. Upon their return home, both men and their families received scores of death threats. Even Australian runner Peter Norman faced a backlash when he returned home after the Olympic Games. Australian Olympic authorities ostracized him and went as far as banning him from participating in the 1972 Summer Olympics despite the fact that he had officially qualified to participate.

The infamous black power salutes became one of the two most lasting images of the Olympic Games; the other, ironically, were the various depictions of Jesse Owens smashing the conceptualization of the superior Aryan athlete during the 1936 Summer Games. Both Smith and Carlos went on to brief stints in the National Football League and have coached track and field teams at various levels. Between 1997 and 2008, both men individually and together received a number of honors in recognition of their courage and commitment to social justice including the Courage of

Conscience Award from the Peace Abbey and the Arthur Ashe Award for Courage, and a statue in their honor has been erected on the campus of San Jose State University. *See also:* Black Athletes; Black Power

Walter C. Rucker

Bibliography
Bass, Amy. *In the Game: Race, Identity, and Sports in the Twentieth Century.* New York: Palgrave Macmillan, 2005.
Bass, Amy. *Not the Triumph but the Struggle: The 1968 Olympics and the Making of the Black Athlete.* Minneapolis: University of Minnesota Press, 2002.
Hoffer, Richard. *Something in the Air: American Passion and Defiance in the 1968 Mexico City Olympics.* New York: Free Press, 2009.
Witherspoon, Kevin B. *Before the Eyes of the World: Mexico and the 1968 Olympic Games.* DeKalb: Northern Illinois University Press, 2008.
Zirin, Dave. *What's My Name, Fool?: Sports and Resistance in the United States.* Chicago: Haymarket Books, 2005.
Zolov, Eric. "Showcasing the Land of Tomorrow: Mexico and the 1968 Olympics." *The Americas* 61 (2004):159–88.

A Negro Nation Within the Nation

When W. E. B. Du Bois wrote "A Negro Nation Within the Nation" in the June 1935 edition of *Current History and Forum,* he was expressing decades of frustration in his longstanding battle against white supremacy, racism, and imperialism. Lynching and other forms of racial violence, the systematic denial of education to black youth, disfranchisement, various economic distresses, and Jim Crow segregation defined the collective condition of African Americans nationwide and demonstrated to Du Bois that, despite the presence and activism of the NAACP, little had actually changed in America. He became extremely disillusioned with the NAACP and left the movement after taking public stands on some rather controversial issues. In 1934, Du Bois wrote a series of editorials in *The Crisis* that seemingly advocated segregation and racial separation. These ideas would coalesce more fully by June 1935. In "A Negro Nation Within the Nation," he called for racial separation, which would foster economic cooperation, organize self-defense initiatives against white repression, and build pride and self-confidence among African Americans.

Black economic development was something that Du Bois began to value after Booker T. Washington's death in 1915 and especially after he visited the Soviet Union in 1926. Although it is true that Du Bois officially joined the Socialist Party as early as 1911, his connection with the party was brief, and he would severe his ties within a year. His ambivalence regarding the Socialist Party was primarily due to his fears that they tended to be short-sighted on the issue of race in America. Du Bois did begin to understand the dangers of ignoring the economic side of black life and, through personal experiences, he began to become extremely critical of the talented tenth. Instead of leading the masses in the movement for liberation, the black educated elite and black intellectuals were more interested in distancing themselves from the masses and adopting the norms and values of white American society. The Bolshevik revolution in Russia and Du Bois's earlier interest in socialism played a role in this reorientation, but another factor was that Du Bois likely saw some value in Washington's emphasis on industry, vocational training, and economic development. Both Marcus Garvey and Elijah Muhammad saw in Washington a man who had the tools, although not the inclination, for nation building, and both the UNIA and the Nation of Islam would serve as quite ironic legacies of Washington's approach.

This emphasis on economic dimensions led Du Bois down the path toward his resignation as the editor of *Crisis* in June 1934. He began to advocate, once again, the need for independence from the white community and reliance on black institutions and organizations. In a series of *Crisis* editorials in 1934, Du Bois made plain his notion of self-segregation. In the April 1934 edition, he wrote that blacks should organize their collective economic and political strength in order to run and support black institutions. After he left the editorial office of the *Crisis,* Du Bois gave a number of speeches that advocated self-segregation. These efforts culminated in the publication of "A Negro Nation Within the Nation" in June 1935. It would be the most sustained treatment on the issue offered by Du Bois to date. He begins the article with a discussion of the social, economic, and political problems facing blacks in the Depression-era South and North. According to Du Bois, the inability to garner a sound economic footing was the principal weakness of black communities in the decades after emancipation and Reconstruction. The failure of Radical Reconstruction was ultimately the failure

to provide freed people with land on which they could base an independent existence in America. This was the revisionist argument that would serve as the basis for his 1935 work *Black Reconstruction in America, 1860–1880.* In essence, Du Bois argued in this work the same thing Thaddeus Stevens predicted 70 years earlier—that without land, the newly freed African American masses might as well remain slaves. Sharecropping, debt peonage, tenant farming, and other forms of labor use in the postbellum South relegated African Americans to subordinate and dependent status. The acquisition of land would effectively and permanently break the chains of bondage and would allow for advances in other arenas, namely black suffrage rights.

In later years Du Bois would claim that the key success of the Bolshevik revolution was the massive land reform effort that fundamentally changed the face of Soviet Russia. The failure to redistribute land in the American South in the wake of the Civil War forced blacks into dependent economic relationships with their former masters. By emphasizing vocational and industrial education, Booker T. Washington hoped to break this cycle of dependency. The main flaw Du Bois saw in Washington's program was that it sought to build a new economic foundation for black southerners by incorporating them into white industry. Washington did not heed the various "glass ceilings" that inhibited the growth and advancement of black men in certain trades and that would relegate the mass of black people into a permanent underclass.

Because he saw few available allies and no forthcoming changes in American society, Du Bois concludes this article by stating that the only plausible solution was voluntary racial separation. This call for "self-segregation" closely mirrors the idea of community-control black nationalism espoused by black power advocates in the 1960s and 1970s. Stokely Carmichael (Kwame Ture) and Huey P. Newton would have found a great deal of resonance with Du Bois's suggestion of a set of cooperative relationships within black communities and the need for self-defense.

See also: Black Nationalism; Black Power; Du Bois, W. E. B.; National Association for the Advancement of Colored People; Self-Segregation

Walter C. Rucker

Bibliography
Bracey, John, August Meier, and Elliott Rudwick, eds., *Black Nationalism in America*. Indianapolis: Bobbs-Merrill, 1970.

Du Bois, W. E. B. *The Autobiography of W. E. B. Du Bois: A Soliloquy on Viewing My Life from the Last Decade of Its First Century.* New York: International Publishers, 1968.

Du Bois, W. E. B. *Black Reconstruction in America, 1860–1880.* New York: Atheneum, 1992.

Moses, Wilson Jeremiah. *The Golden Age of Black Nationalism, 1850–1925.* New York: Oxford University Press, 1978.

Rucker, Walter "'A Negro Nation Within the Nation': W. E. B. Du Bois and the Creation of a Revolutionary Pan-Africanist Tradition, 1903–1947." *The Black Scholar* 32 (2002):37–46.

Abernathy, Ralph David

Ralph David Abernathy (1926–1990) was a leading civil rights activist. He was born on March 21, 1926 in Lindon, Alabama. After serving in the Army in World War II, he became an ordained Baptist minister in 1948. He graduated from Alabama State University in 1950, receiving a BA degree in mathematics. The next year he graduated from Atlanta University with an MA degree in sociology. He married Juanita Jones and they had five children.

In 1951, he became the minister of the First Baptist Church in Montgomery, Alabama. On December 5, 1955, Rosa Parks violated a Montgomery city law when she refused to give up her seat on a municipal bus to a white man. She was promptly arrested. The black community sought to protest her arrest, and they turned to Abernathy for assistance. He met with another local minister, Dr. Martin Luther King Jr., and they formed the Montgomery Improvement Association to organize a boycott of the city's buses. The boycott lasted for 381 days and resulted in the desegregation of the municipal bus system. This protest is generally considered to have sparked the modern Civil Rights movement.

Abernathy helped to organize a meeting of civil rights groups in Atlanta, Georgia in January 1957. During the meeting, Abernathy's home and church in Montgomery were bombed. Groups from 10 states attended the meeting, which culminated in the founding of the Southern Christian Leadership Conference (SCLC). Dr. King was elected president of the organization, and Abernathy was elected secretary-treasurer.

Abernathy, working on behalf of SCLC, assisted in organizing 21 meetings in prominent southern cities as part of the "Crusade for Citizenship" in 1958. The goal of the meetings was to vastly increase the number of black voters throughout the South. In 1960, both Abernathy and Dr. King moved their families to Atlanta, Georgia. The two men worked closely together for the remainder of Dr. King's career. Abernathy participated in the "Freedom Rides" of 1961, in which civil rights activists challenged segregation on buses and in public accommodations throughout the South. That same year he was elected vice-president of SCLC.

In 1963, Abernathy, along with Dr. King, organized a massive protest in Birmingham, Alabama, which many considered to be the most segregated city in America. Both men were arrested for holding a demonstration without a permit and served eight days in jail. Later in 1963, Abernathy helped organize the "March on Washington for Jobs and Freedom," which brought an estimated 100,000 demonstrators to the nation's capital to protest racial discrimination. Abernathy also helped coordinate the "Freedom Summer" of 1964, in which numerous civil rights groups went to Mississippi to increase the number of black registered voters.

In 1965, Abernathy helped organize a large civil rights protest in Selma, Alabama. The protest turned violent when numerous activists were beaten and one was killed. This prompted Abernathy to lobby for passage of the Voting Rights Act to ensure that blacks had equal access to voting polls in the South. Later that year, Congress did pass the Voting Rights Act of 1965. After Dr. King's assassination in 1968, Ralph Abernathy was elected president of SCLC. In the late 1960s, he led several strikes on behalf of black workers. He resigned in 1977 and returned to Atlanta to serve as a church minister. He died on April 17, 1990.

See also: Albany, Georgia Movement; King, Martin Luther Jr.; Montgomery Bus Boycott; Southern Christian Leadership Conference

Gene C. Gerard

Bibliography

Abernathy, Ralph. *And the Walls Came Tumbling Down: An Autobiography.* New York: Harper Collins Publishers, 1989.

Abernathy, Donzaleigh. *Partners to History: Martin Luther King, Jr., Ralph David Abernathy, and the Civil Rights Movement.* New York: Crown Publishing Group, 2003.

Abu Jamal, Mumia

Mumia Abu Jamal (1954–) was convicted and sentenced to death in 1981 for the murder of a police officer named Daniel Faulkner. He is currently serving his sentence at the

State Correctional Institution Greene near Waynesburg, Pennsylvania. His case has received much national and international attention. Abu Jamal's supporters claim that he is not guilty of murder and that his trial had a number of irregularities.

Abu Jamal was born Wesley Cook in Philadelphia, Pennsylvania, on April 24, 1954. In 1968, he started his career at the Philadelphia branch of the Black Panther Party as an assistant spokesman. He dropped out of Benjamin Franklin High School and joined the Panther Party in 1969. He lived and worked with his colleagues in New York City and Oakland. In October 1970, he quit the Black Panther Party and returned to his old high school, but he was suspended for calling for "black revolutionary student power." He studied briefly at Goddard College in Vermont. Between 1975 and 1980, he had been working for several radio stations, pursuing his vocation as a journalist. He became renowned for giving exposure to the anarchist MOVE commune in Philadelphia's Powelton Village neighborhood. In 1981, he was the president of the Philadelphian Association of Black Journalists. At the time of the killing of Daniel Faulkner, he had quit his job at the WUHY public radio station and started working as a taxicab driver in Philadelphia.

On December 9, 1981, officer Daniel Faulkner of the Philadelphia Police Department was shot during a routine traffic stop. The car belonged to Abu Jamal's younger brother, William Cook. In the altercation Faulkner shot Abu Jamal, who collapsed on the side walk. He was taken to Thomas Jefferson University Hospital where his injuries were treated. Abu Jamal was later charged with the first-degree murder of Officer Faulkner.

Three independent eye-witnesses testified that Abu Jamal appeared right at the moment when Faulkner and his brother started to bicker, and he shot the police officer in the back. Before collapsing, Faulkner shot back once and hit Abu Jamal. Despite being injured, Abu Jamal moved over to Faulkner and shot five bullets into his head. The cartridges of the .38 caliber revolver belonging to Abu Jamal were found at the crime scene. The shell castings and the rifling characteristics of his Charter Arms revolver were consistent with the bullet fragments taken from Faulkner's body.

During the turbulent trial, Abu Jamal was evicted from the court room several times. He insisted in proceeding *pro se* and requested defense assistance from John Africa

Mumia Abu Jamal, convicted in 1981 of killing a Philadelphia police officer, is the center of an international movement against the death penalty in the United States. (AP Photo/ Jennifer E. Beach)

of the MOVE organization, but his demands were refused by Judge Albert Sabo, an active member of the Fraternal Order of the Police who, according to the court stenographer in a 2001 interview, had stated that he would help the defense "fry the nigger." On July 3, 1982, the jury delivered a guilty verdict and Abu Jamal was subsequently sentenced to death. During the sentencing phase of the trial, several of Abu Jamal's writings as a member of the Black Panther Party were used to demonstrate his disdain for law enforcement officials.

William Cook did not make any statement at all until 2001, when he claimed that he had not seen who shot the police officer. In May of the same year, Abu Jamal provided a sworn statement, telling for the first time his version of events. He claims that he was sitting in a taxicab across the street when he heard his brother shouting. While running to him, Abu Jamal was shot by a police officer. He does not mention either the gun that was found at the crime scene, nor the gun shoulder holster he was wearing at the time he was arrested.

On December 18, 2001, Judge William H. Yohn Jr. of the U.S. District Court for the Eastern District of Pennsylvania voided Abu Jamal's death sentence as a result of irregularities in the process of sentencing, but he still upheld the conviction. Both the Commonwealth of Pennsylvania, who wanted the original sentence to be upheld, and Abu Jamal, who wanted the conviction overturned, appealed. On May 17, 2007, the case was argued in the U.S. Court of Appeals for the Third Circuit, Philadelphia before a three-judge panel. They affirmed the decision of the District Court on March 27, 2008.

During his imprisonment, Abu Jamal continued his political work. In 1999, he contributed comments for Pacifica Radio Network's "Democracy Now!" He has a weekly column in the German language Marxist daily newspaper *Junge Welt* in which he shares his anti-imperialistic interpretations of world affairs. Besides his journalistic works, Abu Jamal published several books and pamphlets. In *All Things Censored* he examines issues of crime and punishment. *Life from Death Row* describes life in prison. It also includes several commentaries on crime and punishment that should have been broadcast by National Public Radio's "All Things Considered" in May 1994, but were cancelled owing to several complaints. *I Write to Live* is a collection of essays and reflections on social life and individuality. *Death Blossoms: Reflections from a Prisoner of Conscience* deals with religious topics, and *We Want Freedom: A Life in the Black Panther Party* has a strong autobiographical background.

Human Rights Watch, Amnesty International U.S.A., and activist groups criticized his trial for being unfair and not meeting minimum international standards safeguarding the fairness of legal proceedings. Several artists, such as Rage against the Machine, Anti-Flag, or Immortal Technique dedicated songs to Abu Jamal's cause. In April 1999, mass protests were staged in several cities across the United States and the world in opposition to the death penalty and in support of a new trial for Abu Jamal. Since then, Abu Jamal has become an honorary citizen of 25 cities around the world, including Paris, Montreal, and Palermo. In the Parisian suburb St. Denis, a newly paved street was named after him on April 29, 2006. The *rue Mumia Abu-Jamal* commemorates the 25th anniversary of the abolition of the death penalty in France. In December of the same year, 25 years after the murder, the executive committee of the Republican Party of the 59th Ward of the City of Philadelphia

filed two criminal complaints against the City of Paris and the City of St. Denis for glorifying Abu Jamal.

See also: Black Power; COINTELPRO

Carmen De Michele

Bibliography
Bisson, Terry. *On a Move: The Story of Mumia Abu Jamal.* Farmington, PA: Litmus Books, 2000.
Weinglass, Leonard. *Race for Justice: Mumia Abu-Jamal's Fight Against Death Penalty.* Monroe ME: Common Courage Press, 1995.
Williams, Daniel R. *Executing Justice: An Inside Account of the Case of Mumia Abu-Jamal.* New York: St. Martin's Press, 2000.

Accommodationism

Accommodationism is a strategy first outlined by formerly enslaved educator and leader Booker Taliaferro Washington in his famous "Atlanta Compromise" speech delivered at the Cotton States and International Exposition in Atlanta, Georgia on September 18, 1895. In exchange for the white promise to trust blacks with some responsibilities that would lead to a solution of the problems surrounding race relations and the poor social and economic conditions blacks endured in the South, Washington pledged that blacks would strive toward an education that would dignify and glorify common labor, begin to reconcile with and forgive the South, and discourage agitation for equal rights and an integrated society.

Born a slave in Virginia in the spring of 1865, Washington attended Hampton Institute, a school founded by Samuel Chapman Armstrong in Virginia. Here young Washington began to perceive success for blacks in America in the shape of cooperation and hard work. Initially well received and widely discussed in newspapers around the country, the philosophical tenet of accommodationism was soon understood by many blacks as the sacrifice of equality for economic progress and acceptance. Quintessentially surrendering the promise of an integrated society, Washington held that social segregation was fine as long as blacks and whites in the South could come together for things essential for mutual progress.

To carry out the compromise, Washington issued several guarantees. First, accommodationism advocated the cooperation and coexistence of the races in a segregated society through "industrial education" of African American youth. Washington had already begun this element of the accommodationist strategy when he became headmaster of a school in Tennessee called the Tuskegee Normal and Industrial Institute in 1881. As a reaction to the southern antipathy to the education of black children and young adults, Washington developed this program, which led whites to believe that his school was meant to keep blacks in subordinate roles such as cooks, printers, bricklayers, housekeepers, mechanics, carpenters, and factory workers. But in fact, Tuskegee students not only learned to read and write, but many also went on to enroll in universities such as Fisk or Atlanta University, and others became teachers themselves. On the other hand, many feared that the accommodationist philosophy would cause the development of a dual standard of education—one for whites leading to advanced studies and curricula, and one for blacks that trained students to work and contribute to society with little hope of upward mobility or advancement.

In addition to the upkeep and contributions of the students enrolled at Tuskegee, Washington was able to operate the school with unprecedented financial success as a result of the second guarantee he professed in his Atlanta speech. By promising to leave the past behind and move forward, Washington was able to attain the financing to operate the school from the pockets of wealthy whites in the Northeast and Southerners attempting to resurrect the impoverished economic and political landscape in the aftermath of the Civil War and Reconstruction. Regrettably, most of these "philanthropists" had less than benevolent motives. They understood how the structure and programming of an industrial education could directly benefit them by keeping blacks "in their place," not to mention providing a competent labor force for their factories and farms.

The third guarantee the accommodationist philosophy gave whites was the discouragement of protest and agitation for civil rights, including abandoning politics and cooperating with segregation. Washington saw that open protest of Jim Crow laws only further antagonized white Southerners and would exacerbate the condition of blacks living in the South, whether rural or urban.

Ultimately, many blacks saw the compromises of accommodationism as a way of keeping them in a subordinate role in the postemancipation society. In addition, accommodationist thought and action were the ultimate exchange of respect for political power, civil rights, and educational opportunities beyond the industrial type, for all blacks. In fact, the deepest criticisms of Washington's philosophy of accommodationism came from his contemporaries. Perhaps his most significant opponent was scholar and activist W. E. B. Du Bois. According to Du Bois, an advocate of higher education and the assertion of rights and privileges through protest, implementing the guarantees of accommodationism led to total revocation of voting rights for blacks, reinforcement of Jim Crow laws, and removal of support and funding for black institutions of higher education.

Southern whites interpreted accommodationist thought in one of two ways. According to Du Bois, some who were more extreme saw it as a surrender of civil and political rights for blacks. Others that were more conventional saw it as a charitable means for mutual acceptance of a racially divided society.

In the end, Washington's accommodationist philosophy failed to improve race relations in the South and a part of the time period in which it was implemented has been termed the "nadir" or low point in African American history. Still, Booker T. Washington's philosophy of accommodationism and the "Atlanta Compromise" speech still have relevance and remain important to the historical making of America.

See also: Black Nadir; Cotton States Exposition; Jim Crow; Washington, Booker T.

Mary Jo Fairchild

Bibliography

Du Bois, W. E. B. *The Souls of Black Folk.* New York: Bantam Books, 1989.

Fairclogh, Adam. *Better Day Coming: Blacks and Equality, 1890–2000.* New York: Penguin Classics, 2002.

Harlan, Louis R. *Booker T. Washington: The Wizard of Tuskegee, 1901–1915.* New York: Oxford University Press, 1983.

Washington, Booker T. *Up From Slavery.* Oxford: Oxford University Press, 1995.

Affirmative Action

Affirmative action, one of the most contentious outcomes-oriented civil rights policies of the 20th century, first entered the public lexicon on March 6, 1961, when President John F. Kennedy issued Executive Order 10925. Facing mounting pressures from civil rights activists, Kennedy called on employers to engage in "affirmative action" to address the race issue in America. The policy began with the stroke of the presidential pen. Kennedy's vision focused on the need for the federal government to foster and promote fairness and equal opportunity in federal employment practices. Given the expansiveness of government involvement with private employers, the initial efforts focused on businesses that received federal support through lucrative governmental contracts.

On September 26, 1965, President Lyndon Johnson strengthened affirmative action policy when he reaffirmed the government's position in Executive Order 11246. The order prohibited discrimination on the basis of race, creed, color, and national origin, but not sex. At that time, women were not identified as an underrepresented group in need of legislative protection. In 1973, President Richard Nixon amended Executive Order 11246 with 11375 in order to include sex as a protected class. This concluded the presidential initiatives that launched affirmative action policy. Over the next several decades, affirmative action's evolutionary process was marked by the passage of various legislative and regulatory acts, laws, executive orders, and Supreme Court decisions. Its early supporters argued that the concept of equal opportunity for all of America's citizens was grounded by legal mandates of the Constitution, the Fourteenth Amendment, and civil rights acts; and, if aggressively applied, affirmative action could become an important aspect of the nation's civil rights initiative.

In the 1960s, affirmative action was endorsed by many who lauded the government's efforts to increase minority participation in the workforce. Access to blue-collar positions was the primary target of the federal government's enforcement efforts. As businesses and unions began organized forms of resistance, they were rebuffed by liberal politicians and scholars who believed that strong governmental enforcement was an essential component of the policy. As the federal initiative expanded to include hiring and admission practices at institutions of higher education, however, strong public opposition to the policy emerged.

Proponents argued that affirmative action was a morally justified approach to redress the nation's historic practices of racial and sexual discrimination. Opponents advanced the concept of "reverse discrimination," contending that whites, and more specifically white males, were being victimized by college and university efforts to include members of diverse groups on their campuses. Although many

opposing voices acknowledged the devastating impact of past discrimination on African Americans and similarly situated groups, they posited that a "color blind" approach was the only legitimate way to end centuries of social discrimination and social injustice.

Supporters on both sides eagerly waited the 1978 Supreme Court decision in *Regents of California v. Bakke.* Alan Bakke, a 36-year-old, white male engineer, had been denied admission to the University of California's Medical School at Davis. He sued on the basis that the institution's affirmative action program, which used a quota system to guarantee minority inclusion, violated his constitutional rights as an individual. In a split decision, the Supreme Court affirmed that quota systems were a violation of constitutional law; however, the Court also affirmed its support for affirmative action, ruling that race could be used as a factor in the admission and selection process. Thus, the national debate on which criteria would be acceptable under the government's affirmative action policy began. And repeated legal challenges to affirmative action in both the public and private sectors made it difficult for institutions committed to diversity to continue their efforts.

As popularity for affirmative action waned, many looked to the Office of the President to help clarify the nation's direction. The Carter Administration (1976–1980) was supportive of affirmative action policy. By the early 1980s, however, the Reagan Administration's (1980–1988) open opposition to civil rights and race-sensitive solutions to the nation's social problems helped to usher in a new era of social resistance. The Bush Administration's (1988–1992) lack of enthusiasm for affirmative action was consistent with that of his predecessor. The Clinton Administration (1992–2000) offered hope that affirmative action initiatives would be strengthened, particularly as it related to the appointment of federal justices who shouldered primary responsibility for interpreting the nation's policy. Early in his administration, George W. Bush (2000–2008) indicated his opposition to affirmative action as policy, and decision makers continued to muddle through the legal morass. The legal challenge to the University of Michigan's affirmative action program, which finally made its way to the Supreme Court in 2003, was the most anticipated affirmative action ruling in the 21st century. It was the first opportunity for the Supreme Court to rule on affirmative action policy in nearly 25 years.

In two closely related cases (*Grutter v. Bollinger* and *Gratz v. Bollinger*), conservative activists sued the University of Michigan hoping to strike down the school's race-sensitive admission programs at both the undergraduate college and the law school. Support for Michigan's affirmative action program was broad based. Colleges, universities, Fortune 500 companies, and retired military personnel from throughout the nation filed amici briefs (friends of the court) supporting the university. In another split decision (5–4), the Supreme Court affirmed the Bakke ruling, noting that talented and qualified individuals of every race and ethnicity should be given opportunities. Race could be considered. In a related decision, however, the Court invalidated the school's undergraduate policy that used a point system to help diversify its student body, further weakening the institution's diversity efforts.

The debate on the merits of affirmative action continues. For many in the African American community, affirmative action is the unfinished business of the Black Power movement, the Civil Rights movement, Reconstruction, and the Freedmen's Bureau. It is a quest for redistributive justice and will remain a strategic path to equal opportunity until another viable policy option takes it place.

See also: Fourteenth Amendment; Johnson, Lyndon Baines; Kennedy, John Fitzgerald

Patricia Reid-Merritt

Bibliography

Anderson, Terry H. *The Pursuit of Fairness: A History of Affirmative Action.* Oxford: Oxford University Press, 2004.

Curry, George E., ed. *The Affirmative Action Debates.* New York: Perseus Books, 1996.

Eisaguirre, Lynne. *Affirmative Action: A Reference Handbook.* Santa Barbara, CA: ABC-CLIO, 1999.

Kellough, J. Edward. *Understanding Affirmative Action: Politics, Discrimination, and the Search for Justice.* Washington, D.C.: Georgetown University Press, 2006.

Perry, Barbara A. *The Michigan Affirmative Action Cases.* Lawrence: University Press of Kansas, 2007.

African Blood Brotherhood

African Blood Brotherhood (ABB) was a semi-clandestine, militant liberation organization that merged black nationalism with Marxism. Taking its name from the blood brotherhood ceremony of black African tribes, the organization was established after the race riots during the Red Summer of 1919 by Cyril Briggs, a West Indian immigrant of mixed parentage. ABB represented the first independent Communist organization composed solely of people of African descent. It was a defiant response to the perceived shortcomings of numerous contemporary liberation movements. Briggs disavowed the reformist policies of the NAACP. He believed Du Bois's organization had been compromised by white liberalism. He rejected the capitalist orientation of Garvey's UNIA. He was even critical of the Socialist Party's failure to establish an African American policy.

ABB sought to unite radicals around the themes of anticapitalism, anticolonialism, race patriotism, armed defense against racist assaults, and the establishment of an independent black socialist commonwealth. In 1920, Briggs formalized the aims of the ABB with a nine point program: (1) a liberated race; (2) absolute race equality—political, economic, social; (3) the fostering of racial self-respect; (4) organized and uncompromising opposition to the Ku Klux Klan; (5) a united Negro front; (6) industrial development; (7) higher wages for Negro labor, shorter hours, and better living conditions; (8) education; and (9) cooperation with the other darker peoples and with the class-conscious white workers.

The primary propaganda apparatus of the ABB was *The Crusader,* a newspaper Briggs launched in 1918 after he resigned from *The New Amsterdam News* in protest against attempts to censor his editorials that criticized the imperialist foreign policy of the Wilson administration. The readership of *The Crusader* reached nearly 36,000, but the membership of the ABB peaked at less than 3,000. Most of the organization's activities were centered in Harlem. Briggs suggested that although some regional posts were established throughout the country, ABB made few inroads west of the Rockies: "The Brotherhood was more a regional than a truly national organization" (Briggs). ABB gained notoriety outside of Harlem in 1921, when its Tulsa post was linked to the armed resistance of local blacks during the race riots of that summer. Although the ABB's direct role in the riots was later proved to be tenuous, the events in Tulsa resulted in a substantial increase in national support. This, along with Briggs's participation in the Workers Party of America convention in December 1921, signified ABB's transition from an underground to an aboveground organization.

ABB began as an independent organization. It was not originally an adjunct of the Communist Party. Briggs's interest in communism was inspired by the national policy of the Bolsheviks and the anti-imperial orientation of the postrevolution Soviet state. Yet initially, he claimed he was more interested in national liberation revolution than in the social revolution. When Briggs joined the Communist Party in 1921 (as the organization's third black member), however, ABB began to shift away from its staunch black nationalism to embrace class-conscious interracial solidarity. ABB formally dissolved in 1924, when many of its members joined the Communist Party's American Negro Labor Congress. Nevertheless, Briggs's amalgamation of black liberation and revolutionary socialism continued to influence black activists for decades. The ABB's brand of radical black Marxist political thought later manifested itself in black liberation organizations of the 1960s and 1970s, such as the Black Panthers and the Black Liberation Army.

See also: Black Nationalism; Harlem Renaissance

Rob Walsh

Bibliography

Kornweibel, Theodore. *Seeing Red: Federal Campaigns against Black Militancy, 1919–1925.* Bloomington: Indiana University Press, 1998.

Kuykendall, R. A. "African Blood Brotherhood, Independent Marxist During the Harlem Renaissance." *The Western Journal of Black Studies.* 26 (2002):16–21.

Solomon, Mark. *The Cry Was Unity: Communists and African Americans, 1917–1936.* Jackson: University of Mississippi Press, 1998.

African Imperialism

The end of the 19th century heralded the new imperialist scramble for European dominance of Africa, which resulted in the gross economic exploitation of the continent. The stagnant European economy encouraged entrepreneurs and adventures to seek new markets to further Western industrialization and profits. As a result, Europe added almost one-fifth of the land area of the globe to its overseas colonial possessions. European nationalism and racism resulted in numerous atrocities and ethnocentricities on the part of the colonists, such as forced slave labor, mutilations of the native population, and the notion that Africans were uncivilized.

Imperialism was a longstanding practice in Africa, dating from ancient times. In North Africa, Phoenician colonists founded Carthage in modern Tunisia. The city became a Mediterranean power by the fourth century BCE. After the Third Punic War, Carthage fell to the Romans, who made it the capital of their African province. The Vandals established a North African kingdom in the fifth century before its conquest by the Byzantine (Eastern Roman) Empire. The Egyptian empire fell to the Greeks, later passing to the Romans. During the seventh century, Arab invaders conquered North Africa, spreading the Islamic religion and Arabic language. Arab trade with sub-Saharan Africa led to the colonization of East Africa, particularly around Zanzibar.

Early European expeditions established trade bases along the African coastline and colonized previously uninhabited islands such as Cape Verde and Sao Tome. Trade bases later served as the nucleus for slave trading operations. The interior of the continent, however, remained free from European penetration until the 19th century.

Africa became increasingly open to Western exploration during the 19th century. By mid-century, Europeans had mapped most of northwestern Africa. By the end of the century, explorers had charted the source of the Nile and the courses of the Niger, Congo, and Zambezi Rivers. The findings of such expeditions made Europeans aware of Africa's economic potential and vast amount of raw materials necessary for industrialization unavailable in Europe.

From 1876 to 1914, European powers, including Britain, France, Portugal, Belgium, Germany, and Italy, scrambled for control of the African continent with the self-proclaimed goals of spreading civilization, Christianity, and commerce to the "uncivilized" indigenous population. Technological advances in Europe facilitated the new imperialistic onslaught. Industrialization brought advances in transportation and communication in the form of railroads, telegraphs, and steam navigation. Medical advancements allowed Europeans to effectively combat tropical diseases, enabling penetration of the African interior.

Europeans targeted sub-Saharan Africa for several reasons. European governments had not entered into any formal agreements or treaties with the governments of sub-Saharan Africa, which could be argued as giving legal recognition to a particular African government. Absent a legal position acceptable to Europeans, Western nations considered the area available for occupation. In their minds, sub-Saharan Africa was undeveloped and required more capital for industrialization than it could provide by itself. Economic stagnation and protective tariffs in Europe prompted those countries to seek an open market that would garner a trade surplus. Overseas investment became popular as a means of obtaining profit owing to the availability of cheap labor, limited competition, and an abundance of raw materials.

The British occupation of Egypt in 1882 and the acquisition of the Congo by King Leopold II of Belgium were the first major initiatives to launch the European scramble for African territory. From November 1884 to February 1885, the Berlin Conference, initiated by Otto von Bismarck, chancellor of Germany, met to discuss the Africa problem. The conference was concerned with formulating understandings on the freedom of commerce in the Congo basin, the application to the Congo and Niger Rivers of the principles adopted by the Congress of Vienna concerning the preservation of freedom of navigation on international rivers, and the establishment of effective procedures for the occupation of new territory along the coasts of Africa.

Britain was concerned with controlling the African interior to dominate the flow of overseas trade. Securing the Suez Canal in Egypt was essential for security for lucrative British markets. In the 1890s and early 1900s, Britain seized Sudan, Nigeria, Kenya, and Uganda. It used Cape Colony in southern Africa as a base for the subjugation of adjacent African states and the Dutch Afrikaner settlers. Britain desired to construct a railway connecting its southern base at Cape Colony to Cairo. The French penetrated the African interior from its colonies in West Africa eastward in an attempt to establish a link between the Niger and Nile Rivers, and thereby control trade. Increased pressure from investors led colonizers to inflict forced labor conditions on the indigenous population to lower costs of production and increase profits. European manufacturing plants extracted raw materials, developed by an indigenous labor force under European management.

European capitalism revolutionized the economies of Africa, inducing radical social and political changes that forever altered African societies. European efforts to maximize production and minimize costs conflicted with traditional, seasonal patterns of agricultural production, shifting African subsistence-based economies to ones of specialization and surplus accumulation.

The period of European imperialism heightened tensions between the European powers, ultimately paving the way to World War I. Some Europeans perceived the dangers that imperialism posed to Europe and questioned the morality of colonialism.

John Hobson, a British reformer, studied economics in an attempt to solve the problem of poverty.

See also: Berlin Conference, 1884–85; Fanon, Frantz; Pan-Africanism

Eric Martone

Bibliography

Collins, Robert O., ed. *The Partition of Africa: Illusion or Necessity.* New York: John Wiley, 1969.

Offiong, Daniel A. *Imperialism and Dependency: Obstacles to African Development.* Washington, D.C.: Howard University Press, 1982.

Pakenham, Thomas. *The Scramble for Africa: The White Man's Conquest of the Dark Continent from 1876 to 1912.* New York: Random House, 1991.

Sesay, Amadu, ed. *Africa and Europe: From Partition to Interdependence or Dependence?* London: Croom Helm, 1986.

Vandervort, Bruce. *Wars of Imperial Conquest in Africa, 1830 to 1914.* Bloomington: Indiana University Press, 1998.

Williams, Eric. *Capitalism and Slavery.* 2nd ed. Chapel Hill: University of North Carolina Press, 1994.

African National Congress

Since the establishment of majority rule in May 1994, the African National Congress (ANC), which won 63 percent of the vote, has been South Africa's ruling party. Founded in 1912 by John Dube, Pixley Ka Isaka Seme, and Sol Plaatje, along with African chiefs, the body answered a call by Seme to unite. Seme believed that Africans were essentially one people. Formed at a time when the South African economy blossomed because of the discovery of diamonds and gold, respectfully, in 1867 and 1886, the ANC faced problems concerning the prohibition on Africans from buying land except in the reserves, places marked expressly for African occupation. Citizenship, the economy, and the franchise also emerged as other key issues that the ANC lobbied for change. Dube also used his newspaper, *Ilanga laseNatal*, as a forum to discuss and debate the aforementioned concerns in isiZulu. Not until 1944, when many people migrated to the cities, and squatter and bus boycotts abounded, did Nelson Mandela, Walter Sisulu, Oliver Tambo, and others create the ANC Youth

League (ANCYL) and advocated for mass mobilization, did the ANC begin to change its strategies for confronting racial and economic discrimination. With the belief that Africans would be liberated by their concerted efforts, the ANCYL militarized the parent body, causing it to reform by the 1950s.

In the 1950s, the mass movement took off. Initiated by the 1952 Defiance Campaign, when participants publicly burned their passes, the ANC, under the leadership of Dr. James F. Moroka, united disparate political groups as result of its endorsement and involvement. Closer relations developed with the ANC and the South African Indian Congress (SAIC), the South African Coloured People's Organisation (SACPO), and the Congress of Democrats (COD). This merging of political bodies led to the formation of the Congress Alliance, an umbrella organization organizing different political bodies into one unit. Besides unification, the Congress Alliance advocated for better housing, equal pay, better working conditions, and equity in education. The Freedom Charter, a document detailing these demands, was presented at a meeting held in Kliptown in Soweto on June 26, 1955. As an adoption by the four aforementioned political parties, the Freedom Charter documented the political parties' commitment to nonracialism. The document proclaims that South Africa belongs to all who live in it, black and white, and that no government can justly claim authority unless it is based on the will of all the people. The Freedom Charter sought to end oppression orchestrated by either blacks or whites. The document also calls for a government, equality for all national groups, equal distribution of the country's wealth, land equity, equality before the law, the right to human decency, houses for all, end to adult illiteracy, and a government that represents the people.

In calling for democracy, human rights, land reform, nationalization, and labor rights, the Freedom Charter was a radical document for its time. This blueprint for a democratic South Africa aroused suspicion by the government. Officials labeled the Freedom Charter as Communist inspired, resulting in the arrests of ANC and Congress leaders. Arrested leaders faced legal ramifications in the Treason Trial, where 156 people (105 blacks, 21 Indians, 23 whites and 7 coloreds) were indicted, because the state believed that they planned to overthrow the government. The state also concluded that the accused had adopted a policy of violent direct action. They all faced the death penalty. A legal counsel consisting of Bram Fischer, Vernon Berrange, Sydney Kentridge, and Israel Maisels represented the accused, who were supported by a Treason Trial Fund. Two stages delineated the trial. The first was the preparatory examination in a magistrate's court, which determined the sufficiency of evidence to support a trial. If evidence existed then the accused faced trial by the Supreme Court and would be at the state's mercy. It took more than a year for the preparatory examination to conclude; at the end, 61 of the accused were acquitted and the remaining 95, which included people such as Nelson Mandela, Oliver Tambo, and Ahmed Kathrada, still faced trial.

In 1961, all the defendants were found not guilty. Oliver Tambo, who left the country during the trial, faced exile. Other trialists would eventually be arrested at a Rivonia farmhouse and later convicted. Some, like Nelson Mandela, were sentenced to life imprisonment or a specified time period on Robben Island, an Alcatraz-like prison in Cape Town. While the Treason Trial occurred, protests around the country erupted even in the rural areas, and the government forced women to carry passes, resulting in women forming a march in Pretoria where they stormed the Parliament steps and demanded justice. Little did any one know at the time, but the 1960s would usher in a new period of resistance and successful government repression of opposition for 16 years until the 1976 student uprising against the imposition of Afrikaans.

Clamping down against opposition groups began after the Sharpeville Massacre. Organized by the Pan-Africanist Congress (PAC), a splinter ANC group, which opposed nonracialism and called for an "Africa for Africans," the Sharpeville protest originally began as a demonstration against the pass books. Bedlam would soon ensue. Police officials shot running participants in the back and killed 69 people and injured 186. Newspapers captured the carnage. Bodies lay strewn in the positions that they fell. After this violence, government officials banned political organizations. The PAC and the ANC could no longer operate as legal political bodies. A state of emergency also followed, as well as the arrests of Congress and PAC activists. Neither political body lay idle. Both the ANC and the PAC created military wings and engaged in an underground movement. The ANC created Umkhonto we Sizwe (Spear of the Nation) and the PAC established POQO, which means alone in Xhosa. Formed on December 16, 1961, Umkhonto we

Supporters of South Africa's African National Congress (ANC), wearing the colors of their party on their sleeves, gather on August 12, 1952, in Johannesburg as part of a civil disobedience campaign to protest the apartheid regime of racial segregation. The protesters were later arrested. (AFP/Getty Images)

Sizwe launched attacks against government installations. This tactic raised the government's ire. While operating from its base at Rivonia, a Johannesburg suburb, Umkhonto weSizwe was labeled a terrorist organization by both the government and the media.

See also: Antiapartheid Movement; Mandela, Nelson, Pan-Africanism

Dawne Y. Curry

Bibliography

Holland, Heidi. *The Struggle: A History of the African National Congress.* New York: G. Braziller, 1990.

Meli, Francis. *A History of the ANC: South Africa Belongs to Us.* Bloomington: Indiana University Press, 1989.

Walshe, Peter. *The Rise of African Nationalism in South Africa: The African National Congress, 1912–1952.* Berkeley: University of California Press, 1971.

Afrocentricity

Afrocentricity is an intellectual concept and theoretical approach that argues for an understanding and study of world phenomenon from the perspective of people of Africa and the African Diaspora. The approach situates black people as subjects and agents of history, as opposed to objects or props in other people's history.

Although the term was used by Du Bois in the 1960s and by black intellectuals in the 1970s, Molefi Asante, professor of African American Studies at Temple University, is widely credited for coining the term. Asante's book *Afrocentricity: A Theory of Social Change* (1980) represents the first full-fledged attempt to clearly define the term and explore its implications for the study of African people. In the book, Asante outlined a tradition of black intellectuals and activists that he built on in order to construct the idea; the list included Booker T. Washington, Marcus Garvey, Martin Luther King Jr., Elijah Muhammad, Malcolm X, and Maulana Karenga. Along with these figures, Afrocentricity also built on the intellectual work of the Senegalese historian Cheikh Anta Diop and the black arts movement theorists and historians of Africa such as George James, John Henrik Clarke, Yosef Ben Jochannan, Ivan Van Sertima, and Chancellor Williams.

In the late 1980s and early 1990s, afrocentricity garnered mainstream media attention with its challenge to classical European history. Great controversy was caused by two arguments emerging from the Afrocentric school of thought. The first asserted that Egypt was the foundation of black world culture and history, just as Greece was the foundation of Western civilization. The second argument, and the one that caused more controversy, asserted that Egypt was a black civilization that served as the major philosophical, intellectual, and cultural foundation and inspiration for Greece. *Black Athena: Afroasiatic Roots of Classical Civilizations, Volume 1: the Fabrication of Ancient Greece, 1785–1985* (1987) and *Volume II: the Archeological and Documentary Evidence* (1991) by Martin Bernal, the Cambridge trained Orientalist, and Molefi Asante's *KMT, Afrocentricity and Knowledge* (1997) stood at the center of this debate. Although Bernal did not declare himself to be an Afrocentrist, his work gave credence to the group of African historians named here that had largely been excluded from mainstream historical canon.

Afrocentricity became a central aspect of the "culture wars" and debates over "multiculturalism" that raged in all areas of American life, especially education, in the 1980s and 1990s. At the height of the debate, *Newsweek* magazine featured a stone image of Cleopatra wearing a red, black, and green African earring, and the cover read: "Afrocentrism: Was Cleopatra Black? Facts or Fantasies—A Debate Rages Over What to Teach Our Kids About Their Roots" (1991). The leading intellectuals that supported and developed the Afrocentric position through writing, speaking and program development were Molefi Asante; Malauna Karenga, Cal State University Long Beach Black Studies professor and creator of Kwanzaa, the pan-African holiday; Leonard Jeffries, Black Studies professor at City College in New York; Asa Hilliard, black psychologist; Theophile Obenga, African historian and student of Diop; Wade Nobles, black psychologist and professor of Africana Studies

at San Francisco State University; Naim Akbar, black psychologist; and Jacob Caruthers, the founding director of the Association for the Study of Classical African Civilizations (ASCAC). Although several women championed Afrocentricity, four key women produced landmark texts in Afrocentric thought: Vivian Gordon, former professor of Black Studies and author of *Black Women: Feminism and Black Liberation* (1987); Clenora Hudson-Weems, professor of English at the University of Missouri Columbia and author of *Africana Womanism: Reclaiming Ourselves* (1993); Marimba Ani, former SNCC field organizer, professor of Black Studies, and author of *Yurugu: An African-Centered Critique of European Cultural Thought and Behavior* (1994); and Ama Mazama, professor of African American Studies at Temple University and editor of *The Afrocentric Paradigm* (2003).

The major critics of Afrocentricity included Mary Lefkowitz, professor of Classical Studies at Wellesly College and author of *Not Out of Africa: How Afrocentricism Became an Excuse to Teach Myth as History* (1996) and *Black Athena Revisited* (1996); American historian and former Kennedy advisor, Arthur Schlesinger; Stephen Howe, author of *Afrocentricism: Mythical Past and Imagined Homes* (1998); Clarence Walker, author of *We Can't Go Home: An Argument about Afrocentrism* (2000); world-renown professor of African Studies, Ali Mazrui; Henry Louis Gates Jr., professor of Afro American Studies at Harvard University; Paul Gilroy, author of *the Black Atlantic* (1993) and *Against Race* (2000); Kwame Anthony Appiah, Harvard professor and author of *In My Father's House* (1992); and Tunde Adeleke, professor of African American Studies at Iowa State University. Although each of the critics challenged Afrocentricity for different reasons, their collective work represents the major oppositional voices.

Regardless of the strength of its intellectual adversaries, Afrocentricity made a major impact on black popular culture and American institutions in general. During the height of the debate, several Afrocentric schools emerged in Philadelphia, Chicago, New York, Los Angeles, and other major American cities, providing education for children from elementary to high school. Some public schools adopted Afrocentric themes or incorporated black history into the state curriculum, as was the case in Philadelphia and New Jersey. Colleges were impacted the most, as hundreds of Black Studies programs across the country designed their curriculum to adhere to an Afrocentric approach. In fact,

Temple University established the first doctoral program in Black Studies in 1987; under the leadership of Asante the program championed an Afrocentric approach to Africana Studies. In the political sphere, Afrocentricity rode the wave of the antiapartheid movement and gained currency with the development of Kwanzaa and the Million Man March, lead by the Nation of Islam in 1995. The idea also influenced hip-hop music, as Afrocentric themes emerged in the lyrics of Boogie Down Productions, Public Enemy, the Poor Righteous Teachers, Queen Latifah, Ice Cube, Brand Nubain, Arrested Development, and others.

Although the intensity of the intellectual debate has allayed since the 1990s, Afrocentricity remains a lasting ideological fixture in African American thought and culture. Black graduations are still celebrated every year on college campuses, Afrocentric conferences are still held, Kwanzaa themes have become standard for greeting cards, Temple's Department of African American Studies continues to produce graduates, and mud cloth has become a conventional signifier of African American and African Diasporic culture in fashion and interior home decorating.

See also: Asante, Molefi Kete; Karenga, Maulana; Kwanzaa; National Council for Black Studies

Jonathan Bryan Fenderson

Bibliography

Asante, Molefi. *The Afrocentric Idea.* Philadelphia: Temple University, 1987.

Asante, Molefi. *Afrocentricity: A Theory of Social Change.* Buffalo: Amulefe, 1980.

Austin, Algernon. *Achieving Blackness: Race, Black Nationalism, and Afrocentrism in the Twentieth Century.* New York: New York University Press, 2006.

Lefkowitz, Mary. *Not Out of Africa: How Afrocentrism Became an Excuse to Teach Myth as History.* New York: Basic Books, 1996.

Mazama, Ama, ed. *The Afrocentric Paradigm.* Trenton: Africa World Press, 2003.

Moses, Wilson. *Afrotopia: The Roots of African American Popular History.* Cambridge: Cambridge University Press, 1998.

Al-Amin, Jamil Abdullah (H. Rap Brown)

Jamil Abdullah Al-Amin (1943–), also known as Hubert Gerold Brown and H. Rap Brown, was a civil rights activist and proponent of black power who served as the chair of the Student Nonviolent Coordinating Committee (SNCC) and the justice minister of the Black Panther Party. He is, perhaps, best known for his statement that "violence is as American as cherry pie." Born on October 4, 1943, in Baton Rouge, Louisiana, Al-Amin attended Southern University from 1960 until 1964 before becoming an active member of the Non-Violent Action Group (NAG) and SNCC. He became known as H. Rap Brown because of his mastery over playing the dozens and signifying. Al-Amin's quick wit and oratorical skills made him a legendary dozens player, and he often set his verbal jabs to rhymes, earning him the nickname "Rap." While Al-Amin was at Southern, his brother Ed encouraged him to read W. E. B. Du Bois, Frederick Douglass, Marcus Garvey, and Richard Wright; in many ways, this was the beginning of his political education. After joining NAG and then later SNCC, Al-Amin became involved in a series of protest activities including sit-ins, voting rights campaigns, and marches.

In 1965, Al-Amin's transformation into an advocate of black power began when he, along with several other African American leaders, were called to the White House to meet with President Lyndon Baines Johnson. As Al-Amin would later reflect in his book *Die Nigger Die!,* Johnson's impatient arrogance coupled with the passivity of the group of African American leaders meeting with him led Al-Amin to personally engage President Johnson in his typically brash manner. It was after this exchange that Al-Amin would claim that he became a marked man. In rapid succession after this meeting, he would be called up for the draft, he was involved in a shootout with police in Cambridge, Maryland, and he was arrested twice in Virginia. Al-Amin was certainly one of many targets in the FBI's COINTELPRO campaign, particularly after he ascended to the chair of SNCC in 1967. Shortly thereafter, he joined the Black Panther Party to serve as their justice minister in 1968. The potential coalition of two of the most prominent black power organizations—SNCC and the Black Panthers—was actively disrupted by the FBI, and both Al-Amin and his close friend and associate, Stokely Carmichael (Kwame Ture), found themselves in a precarious situation.

In 1970, Al-Amin went underground for 18 months during the course of a trial in Maryland on the charges of inciting riot and carrying a gun across state lines. As a direct result, he appeared on the FBI's Ten Most Wanted List. By 1972, Al-Amin resurfaced and was arrested for attempted robbery of a bar in New York City. Released from

H. Rap Brown (later Jamil Abdullah Al-Amin), national chairperson of the Student Nonviolent Coordinating Committee (SNCC) and a leader in the Black Power movement, holds a press conference on July 27, 1967. Brown was shot and wounded in 1967 after delivering a fiery speech. The Black Power movement encompassed the more strident attempts of African Americans to establish their own political, cultural, and social institutions, independent of white society. (Library of Congress)

prison in 1976, Al-Amin moved to Atlanta, Georgia to open a grocery store. Having converted to Islam in prison, he became leader of the National Ummah and worked to eradicate drugs, gambling, and prostitution in Atlanta's West End. On March 16, 2000, when two sheriff's deputies attempted to serve an arrest warrant, both men were shot and one died the next day from his wounds. The surviving deputy identified Al-Amin as the shooter and, on March 9, 2002, he was convicted of 13 criminal charges including murder. Al-Amin is currently serving a life sentence at the ADX Super Maximum Security Prison in Florence, Colorado.

See also: Black Panther Party; Black Power; COINTELPRO; Student Nonviolent Coordinating Committee

Walter C. Rucker

Bibliography
Al-Amin, Jamil. *Die, Nigger, Die!* New York: Dial Press, 1969.
Al-Amin, Jamil. *Revolution by the Book: (The Rap Is Live).* Beltsville, MD: Writers' Inc.-International, 1993.
Heineman, Kenneth J. Put *Your Bodies Upon the Wheels: Student Revolt in the 1960s.* Chicago: I. R. Dee, 2001.
Thelwell, E. M. "H. Rap Brown/Jamil Al-Amin: A Profoundly American Story." *The Nation* 274 (2002):25–35.

Albany, Georgia Movement

The Albany, Georgia movement refers to both the campaigns to end racial segregation and the organization founded to achieve this goal. The Albany movement began in 1960, as an umbrella group composed of various civil rights organizations in Albany, a town in southwest Georgia. Some of the community groups involved included the Student Nonviolent Coordinating Committee (SNCC), the National Association for the Advancement of Colored People (NAACP), the Federation of Women's Clubs, the Negro Voters League, and various churches. Led by Dr. William G. Andrews and Slater King, the Albany movement sought to dismantle the system of racial segregation that excluded African Americans from full participation in the political, social, and business affairs of their city.

Undaunted by the arrest of some its members, the Albany movement held mass meetings in churches to plan strategies. During the meetings, members sang freedom songs that became a common feature of civil rights marches in the 1960s. These songs demonstrated the spirit and resolve of the protestors while also providing a cultural link between the present day and hundreds of years of African American suffering. SNCC members also instructed Albany residents nightly on nonviolent tactics.

Although the Albany movement had existed for almost a year, it was a demonstration at the city bus depot by five students on November 1, 1961, that served as a catalyst for the acceleration of protests. The Interstate Commerce Commission (ICC) had found racial segregation in interstate transportation facilities unconstitutional with the order to take effect on November 1. As the African American students attempted to enter the waiting room reserved for white Americans, Albany police blocked their way. Threatened with arrest, the students left the bus terminal but vowed to return another day.

Impressed by the demonstrations, the Reverend Dr. Martin Luther King Jr., accepted a one-day invitation to speak at a mass meeting. On December 15, 1961, Dr. King spoke at Shiloh Baptist Church, urging Albany residents to continue their struggle. King eventually decided to stay and participate in a protest march at City Hall planned for the next day, where Albany police arrested him along with more than 250 others. Initially claiming he would remain in jail over Christmas to highlight the treatment of African Americans in the South, Dr. King left jail on bail when city officials announced they had reached an agreement with the Albany movement. The city was to drop the charges levied against the 250 demonstrators and comply with the ICC ruling. It was soon apparent that the city did not plan to keep its part of the bargain.

The decision to leave jail helped Albany Police Chief Laurie Pritchett devise a strategy to defeat the demonstrations. Whenever Dr. King was arrested, Pritchett would now find someone to bail him out, thus preventing King from publicizing the arrests. In addition, Pritchett, who had read King's book on nonviolent direct action campaigns, reserved jail space in surrounding counties so the media in Albany would not see African Americans jailed in overcrowded conditions. Also, he ordered the police force to remain peaceful while arresting demonstrators. In this regard, Pritchett downplayed the violence that lay at the root of racial segregation and appeared somewhat reasonable to the national media. While Pritchett continued to outmaneuver African American leaders, the Albany city government remained committed to racial segregation. In essence, the Albany campaign seemed a stalemate. African Americans would continue to protest, Chief Pritchett would quietly arrest them, and the city government would maintain racial segregation.

The lack of progress led to problems within the campaign. Racial violence erupted on a number of occasions in July 1962 when African American protestors threw stones, bottles, and other items at police. Upset by this turn of events, Dr. King called for a temporary halt in the marches and a day of penance to atone for the violent outbreaks.

There was also dissension between SCLC, led by Dr. King and other nationally prominent leaders, and the other civil rights groups involved in Albany. Some had perceived of the desegregation campaign as a local initiative, only inviting Dr. King and the SCLC to help publicize the situation. Once joining the Albany movement, however, SCLC leaders became assertive in a way that angered the sensibilities of those who thought the Albany movement should remain in the hands of Albany citizens.

In the end, beset with internal problems and a strategy that seemed ineffective against Chief Pritchett, the campaign did not achieve the tangible goal of desegregating city facilities. Nevertheless, the Albany movement did become a sustained effort by local African Americans to end racial inequality. When the SCLC and Dr. King left the area in 1962, the Albany movement continued protesting against discrimination. Before this period, as was common in many communities, the various civil rights groups competed against each other for the allegiances of local African Americans. Under the Albany movement umbrella, there was unity among elites, professionals, and workers that had not existed previously. *See also:* Abernathy, Ralph David; King, Martin Luther Jr.; National Association for the Advancement of Colored People; Southern Christian Leadership Conference; Student Nonviolent Coordinating Committee

David Kenneth Pye

Bibliography

Carson, Clayborne. *In Struggle: SNCC and the Black Awakening of the 1960s* Cambridge, MA: Harvard University Press, 1981.

Chalfen, Michael. "The Way Out May Lead In: The Albany Movement Beyond Martin Luther King, Jr.," *Georgia Historical Quarterly* 79 (1995):560–98.

Garrow, David *Bearing the Cross: Martin Luther King, Jr., and the Southern Christian Leadership Conference* New York: William Morrow, 1986.

Lewis, David L. *King: A Biography.* Urbana: University of Illinois Press, 1978.

Ali, Muhammad

Muhammad Ali (1942–), the three-time heavyweight champion of the world, became an important symbol of black nationalism as a member of the Nation of Islam who refused to serve in the Vietnam War. Born Cassius Marcellus Clay and raised in Louisville's mostly black West End, his family was working-poor. Clay lived in a small house with his brother and parents. His mother worked as a maid and his father was a sign painter. His father was an early influence on the fighter's racial consciousness. Clay Sr. had been influenced by Marcus Garvey's Universal Negro Improvement Association as a young man and believed that racism had kept him from achieving greater heights as an artist. His father also had several run-ins with Louisville's police department and felt that blacks in the city were unfairly targeted by law enforcement. Young Cassius's understanding of race grew when he learned of Emmett Till's murder. In his autobiography, the fighter claimed to be deeply affected by the lynching.

Clay became interested in boxing after his bicycle was stolen. He cried to police officer Joe Martin that he wanted to beat up the offender. Martin, who trained amateur boxers, offered his services to Clay, who accepted them. Clay progressed rapidly, appearing often on a local television show called *Tomorrow's Champions*. Twice he captured the national Golden Gloves title. In 1960, Clay represented the United States in the Rome Olympics, where he won a gold medal in the light-heavyweight division. Clay showed little inclination for political controversy at the time. During interviews, he downplayed America's race problems. He called the United States the greatest country in the world. He told reporters that America's race problems would soon be solved. Clay also favorably compared the living conditions of black Americans to those of Africans, who he characterized as living in mud huts. He would express regret about these comments in later years.

After the Olympics, Clay decided to become a professional boxer. His emerging race consciousness affected his choices when selecting advisors and managers. Clay's first suitor was Billy Reynolds, the Louisville metals magnate. Although Reynolds made a lucrative offer, Clay felt that he would not be treated fairly by someone he considered to be a racist. Clay based his conclusion on experiences he had while working at the Reynolds estate shortly before the Olympics. Members of the Reynolds family treated him poorly, and Clay believed that the abuse was racially motivated. Reynolds also insisted that Joe Martin be Clay's trainer. Clay was against this for two reasons. First, he felt that Martin was not capable of taking him to the top as a professional. Second, he was influenced by his father's distrust of white policemen. These factors led to the rejection of Reynolds's offer to become his manager. While deciding on a team to guide his career, Ali employed blacks in key positions whenever possible. For his first bout, he named

as his manager of record former amateur opponent George King. For his professional debut, Clay's trainer was Fred Stoner, who guided many of Louisville's black fighters, professional and amateur. He also hired Alberta Jones, the first black woman to become a member of the Kentucky Bar Association, as his attorney. Jones was the sole negotiator of Ali's first professional contract.

In October 1960, Clay signed a six-year contract with the Louisville Sponsoring Group, a syndicate of 11 white men from his hometown. Almost all of the partners were millionaires. The terms of the arrangement were fair and generous, giving Ali a large signing bonus and an annual salary, which would grow according to his ring earnings. The partnership also paid all of his living and training expenses. In exchange they received a share of the purses from Clay's fights. It was an excellent arrangement for Clay because the group's wealth ensured him first-class accommodations and allowed him to be brought along without being rushed into profitable but dangerous matches. Local newspapers lauded the fighter's sensibility and praised his choice.

The one problem that many people had with the young fighter was his demeanor. Ali talked loudly, downgraded his opponents, predicted the rounds in which he would win fights, and refused to be silenced by reporters and fans who believed that he needed to be more reserved. Clay's persona sometimes affected his professional relationships. He clashed with Archie Moore, the former light-heavyweight champion who had become his trainer. Angelo Dundee replaced Moore in that role and was with Clay for the remainder of his career. There were also people who enjoyed Clay's bombast. Some found him entertaining and funny. Others saw his defiance as something political. His insistence that he was "pretty," for example, anticipated the Black Power movement mantra "black is beautiful."

Because he evoked strong feelings, Clay's fights did very well at the box office and rejuvenated a sport that had been racked by scandal and government crackdowns. The national press took an interest in him. In his first year as a professional, *Life, Saturday Evening Post,* and *Sports Illustrated* ran features on the young boxer. Shortly thereafter, he appeared in the Anthony Quinn film *Requiem for a Heavyweight*. His eighth and ninth professional bouts were televised nationally. When Clay entered major markets like New York and Los Angeles, his fights did amazing business. His 1962 match with former trainer Moore set a California indoor sporting events box office record. His bout the next January against Charlie Powell set a Pittsburgh indoor attendance record, despite being held on one of the coldest days in the city's history. Two months later, despite a newspaper strike in New York that curtailed coverage of the contest, Clay's fight with Doug Jones became the first boxing event in Madison Square Garden's 38-year history to sell out in advance. The bout created the arena's largest gross receipts for any event of the previous 10 years. Clay made the cover of *Time* magazine. He was more than just a national phenomenon. That summer, his match with British heavyweight Henry Cooper produced England's largest fight crowd since 1935, as 55,000 fans packed Wembley Stadium. Because of his talent and his personality, Clay was an international sensation by the time he landed his chance to fight for the heavyweight championship of the world.

Most people did not know that Clay was already a part of the Nation of Islam. The Nation of Islam was troubling to some people because it espoused the separation of black and white people. According to his longtime best friend Howard Bingham, Clay's membership in the organization went back to 1958. But Clay did not discuss religion or politics with reporters in the first years of his career. He felt that public knowledge of his beliefs would jeopardize his chances to fight for the title. There were some outward signs, however, of his affiliation. Nation of Islam devotees were sprinkled around his early training camps. He wore dark suits, bowties, and white shirts, which was standard Nation garb. He lectured on the evils of pork to a writer who ordered a ham sandwich during a lunchtime interview.

By the time of the Jones bout, Clay was starting to speak more clearly. He told reporters that integration was an ignorant philosophy. He charged that police officers in the South targeted him for harassment. Clay also refused to deny a newspaper report that placed him at a Nation of Islam meeting in Philadelphia. The clearest sign emerged in Miami, where Clay was training for a February 1964 title match with Sonny Liston. There, he spent time with Malcolm X, the Nation of Islam's national spokesman. Clay told the press that he found the organization's meetings to be inspiring.

Opposition to Clay materialized as his relationship with the Nation of Islam came to light and then increased when he defeated Liston. First, the promoter threatened to cancel the fight. But with hundreds of thousands of dollars already invested in the event, it was difficult for him

to do so. Eventually, he and Clay's representatives reached a compromise in which Malcolm X would leave town for the remainder of the training period. Most people did not expect Clay to beat Liston, so they did not worry much about his political and religious leanings. In a surprise outcome, however, Liston refused to answer the bell for the seventh round, claiming to have injured his shoulder. Clay was winning the match up to that point. Afterwards, the new champion told reporters that they were wrong to pick against him. He announced that his name was no longer Cassius Clay, but Cassius X. Like Malcolm X, Clay rejected the name given to his family by slave masters. Soon after, Nation of Islam leader Elijah Muhammad renamed the fighter Muhammad Ali. Newspapers often carried articles that cast Ali in a negative light. A rematch with Liston further turned the public against Ali. Ali won the fight by knockout in the first round, and many people felt the bout was fixed. In addition to those who disliked Ali's demeanor and politics were those who felt that he was a sham champion, one whose confidence did not correspond with his ability.

In his second title defense, Ali took on former champion Floyd Patterson in November 1965. The rivalry between the two fighters focused on their contrasting visions of race relations. Patterson was an integrationist and a supporter of the Civil Rights movement. He moved into an all-white neighborhood and was married to a white woman. Although these things were repugnant to the separatist Ali, it was Patterson who escalated the prefight rhetoric beyond boxing. In a series of articles for *Sports Illustrated,* Patterson wrote that for the good of the country, Ali must be defeated. Patterson referred to him as Cassius Clay, refusing to acknowledge Ali's chosen name. Some sportswriters criticized Patterson's efforts to construct himself as a heroic alternative to Ali, but the majority of the press cast the fighters as Patterson had. Ali responded to this by calling Patterson a white man's champion and promising to punish him. The fight was one-sided, with Ali winning nearly every moment before the referee stopped it in the 12th round.

Muhammad Ali began to phase out the Louisville Sponsoring Group, replacing them with a corporation known as Main Bout, Inc. At a press conference in January 1966, Ali announced that Main Bout would control the ancillary rights to his fights, starting with a bout two months later against contender Ernie Terrell in Chicago. Main Bout's ownership of these ancillary rights gave them access to the vast majority of revenues from Ali's bouts. The major money from big-time boxing matches during this period came from closed-circuit television, which was controlled by the ancillary promoter. Because seating at and revenue from the hundreds of closed-circuit theaters nationwide greatly outnumbered what could be generated at the arena where a given fight took place, such bouts usually had closed-circuit television takes much larger than from other sources.

Main Bout was controlled by the Nation of Islam, which meant that at least some of the revenues from Ali's fights were going to that organization. Main Bout had five stockholders. Herbert Muhammad, son of Nation of Islam leader Elijah Muhammad, was its president. John Ali, the Nation of Islam's national secretary, was Main Bout's treasurer. Together, they shared 50 percent of its stock and half of its board's six votes. The closed-circuit television operator Michael Malitz and his attorney Bob Arum were Main Bout's vice-president and secretary, holding 20 percent of Main Bout's stock and one vote each. Jim Brown, the professional football player and Main Bout's vice-president in charge of publicity, controlled one vote and 10 percent of the company. Malitz and Arum were Main Bout's sole white members. Ali told reporters that he hoped Main Bout would become the linchpin of a larger economic network that would result in the empowerment of large numbers of African Americans.

In February 1966, less than a month after Main Bout's formation, the United States Selective Service reclassified Muhammad Ali as draft-eligible for the Vietnam War. Originally, Ali had failed the mental aptitude portion of the U.S. Army's entrance exam. He had then been retested in front of government psychologists and failed again. Ali had always had trouble with school, and he was not prepared to answer the questions. As a result, he was declared ineligible to serve in the Armed Forces. By this time, however, the government needed more troops to continue the fight in Vietnam. As a result, it lowered the qualifying standard for its mental aptitude exam, and Ali was retroactively declared eligible. Some people saw Ali's drafting as a political act, an attempt to silence an outspoken and militant black man. Others believed it fair, that there should be no reason to prevent a healthy and intelligent person like Ali from serving.

When reporters asked Ali for comment, he declared his opposition to the Vietnam War. Combined with the Nation of Islam's entrance into the promotion of his fights,

it caused a major backlash against him. In Chicago, politicians and the press rallied against the upcoming bout with Terrell, and it was driven out of the city. When Main Bout tried to shop the contest around the United States, it found no takers. Nationwide, mayors in more than 100 cities announced that they would not host an Ali fight. Main Bout was forced to move the fight to Canada, where they made very little money. Furthermore, Ali had to have his next three bouts in Europe, where there had not been a world heavyweight title match in more than 30 years. The movement to ban Ali from fighting in the United States grew.

Ali refused to be inducted into the U.S. Army in May 1967 and was indicted on draft evasion charges. Almost immediately, state athletic commissions around the country indicated their refusal to grant Ali a boxing license. The next month, a federal court convicted Ali and sentenced him to five years in prison. He remained out of jail while appealing the case, but he was barred from fighting. No state would allow him to box, and because he was a convicted felon, the government stripped him of his passport, preventing him from fighting abroad. For three-and-a-half years, as his case made its way to the U.S. Supreme Court, Ali was exiled from the sport. During this time Ali made money by speaking on college campuses, commentating on boxing telecasts, and acting.

Ali tried to resurrect his boxing career. He lobbied Indian tribes to hold fights on reservations, which were outside the purview of state athletic commissions. He asked the government to grant him a one-day visa to fight in Tijuana. A breakthrough finally came for Ali when Georgia State Senator Leroy Johnson led a campaign to hold an Ali fight in Atlanta. Because Georgia had no state athletic commission, Johnson, an African American, knew that white supremacist governor Lester Maddox would have no political oversight of the match. Therefore, Johnson worked within Atlanta's city government and used his contacts and leverage to get the bout made over the objections of a number of state-level politicians. In October 1970, Ali returned to the ring, scoring a victory over Jerry Quarry. About a month later, Ali defeated Oscar Bonavena in New York. He then agreed to terms for a fight with Joe Frazier, who had replaced him as heavyweight champion during Ali's exile from the sport.

Ali's rivalry with Joe Frazier was the most important of both fighters' careers, and their first bout was perhaps the biggest event in boxing history. The March 1971 battle between Ali and Frazier became a key backdrop through which people made meaning of larger political and racial conflicts. Frazier became a symbolic representative to many people who despised Ali's draft resistance, although Frazier did nothing to cultivate their allegiance, unlike a number of Ali's previous opponents. Ali seized on this public sentiment in his treatment of Frazier. Because he had become the heavyweight champion during Ali's exile, Ali framed Frazier as a tool of the establishment, calling him an Uncle Tom. Throughout the buildups for their three matches, Ali insulted Frazier, calling him ignorant, ugly, and comparing him to a gorilla. As a result, Frazier's bad feelings for Ali have endured long after their bouts. Each fighter made a record $2,500,000. Frazier won a 15-round decision and retained the championship in a bitterly fought contest.

That summer, the Supreme Court overturned Ali's draft evasion conviction. Although its decision caused all criminal charges against Ali to be dropped, the Court did not officially exonerate him for his draft resistance. The Court reversed Ali's conviction because the fighter's draft board had never indicated to the defendant why his conscientious objector status had been denied. A technicality, rather than Ali's innocence or the government's mistaken refusal to grant him a ministerial deferment, was the court's given explanation for the reversal. This was an important distinction because by ruling in this manner, the Supreme Court did not set a precedent that would alter the draft status of large numbers of people. At the same time, it seems clear that the Supreme Court's decision was motivated by its belief that Ali's draft resistance was legitimate and that the federal court's ruling was incorrect.

In the next couple of years, Ali pursued the championship. He capitalized on his worldwide popularity, fighting in Switzerland, Tokyo, Vancouver, Dublin, and Jakarta. Most observers, however, questioned whether or not Ali still had what it took to regain the title. A pair of matches in 1973 against little-known Ken Norton seemed to signal Ali's decline. In the first, Norton broke Ali's jaw and won a decision. In the second, Ali narrowly escaped with a decision victory. Ali's struggles against Norton were highlighted by the performances of George Foreman, who had knocked out Joe Frazier in two rounds that year to become the champion. When Norton challenged Foreman for the title, Foreman knocked him out in the second round. Although Ali captured a decision victory over Frazier in their 1974 rematch, it looked improbable for him to regain the title. Foreman had steamrolled the two fighters who had beaten Ali.

The 1974 fight between Muhammad Ali and George Foreman happened because boxing promoter Don King was able to convince Zaire's President Mobutu Sese Seko that hosting the bout would increase his country's fortunes. Mobutu paid $10,000,000 for the honor, which gave King the money to get Ali and Foreman to Kinshasa for record purses of $5,000,000 each. It was the first world heavyweight title fight held in Africa, but it was not Ali's first visit to the continent, and he was the popular favorite of the hometown crowd. The bout cemented Ali's reputation as an all-time great fighter. Although it appeared in the early rounds that Ali was losing the fight, he had in fact devised a strategy in which he would stay along the ropes and cover up while Foreman punched himself into exhaustion. The "rope-a-dope" plan worked as Ali absorbed the seemingly invincible Foreman's best blows and came back to win with an eighth-round knockout. Twenty-two years later, *When We Were Kings,* a film about the Ali/Foreman match, won the Academy Award for outstanding documentary.

With the victory over Foreman came an outpouring of support for the new champion. A number of sportswriters who had always disparaged Ali's boxing skills finally acknowledged his excellence. Later that year, President Gerald Ford invited Ali to visit the White House. TWA Airlines showed films of the Ali-Foreman bout on selected flights. Although Ali still held beliefs about race and religion that many Americans opposed, it was clear that huge numbers of people admired him. Part of this came from the changing public sentiment about the Vietnam War. As the conflict declined in popularity, Ali's position became more acceptable. When Elijah Muhammad died in 1975, Ali chose to align himself with Muhammad's son Wallace, who wanted to take the Nation of Islam in a direction that followed orthodox Islam more closely than his father had. As a result of this move, Ali disassociated himself over the years from the racial separatism he espoused during the 1960s and 1970s. This, too, increased Ali's acceptability to many people.

Ali remained champion until 1978, but his skills declined during this period, and he took a lot of punishment in the ring that would later contribute to serious health problems. A third fight with Joe Frazier in 1975, known as the "Thrilla in Manila," ensured Ali's status as a boxing legend, but also subjected him to severe physical damage. In his final year as champion, Ali lost the title to upstart Leon Spinks, but regained it in a rematch that made Ali the first fighter to hold the heavyweight championship three times. Ali then retired, but came back to challenge Larry Holmes in 1980. Holmes pummeled Ali, who could not answer the bell for the 11th round. Ali fought and lost once more before retiring permanently in 1981. The years immediately following the end of his career were difficult for Ali, as Parkinson's syndrome, probably a result from his years in boxing, depleted him. Although he did not vanish from the public scene throughout the 1980s and early 1990s, his place in American consciousness became somewhat recessed.

During the late 1990s, and into the 21st century, Ali has made a remarkable resurgence into public prominence. There are many causes for this, but three stand out. Ali's 1986 marriage to Yolanda "Lonnie" Williams helped him regain control over his health and finances. Lonnie Ali manages Ali's business decisions and has made their family millions of dollars through her marketing of the fighter's image. Thomas Hauser's best-selling 1991 biography *Muhammad Ali: His Life and Times* is the most thorough of all books about Ali, and it presents Ali as a great man. Hauser's book institutionalized the idea of Ali as a national treasure. Ali's lighting of the ceremonial torch to open the 1996 Olympics in Atlanta showed the fighter struggling with Parkinson's syndrome and positioned him as an American hero in front of a huge television audience. In 2001 a major motion picture called *Ali* was released. Despite health problems, Ali still travels for many weeks every year in pursuit of humanitarian and religious service to the world. The 93,000 square foot Muhammad Ali Center, headquartered in Louisville, will preserve Ali's legend for many years to come. At the turn of the 21st century, Ali's popularity seems unmatched as he stands as a symbol of love and tolerance to billions of people. Tracing his journey to this point from his days as a more controversial figure is an exciting pursuit that can tell us a great deal about American society.

See also: Black Athletes; Muhammad, Elijah; Nation of Islam; Till, Emmett; X, Malcolm

Michael Ezra

Bibliography

Ali, Muhammad, with Richard Durham. *The Greatest: My Own Story.* New York: Random House, 1975.

Bingham, Howard, with Max Wallace. *Muhammad Ali's Greatest Fight: Cassius Clay vs. The United States of America.* New York: M. Evans, 2000.

Cottrell, John. *Muhammad Ali, Who Once Was Cassius Clay.* New York: Funk and Wagnalls, 1968, c.1967.

Early, Gerald. *The Muhammad Ali Reader.* Hopewell, NJ: Ecco Press, 1998.

Gorn, Elliott. *Muhammad Ali: The People's Champ.* Urbana: University of Illinois Press, 1995.

Hauser, Thomas. *Muhammad Ali: His Life and Times.* New York: Touchstone, 1991.

Kram, Mark. *Ghosts of Manila: The Fateful Blood Feud Between Muhammad Ali and Joe Frazier.* New York: HarperCollins Publishers, 2001.

Marqusee, Mike. *Redemption Song: Muhammad Ali and the Spirit of the Sixties.* London: Verso, 1999.

Olson, Jack. *Black Is Best: The Riddle of Cassius Clay.* New York: Putnam, 1967.

Remnick, David. *King of the World: Muhammad Ali and the Rise of an American Hero.* New York: Random House, 1998.

Sheed, Wilfrid. *Muhammad Ali: A Portrait in Words and Photographs.* New York: Crowell, 1975.

Ali, Noble Drew

Noble Drew Ali (1886–1929), born Timothy Drew, ascended from obscurity to become the founder and leader of the Moorish Science movement. Little is known of Ali's early years. According to some reports, he was raised by Cherokee Indians; others claim he wandered with a gypsy tribe. In his adulthood, Ali told various stories to explain his knowledge of Islam and Egyptian mystery cults; for example, he claimed to receive the title of "Ali" from Sultan Abdul Asis Ibn Saud during a visit to Mecca. It is unclear whether he actually traveled abroad or whether he acquired his interest in Islam from American libraries. The first established fact about Ali is that in 1913, he founded the first Moorish Science Temple in Newark, New Jersey.

The temple was organized around Ali's revision of African American history. Ali preached that black people were actually not African, but Asiatic (or Moors). Their true homeland was not West Africa, but Morocco, and their true religion was Islam. Ali's job was to restore African Americans to their rightful status on earth: to restore their true nationality, true religion, and true genealogy. The central text of his movement was a 60-page pamphlet by Ali titled, *Holy Koran,* that included Christian Bible passages, quotations from Marcus Garvey, anecdotes from the life of Jesus, and Ali's own codes regarding dress, diet, and morality.

The primary theme of the *Holy Koran* was a retelling of Jesus' life story, focusing on his exploits in India, Europe, and Africa. Although the book glorified Jesus as a genealogical forebear of the Moors, it still insisted that Christianity was a religion for Europeans and that Islam was the religion of the Asiatics. Ali had been sent by Allah, the god of Islam, to tell black Americans that their identity had been stolen by Christian Europeans. Once their nationality and religion were restored, these newly cast Moors could take over society.

To affirm his followers a new identity, Ali issued them identification cards and encouraged the wearing of fezzes and turbans. Combining aspects of Islam, Freemasonry, Theosophy, and 19th-century black nationalist philosophies, Moorish Science appealed to a new generation of urban black Americans seeking to differentiate themselves from their enslaved ancestors. Ali was convinced that he could change the political and economic destiny of African Americans by recasting their ethnic identity and erasing the stigma of slavery. From the outset, Ali had many competitors within his organization, and in 1923 he removed to Chicago to escape his New Jersey rivals. There he set up the permanent headquarters of the Moorish Holy Temple of Science. In 1928, he changed the name to the Moorish Science Temple of America and finally organized all of his temples under the name of the Moorish Divine and National Movement of North America, Inc. With branches in Chicago, Detroit, Milwaukee, Philadelphia, Pittsburgh, New York, and several southern cities, the Moorish Science movement would, at its height, achieve a membership of nearly 30,000.

Under the auspices of the Moorish Manufacturing Corporation, many became rich selling Asiatic charms, herbal preparations, and literature. Some leaders decided to get rid of Ali and take over the increasing fortune of the organization. In 1929, Ali's leadership was challenged by the murder of his business manager, Sheik Claude Green. Although Ali was out of town at the time of Green's death, he was briefly jailed for the crime. Following his release on bail, he, too, died under mysterious circumstances.

See also: Black Nationalism; Moorish Science Temple

Kathryn Emily Lofton

Bibliography

Ali, Noble Drew. *The Holy Koran of the Moorish Science Temple of America.* 1913.

Curtis, Edward E. *Islam in Black America: Identity, Liberation, and Difference in African-American Islamic Thought.* Albany: State University of New York Press, 2002.

Turner, Richard Brent. *Islam in the African-American Experience.* Bloomington: Indiana University Press, 2003.

Antiapartheid Movement

The African American antiapartheid movement was actually a series of intrarelated and interrelated movements that contested apartheid policies and practices from 1937 to 1994. Apartheid was a political system of separate development that became state policy in South Africa in 1948 and lasted until Nelson Mandela became president in 1994. Based on rigid racial divisions, the purpose of the policy was to privilege the political, cultural, and economic interests of the white minority population in South Africa while maintaining a cheap work force of people of color. The African American antiapartheid movement primarily sought to disrupt the South African economy by appealing to U.S. policymakers and the United Nations to impose sanctions and a trade embargo on South Africa. The movement also consisted of cultural and political sanctions. At the heart of the African American antiapartheid movement was the struggle to end white supremacy both at home and abroad.

The earlier movements against apartheid were part of a larger struggle that aimed to raise awareness about African liberation and help African states gain independence. The earliest organization to address South Africa's racist laws was the Council on African Affairs. Originally organized as the International Committee on African Affairs in 1937, it was renamed the Council on African Affairs by 1943 (CAA). The CAA was composed of internationally renowned African Americans, including W. E. B. Du Bois, singer and activist Paul Robeson, Howard University political scientist Ralph Bunche, Harvard anthropologist Raymond Leslie Buell, and YMCA Baptist missionary Max Yergan. The CAA was a powerful voice for anticolonialism and Pan-Africanism and linked the struggles of African Americans with the struggles of colonized African people. The organization's publications, including *Spotlight on Africa*, were relied on by activists and scholars for credible information about South Africa.

The first notable action of the CAA with regard to apartheid came in 1946 when the CAA, along with India, launched a campaign for international sanctions against South Africa at the first United Nations General Assembly meeting in London. The CAA would maintain a lobby at the UN. Although this campaign was unsuccessful at achieving sanctions, the CAA's activity and sponsored demonstrations and letter-writing campaign gave rise to global consciousness about the plight of millions of oppressed South Africans. The CAA called for the United States to sever relations with South Africa. Apartheid would become the single most important international issue concerning African Americans.

In 1952, the CAA initiated mass protests that coincided with the Campaign of Defiance of Unjust Laws in South Africa. Black and white leaders from churches, labor unions, and civic and peace organizations from New York, Philadelphia, and Boston initiated the CAA campaign. These leaders pledged to obtain 100,000 signatures on a petition and raise $5,000 to assist in relieving some of the suffering and funding some of the legal costs for those South Africans who were arrested in the defiance campaign.

The antiapartheid movement emerged during a period of Cold War and communist hysteria. Anticommunism sentiment curtailed early efforts and took its toll on organizations like the CAA. The hysteria fragmented antiapartheid and African liberation movements. CAA fell victim after it was labeled a communist organization, and several of its members', including its primary financier, Paul Robeson's passports were revoked. CAA collapsed in 1952.

A new organization called Americans for South African Resistance (AFSAR) emerged in that same year. AFSAR was assembled by African American liberals who had been involved in the antiapartheid movement. The secretary, George Houser, was careful not to conflate AFSAR objectives with communist sentiment. One of the first actions of AFSAR was a rally at Abyssinian Baptist Church in Harlem in April 1952 where 800 members were in attendance and a US$300 check was sent to Walter Sisulu as the first installment in a series of contributions in support of the non-European congresses in South Africa. AFSAR was disbanded in 1953 and transformed into an organization that could would relate to the entire anticolonial struggle in Africa. The new organization was named the American Committee on Africa (ACOA) and would include prominent African American activist and leader Martin Luther King Jr.

Martin Luther King Jr. was exposed to South African issues when his father invited Albert Lithuli, the president of the African National Congress, to speak at his church in Atlanta in 1948. As a pastor, King constantly compared South Africa to the Jim Crow South and urged the usage of nonviolent resistance in South Africa. ACOA organized a Declaration of Conscience campaign in 1957 in the United States to protest the unjust arrest of 156 leaders of the liberation movement in South Africa who were being charged with treason. The unveiling of the campaign coincided with Human Rights Day, and Eleanor Roosevelt and Martin Luther King Jr. were cosponsors of the declaration. ACOA organized the South African Defense Fund, which aimed to collect $100,000 to help pay for legal fees for the defendants of the treason trial in South Africa.

During the early 1960s, black nationalism came to prominence, with young leaders like Malcolm X leading the way. Malcolm X visited several heads of states throughout Africa where he laid out a plan to internationalize the black freedom struggle in America by placing it at the level of human rights. His insistence on linking racism in South Africa and the United States and his militancy was a source of contention for some African American antiapartheid leaders.

The independence of many African countries in the 1970s reinvigorated the antiapartheid movement. Many athletes now joined the struggle against apartheid. African American professional athletes became important actors in the antiapartheid struggle. The sports boycotts against South Africa attracted supporters from around the world. World tennis champion, Arthur Ashe was one of the most prominent athletes to oppose apartheid. After being denied a travel visa by the South African government, he used the media to bring focus on the oppressive regime in Pretoria. He became involved with the movement that boycotted South Africa's participation in the 1968 Olympic Games in Mexico City. His further activism resulted in South Africa's expulsion from the governing body of world tennis, the Davis Cup, and from the International Olympics Association. Ashe opposed apartheid and protested the policy throughout the next two decades until his death in 1993.

Besides athletes, African American workers, students, legislators, and activists directed their frustration of pro-apartheid U.S. foreign policy toward corporations with investments in South Africa. Black workers in Boston led a campaign against the Polaroid Corporation, accusing them of supporting apartheid because the passbook identification cards in South Africa were being manufactured using Polaroid cameras and film. The passbooks were one of the most intrusive components of apartheid because it restricted the movement and residential patterns of South African people of color. The anti-Polaroid activists went to the streets using direct-action techniques. They began informing local shop owners of Polaroid's connection to apartheid and insisting that the shops stop selling Polaroid products. They addressed the United Nations, proposing an international boycott of Polaroid products, and lobbied Congress, where they worked with members of the Congressional Black Caucus who soon met with President Richard Nixon about installing sanctions against South Africa. As a result of the Polaroid campaign, the company lost $4 million in sales and pulled out of South Africa by 1977.

The lobbying group, TransAfrica, was formed in 1977 and would become the most important lobby for Africa and the Caribbean ever created by African Americans. This organization was made possible by the sustained mobilization of African American groups throughout the 1960s and 1970s. TransAfrica, which was led by African American liberals who felt a kinship with Africa based on history and shared experiences of racial discrimination, combined direct-action techniques and educational campaigns to influence foreign policy. One of the most prominent leaders was founder Randall Robinson, who served as the president until 2001. Robinson had previously worked for Congressman Charles Diggs, at which time he was engaged in foreign policy activities. TransAfrica met regularly with Congress, conducted press conferences, obtained grants, and published policy statements, reports, and newsletters on apartheid in South Africa and effectively galvanized worldwide support of the antiapartheid movement. TransAfrica built a mass base of supporters by reaching out to the black church, an institution with a long history of community activism for social justice. TransAfrica's profile was raised when President Jimmy Carter, pressured by the organization, decided to maintain sanctions against Ian Smith's minority government in Rhodesia. Antiapartheid sentiment was widespread in the African American community by 1980. White students and religious groups shared this sentiment and TransAfrica quickly became a multiracial organization. The organization came to international attention when Robinson addressed the Organization of African Unity's Heads of

State Summit in Nairobi in 1981. Although Malcolm X had met with the Organization of African Unity (OAU) in 1964, Robinson's address marked the first time since then that an African American had addressed the OAU.

Ronald Reagan administration's constructive engagement policies toward South Africa signaled a sharp contrast from Carter's human rights approach. Many antiapartheid activists considered Reagan to be in full partnership with South Africa's racist regime, and this support became a catalyst for the resurgence of the antiapartheid movement. By 1984, apartheid had become a major issue in African American politics. At this time, Jesse Jackson entered the race for the nomination of the Democratic Party's candidate for president in 1984 and 1988. Jackson, who carried on King's ideas on foreign policy, helped to reshape African American consciousness by providing a link between Africa and the Civil Rights movement of the 1960s and the pan-Africanist movements of the 1980s. His views on apartheid forced the issue onto the national stage of American politics and increased national and worldwide attention on the issue.

TransAfrica's Randall Robinson, Congressman Walter Fauntroy, Civil Rights Commission member Mary Frances Berry, and law professor Eleanor Holmes Norton entered the South African consulate's office on November 21, 1984. They met with the consular and presented their case that all South African political prisoners be released. Afterwards, they occupied the meeting room and refused to leave until their demands were met. They were subsequently arrested. This event led to the formation of the Free South Africa Movement, which brought the issue of apartheid home and declared constructive engagement a failure. There were numerous sit-ins and demonstrations outside the South African embassy, at other federal buildings throughout the country, at businesses with South African interests, and at coin shops that sold the gold Krugerrand. Numerous celebrities and officials participated in these demonstrations and sit-ins including Harry Belafonte, Detroit mayor Coleman Young, Coretta Scott King, Jesse Jackson, Amy Carter, and Gloria Steinem. This movement spread to hundreds of colleges and universities and included a coalition of church, student, civil rights, and women's groups. These actions represented a surge in antiapartheid grassroots activism, and more than 5,000 people were arrested across the country within one year. *Time* magazine and the *Washington Post* compared the new antiapartheid activism with the tactics used during the Civil Rights movement of the 1960s. This increased activity influenced Congress to adopt the Comprehensive Anti-Apartheid Act in 1986 over President Reagan's veto. Before passage of this Act, Representative William Gray of Pennsylvania sponsored a similar bill in the House that called for the cessation of all loans and investment in South Africa and imposed hefty fines and jail time for individuals who ignored the law.

The increase in state violence in South Africa was brought into American living rooms on the evening news, further fueling antiapartheid activists. On the 25th anniversary of the Sharpeville massacre, police opened fire on a funeral procession held to bury three black South Africans who had been killed the week before. Nineteen funeral-goers were killed on that day alone and no less than 400 youth had been killed within a 12-month period. The Free South Africa Movement (FSAM) protest continued outside of the South African embassy every weekday for eight months. These protests and high-profile arrest of former first daughter, Amy Carter, two of Robert Kennedy's children, and Coretta Scott King focused the national spotlight on South African repression. Before the FSAM demonstrations, many Americans knew little about apartheid.

During this time, Jesse Jackson traveled around the country addressing colleges and universities about the importance of the antiapartheid movement. While he visited Princeton University, a sit-in was in progress. Jackson attacked the university administration for refusing to divest financial holdings in South Africa. Similar scenes played out at Harvard University and Rutgers University in New Jersey. Jackson further fought apartheid by touring the front-line states, addressing the United Nations, popularizing the issue of sanctions, and raising awareness about the impact of apartheid. Jackson was very outspoken toward the Reagan administration for their failure to abandon constructive engagement and spoke of the deaths, tortures, and imprisonments perpetrated by the apartheid regime. His efforts played an important role in pressuring Congress to pass the Comprehensive Anti-Apartheid Act of 1986. Fourteen years earlier, this act was originally sponsored by California Representative Ronald Dellums, an antiapartheid activist and member of the Congressional Black Caucus. Dellums was at the center of the African American antiapartheid struggle and cleverly used the legislative machinery, finally gaining a victory with the passage of the act. In 1988, the act was modified and included broader new trade restrictions that eventually took its toll on the South African economy, essentially blocking economic growth. As a result, political prisoners were released, including Nelson Mandela who had been imprisoned for over a quarter of a century. Mandela would go on to become the first freely elected president in the new South Africa, closing the chapter on apartheid and the African American antiapartheid movement.

See also: Ashe, Arthur; Congressional Black Caucus; Jackson, Jesse; King, Coretta Scott; King, Martin Luther Jr.; National Association for the Advancement of Colored People; Pan-Africanism; X, Malcolm

Clay M. Johnson

Bibliography

Baldwin, Lewis V. *Toward the Beloved Community. Martin Luther King Jr. and South Africa.* Cleveland: The Pilgrim Press, 1995.

Culverson, Donald R. *Contesting Apartheid. U.S. Activism, 1960–1987.* Boulder, CO: Westview Press, 1999.

Hostetter, David L. *Movement Matters. American Antiapartheid Activism and the Rise of Mulitcultural Politics.* New York: Routledge, 2006.

Marable, Manning, and Leith Mullings, eds. *Let Nobody Turn Us Around. Voices of Resistance, Reform, and Renewal.* Lanham, MD: Rowman and Littlefield, 2000.

Nesbitt, Francis Njubi. *Race for Sanctions. African Americans against Apartheid, 1946–1994.* Bloomington: Indiana University Press, 2004.

Antilynching Campaign

Between 1882 and 1968, at least 4,743 people, including around 3,450 African Americans, were lynched in America. In the single year of 1892, which marked lynching's peak, at least 230 black people were killed (Brundage, 4). But that year also marked the beginning of the country's first sustained antilynching campaign. Three of the men who died in 1892 were friends of the Memphis-based journalist Ida B. Wells.

Wells began to investigate the lynchings of the previous decade and wrote a controversial editorial challenging the concept that the assault of white women by African American men was at the core of these acts by white mobs. She followed the editorial with a pamphlet, *Southern Horrors,* which discussed consensual interracial sex, connected lynching to slavery, and advocated black boycotts of white businesses, armed self-protection, migration, and legislative action. In another antilynching pamphlet, she asked readers to support the Blair Bill, a resolution coming before the House of Representatives in August 1894.

She continued her work into the 20th century, and, in 1909, she helped to found the National Association for the Advancement of Colored People (NAACP), which launched its own antilynching campaign. Led by Walter White, who personally investigated more than 40 lynchings, the association amassed vast amounts of lynching data. From 1916 onward its Anti-Lynching Committee developed legislative and public awareness campaigns, and in 1919 it documented the deaths of 3,224 people in a 30-year period. Throughout the early 1920s, it advertised lynching statistics in national newspapers and lobbied for the passage of the federal Dyer Bill, which proposed to punish anyone who participated in a lynching or who failed to prosecute lynchers.

Introduced in 1918 and passed by the House in January 1922, the bill was halted by a filibuster in the Senate. But one important legacy of the failed bill was the organizational model of the Anti-Lynching Crusaders. Established in 1922, this group of black women within the NAACP raised money to promote the Dyer Bill and attempted to unite black and white women around a renewed antilynching effort. After the death of the bill, the Anti-Lynching Crusaders' model was taken up by Jessie Daniel Ames's Association of Southern Women for the Prevention of Lynching (ASWPL).

On November 1, 1930, Ames held a meeting in Atlanta, Georgia, for southern white women who wanted to help end lynching. This was an important role, she explained, because lynching was frequently justified in their name, as a method of protecting them from rape. Women from seven of the southeastern states attended the meeting and on November 6, another group of women—from

Members of the National Association for the Advancement of Colored People (NAACP) New York City Youth Council picketing for antilynching legislation before the Strand Theatre in Times Square in 1937. (Library of Congress)

Louisiana, Arkansas, Oklahoma, and Texas—joined with Ames's group to create a South-wide movement. The newly formed association launched an informational campaign condemning lynching and disavowing the notion of "protection" for white womanhood. They followed this with outreach efforts, asking sheriffs to protect the rule of law. Within their communities, southern white women congregated wherever a lynching was rumored to take place and tried to prevent it from unfolding.

Jacquelyn Dowd Hall notes that the ASWPL was deeply subversive to the southern social and sexual hierarchy. By speaking out, its members overturned the patriarchal order that had kept white women in their place and in need of white male "protection." And although results are impossible to quantify with any precision, the ASWPL may have contributed to a 50 percent reduction in the incidence of lynching by 1938. Membership had reached 40,000 by 1939.

Other activism during the 1930s included the campaign to pass the Costigan-Wagner Bill of 1935, led by the NAACP. The bill's text was the same as the Dyer bill, proposing fines and imprisonment for any governmental body that failed to protect an individual from a mob. Some campaigners felt these proposals did not go far enough, and so a coalition of left-wing organizations, including The League of Struggle for Negro Rights, proposed its own legislation— a "Bill for Negro Rights." This made lynching punishable by death and outlawed the Ku Klux Klan. It garnered little support and Congress also failed to pass the Costigan-Wagner Bill. The 200 other antilynching bills introduced between 1882 and 1968 met the same fate.

Yet while their lobbying efforts failed, antilynching campaigners did succeed in challenging both the gender dynamics surrounding lynching (including the stereotype of the black male as a sexual beast) and the white supremacist notion of racially redemptive violence. The legacy of antilynching campaigning was further evident in 2005, when the Senate finally passed a resolution related to lynching. Summarizing the long history of antilynching campaigns, the Senate went on to issue an apology to lynching victims for its own failure to enact antilynching legislation. *See also:* Du Bois, W. E. B.; Ku Klux Klan; National Association for the Advancement of Colored People; National Association of Colored Women; Terrell, Mary Church; Wells-Barnett, Ida; White, Walter

Zoe Trodd

Bibliography

Brundage, W. Fitzhugh, ed. *Under Sentence of Death: Lynching in the South.* Chapel Hill: University of North Carolina Press, 1997.

Duster, Alfreda M., ed. *Crusade for Justice: The Autobiography of Ida B. Wells.* Chicago: University of Chicago Press, 1970.

Hall, Jacquelyn Dowd. *Revolt Against Chivalry: Jessie Daniel Ames and the Women's Campaign against Lynching.* New York: Columbia University Press, 1993.

Royster, Jacqueline Jones, ed. *Southern Horrors and Other Writings: The Anti-Lynching Campaign of Ida B. Wells, 1892–1900.* Boston: Bedford Books, 1997.

Asante, Molefi Kete

Molefi Kete Asante (1942–), scholar, author, and Afrocentric theorist, was born Arthur Lee Smith Jr. in Valdosta, Georgia. The oldest of 16 children, he is the first born son of Lillie Wilkson and Arthur L. Smith. As a child in the small southern town of Valdosta, Asante witnessed firsthand the social injustices perpetrated against black people under a system of de jure segregation. A racist encounter at the age of 11 left an indelible mark on his childhood memories and was the beginning of his quest to end racism and discrimination.

A precocious and gifted child, Asante showed his academic capabilities early in life. Fully cognizant of the suffering around him and mindful of the stories told to him about the powerful role of family and ancestors, Asante often used his intellectual gifts to aid others. His superior academic achievements earned him acceptance at the Nashville Christian Institute. Located in Nashville, Tennessee, it was one of a handful of black boarding schools in the United States dedicated to developing academic excellence in black children. After graduation in 1960, Asante enrolled in Southwestern Christian College. He remained there for two years before transferring to Oklahoma Christian College where he received his BA in Communication in 1964. He received an MA in Communication in 1965 from Pepperdine University, and, in 1968, the PhD from the University of California at Los Angeles (UCLA).

Asante's academic career began in 1968 with his first appointment, albeit brief, at Purdue University as an assistant professor of communication. In 1969, he returned to UCLA to accept the position of associate professor of communication and director of the Center for Afro-American

Studies. During this period Asante began to re-create himself as an African-centered scholar dedicated to the study of black people. Asante played an instrumental role in the establishment of the masters program in African American Studies at UCLA and served as co-founder of the *Journal of Black Studies*. In 1976, before his move to Buffalo, New York (SUNY) to accept the position as professor and chair of the Department of Communication, he legally changed his name from Arthur Smith to Molefi, "keeper of the traditions" in Sotho, Kete, lover of music in Akan, and Asante, a general surname among the Akan.

From 1977 to 1979, Asante served as chair of SUNY's Department of Black Studies, an opportunity that undoubtedly played a role in his decision to switch career focus from communications to African American Studies. He often refers to this decision as indicative of his ability to commit "discipline suicide." Asante believed that this was a critical and necessary choice. Although many colleges and universities appointed faculty to positions in black studies during the formative years of program development, none possessed the traditional prerequisite of a PhD in the discipline. This contributed to a high level of role confusion, as many faculty members straddled the fence, attempting to generate significant scholarly activity in two separate disciplines. Asante rejected this dichotomous confusion.

With the 1980 publication of *Afrocentricity*, his transformation was complete. In this critical work he puts forth his theory based on self-conscious cultural awareness of African-ascended people. Asante rejected the Eurocentric hegemony of Western culture and insisted on recognizing the existence of African epistemologies that existed before European dominance. He built on the works of Carter G. Woodson, Cheikh Anta Diop, Maulana Karenga, Mary McLeod Bethune, and Marcus Garvey. Advocating the need for an African-centered approach to knowledge, understanding, and being would be the focus of his life's work. It was Asante's appointment as chair of the Department of African American Studies at Temple University in 1984, however, that would alter the face of the discipline and gain him national recognition as a leader in the field.

Under Asante's leadership, Temple University created the world's first PhD program in African American Studies in 1988. Its instant popularity was astounding, demonstrating the thirst for knowledge about the African American experience at the most advanced level of study. The program attracted hundreds of students from within the United States and around the world. It also drew heavy criticism from those who challenged its validity as a legitimate field of academic inquiry. Asante's emergence as the preeminent Afrocentric scholar drew praise and controversy. He was seen as a visionary by some and was demonized by others. Asante's views were also frequently attacked by scholars within the discipline who questioned his advocacy of Africology as the primary foundation for the study of African people. Asante ended his chairmanship in 1997, but he remains on the faculty as professor of African American Studies.

With hundreds of publications in the form of books, articles, essays, and editorials, Asante has gained worldwide recognition. He has lectured on college and university campuses throughout the world. Several of his most important works have been translated into French, Portuguese, and Spanish. One of the highest forms of recognition came in 1993 when he was honored as a traditional king of Ghana, Nana Okru Asante Peasah, Kyidomhene of Tafo, in a public ceremony in Philadelphia, Pennsylvania.

An activist scholar, Asante remains committed to the empowerment and liberation of African people. He has distinguished himself as one of the foremost African-centered scholars and intellectuals of the 20th and 21st centuries.
See also: Afrocentricity; National Council for Black Studies

Patricia Reid-Merritt

Bibliography
Asante, Molefi Kete. *Afrocentricity: The Theory of Social Change.* Buffalo: Amulefi Publishing, 1980.

Ashe, Arthur

Arthur Robert Ashe Jr. (1943–1993) was a tennis champion, author, and activist known equally for his accomplishments off the court as on. Ashe was born in Richmond, Virginia, and grew up next to the city's largest playground for the black community and ultimately learned to play tennis there. His tennis playing began to attract attention and his tennis coach Ronald Charity arranged for Ashe to spend the summer with Dr. Walter Johnson, tennis champion Althea Gibson's coach.

After attending segregated schools and competing in segregated tournaments, Ashe transferred to an integrated high school in St. Louis during his senior year. An "A" student who graduated first in his class, Ashe accepted a tennis scholarship to UCLA in 1962. At 20, Ashe was selected to the U.S. Davis Cup team, becoming the first African American on the team. Ashe stayed with the team until 1970 but returned in 1975, 1976, and 1978. He won 27 of 32 cup matches, more than any other American to that point.

In 1965, Ashe helped the Bruins capture the NCAA title by winning the singles tournament. One year later, Ashe graduated from UCLA with a BS in business administration. He then went to West Point to serve a two-year Army commitment as an officer, eventually attaining the rank of second lieutenant. In 1968, while still an amateur, Ashe defeated Tom Okker of the Netherlands to win the U.S. Open men's singles title. The victory made Ashe the first American to win the title since 1955, as well as the first African American to win a men's title at a Grand Slam. Because he was still an amateur, however, he could not collect the prize money totaling $14,000.

One year later, Ashe, along with Charlie Pasarell and Sheridan Synder, established the United State Tennis Association's National Junior Tennis League to introduce tennis to and help develop inner-city tennis players. Ashe won his second Grand Slam, the Australian Open, by defeating Australian Dick Crealy in 1970. At that time Ashe, who was the top-ranked American in the world, applied for a visa to play in the South African Open, but his visa application was denied because he was black. Ashe called for South Africa's expulsion from the tennis tour to protest the country's system of apartheid. The call gained widespread support from both inside and outside the tennis world. Three years later, Ashe was granted a visa and became the first black professional player in South Africa's national championships.

In 1975, Ashe won his last Grand Slam single's title when he upset defending champion Jimmy Connors at Wimbledon, making him the first African American male to win that title. Partially because of the win, Ashe became the No. 1 ranked tennis player in the world. Two years later, Ashe married Jeanne Moutoussamy, a photographer he had met during a tennis tournament.

Ashe suffered a heart attack in July 1979 and underwent quadruple bypass surgery five months later. He retired the next year with a professional record of 818–260 and 51 titles.

Despite the retirement, Ashe continued to stay involved with professional tennis, serving as the Davis Cup captain in 1980. He coached the team from 1981–85. His activism also continued; he served as national chairman of the American Heart Association in 1981. One year later Ashe underwent a double bypass surgery.

In 1985, Ashe was inducted into the Tennis Hall of Fame just months after being arrested outside the South African embassy in Washington during an antiapartheid protest. In 1988, Ashe authored and published the three-volume *A Hard Road to Glory*, which chronicles the history of African American athletes in the United States. That same year, Ashe was hospitalized and learned that he was HIV-positive. His exposure was traced to a blood transfusion received after his double bypass surgery.

In April 1992, believing *USA Today* was about to report that he was HIV-positive, Ashe called a press conference and made the announcement himself. Five months later while protesting the U.S. crackdown on Haitian refugees, Ashe was arrested outside the White House. On World AIDS Day, Ashe addressed the United Nations General Assembly and pled with the delegates to boost funding for AIDS research and to increase knowledge of the disease and its effects. He was later named *Sports Illustrated*'s Sportsman of the Year.

On February 6, 1993, Ashe died of AIDS-related pneumonia in New York at the age of 49. His body lay in state in Richmond where it was viewed by more than 5,000 people. Ashe is the first person to lie in state at the governor's mansion since Confederate General Stonewall Jackson in 1863. In 1996, on what would have been his 53rd birthday, a statue of Ashe was dedicated on Richmond's Monument Avenue. Ashe is depicted carrying books in one hand and a tennis racket in the other. In 1997, the U.S. Tennis Association announced that its centerpiece tennis center would be named in Ashe's honor. In 2005, the U.S. Postal Service honored Ashe with a postage stamp.

See also: Antiapartheid Movement; Black Athletes

Lisa Doris Alexander

Bibliography
Ashe, Arthur. *A Hard Road to Glory: A History of the African American Athlete, 1619–1918.* New York: Warner Books, 1998.
Ashe, Arthur. *A Hard Road to Glory: A History of the African American Athlete, 1919–1945.* New York: Warner Books, 1998.

Ashe, Arthur. *A Hard Road to Glory: A History of the African American Athlete, Since 1945.* New York: Warner Books, 1998.

Ashe, Arthur, and Arnold Rampersad. *Days of Grace: A Memoir.* New York: Knopf, 1993.

Steins, Richard. *Arthur Ashe: A Biography.* Westport, CT: Greenwood Press, 2005.

Association for the Study of African American Life and History

The Association for the Study of African American Life and History (ASALH) is one of the oldest African American professional organizations today. Its continued existence is owed to the extraordinary efforts of its founder, Dr. Carter G. Woodson, the second African American to earn a doctorate in history from Harvard University in 1912. The Association's goal is to research, promote, publish, preserve, interpret, and disseminate scholarly information on the history and culture of people of African descent to a global audience. It counts among its members both academic scholars and history buffs. The organization is responsible for founding a scholarly journal, a publication for primary and secondary educators, and a publishing press; but it is probably best known for creating Black History Month, a national celebration of African American history and achievement during the month of February.

Carter G. Woodson, assisted by four others, founded the Association for the Study of Negro Life and History (ASNLH, later known as Association for the Study of Afro-American Life and History or ASALH) on September 9, 1915 in Chicago, but its headquarters were in Washington, D.C. Its mission was to conduct historical research; publish books on African American life and history; promote its work through black colleges, fraternal organizations, public schools, and churches; and collect and preserve historical documents. An executive council governed the organization and George Cleveland Hall, a physician and civic leader, served as the first president. As executive director, Woodson would single handedly guide and direct the organization as it sought to establish the scientific study of the history and culture of people of African descent as a legitimate endeavor at a time when African Americans were denied their citizenship rights.

The association worked to counter the misrepresentations of African Americans by teaching black folks that they had a history to be proud of while demonstrating to whites that people of African descent made major contributions to the history and culture of the United States and the world. Although the ASNLH, with its devotion to an accurate and truthful rendering of the black past, largely through the efforts of Woodson, did not have a specific political agenda, it could be viewed as an organization of social activism, as it worked incessantly to bolster black pride while eroding white prejudice.

To provide an outlet for the research of Woodson and other scholars of African American history, the Association founded the *Journal of Negro History* on January 1, 1916, with Woodson as editor until his death on April 3, 1950. The journal would be largely responsible for establishing the study of black history and culture as a legitimate field of inquiry, publishing the work of reputable scholars—black and white, male and female, in a range of disciplines—from its inception. Although most of its focus was on African Americans, it did publish articles on Africa, the Caribbean, and Latin America. Starting in 1917, the ASNLH also held annual conferences, usually in October, to bring together scholars to present research papers on various topics to promote both scholarly and popular interest.

One of the association's main goals was to reach a wider audience, particularly young people, and toward that end, it created the event that it is best known for. Taken from the annual celebration of Negro Achievement Week begun in 1924 by Woodson's fraternity, Omega Psi Phi Fraternity, Inc., the Association established Negro History Week in 1926 during the month of February to incorporate the birthdays of Frederick Douglass and Abraham Lincoln, two important figures in African American history, and developed an overall theme for each yearly celebration. The response was tremendous, and branches of the association sprang up across the country to provide history enthusiasts a link to the organization. The association also established the Associated Publishers in 1921 to publish historical materials and in 1937 created the *Negro History Bulletin* as a tool of instruction for primary and secondary teachers.

After Woodson's death, the association continued to grow. Owing to increased black consciousness, the organization changed its name to the Association for the Study of Afro-American Life and History (ASALH) in 1972 and Negro History Week became Black History Month in 1976.

Later on, the name was further changed to the Association for the Study of African American Life and History, the *Journal of Negro History* became the *Journal of African American History* in 2002, and the *Negro History Bulletin* renamed the *Black History Bulletin*. Several prominent African Americans held important positions in the organization during Woodson's tenure and after, and helped to establish the association as the premier African American historical organization, including Mary McLeod Bethune, John Hope, Rayford Logan, Charles Wesley, M. Sammye Miller, Robert Harris Jr., and Bettye Gardner.

Today, the association, still headquartered in Washington, D.C., is under the leadership of President Dr. John Fleming and Executive Director Sylvia Cyrus-Albritton. The *Journal of African American History* is under the editorship of Dr. V. P. Franklin and the *Black History Bulletin* is co-edited by Dr. Alicia L. Moore and Dr. La Vonne I. Neal. It has published the *Woodson Review,* a magazine on the National Black History Theme, since 2005.

See also: Woodson, Carter Godwin

Tony Gass

Bibliography
Goggin, Jacqueline. *Carter G. Woodson: A Life in Black History.* Baton Rouge: Louisiana State University Press, 1993.
Meier, August, and Elliott Rudwick, eds. *Black History and the Historical Profession.* Chicago: University of Illinois Press, 1986.
Smith, Jessie Carney, ed. *Notable Black American Men.* Detroit: Gale Research, 1999.

Atlanta, Georgia, Riot of 1906

The genesis of the Atlanta riot of 1906 lay in the vituperative racist gubernatorial campaign of that year. The two principal candidates, Hoke Smith and Clark Howell, seemed to try to outdo each other in their race-baiting. Already negative white public opinion had been aroused by a series of unconfirmed reports in the city newspapers of physical assaults on white women by black men. Additional racial tensions had surfaced because of increased competition between black and white men for jobs during a period of economic recession.

As tensions grew, both races began to fear an open confrontation. The black mortician, David T. Morgan, for example, smuggled a box of weapons into the city from Chicago in a casket. The actual riot began on the evening of September 22, 1906, in the red-light district of Decatur Street near downtown Atlanta. This was an area frequented by both poor blacks and whites, lured by bars, gambling, prostitution, and other vices. On that evening, a mob of whites paraded through the streets, attacking unsuspecting blacks who were either shopping or traveling through the area. The riot continued for three days, eventually spreading to black residential sections in the southeast, northeast, and southwest quadrants of the city.

When the mob approached the Darktown portion of northeast Atlanta, near the black business district on Auburn Avenue, George White, a black postman and father of future NAACP leader, Walter White, secured weapons and waited in anxious anticipation with his family. As the mob stopped at the White home, the son of a white grocer with whom the black family had done business pointed out where White and his family lived and urged the mob to set fire to the house. George White, then turned to his 13-year-old son, Walter, and told him to shoot the first man to step foot on their lawn. But as the mob moved toward the house, the Whites' neighbors fired and drove them away. The white mob retreated toward downtown.

On their way toward Darktown, the rioters had passed the black First Congregational Church at Houston and Courtland streets. The church's pastor, the Reverend Hugh Proctor, saw the mob as it came into the churchyard. A number of children were sheltered in the parsonage nearby. But the whites scattered when some of the black residents shot out the streetlights.

In southeast Atlanta, in an area called Brownsville, a panic developed as a white mob approached. Several of the residents sought refuge in the Gammon Theological Seminary. On the first night there, many sat up all night praying. The school's president, John W. E. Bowen, later said that he had not been able to sleep for several days in anticipation of the arrival of the mob. On Sunday, he called for police protection, but none was provided. On Monday evening, a squad of county police did arrive, and, even though there had been no trouble reported at the time, they arrested blacks, with the aid of several white citizens, for carrying weapons illegally. During one of these incidents, one white policeman was killed, another was wounded, and several blacks were killed or injured. Although the blacks contended that they had fired on the officers because they mistook them for a mob in the darkness, some were charged with murder. At least two were shot in police custody.

Because of the riot in Brownsville, Clark University delayed its fall opening, which probably served to prevent a dangerous altercation between the mob and black college students. Similarly, on the city's west side, area blacks clustered in refuge with President John Hope at Morehouse College, but the mob was driven away from the campus by neighbors before a melee developed. Nevertheless, President Bowen of Gammon, one of the city's most influential black leaders, was beaten over the head with a rifle-butt by a police officer.

When state and local police, with the aid of a rainstorm and dissipated energies, finally brought turmoil to an end, the best estimates were that at least 25 blacks had been killed, 150 seriously injured, and a thousand had fled the city. At least 2 whites were killed and 10 wounded. W. E. B. Du Bois and others, however, placed the number of black and white casualties much higher and contended that the riot produced at least 5,000 black refugees. The higher white death toll is partially attributed to a statement by the black mortician Howard that no one had an idea of the number of white casualties, as he had been forced to bury an untold number of whites in the black cemetery. This was done to conceal the number of whites being killed by blacks during the course of the riot.

The riot profoundly affected the individual and collective lives of all Atlantans, particularly black Atlantans. Many black families, who were terrified and left unprotected, sold their homes, often at great sacrifices, and fled to the North and West. Labor remained scarce and wages high in Atlanta because of the riot. The roles of such men as Hope at Morehouse and Bowen at Gammon increased their stature in the black communities and fostered closer relations between the colleges and their neighbors. A similar enhancement of influence was accorded to the Reverend Proctor and his First Congregational Church. It became known as the "church that saved a city." But for Walter White, the events produced a transformation of his entire life. For although he had blue eyes and blond of hair and only a fraction of African American blood, he came to know, in the wake of the riot, who he really was—a black man who could be marked for indiscriminate murder by whites. And so, despite his white features, he decided in those hours of racial warfare in Atlanta to cast his lot with the Negro race and to do what he could for its elevation and liberation. He became active in the local NAACP, then assistant secretary in the national office of the civil rights organization, and finally executive secretary from 1931 until his death in 1955. During these years he used his pale complexion to infiltrate the ranks of white lynchers and later exposed the perpetrators to law enforcement authorities.

The calamitous events of the early fall of 1906 also had a sobering and beneficial, if only a temporary, effect on white attitudes and race relations, generally, in Atlanta. The Journalist Ray Stannard Baker, who traveled to the city immediately after the riot, found that the most important and far-reaching effect of the tragedy was that it aroused the white men of the city. Some of these men first met at the Piedmont Hotel on the Sunday after the first rioting and then again at the county courthouse Tuesday afternoon following the news from Brownsville. They resolved that the rioting must stop. Among those in attendance was Sam D. Jones, president of the local chamber of commerce, and Charles T. Hopkins, a businessman. Hopkins decried the financial damage that the events had created in the city.

While Hopkins's statements were replete with paternalism, they represented, at the time, a major metamorphosis in prevailing white attitudes and was a foundation on which better racial harmony could be built. Hopkins's extension of the olive branch on behalf of whites was first met by Dr. W. F. Penn, a prominent black physician, who had graduated from Yale College. He told a meeting of concerned whites of his own experience during the riot. A group of white men, some of whose families he had treated professionally, came to his house to search for weapons. His young daughter had run to them and begged them not to shoot her father. Later, however, a mob appeared, threatened the family, and forced them from their home. He credited a white man passing in an automobile for saving their own lives.

The pleading and conciliatory tone of the Penn speech, which was received as profound, inspired the ex-Confederate veteran and real estate man, Colonel A. J. McBride to stand up and vow that Atlanta would protect such "good" black men as Dr. Penn. Colonel McBride stated that he would even defend such men with his own rifle. Amid these warm feelings, exemplified by the words of Hopkins, Penn, and McBride, Hopkins proposed that the white people of the city express their deep regret for the riot and show their sympathy for the blacks who had suffered at the hands of the mob by raising money to assist them. A total of $4,423 was pledged immediately and the city government later added an additional $1,000.

The group then turned its attention to reconstruction and prevention of a recurrence of racial violence in the city. A committee consisting of some of the most influential men in the city was appointed to work with public officials in restoring order and confidence. Among them were Charles Hopkins and Sam Jones; L. Z. Rossen, president of the board of education; J. W. English, a bank president; Forrest Adair, a leading realtor; W. D. Ellis, an attorney; A. B. Steele, a wealthy lumberman; M. L. Collier, a railroad executive; and H. Y. McCord, a wholesale grocer. Shortly after its formation, this group sent for several of the most prominent black leaders in the city, including Reverend Hugh Proctor, Benjamin Davis, and the Reverends E. P. Johnson, E. R. Carter, J. A. Rush, and Lucius Holsey.

The meeting of the representatives of the two races, the first important occasion in the South on which an attempt was made to get blacks and whites together for any serious consideration of their differences, began with the whites asking the blacks: "What shall we do to relieve the irritation?" Blacks replied that they thought that they were treated with unnecessary roughness on the streetcars by the police. The whites admitted that the claim was justified and promised to take the matter up immediately with the streetcar company and the police department.

From this beginning, Hopkins invited 2,000 additional, influential local whites to join the efforts of racial peace; 1,500 accepted immediately, only two refused outright, and those "anonymously." Five hundred more men, who were not initially invited, asked to join and were accepted. The enlarged group became formally known as the Atlanta Civic League. At the same time, Reverend Proctor and the committee of blacks recruited 1,500 for the "Coloured Co-operative Civic League." Small subcommittees from each group were then appointed to meet together to further the cause of racial goodwill and law and order.

There was some fear, however, that the merriment of the Christmas season might lead to a renewal of racial violence. With the encouragement of the leagues, strenuous preventive efforts were instituted. New policemen were hired and municipal judges Broylee and Roan warned against lawlessness. The leagues secured promises from the local press that it would not publish "sensational news," and they asked that saloons be closed at 4 P.M. on Christmas Eve. Black league members made a special effort to keep members of their race off the streets. The success of the leagues influenced and inspired other movements for improved race relations. Several white ministers promoted the effort in letters to the *Atlanta Constitution*. The newspaper's editor and former gubernational candidate, Clark Howell, responded with a conciliatory editorial entitled, "Shall We Blaze the Trail?" Ex-Governor W. J. Northern called a prayer meeting, attended by 20 whites and 20 blacks, at the black Butler Street YMCA and traveled throughout the state speaking in favor of law and order. He condemned mob violence, including lynching, and predicted that racial problems would not be resolved until African Americans had full justice. The belief that saloons, dives, and other places of vice had contributed to the riot helped to inspire the antisaloon campaign, which took place throughout the state in 1907. The success of this movement led to the temporary closing of every saloon in the state of Georgia on the first of January, 1908.

It is clear, then, that the short-range effects of the riot were generally positive, in the sense that white leaders throughout the state, but especially in Atlanta, seemed to cast aside old prejudices to work for racial harmony and for civil peace. Not all segments of white Atlanta and white Georgia were repentant, but the attitudes and actions of Governor Northern, Governor-Elect Hoke Smith, Editor Clark Howell, Charles Hopkins, and Colonel McBride seemed more representative of white opinion that that of the Atlanta *Evening News*. This newspaper, which had helped ferment the riot, declared in an end-of-the-year editorial that black men who attacked white women will know the vengeance of whites—a not so subtle threat to lynch black men.

As to the lasting consequences of the riot and the reconstruction, it can be said that Atlanta never again witnessed such a distinctive occurrence, even during the racial turmoil of the 1960s. It can also be said, however, that the problems of racial segregation, racial equality, and political rights were barely touched by either the white or black reformers. Most of the whites seemed content with the recent Supreme Court ruling in *Plessy v. Ferguson* (1896), which upheld segregated public facilities for the races; and among the blacks, there were serious divisions among the leaders as to the wisdom of mounting assaults, vocal or otherwise, against Jim Crow.

See also: Disfranchisement; Du Bois, W. E. B.; Jim Crow; White, Walter; White Mob Violence

Alton Hornsby Jr.

Bibliography

Bauerlein, Mark. *Negrophobia: A Race Riot in Atlanta, 1906.* San Francisco: Encounter Books, 2001.

Burns, Rebecca. *Rage in the Gate City: The Story of the 1906 Atlanta Race Riot.* Cincinnati: Emmis Books, 2006.

Godshalk, David Fort. *Veiled Visions: The 1906 Atlanta Race Riot and the Reshaping of American Race Relations.* Chapel Hill: University of North Carolina Press, 2005.

Mixon, Gregory. *The Atlanta Riot: Race, Class, and Violence in a New South City.* Gainesville: University Press of Florida, 2005.

Baker, Ella

Ella Baker (1903–1986) was one of the most influential African Americans in the Civil Rights movement of the 20th century. Born in Norfolk, Virginia, on December 13, 1903, Baker worked throughout her 83 years of life to advance the position of African Americans. An African American herself, Baker worked as both an organizer and an activist in well-known civil rights organizations such as the National Association for the Advancement of Colored People (NAACP), the Southern Christian Leadership Conference (SCLC), the Student Nonviolent Coordinating Committee (SNCC), and the Mississippi Freedom Democratic Party (MFDP).

Baker moved to North Carolina in 1911. Seven years later, she entered Shaw University in Raleigh. In 1927, she graduated valedictorian of her class. Although Baker wanted to enter graduate school, her financial situation would not allow it. She instead moved to Harlem, New York. While there, Baker became actively involved in organizing and promoting the advancement of African Americans. From 1929 to 1932, she was a member of the editorial staffs of the *American West Indian News* and the *Negro National News.* During the Great Depression she accepted a position with the Works Progress Administration (WPA).

In 1938, Baker began working with one of the most renowned civil rights organizations in the country—the NAACP. By 1942, she was named national director of all the NAACP branches. It was in this position that Baker greatly expanded her contacts within the African American community. In 1946, however, she left the national office over a conflict of interests. Baker felt that the NAACP was overly concerned with the opinions and recognition of whites and middle-class blacks. She, on the other hand, thought more attention needed to be given to the lower class black masses.

Although Baker removed herself from the national office, she remained involved on the local level. In 1954, she became president of the New York City branch of the NAACP. As president she aimed to bring the movement back to the masses.

In the mid-1950s, Baker, along with A. Phillip Randolph, Bayard Rustin, and Stanley Levinson, formed In Friendship, a New York-based organization that provided economic assistance for disadvantaged blacks in the South. After the eruption of the Montgomery Bus Boycott, following Rosa Parks' refusal to give up her seat on a Montgomery bus, In Friendship worked to raise funds for the Montgomery efforts. When the boycott ended with the Supreme Court's decision to desegregate transportation, In Friendship united with several other newly created civil rights organizations to form the Southern Christian Leadership Conference (SCLC). Baker became the first full-time executive director of the SCLC. Her involvement in the organization, however, was short lived. As with the NAACP, Baker did not feel she fit in with the SCLC. The organization was primarily composed of clergy. Baker, as a woman, and an older woman at that, knew she had little place within the organization for leadership roles. Furthermore, Baker disliked the leadership style of the SCLC. Baker believed that civil rights organizations should be group centered. The SCLC, like the NAACP, was more individual centered.

Baker's role with the SCLC allowed her to assist in the creation of the Student Nonviolent Coordinating Committee (SNCC). In the late 1950s, the sit-in movement erupted among black college students throughout the South. Initially many of the sit-ins were disconnected; Baker used the numerous contacts she had made through the NAACP and SCLC to bring the detached demonstrations together. In 1960, Baker convinced the SCLC to sponsor a meeting of student activists at her alma mater, Shaw University. The NAACP, SCLC, and Congress for Racial Equality (CORE) all sent representatives to the meeting. The meeting culminated with the creation of SNCC, with Baker as its primary advisor. Other civil rights organizations, like the NAACP, SCLC, and CORE, all wanted in on the action, but Baker worked to keep the students in SNCC independent of other adult civil rights organizations. By 1961, SNCC had become the organization that Baker had been trying to create for several years. Unlike the SCLC, SNCC allowed for the active participation of women and young people. Unlike the NAACP, SNCC took civil rights back to the masses. Most

Ella Baker, an active member of the Southern Christian Leadership Conference (SCLC) and founding member of the Student Nonviolent Coordinating Committee (SNCC), was one of the most important civil rights leaders of the 1960s. (Library of Congress)

Civil Rights movement and bring freedom to her fellow African Americans. Baker's contributions to the advancement of African Americans are immeasurable. She worked with the NAACP in the 1940s, the SCLC in the 1950s, and SNCC and the MFDP in the 1960s. With each organization she enlarged the Civil Rights movement and advanced the African American struggle for freedom and equality.

See also: Carmichael, Stokely (Kwame Ture); Southern Christian Leadership Conference; Student Nonviolent Coordinating Committee

Mindy R. Weidman

Bibliography

Dallard, Shyrlee. *Ella Baker: A Leader Behind the Scenes.* Englewood, NJ: Silver Burdett, 1990.

Grant, Joanne. *Ella Baker: Freedom Bound.* New York: Wiley, 1998.

Ransby, Barbara. *Ella Baker and the Black Freedom Movement: A Radical Democratic Vision.* Chapel Hill: University of North Carolina Press, 2003.

Baldwin, James

Once regarded as the heir to Richard Wright, the preeminent African American novelist, James Baldwin (1924–1987) did not sustain his early achievement. Today, he may be most remembered as an essayist, in particular for several collections of essays published in the 1950s and 1960s that made him one of the most important literary spokespersons for the Civil Rights movement.

Born in Harlem, Baldwin was adopted by his stepfather, a factory worker named David Baldwin, when he was still very young. Although Baldwin would be much influenced by his stepfather's avocation as a street-corner evangelist, they had a very troubled relationship that left scars on Baldwin's sense of self-esteem. His experiences in school had a more salutary effect. From an early age, he had escaped into the local library and into the books that he read voraciously. At Frederick Douglass Junior High School, one of Baldwin's teachers and early mentor's was the poet Countee Cullen, who encouraged the thoughtful reader to become a committed writer. At Frederick Douglass and at DeWitt Clinton High School, Baldwin would publish his first stories and essays in the school newspapers.

During his teens, Baldwin also became a popular preacher at the Fireside Pentecostal Assembly. The leader of

important, SNCC's leadership, unlike either the SCLC or NAACP, was group centered.

Baker remained actively involved with SNCC over the next few years. In 1964, she helped to organize the Mississippi Freedom Democratic Party (MFDP). The MFDP sought to combat the disenfranchisement of African Americans in the South. The organization forced the Democratic Party to elect many black leaders in Mississippi. Baker remained involved in the Civil Rights movement until her death on December 13, 1986.

Ella Baker will forever be remembered for her contributions to the advancement of African Americans. More than anything else, she believed in the power of the masses to organize and demand change. Throughout her life, Baker was the organizational factor behind many of the civil rights organizations of the 1950s and 1960s. She never wanted to make a name for herself, but rather, wished to enlarge the this storefront church in Harlem was Mother Horn, whose influence on Baldwin was profound. Whereas his stepfather had stressed the fear of divine retribution, Mother Horn emphasized the beneficent effects of divine love and Christian fellowship. In addition, Baldwin's experience as a preacher would show itself in the biblical cadences in much of his writing, especially his essays.

After high school, Baldwin moved to New Jersey, where he worked on a construction crew and, for the first time, was exposed for sustained periods to virulent racism. His stepfather's death in an asylum coincided with the outbreak of terrible rioting in Harlem, and this combination of family and public traumas compelled Baldwin to commit himself to his writing. He began living in Greenwich Village, where his exposure to the Bohemian lifestyle and radical activism awakened hedonistic and political impulses in him that would be every bit as intense as his earlier religious fervor.

Baldwin's literary career really began with his receiving the Eugene F. Saxton Memorial Trust Award, on the recommendation of Richard Wright. As his first essays and stories began to appear in magazines, he started to work on his first novel. His progress was slowed by personal issues, primarily his struggle to accept his homosexuality after his relationship with a woman had led to their formal engagement. In the wake of the end of that relationship, Baldwin followed Wright to France. There, as he established relationships with all sorts of writers and artists, his relationship with Wright soured, and for much of his subsequent career, Baldwin would be very conscious of trying to step out of Wright's shadow.

Baldwin's first novel, *Go Tell It on the Mountain* (1953), was a pointedly autobiographical coming-of-age story. Powerfully immediate and intimate, this debut effort is considered by many critics to be Baldwin's most fully realized novel. Set on a single day that provides a microcosm of a family's life together, the novel focuses on the strained relationship between a preacher with a hard temperament and his teenage stepson.

As the Civil Rights movement gathered momentum, Baldwin was inspired to write some of the seminal essays on race in America collected in *Notes of a Native Son* (1955), *Nobody Knows My Name: More Notes of a Native Son* (1961), and *The Fire Next Time* (1963). In these essays, Baldwin managed to combine eloquent and incisive insight with a deep sense of personal and communal rage as he exposed the pernicious causes and effects of the continuing social, economic, political, and cultural oppression of African Americans. He warned white America that the extended quest for equality had very nearly exhausted the patience of African Americans and had pushed them to a revolutionary edge.

In his second novel, *Giovanni's Room* (1956), Baldwin created a sensation with his unsparing exploration of issues of identity related to both race and sexual orientation. After Knopf refused to publish it, the novel was published first in the United Kingdom and then picked up by Dial in the United States. The novel draws on Baldwin's own complicated personal relationships before he emigrated to France, but it is set among expatriates in France and Spain.

Baldwin's later novels include *Tell Me How Long the Train's Been Gone* (1968), *If Beale Street Could Talk* (1974), *Just above My Head* (1979), and *Harlem Quartet* (1987). His short stories are collected in *Going to Meet the Man* (1965), and his best-known plays are *The Amen Corner* (1955) and *Blues for Mister Charlie* (1964).

Over the last two decades of his life, Baldwin continued to produce work in a variety of genres. But increasingly he seemed a prematurely anachronistic figure. In the course of the social revolution of the 1960s, the political and sexual radicalism that he had given voice to in the 1950s suddenly seemed quite dated, even tame. Having spent much of his career trying to step out of Richard Wright's shadow, Baldwin now found himself in the uncomfortable position of seeing his later work overshadowed by his earlier work

See also: Black Folk Culture; Wright, Richard

Martin Kich

Bibliography

Balfour, Katharine Lawrence. *The Evidence of Things Not Said: James Baldwin and the Promise of American Democracy.* Ithaca: Cornell University Press, 2001.

Bloom, Harold, ed. *James Baldwin.* New York: Chelsea House, 1986.

Bobia, Rosa. *The Critical Reception of James Baldwin in France.* New York: Peter Lang, 1997.

Campbell, James. *Talking at the Gates: A Life of James Baldwin.* Berkeley: University of California Press, 2002.

Clark, Keith. *Black Manhood in James Baldwin, Ernest J. Gaines, and August Wilson.* Urbana: University of Illinois Press, 2002.

Kollhofer, Jakob, ed. *James Baldwin: His Place in American Literary History and His Reception in Europe.* New York: Peter Lang, 1991.

Leeming, David Adams. *James Baldwin: A Biography.* New York: Knopf, 1994.

McBride, Dwight A., ed. *James Baldwin Now.* New York: New York University Press, 1999.

Porter, Horace A. *Stealing the Fire: The Art and Protest of James Baldwin.* Middletown, CT: Wesleyan University Press, 1989.

Baraka, Amiri

Amiri Baraka (1934–) is a writer who is perhaps best known as the founder of the black arts movement. Born as Leroi Jones on October 7, 1934, in a lower middle-class neighborhood of Newark, New Jersey, he attended predominately white public schools, then Rutgers University and Howard University, before beginning military service in the U.S. Air Force in 1954. After his release from the military in 1957, he attended graduate school and moved to New York's Greenwich Village, where he met and married a white woman, Hettie Cohen. The couple went on to have two daughters. Baraka lived in the Village from 1957 to 1965, working as an editor, poet, dramatist, and jazz critic. He befriended numerous beat writers, including Allen Ginsberg and Frank O'Hara, and established a beat magazine called *Yugen.* As part of the Village's bohemian, avant-garde crowd, he published his first major collection of poetry, *Preface to a Twenty Volume Suicide Note* (1961). Throughout these poems, Baraka drew on the styles of the beat poets to combine stream of consciousness, projective free verse, and dialect.

By 1962, he was pulling away from Ginsberg and rejecting the otherworldly poetics of beat writers. In his early poetry, Baraka had meditated on the black man's loneliness. Excluded from white America, he was also disconnected from black Africa, and Baraka laid out that racial isolation. His focus on the existential isolation of African Americans would soon translate into the solution of black nationalism, a nation within a nation, and so a home for black people in white America. In 1964 and 1965, he shifted from introspective, semiautobiographical poetry to forge a collective voice in his work. No longer writing out of lyric self-consciousness, he produced poems of lyrical communism.

By 1965, Baraka was celebrating the African heritage of African Americans. Black Americans have African imaginations, are beautiful, and must embrace blackness as he put it in 1966. He offered a shift from dislocated black American to proud African American, declared a hatred for the black middle class (equating its values with Euro-American values), and expressed one of the tenets of black nationalism: the assertion of black Americans' identity as a people of African ancestry.

Baraka began to seek out friendships with black nationalists including Stokely Carmichael. Moving to Harlem in the wake of Malcolm's death, he also married a black poet, Sylvia Robinson, in 1967, and the same year converted to Islam. To express this transformation, he changed his name from Leroi Jones to Imamu ("spiritual leader") Amiri ("warrior") Baraka ("sacrifice"). Becoming more and more engaged with black nationalist politics, Baraka assumed leadership of his own black Muslim organization, Kawaida. From 1968 to 1975, he also chaired the Committee for Unified Newark, a Black United Front organization, and he was a prominent figure in the National Black Political Convention of 1972.

The beat poet had become a black nationalist. Baraka believed that art could create this black "Nation" and he challenged black artists to create a "Black Poem" and a "Black World" in his 1966 poem "Black Art." Explaining that he wanted to go beyond mere poetry to achieve literature as action, he called for art that both described the situation of black people *and* showed how to change it. He also formulated a theory of the "theater of assault." Laying out his manifesto for a new kind of theater in 1965, Baraka explained that revolutionary theater should force change and be a political weapon. To its shocked audiences and dazzled critics, Baraka's play *Dutchman* (1964) perhaps seemed just that kind of revolutionary theater. The story of a deathly encounter between a white woman and a black college student, it depicted a seemingly unstoppable race war between black and white Americans. It went on to win an Obie Award, was proclaimed the best play in America by Norman Mailer, and in 2007 it was controversially revived in New York.

In July 1967, Amiri Baraka was arrested for unlawfully carrying a weapon during the Newark Rebellion. The trial judge read Baraka's poem "Black People" (1967) to the all-white jury. "I'm being sentenced for the poem. Is that what you are saying?" responded Baraka. Although not published until *after* the riots, "Black People" seemed a call to violence: "We must make our own World...and we cannot do this unless the white man is dead. Let's get together and kill him" (*The LeRoi Jones/Amiri Baraka Reader,* p. 224). The poem was admitted as evidence of a plot to ignite violence and on January 4, 1968, Baraka was sentenced to three

Playwright, poet, and figure in the black arts and Black Power movements, Amiri Baraka leads a delegation of Newark public school students from the State House after the group disrupted a session of the State Senate by leaving the chamber chanting. The students were protesting the legislature's failure to enact a tax plan to fund New Jersey's public schools, May 27, 1975. (Bettmann/Corbis)

years in New Jersey's state penitentiary and fined $1,000 (although the conviction was overturned on appeal).

This incident illustrates the longstanding fusion of politics and art at the center of Baraka's work, a canon that encompasses 14 books of poetry, 24 plays, 5 books of essays, 4 anthologies, and a novel. As he explained in a recent interview, "all art is political" and no literature exists in a vacuum. Any suggestion to the contrary is meant "only to have us look away from the real world so that…all's well in the big house while the great majority—slaves, serfs, the generally exploited—suffer out of sight" (*American Protest Literature*, p. 375).

In part because of this insistence on the political nature of art, Baraka is a controversial figure in American literature. Even more controversial is his use of art to advocate violence. As with "Black People," his poems often call for violent action. Not only using art to advocate violence, he

also imagines art *as* violent: in numerous poems he demands that writers be warriors, describes language as a weapon, and fashions poems themselves as daggers, fists, and poison gas.

These calls to violence echo the rhetoric of the black militant leader Malcolm X, as do Baraka's repeated critiques of nonviolence as a continuing with the status quo. In fact, Malcolm's influence on Baraka was profound. Malcolm was killed while speaking in Harlem, on February 21, 1965. Responding to the assassination, Baraka wrote "A Poem for Black Hearts" (1965). Here he celebrates and mourns Malcolm X. Also in response to the assassination, Baraka left his white wife, moved uptown to Harlem from his Greenwich Village home, and embraced black nationalism.

Emphasizing his transformation still further, Baraka published a series of black nationalist poems. His hostility toward all white people appears in numerous other poems from this period, and his rejection of any cross-racial collaboration was even more evident during an infamous encounter with a white woman. She stated her desire to help solve racial tensions, and Baraka replied that she can help by dying. As well, several of his poems discuss raping white women as a way to counterbalance the oppression of black men. Leading to further criticism of his gender politics, Baraka went on to demonstrate an apparent hostility to all women, black or white. For example, he controversially stated that the recovery of healthy African identities depended on distinct gender roles and a submissive femininity.

Another new aesthetic that Baraka explored was the jazz avant-garde. Musical freedom as social activism continued the work of Harlem Renaissance poets Langston Hughes and James Weldon Johnson, and, in a recent interview, Baraka observed that the black arts movement (BAM) was on a continuum with the Harlem Renaissance. But Baraka also noted in the same interview that BAM was a version of Mao's Cultural Revolution. Baraka's references to Mao are in fact representative of his worldview after a second major transformation: from a black nationalist to a third world Marxist, in 1974. A trip to Cuba in 1960 had begun to radicalize his thinking about oppression in the third world, and in the mid-1970s, he proclaimed a complete identification with the artists he had met on his trip. Dissatisfied with Kenneth Gibson's black bourgeois leadership of their Newark organization and newly impassioned by theories of African socialism, he reformed the Congress of African People as the Revolutionary Communist League.

This final transformation came with an unexpected shift to humor. His early work, from the late 1950s and early 1960s, had focused on the themes of death and despair, of moral and social corruption, and of self-hatred. His black nationalist poems of 1965–1975 are militant in tone. And his later poems frequently exhibit a comic sensibility. Baraka's life and art therefore falls into these three periods: beat generation, black nationalism, third world Marxism. But the thread that runs throughout is his stated belief that "ethics and aesthetics are one" (*American Protest Literature*, p. 375).

See also: Black Arts Movement; Black Nationalism; Black Power; Destination, Cuba; X, Malcolm

Zoe Trodd

Bibliography

Baraka, Amiri. *Home: Social Essays.* New York: Morrow, 1966.

Baraka, Amiri. *Raise, Race, Rays, Raze: Essays since 1965.* New York: Random House, 1972.

Baraka, Amiri. *Selected Poetry of Amiri Baraka/LeRoi Jones.* New York: Morrow, 1979.

Harris, William J., ed. *The LeRoi Jones/Amiri Baraka Reader.* New York: Thunder's Mouth Press, 1991.

Trodd, Zoe, ed. *American Protest Literature.* Cambridge, MA: Harvard University Press, 2006.

Watts, Jerry Gafio. *Amiri Baraka: The Politics and Art of a Black Intellectual.* New York: New York University Press, 2001.

Bass, Charlotta Amanda Spears

Charlotta Amanda Spears Bass (1879–1966) was a journalist and activist who fought vigorously to end racial discrimination and injustice for African Americans and other groups in the United States. During her 40-year career, she used her power as owner of the *California Eagle,* at the time the oldest black newspaper on the West Coast, and her affiliation with multiple community and national organizations as vehicles to advance a range of social justice causes. Her grassroots, community-based campaigns galvanized her readers and co-citizens to combat racism, to fight housing and employment discrimination, and to use their vote to empower themselves. In 1952, she made history by becoming the first African American woman to run for vice president of the United States. An independent thinker, her progressive ideas on social justice were sometimes out of step with the black press and African American leaders. Because of her militant activism, she endured character assassinations, lawsuits, a government investigation, and death threats, but she was undeterred in her career-long battle to end racial and social injustice.

Spears was born in Sumpter, South Carolina, in 1874. She was the sixth of 11 children born to Hiram and Kate Spears. After graduating from public schools, Charlotta Spears attended Pembroke College for one semester before moving to Providence, Rhode Island, around the turn of the century. She found employment with the *Providence Watchman,* a local newspaper, but would later migrate to Los Angeles, California because of a health ailment. In September 1910, she took a job selling subscriptions for a struggling African American newspaper, the *Advocate,* later renamed the *Eagle.* Before his death, the owner of the paper, John

Neimore, asked Spears to assume editorship of the *Eagle.* When Neimore died, a benefactor purchased the *Eagle* for $50 and handed it over to Spears. In later years, Spears would reflect that her belief in the Constitution, in the Bill of Rights, and in the idea that all rights "must be defended" induced her to become a newspaper editor and owner. Spears's mission of social justice put her in line with the majority of the black press. Because racial advocacy and uplift were more important than financial gain, Spears's responsibilities at the *Eagle* included publisher, editor, reporter, business manager, distributor, printer, and janitor.

In 1913, Spears hired Joseph Blackburn "J. B." Bass, a 50-year-old veteran journalist as a reporter. Spears became managing editor and the two married in 1914. As a team they tackled different forms of discrimination in Los Angeles, always placing the *Eagle* at the center of any battle. Among their first battles was the campaign to halt the production of D. W. Griffith's 1915 motion picture *The Birth of a Nation.* The movie glorified the Ku Klux Klan and depicted black males as buffoons and racists. For weeks on the editorial pages of the *Eagle,* Bass excoriated the film and the Los Angeles mayor for permitting its production. At the same time she rallied other civic organizations, notably the Los Angeles branch of the National Association for the Advancement of Colored People (NAACP) to stage a "citizen's protest" against making the film. The campaign met with some initial success when the Los Angeles City Council voted to halt production, but the decision was overturned in court. Nevertheless, this campaign established Bass and her husband as bold community activists.

In her zeal to oppose racism and discrimination in the 1920s, Bass aligned herself with two strong national black organizations that adopted divergent strategies for achieving civil rights for African Americans. In addition to joining her local chapter of the NAACP, which adopted integrationist goals and approaches to fighting black oppression, Bass, her husband, and several other prominent African Americans chartered a chapter of the United Negro Improvement Association (UNIA). Created by black nationalist Marcus Garvey, the UNIA promoted racial separatism. Despite their divergent approaches, these national organizations served as resources for Bass in the local battles she waged against discrimination and injustice.

One such battle in the 1920s was defending herself against a leader of the California Ku Klux Klan who sued Bass and the *Eagle* after she exposed a plan by white supremacists to burn down a black family's house. The paper also revealed that the Klan was distributing hate literature in a local neighborhood. The court ruled in favor of Bass and the victory magnified her reputation as a fearless opponent of any form of social injustice.

By the 1930s, Bass's approach to fighting discrimination had crystallized into three main tactics: wage a rhetorical war against her opponents in the pages of her newspaper, enter into diplomatic negotiations with the opposition, and rally citizens to initiate direct action with boycotts or pickets. These tactics won several victories for causes she and her husband pursued in the 1920s and early 1930s. Bass's husband died in 1934, but she continued to use the same tactics for the remainder of her career.

Among the most important and longest battles of Bass's career was her effort to strike down racially restrictive housing covenants designed to bar African Americans and other minorities from living in many areas of Los Angeles. Her first involvement with this issue came early in her career in 1914 when a black woman sought help from the *Eagle* after being thrown out of her home in a predominantly white neighborhood and threatened with jail if she returned. After Bass mobilized dozens of women to form a picket in front of the woman's house, the sheriff relented and she moved back into her home.

By the 1940s, the problem of racially and ethnically restrictive housing covenants, a prevalent and longstanding practice in Los Angeles, became more acute as droves of people of color came to the city looking for employment. Bass fought hard against restrictive covenants by denouncing them in her paper and by cofounding the Home Protective Association to support citizens in standing up against unfair housing practices. For example, in 1942, she fought the residents in the white suburb of Maywood over renewal of their racially restrictive covenant. Bass published an "Open Letter to the Citizens of Maywood" calling for an end to the policy, and she tried to galvanize opposition to the restrictions at public meetings. Bass lost this battle when the community voted to renew its restrictive policy.

Bass did not lose all such battles, however. In 1945, she encouraged wealthy black actors, lawyers, and doctors involved in the "Sugar Hill" case to fight the restrictive covenant their white neighbors passed to force them from their affluent neighborhood. On Bass's advice and with the editorial support she lent through the *Eagle,* the group united, fought, and won the case. Bass also championed middle and lower income citizens' fight against unfair housing practices. Her support of the Laws family in their seven-year battle to occupy the home they purchased in a white neighborhood demonstrated her commitment to the issue and to the victims of discrimination. Bass placed the rhetorical power of the *Eagle* behind them to keep their situation before the community throughout their struggle. Significantly, during this time she expanded her agenda on the housing issue by raising awareness among *Eagle* readers about the struggle of Mexican American families to pressure the city to alleviate slum conditions in their neighborhoods. At the end of World War II, Bass also pushed for desegregated housing for veterans. Bass and other leaders pushed the housing covenant issue through to the California Supreme Court. Finally, in 1948, the United States Supreme Court ruled such covenants to be unconstitutional.

Employment discrimination is another issue that saw the force of Bass's activism. In 1919, when Bass discovered that the Los Angeles County General Hospital refused to hire African Americans, she reported this policy to her readers in the *Eagle,* but also appealed directly to hospital supervisors, who finally agreed to hire blacks for selected positions. Bass waged a successful but longer campaign in 1933 to persuade the South California Telephone Company to hire blacks. In her typical fashion, she fought the company on the rhetorical front calling on her readers to boycott the utility company and engaged in more strategies through the activities of the Industrial Council, an organization she had created in 1930 to generate more employment and business opportunities for African Americans. The telephone company relented and hired blacks three years later.

Bass's uncompromising opposition to employment discrimination is also evident in her staunch support in the 1930s of the "Don't Buy Where You Can't Work Campaign," a national effort among blacks to end unfair employment practices. On the pages of the *Eagle* during World War II, Bass exposed discriminatory practices of California's thriving defense industry that systematically kept African Americans out of the industry's well-paying jobs. One successful effort in this campaign compelled the United States Employment Service to change its practice of excluding black women from holding defense jobs. Bass used her affiliation with the Los Angeles Negro Victory Committee and the *Eagle* to call on African American women to march to the Employment Service in large numbers and consistently insist they be given jobs. The tactic worked and black women were hired.

Although Bass initially represented the grievances only of African American workers like the Brotherhood of Sleeping Car Porters in the mid 1920s, she gradually became a voice for the rights of all industrial workers. In the 1930s, she used her editorial powers to support the strike against the American Tobacco Company, the first interracial strike in American history; in her front-page column, "On the Sidewalk," she informed readers about union and labor movement news including longshoremen strikes and various local CIO campaigns for workers' rights.

Workers' rights and civil rights melded as Bass expanded her advocacy beyond her own racial community. This shift is evident in her board membership on the Civil Rights Congress, a group that advocated on behalf of Mexican Americans and other people of color. This group was largely dedicated to fighting the kind of police brutality witnessed in the "Sleepy Lagoon" case in which several Mexican American youths were beaten, jailed, and charged with murder. Bass and other supporters of the jailed youths charged that the evidence against the youths was based primarily in ethnocentric judgments about the "flamboyant" clothing called "zoot suits" the youths wore. For Bass, the case illuminated the vulnerability to racism all minorities in Los Angeles faced, and she broadened her concern for the rights of all oppressed groups.

Throughout her career, Bass was active in electoral politics. She reported political activities in her newspapers, but she was also a political operative; however, she identified less with parties than with candidates' stance on issues. Although she was a registered member of the Republican Party for most of her career, she would back a Democratic or independent candidate if she felt the candidate demonstrated a stronger commitment to racial justice. This position led her to support Franklin D. Roosevelt in the 1932 presidential elections, as did many African Americans of this period.

Bass ran for public office twice in her career. In 1945, she ran as an independent candidate for the Los Angeles City Council but lost her bid in a run-off election. Frustrated by the failure of both the Democratic and Republican parties to advocate a strong civil rights program, she abandoned them in 1947for the leftwing Progressive Party and became a vocal critic of U.S. foreign policy. She made her second bid for political office in 1950 when she ran for Congress on the Progressive Party ticket. She lost the election.

Toward the end of the 1940s, Bass's positions on domestic issues and foreign policy were out of step with mainstream local and national African American leadership. The Federal Bureau of Investigation (FBI) and some members of the black press leveled charges of communism and subversion against her and, consequently, she lost credibility and readers. Although she publicly denied her support of communism, the financial losses that resulted from the accusations forced her to sell the paper in 1951. After she sold the paper she advanced her social justice agenda by working full-time with the Independent Progressive Party. In 1952, she became the party's vice presidential candidate. She and her white running mate, civil rights attorney, Vincent Hallinan, received less than 1 percent of the vote, but her campaign slogan bespeaks her perspective of the importance the Progressive Party's campaign held for public debate, "Win or Lose, We Win by Raising the Issues," and the issues for her were racism, civil rights, workers' rights, the Korean War, and U.S. imperialism.

After the election, Bass retired to a small community in Los Angeles but continued to support the movement for civil rights that gained momentum in the mid 1950s and extended into the 1960s. She transformed the garage of her home into a community reading room that served as a voter registration site for African Americans. She died of a stroke in 1966.

See also: Brotherhood of Sleeping Car Porters; Cold War and Civil Rights; Garvey, Marcus; Ku Klux Klan; National Association for the Advancement of Colored People; Republican Party; *The Birth of a Nation;* Universal Negro Improvement Association; White Supremacy

Cynthia King

Bibliography

Buni, Andrew, and Carol Hurd Green. "Charlotta A. Bass." In *Notable American Women: The Modern Period: A Biographical Dictionary,* Barbara Sicherman and Carol Hurd Green, eds., 61–63. Cambridge: The Belknap Press of Harvard University Press, 1980.

Freer, Regina. "LA Race Woman: Charlotta Bass and the Complexities of Black Political Development in Los Angeles." *American Quarterly* 56, no. 3 (2004):607–32.

Gill, Gerald R. "Win or Lose—We Win: The 1952 Vice-Presidential Campaign of Charlotta A. Bass." In *The Afro-American Woman: Struggles and Images,* Sharon Harley and Rosalyn Terborg-Penn, eds., 109–19. Baltimore: Black Classic Press, 1997.

Leavitt, Jacqueline. "Charlotta A. Bass, *The California Eagle,* and Black Settlement in Los Angeles." In *Urban Planning and the African American Community: In the Shadows,* Jane Manning Thomas and Marsha Ritzdorf, eds., 167–86. Thousand Oaks, CA: Sage Publications, 1997.

Streitmatter, Rodger. *African-American Women Journalists Who Changed History.* Lexington: The University Press of Kentucky, 1994.

Bates, Daisy

Daisy Bates (1914–1999) was an African American civil rights activist, journalist, author, and National Association for the Advancement of Colored People (NAACP) leader during the Little Rock School crisis of 1957. Bates was president of the Arkansas State NAACP and a publisher of the *Arkansas State Press* during the crisis. She helped direct negotiations between the Little Rock School Board, state, and federal authorities, while focusing primarily on the nine students' well-being.

Born Daisy Lee Gatson in tiny Huttig of southern Arkansas, she grew up with friends of her original parents after her mother was killed by whites and her father fled town. This pushed Daisy to fight for racial equality throughout her life. At 15, she and L. C. Bates began dating and married three years later. Although L. C. Bates was an insurance salesman when he first met Daisy, he received an education in journalism and worked for several black-owned newspapers.

They leased a struggling church-owned press and began printing the *Arkansas State Press.* The Little Rock newspaper focused on civil rights issues. Besides journalism, the Bateses spent time working for the NAACP. Daisy was not a member of Little Rock's black upper crust. She never completed college, did not have a significant role in the African American church, or was not wealthy. Yet she still managed to rise in the organization, eventually becoming president of the state's confluence of local NAACP branches in 1952.

After the *Brown v. Board* case, school desegregation became the Arkansas NAACP's primary focus. Bates and the NAACP Legal Defense Fund brought a lawsuit against the Little Rock School Board in 1956. In *Aaron v. Cooper,* the Supreme Court established that Central High School would desegregate in the fall of 1957. Thereafter, more students and schools would be integrated. On September 2, the day before school was scheduled to begin, Orville Faubus, Arkansas's segregationist governor, ordered the Arkansas National Guard to surround Central High School in order to keep the peace. Desegregation did not begin on September 3 as scheduled.

After more judicial activity, Faubus removed the National Guard and city police took over on September 20. On September 23, the nine students entered Central High through a side door. With the mob growing larger and more unruly, police removed the students from school. The next day President Eisenhower sent the 101st airborne division to keep peace in Little Rock. The next day, soldiers escorted the students to school.

Throughout this period and during the school year, Daisy would serve as a liaison between the students, NAACP lawyers, public officials, and the media. The NAACP's local lawyer, Wiley Branton, relied on Bates to communicate with the students and their families who did not have legal representation of their own. Likewise, the Bates home became an unofficial meeting place for members of the northern media who descended on Little Rock and had also been attacked by segregationist protesters.

Bates continued to be harassed on a nightly basis, becoming a lightning rod for attack from white supremacists. Several crosses were burned on her lawn, her windows were shot out repeatedly, and threatening phone calls offered her little rest at night from 1956 until she moved to New York in 1960 to work on her memoir of the Little Rock crisis. *The Long Shadow of Little Rock* was published in 1962 with a foreword by Eleanor Roosevelt. The enduring work won much acclaim and the American Book Award for a version republished by the University of Arkansas Press in 1982.

Bates lived in Washington, D.C. and worked with Lyndon Johnson's War on Poverty initiative until she had a stroke in 1965. She moved back to Arkansas in 1968, but continued working on local poverty issues in Mitchellville. After the death of L. C., she focused on restarting the *State Press*. The newspaper reappeared in 1984, with Ernest Green (one of the Little Rock Nine) working as its national marketing director. In 1984, she also received an honorary law degree from the University of Arkansas–Fayetteville, where her papers were later deposited.

Daisy Bates will be known for her unwavering devotion to attacking discrimination against African Americans. Her presence also challenged the domination by black male clergyman in the NAACP's leadership roles. She broke the mold of most female civil rights supporters and did not have the deep religious background of other women working in the movement. Unlike Ella Baker, Bates worked in

A civil rights activist since the 1940s, Daisy Bates became famous as the protector of the Little Rock Nine during their successful integration of Central High School in 1957. (Library of Congress)

the foreground, becoming a public face of activism. Finally, Daisy and L. C. did not believe in the nonviolent tactics of Martin Luther King Jr.'s Southern Christian Leadership Conference and kept their home heavily armed. Most important, Daisy Bates did not permit the Little Rock Nine to become sacrificial lambs for the Civil Rights movement. The actions by Bates and President Eisenhower's federal intervention ensured that massive resistance never became an accepted practice and pushed the Civil Rights movement in new directions.

See also: Brown v. Board of Education; Little Rock Nine; National Association for the Advancement of Colored People

Peter Carr Jones

Bibliography

Bates, Daisy. *The Long Shadow of Little Rock*. Little Rock: University of Arkansas Press, 1986.

Jacoway, Elizabeth. *"Turn Away Thy Son": Little Rock, The Crisis That Shocked the Nation.* New York: Free Press, 2007.

Stockley, Grif. *Daisy Bates: Civil Rights Crusader from Arkansas.* Jackson: University Press of Mississippi, 2005.

Belafonte, Harry

Harold (Harry) George Belafonte Jr. (1927–) was born to West Indian parents in Harlem, New York, on March 1, 1927. After his graduation from high school, he joined the Navy. After his military discharge, he worked at various jobs in New York City. Because of his interest in the performing arts, he studied acting at Stanley Kubrick's Dramatic School. He also studied at the New York School for Social Research. Two of his most recognized classmates were Walter Matthau and Marlon Brando. Neither Brando nor Belafonte recognized, at this time, how their professional careers and involvement in political and social issues would intertwine.

Harry Belafonte became successful in the early 1950s when he gained a great amount of recognition as a folk singer. His performance style was appealing and attracted a large following from across the United States. His signature calypso song was titled "Banana Boat Song." Other calypso songs he made popular include "Jamaica Farewell," "Matilda," "Brown Skin Girl," "Come Back Lisa," "Coconut Woman," and "Hold 'Em Joe."

Even though Harry Belafonte was a fan favorite, he experienced racism on several occasions. Such negative experiences played a significant role in his becoming a political activist. He participated with Dr. Martin Luther King Jr. in the march from Selma to Montgomery in support of the bus boycott and later played a significant role in the march on Washington, D.C.

Belafonte was able to maintain a balance between his involvement in issues related to social injustices and his career throughout the 1950s, 1960s and 1970s. His production of the first integrated musical show on television gained him an Emmy in 1960. He was chastised by the network and corporate sponsors, however, because popular singer Petula Clark touched his arm. In fact, Belafonte was fired because of this particular incident. The firing clearly represented the racial divide in the United States.

There are many achievements and career highlights that establish Harry Belafonte as a significant player in the world of entertainment. He earned a Tony Award in 1953 as a cast member in John Murray Anderson's *Almanac.* In 1954, he performed in the revised version of Bizet's Opera *Carmen Jones.* The costar for this production was Dorothy Dandridge. His other film appearances include *Bright Road,* 1953; David Boyer's *Island in the Sun,* 1957; *The Heart of Show Business,* 1957; *The World, the Flesh, and the Devil,* 1958; *Odds Against Tomorrow,* 1959; *Tonight with Belafonte,* 1960; *The Angel Levine,* 1969; *Buck and the Preacher,* 1972; *Uptown Saturday Night,* 1974; *Sometimes I Watch My Life,* 1982; *Say No*—Documentary, 1983; *Three Songs,* 1983; *We Shall Overcome*—Documentary, 1989; *The Payer,* 1992; *Ready to Wear,* 1994; *Hank Aaron: Chasing the Dream*—Documentary, 1995; *White Man's Burden,* 1995; *Jazz '34*—Documentary, 1996; *Kansas City,* 1996; *Scandalize My Name: Stories from the Blacklist*—Documentary, 1998; *Fidel*—Documentary, 2001; and *XXI Century*—Documentary, 2003.

The performing arts medium truly embraced Harry Belafonte for his artistry within the profession and his marketability. He is the recipient of the Donaldson Award, 1953–1954; U.S. Department of State Award, 1958; an Emmy Award for the 1960 TV Special, Tonight with Harry Belafonte; an Honorary Doctorate of Humanities from Park College in Missouri; Martin Luther King Jr. Nonviolent Peace Prize, 1982; Thurgood Marshall Lifetime Achievement Award, 1993; National Medal of Arts, 1994; and recipient of the Bishop John T. Walker Distinguished Humanitarian Service Award from Africa in 2002. He was inducted into the Black Filmmakers Hall of Fame in 1976.

Belafonte became very active in addressing social issues across the globe in the 1980s. The concept behind the song, "We Are the World" was the brainchild of Belafonte. The performance and sale of recordings of this song generated millions of dollars to assist in fighting famine in Ethiopia (1985). In 1987, he was named UNICEF Goodwill Ambassador and was selected to chair the welcome committee for Nelson Mandela's visit to the United States after his release from prison in South Africa. He also performed in Monte Carlo at the Princess Grace Red Cross Ball in 1987 and became the first entertainer to serve on the Advisory Committee of the Peace Corps in 1989.

The following represents a selective discography of Harry Belafonte's recordings: "Calypso" (RCA), 1956; "Mary's Boy Child," 1956; "Coconut Woman," 1957; "Love Is a Gentle Thing," 1959; "Mark Twain and other Folk Favorites," 1959;

and "We Shall Overcome" (video recordings) by Harry Belafonte, 1992.

In addition to his involvement as a social activist, filmmaker, and recording artist, he found time to appear on talk shows as a performer and/or engage in intellectual dialogue related to political and social events. Belafonte appeared on diverse television shows including the Dick Cavett Show, 1972; Mike Douglas Show, 1974; and Paul Robeson (The People), 1976.

Belafonte has also represented the United States on the world stage in speaking of the disenfranchised and those persons or societies whose quality of life does not meet expected standards.

See also: Black Folk Culture; King, Martin Luther Jr.; Robeson, Paul; Student Nonviolent Coordinating Committee

Lemuel Berry Jr.

Bibliography

Estell, Kenneth. *African American: Portrait of a People.* Washington, D.C.: Visible Ink Press, 1994.

Hill, Early G., and James V. Hatch. *A History of African American Theater.* New York: Cambridge University Press, 2003.

Southern, Eileen. *Biographical Dictionary of Afro-American and African Musicians.* Westport, CT: Greenwood Press, 1982.

Southern, Eileen. *The Music of Black Americans.* New York: W. W. Norton, 1997.

Bensonhurst, New York, Incident of 1989

The Bensonhurst incident of 1989 was sparked by the racially motivated murder of Yusuf Hawkins. On the night of August 23, Hawkins, a 16-year-old African American, and three friends traveled from Bedford-Stuyvesant, their predominately black neighborhood, to Bensonhurst, an Italian-American enclave a few miles away. The four teenagers seldom left their neighborhood, but Claude Stanford was eager to inquire about a used 1983 Pontiac automobile that was for sale in Bensonhurst. As they entered the foreign neighborhood, they were surrounded by 20 to 30 white youths, who wielded baseball bats, golf clubs, and at least one gun. The white youths had been lying in wait to ambush a group of African Americans and Latinos whom they believed were involved with a white neighborhood girl, Gina Feliciano. Throughout the day, rumors had

spread that Feliciano arranged for some nonwhite friends to come to Bensonhurst to start trouble. The white youths were resolved to "break out the baseball bats," and "teach the niggers a lesson." Despite realizing that Hawkins and his friends were not the group they were looking for, the white mob challenged their right to be in Bensonhurst. Convinced that beating the four African American teenagers was not enough, Joey Fama pulled a gun and fired four shots. Two of the bullets fatally wounded Hawkins.

The murder of Hawkins was New York City's third killing of a black man by a white mob during the 1980s. In 1982, Willie Turks was beaten to death, without provocation, by 15 to 20 white men in Brooklyn. In December 1986, Michael Griffith was murdered in Queens by a mob of white men armed with baseball bats, tree limbs, and golf clubs. Throughout the 1980s, Bensonhurst earned a reputation for intolerance toward nonwhite minorities; in 1983, three black men were beaten by a group of whites; in 1987, two black men were chased and beaten by a group of whites; also in 1987, anti-Asian fliers were disseminated throughout the neighborhood.

The aftermath of Hawkins's murder brought to the fore the hatred and ignorance of many Bensonhurst residents. On August 26, Al Sharpton led a group of 400 marchers through Bensonhurst, denouncing the neighborhood's racial hostility. This predominately black contingent was met by hundreds of counter-demonstrators who held watermelons above their heads and jeered, "niggers go home!" As demonstrations continued throughout the investigation and subsequent trials, the tone of marchers became more bellicose. On August 31, activist Sonny Carson led 7,500 demonstrators through the streets of Brooklyn. When the demonstrators reached the Brooklyn Bridge, they were met with a wall of police officers in riot gear and with batons ready. Frustrated and determined not to submit, the demonstrators picked up sticks and threw bottles. Forty police officers and unnumbered demonstrators were injured. Many in the African American community felt that the months after Hawkins's murder were more like 1963 than 1989.

Seven Bensonhurst men were eventually charged with crimes related to the murder of Hawkins. All but one was convicted of murder. Joseph Fama, the triggerman, was sentenced to 32 and 2/3 years to life for murder. Keith Mondello, who admitted to rounding up the mob that attacked Hawkins, was acquitted of murder and manslaughter. He was later sentenced to 5⅓ to 16 years in prison for lesser felonies, including rioting, menacing, unlawful imprisonment, discrimination, and possession of a weapon. John Vento, who was also acquitted of murder, was convicted of unlawful imprisonment and sentenced to 2 to 8 years in prison. Joseph Serrano was convicted of possession of a weapon and sentenced to 300 hours of community service. Three others defendants were acquitted of all charges. The acquittals and light sentences ignited additional protests.

The Bensonhurst incident had profound implications for the upcoming Democratic mayoral primary. Ed Koch, the white incumbent, had long been criticized as being an apologist for racially motivated crimes toward African Americans. Koch was subsequently critical of the demonstrations led by Sharpton. His failure to express sympathy for the marchers compromised the city's stance on racial justice. Koch's opponent, David Dinkins, the only black democratic candidate, defended the demonstrations and chastised the racial hostility of Bensonhurst. Dinkins contended that Koch created a racial climate that allowed such an attack to occur. He defeated Koch in the primary and was elected the first and, to date only black mayor of New York City.

Despite the election of Dinkins and the conviction of several of those involved, the wounds of the Bensonhurst incident never fully healed. When Mondello was paroled after serving only 8 years of his sentence, Sharpton and 200 marchers returned to Bensonhurst to protest his early release. Again, white bystanders shouted racist epithets. This response underscored that after a decade, many of the residents of Bensonhurst continued to harbor the bigotry and hatred that led to Hawkins's death. The response of African Americans evinced their continued frustration with the lack of justice in the city.

See also: Sharpton, Al; White Mob Violence; White Supremacy

Rob Walsh

A crowd looks on as the coffin containing Yusuf Hawkins is carried out of Glover Memorial Church in Brooklyn, New York. Hawkins, 16, was shot to death in Bensonhurst on August 23, 1989. (AP Photo/Mario Cabrera)

Bibliography

Barstow, David. 1999. "Decade Later, Grief Returns over Yusuf Hawkins." *New York Times,* August 25, B.3

DeSantis, John. *For the Color of His Skin: The Murder of Yusuf Hawkins and the Trial of Bensonhurst.* New York: Pharos Books, 1991.

Johnson, Kirk. 1989. "A New Generation of Racism is Seen." *New York Times,* August 27, A.32.

Berlin Conference, 1884–1885

The Berlin Conference of 1884–1885 regulated European colonization and trade in Africa. Its outcome, the General Act of the Berlin Conference, is often seen as the formalization of the scramble for Africa. In German it is referred to as *Kongokonferenz* ("Congo Conference"). Although by the end of the third quarter of the 19th century, France, Britain, Portugal, and Germany had acquired commercial interests and were exercising considerable influence in different parts of Africa, their direct political control there was extremely limited.

These European powers preferred informal control and influence in Africa. But this attitude began to change as a result of three major events that occurred between 1876 and 1880. The first was the new interest the Duke of Brabant, crowned a constitutional king (Leopold I) of the Belgians in 1865, proclaimed in Africa. In September 1876, King Leopold II of Belgium convened the Brussels Geographical Conference for the purpose of founding an international society that should promote the exploration of Central Africa. Forty representatives from Great Britain, Belgium, Austria, France, Germany, Italy, and Russia were present.

The conference resulted in the setting up of an organization called "L'Association Internationale pour l'exploration et la Civilisation de l'Afrique Centrale," better known as the International African Association. Its headquarters were at Brussels under the immediate direction of Leopold, and its national committees were spread in practically all the European countries and in the United States. Its aim was to arouse interest in the movement and to raise funds.

The association secured the employment of Henry Morton Stanley in 1879 to explore the Congo in the name of the association. In August of the same year, he had begun to explore the Congo, to make treaties with the native chiefs, to establish stations along the river for the advancement of trade and the protection of the natives, and to try to end the interior slave trade.

In 1882, the association was transformed into a corporation called the International Association of the Congo, with King Leopold as president. An association flag was adopted and an energetic and systematic attempt was made to develop the trade of the Congo Basin. The International Association of the Congo had not been recognized by the powers and had therefore no assured territorial existence. These moves culminated in the creation of the Congo Free State, whose recognition by all the great European nations Leopold managed to obtain before the Berlin West African conference had ended its deliberations.

The second significant series of events was the activities of Portugal from 1876 onwards. For centuries Portugal had claimed the West Coast of Africa and an indefinite amount inland. No country had explicitly recognized the claim to the important northern strip, which included the mouth of the Congo. France, by the Convention of 1786, agreed not to occupy any of that territory herself. Great Britain, on her part, refused to recognize Portuguese jurisdiction. Portugal had never been able to enforce, with any regularity, her commercial monopoly on the Congo, and a complete freedom of trade had been confirmed to France by the Convention of 1786 and was equally enjoyed by other countries, with or without treaty rights.

The third and final factor that helped to set the partition in motion was the expansionist mood that characterized French colonial policy between 1879 and 1880. This was signified by her participation with Britain in the dual control of Egypt (1879), the dispatch of Savorgnan de Brazza into the Congo and the ratification of his treaties with Chief Makoko of the Bateke, and the revival of French colonial initiative in both Tunisia and Madagascar.

The rapid success of Stanley, the penetration of M. Savorgnan de Brazza to the Upper Congo, and the occurrence of several violent conflicts between natives and traders once more compelled Portugal to open negotiations for the recognition of her sovereignty. Accordingly, early in November 1882, Portugal approached both France and Great Britain. The French government was friendly, but apparently wished to postpone the delimitation until de Brazza had had time to consolidate their holdings along the Congo. In February 1883, he was given the powers of a colonial governor and authorized to make such treaties with the native chiefs as were necessary to advance the French influence.

With Great Britain, Portugal was more successful. Great Britain proposed as bases for a treaty in December 1882 the recognition of the Portuguese boundaries; unrestricted commerce on the Congo and the Zambesi; low tariffs in all the African possessions of Portugal; and the equality of British and Portuguese subjects in matters of land, leases, religion, and taxes. A lively correspondence, lasting until February 1884, led to the signing of a treaty along the lines suggested, but with the rights of foreigners much more thoroughly safeguarded. The equality of treatment was carefully defined, elaborated, and extended to all foreigners; freedom of navigation on the Congo was guaranteed; the duties levied in the Congo territory might not for 10 years exceed those of the Mozambique tariff of 1877, and might then be revised only by consent of Great Britain; and Portuguese sovereignty on the Congo was recognized only to Noki. Almost instantly serious opposition arose to this treaty. France knew the treaty was directed against her, and in Germany a score of chambers of commerce appealed to Bismarck for aid. The Woermann Line had a monthly service to the Congo and, from January 1883 to March 1884, inclusive, had sold there 1,029,924 pounds of powder, 2452 tons of liquor, and 555 tons of weapons and rice. There were also many sailing vessels that visited these regions. Otto von Bismarck, German chancellor, imagined that this trade was threatened.

Great Britain had abandoned the treaty; however, negotiations were to be continued. Portugal proposed the calling of an international conference to sort out the territorial disputes arising from European activities in the Congo region. This idea was later taken up by Bismarck who, after sounding the opinions of the other powers, was encouraged to bring it about. The conference was held at Berlin between November 14, 1884 and February 26, 1885. Representatives to the conference were from the United States, Austria-Hungary, Belgium, Denmark, France, Great Britain, Italy, the Netherlands, Portugal, Russia, Sweden-Norway, and Zanzibar.

Officially, the conference ignored the international association until its last session, at which the Independent State of the Congo, or the Congo Free State, was formally welcomed into the family of nations. Many members of the conference, in behalf of their respective governments, had been busy making treaties that established its position

as a state and defined its territory. Bismarck saw in this a means of preventing armed conflict over the Congo Basin, of restricting the Portuguese advance, and of preserving the region to free trade. The association agreed not to levy import duties on goods brought into its territory and to accord to German subjects all rights. On her part, Germany recognized the flag and the boundaries of the independent state to be formed by the association, as given in a map appended to the treaty.

The treaties signed by the other powers were similar, although much European pressure was required to compel Portugal to recognize the north bank of the Congo as belonging to the new state. The south bank as far as Noki was relinquished to Portugal, and the coast province of Kabinda. The Congo territory on the north bank was only a narrow strip west of Manyanga; to the east of that point, France insisted on the Congo and the Ubangi as boundaries.

The association gave its adhesion to the Act of 1885, and proclaimed the neutralization of its territory. The Belgian legislature granted Leopold II permission to become sovereign of the new state. The transformation of the association into the Independent State of the Congo was officially proclaimed in the summer of 1885.

The primary purpose, both of the international association and of the promoters of the Berlin Conference, was to secure free navigation and free trade on the Congo and its tributaries, and to have the development of the region, as well as the protection of the natives, placed in the hands of some responsible but independent organization. To this end the Congo Independent State was created. The conference marked off for free trade all the territory drained by the Congo and its branches. Navigation of every foot of the Congo and its tributaries was to be free; and an international commission, composed of representatives of states signing the act, was to supervise the navigation of the river, the levying of river tolls and pilotage dues, the surveillance of quarantine stations, and all matters necessary for the upkeep of the river.

Conditions on the Congo were well known to many members of the conference, and Stanley was present to explain both the claims of the Association and the needs of the natives. It was therefore provided in the act that all the powers should cooperate to put an end to the slave trade, and it was understood that all were to support the independent state in its efforts to stop these atrocities and to care for the welfare of the natives. All the promoters of the conference, including King Leopold, seem to have been largely actuated by motives of humanity.

The powers bound themselves to suppress the slave trade, but by far the greater portion of their discussions was devoted to the commercial and political questions involved. In the "General Act" itself, only 2 of 38 articles dealt with the humanitarian interests. In Article VI the powers agreed to protect the natives in their moral and material well-being, to cooperate in the suppression of slavery and the slave trade; to further the education and civilization of the natives; to protect missionaries, scientists, and explorers; and to preserve freedom of religion. Article IX reiterates the intention of the European states to abolish the slave trade.

To prevent conflicts among European states and to provide for the proper and regular extension of colonial possessions in Africa, it was agreed that the marking out of all new protectorates must be preceded by due notification to the powers; that to retain titles to lands the occupation must be effective; and that recourse would be had to arbitration in case of differences.

After the conference, the scramble for Africa sped up. Within a few years, Africa was at least nominally divided up south of the Sahara. By 1895, only the settlements in Liberia, Orange Free State, and Transvaal remained independent. The large part of the Sahara was French; after the quelling of the Mahdi rebellion and the ending of the Fashoda crisis, the Sudan remained under joint British-Egyptian rulership. The Boer states were conquered by Great Britain in the Boer wars from 1899 to 1902. Morocco was divided between the French and Spanish in 1911, and Libya was conquered by Italy in 1912. The official British annexation of Egypt in 1914 ended the colonial division of Africa. By this point, all of Africa, with the exceptions of Liberia and Ethiopia were under European rule.

See also: African Imperialism

Moshe Terdiman

Bibliography

Förster, Stig, Wolfgang J. Mommsen, and Ronald Robinson, eds. *Bismarck, Europe, and Africa: The Berlin Africa Conference 1884–1855 and the Onset of Partition.* London: The German Historical Institute and Oxford University Press, 1988.

Harris, Norman Dwight. *Europe and Africa: Being a Revised Edition of Intervention and Colonization in Africa.* New York: Negro Universities Press, 1969.

Oliver, Roland, and G. N. Sanderson. *The Cambridge History of Africa: Volume 6 from 1870 to 1905.* Cambridge: Cambridge University Press, 1985.

BET

Black Entertainment Television (BET) began in 1980 by CEO Robert L. Johnson in Washington, D.C. At its inception, BET network proposed to target African American viewers as an untapped media niche—particularly those interested in shows starring black actors—that marketing executives previously ignored as a consumer base. In its earliest broadcast, BET aired a variety of programs including investigative news show *BET Nightly News with Jacque Reid,* teen-targeted *Teen Summit,* and syndicated comedy shows like *227, Amen,* and *Sanford & Son.* Although it also featured musical programming like *Rap City* and other genre-specific video countdown shows for jazz and R&B listeners, such programs did not yet dominate the network's TV line-up until much later on. Instead, with a Sunday morning line-up of Gospel music and televised Christian church programming, BET set out to be a base for representations of blacks in various mediated context— movies, news, entertainment—and would simultaneously offer advertisers a primary location for reaching African American consumers through commercials.

Since then, during its 28-year history, BET has consistently enjoyed a mixed bag of supporters and detractors on the basis of its original commitments to its founding concepts, as they have shifted within the evolving media landscape. Those who have supported the network have done so primarily from a business perspective, hailing it as an entrepreneurial success, brilliant for its ability to make a black-targeted brand marketable to more mainstream audiences. Alternatively, much of the reception and critique of BET has also been derogatory. Critics of the network cite its subscription-based nature as evidence that capital is its primary motivation, not proper representation. Moreover, many argue that because BET is mostly interested in generating revenue, it does so at the expense of reaching more African American people because, as a cable network, BET fails to reach a larger swath of viewers interested in seeing more images of blacks on television.

Most commonly, BET is critiqued for the representations of African Americans propagated through its programming decisions. In general its content most drastically changed in 2000 when Robert Johnson sold the company to Viacom Incorporated for a reported $3 billion to add to Viacom's media empire along with MTV, Nickelodeon, and Comedy Central. The bureaucratic changes that accompanied the acquisition drastically changed BET's program content, as well as the commercials featured in-between its new shows. The post-Viacom BET features a disproportionate number of ads for liquor and lower priced commodities compared to ads in other networks like ABC or NBC.

The most appreciable difference in BET as a network is manifested through its content, which shifted to solely focus on music programming. Producers developed new shows like *106 & Park* (a music video countdown show that also features live performances and interviews) for younger viewers and moved away from accommodating older audience members. Concomitantly, the additional programming also propagated a greater number of negative images of black men and women featured in music videos as violent and hypersexual. Thus through its change, BET became responsible for the mass dissemination of misogynist and damaging images of African Americans, rather than offering a remedy to the damning images of blackness found elsewhere on television. Of the more hellacious shows was "BET: Uncut" featuring pornographic-like videos reserved for mature audiences viewing television even after late-night viewing slots. As BET has become a bastion of negative portrayals, it has been subject to public outcries for change, ranging from protestors congregating at the homes of BET executives to the cartooned critiques of *Boondocks* creator Aaron McGruder. These opponents argue that the network offers too small a view of African Americans to others and in consequence creates social problems for blacks who do not identify with the images BET offers.

By changing its imagistic investments, BET fails to offer African American viewers any variety in representation and thus mimics (or enhances) the negativity found on other networks. As the power shifted out of the hands of African American executives at BET to instead offer more control and financial interests to media companies, BET's content has been more demeaning to black Americans and renders the network as a chief disseminator of damaging images. In an effort to mitigate these claims the (once) predominantly music channel MTV became a model for BET's new content. In addition to music-centered shows, BET's new line-up mimics programs found on MTV by recreating them with exclusively black casts in order to achieve more socioeconomic variety in black representations. Thus whereas MTV airs *Laguna Beach,* a reality program about wealthy white teens living in California, BET now airs *Baldwin Hills;* showing wealthy black teen personal dramas through the same reality-TV show format. Similarly BET offers shows such as *College Hill* (a Black rendition of MTV's groundbreaking *The Real World*) and *How I'm Living* (a version of MTV's *Cribs*) in an attempt to quench complaints.

As BET's content has changed, it remains vibrant, reaching over 85 million households nationwide. It no longer dominates the network landscape for black representations with the emergence of network competitors like Radio One Inc.'s TVOne, which offers many of the syndicated shows previously found on BET; it also airs lost classics like *Roots* and the political *Sharp Talk with Al Sharpton.* BET, however, does remain a salient location for types of black images on television, and it has branched out to include other venues such as BETjazz network, which features less youth- and urban-oriented programming.

See also: Ebony Magazine; *Jet* Magazine

Jasmine Nichole Cobb

Bibliography

Coleman, Robin R. Means. *African American Viewers and the Black Situation Comedy: Situating Racial Humor.* New York: Garland, 2000.

Entman, Robert M., and Andrew Rojecki. *Black Image in the White Mind: Media and Race in America.* Chicago: University of Chicago, 2001.

McGruder, Aaron. *A Right to be Hostile: The Boondocks Treasury.* New York: Three Rivers, 2003.

Smith-Shomade, Beretta E. "Narrowcasting in the New World Information Order: A Space for the Audience?" *Television & New Media* 5, no. 1 (2004):69–81.

Bethune, Mary McLeod

Mary McLeod Bethune (1875–1955), an educator, civil rights activist, and founder of an historically black college was one of the most important black leaders of the early 20th century. She played an important role in promoting education for blacks, led numerous African American organizations, and also worked as a member of the "black cabinet" in Franklin Delano Roosevelt's presidential administration. Although Bethune played such a significant role in high-level politics, she argued that she wanted to help ordinary African Americans. She fought for racial integration as a means for blacks to gain civil rights.

Mary McLeod was born in Maynesville, South Carolina in 1875, the 15th of 17 children of former slaves. She was born and grew up in the South during the era of Jim Crow segregation and violence. Mary McLeod distinguished herself by her academic ability at a young age and attended a local school run by black educator, Emma J. Wilson. In 1887, she won a scholarship to a boarding school—Scotia Seminary for Negro Girls—in Concord, North Carolina. Mary McLeod would go on to play a prominent role in black education, in large part owing to her early experiences with schools. She believed that education was the key to advancement of African Americans and spent much of her career promoting schools for blacks.

In 1898, Mary McLeod married Albertus Bethune, a clothing salesman. The couple gave birth to their son, Albert, the next year. The family moved to Florida shortly thereafter and opened a school. In 1904, Mary McLeod Bethune founded the Daytona Literary and Industrial Training School for Negro Girls. Like Booker T. Washington at the Tuskegee Institute, Bethune promoted industrial education. In 1907, Albertus left and went back to South Carolina. The couple never divorced, however, and Albertus died in 1918. Mary McLeod Bethune struggled to raise funds to keep the school afloat, and the student population increased tremendously over the next two decades. The school was later renamed the Daytona Normal and Industrial School and, in 1923, it merged with the Cookman Institute of Jacksonville, Florida. The school ultimately became a four-year college, Bethune-Cookman College. Mary McLeod Bethune served as the president of the college from 1923 to 1942 and again from 1946–1947.

Bethune also played a central role in women's political activities in the early 20th century where she focused on her goal of improving the lives of black women. She served as the head of the Florida Federation of Colored Women's Clubs from 1917 to 1925. In this capacity, she founded a home for delinquent black girls in Ocala, Florida. Bethune served as the president of the Southeastern Federation of Colored Women's Clubs from 1920 to 1925 and headed up the National Association of Teachers in

Colored Schools from 1923 to 1924. Bethune was elected president of the National Association of Colored Women (NACW) from 1924 to 1928 after defeating Ida B. Wells-Barnett for the position. She served as the NACW president for two terms.

Bethune was recognized nationally for her work promoting education and political upliftment of African Americans. In 1930, President Herbert Hoover invited her to a conference at the White House to reward her active work within the Republican Party. When Franklin Delano Roosevelt was elected president on the Democratic ticket in 1932, however, Bethune aligned herself with the Democrats. In 1935, Bethune wanted to promote a more radical political agenda, so she formed the National Council of Negro Women (NCNW). Bethune sought to create an organization that would promote the interests of all black women and also make the entire nation recognize the struggles and triumphs of African American women.

Bethune moved to Washington, D.C. in 1936 when she joined the National Youth Administration (NYA), an agency within the Works Progress Administration. The NYA was

Mary McLeod Bethune fought fiercely to achieve social, economic, and educational opportunities for African Americans, and particularly for African American women. (Library of Congress)

founded to spread democratic ideas to American youth and to provide vocational training for youth struggling with the economic ramifications of the Great Depression. In 1939, Bethune's unit of the NYA was moved to the Division of Negro Affairs in the Federal Security Agency, making Bethune the highest ranking African American woman in the federal government. In her role, she promoted college education for black students, as well as training in skills necessary for the war effort.

In 1936, Bethune began to serve on the Federal Council on Negro Affairs, also known as the "black cabinet." The cabinet promoted civil rights for all blacks. In 1937, Bethune helped to organize the National Conference on the Problems of the Negro, a widely publicized conference. Attendees included Eleanor Roosevelt along with other important political figures. The conference promoted the goal of integration and publicized the struggles of African Americans.

After the attack on Pearl Harbor and the entrance of the United States into World War II, Bethune encouraged black Americans to support the war effort. She viewed the war as an opportunity for blacks to fight for their civil rights. She promoted war bonds and also worked to recruit black women to the army through the Women's Army Auxiliary Corps (WAC). She also agitated for equal treatment of black soldiers and protested against unfair treatment for black women in the (WAC). As World War II drew to a close, Bethune assumed a role on the international stage. In 1945, the State Department reluctantly named her an associate consultant to the U.S. delegation to draft the UN Charter in San Francisco. She was the only black woman on the delegation. She also continued to play a prominent role in American politics. From 1936 to 1952, Bethune served as president of the Association for the Study of Negro Life and History, an organization founded by Carter G. Woodson.

Bethune left Washington, D.C. and returned to Florida in 1949, where she continued her work. In addition to taking trips to Haiti and Liberia, she also continued to promote equality for African Americans. She worked with black businessmen to develop beaches that blacks could use under the Bethune-Volusia Project. She also founded the McLeod Bethune Foundation, a charitable organization to house her papers and promote black education. In 1955, Bethune attended the World Assembly for Moral Re-Armament (MRA) conference in Switzerland. The MRA promoted honesty, purity, unselfishness, and love, all traits that appealed to Bethune and her political philosophy. Mary McLeod Bethune suffered a heart attack on May 18, 1955, and died at her home in Florida.

See also: Association for the Study of African American Life and History; Black Cabinet; Historically Black Colleges and Universities; National Association of Colored Women; World War II (Black participation in)

Jane E. Dabel

Bibliography

Collier-Thomas, Bettye, and V. P. Franklin. *Sisters in the Struggle: African American Women in the Civil Rights-Black Power Movement.* New York: New York University Press, 2001.

Hanson, Joyce Ann. *Mary McLeod Bethune & Black Women's Political Activism.* Columbia: University of Missouri Press, 2003.

Holt, Rackham. *Mary McLeod Bethune; A Biography.* Garden City, NY: Doubleday, 1964.

Biko, Steve

Born on December 18, 1946, Steven Bantu Biko (1946–1977) would emerge as one of South Africa's most revered leaders. Biko grew up in King Williams Town in the Eastern Cape. There, his father worked as a government-employed clerk while his mother performed domestic work in surrounding white homes. Early on Biko learned the value of education from his parents who ensured that their youngest child understood its significance. In 1952, at the age of six, Biko began his formal schooling. Later on in 1963, when he matriculated at Lovedale High School, Biko faced expulsion because of his political affiliation with the fledgling Black Consciousness Movement (BCM). Biko became not only a major proponent of the BCM but also one of its chief theorists and practitioners. Despite the banning order that made it unlawful for Biko to speak with more than one person at a time, which was legislated in 1973, he managed to speak publicly and write proficiently. His *I Write What I Like,* for example, details his thoughts on apartheid, his adherence to "black is beautiful," and his ideas on the meaning of black. In Biko's opinion, any oppressed person, whether he represented Asian, European, or African persuasion, represented a black.

By adhering to this philosophy, Biko united disparate groups under a common theme. His public pronouncements against apartheid made Biko a government target. Biko died in September 1977 while in police custody

As a founder of the Black Consciousness movement, Steve Biko inspired blacks in South Africa to express their pride as a people and to confront the apartheid system as a group. (AP/Wide World Photos)

from massive head wounds, not from a self-imposed hunger strike as the state had proclaimed. Biko left behind a wife and four children; two of the children he had by Dr. Mamphela Ramphele. His death led to his martyrdom.

Before Biko met this fate, he attended medical school at the University of Natal in 1966. When Biko realized that his education would not help to bring about integration between black and white, he stopped his studies and began fervently participating in several political organizations to hone his skills as a thinker of repute. Biko was also influenced by other intellectuals such as Frantz Fanon, Aime Cesaire, and Leopold Senghor; Mahatma Gandhi and Martin Luther King Jr. also impacted on Biko's intellectual development. In calling for the restoration of African consciousness, Biko argued that black South Africans had to undergo psychological liberation and physical liberation. With the first stage, Biko advocated that blacks gain a better appreciation of their beauty, intellect, and verve, rather

than adhering to inferiority. Blacks, Biko believed, lacked confidence as a result of the system of apartheid and its degrading impact on the black psyche. In order for blacks to evolve, Biko believed that they had to throw off the psychological shackles that imprisoned them. Once they attained this goal, then physical liberation would follow. In analyzing the psychological effects of apartheid, Biko chose to verbalize what everyday South Africans felt. This was seen as incendiary by the South African government, which instituted a banning order against the freedom fighter.

When Biko was banned, the government restricted his movements to the Eastern Cape. Although he lived under such orders, Biko refused to allow the banning order against his physical mobility to limit his freedom. He traveled to soccer games, and Biko even gave a speech during one of these athletic events, where he first hid from view and then appeared. His trip to Cape Town led to his detainment. On August 18, 1977, police arrested Biko at a roadblock. He had according to officials contravened the Terrorism Act No. 83 of 1967. During his prison tenure, Biko faced torture. For one day, police officials chained Biko to a window grille; they also transported him nude in a Land Rover and drove 1,200 kilometers to Pretoria. Shortly after his arrival in Pretoria, Biko died. The cause of death was massive head wounds, which white South African journalist Donald Woods captured on film. In 1997, the perpetrators who killed Biko, all five of them, admitted their crime before the Truth and Reconciliation Commission for which they were exonerated. Finally, the family could receive some closure. Closure also came when the country and others around the world honored Biko. For example, the main student union building on the University of Manchester's Oxford campus carries his name. In 2004, in a poll conducted in South Africa by SABC3, Biko was named the 13th Greatest South African.

See also: Antiapartheid Movement

Dawne Y. Curry

Bibliography

Arnold, Millard. *Steve Biko: Black Consciousness in South Africa.* New York: Random House, 1978.

Biko, Steve. *I Write What I Like.* San Francisco: Harper & Row, 1986.

Mngxitama, Andile, Amanda Alexander, and Nigel C. Gibson. *Biko Lives!: Contesting the Legacies of Steve Biko.* New York: Palgrave Macmillan, 2008.

Woods, Donald. *Biko.* London: Paddington Press, 1978.

Black Arts Movement

In 1965, the passage of the Voting Rights Bill ended one phase of the Civil Rights movement and, by October 1966, the emergent doctrine of Black Power had concrete political form in the Black Panther Party for Self-Defense. Black power also had an artistic extension in the form of the black arts movement (BAM). Positioning themselves as an alternative to the mainstream Civil Rights movement, BAM poets and black power activists replaced the ideal of integration with that of black cultural particularism.

BAM was led by Amiri Baraka, Ed Bullins, Addison Gayle Jr., Hoyt Fuller, Larry Neal, Ishmael Reed, and James Stewart. It emerged out of Philadelphia, New York, and Oakland during the early 1960s, and by 1964 it had a literary center in the arts journal *Liberator,* founded by Neal and Askai Touré. In 1968, the publication of the *Black Fire* anthology, edited by Baraka and Neal, marked one of the major events in BAM's print culture. BAM reached the peak of its cultural influence in the late 1960s and early 1970s.

Central to the movement was a belief that political action would come through artistic expression. Art had a social value and the artist had a role in political transformation. Black nationalist cultural politics would help answer problems like poverty, police brutality, and substandard education, because imaginative culture could alter the reality of oppressed peoples.

The movement also stressed cultural heritage, the beauty of blackness, and a black aesthetic. It asked that black people no longer see through white eyes, and BAM poets therefore subverted traditional forms and accepted values. If "white" and "black" were signifiers for "good" and "bad," then BAM poets would use the terms differently, celebrating what Baraka frequently termed "black magic." In 1968, Neal described BAM as a cultural revolution, adding that a whole new system of ideas was needed. Neal's poem "Black Boogaloo" (1969) went on to instruct black poets, painters, and musicians: "Take care of business. All get together.... Combine energy.... Calling all Black People" (42).

As part of this revolution, BAM artists embraced the jazz avant-garde. They believed that music articulated an authentic black expression: "Negro music alone, because it drew its strengths and beauties out of the depth of the black man's soul, and because to a large extent its traditions could be carried on by the lowest classes of Negroes, has been able to survive the constant and wilful dilutions of the black middle class," wrote Baraka in 1966 (*Within the Circle,* p. 165). Musical freedom constituted another form of social activism, and BAM poets used the rhythms of black music in their verse. We were "drenched in black music and wanted our poetry to be black music…its rhythms, its language, its history and struggle," remembered Baraka of BAM. "It was meant to be a poetry we copped from the people and gave them right back, open and direct and moving" (*The Autobiography,* p. 237).

Alongside this interest in music as a language of the people, BAM poets stressed the orality of poetry, focused on vernacular speech as a communicative medium, and tried to make art accessible to the whole Harlem community. In 1965, Baraka founded the Black Arts Repertory Theatre/School (BART/S) in Harlem to assist the creation of a black culture. Focused on community art, BART/S produced plays that questioned core American values and provided African Americans with new meanings to their lives. BAM saw the artist-audience relationship as localized and collaborative, and when BART/S closed in 1966, Baraka opened Spirit House in Newark, New Jersey, guided by the same founding principles as BART/S.

Yet for all their efforts, BAM writers failed to resonate beyond a limited group of black urbanites. Nearly all of the movement's theater groups and journals were short-lived, and Gayle began preserving BAM for posterity as early as 1971. In an anthology titled *The Black Aesthetic,* he juxtaposed BAM writers with other major 20th-century theorists of the black aesthetic (including W. E. B. Du Bois and Langston Hughes), as though to ensure BAM's place in the annals of literary history. Then in 1973, Bullins's book *The Theme is Blackness* offered a closing statement of BAM and also expressed admiration for the accomplishments of the mainstream Civil Rights movement. Increasingly criticized for its anti-Semitism and chauvinism, as well as its exclusion of liberal whites and its strident form of nationalism, BAM faded from public view by the mid-1970s.

See also: Baraka, Amiri; Black Power

Zoe Trodd

Bibliography

Baraka, Amiri. *The Autobiography.* New York: Freundlich Books, 1984.

Baraka, Amiri, and Larry Neal, eds. *Black Fire.* New York: Morrow, 1968.

Gayle, Addison Jr. *The Black Aesthetic.* New York: Doubleday, 1971.

Mitchell, Angelyn, ed. *Within the Circle: An Anthology of African American Literary Criticism from the Harlem Renaissance to the Present.* Durham: Duke University Press, 1994.

Neal, Larry. "The Black Arts Movement." *Drama Review* 12 (Summer 1968):29–39.

Neal, Larry. *Black Boogaloo.* San Francisco: Journal of Black Poetry Press, 1969.

Black Athletes

Black athletes have contributed significantly to many sports—most notably basketball, baseball, football, track and field, and boxing—while facing many challenges, including formal segregation policies and/or personal prejudices that often denied them the opportunity to compete against nonblack athletes of their caliber and to make comparable wages. Countless black athletes have nevertheless found creative ways to participate in the sports in which they excelled, oftentimes redefining the game.

Perhaps the sport of basketball most effectively illustrates how black athletes have revolutionized a sport. Invented in 1891, basketball was almost entirely segregated by color, but the Renaissance Big Five—an all-black team formed in 1922 in Harlem, New York—consisted of premiere players who barnstormed across the country for about two decades, challenging teams of white players, thereby providing opportunities for quality racially integrated play.

Talented as the Renaissance team was, it was their contemporaries who founded a team that spread basketball around the world, adding elements of playfulness and showmanship to their athleticism. This all-black team formed in 1926 and first played on January 7, 1927 in Hinckley, Illinois; because of their traveling, originally in the Model T Ford of their promoter, they eventually became known as the Harlem Globetrotters.

They reached their 1,000-game mark in 1934, and played their first professional tournament in 1939. That same year, players began "clowning around" during the games to entertain their audiences and, although they continued to boast a talented roster, the Harlem Globetrotters became known for their skillfully orchestrated slapstick routines.

In 1950, the New York Knicks purchased Nathaniel "Sweetwater" Clifton from the Harlem Globetrotters; the Boston Celtics signed Chuck Cooper; and the Washington Capitols signed Earl Lloyd. These three men were the first black players to cross the color line and play in the National Basketball League (NBA). Over the next two years, the players who remained with the Harlem Globetrotters—and there were many of quality—toured Portugal, Switzerland, England, Belgium, France, Germany, Italy, Morocco, Algeria, and South America, spreading the game of basketball to those countries. They also traveled to Germany; track star Jesse Owens accompanied them.

In 1954, Meadowlark Lemon became one of the Globetrotters' star attractions; he participated on the team for 24 years. That same year, the NBA instituted many rule changes, including the 24-second clock and a revised policy on fouls, that favored the quick athleticism that many black athletes would bring to the game.

In 1959, the Globetrotters toured the Soviet Union and Eastern Europe. "Curly" Neal joined the team in 1963, staying with them for 22 years and demonstrating intricate dribbling patterns to international audiences.

By 1966, the Globetrotters had played 8,945 games, with only 330 losses; they had also traveled to 82 countries. In 1985, they hired their first female player, Olympic gold medalist Lynette Woodard. In 2004, more than 1.3 million people watched Globetrotter games as the team toured Ireland, the United Kingdom, Belgium, Holland, France, and Spain.

Meanwhile, from 1967 until 1976, the American Basketball Association (ABA) challenged the NBA for basketball predominance. The ABA was known for its "outlaw" style of play, and players such as Julius "Dr J" Erving added a new level of excitement to the sport. When this league merged with the more traditional NBA, its players contributed to the level of showmanship and skill in modern professional basketball, and elements such as the sky hook, slam dunk, and extended hang time, owe much to the black players who brought this "showtime" to their fans.

Black basketball players have set many records. Kareem Abdul-Jabbar scored the most career points (38,387), and he blocked 3,189 shots, a record surpassed by Nigerian-born Hakeem Olajuwon, with 3,830; Abdul-Jabbar was also voted the Most Valuable Player a record-breaking six times. Wilt "The Stilt" Chamberlain started his career as a Harlem Globetrotter in 1958, and then switched to the NBA one year later. In the NBA, he set the record for career rebounds (23,924) and served as the leading scorer for seven consecutive seasons. Perhaps most astonishing is his performance on March 2, 1962, when he scored 100 points in one game. Another record is Earvin "Magic" Johnson's 11.2 assists per game.

Other athletes who deserve mention are Bill Russell, who was part of 11 championship NBA teams, and Karl "The Mailman" Malone, the second highest all-time scorer, with 36,374 points. Michael Jordan, perhaps the most successful basketball player in the history of the sport, won the NBA's Most Valuable Player award five times, and he led the Chicago Bulls to six championships. Furthermore, he shares—with Wilt Chamberlain—the record for being the leading scorer during seven consecutive seasons.

Black athletes currently contributing much to the sport include Shaquille O'Neal and Lebron James. Women who have excelled in basketball include Cheryl Miller, Teresa Weatherspoon, Sheryl Swoopes, Lisa Leslie, and Cynthia Cooper.

In the sport of baseball, black athletes began forming their own teams shortly after the inception of the game, in the 1840s, but they had to wait a full century to join the ranks of the most prestigious professional leagues. On occasion during the 19th century, exceptionally determined men, such as John "Bud" Fowler and Moses Fleetwood "Fleet" Walker," played on professional teams otherwise consisting of white players, but they were the exception; in 1887, after National League star Cap Anson refused to play against George Stovey, a black man, players of color were officially banned from participation in the professional leagues populated by white players.

The first all-black professional baseball team, the Cuban Giants, formed in 1885, and other teams of quality followed. These men played scheduled games and also barnstormed across the country in search of opportunities to play baseball. Team owners often lacked funding, so players' wages were uncertain, and prejudices often prevented these men from participating against other players of their ability.

In 1920, Andrew "Rube" Foster created the National Negro League, the most stable all-black baseball league. It collapsed in 1930, however, four years after Foster's death. Revived in 1932, the league lasted into the early 1950s. Men who played their entire careers in the Negro leagues, but who had the skill to play in the all-white major leagues, include "Smokey" Joe Williams, Josh Gibson, "Buck" O'Neil, "Mule" Settles, Oscar Charleston, "Bullet" Joe Rogan, and "Cool Papa" Bell.

Desegregation began in the sport in 1947 when John Roosevelt "Jackie" Robinson began playing for Branch Rickey's Brooklyn Dodgers; that year, Robinson won the Rookie of the Year Award. Also in 1947, Bill Veeck of the Cleveland Indians signed Larry Doby, thereby breaking the color barrier in the American League. Doby participated in All-Star games from 1949–1954.

Other players who successfully transitioned from the Negro leagues into major league baseball include Leroy "Satchel" Paige who, after pitching for black teams for 22 years, joined the Cleveland Indians in 1948 and pitched well into his fifties. Another was catcher Roy Campanella, who also played for Branch Rickey's Dodgers. Hank Aaron signed with the Milwaukee Braves in 1954 and went on to break Babe Ruth's major league home run record (755) and the record for runs batted in (2,297).

Other black baseball players of note include Rickey Henderson, who is the all-time leader in walks, steals, and runs scored, and who successfully hit for the 3,000th time in 2001; Willie Mays, who hit 660 home runs during his 22-year career; and Reggie "Mr. October" Jackson, the first player to hit 100 or more home runs for three different teams. Tony Gwynn successfully hit 3,141 times in his baseball career. Also worthy of mention are Bo Jackson and Deion Sanders, who have succeeded in both professional baseball and football.

In the sport of football, segregation was total until 1946, when Kenny Washington and Woody Strode began playing for the Los Angeles Rams, and the Cleveland Browns' All-America Football Conference team signed Marion Motley and Bill Willis, two future hall-of-fame players. Several black football players hold records of significance. Walter "Sweetness" Payton had the most yards rushing (16,726) until Emmitt Smith broke the record with 18,355; Payton also rushed 100 yards or more in 77 games. In 1997, Barry Sanders rushed for over 100 yards in 14 consecutive games for a total of 2,053 yards; in 1984, Eric Dickerson rushed over 100 yards 12 times for a total of 2,105, which is the most yards gained in a single season. Jerry Rice caught the most touchdown passes (197), with 22 of them in a single season, another record. Jim Marshall played in 282 consecutive games.

Other black athletes worthy of mention include Orenthal James (O. J.) Simpson, Roosevelt "Rosey" Grier, Franco Harris, Lawrence Taylor, "Mean" Joe Green, Gale Sayers, Donovan McNab, and Jim Brown who, at retirement, held

20 NFL records. Doug Williams, the first black quarterback to play in a Super Bowl, led the Washington Redskins to victory in 1988 and was awarded the MVP award.

Besides the skill, power, and speed that these athletes have brought to the game, several black players have been known to increase excitement by end zone celebrations and other sensational and attention-getting moves.

Seldom, however, has an athlete received the type of attention as did Jesse Owens. He was the first American track-and-field athlete to win four gold medals in one single Olympic competition and, in three events, he also set records. Yet, he is best remembered as the black athlete who triumphed in Berlin in 1936, while Nazi Chancellor Adolf Hitler, who believed in the superiority of the white race, watched.

Other black track-and-field athletes of note include Leroy Burrell (100 meters in 9.85 seconds), Butch Reynolds (400 meters in 43.29 seconds), Roger Kingdom (100 meter hurdles in 12.92 seconds), Edwin Moses (400 meter hurdles in 47.02 seconds), Bob Beamon (long jump of 29 feet, 2½ inches), and Willie Banks (triple jump span of 58 feet, 11-1/2 inches). Charles Dumas was the first athlete to jump over seven feet, and Carl Lewis won four Olympic gold medals in 1984, in the same events that Jesse Owens won in 1936.

Female track stars of note include Alice Coachman, the first black woman to receive an Olympic gold medal for the high jump (1948); Wilma Rudolph, who won three Olympic gold medals in one single Olympiad (100- and 200-meter dash, and the 400-meter relay in 1960); and Florence Griffith Joyner who holds the world record for 100-meter dash (10.40 seconds) and for the 200-meter (21.34). Jackie Joyner-Kersee has held the heptathlon world record since 1986, besting her own point totals. Furthermore, Evelyn Ashford won four Olympic gold medals, and Gail Devers won Olympic gold medals in the 100-meter event in 1992 and 1996, besides other accomplishments.

In boxing, Jack Johnson—the first black American to hold the heavyweight title, which he won in 1908 and held until 1915—was a figure of controversy, in part because of his outspokenness, flashy lifestyle, and fondness for white women; and in part because of a bout he fought against Jim Jeffries—the "Great White Hope"—on July 4, 1910. Billed as the "Fight of the Century," Johnson beat the former heavyweight champion, thereby cementing his reputation as a powerful fighter.

Fifty years later, another flamboyant boxer caught the attention of audiences. Muhammad Ali, who won an Olympic gold medal in 1960, combined speed and athletic prowess with a boastfully humorous persona that helped transform boxing into the popular sport that it is today. Other 20th-century black boxers of note include Joe Louis, George Foreman, Floyd Patterson, Evander Holyfield, Sugar Ray Leonard, Joe Frasier, Thomas Hearns, and Mike Tyson. Don King, another controversial figure, deserves credit for promoting the sport of boxing to the masses.

Although the five aforementioned sports—basketball, baseball, football, track and field, and boxing—are the ones in which black athletes have made the most contributions, there are also black athletes of note in soccer, hockey, tennis, golf, and skating, as well as other sports.

Skater Debi Thomas was the first black athlete to win a medal during the winter Olympics. In tennis, women of note include Althea Gibson; in 1957 and 1958, she won both the singles and doubles titles at Wimbledon. Other female tennis stars include Zina Garrison-Jackson, and Serena and Venus Williams. In men's tennis, Arthur Ashe, the first black man to win at the U.S. Open and Wimbledon, deserves particular mention. Ashe once discussed the sports performances of whites, which he labeled "method acting," lacking spontaneity, creativity, and innovation; it was his belief that black athletes brought those elements to various sports.

Edson Arantes Do Nascimento, known simply as Pelé, is perhaps one of the greatest soccer players ever, blessed with extraordinary ball-controlling ability, speed, and balance. Pelé played in four World Cups with Brazil's National Team.

The first black to join the National Hockey League (NHL) was Willie O'Ree, who joined the Boston Bruins in 1958, despite being legally blind in his right eye. O'Ree recalls significant racial taunting, noting that it was worse in the United States than in Canada. It was not until 1974 that another black athlete—Mike Marson—joined the league.

Overall, only 18 players participated in the National Hockey League (NHL) in the years between 1958 and 1991; this was, in large part, because Canadians comprised more than 95 percent of the NHL in 1971, and only .02 percent of the Canadian population at that time was black; that figure is now 2 percent. Moreover, about 15 percent of the NHL players are now from the United States, whereas Canadians make up 60 percent. This partially explains why, in 2003 alone, the number of black hockey players had increased to 13.

Perhaps the most notable black hockey player so far has been goaltender Grant Fuhr, who played with Wayne Gretzky on the Edmonton Oilers team in the 1980s. Fuhr has the sixth most all-time wins for goalies. Another black hockey player of note is Anson Carter, who was the second-leading scorer for the Boston Bruins in the 1999–2000 season; other players include Fred Brathwaite of the Columbus Blue Jackets and Kevin Weekes of the Carolina Hurricanes.

Black golfers began participating in the sport in the late 19th century, and it was a black man, Dr. George F. Grant, who invented the golf tee in 1899. In 1896, John M. Shippen Jr., a laborer who helped build Shinnecock Hills, played in the second U.S. Open Championship at the golf course he helped construct. He placed fifth, seven strokes behind the winner.

That was an exception, though, in the then-segregated sport of golf. During the summer of 1925, a group of black men formed the Colored Golfers Association of America (or, as some report, the United States Colored Golfers Association), in which they sponsored their own tournaments and offered their own awards and prizes. They faced challenges; by 1939, fewer than 20 golf facilities, nationwide, were said to be available for black players. Black players were not admitted to the Professional Golf Association of America (PGA) until 1959, and that was in response to a lawsuit filed as far back as 1943.

Golfers of significance include Charlie Sifford, Calvin Peete, and Lee Elder; the most famous black golfer is unquestionably Eldrick "Tiger" Woods. Among other accomplishments, Woods won the Masters Tournament in 1997, 2001, and 2002; the PGA Championship in 1999 and 2000; the U.S. Open Championship in 2000 and 2002; and British Open Championship in 2000. In 2001, Woods became the first golfer to hold all four major championships during the same year.

It would be impossible to mention all black athletes, or to list all of their accomplishments. It is fair to say, however, that this group of athletes has contributed much to the sports that they have played, combating racism and other challenges, and that they have made each of their sports richer by their presence.

Besides combating segregation, black athletes have had to contend with an evolving series of stereotypes. In the 19th century and much of the 20th century, a significant percentage of people believed that black athletes succeeded because their relatively lower intelligence was compensated by a stronger physical ability. The race of the athlete was nearly always part of any media reporting; for example, Jesse Owens was labeled as "saddle colored" or a "streak of ebony." When Joe Louis won a boxing match against a white man in 1935, it was suggested that someone "not quite human, came out of the jungle last night."

Although fewer people today would say that black athletes succeed more often because of their lower intelligence but greater physical capacities, a more subtle stereotype is displayed whenever it is stated that blacks are more naturally athletic, implying that they do not possess the same intelligence or dedication that white athletes need to perform at the same capacity.

Black athletes who either broke the color line or were one of the first to participate in a particular professional sport faced a duel challenge: while their athletic efforts were under intense scrutiny, so were their personal lives and levels of conduct. Some, such as Jack Johnson, flaunted conventions, but most groundbreakers did not.

Because as many as three-fourths of current NBA and NFL players are black, and as many track-and-field events are dominated by black participants, it is therefore expected that the contributions of these athletes to the world of sports will only continue to increase.

See also: 1936 Summer Olympics, Berlin; 1968 Summer Olympics, Mexico City; Ali, Muhammad; Ashe, Arthur; Owens, Jesse; Robeson, Paul; Robinson, Jackie

Kelly Boyer Sagert

Bibliography

Cottrell, Robert C. *Blackball, the Black Sox and the Babe: Baseball's Crucial 1920 Season.* Jefferson, NC: McFarland, 2002.

James, Bill. *The New Bill James Historical Baseball Abstract.* New York: The Free Press, 2001.

Peterson, R. W. *Cages to Jumpshots: Pro Basketball's Early Years.* New York: Oxford University Press, 1990.

Shouler, K. et al. *Total Basketball: The Ultimate Basketball Encyclopedia.* Wilmington, DE: Sports Media Publishing, 2003.

Black Cabinet

Black cabinet, black brain trust, or Federal Council of Negro Affairs refers to the various men and women appointed to administrative positions in Washington as part of President

Franklin Delano Roosevelt's New Deal shift toward more equitable treatment of African Americans.

Despite its expansive uplift and improvement aims, initially the New Deal with all its promise and promises was marked by an overwhelming indifference and even enmity in regards to issues concerning African Americans. For example, The National Recovery Administration or NRA, which African Americans began to refer to by the negative soubriquet "Negro Run Around," was one of the associations that implemented inauspicious policies concerning African Americans. Under The National Recovery Administration, various codes forced African American workers to become displaced from entrepreneurial endeavors and higher wage jobs in favor of their white counterparts and larger modernized business ventures. The Civilian Conservation Corp (CCC), which employed racial exclusionary and discriminatory practices regarding African Americans in the organization's units and ultimately ill-effected their ability to advance, was another New Deal program that negatively affected blacks. The Agricultural Adjustment Administration (AAA) allowed whites superior representation in county committees and disallowed approximately 400,000 African American sharecroppers and 300,000 black tenant farmers from receiving proportionate distributions of crop reduction payments to which they were entitled while simultaneously consenting to the widespread eviction of tenants whose labor was deemed no longer valuable.

Despite the inequitable treatment that was a mark of early New Deal implementations, after 1934 countervailing forces began to succeed in gradually shifting President Roosevelt in the direction of more just treatment for blacks. Dissatisfaction felt by blacks with the state of race relations throughout the nation at the time began to manifest itself in the form of fervent protests and an immense upsurge in voting registration among African Americans. The active response among African Americans to address the racial ills of the moment was supplemented by calls for policy reform both outside from southern liberals, leftists groups, labor movements, and within the Roosevelt Administration from various persons, including the First Lady Eleanor Roosevelt, Will Alexander, Harry Hopkins, Harold Ickes, and Aubrey Williams, all of which helped to foment and expedite the creation and implementation of policy that was beneficial for African Americans.

As a loosely constituted, unofficial governmental organization, the daily happenings of the black cabinet varied

greatly, but it is an accepted fact that all of the cabinet's work was aimed at uplift of African American people. The black cabinet served both a material and a symbolic function in regard to improving the collective lot of African Americans. The mere existence of such a large constituency of blacks in influential political and governmental positions indicated to the wider African American community that perhaps a needed shift in terms of racial equality was taking place, while materially the presence of African Americans in government as racial advisors allowed the needed space to voice the myriad of concerns of the modal black population to the larger administration. Because of the Federal Council of Negro Affairs loose construction and some of the black cabinet's more logistical aspects, such as specific information about the everyday occurrences, as well as information regarding its members, remain unclear.

Despite a paucity of information regarding all of the inner workings as well as official information on the number of members exact members because of the dynamic influx and outflow of the black cabinet, some of the black brain trust's initiatives and endeavors are revealed through the work of some of its most prominent members such as Robert Weaver, William Hastie (who worked for the Department of Interior as an assistant solicitor), and Mary McCloud Bethune.

Mary McCloud Bethune was perhaps one of the black cabinet's foundational and most visible members, and certainly its most prominent female member. During her work in the club movement, she developed a close friendship with Eleanor Roosevelt, a relationship that would eventually allow her to move into governmental positions. Regarding her role in the Federal Council of Negro Affairs, Bethune was involved in the development of the Fair Employment Practices Commission. Bethune also worked on the Civilian Pilot Training Program, which was focused on training black pilots, and the Women's Army Corp (WAC) and its admittance of black women. Mary McCloud Bethune's work is indicative of the type of projects for African American improvement that the black cabinet was created for and committed to carrying out.

In many ways the black cabinet reflected a material shift in things such as political party affiliation, as African Americans had previously been overwhelmingly Republican began to align themselves more with Democratic politics. The cabinet also indicated perhaps the nascent stage of a national collective ideological shift that would eventually recognize not just inclusion and amelioration, but uplift and equality for African Americans.

See also: Bethune, Mary McLeod; Bunche, Ralph; Roosevelt, Eleanor

Christina Bush

Bibliography

Birnbaum, Jonathan, and Clarence Taylor, eds. *Civil Rights Since 1787: A Reader on the Black Struggle.* New York: New York University Press, 2000.

Franklin, John Hope, and Alfred A. Moss Jr. *From Slavery to Freedom: A History of African Americans.* New York: Alfred K. Knopf, 1994.

Weiss, Nancy J. *Farewell to the Party of Lincoln: Black Politics in the Age of FDR.* Princeton, NJ: Princeton University Press, 1983.

Black Codes

Black Codes, laws enacted in Southern states during Reconstruction, discriminated against blacks and restricted their newly acquired freedom. The laws, which appeared to be neutral and fair to both whites and blacks, were not neutral. The codes became known as Jim Crow laws because they were as deceptive as the minstrel show character, Jim Crow, was deceptive. Crow, a white character, disguised himself with a painted black face and the Black Codes, like the minstrel character, were thought to be based on racial disguise.

Mississippi and South Carolina were the first states to enact Black Codes. South Carolina's newly adopted post-war constitution prohibited African Americans from voting and continued to impose racial qualifications on those who desired to become state legislators. Its legislative enactments prohibited black men from earning a living as artisans, mechanics, or shopkeepers unless they were licensed. Black laborers could be employed under yearly contracts of labor, but if they were terminated from employment, either voluntarily or by the employer, they were required to forfeit all wages earned within the year to any date of the termination.

Mississippi's Black Codes were the most stringent. Freedmen, free negroes, and mulattoes could only own land in cities, were limited in their ability to testify in court proceedings, were punished for leaving employment, and were defined as vagrants if they had no lawful employment or business, were found congregating together at any time of the day of night, or failed to pay any tax levied upon them. Other Southern states had similar legislation and, although the language of the enactments varied from state to state, the Black Codes placed controls on blacks' property ownership, employment, sexual behavior, and voting rights. The laws also limited the rights of blacks to sit on juries, testify at trials, and to own or carry weapons. All states imposed poll taxes on blacks. Unemployment was considered a crime in most states, and most codes defined vagrants as freedmen who were unemployed. The Black Codes were supplemented by additional legislation in some states. States provided separate public transportation for blacks and denied them the use of public education funding.

Louisiana required all freed peoples to obtain comfortable housing and have visible means of support within 20 days of the passage of the legislation or be subject to arrest. Alabama's Black Codes required all Civil War officers to report to the county all the names of black minors whose parents were unable or unwilling to support them. Once the minors' names had been reported, they were subject to fines, arrest, and a sentence that included working for the highest bidder for their services in order to work off the fine. Florida laws prohibited negroes and mulattos from keeping any weapon, firearm, or ammunition without a license. Penalties for noncompliance included whipping the offender's bare back.

Effects of the Black Codes had wide ramifications beyond the everyday lives of the freed blacks. Northern Republicans were successful in getting Congress to pass the Civil Rights Act of 1866 over President Andrew Johnson's veto, and the Fourteenth Amendment was added to the United States Constitution. The federal government also imposed military rule to ensure compliance with Reconstruction measures.

See also: Civil Rights Act of 1866; Fourteenth Amendment; Jim Crow; Johnson, Andrew; Radical Republicans; White Supremacy

Nancy A. McCaslin

Bibliography

Curtis, Michael Kent. *No State Shall Abridge: The Fourteenth Amendment and the Bill of Rights.* Durham: Duke University Press, 1986.

Dickerson, Donna Lee, ed. *The Reconstruction Era: Primary Documents on Events from 1865 to 1877.* Westport, CT: Greenwood Press, 2003.

Moore, Dan. *Black Codes in Georgia*. Atlanta: APEX Museum, 2007.

Wilson, Theodore Brantner. *The Black Codes of the South*. Tuscaloosa: University of Alabama Press, 1965.

Black Conservatives

All politics is involved with promoting the practical means of obtaining the good life. For black conservatives, this means an embracing of such values as hard work and individual responsibility. They reject the current liberal approach that argues for collective action and that states that the prime source for black failure is still institutionalized racism. They are a diverse group who are sometimes called neo-Washingtonians. The history of black conservatism begins in the 1800s, but like all political movements it has changed over the years and has found a resurgence beginning in the 1970s.

In the late 19th century and early 20th century, two opposing political philosophies—liberal and conservative—began to take shape for black Americans. After the Civil War, African Americans supported Republicans, the party of Lincoln and of emancipation. Even after Lincoln's assassination, Republicans continued to support civil rights for blacks. At this time, Booker T. Washington (1856–1915) shaped the conservative views of black Americans.

Washington, a former slave from Franklin County, Virginia, attended Hampton Institute and Wayland Seminary. He then helped to develop the Tuskegee Institute, recruiting its first students and raising money for its first buildings. Two important events happened in his life during these years. First, while he was a student at Wayland, he became convinced that black students who opted for a classical education forgot their roots and became estranged from the experience of black poverty. Second, as the head of the Tuskegee Institute, he encountered strong antipathy from Southern whites who feared that educated blacks would not be willing to enter the agricultural economy that dominated the South. To overcome this, Washington emphasized that the Tuskegee Institute would emphasize "industrial" education, meaning farming, carpentry, etc. These, he believed, would be the most likely avenues of employment for the majority of African Americans.

The basis of his political philosophy was that being productive was a more powerful antidiscrimination tool than protesting or hoping for intervention from the federal government. He argued that no race will ever be marginalized if they can contribute to the economy of the world. In 1895 he gave his famous "Atlanta Compromise" speech in which he further argued against "artificial forcing" of rights and emphasized that white society needed African Americans and that any attempt to stifle the growth of blacks by white society would be counterproductive. His compromise was for there to be a symbiotic relationship between the two races. In 1900, he founded the National Negro Business League. He strongly believed in self-help and hard work as the keys to success.

One of the biggest critics of Washington's approach was W. E. B. Du Bois (1868–1963). Du Bois's ideas have been influential in the shaping of modern-day black liberalism. He was brilliant, well educated, and talented. He was a writer, a teacher, a sociologist, an editor, and an activist. His major complaints against Washington were that Washington believed in a subordinate position for African Americans, that Washington denigrated higher education for blacks, and that he was too conciliatory toward the South. Du Bois was a socialist and believed that government had to become involved in order for equality to become a reality and that social protest and agitation were also necessary. As a socialist, he was skeptical of capitalism and toward the end of his life became a member of the Communist Party.

Both black conservatism and black liberalism have changed over time, and neither is an exact replica of the ideas of either Washington or Du Bois. But certain principles have survived. For modern black liberals, protest, agitation, and federal intervention in the lives of African Americans are still important. For modern black conservatives, self-help, entrepreneurship, and a dislike of the welfare state are still important.

This is best understood in the context of the changes in party affiliations of African Americans during the last century. Black Americans generally continued to support the Republican Party until the Great Depression, when Franklin Roosevelt's left-leaning administration undertook to intervene in the lives of poverty-stricken people, both black and white. As a result, Roosevelt's Democrats won the loyalty of many Americans who now saw the federal government as good and big business as evil.

The 1960s further strengthened black Americans' loyalty to the more liberal Democratic Party. This was the era of active civil rights and school desegregation, and liberals were more clearly identified with this group approach than were conservatives. In addition, Democrat Lyndon Baines Johnson's Great Society legislation offered even more federal intervention in people's lives.

But beginning as early as the 1970s (even earlier, if George S. Schuyler, who lived between 1895 and 1977, is considered), conservative voices in the black community began to assert themselves. Early on, most black conservatives worked for the media. Soon they would create organizations and interest groups and eventually they would move into politics—one even to the U.S. Supreme Court. Taken together, they demonstrate the essence, as well as the diversity, of contemporary black conservative thought.

In the media, newspapers, like *The Chicago Independent Bulletin*, published by Hurley Green Sr., carried important black conservative columnists. Magazines, like *National Minority Politics*, published by Willie and Gwen Richardson; *Issues and Views*, edited by Elizabeth Wright; and *The Lincoln Review*, edited by J. A. Parker began to promote conservative thought. Important black columnists include men like Thomas Sowell, Walter Williams, and Shelby Steele. In general, they argue that the key to success for African Americans is individual effort rather than government intervention.

Thomas Sowell, born in North Carolina but raised in Harlem, never finished high school. He joined the Marine Corp and eventually graduated (magna cum laude) with an economics degree from Harvard and a PhD in economics from the University of Chicago. He is now a nationally syndicated columnist. He has argued against the idolization of ghetto culture by liberals, Hollywood, and the media. He believes that economic lags by African Americans are not entirely due to racial discrimination, and therefore fixable by government intervention, including the intervention of affirmative action. In short, he does not believe that the government—or judicial activism by judges—can solve racial problems. One of his major concerns is education for blacks, but he does not limit his ideas about education, as did Washington. For him, education, including higher education, is the key to success. He is also for education reforms like vouchers.

Walter Williams, also an economist, was born in Philadelphia. He has a PhD in economics from UCLA. He, too, is a believer that education is the key to success for all people.

He is also a believer in the power of such middle class values as stable families and hard work. He is not against the civil rights battles of the past that guaranteed constitutional guarantees, but he is against people forever thinking that they are victims and that the only way to not be a victim is for someone else to do something for them. And he dislikes the paternalistic attitude of white liberals that feeds this victim attitude.

Shelby Steele, with a PhD in English and a master's degree in sociology, was born in Chicago. In 1991, he won the National Book Critics Circle Award for his book *The Content of Our Character*. In this book, he calls for African Americans to work as individuals within the mainstream rather than attempt to reach their goals through collective action that attacks the mainstream. That, he argues, is the way to advance. In *A Dream Deferred: The Second Betrayal of Black Freedom in America,* he defines a black conservative as one who does not accept that victimization is the sole—or the major—reason for black failure.

Black conservatives have also made an impact on radio. A good example is Larry Elder who has a popular radio program in Los Angeles. Elder went to Brown University and received a law degree from the University of Michigan. He appears frequently on television. He is the author of several books, including the best-selling *The Ten Things You Can't Say in America*. He, too, thinks that the belief in victimization is crippling to black progress. He has even coined a word, "victicrat," to describe people who use victimization. He is a strong believer in personal responsibility.

Besides black conservative voices in the media, there are also organizations that promote conservative ideas in the African American community. The National Center for Neighborhood Enterprise is an example. It helps lower income blacks by promoting "self-sufficiency and financial independence." There is also The Brotherhood Organization of a New Destiny that believes in self-help and focuses on the lives of young black men. There are others.

There are also a number of black organizations that promote conservative ideas through political means. One of the most influential is Project 21, located in Washington, D.C. This organization states on its Web site that it is promoting "entrepreneurial spirit, sense of family and commitment to individual responsibility." One of its leaders, Edmund Peterson, has said that Project 21 attempts to fulfill the ideals of the Civil Rights movement by promoting basic middle class values, which he calls the "civil-behavior movement." Petersen believes that the breakup of the family is a major contributor to individual failure, thus his belief in strong family values.

One of the most powerful men in the United States is a black conservative, Supreme Court Justice Clarence Thomas. He was born in Pin Point, Georgia, in 1948, and attended Conception Seminary for a year. He then received his undergraduate degree from Holy Cross College and his law degree from Yale. He practiced law in Missouri before working for the U.S. Department of Education as Assistant Secretary for Civil Rights. He was the chairman of the U.S. Equal Employment Opportunity Commission from 1982 until 1990. He was appointed to the U.S. Court of Appeals for the District of Columbia in 1990. He became a United States Supreme Court Justice in 1991.

In 1980, Thomas, at the invitation of Thomas Sowell, attended a historically important conference, the Fairmont Conference in San Francisco. The sponsors titled it a Black Alternatives Conference and focused on conservative ideas. They discussed education and black priorities, the problems of government interference in the destiny of citizens, and legal barriers to economic success.

Thomas has written since then, in an article titled "No Room at the Inn: The Loneliness of the Black Conservative," about the values that he considers conservative and about how the Fairmont Conference and its aftereffects helped him to clarify them. The values come from his family, especially his grandparents; they are his road map to success in this country. For him, the basis of conservatism lies in the principle of natural Law, which underpins the Constitution. First, there must be respect for each person's freedom. Second, we should never be governed by anyone except with our consent. Third, the individual must take responsibility for his life. He saw this abstraction first in the concrete life of his grandparents who taught him that each person must fend for herself. They could give him values to make this work—God, education, discipline, and a belief in the efficacy of hard work—but it was up to him to make it happen. The government could never be a substitute for personal responsibility. Conservatives, he concluded, must actively protect the rights of individuals while at the same time demand individual responsibility.

Black conservatives may not always agree on every point, but they all share a belief in the American system. For them, the good life is possible, but no amount of government intervention will bring it; only individual effort can do that.

See also: Thomas, Clarence; Washington, Booker T.

William P. Toth

Bibliography

Bracey, Christopher Alan. *Saviors or Sellouts: The Promise and Peril of Black Conservatism, from Booker T. Washington to Condoleezza Rice.* Boston: Beacon Press, 2008.

Cooper, Anthony J., ed. *The Black Experience, 1865–1975: A Documentary Reader.* Dartford, Kent, UK: Greenwich University Press, 1995.

Faryna, Stan, Brad Stetson, and Joseph G. Conti, ed. *Black and Right: The Bold New Voice of Black Conservatives in America.* Westport, CT: Praeger, 1997.

Sowell, Thomas. *Race and Culture: A World View.* New York, Basic Books, 1995.

Steele, Shelby. *The Content of Our Character: A New Vision of Race in America.* New York: St. Martin's Press, 1990.

Williams, Walter E. *More Liberty Means Less Government.* Stanford: Hoover Institution Press, 1999.

Black Nadir

The black nadir traditionally references to the worst period in the African American experience, a period dating from 1877 to 1918. Historian Rayford Logan coined the term in his book *The Negro in American Life and Thought* (1954). This groundbreaking text was important for expanding the discourse of black history in that critical period between Reconstruction and World War I to include a narrative of how blacks were systematically oppressed and stereotyped, while also linking talented tenth activism to the modern civil rights movement.

In the nadir construct, Reconstruction was an era of hope for Southern blacks following centuries of enslavement. They had hoped for freedom and equality through land ownership, socioeconomic independence, reforging the ties within families and communities, and acquiring the ballot and first-class citizenship. This hope was systematically undermined by the reality that they were only quasi-free. Crucial to this narrative was that blacks represented a major threat in tipping the political-economic balance of power in the South to their own (and white liberal) favor. White conservatism curtailed these advances by forming white terrorist groups like the Ku Klux Klan, restricting most freedmen to back-breaking manual labor and domestic work, and restricting them from voting, racial intermingling, serving on juries, and land ownership. Finally, white liberal indifference led to the systematic collapse of the Radical Republican political structure in the South after the economic Panic of 1873. Reconstruction officially ended following the Hayes-Tilden Compromise of 1877, which called for the withdrawal of Union troops from the South, depriving Southern blacks and white liberals of the protection of the federal government.

The failure of Reconstruction set a pattern of Southern white supremacy, which expanded nationwide until it was finally brought to a halt in large part by the Civil Rights movement during the 1960s. From 1877 to 1968, black freedom was opposed by customary and legal discrimination in the forms of Black Codes and states' rights, which nationally extended as Jim Crow (legal) segregation after the *Plessy v. Ferguson* U.S. Supreme Court verdict in 1896. During this period, African Americans were systematically beaten, lynched, raped, disenfranchised, and made to appear stereotypically pathological, immoral, and inferior to whites in entertainment (i.e., minstrel shows) and "science" (i.e., eugenics). Moreover, civil rights legislation established during Reconstruction as well as the Fourteenth Amendment (that guaranteed citizenship and due process) and the Fifteenth Amendment (that conferred the right to vote) were rarely used to protect people of color. Couple this with the federal government's obsession with promoting industry and territorial expansion, and the end result was the loss of hope through socially constructed oppression for people not considered to be U.S. citizens.

The nadir construct marginally addresses how blacks confronted white supremacy using a wide range of strategies that blossomed into a freedom movement after 1945. Central to black self-determination was the formation of black institutions such as churches and schools that fostered leadership, community, and literacy. Blacks also elected their own political leaders, served in the military, and infused politics into art. Moreover, blacks quested after freedom in search of promised lands in the West, North, and abroad such as Nicodemus (Kansas), Pittsburgh, and Liberia. In the early 20th century, freedom strategies increased in intensity over time from the work of Booker T. Washington, who found black salvation in agricultural and domestic industrial pursuits while accommodating the "color-line," to the articulate critique of W. E. B. Du Bois, who opposed racism through his political activism and intellect.

The black nadir reactively centers black oppression without balancing the discourse with a strong understanding of black agency and resistance. In addition, it should reflect the lowest point of the black experience by era, not year. For example, after World War I (1919), severe restrictions on black freedom nationally continued in race rioting, voting, public accommodations, employment, housing, education, and entertainment, which maintained unadulterated white supremacy from 1874 to at least the passing and enforcement of civil rights legislation in the 1960s.

See also: Disfranchisement; Du Bois, W. E. B.; Jim Crow; Lynching; *Plessy v. Ferguson;* Sharecropping; Washington, Booker T.

Herbert G. Ruffin II

Bibliography

Loewen, James W. *Sundown Towns: A Hidden Dimension of Segregation in America.* New York: W. W. Norton, 2005.

Logan, Rayford. *The Betrayal of the Negro: From Rutherford B. Hayes to Woodrow Wilson.* New York: Perseus Publishing, 1997.

Taylor, Quintard. *In Search of the Racial Frontier: African Americans in the West, 1528–1990.* New York: W. W. Norton, 1998.

Trotter, Joe William. *The Great Migration in Historical Perspective: New Dimensions of Race, Class, and Gender.* Bloomington: Indiana University Press, 1991.

Black Nationalism

Black nationalism did not emerge as a coherent movement focused on racial solidarity until the early 20th century. But its origins lie in the philosophies of black abolitionists—namely Martin Delany, who advocated emigration to Africa. Explaining that black Americans were culturally and politically homeless, Delany proposed that they needed to build their own nation in Sierra Leone and Liberia. He also believed that this nation building would raise the social status of those who remained behind in America. Trying to move his plan forward, he led an emigration commission to West Africa in 1859 and explored potential sites for a black nation. While these ideas did not become a reality, later black nationalists, including Huey Newton, found inspiration and historical precedent in his work. They also looked back to Frederick Douglass's more radical speeches (such as his 1857 "West Indian Emancipation" speech) and the plans of the militant white abolitionist John Brown to build a slave-free nation in the Adirondacks.

By the 1920s, the Jamaican immigrant Marcus Garvey had developed radical abolitionist theories into a full-fledged black nationalist movement. In 1914, Garvey founded the Jamaica-based Universal Negro Improvement Association (UNIA), and, in 1917, he opened a first branch in the United States. Tapping into urban discontent after the Great Migration, the UNIA advocated black unity and self-improvement. It sponsored several educational institutions, convened international conventions, and opened more than 1,000 branches. It had 11 million members at its peak, mainly northern working class black people. Garvey's UNIA-affiliated newspaper, *Negro World,* first appeared in 1918 and fast became one of the country's most widely circulated black newspapers. Then, going beyond black self-improvement, Garvey echoed Delany's call for black national independence and emigration from the United States to Africa. In 1919, he established the Black Star Line, a transportation company focused on moving people and property to Africa. The venture failed and Garvey was deported after a mail fraud conviction in 1923. Nonetheless, he had turned the ideas of abolitionists into a movement and developed the first major strand of black nationalism: black separatism through a Back-to-Africa ideology.

His movement also inspired a new black nationalist effort: Farrad Muhammad's Nation of Islam (NOI). Founded and developed during the early 1930s, and with many former Garveyites among its early members, the NOI represented a second major strand in black nationalism: black separatism within the United States (rather a separate nation in Africa). To prepare for this separate black nation, the NOI preached black racial superiority and focused on developing economic self-sufficiency within black communities. Led by Elijah Muhammad after 1934, it entirely rejected white society and demanded several American states—a nation within a nation—as compensation for slavery.

By the late 1950s, Malcolm X had become its most prominent spokesperson. Born Malcolm Little, he had converted to the Black Muslim religion while in prison for armed robbery and changed his name to "X." He later explained that his parents were followers of Garvey and members of the UNIA, thereby giving him an early exposure to black nationalism. As a minister for the NOI, he defined land as the basis of freedom and equality, called for racial independence and a separate black identity, and advocated black self-defense. He also termed American history a *white* history, famously noting that blacks were no more than a

sack of potatoes to the Founding Fathers. He aimed these black nationalist philosophies at a primary audience of young, urban blacks, who were frustrated by what they saw as Martin Luther King Jr.'s embrace of white protest traditions (including civil disobedience) and futile gradualism.

In 1964, Malcolm declared independence from the NOI and formed Muslim Mosque, Inc. He soon expanded his vision of black nationalism to include Africans and made two trips to Africa in 1964 in an effort to solicit support from African leaders. On June 28, 1964, he called a press conference to announce his new project, the Organization of Afro-American Unity (OAAU). Rather than promoting a Back-to-Africa movement, like Garvey's, this would be an organization that sought to achieve a global African community, promote the interests of black people worldwide, fight white supremacy, and link black Americans with Africa.

Malcolm was killed on February 21, 1965, before he could develop the OAAU program any further. But his ideas soon inspired a new black nationalist vision in the form of the Black Panther Party for Self-Defense (BPP). Bobby Seale and Huey Newton founded the BPP at a community center in North Oakland, California, in October 1966, and acknowledged it was a living testament to Malcolm's work. Long frustrated with mainstream civil rights efforts, they were also galvanized by the defeat of the Mississippi Freedom Democratic Party in 1964, the Watts uprising, and the Voting Rights Act of 1965. They believed that King and his supporters paid scant attention to the situation of urban African Americans, including the ongoing problems of high unemployment, substandard housing, and poor education. Now they aimed their new group at a post Civil Rights era.

Adopting Malcolm X's model of armed self-defense, they quickly formed a system of police patrols, aimed at countering police brutality against Oakland's black community. Their new members began to monitor and confront law enforcement officials and to advise Oakland residents of their rights. They began to use the term "black power" as a theory to explain their practices. This represented a new spin on black nationalism. Richard Wright had first used this phrase in his 1954 book of the same title, but it was Stokely Carmichael, the Student Nonviolent Coordinating Committee (SNCC) chairman and eventually the BPP's honorary prime minister, who first developed the idea into a full movement ideology. In 1966, he laid out a philosophy of black power that Newton and Seale adopted for their newly formed organization: black people needed to achieve racial pride and reclaim a black history, as well as building separate black communities, developing economic self-sufficiency, and collectivizing their resources. Black nationalism now meant not only political and economic control but also psychic and historical control. Another part of this black power philosophy was to prohibit whites from joining the liberation movement. Carmichael explained that whites could not relate to the black experience and that an all-black project was needed in order for black people to achieve freedom. He rejected racial reconciliation, nonviolent civil disobedience, and any notion of the American dream as defined by white people.

Newton and Seale translated this philosophy of absolute self-determination into the formation of community programs, rather than attempts to achieve an independent black colony. The BPP therefore represented a third major strand in black nationalism: the development of black community control over political and economic resources, or community nationalism. The BPP "survival programs" tried to combat the institutional racism at the heart of substandard housing, bad diets, poor health care services, and poor education for African Americans. They eventually offered breakfasts for schoolchildren, medical care, pest control, busing to prisons for the families of inmates, sickle cell anemia testing, clothing and shoes, community political education classes, and "liberation schools." In part because of this smaller-scale, practical application of black nationalist philosophy—improving existing black communities rather than reaching for a separate black nation—the BPP's membership had grown to around 5,000 by the end of 1968, with chapters in India, Israel, Australia, and England, as well as 40 chapters in the United States.

But the organization was under attack. In August 1967, the FBI under J. Edgar Hoover had instructed its covert action program—COINTELPRO—to disrupt and neutralize "Black Nationalist Hate Groups," and by July 1969 the Panthers were COINTELPRO's primary focus (although it also targeted the Southern Christian Leadership Conference, SNCC, the Revolutionary Action Movement, and the Nation of Islam). The program attempted to weaken BPP leaders, discredit the organization, and prevent the unification of black nationalist groups. They set other groups against the BPP and created rifts and factions within the BPP itself. A series of FBI raids and prosecutions, including the 1969 indictment and conviction of Seale for protesting

during the Democratic National Convention of August 1968, weakened the BPP's national and regional leadership and diminished its local membership.

By the early 1970s, its leadership was also engaged in a series of internal conflicts over the primary focus of black nationalist activism. Newton wanted to emphasize community service, but another BPP leader, Eldridge Cleaver, believed armed confrontation was more important. Cleaver publicly criticized the BPP as "reformist" rather than "revolutionary," and Seale countered that the survival programs *were* "revolutionary" (412). In early 1971, Newton expelled Cleaver from the Central Committee and stated that his focus on violence alienated the black community and inhibited his potential role in the black nationalist transformation of society.

Before long the BPP was entirely crippled. Internal disputes, infiltration by covert government operations, and the deaths of party members during violent clashes with the police had diminished its energy and support. In March 1978, the membership of the BPP had declined to around 20. But the party's platform did offer a blueprint for other 1960s protest manifestos, including those by the Brown Berets, the Young Lords, the White Panther Party, the Red Guards, and the Gray Panthers.

The BPP represents the last truly influential black nationalist movement in the United States. But elements of black nationalism do persist. As late as 1995, the NOI attracted between 650,000 and 1.5 million people to its "Million Man March" in Washington, D.C. The black nationalism emphasis on racial pride and black history also influenced the emergence of hip-hop as a protest medium. For example, Tupac Shakur embraced the doctrines of black nationalism in songs like "Panther Power" (1989). As well, elements of the "Back to Africa" movement influenced the development of pan-Africanism. Several former Panthers, including Carmichael, shifted direction to embrace pan-African pride, explaining that the only way forward for black nationalism was a socialist pan-African revolution.

As for the strand of black nationalism focused on community development, this persists in two new groups. In the early 1990s, activists inspired by the BPP pointed to new and continuing crises in black America: poverty, AIDS, infant mortality, drugs, high unemployment, and institutionalized racism. They announced the return of black nationalism and in 1994 former members of the original BPP launched The Black Panther Collective. They began to document police brutality in New York and to raise public awareness about political prisoners. The New African American Vanguard Movement was also founded in 1994, with B. Kwaku Duren as its chair. It became the New Panther Vanguard Movement in 1997. The group develops community-based social and cultural institutions, also demanding sentencing reviews and reductions for black prisoners.

But the separatist strand of black nationalism was also taken up by a more high-profile contemporary black nationalist group: the New Black Panther Party (NBPP), founded in 1991. The party's literature references Garvey's separatist movement and calls for independent African-centered schools, more trade with Africa, black tax exemption, and its own provisional government. The NBPP's ultimate aim is black national liberation and a black "liberated zone." But its strong anti-Zionist tendencies have led to accusations of anti-Semitism, and several members of the original BPP have condemned the NBPP, observing that the BPP had operated with love for blacks, not hatred of whites.

See also: A Negro Nation Within the Nation; Black Panther Party; Black Power; Delany, Martin R.; Five Percenters; Garvey, Marcus; Muhammad, Elijah; Nation of Islam; Organization of Afro-American Unity; Universal Negro Improvement Association; X, Malcolm

Zoe Trodd

Bibliography

Bracey, John et al, eds. *Black Nationalism in America.* Indianapolis: Bobbs-Merrill, 1970.

Essien-Udom, E. U. *Black Nationalism: A Search for an Identity in America.* Chicago: University of Chicago Press, 1962.

Gardell, Mattias. *In the Name of Elijah Muhammad: Louis Farrakhan and The Nation of Islam.* Durham: Duke University Press, 1996.

Haines, Herbert H. *Black Radicals and the Civil Rights Mainstream, 1954–1970.* Knoxville: University of Tennessee Press, 1988.

Robinson, Dean E. *Black Nationalism in American Politics and Thought.* New York: Cambridge University Press, 2001.

Seale, Bobby. *Seize the Time: The Story of the Black Panther Party and Huey P. Newton.* Baltimore: Black Classic Press, 1991.

Ullman, Victor. *Martin R. Delany: The Beginnings of Black Nationalism.* Boston: Beacon Press, 1971.

Black Panther Party

Originally called the Black Panther Party for Self-Defense, the Black Panther Party (BPP) was a radical African American political organization established in 1966 in Oakland,

California, by Huey P. Newton (1942–1989), minister of self-defense, and Bobby Seale (1936–), chairman. Although the group's organizational beginnings can be traced to October 1966, with the creation of the "Black Panther Party Platform and Program," a manifesto outlining the group's ideological and political perspectives and goals with respect to housing issues, educational and economic opportunities, police violence, and African American disenfranchisement, the BPP is a continuation of black freedom struggles that began with the first rebellions against slavery and captivity in the barracoons, holding cells for enslave Africans, centuries ago. Black Panther Party members perceived themselves as a vanguard party who mobilized the black lumpenproletariat, those unemployed members of the black working classes without political consciousness, and gave voice to the needs and desires of poor, segregated, urban communities that had not benefited from the legal victories of the Civil Rights movement. Throughout their 16-year existence, from 1966–1982, the party's political perspective and activity marked by ideological flexibility, adaptability, and hybridization—a fusion of ideas from post-World War II black liberation struggles in the United States and anticolonial struggles throughout the third world. Their most ostensible influences were Malcolm X, Frantz Fanon, Mao Zedong, Robert F. Williams, Kwame Nkrumah, Fidel Castro, V. I. Lenin, and Karl Marx.

Violent police brutality, hallmarks of many black, urban communities of the late 1960s, determined the party's initial black nationalist perspective and its political activity. Newton, as the party's theoretician, saw black urban neighborhoods as colonies occupied by the police force whose brutal surveillance were geared toward maintaining black exploitation. This approach led the small group of activists to focus on armed community patrols of the police. Equipped with pistols, shotguns, and law books, Newton, Seale, and Bobby Hutton, the first member and treasurer of the organization, traversed the streets of Oakland to ensure that police officers did not violate residents' rights. During patrols, Panthers, with weapons in plain sight, observed police officers carrying out their duty and questioned the detained resident to see if abuse had taken place. If the suspect was arrested, the patrol would pursue the arresting vehicle to the precinct station and post bail for the individual. Newton observed that patrols had a threefold effect: they taught the community how to protect themselves from the police, they decreased the incidents of police brutality, and they increased the membership of the BPP. As the membership increased so did police patrols of other black neighborhoods in the San Francisco Bay area including Berkeley, Richmond, and San Francisco.

In 1967, the party gained recognition among San Francisco Bay Area communities after it investigated and publicized the fatal police shooting of Denzil Dowell, a Richmond, California resident. During the same year, after providing protection for Betty Shabazz, the widow of the slain leader Malcolm X, the party attracted new members. Perhaps the most prominent person to join that year was Eldridge Cleaver, the renowned ex-convict and writer for the leftist magazine *Ramparts,* who became the organization's minister of information. His writing ability and connections with leftist activists were instrumental in attracting new members and helping the party create the Black Community News Service and *The Black Panther,* a weekly newspaper. The paper was indicative of the BPP's political dexterity in their attempts to empower black communities.

The Black Panther provided a medium through which party leadership and members could connect to the communities they served and raise reader consciousness. By 1970, the paper had a weekly circulation of over 100,000.

In the spring of 1967, the BPP gained national attention. On May 2, 1967, Bobby Seale and a contingent of 30 armed Black Panthers orchestrated a political demonstration when they delivered a public announcement called "Executive Mandate Number One" on the stairs of the Capitol Building in Sacramento, California. "Executive Mandate Number One" was a written response to the Mulford Gun Bill, legislation that would make carrying weapons illegal. As a result of their political demonstration, Bobby Seale and several other Panthers were arrested and accused of conspiracy. Despite its portrayal of the BPP as a black supremacist group and motley crew of thugs, the mainstream media coverage unknowingly acted as a recruiting mechanism for the organization. After the Sacramento incident, requests poured in from across the country for assistance

Members of the Black Panther Party (BPP) march in Manhattan on July 22, 1968, to protest the murder trial of leader and cofounder, Huey P. Newton. (Bettmann/Corbis)

in creating local chapters of the Black Panther Party. By the end of the decade, the BPP had grown to be a national organization with 40 chapters, more than 5,000 members, and tens of thousands of supporters. By 1969, the Black Panther Party comprised individual chapters unified under one central committee.

The Party Goes National

By 1968, the BPP grew to be larger than its founders had imagined. To connect the work being done in the southern states by the Student Nonviolent Coordinating Committee (SNCC) with BPP work in western and northern urban areas, the two organizations attempted a merger. SNCC's Stokely Carmichael was named BPP prime minister; James Forman, minister of foreign affairs; and H. Rap Brown, minister of justice. The merger was short-lived and the appointments were largely symbolic, as the union was destroyed by organizational mistrust, exacerbated by well-placed counterintelligence by the FBI, and differing leadership styles. With Huey Newton as the BPP leader, authority was centralized. SNCC was best known for its decentralized structure and a belief in the leadership ability of all its members. Further, SNCC was moving closer to a black nationalist perspective and was unwilling to work with white groups. The BPP was moving away from its previous black nationalist perspective toward socialism and was willing to work with any organization that held the best interest of black communities to heart, especially the Peace and Freedom Party.

With the merger between the BPP and SNCC undermined, the BPP Central Committee set out to maintain a cohesive national unit. This proved difficult for the young revolutionaries. From 1967 to 1970, Huey P. Newton was imprisoned for allegedly shooting Patrolman John Frey, assaulting Patrolman Herbert Heanes, and kidnapping Dell Ross, a black motorist. Concurrently, Eldridge Cleaver and Bobby Seale were trying to gain popular support to "Free Huey" and were involved in their own court cases. But all chapters, from the most popular in Chicago, New York City, and Los Angeles, to the more obscure in Wilmington, Delaware, Omaha, and Denver, were unified around the survival programs, a willingness to re-envision the party platform and revolutionary activity, and government repression.

Survival programs were instituted with the primary objective of transforming social and economic relations within the United States. The party's survival programs indicate

not a "deradicalization" of the BPP or the substitution of a radical approach for a reformist one, but rather a willingness to supplement ostensibly radical political activities (mainly armed protection of black communities, rallying for self-determination, running political candidates, building interracial coalitions, and critiquing the intersection of racism and capitalism) with radical work that ensured the survival of black communities nationwide. From 1967 to 1974, BPP chapters throughout the country instituted survival programs addressing the multifaceted needs of urban communities. Some of the most popular include the Free Breakfast for School Children, Free Busing to Prisons Program, Sickle Cell Anemia Research Program, Seniors Against Fearful Environment, Free School Program, Free Pest Control Program, Free Food Program, Free Ambulance Program, Free Plumbing and Maintenance Program, and Liberation Schools. The survival programs were also indicative of the ways BPP members were willing to consistently expand the boundaries of their work and the limits of their perspective.

The 16-year lifespan of the BPP, especially the first five years, was marked by ideological expansion for the central committee, as well as the chapters. From 1966 to 1968, the party line was one of black nationalism, in which the primary vehicle for black liberation was understood to be black community control of community resources and institutions. In time, black nationalism as an ideology was too limiting, as it did not consider class issues and was replaced by revolutionary socialism from 1969 to 1970. From this perspective, capitalism did not provide adequate opportunities for the practice of self-determination, even with black community control. Only socialism provided the political and economic spaces for black self-determination and the potential for eradicating racism. By 1970, the party began to understand its freedom struggle as part of a larger global movement against imperialism and exploitation. With internationalism the ascendant philosophy from 1970–1971, as Judson Jeffries purports in *Huey P. Newton: The Radical Theorist* (2002), "the Panthers saw their struggle in the United States as not only necessary for the liberation of blacks and other oppressed people in America but as a struggle whose success was critical for the liberation of nations worldwide (74)." Intercommunalism developed from Internationalism and was the BPP dominant line from 1971 until the party's demise in 1982 and posits the notion that the growth of transnational corporations and economic globalization erased national borders, creating scattered communities loosely connected through commodity exchanges. The intellectual progression from black nationalism to intercommunalism represents the Black Panther Party's attempts to understand and explain forms of subordination and manipulation situated in political and economic realms. In fact, the BPP was one of the first organizations to openly criticize homophobic and sexist tendencies within black political movements.

Repression and Decline of the Black Panther Party

The Black Panther Party's zenith was short lived. As early as August 1967, it was targeted by the FBI's Counter-Intelligence Program (COINTELPRO) for neutralization. The BPP may have posed a political threat to the established mainstream arena by acting as a nucleus around which many New Left organizations could ally themselves, but it did not pose an offensive physical threat to the country. Despite this, in September 1969, J. Edgar Hoover, the director of the Federal Bureau of Investigation (FBI), declared that the BPP was a major threat to the domestic security of the United States. The FBI's repression of BPP chapters was nationwide in scope and used a variety of tactics including, but not limited to, manipulating media coverage of the BPP, interrupting the circulation of the *Black Panther,* disrupting survival programs (especially the Free Breakfast for School Children program), obstructing the creation of political alliances, harassing BPP supporters, creating and intensifying internal BPP conflicts, exacerbating tensions with other political groups, infiltrating chapters, raiding chapter headquarters, preventing due process in the judicial system, and assassinating party members. Moreover, of the 295 counterintelligence operations in 1969, 233 were directed toward crippling the Black Panther Party.

The counterintelligence operations affected chapters throughout the country. In 1969, in San Francisco, California, the FBI office gave fraudulent articles to local Jewish organizations declaring David Hilliard, the National Committee chief of staff, an anti-Semite, causing the organizations to cancel his lecture. On December 4, 1969, using a floor plan created by William O'Neal, an FBI infiltrator and informant, the Chicago police raided Black Panther leader Fred Hampton's home. Although Hampton was unarmed, police killed him with two close range shots to the head.

Throughout the country, FBI operatives convinced grocery stores and supermarkets to stop supporting the Panther's breakfast program, informing managers and owners that the party used the program to disseminate antipolice propaganda to children. Also, parents were told that the party's breakfast food was contaminated and infected with diseases. Further, to create dissension among the chapters, the FBI office in Philadelphia sent a letter to Huey Newton, allegedly from the Philadelphia BPP chapter, questioning his leadership ability. In his published doctoral dissertation, *War Against the Panthers* (1996), Huey P. Newton noted that COINTELPRO programs "anonymously advised the national headquarters that food, clothing, and drugs collected for BPP community programs were being stolen by [Philadelphia] BPP members (58)." Consequently, the national office transferred and expelled members and considered closing the Philadelphia office.

Besides government-sponsored repression, the party's centralized leadership may have contributed to its demise. After his release from prison in 1970, Huey Newton became the sole authority in party matters from 1970 to 1974. Manipulated by government misinformation, Newton publicly censured and dismissed individuals key to the party's history and political activity including Eldridge Cleaver and the International Section of the Party, members of the Los Angeles chapter, and the entire New York chapter. In 1973, at the behest of Huey Newton, the Black Panther Party moved into the political arena with its attempt to get Bobby Seale elected mayor of Oakland. To ensure his victory, Newton proposed that all state offices close and move to Oakland. With members refusing to submit to his decision, chapters across the country closed in protest and individuals resigned from the party. Some, however, moved to Oakland in 1972 and 1973 to assist in Seale's campaign. When Seale lost the election, many of the transplants lost hope and resigned. With state chapters closed and a failed political election, the party's membership fell to 500. In the summer of 1974, after a vehement disagreement with Huey Newton, Bobby Seale resigned followed by other key members of the deteriorating organization, including Audrea Jones.

From 1974 to 1977 with Huey Newton in exile, Elaine Brown assumed the party's leadership, decentralized power, appointed more women to leadership positions, obtained government funding to operate a school—the Oakland Community School—and ran for public office. Upon Newton's return in 1977 with less than 200 members, Newton again took the mantle of leadership until the party's demise in 1982. With Newton's behavior becoming more erratic, perhaps as a result of substance abuse, survival programs were discontinued, funds were mismanaged, and the party's relationship with the community deteriorated. In 1980, *The Black Panther* was discontinued and in 1982, the school was closed, marking the end of the exciting and often turbulent organization.

That the Black Panther Party existed demonstrates that the immediate post Civil Rights era was fraught with problems. Despite the passage of civil rights legislation and face-saving rhetoric of politicians, urban black neighborhoods in the late 1960s and early 1970s were facing the conundrum of being politically and economically ignored by policymakers. As young, black revolutionaries, party members and leaders organized to bring about change and provide services refused by city and state governments. Their militancy provided vivid examples for other communities of color and oppressed groups in the United States and throughout the world. From 1968 to 1987, groups inspired by the names, militancy, and program of the BPP were formed. In 1968 the Black Panther movement was organized in England. One year later, black Bermudans formed the Black Beret Cadre. The White Panther Party was organized in England in 1970, the Black Panther Party of Israel in 1971, the Black Panther Party of Australia in 1972, and the Dalit Panthers of India in 1987.

In the late 1990s, there was also an emergence of militant stylized-Panther groups in the United States. The opening decade of the 21st century finds several former Panthers in exile or imprisoned for the political beliefs. A host of biographies of former Panthers have appeared and historical research has been published about the Panthers, but more needs to be done. By studying the Black Panther Party and other New Left militant organizations, not only does one recover dimensions of working class, radical, and African American history that has been elided from historical texts, but one may also ascertain lessons to more effectively organize the growing impoverished masses who inhabit urban communities.

See also: Black Nationalism; Black Power; Brown, Elaine; Cleaver, Eldridge; COINTELPRO; Fanon, Frantz; Lowndes County Freedom Organization; Newton, Huey P.; Seale, Bobby; Shabazz, Betty X.; Williams, Robert F.; X, Malcolm

Jamie J. Wilson

Bibliography

Brown, Elaine. *A Taste of Power: A Black Woman's Story.* New York: Pantheon Books, 1992.

Churchill, Ward. *Agents of Repression: the FBI's Secret War Against the Black Panther Party and the American Indian Movement.* Boston: South End Press, 1988.

Churchill, Ward. "'To Disrupt, Discredit, and Destroy': The FBI's Secret War Against the Black Panther Party." In *Liberation, Imagination, and the Black Panther Party,* Kathleen Cleaver and George Katsiaficas, eds., 79–117. New York: Routledge, 2001.

Clemons Michael, and Jones, Charles E. "Global Solidarity: The Black Panther Party in the International Arena." In *Liberation, Imagination, and the Black Panther Party,* Kathleen Cleaver and George Katsiaficas, eds., 20–39. New York: Routledge, 2001.

Foner, Philip S. *The Black Panthers Speak.* New York: Da Capo Press, 1995.

Grady-Willis, Winston A. "The Black Panther Party: State Repression and Political Prisoners." In *The Black Panther Party Reconsidered,* Charles E. Jones, ed., 363–90. Baltimore: Black Classic Press, 1998.

Jeffries, Judson. *Huey P. Newton: The Radical Theorist.* Jackson: University Press of Mississippi, 2002.

Johnson, III, Ollie A. "Explaining the Demise of the Black Panther Party: The Role of Internal Factors." In *The Black Panther Party Reconsidered,* Charles E. Jones, ed., 391–414. Baltimore: Black Classic Press, 1998.

Jones, Charles E., and Judson Jeffries. "Don't Believe the Hype": Debunking the Panther Mythology." In *The Black Panther Party Reconsidered,* Charles E. Jones, ed., 25–55. Baltimore: Black Classic Press, 1998.

Newton, Huey P. *Revolutionary Suicide.* New York: Harcourt Brace Jovanovich, 1973.

Newton, Huey P. *To Die for the People: the Writings of Huey P. Newton.* New York: Vintage Books, 1972.

Newton, Huey P. *War Against the Panthers: A Study of Repression in America.* New York: Harlem River Press, 1996.

Seale, Bobby. *A Lonely Rage: The Autobiography of Bobby Seale.* New York: Times Books, 1978.

Seale, Bobby. *Seize the Time: The Story of the Black Panther Party and Huey P. Newton.* New York: Random House, 1970.

Umoja, Akinyele O. "Repression Breeds Resistance." In *Liberation, Imagination, and the Black Panther Party,* Kathleen Cleaver and George Katsiaficas, eds., 3–19. New York: Routledge, 2001.

Black Power

Black power refers to a phase or extension of the Civil Rights movement beginning in the period after 1966 when individual activists and organizations began to articulate the need for black political empowerment and self-defense as a means of achieving a variety of goals. In most historical accounts, black power began as a slogan during the

James Meredith March Against Fear in June 1966. After Meredith's shooting in Jackson, Mississippi, two activists in the Student Nonviolent Coordinating Committee (SNCC), Stokely Carmichael (Kwame Ture) and Willie Ricks (Mukasa Dada), used the slogan as an alternative to "We Shall Overcome," which had been an unofficial anthem of the Civil Rights movement. Although this may have been the genesis of the slogan as it became associated with the Civil Rights movement, it was not the first time that African American leaders or activist articulated a need for black empowerment. On the eve of Ghanaian independence, Richard Wright penned his 1954 book entitled *Black Power* as a reflection on the possibilities of empowerment on the African continent. Both Paul Robeson and Adam Clayton Powell Jr. had articulated the specific need for black power, whereas others, including W. E. B. Du Bois, Malcolm X, Ida B. Wells-Barnett, and Robert F. Williams, epitomized its meaning and ultimate potential in earlier decades.

Pressed for a definition of black power, Kwame Ture, along with political scientist Charles V. Hamilton, published *Black Power: The Politics of Liberation* in 1967 as an answer to the many critics of the concept. In essence, Ture defined black power as mobilizing African Americans to use their newfound political voice—as a result of the passage of the 1965 Voting Rights Act—to create semiautonomous communities in which black police officers patrolled black people, black businesses provided jobs, black elected officials and black-controlled political parties articulated the aspirations of African Americans, and African Americans used armed self-defense to protect their lives. Thus, black power can be seen as a "community-control" form of black nationalism. In many ways, this definition of black power was shaped largely by Ture's organizing activities in Lowndes County, Alabama in 1965 where he and other SNCC organizers had helped create the Lowndes County Freedom Organization (LCFO). In a region that was 97 percent African American, voter registration, the creation of an all-black political party (the LCFO), and mass mobilization could potentially lead to a complete take over of the county and, hence, real black empowerment. Using the Black Panther as the symbol of their political

Stokely Carmichael, head of the Student Nonviolent Coordinating Committee (SNCC), speaks against the draft at the University of California at Berkeley on October 29, 1966. (AP Photo)

party, the LCFO had several candidates vying for political office in the election season of November 1966. Hoping to elect candidates for sheriff, coroner, tax assessor, and in the board of education, all of the LCFO's candidates lost in the general election. Despite this defeat, the idea of community-control black nationalism and the symbol of the Black Panther spread to black communities across the United States.

The example and potential of Lowndes County spread and were articulated by an ever-widening group of individuals and organizations after 1966. Among the many organizations espousing black power that grew between 1967 and 1974 were the Black Panther Party for Self-Defense, SNCC, CORE, the Republic of New Afrika, the Congress of African Peoples, the Deacons for Defense and Justice, and Us. Although these organizations and their leadership differed vastly in goals and tactics, practically all of them were heirs of Malcolm X. In this sense, armed self-defense, as opposed to the nonviolent tactics of Martin Luther King Jr., were generally embraced. Malcolm's life, his many speeches, and his 1965 posthumous autobiography became canonical "texts" for many black power advocates. In addition, Robert F. Williams's *Negroes with Guns* (1962) and Frantz Fanon's *Wretched of the Earth* (1961) were quite influential in giving definition and shape to black power. Although the Black Power movement was eventually split between cultural nationalist and socialist factions, the goal of achieving some semblance of black empowerment and autonomy were concepts that all black power activists continued to embrace.

See also: Black Panther Party; COINTELPRO; Student Nonviolent Coordinating Committee; US Organization

Walter C. Rucker

Bibliography

Carmichael, Stokely, and Charles V. Hamilton. *Black Power; The Politics of Liberation in America.* New York: Random House, 1967.

Jeffries, J. L. *Black Power in the Belly of the Beast.* Urbana: University of Illinois, 2006.

Joseph, Peniel E. *Waiting 'til the Midnight Hour: A Narrative History of Black Power in America.* New York: Henry Holt, 2006.

Ogbar, Jeffrey Ogbonna Green. *Black Power: Radical Politics and African American Identity.* Baltimore: Johns Hopkins University Press, 2004.

Van Deburg, William L. *New Day in Babylon: The Black Power Movement and American Culture, 1965–1975.* Chicago: University of Chicago Press, 1992.

Black Radical Congress

Black Radical Congress (BRC, pronounced "brick") is a progressive grassroots organization that formed in June 1998 at the University of Illinois–Chicago. The BRC was established to revitalize the black freedom movement, which organizers felt had been compromised by liberal integrationists, elitist leaders, and conservative black nationalists. According to its mission statement, the BRC is resolved to build dialogue and alliances, "bringing diverse radical traditions to bear on contemporary realities." At a critical juncture in African American history, the BRC's organizers were determined to forge a liberation agenda for the new millennium. With deteriorating economic conditions, the erosion of civil rights legislation, and an increase in racial violence, the period between the mid-1970s and mid-1990s represented a "new nadir" for black Americans. Yet, although the BRC was a response to the conditions of a specific epoch, it was never intended to be a singular event. In its 11 years of existence, it has served as a national network of radical grassroots activists and organizations. From its inception, it represented a united front determined to construct a new humanity.

The BRC was not meant to replace existing organizations; it was formed to mobilize activists around common concerns. Drawing on the rich tradition of black Marxism, organizers were committed to the creation of an organization that represented the aspirations and interests of the masses. They did not seek to establish a vanguard party run by elites. Organizers also were not interested in creating another reactionary and polemic gathering such as the Million Man March. They did recognize, however, the need for black nationalists, socialists, communists, and feminists to work together to resuscitate the liberation movement. For the BRC's founders, this required the recognition of the interdependence of race-based, class-based, and gender-based oppression. The interconnectedness of these oppressive forces had been long ignored by those leading the liberation movement. This comprehensive approach to liberation was represented by the diverse backgrounds of the more than 100 individuals who endorsed the creation of the BRC. They included Larry Adams (Mailhandlers Local 300), General Baker (auto worker), Amina Baraka (Communist Party, USA), Adolph Reed (Labor Party, Chicago), Yicki Smith (Feminist Action Network), and Makungu

Akinyela and Efia Nwangaza (Malcolm X Grassroots Movement). These radical activists were joined by prominent black scholars including Angela Davis, Dwight Hopkins, Robin D. J. Kelly, Manning Marable, and Cornel West.

A year after the BRC convened, its national council ratified a 15-point "Freedom Agenda for the Twenty-First Century." This document stipulated:

I. We will fight for the human rights of Black people and all people;

II. We will fight for political democracy;

III. We will fight to advance beyond capitalism, which has demonstrated its structural incapacity to address basic human needs worldwide and, in particular, the needs of black people;

IV. We will fight to end the super-exploitation of southern workers;

V. We will struggle to ensure that all people in society receive free public education;

VI. We will struggle against state terrorism;

VII. We will struggle for a clean and healthy environment;

VIII. We will fight to abolish police brutality, unwarranted incarceration, and the death penalty;

IX. We will fight for gender equality, for women's liberation, and for women's rights to be recognized as human rights in all areas of personal, social, economic, and political life;

X. We recognize lesbian, gay, bisexual, and transgender people as full and equal members of society and of our communities;

XI. We support affirmative action;

XII. We will fight for reparations;

XIII. We will struggle to build multicultural solidarity and alliances among all people of color;

XIV. We will uphold the right of the African American people to self-determination;

XV. We support the liberation struggles of all oppressed people.

In 2003, the BRC celebrated its fifth anniversary with a conference at Seton Hall University. The objectives of the conference were to build a movement for peace and justice and to resist repressive domestic policies such as the PATRIOT Act. Chaired by activist Bill Sales, this conference included presenters from Africa, the Middle East, the Caribbean, and Latin America. In June 2008, the BRC convened a 10th Anniversary National Conference. Michael Eric Dyson opened the conference with a presentation on "Electoral Politics in the Struggle for Black Political Power." Continuing the commitment to a comprehensive approach to liberation, workshops included "Black People and the Iraq War," "In Search of a Black Gay Agenda," "Radicalizing the Hip-Hop Political Movement," "Gettin' the Vote Out: The Radical Approach," and "Black Liberation and Student Organizing." Plenary sessions assessed the BRC's past 10 years and developed a direction and strategy for the next 10 years. Despite changes in its programmatic structure and leadership, as outcomes of the plenary discussions, the BRC remains steadfast in its commitment to organizing a critical mass of black radicals to effect meaningful economic, political, and social change.

See also: Baraka, Amiri; Black Nationalism; Davis, Angela; Sanchez, Sonia

Rob Walsh

Bibliography

Cha-Jua, Sundiata Keita. "The Black Radical Congress and the Reconstruction of the Black Freedom Movement." *Black Scholar* 28, no. 3/4 (Fall/Winter 1998):8–21.

Forging a Black Liberation Agenda for the 21st Century. March 25, 2009. Black Radical Congress. March 27, 2009. http://www.blackradicalcongress.org/.

"The Freedom Agenda of the Black Radical Congress (BRC) Ratified by the BRC National Council (NC) April 17, 1999, Baltimore, Maryland." *Black Scholar* 35, no. 1 (Spring 2005):31–35.

Black Self-Defense

Black self-defense against racist violence has played a significant role throughout the history of the African American freedom struggle. Those who attempted to protect themselves or their communities against white aggression, however, generally faced overwhelming odds. In the antebellum South, rigid Slave Codes forbade black bondsmen to carry weapons, and confronting white masters was mortally dangerous. The end of slavery in 1865 and subsequent Constitutional Amendments finally granted all African Americans the right to bear arms, and a large number of former slaves used their newly acquired guns to fight terrorist groups such as the Ku Klux Klan. But black self-defense, which conjured up deep-seated fears of armed insurrection among white southerners, remained a dangerous venture. When armed blacks confronted exploitative employers, white lynch mobs, or abusive police officers in the 1880s and 1890s, their militancy tended to result in swift retaliation against individuals or entire black communities.

In the 1910s and 1920s, a number of militant black activists practiced and publicly advocated self-defense against racist terrorism. In the aftermath of World War I, for example, when numerous race riots rocked American cities, some black veterans used their army training to repel white invaders. Black nationalist leaders Marcus Garvey and Cecil Briggs applauded such examples of black militancy and urged their followers to confront white aggression. World War II further politicized and radicalized African American activists. Between 1942 and 1943, hundreds of racial clashes erupted in cities across the United States. Especially black veterans frequently resorted to armed actions when confronted with racist attackers upon their return to the United States. Still, armed resistance to white violence remained risky, especially in the Deep South, where white supremacy continued to reign supreme.

That changed during the civil rights struggle of the 1950s and 1960s, when organized black self-defense sparked less brutal repercussions and frequently complemented civil rights campaigns in the region. NAACP activist Robert F. Williams emerged as an early proponent of "armed self-reliance." In 1957, the black military veteran founded a black self-defense organization in Monroe, North Carolina to protect the local freedom movement against the revived Ku Klux Klan. Around the same time, a group called the "The Civil Rights Guards" prevented dynamite attacks against the church of local civil rights leader Rev. Fred Shuttlesworth in Birmingham, Alabama, and armed men in Little Rock, Arkansas formed a "volunteer guard committee" to protect the home of NAACP officer Daisy Bates.

When civil rights activists launched massive nonviolent protest campaigns and voter registration drives in the Deep South in the 1960s, the federal government's reluctance to provide protection led to the formation of several black protection agencies. Their armed actions helped local freedom movements survive in the face of white violence, bolstered the morale of civil rights activists, instilled pride in black protectors, and sometimes served as an additional means of coercion in the fight against Jim Crow. In the summer of 1964, for example, black military veterans

in Tuscaloosa, Alabama, organized a highly sophisticated defense squad that guarded nonviolent activists and their white allies. During the Freedom Summer project of 1964, some black Mississippians formed similar groups to repel segregationist attacks on their communities.

That same year, blacks in Jonesboro, Louisiana formed the Deacons for Defense and Justice (DDJ). The armed unit patrolled black neighborhoods, provided armed escorts for white and black activists, and guarded the offices of the Congress of Racial Equality (CORE). In 1965, African American activists formed another DDJ group in Bogalusa, Louisiana, achieving nationwide notoriety after shootouts with the Ku Klux Klan. Although such protective efforts generated frequent debates about their legitimacy among nonviolent activists, many civil rights organizers of CORE and the Student Nonviolent Coordinating Committee (SNCC) came to accept black self-defense as a matter of course.

Southern self-defense groups had disbanded by the end of the 1960s, but black self-defense remained a vital part of the Black Power movement, but it played a fundamentally different role and underwent a process of radical reinterpretation. In contrast to their southern peers, black power militants rarely engaged in armed confrontations with segregationist attackers. Rather black self-defense became a militant symbol of black defiance, which served primarily as a means to affirm and nurture black manhood. As early as 1961, black nationalist leader Malcolm X had denounced Martin Luther King's nonviolent philosophy as unmanly, urging African Americans to repel white attacks. In the aftermath of the James Meredith March of 1966, during which SNCC activist Stokely Carmichael first voiced the slogan black power, an increasing number of black activists heeded his advice.

The most prominent example of this new type of armed militancy was the Black Panther Party (BPP). Founded in Oakland, California in 1966, the BPP initially regarded its armed patrols in urban black communities as a way to confront police brutality. Ultimately, however, the Panthers and other black nationalist groups such as US or the Republic of New Africa reinterpreted traditional concepts of self-defense, arguing that race riots and revolutionary violence constituted a legitimate form of self-defense to confront white supremacy. Despite the largely symbolic nature of black power militancy, the Federal Bureau of Investigation (FBI) considered black power militants a threat to the nation's security, launching a massive counterintelligence program to disrupt their activities. By the mid-1970s, militant groups such as the Panthers had either succumbed to the FBI's destructive tactics or toned down their violent rhetoric.

See also: Black Panther Party; Black Power; Deacons for Defense and Justice; Republic of New Afrika; Student Nonviolent Coordinating Committee; US Organization; Williams, Robert F; X, Malcolm

Simon Wendt

Bibliography

Hill, Lance E. *The Deacons for Defense: Armed Resistance and the Civil Rights Movement.* Chapel Hill: University of North Carolina Press, 2004.

Shapiro, Herbert. *White Violence and Black Response: From Reconstruction to Montgomery.* Amherst: University of Massachusetts Press, 1988.

Strain, Christopher B. *Pure Fire: Self-Defense as Activism in the Civil Rights Era.* Athens: University of Georgia Press, 2005.

Tyson, Timothy. *Radio Free Dixie: Robert F. Williams and the Roots of Black Power.* Chapel Hill: University of North Carolina Press, 1999.

Wendt, Simon. "God, Gandhi, and Guns: The African American Freedom Struggle in Tuscaloosa, Alabama, 1964–1965." *Journal of African American History* 89, no. 1 (Winter 2004): 36–56.

Black Star Line

Incorporated by Marcus Garvey in 1919, the Black Star Line of Delaware was a steamship company founded as an economic venture supported by the Universal Negro Improvement Association (UNIA). The company owned three ships at its height and was working on purchasing a fourth. Despite an enthusiastic response among people of color throughout several countries, the shipping line failed as a result of poor financial management, internal subversion, and the eventual arrest of Garvey on charges of mail fraud.

Garvey believed economic development among African Americans was critical for overcoming white oppression. He saw the Black Star line as an opportunity for African Americans to manage their own business venture, employ and serve persons of color, and offer financial investment opportunities. Shares of the company's stock originally sold for $5 apiece and could not be purchased by whites. Garvey assured investors they would see near boundless returns.

In September 1919, the company purchased its first ship, the *Yarmouth,* for $165,000. Garvey initially hired an African American as captain, although he would later be dismissed for dishonesty and replaced by a white captain. On its voyages the *Yarmouth,* unofficially dubbed the *Frederick Douglass,* was received with large displays of enthusiasm both in American ports and in places like Cuba, Jamaica, and Panama. It hauled several loads of cargo, including cement, fertilizer, logwood, a botched cargo of coconuts, and a hasty shipment of whisky before the enactment of Prohibition laws. In all the *Yarmouth* made three voyages to the West Indies before being sold by the U.S. government in November 1921 for $1,625 to repay several of Garvey's creditors.

The second addition to the Black Star Line was a passenger excursion boat, planned for trips along the Hudson River, called the *Shadyside.* Garvey purchased the boat in April 1920 for $35,000. After completing the summer excursion season, the *Shadyside* docked for the winter at which time it sprang a leak and sank during an ice storm.

In May 1920, the *Kanawha,* a converted yacht unofficially dubbed the *Antonio Maceo,* was purchased for $65,000. When it set sail up the Hudson in June 1920, it blew a boiler, killing one employee. Because of continued mechanical problems, the ship would not leave for the West Indies until March 1921. This voyage was plagued by continual mechanical failures, some only hours apart. The crew, through either neglect, incompetence, or sabotage, had a hand in the continued breakdowns. The ship was abandoned in Antilla, Cuba, where it remained for many years, being stripped of anything of value and sinking into the ocean.

The Black Star Line entered negotiations to purchase a fourth ship, to be dubbed the *Phyllis Wheatley,* intended for passage and trade to Africa. Several ships were pursued to this end, but negotiations stalled out on each. A down payment was made on the *Hong Kheng,* but the ship was never delivered. Offers were also made to the U.S. Shipping Board for the *Porto Rico* and the *Orion,* the latter of which was to be sold to Garvey's company for $200,000. Once the terms of purchase were arranged, Garvey proceeded to place advertisements for the ship's maiden voyage and collect $8,900 in fares from prospective passengers. Unfortunately, the agent handling the purchase, as well as others, misappropriated the organization's funds and the down payment for the ship was not met in full. Ultimately, the shipping board decided not to sell the ship to the Black Star Line based on its inability to pay, Garvey's arrest, and several financial claims against the company. The money offered as a partial down payment was tied up in court claims until March 1929 when the U.S. Senate ruled the court of claims could decide on creditor's claims against the company. The *Orion* was scrapped in 1930 for less than $28,000.

In April 1922 the initial Black Star Line of Delaware was a financial catastrophe and was suspended. By March 1924, however, Garvey had announced a new Black Cross Navigation and Trading Company. Under new auspices, Garvey purchased the *General Goethals,* unofficially dubbed the *Booker T. Washington,* for $100,000. This money was again raised by selling stock, and Garvey claimed that 90 percent of the investors were previous Black Star Line stockholders. The *General Goethals* made one voyage to Cuba, Panama, and Jamaica, which was plagued by many of the same problems of the Black Star Line's ships. In June 1925, the ship docked in New York where it would later be sold to help repay debts.

There is some debate as to who is responsible for the ultimate demise of the UNIA's steamship line ventures. Garvey purchased ships in seemingly poor repair for inflated amounts. He and his subordinates had little knowledge of the industry, and losses and delays were often related to poor contract negotiations or mishandling of business protocol. Outside sources of decline came from the company's explicit enemies, such as the *Chicago Defender* and other publications denouncing the shipping line. Government organizations, such as the FBI, may also have had a hand in the demise of the Black Star Line. Yet many believe that the most significant cause of the company's failure was the underhanded practices of its employees. The financial ruin exacted by theft, sabotage, and negligence was defeating.

In spite of commercial interest in the company, Garvey's Black Star Line was never able to achieve its goals of economic development among peoples of color owing to a number of undermining factors.
See also: Black Nationalism; Garvey, Marcus; Universal Negro Improvement Association

Shawntel Lyn Ensminger

Bibliography
Cronon, E. David. *Black Moses: The Story of Marcus Garvey and the Universal Negro Improvement Association.* Madison: The University of Wisconsin Press, 1955.
Grant, Colin. *Negro with a Hat: The Rise and Fall of Marcus Garvey.* Oxford, UK: Oxford University Press, 2008.
Martin, Tony. *Race First: The Ideological and Organizational Struggles of Marcus Garvey and the Universal Negro Improvement Association.* Westport, CT: Greenwood Press, 1976.

Bloody Sunday

Bloody Sunday was a brutal attack by members of the Alabama state and local police (using tear gas, nightsticks, and bull whips) on 300 predominantly African American civil rights marchers that took place Sunday, March 7, 1965 in Selma, Alabama.

Bloody Sunday took place within the larger context of the African American freedom struggle that has been ongoing before, during, and since the 1960s. Although African Americans were guaranteed the right to vote long before the 1960s, through the Fifteenth Amendment to the U.S. Constitution ratified March 30, 1870, southern states instituted a series of state and local restrictions abridging African American civil rights as bolstered by the Supreme Court decision in *Plessy v. Ferguson* (1896). The Plessy decision upheld the doctrine of "separate but equal," as well as the power of state and local agencies to maintain and regulate under the guise of their "police power" segregation policies also called "Jim Crow" laws. In keeping with a longstanding "organizing tradition," African Americans created self-help agencies and civil rights organizations such as the National Association for the Advancement of Colored People (NAACP) in 1909, the National Urban League (NUL) in 1911, and the Congress of Racial Equality in 1942 to combat restrictions placed on black civil rights. Voting rights were of a particular concern to African Americans because many southern municipalities adopted obstacles that prevented African Americans from voting, such as the grandfather clause, the poll tax, and the literacy test through the turn of the century.

Jim Crow laws were accompanied by regular acts of violence and brutality against African Americans. An estimated 82 percent of the lynchings that took place in the United States between 1890 and 1900 occurred in the American South, with an average of more than 150 lynchings per year. In the first decade of the 20th century (1900–1910), the percentage of lynchings taking place in the South increased by more than 10 percent. Although African Americans were not the only group made subject to lynching, they were certainly the chief victims in overwhelming numbers. In response to continuous violence, disenfranchisement, and segregation in public facilities, African Americans challenged such measures through "sit-down" campaigns in the 1940s to boycotts and marching in the 1950s. The Civil Rights movement expanded and became a mass movement through the 1950s and 1960s to include such organizations as the Southern Christian Leadership Conference created in 1957 and the Student Nonviolent Coordinating Committee in (SNCC) established by black student activists in 1960. Representatives from the aforementioned civil rights organizations felt it necessary to cross the Edmund Pettus Bridge in Selma, Alabama in 1965 to secure voting rights for African Americans.

Although the collective activism of African Americans secured important gains between 1960 and 1965, such as the Civil Rights Act of 1964, which guaranteed equal access to jobs and public facilities, 26 civil rights workers were killed during this time period, and there was no major voting rights legislation in place to guarantee black voting rights. Martin Luther King Jr. (1929–1968) declared that the first important civil right was the right to vote and actively incorporated voting rights as a central issue into his civil rights campaigns beginning in the period between 1963 and 1965. From 1960 to 1965, SNCC students organized several voter registration projects (including the Freedom Summer of 1964) in places such as Mississippi and Alabama in an effort to increase the number of African American registered voters across the South. Only 1 percent of the black population eligible to vote in Mississippi was registered to vote before 1965; about 2 percent of the black population eligible to vote in Alabama before 1965 was registered to vote. Thus, African American civil rights activists such as John Lewis of SNCC along with Hosea Williams and eventually Martin Luther King Jr. decided to surmount a voter's rights demonstration in Selma, Alabama in the spring of 1965. These individuals sought to bring attention to the problems of disenfranchisement, segregation, and vigilantism (African American Jimmy Lee Jackson was shot on February 18, 1965 by an Alabama police officer) on the part of whites in Selma by organizing a 54-mile trek on U.S. highway 80 across the Edmund Pettus Bridge toward Montgomery, Alabama to demand redress for their grievances.

Bloody Sunday occurred as John Lewis and Hosea Williams led 300 marchers across the Edmund Pettus Bridge on March 7, 1965. The marchers were charged by 200 state and local police officers wielding clubs in the form of nightsticks. John Lewis was beaten bloody to the ground. Five women marchers were beaten unconscious. Ultimately, several marchers were attacked and bludgeoned

senseless. Seventeen marchers were hospitalized including civil rights organizer Amelia Boynton Robinson who was almost gassed to death. That this incident was televised and people around the United States were able to see scenes of defenseless marchers attacked by police officials brought national support to the movement. Martin Luther King Jr. called for a continuation of the march on March 9, but decided instead to hold a short ceremonial march to the Edmund Pettus Bridge then turn around until a court order was secured. A white Unitarian minister, James Reeb from Boston, who came to Alabama to join the second march, was attacked the same day by an angry mob and died on March 11. After Reeb's death, a federal judge ruled in favor of Martin Luther King Jr. and SCLC. The number of marchers completing the journey on March 25, 1965 eventually increased to an estimated 25,000.

Bloody Sunday led to the signing of the Voting Rights Act of 1965. This act invalidated any test or device to deny voting, including a poll tax, literacy test, and grandfather clause, and allowed federal examiners to enter states to ensure the registration of African Americans in any state with a history of discrimination. "And we shall overcome," stated President Lyndon Baines Johnson in a speech supporting access to the franchise for African Americans following "Bloody Sunday."

See also: Abernathy, Ralph David; Jim Crow; King, Martin Luther Jr.; Lewis, John; Southern Christian Leadership Conference; Student Nonviolent Coordinating Committee; Selma March; Voting Rights Act 1965; Williams, Hosea

Hettie V. Williams

Bibliography

Branch, Taylor. *At Canaan's Edge: America in the King Years, 1965–1968.* New York: Simon & Schuster, 2006.

Fager, Charles. *Selma 1965: The March That Changed the South.* Boston: Beacon Press, 1985.

Garrow, David. *Protest in Selma: Martin Luther King, Jr. and the Voting Rights Act of 1965.* New Haven, CT: Yale University Press, 1979.

Bombingham

In 1963, Martin Luther King Jr. referred to Birmingham, Alabama as the most segregated city in the United States. To the city's African American residents, it was simply "Bombingham," a place where they had suffered decades of reactionary violence, police brutality, and political emasculation. The city had earned such a sobriquet because of its high frequency of racially motivated bombings—no less than 50 between 1947 and 1965—and because its elected officials did little to impede the carnage. Nearly everyone who lived in or visited Birmingham in the years before the Civil Rights movement noted its oppressive climate and its glaring lack of concern for basic human rights. And it was for these reasons that King and the Southern Christian Leadership Conference (SCLC) targeted the city for their 1963 campaign, thus transforming Bombingham into the main battleground in the postwar struggle for civil rights.

Birmingham was founded in the 1870s, a scion of America's postwar industrial boom. By 1900, thousands of working class whites and blacks called the city home, daily plying their trade in the iron and steel mills that dotted the bleak urban landscape. Few of the business and industrial leaders who controlled the local economy actually resided in Birmingham. Rather, they managed its affairs from New York or Pennsylvania, or they settled in the "over the mountain" communities of Mountain Brook, Homewood, and Vestavia Hills. Hence, the city's political power structure was controlled by working and lower-middle class whites, who composed a majority of the population and who enjoyed all the economic advantages residing with their race. African Americans made up about 40 percent of the population by the late 1950s, yet fewer than 20 percent could cast a vote. A majority of the black populace lived at or below the poverty level, and only a handful worked in trades not classified as unskilled or menial. A strict system of segregation determined the parameters of social interaction between the two races. And if blacks ever endeavored to step beyond the narrow confines of Jim Crow, whites would often react with violence.

After World War II, racial tensions escalated to unprecedented levels in Birmingham. Because of a postwar housing shortage in the city, African American families began moving into residences that either bordered on, or rested in, historically white neighborhoods such as North Smithfield (an area later designated as Dynamite Hill). This not only violated segregated housing ordinances, it drew the ire of working class whites who wanted to maintain the racial integrity of their communities. As a result, there were a number of black residences bombed by night-riding vigilantes in the latter half of the 1940s. The Birmingham Police Department, headed by public safety commissioner Eugene

"Bull" Connor, failed to adequately investigate the attacks, much less arrest those responsible. Consequently, members of the African American community responded to the lack of police protection by posting armed guards in front of their homes and began conducting nightly neighborhood patrols. Their actions probably saved dozens of homes from destruction. But the conflict raged on.

After the 1954 *Brown* decision, racial animosities heightened all over the city. This time, vigilantes began targeting civil rights activists, like the Reverend Fred Shuttlesworth, who headed the Alabama Christian Movement for Human Rights. Twice, in 1956 and 1962, terrorists bombed Shuttleworth's church, Bethel Baptist, coming close to killing the fearless minister. Similar bombings targeted the homes of Attorney Arthur Shores, A. G. Gaston, and A. D. King, the brother of Martin Luther King. In September 1957, Shuttlesworth and his wife were attacked by a mob when they attempted to integrate Phillips High School. Shuttlesworth was severely lashed with bicycle chains and brass knuckles in the melee, and his wife received a stab wound to the hip. In May 1961, Klansmen, with Bull Connor's full blessing, savagely assaulted a busload of Freedom Riders in the downtown Trailways station. Photographs of the attack ran in newspapers around the world, shocking the international community and convincing many Birmingham businessmen that the continued maintenance of white supremacy was both impractical and immoral.

In the spring of 1963, King and the SCLC conducted widespread demonstrations in Birmingham, hoping, among other things, to end discriminatory hiring practices in downtown businesses, desegregate public facilities, and integrate the local school system. The campaign was only marginally successful in Birmingham itself, but eventually influenced Congress and the White House to pass the Civil Rights Act of 1964.

The situation in Birmingham, however, seemed as volatile as ever. On September 15, 1963, days after area schools were desegregated, a bomb was detonated outside the Sixteenth Street Baptist Church, resulting in the deaths of four black children. Withdrawing into their familiar roles, local and state police did little to nab those responsible for the blast. In fact, it was not until the late 1970s that one of the bombers, Robert Chambliss, was brought to justice. More than two decades after Chambliss's conviction, two of his accomplices, Bobby Frank Cherry and Thomas Blanton, were tried and found guilty for their roles in the attack.

Finally, and mercifully, Birmingham could begin the process of healing.

See also: Civil Rights Act of 1964; Jim Crow; King, Martin Luther Jr.; Shuttlesworth, Fred; Sixteenth Street Baptist Church

Gary S. Sprayberry

Bibliography

Eskew, Glenn T. *But for Birmingham: The Local and National Movements in the Civil Rights Struggle.* Chapel Hill: University of North Carolina Press, 1997.

McWhorter, Diane. *Carry Me Home: Birmingham, Alabama, the Climactic Battle of the Civil Rights Revolution.* New York: Simon and Schuster, 2001.

Nunnelly, William A. *Bull Connor.* Tuscaloosa: University of Alabama Press, 1991.

Thornton, J. Mills. *Dividing Lines: Municipal Politics and the Struggle for Civil Rights in Montgomery, Birmingham, and Selma.* Tuscaloosa: University of Alabama Press, 2002.

BPP, Chicago Branch

Founded in late 1967, the Chicago Illinois Branch of the Black Panther Party (C-BPP) was organized by Bob Brown and Bobby Rush. The C-BPP propagated itself through community service projects, weekly political education classes, and rallies. In November 1968, the C-BPP welcomed Fred Hampton (1948–1969). Hampton, a native Chicagoan, quickly became the C-BPP most recognized member. Following Hampton's lead, the C-BPP became an undeniable regional force. In May 1969, Hampton coordinated a non-aggression pact among Chicago gangs. Hampton termed the multihued and politically diverse groups a "rainbow coalition." The teen-age BPP leader eventually assumed the BPP Illinois chapter chairman position. The chairman's position carried with it an ancillary spot as national-level deputy chairman on the BPP policymaking Central Committee. Hampton's ascension to the Central Committee made him a target of the Federal Bureau of Investigation's (FBI) "Counter Intelligence Program" (COINTELPRO).

Hampton was clearly the most charismatic and intelligent of the BPP leadership cadre. FBI Director J. Edgar Hoover acknowledged Hampton's voluminous abilities in bureau memoranda by vowing to prevent his development into a "Black Messiah" capable of politicizing and unifying divergent revolutionary and gang-affiliated blacks. Ongoing surveillance solidified FBI leaders' belief that drastic

measures—wiretaps, fraudulent letters, and agent provocateurs—were needed to subdue Hampton.

Indicative of the importance Hampton held within the late-1960s protest scene was the FBI's creation of a "Racial Matters" squad to coordinate attacks against the C-BPP. Plans began with the introduction of agent provocateurs. Central to bureau plans was William O'Neal. O'Neal came under FBI control as he sought to avoid incarceration for pending charges of interstate car theft and impersonation of a federal officer. Once inside the C-BPP, O'Neal swiftly rose through the ranks. O'Neal, who would become the Bureau's most active agent provocateur, became the C-BPP director of security.

Rationalizing that the C-BPP vulnerability would increase exponentially if it was isolated from its activist peers, FBI agents attacked the "Rainbow Coalition" via myriad activities. For example, "Racial Matters" agents dispensed bogus correspondence to Black Stone Ranger leader Jeff Fort detailing an imminent C-BPP assassination attempt. Agents hoped that Fort would take retaliatory action against the C-BPP; when Fort did not fall for such bait, Bureau agents ordered informant O'Neal to instigate the conflict. O'Neal accomplished this goal on April 2, 1969. As a result of FBI operations, Hampton's "Rainbow Coalition" was decimated.

Amazingly, the Chicago Police Department's (CPD) repression was more blatant than their FBI brethren. Indicative of such aggression was an attack on the C-BPP Monroe Street office. The Monroe Street attack was particularly egregious because of officers' deliberate destruction of C-BPP supplies earmarked for the needy. Incredibly, law enforcement officers set fire to areas storing food and medical supplies, brutally attacked and arrested those present, and as a final insult boarded up the C-BPP office. Toward resisting such blatant attempts of intimidation, Panther Chairman Bobby Seale ordered the office reopened. Impressively, black Chicagoans donated supplies and personnel to the cause. The C-BPP refusal to fold forced "Racial Matters" agents to increase their pursuit of Hampton.

Toward securing a permanent solution to their C-BPP problem, William O'Neal's FBI contacts stepped up communications. O'Neal was ordered to build a criminal case against the C-BPP leader. Despite his best attempts, Hampton was above all criminality. The C-BPP leader, however, did transgress the law on one occasion. Hampton offered opponents a proverbial sword when he stole $72 worth of ice cream as a treat for neighborhood children. Officers pounced on this transgression and arranged for Hampton to be given a two- to five-year prison sentence for the trivial transgression. Hampton, however, was released after several weeks on an appeal bond. Hampton's release solidified opponents' belief that a permanent solution was needed. Toward accomplishing said goals, FBI agents began making specific requests of Agent Provocateur William O'Neal. O'Neal was ordered to provide a detailed map of Hampton's dwelling and provide officers with a legitimate reason to raid the dwelling. O'Neal accomplished both goals with the desired map and information that Hampton's dwelling was used to store the C-BPP weapons caches. Armed with this information, a coalition of FBI agents, state, and local law enforcement officials created a plan to assassinate Hampton. The assassination was set for December 4, 1969, and included myriad elements such as C-BPP head of security William O'Neal who was set to play a critical role in the operation.

After teaching a political education class on the evening of December 3, Hampton retired to his West Monroe Street dwelling. Informant O'Neal had prepared a late dinner for the arriving Panthers. After serving dinner, O'Neal exited the residence. Hampton retired to his bedroom and telephoned his mother. Strangely, an unusually exhausted Hampton drifted into a slumber mid-sentence. At approximately 4:00 A.M. a platoon of 14 officers assembled outside of Hampton's apartment. At 4:45 A.M. officers stormed the building. A slumbering Mark Clark was discovered in a front room. Officer's killed the young Panther instantly; Clark, who was on security detail, had his shotgun discharge after it fell from his lifeless grip. Officers immediately directed their bullets toward the room that O'Neal's map had listed as Hampton's bedroom. Satisfied that no one could have survived their savage attack, officers ceased fire and began their search for what they hoped was Hampton's lifeless body. Hampton, who never stirred from his slumber, was struck in the shoulder. Subsequent coroner reports would indicate that Hampton was drugged with secobarbitol, a powerful barbiturate; all indicators point toward William O'Neal as the source of the drugging. A frightened Deborah Johnson, Hampton's visibly pregnant fiancée, was ordered from the room by raiding officers. Johnson alleged overhearing a disturbing discussion among the raiders. He charged that one officer answered fellow officers' inquiries regarding Hampton's status with the comment that "he is barely alive." Moments later, two additional shots were discharged. Autopsy reports detail that Hampton had two

shots to the back of his head. Raiding officers cryptically mused that "he is good and dead now." After murdering Hampton, raiding officers sprayed the remaining rooms with bullets and beat surviving Panthers before arresting them for aggravated assault and attempted murder. The arrested Panthers would be held on $100,000 bail.

CPD leaders and public officials initially praised officers for their restraint while simultaneously blaming the Panthers for the horrific incident. Only the rallying of progressive-minded Chicagoans, a congressional investigation, and inquisitive reporters would unearth irrefutable proof that Hampton and Clark had been executed. Ballistics experts proved that of the 100 shots fired, only one came from the C-BPP. That particular salvo was discharged from Mark Clark's shotgun. Despite their obvious culpability in the murders, the raiding officers were never prosecuted. The estates of Fred Hampton and Mark Clark would be given a monetary settlement a decade after the incident. Unfortunately, there was no one capable of replicating Fred Hampton's leadership, charisma, and intelligence within the C-BPP. Consequently, the C-BPP drifted into nonexistence. *See also:* Black Panther Party; COINTELPRO; Hampton, Fred

James Thomas Jones III

Bibliography
Brown, Elaine. *A Taste of Power: A Black Woman's Story.* New York: Pantheon Books, 1992.
Churchill, Ward, and Jim Vander Wall. *Agents of Repression: The FBI's Secret Wars against the Black Panther Party and the American Indian Movement.* Boston: South End Press, 1988.
Churchill, Ward, and Jim Vander Wall. *The COINTELPRO Papers: Documents from the FBI's Secret Wars against Domestic Dissent.* Boston: South End Press, 1990.
Jeffries, J. L. *Black Power in the Belly of the Beast.* Urbana: University of Illinois Press, 2006.
Jones, Charles E. *The Black Panther Party (Reconsidered).* Baltimore: Black Classic Press, 1998.
Madhubuti, Haki R. *One Sided Shoot-Out (for Brothers Fred Hampton & Mark Clark, Murdered 12/4/69 by Chicago Police at 4:30 AM While They Slept).* Broadside, no. 33. Detroit: Broadside Press, 1969.

BPP, Los Angeles Branch

The Los Angeles branch of the Southern California chapter of the Black Panther Party was founded in February 1968. Eager to expand Panther operations, Eldridge Cleaver authorized Alprentice Bunchy Carter and Earl Anthony to launch a chapter in Los Angeles. Within a month, the two men (mainly Bunchy) had organized 20 men. Most of the recruits came from the Teen Post, an antipoverty program where Bunchy worked as a counselor. Before long the Panthers were the largest militant group in Los Angeles. Aside from Carter and Anthony, others who helped build the chapter were Raymond "Masai" Hewitt, Gwen Goodloe, Elaine Brown, John and Erika Huggins, and Elmer "Geronimo" Pratt. Pratt had been a member of the Army's 82nd Airborne division and was a decorated Vietnam veteran instrumental in training members of the chapter in combat readiness. Goodloe, Brown, and Erika Huggins were instrumental in putting in place most of the Panthers' survival programs. Masai Hewitt, the well-read street scholar set up the chapter's weekly political education classes, an activity mandated by the national headquarters in Oakland.

The Los Angeles outpost had several offices, making it was one of the largest in the organization. Among the people the Panthers attracted were gang members, dropouts, ex-servicemen, runaways, men and women who lived on the streets, and black youth looking to get involved politically for the first time in their lives. The chapter was composed of three groups: the sociopolitical element, the military, and the underground. The sociopolitical element worked closely with the community. This group was primarily responsible for putting the survival programs in place; they did the day-today grunt work that was necessary to meet the needs of the people. The military sector consisted of the chapters' foot soldiers. They acquired weaponry and trained members in warfare in preparation of the impending revolution. The underground, composed of small cell units, were hardened street types that would do whatever needed to be done for the organization in the name of the revolution. The underground consisted of only those men that Bunchy knew and could trust, men that he had seen fight in the mean streets of LA, men who had been tested—some of whom by him. The underground had its own ethics. For example, it did not rob individuals, it robbed institutions. Bunchy kept the identities of the underground members from the general body for obvious and strategic reasons. For instance, if authorities interrogated someone outside of the underground, he or she could only reveal limited information.

It took the Panthers almost two years to set up its community survival programs. The Panthers were able to serve free dinners from time to time, but not with any regularity because they had no access to a proper facility and, more important, because much of their funds were being used for legal fees, medical treatment for those beaten when arrested, parking fines, and impounded vehicles. Although the Panthers were slow in setting up their survival programs, they were still active in the community. One of the Panthers' more substantive efforts involved ridding the community of drugs. Indeed, the one thing that shop owners and other residents noticed shortly after the party opened its office on Central Avenue was that drug activity waned. Before the Panthers arrived, drug pushers peddled their wares openly. Determined to make the neighborhood safe, the Panthers set out to run the pushers out of the community. Those who ignored the Panthers' appeals were either shaken down until they left on their own accord or were driven out by force.

By 1969, the Panthers were finally able to launch the first of three free breakfast programs. Garnering support for the program proved more difficult than the Panthers had expected. Hundreds of letters were sent to retail and wholesale stores, requesting supplies; the response was dismal. Undeterred, the Panthers came up with a plan. The convinced officials at UCLA's dining halls to donate its leftover items instead of discarding them at the end of each day. The first breakfast program was established in early 1969 at the University Seventh Day Adventists Church, much to the chagrin of the congregation. Despite the parishioners' uneasiness about the Panthers, the Panthers were allowed to use the facility with one stipulation—that no meat be served. Realizing that for many people breakfast is not a complete meal without meat, the Panthers discovered vegeburgers and passed them off as sausages. Dozens of children ranging in age from 3 to 14 were served daily. Among the other Panther offerings included a free clinic, a busing-to-prisons program that catered to black families that did not have the means to visit their loved ones who were often incarcerated in facilities that were hundreds of miles outside the city.

Because of the Panthers' strong community ties, they were able to expand throughout the state. Over the course of a few years Panther offices were set up in Bakersfield, Riverside, Santa Barbara, Pomona, Pacoima, Pasadena, and San Diego. As the Panther operation grew, so did the attacks on them.

No chapter or branch suffered more casualties than did the LA Panthers. Bunchy and John Huggins were killed by members of a rival black organization. Tommy Lewis,

Steve Bartholomew, and Robert Lawrence were shot and killed by police officers at a local gas station in August 1968. Several other Panthers were murdered, the circumstances of which remain mysterious. Panther offices were frequently raided. Given the assault launched against the LA cohort, it is amazing that more Panthers were not killed. Although in a state of siege, Panthers were able to put in place a set of programs that were designed to increase poor people's lot. Although the chapter was obviously unable to uplift the entire black community, many lives were touched by the Panthers' efforts. Not only were people impacted by the breakfast programs, the free clothing giveaways, and the free tuberculosis testing, but both the black and white communities were affected by the example set by the Panthers. *See also:* Black Panther Party; Brown, Elaine; Cleaver, Eldridge; Pratt, Geronimo Ji-Jaga; US Organization

Judson L. Jeffries

Bibliography
Anthony, Earl. *Picking up the Gun.* New York: Dial Press, 1970.
Jeffries, Judson L., ed. *Comrades, A Local History of the Black Panther Party.* Bloomington: Indiana University Press, 2007.

BPP, New York Branch

The New York branch of the Black Panther Party (BPP) existed in Albany, Buffalo, Mount Vernon, Peekskill, and New York City (Brooklyn—its birthplace—the Bronx, Corona, Harlem, Jamaica, and Washington Heights). They were involved in the community from its earliest stages. The New York branch called for a school boycott in Harlem if the educational institutions did not teach heritage and provide better education in addition to hiring black principals. They also supported Ocean Hill-Brownsville's quest for neighborhood-controlled schools. The Panthers outlined goals including becoming a political force by 1968, indicating that the BPP in New York existed earlier than that year. Breakfast programs for children and a health clinic operated in a Brooklyn community center, developed by Panthers.

By 1969, the New York branch was responsible for a third of the national weekly circulation of *The Black Panther* newspaper for a period of time, sending $13,000 to headquarters at one point. The New York Panthers wanted (1) a larger portion of the newspaper profits to benefit the local communities and (2) to continue advocating for better housing and schools. They embraced adopting African names, as many members worked with black nationalists or had backgrounds in such organizations. Their cultural orientation conflicted with the changing ideology of the BPP headquarters. These differences became more evident when headquarters sent reinforcements to the New York branch, after many of their leaders had been arrested. Larry Neal, education director for the New York branch, outlined numerous incidents of police harassment, so the arrests were only a matter a time.

Twenty-one Black Panther members were charged with conspiracy to bomb Penn Station, Morrisania police station, department stores, and the Bronx Botanical Gardens. Because many of the first 16 who were arrested on April 2, 1969 were leaders in the New York branch, this was the beginning of the end. Zayd-Malik Shakur (deputy minister of information), Joan Bird (a nursing student at Bronx Community College), Dr. Curtis Powell (a biochemist at Columbia Presbyterian Medical Center), and Roseland Bennett, among others, described their arrest in *The Black Panther* over the subsequent two years. Bail for most of them was set at $100,000 and ads requesting bail money for those arrested ran in *The Black Panther* in April 1969. Donations were to be sent to Brooklyn. In later months, however, the ads requesting financial support for the Panther 21 included addresses in both Brooklyn and Berkeley, California.

The Panther 21 also included Afeni Shakur (a section leader and the mother of Tupac Shakur), Dhoruba Bin Wahad (section leader), and Sekou Odinga (Bronx section leader). Ms. Shakur had joined the Black Panther Party after hearing Bobby Seale speak. She noted that meeting Odinga and Lumumba Shakur was life-changing, as they were men who respected women. She was released in January 1970; Bin Wahad, Michael (Cetewayo) Tabor, and Joan Bird were released on bail a few months later. By 1971, there were 13 defendants of the original 21 on trial facing 156 charges. All were found not guilty and released in that year.

The New York branch had grown increasingly dispirited with the national headquarters. Not only had they struggled with losses related to the Panther 21, but also other resources such as arson of the Jamaica chapter's building in October 1970. By 1971, the Panther 21 were purged from the BPP, in addition to the New York branch. In February of that year, some East Coast chapters announced in Harlem that Huey Newton and David Hilliard should be expelled from the BPP. They went further by attributing legitimate leadership to Eldridge Cleaver, Kathleen Cleaver, and Donald Cox (all of whom represented the International Section in Algeria), as well as Bobby Seale who was in prison at the time. The FBI forged a letter suggesting that the New York branch and Cleaver were orchestrating Newton's death.

The Newton/Cleaver rift escalated and was played out in New York City. The New York branch demanded accountability after Robert Webb's (former bodyguard for Newton) description of Newton's extravagances and drug use. Webb was killed in Harlem in March 1971; Donald Cox believed that the murder was Newton's revenge for Cox's support of Cleaver. The New York branch received another forged FBI letter intimating the same fate for others affiliated with Cleaver. The next month, *The Black Panther* office was burned and the body of Sam Napier, circulation manager of the newspaper, was found. Napier's tortured death was seen as retaliation for Webb's death. The New York branch began to publish *Right On* because *The Black Panther* was seen as Newton's outlet; publication of *Right On* ceased in 1974. When police began arresting Cleaver-affiliated Panthers en-masse, the New York branch suspected that Newton had been cooperating with law enforcement. The BPP on the East Coast began looking for other options by which to serve the community.

Many members of the New York branch became involved with the Black Liberation Army (BLA) and/or the Republic of New Africa. The BLA was considered the armed force of the BPP. In the late 1990s, former New York Panthers organized the Black Panther Collective, designed to carry out the mission and purpose of the New York branch of the Black Panther Party.

See also: Black Panther Party; Shakur, Assata

Marilyn D. Lovett

Bibliography

Alkebulan, Paul. *Survival Pending Revolution: The History of the Black Panther Party.* Tuscaloosa: University of Alabama Press, 2007.

Cleaver, Kathleen, and George Katsiaficas, eds. *Liberation, Imagination, and the Black Panther Party: A New Look at the Panthers and Their Legacy.* New York: Routledge, 2001.

Jeffries, Judson L., ed. *Comrades, A Local History of the Black Panther Party.* Bloomington: Indiana University Press, 2007.

Shakur, Assata. *Assata: An Autobiography.* Westport, CT: Lawrence Hill, 1987.

BPP, Oakland Branch

The Black Panther Party (BPP) was created October 15, 1966, in Oakland, California, by Merritt Junior College students Huey P. Newton and Bobby Seale. The BPP offered a revolutionary alternative to traditional civil rights tactics, strategies, and goals. Inspired by the revolutionary nationalist theory of Malcolm X, the BPP spiritual and intellectual father, Newton and Seale intended to extend his legacy to its next logical step—revolution. Informing the BPP ideological underpinnings was an international base of political theoreticians and revolutionaries: Frantz Fanon, Mao Tse-Tung, Robert F. Williams, Malcolm X, Fidel Castro, and Che Guevara. Such theory enabled the BPP to avoid oversimplified nationalist doctrines in favor of a Marxist-Leninist politic.

Armed with a ten-point platform of largely reformist wants and goals—housing, full employment, relevant education—Newton and Seale attempted to recruit local collegians, but they were unconditionally rebuffed. Undaunted by such refusal, the Panther's turned toward the lumpen proletariat. To the BPP dismay, marginalized African Americans were equally resistant to their recruitment efforts.

The aforementioned failure forced the Panther's to embrace what many derisively term suicidal tactics. Toward reversing their recruiting problems, the BPP decided to implement point #7 (an immediate end to police brutality and murder of black people) of the ten-point platform and program. Newton sought to exploit California's State Constitution, which allowed citizens to carry armaments via the Panther Patrols. The Panther Patrols were composed of BPP members carrying firearms (for protection), law books (to offer appropriate legal aid), and cameras (to preserve evidence) while following Oakland Police Department (OPD) officers as they performed routine patrols. The BPP could not have wished for better publicity.

Despite its relative popularity, the Panther Patrols failed to translate into a significant membership increase. Bay Area African Americans remained leery of affiliating with the BPP. Central to African–Americans' refusal to enlist in the BPP was the OPD record of unpunished abuse of Bay Area blacks. These police abuses led Bay Area African Americans to theorize that the BPP would be quickly destroyed by OPD officers. As predicted, local officers were determined to destroy the BPP "by any means necessary."

The initial campaign to curtail the BPP was a simplistic plan of harassment and intimidation. The petty harassment campaign proved to be little more than a nuisance to the BPP. Realizing the petty harassment campaign's futility, officers altered their strategy. OPD officials requested the assistance of State Legislator Donald Mulford in early 1967. Representative Mulford immediately drafted a bill removing Californians' Constitutional right to carry armaments.

In response, BPP leaders formulated a unique protest. On May 2, 1967, a cadre of 30 Panthers traveled to the state capitol to protest the pending Panther Bill. The capitol protest, which included the BPP carrying guns onto the legislative floor, was broadcast throughout the nation. The BPP gamble at receiving free publicity via reporters covering capitol proceedings was a phenomenal success. Such exposure led to their being inundated with calls regarding BPP expansion throughout the nation. Unfortunately, the BPP exposure via news snippets gave admirers little hint of their repudiation of parochial race-first politics. Ironically, BPP politics often contradicted would-be Panthers' personal political positions and motivations. Such issues intensified exponentially after Huey P. Newton was involved in an early morning shootout that left him wounded, one officer dead, and a second officer wounded.

Newton's arrest on October 28, 1967 for this offense not only moved the BPP to the center of the American protest scene, but also polarized the nation. One's position regarding Newton's guilt or innocence was usually determined by an individual's acceptance or repudiation of 1960s radicalism. With Newton confined, Minister of Information Eldridge Cleaver assumed an influential leadership position. Cleaver, a public relations genius, mobilized progressives behind a catchy slogan of "Free Huey."

The "Free Huey" campaign created a loose coalition of radicals. Most notable of these groups was the Peace & Freedom Party (P&FP). It was the BPP relationship with the white P&FP that ostracized the Panthers from their racially chauvinistic nationalist peers. Compounding matters was the selection of Charles R. Garry, a white attorney, to represent Newton in his capital murder trial. With the Panthers isolated from fellow nationalists, Newton incarcerated, and the BPP in a general state of disarray, the Federal Bureau of Investigation (FBI) moved against the BPP in a substantive way.

The FBI's modus operandi was the Counter Intelligence Program (COINTELPRO). COINTELPRO was a covert operation aimed at usurping the powers and authority of national level black religious and political leaders. The BPP ascension was particularly troubling to FBI Director J. Edgar Hoover because the BPP chose to align with white leftist groups and propagated revolution instead of parochial race-first reformist politics. Ironically, the COINTELPRO violated laws in its pursuit of African American leaders. Bureau agents attacked via an intricate campaign of wiretaps, fraudulent letters, informants, agent provocateurs, assassinations, murder, and the assistance of friendly jurists.

Unable to defend against such a blitzkrieg, the BPP countered with a flurry of ineffectual decisions, policies, and counterrevolutionary activities. Indicative of such realities was the BPP battling Ron Karenga's US organization, a 1960s cultural nationalist group, and turning in on itself. Although impossible to identify informants, BPP leaders executed an organizational purge. State and local chapters were summarily closed. Loyal Panthers were ordered to Oakland for an unprecedented attempt at capturing the city's bourgeoning Pacific Rim economy. The plan was to elect Bobby Seale to the mayor's position via flooding municipal voting rolls. In the end Bobby Seale and former BPP head Elaine Brown were both unsuccessful in their bids for public office. Despite such failure, the BPP laid the foundation for subsequent electoral success in Oakland. In the wake of its electoral failure, the BPP declined into a former shell of itself. Although the BPP existed into the 1980s with various activities, the organization never reached earlier levels of importance and influence.

See also: Black Panther Party; Brown, Elaine; Cleaver, Eldridge; COINTELPRO; Karenga, Maulana; Newton, Huey P.; Seale, Bobby; US Organization

James Thomas Jones III

Bibliography

Anthony, Earl. *Spitting in the Wind: The True Story Behind the Violent Legacy of the Black Panther Party.* Santa Monica, CA: Roundtable Publishing, 1990.

Carmichael, Stokely (Kwame Ture), and Charles V. Hamilton. *Black Power, The Politics of Liberation.* New York: Vintage Edition, 1992.

Karenga, Maulana Ron. *The Roots of the US-Panther Conflict: The Perverse and Deadly Games Police Play.* San Diego: Kawaida Publications, 1976.

Newton, Huey. *Revolutionary Suicide.* New York: Harcourt Brace Jovanovich, 1973.

Ogbar, Jeffrey O. G. *Black Power: Radical Politics and African American Identity.* Baltimore: The John Hopkins University Press, 2005.

Seale, Bobby. *Seize the Time: The Story of the Black Panther Party and Huey P. Newton.* Baltimore: Black Classic Press, 1991.

Brotherhood of Sleeping Car Porters

The Brotherhood of Sleeping Car Porters was an African American labor union organized in 1925 by A. Philip Randolph. It was the first predominantly African American labor union in the United States to sign a collective bargaining agreement with a major U.S. company and gain charter recognition from the American Federation of Labor (AFL).

Historically, labor opportunities and labor protections for African Americans have been largely exploitative, beginning with slavery and indentured servitude and following with Reconstruction through the early 20th century. African Americans first responded to freedom with migration, moving from one part of the South to another with westward expansion. Those who remained in the South were left bound in a system of debt peonage called the crop lien system as buttressed by the rise of discriminatory laws sanctioned by a series of Supreme Court decisions sanctioning "separate but equal" practices in public facilities, education, and employment. In the mid-19th century and after the Civil War (1861–1865), the process of industrialization and the rise of "big business" dramatically changed the American landscape and the lives of African Americans. The transformation of the American economy from an agrarian to industrial economy redefined the nature of work and society overall as African Americans migrated to northern cities. The development and construction of the railroads (the transcontinental system was built primarily with Chinese immigrant labor) largely after the Civil War became America's first "big business." As Americans flocked to the cities for work, demands for worker protections became more prevalent with the rise of trade unions in the late 19th century.

Most of the major labor unions created amid worker unrest in the late 19th century, such as the Knights of Labor (1869), organized by Uriah Stephens under the guise of "universal brotherhood," and the American Federation of Labor (1886), created by Samuel Gompers (1850–1924), initially made overtures to black workers. The Knights of Labor made efforts to organize workers regardless of race, skill, or nationality. Between 1885 and 1886, the number of African American members swelled to 60,000. Unlike the AFL, the Knights placed less emphasis on worker skills. The AFL focused on coordinating the activities of skilled craft unions throughout the country yet made an overture in the form of a resolution to include African American workers within their ranks in 1893. As both a social and labor movement, the Knights of Columbus declined after the Haymarket Riot (massive rally in support of 8-hour workday that took place in Chicago, 1886) and bombings under the specter of radicalism. Although the AFL made public overtures of inclusion to African Americans, local affiliates customarily barred African Americans from joining; those chapters organized with black membership were segregated. Later attempts to develop unions such as the International Workers of the World (IWW) (1905) were not as successful in terms of numbers in gaining black participation. The IWW never had more than 10,000 members nationwide.

African Americans began to migrate to cities in the North between 1890 and 1930 in a "Great Migration," in search of work and equality. Many times, such as the case with the Pullman Strike of 1894, without work African American served as "strikebreakers." George M. Pullman (1831–1897), founder of Pullman Palace Car Company, began to hire African American workers after the Pullman Strike of 1894. This practice continued after Pullman's death. In fact, African American workers were so pervasive, white passengers who rode in the luxury Pullman railcars often referred to African American male porters who worked the cars as "George." African Americans working as porters and train personnel reached 20,224 by the 1920s; this was the largest category of black labor at the time.

Although the Pullman Company saw itself as "socially progressive" in the hiring of large numbers of African Americans, working conditions and wages remained substandard through the turn of the century. Porters worked long hours, were reliant on passenger tips for satisfactory pay, and spent time on duties such as setup and cleanup that was unpaid. The porters were also responsible for securing their own food, lodging, and uniforms. These costs often consumed significant portions of their pay. They were also charged whenever items went missing from the rail car. Porters were required to work 400 hours per month or 11,000 miles to receive pay. Porters were also not allowed to be promoted to conductor (this job was customarily reserved for whites). These hardships prompted the porters to attempt several efforts to organize, and on August 25, 1925, they commandeered the support of civil rights activist A. Philip Randolph at a meeting in Harlem. Approximately 500 porters agreed to create a union called the Brotherhood of Sleeping Car Porters and adopted the motto "Fight or Be Slaves." A. Philip Randolph became the union's first president.

It was not until the New Deal under President Franklin D. Roosevelt that the Brotherhood of Sleeping Car Porters was formally recognized by the Pullman Company in 1937. This was as a result of the Wagner Act that was created to formally recognize labor unions in the workforce. The principles of collective work, community involvement, and the organizing tradition propelled the Brotherhood to become involved in civil rights activism. Major civil rights leaders such as E. D. Nixon, who was instrumental in developing the Montgomery Bus Boycott in 1956, were members of the Brotherhood of Sleeping Car Porters.
See also: Great Migration; Randolph, A. Philip

Hettie V. Williams

Bibliography

Harris, William H. *Keeping the Faith: A. Philip Randolph, Milton P. Webster, and the Brotherhood of Sleeping Car Porters, 1925–1937.* Champagne: University of Illinois Press, 1977.

Santino, Jack. *Miles of Smiles, Years of Struggle: Stories of Black Pullman Porters.* Champagne: University of Illinois Press, 1989.

Tye, Larry. *Rising from the Rails: Pullman Porters and the Making of the Black Middle Class.* New York: Henry Holt, 2004.

Brown, Elaine

Elaine Brown (1943–), a former chairperson of the Black Panther Party, redefined leadership roles during the 1970s. In 1974, she became the first woman to hold the party's highest honor. She clarified her intent to maintain a unified organization after the departure of Huey P. Newton for Cuba. Brown was born to Dorothy Clark, a factory worker, in a predominately black, low-income area of North Philadelphia on March 2, 1943. Her father, Horace Scott, was a prominent physician who cheated on his wife to conceive Brown with Clark. Scott refused to accept Brown as his daughter during her youth on York Street in North Philadelphia. As a child, Brown grew up singing in various choirs at the Jones Tabernacle African Methodist Episcopal Church and eventually recorded the Black Panthers National Theme in 1969 called "The Meeting." Brown also recorded albums in the 1970s titled *Seize the Time* with Vanguard Records and *Until We're Free* with Black Forum Records, and she also appeared on a 2002 Black Panther record called *The Fugitives.*

During Brown's youth, Brown's mother often bought her pretty dresses and made her take ballet classes as a means to separate her from all things considered black. As a student at Philadelphia High School for Girls, Brown recalled when her mother stated that light skin and straight hair were better features than dark skin and tightly-curled hair. Brown eventually would internalize bourgeois concepts as a child, particularly during a visit with her Aunt Francine in Los Angeles. Nevertheless, she persevered and briefly attended Temple University as a prelaw student. After leaving in 1965, Brown went to Los Angeles and taught piano at the Jordan Downs housing project. While working at the Pink Pussycat Club in West Hollywood, Brown met Jay Kennedy, her eventual mentor and lover. Kennedy, a screenwriter and wealthy patron who is 30 years her elder, introduced her to critical aspects the Civil Rights movement. With the aid of Kennedy and other friends such as Beverlee and Tommy Jacquette, Brown furthered her interest in sociopolitical activism. While in Los Angeles, Brown began a Black Student Union newsletter and organized the Southern California College Black Student Alliance while at the University of California at Los Angeles.

In 1967, Brown became acquainted with the Black Panther Party and by April of the next year, she joined the Southern California chapter. By 1969, Brown became the deputy minister of information and was elevated to the minister of information in 1971. As a result of heightened scrutiny by COINTELPRO of the FBI, many leaders in the Black Panther Party were jailed or killed by the early 1970s. Also in 1971, Brown gave birth to her only child Ericka, who she conceived with former party member Mesai Hewit. Similarly to her father, Horace Scott, Hewit left Brown during her fourth month of pregnancy and later remarried. Before Newton escaped murder charges for Cuba, Brown unsuccessfully campaigned for an Oakland City Council position in 1973, and later would try for the same position in 1976. During Brown's tenure as chairperson, she continued the free medical care, expanded the free breakfast program, and created the renowned Oakland Community Learning Center in the city's poorest neighborhood.

Brown also registered nearly 100,000 new voters and endorsed Governor Jerry Brown and Lionel Wilson, who later would become Oakland's first black mayor. Also, Brown provided jobs to thousands of blacks during the Grove-Shafter freeway expansion that revitalized downtown Oakland. In 1976, Brown was chosen as a delegate to the Democratic Party's national convention, and she also was involved in many Oakland-based community and civic organizations. In 1977, Brown was viewed as a pawn and when Newton returned, neither his cocaine habit nor pressures from the majority male party could save Brown's leadership role. In fact, once Brown witnessed the beating of a female counterpart, she fled with her daughter to Los Angeles. Once there, Suzanne de Passe befriended Brown and allowed her to read scripts and write songs for Motown Records.

Through de Passe, Brown met French industrialist Pierre Elby and later moved to France to write her autobiography and first book, *A Taste of Power*, which she began in 1985 and completed in 1994. In 2002, Brown wrote her second book titled, *The Condemnation of Little B*, which examines the high incarceration rate for black men in the prison industrial complex. Brown currently maintains an active role in prisoner reform as seen by her work with the Mothers Advocating Juvenile Reform and the National Alliance for Radical Prisoner Reform. Brown also lectures throughout the United States, writes articles, and intends to coauthor a book on the life of Jamil Al-Amin. Also, *A Taste of Power* is being optioned for film. In November 2005, Brown ran for mayor of Brunswick, Georgia as a member of the Green Party.

See also: Black Panther Party; BPP, Los Angeles Branch; COINTELPRO; Newton, Huey P.; US Organization

Jamal L. Ratchford

Bibliography

Bray, Rosemary. "A Black Panther's Long Journey: Elaine Brown's Life Is Comfortable Now, but the Passing Years Haven't Quelled the Anger," *New York Times Magazine* 142 (1993):21–24.

Brown, Elaine. *The Condemnation of Little B: New Age Racism in America*. Boston: Beacon Press, 2002.

Brown, Elaine. *A Taste of Power: A Black Woman's Story*. New York: Anchor Books, 1994.

Perkins, Margo V. *Autobiography as Activism: Three Black Women of the Sixties*. Jackson: University of Mississippi Press, 2000.

Brown, Ron

Ronald Harmon Brown (1941–1996) was born in Washington, D.C. As a young boy, the Brown family moved along the eastern seaboard several times from Washington, D.C., to Boston, Massachusetts, to Harlem, New York. In 1947, Brown's father relocated to New York City as part of his job with the Federal Housing and Home Financing Administration (FHHFA). A short time later, he decided to switch from being a government employee to becoming a civilian employee when he took a job as the manager of the famous Hotel Theresa in Harlem. It was in that context that the younger Brown met several prominent African American hotel guests who had a profound influence on him. Among the notable celebrities he met at the hotel were Joe Louis, world champion boxing legend; Dinah Washington, blues/jazz singer great; and Josephine Baker, U.S.-born French entertainer.

After graduating from high school in New York, Brown attended Middlebury College (Vermont), majored in political science, and graduated in 1962. While at Middlebury, Brown pledged and became a member of a white fraternity. His entrance into the fraternity helped to abolish obstacles for membership in campus groups based on race. Brown's next stop after college was the U.S. Army, where he served from 1962 until 1967 in several leadership capacities commanding troops in the United States, Germany, and South Korea.

After his honorably discharge from the Army in 1967, Brown began studying law at St. John's University (New York) and in 1970, he received his law degree. One year later, he was admitted to the New York bar. While attending law school, Brown worked for the National Urban League as a job developer. Then, in 1973, after several promotions at the National Urban League, he was selected as the director of the organization's Washington, D.C. office. Three years later, in 1976, he was promoted to deputy executive director for programs and governmental affairs. Brown remained at the National Urban League until 1979, when he resigned from his position to work as Massachusetts Senator Edward (Ted) Kennedy's deputy campaign manager to secure the 1980 presidential nomination of the Democratic Party for Kennedy. In that role, Brown served as a political strategist to help secure the "black vote" for Kennedy's bid for the party's presidential nomination.

After his work on the Kennedy campaign ended, Brown decided to remain in Washington, D.C. In 1981, he was hired as an attorney and lobbyist for Patton, Boggs & Blow, one of the capital's most influential law firms. His new position there allowed him to extend his sphere of influence through political networking and to develop some close relationships with elite members of the Democratic Party. Brown was also the first African American to make partner at the powerful law firm.

From 1981 through 1985, Brown served as the deputy chairman of the Democratic Committee. In 1988, he was a convention campaign manager for the Rev. Jesse Jackson who was running for president of the United States. Brown also became a candidate for the position of chairman of the Democratic National Committee (DNC). One year later, in 1989, Brown was elected chairman of the DNC and became the first African American to lead a major political party. From 1989 through 1992, as chairman of the DNC, he led the Democratic Party with distinction.

Brown has been credited with getting Bill Clinton elected as U.S. President in 1992. President Clinton nominated Brown as the United States Commerce Secretary, a cabinet level position, and on January 22, 1993, Brown was sworn in as the 319th commerce secretary. Brown, as secretary of commerce, led one of the largest, complex governmental agencies with a multibillion dollar budget. Like many previous appointments throughout his life, Brown was a trailblazer; not only was he the first African American to serve as a commerce secretary, but he also significantly changed the role of that cabinet position.

Unlike his predecessors, who viewed the position as a formal, ceremonial one, Brown took an active role in reshaping the position. He expanded global business and commerce between the United States and other major international players in economic markets through his worldwide travels with governmental officials and business executives. Brown made multiple visits to several Asian, South American, and Middle Eastern countries that were eager to conduct commercial activities with business in the United States. He received high marks from a bipartisan business community for his efforts.

In office for slightly more than three years, Brown, along with a group of governmental officials and business executives, was killed when their Boeing T-43A military airplane crashed on April 3, 1996, in Dubrovnik, Croatia, during a tour of several countries in the Balkans to communicate his vision about developing possible investment opportunities in the region. Despite the speculation by some conspiracy theorists about the cause of his death, official sources state that Brown, as a result of pilot error resulting from poor weather conditions, was killed when his airplane crashed into the side of a mountain.

Brown's remains are buried at Arlington National Cemetery, Arlington Virginia. He left a wife, Alma Arrington; a son, Michael Brown; and a daughter, Tracey Brown. In December 1996, as a testimony to his memory and life work, the CAP Charitable Foundation, a private philanthropic foundation, established the Ron Brown Scholar Program. The mission of the program is to provide financial scholarships for talented African American high school seniors who may be financially unable to pay for college. In addition to their academic aptitude and desire to attend an institution of higher education, Ron Brown scholars should possess leadership abilities and demonstrate a willingness to engage in various types of community activities.

See also: Clinton, William Jefferson; Jackson, Jesse

Joseph C. Santora

Bibliography

Brown, Tracey L. *The Life & Times of Ron Brown*. New York: William Morrow, 1998.

Holmes, Steven, A. *Ron Brown: An Uncommon Life*. New York: Wiley, 2000.

Brown v. Board of Education

Brown v. Board of Education in Topeka Kansas (1954, 1955) are the landmark Supreme Court decisions that declared segregated educational institutions illegal. Even before the Supreme Court upheld the separate but equal doctrine decree in *Plessy v. Ferguson* (1896), individual parents challenged separate educational facilities via the courts, mostly because separate schools were rarely equal. Pursuant to their goal of eliminating segregation in all public facilities, the National Association for the Advancement of Colored People (NAACP) began the process of challenging segregation by laying the groundwork for Brown. To do so, the NAACP tried cases dealing with desegregation in graduate and professional schools. Two of the most significant cases include *Sweatt v. Painter* (1950), which found that segregated law schools deprived black students of certain intangible qualities, and *McLaurin v. Oklahoma State Regents* (1950), which mandated that black graduate students be treated the same as white graduate students.

The Kansas segregation statute permitted cities with a population greater than 15,000 to maintain separate elementary schools despite the fact that high schools, except in Kansas City, were desegregated. The Topeka Board of Education decided to operate segregated elementary schools, which provided the NAACP an opportunity to take legal action. The District Court ruled that while segregated schools did have a detrimental effect on African American children, the schools were substantially equal and therefore compliant with Plessy.

The NAACP lawyers, including Thurgood Marshall, Robert L. Carter, and Jack Greenberg, originally argued the case before the Supreme Court in 1952, but a decision was not reached because there were similar cases pending. As a result, the Brown case is actually an amalgam of four class action school segregation cases in Kansas, South Carolina (*Briggs v. Elliott*), Virginia (*Davis v. County School Board of Prince Edward County*), and Delaware (*Gebhart v. Belton*) representing approximately 200 plaintiffs. The NAACP legal team argued that segregated schools violated the equal protection clause of the Fourteenth Amendment. Using evidence supplied by Kenneth Clark and Mamie Phipps's doll experiments, the legal team also argued that segregated schools deprived them of the opportunity to learn to adjust personally and socially in an integrated setting, lowered

Mrs. Nettie Hunt and daughter Nickie on the steps of the U.S. Supreme Court in 1954. Hunt holds a paper announcing the Brown v. Board of Education *decision to ban segregation. (Library of Congress)*

black children's level of aspiration, instilled feelings of insecurity and inferiority in them, and retarded their mental and educational development.

The unanimous Brown decision, written by Chief Justice Earl Warren, declared that to separate children from others of similar age and qualifications solely because of their race generates a feeling of inferiority as to their status in the community that may affect their hearts and minds in a way unlikely ever to be undone. Most important, the Court found that maintaining separate educational facilities violated the equal protection clause of the Fourteenth Amendment and therefore declared that in the field of public education the doctrine of 'separate but equal' has no place. Separate educational facilities are inherently unequal.

Although the 1954 Brown decision overturned *Plessy v. Ferguson,* it did not provide guidance as to how the schools should desegregate. The Court decided that because the situations were so diverse, the remedies were best decided at the local level. Brown II (1955) mandated that the district courts should oversee the desegregation process "with all deliberate speed." Without a specific timeline in place, desegregating public schools was a slow-moving process. Only two southern states, Texas and Arkansas, began desegregation in 1954. Some other school districts circumvented the ruling by closing all the public schools. The process was so sluggish that it was 1957 when children attempted to desegregate schools in Little Rock, Arkansas, only to be met by angry mobs and National Guard troops. In other areas of the country, it was more than a decade before schools and school districts began the arduous process of desegregation. The most immediate success of the Brown ruling was that it set the stage for civil rights groups to challenge segregation in other public arenas including public transportation.

See also: Fourteenth Amendment; Houston, Charles Hamilton; Little Rock Nine; Marshall, Thurgood; National Association for the Advancement of Colored People; *Plessy v. Ferguson*

Lisa Doris Alexander

Bibliography

Bell, Derrick. *Silent Covenants:* Brown v. the Board of Education *and the Unfulfilled Hopes for Racial Reform.* Oxford: Oxford University Press, 2004.

Olgetree, Charles. *All Deliberate Speed: Reflections on the First-Half Century of* Brown v. Board of Education. New York: W. W. Norton, 2004.

Patterson, James T. Brown v. Board of Education: *A Civil Rights Milestone and Its Troubled Legacy.* Oxford: Oxford University Press, 2001.

Robinson, Mildred Wigfall, and Richard J. Bonnie, eds. *Law Touched Our Hearts: A Generation Remembers* Brown v. Board of Education. Nashville: Vanderbilt University Press, 2009.

Whitman, Mark. *Removing a Badge of Slavery: The Record of* Brown v. Board of Education. Princeton, NJ: Markus Wiener, 1993.

Bruce, Blanche K.

Blanche Kelso Bruce (1841–1898) was the first African American senator to serve a full term in the United States Senate. Born March 1, 1841, in Farmville, Virginia, Bruce was born into servitude. He spent his younger years in Virginia, Mississippi, and then Missouri. Although Bruce was a slave, he grew up similar to white Southern children. As a light-skinned biracial man, under a relatively benign master and mistress, Bruce's years in servitude were less harsh than those of other enslaved African Americans. He was both well educated and relatively well treated during his early years.

After the Civil War, Bruce moved to Mississippi where he became a wealthy landowner and heavily involved in the political scene. After just a few months in Mississippi, Bruce gained the attention of the Republican hierarchy. In his first few years in the state, Bruce held important positions including sergeant-at-arms in the state senate and tax assessor of Bolivar County. In 1871, when the first election following the adoption of Mississippi's Reconstruction constitution was held, Bruce was elected to the combined position of sheriff and tax collector. A few weeks later he was awarded the office of county superintendent of education. In 1872, Bruce was awarded a position on the board of levee commissioners. In these various positions Bruce gained popularity and notoriety throughout the state.

There were other notable African American politicians in Mississippi, but Bruce was especially appealing because he had not aligned himself with either faction of the Republican Party. Instead, he had chosen to stay on the good side of both the radicals and moderate factions of the party. In doing so, he furthered his popularity in the organization on both the state and national level. Furthermore, his actions in the various offices he held in the state had pleased many whites. Thus, Bruce was favorable to both whites and blacks in the state.

In 1874, Bruce's popularity awarded him a place in the United States Senate where he served from 1875 to 1881. During this period he strongly advocated for the education and equality for African Americans. In 1881, Bruce was unseated when the Democrats took control of the Mississippi legislature. He was replaced by Democrat James Z. George.

After Bruce left the Senate, President Garfield offered him the position of minister to Brazil or postmaster-general. Bruce turned both positions down and instead asked to be appointed minister of the treasury. Garfield agreed and the Senate, filled with Bruce's former colleagues, confirmed Garfield's selection. In the position of the minister of treasury, Bruce was awarded the highest appointed position that an African American had ever received. Bruce's term ended in 1885 when the Republican Garfield was replaced by newly elected Democrat Grover Cleveland. For the next few years, Bruce lectured and campaigned for the Republicans. In 1888, when the Republicans successfully regained the presidency with Benjamin Harrison, Bruce was again awarded a position of respect, this time as recorder of deeds for the District of Columbia. When Cleveland reclaimed the presidency in 1892, Bruce was again out of office. In 1896, Bruce finally regained his position as minister of the treasury under newly elected President McKinley. Bruce held this position until his death on March 17, 1898.

Blanche Kelso Bruce was an influential African American. He held numerous positions on the local, state, and national level. In these positions he advocated and fought for black equality. While fighting for his African American brothers and sisters, Bruce stayed on the good side of whites as well. This helped to make Bruce the first African American to serve a full term in the United States Senate and forever a part of the history books.

See also: Radical Republicans; Reconstruction Era Black Politicians; Republican Party

Mindy R. Weidman

Bibliography

Harris, William C. "Blanche K. Bruce of Mississippi: Conservative Assimilationist." In *Southern Black Leaders of the Reconstruction Era,* Howard N. Rabinowitz, ed., 3–38. Urbana: University of Illinois Press, 1982.

Shapiro, Samuel. "A Black Senator from Mississippi: Blanche K. Bruce (1841–1898)." *Review of Politics* 44 (January 1982): 83–109.

Blanche K. Bruce was the second African American ever to serve in the U.S. Senate. (Library of Congress)

Buffalo Soldiers

After the Civil War, when the massive Union army of about 1 million was disbanded, Congress could not ignore the contributions of the large number of black volunteers to the Union victory. So when the army was reduced and reorganized in 1866, blacks had a place in the regular army for the first time. Congress designated six post-Civil War regiments for black enlisted men in the Reorganization Act of July 28, 1866—the 9th and 10th Cavalry and the 38th, 39th, 40th, and 41st Infantry regiments (consolidated in 1869 into two infantry regiments, the 24th and 25th). The act marked the first inclusion of black men in the regular army. Soldiers who served in these regiments during the period of the frontier wars and the overseas wars at the turn of the 20th century have come to be called "Buffalo Soldiers." Since 1866, African Americans have remained a continuous presence in the armed forces, and their inclusion in the regular force has been considered a positive step toward equal opportunity. The creation of this segregated place for black soldiers, however, anticipated by a generation the spread of segregation as the mode of race relations imposed by whites in the South—usually called "Jim Crow"—and foreshadowed by two generations the formal segregation of civilian employment in the federal government by President Woodrow Wilson.

The officers of the black regiments were white. In the 50 years between the Civil War and World War I, only five African Americans received commissions in the regular army and served with the black regiments. Three were West Point graduates: Henry Flipper was the first in 1877, followed by John Alexander in 1887 and Charles Young in 1889. The other two were former enlisted men, Benjamin O. Davis and John E. Green, commissioned at the turn of the 20th century. Davis ultimately became the first black general officer.

The law of 1866 required that a chaplain be assigned to each new black regiment. This departed from the normal army practice of appointing chaplains to specific posts rather than units. Their responsibilities included the common school education of the men, many of whom were illiterate former slaves who had been denied access to education, as well as their spiritual needs. The first chaplains were white. Henry Vinton Plummer, a Baptist minister who

Soldiers with the 9th Cavalry, about 1898. The 9th Cavalry was one of six regiments for black enlisted men organized after the Civil War. In time, these regiments became known collectively as the Buffalo Soldiers. (Library of Congress)

had served in the Navy during the Civil War, became the first black chaplain and served 10 years (1884–1894) before he was dismissed from the service on spurious charges of conduct unbecoming an officer and a gentleman. By 1898, all four regiments had black chaplains: George Prioleau (9th Cavalry), William T. Anderson (10th Cavalry), Allen Allensworth (24th Infantry), and Theophilus Gould Steward (25th Infantry). They were a distinguished group of clergymen and scholars.

Like the white soldiers of their time, Buffalo Soldiers participated in central episodes of the American experience. They made many essential contributions to western settlement, making maps, blazing trails, and improving roads; guarding settlements, roads, and stage stations; and providing the reassuring military presence that helped encourage development. They also fought in some major wars against Indians, from the conflicts against the Cheyenne in Kansas just after the Civil War to the last big campaign on the Pine Ridge against the Sioux in South Dakota during 1890–1891. Most notably they were at the center of the arduous campaign against the Apaches Victorio and Nana in a wide belt of the Southwest covering western Texas, much of New Mexico, and eastern Arizona during 1879–1881.

During the period of the frontier wars, the black regiments made up about 12 percent of the very small Indian fighting army, which sometimes included a mere 25,000 or so soldiers, and participated in about 13 percent of the combat engagements against Indians. The 9th Cavalry, commanded by Colonel Edward Hatch from 1866 to 1887, was organized at New Orleans, Louisiana. It served in Texas through the mid-1870s, then moved west to New Mexico. In the 1880s, the regiment moved first to Kansas, then farther north to stations in Nebraska, Wyoming, and Utah. The 10th Cavalry started at Forts Riley and Leavenworth, Kansas. Colonel Benjamin Grierson, who, like Hatch, had distinguished himself as a leader of mounted troops during the Civil War, remained in command until 1889. His regiment served in Kansas and what later became Oklahoma into the 1870s, then moved to Texas and later to Arizona, where it participated in the campaign against Geronimo in 1886 and remained until 1892. It spent the rest of the 1890s at Montana stations. The 24th Infantry, the product of the merger of the 38th and 41st in 1869, spent many years at remote Texas posts before the war with Spain. The unit's arrival at Fort Douglas, Utah, outside Salt Lake City, in 1896 marked a rare instance of the stationing of a black regiment near a center of population. The 25th Infantry, consolidated from the 39th and 40th, also spent its first decade in isolated parts of Texas before moving to equally remote posts on the northern plains in Minnesota, the Dakotas, and Montana. A total of 37 of the 61 Buffalo Soldiers killed in Indian fighting during the period 1867 to 1890 fell against the Apaches during 1877–1881. Eight of the 18 who received the Medal of Honor during the period of frontier warfare earned recognition for conspicuous bravery in this bitterest of American frontier wars. Sergeant Emanuel Stance of the 9th Cavalry was the first Buffalo Soldier to receive the medal for leadership and bravery in 1870.

All four regiments fought in the two foreign wars of the turn of the 20th century. They achieved prominence in the war against Spain in the summer of 1898, participating in the attack on San Juan Hill Cuba, alongside Theodore Roosevelt and his Rough Riders. They also served in the harsh guerilla struggle in the Philippines against a native independence movement during 1899–1902; 29 were killed in Cuba, 23 in the Philippines. Later, they participated in General John Pershing's 1916 punitive expedition into Mexico. Five black soldiers received the Medal of Honor for valor in Cuba.

Although Buffalo Soldiers and white soldiers carried out the same duties, they did so under different circumstances. Black soldiers often faced discrimination and hostility from the people they were assigned to protect. Through the entire period from the creation of the regiments to World War I, Texas represented the most dangerous racially charged environment, but soldiers lost their lives to racist attacks in a number of places including Fort Concho, Texas (1881), Sturgis, South Dakota (1885), and Suggs, Wyoming (1892). The two most serious racial incidents took place in Texas. A shooting incident at Brownsville, Texas, in 1906 resulted in the dishonorable discharge of an entire battalion of the 25th Infantry, and a riot in Houston, Texas, in 1917 led to the hanging of 14 soldiers of the 24th. Despite the difficulties, black soldiers rarely deserted and were much more likely than white soldiers to reenlist, reflecting the paucity of viable options in an era of increased segregation and lack of respectable mainstream employment. Moreover, black civilians considered the Buffalo Soldiers important and followed their activities avidly in weekly newspapers.

Black regulars from the period of the frontier wars are now widely known as Buffalo Soldiers. It is generally supposed that the Indians, either the Comanche or Cheyenne,

first called the troopers "buffalo soldiers," and the best guesses are that the name reflected a perceived resemblance between the brown skins and nappy hair of some of the men and the color and texture of the fur of the bison. The earliest known user of the phrase was Frances Roe, the wife of an officer who served at a post with the 10th Cavalry in Indian Territory during 1872–1873. Her letters were dated 1872 but not published until 1909. Some historians, including William Leckie in his path-breaking book *The Buffalo Soldiers: a Narrative of the Negro Cavalry in the West,* claimed that, because the buffalo was so important to these tribes, the term was probably a sign of respect and that the soldiers so comprehended it. The assumption that the term Buffalo Soldier was somehow honorific and that the Indians considered the black troopers to be exceptional has sometimes led to another, that the Buffalo Soldiers and the Indians viewed each other with empathy and respect. This cannot be proved, and the origins, significance, and prevalence of the phrase are not clear. Moreover, evidence that the soldiers themselves used or even referred to this title—in pension affidavits, black newspapers, or other venues—has not turned up, so claims concerning their views of the usage remain unproved suppositions. The 10th Cavalry adopted the buffalo as a central element of its unit crest, but not until 1911.

The improbability of any special bond between Indians and Buffalo Soldiers is underscored by the soldiers' use of the same dismissive epithets—"hostile tribes," "naked savages," and "redskins"—used by whites. Overall, the quest of Buffalo Soldiers for recognition as citizens in a racist country and the struggle of Native Americans for cultural and physical survival were not compatible. The strongest modern challenge to the emerging myth came from Indians, who were especially angered over the publicity that attended the issue of a buffalo-soldier postage stamp in 1994 and resented suggestions regarding some special bond between their warrior ancestors and the soldiers.

General awareness of the participation of black soldiers in the westward movement dates from the 1960s, the period of the civil rights revolution. The process started in 1960, with the release of John Ford's "Sergeant Rutledge," a subtle and insightful film featuring Woody Strode as a black cavalry sergeant accused of rape and murder. The Civil War centennial joined with the Civil Rights movement to provoke reconsideration of the Civil War and a new focus on black soldiers as well as expanded general interest in black history. Leckie's book appeared in 1967. General Colin

Powell, a black four-star army general who, as chairman of the Joint Chiefs of Staff, served as the military advisor to the President of the United States between 1989 and 1993, was instrumental in promoting this knowledge, dedicating a larger-than-life statue of a mounted Buffalo Soldier by sculptor Eddie Dixon at Fort Leavenworth Kansas on July 25, 1992. The well-publicized ceremony, the declarations by both houses of Congress that July 28, 1992 was "Buffalo Soldiers Day," and the imposing permanent presence of the statue (the first of at least five at western forts), triggered a flood of commemorations, displays, and publications; stimulated formation of reenactment societies; and created a market for souvenirs and memorabilia. Between 1960 and 1992, the Buffalo Soldier emerged from obscurity in the United States. By the end of the 1990s, he was a well-known, widely recognized cultural icon.

See also: Jim Crow; Union Army

Frank N. Schubert

Bibliography

Leckie, William H. *The Buffalo Soldiers: A Narrative of the Negro Cavalry in the West.* Norman: University of Oklahoma Press, 1967.

Schubert, Frank N. *Black Valor: Buffalo Soldiers and the Medal of Honor, 1870–1898.* Wilmington, DE: SR Books, 1997.

Schubert, Frank N. *On the Trail of the Buffalo Soldier: Biographies of African Americans in the U.S. Army, 1866–1917.* Wilmington, DE: Scholarly Resources, 1995.

Schubert, Frank N. *On the Trail of the Buffalo Soldier II: Biographies of African Americans in the U.S. Army, 1866–1917.* Lanham, MD: SR Books, 2004.

Schubert, Frank N. *Voices of the Buffalo Soldier: Records, Reports, and Recollections of Military Life and Service in the West.* Albuquerque: University of New Mexico Press, 2003.

Bunche, Ralph

Ralph (Johnson) Bunche (1904–1971) was born in Detroit, Michigan, the son of a barber. He moved from Detroit to Toledo, Ohio with his parents as his father searched for work. He attended elementary school in Ohio. In 1917, when his mother died, Bunche, then 13 years old, and his sister became orphans. His maternal grandmother, Lucy Taylor Johnson, took charge of the children who went to live with her in Los Angeles, California.

After graduating from a Los Angeles, California, high school with honors in 1922 where he excelled in academics

and sports, Bunche attended UCLA. He continued to be an outstanding student. He was both a Phi Beta Kappa and summa cum laude graduate at UCLA. In 1927, he received an undergraduate degree in political science. Based on his academic prowess, he was awarded a fellowship to attend Harvard University to study political science in the department of government.

In 1928, Bunche graduated from Harvard University with a master's degree in political science. He then took a position as an instructor at Howard University in Washington, D.C., where be founded and became chair of its political science department. At Howard, Bunche played a major role as an academic and quasi-university administrator when he served as assistant to the university president. Bunche's work at Howard was rewarding, but he wanted to pursue his terminal degree. He enrolled in a PhD program in political science at Harvard and began working on his doctoral studies during summers from 1929 through 1934. While at Harvard, Bunche met Ruth Harris, whom he married in 1930. One year later, Ruth gave birth to Joan, the first of his three children. The Bunche family would include two additional children: Jane and Ralph Jr. In 1934, five years after he began his formal doctoral studies, Bunche fulfilled all the requirements for his PhD degree in the department of government, when the faculty accepted his dissertation "French Administration in Togoland and Dahomey." He had the unique distinction of receiving the William Toppan Prize, an annual award bestowed on doctoral students who submitted the best dissertation in political science. Bunche was also the first African American to receive a PhD from Harvard, or from any institution of higher education in political science. With his newly minted PhD, Bunche was identified as a rising star in the academic community. He was considered someone who could make a major contribution to the field. But Bunche opted to publish a few short articles from his research instead of turning his dissertation into a major book.

Bunche held some interesting views about poverty and political powerlessness. At the outset of his career, he believed that capitalism was the root of poor political and economic conditions for blacks. He advocated the position that blacks and whites should work together for "economic and political justice," which would ultimately result in the creation of a new, more equal, society. In 1939, Bunche had the unique opportunity to work part-time with Gunnar Mydal, the noted Swedish economist and sociologist, on the issue of race in the United States. This field of research culminated in the 1944 landmark publication *The American Dilemma: The Negro Problem and Modern Democracy*.

Bunche left academic life to embark on a new career. In 1941, President Franklin Delano Roosevelt created the Office of Coordination of Information, later renamed the Office of Strategic Service or OSS. Needing a specialist on Africa, Roosevelt reached out to his alma mater Harvard University for a recommendation for the position; Bunche was recommended and Roosevelt accepted him.

Over the next three decades, Bunche would play a significant role in shaping government and international affairs. In 1942, Bunche moved from OSS to the U.S. State Department. In addition, he participated in preparing those chapters of the United Nations Charter that dealt with colonial territories. In 1946, Bunche became the director of the UN Trustee Division to help monitor the progress of autonomy in the UN Trust Territories and thus began his illustrious career at the UN.

In 1948, UN Secretary General Trygve Lie appointed Bunche his representative in Palestine, but he soon became acting mediator for the crisis. His diplomatic skills were instrumental in hammering out an armistice agreement on Palestine between Israel and several Arab countries. For his efforts in defusing the conflict and in brokering a deal in the Middle East, on December 10, 1950, Bunche became the first African American to receive the Nobel Peace Prize.

In the 1950s, the economic plight of African Americans was still very much on his mind. At this time, Bunche changed his political philosophy about capitalism, as he no longer blamed capitalism for economic disparity. He now believed that economic inequities were based on racism. In 1953, UN Secretary General Dag Hammarskjold appointed Bunche the undersecretary general for Special Political Affairs. For more than a decade, Bunche participated in peacekeeping missions in the Middle East and Africa.

In the 1960s, Bunche believed strongly in civil rights and sought integration and equality for African Americans. He supported Dr. Martin Luther King Jr. and participated in the March on Washington in 1963 and the 1965 march from Selma to Montgomery (Alabama). In 1963, President Lyndon B. Johnson presented Bunche with the Medal of Freedom. The urban unrest of the 1960s, starting with the 1965 Watts riots in particular, solidified his views on the need for integration; as a result, black radicals of the time called him an "Uncle Tom." Bunche was also vehemently against the Vietnam War. He saw irony in the fact that African American soldiers were fighting for the rights of the South Vietnamese, yet they had limited rights in their own country.

In the later part of the 1960s, Bunche suffered a number of personal tragedies. In October 1966, one of his two daughters committed suicide. In addition to this devastating event, his personal health began to fail. He was diagnosed with diabetes, which had an impact on his eyesight. In early 1967, Bunche wanted to resign from his UN position, but then Secretary General U Thant refused to accept his resignation. His career and his family obligations were at odds: his wife accused him of deserting his family for his career. He resigned from the UN on October 1, 1971 because of ill health.

Slightly two months later, on December 9, 1971, Bunche died in New York Hospital from complications connected with diabetes. As a lasting tribute to Bunche, in 1980, a park facing the United Nations building in New York City was named "The Ralph Bunche Park for Peace" in his honor.

See also: Black Cabinet; Vietnam War (Black Participation in)

Joseph C. Santora

Bibliography

Henry, Charles P. *Ralph Bunche: Model Negro or American Other?* New York: New York University Press, 1999.

Holloway, Jonathan Scott. *Confronting the Veil: Abram Harris, Jr., E. Franklin Frazier, and Ralph Bunche, 1919–1941.* Chapel Hill: University of North Carolina Press, 2002.

Keppel, Ben. *The Work of Democracy: Ralph Bunche, Kenneth B. Clark, Lorraine Hansberry, and the Cultural Politics of Race.* Cambridge, MA: Harvard University Press, 1995.

Lindsay, Beverly. *Ralph Johnson Bunche: Public Intellectual and Nobel Peace Laureate.* Urbana: University of Illinois Press, 2007.

Rivlin, Benjamin, ed. *Ralph Bunche: The Man and His Times.* New York: Holmes & Meier, 1990.

Urquhart, Brian. *Ralph Bunche: An American Life.* New York: W. W. Norton, 1993.

Busing

Busing, the act of moving students outside of their school district to end de facto segregation of public schools, became a controversial integration strategy ordered by the Supreme Court during the 1960s and 1970s. In 1954, the Court determined in *Brown v. Board of Education* that de jure segregation violated the Fourteenth Amendment. Despite the Court's ruling to end segregation, whites resisted desegregation in the North and in the South.

In 1968, the Supreme Court, unsatisfied with the slow pace of desegregation, ruled in *Green v. County School Board of New Kent County* that open enrollment desegregation programs did not comply with the *Brown* decision. School districts were required to take affirmative steps to achieve racial balance. Three years later, in *Swann v. Charlotte-Mecklenburg,* the Court ordered busing as a valid means to reach racial integration.

The public responded in protest. In June 1974, U.S. District Judge W. Arthur Garrity ordered the Boston Public School System to begin busing several thousand students between predominantly white South Boston, Hyde Park, and Dorchester and mostly black Roxbury. White opponents of busing demonstrated to prevent black children from entering white schools and withheld their own children from being bused into black schools. For weeks violence and hostilities ensued.

Integration efforts were damaged further when white parents moved their families to the suburbs, leaving behind overwhelmingly black urban enclaves. A month after Garrity's decision, the Court assessed the consequences of "white flight" on urban schools and overturned a Detroit busing plan in *Milliken v. Bradley.* In the 1990s, the Supreme Court redefined school desegregation, prohibiting racial discrimination, but relieved school districts of integration requirements.

See also: Brown v. Board of Education

John Matthew Smith

Bibliography

Dimond, Paul R. *Beyond Busing: Inside the Challenge to Urban Segregation.* Ann Arbor: University of Michigan Press, 1985.

Graglia, Lino A. *Disaster by Decree: The Supreme Court Decisions on Race and the Schools.* Ithaca, NY: Cornell University Press, 1976.

Schwartz, Bernard. *Swann's Way: The School Busing Case and the Supreme Court.* New York: Oxford University Press, 1986.

Wolters, Raymond. "From *Brown* to *Green* and Back: The Changing Meaning of Desegregation," *The Journal of Southern History* 30 (May 2004):317–26.

Carmichael, Stokely (Kwame Ture)

Stokely Carmichael (1941–1998) was a charismatic and controversial leader of the Civil Rights movement in the 1960s and 1970s. He is best known as an activist and chairman of SNCC and a leader in the Black Power movement, which marked a turning away from the nonviolent tactics of leaders like Martin Luther King Jr. in favor of a more militant brand of activism.

Carmichael was born in Port of Spain, Trinidad on July 29, 1941 to Mabel and Adolphus Carmichael. Carmichael's parents moved to New York City when he was three years old, and in 1952, he and his three sisters joined them there. The family first settled in Harlem, a predominantly black part of the city, before relocating to the Bronx, where Adolphus worked as a cab driver and carpenter and Mabel worked as a maid. Carmichael attended the Bronx High School of Science, one of the most prestigious schools in New York City, where he was one of only two black students, and graduated in 1960.

Before graduating from high school, Stokely experimented with political activism by participating in a sit-in sponsored by the New York chapter of the Congress of Racial Equality (CORE). He was beaten up during the sit-in, which only fueled his desire to further participate in the Civil Rights movement. Through CORE, he participated in boycotts of Woolworth stores in New York, which the organization targeted because of the company's policy of segregating their southern locations. Although Carmichael received scholarship offers from a number of universities, including Harvard, he chose to attend Howard University, an all-black institution in Washington, D.C. Because he did not receive a scholarship, Carmichael's parents had to pay his tuition.

While at Howard, he continued to work closely with CORE, as well as the Nonviolent Action Group (NAG), a local organization that planned demonstrations and sit-ins in the Washington, D.C. area. In 1961, Carmichael expanded his involvement in the Civil Rights movement by joining the Freedom Riders, a group of protesters who traveled to southern cities via bus (with whites riding in the back and African Americans in front), challenging segregation and attempting to integrate public places that upheld the practice. He and his fellow riders were arrested for these actions in Mississippi and spent 53 days in Parchman Penitentiary, a notoriously brutal state prison. During this period of incarceration, the prison guards subjected the prisoners to terrible food, dirty mattresses, and constant harassment. The prisoners sang protest songs as a way of keeping up morale, but their songs only brought more harsh punishment from the guards.

Stokely Carmichael (later Kwame Ture), an effective leader of the Student Nonviolent Coordinating Committee (SNCC), became an advocate of black power by 1965. He eventually joined the Black Panthers in 1967 and, while in exile, founded the All African People's Revolutionary Party (AAPRP) in Guinea. (Library of Congress)

Carmichael was released from prison in time for his second year at Howard, where he changed his major from pre-med to philosophy. He continued his education while also constantly participating in civil rights demonstrations. Carmichael finally finished his degree in the spring of 1964, and, although he received a scholarship offer from Harvard for graduate school, he passed in favor of joining the Mississippi Freedom Summer Project (MFSP), which aimed to increase black voter registration, organize a legal Democratic party that included blacks, establish schools for teaching basic literacy skills to black children, and open community centers where poor families could receive legal and medical assistance. He headed the Student Nonviolent Coordinating Committee (SNCC), the organization sponsoring the project, for one of the voting districts in Mississippi. His responsibilities included finding and training staff members, registering people to vote, distributing funds, and holding community meetings. The job was dangerous, and a number of students were injured

and even killed because of their involvement with the project.

Stokely left the MFSP at the end of the summer in search of a new project that would allow him to work solely with other African Americans. He did not like that the Mississippi Freedom Summer Project encouraged alliances with whites and felt there needed to be an all-black political party in order to achieve real political power. Carmichael also believed that leaders like Martin Luther King Jr., who advocated peaceful resistance, were too focused on integration and were getting in the way of establishing strong and independent black communities. Carmichael preferred more militant leaders such as Malcolm X, who encouraged African Americans to defend themselves, through violence if necessary, and to learn about and embrace their African heritage. In 1965, Carmichael went to Lowndes County, Alabama, in the hopes creating a strong, all-black resistance movement there. The number of blacks in Lowndes County outnumbered the whites, yet whites held all the positions of power, and the intense racial oppression there left black citizens living in fear. Carmichael felt that this town provided the ideal setting for incubating a black rights movement. Dressed in overalls so that he fit in with his surroundings, the charismatic Carmichael convinced black citizens in the county that they should vote, despite violent resistance from local whites, and managed to register nearly 300 black voters. Once registered, however, these black voters did not know who to vote for. There were no black members of either the Republican or Democratic Parties in Lowndes County, and black voters did not trust any white politicians to protect their interests. Carmichael decided to create a new party, the Lowndes County Freedom Organization, which soon became known as the Black Panthers because of its mascot. Several members of the Black Panthers ran for office in the next election, and although none of them won, the black community in Lowndes felt they had more power and were better organized to protect their rights in the future.

After his success in organizing Lowndes County, Carmichael ran for and won the chairmanship of SNCC in 1966. His election marked the beginning of a new, more militant chapter of the organization's history. Like Carmichael, many members of the SNCC felt that nonviolent protest had not achieved any results and that stronger action was necessary. Shortly after his election, Carmichael found a national platform for his ideas. In June 1966, James Meredith was shot during his solitary "March Against Fear." While Meredith recuperated from his wounds, Carmichael joined Martin Luther King Jr., NAACP president Roy Wilkins, and other civil rights activists to finish the march. At the end of the march, Carmichael gave a rousing speech in which he invited African Americans to embrace "black power," meaning that they should be prideful of their race while also striving to achieve socioeconomic independence from the white community. The term became a rallying cry for young blacks across the country, with the most public example being the 1968 Olympics, when two African American track-and-field medalists raised their fists in the black power salute while standing on the award podium. SNCC, which valued a group ethic over individual merit, became displeased with Carmichael's growing celebrity, and, in response, he stepped down from his position of leadership in 1967. He traveled the country, becoming more closely identified with the Black Panthers and writing a book entitled *Black Power* (1967).

In 1968, Carmichael married South African singer Miriam Makeba, and the following year, the two moved to Guinea, where he became an aide to Prime Minister Ahmed Sekou Toure and a student of exiled Ghanaian president Kwame Nkrumah. Shortly after his arrival in Guinea, Carmichael published a formal rejection of the Black Panthers, citing their increasing willingness to form alliances with whites. In 1970, he returned to the United States in order to appear before the Subcommittee to Investigate the Administration of the Internal Security Act and Other Internal Security Laws. The subcommittee asked him to provide information on organizations and people that might be trying to overthrow the U.S government, including the Black Panther Party and SNCC. They also asked Carmichael to provide details of his activities while outside the United States. He pleaded the Fifth Amendment throughout the hearing.

In 1971, Carmichael published another book entitled *Stokely Speaks: Black Power Back to Pan-Africanism,* which contained many of his speeches during his years with the SNCC and the Black Panthers. In 1978, he divorced his wife and changed his name to Kwame Ture in honor of his two new patrons, although many people continued to refer to him by his birth name. He then married Marlyatou Barry, a doctor whom he divorced several years later. He became a member of the All African Peoples Revolutionary Party (AAPRP), a group that advocated Pan-Africanism, or the uniting of all African peoples inside and outside of Africa

to form a single political entity. Ture traveled the world organizing new chapters of AAPRP for nearly a decade.

After the death of Ahmed Sekou Toure in 1984, the military regime that took his place arrested Ture several times on suspicion of trying to overthrow the government, although the reasons behind these allegations remain a mystery. He was jailed for several days for these charges, marking his final encounter with the law. By the mid-1980s, Ture grew disillusioned with the Civil Rights movement. Although there were 255 African American mayors in the United States by 1984, he felt that blacks had never truly organized effectively enough to gain real political power. Even so, he continued to visit the United States several times a year in efforts to promote Pan-Africanism. After receiving treatments for prostate cancer over a period of two years, Kwame Ture died in 1998 in Conakry, Guinea, at the age of 57.

See also: Black Nationalism; Black Panther Party; Black Power; CORE; King, Martin Luther Jr.; Lowndes County Freedom Organization; MFDP; Mississippi Freedom Summer, 1964; Nkrumah, Kwame; Pan-Africanism; Student Nonviolent Coordinating Committee

Sara K. Eskridge

Bibliography

Carmichael, Stokely. *Stokely Speaks: Black Power Back to Pan-Africanism.* New York: Random House, 1971.

Carmichael, Stokely, and Charles V. Hamilton. *Black Power, Politics of Liberation in America.* New York: Random House, 1967.

Carmichael, Stokely, and Ekwueme Michael Thelwell. *Ready for Revolution: The Life and Struggles of Stokely Carmichael {Kwame Ture}.* New York: Scribner, 2003.

Dittmer, John. *Local People: The Struggle for Civil Rights in Mississippi.* Urbana: University of Illinois Press, 1994.

Johnson, Jacqueline. *Stokely Carmichael: The Story of Black Power.* Englewood Cliffs, NJ: Silver Burdett Press, 1990.

Wayne, Bennett, ed. *Black Crusaders for Freedom.* New York: Garrard, 1974.

Castro, Fidel

Fidel Alejandro Castro Ruz (1926–) was the leader of the Cuban Revolution, the prime minister of Cuba from February 1959 to December 1976, and the president of the Council of State of Cuba until February 2008 when power was transferred to his brother Raúl Castro. During his 50 years as the head of state of Cuba, Castro worked diligently to support, and gain the support of, civil rights activist in the United States and anticolonial revolutionaries in Africa. As a result, Castro has met with a large number of political activist spanning the African Diaspora and, as such, both Cuba and Castro have become iconic figures in the various struggles led by people of African decent. Castro's role in this regard began in 1960, just a year after the successful coup against the U.S.-backed regime of Fulgencio Batista, when he invited a group of African American intellectuals including John Henrik Clarke, Julian Mayfield, Amiri Baraka (Leroi Jones), and Harold Cruse to see, first hand, Revolutionary Cuba and its progress.

In October 1961, Castro and a delegation of Cuban government representatives came to New York to address the United Nations. When the delegation balked at staying in a plush mid-Manhattan hotel, the Fair Play for Cuba Committee arranged for Castro and his delegation to be moved to the black-owned Hotel Theresa in Harlem. During his stay in Harlem, Castro had a 30-minute conversation with Malcolm X and the picture taken during their meeting may have been the genesis of the positive association between Castro and African American leaders. Between 1960 and 1961, militant civil rights activist Robert F. Williams visited Cuba three times to the dismay of the NAACP. Williams's visits to Cuba and, along with Malcolm X, his October 1960 meeting with Castro in Harlem forged the first links between militant black activists and Cuban revolutionaries. As Cuba spiraled further away from the orbit of the United States, it became even more attractive to a number of radical organizations. Cuba alone stood against the combined might of the most powerful military in the world; Castro successfully repulsed an invasion, avoided several assassination attempts, and effectively became the unmovable object to the unstoppable force of U.S. domination in the Western Hemisphere.

This positive affiliation between African American radicals and Cuban revolutionaries, solidified even further by Castro's efforts in Angola, Namibia, Mozambique, and South Africa, explains why Cuba became a haven for African American activists during the era of political persecution and COINTELPRO operations in the United States. Beginning with Robert F. Williams in August 1961, a long secession of African American activist escaped to Cuba to seek political asylum, including Assata Shakur, Huey Newton, and Nehanda Abiodun (Cheri Dalton), William Lee Brent, and Charlie Hill among many others. While he and his family lived in Cuba, Williams joined the staff of join the staff of Radio Progresso in July 1962, and was given access to a 50,000-watt radio station with enough power to reach Saskatchewan, Canada. Airing three days a week, listeners heard "Radio Free Dixie" broadcasts in Monroe, Harlem, and Detroit. Williams's continued publication of his monthly newsletter, The Crusader-in-Exile, and his "Radio Free Dixie" broadcasts between 1962 and 1965 solidified the notion that Castro was a friend to African Americans in the minds of millions throughout the United States.

In 1995, Castro made a return visit to Harlem during the UN's 50th anniversary celebration, delivering a speech to 1,300 people at Abyssinian Baptist Church. Citing the achievements of the Cuban Revolution, he noted that in terms of infant mortality, access to health care, and literacy, Cuba has quantifiably better statistics than New York City, despite decades of the U.S.-imposed trade embargo. He also reminded the audience of Cuba's longstanding fight against imperialism and neocolonialism in Latin America and Africa and that, specifically, Cuban soldiers had shed blood on behalf of Angola in repulsing the CIA- and apartheid-backed effort led by Jonas Savimbi and the Republic of South Africa to invade and control the former Portuguese colony. More recently, Castro visited the United States again in September 2000 to deliver a four-hour speech at Harlem's Riverside Church. Finally, six members of the Congressional Black Caucus made a trip to Cuba in April 2009 to meet with the Castro brothers, a signal that relations between the United States and Cuba may be thawing under President Barack Obama after a half-century of tension and distrust. Perhaps it is fitting that African American political leaders are playing principal roles in creating new diplomatic relations with Cuba.

See also: Destination, Cuba; Williams, Robert F.; X, Malcolm

Walter C. Rucker

Bibliography

Baraka, Imamu Amiri. Home; Social Essays. New York: Morrow, 1966.

Castro, Fidel. We Stand with the People of Africa. New York: Venceremos Brigade, 1976.

Cruse, Harold. The Crisis of the Negro Intellectual. New York: Morrow, 1967.

Mandela, Nelson, and Fidel Castro. How Far We Slaves Have Come!: South Africa and Cuba in Today's World. New York: Pathfinder, 1991.

Mealy, Rosemari. *Fidel & Malcolm X: Memories of a Meeting*. New York: Ocean Press, 1993.

Rucker, Walter. "'Crusader in Exile': Robert F. Williams and the Internationalized Struggle for Black Freedom in America." *Black Scholar* 36 (2006):19–34.

Tyson, Timothy B. *Radio Free Dixie: Robert F. Williams and the Roots of Black Power*. Chapel Hill: University of North Carolina Press, 1999.

Young, Cynthia Ann. *Soul Power: Culture, Radicalism, and the Making of a U.S. Third World Left*. Durham, NC: Duke University Press, 2006.

Chicago Defender

Characterized as the "world's greatest weekly" by founder Robert S. Abbott, the *Chicago Defender* emerged as a leading newspaper advocate for black rights in the 20th century. Throughout its–100-year history, the *Defender* spurred on the Great Migration, fought Jim Crow and lynching, campaigned for equal opportunity, and believed that American racism must be eliminated.

Founded on May 5, 1905 by Robert Sengstacke Abbott, a black entrepreneur and millionaire who was born to former slaves, the *Defender* began with a budget of 25 cents and was only four pages long. Abbott originally could not afford to hire a staff and therefore managed the entire news reporting, editing, and distribution processes. He would not be dismayed and sold more than 200 copies at two cents a paper in 1905. Unfortunately, times were not always easy and the *Defender* nearly folded owing to economic hardship. The *Defender* endured, however, because of the sincerity of patrons such as Henrietta Plummer Lee. It was Lee, Abbott's landlady, who allowed him to use her dining room in her home at 3159 State Street in Chicago, Illinois; and so, the first headquarters of the *Defender* commenced on June 5, 1905. In fact, Lee, who was moved by Abbott's initiative to champion black-related issues, accepted token payments for rent and food. Later, Abbott would honor her patronage with an eight-room brick house that he bought in 1918. Despite early economic challenges, Abbott instilled confidence into a people whom he referred to as the "Race" rather than "Negro," "Afro-American," or "Black." With World War I looming and thus need of coverage in addition to the aid of people such as J. Hockley Smiley, the managerial editor who used captivating headlines, and Jesse Binga, founder of Binga State Bank and a financial consultant who

also helped Abbott manage his bills, the *Defender* was able to mobilize toward success.

Robert Abbott was born on November 24, 1868, in Frederica, on St. Simons Island, Georgia, to Thomas and Flora Butler Abbott. While Thomas was a butler on the Charles Stevens' plantation, Flora Butler was a hairdresser in the Savannah Theater. When Thomas Abbott died of tuberculosis in 1869, Flora later moved back to Savannah and eventually met John Herman Henry Sengstacke. In 1874, Sengstacke married Flora Butler and they had seven children together. Sengstacke became a key mentor to young Abbott and subsequently paid for his education at Beach Institute, an American missionary school in Savannah, Claflin University, and later Hampton Institute. In fact, Robert Abbott would change his name to Robert Sengstacke and would change it once more by adding Abbott to the end in 1897 before enrolling in the Kent College of Law. Abbott learned that law was not his passion and thus decided to remain in Chicago to begin a newspaper. Nevertheless, Abbott noted that his adopted father, Rev. John H. H. Sengstacke, who indoctrinated him to the craft of printing, told him that to be a newspaperman, he must study not only his own needs, but the needs of those about him.

By 1910, Abbott noted that 25,350 people had read Chicago's only weekly paper. These numbers would steadily rise as a result of the horrors of lynching and Jim Crow, after which southern blacks sought information about the Great Migration to the North. In 1913, the *Defender* was sold to Daw's Steamship agency in London, England, marking the emergence of an international market. Also, in 1919, the *American Newspaper Annual and Directory* reported the *Defender's* circulation as 120,000. The overall readership may have been higher, as a particular family and surrounding community might share a newspaper for financial reasons. Thus, an estimated circulation of the *Defender* during the early 1920s went as high as 600,000, as Abbott's dream of an influential paper took shape. In 1921, the *Defender* moved into its 3435 Indiana Avenue address that featured a $100,000 Goss straight-line sextuple press that could turn out 72,000 papers per hour. Nevertheless, all was not well in Chicago during 1919; in that year the infamous riots swept the city. During this tumultuous period, Abbott urged blacks to stay off the streets and allow the police to conduct order. The riot came about as a result of racial and class tensions between southern migrants and immigrants for labor and housing space in Chicago. Although Abbott noted the presence of tension between Irish and blacks in addition to northern racism that transcended the city, he halted attempts to settle the race question so that order could be restored.

Abbott promoted the *Defender* as a race-pride advocate, of which readers would recognize a black-owned business rooted in professionalism. In 1910, the *Defender* claimed to be the only weekly that telegraphed Jack Johnson at Reno during his defeat of Jim Jeffries. When Booker T. Washington died in 1915, the *Defender* claimed that its extra-last Sunday beat the newspaper world by 24 hours in announcing his death. Similarly, on October 2, 1920, the *Defender* and its headline, "Expose Reign of Terror in Haiti," claimed to beat the daily press by 12 full days. Abbott's articles, headlines, and even cartoons depicted the *Defender's* role as the guiding light for blacks. While a 1916 cartoon titled "Backbone" depicts a *Defender*-sponsored doctor injecting a black man with a shot of backbone, Oscar De Priest's nomination for Congress was seen as the race being put back into Congress. During the Progressive Era, the *Defender* continued its promotion of honesty, persistence, education, and morality so that blacks could equally participate and rise in American society.

Abbott spurred the *Defender's* Great Migration Northern Drive in order to end the tyranny of lynching and peonage for southern blacks. Although tens of thousands of blacks departed for Chicago, the *Defender* met challenges from various southern cities that prohibited distribution of the paper. Particularly, as the United States was engaged in World War I and sought complete allegiance to patriotism, the *Defender's* stances against disfranchisement, segregation, mob violence, and now migration were viewed as threats to national security. Surveillance from the Bureau of Investigation began as early as 1916; national laws such as the Espionage Act of 1917, the Trading with the Enemy Act also of 1917, and the Sedition Act of 1918 allowed government officials to regularly monitor the *Defender*. Also, the government received complaints from as far west as San Antonio, Texas, Tucson, Arizona, and Columbus, New Mexico, for local whites believed that the *Defender* made blacks antagonistic toward them. Similar accusations were made in the South, as seen by petitions from residents of Madison County, Mississippi. With an endorsement from their senator, John Sharp Williams, the *Defender* was charged with instigating lies and causing race trouble. The *Defender* also was accused of being antipatriotic by Colonel Ralph

Van Deman, head of the Military Intelligence Branch. Thus, Major Joel E. Spingarn, a white chairman of the NAACP board of directors led a cooperative meeting of negotiation among 41 black leaders, of which it was agreed to tone down all race arguments during the war with the exception of lynching. Ironically, governmental suppression of the *Defender* would once again challenge its existence during World War II, under the leadership of John H. Sengstacke Jr.

Abbott and the *Defender* also promoted Bronzeville, the center of the Chicago Renaissance during the 1920s, in addition to the Bud Billiken Club for city youth, the *Defender's* 1930 massed chorus as examples of cordiality that southern blacks could find in Chicago. Also, the *Defender* promoted religious institutions such as the Olivet and Pilgrim Baptist Churches, as well as the many jazz clubs and labor opportunities, all of which provided alternatives to Southern Jim Crow and lynching. Abbott also donated thousands of Christmas baskets to needy families as an extension of his *Chicago Defender* Goodfellow club. Most Southern blacks thus could depart for Chicago on an Illinois Central Railroad line.

After Robert Sengstacke Abbott died on February 29, 1940 from tuberculosis and Bright's disease, his nephew John H. Sengstacke Jr. took the helm as editor of the *Defender*. In fact, Sengstacke Jr. remained editor for 43 years until he retired in 1983 and later died in 1987. The *Defender* would remain in the Sengstacke family under the leadership of Frederick Sengstacke until 2000. Under Sengstacke Jr., the *Defender* continued to prosper, as he kicked off their 50-year anniversary by awarding President Dwight D. Eisenhower with the ninth annual Robert S. Abbott award. Sengstacke Jr. continued Abbott's legacy and expanded the *Defender* during his reign by creating a seven-paper consortium titled the *Defender* publications. Sengstacke Jr. also made the *Defender* a daily paper in 1956. Although the *Defender* did not officially recognize its 50-year anniversary until the August 13, 1955 issue, Sengstacke Jr. spared no expense and published a detailed commemorative edition of the *Defender* that included articles from distinguished guests such as A. Philip Randolph, Charles Johnson, Langston Hughes, W. C. Handy, and Adlai Stevenson, former governor of Illinois.

Langston Hughes, commonly known as the poet laureate of the black race, joined a distinguished list of past contributors to the *Defender* including Walter White, executive secretary of the NAACP, and S. I. Hayakawa. For Hughes, who served from 1942 to 1962, the *Defender* was the "journalistic voice of a largely voiceless people," as he sought to eradicate racism and examine citizenship in the United States. In addition to outspoken articles and poems related to race, Hughes dedicated one-fourth of his columns to Jesse B. Semple, a fictional character who represented the joy and pain of being African American.

By 1980, during the week of the *Defender*'s 75th anniversary, the State of Illinois Governor James P. Thompson declared May 5 through May 11 as the *Chicago Daily Defender* Week in hopes that all people of Illinois would honor its journalistic persistence and achievements. Mayor Richard Daley and Governor Rod Blagojevich also honored the *Defender* in 2005 during its centennial by declaring May 5 as "*Chicago Defender* Day" in the city and state. While fourth editor of the *Defender,* Colonel Eugene Scott, continued the tradition and cited the need for increased labor among black men and women in 2000, current leaders Roland Martin, executive editor, and Thomas Picou, CEO of Real Times Inc., noted the *Defender's* futuristic goals of becoming a versatile multimedia company that will be the leading source for black news.

See also: Destination, Chicago, Illinois; Great Migration; National Association for the Advancement of Colored People; White, Walter

Jamal L. Ratchford

Bibliography

De Santis, Christopher C., ed. *Langston Hughes and the Chicago Defender: Essays on Race, Politics, and Culture, 1942–62.* Urbana: University of Illinois Press, 1995.

Doreski, C. K. "Chicago, Race, and the Rhetoric of the 1919 Riot." *Prospects* 18 (1993):283–309.

Grossman, James R. *Land of Hope: Chicago, Black Southerners, and the Great Migration.* Chicago: University of Chicago Press, 1989.

Grossman, James R. Ann Durkin Keating, and Janice L. Reiff., eds. *The Encyclopedia of Chicago.* Chicago: The University of Chicago Press, 2004.

Kornweibel, Theodore Jr. "The Most Dangerous of All Negro Journals: Federal Efforts to Suppress the *Chicago Defender* during World War I." *American Journalism* 11 (1994):154–68.

Ottley, Roi. *The Lonely Warrior: The Life and Times of Robert S. Abbott.* Chicago: Henry Regnery, 1955.Presley, James. "The Birth of Jesse B. Semple." *Southwest Review* 58 (1973):219–25.

Smith, Jessie Carney., ed. *Notable Black American Men.* Detroit: Gale, 1999.

Stovall, Mary. "The *Chicago Defender* in the Progressive Era." *Illinois Historical Journal* 83 (1990):159–72.

Washburn, Patrick S. *A Question of Sedition: The Federal Government's Investigation of the Black Press during World War II.* New York: Oxford University Press, 1986.

Chicago Race Riot of 1919

During the first two decades of the 20th century, thousands of African Americans migrated from the cotton fields of South to the cities of the North. This trend accelerated during World War I as African Americans took industrial jobs they had previously been excluded from. The African American population of Chicago doubled between 1910 and 1919. African Americans escaping the racial system of the South sadly discovered segregation existed in Chicago. Residentially, African Americans were confined to a small area of the city referred to as the black belt. Other facilities, such as beaches, were also de facto segregated by color. Conditions inside the black belt steadily deteriorated as more and more people moved in.

Postwar competition for housing and jobs further exacerbated tensions. African American veterans felt they had earned their place as equal citizens and had proven their loyalty to their country. Instead of equality, they met discrimination when they returned. They challenged the confines of the black belt by moving to other areas of Chicago. White resistance led to almost two dozen instances of violence against African Americans and their homes. Competition for jobs was equally as rough. The transition from a wartime to a peacetime economy caused significant dislocation. In the factories, African Americans were let go to make place for returning white veterans. When the unions in the meat packing industry struck, the packers employed desperate African Americans as strikebreakers.

In the summer of 1919, Chicago's racial tensions became enmeshed in the waves of hysteria that swept through the United States in the wake of strikes and fears of Communist terrorists. This volatile powder keg required only a spark to ignite. On June 21, 1919, two African Americans were killed in separate incidents. Failure by the police to make any arrests led to a feeling among African Americans that an injustice had been committed against their community. City and neighborhood leaders worked to keep the peace, but the ratcheting up of racial tensions could not be overcome.

On Sunday July 27, 1919, a group of black teenagers were swimming at a Lake Michigan beach on a hot summer day. They drifted from the black beach to the white side. White youths who had only minutes before chased away other African Americans from the 29th Street Beach

White children cheer outside an African American residence that they have set on fire in Chicago during the summer of 1919. The police arrived soon after. (Bettmann/Corbis)

responded by throwing rocks at the blacks in the water. They struck Eugene Williams in the head, causing him to drown. The police failed to arrest any of the perpetrators and riots broke out in Chicago. That night, 27 African Americans were assaulted. Among those, seven were stabbed and four were shot. Monday morning was quiet and it appeared that the worst might be over, but violence resumed in the afternoon. A transit strike on Tuesday left many with no quick route home. They had to pass through hostile territory. Rain on Wednesday and Thursday dampened the rioting. Friday passed without significant incident. The final flurry of activity was an arson wave on Saturday that burned down 49 homes, leaving more than 900 Polish and Lithuanian immigrants homeless.

Throughout the five days, local authorities struggled to regain control of the city. Inflammatory newspaper headlines and outrageous rumors further exacerbated animosity. For reinforcements, the overwhelmed city police force belatedly called in the state militia. Most of the violence was perpetrated by gangs who roamed the street committing assault, battery, arson, home invasions, vandalism, and murder. They pulled African Americans off trolley cars and beat them in the middle of the street. Whites sped through black areas shooting from moving cars, and African Americans stationed armed men to ambush the cars. The violence was not continuous or sustained; it was, instead, episodic and often random. The police made almost 400 arrests during the riots, with African Americans being disproportionately among the ranks of the arrested.

In all, 38 people were killed, 25 African Americans and 13 whites, and more than 500 were injured. Chicago had been fortunate to avoid the wave of race riots that struck in 1917, but its racial tensions were not unique. Chicago was the site of one of more than 20 race riots in 1919 in the United States. Significant race riots broke out in Europe and Africa as well.

After the riot, Chicago struggled to understand what had happened. The coroner compiled a report and Illinois Governor Frank Lowden created the Chicago Commission on Race Relations. To ease racial tensions, the commission recommended that the city eliminate segregation and improve services inside the black belt. Throughout the 1920s, however, the situation only got worse. The Chicago Real Estate Board established a system of restrictive covenants in deeds that prevented a homeowner from selling property to an African American. Almost no housing was built inside the black belt over the course of the decade following the riot of 1919 and conditions worsened.

See also: Destination, Chicago, Illinois; Great Migration; "If We Must Die"; Jim Crow; Red Summer Race Riots; White Mob Violence

Gregory J. Dehler

Bibliography

Chicago Commission on Race Relations. *The Negro in Chicago: A Study of Race Relations and a Race Riot.* Chicago: University of Chicago Press, 1922.

Philpot, Thomas Lee. *The Slum and the Ghetto: Immigrants, Blacks and Reform in Chicago, 1880–1930.* Belmont, CA: Wadsworth Publishing, 1978.

Sandberg, Carl. *The Chicago Race Riots.* New York: Harcourt, Brace, and Howe, 1919.

Spear, Allan H. *Black Chicago: The Making of a Negro Ghetto, 1890–1920.* Chicago: University of Chicago Press, 1967.

Tuttle, William M. Jr. *Race Riot: Chicago in the Red Summer of 1919.* Urbana: University of Illinois Press, 1997.

Chisholm, Shirley

Best known as the first African American woman to run for President of the United States, Shirley Chisholm (1924–2005) was also the first African American woman to be elected to the U.S. Congress. She served seven terms as a representative from New York's 12th district, from 1969 until her retirement in 1982.

Originally named Shirley Anita St. Hill, she was born on November 30, 1924 in Brooklyn, New York, in the notoriously impoverished neighborhood of Bedford-Stuyvesant. Her parents were both immigrants to the United States; her father, Charles Christopher St. Hill, was born in British Guiana and arrived in New York in 1923 in New York City; her mother, Ruby Seale, was born in Barbados and arrived in New York City in 1921. Although young Shirley lived her early life in Brooklyn, she was sent, at age three, to live with her maternal grandmother in Barbados. Her parents, who were struggling to save money for their children's education, sent Shirley and her three sisters to live in Barbados for nearly eight years. At the age of 11, however, she returned to New York City and was enrolled in an all-girls highschool in Brooklyn.

After graduating from highschool, she won tuition scholarships to Oberlin, Vassar, and Brooklyn College; she ultimately decided to remain at home and attend Brooklyn College, where she pursued a degree in sociology. Young Shirley had been exposed to politics throughout her life, especially since her father was a reputed follower of activist Marcus Garvey, who advocated black pride and unity among blacks to achieve economic and political power. As a result, during her years in college, she became active in many black organizations including the Harriet Tubman Society, the Urban League, the National Association for the Advancement of Colored People (NAACP), and Delta Sigma Theta Sorority, Inc. As her participation in the black community expanded, she began to attend city meetings, which eventually prompted her to raise questions about the conditions plaguing her predominately black neighborhood. Even so, Shirley did not immediately consider becoming a politician.

Instead, in 1946, she graduated cum laude from Brooklyn College and began working as a teacher. For the next few years, she worked in a nursery school and pursued a graduate degree in elementary education at Columbia University. In 1949, she married Conrad Chisholm, and two years later she earned her master's degree. Upon graduating from Columbia, Chisholm continued to work in the educational sector; she served as the director of the Friends Day Nursery in Brownsville, New York, and, from 1953 to 1959, as the director of the Hamilton-Madison Child Care Center, in Lower Manhattan. For the next several years, from 1959 to 1964, she worked as an educational consultant in New York City's Bureau of Child Welfare.

Yet despite her important work in the field of education, Shirley Chisholm never lost her interest in community

Congresswoman Shirley Chisholm announces her candidacy as the first African American woman to run for a presidential nomination on January 25, 1972. (Library of Congress)

and political matters. She served on the board of directors of the Brooklyn Home for Aged Colored People and became a prominent member of the Brooklyn branch of the NAACP. She likewise volunteered for various political organizations including the Democratic Women's Workshop, the League of Women Voters, and the Bedford-Stuyvesant Political League, an organization formed to support black candidates.

By 1964, Chisholm had earned a name in Brooklyn's political scene, which inspired her to consider a run for the New York State Assembly. To the surprise of many in the Democratic political machine, Chisholm won the election and served as an assemblywoman from 1964 to 1968. During her time in office, Chisholm sponsored 50 bills, most of which reflected her interest in the cause of blacks and the poor, women's rights, and educational opportunities. Although most of the bills failed to gain sufficient support, at least eight of them became law and made significant changes in her community. One of the

successful bills provided an opportunity for poor students, particularly students of color, to gain financial support to pursue higher education. Another provided employment insurance coverage for personal and domestic employees. Still another reversed a law that caused female teachers in New York to lose their tenure while they were out on maternity leave.

In 1968, Chisholm made the bold decision to campaign for a seat in Congress. Ironically, she ran against seasoned civil rights leader James Farmer, but she easily won the election and became the first African American woman to earn a seat in the U.S. Congress. Ultimately, she spent 13 years in the halls of Congress; she was a member of the U.S. House of Representatives from the 91st through the 97th Congress (1969–1982). As she had in the New York State Assembly, Chisholm fought persistently to represent the needs of her community. Perhaps the most famous demonstration of her commitment came when she was assigned to the Forestry Committee, an appointment she strongly opposed on the grounds that she would rather serve on a committee that would allow her to grapple with issues of racism, social justice, and poverty. During her years in Congress, Chisholm served on several House committees including Agriculture, Veterans' Affairs, Rules and Education, and Labor. More specifically, she supported bills that sought to address tangible issues such as housing, education, discrimination, and abortion. She became a particularly outspoken advocate of women's rights, and, in 1971, she joined other feminists such as Gloria Steinem to establish the National Women's Political Caucus.

Perhaps Chisholm's most bold political decision came on January 25, 1972, when she announced her candidacy and became the first African American woman to run for President of the United States. Her platform encompassed a wide variety of issues including civil rights, prison reform, economic justice, gun control, and opposition to police brutality and drug abuse. Even so, the primary issue that drove her campaign was her vehement opposition to the Vietnam War and President Richard M. Nixon's policies nationally and abroad. As a result, Chisholm gained only limited support. Many black leaders were hesitant to endorse her, and although she got significant encouragement from women and young people, Chisholm struggled from insufficient funding. In the end, George McGovern won the presidential nomination at the Democratic National Convention, but Chisholm managed to capture 10 percent of the delegates' votes, particularly after Hubert H. Humphrey released his black delegates to vote for her.

Although Chisholm lost her bid for the presidency, she was reelected to her position in the House of Representatives in 1972 and faithfully served in that role for the next 10 years. In the early 1980s, however, the political climate in the United States changed dramatically. With the election of Ronald Reagan in 1980, liberals and the Democratic Party steadily lost their foothold in Congress. Thus, when Chisholm announced her retirement in February 10, 1982, she openly expressed her frustration with the rise of the Reagan era and President Reagan's domestic and international policies and lamented the decline of progressive politicians. Chisholm's decision to retire, however, was also motivated by personal considerations. After divorcing her first husband in 1977, she married Arthur Hardwick, a businessman from Buffalo, New York. After Hardwick was seriously injured in a car accident, Chisholm wanted to spend more time assisting with his recovery; Hardwick died several years later in 1986.

Even after her retirement from Congress, Chisholm remained publicly active. She joined the faculty at Mount Holyoke College, the oldest women's college in the United States, where she taught courses in political science and women's studies until 1987. She also spent a year as a visiting scholar at Spelman College in 1985 and, in that same year, she became the first president of the newly formed National Political Congress of Black Women. She also campaigned for Jesse Jackson when he sought Democratic Party's presidential nomination in 1984 and 1988.

Even after Chisholm moved to Florida in 1991, she remained outspoken on political matters, particularly her strong opposition to the Persian Gulf War. In 1993, President Bill Clinton nominated Chisholm as Ambassador to Jamaica, but because of declining health, she withdrew her name from further consideration. After suffering many strokes, Chisholm died on January 1, 2005, at the age of 80.

See also: Clinton, William Jefferson; Jackson, Jesse; National Association for the Advancement of Colored People

Leslie M. Alexander

Bibliography

Chisholm, Shirley. *The Good Fight.* New York: Harper Collins, 1973.

Chisholm, Shirley. *Unbought and Unbossed.* New York: Houghton Mifflin, 1970.

Gill, Laverne McCain. *African American Women in Congress: Forming and Transforming History.* Piscataway, NJ: Rutgers University Press, 1997.

Scheader, Catherine. *Shirley Chisholm: Teacher and Congresswoman.* Berkeley Heights, NJ: Enslow Press, 1990.

Civil Rights Act of 1866

Despite two presidential vetoes from Andrew Johnson, on April 19, 1866, Congress passed the Civil Rights Act of 1866, which was designed to protect the rights of newly freed slaves. When Congress passed the Thirteenth Amendment to the Constitution, Southern states, such as Mississippi and South Carolina, responded by passing a series of local Black Codes, which restricted the rights of freedmen. Unhappy with such local legislation and President Andrew Johnson's conservative reconstruction policies, Congress drafted a bill designed to protect the freedmen's natural rights, among which included citizenship, the right to secure employment, and the right to receive compensation. Congress drafted two bills designed to give meaning to the Thirteenth Amendment and crush the Black Codes.

In February 1866, Congress passed the Freedman's Bureau Bill and in March it passed the Civil Rights Act of 1866. The Civil Rights Act of 1866 stipulated that all native-born persons (except Native Americans), regardless of race, color, or previous condition (slavery), were U.S. citizens. As citizens, they could enter into contracts, sue and be sued, give evidence in court, and own, as well as sell, private property. If anyone denied such rights to U.S. citizens, then they would be subject to federal prosecution, and if they were found guilty, they faced a fine up to $1,000 and a year in prison.

President Johnson gave the bill's author, Illinois Republican Senator Lyman Trumbull, every indication that he would sign it; however, on February 19, 1866, Johnson issued a presidential veto. Three days later, the president spoke to a group outside the White House and outlined his reasons for issuing the veto. First, because the bill aimed to protect the rights of African Americas, he claimed that it unfairly discriminated against whites. Second, he argued that the bill was unconstitutional because Congress had passed it without consulting the still unseated representatives from Southern states. Third, the federal government, at the expense of individual states, was presuming too much power. Democrats held mass meetings and celebrated the president's veto, while the Republicans chided the president and revised the bill.

The revised version of the Civil Rights bill resembled the previous version. It granted citizenship to African Americans, as well as to all native-born persons (still Native Americans were excluded). It granted property ownership, as well as the right to sue and be sued in court, to African Americans and, most important, it nullified the Black Codes. The bill stopped short of allowing all citizens to vote, however; nor did it allow all citizens to sit on juries. Similarly, the bill did not desegregate schools or public facilities. On March 13, 1866, the bill overwhelmingly passed both Republican-controlled houses of Congress and was submitted to the president.

On March 27, 1866, Johnson again vetoed the bill. Like the first veto, Johnson cited his reasons. The president repeated his previous criticisms, but added that the Civil Rights Act was not fair to immigrants because it granted immediate citizenship to newly born freedmen, but newly arrived immigrants had to wait five years to become citizens.

Johnson's veto carried significant consequences. First, Republicans vowed to pass the bill despite the president's veto. They worked through the spring and on April 9, 1866, Congress passed the Civil Rights Act of 1866 with a two-thirds majority, successfully overriding the presidential veto. Second, Senator Trumbull never forgave Johnson for his actions concerning the Civil Rights bill. Because he was the chair of the Senate Judiciary Committee, Trumbull was certainly not a good enemy to have. Trumbull and the Republicans took the lead in Reconstruction from 1867 onward and, by 1868, they impeached the president, who survived removal by only one vote. Third, in June 1867, Congress incorporated many of the provisions of the Civil Rights Act of 1866 into the Fourteenth Amendment to the Constitution, which was designed to protect the rights of freedmen from state legislatures, federal courts, and future presidential vetoes. By June, Congress passed the amendment and submitted it to the president. When the Fourteenth Amendment became law, the constitutionality of the Civil Rights Act of 1866 was upheld, and it was reenacted

in 1870. Fourth, the Civil Rights Act of 1866 marked the beginning of a trend in American constitutional history. Congress strengthened the power of the federal government at the expense of traditionally powerful state governments by granting national citizenship to the very people whose rights the state governments were trying to limit via the Black Codes.

The Civil Rights Act of 1866 was revolutionary because it gave meaning to the Thirteenth Amendment, it worked against the Black Codes, it expanded the power of the federal government at the expense of the state governments, and it provided the basis for the Fourteenth Amendment to the Constitution. Yet conservative Southern governments found ways around it. Because it protected against public, rather than private abuses, it was difficult to enforce, and organizations like the Ku Klux Klan successfully intimidated not only African Americans but also local officials. As a result, Congress passed a series of Civil Rights Acts throughout the 1870s and into the 19th century that reinforced and built on the successes of the Civil Rights Act of 1866.

See also: Black Codes; Disfranchisement; *Dred Scott v. Sandford;* Fourteenth Amendment; Jim Crow; Johnson, Andrew; Ku Klux Klan; Radical Republicans; Thirteenth Amendment

Samuel Paul Wheeler

Bibliography

Foner, Eric. *Reconstruction: America's Unfinished Revolution.* New York: Harper & Row, 1988.

McKitrick, Eric. *Andrew Johnson and Reconstruction.* Chicago: University of Chicago Press, 1960.

McPherson, James. *Ordeal by Fire.* New York: McGraw-Hill, 1993.

Civil Rights Act of 1875

The Civil Rights Act of 1875 was adopted by the 43rd Congress in February 1875 and signed into law the following month by Ulysses S. Grant, the 18th president and commanding general of Union armies. The chief legislative sponsors were the Senate's staunchest abolitionist, Charles Sumner (R–MA), and Representative Benjamin F. Butler (R-MA), a controversial major general of the Civil War.

The act represented a final effort by Reconstruction Republicans to reinforce civil rights legislation (1866, 1870, and 1871) that asserted Congress' statutory authority to enforce provisions of the Thirteenth (1865), Fourteenth (1868), and Fifteenth (1870) Amendments. These constitutional and statutory expansions of federal authority secured the civil and political rights of African Americans and challenged efforts by defeated Southern states to reinstitute white supremacy through racial violence and Black Codes.

The law's most controversial feature was the provision for criminal and civil penalties for denying, or abetting the denial of, access to public accommodations (including inns, public transportation, and entertainment venues) on the basis of race. Violators could be imprisoned for 30–365 days and fined $550-$1,000 for each offense.

The act's significance was undermined by Congress's failure to enact prohibitions against racial segregation in public education, weak federal enforcement, and the difficulty of pursuing private litigation in federal courts. In an 1883 landmark decision, the Supreme Court ruled that the Fourteenth Amendment's prohibition against race-based discrimination by state governments does not authorize Congress to statutorily regulate similar action by private individuals.

See also: Disfranchisement; Fourteenth Amendment; Jim Crow

Michael S. Rodriguez

Bibliography
Gunther, Gerald. *Constitutional Law.* New York: The Foundation Press, 1985
McPherson, James M. "The Abolitionists and the Civil Rights Act of 1875." *Journal of American History* 52, no. 3 (1965):493–510.

Civil Rights Act of 1957

President Dwight D. Eisenhower's signature of the Civil Rights Act of 1957 marked the first time since the end of Reconstruction that Congress successfully enacted, albeit in limited form, federal protections for the voting rights of African Americans. As originally formulated, the act also prohibited discrimination and segregation in education and public accommodations on the basis of race, nationality, or religion. Segregationist Democrats in Congress, however,

successfully pressured the act's proponents, including major civil rights organizations, to endorse a version of the legislation that eliminated these prohibitions and substantially limited the federal government's authority to enforce voting rights. Senate Majority Leader Lyndon B. Johnson successfully maintained a fragile coalition to ensure passage of the act and thereby enhanced his national profile for the 1960 presidential election.

The act's three main features are the creation of the Commission on Civil Rights to investigate voting rights violations in federal elections (Part I), the establishment of an Assistant Attorney General for Civil Rights and the formation of the Civil Rights Division of the Department of Justice (Part II), and the provision for injunctive relief and contempt proceedings against violators of federal voting rights (Part IV & V). Notwithstanding concerns that the Civil Rights Act of 1957 lacked substantive enforcement authority, it represented an important departure from the decades-long intransigence of southern Democrats to accept even symbolic civil rights legislation for African Americans. The act laid the groundwork for significant civil rights legislation throughout the 1960s.

See also: Disfranchisement; Fourteenth Amendment; Jim Crow; Johnson, Lyndon Baines

Michael S. Rodriguez

Bibliography
Caro, Robert. *Master of the Senate: The Years of Lyndon Johnson.* New York: Alfred A. Knopf, 2002.
Walton, Hanes, Jr., and Robert C. Smith. *American Politics and the African American Quest for Universal Freedom,* 4th ed. New York: Pearson Longman, 2008.

Civil Rights Act of 1960

The Civil Rights Act of 1960 advanced the struggle for African American freedom by responding, albeit in limited form, to the "massive resistance" of southern segregationists. The legislation criminalized the obstruction of federal [desegregation] court orders (Title I) and the crossing of state lines to engage in racially motivated violence against religious and civic institutions (Title II). For the children of military personnel living on federal property, the act provided for their education if public schools closed to avoid racial integration (Title V). The legislation also mandated the preservation of registration and voting records in federal elections (Title III), the judicial appointment of "voting referees" to compile evidence of voting rights violations (Title VI), and the authority for the Commission on Civil Rights to take sworn testimony.

The legislation had symbolic and strategic implications for subsequent, landmark legislation (the Civil Rights Act of 1964 and the Voting Rights Act of 1965). President Dwight Eisenhower's enactment of the legislation symbolized a critical juncture in American federalism. Henceforth, the national government's authority would be deployed against efforts by states to deny citizenship rights to racial minorities.

The strategic acumen developed by (congressional) civil rights proponents during the act's passage neutralized southern obstructionism in subsequent civil rights legislation. Congress also invoked its authority to regulate interstate commerce as the constitutional basis for prohibiting racial violence by private individuals (Title II), thereby insulating the act from the sort of constitutional challenge that invalidated the Civil Rights Act of 1875. The legislation therefore prefigured a significant broadening of Congress's authority to ban racial discrimination in public accommodations in 1964.

See also: Civil Rights Act of 1875; Disfranchisement; Fourteenth Amendment; Jim Crow; Voting Rights Act of 1965

Michael S. Rodriguez

Bibliography

Berman, Daniel. *A Bill Becomes A Law: The Civil Rights Act of 1960.* New York: Macmillan, 1962.

Civil Rights Act of 1964

The Civil Rights Act of 1964 ushered in a relatively brief period (1964–1968) of progressive legislation that rectified the post-Reconstruction evisceration of statutory and constitutional protections for African Americans. The act (and subsequent amendments), the Voting Rights Act of 1965, the Immigration Act of 1965, and the Fair Housing Act of 1968 established the statutory and bureaucratic enforcement mechanisms that substantially expanded the national government's authority to protect the civil rights of African Americans and other groups who endured historical patterns of discrimination on the basis of race, national origin, language, religion, disability, age, or sex. This era of landmark legislation is often characterized as the Second Reconstruction because it dismantled the (Jim Crow) system of racial hierarchy and privilege and produced unprecedented levels of federal intervention into areas of social relations traditionally within the jurisdiction of state governments.

President Lyndon B. Johnson demonstrated extraordinary political courage and prescience for understanding that his signature on the act (July 2, 1964) would exacerbate the fracturing of the New Deal coalition. The act also marked the nadir of legislative obstructionism by southern Democrats on proposed civil rights legislation. For the first time in the Senate's history, a successful cloture vote by a coalition of northern Democrats and Republicans defeated a civil rights filibuster by southern Democrats. In the subsequent presidential elections of 1968 and 1972, the Democratic nominee won the electoral votes of only one of the former states of the Confederacy (Texas in 1968).

Although President Johnson demonstrated exceptional leadership and moral conviction in championing the act (and voting rights legislation a year later), the Johnson Administration was also responding to an emerging national consensus that meaningful civil rights legislation was an urgent national priority. A "window of opportunity" for a major breakthrough in civil rights legislation was precipitated by several factors: the paroxysms of racial violence against African American churches, civic organizations, and civil rights activists; the moral urgency President John F. Kennedy attached to civil rights legislation before his assassination; urban unrest in northern cities often triggered by incidents of policy brutality; and the increasing unease in the national security establishment that the international status of the United States was severely undermined by government repression of nonviolent civil rights protesters.

The act also indirectly corrected a longstanding Supreme Court precedent that invalidated congressional authority to prohibit racial discrimination in public accommodations. In the Civil Rights Cases (1883), the Court ruled that the Fourteenth Amendment was limited to prohibitions against racial discrimination by state governments (the state action doctrine). Congress anticipated similar challenges and instead anchored the act's constitutional authority on the

Interstate Commerce Clause. That approach was affirmed by the Supreme Court in two companion cases decided just five months after the passage of the act (on December 14, 1964). In a concurring opinion for both cases, Justice William O' Douglas signaled a potential willingness by the Court to revisit Congress's 14th Amendment authority to protect civil rights through enabling legislation.

In its initial formulation, and subsequent amendments, the Civil Rights Act of 1964 constituted a substantial expansion of federal authority in protecting civil rights by prohibiting differential standards for voter eligibility in federal elections (Title I); prohibiting discrimination in public accommodations (Title II); empowering the attorney general to bring lawsuits against states that maintained racially segregated public school systems (Title III); outlawing discrimination in federally funded programs (Title VI); prohibiting employment discrimination on the basis of race, color, national origin, language, religion, age, sex, and disability (Title VII); establishing the Equal Employment Opportunity Commission to investigate employment discrimination and mandate the collection of workforce demographic data (also Title VII); and ban gender-based discrimination in educational programs that receive federal funding (Title IX).

Enactment of the Civil Rights Act of 1964 contained several far-reaching implications for the development of civil rights policy in American society. The act underscored the necessity for congressional legislation and executive branch action (enforcement mechanisms) to fully implement landmark judicial opinions such as *Brown v. Board of Education*. It established the legislative and bureaucratic framework for the subsequent promulgation of Affirmative Action policies and programs in federal contracting, public sector employment, and higher education. The act's inclusion of prohibitions against discrimination on the basis of sex, age, language, and disability suggests that the national government's responsiveness to civil rights claims is not exclusively predicated on mass mobilization by historically marginalized groups. For instance, key policy entrepreneurs within government contributed significantly to the adoption of Section 504 of the Rehabilitation Act of 1973 and the Americans With Disabilities Act, two major achievements of the disability rights movement. Perhaps the most enduring legacy of the act is the proposition that the full legislative, administrative, and judicial authority of the national government can be deployed to dismantle longstanding patterns and practices of discrimination in civil society and state and local governments.

See also: Affirmative Action; *Brown v. Board of Education;* Civil Rights Act of 1968; Disfranchisement; Fourteenth Amendment; Jim Crow; Johnson, Lyndon Baines; Kennedy, John Fitzgerald; March on Washington, 1963; Voting Rights Act of 1965

Michael S. Rodriguez

Bibliography
Berry, Mary, Frances. *Black Resistance White Law: A History of Constitutional Racism in America.* New York: The Penguin Press, 1994.
Skrentny, John, D. *The Minority Rights Revolution.* Cambridge: Harvard University Press, 2002.
Walton, Hanes, Jr., and Robert C. Smith. *American Politics and the African American Quest for Universal Freedom,* 2nd ed. New York: Longman Press, 2003.

Civil Rights Act of 1968

The Civil Rights Act of 1968, often referred to as the Fair Housing Act, was designed to prohibit discrimination in the sale, rental, advertising, and financing of housing. President Lyndon B. Johnson signed it into law on April 11, 1968, but the bill was delayed for several years before it was eventually passed in Congress. The original legislation was intended to extend federal government protection to civil rights workers, many of whom had been injured or killed in the struggle to obtain basic civil rights, but it was later amended to provide for fair housing throughout the United States regardless of one's race, color, religion, or national origin. It stands as one of the last major civil rights statues passed in America during the 1960s.

The act came in the wake of other key civil rights legislation, the most widely known of which is the Civil Rights Act of 1964. Of its many provisions, this act created an equal employment commission, required businesses that wanted federal business to have a procivil rights charter, enforced the constitutional right to vote, and barred discrimination in federally assisted programs. It was evident, however, that housing was an issue that had otherwise been insufficiently addressed by prior legislation, despite provisions outlawing discrimination in public places and venues. The segregation existing in many parts of the country, the failure of banks to provide loans to African Americans, and the refusal of landlords to rent to individuals and families on the basis of race helped create a hostile housing climate that severely limited most African Americans' fair access to housing.

It is argued that the Civil Rights Act of 1968 had it roots in President John F. Kennedy's Executive Order 11063, which he set out in 1962. This order directed all departments and agencies of the U.S. government to take necessary action to prevent discrimination on the basis of one's race, creed, or national origin in the sale, rental, or leasing of federally owned or operated residential property. It also prohibited racial discrimination in public housing built with federal funds and in new housing built with loans from federal agencies. Kennedy's order notwithstanding, it remained clear that the legislation needed to be strengthened and broadened in its chief aims if it was to substantially alter the lack of parity African Americans faced when trying to purchase real estate and secure housing.

Clarence Mitchell Jr., the Washington director of the NAACP, is credited with spearheading the effort to secure the 1968 bill. Mitchell, dubbed by some as the "101st Senator," was a leading force in the battle to obtain civil rights legislation, and his efforts to ensure that this particular bill would become law were critical. A conservative legislative branch used several procedural tactics to delay the passage of the bill for a number of years, but it gained increasing support when Senate Republican minority leader Everett Dirksen strongly backed its enactment. Senator Dirksen generally had a conservative position on domestic legislation and held weekly broadcast news conferences to voice Republican opposition to Kennedy's administration. Yet he had previously been a designer and supporter of civil rights bills and firmly backed the 1968 fair housing bill. After Dirksen announced his support, the Senate voted to pass the bill by a tight 65 to 32 margin on March 4, 1968, but it was thought to be impassable in the House unless it was amended, and likely weakened, in committee.

The assassination of Dr. Martin Luther King Jr. on April 4, 1968, just one month after the bill was voted on in the Senate, contributed to mounting pressure to pass the bill in its entirety. The riots, burnings, and looting occurring in

Lyndon B. Johnson signs the Civil Rights Act on April 11, 1968. Thurgood Marshall stands to Johnson's right. (Library of Congress)

the wake of his assassination in more than 100 cities across the United States marked 1968 as a particularly tumultuous year and served as a powerful indication that advocates of racial justice would continue to resist social, judicial, economic, and political inequalities under the law. The House Rules Committee voted to send the fair housing bill straight to the House floor, permitted only one hour of debate without any further amendments, and the bill went on to pass swiftly the day after Dr. King's funeral. President Johnson signed it into law the next day as the nation continued to mourn the loss of a renowned civil rights leader.

The act was amended in 1974 to include sex as a protected class in fair housing, and, in 1988, disability and familial status were added to make it more comprehensive in its aims and scope. The U.S. Department of Housing and Urban Development, state and local governmental agencies, and nonprofit fair housing advocacy organizations now exist throughout the country to assist those who feel they have been subjected to housing discrimination. This network of agencies and organizations also exists to help ensure that housing does in fact remain fair to African Americans and all those who seek to establish a residence. *See also:* Civil Rights Act of 1964; Disfranchisement; Fourteenth Amendment; Jim Crow; Johnson, Lyndon Baines; Kennedy, John Fitzgerald; King, Martin Luther Jr.; National Association for the Advancement of Colored People

Amanda J. Davis

Bibliography

Carson, Clayborne, D. Clar, David. J. Garrow, Gerald Gill, Vincent Harding, and Darlene Clark Hine, eds. *The Eyes on The Prize Civil Rights Reader: Documents, Speeches, and First-hand Accounts from the Black Freedom Struggle.* New York: Penguin, 1991.

Klarman, Michael. *From Jim Crow to Civil Rights: The Supreme Court and the Struggle for Racial Equality.* New York: Oxford University Press, 2004.

Lawson, Steven F., and Charles Payne. *Debating the Civil Rights Movement: 1945–1968.* Lanham, MD: Rowman & Littlefield Publishers, 1998.

Clark, Septima

Septima Poinsette Clark (1898–1987), educator and civil rights activist, was born in 1898 in Charleston, South Carolina. Her father, Peter Porcher Poinsette, was a caterer, and her mother, Victoria Warren Anderson, was a washerwoman. In 1920, she married Nerie Clark, a sailor from Hickory, North Carolina, with whom she had one surviving son, Nerie Clark Jr. Her husband died as a result of kidney failure five years later, and her son spent much of his youth living with her in-laws in Hickory while she worked in South Carolina.

Septima Poinsette attended private and public schools for African Americans in Charleston, including Avery Normal Institute. She claimed that she always wanted to be a teacher, a desire nurtured by her parents' strong emphasis on education. After graduation from 12th grade with a teaching certificate in 1916, Poinsette took her first job teaching on St. John's Island, near Charleston. There she earned $30 monthly teaching 132 children with only one other teacher, while in comparison, white teachers on the island averaged $85 for teaching approximately 10 students. Clark then taught at various schools in North and South Carolina, eventually moving to Columbia, where she taught for 18 years.

Clark first contributed to organized civil rights activism when she participated in a movement demanding that black teachers be allowed to teach in black public schools in Charleston. Clark argued that the white teachers assigned to black schools were of poor quality and were not interested in African American achievement. She helped gather more than 10,000 signatures for the victorious NAACP petition drive. In Columbia, she continued her activism by participating in a successful legal challenge to force the school system to equalize salaries between similarly qualified black and white teachers. Clark also resumed her education, earning her BA from Benedict College in Columbia and her MA from Hampton Institute in Virginia. She returned to Charleston to teach from 1947 to 1956, when her teaching contract in the public schools was not renewed because of her membership in the NAACP.

Through the encouragement of Anna Kelly, executive secretary of the Charleston African American YWCA, Septima Clark attended a workshop on desegregation at the Highlander School, in Monteagle, Tennessee, in 1954. Highlander School, founded by Miles Horton in the 1930s, initially trained southern labor organizers and then turned its attention to civil rights, holding a series of workshops in 1953 and 1954 on strategies for peaceful school desegregation. Clark then took Esau Jenkins and other community members from St. Johns Island to Highlander, ultimately resulting in the establishment of the first citizenship school on the island in January, 1957. Clark and the first citizenship school teacher, Bernice Robinson, designed the curriculum and materials based on what participants asked to learn on the first day. They taught students how to sign their names, fill out money orders, and how to read and write using lessons on citizenship and democracy. This model for citizenship schools quickly expanded, and Clark assisted other communities in designing their own citizenship schools.

When Septima Clark's teaching contract was not renewed, Horton asked her to become director of education at Highlander school, where, in addition to her work establishing citizenship schools, she ran workshops designed to help community leaders address illiteracy, desegregation, and other issues. When the Tennessee General Assembly tried to revoke the schools tax-free charter on trumped-up charges of alcohol possession, the Southern Christian Leadership Conference (SCLC), the civil rights organization founded by Dr. Martin Luther King Jr., took over the citizenship school program, and Clark moved to Atlanta. As supervisor of teacher training, Clark traveled around the South recruiting teachers to attend a five-day workshop at the Dorchester Cooperative Community Center in McInstosh, Georgia, 300 miles outside Atlanta. Clark also spent time in various communities assisting local volunteers setting up citizenship schools, forming 897 schools between 1957 and 1970. In 1962, SCLC joined with the NAACP, Congress of Racial Equality (CORE), Student Nonviolent Coordinating Committee (SNCC), and the Urban League to form the Voter Education Project. Between 1962 and 1965, this project trained about 10,000 teachers for citizenship schools, resulting in about 700,000 black voters registering in the South. After passage of the Voting Rights Act of 1965, more than 1 million black voters registered before 1970. Andrew Young credited the citizenship schools as being the base on which the entire Civil Rights movement was built.

Septima Clark's activism was driven by her belief that one had to empower local leaders to organize their own communities. She wrote to Dr. King, suggesting that he allow more local activists to lead marches in order to facilitate grassroots leadership. Clark later recalled that the executive staff laughed at her suggestion because it came from a woman. As the first woman on the executive staff of SCLC, she and Ella Baker faced opposition from the mostly male ministers who dominated SCLC and did not respect the contributions of women according to Clark. In 1958, at the invitation of white civil rights activist Virginia Foster Durr, she attended the organizational meeting of the National Organization for Women. Clark argued that both black and white southern women were constrained by the authority of their husbands. Notwithstanding her differences with Dr. King regarding women's roles, Clark respected and admired him deeply and strongly believed in his philosophy of nonviolence. Despite the dangers of arrest, violence, harassment, and threats to her ability to earn a living, Clark always insisted that she was not afraid because she understood the importance of the work she did.

In addition to her work in the NAACP and SCLC, Clark was also involved in the South Carolina Federation of Colored Women's Clubs, the Charleston Tuberculosis Association, the YWCA, and her sorority, Alpha Kappa Alpha, with whom she worked on a health campaign for St. Johns Island. After retiring from SCLC in 1970, she volunteered for the American Field Service, helped organize day care facilities, and was elected a member of the Charleston school board, the same board that had fired her for her political beliefs years earlier. In 1979, President Jimmy Carter presented her with a Living the Legacy Award for her dedication to civil rights and to the nation. She died on December 15, 1987.

See also: Baker, Ella; Du Bois, W. E. B.; National Association for the Advancement of Colored People; Parks, Rosa; Southern Christian Leadership Conference

Joan Marie Johnson

Bibliography

Brown, Cynthia Stokes, ed. *Ready From Within: Septima Clark and the Civil Rights Movement*. Navarro, CA: Wild Trees Press, 1986.

Clark, Septima. *Echo in My Soul*. New York: E. P. Dutton, 1962.

Ling, Peter. "Local Leadership in the Early Civil Rights Movement: The South Carolina Citizenship Education Program of the Highlander Folk School." *Journal of American Studies* 29 (1995):399–422.

McFadden, Grace Jordan. *Oral Recollections of Septima Poinsette Clark*. Columbia: University of South Carolina Instructional Services Center, 1980.

Oldendorf, Sandra B. "The South Carolina Sea Island Citizenship Schools, 1957–1961." In *Women in the Civil Rights Movement: Trailblazers and Torchbearers, 1941–1965*, Vicki L. Crawford, Jacqueline Anne Rouse, and Barbara Woods, eds., 169–82. Brooklyn: Carlson Publishing, 1990.

Cleaver, Eldridge

Leroy Eldridge Cleaver (1935–1998) was a writer, an advocate of black power, and a member of the Black Panther Party for Self-Defense, serving in the capacity of minister of information in the organization for several years. Cleaver, the son of a nightclub piano player, was born on August 31, 1935, in Wabbaseka, Arkansas and moved with his family to Phoenix and, by 1946, Los Angeles. While in California, Cleaver began to have early encounters with law enforcement as a teenager with arrests for stealing a bicycle and selling marijuana. After a brief stint in a reform school, he was arrested again for selling marijuana and was sentenced to 30 months in Soledad Prison. After his release in 1957, Cleaver again turned to a life of crime, committing a series of rapes, and, by 1958, he was convicted of

Eldridge Cleaver led a life of transformations: early years of crime and imprisonment; a decade as a radical African American activist and writer; a period of exile; and his later years as an outspoken Republican and conservative Christian. (Library of Congress)

assault and attempted murder and was sentenced to serve an indeterminate sentence of 2 to 14 years in San Quentin Prison. Before leaving prison in 1966, Cleaver read a number of books on African American history and the civil rights struggle. He became an ardent supporter of the late Malcolm X, and he wrote a series of articles for *Ramparts* magazine.

Upon his release from San Quentin, Cleaver did a number of things in rapid succession. He published his *Ramparts* magazine articles as a book entitled *Soul on Ice;* he married Kathleen Neal in December 1967; he joined the newly formed Black Panther Party for Self-Defense and was appointed as the minister of information; and, in 1968, Cleaver was a presidential candidate for the Peace and Freedom Party. He is most famous for his actions after the assassination of Dr. Martin Luther King Jr. On April 6, 1968, Cleaver, along with Bobby Hutton and David Hilliard, were involved in an altercation with Oakland, California police that left Hutton dead and Cleaver injured. Apparently, Cleaver led this small group in a purposeful attempt to initiate a violent altercation with police. He was subsequently arrested and charged with attempted murder. Fearing a lengthy stay in prison, Cleaver skipped bail and fled the country. His escape route took him through Mexico to Cuba, although he also spent time in exile in Algeria and France.

While in exile, Cleaver continued to write for *Ramparts, The Black Scholar,* and other publications. Because of a series of disagreements between him and Huey P. Newton, Cleaver was expelled from the Black Panther Party in 1971. After seven years in exile, he returned to the United States, immediately renouncing the Black Panther Party and experiencing a profound religious and political transformation. Not only did Cleaver renounce the Panthers and their philosophy, he rejected socialism, communism, and radicalism. He became an evangelical Christian, and later a Mormon, and even endorsed Ronald Reagan, a former arch enemy of the Panthers, as president in 1980 and 1984. In 1986, Cleaver even made an unsuccessful run for the Republican Party Senate seat in California. Throughout the 1980s and early 1990s, Cleaver was an ardent and dedicated conservative Republican and evangelical Christian, in diametric opposition to his prior activities as a Black Panther. He was also addicted to crack cocaine during this period and was arrested on at least two occasions for burglary and cocaine possession. At the time of his death in 1998, Cleaver was a diversity consultant for the University of La Verne in southern California.

See also: Black Panther Party; Cleaver, Kathleen Neal; Newton, Huey P.; Seale, Bobby

Walter C. Rucker

Bibliography
Cleaver, Eldridge. *Soul on Ice.* New York: McGraw-Hill, 1967.
Cleaver, Eldridge, and Kathleen Cleaver. *Target Zero: A Life in Writing.* New York: Palgrave Macmillan, 2006.
Cleaver, Eldridge, and Robert Scheer. *Eldridge Cleaver: Post-Prison Writings and Speeches.* New York: Random House, 1969.
Jones, Charles E., ed. *The Black Panther Party (Reconsidered).* Baltimore: Black Classic Press, 1998.
Otis, George. *Eldridge Cleaver: Ice and Fire.* Van Nuys, CA: Bible Voice, 1977.

Cleaver, Kathleen Neal

Kathleen Neal Cleaver (1945–) was born May 13, 1945, in Dallas, Texas, and in 1967 became the first woman member of the Black Panther Party's Central Committee. As the party's communication secretary, Kathleen Cleaver was a central figure in the early development of the Black Panther Party and a significant figure in the black liberation struggle since the mid-1960s.

Cleaver's father, Ernest Neal, was a professor of sociology at Wuley College in Marshall, Texas, when Kathleen was born. In 1948, the Neals moved to Tuskegee, Alabama, where Cleaver's father taught sociology and served as director of the Rural Life Council at Tuskegee Institute. In 1954, Cleaver's father joined the Foreign Service, which took the family to India, Liberia, Sierra Leone, and the Philippines. In 1958, Kathleen began attending high school in the United States. After high school, she attended Oberlin College, transferred to Barnard College, and in 1966 left Barnard to join the New York office of the Student Nonviolent Coordinating Committee (SNCC). In January 1967, Cleaver began working at the SNCC headquarters in Atlanta, Georgia.

While organizing a student conference at Fisk University in Nashville, Tennessee in April 1967, Kathleen met Eldridge Cleaver, minister of information for the Black Panther Party. The Black Panther Party was cofounded in Oakland, California in 1966 by Huey Newton and Bobby Seale. The party advocated a comprehensive agenda for black liberation detailed in their ten point program, "What We Want, What We Believe." Eldridge Cleaver had just recently been paroled from Soledad Prison where he had written the bestselling book *Soul on Ice.* In November 1967, Kathleen left SNCC and moved to California to join the Black Panther Party. In December 1967, Eldridge and Kathleen were married.

Kathleen Cleaver was the first woman member of the Black Panther Party's Central Committee where she served as the Party's communication secretary. Serving in this position from 1967 to 1971, Cleaver provided press releases, delivered public speeches, wrote articles about the party, and was the assistant editor of the party newspaper, *The Black Panther.* With the imprisonment of the party's minister of defense, Huey Newton, in 1968, on charges of killing an Oakland police officer, Kathleen Cleaver crusaded for Newton's release through the "Free Huey Campaign." In late 1967, the Black Panther Party formed a coalition with the Peace and Freedom Party to run alternative candidates to the Democrats and Republicans in California. In 1968, Cleaver ran for the 18th District seat in the California State Assembly as a Peace and Freedom Party candidate on a ticket that included other prominent Black Panther Party members and peace activists.

In 1968, Eldridge Cleaver was wounded by San Francisco police, was arrested and charged with parole violation, and was to subsequently return to prison. In November 1968, however, Eldridge Cleaver fled to Cuba and then Algeria. In the summer of 1969, Kathleen Cleaver and Black Panther Party Minister of Culture Emory Douglas joined Eldridge Cleaver in Algeria, where they organized and led the International Section of the Black Panther Party. In July 1969, Kathleen Cleaver gave birth to her son, Maceo, in Algeria; in 1970 her daughter Joju was born in North Korea while Kathleen and Eldridge Cleaver served on the American Peoples Anti-Imperialism Delegation to the International Conference of Revolutionary Journalists.

In 1971, as a result of a dispute between Huey Newton and Eldridge Cleaver, the International Section of the Black Panther Party was expelled from the Party. Following their expulsion from the Party, the International Section members reorganized to form the Revolutionary Peoples Communications Network (RPCN). In 1971, Kathleen Cleaver established the organization's headquarters in New York and traveled throughout the United States building support for the RPCN.

In January 1973, the Cleavers left Algeria and moved to Paris. From Paris, Kathleen Cleaver returned to the United States to arrange for the safe return of her husband and to coordinate his legal defense. In November 1975, Eldridge Cleaver returned to the United States, surrendered to authorities, and served eight months in prison before being released on bail.

In 1981, Kathleen Cleaver separated from her husband and moved with her children to New Haven, Connecticut, where she attended Yale University. She graduated Phi Beta Kappa and summa cum laude with a degree in history in 1984 and entered Yale Law School. In 1987, the Cleavers were divorced; the next year Kathleen Cleaver earned her law degree.

Kathleen Cleaver became an associate at the law firm Cravath, Swaine, and Moore in New York City and, in 1991, was a law clerk in the United States Third Circuit Court of Appeals in Philadelphia. Cleaver also served on the Georgia Supreme Court Commission on Racial and Ethnic Bias in the Courts and as a board member of the Southern Center for Human Rights. She has taught at several universities including Emory University and Yale University and has received numerous fellowships at leading institutions including the Bunting Institute of Radcliffe College, the W. E. B. Du Bois Institute of Harvard University, and the Schomburg Center for Research in Black Culture in New York. In addition to teaching, Cleaver continues her activism for human rights and justice, and for the release of political prisoners.

See also: Abu Jamal, Mumia; Black Nationalism; Black Panther Party; Black Power; BPP, Chicago Branch; BPP, Los Angeles; BPP, New York Branch; BPP, Oakland Branch; Cleaver, Eldridge; Pratt, Geronimo Ji Jaga; Newton, Huey P.; Shakur, Assata

Kenneth S. Jolly

Bibliography

Cleaver, Kathleen, and George Katsiaficas, ed. *Liberation, Imagination, and the Black Panther Party: A New Look at the Panthers and Their Legacy.* New York: Routledge, 2001.

Foner, Philip S., ed. *The Black Panthers Speak.* New York: De Capo Press, 1995.

Jones, Charles E., ed. *The Black Panther Party Reconsidered.* Baltimore: Black Classic Press, 1998.

Seale, Bobby. *Seize the Time: The Story of the Black Panther Party and Huey Newton.* Baltimore: Black Classic Press, 1991.

Clinton, William Jefferson

William Jefferson Clinton (1946–), the 42nd President of the United States from 1993 to 2001, was born in 1946 in Hope, Arkansas. Before his presidency, Clinton served five terms as the governor of Arkansas. As a young man, he attended University of Oxford on a Rhodes scholarship and later attended Yale Law School. Clinton taught constitutional law at the University of Arkansas and served as the attorney general of Arkansas before becoming governor. Clinton already had a wonderful relationship with the African American community in Arkansas when he served as governor. Clinton had more African Americans working for him in his cabinet and state boards than any other governor in Arkansas history.

Bill Clinton has had a relationship with the African American community that has never been experienced by any other president in U.S. history until the recent election of President Barack Obama—so much so that writer Toni Morrison and others have said that Clinton was "the first black president." Their reasoning partially lies in the fact that his humble beginnings are likened to the experiences felt by many African Americans. In August 1998, an African American owned survey group found that Clinton's approval rating among African Americans was 93 percent while his approval rating with whites was only 70. In January 2001, Clinton left office with a 93 percent approval rating among African Americans and a 62 percent approval rating with whites.

Clinton's policies as president also reflect sensitivity to African American causes. Clinton appointed more African Americans to the federal bench than any other president in history. Taken as a whole, his cabinet, agencies, and staff contained more African Americans than any other presidential administration in the history of the United States. Clinton promoted peace in international relations. Many African Americans have indicated their admiration for Clinton's increased concern and several visits to the continent of Africa. Clinton attended more celebrations for leading African American figures and addressed the needs of minorities and race relations more than any other president in the history of the United States.

Clinton's administration saw one of the longest periods of economic growth and expansion in history. During his tenure as president, Clinton's domestic triumphs included policies to upgrade education, a restriction of handgun accessibility, stricter environmental laws, and protection of the jobs of parents who must care for sick children. Characteristics of his presidency include lower interest rates, lower inflation, lower unemployment, and high rates of economic growth. Clinton pushed for additional funds to be allocated for public education and allocated more money for young adults to go to college, all of which benefited the vast majority of African Americans. Clinton continued to promote and defend affirmative action programs while he was attorney general, governor, and president.

Clinton made improving race relations a major theme of his presidency. As president, Clinton was characterized as being a much more "hands on" president than most of the previous presidents. His management style allowed him to get in touch with many African Americans where previous Presidents failed to make the connections. This benefited Clinton in two ways. First, it projected the image to African Americans that he was sensitive to their concerns and needs. Second, it gave him real life experience and perhaps more sensitivity to the needs of the African American community. Bush and Reagan had management styles more suited for bureaucracy. Internationally, his priorities included opening up trade and world peace. Clinton sought to bring peace to various regions and especially Africa, which a great deal of African Americans regard as important.

Clinton's presidency is characterized by most scholars as open and perhaps a little more sensitive to working cooperatively with foreign governments than previous or later administrations. Several prominent African Americans have indicated their approval and admiration for Clinton's focus and philosophy in foreign relations. At times his approval rating was very low, setting a record low in his first year, but on leaving office, it was the highest for a retiring president in modern U.S. history. Paradoxically, the majority of Americans were happy he was leaving office, and even less thought he was trustworthy and honest. Ironically, many African Americans felt the opposite and were very sad by his departure. It retrospect, the African American community was better off when Clinton left office than they had been when he took office. African Americans had better access to health care, employment rates were up, additional educational opportunities were provided, and even more important, crime rates were down. Clinton was most instrumental in reducing racial profiling and relieved some of the discriminatory policies of previous administrations that

were disadvantageous to African Americans. Throughout the 1980s, many more black men and women were placed behind bars in greater percentages than whites. Clinton pushed to have the laws changed that would administer the same amount of punishment for the possession of an ounce of cocaine or crack. He was elected twice with the highest percentage of the popular vote among his opponents, but never more than 50 percent.

Clinton made several appearances on *The Tonight Show* before, during, and after leaving the White House. This measure enabled him to be more in touch with common people including African Americans. His relationship with African Americans continued to grow after he left office and opened his office in Harlem. Clinton assisted his wife Hillary Clinton in her campaign for the U.S. Senate where concerns of the African American community were continued to be addressed. It is still somewhat too early to place Clinton's presidency in historical perspective. Some believe it is a half-century or more before a president may be viewed in their true historical context.

See also: Brown, Ron; Obama, Barack

Steven Napier

Bibliography

Clinton, Bill. *My Life.* New York: Alfred A. Knopf, 2004.

Clinton, Hillary Rodham. *Living History.* New York: Simon & Schuster, 2003.

Hamilton, Nigel. *Bill Clinton: An American Journey.* New York: Random House, 2003.

Klein, Joe. *The Natural: The Misunderstood Presidency of Bill Clinton.* New York: Doubleday, 2002.

Maraniss, David. *First in His Class: A Biography of Bill Clinton.* New York: Simon & Schuster, 1995.

Morris, Roger. *Partners in Power: The Clintons and Their America.* New York: H. Holt, 1996.

Shields, Todd G., Jeannie M. Whayne, and Donald R. Kelley. *The Clinton Riddle: Perspectives on The Forty-Second President.* Fayetteville: University Of Arkansas Press, 2004.

Wickham, DeWayne. *Bill Clinton and Black America.* New York: Ballantine Books, 2002.

COINTELPRO

Between 1956 and 1971, the Federal Bureau of Investigation (FBI) conducted a series of domestic covert action programs, COINTELPROs, which discredited, disrupted, and neutralized leaders, members, and supporters of social movements that threatened the social, political, and economic status quo. Launched in 1961, COINTELPRO-Socialist Worker's Party (SWP) singled out black SWP political campaigns for disruption and attempted to block a developing political alliance with Malcolm X's Organization of Afro-American Unity. Launched on August 25, 1967, the COINTELPRO-Black Nationalist Hate Group operation formally institutionalized previously ad hoc covert operations that had targeted groups such as the Nation of Islam (NOI) and the Southern Christian Leadership Conference (SCLC). These operations had aggravated factionalism in the NOI, exposed "links" between SCLC activists and the Communist Party, and attempted to expose Martin Luther King Jr.'s sexual affairs to induce him to commit suicide. Consisting of 360 documented operations, COINTELPRO-BNHG targeted groups that engaged in civil disobedience, picketing, or antiwar activity; advocated separatism, self-defense, or revolution; or associated with other COINTELPRO targets. This included the Student Nonviolent Coordinating Committee (SNCC), the Revolutionary Action Movement (RAM), the Junta of Militant Organizations, the Black Liberators, the Invaders, Black Student Unions, and the US Organization; 79 percent of all operations targeted the Black Panther Party (BPP).

FBI agents used surreptitious entry, electronic surveillance, and informants to acquire and covertly distribute material to police, Congress, the media, elected officials, landlords, college presidents and the Internal Revenue Service. By covertly distributing intelligence information and mailing derogatory and scurrilous communications, agents prevented activists from gaining respectability among white liberals, moderate blacks, and other movement people. To discredit activists and organizations, agents alerted local police forces to targets' plans and activities so that they could arrest activists on pretext. To disrupt personal lives, agents sent anonymous communications to spouses alleging infidelity with traveling companions and co-workers. These operations thwarted fund raising, recruiting, organizing, and favorable publicity; prevented coalition building; and harassed movement leaders.

To capitalize on ideological, organizational, and personal conflicts; create factionalism; and provoke conflict between organizations, FBI agents made anonymous telephone calls and created counterfeit movement literature, cartoons, and other notional communications. Alleging misconduct, provoking ridicule, snitch-jacketing activists

as informants, and alleging the existence of assassination plots, such communications framed effective movement leaders as embezzlers, charlatans, informants, and provocateurs. Such tactics exacerbated divisions among white leftists and black revolutionaries, between moderates and radicals, and between advocates of public positions on nonviolence versus self-defense. COINTELPRO operations also exacerbated and provoked violent conflicts such as those between the Huey Newton and Eldridge Cleaver factions of the BPP, and between the BPP and Jeff Fort's Chicago-based Blackstone Rangers. Similar operations provoked internecine violence in the streets of New York and San Diego. COINTELPRO operations even helped to provoke members of Ron Karenga's Los Angeles-based US organization to kill four Panthers.

FBI informants raised controversial issues, led factional fights, embezzled funds, provoked violence, and supplied information to justify police raids. A provocateur set up a black man named Larry Ward, offering him money to commit a bombing, and Seattle police killed him in an ambush. William O'Neal facilitated the police killings of Chicago Panthers Fred Hampton and Mark Clark, and George Sams engineered the torture-murder of Alex Rackley by labeling him an informant. FBI and police operations are to blame for perhaps 25 other killings. Informants also committed perjury, even as the FBI suppressed exculpatory evidence, enabling convictions and incarcerations on trumped-up charges. Some black activists fled overseas or went underground; BPP members Dhoruba bin Wahad and Geronimo Pratt were incarcerated for decades before their lawyers exposed the police and FBI misconduct that underlay their convictions. COINTELPRO's legacy includes the devolution of some black power organizations into terrorist cells in the 1970s, as well as a sense of political disempowerment, personal disillusionment, antisocial behavior, and nihilistic violence that has plagued America's urban ghettos ever since.
See also: Black Panther Party; Black Power; Carmichael, Stokely (Kwame Ture); Hoover, J. Edgar; King, Martin Luther Jr.; Muhammad, Elijah; Southern Christian Leadership Conference; Student Nonviolent Coordinating Committee; US Organization; X, Malcolm

John Drabble

Bibliography
Blackstock, Nelson. *COINTELPRO: The FBI's Secret War on Political Freedom.* New York: Pathfinder, 1988.

Churchill, Ward, and Jim Vander Wall. *The COINTELPRO Papers: Documents from the FBI's Secret Wars Against Dissent in the United States.* Boston: South End Press, 1990.

Garrow, David J. *The FBI and Martin Luther King, Jr.: From "SOLO" to Memphis.* New York: W. W. Norton, 1981.

Jones, Charles E., ed. *The Black Panther Party Reconsidered.* Baltimore: Black Classic Press, 1998.

O'Reilly, Kenneth. *Racial Matters: The FBI's Secret File on Black America, 1960–1972.* New York: Free Press, 1989.

Theoharis, Athan, ed. *COINTELPRO: The FBI's Counterintelligence Program.* Wilmington, DE: Scholarly Resources, 1978.

Cold War and Civil Rights

The Cold War greatly influenced American race politics and the African American quest for civil rights. On one hand, the struggle with the Soviet Union brought questions of racial equality to the forefront and improved the government's civil rights record. It provided the Civil Rights movement with leverage with the government. On the other hand, it restrained the Civil Rights movement in its activities. The Cold War made civil rights an international issue.

With the victory in World War II, the alliance between the United States and the Soviet Union ended and developed into a stalemate between the two new superpowers. They both longed to fill the new power vacuum. Europe was weakened. The colonial empires of Europe in Asia and Africa disintegrated and new nations evolved. The Soviet Union and the United States struggled for zones of influence throughout the world. Their views of and plans for the world and its future were seemingly irreconcilable. The Soviet Union aspired to expand communism and combat capitalism. The United States feared this expansion and sought instead to spread democratic capitalism in the world. Within the contest for allegiance against communism, the question for civil rights and racial equality became of great importance to the U.S. government. During the Cold War, the world audience became a great factor in shaping American domestic race relations and politics.

The war and the disclosure of the horrors of the Holocaust had discredited ideas of racial superiority. Racism in any form grew to be less acceptable around the world. The assurance of equal human rights for all that was included in the United Nations charter turned into a major principle of world and domestic politics. In the escalating struggle for world leadership and allegiance in the destabilized or newly evolving nations, propaganda and image played an ever-growing role.

To influence emerging nations in Asia and Africa, the Soviet Union attempted to spread distrust of the United States and its claim of world leadership of freedom and democracy. Because of their colonial past, these contested nations were already distrustful of the West. The Soviet Union disseminated America's persistent human rights violations. According to the State Department, in the early 1950s, half of the Soviet propaganda pieces were on racist practices in the United States. The spread of racial violence and the mounting numbers of lynchings after the war were living proof of the American disregard for people of color within and outside the United States.

Not only did the Soviet Union tout the appalling position of African Americans, but newspapers all over the world reported on racial violence in the United States. Foreign countries were appalled by the cruelty and the American government's reluctance to intervene. American racist practices became a worldwide embarrassment for the United States and called into question its legitimacy as a world leader. In late 1947, the report "To Secure These Rights" by the President's Committee on Civil Rights pinpointed the negative influence of American racial inequality on American diplomatic endeavors and image in foreign countries. It underscored the international significance of ending domestic segregation and racism. The Cold War and growing international interest in American domestic policy pressured the United States to adapt its aspired image as the paradigm and bearer of democracy and equality.

As a result of these developments, the White House, the State Department and the Justice Department turned to pro-civil rights and desegregation policy reform to improve its standing in the world and prove its superiority to the Soviet Union. From President Truman through President Johnson's term, the link between the Cold War and international interest in American equal rights and civil rights is most visible. With the Vietnam War, the attention shifted away from the image of domestic racial equality. Although not downplaying the essential importance of the Civil Rights movement and the black vote, foreign policy considerations also undeniably influenced the government's civil rights agenda during the Cold War. Despite the protest of southern whites, the United States began to advance its record on civil rights regulations and launched an image campaign in an effort to counter Soviet propaganda.

The White House, pressed for governmental action on civil rights. The State Department, in particular, was aware of the importance of international opinion in the success of American Cold War foreign policy. Its officials all over the world in their meetings with international audiences, especially at the United Nations, called increased attention to the precarious standing of the United States in the world with respect to race relations. They sought to change the record. The responsible forces, however, also knew that a majority in Congress would not be willing to embrace these plans. Southern Congressmen, who had enormous power in Congress, used the Cold War as a reason for opposing equal rights for minorities. Explaining their opposition to civil rights reform, Southerners primarily argued that a change of race relations was a threat to national security and a hindrance to the aims of American foreign policy. Civil rights reform had to be accomplished mainly without the help of Congress.

Beginning with President Harry S Truman, the civil rights record of the federal government improved. Truman issued executive orders restricting segregation in America. The integration of the American military, accelerated by the Korean War, was internationally one of his most visible civil rights reforms. Truman began to increase the number of African Americans in the State Department and foreign service, a development continued by all subsequent presidents. The State Department also regularly financed trips of African American activists to spread a positive outlook on American race relations and politics.

During Dwight D. Eisenhower's presidency, the decision in *Brown v. Board of Education* officially ended school desegregation. *Brown* and the following Little Rock crisis were international issues and stories that highly affected the American image of race relations. Before *Brown*, the Justice Department had already decided in some cases that racial segregation violated the United Nations Charter and seriously hurt American foreign policy. Its *amicus curiae* briefs displayed concern for the global implications of the American race problem. The racial integration of Washington, D.C., as representative of the nation, took on a special role and would soon be implemented.

The civil rights reforms undertaken during the Cold War, especially early on, contained a considerable amount of tokenism and window dressing. Although the civil rights reforms were issued and celebrated as a proof of change, their implementation lagged. The government claimed their success in improving civil rights and used it as proof of continuous racial progress, but did not force implementation. Political civil rights advocacy and activism was often designed more for impressing the international audience than for revolutionizing domestic race relations.

Propaganda and communication were key elements in the international endeavor to gain supporters for the United States in the Cold War struggle. The propaganda was intended to influence the world audience. It was to counter Soviet propaganda that constantly played on the chasm between the American claim of freedom and the situation of African Americans. American propaganda constructed a story of constant racial progress. The government argued that only in a democracy could these changes come about. The newly founded United States Information Agency (USIA) had primary responsibility for spreading information of American racial progress internationally. Civil rights progress was also examined for its propaganda value. The continued existence of segregation and the recurring protest and violence against African American civil rights, particularly in the South, created problems with the constructed image of racial change and progress. These incidents, however, were incorporated into the image of America's constant change to the better. It was argued that these were individual cases in restricted areas that proved racial progress was only possible in a democracy.

Although the world audience was the main aim of American propaganda, the domestic audience was also to be convinced of the necessity of civil rights reforms and improvements with the Cold War discourse. Civil rights advocates argued that civil rights were essential to a successful fight against communism, although individual states and people were often not too interested in the claim that civil rights advocacy could support the anticommunist struggle.

As much as segregationists used the Cold War as a tool to protest civil rights reform, the African American Civil Rights movement also attempted to use the Cold War and the international attention as leverage for racial progress. Many African Americans believed that supporting the American anticommunist foreign policy would result in the government fighting domestic discrimination. In their civil rights activism, the African American community felt connected to the emerging third world nations' struggle against colonialism that simultaneously took place. The African American Civil Rights movement was well aware of the international interest in and importance of American race relations. The creation of the United Nations was of service to the African American Civil Rights movements. Although the United Nations would not interfere in U.S. domestic affairs, and the U.S. government did not intend to justify its domestic race relations in front of the UN, the Civil Rights movement used it as a multiplier of information on the African American situation. Petitions on American segregation and racial discrimination to the UN furthered the internationalization of racial issues in the United States. The documents were widely published and discussed in the world press, augmenting the pressure on the American government to improve its standing on racial issues.

In its activism, the Civil Rights movement attempted to make use of the Cold War discourse to pressure for civil rights actions of the government. From Walter White and the NAACP to Martin Luther King, major civil rights leaders made use of the Cold War discourse to influence the domestic audience on issues of civil rights. They argued for the necessity of racial reform if the United States wanted to win the support of the international community, the newly emerging nations of Asia and Africa in particular, and effectively contain the international and national spread of communism.

As much as the Cold War might have informed the Civil Rights movement and its goals, it also seriously restricted it. Anticommunist hysteria, fear of Communist conspiracy, and McCarthyism constrained the leeway for civil rights activism. The infringement of constitutional rights during the Cold War seriously affected the African American Civil Rights movement in particular. Suspecting a Communist threat, the Federal Bureau of Investigation put all civil rights organizations under close scrutiny. As a result of these political and societal pressures, the successful use of mass movement activism and any cooperation with left-leaning organizations were suspicious and nearly impossible. The Civil Rights movement had to spend considerable effort and money to fight any public association with communism assigned to them, a serious allegation that slowed down, seriously weakened, and divided the Civil Rights movements. Only with the decline of the Cold War in the late 1960s could the Civil Rights movement radicalize and step up its activism.

See also: Brown v. Board of Education; Bunche, Ralph; Du Bois, W. E. B.; King, Martin Luther Jr.; Little Rock Nine; National Association for the Advancement of Colored People; Robeson, Paul; White, Walter; Wright, Richard

Christine Knauer

Bibliography

Anderson, Carol. *Eyes Off the Prize: The United Nations and the African American Struggle for Human Rights, 1944–1955.* Cambridge, UK: Cambridge University Press, 2003.

Borstelmann, Thomas. *The Cold War and the Color Line: American Race Relations in the Global Arena.* Cambridge, MA: Harvard University Press, 2001.

Dudziak, Mary L. *Cold War Civil Rights: Race and the Image of American Democracy.* Princeton, NJ: Princeton University Press, 2000.

Horne, Gerald. *Black & Red: W. E. B. Du Bois and the African Response to the Cold War, 1941–63.* Albany: State University of New York Press, 1986.

Laville, Helen, and Scott Lucas. "The American Way: Edith Sampson, the NAACP, and African American Identity in the Cold War." *Diplomatic History* 20 (1996):565–90.

Plummer, Brenda Gayle. *Rising Wind: Black Americans and U.S. Foreign Affairs, 1935–1960.* Chapel Hill: University of North Carolina Press, 1996.

Plummer, Brenda Gayle, ed. *Window on Freedom: Race, Civil Rights, and Foreign Affairs, 1945–1988.* Chapel Hill: University of North Carolina Press, 2003.

Skrentny, John David. "The Effect of the Cold War on African-American Civil Rights: American and the World Audience, 1945–1968." *Theory and Society* 27 (1998):237–85.

Von Eschen, Penny M. "Commentary: Challenging Cold War Habits: African Americans, Race, and Foreign Policy." *Diplomatic History* 20 (1996):627–38.

Von Eschen, Penny M. *Race Against Empire: Black Americans and Anticolonialism, 1937–1954.* Ithaca, NY: Cornell University Press, 1997.

Coleman, Bessie

Elizabeth "Bessie" Coleman (1896–1926) was the first African American licensed pilot. Her early life prepared her for the struggle she would face with race. When she was two, the family moved to the cotton capital of the West, Waxahachie, Texas. Her father built a three-room house in the black area of town, Mustang Creek, where family life revolved around school, the Baptist Church, and the cotton fields. The racial barriers in this city led to her father's move in 1901 to Indian Territory (Oklahoma) seeking better opportunities as a man and as a provider. Susan Coleman remained behind finding work as a cook and housekeeper for a white family. To ease the burden on their mother, Bessie's older brothers moved away, leaving Bessie and her sisters at home.

Her intelligence and tenacity appeared early. At age six, she walked four miles to a one-room segregated schoolhouse. Her abilities in math led to her becoming the family's bookkeeper. Nightly Bible reading sharpened her reading skills. At age 12, Bessie was baptized into the Missionary Baptist Church. By age 14, she used her savings to attend the Colored Agricultural and Normal University in the black town of Langston, Oklahoma. She was unable to continue her education because of lack of money so she returned to her mother's home the next year and worked as a laundress.

World War I opened opportunities and employment in the cities of the North, leading to the Great Migration. Coleman left for Chicago in 1915 to join her brother, Walter. She found employment as a manager of a chili parlor and as a manicurist in a barbershop, where she heard soldiers relate stories of their exploits flying in Europe. Despite taunts from her brother about superior French women who flew airplanes, she continued to save money for flight training.

Coleman proceeded to find aviation schools. Only a few wealthy, white women held a license to fly in 1918. Race was another barrier. As one after another flying school rejected her applications, she turned to Robert Abbott, owner/editor of the *Chicago Defender*. Impressed with her tenacity and opposed to barriers of race, gender, and class, Abbott and his friend, Jesse Binga, founder/president of Binga State Bank, helped finance her dream of going to France for her training. She studied French at Chicago's Berlitz School, withdrew her savings, and left the United States on November 20, 1920 for Paris. For seven months, she trained at the Federation Aeronautique Internationale on a 27-foot biplane. On June 15, 1921, she received her international pilot's license, making her the first of her race to be licensed.

When she returned to the United States in September, she was a curiosity to the media. Reporters met her plane in New York City. The black press told the tale of her undaunted quest to fly. The *Air Service News* reported that she had achieved the first license for her race. Black leaders celebrated her achievement. As the guest of honor at the all-black musical, *Shuffle Along,* Bessie Coleman received a standing ovation from both blacks and whites in attendance.

Coleman started her career as a barnstormer, performing aerial stunts in the Midwest and North. Film of her performances regularly appeared in the black theaters of the North and South. In the South, she performed on the Theatre Owners and Booking Association (TOBA) at circuses, carnivals, and fairs. To change segregation practices, she refused to perform until her audiences were desegregated. This refusal led to desegregated audiences in her hometown and at a major event in Orlando, Florida.

Bessie Coleman encouraged others to pursue flying. She lectured at churches, schools, and clubs to encourage young people to follow her lead and to raise money for her aviation school. The Negro Welfare League invited her to perform at their Field Day on May 1, 1926. Plane owners in Jacksonville, Florida refused to rent, sell, or loan her an airplane, so she had a mechanic fly in her Jenny biplane for the performance. She and the mechanic took a test flight. Aloft, the plane malfunctioned, throwing her out of the plane to her death on April 30, 1926. The mechanic also died in the crash.

Her death brought a tremendous amount of recognition. Her funeral in Chicago drew 10,000 mourners and Ida B. Wells-Barnett led the service. In 1929, an aviation school for blacks opened when William J. Powell established the Bessie Coleman Aero Club in Los Angeles. In

Bessie Coleman, the world's first licensed black aviator (in 1921) tragically died on April 30, 1926, after a plane malfunction. (AP Photo)

1931, Chicago's black Challenger Pilots' Association started the annual tradition of flying over her grave at Lincoln Cemetery. African American female pilots honored her in 1977 by establishing the Bessie Coleman Aviators Club. The United States Postal Service issued a commemorative stamp in her honor in 1995.

See also: Chicago Defender; Destination, Chicago, Illinois; Great Migration; Wells-Barnett, Ida B.

Dorothy Salem

Bibliography
Freydberg, Elizabeth Hadley. *Bessie Coleman, the Brownskin Ladybird.* New York: Garland Publishing, 1994.
Holden, Henry M., with Griffith, Lori. *Ladybirds: The Untold Story of Women Pilots in America.* Freedom, NJ: Blackhawk Publishing, 1993.
Jaros, Dean. *Heroes Without Legacy: American Airwomen, 1912–1944.* Niwot: University Press of Colorado, 1993.
Rich, Doris. *Queen Bess, Daredevil Aviator.* Washington, D.C.: Smithsonian Institution, 1993.
Walker, Sallie. *Bessie Coleman: Daring to Fly.* Minneapolis: Carolrhoda Books, 2003.

Colored Farmers Alliance

The Colored Farmers Alliance was an organization of African American farmers that promoted agrarian economic advancement through cooperative ventures, agricultural wage scales, and electoral political action across the U.S. South in the late 19th century. First organized in 1886 in Houston County, Texas, the Colored Farmers National Alliance and Cooperative Union was the strongest of three rival organizations that emerged around this time in eastern Texas. Officially chartered in 1888, the alliance elected J. J. Schufer as its first president, although R. M. Humphrey, a white preacher and landowner, served as the order's national spokesman. The alliance had deep roots in black agrarian movements that developed in the early 1880s in Texas, Arkansas, and North Carolina. These earlier organizations, such as the Arkansas-based Sons of the Agricultural Star, relied on ties to the benevolent, church, and political associations that shaped rural black life in the postemancipation South.

The Colored Farmers Alliance shared the concerns and ideas of its organizational ally, the white Farmers Alliance. Members of the order advocated cooperative exchanges where independent agricultural producers could buy goods and market their crops without becoming indebted by crop liens, furnishing merchants, and railroads. In 1890, the Alliance endorsed Henry George's Single Tax, as well as the subtreasury plan put forward by the Farmers Alliance that called for federal intervention to protect the independence of small farm producers. The Colored Alliance differed with its white counterpart on many issues, particularly over the public role of blacks and the wages paid to seasonal cotton workers.

Organizers for the Colored Alliance, most of whom were African American, gathered support from thousands of farmers throughout the Southeast soon after the formation of the order. Racial hostility forced these organizers to work covertly. Instead of holding public meetings, black organizers introduced the idea of the Alliance to community leaders, such as preachers, and then used their trusted networks to build grassroots support. Many women joined the order and in some areas assumed leadership positions in local meetings. By 1890, the alliance claimed more than 250,000 members in 16 states, including 90,000 in Texas, 55,000 in North Carolina, 50,000 in Alabama, 50,000 in Louisiana, 30,000 in South Carolina, and 20,000 in Arkansas, although these figures may be exaggerated. Farmers from plantation belts, small farming areas, and near small towns joined. In the Carolinas and the Mississippi Valley, many Alliance members also belonged to the Knight of Labor. The alliance formed cooperative exchanges in New Orleans, Mobile, Charleston, Norfolk, and Houston. White members of the Farmers Alliance controlled the exchanges, at least publicly.

The rise of Jim Crow in the 1890s complicated the activities of the Colored Alliance and its relationship with the Farmers Alliance. In Mississippi and Arkansas, white elites directed violent attacks on Colored Alliance members who had made public attempts to exert their collective strength. These assaults killed more than 40 African Americans. Pessimistic about mainstream politics, the Colored Alliance, along with the Knights of Labor, led the call for a third-party political challenge in 1891. Where and when the Farmers Alliance decided to support reform candidates, Colored Alliance members voted to support them, despite the opposition of many black Republicans and white Democrats. Little is known about what happened to the Colored Alliance after 1892, although disfranchisement and rising white violence hastened its demise.

See also: Black Nationalism; Jim Crow; Populist Party; Share-croppers Union

Jarod H. Roll

Bibliography

Goodwyn, Lawrence. *Democratic Promise: The Populist Moment in America.* New York: Oxford University Press, 1976.

Hahn, Steven. *A Nation under Our Feet: Black Political Struggles in the Rural South from Slavery to the Great Migration.* Cambridge, MA: Harvard University Press, 2003.

McMath Jr., Robert C. *American Populism: A Social History, 1877–1898.* New York: Hill and Wang, 1993.

Compromise of 1877

The Compromise of 1877 was a behind-the-scenes deal made between Republicans and Democrats following the disputed presidential election of 1876. This deal allowed the Republican nominee, Rutherford B. Hayes, to win the election over his Democratic rival, Samuel J. Tilden, in exchange for numerous concessions to Tilden's main backers, white Democrats from the South. This compromise is traditionally viewed as the end of Reconstruction in the South. As such, it meant the completion of the return of "home rule" to native white Southerners and the abandonment, by most northerners and the federal government, of a policy of defending African American rights in the region.

After the South's defeat in the U.S. Civil War (1861–1865), Republicans, especially Radical Republicans in Congress, pushed for full rights of citizenship to be given to the newly freed slaves. Republicans in Congress passed the Thirteenth Amendment to the U.S. Constitution, which abolished slavery, in 1865. Within another five years, there were two more monumental amendments to the Constitution: the Fourteenth Amendment in 1868 gave full citizenship rights and equal protection under the law to freedmen, and the Fifteenth Amendment in 1870 gave black males the right to vote. Beginning in 1867, Radical Republicans in Congress took charge of the postwar South and a 10-year period of Congressional Reconstruction of the Southern states began. Federal troops were stationed in the defeated states and Republicans, mostly white Northerners and black Southerners, headed Southern state governments. Southern states were given a list of requirements for their readmittance to the Union, and several Southern states were in fact readmitted to the Union by the early 1870s.

Being ruled by their former slaves and their former enemies was anathema to most white Southerners. After native whites regained control of the state government in Mississippi in 1875 through the use of force, only three Southern states remained under Republican rule: Florida, Louisiana, and South Carolina. By 1876, the year of the nation's centennial, an important presidential election would occur, as for the first time since the Civil War it seemed that a Democrat might be elected to the White House.

The election of 1876 hinged on the issue of reform. Democrats painted Republicans, especially the scandal-prone Ulysses Grant administration, as corrupt and connected this image of national corruption to their image of corrupt "Negro rule" in Republican-run state governments in the South during Reconstruction. For Republicans in the North, the Democratic Party was still the party of traitors, as memories of secession and the Civil War still lingered; many Republicans believed it was also the party that would roll back the work of Reconstruction by ignoring black civil rights.

Both major parties chose "safe" candidates for the election. Republicans chose Rutherford B. Hayes, a Cincinnati lawyer, Ohio governor, and a Union general during the Civil War. Democrats chose Samuel J. Tilden, the New York governor who had been instrumental in bringing in many reforms in his home state. Both candidates promised reforms, including more honest government. Tilden publicly called for an end to Reconstruction and the return of "home rule" in the South. Although he did not say so publicly, privately Hayes also believed that "bayonet rule" was a failing policy and that federal troops should no longer prop up Republican governments in the South.

In November 1876, as the election returns came in, it seemed clear to most observers that Tilden had won the election. In order to do so, he needed the "solid South" to remain solidly in the Democratic camp and to win a few northern states as well. After winning New York, Connecticut, New Jersey, Indiana, and apparently all of the former slave states, it seemed that Tilden would be the nation's next president, the first Democrat in the White House since the Civil War. But Hayes's Republican backers contested the election results in the three Southern states still under Republican rule: Florida, Louisiana, and South Carolina. In all other Southern states Democrats controlled the election machinery, but in those three states, Republicans still had some power and, at least in Louisiana and South Carolina, were backed by federal troops at the statehouse. Republicans claimed that white Southerners intimidated blacks at the polls or coerced them into staying away in voting districts in the three contested states. Without counting the three contested states, Tilden led in the Electoral College 184 to 165; he needed only one more electoral vote to win the election. Hayes needed to win all 19 electoral votes from the three contested Southern states (as well as the one contested electoral vote from Oregon) in order to win.

After a couple of months of bickering, Congress took charge in January 1877 by establishing an electoral commission made up of five U.S. senators, five U.S. representatives, and five justices from the U.S. Supreme Court. There were supposed to be seven Republicans, seven Democrats, and one independent on the commission, but the independent voted with the Republicans and Hayes was handed the presidency. Both houses of Congress were then supposed to certify the election results, but the Democratic-controlled House stalled until about a week before the inauguration, scheduled for March 4, 1877. Hayes's Republican backers met secretly with Democratic leaders from the South to broker a deal that would lead to Hayes's ascension to the presidency. In exchange for accepting Hayes as president, Southern Democrats were promised, among other things, more federal money for economic development in the region, a cabinet post for a Southerner, and most important "home rule" in all of the former Confederate states. The last would have the most far-reaching consequences, especially for African Americans in the South. In return for accepting Hayes's election, white supremacist governments run by native Southern "redeemers" became a reality in all former Confederate states.

See also: Black Nadir; Confederate States of America; Hayes, Rutherford B.; Republican Party; Union Army; White Supremacy

David Turpie

Bibliography
Hoogenboom, Ari. *Rutherford B. Hayes: Warrior and President.* Lawrence: University Press of Kansas, 1995.
Lobrano, Gustav S. *Samuel Jones Tilden: A Study in Political Sagacity.* New York: Dodd, Mead, 1939.
Polakoff, Keith Ian. *The Politics of Inertia: The Election of 1876 and the End of Reconstruction.* Baton Rouge: Louisiana State University Press, 1973.
Rable, George. "Southern Interests and the Election of 1876: A Reappraisal." *Civil War History* 26 (1980): 347–61.
Woodward, C. Vann. *Reunion and Reaction: The Compromise of 1877 and the End of Reconstruction.* Boston: Little, Brown, 1951.

Congressional Black Caucus

Founded in January 1969, the Congressional Black Caucus (CBC) is a nonpartisan organization of black Congressional representatives. Although it is ostensibly nonpartisan, the CBC has, in reality, functioned as part of the left wing of the Democratic Party since its inception. Initially formed as a "Democratic Select Committee" in January 1969, the organization was renamed the Congressional Black Caucus in February 1971. Among the founders of the CBC were Representatives John Conyers and Charles Diggs of Michigan, Ron Dellums and Gus Hawkins of California, Charlie Rangel and Shirley Chisholm of New York, Louis Stokes of Ohio, Ralph Metcalf and George Collins of Illinois, Parren Mitchell of Maryland, Robert Nix of Pennsylvania, William Clay of Missouri, and Walter Fauntroy, the delegate from Washington, D.C. Since 1969, only African American members of Congress have been part of the CBC.

From its beginning in 1969 through 1994, the CBC was considered an official office of Congress and had its own offices, staff, and budget. When Republicans became the majority party in the House of Representatives in 1994, these privileges were ended and, since that time, the CBC claims as its official address the office of the member serving as chair. The principal goals of the CBC are to close achievement and opportunity gaps in education, to help provide quality and universal health care, to achieve equity for African Americans in all areas of American life, to establish retirement security and welfare funding, and to create foreign policy equity, particularly as it relates to the African Diaspora. In addition to these goals, members of the caucus have endorsed and taken part in the antiapartheid movement, the 1995 Million Man March in Washington, D.C., and the 2009 "Fast for Life" campaign to bring attention to the Darfur crisis.

Most recently, in April 2009, seven members of the CBC traveled to Cuba to meet with former Cuban president Fidel Castro as part of an effort to facilitate more positive and normalized relationships with the new Cuban government. Praising Castro as a courteous and hospitable host,

Illinois state representative Bobby Rush speaks during a news conference in Havana on April 7, 2009. Cuba's president Raul Castro met with six visiting members of the Congressional Black Caucus, his first face-to-face discussions with U.S. leaders since he became Cuba's president in 2008. (AP Photo/Javier Galeano)

this delegation called for an end to the travel ban and the longstanding trade embargo imposed on Cuba during the visit and upon their return to the United States. The CBC delegation also noted that Castro was seemingly receptive to the current president—and former CBC member—Barack Obama's overtures to the people and government of Cuba, as well as to Cuban Americans. These moves toward reconciliation may have been a factor in the June 3, 2009 decision by the Organization of American States to lift its suspension of Cuba, which barred the Communist nation from sending representatives for the last 47 years.

Currently, the CBC has 44 members—1 senator and 43 representatives—including two nonvoting members of the House representing Washington, D.C. (Eleanor Holmes Norton) and the U.S. Virgin Islands (Donna Christian-Chistensen). In the 111th Congress, Representative Barbara Lee of California serves as its chair. On a host of issues, the CBC joins with the Progressive Caucus (with whom it shares many members), the Congressional Hispanic Caucus, and the Congressional Asian Pacific American Caucus.

See also: Antiapartheid Movement; Castro, Fidel; Chisholm, Shirley; Million Man March; Norton, Eleanor Holmes; Obama, Barack

Walter C. Rucker

Bibliography

Copson, Raymond W. *The Congressional Black Caucus and Foreign Policy.* New York: Novinka Books, 2003.

Freedman, Eric, and Stephen A. Jones. *African Americans in Congress: A Documentary History.* Washington, D.C.: CQ Press, 2008.

Singh, Robert. *The Congressional Black Caucus: Racial Politics in the U.S. Congress.* Thousand Oaks, CA: Sage Publications, 1998.

Congressional Reconstruction

Congressional or Radical Reconstruction refers to the period beginning in 1867 when Radical Republicans successfully gained control over Reconstruction from President

Andrew Johnson. In the aftermath of President Abraham Lincoln's assassination, Johnson, Lincoln's vice president and a slave-owning Southerner, initially directed Reconstruction efforts without sufficient checks and balances. This was due to the fact that Congress was in recess from April to December 1865. In the Presidential Reconstruction plan, Johnson offered amnesty to any ex-Confederate who took an oath of loyalty; he did not support African American suffrage; and he insisted that each Confederate state accept the Thirteenth Amendment. His plan did not punish Confederates. In issuing 7,000 pardons by January 1866, Johnson allowed high-ranking Confederate officials to reassume their previous political and economic domination over the South. In turn, these officials helped erect the so-called Black Codes, which were blanket denials of civil rights and citizenship for African Americans in the South. In sum, those who were in power before the Civil War were back in power under Johnson's plan for Reconstruction. Likewise, those who were enslaved before the war were still to be oppressed and denied the basic rights of citizenship guaranteed by the U.S. Constitution.

When Congress reconvened in December 1865, they moved to immediately address Johnson's conciliatory policies. The Republican sweep during the 1866 congressional elections, in which they won two-thirds majorities in both the House of Representatives and the Senate, granted them ability to override any of Johnson's presidential vetoes. With this immense power and driven by the zeal of the Radical Republicans, Congress passed the first of three Reconstruction Acts in March 1867. Under the terms of this act, all of the Confederate states. with the exception of Tennessee, were to be divided into five military districts and placed under the authority of a Union general. Martial law would be strictly enforced in these districts and military personnel would protect African Americans and others. In addition, each state had to draft new constitutions and submit them to voters for approval. In the process of electing delegates to draft new constitutions and having each state vote to approve them, the Reconstruction Act granted universal male suffrage. For the first time in Southern history, African American men were granted the right to vote and participate in politics. Finally, every Southern state had to accept the Fourteenth Amendment, which granted African Americans citizenship rights and stripped away the right to vote and hold political office from high-ranking Confederates.

As a result of Congressional Reconstruction, the South experienced some semblance of democracy for the first time in its history. Despite the claims of "Negro domination" and "black supremacy," the work of the biracial delegations that rewrote Southern constitutions resulted in state governments that created and passed progressive legislation throughout the South. For example, these state governments created the first public schools in Southern history; expanded the political franchise by eliminating property qualifications for voting; and rebuilt railroads, bridges, and roads destroyed throughout the South during the Civil War. Unfortunately, Radical Reconstruction lasted for only a decade. With the Election of 1876, Rutherford B. Hayes ended Reconstruction by withdrawing federal troops from the South. With the return of home rule, much of the gains African Americans witnessed during Reconstruction were reversed. After 1877, Southern states moved aggressively to undercut the rights African Americans had enjoyed for just over a decade. By the 1890s, Jim Crow segregation, political disfranchisement, lynching, race riots, and general lawlessness characterized white redemption and white Democratic control of the South.

See also: Black Codes; Compromise of 1877; Fourteenth Amendment; Johnson, Andrew; Lincoln, Abraham; Radical Republicans; Reconstruction Era Black Politicians; Thirteenth Amendment

Walter C. Rucker

Bibliography

Dickerson, Donna Lee, ed. *The Reconstruction Era: Primary Documents on Events from 1865 to 1877.* Westport, CT: Greenwood Press, 2003.

Foner, Eric. *Reconstruction: America's Unfinished Revolution, 1863–1877.* New York: Harper & Row, 1988.

Hume, Richard L., and Jerry B. Gough. *Blacks, Carpetbaggers, and Scalawags: The Constitutional Conventions of Radical Reconstruction.* Baton Rouge: Louisiana State University Press, 2008.

Cooper, Anna Julia

Anna Julia Cooper's (1858–1964) life spanned the antebellum period to the Civil Rights movement, and from her early childhood to her death she was committed to the causes of women's and racial equality. She was a teacher, principal, feminist, clubwoman, community activist, scholar, social theorist, and mother. Anna Julia Cooper was born Anna Julia Haywood, the daughter of an enslaved woman, Hannah Stanley Haywood, and her white master, George Washington Haywood, in Raleigh, North Carolina, on August 10, 1858. She was raised by her mother and later credited many of her successes to her mother's devotion. Like most antebellum mulatto children, Cooper had very little contact with her father. Growing up during the era of Reconstruction, however, meant that Cooper was among the first generation of educated freed black children. The schoolhouse and the church were the two primary institutions Cooper interacted with throughout her life. In 1865, just after the Civil War's conclusion, and at the age of nine, she was admitted on scholarship to St. Augustine's Normal School and Collegiate Institute, an Episcopalian institution for freedpersons. Cooper remembered St. Augustine's as embodying the perfect balance between intellectual rigor and spiritual guidance. Like many of her free and newly freed contemporaries, Cooper was raised to believe that education was essential to racial progress. Just three years after enrolling in St. Augustine's College, she was already tutoring older students. From 1871 to 1881, she also taught Latin, Greek, and mathematics.

At St. Augustine's College, Anna Julia Haywood met an aspiring young Protestant Episcopal minister George Cooper. In 1877, at nineteen years of age, she married him and became Anna Julia Cooper. But just two years later, she was widowed, and it was this misfortune that enabled her to seriously pursue a career in education—a field closed to most married women. While marriage and family were the major hallmarks of most 19th-century women's lives, for Cooper the former was buried with her husband and the latter did not arrive until mid-life, when she became the primary caregiver to two foster youth and five orphaned children.

Completing her education at St. Augustine's in 1881, she applied to Oberlin College. In her mid-twenties, she moved to Ohio to attend Oberlin where she received both a bachelor's degree in math (1884) and later a master's degree in college teaching (1887). Between receiving her degrees from Oberlin she taught first at Wilberforce, in Ohio, and again at St. Augustine's. Her distinction as one of Oberlin's few black graduates—only five black women earned degrees from Oberlin by 1899—in conjunction with her years of classroom experience, made her a particularly attractive

teaching candidate. The superintendent of Colored Schools in Washington, D.C., invited her to teach at the Colored Preparatory School in 1887. Cooper served her school in numerous capacities during her tenure, first, as a math and science teacher, eventually as principal, and later as a Latin teacher.

Her teaching responsibilities, however, did not stifle her scholarly instinct or prohibit her from examining and contesting the racial and gender constraints of Southern Jim Crow. Cooper was an active participant in the women's and Civil Rights movements of the late-19th century. She delivered numerous addresses and speeches before diverse audiences, ranging from the colored clergy of the Protestant Episcopal Church, to educators, and feminists. At 34 she published *A Voice from the South* (1892), a series of lectures and essays delivered and written between 1886 and 1892. The first set of essays in *A Voice from the South*—"Womanhood: A Vital Element in the Regeneration and Progress of a Race," "The Higher Education of Women," "'Woman versus the Indian,'" and "The Status of Woman in America"—examining the historical status and contemporary significance of womanhood, have garnered the most scholarly attention. While emphasizing women's domestic responsibilities and the need for a womanly influence in a masculine world, Cooper simultaneously asserted men's and women's moral equality and advocated women's self-development and broad entrance and incorporation into society. While arguing that all racial progress lay on the shoulders of women, she appeared most comfortable with women shouldering that burden at home. Highly critical of southern white women and the women's movement on account of their racism, she pushed all women to embrace their public responsibilities as racial intermediaries and peacemakers. Higher education would be central to women's new role. In the same breath that she advocated higher education, however, she deflected the new public possibilities this education might offer women. Yet recalling and praising her feminist foremothers—Sojourner Truth, Sarah Woodson Early, Charlotte Forte Grimké, Hallie Quinn Brown, and Frances Watkins Harper—Cooper argued that the domestic realm was no longer women's only sphere; rather every area was open to women in the new era.

Although the 1890s witnessed southern black male disenfranchisement, rampant labor discrimination, and the proliferation of public and private segregation, Cooper and her black feminist contemporaries were hopeful that the new spaces created by and for women would benefit all African Americans. Rather than seeing the nadir of African American civil rights as a separate phenomenon from what she and her contemporaries called the "woman's era," Cooper envisioned the woman's era as opening the door to rapid racial progress for both sexes. Her conception of womanhood echoed the sentiments of a growing cadre of women who stood with her in the African American club women's movement. These women reclaimed the word "womanly," extending its meaning beyond the hollow platitudes of soft, fragile, shallow, and submissive to denote rationality, ambition, education, and leadership.

The second set of essays in *A Voice from the South*— "Has America a Race Problem? If so, How Can It Best Be Solved?," "The Negro as Presented in American Literature," "What Are We Worth?" and "The Gain from a Belief"—are directed less toward the woman question and more toward the race question, although Cooper clearly saw the two as interdependent and inextricably connected. In these essays, she asserted that racial diversity was not a weakness, but the nation's greatest strength. She challenged negative literary portrayals of African Americans, arguing that cruel stereotypes revealed more about white racism than about African Americans. Contesting Henry Ward Beecher's claim that the world would not be poorer if the African continent sank, she argued that African Americans had a heritage deserving of respect and that Christian manhood and womanhood, the true measures of one's worth, were not limited by race or class.

As much as Cooper was a scholar, she was equally an activist. Her scholarship was nearly always in service to social activism and dedicated to the causes of women's and racial equality. Shortly after the publication of *A Voice from the South,* Anna Julia Cooper, Mary Church Terrell, and Mary Jane Patterson founded the Colored Women's League of Washington, D.C. She was also active in the National Association of Colored Women when the Colored Women's League became one of its first affiliates, in 1894. Black clubwomen, like Cooper, advocated a racial uplift philosophy premised on self-help; were active proponents and defenders of black womanhood and of women as racial redeemers; and offered critical appraisals of both Jim Crow and patriarchal policies. As much as Cooper's essays can be read as scholarly articles, they were equally declarations of a black Christian feminist worldview and movement. Cooper was also an active participant in local and international conferences such as the Pan-African Conference held in London in 1900. She was a YWCA Life Member, serving on their board of directors for a decade. She also worked with the Colored Social Settlement, 1901–1907, 1911–1918, and was a Guardian for the Camp Fire Girls.

In 1901, Cooper was appointed principal of M Street High School in Washington, D.C. A fervent advocate of both industrial and higher education, she encouraged her students to be true to themselves whether it was as craftsmen or professionals. Her students were very successful; several were granted admission to prestigious universities. Cooper's efforts to have her school accredited, in a time when African American advances were being rolled back, proved to be her undoing. Racism, sexism, sexual innuendoes, and the hostile force of Booker T. Washington's Tuskegee machine contributed to her eventual dismissal. Around 1906, she was removed from her position as principal. That same year, she moved to Missouri and began teaching at Lincoln Institute. This painful setback, however, did not squelch Cooper's fire or commitment to education. In 1911, she returned to Washington, D.C., taking a teaching position at the school she once presided over.

In her mid-fifties, Cooper embarked on several new and significant adventures. She began two doctoral programs, one at Columbia University, in 1914, and the other at the Sorbonne, in 1924. Between teaching and studying, she took on the added responsibility of becoming the legal guardian to five small children in 1915. Caring for five children, teaching at M Street School, and taking only one short and highly contested sabbatical leave, Cooper managed to defend her doctoral thesis at the Sorbonne, in 1925 at 66 years of age. That same year, she received a doctoral degree from Howard University.

Five years later, in 1930, she retired from her M Street teaching position and began another career as president of Frelinghuysen University for adult education in Washington, D.C. She moved the school to her home and spent most of her seventies presiding over it. In her eighties, she resigned from the presidency, but continued to teach at the school, and published two works of great personal importance. First, around 1945, Cooper published *The Third Step,* an autobiographical essay. Then, in 1951, she published her *Personal Recollections of the Grimké Family.* Cooper lived not only to celebrate her 100th birthday, but to the age of 105. She died peacefully in her home and was buried in her birthplace, Raleigh, North Carolina on March 4, 1964.

See also: Du Bois, W. E. B.; National Association of Colored Women; Terrell, Mary Church; Truth, Sojourner; Tuskegee Institute; Washington, Booker T.

Daniel P. Kotzin

Bibliography

Alexander, Elizabeth. "'We Must Be about Our Father's Business': Anna Julia Cooper and the Incorporation of the Nineteenth-Century African-American Woman Intellectual." *Signs* 20, no. 2 (1995):336–56.

Baker-Fletcher, Karen. *A Singing Something: Womanist Reflections on Anna Julia Cooper.* New York: Crossroads Press, 1994.

Carby, Hazel. *Reconstructing Womanhood: The Emergence of the Afro-American Woman Novelist.* New York: Oxford University Press, 1987.

duCille, Ann. *The Coupling Convention.* New York: Oxford University Press, 1993.

Gabel, Leona. *From Slavery to the Sorbonne and Beyond: The Life and Writings of Anna J. Cooper.* Northampton: Department of History of Smith College, 1982.

Gaines, Kevin. *Uplifting the Race: Black Leadership, Politics, and Culture in the Twentieth Century.* Chapel Hill: University of North Carolina Press, 1996.

Giddings, Paula. *When and Where I Enter: The Impact of Black Women on Race and Sex in America.* New York: Bantam Books, 1984.

James, Joy. *Transcending the Talented Tenth: Black Leaders and American Intellectuals.* New York: Routledge, 1997.

Johnson, Karen Ann. *Uplifting the Women and the Race: The Educational Philosophies and Social Activism of Anna Julia Cooper and Nannie Helen Burroughs.* New York: Garland, 2000.

May, Vivian. "Thinking from the Margins, Acting at the Intersections: Anna Julia Cooper's *A Voice from the South.*" *Hypatia* 19, no. 2 (2004):74–91.

Tate, Claudia. *Domestic Allegories of Political Desire.* New York: Oxford University Press, 1992.

CORE

The Congress of Racial Equality (CORE) was an early pioneer of nonviolent direct-action campaigns that took place during the Civil Rights movement during the 1950s and 1960s. The organization grew out of the Christian pacifist student organization, the Fellowship of Reconciliation (FOR), which was started in 1942. At the outset, the group's goal was to foster improvement in race relations. CORE's nonviolent, direct-action ideology was used a number of times within urban African American communities during the era in their struggle against racial discrimination. These protests developed out of a long-established protest tradition that ranged from the "Don't Buy Where You Can't Work" campaigns in Chicago and New York City during the 1930s, A. Philip Randolph's March on Washington movement of the 1940s, and the more militant mood among African Americans over the obvious contradictions between American's democratic war propaganda and its violation of democratic principles at home. Each of these campaigns came in response to inadequate housing opportunities, job segregation, and discrimination in public accommodations and public spaces that resulted from white resistance to the growing number of black migrants moving north in search of better economic and social opportunities in the World War II and postwar periods.

The first CORE chapter, the Chicago Committee of Racial Equality, was formed in 1942 at the University of Chicago. The leaders of this new, interracial organization, which included future national directors James Farmer and James A. Robinson, were skeptical and critical of conservative actions of older civil rights groups like the National Association for the Advancement of Colored People (NAACP) and the National Urban League, which often insisted on lengthy legal battles to fight Jim Crow. They instead embarked on campaigns that directly confronted discrimination in housing, employment, and public accommodations. In March 1942, for instance, the group chose the White City Roller Rink as its first site to test Illinois's civil rights law. Here, 24 CORE members sought entry into the facility. When the African Americans in the group were denied entry, the group negotiated with the manager to end segregation at the location. Later that same year, the group targeted discrimination in housing at the University of Chicago Hospital and Medical School and at the university barbershop.

After changing its name to the Congress of Racial Equality in 1943, CORE expanded its operations and affiliated with other civil rights groups across the country. This proved difficult because CORE affiliates resisted centralized leadership out of the belief that a central structure would deprive local chapters of valuable, and often limited, financial resources. Moreover, problems in northern urbanized areas transcended mere segregation and encompassed a myriad of other issues, in particular, residential and employment discrimination. Many chapter leaders believed that creating a bureaucracy unfamiliar with local issues would severely limit the type of activism that could be used.

Despite this resistance, throughout the late 1940s and early 1950s, local CORE groups managed some substantial

James Farmer, national director of the Congress of Racial Equality (CORE), leads a demonstration at New York's World Fair. (Library of Congress)

victories. In 1949, St. Louis CORE, operating in a locale whose African American populace had increased during wartime migration, launched a successful campaign to desegregate Woolworth lunch counters through sit-ins and picketing. In another example, CORE operations in Omaha, Nebraska, successfully pressured a local Coca-Cola plant to agree to more equitable hiring practices. Unfortunately, the successes of these campaigns were not enough to maintain morale and activism among CORE affiliates across the nation. By 1954, while the NAACP was enjoying success as a result of the *Brown v. Board of Education* case, and 1955, when Martin Luther King Jr., and the Montgomery bus boycott gained national attention, CORE suffered from organizational disarray and growing anti-Communist investigations.

In 1961, CORE reached an important point in its organizational history when James Farmer, after a brief time working for the NAACP, became its national director. Farmer's influence on CORE's activism developed after he attended Howard University's Divinity School. Farmer refused ordination as a Methodist minister, citing that he could not preach in a church that practiced discrimination. Subsequently he began work for a number of pacifist and socialist groups, applied for conscientious objector status, and was deferred from the draft during World War II because of his divinity degree. During his early career as an activist, Farmer worked for two Chicago organizations, a pacifist group, the Fellowship of Reconciliation (FOR), in 1941, and later CORE from 1942 to 1945. With FOR, Farmer helped draft responses to such social ills as war, violence, bigotry, and poverty. With CORE, where he served as the group's first chair, Farmer proposed a new strategy based less on religious pacifism and more on the principle of nonviolent direct action that was used in northern urban areas during the Great Migration and World War II eras as African Americans increasingly questioned the contradictions between American racism and the nation's war for democracy.

Before Farmer, whose charisma proved invaluable in strengthening CORE's ability to increase its profile within the African American community, CORE had begun to develop a reputation as being a predominately white organization. With Farmer as its leader, the group moved into a more influential position among African American protest organizations because of its willingness to directly confront racial inequality.

On May 4, 1961, CORE brought its confrontational style to the Deep South when 13 CORE members departed via bus from Washington, D.C., in two interracial groups as part of the Freedom Rides. The endeavor was modeled after the 1946 Journey of Reconciliation, which tested the limits of a Supreme Court ruling banning discrimination in interstate travel sponsored by CORE and FOR. The Freedom Rides, a demonstration that Farmer had long pushed the NAACP to undertake, was aimed at challenging southern segregation in interstate travel and testing a recent Supreme Court ruling, *Boynton v. Virginia*, that extended nondiscrimination in interstate travel to bus terminal accommodations. On May 13, outside Birmingham, Alabama, an armed mob attacked the buses carrying a group of Freedom Riders and firebombed one of the buses. These incidents prompted CORE activists to abandon the remainder of their trip, and the riders were transported to New Orleans under the protection of the Justice Department. These actions, although initially disappointing, stimulated other freedom rides throughout the South and demonstrated how a protest strategy, tested and proven in northern states, could be implemented in the South. In the end, the Freedom Rides and voter registration drives in the South succeeded in moving CORE into a better position to fight racism throughout the North and South.

The visceral hatred demonstrated by southern whites and the extreme racial violence aimed against the Freedom Riders made national news and thrust CORE into the national spotlight. The events surrounding the Freedom Rides transformed the national profile of the group in civil rights circles. During Farmer's tenure, CORE soon developed a reputation of being one of the "Big Four" in the Civil Rights movement, along with Roy Wilkins of the NAACP, Whitney

Young, of the National Urban League, and Martin Luther King Jr. of the Southern Christian Leadership Conference, and was considered by most to be the spiritual leader of the movement.

In 1962, CORE, the Student Nonviolence Coordinating Committee (SNCC), and the NAACP organized its Freedom Summer campaign. The primary objective was to attempt to end the political disenfranchisement of African Americans in the Deep South. Volunteers from these three groups concentrated efforts in Mississippi where, in 1962, only 6.7 percent of African Americans in the state were registered to vote, the lowest percentage in the country. This activism included the formation of the Mississippi Freedom Democratic Party (MFDP). CORE, along with SNCC and NAACP, also established 30 Freedom Schools in towns throughout Mississippi. Volunteers taught in the schools and the curriculum now included black history and the philosophy of the Civil Rights movement. During the summer of 1964, more than 3,000 students attended these schools and the experiment provided a model for future educational programs such as Head Start.

White mobs frequently targeted the Freedom Schools but also attacked the homes of local African Americans involved in the campaign. During the summer months 30 black homes and 37 black churches were bombed, and more than 80 volunteers were beaten by white mobs or racist police officers. Also, there was the murder of three men, James Chaney, Andrew Goodman, and Michael Schwerner by the Ku Klux Klan on June 21, 1964. These deaths created nationwide publicity for the campaign.

The year 1963 ushered in a new philosophy in the Civil Rights movement—"Freedom Now!" For many activists within CORE, the achievements won between 1960 and 1963 brought only token success. This new philosophy brought organizations like CORE into more substantial debates with the NAACP and Urban League, which were devoting much of their resources to ending segregation in the public space and less attention to economic freedom. Nowhere was this more important than in the 1963 March on Washington. In the initial planning of the 1963 march, CORE was approached by A. Philip Randolph to cosponsor the event. As the event grew and more organizations agreed to participate, however, the original impetus of the march—jobs—became a secondary focus behind the passage of the 1964 Civil Rights Act. Moreover, the NAACP, the Urban League, and the Southern Christian Leadership

Conference (SLC) openly argued against militant direct action or sit-ins in exchange for CORE's participation. This conflict accentuated an already contentious relationship between CORE and these other groups over such issues as membership, funding, and prestige.

By 1964, civil rights activists found it increasingly difficult to coordinate activities with other groups. For CORE, this cooperation was made more difficult, as the organization developed a more militant critique of the Vietnam War and American society began to publicly distance itself from an integrationist platform and membership such as those in more moderate organizations like the NAACP and SCLC. This conflict gained growing momentum within CORE when Floyd McKissack succeeded James Farmer in 1966. McKissacks' ascension marked a shift from an adherence to Gandhian principles of nonviolent direct action to a philosophy of black nationalism.

This nationalist shift of CORE modeled that of other groups of the period, particularly, SNCC. For CORE this position was not only a marked departure from the group's origins but also alienated white members and financial support. Although during McKissack's tenure whites were not expelled from the organization, during the 1967 CORE convention, McKissack's opponents within the group demanded the dismissal of all white members from the organization. In 1968, Roy Innis became national director, and the transition of CORE into a black nationalist body was complete. White financial support virtually disappeared, and CORE found itself at the brink of bankruptcy.

After 1968, political developments within the organization caused CORE to create a more politically conservative platform. For example, CORE supported the presidential candidacy of Richard Nixon in 1968 and 1972. More recently, CORE commented on same sex marriage and black health, calling the issue not something that is a civil right but a human one. Moreover, COREcares, an HIV/AIDS advocacy, education, and prevention program for black women, was dismantled; and Innis is on the board of Project 21, a conservative public policy group that provides broadcasters and the print media with prominent African American conservative commentators as columnists and guests. The organization refers to itself as "The National Leadership Network of Black Conservatives."

See also: Black Conservatives; Black Nationalism; Black Power; *Brown v. Board of Education;* Freedom Rides; Jim Crow; March on Washington Movement, 1941; March on Washington, 1963; National Association for the Advancement of Colored People; Southern Christian Leadership Conference

Lionel Kimble Jr.

Bibliography

Farmer, James L. *Freedom, When?* New York: Random House, 1966.

Farmer, James L. *Lay Bare the Heart: An Autobiography.* New York: Arbor House, 1985.

Meier, August, and Elliott Rudwick. *Core: A Study in the Civil Rights Movement, 1942–1968.* Urbana: University of Illinois Press, 1975.

Noble, Phil. *Beyond the Burning Bus: The Civil Rights Revolution in a Southern Town.* Montgomery, AL: New South Books, 2003.

Rachal, John R. "'The Long, Hot Summer': The Mississippi Response to Freedom Summer, 1964." *Journal of Negro History* 84, no. 4 (1999):315–39.

Cosby, Bill

William Henry CosbyJr. (1937–), comic, actor, and social commentator, was born in Philadelphia, Pennsylvania. His mother, Annie "Anna" Pearl Cosby, worked as a housekeeper. His father, William Cosby Sr., worked as a welder and then became a mess steward in the U.S. Navy. Cosby shined at Channing Wister Elementary School and became captain of the baseball and track teams and class president. He continued his dedication to sports at Fitz-Simmons Junior High and Central High School. While in high school, Cosby also helped his family financially by shining shoes and delivering groceries. With so many pursuits, his grades suffered and Cosby transferred to Germantown High School in 1956. After failing the 10th grade, Cosby left school and joined the Navy. While in the Navy, Cosby ran track and completed high school. He was honorably discharged in 1960 and went to Temple University on an athletic scholarship.

To have supplemental money in college, Cosby worked as a bartender in a café called The Underground. When the local comedian failed to perform his acts at the café, Cosby stood in and gained a quick following. Using material from the popular comedians Nipsey Russell and Flip Wilson, Cosby also added his amusing tales of life experiences. His first major performance quickly followed in 1962 at the Gaslight Café, a popular coffeehouse. Cosby left Temple to pursue comedy full time and performed throughout the United States. He was later awarded his bachelor's degree by Temple in 1971 and received his master's degree in 1972 and doctorate degree in 1977 from the University of Massachusetts.

While performing in a local club in Maryland in 1963, he met Camille Olivia Hanks. Hanks and Cosby soon dated and were married on January 25, 1964, in Olney, Maryland. Soon after the wedding, Cosby completed his first comedy album called *Bill Cosby Is a Very Funny Fellow...Right!* The album won a Grammy Award and was followed by a host of other Grammy Award-winning albums: *I Started Out as a Child*, 1965; *Why Is There Air?*, 1966; *Wonderfulness*, 1967; *Revenge*, 1967; and *Russell, My Brother, Whom I Slept With*, 1969.

Cosby parlayed his stage and recording success into acting. In 1965, he accepted a role on the television show *I Spy* and was the first African American in a national prime-time drama. Because of his talent in the series, Cosby garnered Emmy Awards in 1966, 1967, and 1968. He left *I Spy* to work on *The Bill Cosby Show*, which ran from 1969 to 1971. Cosby then turned to animation and used his childhood experiences to create the successful children's series named *Fat Albert and the Cosby Kids*. Critics praised the show's promotion of morals and ethics. After airing from 1972 to 1979, the show was renamed *The New Fat Albert and the Cosby Kids*. Cosby won another Emmy Award in 1981 for outstanding achievement in children's programming.

In 1984, Cosby started his next television series *The Cosby Show*, which boosted his appeal worldwide. He also demonstrated his talent as the lead actor, co-producer, and executive consultant of the show. The show's positive images of African Americans, encouragement of attending black colleges, and universal life scenarios generated millions of viewers. The series won three Emmy Awards, and Cosby won a NAACP Spingarn Medal in 1985. After *The Cosby Show* ended in 1992, Cosby starred in *You Bet Your Life* (1992–1993) and *The Cosby Mysteries* (1994). In 1996, he returned to a comedic sitcom called *Cosby* and teamed again with Phylicia Rashad from *The Cosby Show*. The show ran until 2000.

In addition to television, Cosby also earned some prestige in movies. He co-starred with Sidney Poitier in *Uptown Saturday Night* in 1974 and *A Piece of Action* in 1977. His later works, though, were not so well received. Critics had mixed reviews of his work in *California Suite* (1978), *The Devil and Max Devlin* (1981), *Leonard Part VI* (1987), *Ghost Dad* (1990), *The Meteor Man* (1993), and *Jack* (1996).

Cosby returned to the spotlight with his 1994 induction into the Academy of Television Arts and Sciences Hall of Fame and lifetime achievement award at the prestigious Kennedy Center Honors in 1998. A year later, he created a children's book series called "Little Bill." Cosby dedicated the books to his son Ennis, who was killed in 1997. The book series was soon turned into a television program on Nickelodeon. Cosby also wrote the humorous guide for college graduates titled *Congratulations! Now What?: A Book For Graduates* in 1999. As they did with his previous successful texts *Fatherhood* (1986), *Time Flies* (1987), *Love and Marriage* (1989), and *Childhood* (1991), readers enjoyed Cosby's entertaining stories and amusing insights. His next text *Cosbyology* (2001) featured his comical opinions about life. Cosby also shared his thoughts about healthy eating in *I Am What I Ate...And I'm Frightened* in 2003.

Cosby continues to be recognized for his contributions to the arts. He received the notable Presidential Medal of Freedom in 2002 and the Lifetime Achievement Emmy Award in 2003. He is also active in the film industry and oversaw the movie production of *Fat Albert* in 2004. Cosby also speaks at college graduation ceremonies and donates money to several African American colleges.

See also: BET; Black Athletes; Historically Black Colleges and Universities; National Association for the Advancement of Colored People; Poitier, Sidney

Dorsia Smith Silva

Bibliography
Cawley, Janet. "Bill Cosby." *Biography* 2, no. 6 (1998):52–58.
Smith, Ronald. L. *Cosby: The Life of a Comedy Legend*. Amherst, NY: Prometheus Books, 1997.

Cotton States Exposition

In 1894, civic leaders in Atlanta, Georgia, inspired by the 1893 Chicago Worlds Fair, decided to highlight the progress made in the South in a grand affair called the Cotton States Exposition. Two previous expositions were held in 1881 and 1887. The 1895 event is the most well known.

Realizing they needed additional funding for this event, white leaders took a contingent of black leaders to Washington, D.C., to lobby Congress for funds. The three black men, Bishop W. J. Gaines, Bishop Abram L. Grant, and Booker T. Washington, explained the benefits such a fair would be to black Americans. The group mentioned that blacks were unable to participate fully in the Chicago Worlds Fair. In contrast, they said, the 1895 Atlanta Cotton States Exposition would allow blacks to prove their worth to the world. The exposition would be the first to feature blacks prominently in displays, thus proving to Congress that the event could help improve southern race relations.

Booker T. Washington, the founder and head of the Tuskegee Institution in Alabama, soon found himself thrust into the national spotlight. White leaders decided to have Washington offer a speech during the inaugural ceremony of the Atlanta Exposition. Washington had delivered speeches to audiences of blacks, northern whites, and southern whites before. In fact, southern conservative whites chose him to speak at the exposition partly because they had heard him speak on two previous occasions. In Atlanta, he would have to speak to all of these groups simultaneously.

In what scholars have labeled the "Atlanta Compromise Speech," Washington addressed the issues facing the South entering the 20th century. He called for blacks to forego politics, traditionally the domain of white males, in favor of economic advancement. But as his critics would mention, for a people with little resources, doing so would entail working for others with the mere hope of one day accumulating enough money to open a business. Washington, however, perceived of the South as home and thought blacks needed to stay put in the region they knew best.

The "Atlanta Compromise Speech" also addressed white Southerners. Conjuring up images of friendly race relations during slavery and black loyalty during the Civil War, Washington implied that the extra-legal violence against blacks advocated by some southern whites was unprovoked. Instead, he thought blacks and southern whites knew each other intimately and should be the best of friends. To rich, conservative whites, those who owned the businesses that employed blacks, Washington promised blacks would continue to be nonparticipants in strikes and labor disputes. Given the rising number of European immigrants who would compete with blacks for jobs, it is clear Washington meant to compare blacks favorably against the perception of these immigrants as labor radicals. This five-minute speech met widespread approval among most Americans.

After the Atlanta Cotton States Exposition, Booker T. Washington became the unquestioned "leader" of black America. Fredrick Douglass had died earlier in the year, and there seemed to be no black American poised to speak for the race in an era of increasing racial discrimination. Washington served as the nonthreatening spokesperson for blacks, whom whites in the North and the South could accept. Since 1877, the apparent end of Reconstruction, the North had allowed southern whites to decide how best to handle the race situation. As a result, southern blacks gradually lost most of the social and political gains made since emancipation. It was with this reality in mind that Washington delivered this speech.

Within the black community, Washington gained enemies among those who thought his public acceptance of the status quo in race relations further harmed African American attempts to end discrimination; W. E. B. Du Bois and William Monroe Trotter were the most focal this group. Washington possessed the power to dispense political appointments and award financial backing for projects via his friendship with rich, industrial philanthropists. To enemies, Washington was a charlatan who traded black political rights for personal gain. To friends, Washington was a sensible leader in a time of racial discord.

It has become clear that despite the rhetoric of the Atlanta Compromise Speech, Washington secretly funded court cases aimed at challenging Jim Crow segregation laws in the South. Southern civic leaders proposed the Atlanta Cotton States Exposition as a means to highlight their perception of progress in the New South. Part of this progress was the continued racial subjugation of African Americans. The Atlanta Compromise Speech by Booker T. Washington acknowledged this attempt by elite whites to include African Americans in the southern social system, albeit in a subordinate position. Perceiving the continued disfranchising of black citizens in the South, Washington chose to accept the system in his public speeches while privately working to some extent to eradicate racial segregation.

See also: Accommodationism; Du Bois, W. E. B; Trotter, William Monroe; Washington, Booker T.

David Kenneth Pye

Bibliography
Davis, Harold E. *Henry Grady's New South: Atlanta, a Brave and Beautiful City.* Tuscaloosa: University of Alabama Press, 1990.

Du Bois, W. E. B. *The Souls of Black Folk.* New York: New American Library, 1982.

Harlan, Louis R. *Booker T. Washington: The Making of a Leader, 1856–1901.* New York: Oxford University Press, 1972.

Washington, Booker T. *Up from Slavery: An Autobiography with Related Documents.* Boston: Bedford/St. Martins, 2003.

Daddy Grace

Charles Manuel "Sweet Daddy" Grace (1881–1960) was the founder of the United House of Prayer for all People of the Church on the Rock of the Apostolic Faith (shortened as United House of Prayer or UHOP), an ecumenical and racially integrated Christian group with deep roots in Pentecostalism. Daddy Grace was born Marceline Manuel DaGraca in the Portuguese territory of Brava, Cape Verde. His family immigrated to America when he was 22 and settled in Bedford, Massachusetts, where Marceline DaGraca changed his name to Charles Grace. In Massachusetts, Grace was drawn to Protestantism (although he was baptized Catholic in Brava) and quickly became conscious of racial divisions in the churches he attended. In the face of this religious crisis, Grace called for a revival that would erase all divisions within Christianity, specifically divisions among the denominations and races. By 1919, Grace had gathered a number of followers and opened the first United House of Prayer in Wareham, Massachusetts. In 1926, the United House of Prayer for all People of the Church on the Rock of the Apostolic Faith was incorporated in Washington, D.C. with the mission of maintaining places of worship open to all people regardless of denominational affiliation or race.

During the 1920s and 1930s, the United House of Prayer grew dramatically under Grace's charismatic leadership. Grace regularly preached to integrated congregations, and his message was especially well received in urban areas. As an evangelical Christian, Grace believed that human beings were living in the end times and taught that miracles and other supernatural events occurred regularly. Grace performed healings and encouraged his followers to heal themselves by faith. Worship in the United House of Prayer was, and still is, charismatic, characterized by tongues speaking, ecstatic praise, shouting, dancing, and lively music performed by choirs, bands, and congregants. Members were encouraged to invest their time in church activities and attend daily religious services.

Under Grace, UHOP facilities operated as community centers and offered congregants access to economic opportunities. One of the greatest successes and attractions of the United House of Prayer was its economic stability. Grace invested money from his congregants in a diversity of businesses and real estate ventures. Members bought and sold community manufactured products like Daddy Grace toothpaste, Daddy Grace cold cream, and Daddy Grace hair straightener. The ministry also published *Grace Magazine.* The wealth generated from these projects allowed the church to offer pension plans and insurance to its preachers and the elderly. During the Great Depression, United House of Prayer churches helped to stabilize black communities and provided jobs, food, and resources.

A flamboyant and extravagant personality, Grace portrayed himself as a man of means, traveling with an extensive entourage of assistants, bodyguards, and a chauffeur. With a thin mustache, long hair, and nails painted red, white, and blue, Daddy Grace was always seen wearing new bright suits and expensive jewelry. Frequent UHOP celebrations, baptisms, festivals, and parades thrust the group further into the public eye. Grace's persona both attracted and repulsed onlookers. Skeptics viewed Grace as a cult leader and portrayed his followers as naive victims of economic and religious exploitation. Others saw Grace's displays of wealth and power as evidence of divine blessing from God. For many people, especially African Americans, Grace's success attracted attention and offered hope that social mobility and economic prosperity were possible. Moreover, Grace's community was a social utopia where people of all backgrounds could worship together freely and equitably. In a world where outside forces limited individual freedoms and prohibited equal access to resources, Grace's interpretation of Christianity challenged the social order through supernatural and real-world activities.

Like his contemporary, Father Divine, Daddy Grace offered believers structure, community, and economic support during uncertain times. During the Great Depression, Divine and Grace were able to provide for their members and secure wealth, an accomplishment that particularly incensed struggling whites. During their lives, Grace and Divine faced public controversy and legal challenges that were, at least in part, instigated by white fear. Paving the way for the Civil Rights movement, both Grace and Divine disrupted the status quo and carved out religious and cultural space for challenging racial stratification.

At the time of Daddy Grace's death in 1960, there were nearly 100 United Houses of Prayer in America. Having built UHOP through his charismatic leadership, Grace's death resulted in a religious crisis. Concerns over who would take over leadership led to a small schism. Eventually the community recognized Walter McCollough as its new leader, and under his direction, UHOP turned its financial and community efforts toward civil rights and social justice. Church funds were invested in social assistance programs, subsidized housing, and scholarships. Without the drama that surrounded Grace and his controversial public persona, the United House of Prayer became more accepted as a part of mainstream Christianity. At his death in 1991, McCollough was replaced by S. C. Madison and, in 2008, Madison was succeeded by Bishop C. M. Bailey. Today UHOP boasts 131 American churches with approximately 1.5 million members. The church continues to invest in progressive social programs, providing homes for the elderly, scholarship funds, and community shelters.

See also: Black Churches; Evangelism

Kathleen Hladky

Bibliography
Dallam, Marie. *Daddy Grace: A Celebrity Preacher and His House of Prayer.* New York: New York University Press, 2007.
Fauset, Arthur. *Black Gods of the Metropolis: Negro Religious Cults of the Urban North.* Philadelphia: University of Pennsylvania Press, 1944.
Robinson, John W. "A Song, a Shout, and a Prayer." In *The Black Experience in Religion,* ed. C. Eric Lincoln. 212–35. Garden City, NY: Anchor Press, 1974.

Davis, Angela

Angela Yvonne Davis (1944–) is a well-known lecturer and writer, a member of the central committee of the American Communist Party, a philosophy professor who was appointed to a presidential chair, and a political activist who consistently advocates the elimination of the whole panoply of oppressions that damage people in the prison systems. In the late 1960s, Davis became entangled in controversy as a result of her political affiliations and commitment to prison reform. This controversy was reminiscent of the second red scare of the McCarthy era during the mid-to late 1950s after World War II.

The lessons of the McCarthy era indicate that the guarantees of the Bill of Rights are highly context dependent. Under the guise of preventing communist subversion, U.S. Senator Joseph McCarthy (R, Wisconsin) and other politicians encroached on the freedoms of speech, assembly, and self-incrimination with little or no evidence. These endeavors ultimately cost an estimated 10,000 American citizens their jobs. During Chief Justice Earl Warren's tenure, the Supreme Court eventually made a distinction between mere advocacy and incitement, ruling that citizens can be punished for inflammatory rhetoric only if it urges immediate action to violate any laws.

Davis was indicted for crimes she did not commit and consequently became the third woman to be placed on the FBI's "Ten Most Wanted List." She emerged from this controversy as an international symbol of courage and political repression. A jury of 1 Mexican-American and 11 whites acquitted her in 1972. Throughout the whole tragedy, the media did not succinctly explain that Davis was influenced by a history of "uplifting the race." Her political development was a product of the social and political reality in which she lived.

She was born on January 26, 1944 to her proud parents B. Frank and Sallye E. Davis, in Birmingham, the oldest of four children. Her parents were schools teachers. Because of his meager salary, her father left the teaching profession, became an automobile mechanic, and bought his own gas station. His actions empowered him to provide a financially comfortable lifestyle for his family in a middle-income neighborhood, initially zoned for whites, and eventually referred to as Dynamite Hill because the Ku Klux Klan frequently bombed it.

Angela's mother taught her to read, write, and do arithmetic before she started the first grade. She was regarded highly in her Girl Scout troop and was able to have dance, piano, and clarinet lessons. While she was a child, she became conscious of racism and social differences between the poor and rich. Her maternal grandmother instilled in her a sense of outrage over the peculiar institution of slavery. Davis had ample opportunity to observe the interplay and impact of classism, sexism, and racism in Birmingham, Alabama. Therefore she developed a lift-up-the-race mentality because her parents were activists well before she was born; they instilled in her an appreciation for human beings and a desire for a more humane society.

During their college days, Angela's parents were members of the Southern Negro Youth Congress, which was concerned with public issues and addressing unjust activity. In 1931, they participated in the campaign to free the Scottsboro boys who were wrongly sentenced to the electric chair for the rape of two white girls. In elementary school, she attended civil rights demonstrations with her mother. In high school, Angela helped to organize interracial study groups that were disbanded by the police.

Davis often spent summers in Manhattan with her mother while she worked toward a master's degree at New York University. When Davis was 15, she earned a scholarship from the American Friends Service Committee to attend the Elizabeth Irwin High School, a progressive private

Civil rights activist Angela Davis addresses the press in 1969, in response to regents at the University of California, Los Angeles, who had banned her employment as a faculty member due to her political views. (AP Photo/David F. Smith)

school in Greenwich Village. Many of this school's teachers were banned from working in the public schools because of their radical political ideology. During this time, Davis was introduced to socialist ideology and joined the Marxist-Leninist group, Advance.

This school was more challenging than Parker High School in Birmingham where Davis made straight "As." She had to struggle at Elizabeth Irwin High School to achieve the same grade point average. During this time, she lived with the family of William Howard Melish, a winner of the 1956 Stockholm Peace Prize and an Episcopalian minister. In 1961, she graduated and enrolled in Brandeis University in Waltham, Massachusetts on a scholarship.

Davis was an excellent student, majoring in French literature at Brandeis. Her junior year was spent at the Sorbonne where she met and talked with students from Algeria, who were involved in the struggle against French colonialism. Their interpretations of discrimination in their homeland and the 1963 Birmingham church bombing killing of four girls Davis knew personally enhanced her commitment to social change.

In her senior year, she studied under the philosopher Herbert Marcuse. She was impressed with his analysis of modern industrial society of the West and with his suggestion that it was the individual's responsibility to resist and rebel against the oppression of capitalism. Davis wrote in her autobiography that she was particularly impressed with the idea that emancipation of the proletariat would set the foundation for the freedom of all oppressed groups in society.

The next year, 1965, Davis graduated magna cum laude from Brandies with Phi Beta Kappa membership. From 1965 to 1967, she attended graduate school at the Institute for Social Research at the Johan Wolfgang von Goethe University in Frankfort, West Germany. This graduate school was the most prestigious center in the world for the study of Marxism and German idealism. Professors Oskar Negt and Theodore Adorno were impressed with her scholarship. At this point, Davis spoke both French and German. In Frankfurt, she became a member of a socialist student group, which was opposed to the Vietnam War.

In 1967, Davis returned to the United States of America to complete the requirements for her master's degree and study again under Marcuse who was now at the University of California at San Diego. She joined several organizations, among then Dr. Maulana Karenga's group "US," the Black Panthers, and Student Nonviolent Coordinating Committee (SNCC), and resumed her participation in the Civil Rights movement. That same year, she attended an "Economics and the Community" workshop sponsored by SNCC. At the work she met Franklin Alexander and his wife Kendra who were active in SNCC, the Black Panthers, and the Communist Party.

Franklin's sister Charlene was the leader of the Che-Lumumba All Black Collective of the Communist Party of Southern California. This organization was focused on the third world and away from the Soviet Union. In 1969, Davis moved to Los Angeles and joined Che-Lumumba because she was disappointed with the sexism in SNCC, the Black Panthers, and US.

Davis earned her masters degree, made her pilgrimage to Cuba in 1969, and completed her PhD comprehensive exams in 1970. She was hired by the University of California at Los Angeles as an assistant professor of philosophy in 1969. Davis taught courses in literature, philosophy, and political theory. William Tulio Divale, a graduate student in anthropology and a paid FBI informer, published a letter in the UCLA *Daily Bruin* announcing that there was a communist on the faculty. Eight days later, on July 9, 1969, Ed Montgomery published an article in the San Francisco *Examiner* naming Angela Davis as the person Divale alleged was a communist in the *Bruin.* At the insistence of Governor Ronald Reagan, the university regents dismissed Angela Davis from her post. This firing was done in spite of the fact that the students, faculty, President of the University Charles Hitch, and the UCLA Chancellor Charles Young supported her and academic freedom.

She challenged the dismissal in court and was instated because the dismissal violated her constitutional right to teach regardless of political affiliation. The UCLA administration continued to monitor her courses; students rated the instruction as excellent and unbiased. When the 1969–1970 academic year came to an end, the board refused to renew her contract because of her inflammatory speeches in the community and the fact that she had not completed the requirements for her doctorate.

Davis had become actively involved in the cause of the Soledad Brothers, George Jackson, John Clutchette, and Fleeta Drumgo, who had been treated harshly because they organized a Marxist group among the prisoners. She delivered speeches and led demonstrations calling for their parole.

On January 13, 1970, a mixture of 15 militant black and racist white inmates started fighting on the exercise yard at the Soledad Prison in Salinas, California. Prison guard O. G. Miller killed one white and three black convicts in order to stop the fight. The district attorney of Monterey County ruled Miller's action justifiable homicide and the grand jury confirmed this verdict. On that same day, prison guard John Mills was beaten and thrown over the jail's third tier railing, falling to his death. All 137 convicts in Y Wing where the murder occurred were confined to their cells. The prison authorities assumed that only the militants could have organized the revenge and blamed the Soledad Brothers.

Davis's public comments in defense of the Soledad Brothers drew anonymous threats on her life by mail and telephone. Therefore, she purchased several weapons and secured them in the Che-Lumumba Club headquarters. George's teenage brother Jonathan Jackson decided to be her bodyguard.

On August 7, 1970, Jonathan used these weapons to rescue James McClain who was on trial for assaulting a San Quentin guard from California's Marian County Courthouse. Jackson, McClain, two inmate witnesses (Russell Moore and William Christmas) took hostages: three jurors, Assistant District Attorney Gary Thomas, and Judge Harold Harley. Jonathan intended to trade the hostages for the Soledad Brothers. The effort was stymied by a barrage of shooting by the San Quentin guards, in defiance of the sheriff and his instructions not to shoot, which killed the judge, two prisoners, and Jonathan. A federal warrant was issued for Davis, because the weapons were registered in her name. She fled into hiding rather than surrender to the authorities.

The State of California charged her with kidnapping, conspiracy, and murder; the FBI placed her on the 10 most wanted fugitive list and undertook a massive two-month search for her. She was arrested in New York, extradited to California, and placed in jail without bail. An international "Free Angela" movement ensued. On February 23, 1972, a judge released Davis on $102,000 bail, which was paid by singer Aretha Franklin. This position of separating Davis from her politics was taken by many middle- to upper-income African Americans. The subsequent trial received worldwide attention; Davis was acquitted of all charges.

Acting as co-counsel, Angela explained that she had been involved in the liberation struggle of minority groups, in the opposition to the Vietnam War, in the fight to raise the status of women, and in the defense of academic freedom. She went underground because of fear. Her chief counsel Howard Moore, an Atlantan who defended the black power leaders Rap Brown and Stokely Carmichael, argued that there was insufficient evidence to prove Angela Davis was part of the murder plans, as she was not at the scene of the murders.

Her defense committee was renamed the National Alliance against Racism and Political Repression. It has provided help in the defense of political cases, the majority of which have involved blacks and Hispanics. Davis has remained politically active. She has delivered speeches on behalf of the organization and led demonstration on numerous issues since 1972. In 1980 and 1984, she ran for vice president of the United States on the Communist Party ticket. Ronald Reagan and the California State Board of Regents voted in 1972 that she would never teach at a state-supported university because of her militant activities. The American Association of University Professor censured UCLA for lack of due process when it failed to renew her contract. Davis has taught at a number of California universities including UCLA, despite Ronald Reagan's admonitions. Today, Davis continues to write, give speeches and lectures, and is still an advocate of penal reform and an opponent of racism and classism in the criminal justice system. She is currently a professor of historical consciousness at UC Santa Cruz.

See also: Black Panther Party; Student Nonviolent Coordinating Committee; Soledad Brothers

Marva Strickland-Hill

Bibliography

Aptheker, Bettina. *The Morning Breaks: The Trial of Angela Davis.* Ithaca: Cornell University Press, 1999.

Davis, Angela Y. *Angela Davis—an Autobiography.* New York: Random House, 1974.

Nadelson, Reggie. *Who Is Angela Davis? The Biography of a Revolutionary.* New York: P. H. Wyden, 1972.

Perkins, Margo V. *Autobiography as Activism: Three Black Women of the Sixties.* Jackson: University Press of Mississippi, 2000.

Deacons for Defense and Justice

Founded in 1964 in Louisiana, the Deacons for Defense and Justice (DDJ) was an African American self-defense organization that protected civil rights activists against racist

terrorism. The history of the Deacons began in the small town of Jonesboro, Louisiana. In June 1964, organizers of the Congress of Racial Equality (CORE) and local black activists launched nonviolent protest campaigns and voter registration drives to challenge the town's tradition of white supremacy. When white residents and the area's Ku Klux Klan responded with a wave of violence and intimidation, a group of armed black men began to guard the CORE office against white attacks. Although Jonesboro's police department deputized five black men, ostensibly to provide more security, the new police officers could do little to stop white violence. When Klansmen staged a nightly parade through Jonesboro's black neighborhood in late July 1964, members of the informal protective squad decided to establish an official defense unit to halt the Klan's reign of terror. This organization came to be known as the DDJ.

In the following months, the DDJ evolved into a highly sophisticated and disciplined protection agency. The Deacons consisted mostly of working-class military veterans who had to conform to strict membership criteria. The organization's president, a stockroom worker named Percy Lee Bradford, and co-founder Earnest Thomas, a mill worker and handyman, accepted only American citizens who were at least 21 years old. They preferred married men and registered voters. Applicants who had a reputation for being hot-tempered were quickly rejected. In this strictly defensive spirit, the new organization continued to guard the CORE headquarters and began to patrol the black neighborhood with rifles and shotguns. Armed men also guarded civil rights meetings and provided escorts for white and black activists who were canvassing in the dangerous areas of the surrounding Jackson parish. Walkie-talkies facilitated the coordination of guard duties. When Jonesboro's police department disbanded the group of black deputies in October 1964, the Deacons remained the only protection against white violence. Ultimately, the DDJ's activities put an end to Klan intimidation in Jonesboro and effectively stemmed the tide of white harassment.

The formation of another Deacons chapter in Bogalusa, Louisiana marked the beginning of the defense unit's rise to national fame and notoriety. Located 60 miles north of New Orleans, the city was a stronghold of the Ku Klux Klan. As in Jonesboro, segregationists resorted to violent terror when, in January 1965, local blacks sought the assistance of CORE to challenge Jim Crow. In February, the necessity of protecting the black community and CORE's field workers from the Klan's wrath prompted several men to organize a DDJ branch in Bogalusa. The Jonesboro Deacons assisted in the formation and, after receiving a charter from the state of Louisiana in March 1965, granted the new branch an official certificate of affiliation. Although protection was the key rationale behind its activities, the defense group also became an enormous source of pride among black activists. Defying the Southern myth of the submissive and contented Negro, the Deacons powerfully asserted blacks' dignity and their legitimate claim to the rights of American citizenship. Its members considered their armed actions an important affirmation of black manhood.

In April 1965, when a new round of nonviolent demonstrations exacerbated racial tensions in Bogalusa, a shootout between Klansmen and a group of Deacons catapulted the defense squad into the national spotlight. By that time, the Federal Bureau of Investigation (FBI) had launched a large-scale investigation into the activities of the defense squad. Although FBI agents and white journalists tended to regard the militant group as the harbinger of racial warfare, the Bogalusa Deacons worked side by side with CORE, complementing its nonviolent protest campaigns and ultimately enhancing its effectiveness in Bogalusa. In part, white concerns stemmed from the defense unit's strategy to exaggerate its actual strength to deter white terrorists. Media accounts put the Deacons' membership at several thousand in 59 chapters across the South, but the real number of members was never larger than several hundred, and the Deacons established only three official chapters in Louisiana. Despite its hyperbole, the Deacons did have expansionist ambitions and inspired the formation of loosely affiliated groups in 14 southern and 4 northern cities. Amidst the media frenzy about the defense unit, CORE was hard pressed to justify its alliance with the Deacons. CORE's leadership accepted self-defense but reassured the concerned media of the organization's unwavering commitment to nonviolence.

By 1968, however, as segregation and disfranchisement were on the wane and state and local authorities in the South finally appeared to take seriously their responsibility to protect civil rights protest, black self-defense groups such as the Deacons had outlived their usefulness. Until the summer of 1967, the Bogalusa Deacons continued to patrol the city's black neighborhood and guarded a last round of nonviolent demonstrations. By November 1967, the Bogalusa Deacons no longer held official meetings. Four months later, the FBI ascertained that the Deacons and affiliated chapters had ceased their activities.

See also: Black Nationalism; Black Power; CORE; Ku Klux Klan

Simon Wendt

Bibliography

Hill, Lance E. *The Deacons for Defense: Armed Resistance and the Civil Rights Movement.* Chapel Hill: University of North Carolina Press, 2004.

Honigsberg, Peter Jan. *Crossing Border Street: A Civil Rights Memoir.* Berkeley: University of California Press, 2000.

Wendt, Simon. "'Urge People *Not* to Carry Guns': Armed Self-Defense in the Louisiana Civil Rights Movement and the Radicalization of the Congress of Racial Equality." *Louisiana History* 45, no. 3 (Summer 2004):261–86.

Destination, Chicago, Illinois

Chicago, Illinois, has played a central role in attracting African American migrants from the South. In 1910, before the onset of the first wave of the Great Migration, fewer than 50,000 blacks lived in Chicago, roughly 2 percent of the city's population. Sixty years later a million blacks, the majority born in the South, resided there, nearly one-third of the total population. By 1970, more blacks called Chicago home than the state of Mississippi, a fact that dramatically illustrates its importance to the southern exodus.

In the late-19th and early-20th century, Chicago was a transportation, commercial, and manufacturing giant. As a result, heavy factories and other industries had an insatiable need for a cheap and reliable labor force. When World War I began in 1914 and halted the influx of immigrant laborers, Chicago's industrialists actively recruited southern black workers. This employment draw made the city a primary destination for black migrants racial repression and declining prospects in agriculture in the Jim Crow South. During World War I, an estimated 50,000 to 70,000 black migrants lived in Chicago. Of this total, the majority came from Louisiana, Tennessee, Alabama, and, above all, Mississippi. The Illinois Central Railroad Line ran directly from Chicago to New Orleans, helping connect the city to the South, and the *Chicago Defender,* a vigorous advocate of the southern exodus and widely circulated in the South, helped link the image of Chicago with "the land of hope" in the psyche of many black southerners.

Life in Chicago was far from ideal. Newcomers were generally restricted to the least desirable work in processing and manufacturing jobs. Moreover, because of housing discrimination, they were concentrated in areas not located near the city's plants and factories. They faced high rents and overcrowding, as apartments and tenements were subdivided into smaller units, many of which were known as kitchenettes. Established black residents could not ignore the changing composition of their community. Some were alarmed by the appearance and manners of the southern migrants, and they did not keep their opinions to themselves. Most black Chicagoans, however, followed the lead of the *Chicago Defender* and lent a supportive hand to the newcomers.

The migration triggered more competition between blacks and whites for housing, jobs, and access to public accommodations. Whites in neighborhoods adjacent to the growing Black Belt sought to stymie neighborhood integration through restrictive covenants and intimidation. At work, whites viewed blacks as rivals for jobs and as enemies of unions. These tensions culminated in July 1919 with the Chicago race riot when a black teenager drowned in Lake Michigan after whites had thrown rocks at him and four friends while their raft drifted near a beach claimed by whites. For five days, blacks and whites battled one another leaving 23 blacks and 15 whites dead and millions of dollars in property damage.

The downturn in Chicago's economy in the post-World War I era slowed, but did not stop, the influx of black southerners. By 1921, the migration had resumed with great velocity. Nearly 100,000 newcomers arrived in Chicago over the next decade, and, by 1930, more than 225,000 African Americans lived in the city. Even as northern factories shed jobs and long lines formed at soup kitchens during the Great Depression, the population of black Chicago grew slightly. Between 1940 and 1970, growing mechanization of cotton production displaced hundreds of thousands of black workers in the South. Moreover, World War II labor shortages brought roughly 60,000 black migrants to the city. These newcomers had the advantage of established kinship networks in the city.

Many newcomers settled on the South Side; others moved into the growing West Side ghetto. The West Side had been home to roughly 25,000 blacks until 1940, but as Jews and other ethnic groups left settlements for better housing elsewhere, black migrants packed into the available housing in East Garfield Park, North Lawndale, and Near West Side. By 1960, the West Side was home to more than 200,000 African Americans.

Chicago turned into an intensely segregated city in the early 20th century as ghettos maintained by white racism and local, state, and federal policies. Black newcomers as well as native black Chicagoans were excluded from the proliferating postwar suburban housing, and many found themselves living in high-rise public housing projects stacked within the confines of the ghetto. If blacks sought to live in white neighborhoods in the city or suburbs, they often faced white violence. By the early 1960s, big public housing projects like the Robert Taylor Homes, hailed by its first residents, had become increasingly warehouses of human misery. The low-skill and semiskilled manufacturing jobs that had done much to lure migrants and raise their standards of living were no longer available.

See also: Chicago Race Riot of 1919; Great Migration; Red Summer Race Riots; Urbanization

Lionel Kimble Jr.

Bibliography

Black, Timuel. *Bridges of Memory: Chicago's First Wave of Black Migration.* Evanston, IL: Northwestern University Press, 2003.

Drake, St. Clair, and Horace Cayton. *Black Metropolis: A Study of Negro Life in a Northern City.* New York: Harcourt, Brace, and World, 1970.

Grossman, James R. *Land of Hope: Chicago, Black Southerners and the Great Migration.* Chicago: University of Chicago Press, 1989.

Hirsch, Arnold R. *Making of the Second Ghetto: Race and Housing in Chicago, 1940–1960.* New York: Cambridge University Press, 1983.

Spear, Allan H. *Black Chicago: The Making of a Negro Ghetto.* Chicago: University of Chicago Press, 1967.

Tuttle, William M. *Race Riot: Chicago in the Red Summer of 1919.* Urbana, IL: University of Illinois Press, 1996.

Destination, Cuba

The Republic of Cuba is an archipelago of islands in the Caribbean Sea, located approximately 90 miles south of the U.S. state of Florida. The only socialist republic in the Americas since the success of the 1959 revolution, Cuba also has the largest population of any Caribbean nation.

The history of Cuba cannot be separated from the development of the sugar plantation industry in the Americas. On October 7, 1886, Cuba became one of the last nations to formally abolish slavery. The late termination of the importation of slaves to the island is considered to be a key determinant of the strong African legacy in the country's cultural and national development. Prized by generations of U.S. leaders as "the Pearl of the Antilles" for both strategic and ideological reasons, Cuba has faced a long and complicated history of American overinvolvement in its national affairs.

The entangled issues of slavery and colonialism for centuries overshadowed all aspects of Cuban life. The island was quickly occupied and settled by Spaniards in 1511; it was used as a base for military conquest of the American mainland. It was only when Cuba developed from a naval way station and small-scale coffee producer into a sugar plantation colony, that the importation of African slaves in great number commenced, after the brutal decimation of the indigenous Indians. Furthermore, with the shipment of African slaves to Cuba continuing until long after slavery had been abolished in British and French colonies, cultural links between Cuba and Africa were maintained to a degree unparalleled in the region.

The Spanish system of slavery was heavily influenced by metropolitan norms and culture. Inasmuch as provenance was celebrated by the colonizers within associations known as *cabildos,* African slaves were given leave to form similar groups according to social custom and ancestral ties. This practice allowed the flourishing of African religious cult activity (such as *santeria, palo,* and *lucumí*) that continues to enjoy widespread popularity to this day. Ties to individual ethnic and tribal origins were likewise conserved by the white slaveowners' custom of identifying and characterizing their captives according to place–of origin.

When Cuban-born Spaniards, known as Creoles, began to press for independence from Spain, their efforts at times intersected with slaves' struggles against bondage. Some Creoles saw independence and the abolition of slavery as desirable, but the authorities kept many of them loyal by warning of the "Africanization" of Cuba that would result.

The outstanding military career of Antonio Maceo, a Cuban of mixed race, known as *El Bronce Titan* (the Bronze Titan), began with the outbreak of the War of Independence in 1868. Carlos Manuel de Céspedes emancipated the slave population, and soon black soldiers outnumbered white troops in the revolutionary armies. Before long, the real objectives of Maceo, then second–in command of the independence army, became the subject of suspicion. He was charged with harboring designs for black rule, rumors that persisted until his death in battle in 1896. In fact, Maceo refused to recognize the Pact of Zanjón, which ended the first revolutionary war, also called the Ten Years War. He and other *mambi* (independence) officers vowed to continue fighting until complete independence for Cuba and the universal abolition of slavery had been achieved. The pact meanwhile offered liberty only for slaves who had fought in the independence armies. This event is known as *La Protesta de Baraguá* (the Protest of Baraguá).

During the era of the independence struggles against Spain, the concept of "racelessness" was constructed by Cuban intellectuals who sought to transmute the inherent violence of a socially stratified plantation society into the all-embracing concept of Cubanness (*cubanidad*). White and nonwhite intellectual elites asserted that the struggle against Spain had produced a new kind of individual and a new kind of collectivity. The experience of war, it was claimed, had united black and white into nothing more or less than Cuban. Jose Martí, often described as the "Apostle" of Cuban independence, went even further by denying the existence of races. Popular nationalist readings of Martí's ideals of racial fraternity and social unity have inspired all Cuban independence struggles since this time. Accordingly, independent black Cuban mobilization has without exception been strongly condemned, beginning with the brutal crushing of the Partido Independiente de Color (PIC) rebellion in 1912.

After independence from Spain, U.S. dominance was predicated on the belief that racial inferiority rendered Cubans incapable of self-government. Americans considered Cuba to be a black nation not only because of the skin color of a large percentage of its population, but also because of the strong African influence in its culture, and the island's history as a colonial possession. Thus, beginning in the 1890s, the movement to form a new Cuban identity simultaneously responded to the need to challenge U.S. racist stereotypes that associated blackness with debasement.

By 1930, this new national paradigm celebrated black Cubans' cultural contributions and claimed *mestizaje* (racial mixing) as the very essence of Cubanness. In the image of similar movements in the United States (the Harlem Renaissance) and France (*Négritude*), black culture in

Cuba was celebrated by artists and intellectuals responding to the rallying call of "Afrocubanism." Nicolas Guillen first made mention of "Cuban color" in the prologue to his 1931 collection of poems *Sóngoro Cosongo.* Later, in a speech given at the University of Havana on November 28, 1939, white Cuban anthropologist, Fernando Ortiz, one of the guiding lights of Afrocubanismo, elucidated the distinct quality of Cubanness, which he likened to the national dish—*el ajiaco*—a simmering stew that reduces separate ingredients until each becomes indistinguishable from the other.

As the dictatorship of Gerardo Machado collapsed in September 1933, a wave of mass protests took hold across the island. In the countryside of the eastern provinces, one sugar mill after another was seized by laborers demanding an improvement to appalling working conditions. Many were migrants from Jamaica and Haiti, often employed by American-owned companies. These African-Caribbean workers would soon become the first victims of the newly installed anti-imperialist government of Dr. Ramón Grau San Martín. As one of a series of nationalization measures, the short-lived revolutionary administration made it illegal for a business to employ more foreign nationals than Cubans; at least 50 percent of the workforce had to be native-born. Soon tens of thousands of Haitians were cruelly deported, while Jamaicans, enjoying a slightly higher social status and more vigorous diplomatic representation, more successfully withstood the tide of discrimination and economic adversity.

Until this period, the Communist Party of Cuba (PCC) had no prior experience with the rural populations and very little contact with black labor. The strikes that threatened to cripple the sugar industry between 1930 and 1933, however, focused the class struggle in the countryside, and soon the PCC were striving to organize and unite the plantation workforce. Most of the success the communists enjoyed was among skilled workers in the *ingenios* (mills), where blacks and whites were organized across racial and ethnic lines. In December 1932, the organization of labor in the rural districts culminated in the formation of the National Union of Sugar Workers (SNOIA), initiating the link in Cuban politics between the struggle for racial equality and proletarian ideology. Alone among Cuba's political parties the PCC fought against segregation and racial discrimination. Cuban communists also mounted campaigns against racism in the United States, including raising awareness of

the Scottsboro Boys case. The party also offered black Cubans their first experience of political leadership.

On January 1, 1959 Fidel Castro's July 26th Movement triumphantly heralded a new chapter in Cuban history, a day after the harsh reign of General Fulgencio Batista concluded with his hasty flight from the island. The revolution was ushered in on a nationalistic wave of hope for an end to the ills of hegemonic domination: corruption, poverty, illiteracy, bad housing, and discrimination.

Before the revolution black and *mestizo* (mixed-race) Cubans were among the most economically-disadvantaged, typically receiving lower wages than whites. The first and second Agrarian Reform Laws improved the lot of black farmers and agricultural workers, and the Urban Reform Law guaranteed the right to decent housing for black Cubans who lived in the cities. However, a twin assault from the literacy campaign and educational reform policies dealt the most deadly blows to the institutionalized racism that had impoverished so many. Antiracism was instrumental in strengthening the revolutionary government and discrediting the opposition. As early as September 1959, a U.S. State Department report considered support from black Cubans crucial to the survival of the revolutionary government.

From the early days of the revolution Fidel Castro reached out to black America for support against the common enemy of U.S. imperialism. If Cuba had succeeded in liberating itself from U.S. hegemonic control then it could obviously serve as a powerful role model for black emancipation in the North. Joe Louis was engaged to spearhead a public relations campaign to encourage black tourism to 'racism-free' Cuba, which was met with mild interest. Reverend Adam Clayton Powell Jr., an ardent early supporter of the revolution, remained loyal until signs of the revolution's commitment to socialism proved hard to ignore. Poet Amiri Baraka (at the time Leroi Jones) credits his 1960 visit to Cuba for an increased racial and third-world consciousness.

Indeed, African American support for the Cuban Revolution has a long and intricate history. For if it is true that in North America blacks comprise the only group consistently to identify with the revolution's anti-imperialist goals, some of the most scathing denouncements of Cuba's racial policies came from black nationalists such as Stokely Carmichael and Eldridge Cleaver. Harlem residents may still in some quarters cherish the memory of Fidel Castro and the

Cuban delegation to the United Nations during their week-long stay at the Hotel Theresa in September 1960, when Malcolm X, Robert F. Williams, Egyptian president Gamal Nasser, and Russia's Nikita Khrushchev paid court to the revolutionaries. While Assata Shakur and other members of the Black Panther Party found refuge from U.S. judicial persecution on the island. However African Americans have at times been challenged to reconcile their own socially-alienated experience of race, with the culturally integrated racial attitudes of black and white Cubans.

Links between black Cubans and African Americans are of long-standing, and have particularly flourished in the areas of music and sport. Cuban teams competed against the segregated teams of the American Black baseball league, and fans were well informed about Cuban players through the sports columns of black newspapers. Poets, musicians and other artists routinely collaborated, and mutually supported each others' work. The Afro-Cuban style of jazz grew out of the musical partnership of Mario Bauzá and Dizzy Gillespie, which, under the influence of Charlie Parker, branched out into the Cubop movement.

Despite the austerities imposed by the continuing U.S. blockade, and the absence of Soviet support since 1990, Havana continues to pursue an active internationalist foreign policy. The revolutionary government's early interest in Africa was spearheaded by Ernesto "Che" Guevara, who made an extended tour of the continent between December 1964 and March1965. Guevara made contact with potential allies in, among other nations, Algeria, Ghana, Guinea, Mali, and Congo-Brazzaville. Fidel Castro embarked upon his own African tour in the early 1970s, and in April 1976 he declared Cuba a "Latin-African" nation.

From the 1960s Cuba sent military advisers to support African revolutionary movements and governments in Sierra Leone, Guinea, Mozambique and South Yemen. In the 1970s Cuban troops served in Angola and in the Horn of Africa.

After the Organisation of American States (OAS) lifted its ban on member states' interaction with Cuba in 1975, Cuba established diplomatic relations with several newly independent countries in the Caribbean, and developed close relations with Barbados, Guyana, Jamaica, and Trinidad and Tobago. In recent times Cuba has forged closer ties with CARICOM countries. Cuban doctors, educators and engineers have served in the Caribbean and Africa.

See also: Baraka, Amiri; Black Nationalism; Black Panther Party; Castro, Fidel; Harlem Renaissance; Negritude; Shakur, Assata; Williams, Robert F.; X, Malcolm

Christabelle A. Peters

Bibliography

Brock, Lisa, and Digna Castañeda Fuertes, eds. *Between Race and Empire: African-Americans and Cubans before the Cuban Revolution.* Philadelphia: Temple University Press, 1998.

De La Fuente, Alejandro. *Race, Inequality, and Politics in Twentieth-Century Cuba.* Chapel Hill: University of North Carolina Press, 2001.

Domínguez, Jorge I. *To Make a World Safe for Revolution: Cuba's Foreign Policy.* Cambridge: Harvard University, 1989.

Ellis, Keith. *Cuba's Nicolás Guillén: Poetry and Ideology.* Toronto: University of Toronto Press, 1983.

Ferrer, Ada. "Rethinking Race and Nation in Cuba." In *Cuba, the Elusive Nation: Interpretations of National Identity,* ed. Damián J. Fernández and Madeline Cámara Betancourt. Gainesville: University Press of Florida, 2000.

Franco, José Luciano. "Africanos y sus Descendientes Criollos en las Luchas Liberadoras, 1533–1895." *Casa de las Americas* 93 (1975):12–21.

Gott, Richard. *Cuba: A New History.* New Haven, CT: Yale University Press, 2004.

McLeod, Marc C. "Undesirable Aliens: Race, Ethnicity, and Nationalism in the Comparison of Haitian and British West Indian Immigrant Workers in Cuba, 1912–1939." *Journal of Social History* 31, no. 3 (1998):599–623.

Tyson, Timothy B. *Radio Free Dixie: Robert F. Williams and the Roots of Black Power.* Chapel Hill: University of North Carolina Press, 1999.

Destination, Detroit, Michigan

During the phase of African American history, typically referred to as the Great Migration, the black population of Detroit, Michigan increased from less than 6,000 in 1910 to more than 40,000 a decade later in 1920, a percentage increase of 600 percent. During World War I and the decades that followed, Detroit was an extremely popular destination for refugees from the South. Beginning in 1915, approximately 1,000 African Americans arrived monthly from Georgia, Alabama, Mississippi, Arkansas, and other Southern states. The influx in 1915 was largely due to the decision by Henry Ford to pay employees, including African Americans, of Ford Motor Company in Detroit the unprecedented amount of $5 per day. By 1916, the rapidly expanding defense industries created more demand for labor and served as additional inducement for African Americans looking for better lives in the North.

A brief recession in 1920–1921 served as a slight discouragement to the numerous migrants in the city as some struggled to find gainful employment. With a reduction in the amount of foreign immigration, however, the need for African American migrants from the South grew even during the recession. In 1923 alone, about 14,000 African Americans arrived in Detroit. By 1930, at the onset of the Great Depression, Detroit had a black population of 120,066, an astounding increase from the 1910 total of less than 6,000.

In addition to the "pull" factors of jobs in the automobile and defense industries, the Great Migration was also a product of a number of forces that actively pushed African Americans from the South. The suffocating combination of sharecropping, Jim Crow, disfranchisement, and lynching—the various dimensions of the Black Nadir—provided more than enough incentive for millions of African Americans to relocate to the North in the period between 1910 and 1940. Far from the "Promised Land" of their collective hopes and dreams, however, the North was rife with significant problems as epitomized by the 1919 Chicago race riot. Although Detroit did not witness a large-scale race riot until 1943, the massive influx of African Americans led to occasional violent interactions with other emigrant and native-born groups vying for jobs.

Segregated living patterns was the principal problem faced by early African American migrants. Like practically all northern cities, Detroit had a long tradition of segregated housing. Restrictive covenants, redlining, and other mechanisms were used to maintain segregated communities. During the World War I era, only 20 percent of all African Americans purchased homes in Detroit. The majority of the migrants were limited to dilapidated tenements in areas customarily set aside for African Americans. Despite poor housing, high unemployment, and social marginalization, many African Americans originating from the South would still view Detroit and other northern cities as far superior to the daily hostilities they faced in southern states. In this instance, African Americans voted with their feet and the influx of southerners into Detroit continued throughout much of the 20th century. In the aftermath of the 1967 Detroit riot, whites fled to the suburbs in large numbers, leaving behind a black numerical majority in Detroit and making it one of many so-called Chocolate Cities.

See also: Black Nadir; Detroit, Michigan, Riot of 1943; Great Migration; Muhammad, Elijah

Walter C. Rucker

Bibliography
Marks, Carole. *Farewell—We're Good and Gone: The Great Black Migration.* Bloomington: Indiana University Press, 1989.

Martin, Elizabeth Anne. *Detroit and the Great Migration, 1916–1929.* Ann Arbor: Bentley Historical Library, University of Michigan, 1993.

Sernett, Milton C. *Bound for the Promised Land: African American Religion and the Great Migration.* Durham: Duke University Press, 1997.

Trotter, Joe William, ed. *The Great Migration in Historical Perspective.* Bloomington: Indiana University Press, 1991.

Destination, Harlem, New York

Located in Upper Manhattan, Harlem has been a destination for non-native Americans since 1658. Named Nieuw Haarlem by the Dutch in honor of the Dutch city of Haarlem, Harlem has been variously a magnet for farmers, aristocrats, immigrants, and African Americans. During the 1920s, it was the site of a great blossoming of African American culture—the Harlem Renaissance. It has been the home to many African American luminaries such as W. E. B. Du Bois, Walter White, Roy Wilkins, Thurgood Marshall, and Zora Neale Hurston, as well as many other artists, musicians, and writers.

The Dutch, the English, and post-Revolutionary Americans farmed the land on the eastern side of Harlem and built country estates. Then around 1830, when the rich farmland became depleted, the area became a haven for those seeking cheap housing, including immigrants who built shantytowns. But as transportation to Harlem improved (an elevated railroad was built between 1878 and 1881; the subway was soon to come), developers began to meet the growing demand for housing in Manhattan by building row houses, tenements, and luxury apartments in Harlem. In fact, many of the buildings in Harlem today were built between 1870 and 1910.

Development led to speculation and by 1904, prices became seriously inflated. Owners were finding it difficult to find tenants able to pay the high rent required to make a profit. As a result, banks were foreclosing on property owners. In the midst of this situation, black real estate manager Philip Payton Jr. saw an opportunity. He was able to lease buildings from white owners and then rent them at 10 percent above the deflated price to African Americans. Experiencing immediate success, he soon created the African-American Realty Company. Other black entrepreneurs, such as John E. Nail and Henry C. Parker, as well as black churches (like St. Philip's Church), were also able to capitalize on property in Harlem, and in doing so they met a growing demand by African Americans for decent housing.

Initially, this demand for new housing came from African Americans living in other parts of Manhattan. In 1900, most of the black population in Manhattan was located in the midtown neighborhoods known as Hell's Kitchen, the Tenderloin, and San Juan Hill. But many of the residents in these areas were displaced by the building of Pennsylvania Station and by the expansion of commercial enterprises in the area. Beginning in about 1904, Harlem offered even better housing than they had had. Soon, though, this demand came from outside Manhattan as well.

Of prime importance was the black migration from the South. Usually associated with World War I, this migration had, in fact, already begun before the war, as blacks moved to the North to avoid violence, oppression, and lack of opportunity. By 1910, 61 percent of blacks in Manhattan were from the South. Added to this were migrations from the British West Indies, Latin America, French West Indies, and the American Virgin Islands (in 1925, the foreign-born blacks in Harlem were estimated to number 35,000).

This was a cultural migration as well. Many black churches from other parts of Manhattan, such as the Abyssinian Baptist Church, moved there as well as the local offices of the NAACP and the Urban League. In addition, black writers, intellectuals, musicians, painters, sculptors, poets, and novelists were drawn to Harlem, especially during the 1920s. Writers like James Weldon Johnson, Langston Hughes, Countee Cullen, and Claude McKay, as well as painters like Aaron Douglass and sculptors like Sargent Johnson made Harlem their home. And jazz flourished in Harlem at such clubs as the Savoy, where Duke Ellington played and Ella Fitzgerald sang, and Minton's Playhouse, which is often considered the birthplace of Bebop and the meeting place for musicians like Thelonius Monk, Dizzy Gillespie, and Charlie Parker. It was from Harlem that the Silent March of 1917—in protest for the murders of African

Americans during the East St. Louis race riot—emanated. Social activist W. E. B. Du Bois, who helped to found the NAACP and who founded and edited *Crisis* magazine—the official magazine of the NAACP—lived and wrote in Harlem.

Writing in 1925, James Weldon Johnson called Harlem the "greatest Negro city in the world." It has had its ups and downs since then (it has been a famous black neighborhood for nearly a century), and the hopes of many were not always realized. The Great Depression had its effect on Harlem as it did on other parts of the country. And Alain Locke, a professor of philosophy at Howard University, also writing in 1925, prematurely called Harlem "another statue of liberty." In truth, there were many more social battles yet to be fought in the Civil Rights movement before liberty could be considered. Nevertheless, Harlem famously exemplifies the shift from a rural to an urban way of life, and it remains a historic symbol of cultural excellence.

See also: Du Bois; W. E. B.; Garvey, Marcus; Great Migration; Harlem Renaissance; Urbanization

William P. Toth

Bibliography
Domingo, W. A. "The Tropics in New York." *The Survey Graphic* 6 (1925):648–50.
Huggins, Nathan Irvin. *Harlem Renaissance.* New York: Oxford University Press, 1971.
Johnson, James Weldon. *Black Manhattan.* New York: Knopf, 1930.
Johnson, James Weldon. "The Making of Harlem." *The Survey Graphic* 6 (1925):635–39.
Locke, Alain. "Harlem." *The Survey Graphic* 6 (1925):629–30.
Marberry, Craig, and Michael Cunningham. *Spirit of Harlem.* New York: Random House, 2003.
Osofsky, Gilbert. *Harlem: The Making of a Ghetto.* New York: Harper, 1964.

Detroit, Michigan, Riot of 1943

The Detroit Riot of 1943 was one of the biggest and bloodiest race riots in the history of the United States. It was a culminating event in the early Civil Rights movement, as it raised the American consciousness about the explosive nature of growing racial tensions fueled by racial inequalities in this thriving northern metropolis. In the 1940s Detroit experienced a growth splurge burgeoned by the need for workers in the defense industry. The growing economic base attracted both black and white workers, leading to a rapid increase in the population and putting a strain on housing, transportation, education, recreation facilities, and most portentously, race relations.

By 1943, the number of blacks in Detroit had doubled, and racial tensions in the city increased accordingly. On June 20, more than 1,000 Detroiters gathered on Belle Isle, one of Detroit's largest parks. Two young black men who had became angry as a result of their expulsion from Eastwood Park five days previously, traveled to Belle Isle to try to even the score. Their anger grew as police conducted searches of the cars of blacks crossing to Belle Isle but did not search cars driven by whites. In *Harper's Magazine*, a record of the riot states that Leo Tipton, a black man, announced in a nightclub that whites had thrown a black woman and her baby off the Belle Isle Park Bridge. Tipton urged the nightclub customers to assist in the fighting.

A number of sources report that another rumor simultaneously circulated in the white community that blacks had murdered and raped a white woman on the Belle Isle Park Bridge. Fights broke out between blacks and whites and some erupted on the bridge connecting Belle Isle to Southeast Detroit. Rumors of a race war roused whites and blacks, who both took to the streets near Belle Isle and in the downtown area. The mixed race mob attacked passersby, streetcars, and property. Blacks in Paradise Valley, also known as the Black Bottom, looted white-owned shops; whites overturned and burned cars of black drivers on Woodward Avenue. Breaking and entering occurred involving both black and white merchants. Differing opinions arose regarding the Detroit police and their handling of the rioters. Blacks saw it as police brutality and racist attacks, whereas whites characterized it as justifiable.

The riot came to an end once Mayor Edward Jeffries Jr. and Governor Harry Kelly asked President Roosevelt for help. In response, federal troops in armored cars and jeeps with automatic weapons drove down Woodward Avenue. The appearance of the troops with their overwhelming firepower succeeded in dispersing the mobs. The aftermath of the Detroit Riots that lasted for three days included the

A female passenger climbs out of the rear window of a tram in Detroit, Michigan, on June 21, 1943, after a mob halted the car in an effort to assault the black passengers on board during the race riots. (Library of Congress)

following statistics: 34 persons were killed (25 blacks and 9 whites), 765 suffered injuries that required hospital treatment, 1,893 persons were arrested, an estimated $2 million in property damage was due to vandalism, looting, and fire; a million hours of labor was lost totaling $115,000 a day for federal and state troops.

Depending on the vantage point, a number of theories emerged regarding those who held the greatest responsibility for the riots. The media espoused the belief, through photos, nightly news reports, and news articles, that those most responsible were angry black males. Many of the locals blamed southern newcomers, ethnic groups, communists, and hate groups. The federal government endorsed a fact-finding committee that produced an 8,500-word, fact-finding committee appraisal, known as the *Dowling Report.* The *Dowling Report* placed the blame on black hoodlums and identified whites as victims who reacted with violence only as a reaction to black bloodshed.

In reality those who rioted included the following groups:

1. Black men: The majority were married, stable, older, and acted out during the riots to protect themselves and their families. They acted as individuals rather than groups within the ghetto. Most were not Detroit natives but had lived there for five years or more before the riot and worked in the unskilled positions of industrial labor.
2. Black women: Many were single, unemployed or holding low-paying servile jobs. The offense they were most often convicted of was looting.
3. Black youth: They were mainly male, younger than white juveniles, and engaged more in felonies involving theft, breaking and entering, looting, carrying concealed weapons, assaulting someone, or destroying property inside their own neighborhoods.
4. White men: These men held skilled and semiskilled jobs in the factories, traveled far from home to riot, were younger than their black counterparts, were from Michigan, rioted in groups rather than as individuals, represented various class, ethnic, and religious communities, and battled for white dominance in the city.
5. White youth: They were older than their black counterparts and, along with black youth, were largely responsible for igniting the riot on Belle Isle and spreading it through Paradise Valley and beyond.

See also: Destination, Detroit, Michigan; Great Migration

Jill E. Rowe-Adjibogoun

Bibliography

Brown, Earl. "The Truth About the Detroit Riot." *Harper's Magazine* 187 (November 1943):488–90.

Capeci, Dominic J. Jr., and Martha Wilkerson. *Layered Violence: The Detroit Rioters of 1943.* Jackson: University Press of Mississippi, 1991.

Shogan, Robert, and Tom Craig. *The Detroit Race Riot: A Study in Violence.* Philadelphia: Chilton, 1964.

Sitkoff, Harvard. "The Detroit Race Riots of 1943." *Michigan History* 53 (Fall 1969):183–206.

Sugrue, Thomas J. *The Origins of the Urban Crisis.* Princeton: Princeton University Press, 1996.

Detroit, Michigan, Riot of 1967

In what became the deadliest urban disturbance during the 1960s, the Detroit riot of July 23–27, 1967, resulted in 43 deaths, 1,200 injuries, more than 7,000 arrests, and in excess of $300 million in damaged property. Ongoing violence, looting, arson, and gun battles convulsed the city and, for the first time in a quarter-century, the U.S. Army had to be used to contain civil strife.

The precipitating event leading to the violence occurred before 4 A.M. on July 23 when Detroit police raided an after-hours and illegal drinking club, referred to locally as a "blind pig," on 12th Street. A blind pig operated in open violation of city ordnances, which prohibited the sale of alcohol at bars after midnight. When the police arrived, they expected to encounter a small crowd. To their surprise, this particular blind pig had close to 80 people who were attending the celebration of two returning African American soldiers from the Vietnam War. Typically in raids on blind pigs, Detroit police would have simply arrested the proprietors and a handful of customers caught with illicit drugs. In this instance, they arrested all 73 African American patrons and the bartender. Rumors quickly spread that some of those arrested had been beaten by police officers. Given the number of individuals arrested, it took about a half-hour before police vans arrived and, in the interim, a small crowd of local residents began to gather outside the blind pig.

Rumors of police brutality, coupled with the political volatility of the times and the depressed local economy, explains, in part, the events that followed. As the police vans departed with the arrested partygoers, the crowd that formed outside the bar began throwing rocks and bricks into store windows, and about 50 people began looting a clothing store. With no police in sight, the looting spread to other nearby stores and, within an hour, dozens of stores in a 16-block radius were looted and set on fire. Within the next 24 hours, African Americans and whites in the thousands were roaming the streets, moving from Detroit's West Side to the East Side neighborhoods and into downtown. The rioters moved quickly along large sections of Grand River and Woodward Avenues and 12th Street in the downtown area of Detroit and ranged as far as seven miles toward the outer edge of the city.

In an attempt to prevent the riot from spreading further, Governor Hugh Romney and Detroit Mayor Jerome Cavanagh acted quickly to call up 600 Detroit police, 800 state troopers, and 1,200 National Guardsmen to seal off large areas of the city and to disperse the rioters. These actions were not sufficient and the violence of the riot intensified. By Monday, July 24, the first three fatalities of the riot occurred. All three were white. One was beaten to death by a group of African American youths while protecting his store. Another was killed by a stray bullet. The third was a rioter killed by a storeowner. Ironically, the vast majority of those killed during the five full days of rioting were African American, and many of their deaths are attributed to the police and National Guard.

When it became clear that local and state law enforcement resources were insufficient, Governor Romney requested federal assistance from U.S. Attorney General Ramsey Clark. Clark informed Romney that before federal troops could be sent, the governor had to declare that a civil insurrection was taking place. Romney balked at this, fearing that insurance companies would not compensate residents of Detroit for their property losses if the cause was insurrection. When the situation in the city became progressively worse, President Lyndon Baines Johnson stepped in and sent Army paratroopers from the 101st Airborne.

While the paratroopers assisted in restoring order to the city, a number of disturbing incidents occurred that further enraged African American residents in Detroit. In one incident, National Guardsmen fired .50-caliber machine gun rounds into an apartment building, killing a four-year-old girl. In a more publicized case, three unarmed African American teenagers—Aubrey Pollard, Fred Temple, and Carl Cooper—were shot and killed at Algiers Motel by three Detroit police officers. The three officers were later exonerated by an all-white jury, and two of them returned to the police force by 1971.

By Thursday, July 27, the riot was effectively over and federal paratroopers were withdrawn. President Johnson appointed a Special Advisor Commission on Civil Disorders on July 27, 1967 to help discern the origins of the Detroit riot and other civil disturbances occurring during the so-called long, hot summer of 1967. Pointing to economic disparities and despair in urban "ghettoes," the commission headed by Illinois Governor Otto Kerner concluded that America was sharply divided into two societies—one white, one black—which were separate and increasingly unequal. In the aftermath of the riot, white flight to the suburbs of Detroit accelerated at an alarming rate to the point that the city had a majority African American population by the early 1970s. The removal of whites to Detroit's suburbs and the creation of an impoverished and black urban core provided additional proof of the Kerner Commission's assessments of the growing economic and even spatial divides in the United States.

See also: Johnson, Lyndon Baines; Kerner Commission Report; League of Revolutionary Black Workers; Long Hot Summer Riots, 1965–1967; Vietnam War (Black Participation in)

Walter C. Rucker

Bibliography

Buchanan, Heather, Sharon Stanford, and Teresa Kimble, eds. *Eyes on Fire: Witnesses to the Detroit Riot of 1967.* Detroit: Aquarius Press, 2007.

Fine, Sidney. *Violence in the Model City: The Cavanagh Administration, Race Relations, and the Detroit Riot of 1967.* East Lansing: Michigan State University Press, 2007.

Locke, Hubert G. *The Detroit Riot of 1967.* Detroit: Wayne State University Press, 1969.

Diallo, Amadou

Amadou Bailo Diallo (1975–1999) was a 23-year-old immigrant from Guinea living in the Bronx. On the evening of February 4, 1999, on his way home from dinner, Diallo was shot and killed by four New York City police officers. The shooting took place at Diallo's apartment at 1157 Wheeler Avenue. Diallo was allegedly unarmed and innocent of committing any crime. Nonetheless, he was pursued by officers dressed in civilian clothing—Sean Carroll, Richard Murphy, Edward McMellon and Kenneth Boss—when they mistook him for a rapist who the police were looking for at the time. Afraid of the men, Diallo ran to the door of his apartment and reached into his coat to grab his wallet. The officers, who believed him to be reaching for a gun, opened fire. A total of 41 rounds were fired by the four officers, 19 of which were lodged in Diallo's body.

Diallo's mother, Kadiatou Diallo, and his stepfather, Sankarella Diallo, filed a $61,000,000 ($20 million plus $1 million for each shot fired) lawsuit against the City of New York and the four officers, claiming negligence, wrongful death, racial profiling, and myriad other violations of Amadou Diallo's civil rights. After years battling in court, they accepted a $3,000,000 settlement. Kadiatou Diallo has since published a novel entitled: *My Heart Will Cross This Ocean: My Story, My Son, Amadou* with the collaboration of Craig Wolff.

Amadou Diallo was born in 1975 in Sinoe, Liberia. As a youth, Amadou traveled and lived with his family in many parts of the world, including Togo, Guinea, Bangkok, and Singapore. Diallo was a devout Muslim and a talented student. By the time he arrived in the United States in 1996, with the intention of studying computer science, he had already attended The French International School, London's Cambridge University, and The British Consulate College in Thailand. Trying to establish himself in New York, he worked as a delivery person and also sold videotapes, gloves, and socks on a street corner in Manhattan. After the shooting, Diallo's body was returned to Guinea where he was laid to rest in the village of Hollande Bourou, located in the Fouta Djallon region.

Diallo's death and subsequent trial caused a large amount of controversy throughout the nation. These events sparked discussions of racial profiling and discrimination, as well as a series of protests. Diallo's death also revealed the substantial presence of West African immigrants in New York City (in 1999, there were approximately 50,000). Shortly after Amadou's death in 1999, his father, Sakou A. Diallo, founded The Amadou Diallo Educational, Humanitarian & Charity Foundation. The foundation aims to memorialize Diallo's life by aiding educational and humanitarian organizations that meant a great deal to Amadou. The foundation also supports organizations dedicated to putting a stop to police beatings and racial profiling.

See also: Racial Profiling

Jen Westmoreland Bouchard

Bibliography

Diallo, Kadiatou, and Craig Thomas Wolff. *My Heart Will Cross This Ocean: My Story, My Son, Amadou.* New York: Ballantine Books, 2004.

Fireside, Bryna J. *The Trial of the Police Officers in the Shooting Death of Amadou Diallo: A Headline Court Case.* Berkeley Heights, NJ: Enslow Publishers, 2004.

Roy, Beth. 41 *Shots—and Counting: What Amadou Diallo's Story Teaches Us About Policing, Race, and Justice.* Syracuse, NY: Syracuse University Press, 2009.

Disfranchisement

The term "disfranchisement" may refer to any systematic removal and denial of the right to vote; here it refers to the aggressive movement by southern states to eliminate African American political participation accompanied the rise of segregation between the late 1880s and the beginning of the 20th century. Legislatures throughout the region enacted statutory measures and reformed state constitutions with provisions designed to circumvent the Fifteenth Amendment guarantee of universal manhood suffrage. The sum of these measures, from poll taxes to literacy tests and property requirements, amounted to a near complete purge of African Americans and a substantial number of poor whites from voting rolls, inaugurating a new era in southern political history marked by one-party domination and social conservatism that lasted into the 1940s.

Early accounts have suggested that these restrictive laws and provisions merely legalized what had already been accomplished through fraud, intimidation, and coercion immediately after the end of Republican rule in 1877. But "legal disfranchisement" actually constituted a significant departure from an era of dynamic African American electoral participation after Reconstruction. Throughout the South, blacks had used a variety of strategies to win office and gain local influence. Ranging from fusion with local Democrats to continual support for Republican and aggressive third-party movements, this well-organized black political activity provoked concerns among southern whites over what the latter called "Negro domination." The return to Republican control of the White House and Congress by 1888, along with the rise of the Populist movement of agrarian reformers—African American and white—against planter elites and industrialist classes, further incited fears that white Democratic leaders could no longer control the black vote by either courting it or suppressing it through extralegal or statutory means. The only answer, they believed, was a constitutional reform movement that took blacks "out of politics" altogether.

Beginning in the 1880s, several southern states had passed laws that tightened registration regulations and/or reformed the ballot system. Justified as mainly "electoral reforms" to prevent fraud, such regulations disproportionately affected the poor, illiterate working classes that usually threatened Democratic dominance. The "secret ballot," for instance, while cutting down on intimidation and corruption, also effectively disfranchised those unable to read the new ballots, which usually contained a lengthy list of candidates from all parties. Combined with regulations calling for greater accuracy in age, place of birth, and occupation on registration forms, such statutory measures in Tennessee, North Carolina, and other states effectively restricted the ballot to a shrinking number of "desirable" voters.

But in 1890, Mississippi set the standard of "legal disfranchisement" when it convened a new constitutional convention to remove this last vestige of Reconstruction. Although white support was far from unanimous, delegates ratified a new constitution that placed the power to enfranchise entirely in the hands of state-appointed officials. Such a move forestalled potential voters' ability to seek registration through local or federal channels. In addition to property and educational requirements, the constitution also contained several supposedly "color blind" provisions. Potential voters had to live in the state for two years and the election district for one year. They also had to prove payment of a $2 poll tax for the previous two years. To these regulations, the convention added a so-called "understanding clause," in which a registrant had to either read a section of the state constitution or to understand what was read to him by offering a "reasonable interpretation thereof."

Reducing the number of eligible black voters from 190,000 to 8,615 by 1892, the "Mississippi Plan" became the model for disfranchisement throughout the South. South Carolina followed suit in 1895 with a similar constitution. Other states, facing more substantial populist revolts that undermined white unity until the end of the decade, eventually passed their own measures once this agrarian challenge dissipated. Between 1898 and 1908, Louisiana, Alabama, and Virginia also rewrote constitutions while North Carolina, Texas, and Georgia amended existing ones. All southern states followed a general pattern, but

some variations did exist depending on the intended targets of disfranchisement. Louisiana, for instance, enacted a "grandfather clause" that maintained the franchise for anyone who was either an eligible voter or was the son or grandson of one on January 1, 1867. Like the "understanding clause" test that could be applied with varying degrees of rigor at the registrar's discretion, such measures offered a loophole for poor, illiterate whites. Even if African Americans managed to meet these requirements, the white primary became a final obstacle. Since disfranchisement decimated support for Republican and third-party movements by the 1900s, local regulations limiting the Democratic primary to whites effectively excluded even registered voters from participating in what had become the only true election.

Despite such deliberate efforts to target the black vote, resistance to the movement was scarce. Northern Republicans, long since abandoning the "equal rights" ideals of Radical Reconstruction to embrace a gospel of economic prosperity and political efficiency, largely ignored the measures. Throughout the 1890s, Congress defeated attempts to establish federal control over elections and repealed existing regulations. Yet nothing seemed to demonstrate a rising national mistrust of government by "the masses" more than the 1898 *Williams v. Mississippi* decision, in which the Supreme Court upheld the state constitution's franchise restrictions.

Poor white farmers, who had previously benefited from black support, also largely acquiesced to disfranchisement. White populist ties to African American agrarian activists were often tenuous, and, as some historians have argued, poor whites essentially bought into Democratic elites' rhetoric of racial antagonism. As the latter—representing the Black Belt region of influential planters—and their allies moved to solidify their political power, they often targeted white farmers for disfranchisement as well. This would suggest that the movement was often a partisan endeavor rather than one motivated by race. Other historians, however, have suggested that poor whites themselves actually propelled the movement through their belief that the black vote bred the corruption that ensured elite Democrats' dominance. Populist leaders like Tom Watson of Georgia, for instance, not only converted to the necessities of disfranchisement, but also became one of the most ardent propagators of "Negrophobia" by the 1900s. Thus, disfranchisement is often seen as part of a larger wave of white supremacy, marked by the rise of Jim Crow and the increase of violence against African Americans, throughout the South in the 1890s.

Whatever the identity and motivation of the disfranchisers, response by the movement's victims also varied. Some African Americans sought to mobilize against ratification of the new constitutions. But, given the climate of intimidation in the late 19th century South, most hoped to simply mitigate the results of these provisions by calling for equal application of franchise restriction to blacks and whites alike. The most famous moment of accommodation to the new political order, however, came in 1895 when Booker T. Washington, in a speech to the Cotton States Exposition in Atlanta, argued that African Americans could trade their political aspirations and social integration for an equal share in the economic progress of the South. Although many black leaders excoriated what became known as the "Atlanta Compromise," the realities of disfranchisement and the rise of segregation effectively transformed the political and social world that southern blacks inhabited. It also gave rise to the emergence of new forms of political participation. For instance, African American women, through their rising participation in social agencies established during the Progressive Era, ensured that black protest would not fall silent in the early decades of the 20th century.

See also: Fifteenth Amendment; Grandfather Clause; Jim Crow; Voting Rights Act of 1965; Washington, Booker T.; White Primaries

Justin D. Poché

Bibliography

Ayers, Edward L. *The Promise of the New South: Life after Reconstruction.* New York: Oxford University Press, 1992.

Gilmore, Glenda. *Gender and Jim Crow: Women and the Politics of White Supremacy in North Carolina, 1896–1920.* Chapel Hill: University of North Carolina Press, 1996.

Hahn, Steven. *A Nation Under Our Feet: Black Political Struggles in the Rural South from Slavery to the Great Migration.* Cambridge, MA: Belknap-Harvard University Press, 2003.

Kousser, J. Morgan. *The Shaping of Southern Politics: Suffrage Restriction and the Establishment of the One-Party South, 1880–1910.* Baton Rouge: Louisiana State University Press, 1971.

Nieman, Donald G., ed. *African Americans and Southern Politics from Redemption to Disfranchisement.* New York: Garland Publishing, 1994.

Perman, Michael. *Struggle for Mastery: Disfranchisement in the South, 1888–1908.* Chapel Hill: University of North Carolina Press, 2001.

Woodward, C. Vann. *Origins of the New South, 1877–1913.* Baton Rouge: Louisiana State University Press, 1971.

Woodward, C. Vann. *The Strange Career of Jim Crow.* New York: Oxford University Press, 1955.

Double V Campaign

In February 1942, the African American newspaper the *Pittsburgh Courier* began the "Double V" campaign to promote victory against the Axis abroad and victory against racism and discrimination at home. In the months preceding the outbreak of war, and particularly after the United States entered World War II, the black press had been repeatedly criticized for its lack of sufficient patriotism—sometimes outright disloyalty—and African Americans had demonstrated a noticeable apathy toward the war effort. To counter this, the *Courier*'s Double V campaign encouraged African Americans to support the war effort but not to abandon their struggle for greater civil rights. To this end, the Double V campaign succeeded: it rallied African American support for national defense, and it kept the idea of civil rights front and center. Yet the *Courier*'s campaign, in the end, did not change the reality of the discrimination against, and exclusion of, blacks in American society.

The *Pittsburgh Courier* drew its inspiration for the Double V campaign from a letter by James G. Thompson of Wichita, Kansas, published in the issue of January 31, 1942. Thompson, in his letter titled "Should I Sacrifice to Live 'Half American?,'" advocated for a "double VV" for a dual victory over enemies to the country and enemies—opposed to equality, justice, and democracy—at home. In its next issue, on February 7, the *Courier* displayed Double V drawings emphasizing the theme "Democracy, At Home, Abroad." The paper announced the Double V campaign the next week, declaring its support for the defeat of totalitarianism abroad and inequality at home.

African Americans faced discrimination in every aspect of society, but their exclusion from the war effort, particularly from national defense industries, particularly stung, especially since the United States government promoted the war as being for the preservation of democracy. President Franklin D. Roosevelt's stated goals of the war, the Four Freedoms, did nothing to alleviate the racism and discrimination that African Americans faced. The disjunction between the rhetoric and the practice of liberty and democracy in the United States only fostered black apathy toward the war effort. Indeed, only a couple of weeks before the Thompson letter appeared in print, the *Courier* reported on the lukewarm support for the war among African Americans. Although many African Americans, and certainly those in the black press, accepted the premise that the war should be vigorously prosecuted abroad, they also believed that the same should apply for the struggle for black civil rights. The *Courier*'s Double V campaign captured that belief in bold print.

Among all of the black weekly newspapers in the United States during World War II, the *Pittsburgh Courier* had the largest circulation at 350,000, far outpacing the *Chicago Defender* whose circulation reached 230,000. The influence and circulation of the black press reached greater proportions during the war than at anytime in its history, and other black newspapers across the United States—the *Chicago Defender* and *Amsterdam Star-News* among others—embraced the Double V, making the *Courier*'s campaign a national effort. The Double V became a ubiquitous symbol in the pages of many black newspapers, and Double V clubs formed across the nation. African American celebrities of the time, such as Marian Anderson, Adam Clayton Powell Jr., and the NAACP's Roy Wilkins all appeared in photographs supporting the campaign. The *Courier* also offered integrated images of whites along side African Americans, promoting at once racial unity and the idea that the struggle for democracy was not just a black concern. The Double V resonated with the African American public, and its popularity helped to increase the circulation of black newspapers.

Yet, not everyone viewed the Double V campaign as a unifying force. Many white newspapers, especially those in the South, characterized the *Courier*'s crusade as an attempt to foment revolution. Although southern whites had long condemned the black press as a radical, destabilizing force in race relations, the U.S. government viewed the Double V as actually causing disunity and harm to black morale. Governmental surveillance and pressure on the black press to cease the agitation for greater rights, at least during wartime, proved unsuccessful, as black editors stood their ground and maintained their demands for equality and civil rights.

The *Pittsburgh Courier* promoted the Double V campaign throughout 1942. By early 1943, the campaign had died down significantly, as the paper gradually ceased emphasizing it. In its place, the *Courier* published numerous articles demonstrating the gains that African Americans had made because of the Double V campaign. There is no question that the Double V campaign energized many African Americans who sought greater rights and greater opportunities, but by war's end, the campaign had not achieved its desired goal: a double victory abroad and at home. The United States had won the war abroad, but racism and discrimination at home continued. In September 1945, the *Courier* removed the Double V from its masthead but left a single V to signify the war still to be waged. It was removed in 1946, the war at home still unfinished.

See also: Anderson, Marian; Powell, Adam Clayton Jr.; Randolph, A. Philip; Wilkins, Roy; World War II (Black Participation in)

Dan J. Puckett

Bibliography

Finkle, Lee. *Forum for Protest: The Black Press During World War II.* Rutherford, NJ: Fairleigh Dickinson University Press, 1975.

Simmons, Charles A. *The African American Press: A History of News Coverage During National Crises, with Reference to Four Black Newspapers, 1827–1965.* Jefferson, NC: McFarland Publishers, 1998.

Steven, John D. "World War II and the Black Press." In *Perspectives of the Black Press: 1974*, ed. Henry G. La Brie III. Kennebunkport, ME: Mercer House Press, 1974.

Washburn, Patrick S. "The *Pittsburgh Courier*'s Double V Campaign in 1942." *American Journalism* 3 (1986):73–86.

Washburn, Patrick S. *A Question of Sedition: The Federal Government's Investigation of the Black Press During World War II.* New York: Oxford University Press, 1986.

Du Bois, W. E. B.

Dr. William Edward Burghardt Du Bois (1868–1963) was a scholar, civil rights activist, editor, and novelist. Born February 23, 1868 to Alfred Du Bois and Mary Silvina Burghardt, Du Bois grew up in Great Barrington, Massachusetts, where less than 1 percent of the predominately Dutch and English population was of African descent. After graduating from high school, Du Bois earned an AB from Fisk University and a BA in philosophy and an MA in history from Harvard University. In 1892, he continued graduate studies at the University of Berlin, Germany, as a Slater Fund Fellow. He returned to the United States in 1894 and taught classes at Wilberforce University. In 1895, Du Bois became the first African American to receive a doctorate from Harvard. During the next 65 years, he was a professor of history, economics, and sociology at the University of Pennsylvania and Atlanta University, a leader of the NAACP, and an advocate of peace and civil rights. He also wrote two novels, edited several periodicals, and received numerous awards and honorary degrees. He died in 1963 as a citizen of Ghana.

Analyses of race and racism were prominent themes throughout Du Bois's career and were shaped by his education, worldwide travels, and experiences of the effects on African Americans of race riots, lynching, war, imperialism, and capitalism. His evolving racial consciousness impacted the scholarship he produced and the professional and political activities in which he participated. Du Bois made significant contributions to African American and American history, culture, politics, and scholarship. He developed ways to understand African Americans' racial identity, established the field of sociology, elucidated the historical significance of race, and fought internationally for freedom, equality, and peace.

Du Bois's most famous scholarly contributions were his interpretations of African American racial identity. In *The Souls of Black Folk,* published in 1903, Du Bois described African Americans' spirituality and history from 1861 to the early 20th century to explain the peculiar character of their identity as a race. He identified this race identity as "double consciousness," or the simultaneous presence in African Americans' minds of two conflicting "souls"—a longing to be a part of mainstream American society coupled with an equally strong feeling of kinship with African and African American culture. In this book, he discussed how double consciousness colored African Americans' contributions to American labor, music, economics, and religion. As a continuation of *The Souls of Black Folk, Darkwater*—a mixture of poetry, autobiography, and prose published in 1920—he described the effects of racism, imperialism, economic greed, sexism, and war on African Americans' racial identity.

Du Bois also contributed to academic research through pioneer sociological studies. In *The Philadelphia Negro,* he examined the economic and health statistics, education, and social experiences of black Americans in Philadelphia in the late 1890s. From 1897 to 1911, Du Bois directed the Atlanta University Studies of the Negro Problem, the only

W. E. B. Du Bois, considered the father of Pan-Africanism for his work to undermine European Imperialism in Africa, devoted his life to the struggle for equality for African Americans and all people of color. (Library of Congress)

scientific social studies of aspects of African American life and culture in the world during the late 19th and early 20th centuries. During the 1940s, he founded and edited *Phylon,* a journal published by Atlanta University that interpreted racial and cultural issues from the perspectives of the social sciences.

Du Bois made major contributions to historiography by interpreting American history through the lens of race relations, particularly as pertained to Africans and African Americans. Du Bois's historiography challenged historians' refusal to acknowledge facts regarding the significance of Africans' achievements and struggles in America and the world. *The Suppression of the African Slave-Trade,* published in 1896, and *Black Reconstruction in America, 1860–1880,* published in 1935, clarified and scrutinized two misconstrued and overlooked epochs in American history. *The World and Africa,* published in 1947, expanded the work of the aforementioned publications to a global scale, emphasizing Africans' crucial roles in the history of humankind from prehistoric times through modernity.

By editing mass-circulated publications, Du Bois extended his scholarship into African American communities. He created the NAACP's official monthly news magazine, *The Crisis,* and edited it from 1910 to 1934. In the early 1920s, Du Bois founded and edited *Brownie's Book,* a magazine for African American children containing visual images and literature.

Civil rights activism was integral to Du Bois's life. In 1905, he established the Niagara Movement to organize black intellectuals committed to black freedom. In 1909, he helped found the NAACP, a civil rights organization consisting of black and white liberals of various professions. On behalf of the NAACP, Du Bois investigated black American troops' experiences of racism in Europe during World War I and presented to the United Nations *An Appeal to the World* denouncing American segregation.

Ultimately, Du Bois epitomized his idea of the "talented tenth" and was one of the earliest practitioners of American Studies and Africana Studies. As a member of the talented tenth, or the top 10 percent of African Americans responsible for training and serving the masses of black communities, Du Bois devoted his professional career, scholarship, and political activism to the causes of racial uplift and equality. Decades before the establishment of an American Studies discipline, Du Bois conducted interdisciplinary research to illuminate various aspects of American culture. He incorporated physiology, psychology, sociology, economics, history, and philosophy into analyses of the significance of race in America. Du Bois's interpretations of the experiences of members of the African Diaspora created ways to understand black American identity and culture that remain among the premier scholarship of Africana Studies.

See also: African Diaspora; Double Consciousness; National Association for the Advancement of Colored People; Niagara Movement; Pan-Africanism; Pan-African Congresses

Kimberly M. Curtis

Bibliography

Bruce, Dickson D. Jr. "W. E. B. Du Bois and the Idea of Double Consciousness," *American Literature* 64 (June 1992):299–309.

Du Bois, W. E. B. *The Autobiography of W. E. B. Du Bois.* New York: International Publishers, 1968.

Du Bois, W. E. B. *The Souls of Black Folk.* New York: Penguin Books, 1996.

Lewis, David Levering. *W. E. B. Du Bois: Biography of a Race, 1868–1919.* New York: Henry Holt, 1993.

Lewis, David Levering. *W. E. B. Du Bois: The Fight for Equality and the American Century, 1919–1963.* New York: Henry Holt, 2000.

East St. Louis, Illinois, Riot of 1917

From 1910 and the U.S. entry into World War I in April 1917, East St. Louis, Illinois, grew rapidly. It developed as an important center of food processing, as well as manufacturing. The population similarly expanded. It had only 59,000 residents according to the 1910 census; approximately 10 percent were African American. By the time of the 1920 census, there were 66,000, of whom 7,200 were African American.

The rapid increase in population led, naturally, to increased contact between African Americans, native-born whites, and immigrants. That conflict was exacerbated by the competition over jobs. Several of the leading manufacturing companies in East St. Louis were believed to be encouraging African American migration from the South as a way of driving down labor costs. There was widespread talk that companies like the American Ore Company had sent recruiters to Mississippi and Alabama promising employment to African Americans who would relocate to East St. Louis.

Violence first appeared on May 28 when a rumor circulated among white workers that an African American man had robbed a white man. Throughout the night, whites randomly attached African Americans on the streets. Those tensions boiled over again on the evening of July 1, 1917, when a car road through the African American section of East St. Louis and indiscriminately fired into homes. The African American community quickly assembled. The next time a car was spotted with armed men inside, those community members fired on it. Unfortunately, the occupants were police officers and a newspaper reporter.

A congressional committee convened to investigate the riot reporting the extent of the damage; many black workers were killed, thousands driven from their homes, and dozens of railroad cars destroyed. The committee laid the blame on the bitter feelings between the races. The Aluminum Ore Company had used the new immigrants as strikebreakers, which led to particular animosity.

On the morning of July 2, as news of the deaths of the two police officers spread, riot swept East St. Louis. The bullet-riddled police car was left on display outside police headquarters, stirring anger. During the morning of July 2, there was confusion about what was happening. The congressional committee implied that blacks instigated violence without provocation and, in response, white residents formed into mobs to retaliate. Yet, even the committee acknowledged that the violence turned on East St. Louis blacks, and with a vengeance. The city police stood by while helpless blacks were mobbed. Sometimes they joined in the terror.

The congressional committee saw the city government as corrupt. They took bribes to protect bars, prostitution businesses, and gambling businesses. The committee's report, which was based on volumes of testimony taken in East St. Louis, aimed to lay blame on business and to clean up the city. But even as the committee blamed industry, white rioters, and the local authorities, as well as some African Americans, the local prosecutor was placing much blame on African Americans. A number of community leaders were charged with conspiracy to arm themselves and attack any white men who came into the African American section of East St. Louis. The prosecution turned the community's self-defense into a crime.

East St. Louis stands as an important reminder that African Americans faced enormous hurdles in trying to obtain economic success. Even in places where they worked hard and began to succeed, their communities might be destroyed.

See also: Great Migration; White Mob Violence

Alfred L. Brophy

Bibliography
Barnes, Harper. *Never Been a Time: The 1917 Race Riot That Sparked the Civil Rights Movement.* New York: Walker, 2008.
Lumpkins, Charles L. *American Pogrom: The East St. Louis Race Riot and Black Politics.* Athens: Ohio University Press, 2008.
Rudwick, Elliott. *Race Riot at East St. Louis.* Carbondale: Southern Illinois University Press, 1964.

Ebony Magazine

Ebony first appeared on November 1, 1945, at a cost of 25 cents. That original issue sold 50,000 copies. The magazine served as a "black" counterpart to the largely "white" photographic magazines of *Life,* founded in 1936, and *Look,* founded in 1937, and originally retained the oversize format of those publications. From its inception, it depicted the accomplishments of African Americans in business and their celebrity in the entertainment industry, demonstrating success stories that met the standards of the white middle class, a policy later criticized by some as creating false goals.

John Harold Johnson created *Ebony* in Chicago, Illinois, the second publication of his Johnson Publishing Company. Born in the small Mississippi delta community of Arkansas City, Arkansas on January 19, 1918, Johnson and his mother moved to Chicago in 1933 to experience the World's Fair and to give the teenager an opportunity to attend high school. While attending DuSable High School, Johnson met Harry Pace of the Supreme Life Insurance Company, who employed the graduate as he continued his education at the University of Chicago. Johnson excelled in his work with Supreme's company magazine and eventually became its editor. The small publication carried information about the African American populace in a style similar to that of *Reader's Digest.* Believing there was a commercial market for such a publication, Johnson gained a $500 loan using his mother's furniture as collateral in November 1942. With that initial investment, Johnson created *Negro Digest* and the Johnson Publishing Company. *Negro Digest* began a consistent trend throughout the history of the company of mimicking successful periodical models of the mainstream "white" press and reformulating them with stories and photographs of interest to the black community. The new publishing company's first office was on the second floor of the Supreme Life Insurance Company building.

Within a year of *Negro Digest*'s inception, its sales reached $50,000. That success, coupled with Johnson's concern with the popular portrayal of African Americans, led him to believe that a new publication was in order. Johnson saw black achievement in business, and in entertainment in the returning African American veterans after the close of World War II. Perhaps more important, he saw such achievement underrepresented by mainstream "white" periodicals. The growth of photojournalism in the late 1930s and early 1940s prompted Johnson to create *Ebony,* a publication saturated with photographs to portray the successes of African Americans and their contributions to American culture.

Johnson announced that he would not seek advertising revenue until the magazine's circulation grew to 100,000 copies, which took seven months to accomplish. When he did reach his advertising threshold, he found that many black businesses were either unable to afford national advertising space or reluctant to devote such substantial portions of their advertising budgets to *Ebony* full-page ads. Johnson responded by writing letters to the presidents of large corporations in an attempt to convince them of the benefits of advertising in the African American press. His argument swayed Eugene McDonald, president of the Zenith Corporation. McDonald was a former military commander and Arctic explorer who had known the African American polar explorer Matthew Henson. Johnson gave Zenith's president an autographed copy of a Henson biography, began a friendship of his own with the leader, and secured an advertising contract. The Zenith account stabilized *Ebony*'s finances and gave entrée into the boardrooms of other "white" companies.

Ebony early avoided "the race question," choosing instead to present a portrait of black success that others in the community could strive toward. Hard work would breed success, argued the Johnson Publishing Company, and the success of some would breed the success of others. *Ebony* revived the Booker T. Washington model of social progress. To boost sales in the late 1940s and early 1950s, the magazine included sexier, more sensational photographs, but recession slowed sales and returned the publication to a more moderate position. By using a white middle class model for success, Johnson and *Ebony* alienated some, but the tone of the magazine changed as the Civil Rights movement's militancy increased. *Ebony* included news on the fight for integration, often praising the activism of African American college students. Along with its profiles of black celebrities, the periodical featured profiles of government officials, legislators, and visiting dignitaries. As the movement's issues changed, so did *Ebony*'s coverage, moving in the 1960s to cover impoverished inner-city living conditions, the racial inequity in educational and hiring practices, and the misapplication of drug laws to entrap African Americans. From the first presidential election of the magazine's tenure, the 1948 Harry Truman victory over Thomas Dewey, *Ebony*'s publisher used the magazine to endorse Democratic candidates. The moves did not exonerate the periodical from further criticism, however, as editorials denouncing militant violence and continued success-story profiles alienated the more radical among the black nationalist and black power communities.

Despite the criticism, *Ebony* featured the writing of many leading African Americans from the liberal intellectual community. Carl T. Rowan and Kenneth Clark contributed articles. Martin Luther King Jr., wrote a column for the periodical called "Advice for Living By." Through the close of the Civil Rights movement proper, and its continuing reverberations in the 1980s, 1990s, and 2000s, *Ebony* has maintained its attempt to represent the black middle class and the successes that lifestyle creates. *Negro Digest* came and went, but *Ebony* remained the backbone of the Johnson Publishing Company. John Johnson parlayed the success of the periodical into a publishing empire, adding magazines such as *Jet, Ebony Man, Ebony Jr!, Ebony International,* and others. Today, the magazine carries a readership of more than 6 million, with almost 2 million subscribers, and remains the pinnacle in its genre. In 1969, Moneta Sleet Jr., an *Ebony* photographer, became the first African American male to win the Pulitzer Prize. His photos and those that followed continue to demonstrate the great African American success story.

See also: BET; *Jet* Magazine

Thomas Aiello

Bibliography

Daniel, Walter C. *Black Journals of the United States.* Westport, CT: Greenwood Press, 1982.

Johnson, John H., and Lerone Bennett Jr. *Succeeding Against the Odds.* New York: Warner Books, 1989.

"The Story of *Ebony*," *Ebony* (November 1953):122–24.

Wolseley, Roland E. *The Black Press, USA,* 2nd ed. Ames: Iowa State University Press, 1971.

Elaine, Arkansas, Riot of 1919

During and after World War I, a series of violent confrontations, known as "race riots," erupted across the country. Along with Houston, East St. Louis, Chicago, Washington, D.C., Omaha, Knoxville, Charleston, Indianapolis, and other cities, Elaine, Arkansas captured national headlines, as racial violence exploded in this rural Mississippi Delta community. More accurately termed a massacre than a riot, whites overwhelmingly perpetrated the violence against African Americans who died in far greater numbers and who, ironically, were the only ones charged with a crime.

On September 30, 1919, a secret meeting of local African Americans gathered late at a church in Hoop Spur, a rural area in Phillips County located three miles north of the small town of Elaine, Arkansas. Protected by armed guards, those attending were members of the Progressive

Farmers and Household Union. This secretly organized union of black farmers wanted a greater share of the profits for cotton tenant farmers and fairer, more open debt terms for sharecroppers. Although African Americans accounted for three-fourths of the population of this southeastern Arkansas county, situated on the west bank of the Mississippi, the landowners were overwhelmingly whites who leased the land to the county's black majority under exploitive terms that greatly favored the landowners. Frustrated by their long-term economic oppression and emboldened by their recent participation in the war fought to make the world "safe for democracy," African Americans organized the Farmers Union to effect change and improve their lives. Yet their opponents' knowledge of these bold plans influenced law enforcement's intervention. Outside the church that night, a gun fight between union members and two law enforcement officers left one of the white officers dead and sparked the violent retaliation that ensued the next few days.

A law enforcement posse arrived in Hoop Spur from Helena, the county seat, to investigate the shooting. More deaths—white and black—occurred during this confrontation. Shocked that African Americans fought back, the sheriff issued before dawn a panic call for help to whites in surrounding Delta counties in Arkansas and Mississippi. By sunset October 1, 600 to 1,000 whites had arrived armed and ready to kill any African American who moved. For two days whites aggressively hunted and killed African Americans. They also captured, interrogated, and forced false confessions from terrified blacks. Meanwhile Governor Charles Brough requested troops from nearby Fort Pike to quell the violence. After some delay, the troops arrived by train early on October 2. Some accounts credit the soldiers with disarming rampaging whites and restoring order. Other witnesses reported that some soldiers, armed with machine guns, also engaged in indiscriminate killing before disarming white civilians.

Once the violence subsided, official reports acknowledged 25 black and 5 white deaths. Yet widely circulated, unofficial accounts reveal that white mobs killed many more blacks; frequently reported estimates range from scores to hundreds. Local whites and soldiers who perpetrated this retaliatory violence had no interest in securing an accurate death count that reflected large number of black victims. The white power structure immediately began constructing a narrative that blamed African Americans for the riots, alleging that blacks were plotting to kill their white landowners. This explanation, they reasoned, justified whites' violence as a preemptive defense. Although no evidence ever emerged to support this alleged plot, when the killing stopped, the arrests began, but only for the alleged killers of white victims. Within weeks, 122 African Americans were charged with crimes associated with the riots. Arkansas never arrested or charged any whites with a crime, nor did the state seek justice for any of the black victims.

In all, 67 indicted blacks pled guilty to reduced charges and began their prison terms immediately. The grand jury indicted 12 blacks with first-degree murder on October 31, and the trials began on Monday, November 3, one month after the massacre. Court-appointed attorneys never met with defendants, questioned jurors, or called witnesses. Outside the court house a white mob gathered, threatening to lynch any defendants that jurors failed to convict. Each jury deliberated no more than eight minutes before delivering a guilty verdict. By week's end all 12 men had been found guilty and sentenced to death. The white power structure of Arkansas considered the matter closed, but a black attorney from Little Rock and the NAACP, independent of each others' actions, simultaneously challenged this gross injustice.

Scipio Africanus Jones, a successful black attorney from Little Rock, organized the local black community to support an appeal for the Elaine Twelve. Unknown to Jones, the NAACP was also preparing an appeal and had already hired a local white attorney, Colonel George Murphy. The NAACP's involvement began earlier when it sent Walter White to investigate the riot. White, the NAACP's executive secretary who could "pass" for white with his fare skin and blue eyes, posed as a Chicago *Daily News* reporter interested in a good story. White's investigation garnered candid information from whites that the NAACP used to counter the cover-up interpretation that the white power structured offered the local press. Murphy and Jones partnered their efforts on the appeal process until Murphy died two years later. Jones continued with Murphy's partner and later with Moorefield Storey, president of the NAACP.

After several years of determined effort, close calls, and frustrating results, the case eventually appeared before the United States Supreme Court as *Moore v. Dempsey.* Jones and Storey argued on appeal that mob intimidation at the trial denied the defendants a fair trial. In February 1923, Oliver Wendell Holmes, speaking for the majority, issued a landmark decision supporting their argument.

All 12 condemned men were released and all others imprisoned from the Elaine riots were set free.

See also: National Association for the Advancement of Colored People; Red Summer Race Riots; Wells-Barnett, Ida B.; White Mob Violence

Janet G. Hudson

Bibliography

Cortner, Richard C. *A Mob Intent on Death: The NAACP and the Arkansas Riot Cases.* Middletown, CT: Wesleyan University Press, 1988.

Stockley, Grif. *Blood in Their Eyes: The Elaine Race Massacres of 1919.* Fayetteville: University of Arkansas, 2001.

Whayne, Jeannie M. "Low Villains and Wickedness in High Places: Race and Class in the Elaine Riors." *Arkansas Historical Quarterly* 58 (1999):285–313.

Ellison, Ralph

Born in 1913 in Oklahoma City, Oklahoma, Ralph Waldo Ellison (1913–1994) authored *Invisible Man,* one of the most read novels of the 20th century. Published in 1952 and hailed as one of the great "protest novels" of American history, *Invisible Man* depicted the saga of an unnamed protagonist on his journey from his boyhood home to college to New York City. The odyssey allows the protagonist to discover his identity, as a member of a caste and as a human.

Invisible Man opens with the protagonist (known as Invisible Man or IM) living in a garret in New York City, lighting his apartment with 1,369 light bulbs using stolen electricity. Yet, IM seems immune from liability for stealing the electricity and for assaulting a man he meets on the street. This was strange to modern readers, who were so used to seeing African Americans as the objects of intense scrutiny by police and prosecutors. But people visible for some reasons still may not be *seen;* their humanity may be completely ignored, as Ellison reminds us in his 1981 introduction. Lynching victims, for instance, can be "illuminated by flaming torches and flashbulbs," but they are mere objects, not humans. The Invisible Man understands that principle of remaining invisible to the police. At one point during the novel he is told, "The longer you remain unknown to the police, the longer you'll be effective." (*Invisible Man,* p. 284)

The novel then narrates how IM arrived in New York. It returns to his home in Greenwood. The name is an allusion

to the Greenwood section of Tulsa, Oklahoma, which witnessed a terrible riot in 1921. IM witnesses the last words of his grandfather. The grandfather—who is notorious in the community as an agreeable black man who is complicit with whites—changes temperament on his deathbed. The grandfather tells IM to agree the white man to death. All of that sets up a battle royale of blindfolded, adolescent black boys fighting against each other for the amusement of a white audience. Those who survive the contest of all against all are given the chance to scramble for worthless coins. In essence, there is no way to "win." Shortly after that, IM dreams that there is a letter inside his briefcase with instructions that say "keep this Nigger-boy running."

IM then goes to a black college (believed to be modeled on Tuskegee), where he serves as a chauffeur to a wealthy white donor on the board of trustees. He follows the instructions given him by the donor to show the poor neighborhoods. That angers the college president, who is surprised that IM would be honest with a white man. IM is then sent to New York City by the college president. He is given letters of reference that, in effect, say "keep this nigger boy running."

It is in New York that IM searches for his humanity and individuality. In one important scene, for instance, IM helps an elderly couple who are being evicted from their apartment. IM sees the evidence of their humanity strewn on the sidewalk—emancipation papers, a picture of Lincoln, a souvenir from the World's Fair, a breast pump, a card addressed to grandma—and realizes that the couple represents common humanity. What are they being evicted from, IM asks? For they have little. All they have is the "great constitutional dream book." And even that they could not read. The "laws" failed to protect the community. IM's refrain was "we're a law abiding people." But the elderly couple was being evicted and how could that be consistent with law? Well, it was what was demanded by the police officers:

> [L]ook up there in the doorway at that law standing there with his forty-five. Look at him, standing with his blue steel pistol and his serge suit, or one forty-five, you see ten for every one of us, ten guns and ten warm suits and ten fat bellies and ten million laws. *Laws,* that's what we call them down South! Laws! (*Invisible Man,* p. 278)

The eviction scene juxtaposes "law" as imposed by white police officers, prosecutors, and judges with justice. It also juxtaposes law with religion. IM asked, "They don't want the world, but only Jesus. They only want Jesus, just fifteen minutes of Jesus on the rug-bare floor…How about it, Mr. Law? Do we get our fifteen minutes worth of Jesus? You got the world, can we have our Jesus?" (*Invisible Man,* p. 279)

In another scene, IM is working in a paint factory, where he mixes a batch of "National Monument White" paint. He makes it whiter by dropping black paint into a vat of white paint. In an almost transparent way, Ellison alludes to the ways that black and white culture are mixed and how some parts of white culture originate (and draw from) black thought.

Another theme is that of insider versus outsider (or power versus individuality). In one scene, for instance, Brother Clifton, who is selling paper dolls on the street, is shot by a police officer. Brother Clifton died "resisting reality in the form of a.38 caliber revolver in the hands of the arresting officer, on Forty-second between the library and the subway" The shooting of Brother Clifton illustrates the conflict between myth and history. Although Ellison believed that Clifton was an innocent victim, others who were not there might not. "[I]t is only the known, the seen, the heard and only those events that the recorder regards

Ralph Ellison, whose novel Invisible Man *has become a classic of modern American fiction, wrote compellingly of the experience of African Americans in a society that has tended to ignore their problems. (National Archives)*

as important that are put down, those lies his keepers keep their power by….Where were the historians today? And how would they put it down?" (*Invisible Man,* p. 439)

That problem of history as written and history as it happened, of myth versus reality, was a critical part of Ellison's thought. He spoke about it in a talk, "Going to the Territory," at Brown University in 1979. There he reminded listeners that myth controls our vision of ourselves and shapes how we behave, but that grim and complex reality of the past also affects us. It was from that interaction of myth and reality—of mixing and interdependence of black and white—that concerned Ellison.

Now that we have passed the 50th anniversary of the publication of *Invisible Man,* we are gaining the distance that is necessary to evaluate dispassionately the novel and the civil rights revolution that surrounds it. After the initial, warm embrace of the novel, Ralph Ellison was seen as a conservative in the 1960s and early 1970s and consequently, given the political double standard applied to African American intellectuals, was viewed with suspicion. In more recent times, we have been able to view his accomplishments more accurately.

Perhaps part of the explanation for the criticism of Ellison was his faith in the idea of law to overcome inequality. Many others, faced with laughably biased mechanisms of law enforcement, did not share Ellison's optimism in law. At times even Ellison could not share that optimism. As he tells in his meditation on law and literature, "The Perspective of Literature," as a young man he had little respect for law. He recalled of his youth in Oklahoma City that law meant the arbitrary dictates of law enforcement officers. Those men followed their own caprice and left the black community with unequal schools, little protection against violence, and little access to the rights of citizens to participate in democracy. They even participated in lynchings on occasion. Thus, there were two concepts about "law" in the Oklahoma of Ellison's youth: the rule of law as imposed by white society on African Americans and the rule of law as it ought to exist. In his notes on *Juneteenth,* Ellison further elaborated the distinction. The law defined African Americans in certain ways that were inconsistent with the facts and that was inconsistent with religion:

The law deals with facts, and down here the facts are that we are weak and inferior. But while it looks like we are what the law says we are, don't ever forget that we've been put in this position by force, by power of numbers, and the readiness of those numbers to use brutality to keep us within the law. Ah, but the truth is something else. We are not what the law, yes and custom, says we are and to protect our truth we have to protect ourselves from the definitions of the law. Because the law's facts have made us outlaws. Yes, that's the truth, but only part of it;....we're outlaws in Christ and Christ is the higher truth. (*Juneteenth,* p. 354)

Ellison looked forward in *Invisible Man* to a new understanding of multiracial humanity. He wrote of a symbolic poster of a heroic figure:

An American Indian couple, representing the dispossessed past; a blond brother (in overalls) and a leading Irish sister, representing the dispossessed present; and Brother Tod Clifton and a young white couple (it had been felt unwise simply to show Clifton and the girl) surrounded by a group of children of mixed races, representing the future (*Invisible Man,* p. 385)

In Ellison's Oklahoma, there was segregation in housing and schools and extreme examples of racial violence, particularly the Tulsa Race Riot of 1921. And yet somehow Ellison, like the Oklahoma black community more generally, found an optimism in the idea of justice. Perhaps that optimism came from Roscoe Dunjee, editor of the *Oklahoma City Black Dispatch.* Dunjee had a faith in the Constitution and the rule of law, if properly administered, to remake American society. Dunjee advanced the idea of equal treatment under law—that people should be able to vote regardless of their race, that everyone had the right to adequate schools, that the police should protect all communities.

We should avoid too much of a temptation to read subsequent history back onto the novel, but it seems that some of Ellison's optimism in the Constitution's possibilities appears in *Invisible Man,* particularly in its call for a recognition of humanity and individuality. Ellison was working on the novel at the same time that the decisions that brought us to *Brown v. Board of Education* (several of the most important of which arose in Oklahoma, largely through the efforts of Roscoe Dunjee) were being written. *Invisible Man* and the Supreme Court drew on the common reservoir of cultural opposition to group identity and racial caste. At long last, the Court awoke to the realities of segregation and allowed African Americans to have a legal status other than that of invisible people. Maybe Ellison's most important contribution comes in his shaping of a humanity that undermined the segregation mentality. Thus, a nonlegal

document, concerned about people who are left outside the law, has implications for law. And in that era of the early 1950s, Ellison's optimistic call for seeing through—seeing humanity—was fulfilled in some important ways in the decision of the United States Supreme Court in *Brown v. Board of Education.*

In Ellison's other work, we see similar themes. In his posthumously published novel, *Juneteenth,* Ellison explored the life of jazz musician-turned preacher, Alonzo Hickman. Hickman became a preacher after his brother was falsely accused of raping a white woman and then lynched. Hickman raised that woman's baby, Bliss, in the hopes that Bliss (a boy of ambiguous racial identity) might bring African American values to the white community. Bliss, however, grows into a race-baiting politician who is elected senator from a southern state. When Reverend Hickman gets wind of a plot to assassinate Bliss (now Senator Sunraider), he comes to warn the senator. But Hickman is prevented from seeing Senator Sunraider by a "law" (a law enforcement officer) who stands guard outside the Capitol building. And, thus, Sunraider is shot on the Senate floor by an assassin (who is also his black son)!

Through *Invisible Man,* we can see how African Americans created lives despite segregation, how elegant ideas like equality and humanity remade the law, and how that story is at the center of our continuing American struggle. *See also:* Wright, Richard

Alfred L. Brophy

Bibliography
Brophy, Alfred L., ed. "Ralph Ellison and the Law." *Oklahoma City University Law Review* 26 (2001):823–1081.
Callahan, John F. ed. *The Collected Essays of Ralph Ellison.* New York: Modern Library, 1995.
Ellison, Ralph. *Invisible Man.* New York: Random House, 1952.
Ellison, Ralph. *Juneteenth.* New York: Random House, 1999.
Morel, Lucas, ed. *Ralph Ellison and the Raft of Hope: A Political Companion to Invisible Man.* Lexington: The University Press of Kentucky, 2004.

Emancipation Proclamation

When Abraham Lincoln delivered his inaugural address on March 4, 1861, he struck fear into many abolitionists and free blacks when he stated he would not do anything to interfere with the institution of slavery in the states where it already existed; rather he would just prevent the expansion of slavery into the country's territories. Abolitionists were outraged at Lincoln's stance. After the inauguration, leading advocates of immediate emancipation, such as Massachusetts Senator Charles Sumner, tried to convince Lincoln that emancipation needed to be immediate and swift. Lincoln disagreed. He knew that any sudden change in slavery would have dramatic consequences. Initially, Lincoln favored gradual emancipation and financially compensating slave owners. Lincoln also preferred colonization of emancipated slaves—sending them beyond the borders of the United States to live out the rest of their lives.

After the Civil War began on April 12, 1861, with the bombardment of Fort Sumter, Lincoln's primary concern was the preservation of the Union. He did believe, however, that his actions of reuniting the country would ultimately lead to the abolition of slavery throughout the nation, as he recognized slavery to be the root cause of the conflict. Although Lincoln's view of how emancipation would occur was pragmatic, many abolitionists believed that the Civil War provided an opportunity for immediate emancipation. Emancipation, however, was a divisive issue and Lincoln did not want to do anything to alienate the border states—Kentucky, Missouri, Maryland, and Delaware—which still maintained slavery and allegiance to the United States.

Although Lincoln was careful in the war's first year to convey to slave owners that he would not abolish slavery where it existed, some abolitionist Union officers cared little. General John C. Fremont, commanding Union forces in Missouri in 1861, used the Confiscation Act, federal legislation stating that the property of anyone in rebellion could be seized by the United States government, to emancipate slaves. The next year, General David Hunter created more problems for the Lincoln administration on the South Carolina Sea Coast Islands when he armed former slaves and used them as contraband soldiers. Lincoln ordered both of these generals to return the slaves to their masters, fearing these actions might make the border states fearful of Lincoln's intentions to end slavery, thus driving them to secede.

Despite Lincoln's desire to emancipate slaves gradually, pressure for abolishing slavery increased by the end of his first year in office. In November 1861, Lincoln took the first steps toward emancipation when he drafted a plan of gradual, compensated emancipation for Delaware. Lincoln proposed that Delaware free all of its slaves over the age of 35 and when other slaves reached that age, they, too, would be free. In return the federal government would pay Delaware more than $700,000 spread out over a period of 31 years. Lincoln further promised Delaware that, if it would agree to eliminate slavery by 1872, the government would make payments in excess of $70,000 each year for the next decade. Ultimately Lincoln wanted to use money to end slavery. He believed that if the government could compensate slave owners, slave owners would have two choices. They could either accept payment for their slaves or they could leave and go to another slave state. This, however, would drive the supply of slaves in each state up, and therefore the value of slaves as a commodity would decrease. Lincoln surmised that as the price of slaves plummeted, masters would look for a way to rid themselves of their slaves; therefore over the course of time slaves would be freed as an economic necessity.

Lincoln's plan of gradual and compensated emancipation, although in theory might have worked, did not comply with the emancipationist vision of abolitionists and free blacks who demanded immediate action. That swift action began in the summer of 1862 when Lincoln signed the Militia Act. This legislation not only gave the chief executive the authority to call 300,000 state militia troops for a period of nine months, but also gave the president the right to accept the service of African Americans. Even though Lincoln was not yet ready in the summer of 1862 to accept the widespread armed service of African Americans, he was prepared to accept them in limited numbers. Furthermore and most important, the Militia Act empowered the president to emancipate any slaves who enrolled into the service.

The giant step toward emancipation came on July 22, 1862, less than one week after the Militia Act passed both houses of Congress, when Lincoln informed his cabinet that he intended to issue a proclamation to end slavery. Reaction to Lincoln's proposed decree was mixed among his cabinet, but Lincoln explained to them that abolishing slavery was critical to the Union war effort. After all, hundreds of thousands of slaves throughout the Confederacy labored in war industries, built fortifications, and aided in running farms, freeing up a considerable amount of the white male population to enlist and fight for the Confederacy. If these slaves could be freed, it would have a dramatic impact on the Confederate labor supply and ability to support the troops in the field. His cabinet now stood behind him, but his Secretary of State, William Seward, advised Lincoln to not issue the Emancipation Proclamation until the Union Army of the Potomac, operating in the east, won a battle. Despite Union victories in the west in 1861 and 1862, the central focus of the war was in Virginia. If Lincoln issued his proclamation amid Union defeat in Virginia, it would have little weight, as the success of the proclamation depended on whether or not the Union forces could win the war. Lincoln agreed and decided to wait for a Union victory in the East.

The long-awaited victory came on September 17, 1862, at the battle of Antietam (Sharpsburg) in Maryland. Although considered a victory by the Lincoln administration, Antietam was in reality a tactical draw—neither side won. It could be portrayed as a victory, however, because General Robert E. Lee's Army of Northern Virginia retreated south across the Potomac River and into Virginia. On September 22, five days after the battle, Lincoln issued his preliminary Emancipation Proclamation.

The preliminary proclamation announced that on January 1, 1863, Lincoln would declare slaves in areas in rebellion against the United States free; border states would not have their slaves emancipated. Lincoln's Emancipation Proclamation parted drastically with his earlier idea of gradual, compensated emancipation as well as colonization. Nothing in his proclamation said it would be gradual or compensated; rather it would be swift and decisive—if the Union army of course won the Civil War. He also included a provision in the document allowing for the enlistment of African Americans into the army and navy.

When Lincoln's Emancipation Proclamation was announced after Antietam, it met mixed reactions among soldiers in the Union Army. General George B. McClellan, who at the time commanded the Union Army of the Potomac that fought Lee at Antietam, condemned the proclamation and many soldiers were outraged as they claimed to have not enlisted in the Union army to fight for the freedom of the slaves. Internal rage among Union soldiers escalated into near scenes of mutiny in some regiments. Entire units

The first reading of the Emancipation Proclamation before the cabinet on July 22, 1862, after a painting by F. B. Carpenter. Abraham Lincoln, seated next to table, is surrounded by members of his cabinet. (Library of Congress)

condemned Lincoln's measure and signed petitions to be sent to President Lincoln stating that they refused to fight. Union soldiers vented their frustration in other ways as well. In December 1862, as the Union Army of the Potomac crossed the Rappahannock River and entered Fredericksburg, they destroyed much of the town. Some soldiers explained that one of the reasons they lashed out was that they did not approve of emancipation.

Soldiers aside, many politicians criticized Lincoln's measure. For example a former associate justice of the United States Supreme Court, Benjamin Robbins Curtis, argued in a pamphlet he published in late 1862, *Executive Power,* that the president did not have the power to issue an executive order eliminating slavery—something that was legally allowed in the states under the Constitution. Other prominent figures such as Joel Parker, a Republican judge from Massachusetts, and former Speaker of the House of Representatives, Robert C. Winthrop, criticized the Emancipation Proclamation and stated that Lincoln had overstepped his powers as chief executive.

Many southern Unionists—those who lived in the Confederacy, but swore allegiance to the United States government—were also outraged at the Emancipation Proclamation. They believed that it contradicted Lincoln's first inaugural address and that the war should not be turned into a war of emancipation. Despite the disapproval of many Unionists, they eventually recognized the importance of slavery as a major resource for the Confederacy and viewed the abolition of slavery as a means to achieve Union victory in the Civil War.

A barrage of antiemancipation editorials appeared throughout the country. Even though these might have concerned Lincoln and served as a good indicator of what many felt about emancipation, Lincoln knew the real test would be the 1862 elections. Republicans who supported emancipation failed the test miserably. The Republicans lost seats in the United States House of Representatives when Democrats won the majority of seats for Pennsylvania and Ohio. In the New York and New Jersey gubernatorial elections, the citizens elected Democrats. In Lincoln's home state of Illinois, 11 of the 14 seats in the House of Representatives would be occupied by Democrats. The Democrats also won a 28-seat majority in the Illinois state legislature. In all, the interim election of 1862 was a dismal failure for Lincoln and the Republicans, as 31 Republican seats were lost in Congress. Many Northerners had sent a clear message

to Lincoln—they would not support an administration and party who made emancipation a war aim.

Even though Lincoln had early enemies of emancipation in the North, there were some who supported him and recognized the importance of emancipation as a way to bring the conflict to an end. General Henry Halleck, who at the time served as Lincoln's general-in-chief, believed emancipation was a great weapon in the Union arsenal. Halleck argued that every slave taken from the South and out of the Confederacy's labor supply was the equivalent of one Confederate soldier being taken from the battlefield. Lincoln had other supporters as well. Horace Greeley's *New York Tribune* praised the Emancipation Proclamation and hailed it as the beginning of the end of the Confederacy.

Despite the criticism of both Republicans and Democrats, Lincoln proceeded with his Emancipation Proclamation and formally issued it on New Year's Day, 1863. On the date the Emancipation Proclamation went into effect, African Americans, both slaves and free blacks, rejoiced. Crowds gathered around the White House and praised Lincoln. African Americans and abolitionists throughout Northern cities celebrated. African American troops already in service as a result of the Militia Act signed in 1862 celebrated as well. For example troops in the First Kansas Colored Volunteer Infantry held a ceremony and celebration at Fort Scott Kansas in honor of the Emancipation Proclamation. Despite the joy that many African Americans felt on January 1, 1863, many understood that the only way their freedom would be guaranteed was that if the Union army won the Civil War.

By the time Lincoln issued the formal declaration, he still had his detractors, but many of the soldiers, initially outraged at the prospect of fighting to free the slaves, had calmed their anger. Regardless of their feelings toward slavery and emancipation, many Union troops began to understand that emancipation was a great weapon to defeat the Confederacy, as it would strip away thousands of workers from the Confederate labor force. Although not all soldiers were eager to enforce emancipation, some of them were. Among those enthusiastic to implement emancipation were the large majority of troops commanded by Union General Robert H. Milroy. On January 1, 1863, Milroy marched his troops into Virginia's northern Shenandoah Valley. Milroy, an Indiana native with abolitionist leanings, established headquarters in Winchester, Virginia, on the date the Emancipation Proclamation took effect. General Milroy issued his own proclamation on January 5—"Freedom to Slaves"—informing the citizens of the northern Shenandoah Valley that he would do everything in his power to enforce emancipation, and those who interfered would be arrested and sent beyond Union lines. Furthermore, and just as Lincoln had explained in his Emancipation Proclamation, Milroy informed the former slaves that he expected them to behave themselves and to occupy themselves with some task. The Indiana general took great pride in enforcing emancipation in a town that boasted as residents Senator James Mason, author of the 1850 Fugitive Slave Law, and Judge Richard Parker, who presided over John Brown's trial in Charles Town, Virginia, in 1859. Milroy freed hundreds of slaves and put them to work for his command or put those who wanted to go north on trains.

News of Lincoln's Emancipation Proclamation and the actions of generals such as Milroy, who took an active roll in seeing that emancipation was carried out, created fear among many Confederate officials. Virginia's Governor John Letcher branded Lincoln and Milroy as war criminals attempting to incite a slave insurrection. It was even ordered that if Milroy were captured, he should be executed without any trial.

Even though Union generals such as Milroy spread the word about emancipation, there were many areas throughout the Confederacy that Union troops were unable to reach, and slave owners withheld news of the Emancipation Proclamation from the slaves. Fearing that slaves would not hear of their liberation, Lincoln called on Frederick Douglass in the summer of 1863 to organize a group of African American scouts to go throughout the South, spread the news of emancipation, and help the slaves to come into Union lines. Douglass thought the measure of carrying off large numbers of slaves, without proper military support, in Confederate territory was too risky. Instead, Douglass suggested that Lincoln use special agents who would go into the South and tell the slaves that the president had issued a proclamation declaring their freedom, but that the slaves should remain where they were and that they should plan their own escape. Lincoln agreed with Douglass's plan.

Confederate officials became enraged further with Lincoln's Emancipation Proclamation because it not only freed slaves, but it opened the door for the widespread recruitment of African Americans—many of whom were former slaves—into the Union army. Even though African American troops had been serving in the Union Army as a result of the Militia Act, Confederate officials understood that the Emancipation Proclamation would dramatically swell the ranks of African Americans in the federal army. The thought of armed African Americans struck fear into many white Southerners. The Confederate government aimed to do something about it. To discourage African Americans from enlisting, Confederate President Jefferson Davis and the Confederate Congress ordered that captured African Americans would not be treated as prisoners of war; rather they would be regarded as slaves in armed rebellion in the state where they were captured and would be subject to the punishment of that state for being involved in a slave rebellion. The punishment was always death. Davis also encouraged the execution of captured white officers who commanded African American regiments. Furthermore, Davis recommended that African American sailors captured from the Potomac Flotilla be executed by hanging. These threats did little to deter African Americans from enlisting and fighting for their freedom. Nearly 200,000 African Americans volunteered for service in the U.S. Army and Navy.

As 1863 came to a close and the presidential election year of 1864 approached, Lincoln made every effort to pass the Thirteenth Amendment, formally abolishing slavery. Lincoln understood that the Emancipation Proclamation was a war measure and that to officially outlaw slavery, which was protected under the Constitution, the Constitution needed to be amended. After he won reelection, Lincoln pressured Congress to act. He believed that the passage of a constitutional amendment abolishing slavery would have a tremendously positive impact on the course of the Civil War. Furthermore, Lincoln surmised that if the border states, which still maintained slavery, ratified the amendment, it would break Confederate morale even further. The amendment passed Congress on January 31, 1865, and became law on December 6, 1865, when states ratified the amendment. Unfortunately, Lincoln, who had been assassinated in April 1865, would not live to see the ultimate achievement of his Emancipation Proclamation.

The Emancipation Proclamation marked a major turning point in American history and was perhaps the greatest legacy of the American Civil War. Abraham Lincoln was revered among African Americans as their great emancipator. Even years after the Civil War ended, January 1 held special meaning for African Americans and they celebrated emancipation day in both North and South well into the 20th century.

See also: Abolition, Slavery; Douglass, Frederick; Lincoln, Abraham; Thirteenth Amendment

Jonathan A. Noyalas

Bibliography

Berlin, Ira, Leslie S. Rowland, and Steven F. Miller. *Slaves No More: Three Essays on Emancipation and the Civil War.* New York: Cambridge University Press, 1992.

Blight, David W., and Brooks D. Simpson, eds. *Union and Emancipation: Essays on Politics and Race in the Civil War Era.* Kent, OH: Kent State University Press, 1997.

Guelzo, Allen C. "Defending Emancipation: Abraham Lincoln and the Conkling Letter, 1863." *Civil War History* 48 (2002): 313–37.

Guelzo, Allen C. *Lincoln's Emancipation Proclamation: The End of Slavery in America.* New York: Simon and Schuster, 2004.

Jenkins, Wilbert L. *Climbing Up to Glory: A Short History of African Americans During the Civil War and Reconstruction.* Wilmington, DE: Scholarly Resources, 2002.

Klingaman, William K. *Abraham Lincoln and the Road to Emancipation.* New York: Viking, 2001.

Krug, Mark M. "Lincoln, the Republican Party, and the Emancipation Proclamation," *The History Teacher* 7 (1973):48–61.

McConnell, Roland C. "From Preliminary to Final Emancipation Proclamation the First Hundred Days," *The Journal of Negro History* 48 (1963):260–76.

McPherson, James M. *Antietam: The Battle That Changed the Course of the Civil War.* Oxford, UK: Oxford University Press, 2002.

Quarles, Benjamin. *Lincoln and the Negro.* Oxford, UK: Oxford University Press, 1962.

Wiggins, William H. *O Freedom!: Afro-American Emancipation Celebrations.* Nashville: University of Tennessee Press, 1987.

Ethiopian Peace Movement

The Italo-Ethiopian War (1935–1936) and the Italian occupation of Ethiopia (1936–1941) sparked a support movement among African Americans for Ethiopia that led to variety of actions and reactions. Along with Liberia, Ethiopia was one of only two independent African nations by the early 20th century, and it was the only independent African nation run by indigenous Africans. As such, Ethiopia became a symbol for many in the African Diaspora, including African Americans in the United States. In the imperialist fervor of the 1890s, Italy had sought to conquer Ethiopia, but had lost badly in its attempt to do so, culminating in its loss at the Battle of Adowa (1896). Ethiopia thus remained independent throughout the first third of the 20th century.

When the Fascist leader Benito Mussolini came to power in Italy in the 1920s, he promised a program of nationalist glory, including a more vigorous foreign policy. By the early 1930s, Mussolini began to covet Ethiopia in order to expand the Italian empire in northeastern Africa and to seek revenge for the Italian setbacks of the 1890s. After a brief skirmish along the Ethiopian border with Italian Eritrea in November 1934, the Italian government demanded an apology and an indemnity from Emperor Haile Selassie and the Imperial Ethiopian government. Selassie refused and tensions mounted; the emperor pleaded for help from the League of Nations, of which Ethiopia was a member, but the League did very little to stop Italian aggression. The League was led by the British and French, who feared pushing Mussolini into Adolf Hitler's camp. Hitler, however, learned a lesson from this episode about the use of a policy of appeasement by the British and the French.

Unhampered by the League of Nations, Italy invaded Ethiopia on October 3, 1935, with an army of 120,000 men. The Italians quickly captured Adowa, the site of their humiliating loss in the 1890s. The Ethiopians held out as long as they could, but, unlike in the 1890s, this time Italy had a superior fighting force and superior technology. The Italians used modern weapons such as tanks, airplanes, and even used poison gas on Ethiopian combatants and civilians. In May 1936, Emperor Selassie went into exile, eventually settling in London. During World War II, Italian Ethiopia was invaded by an Allied force of mostly African colonial troops led by the British. In May 1941, Italy was ousted from Ethiopia, and the British reluctantly installed Haile Selassie on the throne of the independent nation of Ethiopia.

African Americans responded vigorously to the Ethiopian crisis of the mid-1930s. As Italy began threatening Ethiopia in 1934, Africans and people of African descent around the world spoke out in support of Ethiopia and against Italian aggression. The Italo-Ethiopian conflict thus led to an outpouring of black nationalism (in Africa and in the Diaspora), pan-Africanism, and a general philosophy of anti-imperialism. In the United States, the conflict led African Americans to organize in support of Ethiopia: sometimes for peace, sometimes for Ethiopian independence, and sometimes to support the Ethiopian military in its war against Italy.

A number of African American, women's, religious, and peace organizations attempted to influence U.S. policymakers, international organizations like the League of Nations, and public opinion in favor of Ethiopian independence. The peak of organizational activity occurred between the opening of hostilities in 1934 and the Italian victory in 1936. For example, in March 1935, the NAACP sent a telegram to the League of Nations and the U.S. State Department outlining its opposition to an Italian takeover of Ethiopia. Between December 1934 and May 1935, the Women's International League for Peace and Freedom (WILPF) sent three telegrams to the League of Nations calling for League action to ensure a peaceful resolution to the Italo-Ethiopian border dispute.

Besides already existing organizations like the NAACP and the WILPF, new organizations were created to support peace initiatives and give any support they could to Ethiopia. Among the many new organizations founded during the Ethiopian crisis of the mid-1930s were the Provisional Committee for the Defense of Ethiopia (Harlem), the Friends of Ethiopia in America (New York), the Committee for Ethiopia (New York), the Joint Committee for the Defense of Ethiopia (Chicago), the Chicago Society for the Aid of Ethiopia, and many others around the country. These organizations were created to give support to Ethiopia, whether moral, monetary, or otherwise. These new organizations, along with the older ones like the NAACP, worked to raise funds to send to Ethiopia, usually for military or aid purposes. Sometimes in lieu of money, specific items were sent: an ambulance, medical supplies, or weapons. Besides fundraising, these organizations worked to raise awareness about Ethiopia as well. Numerous African American individuals contacted these organizations, the federal government, or members of the Ethiopian government to volunteer their services or give money to the Ethiopian cause.

Throughout the Italo-Ethiopian conflict, the U.S. government remained officially neutral, although, like the League of Nations, the U.S. government enacted a partial embargo against the Italians. In 1934 and 1935, many African Americans worked to pressure policymakers in Washington and in Europe into seeking a peaceful resolution to the conflict. Many pointed to the Kellogg-Briand Pact (1928), of which the U.S. was a signatory, which had attempted to outlaw war. The pressure worked to an extent. In August 1935, Secretary of State Cordell Hull asked American diplomats in London and Paris to find out whether or not the United States could help in the peace process. On August 19, 1935, President Roosevelt got involved and sent a message to Italian Premier Benito Mussolini calling for a peaceful resolution to the conflict. The U.S. government gave only minimal rhetorical support to the Ethiopian cause, but support for Ethiopia among African Americans and others continued throughout the war, although it waned by the war's end in 1936. Many African Americans and peace activists continued to oppose the Italian takeover of Ethiopia throughout the late 1930s, and these diehards remained hopeful for the return of the Ethiopian empire, which came about in 1941.

See also: African Diaspora; Black Nationalism; National Association for the Advancement of Colored People; Pan-Africanism; Selassie, Haile

David Turpie

Bibliography
Del Boca, Angelo. *The Ethiopian War, 1935–1941.* Chicago: University of Chicago Press, 1965.
Du Bois, W. E. B. "Inter-Racial Implications of the Ethiopian Crisis." *Foreign Affairs,* 14, no. 1 (1935):82–92.
Harris, Joseph E. *African-American Reactions to War in Ethiopia, 1936–1941.* Baton Rouge: Louisiana State University Press, 1994.
Plummer, Brenda Gayle. *Rising Wind: Black Americans and U.S. Foreign Affairs, 1935–1960.* Chapel Hill: University of North Carolina Press, 1996.
Scott, William R. *The Sons of Sheba's Race: African-Americans and the Italo-Ethiopian War, 1935–1941.* Bloomington: Indiana University Press, 1993.

Evers, Medgar

Medgar Evers (1925–1963) was a prominent Mississippi civil rights leader who pushed for black equality without confrontation. Assassinated in June 1963, at the young age of 37, Evers became a national hero for African Americans across the United States.

Medgar Wiley Evers was born on July 2, 1925 in Decatur, Mississippi. He was born into a typical Southern farming family. His father James and his mother Jessie raised him and his six brothers and sisters to be self-sufficient, hard working, and proud. Throughout his younger years, Evers was taught the importance of education. Although most southern farming families took their children out of school during the harvesting season, the Everses did not. In 1942, Evers dropped out of Newton High School to join the army. After spending a few years in the service, he returned to Newton in 1947 to complete his high school degree. In the same year, Evers successfully voted in the local county election. He had attempted to vote the year before, but was unsuccessful because of white opposition.

After completing high school, Evers enrolled in Alcorn State University, one of only two black universities in Mississippi. Although many African Americans chose a path in teaching, Evers decided to take a different and more radical route, as a business major. At Alcorn, Medgar met his future wife Myrlie Beasley. On Christmas Eve 1951 the two married. The next year Evers graduated from Alcorn. He was instantly hired by a newly created black business—Magnolia Mutual Insurance Company.

While employed by the insurance company, Evers spent most of his time visiting poor black sharecroppers and other southern black families in an attempt to sell them insurance. Medgar always defied the white power structure, but it was not until his experience with the poor blacks of Mississippi that Evers became more directly involved in the civil rights struggles of blacks in the South. Seeing the dreadful conditions of many of the poor southern blacks Evers immediately joined the National Association for the Advancement of Colored People (NAACP). The NAACP, founded in 1909, was one of the most prominent civil rights organizations in the country. The NAACP, however, did not have a Mississippi branch. Evers's efforts changed this. By 1953 the NAACP had 21 branches in Mississippi.

Mississippi was a strongly segregated southern state. Even after the *Brown v. Board of Education* decision, in which the U.S. Supreme Court ruled school segregation unconstitutional, segregation remained strong in Mississippi. To test the *Brown* decision, Evers applied to the University of Mississippi Law School but was denied admission on the basis of his race. Evers fought for admission but was unsuccessful, and the university remained segregated. Despite this setback, the NAACP, impressed with Evers's actions, awarded him the newly created position of field secretary for the state of Mississippi. In this position, Evers became the national NAACP's representative for the state of Mississippi.

With the NAACP, Evers worked emphatically to educate blacks and bring them the right to vote. When segregation continued to run rampant in Mississippi, Evers encouraged blacks to patronize only black-owned businesses. This angered many whites throughout the state. In 1962, James Meredith applied to the University of Mississippi Law School. Meredith was originally denied admittance, but he fought, with the support of Evres and the NAACP, and was awarded admission in September,—a privilege denied to Evers eight years earlier.

Evers's high position with the NAACP and support of black equality decreased his standing within the white community. Increasingly whites in Mississippi were becoming more and more hostile to him. In May 1963, Evers's home was firebombed. Evers was at a nearby church when the firebombing occurred, but his wife Myrlie and their three children, Darrell, Rena, and Van, were at home. The firebombing was deemed an assassination attempt on Evers's life. Nevertheless, he continued in his civil rights battles. The next month, on June 12, 1963, Medgar Evers was shot in front of his home after returning home from a civil rights rally. He died within an hour.

More than 4,000 people came to Evers's funeral both to honor and remember the civil rights activist who died for the battle he fought. He was buried at Arlington National Cemetery in Virginia. Eleven days after Evers's assassination, Byron de la Beckwith was arrested and charged with the murder of Medgar Evers. Beckwith was tried twice by all-white juries and both cases ended in mistrial. Despite strong evidence incriminating Beckwith, neither jury could unanimously decide Beckwith's guilt or innocence. The case was dropped and Beckwith was released. In 1989, evidence surfaced that the juries of the first two trials were tampered with. Consequently, in February 1994, a third trial was held with a biracial jury. This time Beckwith was found guilty of the murder of Medgar Evers.

Evers may not have lived to see the civil rights advances he had long fought for, but he played a large role in bringing them about. His untimely death increased the popularity of the Civil Rights movement. Furthermore, as one of the first martyrs of the cause, his death angered many blacks in the South. No longer would blacks be afraid to stand up against their white counterparts. Instead, the majority of blacks decided to stand up against their opposition and demand equality. On July 2, 1964, the Civil Rights Act of 1964 was passed. Similarly, in August 1965, a Voting Rights Act was passed. With these two acts, Evers's battle had been won. Blacks in both Mississippi and across the nation were awarded the civil rights they had long fought for.

See also: Ku Klux Klan; National Association for the Advancement of Colored People; World War II (Black Participation in)

Mindy R. Weidman

Bibliography
Brown, Jennie. *Medgar Evers.* Los Angeles: Melrose Square Publishing, 1994.
Nossiter, Adam. *Of Long Memory: Mississippi and the Murder of Medgar Evers.* Reading, MA: Addison-Wesley, 1994.

Exoduster Movement

The push for southern blacks to move to Liberia or the mass migration of blacks to the northern United States, otherwise known as the Great Migration, are the most well-known attempts at mass relocation by blacks. Yet, in 1879–1881, approximately 20,000 blacks from southern states such as Mississippi, Louisiana, and primarily Tennessee, moved to Kansas seeking opportunities and hoping to escape the racial discrimination they experienced in the post-Civil War South. Today, little remains of the dozens of towns that these black migrants founded. These migrating blacks were known as "Exodusters." This term drew parallels between the experiences of the Hebrews who left Egypt in search of freedom and the Promised Land with that of blacks who fled the South for their own "Promised Land" in Kansas.

Although the Exoduster movement officially began in 1879, it really began when Abraham Lincoln issued the Emancipation Proclamation, which, in essence, freed the slaves. Although most slaves desperately wanted freedom, a vast majority of the former enslaved had no formal education, were illiterate, had no financial resources, and had nowhere to go. As a result, a number of former enslaved negotiated deals with their former masters that allowed them to stay on the land and share in the profits from the crops produced. These deals greatly benefited the southern landowners, many of who were left destitute after the war and were unable to afford to hire employees to work their land. This tenant farming system was also known as a land-tenant system or sharecropping.

It was nearly impossible for sharecroppers to make a profit in this system. Similarly, the option for them to own land and/or open their own business was a difficult venture, if not impossible in many areas. If they owned the land or had their own businesses, whites routinely harassed them. To secure freedom for southern blacks, a number of leaders emerged to ensure that black men were able to exercise their voting rights and not be tormented by whites.

A growing number of black leaders believed that leaving the South would provide blacks with opportunities and a true sense of freedom. Two key leaders that emerged were Henry Adams of Louisiana and Benjamin "Pap" Singleton of Tennessee.

Henry Adams was born a slave in 1843 in Georgia. His initial foray into politics occurred in 1870 when he voted Republican for the first time. At the time, a vast majority of black men voted Republican, as that was the party of Lincoln and the party that gave the most amount of aid to the poor. He did not think of himself as a political activist, yet Adams encouraged blacks not to vote for the Democratic Party, as they would have their rights slowly diminished and would eventually become slaves again.

In 1875, Adams attended a conference in New Orleans with a number of black ministers and leaders. Their goal was to come up with solutions for the increasing debt that black sharecroppers were accumulating, which prevented them for owning their own land. Blacks also faced staunch opposition when exercising their voting rights. This delegation, otherwise known as The Committee, decided that leaving the South for other parts of the United States, U.S. territories, or Liberia was their best option. Adams and other members of The Committee traveled throughout Louisiana, Texas, and other southern states and found a number of blacks who were willing to leave the South if their voices were not heard in the election of 1876.

The Republican defeat in the 1876 Louisiana state elections was the catalyst that encouraged The Committee to begin preparations to emigrate from the South. The Committee became known as The Colonization Council. Almost 100,000 blacks from Arkansas, Texas, Mississippi, and Louisiana agreed to move to either Liberia or an American territory if President Hayes agreed to the petition to have the federal government pay for the relocation.

This was not the first time that blacks sought to emigrate from the United States. In 1817, the American Colonization Society was organized by whites to encourage freed blacks to move to Liberia. Adams began to solicit aid from the American Colonization Society in 1877 after his requests for aid from President Hayes and Congress went ignored. In 1878, The Colonization Council made attempts to travel to Liberia to inspect it; however, they could not raise enough funds to do so. When it became apparent that neither The Colonization Council nor the individuals emigrating would be able to afford the move to Liberia, their travel options became limited to the United States. Henry Adams began to lose popularity and slowly began to fade from the limelight; however, he was able to encourage thousands of blacks to leave the South for more opportunity elsewhere and many moved to Kansas.

Tired of the treatment that blacks were experiencing, Benjamin "Pap" Singleton began encouraging them to leave their homelands. Unlike other black political leaders, such as Henry Adams, however, Singleton did not think that Liberia was a practical option, and he encouraged blacks to move to Kansas instead. Singleton realized that leaving the South was imperative for black liberation.

Pap Singleton, the central figure in the Exoduster movement, was born a slave in 1809 and raised in Nashville, Tennessee. Singleton eventually escaped slavery and fled to Ontario, Canada, and later to Detroit. While in Detroit, he regularly helped fugitive slaves escape to Canada. Longing for Tennessee, however, he moved back to Nashville after the end of the Civil War. Not much is known about his early life; however, in his early seventies, Singleton began the tireless fight to encourage blacks to leave the South to find more opportunities elsewhere. Singleton did not try to politically mobilize the blacks in Tennessee. The state of Tennessee was far more Democratic and had a significantly smaller black population than other southern states where active attempts at political mobilization were made. Instead, Singleton began to encourage blacks to purchase their own farmlands. In 1874, Singleton helped to form the Edgefield Real Estate Association. This would be quite difficult to do in Tennessee, however, where whites routinely overcharged for the land and refused to sell to black farmers. As a result, Singleton saw more opportunity in the prairie lands of the Midwestern states, especially in Kansas.

Singleton was drawn to Kansas because of the 1862 Homestead Act signed by Abraham Lincoln. This act encouraged farmers to begin to settle the western states and decreed that any American citizen could have up to 160 acres. Having visited Kansas earlier in 1873, in what was then Cherokee County, Singleton thought it the perfect place for blacks in Tennessee to move to. Consequently, in 1875, Singleton later renamed his organization, Edgefield Real Estate and Homestead Association (EREHA). Singleton also firmly believed that racial equality would not be achieved in Tennessee until the blacks were removed from the land and whites were forced to live without blacks, then realizing the importance that blacks played in the area.

Singleton and Columbus M. Johnson, a black minister from Nashville and his EREHA co-founder, began by contacting Tennessee politicians to aid in the cost of transportation for the blacks who wanted to leave for Kansas. After no response from these politicians, Singleton and Johnson began to hold meetings open to blacks and whites, explaining the importance of the plan and to raise enough money for those interested in moving. So much money was raised, in fact, that in 1879, the EREHA began to leave Tennessee with black homesteaders for southern Kansas. Once settled, they incorporated a town they called Singleton Colony near the town of Dunlap in Morris County, Kansas. Approximately 2,400 settlers moved to Singleton Colony, and most of them lived in tents and other makeshift housing.

As word of the Exoduster movement spread, blacks from states such as Louisiana, Missouri, Illinois, Texas, Indiana, and Mississippi joined those from Tennessee in Kansas. Although those blacks were not associated with those from Tennessee, Singleton and the Exodusters from Tennessee helped the movers from other states, especially when white settlers emphasized they did not want so many blacks moving to Kansas.

Singleton testified before the United State Senate in 1880. He told of the poor conditions that led to the migration to Kansas and the success of the black colonies in Kansas, making him the most well-known figure in the Exoduster movement or the "father of the Kansas migration." As much as Singleton wanted to retire and let his colleagues handle the Exodusters, he realized that, although in his seventies, it was his job to remove blacks from Tennessee until the whites there could learn to appreciate them and to then lead them back to Tennessee. Singleton did not retire. Instead, he helped to organize United Colored Links (UCL) in Tennessee Town, a town outside of Topeka named for the large number of blacks who moved from Tennessee. Among the goals of the UCL was racial equality in the United States. After working with the local Republican Party and even Greenback Party presidential candidate James B. Weaver, the UCL was disassembled.

When the UCL failed, Singleton was so discouraged that the decided to encourage blacks to move to Cypress, off the coast of Greece. Later he worked to encourage blacks to move back to Africa. In 1889, Singleton called for Oklahoma to be reserved for blacks; however, soon afterwards, he, too, faded from the limelight and died in 1892.

Throughout the 1870s, blacks began moving to Kansas, but the zeal with which Singleton spoke of migrating to another place certainly inspired blacks to leave states such as Tennessee and Missouri. In fact, more blacks migrated to Kansas during the 1870s than they did during the migration years of 1879–1881. Among the first black colonies, Nicodemus, a black colony founded by colonists from Kentucky in 1877, was thriving when Singleton began the move to Kansas.

In 1878, the Hinds County *Gazette* in Kansas tried to encourage blacks to move to Kansas. Also, the *Colored Citizen,* a black publication based in Kansas, reported on the families who had moved to Kansas and described their positive experiences. As more and more blacks came to settle in Kansas, word spread back to their original homelands telling their friends and family about the opportunities in Kansas. Unlike Nebraska and the other Midwestern states, Kansas played an important role in abolitionist John Brown's battle against slavery and slave states. During the 1850s, this struggle, known as "Bleeding Kansas," took the lives of dozens of people, but Kansas became known as a place where people fought for equality and freedom and a place where blacks had opportunity.

For the most part, although blacks moved to Kansas on their own in large numbers beginning in the early 1870s, and a more organized move followed with Singleton's push to Kansas, the Republican Kansas government never officially welcomed them to the state. Kansas extended the same call to black migrants as they did to whites who were planning the move out West. Although blacks were largely settled in Nicodemus and Singleton Colony, they soon spread throughout Kansas to cities such as Dodge City and Topeka.

As more Exodusters moved to Kansas, many were unable to afford the long trip. Many had a difficult time leaving their home state or even making it past St. Louis, Missouri. There was no free transportation or even free land. These migrants were unable to continue the trip into Kansas. As a result, a number of Exodusters were forced to stay in St. Louis, in what became known as "the Red Sea." Nonetheless, many communities in Kansas continue to have thriving black communities as a result of the thousands of blacks who left the South for Kansas.

See also: Nicodemus, Kansas; Singleton, Benjamin "Pap"; Wells-Barnett, Ida

Angelique Harris

Bibliography

Meacham, M. "The Exoduster Movement." *The Western Journal of Black Studies.* 27 (2003):108–17.

Painter, Nell Irvin. *Exodusters: Black Migration to Kansas After Reconstruction.* New York: Knopf, 1977.

Williams, Nudie E. *Black Newspapers and the Exodusters of 1879.* Topeka: Kansas State Historical Society, 1985.

Fanon, Frantz

Dr. Frantz Fanon (1925–1961) was a psychiatrist, cultural critic, political theorist and diplomat who published on issues of black identity, decolonization, nationalism, and psychology and devoted much of his professional career to fighting for the freedom of Algeria from French colonial rule. Born in Fort-de-France on the island of Martinique in the West Indies in 1925, Fanon was the son of a civil servant and a shopkeeper, whose combined income made them comfortable members of the majority black middle class. Fanon attended French state school where he learned the virtues of the French language, literature, philosophy, and worldview. At the school in Fort-de-France, Fanon studied under Aimé Césaire, who would become a well-known negritude poet and local politician. In 1944, Fanon enlisted in a small battalion of Antillean soldiers and boarded a ship bound for France to fight beside the allies in World War II. He was wounded later that year in France and received a metal for his bravery. Fanon spent his convalescence near Lyon where he would return to study after the war. After completing his formal education in Martinique, Fanon again left for France and, in 1947, entered the school of medicine and pharmacology at the University of Lyon on a government scholarship that granted veterans free tuition and living stipends.

Fanon began work on his first book, *Peau noire, masques blancs (Black Skin, White Masks)* around the time he entered the university. It characterizes his early development as a thinker and his awakening to the meaning behind the subtle racial categorization he experienced as a marginalized subject at home and even more poignantly in France. First published in 1952, *Peau noire, masques blancs* combines elements of literary and social criticism, philosophy, and phenomenology with a psychology of race relations, paying particular attention to the situation of Martinique and its black, French middle-class mentality.

Fanon completed his studies in 1951 with a specialization in psychiatry, began clinical work the same year, and married Marie-Josephe Dublé in 1952. In 1953, Fanon passed the competitive postgraduate qualifying exams that made him a doctor of psychiatry. He took a position in Algeria as the *Chef de service* at the Blida-Joinville psychiatric clinic. While working on his dissertation and in his clinical practice in Lyon, Fanon had treated many North Africans and this, combined with a brief period of training he spent there while in the army, convinced him that there was much humanitarian work awaiting him in the French colony.

In Algeria, Fanon was confronted by a corrupt, indoctrinated, and malpractice-ridden French medical institution that was at best held highly suspect in the eyes of the Algerian citizens. Nevertheless, Fanon diligently worked at his practice, testing experimental methods of social therapy to determine the specific needs of his Algerian clientele and to develop his own firsthand understanding of the extent of psychological pathology produced by colonialism. A year after Fanon's arrival in Blida, the Algerian revolution officially began, and as early as 1955, Fanon started to aid the Front de Libération Nationale (FLN), one of the Algerian nationalist group that led the armed insurrection against French colonial rule, by providing services for them at the hospital. In 1956, as the war escalated and Fanon's participation with the FLN became more involved and publicly suspect, it became clear that continuing his psychiatric practice under any semblance of normal operation was out of the question. Later that year, Fanon officially resigned from his post in Blida and entered exile, not only from Algeria, but also from France and any hope of professional involvement in the French medical community.

Fanon settled in Tunis, where the FLN had set up its operations and where Fanon could work as a psychiatrist in top hospitals and lecture at the university. He was also able to openly write for the FLN's paper *El Moudjahid,* later becoming a spokesman for the party. In 1958, the Provisional Government of the Republic of Algeria (GPRA) formed to lead the nation until independence, and Fanon began to represent the FLN and the GPRA on the international stage, most notably at the All-African People's Congress in Accra. In 1959, on a trip to Morocco to reorganize the FLN's medical services in the west, Fanon suffered a spinal injury in a car accident and subsequently dodged an assassination

Frantz Fanon was a leading ideologist of the anticolonial and Pan-Africanist movements of the 1950s and 1960s. In addition to his intellectual contributions to colonial liberation movements around the world, he also worked with the National Liberation Front during Algeria's struggle for independence. (Algerian Ministry of Information)

attempt in an Italian hospital, but he was back in Tunis less than a month later meeting on FLN policy issues.

Fanon published his second book, *L'An V de la Révolution algérienne (Year V of the Algerian Revolution)* later that year, which contained short studies of five aspects of the war. In 1960, the GPRA sent Fanon to Accra to permanently head a delegation representing them in sub-Saharan Africa, and he traveled all over Francophone Africa in an effort to garner support for the Algerian cause. In late 1960, Fanon was diagnosed with leukemia and underwent treatment in Russia and finally the United States, where he died on December 6, 1961. His body was flown back to Tunis, snuck across the boarder, and buried on Algerian soil to remain there as a martyr of the revolution.

Fanon's final book, *Les Damnés de la terre (The Wretched of the Earth),* appeared just before his death and was an impassioned defense of third-world struggle for equality and independence. Much of Fanon's corpus has been published since his death, and his legacy has had a tremendous impact on political thought, cultural criticism, and race theory over the last 45 years. His ideas are still at the forefront of academic debates in various disciplines.

See also: African Imperialism

Matthew Evans Teti

Bibliography

Fanon, Frantz. *Black Skin, White Masks.* Trans. Charles Lam Markmann. New York: Grove Press, 1967.

Fanon, Frantz. *Studies in a Dying Colonialism.* Trans. Haakon Chevalier. New York: Grove Press, 1967.

Fanon, Frantz. *The Wretched of the Earth.* Trans. Constance Farrington. New York: Grove Press, 1965.

Gibson, Nigel C., ed. *Rethinking Fanon: The Continuing Dialogue.* Amberst, NY: Humanity Books, 1999.

Macey, David. *Frantz Fanon: A Biography.* New York: Picador, 2000.

Farrakhan, Louis

Minister Louis Farrakhan (1933–) was the principal architect of the Million Man March and is the current leader of the Nation of Islam. Farrakhan was born Louis Eugene Walcott in 1933 in Bronx, New York. His mother raised him in Roxbury Massachusetts. He adopted the surname, Farrakhan after his conversion to Islam. In his youth, Farrakhan's greatest ambition was to attend New York's Julliard School of Music. Although he was a talented singer, he was denied admission to the prestigious institution. As an alternative, he enrolled at a teachers colleges for African Americans located in Winston-Salem, North Carolina. Within a few years, he withdrew from the college and became a calypso singer in a Boston nightclub. He was nicknamed "The Charmer."

Throughout the earlier part of his life, Farrakhan was a devout member of the Episcopal Church. In 1955, however, having grown disillusioned with the presumed "hatred" that white Christians showed toward black Christians, he severed his church affiliation. Frustrated with the racial inequality that persisted throughout the United States during this period, Farrakhan began seeking an alternative religious and spiritual outlet. During the early 20th century, many African Americans began aligning themselves with the black nationalist movement. The movement in America was chiefly designed to eradicate the "race problem" of the 20th century. Some nationalists, including members of the Nation of Islam (NOI), purported that abolition of white supremacy would include the defrayal of a separate space whereby blacks could control their economic, social, and political fate through "external emigration" to Africa or by disconnecting from the white masses in the United States. Farrakhan's initial reaction to the black nationalist agenda, and specifically the NOI, was one of disinterest.

At first glance, Farrakhan regarded the NOI as a peculiar and undesirable resolve to his animosity for the prejudice and discrimination persistent in the Christian church. On meeting Malcolm X, former NOI spokesperson and influential religious leader, in 1955, however, his feelings permanently changed. Farrakhan was immediately drawn to Malcolm's rhetorical abilities and within a short time, he enlisted in the NOI. Malcolm X began to train minister Farrakhan and, after Malcolm X's assassination in 1965, Farrakhan ascended as the NOI's primary representative and became minister of New York's temple number seven where Malcolm X had been preaching.

After the death of Elijah Muhammad, the original leader of the NOI from 1934–1975, the organization fell to the leadership of his son, Wallace Muhammad. Wallace Muhammad was a Sunni Muslim who sought to integrate the organization with orthodox Islamic values. To revitalize and reform the original precepts of the NOI, and to refurbish the socialization process that the organization was noted for, Farrakhan broke away from Muhammad's "new nation" in 1978. He subsequently began establishing another branch of the NOI modeled after the teachings of Elijah Muhammad and Master Farad Muhammad, the original founder of the NOI. Elijah Muhammad had been trained by Farad Muhammad who believed that African Americans were the original members of the *Tribe of Shabazz,* wrongfully exploited and enslaved in the United States. Farad is revered by NOI members as a prophet sent by God to teach African Americans a thorough and "true" knowledge of themselves and God.

With the NOI physically and ideologically splintered, Farrakhan assumed the arduous task of attempting to rebuild the NOI as it existed before the break. He successfully secured a large following and gained the interest of members of the African American community, just as his predecessors had attempted to do. Throughout his career, he has enjoyed monumental successes. His newspaper, *The Final Call,* was established in 1979 and modeled after Elijah Muhammad's *Muhammad Speaks.* The newspaper has a circulation of more than 500,000 per edition. Farrakhan has participated in numerous political, religious, and civic organizations and has become an international voice to promote peace and enfranchisement for marginalized groups in America and abroad. The building of the Salaam restaurant in Chicago in 1995 and the expansion of Muhammad Farms, a black-owned independent agricultural system, are also included among his successes.

Farrakhan has enjoyed an extensive career and continues to add to his record colossal achievements including the 1995 Million Man March. The march represented one of the largest assemblies of African Americans in U.S. history. It was designed to inspire black men about atonement, reconciliation, hard work, and responsibility, bringing them together to make solemn oaths to be better husbands, fathers, sons, and citizens. The televised event challenged the viewing public to analyze their social and racial perspectives. After the march there was a tremendous increase in voter registration among African Americans, as well as church and mosque memberships.

In 2000, Farrakhan organized the Million Family March to fulfill similar objectives as the Million Man March and to bring African American families together in harmony. Both marches were intended to be different from the civil rights demonstrations of the 1950s. NOI officials purposefully designed the marches to focus on blacks helping themselves without interracial cooperation.

Much like his forbear, Elijah Muhammad, Farrakhan is considered one of the most controversial African American religious leaders to date. Holding fast to the tenets of black nationalism, much of Farrakhan's vision is geared toward racial solidarity, uplift, and self-efficacy. He is often scrutinized for his *radical* beliefs and charged with being anti-Semitic. Nonetheless, Farrakhan has situated himself in U.S. history as one of its most ardent and influential leaders.

See also: Black Nationalism; Million Man March; Muhammad, Elijah; Nation of Islam; X, Malcolm

Talitha L. LeFlouria

Bibliography

Alexander, Amy, ed. *The Farrakhan Factor: African American Writers on Leadership, Nationhood, and Minister Louis Farrakhan.* New York: Grove Press, 1998.

Banks, William Jr. *The Black Muslims.* Philadelphia: Chelsea House Publishers, 1997.

Gardell, Mattias. *In the Name of Elijah Muhammad: Louis Farrakhan and the Nation of Islam.* Durham, NC: Duke University Press, 1996.

Levinsohn, Florence Hamlish. *Looking for Farrakhan.* Chicago: Ivan R. Dee, 1997.

Van Deburg, William L., ed. *Modern Black Nationalism: From Marcus Garvey to Louis Farrakhan.* New York: New York University Press, 1997.

Father Divine

Father Divine (1877?–1965), born George Baker, founded an interracial religious community called Father Divine's International Peace Mission Movement that came to prominence in America in the 1930s. Many of the details of George Baker's life before becoming Father Divine are disputed. Most sources cite his birthplace as Savannah, Georgia in 1877 or Rockville, Maryland in 1879, but legal documents state that he was born in Providence, Rhode Island in 1880. Members of the Peace Mission Movement, however, mark June 6, 1882 as the date of his first marriage to Peninniah. As a child, his mother, Nancy Baker, took him and his siblings to Jerusalem Methodist Church. After his mother died in May 1897, Baker's whereabouts are largely unknown until 1899, when he attended a series of storefront churches in Baltimore and, in 1902, did missionary work in the South.

Divine was influenced by a number of religious thinkers and events including Charles Fillmore's Unity School of Christianity and the Azusa Street Revival in 1906. In 1907, he joined a Baptist storefront in Baltimore, whose leader, Samuel Morris, referred to himself as Father Jehovia. Shortly thereafter, Baker became known as the Messenger. As Baker's oratorical skills grew and his number of followers swelled, he began to assert that he was the only incarnation of the divine. By 1912, Baker had formed his own ministry, leaving Baltimore for Georgia. Baker clashed often with the local ministers and was arrested several times for vagrancy and "lunacy" based on the observations of outsiders that his religious services were too enthusiastic and practiced glossolalia, or speaking in tongues. After traveling around the country, in 1917, Baker settled in New York, specifically a mostly white community, Sayville in Suffolk County, Long Island, and took the name the Reverend Major Jealous Divine. In addition to Divine's teachings and writings, which were considered sacred, members followed the *International Modest Code* that prohibited tobacco, alcohol, and profanity and established dress codes for men and women. Divine had a diverse following that included both African Americans and whites, and members of the upper and lower class. At the height of the movement, the community had about 50,000 members.

On November 15, 1931, responding to a disturbing the peace complaint, officers arrested 80 members attending Divine's service. Fifty-five members pleaded guilty and paid a $5 fine. Father Divine and others pleaded not guilty and stood trial. Most were found guilty and were forced to pay the fine. Justice Lewis J. Smith sentenced Divine to a year in jail and a $500 fine. Two days later, an apparently healthy Smith died of cardiac arrest. For many of Divine's followers, the event confirmed his divinity. A new trial was ordered, but never took place. After 33 days, Divine was released from jail.

Divine's Peace Mission Movement opened hotels, restaurants, stores, and many other businesses, while providing jobs, housing, and free meals during the dire Depression years. Divine became famous for his elaborate "Love Feasts," communion banquets, and services. In the mid-1930s, Divine moved his community to Harlem. In January 1936, Divine issued his "Righteous Government Platform," which called for the elimination of racial segregation, lynching, and capital punishment and advocated for additional government funds to end unemployment and poverty. In 1940, the movement petitioned for more stringent federal prosecution of lynching. Throughout his ministry, Divine had a number of accusations leveled against him including racketeering charges; however, the movement grew steadily in the 1930s, with more than 150 communities across the country.

After the death of his first wife, Divine married Edna Rose Ritchings, also known as Sweet Angel, on April 29, 1946. After the wedding, she assumed the title of Mother Divine. In 1947, the community moved to Woodmount, a suburb in Philadelphia. While the community held a variety of beliefs and practices, they emphasized racial and gender equality, patriotism to the United States, economic independence, and celibacy. As his health declined, Father Divine put institutional structures in place for the continuation of the movement such as developing new orders with

their own codes of conduct such as the "Rosebuds" for young girls, "Lily-buds" for women, and "Crusaders" for men. Despite his death on September 10, 1965, the community was able to continue under the direction of Mother Divine. Mother Divine currently handles the affairs of the community from Woodmont, which still operates several businesses. Their newspaper the *New Day*, which appeared weekly during the 1930s, suspended publication in 1992; however, Father Divine's teachings and writings remain sacred to his followers. There are currently several hundred members of the Peace Mission Movement, with the largest communities in Philadelphia and Newark, but there are followers across the United States and around the world.

See also: Destination, Harlem, New York; Evangelism

Julius H. Bailey

Bibliography

Burnham, Kenneth. *God Comes to America: Father Divine and the Peace Mission Movement.* Boston: Lambeth Press, 1979.

Watts, Jill. *God, Harlem, U.S.A.: The Father Divine Story.* Berkeley: University of California Press, 1992.

Weisbrot, Robert. *Father Divine and the Struggle for Racial Equality.* Chicago: University of Illinois Press, 1983.

Fifteenth Amendment

Most Americans take voting for granted, but the right to vote was not given to African Americans, women, and American Indians until sustained legislative and legal battles had been fought. The first such victory was the enactment of the Fifteenth Amendment. Passed by Congress on February 26, 1869 and ratified on March 30, 1870, the Fifteenth Amendment prohibited states from denying the right to vote (to African American males) on the basis of race, color, or previous condition of servitude.

The Fifteenth Amendment was a catalyst of suffrage extensions. Tracing the evolution of American voting rights, it took a half-century to extend this same right to women under the Nineteenth Amendment in 1920, with American Indians receiving the right to vote in 1924. Not surprisingly, the Fifteenth Amendment's color-blind language ("race, color, or previous condition of servitude") was acutely color-conscious. Thus, one lingering "badge of slavery" was what one might call "political slavery," in the sense that blacks, prior to the Fifteenth Amendment (and after), were barred from balloting, had no political representation, and perforce followed the laws of the white political establishment. In 1870, African Americans comprised around 10 percent of the nation's population (an estimated 4,000,000 out of 40,000,000). African Americans make up 14 per cent of Americans today, along with an equal number of Hispanic Americans.

Civil rights must first be recognized in principle. Then they must be realized in practice. After slavery was abolished by the Thirteenth Amendment in 1865, the question of the right of blacks to vote had ignited a national controversy. In spite of the adoption of the Fifteenth Amendment five years later, it took nearly a century to effectively enforce it under the Voting Rights Act (1965), which is the most successful civil rights legislation ever passed by Congress. This follows a pattern whereby the Civil War Amendments were not fully implemented until civil rights acts had been passed and enforced by direct federal intervention.

Partisan politics played a major role in establishing universal suffrage among African American men. Three years before ratification of the Fifteenth Amendment, Congress passed the Reconstruction Act of 1867, requiring Southern states to grant blacks suffrage rights. Yet in 1868, 11 of the 21 Northern states denied blacks the right to vote. This was not simply a regional problem. It was national in scope and called for a nationwide solution. Amending the Constitution was the surest way to enact this legislative reform. As the law of the land, the Fifteenth Amendment was binding on all states. Yet they were not bound by it for historical reasons. The Southern states were forced to accept what they had long opposed, for the simple reason that they were obliged to ratify both the Fourteenth and Fifteenth Amendments as a condition to their readmission into the Union after the Civil War.

The Southern states ratified these constitutional reforms grudgingly. While the Confederacy lost the Civil War, Southern states gained national power. The way that they exercised that power was to effectively deconstruct Reconstruction. After Reconstruction, Southern states did not honor the Fifteenth Amendment. Instead, they did all within their power to systematically disenfranchise blacks

African Americans march in New York City on April 8, 1870, in celebration of the passage of the Fifteenth Amendment. The Fifteenth Amendment, which gave African American men the right to vote, was adopted by Congress on February 26, 1869, and officially ratified on March 30, 1870. (Library of Congress)

through imposing literacy and character tests ("voter qualifying tests"), registration and poll tax requirements, along with white primaries, grandfather clauses, outright racial gerrymandering, and other restrictive devices, thereby rendering the Fifteenth Amendment a dead letter in a living document. Later, in *Smith v. Allwright,* 321 U.S. 649 (1944), the Supreme Court found that voting rights discrimination in primaries was unconstitutional on the basis of the Fifteenth Amendment. In *South Carolina v. Katzenbach,* 383 U.S. 301 (1966), the Supreme Court held that Congress, in enforcing the Fifteenth Amendment through the Voting Rights Act of 1865, may prohibit literacy tests in an effort to eliminate racial discrimination in voting. Notwithstanding such judicial enforcement, a paradox of national-historical proportions is this: Not until the passage of the Voting Rights Act of 1965 could the majority of African Americans in the South register to vote.

See also: Disfranchisement; Radical Republicans; Voting Rights Act 1965

Christopher Buck

Bibliography

Chin, Gabriel J. "Reconstruction, Felon Disenfranchisement and the Right to Vote: Did the Fifteenth Amendment Repeal Section 2 of the Fourteenth Amendment?" *Georgetown Law Journal* 92, no. 2 (2004):259–316.

Darling, Marsha J. Tyson, ed. *Race, Voting, Redistricting, and the Constitution: Sources and Explorations on the Fifteenth Amendment.* New York: Routledge, 2001.

Gillette, William. *The Right to Vote: Politics and the Passage of the Fifteenth Amendment.* Baltimore: Johns Hopkins Press, 1969.

Katz, Ellen D. "Reinforcing Representation: Congressional Power to Enforce the Fourteenth and Fifteenth Amendments in the *Rehnquist* and *Waite* Courts." *Michigan Law Review* 101 (2003):2341–408.

Maltz, Earl M. *Civil Rights, the Constitution, and Congress, 1863–1869.* Lawrence: University Press of Kansas, 1990.

Mathews, John Mabry. *Legislative and Judicial History of the Fifteenth Amendment.* Union, NJ: Lawbook Exchange, 2001.

Richardson, James D., ed. *A Compilation of the Messages and Papers of the Presidents, 1789–1897.* 10 vols. Washington, D.C.: Bureau of National Literature and Art, 1897, VII, 55–56.

Five Percenters

The Nation of Gods and Earths (NGE) is the official name of an organization popularly known as the Five Percenters. Headquartered in Harlem, with members in major cities across the United States, the organization originated as a splinter group that broke away from the Nation of Islam (NOI) circa 1964, under the leadership of Clarence Jowars Smith, who is better known by his NOI alias, Clarence 13 X and his nickname "Puddin." The latter moniker so-called attested to his legendary powers of persuasion. He was a gifted conversationalist with a hypnotic speaking style. Thus in street parlance his "rap," or "game" was so sweet and smooth that people would swallow his words like pudding. The organization's official name stems from the designation of male members as "Gods" and female members as "Earths" (analogous to the familiar gendered constructions "God the Father" and "Mother Earth"). The popular name is derived from the members' belief that 85 percent of humanity are mentally dead, uncivilized slaves who are unaware of their true identity or the true God; 10 percent are the wealthy enslavers of the poor who use lies to teach that the true and living God is an invisible, ghostlike "spook," and that they, in contrast, are the 5 percent of humanity who are the poor righteous teachers who do not believe in the teachings of the 10 percent and who know and teach that the Living God is the Asiatic black man.

These beliefs come directly from the *Lessons* of the NOI, the catechism-like sets of questions and answers (Q & A) that all NOI members must master (e.g., "Who is the Original Man? The Original Man is the Asiatic Black Man, the Maker, the Owner, the Cream of the Planet Earth, the father of Civilization, and God of the Universe.") The NGE, as an offshoot of the NOI, retains many of the NOI's teachings and heterodox Islamic beliefs, chief among them the idea that God (Allah) exists in a human form, an anathema to orthodox (Sunni and Shi'a) Muslims for whom *shirk* (associating partners with God) is the most grievous and unpardonable sin. There are several contrasts between the NOI and NGE, however. Diverging from the NOI's creed that Allah appeared in the person of Master W. D. Fard (also known as W. D. Farrad and Farrad Muhammad), the mysterious Middle Eastern peddler who was mentor of the Honorable Elijah Muhammad, the NGE holds that it is not Fard Muhammad who is Allah but the black man collectively. While the NOI proclaims that it is a religious organization, and has made attempts to mainstream some of its deviant beliefs and practices so that they are in more in alignment with the orthodox Muslim world, the NGE adamantly states that it is not a religious organization, and the members do not consider themselves Muslims but gods. While a Black Muslim takes on the letter X appended before his or her surname to indicate his "ex-slave name," as well as his unknown African or Asiatic name, the Gods adopt divine or "righteous" names such as "Universal God Allah," "Born Islam," "Allah Supreme," "Eternal Allah," or even "Bisme Allah" (a transliteration of the Qur'anic [Koranic] invocation translated as "In the Name of Allah"). While the NOI has a prominent or highly visible charismatic leader, the Minister Louis Farrakhan, who maintains a tight paramilitary chain of command through the Fruit of Islam (FOI) and has a uniform dress code, the NGE has a very loose organizational structure, with no formal leader and a very relaxed style of dress. Unlike the NOI, which witnessed a struggle for leadership upon the death of "the Messenger," Elijah Muhammad, since the mysterious, unsolved murder of "the Father," Clarence Puddin' 13X, in 1969 there have been no claimants to his mantle of leadership, although the Father's close comrade Justice and the First Nine Born (first nine followers of the Father) held a place of esteem. In recent years (circa 2000), a position entitled national spokesperson has been created, but a highly centralized leadership is eschewed, as it is not in keeping with the philosophy that each of the (male) members is a god. Absent also are the small business enterprises (restaurants, bakeries, barbershops, etc) of the NOI; although the NGE stresses the importance of individual entrepreneurship, actual economic development exists primarily at the street vending level. Finally, and perhaps most important, the NGE appeals to a much younger population than the NOI, recruiting many of its new members when they are adolescents. Although many recruits from decades past have remained with the organization for life, celebrating 50th and 60th birthdays as proud members of the NGE, the strength and character of the NGE are that it is a youth-oriented organization. Its social mission is to save the inner-city youth from violence, drug abuse, criminalization, and incarceration. The ranks of the organization are swollen with members who are under the age of 30. This demographic characteristic has a bearing on all the facets of the organization: divine names, loose organizational structure, informal dress code, and vendor-level business operations, as well as the organization's fascination with mastery of the spoken word or "rap" for which Clarence Puddin' 13X was famous.

Hip-hop culture has long been intertwined with Five Percenter ideology, and the appeal the NGE exerts on disenfranchised African American youth is the uncanny gift of gab that was the "Father's" legacy. Unexcelled as masters of the inner-city black idiom, Five Percenters can only be described as eloquent, mesmerizing, and spell-binding in their usage of Ebonics or African American inner city slang. Using the potency and the vitality of the black dialect, they open up new avenues of logic and thinking, or original ways of perceiving the world. As an expression of awe and wonderment at their verbal agility and conceptual ingenuity, NOI members refer to the Five Percenters as "scientists" because "they science out the Lessons," i.e., because the Five Percenters provide elaborate and insightful commentary on catechism Lessons they inherited from the NOI. The central theme of the Lessons is the allegorical tale of the rise, fall, and eventual resurrection or reascension of a self-created race of black gods. The downfall of their highly advanced divine civilization was due to the machinations of Yakub, a disgruntled evil scientific genius, who, with the aid of his followers, created or "grafted" a genetically mutated race of white devils who were destined to rule over the black man for 6,000 years. While the NOI and the NGE share the same Lessons texts, the NGE's unique contribution to the understanding of the texts is its extensive and unique brand of word-play commentary, which has its foundations in a numerology known as the Supreme Mathematics and occult science of letters known as the Supreme Alphabet. In the context of the Supreme Alphabet, A is Allah, B is Be or Born, C is See, D is Destroy, E is Equal Equality, etc., on down to Y is Why, X is Unknown, and Z is Zig Zag Zig (representing those who stray from the straight path). Using the Supreme Alphabet—and discretionary poetic license—words can be "scienced out" or "broken down" (i.e., analyzed) such that ISLAM means "I Self-Lord Am Master" or "I Surely Love Allah and Mathematics," whereas ALLAH may be deciphered as "Arm Leg Leg Arm Head" and MAN may be viewed as an acronym for "My Almighty Name," the esoteric "etymology" of each of these words indicating the NGE belief in the black man's divine nature or the anthropomorphic nature of God. The Supreme Mathematics is a corresponding numerological system in which 1 is Knowledge, 2 is Wisdom, 3 is Understanding…9 is Born, and 0 is Cipher. Furthermore, an uncanny streetology or street corner logic is an inherent NGE analytical tool, in which, for instance, "knowledge" connotes "know the ledge" (i.e., know one's limitations); and "wisdom" means "wise the dome" or "wides the dome" (make the head or brain wise or wide). The Five Percenters use this streetology, along with their esoteric Supreme

Mathematics and Supreme Alphabet to "science out the *Lessons*" (profoundly elaborate on the NOI mythology) and thus "show and prove" that they are "gods." Each "god" has the opportunity to "show and prove" before an audience of hundreds of gods and earths at their lively monthly Sunday afternoon rallies called Parliaments. Earths, whose modest dress and head-covering often mimic that of orthodox Muslim women, take on names such as "Queen Asia Peace Refinement," or "Everlasting Star Light," sell dinners at the Parliaments and generally play a subdued wifely and maternal role, each woman revolving around her mate or "god "as the earth revolves around the sun." Five Percenter hip-hop artists (see Aidi, 2004 and Allen, 1996) have included Poor Righteous Teachers, Rakim (of Eric B. and Rakim), Big Daddy Kane, Lakim Shabazz, Busta Rhymes, Mobb Deep, and the Wu Tang Clan. Official organs over the decades have included the two defunct newspapers, *Behold The SUN OF MAN* and *The WORD,* and two current newspapers, *The Five Percenter* and *NGE Power.* Dumar Allah is the current national spokesman. The headquarters at 126th St. and Adam Clayton Powell Blvd. proclaims the title, The Allah School in Mecca (i.e., Harlem) and is easily recognized by its symbol the numeral 7 (embedded in a stellated circle), which, in the Supreme Mathematics system, stands for Allah.

See also: Black Nationalism; Nation of Islam

Yusuf Nuruddin

Bibliography

Aidi, Hisham. "'Verily There is Only One Hip Hop Umma,': Islam, Cultural Protest and Urban Marginality." *Socialism and Democracy* 18, no. 2 (2004):107–26.

Allen, Ernest Jr. "Making the Strong Survive: The Contours and Contradictions of Message Rap." In *Droppin' Science: Critical Essays on Rap Music and Hip Hop Culture.* ed. William Eric Perkins, 159–91. Philadelphia: Temple University Press, 1996.

Nuruddin, Yusuf. "The Five Percenters: A Teenage Nation of Gods and Earths." In *Muslim Communities in North America.* Yvonne Yazbeck Haddad and Jane Idleman Smith, ed., 109–32. Albany: SUNY Press, 1994.

Fortune, T. Thomas

(Timothy) T. Thomas Fortune (1856–1928) was, arguably, the preeminent African American journalist of the early 20th century. Fortune was born a slave in Marianna, Florida, on October 3, 1856. Aside from the rudimentary education he received from his father who was a Reconstruction politician, Fortune was largely self-taught and acquired early school training in the South in a variety of sectors. He attended an underdeveloped Freedman's Bureau school in Florida, and when he was 13, Fortune served as a page in the state senate. (Fortune also possessed strong Anglo-American features that helped facilitate experiences that were fairly uncommon for recently emancipated slaves.) At age 19, Fortune would go on to attend Howard University in Washington, D.C., between 1876 and 1877, but more important, he would meet John Wesley Crommel there who would help launch and inspire Fortune's career in journalism. At the time of their meeting, Crommel was editor of the *People's Advocate;* he would go on to assemble the first Colored Press Association convention in 1880 and would become a founding member of Alexander Crummell's American Negro Academy in 1897. Fortune worked briefly for the versatile Crommel before deciding to move to New York to begin his own storied journalistic career.

When Fortune arrived in New York around 1880, he began working in the printer's trade for John Dougall's *Weekly Witness,* a religious paper. Shortly thereafter, he met African Americans whose intellectual interests were similar to his own. One of these was George Parker who had recently begun a little weekly tabloid entitled *The Rumor.* Parker's tabloid quickly came under financial pressures and Fortune, along with Walter Sampson, who helped secure Fortune's job at the *Weekly Witness,* worked evenings writing copy and setting type for *The Rumor* while still working for Dougall's paper in the day. After about a year, by which time he was clearly recognized as a far superior writer and editor to either Parker or Sampson, Fortune became a partner and insisted on changing the paper's name from *Rumor* to *New York Globe* in July 1881. The *New York Globe* continued operating under the joint partnership of Fortune and Parker. In a short period, the *New York Globe* achieved national prominence and Fortune quickly became the most able African American journalist.

The *New York Globe* was only a four-page weekly and had a staff of able correspondents in many cities in the North and South who reported news of race conditions and political developments related to the race. In keeping with its name, the *New York Globe* thought its mission to be broad and universal in scope—insofar as African American readership was concerned—and the newspaper sought to provide as much information pertaining to African Americans as possible within its four pages. (Incidentally, the paper was heralded in the white press for Fortune's intelligent editorials and for being remarkably free from the kind of grammatical errors that marked a newly established African American press tradition that was cropping up throughout the nation.) Also, news letters from smaller communities reported local trivia including activities of churches and fraternal organizations. One reporter of such information was the teenager William Edward Burghardt Du Bois. The paper's popularity was singly due to Fortune's editorials. Fortune was vastly admired for his frank expression, intelligent opinion, and, above all else, his sophisticated writing about issues confronting African American life. The ferocity of Fortune's editorials knew no bounds in their denunciation of hindrances facing the African American community.

In spite of his reputation, Fortune never formally secured legal proprietorship, and after the paper was besieged by turmoil, Parker mortgaged the paper without Fortune's knowledge. Shortly thereafter, Fortune was able to reverse his circumstances, and, in 1884, the *New York Globe* became the *New York Freeman* under his sole proprietorship until 1887, when the name was changed to *New York Age*. Fortune left the newspaper briefly to the management of his brother while freelance writing, and upon his brother's death, he resumed as editor. Fred Moore eventually purchased the *New York Age* from Fortune in 1907.

Fortune's tenure was marked by both successes and controversy. In addition to his reputation as a fiercely eloquent editorial writer, his efforts on behalf of African Americans were just as practical. He assisted Ida B. Wells's crusade against lynching by offering her use of the *New York Age* and providing her with contacts when he learned that her newspaper had been burned and that her life was in danger. Fortune's efforts to assist African Americans, particularly women, are also signaled by his participation in the first meeting of the National Federation of Afro-American Women, where he was one of three invited male speakers. Fortune would also rise to the presidency of the Colored Press Association that his former mentor Cromwell organized in the late 1890s. From this position, Fortune became widely recognized as an African American leader of national importance, and his opinions on uplift, religion, education, race, and a host of other issues became well known.

Fortune was brought into contact with, arguably, the most influential African American leader of the early twentieth-century, Booker T. Washington. This relationship would lead to many disappointments in an otherwise stellar career. After their meeting, Washington would begin subsidizing Fortune's *New York Age*, which was viewed by Washington's critics as an endorsement of his accommodationist policies. (Fortune would also serve as Washington's ghost writer on a number of projects.) This relationship would wear on Fortune, for although he agreed with Washington that African Americans were in need of reform, he did not necessarily agree with Washington's unwillingness to fight for social equality. It would prove too difficult to remain ideologically at odds with a benefactor whose money was necessary for his financial security. In choosing the latter, he lost the respect of many of his intellectual cohorts such as Du Bois, and perhaps most important, himself. He withdrew from public life for a period of time, having several bouts with alcoholism. After the unexpected death of Washington, Fortune returned to public life, serving as editor for various newspapers such as the *Colored American Review* and the *Negro World,* organ of Marcus Garvey's UNIA, which Fortune edited until his death in 1928.

See also: Du Bois, W. E. B.; Garvey, Marcus; Universal Negro Improvement Association; Washington, Booker T.; Wells-Barnett, Ida

Brian Lamont Johnson

Bibliography

Detweiler, Frederick. *The Negro Press in the United States.* College Park: McGrath Publishing, 1968.

Du Bois, William Edward Burghardt. *The Autobiography of W. E. B. Du Bois.* New York: International Publishing, 1968.

Penn, I. Garland. *The Afro-American Press and Its Editors.* New York: Arno Press, 1969.

Pride, Armistead S., and Clint C. Wilson III. *A History of the Black Press.* Washington, D.C.: Howard University Press, 1997.

Thornbrough, Emma Lou. *T. Thomas Fortune: Militant Journalist.* Chicago: University of Chicago Press, 1972.

Forty Acres and a Mule

This phrase refers to the widespread belief that slaves freed after the Civil War were promised by the federal government a parcel of free land (40 acres) and farm animals (a mule) to begin their new lives. The idea is that promise of the government was broken and that African Americans are, therefore, still owed this debt to the present day. While untrue, the myth embodies the historical resentment of black Americans that slaves were never compensated for their labor as bondsmen, but were simply set free and left to their own devices. It also represents an undeveloped demand for present-day reparations for slavery in the United States.

The origins of the myth are unknown. It appeared among freed slaves immediately after the Civil War and persists until today. Shortly after the fall of Richmond in 1865, a freedman named Cyrus explained the meaning of the Northern victory to his former mistress: "Der ain't goin' ter be no more Master and Mistress, Miss Emma. All is equal. I done hear it from de cotehouse steps....All de land belongs to de Yankees now, and dey gwine to divide it out 'mong de colored people." (*Been in the Storm So Long*, p. 399) In November 1865, an official of the Freedmen's Bureau in Mississippi reported that freed blacks believed that planters' lands and other properties were to be confiscated and distributed to them by Christmas that same year. Similar rumors circulated at the time among blacks in other parts of the defeated South.

The idea that ex-slaves would receive confiscated lands after the North won the war, although it was advocated by some abolitionists, may have had its origins in Confederate propaganda. The Freedmen's Bureau blamed such false hopes on precisely that. But in fact, there had been numerous wartime confiscations of Confederate properties, which Union generals and officers had often distributed among freed slaves in numerous states. The most famous of these was "Special Field Order No. 15," issued January 16, 1865, by which General Sherman, after meeting with a delegation of black ministers, set aside the Carolina Sea Islands; the rice coast south of Charleston, extending 30 miles inland, and the country bordering the St. John's River, Florida, for the exclusive resettlement of ex-slaves. Each family was to receive 40 acres of land, although there was no mention of animals. The army did in fact assist some settlers with temporary loans of mules. All such ad hoc, wartime grants of land to freedmen were quickly rescinded, however, after the war and after the assassination of Lincoln, by President Andrew Johnson. Johnson issued extensive presidential pardons to white planters that restored to them full rights to all their properties.

The idea that slaves were owed land and mules that were never given to them remains alive in popular culture.

A scene in the film *Gone With the Wind* (1939) shows a carpetbagger promising 40 acres and a mule to ex-slaves. Spike Lee's production company is named "Forty Acres and a Mule." Oscar Brown Jr. produced a song entitled "Forty Acres and a Mule" (1964) that wryly demands this compensation plus interest. In his song, "Letter to the President," (1999) Tupac Shakur asks about 40 acres and a mule. Kanye West's song "All Falls Down" (2004) mentions 40 acres. *See also:* Field Order No. 15

Anthony A. Lee

Bibliography
Du Bois, W. E. B. *The Souls of Black Folk*. New York: Bantam Books, 1989 (1903).
Foner, Eric. *Reconstruction: America's Unfinished Revolution, 1863–1877*. New York: HarperCollins, 1988.
Litwack, Leon F. *Been in the Storm So Long: The Aftermath of Slavery*. New York: Vintage Books, 1979.
Oubre, Claude F. *Forty Acres and a Mule: The Freedmen's Bureau and Black Land Ownership*. Baton Rouge: Louisiana State University Press, 1978.
Patrick, Rembert W. *The Fall of Richmond*. Baton Rouge: Louisiana State University Press, 1960.

Fourteenth Amendment

The Fourteenth Amendment is among the most important provisions of the United States Constitution. When Americans think of their rights, provisions of the first eight amendments commonly come to mind. What they do not realize, however, is that it is only the Fourteenth Amendment that has been held to make those provisions applicable by courts against state and local governments.

This is a far cry from the original understanding or purpose of the Fourteenth Amendment. Rather, that amendment owes its genesis to the clash between the Reconstruction Congress and President Andrew Johnson. In the wake of the Civil War, Johnson proved unwilling to ratify the change in the structure of the federal system the majority of Northern politicians favored. Thus, when Congress responded to the Black Codes by passing the Civil Rights Act of 1866, the president vetoed it; the Act was, Johnson said, clearly not consistent with the traditional allocation of powers between the state and federal governments.

Congress then sent out to the states a grab-bag amendment with provisions responding to many of the issues that then concerned the Republican Party. It secured a dubious ratification in 1868. First, in Section I, the amendment makes a citizen of the United States and of the state wherein he resides each person born in the United States—and thus overturns part of the holding in *Dred Scott v. Sandford* (1857). The section goes on to say that no state may abridge the privileges or immunities of citizens of the United States. In its decision in *The Slaughterhouse Cases* (1873), the Supreme Court would read this provision as protecting only those few rights (the right to travel to the federal capital, for example) that were attributes specifically of federal citizenship, which means that there has been very little litigation of this clause since.

Section I's two other provisions, however, have proven extremely significant. The first of them (the due process clause) says that no state may deprive anyone of life, liberty, or property without due process of law; the second says that no state may deny anyone equal protection of the law. These two clauses have effectively swallowed up the old notion of the reserved powers of the states in the areas of criminal procedure, church-state relations, punishment, contraception, abortion, lewdness, public speech, press freedom, "expressive" conduct, sex discrimination, and others, because it was through the due process clause that the Supreme Court gradually began to apply notions found in the first eight amendments (or, in some cases, in penumbras of emanations of those amendments) against entities of state government.

One might have thought from reading the due process clause that it was intended to guarantee that people would receive a fair hearing before being executed, imprisoned, or fined; and, indeed, there is abundant extratextual evidence to support that reading. In the late 19th century, however, the federal courts began to read substance into the due process clause, just as Chief Justice Taney had read a substantive component into its Fifth Amendment analogue in his opinion in *Dred Scott*. The first type of substance the federal courts found in that clause is captured by the term "The *Lochner* Era," and generally related to the right to contract freely without government restrictions on wages, hours, or working conditions.

With the Supreme Court's 1937 change of heart concerning the New Deal, however, the Court gave up preventing government from adopting wage, hours, working conditions, and other labor regulations; instead, as foreshadowed in footnote 4 of *United States v. Carolene Products*

Co. (1938), the Court began to apply other limitations on legislative authority related to discrimination against judicially favored minorities and to a different set of individual rights.

The equal protection clause was understood in the 19th century as allowing "separate but equal" accommodations for blacks (*Plessy v. Ferguson* (1896)). In the 20th century, however, the Supreme Court decided that segregation of the races was inherently unequal, first in public education (*Brown v. Board of Education I* (1954)), and later in other areas of life. In his opinion for the Court in *Brown*, Chief Justice Warren tacitly conceded that the Court's opinion that day amounted to an amendment of the Constitution when he said that the understanding of the equal protection clause that existed in the 1860s could not guide the Court in 1954; what he meant was that it would not.

This new pronouncement from the Court spurred the advent of the Civil Rights movement of the 1950s and 1960s; its perceived constitutional illegitimacy also inflamed southern white resistance, which reached its height in the Southern Manifesto and Massive Resistance. The result of the concerted southern political opposition to desegregation was a delay of more than a decade in ending segregation, which only began to be dismantled in earnest across the Gulf South in the wake of the Civil Rights Act of 1964.

Once Congress began to legislate in favor of the rights of blacks and (on their coattails) historically mistreated minorities, it soon moved into the area of granting preferences in contracting, hiring, promotions, licensing, and other areas to members of those groups. This development spawned a new group of equal protection clause cases dealing with the question whether they allowed any racial or ethnic group to be preferred on the basis of past barriers to its advancement. The Supreme Court's decisions in this area have been somewhat inconsistent, as for example in saying that preferences were permissible but quotas were not. The existence of this group of decisions, like that of the Court's decisions respecting sex discrimination, shows how far the equal protection clause has come since the *Slaughterhouse* majority's statement that it was unlikely any group other than blacks would ever be able to claim its protection.

See also: Civil Rights Act of 1866; *Dred Scott v. Sandford*; *Plessy v. Ferguson*; Radical Republicans

Kevin R. C. Gutzman

Bibliography

Curtis, Michael Kent. *No State Shall Abridge: The Fourteenth Amendment and the Bill of Rights*. Durham, NC: Duke University Press, 1986.

Epps, Garrett. *Democracy Reborn: The Fourteenth Amendment and the Fight for Equal Rights in Post-Civil War America*. New York: H. Holt, 2006.

Labbe, Ronald M., and Jonathan Lurie. *The Slaughterhouse Cases: Regulation, Reconstruction, and the Fourteenth Amendment*. Lawrence: University Press of Kansas, 2003.

Franklin, John Hope

John Hope Franklin (1915–2009), American historian, was born in Rentiesville, Oklahoma. His mother, Mollie, a teacher, and his father, Buck, a lawyer, named him after educator and activist John Hope. Franklin moved with his family to Tulsa in 1925, four years after the terrible race riot in that city. In his autobiography, he told of the prejudice and discrimination he and his family faced there and elsewhere.

Franklin graduated from Fisk University (where he met Aurelia Whittington, his future wife) in 1935. After receiving his PhD from Harvard in 1941, Dr. Franklin held teaching positions at North Carolina College at Durham (now North Carolina Central University), Howard University, Brooklyn College (where, in 1956, he became the first African American to chair an academic department in a predominantly white institution), the University of Chicago (where again he served as chair), and Duke University. In addition to these, Franklin has received more than 100 honorary degrees and held a number of temporary and visiting professorships.

Franklin has written widely in American history. His dissertation, "The Free Negro in North Carolina, 1790–1860," became his first book in 1944. *The Militant South, 1800–1861* (1956) described the South's martial culture, including its ties to slavery and its contribution to secession and the Civil War. *Reconstruction after the Civil War* (1961), the first comprehensive revisionist history of Reconstruction, gave African Americans a major role in shaping their position in the postwar South. Perhaps the germ of this book was a review Franklin wrote over a decade earlier of E. Merton Coulter's history of Reconstruction. In the review, Franklin not only criticized Coulter for repeating the racist history of William Archibald Dunning and others, he denounced the white historians who accepted and praised Coulter's work.

Among his dozen or so other books are *A Southern Odyssey: Travelers in the Antebellum North* (1976), *George Washington Williams* (1985), and *Runaway Slaves: Rebels on the Plantation* (1999; written with Loren Schweninger). This last book put the final nail in the coffin of the image of the happy slave. Most recently, Franklin published *In Search of the Promised Land: A Slave Family of the Old South* (2006), on the Thomases of Tennessee.

Franklin is perhaps best known for *From Slavery to Freedom* (1947). There had been general histories of African Americans published before this (such as the one by George Williams, whose story Franklin penned in his prize-winning biography cited previously), but Franklin's was the first to combine comprehensive coverage, an unquestionably scholarly approach, and a wonderful readability. *From Slavery to Freedom* became almost the cornerstone of modern African American Studies.

According to Franklin, historians should become scholar activists, using their knowledge and abilities for more than writing books and teaching classes. Franklin filled that role throughout his career, from working with the National Association for the Advancement of Colored People's Legal Defense Fund in 1953 (tracing the original intent and early understanding of the Fourteenth Amendment, thus helping pave the way for the Supreme Court's decision in *Brown v. Board of Education*) to chairing the advisory board for President William Clinton's Initiative on Race in 1997–1998.

John Hope Franklin is one of the most honored historians the nation has known. He was elected president of the American Studies Association, the Southern Historical Association, Phi Beta Kappa, the Organization of American Historians, and the American Historical Association.

He won the Presidential Medal of Freedom in 1995. In 2000, Duke University established the John Hope Franklin Center for Interdisciplinary and International Studies in his honor. With the historian Yu Ying-shih, Franklin received the million-dollar John W. Kluge Prize for lifetime achievement in the study of humanity in 2006. On March 25, 2009, Franklin died of congestive heart failure at Duke Hospital.

See also: Association for the Study of African American Life and History; Tulsa, Oklahoma, Race Riot of 1921

David B. Parker

Bibliography

Franklin, John Hope. *From Slavery to Freedom,* 8th ed., with Alfred Moss, New York: Alfred A. Knopf, 2000.

Franklin, John Hope. *Mirror to America: The Autobiography of John Hope Franklin.* New York: Farrar, Straus and Giroux, 2005.

Franklin, John Hope. *Race and History: Selected Essays, 1938–1988.* Baton Rouge: Louisiana State University Press, 1989.

Jarrett, Beverly, ed. *Tributes to John Hope Franklin: Scholar, Mentor, Father, Friend.* Columbia: University of Missouri Press, 2003.

Freedmen's Bureau

The Bureau of Refugees, Freedmen, and Abandoned Lands, commonly known as the Freedmen's Bureau, was created on March 3, 1865. It was supposed to last for only one year after the Civil War's end. As an extension of the War Department, the Freedmen's Bureau was supposed to perform a variety of tasks including distributing food, land, clothing, medicine, creating schools, negotiating contracts, and establishing hospitals for freed people as well as white refugees. Although the task of the bureau was monumental, it was given no resources to operate. The War Department had to use its budge and staff to support the Bureau.

In May 1865, General Oliver O. Howard was chosen to lead the new agency. A native of Maine, Howard believed the Freedmen's Bureau should not show favoritism to either African Americans or whites; rather it should act as a moderator between both parties. Furthermore, Howard did not view the Freedmen's Bureau as an institution that would allow freedmen to be idle and lazy. He wanted to protect their social and political rights, but he also wanted those who were able to work. Despite Howard's view, the Bureau met a tremendous amount of resistance from Southern whites. Even Northern Democrats portrayed the Freedmen's Bureau as an institution that would promote laziness among African Americans.

Southern whites resisted the Freedmen's Bureau because it was attempting to put African Americans on an equal plane with whites. Furthermore, some of the border states, such as Kentucky, resisted the Bureau's presence because they believed that it should have only been established in states that had seceded from the Union. White Southerners also opposed the idea of the bureau educating African Americans.

Some African Americans also had problems with the bureau. Although one of the bureau's primary responsibilities was negotiating contracts between freedmen and their former masters, on many occasions the contracts appeared to be more favorable to the former master. Under most circumstances slaves who worked for their former masters entered into contracts for one year, were paid little for their work, given a food ration, and allowed to live in old slave cabins. African Americans, for example in Louisiana, protested the Freedmen's Bureau because they felt that it was forcing freedmen into contracts to simply put them to work and not allowing them freedom to explore their options.

Other African Americans protested the bureau's inability to provide them with land. According to the law that established the bureau agents, were permitted to set aside no more than 40 acres for freedmen as well as loyal white refugees to rent for three years with the prospect of purchasing the land. This strengthened the myth that every former slave would be given 40 acres and a mule. The amount of land, however, that bureau agents had to draw from was limited dramatically when President Andrew Johnson ordered General Howard to restore all land to former Confederates in August 1865.

Johnson's order to return land to former Confederates was only one way in which he tried to block the Freedmen's Bureau. When Congress tried to extend the bureau's life in February 1866, Johnson vetoed the bill. In July Congress overrode the veto and extended the institution's existence.

Although Johnson, Northern Democrats, white Southerners, and some African Americans had problems with the Freedmen's Bureau, it did perform valuable work, namely in educating African Americans. General Howard believed that the best tool the newly freedmen could have was a proper education. With limited government aid and nearly $800,000 in private contributions from African Americans, approximately 4,000 schools were opened educating in excess of 250,000 students. Teachers, the lion's share of whom came from New England, performed invaluable work, but were lambasted by whites and oftentimes were refused services such as rooms or meals.

The Freedmen's Bureau also played an important role in helping to reunite families—perhaps the item of greatest concern to freedmen. Agents, teachers, and missionaries in the Freedmen's Bureau aided in writing letters and assisted in locating former slaves' loved ones. The bureau also made certain that African Americans met no resistance when they registered to vote. The Freedmen's Bureau also acted as a mediator in family disputes, namely spouse abuse. On numerous occasions of spouse abuse, the Freedmen's

A classroom at the Freedmen's Bureau in Richmond, Virginia. Formally known as the Bureau of Refugees, Freedmen, and Abandoned Lands, the Freedmen's Bureau was a federal agency within the War Department that was charged with supervising the transition from slavery to freedom in the erstwhile Confederacy. (Library of Congress)

Bureau ordered the guilty party to pay child support or a sizable fine.

Even though the bureau had some successes, it had many drawbacks. A portion of the bureau's agents were corrupt. On numerous occasions agents forced freedmen out of towns, made them sign contracts that were unfavorable, and sought sexual favors from African American females who came to the bureau for assistance. It was also viewed negatively by some because its presence created a deeper hatred of African Americans among whites.

Despite the shortcomings of the bureau, many African Americans believed it was important for their own protection. When the Bureau's role became limited in 1868 when certain states were readmitted into the Union, African Americans petitioned government officials to keep the bureau operating as it had since 1865. The pleas did not work. The bureau was formally abolished on June 10, 1872.

See also: Historically Black Colleges and Universities; Johnson, Andrew; Joint Committee of Fifteen; Radical Republicans

Jonathan A. Noyalas

Bibliography

Cimbala, Paul A. *The Freedmen's Bureau: Reconstructing the American South after the Civil War.* Malabar, FL: Krieger Publishing, 2005.

Cimbala, Paul A., and Randall M. Miller, eds. *The Freedmen's Bureau and Reconstruction: Reconsiderations.* New York: Fordham University Press, 1999.

Foner, Eric. *Reconstruction: America's Unfinished Revolution, 1863–1877.* New York: Harper Collins, 1988.

Freedom Rides

The Congress of Racial Equality (CORE) organized the Freedom Rides as a bus journey through the South to test President Kennedy's commitment to civil rights in America. These Freedom Riders, an interracial group, decided to specifically test Kennedy's commitment to enforce two Supreme Court decisions banning segregated interstate travel by forcing Kennedy to take a public stand against segregation. To achieve their goal, the Freedom Riders would travel throughout the South, stopping at various stations, with white riders going into "black only" areas and black riders going into "white only" areas. Their route would take them from Washington, D.C. to New Orleans in little less than two weeks. On May 4, 1961, two buses left Washington, D.C. in route to New Orleans.

The Freedom Riders faced little resistance compared to what they would face in the lower South. From Atlanta, Georgia to Birmingham, Alabama the riders were met by violent white mobs. Outside of Anniston, Alabama, with riders still aboard, their bus was firebombed. As riders fled through the back of the bus, they were attacked by a white mob. Many were injured and several were left with permanent injuries, including white riders.

A second bus headed from Atlanta into Birmingham and was also greeted with violence. On their way to Birmingham, riders hoped they would be protected by local police or even the FBI. The riders were unaware that the FBI knew of Ku Klux Klan activity in Birmingham and did nothing to prevent violence. Furthermore, the local police had received the riders' itinerary ahead of time and passed it on to the Klan, knowing an attack would occur. A white mob was waiting for the riders and attacked them as they got off the bus. Several minutes later the attackers dispersed and police appeared.

To prevent further violent incidents, the U.S. Justice Department flew the riders to New Orleans, as buses proved to be too dangerous. The Student Nonviolent Coordinating Committee (SNCC) decided to take over for CORE riders despite the immense risk of violence and even death. According to Stokley Carmichael, one of the Freedom Riders, SNCC felt "if the freedom rides were stopped because of violence, and only because of violence, then the nonviolent

Freedom Riders enroute to Washington, D.C., from New York City hang signs from their bus windows to protest segregation. During the summer of 1961, hundreds of Freedom Riders rode in interstate buses into the prosegregationist South to test a U.S. Supreme Court decision that banned segregation of interstate transportation facilities. (Library of Congress)

movement was over. We might as well disband SNCC. Our movement is over. Give the racist this victory and it sends the clear signal that at the first sign of resistance, all they have to do is mobilize massive violence, the movement will collapse and the government won't do a thing. We can't let that happen" (*Ready for Revolution*, p. 186).

The new group of Freedom Riders left Nashville and headed to Birmingham where they were arrested. They were then driven to the state line and dropped off, having to fend for themselves. After making their journey back to Nashville, they again decided to head back to Birmingham. United States Attorney General Robert Kennedy wanted assurances from Alabama that they would protect the riders; if Alabama would not make those assurances, the federal government would have to intervene. Robert Kennedy sent in his assistant, John Seigenthaler, to negotiate with state officials. After intense discussion, Alabama decided they would provide protection. Alabama placed state patrol cars every 10–15 miles along the highway toward Montgomery. In addition, a plane followed overhead and two officials from Greyhound were on each bus. Despite the protection, about 40 miles outside of Montgomery, all protection disappeared. As the bus entered the Montgomery bus stations, it was eerily quiet.

Without warning, whites rushed the bus with "sticks and bricks." The first to come off the bus was a white man, Jim Zwerg, The mob took him and severely beat him, allowing other riders to disembark the bus, going unnoticed. Riders and whites sympathetic to the riders were beaten, including Seigenthaler. Later that evening, Dr. Martin Luther King spoke at a local church when a white mob surrounded the church. Federal marshals had been sent in by Robert Kennedy, but Goverson Patterson declared martial law, and National Guardsmen were sent in to control rioters and help federal marshals.

On May 24, the Freedom Riders continued to Jackson, Mississippi with adequate and constant protection. Once in Jackson, the riders were allowed to walk through the white sections of the bus stop but were subsequently arrested for trespassing. The local court was not sympathetic to the Freedom Riders, and they were sentenced to 60 days in a maximum security prison. Hundreds had been arrested and sentenced as more freedom riders came into Jackson. Some riders, including Carmichael, spent more than a month in jail before having their bonds posted. Jail had halted the Freedom Riders, but their goals had been achieved.

Robert Kennedy petitioned the Interstate Commerce Commission to pass a regulation making segregation illegal in interstate travel. In September 1961, the commission complied and the Freedom Riders had their victory. This victory was not only important because it showed what a direct action protest could achieve, but also because it signaled the importance of student organizations in the freedom movement.

See also: CORE; Lewis, John; Nash, Diane; Student Nonviolent Coordinating Committee

Cristy Casado Tondeur

Bibliography
Carmichael, Stokely. *Ready for Revolution: The Life and Struggles of Stokely Carmichael.* New York: Scribner, 2003.
Carson, Claiborne. *Eyes on the Prize.* New York: Penguin Books, 1987.
Payne, Charles. *I've Got the Light of Freedom: The Organizing Tradition and The Mississippi Freedom Struggle.* Berkeley: University of California Press, 1995.

Freedom Schools

Freedom schools were created in 1964, during the Student Nonviolent Coordinating Committee's (SNCC) Mississippi Freedom Summer Project. One of SNCC's goals during this incredibly ambitious civil rights campaign was to create a homegrown movement among African American youths in Mississippi. To achieve this goal, SNCC organized more than 40 Freedom schools throughout the state, which ran from late June through mid-August, and was staffed by hundreds of volunteers who were mostly white, female college students.

A young African American SNCC worker named Charlie Cobb initially proposed the Freedom school idea in November 1963. When observing black Mississippi schools, Cobb noticed that there was a complete absence of academic freedom. African American students in Mississippi were not allowed to openly discuss the situation facing them, despite how poverty-stricken and disenfranchised their parents were. There were multiple instances where black teachers were fired for telling students about the National Association for the Advancement of Colored People (NAACP) or discussing the nationwide battle for civil rights. Furthermore, it was frowned on to teach black children anything about the functions of the U.S. government or the world outside of Mississippi. During the first days of

Freedom schools, many of the volunteer teachers recorded that their students did not know basic things such as the nation's capital, or how many states composed America. This lack of access to education, Cobb observed, created an intellectual vacuum among black students and often fulfilled its goal in rendering them powerless.

After leaders of SNCC accepted Cobb's Freedom school proposal, a conference was held in New York City to discuss the curriculum to be taught in these schools. Veteran civil rights activists such as Myles Horton, Septima Clark, Bayard Rustin, and Ella Baker, combined with young SNCC leaders and academics such as Stoughton Lynd, to create an impressive and comprehensive core curriculum for the schools. The group decided that the Freedom schools should be based on a model of participatory education. This structure called for a great deal of classroom discussion during which students would raise questions and provide answers. Teachers would merely provide background information and facilitate conversations. The conference also called for the development of remedial programs to fill basic educational gaps, and leadership training exercises that taught the students not only how to lead, but how to conduct civil rights protests by writing letters, organizing, and using modern nonviolent tactics.

As the Summer Project began in late June, volunteers noticed an incredible response to Freedom schools. Community members of all ages helped SNCC workers construct the schools, and men stood guard outside their doors at night. When a school would be bombed or burnt by racist local whites, entire communities would turn out to construct another building while school sessions continued under the shade of an old tree or inside someone's house. Within two weeks, Freedom school attendance surpassed all estimations, and by the time the summer was over, Freedom schools had more than 2,000 attendees. The Freedom schools were incredibly successful. Toward the end of the Freedom Summer, Freedom school students had started canvassing potential black voters, conducting nonviolent protests, and forming their own organizations. Freedom school students remained the most important legacy of the Freedom Summer, and they would continue the fight for civil rights in the state long after the SNCC summer project ended.

See also: Mississippi Freedom Summer, 1964; Student Nonviolent Coordinating Committee

William Mychael Sturkey

Bibliography
Carson, Clayborne. *In Struggle: SNCC and the Black Awakening of the 1960s.* Cambridge, MA: Harvard University Press, 1981.
Dittmer, John. *Local People: The Struggle for Civil Rights in Mississippi.* Urbana: University of Illinois Press, 1994.

Garvey, Marcus

Marcus Mosiah Garvey (1887–1940), a black nationalist, was born August 17, 1887 to Marcus and Sarah, the youngest of 11 children. Proud of his racial heritage, Garvey led the largest movement of people of African descent in the world to this day. His movement, Garveyism, generated racial pride, uplift, economic independence, and, most important, a return to Africa. To that end, Garvey was influential in establishing black businesses and the first black international organization for blacks, the United Negro Improvement Association and African Communities League (UNIA), established in 1914. UNIA was formed to draw blacks across the world to promote racial pride, worldwide industry, the development of Africa, and educational opportunities.

Garvey's parents were Jamaicans of unmixed African stock, descendants from the Maroons, a group of slaves who escaped the Jamaican slave regime. The Maroons established independent communities after being rewarded with a treaty of independence from Britain in 1739. Marcus Garvey was raised in St. Ann's Bay on the northern coast of Jamaica. Trained as a printer's apprentice, he attended elementary school but was forced to drop out at the age of 14 to help with his family's finances. His activism started early in life. While working as a foreman printer, the union went on strike and Garvey was elected as their leader. The strike failed and Garvey was blacklisted. It was at this time he became skeptical about the use of labor unions and socialism as a form of government to assist blacks.

After his first opportunity to become active, Garvey traveled extensively to find that black people throughout the world were being treated unfairly. From Costa Rica to Venezuela, everywhere Garvey traveled he was able to observe firsthand the harsh conditions of black people across the world. As a result of this new knowledge and his desire to right the injustices of black people, Garvey used his skills to publish several newspapers. The first newspaper was started in 1910, *Garvey's Watchman,* with a weekly circulation of 3,000 copies. He founded his second paper in Costa Rica, *La Nacion.* Garvey used his papers to attack the British consul for their indifference to the conditions of blacks. In Panama, he published *La Prensa.*

Garvey solicited support from the British, but they were indifferent to his initial concerns; thus he concluded that black people could not rely on whites to provide equality. The lack of support from the British government prompted Garvey to travel to Europe. He settled in London where he met Duse Mohammed Ali, who sparked his interest in pursuing African freedom. The turning point in Garvey's life during this time was his exposure to Booker T. Washington. After reading Washington, Garvey's quest to become a race leader began.

In 1914, Garvey returned to Jamaica where, on August 1, 1914, he established the UNIA whose motto was "One God! One Aim! One Destiny! The UNIA had several objectives. As defined by Garvey these objectives were to unify the race, inspire a spirit of pride and love, attend to the needs of the poor, undermine imperialism on the African continent, and help facilitate commerce and industrial development throughout the African world. The work of Booker T. Washington heavily influenced Garvey. Much like Washington, Garvey argued that although blacks are handicapped by circumstances, they are keeping themselves back, which causes other races to refuse to notice them. In an effort to deal with these handicaps, Garvey sought to begin an industrial and technical school in Jamaica similar to the Tuskegee Institute. In an effort to begin the school, Washington extended an invitation to Garvey to meet with him in Tuskegee, a meeting that never took place because Washington died.

By 1916, at the age of 28, Garvey set up a UNIA chapter in Harlem to recruit members. To keep up with the growing membership of the UNIA throughout the world, Garvey began to publish *Negro World,* the official newspaper of the UNIA, his greatest publishing venture. It quickly became one of the leading American black weeklies, with a regular circulation around the world of about 200,000. The *Negro World* refused to accept any advertisement that would degrade the black race, such as hair-straightening or skin-whitening compounds. On the first page of each issue was an editorial by Garvey in which he reminded blacks of their rich history. The remaining parts of the newspaper carried articles on black history and culture, UNIA activities, and racial news. The program of the UNIA was communicated in an eight-point platform in the *Negro World.*

1. To champion Negro nationhood by redemption of Africa.
2. To make the Negro race conscious.
3. To breathe ideals of manhood and womanhood into every Negro.
4. To advocate self-determination.
5. To make the Negro world-conscious.
6. To print all the news that will be interesting and instructive to the Negro.
7. To instill racial self-help.
8. To inspire racial love and self-respect. (*Black Leadership in America,* p. 84).

Much to the fascination of whites, Garvey was a force to reckon with. He was a dominant power with a rapidly growing movement. His message of uplift, international solidarity, and support for Irish, Indian, and Egyptian independence was a threat to international order. As such, British and American intelligence agencies began to accuse Garvey of racial strife.

By 1919, there were UNIA chapters chartered in most American cities with large black populations. The headquarters of UNIA was established in Harlem. The organization had saved enough money to purchase an auditorium, which Garvey named Liberty Hall, that was used for various purposes including meetings, dances, and feeding the hungry. The UNIA also established the Negro Factories Corporation (NFC), a black business that produced a variety of commodities and provided jobs to black people, ultimately employing 300 people.

Garvey's business ventures expanded and also included the Black Star Line (BSL), a fleet of black-owned and operated steamships. The BSL was incorporated in Delaware and capitalized at $500,000 with 100,000 shares at $5 a share only to be sold to blacks, with no individual able to purchase more than 200 shares. The BSL was authorized to own, operate, and charter ships and to carry freight, passengers, and mail. The line was different from the NFC. It offered blacks three distinct opportunities: to invest in a black-owned business, to make money, and to make history. Although many laughed at the idea of the BSL, it was able to purchase several ships, the *S. S. Yarmouth, S. S. Shadyside,* and *Kanawha.* Blacks everywhere marveled at the accomplishment of Garvey's BSL.

Black separatist Marcus Garvey, in uniform as the president of the Republic of Africa. Marcus Garvey founded the Universal Negro Improvement Association (UNIA) to realize the ideals of Pan-Africanism and African repatriation. Garvey's rallying call for the UNIA was, "Up, you mighty race, you can accomplish what you will!" (Library of Congress)

At UNIA's pinnacle, Garvey called for the First International Convention of the Negro Peoples of the World. The delegates attending the convention represented 48 states, 25 countries, and 3 continents. Dignitaries at the convention included an African prince, the mayor of Monrovia, Liberia, and tribal chiefs. The event was a momentous occasion where the various units of the UNIA were amassed together. In a parade through Harlem, the Black Cross Nurses, ready to come to the aid of black people, were dressed in white. The African Legion, which included many World War I veterans dressed in dark blue uniforms with red stripes, were mounted on horseback and marching with precision, indicating to the world that the organization would be prepared to use force to gain black redemption. The white press took notice of the pageantry, which displayed the might and organization of Garvey's group.

Flying high in the midst of the crowd were the crimson, black, and green banners of the delegates that welcomed Garvey with a five-minute standing ovation. His opening statement preached black nationalism calling for the freedom of Africa. Garvey stated:

> We are the descendants of a people determined to suffer no longer. We shall now organize the 400,000,000 Negroes of the world into a vast organization to plant the banner of freedom on the great continent of Africa.... We do not desire what has belonged to others, though others have always sought to deprive us of that which belonged to us...If Europe is for the Europeans, then Africa shall be for the black peoples of the world. We say it; we mean it...The other races have countries of their own and it is time for the 400,000,000 Negroes to claim Africa for themselves (*Great Lives Observed*, p. 65).

The convention designated Garvey as the provisional president of the African Republic, an exile government. Other officers in this government included the titles of supreme potentate, supreme deputy potentate, and an entire cabinet. The Declaration of the Rights of the Negro Peoples of the World, a statement of protest and plan of action for blacks, was also adopted at the convention.

By 1922, Garvey's momentum took an incredible turn downward. The black establishment waged mounting attacks against the business activities of the UNIA because of the large sums of money it had collected from blacks. A few disgruntled stockholders also lodged complaints and accused the BSL of mismanagement. As a result, Garvey and several associates were arrested and charged with 12 counts of mail fraud in promoting the stock of the BSL. Shortly after his arrest, with an operating budget of merely $31.12, Garvey announced BSL's operational activities would desist. The trial was delayed and Garvey was released on bond.

While awaiting trial, Garvey promised to return to the UNIA. Much to the dismay of the America's black elite, Garvey maintained a faithful following; however, disgruntled BSL stockholders and employees sued him. At his trial, Garvey denied overstating the profits of the BSL. He did admit that there were no assets and the corporation had more than $600,000 in operating expenses. The trial also revealed that the BSL never paid dividends to stockholders. The judge stated that Garvey had preyed on his own people. In addition to the business troubles faced by Garvey, there were also domestic troubles that became the center of attention for the black elite in mounting attacks against Garvey.

By 1922, when the third annual convention of the UNIA met in Harlem, his opposition had mobilized and called its own meeting. A group called Friends of Negro Freedom, organized by the editors of *Messenger* magazine, Chandler Owen, and A. Philip Randolph, adopted the slogan "Garvey must go!" This group also called for his immediate deportation. Another major argument against Garvey were various rumors that he had made an agreement with the Ku Klux Klan. The opposition's most fatal move against Garvey was a letter written to the United States attorney general in 1923 protesting the delay of Garvey's trial.

Although no one knows the influence of the letter, Garvey's trial began within six months after the letter was written. Garvey mounted his own defense by blaming his critics and competitors for BSL's demise. The trial revealed that Garvey had used the BSL for promoting the sale of stock rather than using it as a business enterprise. It also revealed that funds were transferred between the BSL and other UNIA business ventures without proper accounting methods. Garvey was found guilty of promoting the sale of BSL stock knowing the company was in financial trouble. He was sentenced to five years in prison and a $1,000 fine. The codefendants were acquitted. Garvey's attorneys made plans for appeals as he was remanded to Tombs Prison in New York.

Garvey was released on bail in September 1923. While waiting appeal, he pursued another maritime venture, the Black Cross Navigation and Trading Company, which purchased one ship, the *General G. W. Goethals*. At the 1924 convention, Garvey declared the ship to be named the *Booker T. Washington*. He hoped it would be the vessel to carry blacks back to Africa. The UNIA sent machinery and technical experts to Liberia to claim the land that had been promised them for colonization only to find that the goods had been confiscated by the shipping company for lack of payment. The experts were also immediately deported amid fears from Liberians that they would be a domestic threat. Garvey's hopes for the *Booker T. Washington* never came to fruition.

By 1925, Garvey's appeals were rejected and the Supreme Court refused to hear the case. On February 8, 1925, he entered the Atlanta penitentiary to begin serving a five-year prison term. Although efforts were made to continue the work of the UNIA, they fell short because of a lack of a flamboyant leader. Surprisingly during Garvey's time in prison, even those who had never supported him became increasingly aware that he had fallen victim to a contentious America. After supporters urged clemency for Garvey, in 1927, President Coolidge commuted his sentence. As an alien, United States law required nonresidents convicted of a felony to be deported. So on release, without having an opportunity to visit UNIA headquarters in New York, Garvey was taken to New Orleans and put aboard the *S. S. Saramacca* headed for Panama and the West Indies.

Even in his homeland of Jamaica, Garvey continued the work of the UNIA by visiting local chapters. The *Negro World* also continued to publish editorials to be sent to his American following. With the support of his wife, in 1928 he traveled to Europe and established new UNIA headquarters in London and Paris. He also presented a petition to the League of Nations at Geneva and urged them to create a "free Negro state in Africa."

By 1929, Garvey issued a call for the Sixth International Convention of Negro Peoples of the World to be held in Kingston, Jamaica. Similar to the first international convention, this was the last major UNIA convention that garnered great attention. Most of the discussion at the conference involved improving the conditions blacks around the world. The delegates established a department of health and public education to improve the health conditions of blacks through the world, and it also sought to establish UNIA consulates in black population centers and to publicize grievances and to protect the rights of blacks. Much to the dismay of critics, even after serving jail time and being deported, Garvey continued to be a force among blacks.

Garvey also seemed to become a dominant force in Jamaican politics by organizing the Jamaican Peoples Political Party. He ran an unsuccessful bid for the Jamaican legislature, which could have been derailed by the lawsuits and complaints by American chapters of the UNIA when he moved the headquarters to Jamaica. By the 1930s, the Garvey movement slowed significantly because the Depression left black Americans in disarray. Just as conditions in America supported Garvey's elevation as a race leader, other conditions in America accompanied his decline.

The seventh convention proved to be a disappointment and Garvey moved the headquarters to London in 1935. Although small meetings of the UNIA were held in the mid-1930s, Garveyism had declined. By the late 1930s, Garvey's health was failing after suffering with pneumonia and a stroke that left him paralyzed. On June 10, 1940, Garvey died. In London, Garvey's death went unnoticed, but in the United States, black and white newspapers paid tribute to him. With mixed reviews on his triumphs and setbacks, they all agreed, it was unlikely that black America would see another Garvey.

See also: Black Star Line; Pan-Africanism; Universal Negro Improvement Association

Angela K. Lewis

Bibliography

Cronon, E. David., ed. *Black Moses: The Story of Marcus Garvey and the Universal Negro Improvement Association.* Madison: University of Wisconsin Press, 1955.

Cronon, E. David., ed. *Great Lives Observed.* Englewood Cliffs, NJ: Prentice-Hall, 1973.

Garvey, Amy Jacques *Garvey and Garveyism.* New York: Collier, 1970.

Garvey, Amy Jacques. *The Philosophy and Opinions of Marcus Garvey, or Africa for the Africans.* Dover, MA: Majority Press, 1986.

White, John. "Marcus Garvey: Jamaican Messiah." In *Black Leadership in America.* John White, ed., 75–108. New York: Longman, 1985.

Wintz, Cary D., ed. "Marcus Garvey." In *African American Political Thought 1890–1930: Washington, Du Bois, Garvey and Randolph.* Carl D. Wintz, ed., 167–242. Armonk, NY: M. E. Sharpe, 1996.

Georgia Educational Association

By August 1865, black Georgians helped organize the Georgia Educational Association (GEA) in Augusta. An offshoot of the Georgia Equal Rights Association (GERA), this organization began when a group of African American farmers from Wilkes County attempted to purchase a large plot of land in neighboring Dougherty County in the fall of 1865. Pooling together more than $7,000, this group, led by Lawrence Speed and Wallace Sherman, sought the assistance of the Freedmen's Bureau to facilitate the sale. Although the black farmers had sufficient funds and the power of the federal government behind them, they only managed to rent 500 acres of land on the Whitlock Place Plantation in Dougherty County. This disappointment represented the first of many defeats in the attempt to redistribute land and wealth in the postbellum South.

The Wilkes County farmers sought the creation of an independent African American community, completely removed from the controls and limitations imposed by white Southerners. Movements of this nature were rampant in the South during the 1860s and 1870s. Just four years earlier in Port Royal, South Carolina, General William T. Sherman occupied the region and freed thousands of slaves. Once liberated and granted land, they immediately became yeomen farmers seeking to grow crops and sustain their community. Of importance, they actively distanced themselves from "slave crops," refusing to grow cotton and indigo. Hardworking and eager to maintain their freedom, this community made a collective decision to grow food crops for internal consumption. This decision meant they sought removal from a white-controlled market economy and from white society in general.

The Port Royal example was repeated in the 245-mile tract of land Sherman granted to African Americans in his Special Field Order No. 15. Issued on January 16, 1865, the order mandated that the 400,000 acres of abandoned and confiscated land be divided among former slaves. On receipt of this land, more than 40,000 freed people settled and cultivated this region, which encompassed the South Carolina and Georgia Lowcountry and Sea Islands. Again, they refused to grow cotton, opting instead for the independent existence guaranteed through the cultivation of nonmarket food crops.

While the Wilkes County freed people failed to purchase their own land, they did succeed in creating an organization that continued to seek self-determination for black Georgian communities. In August 1865, they helped organize a statewide convention held in Augusta. Delegates from black communities throughout the state attended to discuss their fate and future. Out of this convention emerged the GERA, which sought to address all of the major issues of the Reconstruction Era—social rights, land reform, and literacy. Moreover the GERA, as historian Lee Formwalt contends, sought to achieve its goals without the aid of the federal government, Northern progressives, or Radical Republicans.

Within a year of its founding, the GERA formed the GEA as its education and literacy wing. One of the primary purposes of the GEA was to create and financially support elementary schools for African Americans in local communities throughout the state. Local auxiliaries held regular meetings and primarily raised funds to pay for school supplies and teacher salaries while the statewide association held a series of conventions to publicize its mission and garner additional financial and political support. By late 1867, 120 black elementary schools were erected by the GEA in 53 counties. Black communities in Georgia purchased 57 school buildings to meet their own education needs. In Augusta, the Wilkes County farmers, who helped found the Dougherty County Educational Association, opened its first elementary school on the Gintown plantation in 1866. Members of the Dougherty County branch of the GEA taught at both of the local black elementary schools and played a determining role in the curriculum. The Albany, Georgia branch of the GEA opened its elementary school in 1866 and freedmen Jack Mallard, an active member of the Association, instructed 23 students in a building constructed and owned by the African American community. In Savannah, 16 of the 28 black elementary schools were established in 1866 by the GEA. Through the Association's publication, the *Loyal Georgian,* the GEA explicitly voiced its goals and nationalist leanings. In 1866, the paper reported that GEA schools were controlled and taught by African Americans for the benefit of freed people whose donations and drive sustained these schools.

Clearly, then, the GEA rejected paternalist appeals and approaches to the education of African Americans in Georgia and sought to actively define the role of schools within the many black communities throughout the state. They established a model for community-based schools in which the GEA generated funds to purchase or rent land, erected schools, determined the curriculum, and hired teachers. Unlike the situation practiced later under segregation, the locus of control and power in the community-based model was not in the hands of an outside and hostile group. Thus in many ways, the GEA epitomized black self-determination, autonomy, and sovereignty in the post-Civil War South.

Several prominent black leaders and politicians in Georgia played important roles in the association, including James Porter, Jefferson Franklin Long, William Jefferson White, and Tunis George Campbell. Each used their activism in the GERA/GEA to launch impressive political careers. Despite a political platform calling for "Relief, Homesteads and Schools for the People," the Republican party did nothing to directly support the efforts of the GEA and was more interested in gaining political support than supporting the GEA in its continued efforts to establish schools in local communities. Joining this political tug-of-war, the Freedmens' Bureau had long been an obstacle to the goals of the GEA. Although the bureau provided invaluable service in mediating the sale and transfer of land and buildings used by the GEA to erect schools, members

of the association voiced significant concerns because some of the local agents of the Freedmen's Bureau in Albany came from slave-holding families.

Even many of the Northern whites in the bureau dealt with freed people in a condescending and abusive manner. As a result, many African Americans in Dougherty County knew that they could not expect any real support from the federal government. On this note, GEA leaders contended that its African American members should be accountable only to people of their own selection, but not to whites. Thus, the GEA fostered a nationalist, race-conscious perspective as a result of the justifiable suspicions its members had of both Northern and Southern whites. As a result, local auxiliaries of the GEA often debated about whether to even hire white Northern teachers even in the absence of other viable options. Although efforts like this were relatively short-lived, they did represent the collective strivings of black communities in the postbellum South as they sought to carve out autonomous spaces in the midst of racial hostility and intolerance.

See also: Black Nationalism; Freedmen's Bureau; Port Royal Experiment; Reconstruction Era Black Politicians

Walter C. Rucker

Bibliography
Anderson, James A. *The Education of Blacks in the South, 1860–1935.* Chapel Hill: The University of North Carolina Press, 1988.
Blassingame, John. "Before the Ghetto: The Making of the Black Community in Savannah, Georgia, 1865–1880." *Journal of Social History* 6 (1973):463–88.
Du Bois, W. E. B. *Black Reconstruction in America, 1860–1880.* New York: Atheneum, 1992.
Formwalt, Lee W. "The Origins of African-American Politics in Southwest Georgia: A Case Study of Black Political Organization During Presidential Reconstruction, 1865–1867." *Journal of Negro History* 77 (1992):211–22.
Jones, Jacqueline. *Soldiers of Light and Love: Northern Teachers and Georgia Blacks, 1865–1873.* Chapel Hill: The University of North Carolina Press, 1980.

Grandfather Clause

In 1870, after the Civil War, the United States government added three new amendments to the Constitution. The Thirteenth Amendment outlawed slavery. The Fourteenth Amendment guaranteed due process and equal protection to all citizens, regardless of race or color. The Fifteenth Amendment guaranteed the right to vote to all citizens regardless of "race, color, or previous condition of servitude." Although many Southern states still held their Civil War mentality of white superiority, these amendments forced the states to accept African Americans as equal—at least under the law.

Many of the Southern states wished to evade the newly instituted amendments, especially the Fifteenth Amendment. To circumvent this amendment, some Southern states implemented new laws that prevented African Americans from voting. Educational and property qualifications were often installed for this purpose. More specifically, literacy tests were implemented, poll taxes were added, and grandfather clauses were administered. A grandfather clause countered the government's implementation of the Fifteenth Amendment by forbidding any African American from voting unless he was a citizen, or descendant of a citizen, that had the right to vote before 1867. This stipulation eliminated all African Americans from voting because African Americans were not given the right to vote until after 1867. These clauses were adopted into state constitutions so as to legally prevent African Americans from voting.

Grandfather clauses were seen as the most beneficial way to prevent African Americans from voting. Educational and property qualifications often prevented poor whites from voting, but grandfather clauses hampered only African Americans. Furthermore, by the 1890s, a good number of African Americans were able to pass the literacy tests, pay the poll taxes, or circumvent any other regulation Southern governments tried to impose on newly independent African Americans. By implementing grandfather clauses Southern governments were able to prevent all African Americans from voting, even those that could pass the educational, property, or financial qualifications.

Seven Southern states implemented grandfather clauses in the late 1890s to early 1900s. Although many African Americans objected to these clauses, they remained in place until 1915 when the United States Supreme Court declared them to be unconstitutional in *Guinn v. United States.*

The use of grandfather clauses was part of a larger picture that included Jim Crow laws and Black Codes. Jim Crow laws were passed in the Southern United States at the end of Reconstruction, the period of rebuilding in the South after the Civil War. These laws discriminated against African Americans and restricted them from voting, and other fundamental rights, through constitutional and legal means. Like grandfather clauses, Jim Crow laws were found to be legal until 1915. Similarly, Black Codes were implemented after the conclusion of Reconstruction in the South. These codes sought to return African Americans to a position of bondage or servitude. Although African Americans were free in terms of terminology, the Black Codes returned them to a position of servitude in actuality. Jim Crow laws and Black Codes in general, as well as grandfather clauses in particular, were held to be legal by both the Southern state governments and the national government until 1915 with *Guinn v. United States.*

Grandfather clauses, Jim Crow laws, and Black Codes all undermined the legislation the national government put in place at the conclusion of the Civil War. By implementing these discriminatory laws, the Southern states were able to successfully continue in their practice of putting down African Americans and restricting their advancement. These acts, therefore, prevented African Americans from receiving the equality they so desired. It would take almost another hundred years, and endless civil rights battles, to bring the legislation and equality that African Americans so desired.

See also: Black Codes; Disfranchisement; Fifteenth Amendment; Jim Crow

Mindy R. Weidman

Bibliography

Lewis, Thomas T. *The U.S. Supreme Court.* Pasadena, CA: Salem Press, 2007.

Perman, Michael. *Struggle for Mastery: Disfranchisement in the South, 1888–1908.* Chapel Hill: University of North Carolina Press, 2001.

Schmidt, Benno C. Jr. "Principle and Prejudice: The Supreme Court and Race in the Progressive Era, Part 3: Black Disfranchisement from the KKK to the Grandfather Clause," *Columbia Law Review* 82 (1982):835–905.

Great Migration

The Great Migration was the mass exodus of more than 1 million African Americans from below the Mason-Dixon Line to the North between 1916 and 1930. This migration produced a massive demographic shift, resulting in significant economic, social, and political changes for the United States. The highest rates of migration occurred from 1916 to 1918, when approximately 400,000 African Americans moved to the North. Between 1910 and 1930, the African American population in the North increased by 20 percent; however, most African Americans did not leave the South. Many moved from rural areas to southern cities and many others did not move at all.

The first blacks to move north were predominantly young, unskilled, and male. Many of these men went with the intention of settling in the North and sending for their families when they could save enough money. Others planned to earn some money and then return to the South. Another surge in migration, beginning in 1920, brought more black intellectuals and professionals to the North. In fact, by the end of the 1920s, Harlem and Chicago became centers for the black intelligentsia and black culture. Most migrants settled in cities like Chicago, New York, Philadelphia, Boston, Detroit, and others because of cheaper, easier transportation via train, as well as numerous job opportunities. Many black women had already traveled north before World War I to work as domestic servants.

Numerous forces compelled African Americans to leave the South during this period. A major factor was the lack of job opportunities in the South, as well as increased opportunities for employment in the North. Because of segregation and the systems of sharecropping and tenant farming in the largely agricultural South, African Americans had few chances to advance in the jobs they did have and barely any chance to break into more prestigious careers reserved for whites. Moreover, this period saw many changes in southern agriculture, among them increased use of machinery to replace human labor, which further limited blacks' likelihood for financial well-being.

Environmental factors contributed to a fiscal downturn in the farming economy. The boll weevil, a beetle that feeds on cotton, infested and destroyed cotton fields throughout the South during the 1910s and 1920s, causing many people to lose their source of income. Ultimately, the South was forced to diversify its agriculture, ending its dependence on cotton as the primary crop. Another significant environmental factor that affected the southern economy was the Great Mississippi flood of 1927, which destroyed many homes and plantations. As a result of substantial rainfall in the summer months of 1926, the Mississippi River overflowed, flooding more than 270,000 square miles in the states of Arkansas, Illinois, Kentucky, Louisiana, Mississippi, and Tennessee. By 1927, migration to the North had begun to slow, but the desperate situation this flood created for many families encouraged more people to go north.

By contrast, more jobs became available in the North during this period, and northern industries actively recruited southern labor. By 1914, many European countries, although not the United States, were involved in World War I. Many Europeans living in the United States returned to their homelands to contribute to the war effort. European immigration to the United States also slowed considerably. In 1900, Europeans entered the United States at a rate of more than 500,000 per year; by 1916, the immigration rate from European countries was less than 300,000 per year. The Selective Service Act of 1917 created even more job opportunities for unskilled laborers in the North. This law, passed the year the United States entered World War I, required that all men 21 to 30 years old register for service in the U.S. military. Ultimately, 4.8 million men served in World War I (more than half were drafted), leaving many jobs open.

By 1917, Congress also began passing legislation to halt immigration. The United States's exclusionary stance on immigration culminated in the Immigration Act of 1924, which limited the number of immigrants from any country to 2 percent of the total number of people from that country already in the United States. This federal law, also known as the Johnson-Reed Act, also excluded the immigration of individuals from Asian countries. The Immigration Act of 1924 was aimed chiefly at limiting the influx of individuals from southern and eastern European countries, the majority of whom were industrial workers and had been immigrating since the 1850s.

The dwindling number of immigrants and loss of many men to the military encouraged northern businesses to recruit African Americans in the South as cheap sources of labor. Northern agents went south and offered African American men jobs and train fare to northern cities. Also, black newspapers advertised jobs and published articles about opportunities for blacks in the North. Ministers often read letters in their churches from African Americans who found better opportunities in the North. So many African Americans headed to the North that many companies eventually stopped recruiting because they did not need to.

African Americans were driven north by more than economic prospects. The end of Reconstruction in 1877

Painting by African American visual artist Jacob Lawrence depicting African Americans migrating north during World War I. (National Archives)

saw the reinstitution of white control of the South, replacing African Americans who held political office after the Civil War with whites and ushering in the period commonly referred to as the nadir of race relations. The post-Reconstruction South was particularly violent and oppressive for blacks. Jim Crow laws, reified by the Supreme Court's *Plessy v. Ferguson* (1896) decision, segregated public spaces, invoking the "separate but equal" doctrine. African Americans were offered subpar educational resources. Blacks were politically disenfranchised and could not serve on juries. Moreover, the South was rife with racial violence, including lynching. Also, the Ku Klux Klan began a second wave of violence and intimidation in the 1910s and 1920s, which eventually extended to the North. Many blacks went North in hopes of escaping the repressive South.

The Great Migration had significant and longlasting implications for the North and for African Americans. The abrupt arrival of thousands of African Americans in northern cities produced a new kind of white discrimination in the North, as whites attempted to segregate neighborhoods,

schools, workplaces, and leisure spaces. To keep blacks out of all-white neighborhoods, whites used violence or collaborated with realtors to create racially restrictive covenants. Moreover, it was nearly impossible for African Americans to secure mortgages in order to purchase homes in black neighborhoods owing to a practice called "redlining," in which neighborhoods deemed least desirable and too risky for mortgages were circled in red on city maps. These neighborhoods tended to be older, inner-city neighborhoods, populated mostly by blacks and ethnic minorities.

In several cities throughout the North (and South as well), ethnic and racial tensions were exacerbated by postwar economic anxieties. During the Red Summer of 1919, 25 cities experienced race riots. The riot in Chicago, which lasted a week, was among the worst; 23 African Americans and 15 whites were killed. In addition, 342 blacks and 195 whites were injured. More than 1,000 people were left homeless from the fires that ravaged the city. The Great Migration also contributed to white flight from the cities into the suburbs as a result of to racial tension. Whites were able to move to the suburbs because of highway expansion, as well as mortgages from the Federal Housing Authority and the Veterans Administration. The result of white flight was fewer tax dollars for the city, where blacks remained, and a shift in political power.

African Americans, particularly migrant blacks, tended to get the worst jobs at the lowest rates of pay. Even by the 1960s, unions were still predominantly white: northern plumbers unions were 99.8 percent white, electrical workers unions were 99.4 percent white, and carpenters unions were 98.4 percent white. Still, it seems that African Americans migrating from the South fared better that African Americans born in the North. Migrant blacks in the North made more money overall, were more likely to be married, and had lower rates of nonmarital childbearing than northern-born African Americans. Also, migrant children were more likely to live in two-parent households than nonmigrant children.

The mass migration of African Americans to the North coincided with, and helped produce, a new age of modernity. One of the most significant cultural results of the Great Migration was the Harlem Renaissance. The development of a black middle class in Harlem, as well as the influx of blacks into the city, contributed to this cultural revolution, which occurred during the 1920s and ended with the Great Depression. The Harlem Renaissance spanned many genres, including music, drama, literature, and poetry, and articulated what was unique about the black experience in America. The Great Migration introduced the North to blues and jazz music and southern food as well. The dissemination of southern culture was aided in this period, as it could not have been previously, by the popularity of newspapers and advances in radio and film technologies.

One of the most substantial effects of the Great Migration was the restoration of African Americans' political rights. Blacks did not suffer the same kind of systematic disfranchisement in the North that they had in the South. Because African Americans were able to vote, and did vote, politicians were forced to consider their demands. In the North, African Americans were afforded better economic opportunities, which allowed them to contribute to various organizations that worked for civil rights. Moreover, blacks' shared experiences provided a milieu for alliances, fostered by their proximity to one another. City dwelling encouraged organized protest among African Americans that was highly visible. Thus by using their newfound electoral leverage in the North, African Americans were able to defeat Jim Crow in the South.

See also: Black Nadir; Destination, Chicago, Illinois; Destination, Detroit, Michigan; Destination, Harlem, New York; Harlem Renaissance; Urbanization

Laurie Lahey

Bibliography
Baldwin, Davarian L. *Chicago's New Negroes: Modernity, The Great Migration, and Black Urban Life.* Chapel Hill: University of North Carolina Press, 2007.
Gregory, James N. *The Southern Diaspora: How the Great Migration of Black and White Southerners Transformed America.* Chapel Hill: University of North Carolina Press, 2005.
Marks, Carole. *Farewell, We're Good and Gone: The Black Migration.* Bloomington: Indiana University Press, 1989.
Sernett, Milton C. *Bound for the Promised Land: African American Religion and the Great Migration.* Durham, NC: Duke University Press, 1997.
Stewart, Jacqueline Najuma. *Migrating to the Movies: Cinema and Black Urban Modernity.* Berkeley: University of California Press, 2005.
Tolnay, Stewart E. "The African American 'Great Migration' and Beyond," *Annual Review of Sociology* 29 (2003):209–32.

Griggs, Sutton

E. Sutton Griggs (1872–1933), an African American preacher and writer, was one of the few outspoken critics of anti-black propaganda in the South who turned to racial accommodation during the early decades of the 20th century. Born in Chatfield, Texas, Griggs was the son of Reverend Allen R. Griggs Sr., a former slave, who rose to prominence as the president of the Baptist National Convention.

Griggs graduated from Richmond Theological Seminary in Virginia in 1893 and served as a pastor of the First Baptist Church in Nashville until 1913. During this time, he was instrumental in establishing the American Baptist Theological Seminary and was its president for one year, from 1925 to 1926. The reverend established the Tabernacle Baptist Church and built an institutional church in Memphis with the intention to provide spiritual help and employment opportunities to the local people.

Griggs was one of the well-published black authors of the Jim Crow South. His novels and treatises informed his theological and sociological perspective on southern race relations. His fictional work, *Imperium Imperio,* published in 1899, introduced the new and self-respecting African American and defended black Americans' basic rights, including the right to vote. Three years later, he wrote another book, *Unfettered, Dorlan's Plan* that elaborated his objectives to achieve racial equality and said that this racial parity would eventually tear down racial barriers.

Disappointed with his community's unwillingness to rally behind these works, Griggs temporarily abandoned his writings until the National Baptist Convention came forward to finance his next novel, *The Hindered Hand.* In this book published in 1905, Griggs strongly denounced the racist writings of Reverend Thomas Dixon Jr., whose works supported white brutality and segregation. Along the same lines he published a pamphlet, *The One Great Question: Study of Southern Conditions At Close Range,* in 1907. It forecasted a gloomy scenario of human rights violations in the South. In this social and political treatise, he condemned the racist attitudes of the city fathers of Nashville and their policy of encouraging white brutality on African Americans. Frustrated with the lack of response from the city black community, Griggs converted to racial accommodation and directed his message on racial collaboration to the white community.

He published a series of articles in 1911 under the title *Wisdom's Call* that urged African Americans in the South not to migrate to the North. This work made him popular with the members of the white established Memphis Industrial Committee. It was their support and the backing of the Memphis Chamber of Commerce that facilitated Griggs to spread his ideas. He published a little newspaper, *The Neighbor,* in 1919 in which he advised his community to maintain good relations with the white community and supported lynching as a means to control violence and crime. This stand contradicted his earlier works that condemned such brutality. The white press appreciated his message but did not publish the criticism from the local black community and the NAACP regarding his position on lynching.

Griggs published his next work, *The Science of Social Efficiency,* in 1923. The conciliatory tone of Reverend Griggs is evident in this work that advised African Americans to move ahead as a group and adopt Christian virtues and subordinate themselves to the white establishment. To carry this message to black public schools, Griggs sought endorsements of educators, school board presidents, and state teachers associations. He traveled to several southern states where he lectured on the retarding forces that impeded the progress of his community. In a span of four years, from 1925 to 1929, Griggs published *The Stepping Stones to Higher Things, The Winning Policy,* and *the Cooperative Nature and Social Education.* Despite his efforts to convey his message of biracial harmony and cooperation, these works were not prescribed in the curriculum.

African Americans did not purchase his books because they believed that these works damaged their racial pride. Lacking financial and moral support from his community and receiving inadequate funding from the white community, Reverend Griggs was caught in a financial squeeze. He could not make the church mortgage payment and was forced to sell his church in a Memphis public auction. He relocated to Denison, Texas, where he spent his last three years as a pastor in the church, which his father established, and died in Houston on January 1933.

Griggs represented a segment of courageous African American intellectuals who adopted different strategies in attacking racism in the South during the period that witnessed lynching, black disenfranchisement, and the ascendancy of the Ku Klux Klan. Whether he succeeded or not in his attempts to grapple with the social evils, he stands as one of the shinning stars in the galaxy of black scholars before the 1920s Harlem Renaissance.

See also: A Negro Nation Within the Nation; Accommodationism; Black Nationalism; Jim Crow; Self-Segregation

Sivananda Mantri

Bibliography

Griggs, Sutton E. *Imperium In Imperio: A Study of the Negro Race Problem.* New York: Arno Press and the New York Times, 1969.

Griggs, Sutton E. *Overshadowed.* Nashville, TN: Orion Publishing, 1901.

Griggs, Sutton E. *The Science of Collective Efficiency.* Memphis, TN: The National Public Welfare League, 1923.

Griggs, Sutton E. *Wisdom's Call.* Nashville, TN: Orion Publishing, 1911.

Tucker, David M. *Black Pastors and Leaders: The Memphis Clergy, 1819–1972.* Memphis: Memphis State University Press, 1975.

Walker, Randolph M. *The Metamorphosis of Sutton E. Griggs.* Memphis: Walker Publication, 1991.

Haley, Alex

Alex Haley (1921–1992) was a biographer, novelist, and genealogist who is most noted for the book and miniseries *Roots* and *The Autobiography of Malcolm X.* Born in Ithaca,

New York, on August 11, 1921, he moved with his family to Henning, Tennessee, the year he was born and he spent five years there. At the time of Haley's birth, his mother, Bertha George Palmer Haley, was a music teacher and his father, Simon Alexander Haley, was a graduate student at Cornell University. After moving to Tennessee, Haley's father served as a professor of agriculture at a number of black colleges. While they were living in Henning, Haley's maternal grandmother, Cynthia Palmer, told stories about the family's genealogy, which could be traced back to an African named "Kin-tay" who would be Haley's great-great-great-great-grandfather. In 1937, Haley briefly attended Elizabeth City Teachers College in North Carolina, a stint that lasted until 1939. After dropping out of college, Haley enlisted in the Coast Guard as a messboy. This would begin a 20-year association with the Coast Guard.

During World War II, Haley rose in the rank of petty officer third class and began volunteering to write love letters for his fellow sailors, which they sent to girlfriends and wives. By 1949, Haley became the first member of the Coast Guard with a journalist rating, eventually advancing to chief petty officer and chief journalist through his retirement in 1959. Having honed his writing during his years in the Coast Guard, Haley began publishing in the private sector. He became a senior editor for *Reader's Digest* and wrote articles for a number of other publications. In September 1962, he began a long and lucrative relationship with *Playboy* magazine, interviewing such notable figures as Miles Davis, Martin Luther King Jr., Muhammad Ali, Jim Brown, and Malcolm X. Haley's work and association with *Playboy* was literally the genesis of the joke about men reading the magazine just for the interviews. His interview of Malcolm X was the beginning of a project that grew, over time, to the publication of *The Autobiography of Malcolm X* in 1965. Within a decade, this book had sold more than 6 million copies.

The work for which Haley is best know is the novel *Roots: The Saga of an American Family* published during the bicentennial of the United States in 1976. Although mostly fictional and only loosely based on Haley's family, this work initiated serious interest in African American genealogy. Moreover, when ABC aired the first *Roots* miniseries, 130 million people in the United States watched the eight episodes, shattering previous records for television viewers of a U.S. miniseries. Approximately 85 percent of all television homes saw all or part of the miniseries. After winning a National Book Award, the Spingarn Medal, a Pulitzer Prize, and more than 200 other awards for *Roots*, Haley became the source of controversy, as allegations of plagiarism were raised by Harold Courlander. In 1978, Courlander went to U.S. District Court, claiming that Haley lifted more than 80 passages from his 1967 work entitled *The African*. Haley's principal defense was that he had never read Courlander's book, but this was proven false when Joseph Bruchac provided an affidavit claiming that he had personally provided Haley a copy of *The African* five or six years before *Roots* was published. In the end, Haley settled out of court for $650,000 and issued a public acknowledgment of his wrongdoing.

After *Roots*, Haley's next major project, *Queen*, was to be based on a grandmother who was the daughter of an enslaved woman and her white owner. Haley died of a heart attack on February 10, 1992 in Seattle before finishing *Queen*. Per a prior agreement, David Stevens completed the work, and it was made into a 1993 movie. Haley has earned a number of posthumous awards, including having a U.S. Coast Guard cutter named in his honor in 1999; he was the recipient of the Korean War Service Medal in 2002.

See also: Atlantic Slave Trade; Senegambia; X, Malcolm

Walter C. Rucker

Bibliography

Gonzales, Doreen. *Alex Haley: Author of Roots.* Hillside, NJ: Enslow Publishers, 1994.

Haley, Alex. *Roots: The Saga of an American Family.* Garden City, NY: Doubleday, 1976.

Shirley, David. *Alex Haley.* New York: Chelsea House, 1994.

Hamer, Fannie Lou

Fannie Lou (Townsend) Hamer (1917–1977) was born October 6, 1917, in Ruleville, Mississippi. She was the last of 20 children of Lou Ella and James Townsend. Residing in the Mississippi Delta, the Townsend family were descendants of Mississippi's enslaved population. Like most black families of the era, they were sharecroppers. Sharecropping generally bound most workers to the land; workers who were born poor, lived poor, and died poor. Fannie Lou's early life was no exception.

At the age of six, Fannie Lou joined her parents in the cotton fields. By the time she was 12, she was forced to drop out of school and work full time to help support her family. She endured hard labor with few rewards throughout her teens and young adult years. At age 27 she married another sharecropper named Perry "Pap" Hamer and went to work on the plantation that employed her husband. Later, Fannie Lou and Pap adopted two children, Dorothy Jean and Virgie Lee.

In August 1962, Mrs. Hamer attended a meeting of the Student Nonviolent Coordinating Committee (SNCC) in her hometown of Ruleville, Mississippi. From that moment on, her life's path was forever altered. Inspired by the youthful enthusiasm of the student organizers, this is where she made the fateful decision to attempt to register to vote. Her earlier attendance at several conferences sponsored by the Regional Council of Negro Leadership had prepared her to move forward in her own personal struggle for civil rights. She had become part of the movement that would later lead to her activism as a civil rights worker and organizer. Upon learning of Mrs. Hamer's decision to register to vote, her landlord forced her to leave the plantation and denied her further opportunity to work. Mrs. Hamer was not deterred. She traveled to local communities to help spread the word about voter registration. During this period of history, blacks who attempted to vote or who were involved in voter registration efforts were threatened with violence, loss of job, harassment, and murder. In June of the following year, Mrs. Hamer and several SNCC colleagues traveled to Charleston, South Carolina to participate in voter registration and literacy workshop activities. On their return home, they stopped in Winona, Mississippi. Here they were jailed and brutally beaten by law enforcement officers. This beating left her blind in her left eye and her kidneys permanently damaged.

As a leader and organizer of the Mississippi Freedom Democratic Party (MFDP) that was formed in April 1964, Mrs. Hamer was selected as a delegate to attend the 1964 Democratic National Convention in Atlantic City, New Jersey. It was here, during her electrifying testimony before the convention's credentials committee, that she rose to national prominence as she sought to prohibit the seating of the all-white Mississippi delegation. An attempt at compromise would offer the MFDP two delegate seats. The compromise was rejected by the party. The overall effort to seat the MFDP failed, but the Democratic Party agreed that, in the future, no delegation would be seated from a state where anyone was illegally denied the vote. Mrs. Hamer would forever be remembered as a powerful voice of the civil rights struggle who so precisely articulated the pain and frustration of millions of African American citizens. The Democratic Party and the nation took note. Roughly a year later, the 1965 Voting Rights Act was passed.

After her memorable experience in Atlantic City, Mrs. Hamer turned her attention to building strong institutions for addressing problems at the local level. She continued her work in Mississippi, ran for Congress in 1964 and 1965, and was seated as a member of Mississippi's legitimate delegation to the Democratic National Convention in 1968 in Chicago, Illinois. She played an active role in antipoverty programs, especially Head Start, and in 1969 founded the Freedom Farms Corporation, designed to help poor farming families—black and white—become economically self-sufficient. In addition, she was a local

Fannie Lou Hamer, a Mississippi field hand for most of her life, became a prominent advocate of civil rights. As Mississippi's Democratic Party refused African American members, Hamer helped form the Mississippi Freedom Democratic Party (MFDP) whose members attempted to unseat the regular party delegation at the Democratic National Convention in 1964. (Library of Congress)

leader in Dr. King's Poor Peoples Campaign. In 1971 she sought, unsuccessfully, to become a Mississippi state senator as an independent.

The last six years of Mrs. Hamer's life were marked by severe health and financial problems, but during this times she received numerous honors and awards that recognized a lifelong role in the Civil Rights movement. She died on March 14, 1977. The official cause of death was breast cancer. Her funeral in Ruleville drew a cross section of national dignitaries who came to sing her praises. And rightfully so: Mrs. Hamer was one of the most significant participants in the struggle to achieve freedom and social justice for African Americans in the 20th century. In July, 2008, a coalition of local civil rights activists, lead by Alderwoman Hattie Jordan and Patricia Thompson, national scholars, and concerned citizens dedicated the Fannie Lou Hamer Memorial Garden, in Ruleville, Mississippi, marking the final resting place of Mrs. Hamer and her beloved husband, Pap.

See also: Johnson, Lyndon Baines; MFDP; Poor People's Campaign; Student Nonviolent Coordinating Committee

Patricia Reid-Merritt

Bibliography
Lee, Chana Kai. *For Freedom's Sake: The Life of Fannie Lou Hamer.* Athens: University of Georgia Press, 1999.
Mills, Kay. *This Little Light of Mine: The Life of Fannie Lou Hamer.* New York: Dutton, 1993.
Nies, Judith. *Nine Women: Portraits from the American Radical Tradition.* Berkeley: University of California Press, 2002.
Wright, Giles R. *40th Anniversary Celebration: Fannie Lou Hamer, Atlantic City and the Democratic National Convention.* Pomona, CA: Richard Stockton College, 2004.

Hampton, Fred

Fred Hampton (1948–1969) was one of the greatest young political activists to emerge during the Black Power movement. Hampton, chairman of the Illinois Black Panther Party for Self-Defense (BPP), was brutally murdered in his prime by the Chicago police and the FBI.

Hampton was born in Blue Island, Illinois, on August 30, 1948. He started his political career while he was a student at Proviso East High School. He helped found the Maywood NAACP and was admired by both blacks and

whites as an influential youth leader. He attended Triton Junior College in 1966, and, by the fall of 1967, Hampton attended Crane Junior College on Chicago's west side. Crane Junior College, later known as Malcolm X College, was a central meeting place for black activists.

In 1968, Fred Hampton founded the Illinois and Chicago Chapters of the BPP. The BPP was a national organization dedicated to the liberation of black people. He was a gifted leader that made the Chicago BPP one of the most prominent branches in the country. Hampton strove to alleviate the oppression of black people and improve their living conditions. He established several community service programs that included free breakfasts for children, a free medical clinic, and political education classes.

Hampton was a charismatic public speaker who instilled hope and pride in many Chicagoans throughout the city. He spoke out against police brutality and advocated that members of the community defend themselves. Hampton created coalitions with other socially active groups such as the Students for a Democratic Society (SDS). He also reached across racial boundaries to build coalitions between black, white, and Latino street gangs.

Hampton and other BPP members gained national attention because they publicly advocated the use of weapons for self-defense and patrolled the community in an effort to prevent abuse by the police. J. Edgar Hoover, director of the FBI, stated that the Black Panther Party was "the greatest threat to the internal security of the country." The FBI's COINTELPRO (counterintelligence program) was established to neutralize black political activists and destroy their organizations. Many activists were killed or unjustly incarcerated as a result of COINTELPRO. Hampton was sent to Menard Prison for an alleged theft charge but was released on appeal after only a few months.

As a result of COINTELPRO, the Chicago BPP headquarters, located at 2350 W. Madison, was ransacked several times by the police. On December 4, 1969, Chicago police raided a nearby apartment at 2337 W. Monroe where many BPP members slept. The police fired shots into the apartment to deliberately kill BPP leaders. Mark Clark, BPP defense captain of the Peoria, Illinois branch, was killed first with a single shot to the heart. Fred Hampton was killed next. Fellow BPP members heard two shots immediately before the police confirmed that Hampton was dead. There were seven survivors of the raid including Hampton's beloved Deborah Johnson who was pregnant with their son.

Johnson was uninjured, but four other members sustained gunshot wounds. All of them were arrested and charged with attempted murder.

Thousands of community members visited the crime scene and were appalled by the apparent slaughter of these young leaders. Many concerned citizens demanded an investigation. The initial investigation, however, exonerated the police. Although no law enforcement officials were ever convicted of the crimes, subsequent investigations established that the raid was in fact a successful assassination attempt that was approved and sanctioned by the FBI. Eventually, 25,000 pages emerged that confirmed that FBI involvement had been suppressed from the evidence.

The investigations also proved that FBI informant William O' Neal was paid handsomely for his efforts and avoided incarceration for prior criminal activity. O'Neal infiltrated the Chicago BPP and served as the chapter chief of security and Hampton's bodyguard. O'Neal supplied the FBI with a floor plan of the apartment that was critical in the assassination plot because it indicated where members slept. Many BPP members believed that O'Neal drugged Hampton so that he would be unable to defend himself during the raid.

Ballistics evidence proved that the police shot at least 200 bullets into the apartment. BPP members were ambushed and therefore unable to successfully defend themselves. As a result of the findings, the murder charges against the BPP members were dismissed. The Clark and Hampton families filed a multimillion dollar lawsuit that was eventually settled for $1.85 million.

Deborah Johnson, now know as Akua Njeri, and Fred Hampton Jr. work together with the December 4th committee to keep Fred Hampton's legacy alive.

See also: Black Panther Party; BPP, Chicago Branch; COINTELPRO; Hoover, J. Edgar

Claudette L. Tolson (Ayodele Shaihi)

Bibliography

Fred Hampton's House: A Statement Provided December 26, 1970 by a Film-maker Present in Fred Hampton's Apartment a Few Hours after the Killings of December 4, 1969: A Reminder. San Francisco: Hermes Free Press, 1970.

Hampton, Fred. *We Don't Want You Coming Here Clapping and Leaving Here Not Doing Nothing—You've Got to Make a Commitment!* Chicago: Peoples Information Center, 1979.

Hampton, William E., and Templeton, Rini. *The Essence of Fred Hampton.* Chicago: Salsado Press, 1994.

Madhubuti, Haki R. *One Sided Shoot-out (for Brothers Fred Hampton & Mark Clark, Murdered 12/4/69 by Chicago Police at 4:30 AM While They Slept).* Detroit: Broadside Press, 1969.

December 4th Committee. *Fred Hampton 20th Commemoration.* Chicago: Salsado Press, 1989.

Harlem Renaissance

For all its failings, the Harlem Renaissance (1917–1934) (originally called the "Negro Renaissance"), was a spectacular success—spectacular because it was, in fact, a spectacle, a public exhibition of African American poetry, prose, drama, art, and music. This was not just "art for art's sake," but art to redraw the public image of "colored" people in America. Enjoying a "double audience" of black and white, the Harlem Renaissance was the fairest fruit of the New Negro movement, whose mission it was to bring about racial renewal through cultural diplomacy. The Harlem Renaissance was not only a golden age of African American arts but a valiant effort to remove the masks of racial stereotypes in order to put a new face on African Americans. To a certain degree, it not only improved race relations somewhat (a nearly impossible task, given the entrenched racial prejudices of the day), but instilled a racial pride and nobility among African Americans whose lives the Harlem Renaissance touched.

The chief strategist and "voice" of this cultural movement was philosopher Alain Locke (1885–1954), who edited the premiere and pivotal anthology of the Harlem Renaissance, *The New Negro: An Interpretation* (1925), which is described later. As the first African American Rhodes Scholar in 1907, Locke studied abroad in Oxford (1907–1910) and the University of Berlin and the College de France (1910–1911), before receiving his PhD in philosophy from Harvard in 1918. Locke figures prominently in the Harlem Renaissance and served as its principal art critic, promoter, and power broker.

One can say that Alain Locke further democratized American democracy in paving the way for the Civil Rights movement. During the Jim Crow era of American apartheid, when civil rights were white rights (under *Plessy v. Ferguson's* "separate-but-equal" doctrine), Locke was the real genius behind the Harlem Renaissance, which David Levering Lewis (Pulitzer Prize-winning biographer of W. E. B. Du Bois) aptly characterized as a movement that sought to achieve "Civil Rights by Copyright." As the acknowledged "dean" of the Harlem Renaissance, Locke may well be regarded as the Martin Luther King of African American culture. Locke's anthology, *The New Negro*, has been hailed as the first "national book" of African Americans. He ingeniously used culture as a strategy for ameliorating racism and for winning the respect of powerful white elites as potential agents for social and political transformation.

The arc of the rise and fall of the Harlem Renaissance is imprecise. Coexisting with the Jazz Age, the Harlem Renaissance was made possible in part by powerful social forces that effected sweeping changes in America at this time, beginning with the end of World War I in 1918. Foremost among these forces was the Great Migration, a massive exodus of an estimated 13 million African Americans from the rural South to the urban North in the period between 1910 and 1930. These shifts in American demography resulted in the rise of a black middle class in major American cities, particularly in the Northeast. In the midst of this status revolution, one place stood out in particular: Harlem. With this sudden influx of blacks and capital, Harlem became the race capital of black America.

Harlem is a large sector of upper Manhattan in New York City. What was taking place in Harlem was the formation of a distinct racial consciousness. Locke characterized this psychic event in that "American Negroes have been a race more in name than in fact" or "more in sentiment than in experience," reflecting a "common condition rather than a common consciousness." In response to this "problem in common rather than a life in common," the Harlem Renaissance offered African Americans their "first chances for group expression and self-determination" (*The Critical Temper of Alain Locke*, p. 6). The Harlem Renaissance succeeded in the first objective, but failed in the latter.

Parties played a major role both in Harlem night life and in the Renaissance itself, whose official inaugural began with a formal banquet. On March 21, 1924, *Opportunity* editor and sociologist Charles S. Johnson had invited a group of young writers and artists to a dinner party of the Writers Guild held in the Civic Club, a restaurant on 14 West Twelfth Street near Fifth Avenue in Harlem. The Civic Club was the only "upper crust" New York nightclub free of color or sex restrictions. The party was called to celebrate Jessie Redmon Fauset's first novel, *There is Confusion*, and to recognize a newer school of writers that included Eric Walrond, Countee Cullen, Langston Hughes, and Gwendolyn Bennett.

Evidence suggests that it was Alain Locke himself who originally used the term "Renaissance" to characterize the Harlem cultural movement. In 1928, Locke revealed that, in 1924–1925, "the present writer [Locke] articulated these trends as a movement toward racial self-expression and cultural autonomy, styling it as the New Negro movement" (*The Critical Temper of Alain Locke*, p. 446). Published in 1925, *Harlem: Mecca of the New Negro* was an instant success. It sold an estimated 42,000 copies in two printings.

Capitalizing on this success, Locke expanded the special issue and recast it as an anthology in book form. *The New Negro: An Interpretation* (1925) was the inaugural and the epochal centerpiece of the New Negro movement. *The New Negro* featured 34 contributors, 4 of whom were white. The volume showcased most of the stellar figures of the Harlem Renaissance who went on to pursue independent literary and artistic careers in their own right. W. E. B. Du Bois contributed the final essay. Locke proclaimed *The New Negro* to be "our spiritual Declaration of Independence" (*The Critical Temper of Alain Locke*, p. 43).

The prime movers of the Harlem Renaissance believed that art held more promise than politics in bringing about a sea change in American race relations. Although their philosophies of art had shades of differences, their overlap intensified their commonality. As the chief proponent of the "talented tenth," W. E. B. Du Bois was staunch in his conviction that art should serve the interests of the race. In "Criteria of Negro Art" (1926), Du Bois bluntly demands that art should be used explicitly for propaganda. In Locke's view, the problem with propaganda is that it "harangues, cajoles, threatens, or supplicates" (*The Critical Temper of Alain Locke*, p. 27). It operates from a defensive posture. In his classic essay, "The Legacy of the Ancestral Arts," in *The New Negro*, Locke proclaims what the function of art must be: "Art must discover and reveal the beauty which prejudice and caricature have overlaid. And all vital art discovers beauty and opens our eyes to that which previously we could not see" (*The Critical Temper of Alain Locke*, p. 258). Although it was true that the Harlem Renaissance enjoyed a "double audience," the primary audience was white. In its purest form, beauty will be the vehicle of truth: "After Beauty, let Truth come into the Renaissance picture" (*The Critical Temper of Alain Locke*, p. 28).

In 1926, Langston Hughes published his manifesto, "The Negro Artist and the Racial Mountain," in the *Nation*, cited as a sacred text by the Black Arts Movement of the 1960s. Hughes takes a diffident, almost devil-may-care approach: "We younger Negro artists who create now intend to express our individual dark-skinned selves without fear or shame. If white people are pleased we are glad. If they are not, it doesn't matter. We know we are beautiful. And ugly too." Locke praised the essay as a "declaration of cultural independence" (*The Critical Temper of Alain Locke*, p. 446). In his preface to *The Book of American Negro Poetry* (1931), editor James Weldon Johnson wrote that each people is judged by the standard of its own culture. In his November 1928 *Harper's Magazine* essay, "Race Prejudice and the Negro Artist," Johnson argues that, while racism was being fought on educational, economic, political and sociological fronts, it is the African American artist who was charged with undermining racial prejudice. Johnson's philosophy of art accords with and synthesizes those of Du Bois and Locke in that producing "great" black art is a key to gaining a reciprocity of respect.

Art is a surplus of creative energy. Art requires support. Thus much of the creative work of black artists and writers was dependent on white patrons and persons of influence, who were key protagonists of the Harlem Renaissance. This is a remarkable fact. Legally barred from congregating socially, it was practically illegal for blacks and whites to have social relationships beyond the most impersonal kinds of interactions. White patrons played a key role in publishing for and marketing black arts to white consumers for their mutual enrichment. Carl Van Vechten was probably the pivotal white promoter of the Harlem Renaissance. In 1926, he published *Nigger Heaven*, a controversial novel about black life in Harlem. Van Vechten was often excoriated for the title. *Nigger Heaven* was partly a collaborative black-white effort: James Weldon Johnson and Walter White read the galley proofs, and poet Langston Hughes wrote verses to replace song lyrics that Van Vechten had used without permission, which prompted a lawsuit.

A patron of Alain Locke, Langston Hughes, Zora Neale Hurston, and others, Charlotte Osgood Mason was a secret benefactor of major Harlem Renaissance artists and writers. She eschewed publicity and forbade the very mention of her name. Instructing her patrons to refer to her affectionately as "Godmother," her purse had strings attached. This fact has jaundiced Harlem Renaissance art

in the eyes of its critics, for Mason's obsession with African primitivism had to be satisfied. Nonetheless, Mason's patronage was the lifeblood of some of the key Renaissance figures.

"Negro poets and Negro poetry are two quite different things," Locke wrote in 1926. "Of the one, since Phyllis Wheatley, we have had a century and a half; of the other, since Dunbar, scarcely a generation" (*The Critical Temper of Alain Locke*, p. 43). The advent of a self-conscious "Negro poetry" by "Negro poets" helped cultivate the group consciousness that Locke found to be singularly lacking among African Americans historically yet developing rather suddenly in his generation. As Locke predicted, the Harlem Renaissance poets have entered into the canon of mainstream American literature.

A West Indian and British citizen, Claude McKay contributed the poem, "White House," to The *New Negro* anthology. Because of its politically sensitive nature, Locke changed the title to "White Houses." In his social protest poem, "To America," McKay personifies the United States as a tiger, racially terrible yet magnificent in its awesome power. McKay's greatest claim to fame is his military sonnet, "If We Must Die," which appeared in the July issue of the *Liberator* during the Red Summer of 1919, when race riots swept across 25 of the nation's inner cities like a firestorm. The poem, McKay says, "exploded out of me" and is now considered to be the inaugural address of the Harlem Renaissance. This poem took on the power of an anthem: it was reprinted by virtually every leading African American magazine and newspaper. McKay's sonnet surpassed his race when Winston Churchill used "If We Must Die" to rally British soldiers in battles against the Nazis in World War II.

Disinclined to identify himself as a Negro poet, Countee Cullen could not ignore the pain of the black experience. With Keats as his poetic idol, Cullen used white poetic forms, such as the sonnet, to solemnify that angst. Harper and Brothers published his first volume of poems, *Colors*, in 1925, which won the first Harmon Foundation Award in Literature in 1926. In Harvard Graduate School in 1926, Cullen took a course in versification from Robert Hillyer, who paid tribute to Cullen as the first American poet to publish a poem in rime royal. In 1926, Countee Cullen became assistant editor of *Opportunity* magazine, and began to write a regular column, "The Dark Tower." On April 9, 1928, Cullen married Nina Yolande, daughter of

W. E. B. Du Bois, in an event hailed as the social event of the decade. But the marriage was short-lived.

Acclaimed by many as the poet-laureate of the Harlem Renaissance, Langston Hughes was "discovered" in 1924 by poet Vachel Lindsay, who was Hughes's literary idol. Hughes was a busboy at the time and had seized the opportunity to give Lindsay some poems when the latter dined at the Washington, D.C. hotel where Hughes worked. At a formal banquet hosted by *Opportunity: A Journal of Negro Life* (organ of the National Urban League) to present awards for its annual poetry contest, Langston Hughes won second prize for "The Weary Blues," which became the title of the collection of poems published by Knopf in 1926 on the recommendation of Van Vechten, who personally hand-delivered the manuscript to the publisher and wrote the foreword as well. Locke credits Hughes with bringing about, for the first time, a "revelation of the emotional color of Negro life, and his brilliant discovery of the flow and rhythm of the modern and especially the city Negro, substituting the jazz figure and personality for the older plantation stereotype" (*The Critical Temper of Alain Locke*, p. 53).

Locke recognized the contribution of visual artists to the Harlem Renaissance: "The Negro artist thus found his place beside the poets and writers of the 'New Negro' movement, which in the late Twenties and through the Thirties galvanized Negro talent to strong and freshly creative expression" (*The Critical Temper of Alain Locke*, p. 192). Harlem Renaissance artists helped develop a visual vocabulary and grammar of images representing African Americans. In the 1925 *Harlem* issue of the *Survey Graphic*, Locke published seven portraits of Harlem folk, sketched by Winold Reiss. Son of Fritz Reiss, a landscape painter, Winold studied under Franz von Stuck of Munich. "Winold Reiss has achieved," Locke claims, "what amounts to a revealing discovery of the significance, human and artistic, of one of the great dialects of human physiognomy, of some of the little understood but powerful idioms of nature's speech" (*The Critical Temper of Alain Locke*, p. 17). Locke praises Reiss for achieving, through painting locally in Harlem, a "universality" of the human experience.

Acknowledged by some as the father of Black American visual art, Aaron Douglas was recognized by Locke as "the pioneer of the African Style among the American Negro artists" (*The Critical Temper of Alain Locke*, p. 177). In addition to being an illustrator, whose work first appeared in the *Harlem* issue and then in *The New Negro*, Douglas was a muralist, whose work appeared in Club Ebony in New York, in the Sherman Hotel in Chicago, and in Fisk University. In developing his distinctive style, Douglas contributed the illustrations to *God's Trombones* (1927), by James Weldon Johnson, which features cycles of sermon-poems. Douglas drew on Egyptian and African art and was influenced by cubism, art deco, and art nouveau as well. These illustrations are considered to be Douglas's finest work.

A bodybuilder as well as a writer, Jean Toomer was a biracial man, who could pass for white and ultimately did. In 1923, he published *Cane,* a novel set in Georgia, which Langston Hughes praised as the best prose ever written by an African American, and which Locke hailed as "a brilliant performance" (*The Critical Temper of Alain Locke,* p. 447). Toomer was a one-book author, whose career was abortive for personal reasons. In spiritual pursuit of the "four-conscinal" and "illuminant" Absolute, Toomer subsequently became a follower of the mystic Gurdjieff and married a wealthy white woman, Margery Latimer. When James Weldon Johnson invited Toomer to contribute to a revised edition of *The Book of American Negro Poetry* (1931), Toomer refused, no longer wishing to identify himself as a Negro.

Born of a Danish mother and a West Indian father, Nella Larsen won the Harmon Foundation's Bronze Medal for Literature in 1929 for her novel *Quicksand* (1928), which W. E. B. Du Bois acclaimed as comparable in quality to the fictional works of Charles Chesnutt. Although legally black, she had loyalties to both races, a theme of racial fusion and confusion explored in *Quicksand,* in which the main character, Helga Crane, is a full projection of Larsen herself. Locke describes *Quicksand* as a "study of the cultural conflict of mixed ancestry" and hails it as a "truly social document of importance" illuminating "the problem of divided social loyalties and…the conflict of cultures" (*The Critical Temper of Alain Locke,* p. 202–3). In 1930, she became the first black woman to win a Guggenheim Fellowship.

There are more than 130 published plays by 37 Harlem Renaissance authors. On May 22, 1921, *Shuffle Along* opened on Broadway's David Belasco Theater. With lyrics written by Noble Sissle and music by Eubie Blake, *Shuffle Along* became the first musical revue scored and performed by African Americans. It launched the careers of Josephine Baker and Florence Mills. Locke distinguished three plays as "outstanding": Eugene O'Neill's *Emperor Jones,* Paul Green's

Pulitzer Prize-winning *In Abraham's Bosom,* and DuBose Heyward's Charleston folk-drama, *Porgy.*

The year 1929 was a big one for Harlem renaissance drama: the Negro Experimental Theatre founded in February, the Negro Art Theatre formed in June, and the National Colored Players was created in September. That same year, Wallace Thurman collaborated with white journalist and playwright, William Jourdan Rapp to write a murder melodrama, *Harlem.* Produced with an all-black cast (except for a white policeman), the Broadway performances of *Harlem* proved a significant milestone in the development of black drama. It opened at the Apollo Theater on Broadway and was a huge success.

The Harlem Renaissance arose during the period of American progressivism, with its faith in the reform of democracy. Ultimately, the Harlem Renaissance crashed along with the stock market in the early years of the Great Depression, and its failure to effect any real social change was dramatically underscored by the Harlem riot of 1935. Without a unifying ideology, it was given over to exoticism and exhibitionism and failed in its stated mission to solve the racial crisis through cultural diplomacy. It was not so much that the Harlem Renaissance failed; rather it was America that failed the Harlem Renaissance. This failed impact was the fate of modernist movements in general, which sought to create a social conscience for the age of modernity. Yet Houston A. Baker sees the publication of Locke's *The New Negro* (1925) as a success in its own right. The Harlem Renaissance created a place in the national literary tradition, officially recognized in the March 13, 2002 "White House Salute to America's Authors" event, which paid tribute to writers of the Harlem Renaissance who created rich art and became agents of social change. Its cultural diplomacy became a cultural legacy.

See also: Du Bois, W. E. B.; Father Divine; Garvey, Marcus; Hughes, Langston; Hurston, Zora Neale; Locke, Alain; New Negro Movement

Christopher Buck

Bibliography

Baker, Houston A. Jr. *Modernism and the Harlem Renaissance.* Chicago: The University of Chicago Press, 1987.

Balshaw, Maria. "'Black Was White': Urbanity, Passing and the Spectacle of Harlem." *Journal of American Studies* 33, no. 2 (1999):307–22.

Buck, Christopher. *Alain Locke: Faith and Philosophy.* Los Angeles: Kalimat Press, 2005.

Favor, J. Martin, *Authentic Blackness: The Folk in the New Negro Movement.* Durham, NC: Duke University Press, 1999.

Harris, Leonard, ed. *The Philosophy of Alain Locke: Harlem Renaissance and Beyond.* Philadelphia: Temple University Press, 1991.

Holmes, Eugene C. "Alain Locke and the New Negro Movement." *Negro American Literature Forum* 2, no. 3 (Fall 1968):60–68.

Krasner, David. *A Beautiful Pageant: African American Theatre, Drama, and Performance in the Harlem Renaissance, 1910–1927.* New York: Palgrave Macmillian, 2002.

Locke, Alain, ed. *The New Negro: An Interpretation.* New York: Albert and Charles Boni, 1925 and 1927. Reprinted with a new preface by Robert Hayden. New York: Atheneum, 1969.

Long, Richard A. "The Genesis of Locke's *The New Negro.*" *Black World* 25, no. 4 (1976):14–20.

Medina, José. "Pragmatism and Ethnicity: Critique, Reconstruction, and the New Hispanic." *Metaphilosophy* 35, no. 1/2 (2004):115–46.

Nadell, Martha Jane. *Enter the New Negroes: Images of Race in American Culture.* Cambridge, MA: Harvard University Press, 2004.

Scholz, Sally J. "Individual and Community: Artistic Representation in Alain L. Locke's Politics." *Transactions of the Charles S. Peirce Society: A Quarterly Journal in American Philosophy* 39, no. 3 (Summer 2003):491–502.

Spencer, Jon Michael. *The New Negroes and Their Music: The Success of the Harlem Renaissance.* Knoxville: University of Tennessee Press, 1997.

Stewart, Jeffrey C., ed. *The Critical Temper of Alain Locke: A Selection of His Essays on Art and Culture.* New York: Garland Publishing, 1983.

Watts, Eric King. "African American Ethos and Hermeneutical Rhetoric: An Exploration of Alain Locke's *The New Negro.*" *Quarterly Journal of Speech* 88, no. 1 (2002):19–32.

Wintz, Cary D., and Paul Finkelman, eds. *Encyclopedia of the Harlem Renaissance.* London: Routledge, 2004.

Hayes, Rutherford B.

Rutherford Birchard Hayes (1822–1893) was the 19th president of the United States from 1877–1881. He was born in Delaware County, Ohio, on October 4, 1822. Hayes graduated from Kenyon College and Harvard Law in 1842 and 1845, respectively. He began practicing law in Lower Sandusky, Ohio in 1845. In 1849, Hayes moved to Cincinnati where he built a lucrative law practice and worked in city government.

Once the civil war began, Hayes became commander of the Ohio Volunteer Army on the side of the Union He fought on the side of the North throughout the entire Civil War conflict. Hayes served in the U.S. House as a Republican representative from 1865 to 1867. He had a reputation throughout his entire life for honesty. He had refused to leave his command in the Civil War in order to campaign for Congress. While Hayes served in the U.S. Congress, he openly supported the Fourteenth Amendment that extended civil rights to African Americans and the passage of Freedman's Bureau Bill. He also supported the amendment to override President Andrew Johnson who Hayes felt had succumbed to the pressures of former confederates.

Hayes served two nonconsecutive terms as governor of Ohio from 1868 to 1872 and from 1876 to 1877. He campaigned and fought hard against tremendous opposition as governor for universal suffrage of African American males and for their fair treatment. As governor of Ohio, Hayes supported President Ulysses S. Grant's sympathetic policies toward minorities, such as the use of the army to break up the Ku Klux Klan. Hayes attempted to generate support in the U.S. Congress for Grant's attempt to peaceably acquire Santo Domingo as a voluntary place of refuge for African Americans to escape the racism of the South.

Hayes became President of the United States in 1877, largely because of the votes of African Americans; however, most predicted that Democrat Samuel J. Tilden would win the presidential election of 1876. Tilden actually won the popular vote by about 250,000 votes. The Electoral College votes were contested in the states of South Carolina, Louisiana, Florida, and Oregon, which were states with large numbers of African American voters. Either candidate had to have at least 185 Electoral College votes to win. Initially, Tilden had 184; Hayes had 165. A total of 20 Electoral College votes were from the contested states. After several weeks of negotiations, Hayes won the election after he agreed to remove Union troops from the South, appoint at least one Southerner to a cabinet post, and to construct a transcontinental railroad through the South to rebuild its economy. This agreement is known as the Compromise of 1877 and it brought about an end to Civil War Reconstruction.

After the Compromise of 1877, the South, with the exception of African Americans, almost entirely voted Democratic until the Presidency of Lyndon B. Johnson. The compromise proved to be a step backward for African Americans. Contrary to Hayes's approval, many of the reforms instituted since the Civil War were rescinded. Jim Crow laws were instituted and upheld as constitutional under a "separate but equal" jurisprudence. Hayes

continued throughout his entire presidency to fight against the suppression of the rights of African Americans. He was successful during his presidency in getting legislation passed in 1879 that allowed female attorneys, regardless of race, to argue cases before the Supreme Court. He did not seek reelection in 1880, keeping his pledge that he would not run for a second term. Hayes left office on March 4, 1881. He died on Tuesday January 17, 1893.

See also: Black Nadir; Compromise of 1877; Republican Party; White Supremacy

Steven Napier

Bibliography

Barnard, Harry. *Rutherford B. Hayes, and His America.* Indianapolis: Bobbs-Merrill, 1954.

Davison, Kenneth E. *The Presidency of Rutherford B. Hayes.* Westport, CT: Greenwood Press, 1972.

Hoogenboom, Ari. *Rutherford B. Hayes: Warrior and President.* Lawrence: University Press of Kansas, 1995.

Logan, Rayford Whittingham. *The Betrayal of The Negro, From Rutherford B. Hayes to Woodrow Wilson.* New York: Collier Books, 1965.

Hill, Anita

Anita Faye Hill (1956–), currently a professor in the Heller School for Social Policy and Management at Brandeis University, was a former colleague of Supreme Court Justice Clarence Thomas who courageously accused him of sexual harassment and gave testimony in this regard during Thomas's 1991 Senate confirmation hearing. Born on a farm in Murris, Oklahoma, on July 30, 1956, Hill earned an undergraduate degree in psychology from Oklahoma State University in 1977. During her matriculation at Oklahoma State, Hill had served as an intern for a local judge, and this experience spawned her interest in law. In 1980, she earned her JD degree from Yale University and, in the same year, Hill was admitted to the DC Bar. She became a practicing lawyer with the firm of Ward, Hardraker, and Ross in Washington, D.C. By 1981, Hill was special counsel to the assistant secretary of the Department of Education's Office for Civil Rights where she began working, for the first time, with Clarence Thomas. According to her sworn testimony 10 years later, Thomas began making repeated sexual advances and lewd remarks to her.

When Thomas became chair of the Equal Employment Opportunity Commission, Hill served as his adviser and, according to her testimony, his sexual harassment of her intensified. The lewd and vulgar remarks Hill recalled during the Senate confirmation hearing including vivid descriptions of pornographic movie scenes and an infamous joke about a pubic hair Thomas claimed to have found on a Coke can. Hill served as Thomas's assistant from 1982 to 1983 before accepting a faculty position at Oral Roberts University in Tulsa, where she served as an assistant professor of civil rights from 1983 to 1986. In 1986, Hill accepted a position as a professor specializing in contract law at the University of Oklahoma. By 1991, she quickly became a household name when President George H. W. Bush nominated Clarence Thomas to replace Thurgood Marshall on the U.S. Supreme Court. On September 3, 1991, Hill was approached by the Senate Judiciary Committee to provide background information on Clarence Thomas. Although she initially did not divulge details, when prompted by investigators to discuss rumors of sexual harassment and improper conduct on the part of Thomas, Hill cooperated with the Senate Judiciary Committee on September 9. She was later interviewed by the FBI in the midst of the confirmation hearings. Thomas denied all allegations made by Hill and claimed that he was the victim of a "high-tech lynching." After extensive investigation and debate, the Senate confirmed Thomas by the narrow margin of 52–48.

In March 1992, *American Spectator* published an article by David Brock that claimed Hill had lied and exaggerated during the hearings and infamously stated she might be "a bit nutty and a bit slutty." In 1993, Brock expanded these claims into a book-length diatribe entitled, *The Real Anita Hill*. After repudiating his own book and personally apologizing to Hill, Brook published a book-length commentary on the entire affair entitled *Blinded by the Right: The Conscience of an Ex-Conservative* (2002). Hill's own book, *Speaking Truth to Power* (1997), offers an insightful view of the events surrounding the Thomas confirmation and the experiences Hill had with sexual harassment. Most recently, Hill serves as a professor of Social Policy, Law, and Women's Studies at Brandeis University in Massachusetts and, in 2008, she was awarded the Louis P. and Evelyn Smith First Amendment Award by the Ford Hall Forum.
See also: Thomas, Clarence

Walter C. Rucker

Bibliography

Brock, David. *Blinded by the Right: The Conscience of an Ex-Conservative.* New York: Crown Publishers, 2002.

Brock, David. *The Real Anita Hill: The Untold Story.* New York: Free Press, 1993.

Chrisman, Robert, and Robert L. Allen. *Court of Appeal: The Black Community Speaks Out on the Racial and Sexual Politics of Clarence Thomas vs. Anita Hill.* New York: Ballantine Books, 1992.

Hill, Anita. *Speaking Truth to Power.* New York: Doubleday, 1997.

Phelps, Timothy M., and Helen Winternitz. *Capitol Games: Clarence Thomas, Anita Hill, and the Story of a Supreme Court Nomination.* New York: Hyperion, 1992.

Smitherman, Geneva. *African American Women Speak Out on Anita Hill-Clarence Thomas.* Detroit: Wayne State University Press, 1995.

Hip-Hop

When someone mentions the term "hip-hop," it either garners interest, disdain, or indifference. Many people are curious about what it is, what it does, and how it functions. People often mistake hip-hop as a music form, but it is not. Hip-hop is a culture, with its own lexicon, ideology, and aesthetic. Simply put, hip-hop includes a dance style (breaking and pop locking, among others), graffiti and tagging, and rap music. Founded in New York City's area of the South Bronx in the 1970s, rap music was the cultural backlash to disco's prominence in the national and urban music scene. Before rap music emerged onto the music scene of New York City's Harlem and South Bronx streets, there was already a counterculture—a subculture—that was percolating. Urban art was in full expression, whether it was dance, music, poetry, or painting. Amidst the ugliness and the decay of New York City that existed as a result of several failed economic policies and the many aftereffects of the Vietnam War, many already marginalized black, Asian and Latino youths found beauty in their new meaning for existence, their new voice. It was performed with passion and pursued with a vision for having something to call their own, something no one could take from them, something different and unique. This energy is what contributed to the creation of a new culture: hip-hop.

Considered the founding father of rap music and hip-hop culture, DJ Kool Herc had no initial intentions of creating a musical and cultural phenomenon. What was supposed to be a commonplace back-to-school party turned into the beginning of a cultural revolution. What Kool Herc created in the park of Sedgwick and Cedar Streets in the South Bronx simply evolved out of innovation and invention. His crew, the Herculords, included his famous sound system, MCs and dancers, while he managed the turntables. During intermissions, Kool Herc would maintain the crowd's interest by keeping them on the dance floor. Breakdancing, called B-Boying (and B-Girling), was an opportunity for dance crews to battle and flaunt new moves and styles. Herc's use of the break beat, the instrumental break in a song, was a highlight at his parties and shows. Another of Kool Herc's highlights was his ability to rap to the crowd. "Rap" is the slang term for "talk," and Herc's West Indian (Jamaican) cultural roots influenced the way he deejayed. In the Caribbean tradition of "toasting," the deejay raps over a break beat to keep the crowd motivated. In addition, the important aspect of toasting is the call-and-response element, which connects the deejay to his audience and vice versa. Herc's rival deejay was Flash, who also excelled in using break beats. Flash's advantage was that he could mix and scratch faster than anyone else, hence his name. His prowess earned him the title grandmaster, which indicates that he is the best at his skill. Grandmaster Flash and his crew, The Furious Five, were the stuff of legend. With Flash and his crew making history in Harlem and Herc's crew controlling the Bronx, interested people from every corner of New York City's five boroughs (Manhattan, Bronx, Brooklyn, Queens, Staten Island) would flock to sold-out, thereby spreading the culture and its elements.

Hip-hop is an organic culture that is steeped in the art of improvisation and innovation, creative intelligence, and artistic flair. Deemed as a culture by Afrika Bambaataa of the Zulu Nation, hip-hop exists as a cultural entity that requires active participation and involvement in order for it to thrive. Similar to the theological tenets of Christian and Muslim faiths, hip-hop culture also had its tenets, termed the five elements. It was determined that there are five elements of the culture, which are requisite for its existence: the deejay, the MC, the B-Boy (or B-Girl) breaker, the graffiti artist, and the knowledge of self. The five elements were not instantaneously identified and labeled until after the establishment of hip-hop as a culture. Afrika Bambaataa and the Zulu Nation were supporters of the Five Percent Nation of Islam, which was an offshoot of the Nation of Islam. The religion was founded by Clarence 13X, a former disciple of the Nation of Islam. It is also noted that the Zulu Nation is the world's oldest and largest grassroots hip-hop organization; its primary purpose is to promote knowledge, peace, and understanding among those within the hip-hop community.

Deejays (DJ = disk jockey) are the focal point of the culture, because without them, there is no music. Interestingly, it was the famed DJ Luvbug Starski who coined the term "hip-hop." There were many aspiring MCs and dancers, but they needed the deejay's permission to perform for the crowd. If the deejay thought a person's skills were lacking, s/he was instantly dismissed. Therefore, the deejay functioned as a filter, controlling who was going to be heard and who was not. By the time hip-hop gained enough attention to be on the radio, New York City deejays such as Red Alert and Mister Magic used their positions on rival radio stations to promote their respective crews, Boogie Down Productions (BDP) and the Juice Crew. Another important element of deejaying is being able to perform on the turntables. Grand Wizzard Theodore invented the scratch entirely by accident. While in his room practicing, his mother called him and he simply scratched the record by stopping it from spinning—hence the beginning of what DJ Babu of the Dilated Peoples later termed as "turntablism," or turntable arts.

Turntable arts have progressed significantly since the advent of Grandmaster Flash. Other than the ones already mentioned, notable DJs are Jam Master Jay of RUN-DMC, DJ Scratch of EPMD, Master Don, DJ Bobcat, Spinderella of Salt-n-Pepa, Q-Bert, the X-ecutioners, DJ Jazzy Jeff, DJ Steve Dee, and Cocoa Chanelle. A quality hip-hop deejay must also be able to function as the catalyst at parties. If the deejay was in a rap group, s/he often had the responsibility of producing the songs. Because of this overlap, several of the aforementioned producers are also deejays; however, some producers are better recognized for their music production, such as DJ Premier, Dr. Dre, DJ Marley Marl, Da Beatminerz, and DJ Quik. The DJ and production duo the Awesome 2 are also recognized by the Paley Center for Media (Museum of Television and Radio) for having the longest running hip-hop radio program in radio history.

If the deejay is the focal point, the MC is the second in command. The abbreviation MC has been said to stand for master of ceremony, microphone controller, microphone checka', move the crowd, and microphone commander. Whatever the case, anyone who considers himself or herself an MC has to prove lyrical prowess and deftness. Because of the fierce competition, it was common to witness a battle between aspiring MCs. The title MC had to be earned, not simply applied. Unbeknownst to them, the historic battle between MC Busy Bee and Kool Moe Dee of the Treacherous Three determined which standard and criteria aspiring MCs were going to follow. Moe Dee's aggressive, witty, and rapid-fire lyrics set the precedent for future MCs to this day. Similar to playing the dozens, MC battles required lyrical skill and wit in the form of signifying; they were unscripted and unrehearsed lyrical contests in which the crowd decided the winner. There are many rappers who are not MCs, but every MC is a rapper. In current times, the MC garners so much attention that the DJ's visibility has fallen by the wayside.

In the 1990s, it became common to see rap groups sans a DJ; however, some groups still adhere to the tradition. Some notable MCs are Pebblee Poo, Melle Mel, MC Lyte, Rakim, KRS-ONE, Queen Latifah, LL Cool J, Ice Cube, Scarface, Lauryn Hill, Big L, Buckshot of Black Moon, Too $hort, Nas, Big Daddy Kane, Common, Ludacris, Roxanne Shante, Mos Def, Wu-Tang Clan, Jay-Z, Ice-T, T. I., Big Punisher, Tupac, Bahamdia, Notorious B.I.G, Da Brat, the LOX, Grandmaster Caz, and Black Thought of the Roots. Being a quality MC means that one has to be original and authentic and possess a style atypical of the mainstream. There is a difference between being unique and being odd or strange; if an MC's style is too farfetched, it will not be readily accepted, but if it is intriguing, it will be a signature style. For example, Wu-Tang Clan's late member Old Dirty Bastard named himself as such because there was no father to his style. The MC has been made synonymous with the West African griot or storyteller, and, like the griot, s/he has the responsibility of properly representing his/her people and their history. MCs that appropriate or misuse their talents are harshly criticized as sellouts and are demoted to being considered as mere rappers.

Much like the generational and controversial dances of years past, such as the jitterbug and the twist, breaking itself became a cultural phenomenon. Breaking in its current form involves many sophisticated movements and

Rappers Fat Joe, left, and Terror Squad perform during the UrbanAID2 concert in New York, on Tuesday April 9, 2002. (AP Photo/Bebeto Matthews)

techniques that emphasize finesse and acrobatics. Moves such as top rocking, down rocking, power moves, and freezes are standard basics of the dance form. The term "B-Boy" stands for Bronx boy, break boy or beat boy, but because dancers waited for the break beat in a song play to showcase their moves, the term break dancing became synonymous with B-noying. It is debatable whether there is an historical, concrete location of place for the history of breaking; however, it has always been considered a manifestation of African dance. Its modern form was first noticed in the late 1960s and early 1970s in California and New York. After gaining much visibility performing in public places, such as sidewalks, public parks, subway platforms, breaking New York City was almost commonplace. The interest in breaking, which the mainstream considered a new dance craze, quickly caught the attention of corporate America and Hollywood.

In 1983, the films *Flashdance, Style Wars,* and *Wild Style* were released nationwide. The 1984 film *Beat Street* was also released with much success. The West Coast style of breaking was also on the scene and was made more popular in the 1984 Hollywood films *Breakin'* and *Breakin' 2: The Electric Boogaloo.* Before the films, breaking was already gaining national attention. The 1976 television series *What's Happening!* also brought the early forms of breaking into America's homes, with the character Rerun, who was a breaker that specialized in popping and locking. The actual character, Fred Berry, was a member of a breaking crew. James Brown was also credited with inspiring breaking with his 1969 hit, "The Good Foot," which many breakers danced to. James Brown himself also danced with a remarkable flair, which laid the foundation for classic footwork moves.

It is important to note that the history of African American dance was steeped in the inventive and creative spirit. Whether it was a classic jitterbug or softshoe step, African American dance embodied a unique spirit and essence, which many have linked to the history of slavery and oppression. Breaking's ethnic origins have been linked to Brazilian capoeira, a traditional martial arts dance that was performed by African slaves. The spirit and inventiveness of breaking, however, has an apparent connection to that of African American tap dancing. The tap dance challenges and routines made famous by notable figures like the Nicholas Brothers and Howard "Sandman" Sims were equally inventive and uncharacteristic, and they were constantly evolving and developing new movements. Breaking

is an ever-evolving dance form, but it remains true to its roots and traditional structure. Offshoots of breaking that have gained popularity are clown dancing and krumping. Similar to B-Boy culture, their crews are called fam (short for family), and they are predominantly based on battling and street/public performance. All of these dance forms have gained an international audience, and there are films and performers that hail from many nations and continents. One B-Boy crew that arguably has the most recognition worldwide is the Rock Steady Crew, which was founded in 1977 in the Bronx. They have members nationwide and in several international locations, such as Japan, Italy, and the United Kingdom.

Graffiti became tied to hip-hop culture, but it is not exclusive to it. The meaning of graffiti is simply illicit writing on public property. Examples of graffiti have also been found in ancient sites in Turkey, Egypt, Syria, and Greece. Some art historians, anthropologists, and archeologists have classified historical artifacts and places such as cave paintings, tomb writings, and the landmark El Morro National Monument as representations of historic graffiti forms; however, in its modern form, it was considered a cultural nuisance. As urban graffiti became more popular, artists looked for ways to make their work more technologically advanced and noticeable. In New York City, the trains became mobile canvases for graffiti artists; some painted entire sides of subway cars (called bombing) with their trademark designs and signatures (known as tags).

Two graffiti artists who are credited with starting the New York City graffiti movement are Julio 204 and TAKI 183, whose scrawlings were visible throughout parts of the city. In addition to featuring legendary MCs and breakers, the film *Wild Style* also featured legendary graffiti artists such as Dondi (Donald White), Lady Pink (Sandra Fabara), and Lee Quiñones. These artists have since gained prominence and recognition for their talent and have had their works displayed in some of the most notable museums and art galleries, such as the Metropolitan Museum of Art, the Whitney Museum, and the Brooklyn Museum of Art. Dondi was incredibly prolific before his untimely death in 1998. Fabara and Quiñones also have a wealth of material that remains on display in permanent collections. Lady Pink was considered a trailblazer for women graffiti artists, which, like other hip-hop elements, tends to be predominantly male. Her presence paved the way for current graffiti artists of fame and infamy such as Los Angeles's graffiti queen Tribe. Because it is illegal and considered a form of vandalism, many graffiti artists work under an alias.

In the August 2008 arrest of Danielle Bremner (aka "Dani" and "Utah") and her husband Jim Clay Harper (aka "Ether") for graffiti vandalism, they were listed as wanted criminals in the cities of New York, Boston, Pittsburgh, Chicago, London, Madrid, Frankfurt, and Hamburg. Graffiti culture is its own subculture, and it will likely never be accepted as art in mainstream society. It has been termed street art and guerilla art, but neither term has further legitimized it. Because hip-hop is a culture that is lived and not performed, it is not uncommon for deejays and breakers to also be graffiti artists; when people engage with the culture, they often explore its various facets and components. For example, Rock Steady Crew DJ JS-1 was well known as a graffiti artist under the alias "Jerms," and the rap group the Artifacts were known taggers and bombers. The 2007 documentary film *Bomb It!* features many notable and legendary graffiti artists who talk about graffiti's history from ancient eras to contemporary times.

Hip-hop culture has often been criticized for its commercial value, but it also has plenty of substance. Brand Nubian's 1998 album *Foundation* featured in its liner notes the phrase "Do the Knowledge." Similar to the beliefs espoused by African American intellectuals such as W. E. B. Du Bois and Mary Church Terrell, many figures in hip-hop culture also espouse the values of pursuing an education. Furthermore, emphasis is placed on learning African American history and culture, which was considered necessary for understanding one's place in American society.

During the politically volatile 1980s and 1990s, ideologies from the black arts movement and the Black Power movement were particularly celebrated and acknowledged as important beliefs. Groups such as Public Enemy, Boogie Down Productions, and X-Clan were vocal about the miseducation in the nation's school systems, where European history and values were taught, almost exclusively. RUN-DMC was known for their crossover hit "Walk This Way" on the 1986 album *Raising Hell*. The album's final track, however, is "Proud to Be Black," which celebrates the successes and triumphs of key African American such as George Washington Carver, Rev. Dr. Martin Luther King, Benjamin Banneker, Malcolm X, Harriet Tubman, Jesse Owens, and Muhammad Ali. Boogie Down Productions' frontman, KRS-ONE, often promoted black empowerment in his lyrics. His song "You Must Learn" on his 1989 *Ghetto*

Music album also talks about African American inventors not taught in schools such as Eli Whitney, Madame CJ Walker, Garrett Morgan, and Charles Drew. On this album KRS vehemently attacks the education system posing rhetorical questions in songs "Why Is That?" and "Who Protects Us from You?"; the former song discusses the history of blacks being intentionally omitted from Western history, including the Bible, and the latter was inspired by the ever-present police brutality and Tiananmen Square incident in China. In both songs, KRS encourages his audience to ask important questions to those persons who are considered to have authority, and he asserts that blacks have to take responsibility for their education and safety.

During the 1980s and 1990s, there were concerted efforts to organize hip-hop political movements. Two successful movements were the Stop the Violence Movement, which was the proponent of ending street violence and the gold boycott, which was to force the jewelry industry to divest from Apartheid South Africa. Instead, many sported African medallions, Kente cloth clothing, and also made music about worldwide racial discrimination. The energy of the teens and young adults in the hip-hop community was fueled by their affinity for rebellion and resistance. Some rappers, like Paris, endorsed the Black Panther Party's ideologies. X-Clan showed photos of Patrice Lumumba, an armed Harriet Tubman, and Fidel Castro in their video "Heed the Word of the Brother." In this song, they also accuse Aristotle, Plato, and Socrates of stealing their knowledge from Africans and are told to "step off" at the song's conclusion. Queen Latifah's 1989 album *All Hail the Queen* has an insignia of Africa, colored in black, with red and green lettering encircling it. Her music video for the song "Ladies First" shows footage of antiapartheid protests in South Africa and features a slideshow of African American civil rights leaders, such as Harriet Tubman and Angela Davis. The fervor of Nelson Mandela's 1990 release also encouraged many in the hip-hop community to struggle for civil rights. Ice Cube's monumental 1990 album *AmeriKKKa's Most Wanted* champions Maoist ideologies for political resistance. Education was considered a civil right, and in addition to the aforementioned groups, others such as Dead Prez, Black Star, A Tribe Called Quest, The Roots, LL Cool J, Nas, GangStarr, Dilated Peoples, Arrested Development, Chamillionaire, Master-P, Eve, and Native Tongues have released material that focuses on pertinent issues in the African American community (violence, education, racism and discrimination, the HIV/AIDS epidemic, etc.). Recent political topics have included the 2005 Hurricane Katrina devastation, the 2006 Shawn Bell shooting in New York City, and Barack Obama's 2008 presidential campaign and election win.

Although it was once deemed a fad, hip-hop has proven to be a viable cultural institution. More than three decades have passed since its inception and it is likely to persevere for generations to come. Representations of hip-hop culture can be seen throughout the world, whether DJ Honda from Japan or the Cookie Crew from London, the first international female MCs. There is also a strong hip-hop presence in Germany and other parts of Eastern Europe where graffiti artists and B-Boys are everpresent at parties and showcases. India's Panjabi MC has had two major U.S. hits with MCs Sha Stimuli ("Stop What You Doin'," 2004) and Jay-Z ("Beware the Boys," 2005). British singer M.I.A., who is of Sri Lankan Tamil descent, creates music that has obvious connections and ties to hip-hop culture. There is a Hispanic hip-hop presence throughout most of the Americas and the Caribbean, which has allowed for the success of the hip-hop-infused Reggaeton, a Rap-Reggae-Spanish hybrid form of music. MCs such as Ivy Queen, Tego Calderón, Don Omar, and Daddy Yankee have established themselves as iconic figures; however, it was Panama's El General who pioneered the genre in the early 1990s. In the United States, there have been creative attempts to fuse rap with jazz (American classical music), techno, country music, gospel, blues, and European classical music.

Just as jazz music was controversial in its beginnings, hip-hop has also encountered naysayers and critics. As a form of African American artistic expression, hip-hop culture continues to thrive and excel beyond people's expectations. It is a multibillion dollar industry; however, it is still marginalized as a culture by the mainstream. Furthermore, there are more concerted attempts for black artists to have legal ownership of their art and to have more creative control than black artists had in the past. Still, there is a significant gap between hip-hop as product and hip-hop as culture. Those who consume hip-hop as product are likely disconnected from the culture and the people who live it. Although the product is important and allows for creative exposure, it has too often been the target of criticism for celebrating misogyny, violence, materialism, and use of the word "nigger" or "nigga." Many producers' sample music also leaves distaste in musical purists' mouths. Hip-hop

culture has a different focus, in which the culture is not defined by acts of social deviancy and self-denigration. Because of the financial incentive, there are irreconcilable differences between those who wish to preserve the integrity of the culture and those who continue to exploit it for personal gain. Whatever hip-hop culture's future, it will certainly remain a viable and influential form of black artistic expression.

See also: Black Folk Culture; Shakur, Tupac; Urbanization

Shamika Ann Mitchell

Bibliography

Chang, Jeff. *Can't Stop, Won't Stop: A History of the Hip-Hop Generation.* New York: St. Martin's Press, 2005.

Cobb, William Jelani. *To the Break of Dawn: A Freestyle on the Hip Hop Aesthetic.* New York: New York University Press, 2007.

Ganz, Nicholas. *Graffiti World: Street Art from Five Continents.* New York: H. N. Abrams, 2004.

George, Nelson. *Hip Hop America.* New York: Viking, 1998.

Hess, Mickey. *Icons of Hip Hop: An Encyclopedia of the Movement, Music, and Culture.* Westport, CT: Greenwood Press, 2007.

Mitchell, Tony. *Global Noise: Rap and Hip-Hop Outside the USA. Music/Culture.* Middletown, CT: Wesleyan University Press, 2001.

Moe Dee, Kool, and Ernie Paniccioli. *There's a God on the Mic: The True 50 Greatest MCs.* New York: Thunder's Mouth Press, 2003.

Price, Emmett George. *Hip Hop Culture.* Santa Barbara, CA: ABC-CLIO, 2006.

Rose, Tricia. *Black Noise: Rap Music and Black Culture in Contemporary America.* Hanover, NH: Wesleyan University Press: University Press of New England, 1994.

Historically Black Colleges and Universities

These institutions were created under the laws of segregation and before 1964 with the express purpose of educating African Americans. From their arrival on the shores of the United States, black people have thirsted for knowledge and viewed education as the key to their freedom. These enslaved people pursued various forms of education despite rules, in all Southern states, barring them from learning to read and write. A few black colleges appeared immediately before the Civil War, such as Lincoln and Cheyney Universities in Pennsylvania and Wilberforce in Ohio. With the end of the Civil War, the daunting task of providing education to more than 4 million formerly enslaved people was shouldered by both the federal government, through the Freedman's Bureau, and many northern church missionaries. As early as 1865, the Freedmen's Bureau began establishing black colleges, resulting in staff and teachers with primarily military backgrounds. During the postbellum period, most black colleges were so in name only; these institutions generally provided primary and secondary education, a feature that was true of most historically white colleges—starting with Harvard—during the first decades of their existence.

As noted, religious missionary organizations—some affiliated with northern white denominations such as the Baptists and Congregationalists and some with black churches such as the African Methodist Episcopal and the African Methodist Episcopal Zion—were actively working with the Freedmen's Bureau. Two of the most prominent white organizations were the American Baptist Home Mission Society and the American Missionary Association, but there were many others as well. White northern missionary societies founded black colleges such as Fisk University in Nashville, Tennessee, and Spelman College in Atlanta, Georgia. The benevolence of the missionaries was tinged with self-interest and sometimes racism. Their goals in establishing these colleges were to Christianize the freedmen (i.e., convert former enslaved people to their brand of Christianity) and to rid the country of the "menace" of uneducated African Americans. Among the colleges founded by black denominations were Morris Brown in Georgia, Paul Quinn in Texas, and Allen University in South Carolina. Unique among American colleges, these institutions were founded by African Americans for African Americans. Because these institutions relied on less support from whites, they were able to design their own curricula; however, they also were more vulnerable to economic instability.

With the passage of the second Morrill Act in 1890, the federal government again took an interest in black education, establishing public black colleges. This act stipulated that those states practicing segregation in their public colleges and universities would forfeit federal funding unless they established agricultural and mechanical institutions for the black population. Despite the wording of the Morrill Act, which called for the equitable division of federal funds, these newly founded institutions received less funding than their white counterparts and thus had inferior facilities. Among the 17 new "land grant" colleges were institutions such as Florida Agricultural and Technical University and Alabama Agricultural and Mechanical University.

At the end of the 19th century, private black colleges had exhausted funding from missionary sources. Simultaneously, a new form of support emerged, that of white northern industrial philanthropy. Among the leaders of industry who initiated this type of support were John D. Rockefeller, Andrew Carnegie, Julius Rosenwald, and John Slater. These industry captains were motivated by both Christian benevolence and a desire to control all forms of industry. The organization making the largest contribution to black education was the General Education Board (GEB), a conglomeration of northern white philanthropists, established by John D. Rockefeller Sr. but spearheaded by John D. Rockefeller Jr. Between 1903 and 1964, the GEB gave more than $63,000,000 to black colleges, an impressive figure, but nonetheless only a fraction of what they gave to white institutions. Regardless of their personal motivations, the funding system that these industrial moguls created showed a strong tendency to control black education for their benefit—to produce graduates who were skilled in the trades that served their own enterprises (commonly known as industrial education). Above all, the educational institutions they supported were extremely careful not to upset the segregationist power structure that ruled the South by the 1890s. Black colleges such as Tuskegee and Hampton were showcases of industrial education. It was here that students learned how to shoe horses, make dresses, cook, and clean under the leadership of individuals like Samuel Chapman Armstrong (Hampton) and Booker T. Washington (Tuskegee).

The philanthropists' support of industrial education was in direct conflict with many black intellectuals who favored a liberal arts curriculum. Institutions such as Fisk, Dillard, Howard, Spelman, and Morehouse were more focused on the liberal arts curriculum favored by W. E. B. Du Bois than on Booker T. Washington's emphasis on advancement through labor and self-sufficiency. Whatever the philosophical disagreements may have been between Washington and Du Bois, the two educational giants did share a goal of educating African Americans and uplifting their race. Their differing approaches might be summarized as follows: Washington favored educating blacks in the industrial arts so they might become self-sufficient as individuals, whereas Du Bois wanted to create an intellectual elite in the top ten percent of the black population (the "talented tenth") to lead the race as a whole toward self-determination.

Beginning around 1915, there was a shift in the attitude of the industrial philanthropists, who started to turn their attention to those black colleges that emphasized the liberal arts. Realizing that industrial education could exist side by side with a more academic curriculum, the philanthropists opted to spread their money (and therefore their influence) throughout the educational system. The pervasive influence of industrial philanthropy in the early 20th century created a conservative environment on many black college campuses—one that would seemingly tolerate only those administrators (typically white men) who accommodated segregation. But attention from the industrial philanthropists was not necessarily welcomed by institutions like Fisk University, where rebellions ensued against autocratic presidents who were assumed by students to be puppets of the philanthropists. In spite of these conflicts, industrial philanthropists provided major support for private black colleges up until the late 1930s.

At this time, the industrial philanthropists turned their attention elsewhere. In response, Frederick D. Patterson, then president of the Tuskegee Institute, suggested that the nation's private black colleges join together in their fundraising efforts. As a result, in 1944, the presidents of 29 black colleges created the United Negro College Fund (UNCF). The UNCF began solely as a fundraising organization but eventually took on an advocacy role as well.

Until the *Brown v. Board of Education* decision in 1954, both public and private black colleges in the South remained segregated by law and were the only educational option for African Americans. Although most colleges and universities did not experience the same violent fallout from the *Brown* decision as southern public schools, they were greatly affected by the decision. The Supreme Court's landmark ruling meant that black colleges would be placed in competition with white institutions in their efforts to recruit black students. With the triumph of the idea of integration, many began to call black colleges into question and label them vestiges of segregation. Desegregation proved slow, however, with public black colleges maintaining their racial makeup well into the current day. In the state of Mississippi, for example, the *Fordice* case was mired in the court system for almost 25 years, with a final decision rendered in 2004. The case, which reached the United States Supreme Court, asked whether Mississippi had met its affirmative duty under the Fourteenth Amendment's Equal Protection Clause to dismantle its prior dual university system. Despite ample evidence to the contrary, the high court decided that the answer was yes. Although the *Fordice* case applied only to those public institutions within the 5th District, it had a rippling effect within most southern states, resulting in stagnant funding levels for public black colleges and limited inroads by African Americans into predominantly white institutions.

After the *Brown* decision, private black colleges, which have always been willing to accept students from all backgrounds if the law would allow, struggled to defend issues of quality in an atmosphere that labeled anything all black as inferior. Many black colleges also suffered from "brain drain," as predominately white institutions in the North and some in the South made efforts to attract the top 10 percent of their students to their institutions once racial diversity became valued within higher education.

The black college of the 1960s was a much different place than that of the 1920s. The leadership switched from white to black and, because blacks had more control over funding, there was greater tolerance for dissent and black self-determination. On many public and private black college campuses throughout the South, students were staging sit-ins and protesting against segregation and its manifestations throughout the region. Most prominent were the four black college students from North Carolina A & T who refused to leave a segregated Woolworth lunch counter in 1960.

During the 1960s, the federal government took a greater interest in black colleges. In an attempt to provide clarity, the 1965 Higher Education Act defined a black college as an institution whose primary mission was the education of African Americans. The recognition of the uniqueness of black colleges implied in this definition has led to increased federal funding for these institutions.

Another federal intervention on behalf of black colleges took place in 1980 when President Jimmy Carter signed Executive Order 12232, which established a national program to alleviate the effects of discriminatory treatment and to strengthen and expand black colleges to provide quality education. Since this time, every U.S. president has provided funding to black colleges through this program. President George H. W. Bush followed up on Carter's initiative in 1989, signing Executive Order 12677, which created the Presidential Advisory Board on Historically Black Colleges and Universities to advise the president and the secretary of education on the future of these institutions.

Currently, more than 300,000 students attend the nation's 105 historically black colleges (40 public four-year, 11 public two-year, 49 private four-year, and 5 private 2-year institutions). This amounts to 28 percent of all African American college students. Overall, the parents of black students at black colleges have much lower incomes than those of parents of black students at predominantly white institutions. Many researchers who study black colleges, however, have found that African Americans who attend black colleges have higher levels of self-esteem and find their educational experience more nurturing. Moreover, graduates of black colleges are more likely to continue their education and pursue graduate degrees than their counterparts at predominantly white institutions. Despite the fact that only 28 percent of African American college students attend black colleges, these institutions produce the majority of our nation's African American judges, lawyers, doctors, and teachers.

Black colleges in the 21st century are remarkably diverse and serve varied populations. Although most of these institutions maintain their historically black traditions, on average 13 percent of their students are white. Because of their common mission (that of racial uplift), they are often lumped together and treated as a monolithic entity, causing them to be unfairly judged by researchers, the media, and policymakers. Just as predominantly white institutions are varied in their mission and quality, so are the nation's black colleges. Today, the leading black colleges cater to those students who could excel at any top tier institution regardless of racial makeup. Other institutions operate with the needs of black students in the surrounding region in mind. And some maintain an open enrollment policy, reaching out to those students who would have few options elsewhere in the higher education system.

See also: Freedmen's Bureau

Marybeth Gasman

Bibliography
Betsey, Charles L. *Historically Black Colleges and Universities.* New Brunswick, NJ: Transaction Publishers, 2008.
Drewry, Henry N., Humphrey Doermann, and Susan H. Anderson. *Stand and Prosper: Private Black Colleges and Their Students.* Princeton, NJ: Princeton University Press, 2001.
Jackson, Cynthia L., and Eleanor F. Nunn. *Historically Black Colleges and Universities: A Reference Handbook.* Santa Barbara, CA: ABC-CLIO, 2003.
Ricard, Ronyelle Bertrand, and M. Christopher Brown. *Ebony Towers in Higher Education: The Evolution, Mission, and Presidency of Historically Black Colleges and Universities.* Sterling, VA: Stylus Publishers, 2008.
Wenglinsky, Harold. *Historically Black Colleges and Universities: Their Aspirations and Accomplishments.* Princeton, NJ: Educational Testing Service, 1999.

Hoover, J. Edgar

The longest serving bureaucrat in history, Federal Bureau of Investigation Director J. Edgar Hoover (1895–1972) presided over the erection of a domestic security state in the United States between 1919 and 1972. Born into the respectable racism of segregated Victorian society, Hoover was obsessed by fear of racial miscegenation and consistently responded to African American demands for justice and equality as threats to moral propriety and social order. Ignoring the pervasive violations of federal civil rights laws that characterized the American South, Hoover exploited moral panics to repress African American political movements.

During World War I, as Hoover rounded up enemy aliens, the Bureau of Investigation (BI) had launched a large-scale investigation into the activities of black civilians and soldiers, and equal rights organizations and publications. Federal bureaucrats were most alarmed by the radical syndicalists of the International Workers of the World (IWW), an industrial union that engaged in general strikes, attempting to organize all workers irrespective of race or nationality, on the basis of economic radicalism and opposition to the war. In 1918, BI investigations facilitated the incarceration of Benjamin Harrison, the IWW's most prominent black activist.

During the 1919–1920 Red Scare, Hoover was appointed to head the antiradical General Intelligence Division (GID) of the BI and launched investigations into political associations among African Americans. His agents reached entirely erroneous conclusions regarding relationships between the IWW and African American publications like the socialist *Messenger,* the procommunist *Crusader,* and the National Association for the Advancement of Colored People's *Crisis.* BI agents even investigated anticommunist groups such as the African Blood Brotherhood and Marcus Garvey's Universal Negro Improvement Association. Finding no evidence for tax-violation or white slavery charges against Garvey, Hoover obtained a conviction on mail fraud in 1922 and, after five years of incarceration, secured his deportation from the United States.

Dragnet raids, alliances with vigilantes, *agent provocateur* activities, and partisan use of BI agents brought about the abolishment of the GID in 1924, when Hoover rose to the position of director. His agents secretly continued to monitor outspoken black organizations such as the NAACP and the Moorish Science Temple. When Hoover gained authority to investigate subversive activities among Communists and Fifth Columnists in the years before World War II, the FBI investigated and reported to the White House on organizations such as the Southern Conference for Human Welfare and A. Philip Randolph's March on Washington movement.

The FBI launched a systematic investigation of African American life during WWII, monitoring all black-owned newspapers, recruiting paid black informants, and conducting electronic surveillance against groups ranging from the National Negro Congress to the NAACP. Attempting to stem a tide of racial protest, Hoover even ordered his agents to find out if black female domestic servants were demanding a voice in their working conditions. As the Justice Department was drawn into minimal enforcement of black civil rights for the first time, Attorney General Nicholas Biddle ordered Hoover to investigate lynching and pogroms against black defense workers. Hoover resisted. FBI reports tried to deflect responsibility for racial conflict to agitation by pro-Axis subversives.

During the Cold War, the FBI investigated any group that adopted positions on peace, civil liberties, racism, or economics that paralleled the Communist Party line. Hoover viewed the Civil Rights movement as a target for Communist infiltration, so FBI agents and informants penetrated liberal groups such as the NAACP, American Friends Services Committee, Southern Christian Leadership Conference, Congress for Racial Equality, and Students for a Democratic Society. They collected and disseminated information on political opinions, plans, and activities of sympathetic university professors, student groups, civil rights activists, and labor unions. Racist police departments and citizens councils received scant attention.

As the *Brown* decision and nonviolent direct action campaigns provoked racial backlash, Hoover was forced to investigate anti-civil rights bombings and killings. Between 1960 and 1964, FBI agents merely took notes as police brutalized civil rights demonstrators, and an FBI informant even led the Klan beating of the Freedom Riders in Birmingham, but the Civil Rights Act and the Voting Rights Act forced change. After 1964, agents helped local police prevent Klan terrorism and launched a successful covert operation against the Klan. At the same time, however, the bureau also provided political intelligence to President Johnson on the Mississippi Freedom Democratic Party challenge, launched covert action against nonviolent groups such as the Poor People's Campaign, and systematically repressed militant groups such as the Black Panther Party, committing some of the grossest violations of civil liberties that have ever occurred in the United States.

See also: Black Panther Party; COINTELPRO; Garvey, Marcus; King, Martin Luther Jr.; National Association for the Advancement of Colored People

John Drabble

Bibliography
Gentry, Curt. *J. Edgar Hoover: The Man and the Secrets*. New York: W. W. Norton, 1991.
Hill, Robert A. *The FBI's RACON: Racial Conditions in the United States During World War II*. Boston: Northeastern University Press, 1995.
Kornweible, Theodore Jr. *"Investigate Everything": Federal Efforts to Compel Black Loyalty During World War I*. Bloomington: Indiana University Press, 2002.
Kornweible, Theodore Jr., *"Seeing Red": Federal Campaigns Against Black Militancy, 1919–1925*. Bloomington: Indiana University Press, 1998.
O'Reilly, Kenneth. *Racial Matters: The FBI's Secret File on Black America, 1960–1972*. New York: Free Press, 1989.
Powers, Richard Gid. *Secrecy and Power: The Life of J. Edgar Hoover*. New York: Free Press, 1987.
Theoharis, Athan, and John Stewart Cox *The Boss: J. Edgar Hoover and the Great American Inquisition*. Philadelphia: Temple University Press, 1988.

Houston, Charles Hamilton

Attorney and educator Charles Hamilton Houston (1895–1950) was born in the District of Columbia, to William LePre Houston, a lawyer and part-time professor, and Mary Ethel Hamilton, an accomplished hairdresser and former school teacher. A bright youngster, Houston enjoyed a middle-class upbringing and had great pride in his heritage. He attended the racially segregated Washington, D.C. public school system, where he graduated from M Street

High School at the age of 15, before enrolling at Amherst College in Massachusetts in 1911.

Houston graduated with a BA degree, *magna cum laude,* as one of Amherst's six valedictorians. He was the only black student in the Amherst class of 1915 and was elected to Phi Beta Kappa. After briefly teaching English at Howard University, Houston enlisted in the army in 1917 and was sent to Camp Fort Des Moines in Iowa in June 1917. While there, he sought training in the artillery corps, but black officers were trained to serve only in the infantry. Thus, Houston was commissioned first lieutenant of infantry, a position he resigned in June 1918 to attend artillery school. Later he reported to Camp Meade, Maryland, where he won his commission as a second lieutenant of artillery. Houston and other black officers were sent to France where they encountered racism and segregation in the army.

After being honorably discharged from the army in 1919, Houston returned to Washington, D.C. Disturbed by the discrimination he and other black officers encountered and experienced in the army, he decided to follow in the footsteps of his father who was then a leading member of the Bar of the District of Columbia. Houston entered Harvard Law School in the fall of 1919, and, after his first year, distinguished himself among his fellow students and was honored by becoming the first black to serve as editor of the *Harvard Law Review.* Houston earned a bachelor of law degree (*cum laude*) in 1922, and made history again in 1923, when he became the first black person to be awarded a Doctor of Juridical Science at Harvard.

Houston was then awarded a one-year fellowship to study law in Europe at the University of Madrid in Spain, from which he earned a Doctor of Civil Law degree (1924), before returning to Washington, and was admitted to practice law in the District of Columbia that same year. After a short period, he began a lifelong law partnership with his father in Washington, D.C., while also teaching at Howard University Law School. During his distinguished legal career, Houston answered numerous calls, but he remained closely associated with his father. On August 23, 1924, he married his first wife, Margaret Gladys Moran, but they were divorced in 1937. He married his second wife, Henrietta Williams, in August of that same year, with whom he had one child.

In 1929, Houston was appointed vice dean of Howard University Law School, where he also served as a professor of law. He directed the work of the law school as the chief administrative officer until 1935, and, during his administration, Howard Law School trained most of the nation's blacks who entered the legal profession. The law school, however, lacked national recognition, and Houston worked tirelessly and provided leadership that helped transform Howard into a nationally distinguished legal training ground with a mission of racial advancement. His hard work paid off by 1931, when Howard University Law School was fully accredited by the American Bar Association and had gained membership in the Association of American Law Schools. During his tenure, Howard University Law School graduated and trained almost three-fourths of the nation's black law students. Many of the lawyers Houston mentored and trained carried on the struggle for equal justice and won numerous important cases after his death. Thurgood Marshall, the first black Supreme Court Justice, Oliver Hill, and William Bryant, all of whom were distinguished civil rights litigators and later federal jurists, are examples of the national litigators that Howard Law School produced.

Charles Hamilton Houston was the special counsel for the NAACP who led the judicial fight for civil rights from 1929 until his death just four years before the historic Brown v. Board of Education *decision in 1954. (Library of Congress)*

In 1935, Houston left Washington, D.C., to become the first full-time paid special counsel for the National Association for the Advanced of Colored People (NAACP), headquartered in New York City. As head of the legal department, Houston launched a campaign against racial segregation in public schools that would later help to dismantle segregation. Houston handled and won numerous important cases during the 1930s and 1940s, some of which helped to lay the groundwork for the landmark cases of the 1950s. For example in 1938, Houston won his first case for equality in educational opportunity, *Missouri ex rel. Gaines v. Canada* (1938). To protect the rights of persons accused of crimes, Houston litigated *Hollins v. Oklahoma* (1935) and *Hale v. Kentucky* (1938), in which the U.S. Supreme Court overturned the convictions and death sentences of African Americans who had been tried by juries from which African Americans were excluded on the basis of their race. As the major architect and the dominating force behind the NAACP's legal program, Houston aimed high and made heavy inroads. In 1940, he left the organization and returned to private practice in Washington, D.C., but he remained involved in the fight for the rights and welfare of African Americans including discrimination in education, labor, and housing. He was succeeded as NAACP special counsel by his former student, Thurgood Marshall.

Thereafter, he rejoined his father and formed the firm of Houston & Houston, later known as Houston, Houston, Hastie, & Bryant. His work in the firm covered many areas including discrimination in employment, housing, the rights of the accused, and other aspects of discrimination. Houston also won victories as a civil rights litigator in private practice, successfully arguing and winning cases before the United States Supreme Court, including *Steel v. Louisville & Nashville Railroad Co.,* and *Tunstall v. Brotherhood of Locomotive Firemen and Enginemen* (1944), when he challenged discriminatory actions by government negotiators and contractors with regard to fair representation regardless of race or union affiliation. In 1948, Houston assisted the NAACP in preparation for a housing discrimination case, *Shelley v. Kraemer,* and was the chief counsel before the Supreme Court in *Hurd v. Hodge* (1948), in which the Supreme Court ruled against judicial enforcement of racially restrictive covenants in the District of Columbia. Throughout his career, Houston was involved in numerous civic duties including National Legal Aid Committee (1940–1950); he was

vice president for the American Council of Race Relations (1944–1950), vice president of the National Lawyer Guild, a member of the National Board of Directors and chairman of the national Legal Committee of the NAACP, two years a member of the Board of Education in the District of Columbia, and a member of the President's Committee on Fair Employment Practices (1944), before resigning the next year. An active participant in the civil rights struggle beyond academia, Houston was also engaged in political activism during his lifetime, including marching in the 1930s for the freedom of the Scottsboro boys and testifying before congress against lynching and other forms of racial inequality. An incredibly high-energy educator and lawyer, Houston inspired faculty and students with his philosophy of social engineering.

Historically, Charles Houston's most important impact was his strengthening of Howard University Law School, as well as his tireless work as a civil rights litigator for the NAACP. Houston's extensive work and dedication to improving legal education at Howard is notable, and achieving accreditation for the law school was one of the greatest accomplishments for Houston and those who shared his vision. During his administration, Houston commanded and encouraged the legal army to fight and seek equality for African Americans, and many of the cases that Houston argued were instrumental in setting precedents that were later used in the Supreme Court's landmark decisions of *Brown v. Board of Education* (1954) and *Bolling v. Sharpe,* which declared racial segregation in public schools unconstitutional.

Charles Hamilton Houston muddled through the forests of oppression and discrimination seeking equal protection and justice for those who could not fight for themselves. Among the early builders of the road to freedom that later activists such as Martin Luther King Jr. significantly expanded and strengthened, no one played as major a role as Charles Hamilton Houston. He was the chief engineer and the dominant force on the civil rights legal scene. One of the greatest civil rights activist in American history, Houston was the primary force behind the ultimate success of the long struggle that led to an end of the legalized discrimination and in particular, the notion of "separate but equal."

Houston was instrumental in training a generation of fearless civil rights lawyers throughout the country, who carried on the struggle and remained an inspiration to those dedicated to social justice today. Aside from training the great Thurgood Marshall, he was also a close advisor to Marshall. The magnitude of Houston's contributions toward the quality of justice in American society today is tremendous. This civil rights icon was a giant of a man who dedicated his life to the cause of freedom that all Americans enjoy today. Houston made marked contributions to the Civil Rights movement and the struggle against oppression of African Americans, for which he was posthumously, awarded the coveted Spingarn Medal by the NAACP. In 1958, Howard University renamed its law school building in honor of Charles Hamilton Houston.

Throughout his legal career Houston was a pillar for African Americans. For three decades, Charles Houston's civil rights advocacy focused on achieving recognition of equal rights and opportunities, legal guarantees, and elimination of legalized racial discrimination. In spite of the increasing prominence of black scholars, legal academia does not recognize the Houstonian intellectual heritage. This deeply committed strategist, legal counsel, educator, mentor, and adviser in the struggle against racial discrimination remains a model for activists in the cause for justice and equality.

Charles Houston's fast pace in the struggle for racial justice and equality was eventually cut short by a heart ailment. He was first hospitalized for exhaustion and suffered a severe heart attack in 1948, but he never recovered. Houston died on April 20, 1950, in Washington, D.C., four years before fully realizing his struggle against "separate but equal." He left behind his second wife, Henrietta Williams Houston, and their only child, Charles Hamilton Houston Jr. The death of this civil rights icon brought an irreparable loss to the black community and to America. Houston was buried in Lincoln Memorial Cemetery in Suitland, Maryland.

See also: Brown v. Board of Education; Jim Crow; Marshall, Thurgood; National Association for the Advancement of Colored People; *Plessy v. Ferguson*

Njoki-Wa-Kinyatti

Bibliography

Carter, Robert L. "In Tribute: Charles Hamilton Houston." *Harvard Law Review* 11, no. 8 (1998):2149–79.

Hastie, William H. "Charles Hamilton Houston." *Journal of Negro History* 35, no. 3 (1950):355–58.

Klebanow, Diana, and Franklin L. Jonas. *People's Lawyers: Crusaders for Justice in American History.* New York: M. E. Sharpe, 2003.

McNeil, Genna R. *Ground Work: Charles Hamilton Houston and the Struggle for Civil Rights.* Philadelphia: University of Pennsylvania Press, 1983.

Houston, Texas, Mutiny, 1917

On the night of August 23, 1917, more than 100 African American soldiers from the 24th Infantry, in defiance of their white officers, marched from Camp Logan to nearby Houston armed and angry. In a frenzied state fueled by mounting frustrations and fear, these men believed Corporal Charles Baltimore, a military police officer and model soldier, had been killed that afternoon by local police, and they wanted answers. At the conclusion of their two-hour march on Houston, 16 whites, which included five police officers, and 4 black soldiers had been killed. Serious consequences awaited those perceived to be responsible for the Houston riot. This racial violence occurred in the early months of the U.S. mobilization for World War I and weeks after the East St. Louis massacre where white mobs invaded black neighborhoods without law enforcement protection, killing nearly 40 African Americans.

In late July, 654 career black soldiers who made up the 3rd Battalion of the 24th Infantry traveled from New Mexico to their new assignment at Camp Logan, a newly created military training camp located three-and-one-half miles from downtown Houston, Texas. Washington assigned these soldiers the responsibility of guarding construction of the military camp. Immediately, these African American soldiers of the 24th Infantry experienced racial hostility and discrimination. White construction workers on the camp site they guarded resented the black soldiers' authority and regularly harassed them and hurled racial slurs. White Houstonians, strongly committed to white supremacy, refused the newly arrived black soldiers the same respect they accorded white soldiers. Local whites reasoned that respecting these soldiers would imply equality and would raise the expectations of local blacks for similar consideration. Also, Houston's police force had a notorious reputation for brutality to its black population, the largest of any city in Texas. During the soldiers' off-duty visits to town in the weeks that preceded the riot, Houston police regularly insulted, beat, and arrested black soldiers for minor infraction of local customs. Members of the 24th Infantry resented the disrespectful behavior, the police brutality, and fastidious enforcement of Houston's segregation statutes. As proud and self-confident men who had spent the last few years in western states, the soldiers were not accustomed to the South's Jim Crow mores and regularly defied the injustice.

Whether the soldiers reacted spontaneously to mounting frustrations, anger with repeated police abuse, and fear of white mob violence or secretly plotted revenge is disputed, but on the evening of August 23, emotions exploded. That day two police officers beat and arrested an enlisted man, Alonzo Edwards, who tried to protect a local black woman from police harassment. Unlike local whites, Houston's black residents welcomed and revered the soldiers. Viewed as heroes and leaders, black Texans expected the soldiers to protect them. These expectations intensified the soldiers' humiliation, for recent incidents revealed they had been unable to protect even themselves from police brutality. To quell escalating tensions between soldiers and the police, a negotiated agreement assigned 12 black, non-commission officers as military police to monitor soldiers' behavior in town. Consistent with the agreement, Corporal Baltimore inquired about Edwards's arrest to a police officer who asserted that he did not answer to "niggers." The police officer struck Baltimore in the face with his pistol and shot at him three times as he chased him into a vacant building. Although Baltimore escaped with his life, word reached camp that this highly respected MP had been killed.

Cooler heads did not prevail in this difficult situation. Experienced leadership from the 3rd Battalion—black and white—had recently been transferred, and their replacements, especially the white commissioned officers, had not earned the men's trust and proved inadequate for this challenge. Anger, confusion, and fear prevailed in the camp that evening. Rumors of pending trouble led white officers to plead for calm, but shouts that the white mob was coming transformed the chaos into action. More than 100 soldiers, following Sergeant Vida Henry's lead, scrambled for weapons and ammunition and marched to Houston, targeting the police station in the Fourth Ward as their destination. The next two hours altered many lives and Henry killed himself before dawn.

After the Houston riot of 1917 the army launched an extensive and hasty investigation that led to the largest court-martial in American military history—the prosecution of 118 soldiers. The first of three court-martials found 54 men guilty of mutiny and murder. In all, 13 men, perceived as the leaders, were sentenced to death, and 41 others to life in prison. The army quickly carried out the mass execution of these 13 soldiers before Secretary of War Newton Baker or President Woodrow Wilson could review the sentences. Two subsequent court-martials convicted 52 more soldiers; 6 of these men were ultimately executed and 22 more received life sentences. White officers were not prosecuted nor were any white civilians tried. News of the Houston riot traveled rapidly across the South, fueling existing racial animosity. Southern governors, who did not want black soldiers training in their states' new military camps, used the Houston riot to support racist contentions that integrated military training would never work, especially in the South. The NAACP petitioned for many years to have the life sentences of convicted soldiers reduced. As a result of these petitions, most of the men facing life sentences were released throughout the 1920s. The last prisoner was paroled in 1938.

See also: Jim Crow; National Association for the Advancement of Colored People; World War I (Black Participation in)

Janet G. Hudson

Bibliography
Haynes, Robert V. *A Night of Violence: The Houston Riot of 1917.* Baton Rouge: Louisiana State University, 1976.
Smith, C. Calvin. "The Houston Riot of 1917 Revisited." *Houston Review* 13 (1991):85–102.

Howard Beach Incident, 1986

In the 1980s, several racially motivated attacks dominated the headlines of New York City newspapers. The city had a legacy of race bias murders. On September 15, 1983, artist and model Michael Stewart died on a lower Manhattan subway platform from a chokehold and beating he received from several police officers. A year later, on October 29, an elderly grandmother, Eleanor Bumpers, was murdered by a police officer in her Bronx apartment as he and other officers tried to evict her. Later that year, on December 22, a white man, Bernhard Goetz, shot and seriously wounded four black teenagers he thought were going to rob him on a subway train in Manhattan. The Howard Beach racial incident in late 1986 propelled the predominantly Italian and

Jewish community into the national spotlight, exposing racial hatred in New York City.

On the early morning of December 20, 1986, a white mob attacked three stranded African Americans in Howard Beach, an insular community in the borough of Queens. On that night, four African American men—Cedric Sandiford, 36; Timothy Grimes, 20; Michael Griffith, 23; and the car's owner, Curtis Sylvester, 20—were traveling from their home base in Brooklyn to Queens to pick up Griffith's paycheck. On the northbound trip back home, the 1976 Buick they were traveling in stalled on Cross Bay Boulevard, near Howard Beach. Griffith, Sandiford, and Grimes decided to walk to Howard Beach, a few miles away, to locate a pay phone.

At midnight, after entering Howard Beach, the three were initially confronted by a small group of white pedestrians, who yelled racial slurs and told them to get out of their neighborhood. By then hungry and tired, the men decided to dine and rest at the New Park Pizzeria on Cross Bay Boulevard. When Sandiford, Grimes, and Griffith left the restaurant at 12:40 A.M., a mob of 12 white youths were awaiting them with baseball bats, tire irons, and tree limbs. The gang, led by Jon Lester 17, included Salvatore De-Simone, 19; William Bollander, 17; James Povinelli, 16; Michael Pirone, 17; John Saggese; 19, Jason Ladone, 16; Thomas Gucciardo, 17; Harry Bunocore, 18; Scott Kern, 18; Thomas Farino, 16; and Robert Riley, 19.

The white youths began harassing the African Americans. Ladone, another of the ringleaders, yelled taunts and racist epithets. The mob then attacked Griffith and Sandiford, but Grimes brandished a knife on the angry mob and he escaped with minor injuries. Sandiford begged them not to kill him before Lester knocked him down with a baseball bat. With the mob in hot pursuit, the severely beaten Griffith managed to run. He ran several blocks to the nearby Belt Parkway, where he jumped through a small hole in a fence adjacent to the highway. As he staggered across the busy six-lane expressway, trying to escape his attackers, he was hit and instantly killed by a car driven by Dominic Blum, a court officer and son of a New York police officer.

At 1:00 A.M. when the police arrived at the scene, they encountered a bloody and dazed Sandiford nearby, walking west on the parkway. The officers brought him back to Griffin's lifeless body on the parkway. They treated him like a suspect, ripping off his jacket and subjecting him to a spread-eagle search. After being interrogated, a badly bloody and bruised Sandiford was placed in a squad car.

The officers refused him medical attention and forced him to tell his version of the assault several times until dawn.

That morning, an incensed New York Mayor Edward Koch and African American police Chief Benjamin Ward condemned the crime in the media. Koch compared the incident to a lynching, and Ward scolded the Queens commanding officer for his officers' insensitivity toward Sandiford, who by then was receiving legal representation from experienced civil rights attorneys C. Vernon Mason and Alton Maddox.

The incident sparked immediate outrage in the African American community, prompting black civil rights activist Reverend Al Sharpton to organize several protests in Howard Beach, as well as the Carnarsie and Bath Bay sections of Brooklyn. Groups of mostly African Americans marched through the streets with signs comparing the racial climate in Howard Beach to apartheid in South Africa. White residents greeted them with signs that read, "Niggers Go Home," "White Power," and "Bring Back Slavery."

In addition to the leadership of Sharpton, Reverend Floyd Flake, who had just been elected to Congress, Sonny Carson of Black Men Against Crack, and Reverend Herbert Daughtry of the Black United Front publicly criticized the racially motivated incident and the law officials handling of the case. They issued calls for boycotts on all white-owned Howard Beach businesses and New York City pizzerias. Because of the racial sensitivity of the case, New York Governor Mario Cuomo assigned Special Prosecutor Charles J. Hynes. Four of the white youths—Kern, Lester, Ladone, and Pirone—were brought to trial on manslaughter, second-degree murder, and first-degree assault charges. The others were charged with lesser offenses.

During the trial, which began on October 7, 1987, State Supreme Court Justice Thomas Demakos and the jury listened to Lester's attorney deny that his client was a racist. He stressed that Lester had a cordial relationship with African Americans. Lester's mother insisted that he was not racist because he once dated a black female. Attorneys for the other defendants tried the same strategy, portraying their clients as compassionate individuals. The defense team said one of the stranded motorists was a drug addict who instigated the entire incident.

On December 21, 1987, after lengthy deliberation, the jury found three of the four principal defendants guilty of second-degree manslaughter and first-degree assault, but innocent on attempted murder and riot charges. The jury

Protesters, including Al Sharpton (center) and James Bell (third from right), president of the Coalition of Black Trade Unionists, organized a rally held in Howard Beach, Queens, New York, to bring attention to a white mob attack on three black youth. (AP Photo/Ed Bailey)

acquitted Michael Pirone of all charges. The other participants received lighter sentences and, in most cases, received community service.

During Lester's sentencing on January 22, 1988, Judge Demakos said that the teenager and his community failed to display remorse or a sense of guilt for his role in the crime, and sentenced him to 10 to 30 years in prison. The following month, Ladone received a 5- to 15-year sentence, and Kern was sentenced to 6 to 18 years in prison.

The verdict upset the defendants' families and friends, but the decision satisfied most of those who supported the victims. Jon Lester was freed from prison on May 29, 2001, and moved to London. Ladone was released in spring of the same year and Kern was set free the next year. After the Howard Beach incident, race-related crimes continued to plague New York City. Howard Beach was followed in 1989 by the brutal killing of an African American teenager, Yusuf Hawkins, by a gang of white youths in the Bensonhurst section of Brooklyn.

See also: Bensonhurst, New York, Incident of 1989; Sharpton, Al; White Mob Violence

Dwayne A. Mack

Bibliography

Fried, Joseph. "Howard Beach Defendant Given Maximum Term of 10 to 30 Years." *New York Times,* January 23, 1988:1.

Hynes, Charles J., and Bob Drury. *Incident at Howard Beach: The Case for Murder.* New York: G. P. Putnam's Sons, 1990.

McFadden, Robert. "Black Man Dies After Beach Beating by White in Queens." *New York Times,* December 21, 1986:1.

Pickney, Alphonso. *Lest We Forget . . . White Hate Crimes: Howard Beach and Other Racial Atrocities.* Chicago: Third World Press, 1994.

Hughes, Langston

Known as the "poet laureate of Harlem," Langston Hughes (1902–1967) was an African American poet, playwright, short-story writer, novelist, and columnist. Largely associated with the Harlem Renaissance of the late 1920s and early 1930s, he continued to write prolifically well beyond this period. His engagement with ideas of racial consciousness was influential on poets such as Aimé Césaire and Léon Damas and the development of the French Negritude movement of which they were part. Hughes's literature focused on the social uplift of poor African Americans, combated against racial stereotypes, and celebrated black identity, even as it acknowledged its seemingly insurmountable problems.

Langston Hughes was born in Joplin, Missouri, on February 1, 1902, the son of James Nathaniel Hughes, a lawyer, and his wife Carrie Langston Hughes. A year after Hughes's birth, his father, faced with the problems of American racism, unrelenting poverty, and an 18-month-old child to support, moved to Mexico. He subsequently prospered and thus was able to send money back to the United States for the support of his son. Hughes went to live with his grandmother Mary Leary Langston in Lawrence, Kansas, whose first husband had been killed during John Brown's slave rebellion at Harpers Ferry in 1859. Her second husband, Hughes's maternal grandfather, was an abolitionist. Mary Langston instilled a great deal of this racial pride in her grandson. Although he lived briefly with his mother in Topeka, Kansas and Colorado and visited his father in Mexico with her in 1908, she had to move around, seeking work in several different states, and Hughes spent the majority of his first nine years with his grandmother.

Hughes cultivated his love for books and reading after a visit with his mother to the library in Topeka in 1907. As a teenager his passion and talent for writing developed. He contributed to his high school literary magazine the *Belfry Owl* and was elected class poet in his senior year. From 1915 until he graduated high school in 1920, Hughes lived with his mother, first in Lincoln, Illinois, and then in Cleveland, Ohio, cultivating his poetic ability and reading the works of Paul Lawrence Dunbar and Carl Sandburg who would heavily influence his own work. It was also during his high school years that his fellow students introduced him to the socialist ideas that would shape his political leanings and inspire the commitment to the poor that he demonstrated throughout his life.

Hughes had a strained relationship with his father, who did not support his son's decision to become a writer. During the summer of 1919, Hughes had lived with his father in Mexico, but while there he became depressed and had suicidal thoughts. After graduating from high school in 1920, Hughes spent a year in Mexico with his father, writing one of his most well-known poems, "The Negro Speaks of Rivers" on the train ride there. The poem was subsequently accepted for publication in 1921 by *Crisis,* the magazine of the National Association for the Advancement of Colored People (NAACP). Hughes gained further publishing success that year in the *Crisis* affiliated publication *The*

For more than five decades, from the 1920s through the 1960s, Langston Hughes wrote poetry, fiction, and plays that were meant to capture the essence of the black experience in America. (Library of Congress)

Brownies Book with two poems, a children's one act play, and the essay "In a Mexico City."

Although his father wanted to him to attend a European university, Hughes enrolled at Columbia University in 1921 to follow a course of study in engineering. He soon became disillusioned, however, with both the college program and his fellow students, preferring instead to spend his time at Broadway shows and in uptown Manhattan's Harlem district. After only a year he dropped out, owing to a combination of his own disinterest and the racism he experienced at the institution. He took up odd jobs, including one as a crew member of a merchant freighter, the S. S. Malone, sailing along the west coast of Africa. Hughes continued to write poetry as he traveled. In 1923, he penned "The Weary Blues," which would eventually give its name to the first collection of his poetry. He continued to publish work in *Crisis* and in the National Urban League's *Opportunity: A Journal of Negro Life.* In 1924, he sailed to Europe, where he lived in Paris, working in a restaurant and listening to jazz. While he was there, Alain Locke, professor of philosophy at Howard University, invited him to Venice to procure poems from him for the special edition of *Survey Graphic* magazine that would, in 1925, become *The New Negro,* the written manifesto of the Harlem Renaissance.

By this time, Hughes was becoming an integral part of the group of artists, writers, and thinkers that made up this cultural movement. After returning home from Paris, Hughes returned to New York where he met the poet and children's book author Arna Bontemps with whom he was to collaborate on a number of projects. At this time he also met many of the major players in the Harlem scene including Wallace Thurman, Zora Neale Hurston, and James Weldon Johnson, and he renewed his acquaintances with Countee Cullen and Carl Van Vechten. He enjoyed more literary success as his poem "The Weary Blues" won *Opportunity* magazine's first prize for poetry. The year 1926 saw the publication of his anthology of the same name, a collection filled with a mixture of jazz, blues, and traditional verse that celebrated African American experience and creativity. Although Hughes often garnered criticism from black middle class reviewers because of his refusal to comply with what he viewed as an excessive reliance on an ideology devoted to the assimilation and accommodation of Eurocentric values and racial integration, both this text and his subsequent publication *Fine Clothes to the Jew* (1927) established Hughes as a major name in the Harlem Renaissance community.

Hughes enrolled at Lincoln University, Pennsylvania, in February 1926, becoming a member of the first black fraternity Omega Psi Phi. That summer he stayed in New York joining with Wallace Thurman, Zora Neale Hurston, Aaron Douglas, Claude McKay, Countee Cullen, and Richard Bruce Nugent to found *Fire!!,* a black periodical for young African American artists. Only one issue was published. In 1927, Hughes met Charlotte Mason, popularly known as the "Godmother." Mason, a wealthy white woman, became Hughes's literary patron, a relationship that became troublesome for Hughes. Mason desired Hughes to align himself and his work with her ideas of the primitive, a view of his work that Hughes did not share. After graduating from Lincoln University in 1929, however, Hughes proceeded to complete the manuscript for his first novel, *Not Without Laughter,* a book influenced by, but not entirely based on, Hughes's childhood growing up in the Midwest, with

the financial support of Mason. The book was published in 1930, but shortly thereafter Mason and Hughes quarreled, causing Hughes to sever his connection with his benefactress. His relationship with Zora Neale Hurston (also under Mason's patronage) also suffered, as they argued over the financial details and authorship of their collaborative play *Mule Bone.* This disagreement ended their friendship, the play was abandoned, and Hughes sunk into another period of intense depression and disillusionment.

After his breakups with Mason and Hurston, Hughes traveled to the American South and to Haiti. After receiving a grant in 1931 for $1,000 from the Rosenwald Fund, Hughes embarked on a poetry reading tour of southern black colleges. During his trip he visited the Scottsborough boys, who had been unjustly incarcerated in an Alabama jail for the alleged rape of two white women. *Dear Lovely Death* and *The Negro Mother* were published in this year, as was his highly controversial poem "Christ in Alabama," which attacked black colleges for failing to speak out against the Scottsborough boys situation. It was published without his consent in *Contempo,* a Chapel Hill college magazine, and drew an angry crowd to his subsequent reading at that college. This did not deter Hughes, however, and he was met at many other colleges in the South with admiration and enthusiasm.

In 1932, Hughes traveled to the Union of Socialist Soviet Republics (USSR) as part of an African American group, with the aim of participating in a film project entitled *Black and White.* Although the project was unsuccessful, Hughes stayed in the Soviet Union for a time where his leftist engagement was reinvigorated and he wrote some of his most political poetry. At this time another of Hughes's highly controversial poems, "Goodbye Christ," was published in the communist journal *Negro Worker* and was met with public indignation. Upon his return to the United States in 1933, Hughes, as well as suffering from illness, became depressed at the public reaction to "Goodbye Christ." Instead of returning to New York, he stayed in Carmel, California, where he wrote his first volume of short stories *The Ways of White Folks* (1934), a negative take on race relations. On October 22, 1934, Hughes's father died in Mexico. Hughes found out too late to attend the funeral, but he traveled to Mexico in January 1935 to organize his father's affairs.

In 1937, Hughes traveled to Spain as a correspondent for the *Baltimore Afro-American,* reporting on the Spanish Civil War and socializing with writers and critics such as Ernest Hemingway, Nancy Cunard, and Pablo Neruda. Upon his return in 1938, the International Workers Order published his most politically charged and socially engaged work to date, *A New Song*. Sadly, Hughes's mother died from cancer this same year.

The second half of the 1930s brought great literary success for Hughes as he penned a number of well-received plays. *Mulatto*, written several years earlier, was produced at the Vanderbilt Theatre in New York City in 1935 and enjoyed an extensive run on Broadway; the Karamu Theatre in Cleveland produced *Little Ham* and *Troubled Island* in 1936, *Joy to My Soul* in 1937, and *Front Porch* in 1938; and the Harlem Suitcase Theatre produced *Don't You Want to Be Free?* (1938). In 1939, Hughes extended his literary repertoire to screenplays, collaborating with Clarence Muse on the script for the film *Way Down South*. After having met Richard Wright in 1938, the pair collaborated on a poem titled "Red Clay Blues," which was published in 1939 in *New Masses* magazine.

The 1940s began for Hughes with the publication of his autobiography, *The Big Sea* (1940), which documents the story of his childhood, as well as providing an extensive commentary on the Harlem Renaissance and his involvement in it. He founded a play company in 1942 called the Skyloft Players and continued his success as a playwright with the Chicago production of *The Sun Do Move*. His seventh volume of poetry, *Shakespeare to Harlem*, also appeared in this year, but received mixed reviews. Some critics accused Hughes of producing a poetry that was superficial and old fashioned and that failed to respond to the social context of World War II, whereas others praised him for his artistic subtlety. At the end of this year, Hughes began writing what would become a weekly column for the *Chicago Defender*. In 1943, he introduced his now famous Jesse B. Semple (later known as "Simple") character to the column. A comic figure, representative of the black "everyman" in America, Simple had moved from Virginia to Harlem, and each week, despite his lack of formal education, he would philosophize on the important issues of the day.

In 1946, the American Academy of Arts and Letters bestowed Hughes with a prize for $1,000, illustrating his importance as an American writer. Throughout the remainder of the 1940s, Hughes continued to publish work of a mixed variety. In 1947, he wrote the lyrics for a Broadway production entitled *Street Scene*, a commission that finally enabled him to become financially solvent and purchase

the house in Harlem in which he would live until his death in 1967. Another collection of poetry, *Fields of Wonder*, appeared in 1947. *One-Way Ticket* (1949), a collection of verse that was typical of Hughes's tragic-comic style, but that disappointed critics by being far from groundbreaking, followed two years later. The year 1949 proved to be a busy one for Hughes. Aside from his own poetry, he co-edited *The Poetry of the Negro 1746–1949* with Arna Bontemps, an important poetic anthology and an endeavor that showed his continuing commitment to demonstrating the richness of black poetry. In addition, his translation of *Cuba Libre: Poems by Nicolás Guillén* was published, and his 1936 play, *Troubled Island*, was converted into an opera by William Grant Still. The following year he had more musical success when another of his plays, *Mulatto*, became the basis for the opera *The Barrier*, performed at Columbia University and written by Jan Meyerowitz who Hughes met in 1947.

By the 1950s, Hughes's Jesse B. Simple column in the *Chicago Defender* had proved so successful that Hughes brought out his first collection of Simple stories: *Simple Speaks His Mind*. During the rest of his life, Hughes produced four more Simple books featuring his "everyman" protagonist, including *Simple Takes a Wife* (1952) and *The Best of Simple* (1961), and an off-Broadway play, *Simply Heavenly* (1957). During the first half of the 1950s, Hughes published consistently in various artistic forms. *Montage for a Dream Deferred* (1951), his first book-length poem, used the rhythms of bebop jazz and demonstrated his ability to break new ground in poetry. A translation of Garcia Lorca's *Gypsy Ballads* (1952); *Laughing to Keep from Crying* (1952), a short story collection; three children's books; and *Five Foolish Virgins* (1954), an oratorio with Jan Meyerowitz demonstrated Hughes's continued literary output and wide artistic range, despite the personal difficulties he was facing at this time as a result of his previous engagements with leftist politics. Although Hughes associated himself with the Left, published in communist magazines, and participated in communist protests run by organizations such as the John Reed Club, he never joined the Communist Party. In 1953, however, he was called on to testify before Senator Joseph McCarthy's Permanent Subcommittee on Investigations in Washington, D.C. The charges did little to upset his career, however.

A year after the landmark *Brown v. Board of Education* (1954) decision, which outlawed segregation in schools, *The Sweet Flypaper of Life* was published, featuring photographs by African American photographer Roy DeCarava and an accompanying text by Hughes. Hughes's text and DeCarava's beautifully intimate photographic portraits captured the essence of everyday African American life in Harlem. Published by Simon and Schuster, it was incredibly well received and firmly established the reputations of both men to adeptly explicate the intricacies of black life in America.

The second volume of Hughes's autobiography was published in 1956. Entitled *I Wonder as I Wander,* it moves beyond Hughes's experiences in the Harlem Renaissance and discusses his experiences with leftist politics and his travels in the Soviet Union. He finished off the decade with the production of another opera with Jan Meyerowitz, *Esther; The Book of Negro Folklore* (1958), co-edited with Arna Bontemps; and *The Selected Poems of Langston Hughes* (1959), which received harsh criticism in the *New York Times* from James Baldwin. Hughes remained productive throughout the 1960s. The book-length poem, *Ask Your Mama* (1961), a fusion of jazz rhythms, myth, and history, mused on issues including humanism, pan-Africanism and free speech. Deeply invested in ideas central to the black arts movement, it received mixed responses from critics, suggesting that Hughes's universal literary appeal was waning.

The final years of Hughes life saw no letup in his literary output. A commissioned history of the NAACP in 1962, three more plays, another collection of short stories, and an edited collection of stories by African American writers were among his final artistic endeavors. The final Simple story appeared in the *Chicago Defender* in 1966. On May 22, 1967, Hughes died in a New York City hospital from postsurgical complications and a diseased prostate gland. His ashes were placed under the floor of the foyer of the Schomberg Center for Research in Black Culture in Harlem, demonstrating his lasting centrality in the African American cultural imagination. His final poetic collection, *The Panther and the Lash,* an exploration of the Black Power and Civil Rights movements, was posthumously published in 1967. Hughes's work enjoyed a literary renaissance in the 1980s with a series of conferences and programs dedicated to his work and legacy.

Langston Hughes was one of the most influential and inspirational African American writers of the 20th century. Able to capture the intricacies and nuances of the lives of everyday African Americans and dedicated to a view of the world that was inclusive of the most impoverished and unfortunate, Hughes's work and life reflect commitment to art that supports racial, social, and personal uplift.

See also: Harlem Renaissance; Hurston, Zora Neale; Locke, Alain; National Association for the Advancement of Colored People; New Negro Movement

Rebecca L. K. Cobby

Bibliography
Gates, Henry Louis, and K. A. Appiah, eds. *Langston Hughes: Critical Perspectives Past and Present.* New York: Amistad, 1993.
Hughes, Langston. *The Collected Poems of Langston Hughes.* ed. Arnold Rampersad. New York: Vintage Books, 1995.
Hughes, Langston. *Langston Hughes and the Chicago Defender: Essays on Race, Culture and Politics, 1942–62.* ed. Christopher C. De Santis. Urbana: University of Illinois Press, 1995.
Ostrom, Hans A. *A Langston Hughes Encyclopedia.* Westport, CT: Greenwood Press, 2002.
Rampersad, Arnold. *The Life of Langston Hughes. Vol. 1: I Too, Sing America.* New York: Oxford University Press, 1986.
Rampersad, Arnold. *The Life of Langston Hughes. Vol. 2: I Dream a World.* New York: Oxford University Press, 1988.
Tidger, John Edgar, and Cheryl R. Ragar, eds. *Montage of a Dream: The Art and Life of Langston Hughes.* Columbia: London: University of Missouri Press, 2007.
Tracy, Steven C. *Langston Hughes and the Blues.* Urbana: University of Illinois Press, 1988.
Trotman, C. James, ed. *Langston Hughes: The Man, His Art and His Continuing Influence.* New York: Garland, 1995.

"If We Must Die"

Claude McKay wrote "If We Must Die" in 1919. It was his most famous sonnet and, according to many, it inaugurated the Harlem Renaissance. McKay was born in Jamaica in 1890 and immigrated to the United States in 1912. He was a well known Harlem Renaissance author and wrote many novels, short stories, and poems.

"If We Must Die" first appeared in the July 1919 issue of the *Liberator.* It was hugely popular and was reprinted dozens of times. McKay wrote this sonnet in the midst of the Red Scare and the Red Summer of 1919. Shortly after World War I, tensions flared between American employers and laborers, and race riots broke out in a number U.S. cities. McKay was working as a waiter for the Pennsylvania Railway Company during this time, and he and his co-workers were acutely aware of the growing racial tension and violence. They were particularly anxious because they traveled from one city to the next with no way to gauge the racial tensions they would encounter in unfamiliar towns. McKay wrote "If We Must Die" in this context. He read it to the other men working in his dining car, and their enthusiastic and emotional response encouraged him to take the poem to Max Eastman for publication in the *Liberator*. Shortly after the initial publication, the sonnet was reprinted in the *Crusader*. It appeared in the September 1919 issue, and the editors hoped the republication would encourage members of the African American community to engage in the fight for racial empowerment and equality.

While confronting the political climate of the time, McKay presented a model of African American masculinity in "If We Must Die." It called for black men to battle courageously against racial oppression, and it developed out of the difficulty that McKay encountered when attempting to create a masculine identity while experiencing degrading racial oppression. In this work, the role that women should play in the battle for racial uplift was noticeably absent, reaffirming the importance that McKay and his publishers placed on reestablishing a masculine racial identity. The author's use of a communal voice was also notable. In this work he attempted to speak to and for the entire African American community and presented a collective African American voice. The work stressed the importance of camaraderie and the willingness to die an honorable death for the cause of racial uplift. McKay also emphasized African American humanity by referencing animals. Rather than dying like "hogs," McKay said African Americans would die "like men." While calling African Americans to fight bravely, this imagery also illustrated the degree to which McKay understood and experienced the dehumanizing effects of racism.

Although race was at the center of "If We Must Die," explicit reference to race was notably absent. McKay did not disclose the racial makeup of the "kinsmen" or the "common foe." This did not keep Americans from recognizing that the poem was about race, but it did allow other groups to appropriate the sonnet. For example, Winston Churchill used "If We Must Die" to call British troops to fight against the Nazis in World War II. Although the sonnet was written in response to racial tension and violence in the United States and was directed to the African American community, it was well known outside the African American community and gained McKay international prestige.

See also: Black Self-Defense; Chicago Race Riot of 1919; Harlem Renaissance; McKay, Claude; Red Summer Race Riots

Monica C. Reed

Bibliography

Cooper, Wayne F. *Claude McKay: Rebel Sojourner in the Harlem Renaissance, a Biography*. Baton Rouge: Louisiana State University Press, 1987.

James, Winston. *A Fierce Hatred of Injustice: Claude McKay's Jamaica and His Poetry of Rebellion*. London: Verso, 2001.

Locke, Alain LeRoy. *The New Negro*. New York: Simon & Schuster, 1997.

Maxwell, William. *New Negro, Old Left*. New York: Columbia University Press, 1999.

McKay, Claude. *A Long Way Home*. New York: Arno-New York Times, 1969.

Tuttle, William M. *Race Riot; Chicago in the Red Summer of 1919*. New York: Atheneum, 1970.

Jackson, Jesse

The Reverend Jesse Louis Jackson Sr. (1941–) emerged as a leader during the Civil Rights movement. In a long career alternately marked by success and controversy, Jackson founded economic justice organizations, ran for president twice, and negotiated with a host of foreign leaders. Jackson's distinctive and powerful speaking style is characterized by wordplay, rhyming couplets, and the phrase "I am somebody," a refrain aimed at cultivating the self-worth of dispossessed youth.

Jackson was born Jesse Louis Burns in Greenville, South Carolina, on October 8, 1941. His mother, Helen Burns, was an unwed 16-year-old. Her pregnancy dashed the hope of her mother, Matilda "Tibby" Burns, that Helen, born when she herself was only 13, would attend college on a singing scholarship. Jesse's biological father, Noah Robinson, was a married man who lived next door with his wife and stepchildren. In 1943, Jesse's mother married Charles Jackson, who later adopted Jesse when he was about 15. They had one child, Charles Jackson Jr.

Robinson, a former boxer and a well-known figure in Greenville's black community, acknowledged his paternity. He had little contact with Jesse, however, who has since said that as a child he would stand staring at the Robinsons' house hoping for a glimpse of his father. Subsequently, Robinson's wife gave birth to three sons, the eldest of whom, Noah Robinson Jr., went on to earn an MBA and become a young standout in the business world but was imprisoned for defrauding the IRS and being an accessory to attempted murder. Questions about these convictions dogged his half-brother on the 1988 campaign trail.

Jackson graduated from Sterling High School in Greenville in 1959. A distinguished student leader and athlete, he chose a football scholarship to the University of Illinois at Champaign-Urbana over a professional baseball contract. Jackson traced his first integration protest to his attempt to take books out of the Greenville library over winter break. He left Illinois after one year and transferred to the historically black North Carolina Agricultural and Technical College in Greensboro. Jackson maintained he was not allowed to quarterback at Illinois because he was black. This comment caused controversy when it came to light that the school's starting quarterback that year was also black. At his new school, Jackson became student body president and met Jacqueline (Jackie) Lavinia Brown, who became his wife. The two participated in sit-in movements to integrate public facilities in Greensboro. Jackson graduated with a sociology degree in 1964.

Jackson has five children with his wife, Jackie: Santita, Jesse Jr., Jonathan, Yusef DuBois, and Jacqueline Lavinia. Santita attended Howard University and sang in a backup group for Roberta Flack. Jesse Jr. attended his parents' alma mater, as did Jonathan and Jacqueline, and in 1995 was elected to the United States Congress representing the second district of Illinois. Yusef attended the University of Virginia on a football scholarship and became a lawyer. In 2001, it came to light that Jackson had fathered a sixth child, Ashley Laverne Jackson, in an affair with Karin Stanford, a former staffer who was being paid through Jackson's organizations.

After a stint with the Congress of Racial Equality (CORE), Jackson moved his growing family north to attend Chicago Theological Seminary. He became increasingly interested in the Civil Rights movement, participating in the 1965 march on Selma, Alabama, and dropped out of seminary in 1966 six months shy of graduating to become a member of the Southern Christian Leadership Conference (SCLC) staff under Martin Luther King Jr. He was later ordained a Baptist minister by Clay Evans and C. L. Franklin, Aretha's father. Chicago Theological Seminary awarded him a Master of Divinity degree in 2000 based on credits plus experience.

In 1966, King named him the head of SCLC's Chicago branch of Operation Breadbasket, an organization founded to persuade businesses such as grocery stores and bakeries to hire more blacks and carry more products from black businesses. Under Jackson's leadership, the organization struck deals with several businesses that resulted in hundreds of jobs for blacks.

In April 1968, Jackson was traveling with King's retinue in Memphis to support a garbage workers' strike when King was gunned down outside his hotel room. There seems little dispute that Jackson was at the hotel when the shooting happened, but some of the tales told about the event were contested. Other civil rights leaders present became angry when Jackson claimed he cradled the dying leader's head in his arms and when he appeared on television the next day in a blood-spattered sweater. To many, Jackson's attempt to emerge as a major black leader after King's death was an insensitive grab for power. Jackson stayed with SCLC for three-and-a-half years but left after a suspension resulting from his independent incorporation of the first Black Expo, which was meant as an SCLC fundraiser.

In the early 1970s, Jackson founded his own organization, Operation PUSH, or People United to Save Humanity ("Save" later became "Serve"). He also began speaking at high schools to African American youth to promote hard work, education, and responsibility. Jimmy Carter's administration rewarded Jackson's school ministry, named PUSH for Excellence, with grants that later dried up under Ronald Reagan's presidency. Jackson also began to travel abroad, developing a vision that incorporated all the world's oppressed poor. In 1972, he initiated such travel with a trip to Liberia. In 1979, he spoke in South Africa against apartheid. The same year, he traveled to the Middle East and compared the conditions of the Palestinians to African Americans' plight in the United States. A picture of him hugging PLO leader Yasser Arafat caused a major controversy and became for many American Jews a lingering source of distrust of Jackson. During that visit the Israeli government refused to see him, but he made several return trips in which he met with both governments and attempted to spread the Civil Rights movement's concepts of nonviolent resistance and radical love as a political weapon to the Palestinian-Israeli conflict.

Although he had never held public office, Jackson made two noteworthy bids for the Democratic nomination for president in the 1980s,. In 1967, King had proposed the Poor People's Campaign, a movement that would bring together the country's economically dispossessed regardless of ethnicity. The idea foundered after King's assassination but later found new life as Jackson's Rainbow Coalition, an organization he later merged with PUSH. Jackson's

Reverend Jesse Jackson, founder of Operation PUSH (People United to Save Humanity), addresses supporters of the Humphrey-Hawkins bill for full employment, January 1975. (Library of Congress)

economic populism made substantial inroads with white farmers and factory workers. He also toured the country promoting voter registration and likely can be credited with the registration of millions of new voters in the 1980s. These new voters provided the margin that elected a contingent of black congresspeople and mayors in that decade.

Jackson's first presidential bid got a boost from his negotiation to release Robert O. Goodman Jr., a black lieutenant shot down and captured by Syria. Jackson accused the government of working less assiduously for Goodman's release than they would have if he were white. The Reagan administration decried his trip as reckless, but Jackson succeeded in obtaining the release.

Nation of Islam leader Louis Farrakhan traveled with Jackson to Syria, where his status as an American Muslim impressed the Syrians. Before Jackson received Secret Service protection as a presidential candidate, Farrakhan supplied him with Fruit of Islam guards from his organization. Not long after the Syria trip, Jackson's close relationship with Farrakhan fed into the black-versus-Jew controversy

that seemed to haunt Jackson's career. Jackson's growing support and appeal following Goodman's release came to an abrupt halt when he referred to Jews as Hymies and called New York Hymietown in an off-the-record conversation with *Washington Post* reporter Milton Coleman, creating possibly the most intractable controversy of Jackson's entire career. Farrakhan, already an unpopular associate given his organization's association with a theology of the intrinsic evilness of the white race, threatened to have the black journalist who reported on the conversation killed. Setting aside Farrakhan's militance and black-supremacist theology, however, he and Jackson shared a platform of economic justice, self-reliance, and education, and both surprised white observers in the 1980s with their ability to draw large black crowds. Jackson only reluctantly distanced himself from Farrakhan after Farrakhan called Judaism a "dirty" religion.

Jackson tried to bounce back from the Hymietown affair with a trip to Cuba and South America. The highlight was an eight-hour session with Fidel Castro in which he persuaded the Cuban leader to release 22 Americans held on drug charges and 27 Cubans held for political activities. Jackson finished third in the 1984 primary season behind eventual nominee Walter Mondale and Gary Hart. He garnered just over 3 million votes.

Gary Hart's 1988 bid met an early demise after an affair came to light. Jackson, often rumored to have a series of amorous relationships, risked a similar disclosure but nevertheless entered the race with polls showing him to be a leading prospect for the nomination. The crowds he drew wherever he went seemed to indicate the same. When 800 townspeople in Greenfield, Iowa, forewent the Super Bowl to hear Jackson speak, he made Greenfield his Iowa headquarters and soon was running second only to Richard Gephardt in the 97 percent white state. He won about 10 percent of the caucus share in that state and 10 percent of the votes in the New Hampshire primary. Jackson did better than expected on Super Tuesday, ending the day with more of the popular vote than any other Democrat. He followed that performance by claiming 55 percent of the vote in Michigan and briefly looked like the frontrunner. Ahead of the New York primary, New York City Mayor Ed Koch resurrected the Hymietown comments and the Arafat hug, which hurt Jackson in that state even though he had spent the previous four years repairing relationships with the Jewish community. Jackson eventually lost the nomination to Michael Dukakis, but along the way, he finished second with almost 7 million primary votes, about 2 million of them from whites. Jackson was disappointed not to be offered the vice presidential slot. Nevertheless, he threw himself into the Democratic campaign, logging more miles on Dukakis's behalf during the general election campaign than the candidate did.

Jackson declined to run in subsequent elections and was often critical of Democratic candidates. In March 2007, he endorsed Barack Obama, who went on to be the first African American to become a major party's nominee. Despite the endorsement, Jackson made headlines for grumbling that Obama did not give enough attention to racial issues, and in a particularly fraught incident, he was caught wearing an open mike and making a vulgar comment about Obama because of the way he talked about African Americans.

Jackson's commitment to global diplomacy long outlasted his official political career. In 1990, Jackson traveled to meet with Iraqi President Saddam Hussein after his invasion of Kuwait and negotiated the release of hundreds of captives during the runup to war between Iraq and a U.S.-led coalition. In 1999, he negotiated the release of three U.S. military personnel captured by Slobodan Milosevic's regime. In 2004, he traveled to Libya and Sudan in an effort to end the Sudanese civil war. In 2005, Jackson met with the president of Venezuela, Hugo Chavez, and condemned evangelist Pat Robertson's comment that Chavez should be assassinated.

From 1991 to 1997, Jackson served in his only elected office, as one of two District of Columbia statehood senators, often known as "shadow senators," a position created to lobby for the district's statehood. In 1997, President Bill Clinton and Secretary of State Madeleine Albright gave Jackson the title Special Envoy for the President and Secretary of State for the Promotion of Democracy in Africa. In 2000, Clinton honored Jackson with the Presidential Medal of Freedom, the country's highest civilian honor, for his lifetime of work on behalf of the poor and minority communities.

See also: Abernathy, Ralph David; CORE; Farrakhan, Louis; King, Martin Luther Jr.; Obama, Barack; Operation PUSH; Southern Christian Leadership Conference

Brooke Sherrard

Bibliography
Clemente, Frank, and Frank Watkins, eds. *Keep Hope Alive: Jesse Jackson's 1988 Presidential Campaign*. Boston: South End Press, 1989.
Frady, Marshall. *Jesse: The Life and Pilgrimage of Jesse Jackson*. New York: Simon & Schuster, 1996.
Hertzke, Allen D. *Echoes of Discontent: Jesse Jackson, Pat Robertson, and the Resurgence of Populism*. Washington, D.C.: CQ Press, 1993.
Jackson, Jesse L. *Straight from the Heart*. Philadelphia: Fortress, 1987.

Jackson, Maynard

Maynard Jackson (1938–2003) served as the first African American mayor of a major southern city. Elected mayor of Atlanta, Georgia, in 1973, Jackson held this position for the maximum of eight consecutive years after being reelected in 1977. In 1989, he won a third term as Atlanta mayor working with community leaders to bring the 1996 Summer Olympic Games to the city. Jackson was born on

March 23, 1938, in Dallas, Texas, to Maynard H. Jackson Sr., a local minister, and Irene Dobbs, who hailed from a socially prominent black family in Atlanta. John Wesley Dobbs, the Dobbs family patriarch, was one of the major political figures in the Atlanta black community. At the age of seven, Maynard Jackson Jr. and his family moved to Atlanta where his father had accepted the pastorship of Friendship Baptist Church.

As did most southern blacks in this era, Jackson attended racially segregated schools. In this environment, Jackson bonded with friends he would maintain for a lifetime. At the age of 14, Jackson entered Morehouse College, graduating in 1956 with academic honors. A Ford Fellow while at Morehouse, he graduated at 18 years of age and decided to become a lawyer rather than a minister like his father. Living outside the South for the first time, Jackson attended Boston University Law School. Although successful in all of his previous educational endeavors, Jackson could not manage to keep up in his studies at Boston. The family had placed pressure on the teenager to become a legal giant and Jackson thought he failed them. Years later, he still found it difficult to discuss the problems he faced in Boston. In 1961, still embarrassed about his problems in law school, Jackson transferred to North Carolina Central Law School in Durham, North Carolina, determined to make amends for the earlier disappointment. Jackson worked hard at Central Law School, graduating in 1964.

Jackson began his family a year after law school when he married Burnella "Bunnie" Hayes Burke. The couple raised three children: Elizabeth, Brooke, and Maynard III. Given the energy required to complete law school and start a family, Jackson did not find the time to participate in formal civil rights demonstrations. Moreover, doing so might have compromised his standing in the legal profession, especially in the Deep South where he planned to practice. Instead, Jackson worked within the system to effect change, beginning his career at the National Labor Relations Board. He also offered his services to the poor through a legal clinic.

Politics was the next major hurdle for Jackson. Believing that it was time for African Americans to think big when it came to Southern politics, Jackson entered the race for the United States Senate in 1968. In this election he ran against incumbent senator Herman Talmadge, the segregationist former governor of Georgia. Lacking adequate funding, Jackson lost the election handily, but there were positive

signs in this defeat. A certain anti-Atlanta sentiment had long characterized Georgia politics, a fact reflected in the less than one-third of the total vote that went to Jackson in the election. Losing statewide contests in Georgia did not always speak to how one might perform in a city election. In fact, Jackson did win the popular vote in Atlanta that year, something that encouraged him to consider entering city politics. In 1969, Jackson won the elected position of vice mayor of Atlanta, beginning his political career.

Although white mayors in Atlanta had at times attempted to serve the needs of the black community, there remained in the 1970s a lingering belief that only a black mayor could adequately address the desperate situation black people faced after decades of Jim Crow racial discrimination. In 1969, the city elected Sam Massell as mayor. Jackson soon found the vice mayoral job weakened by amendments to the city charter. In 1973, he decided to run for mayor against the incumbent. Massell had received the support of black community leaders in the last election and expected the same when he ran for a second term, forcing blacks to choose between him and Jackson. Initially black business leaders asked Jackson to wait another four years before running for mayor, but Jackson convinced them that now was the time. Eventually, prominent black business executives, such as Jesse Hill of Atlanta Life Insurance Company, decided to back Jackson against Massell. Fearing he would lose the election if blacks stood by Jackson while whites split their votes, Massell resorted to negative advertising to increase his appeal to some voters. In these ads, entitled, "Atlanta, too Young to Die," Massell depicted an Atlanta overrun with trash and desolate of life. The implication, despite later protestations by Massell, was that a black mayor would ruin the city. The 1973 mayoral campaign highlighted two problems Maynard Jackson experienced as mayor: exaggerated black expectations of a black mayor and exaggerated white anxiety over a black mayor. In the end, Jackson won the 1973 race with 95 percent of the black vote and 17.5 percent of the white vote.

In its first two terms, the Jackson administration changed the racial complexion of City Hall, increased the number of black businesses receiving municipal contracts, and proved that Atlanta would not suffer dire consequences under black leadership. The same policies that resulted in these changes, however, also brought Jackson the ire of the Atlanta business establishment that had traditionally controlled City Hall. In Atlanta, a major city without a seaport, commerce had always taken a leading role in city affairs. Economic conservatism seemed a natural outgrowth in a city continuously facing challenges from other southern metropolitan areas to its role as leader of the New South, a name given to the region to emphasize the progress southerners had made since the Civil War. During the Civil Rights movement, while Birmingham, Alabama, and other southern cities received negative publicity after outbreaks of violence toward blacks, Atlantans reveled in the knowledge that their city remained peaceful, or as former Mayor William Hartsfield had proclaimed, Atlanta was a city "too busy to hate."

To increase the number of black businesses involved in city ventures such as the expansion of the Metropolitan Atlanta Rapid Transit (MARTA) system and construction of the new Hartsfield Atlanta Airport terminal (subsequently to become the busiest airport in the world), Jackson founded the Atlanta Minority Business Enterprise (MBE) program. MBE mandated that from 25 to 35 percent of city contracts awarded had to go to minority-owned firms. Joint ventures between white firms and those owned by minorities also qualified under the program to ensure that all could directly benefit from MBE. When the mainstream business community expressed outrage that MBE rules applied to the construction of the international airport, a project deemed crucial to the future of the city, Jackson remained committed to his stated goals. In a standoff between Jackson and white business leaders, Jackson refused to issue any contracts until black firms received the same type of consideration historically given to white firms. Jackson halted all construction for a year until white business elites agreed to work along with black firms. By the end of Jackson's second term, MBE had succeeded in awarding 34 percent of all city contracts to firms with significant minority involvement.

Although Jackson would see MBE as a success, in the early years the white business community often thought of him as a reverse racist. Long used to controlling city projects, mainstream white leaders had usually considered blacks only when there was an apparent effect on the city as a whole. Otherwise, black neighborhoods remained ignored. Jackson changed things by acknowledging that the black community was an integral part of Atlanta that required some special attention to address decades of neglect. To some white leaders, however, the affirmative action plans proposed by Jackson were proof that Atlanta would soon reach the "death" that Sam Massell had preached during the 1973 campaign. In the end, Atlanta continued to prosper economically as the majority of Atlantans supported Jackson Administration policies.

When elected Atlanta mayor in 1973, Jackson proclaimed he would never "sellout" his city. Blacks believed that Jackson had to improve their everyday lives. But it became apparent that major changes were difficult, if not impossible, to implement on a local level. For example, Jackson had limited control over the allocation of funds by the federal government for low-income housing. And with the movement of white businesses from the inner city to the suburbs in the 1970s, a process known as "white flight," the urban tax base declined. In 1977, when city sanitation workers went on strike, demanding a pay raise, Jackson realized he had no choice but to stop the attempt by the mostly black workers to force him to submit to their demands. Jackson fired 1,000 sanitation workers, ultimately concluding the strike was a manifestation of the belief by some blacks that a black mayor was in office primarily to offer redress for the inequality they suffered. Jackson knew that the city faced financial constraints that prevented the pay increase at the time and chose to break the strike.

In 1982, Jackson left the political arena to work as a municipal bond attorney. He also served on various corporate boards. Back in 1976, Jackson and Bunnie had divorced. The next year, Jackson married Valerie Richardson, a New York business executive. The two had two children, Valerie and Alexandra. Before leaving office, Jackson persuaded Andrew Young to succeed him as mayor. Young continued Jackson administration policies for two consecutive terms. Still interested in politics and now more seasoned in the corporate boardroom, Jackson ran for a third term in 1989. In this election, he managed to receive the support of the mainstream Atlanta business community in his win against civil rights leader Hosea Williams. Jackson suffered from heart problems and in 1992 he underwent surgery. The next year, deciding he needed to spend more time with his family and recuperate from his surgery, Jackson announced he would not seek a fourth term as Atlanta mayor despite his popularity.

After leaving office, Jackson remained involved in the Atlanta business community via Jackson Securities, the firm he founded in 1994. He also continued to work for the Democratic Party, serving as a vice-chair and almost becoming Democratic Party chair in 2001. Jackson died in Washington, D.C., on June 23, 2003 of a heart attack.

See also: Williams, Hosea

David Kenneth Pye

Bibliography

Allen, Frederick *Atlanta Rising: The Invention of an International City, 1946–1996.* Atlanta: Longstreet Press, 1996.

Colburn, David R., and Jeffrey S. Adler, eds. *African American Mayors: Race, Politics, and the American City.* Urbana: University of Illinois Press, 2001.

Pomerantz, Gary M. *Where Peachtree Meets Sweet Auburn: The Saga of Two Families and the Making of Atlanta.* New York: Scribner, 1996.

Stone, Clarence N. *Regime Politics: Governing Atlanta, 1946–1988.* Lawrence: University of Kansas Press, 1989.

Jet Magazine

Jet first appeared on November 1, 1951, at a cost of 15 cents. The magazine served as a black version of the largely white *Quick,* a small news publication founded in 1949 by Gardner Cowles, the creator of *Look* magazine. *Jet,* like its white counterpart, was approximately four inches by six inches and featured brief encapsulations of the pertinent news of the day. In 1970, its dimensions were broadened to approximately five inches by eight inches. According to John Johnson, its creator, *Jet* was designed to summarize "the week's biggest Negro news in a well-organized, easy-to-read format."

John Harold Johnson created *Jet* in Chicago, Illinois, the third publication of his Johnson Publishing Company. Born in the small Mississippi delta community of Arkansas City, Arkansas on January 19, 1918, Johnson and his mother moved to Chicago in 1933. While attending DuSable High School, Johnson met Harry Pace of the Supreme Life Insurance Company, who employed the graduate as he continued his education at the University of Chicago. Johnson excelled in his work with Supreme's company magazine and eventually became its editor. The small publication carried information about the African American populace in a style similar to that of *Reader's Digest.* Believing there was a commercial market for such a publication, Johnson gained a $500 loan using his mother's furniture as collateral in November 1942. With that initial investment, Johnson created *Negro Digest* and the Johnson Publishing Company. *Negro Digest* began a consistent trend throughout the history of the company of mimicking successful periodical models of the mainstream white press and reformulating them with stories and photographs of interest to the black community.

Within a year of *Negro Digest*'s inception, its sales reached $50,000. Johnson parlayed that success into his creation of *Ebony,* a photography-heavy periodical in the tradition of *Life* and *Look* that celebrated the successes of African Americans. *Ebony*'s growth prompted Johnson to create a convenient, succinct publication to give readers easy access to the news of African Americans in politics, society, and entertainment. The first known black newsmagazine, *Heebie Jeebies,* appeared in Chicago in 1925 under the leadership of P. L. Prattis. The publication was short-lived, and the next national attempt was Johnson's *Jet.* The magazine's scope was broad and its news coverage brief and readable, allowing it to give a sweeping portrait of the state of the national African American community. In 1951, *Ebony*'s executive editor, Ben Burns, took on the additional duties of serving as executive editor for *Jet. Ebony*'s associate editor, Edward Clayton, became *Jet*'s managing editor.

From its inception, *Jet* presented interesting logistical problems. The small size of the magazine's white predecessor, *Quick,* led to difficulty in retaining advertisers who were forced to produce separate, smaller advertising copy for presentation in the magazine. The periodical discontinued publication in 1953, four years after its creation, primarily because of lack of advertising revenue. Johnson anticipated the problem, diverting the profits from the successful *Ebony* to the new publishing venture until advertisers realized the benefits of advertising in a small magazine. Although initially successful, *Jet,* like *Ebony* and most periodicals of the decade, suffered from a mid-1950s recession that hurt both subscription and newsstand sales. The Johnson Publishing Company, however, gave *Jet* more exposure than *Negro Digest* or any of its other publications, save *Ebony,* and the small magazine recovered. *Jet* quickly gained a reputation for accurate, accessible coverage, which kept it viable through economic downturns.

That reputation only grew with *Jet*'s coverage of the events of 1955. In August of that year, 14-year-old Chicago native Emmett Till was accused of whistling at a white woman in Money, Mississippi. He was subsequently lynched, his body mangled and mutilated after his death. Once the boy's corpse was returned to Chicago, photographers documented the wounds, and in the September 15, 1955 issue of *Jet,* the pictures appeared. The issue sold out.

Johnson Publication Company reporters covered the resulting trial of Till's accused murderers, and *Jet*'s photos and subsequent coverage alerted the African American public and the national news media to the poor state of race relations in the South. As the Civil Rights movement grew, *Jet* maintained its coverage, offering descriptions of the Montgomery bus boycott and resulting civil rights activism without editorial comment.

Jet, in fact, never offered editorial comment, but it did use the draw of sensational headlines to attract readers. Among its coverage of civil rights injustices in the South, *Jet* interposed articles with titles such as "One of the Sexiest Men Alive, Says Miles Davis' New Bride" and "Ten Ways to a Mink Coat." Although editorials remain absent from *Jet*'s pages, the magazine's tone remains celebratory and positive. Like its fellow Johnson publication *Ebony,* the smaller newsmagazine reflected its owner's conservative devotion to the possibilities of free market capitalism to grow the infrastructure of the African American community, but never as overtly as its sister periodical.

Jet's resources allowed it to cover the national happenings of African Americans, and its effectiveness led to the shift in focus of black newspapers away from national coverage. Although *Jet*'s coverage was often cursory, its scope pushed city publications to focus on state and local issues. Its staying power was also manifest within the Johnson Publishing Company, as *Jet* has outlived other Johnson publications such as *Tan, Black Stars, Black World,* and the original *Negro Digest.* The success of *Jet* led Johnson to attempt another periodical of similarly small dimensions, a monthly called *Hue.* Although *Hue* was initially successful, the advertising problems that felled *Quick* and threatened *Jet* soon combined with the recession of the mid- and late 1950s to end the life of *Hue.* The circulation of its predecessor, however, has remained strong. *Jet*'s circulation was close to 800,000 by the close of the 1980s, and today that number is almost 1 million. The modern incarnation of *Jet* features a compendium of notable births and deaths, sections on black history, celebrity gossip, and sports, along with music and television listings and the "Jet Beauty of the Week." The brief and accessible news coverage that made the periodical relevant, of course, still forms the core of *Jet*'s copy.

See also: *Ebony* Magazine; King, Martin Luther Jr.; Montgomery Bus Boycott; Till, Emmett

Thomas Aiello

Bibliography
Daniel, Walter C. *Black Journals of the United States.* Westport, CT: Greenwood Press, 1982.
Johnson, John H., and Lerone Bennett Jr. *Succeeding Against the Odds.* New York: Warner Books, 1989.
"New Hue, New Color," *Newsweek,* October 9, 1953:93.
Wolseley, Roland E. *The Black Press, USA,* 2nd ed. Ames: Iowa State University Press, 1971.

Jim Crow

"Jim Crow" was the American social practice of racial segregation, most prevalent from the 1880s to the 1960s, that robbed African Americans of their basic civil and civic rights and assaulted black people's humanity. This method of segregation allowed African Americans and whites to live within the same cities and towns, while still maintaining white economic, political, and social superiority. Through a series of social customs and state and federal laws, white Americans created "white only" public spaces designed to link free African Americans to their previously enslaved status. For example, the practice of "Jim Crow" required that newly freed African Americans ride in separate sections of public transportation vehicles and sit in separate sections of church, and that black children attend different schools from their white counterparts. By 1896, a racist Louisiana state law, requiring that white and black people sit in separate compartments on trains was upheld by the United States Supreme Court in the case of *Plessy v. Ferguson,* which institutionalized the doctrine of "separate but equal" accommodations and embedded "Jim Crow" segregation into southern culture and law for the next 60 years.

Although the term "Jim Crow" is most frequently associated with racial segregation in the 20th century, it was first harnessed as a racial and spatial epithet in 1830s antebellum Massachusetts. A white actor, Thomas Dartmouth Rice, performing with black cork make-up on his face, made "Jim Crow"—the likeable yet derogatory African American slave he played on northern stages—a national and international sensation. The cultural impact of the show was so great that by 1834, Northerners from all classes—from street urchins to congressional politicians to newspaper editors—alluded to "Jim Crow's" oft quoted refrain: "Weel about and turn about and do jis so, Eb'ry time I weel about and jump Jim Crow." The popularity of both the tune and the character prompted Massachusetts's railroad conductors, when segregating black travelers on the newly minted trains, to name the dirty, drafty, and unkempt compartments reserved for drunken men, poor whites, and African Americans as the "Jim Crow car." The first record of this usage is 1838.

As early as the 1820s, free people of color vigorously protested segregation on public transportation in newspaper editorials. They further organized their protest strategies against the "Jim Crow car" and launched a concerted battle against the Massachusetts railroads from 1838 to 1843. African American abolitionists such as Charles Lenox Remond, Frederick Douglass, and David Ruggles refused to move from first-class seats, prompting violent confrontations between themselves and the railroads' cronies. These abolitionists and their white advocates demanded equal accommodations and argued that receiving equal treatment on public transportation was a right of citizenship.

Furthermore, black activists developed a sophisticated analysis of such racial segregation. They debunked the notion that African American travelers were set apart from whites because they smelled or were disrespectful to white women. Pointedly, black abolitionists highlighted the fact that during the antebellum period, white American men and women traveled alongside enslaved African Americans frequently and never made complaints. Instead activists argued that what whites found so odious about black travelers in the antebellum North was not their skin color or their mere presence, but the social implications of their freedom. They argued that whites feared black political and economic success and imagined that black men sought sexual liaisons with white women because for so long, white men had exploited enslaved African American women in the South. Black freedom threatened social order. Segregation in public spaces such as the "Jim Crow car" was a way for Anglo-Americans to minimize the impact of African American freedom and to cripple black citizenship.

After 4 million African American slaves were freed in the South in 1865, it took just decades for the Southern states to produce laws that echoed the customs of the antebellum North. In the decades after enslavement, and throughout the 20th century, a new generation of black activists, emboldened by a legacy of African American activism against "Jim Crow," believed that segregation threatened the meaning of freedom and citizenship and fought to overturn *Plessy v. Ferguson* through multiple protest strategies, including the courts.

In 1954, through a series of protracted legal battles, the legal arm of the National Association for the Advancement of Colored People (NAACP) successfully overturned *Plessy* in the public schools. The famous U.S. Supreme Court case, *Brown v. Board of Education of Topeka, Kansas,* is largely considered the first victory of the modern Civil Rights movement Soon after, a grassroots movement to desegregate public transportation in Montgomery, Alabama culminated in the successful Montgomery bus boycotts of 1956. Even as white supremacists in the South resisted "Jim Crow's" demise through deadly violence against African American and other activists, President Lyndon B. Johnson signed the Civil Rights Act of 1964 into law, which outlawed racial segregation and gender discrimination in public schools, public places, and employment. These laws profoundly changed the face of "Jim Crow" in the United States, but many argue that the process of racial equality and integration is not yet complete. "Jim Crow" may no longer be an explicitly legal practice of racial exclusion, but socioeconomic factors that relegate African Americans and other Americans of color to poorer neighborhoods with less well-equipped schools and less chance for economic opportunity have fostered a reincarnation of "Jim Crow" into the 21st century.

See also: Black Nadir; *Brown v. Board of Education;* Civil Rights Act of 1964; Montgomery Bus Boycott; *Plessy v. Ferguson*

Elizabeth Stordeur Pryor

Bibliography

Lhamon, W. T. Jr. *Jump Jim Crow: Lost Plays, Lyrics and Street Prose of the First Atlantic Popular Culture.* Cambridge: Harvard University Press, 2003.

Litwack, Leon F. *Trouble in Mind: Black Southerners in the Age of Jim Crow.* New York: Knopf, 1998.

Medley, Keith Weldon. *We As Freemen:* Plessy V. Ferguson. Gretna, LA: Pelican Publishing, 2003.

Packard, Jerrold M. *American Nightmare: The History of Jim Crow.* New York: St. Martin's Press, 2002.

Woodward, C. Vann. *The Strange Career of Jim Crow.* 1955. Revised Edition, London: Oxford University Press, 2002.

Johnson, Andrew

Andrew Johnson (1808–1875), the 17th president and regarded as no ally of African Americans during Reconstruction, was born in North Carolina. Growing up in an extremely poor family, Johnson became an indentured servant to a tailor at age 14. By the time he was 17, his family had settled in Tennessee. His early experience in poverty and as an indentured servant later shaped his policies toward African Americans during Reconstruction.

A successful politician before the Civil War, Johnson was viewed during the conflict as a champion of freedom for slaves in Tennessee. When President Abraham Lincoln appointed Johnson military governor of Tennessee in 1862, Johnson did all he could to abolish slavery in the state. Abolitionists and African Americans applauded Johnson's efforts. His fame continued to rise and, in October 1864, he endeared himself to all who believed in the abolition of slavery when he delivered his "Moses" speech in Nashville. In it he proclaimed that he would lead the slaves of Tennessee out of bondage. What the African Americans and abolitionists did not realize was that his motivations for eliminating slavery in Tennessee were not fueled by sympathy for slaves, but rather were energized by hatred of large slave owners. Johnson, who had grown up in poverty and owned five slaves before the Civil War, held a hatred for slave owners common among poor Southern farmers.

In the presidential election of 1864, Johnson became Lincoln's choice for vice president. When Johnson became president on April 15, 1865, after Lincoln's death, many abolitionists and African Americans felt confident that he would carry the same attitude toward slavery as president as he had as military governor of Tennessee. During the early weeks of his administration, however, Johnson made it clear that, although he would recognize the freedom of former slaves, he did not believe they should play any important part in the rebuilding of the nation. Johnson's proclamations of amnesty and reconstruction for the former Confederate states were lenient and excluded African American involvement. Johnson's reconstruction policy opened the door for the creation of Black Codes, restrictive measures created by states to take away the few rights of African Americans.

Furthermore, Johnson blocked every congressional effort to extend political suffrage to the newly freed men. Johnson firmly believed that the majority of former slaves did not have the mental capacity to be involved in the political process. Johnson also believed that political suffrage for former slaves would create extremely hostile racial tensions throughout the South. Although he felt the majority of former slaves did not have the ability to assume the

responsibility of citizens, he did believe that a limited number of African Americans could vote—if they served in the army, if they were literate, or if they owned property.

Radical Republicans in Congress did not approve of Johnson's plan of limited suffrage. Johnson, however, informed them that he did not believe it was within the boundaries of his constitutional power to impose universal African American suffrage on the states. He stated that he could merely advise states of what to do, but not actually order them to do it. Johnson argued further that an extension of universal suffrage to African Americans would hurt the status of poor whites in the South. Johnson concluded that if all former slaves were allowed to vote, they would be heavily influenced by their former masters and therefore the wealthiest individuals in the South would control politics. Ultimately Johnson believed this problem could be solved with the removal of African Americans from the South.

In 1866, Johnson hampered conditions for African Americans more when he restored much of the land confiscated by the U.S. government to its white owners. This was a major blow to the Freedmen's Bureau, as it was supposed to use that land to help promote African American land ownership. Johnson defended his position by stating that much of the land seized by the government belonged to poor farmers and it was not them, rather the rich, large slave owning planters who ought to be punished by having their land seized, as they were the ones responsible for the Civil War.

Johnson alienated himself further from the Radical Republicans when he blocked legislation for a civil rights act and an extension of the Freedmen's Bureau. Johnson vetoed both measures claiming that they would promote laziness among African Americans. Furthermore, Johnson felt that it was improper to vote on such important legislation when the 11 former Confederate states had no representation in Congress.

Johnson's anti-African American policies during Reconstruction came partially from his experiences as a poor child and undoubtedly ruined his presidency. Many allies of African American suffrage demanded Johnson's removal. Less than a year after Johnson became president, Republicans in Congress began to override his vetoes and made him powerless. His presidential control became further depleted in 1868 when he missed being removed from office by one vote for violation of the Tenure of Office Act. He died in 1875, the same year he reentered politics as a U.S. Senator from Tennessee.

See also: Black Codes; Freedmen's Bureau; Joint Committee of Fifteen; Lincoln, Abraham; Radical Republicans

Jonathan A. Noyalas

Bibliography

McKitrick, Eric L. *Andrew Johnson and Reconstruction.* New York: Oxford University Press, 1960.

McPherson, James M. *The Struggle for Equality: Abolitionists and the Negro in the Civil War and Reconstruction.* Princeton, NJ: Princeton University Press, 1964.

Trefousse, Hans L. *Andrew Johnson: A Biography.* New York: W. W. Norton, 1989.

Johnson, Lyndon Baines

Lyndon Baines Johnson (1908–1973), was the 36th president of the United States. He ascended to the presidency on November 22, 1963, when President John Fitzgerald Kennedy (1917–1963) was assassinated while on a political trip in Dallas, Texas. Johnson completed Kennedy's term and, in 1964, was elected to a term in his own right in a landslide.

Little about his early life suggested that Johnson would become known as one of the most powerful politicians in American history and the civil rights president. Johnson was born one of five children in Stonewall, Texas, to Samuel Ealy Johnson Jr. and Rebekah Baines in a farmhouse located on a poor part of the Pedernales River. His father served in the Texas legislature, and young Lyndon was steeped in politics from the time he was a small boy. The family was poor, however, and by the time Lyndon was a teenager, his father was trapped in debt and lost the family home. The elder Johnson struggled financially for the rest of his life. Family, friends, and biographers agree that this is when Johnson developed his affinity for the poor and disadvantaged, regardless of race.

Johnson did poorly in school and was unable to get into college. He worked odd jobs for a few years after high school and was finally admitted to Southwest Texas State Teachers College, now Texas State University, San Marcos, in 1927. Miserable there, he left college and went to Welhausen School, where he taught fifth through seventh grades and served as the principal to a student body made up of poor Mexicans and blacks. He returned to college and graduated in 1930. He later took a job at Pearsall High School, where he taught public speaking and advised the district championship debate team.

A gregarious person, Johnson gained the attention of United States Congressman Richard Kleberg who asked him to be the secretary in his Washington office. It was here Johnson blossomed; he learned the arcane rules of Congress and was elected speaker of an organization of congressional workers known as the Little Congress. Johnson also caught the eye of his political idol, President Franklin Delano Roosevelt, who appointed him as the Texas director of the National Youth Administration (NYA). Johnson was a most energetic NYA director and was very helpful to African Americans caught in the vice grip of the Depression. He was described as "warmly disposed to giving disadvantaged blacks opportunity for education and work" so that they could help themselves. While he blocked the representation of African Americans to the Texas NYA, he did appoint a black advisory board and enjoyed great success in the black community. He resigned from the NYA in 1937 to run in a special election for the Tenth Congressional District to the House of Representatives.

After the bombing of Pearl Harbor, FDR helped him obtain a commission to the United States Naval Reserve, where he won a Silver Star. He left the military after FDR ordered members of Congress to leave the active service and won a second run for the United States Senate in 1948 by a mere 87 votes. There were allegations of voter fraud, and for the rest of his life he could not shake the ironic nickname "Landslide Lyndon."

Johnson eventually became one of the most powerful Senate majority leaders in history. He did this by prodigious hard work, developing powerful alliances, mastering the byzantine rules of the Senate, and knowing his colleagues as well as they knew themselves. He understood their ambitions, remembered their families, and kept track of their strengths, weaknesses, and peccadillos. He used this information to develop what came to be called the *Johnson treatment.* Through the use of flattery, cajolery, intimidation, doublespeak, humility, and the sheer force of his personality, Johnson so overwhelmed people he was almost always able to enlist them to further his goals.

While in Congress, he was an ardent supporter of FDR and typically voted, as did his Southern colleagues, against the federal antilynching bill, eliminating the poll

President Lyndon B. Johnson meets with civil rights leader Martin Luther King Jr. at the White House in March 1966. (Lyndon B. Johnson Library)

tax, denying federal funds for lunch programs at black schools, and denying the federal government the right to send absentee ballots directly to soldiers stationed overseas, effectively disfranchising thousands of African American servicemen and servicewomen. He explained that his votes were not based on racial prejudice, but on upholding states' rights.

Johnson held the conventional views of his time as they applied to blacks. He was not above repeating racists jokes, and he routinely called blacks, including those who worked for him "nigger," especially when he was in the company of other Southerners. On the other hand, he often helped his black constituents or individual blacks he happened to meet. For example, he hired Zephyr Wright, a college graduate who could not find a job, as the Johnson family cook and spoke sorrowfully about how difficult it was for her to travel with the Johnsons when there were virtually no public accommodations available to blacks.

Privately, he often supported the concept of equal opportunity. Although he refused to support a federal

antilynching bill, on occasion he publicly expressed his horror of the crime. He opposed the poll tax, seeing it not as a racial issue, but something that hurt all those who were disadvantaged, regardless of race. LBJ also supported the civil rights plank in the 1948 Democratic platform, and he refused to ally himself with the Dixiecrats, white segregationists who bolted the Democratic party and formed the States' Rights Party. Nevertheless, he repeatedly made the distinction between passing civil rights laws and attacking poverty, which he thought more helpful to minorities.

Events of the 1950s, however, forced civil rights matters to the forefront of American politics. In the case of *Brown v. Board of Education of Topeka, Kansas* (1954), the United States Supreme Court declared segregated schools unconstitutional. In 1955, Emmett Till, a black teenager from Chicago, was murdered for allegedly whistling at a white women when he was visiting relatives in Money, Mississippi, sparking an international outcry. In 1955, blacks in Montgomery, Alabama, led by a young minister named Dr. Martin Luther King Jr., protested against segregated seating on city buses by boycotting the bus company for more than a year, and the Supreme Court supported their position by declaring segregation in public transportation unconstitutional.

Johnson also recognized earlier than most of his Southern colleagues that there was a shift in the public perception regarding racial equality; he knew that the South as a region would never prosper if it continued to focus on the old bugaboo of race. Furthermore, by the late 1950s, his own political ambitions were such that he began to think of running for the presidency, and he knew it would require him to prove that he was not just a southern leader, but a national one. To this end, he determined that his political fortunes would be advanced by helping to pass a civil rights bill.

In 1956, the administration of President Dwight D. Eisenhower sent a sweeping civil rights bill to Congress. It provided for creation of a bipartisan United States Commission on Civil Rights that would be empowered to investigate racial discrimination and recommend remedies for its eradication; aimed to turn the small civil rights section of the Department of Justice into a full-fledged division led by an assistant attorney general; proposed that the United States attorney general be given the power to obtain injunctions in civil rights cases and that those cases be moved from state courts to federal courts; and sought to expand the power of the Justice Department to ask for injunctions against those who threatened or interfered with the right to vote.

After some pruning by congressmen, a weaker bill passed in the House and moved over to the Senate, where it faced a buzz saw of criticism in the chamber long dominated by segregationist Democrats. As majority leader, Johnson knew that the bill could tear apart the Democratic party for years to come as it pitted anti- and pro-civil rights supporters against each other. Flexing his parliamentary muscles, he sent the bill to the Judiciary Committee, where Democrat and segregationist Senator James O. Eastland of Mississippi eviscerated and then buried it in committee. Legislators who supported civil rights eventually agreed to drop their request for moving cases from state to federal courts, and enough southern senators grudgingly agreed to support it. Still, Senator Strom Thurmond, an ardent segregationist, conducted what was then the longest filibuster ever when he spoke for more than 24 hours straight against the bill. Greatly weakened and watered-down, the bill finally passed both chambers on August 29 and was signed

into law by President Eisenhower on September 9. Through it all, Johnson proved he could rise above partisan, sectional interests and think of the nation as a whole.

In 1959, Eisenhower sent another civil rights bill to Congress. This bill aimed to allow the federal government to inspect local and state voter registration polls and levy penalties against anyone who interfered with the right to register or vote. Once again LBJ aimed for a bill that was narrowly focused so as to protect the rights of African American voters but would not alienate his southern colleagues. This bill aimed to allow the federal government to inspect local and state voter registration polls and levy penalties against anyone who interfered with the right to register or vote. LBJ again aimed for a bill that was narrowly focused so as to protect the rights of African American voters but not alienate his southern colleagues.

The bill passed the House and moved to the Senate. The Senate began debate on February 29, 1960; however, a group of 18 southern Democrats split into three teams of six each so as to create a continuous filibuster. By using this method, each senator would be required to speak for only four hours every three days. To blunt the impact of the filibuster, Johnson began requiring the Senate to meet in 24-hour sessions. A 15-minute break was allowed before the Senate sat for another 82 hours on March 2. The filibuster was then broken, and Congress passed the bill. President Eisenhower signed the bill into law on May 6, 1960. Both bills had been so weakened in the process that they were more symbolic than substantive. They did, however, prove that Congress could deal with such a volatile issue as civil rights without tearing the nation asunder, and Johnson again demonstrated his prowess as a national leader.

Emboldened by his success, Johnson began actively seeking the 1960 Democratic nomination for the presidency. He was outmaneuvered, however, by Senator John F. Kennedy, the junior senator from Massachusetts and a man Johnson felt to be unqualified for the presidency, particularly in the field of civil rights. In a somewhat surprising move, Kennedy offered Johnson the post of vice-presidential running mate, and even more surprisingly to some, Johnson accepted. It is certain that Kennedy could not have won the presidency without Johnson; his presence on the ticket ensured that several southern states that had gone over to the Republican party during the Eisenhower years returned to the Democratic fold.

Civil rights activity bubbled to the surface from the beginning of the Kennedy administration. The president had raised expectations during the campaign by implying that civil rights reform could be achieved in part through vigorous activity by the executive branch. Thousands of demonstrations in favor of racial equality took place across the country. In 1961, the Freedom Rides tested compliance with the Interstate Commerce Commission's directive against segregation in interstate travel. The violence unleashed against the riders drew the personal intervention of Robert F. Kennedy, the United States attorney general. In 1962, the administration sought to enforce a federal court order requiring the University of Mississippi to admit James Meredith as its first African American student. When it was clear that the local and state police would not maintain order, Kennedy federalized the Mississippi National Guard. A riot ensued and two people were killed. On June 11, Alabama governor George C. Wallace fulfilled a campaign promise to stand in the schoolhouse door to prevent the admittance of two black students, Vivian Malone and James Hood, to the University of Alabama. President Kennedy federalized the Alabama Guard, and both students were admitted without violence or bloodshed. On June 12, Medgar Evers, field secretary for the National Association for the Advancement of Colored People (NAACP), was assassinated in the driveway of his home. On August 28, 1963, the March on Washington, which focused on civil rights and economic justice, brought 200,000 people to the nation's capital. These events appear to have been tailor-made for a man with the ambition and legislative skills of Lyndon Johnson. Yet Kennedy rarely sought the advice of his vice president on civil rights.

Kennedy did recognize, however, that his administration could no longer rely on ad hoc solutions to individual civil rights crisis. On June 19, he sent a far-reaching civil rights bill to Congress. The Kennedy civil rights bill was a multiprong attack on racial discrimination designed to outlaw discrimination in public accommodations, expand and protect the right to vote, and bar employment discrimination. It also contained a provision to cut off government funding to institutions who engaged in racial discrimination. In a nationwide television address, he labeled civil rights a moral issue and urged Congress and the American people to act to ensure equal rights for all Americans

After President Kennedy was assassinated, several months later, Johnson told a joint session of Congress that passage of the Kennedy civil rights bill would be the most fitting memorial to the slain president. As president, he placed his reputation on the line and worked tirelessly to get the Civil Rights Act passed. The success of his career in Congress was of great benefit in this area, and he relished using the Johnson treatment at the presidential level.

In the House the bill had been bottled up in the Rules Committee by segregationist chairman Howard W. Smith, who refused to release it. Over the course of the winter recess, public opinion moved toward support of the bill, and Smith finally released it from the Rules Committee. On February 10, 1964, the House passed the bill 290 to 130 and sent it to the Senate. Parliamentary maneuvers on the part of Democratic Majority Leader Mike Mansfield sent the bill to the full Senate for debate, bypassing the Judiciary Committee where it was sure to be stalled by southern segregationists. Southern Democrats launched a 54-day filibuster, but the liberal Democratic Whip Hubert Humphrey led the movement to invoke, breaking the filibuster. The bill passed the Senate by a vote of 73 to 27, and Johnson signed the bill on July 2, 1964. He was said to have predicted that the Democratic party had lost the southern vote for years to come. The impact of the bill was such that racial discrimination in public accommodations was virtually wiped out.

The right to vote, however, was still in question. Several civil rights organizations had been leading voter registration activities in Alabama since 1963. Demonstrators and activists were met with violence perpetrated by law enforcement officials and citizens. In response to the situation, the Johnson administration sent a voting rights bill prohibiting states from interfering with or denying the right to vote to Congress in mid-March 1965. The act also proposed to outlaw literacy tests and extend federal oversight of elections.

On February 18, an Alabama state trooper shot a young black man named Jimmie Lee Jackson who was trying to protect his mother and grandfather from the police. Jackson died on February 24, and civil rights worker James Bevel suggested a march from Selma to Montgomery to confront Governor George Wallace about Jackson's death. Instead, the march became an outlet for black anger and a memorial to Jackson. Wallace declared the march a threat to public safety and vowed to prevent it. On March 7, about 600 marchers made their way across the Edmund Pettus Bridge where they were met by law enforcement officials who charged into the crowd on foot and horseback, beating demonstrators. The scene, referred to as Bloody Sunday, was captured by the media and beamed throughout the world.

King organized a second march, but federal district judge Frank M. Johnson issued a restraining order until additional hearings could be held. On March 9, King led a ceremonial march to the Edmund Pettus Bridge, stopped to pray and then turned back. That same evening, three white ministers who had traveled to Selma for the march found themselves in front of the Silver Moon Café, a gathering point for segregationist whites. The three were brutally attacked by several whites, and James Reeb, a Unitarian minister, died of his injuries.

Judge Johnson lifted the restraining shortly thereafter, and a third march was planned for March 21–24. Citizens, college students, civil rights activists, religious leaders, and celebrities joined the three-day effort. On March 25, King dazzled the crowd of 25,000 with a speech beside the state capital. Later that night, Viola Liuzzo, a white Chicago wife and mother of five, was murdered by Ku Klux Klansman as she transported volunteers to their homes. Her passenger, a young black man named Leroy Moton, was not hurt, and played dead while Klansman searched the car.

It is widely believed that the murders of Rev. Reeb and Mrs. Liuzzo, both of whom were white, forced Congress to act quickly on the voting rights legislation. After a Senate filibuster, cloture was invoked, and the bill passed on May 11; the House passed the bill on July 10. Conference committees resolved the differences in the two bills and sent it to President Johnson, who signed the act on August 6, 1965. The impact of the law was immediate; the number of black registered voters in the 11 states of the Old Confederacy soared.

The Civil Rights Act of 1964 and the Voting Rights Act of 1965 did not resolve the persistent poverty, police brutality, overcrowding, poor health care, and a lack of public transportation for millions of African Americans, especially in the urban North. Beginning in the summer of 1965, a series of rebellions broke out in inner cities across America. The first major riot was in the East Los Angeles neighborhood of Watts in August, 1965. That rebellion lasted almost a week, and Governor Pat Brown was forced to call out the National Guard. Thirty-four people were killed, and property damage was estimated at more than $30 million. Major disturbances also happened in Newark, New Jersey, and Detroit, Michigan, and 57 other cities in 1967. President Johnson ordered about 5,000 troops from the 82nd and 101st Airborne units into Detroit when Governor George Romney reported that the Michigan Guard was unable to restore civil order.

In the wake of the rebellions, Johnson formed the National Advisory Commission on Civil Disorders, chaired by Illinois governor Otto Kerner. The so-called Kerner Commission issued a bleak report on American race relations, stating the root causes of the rebellions were poverty, discrimination and injustice, and recommending that the federal government mount a vigorous attack on those fronts. The Commission also famously reported that America was splintering into two societies, one black and one white.

The racial rebellions that occurred in the latter part of the 1960s caused a severe backlash among white Americans who thought that Johnson had moved too quickly on racial equality, and endangered his most important program, the War on Poverty, the foundation of what he called the Great Society. Johnson had signed the Economic Opportunity Act in 1964. The Act created the Office of Economic Opportunity, which was the administrative arm of several programs. Head Start was designed to help disadvantaged preschoolers, Volunteers in Service to America (VISTA) was a domestic Peace Corps whose purpose was to help the poor across America, and Upward Bound sought to prepare poor teenagers for college. The Education Act funneled more federal money to colleges and universities and provided low-interest loans to financially strapped students. Funding for the first stage of the act was a modest $1 billion.

The War on Poverty was the first government program to involve poor communities in planning and implementing the programs that served them. In this respect, it taught leadership and organizing skills and gave meaningful paid work to hundreds of thousands of poor Americans. Increasingly, however, it was buffeted by disagreements among politicians, anger from white Americans who thought that the program rewarded shiftless and lazy blacks, and ever rising expectations by African Americans. The biggest obstacle to the program, however, was increased spending on the war in Vietnam, where 25 percent of the frontline troops were African American.

In 1968, a presidential election year, it was assumed that President Johnson would run for a second term. The United States, however, was mired in an increasingly unpopular war in Vietnam; thousands of young people took to the streets in demonstrations—some of them outside the White House—and burned their draft cards in protest. The Tet offensive in January of that year showed that the administration had not been truthful about the war, and for the first time, it seemed to be admitting that the war was unwinnable. Urban rebellions continued, and many young people seemed to be inhabitants of a counterculture that was a maze of sex, drugs, and rock 'n roll.

Senator Eugene McCarthy, the liberal Democrat from Minnesota, had come out against the war and entered the presidential race, and hundreds of college student volunteers cut their hair, shaved their beards, and became "Clean for Gene." Although he lost the New Hampshire primary to LBJ by 42 to 49 percent, he was able to show how vulnerable the sitting president was. After McCarthy's strong showing, Robert Kennedy, the junior U.S. senator from New York and brother of the slain president, announced his candidacy, a move LBJ had always feared. On March 31, in a televised news conference, Johnson announced that he would not run for, nor accept, the nomination of the Democratic party for a second presidential term.

On April 4, civil rights leader and Nobel Prize winner Martin Luther King Jr. was assassinated in Memphis, Tennessee, where he had gone to support sanitation workers in their fight for better wages and working conditions. Riots broke out in dozens of cities as angry and frustrated blacks sought to avenge King's death. On June 4, Robert Kennedy was assassinated after he had claimed victory in the California primary. Kennedy had been one of the few whites in public life who understood the plight of minorities and the underclass. The country was spinning out of control.

The death of King heightened a sense of urgency in Congress as it debated a third piece of civil rights legislation. On April 11, Johnson signed the Civil Rights Act of 1968, which prohibited racial discrimination in the advertisement, sale, or rental of housing. It was the last piece of civil rights legislation he would sign. When Johnson turned the White House over to Republican Richard M. Nixon on January 20, 1969, he was one of the most unpopular presidents in history. He had, however, done what he sought to do; he had built on the work of his longtime idol, Franklin D. Roosevelt, and gone so much further. He had created the Great Society—a society that made racial equality not merely a dream, but a reality.

See also: Civil Rights Act of 1964; Civil Rights Act of 1968; Hoover, J. Edgar; Kennedy, John Fitzgerald; Kerner Commission Report; King, Martin Luther Jr.; Voting Rights Act of 1965; War on Poverty

Marilyn K. Howard

Bibliography

Caro, Robert A. *Master of the Senate: The Years of LBJ, Vol. 3.* New York: Knopf Publishing Group, 2003.

Dallek, Robert. *Lone Star Rising: LBJ and His Times, 1961–1973.* New York: Oxford University Press, 1998.

Goodwin, Doris Kearns. *Lyndon Johnson and the American Dream.* New York: St. Martin's Griffin, 1991.

Kotz, Nick. *Judgment Days: LBJ, MLK, Jr. and the Laws That Changed America.* Boston: Houghton Mifflin, 2005.

Mann, Robert. *The Walls of Jericho: Lyndon Johnson, Hubert Humphrey, Richard Russell and the Struggle for Civil Rights.* New York: Harcourt Brace, 1996.

Joint Committee of Fifteen

When the Thirty-ninth Congress convened in December 1865, it faced the monumental task of opposing the Presidential Reconstruction plan crafted by Andrew Johnson. After preventing senators and representatives from the 11 Southern ex-confederate states from taking their seats in Congress, radical and moderate congressmen formed the Joint Committee on Reconstruction to investigate conditions in the South and to report whether any of the ex-confederate states should be entitled to congressional representation. This committee of 15 congressmen, was composed of six senators and nine representatives, of which 12 were Republicans and the remaining 3 were Unionist Democrats. These 15 members of Congress oversaw a massive investigation that called 144 witnesses and generated more than 700 pages of testimony. The committee concentrated its efforts primarily on the treatment of African Americans and Northern whites in Southern states, the continued necessity of the Freedmen's Bureau and federal troops in the South, and the lasting hostilities of former Confederates toward the U.S. government.

On April 28, 1866, the Joint Committee submitted its findings. Their report claimed that the South was still in disarray in the aftermath of the Civil War and that the former confederate states should not actively participate in the federal government until civil rights of all their citizens were guaranteed and high-ranking confederate officials were barred from political office. These recommendations led directly to a bill that extended the life and enlarged the functions of the Freedmen's Bureau and a proposal that would grant civil rights to African Americans in the South. The two measures were vetoed by President Johnson, but Congress eventually overrode both vetoes. The extension of the Freedmen's Bureau and the passage of the Civil Rights Act in 1866 signaled the beginning of radical Republican ascension and the end of Johnson's absolute control over Reconstruction. The most lasting legacy of the Joint Committee's efforts was a set of resolutions drafted on April 30, 1866 that became the Fourteenth Amendment. Passed by Congress on June 16, 1866, this amendment made African American citizenship a Constitutional fact, but every Southern state, with the exception of Tennessee, refused to ratify the measure. Preparing for a protracted political fight, Radical Republicans called for a convention to be held in Philadelphia of Unionists from the South to denounce the doctrine of state sovereignty and support the ratification of the Fourteenth Amendment. Among the Northern representatives at this convention was Frederick Douglass who successfully persuaded the convention to also support granting the right to vote to South African American men. The Fourteenth Amendment was eventually ratified and Douglass's appeal for black suffrage became the basis for the Fifteenth Amendment passed by Congress on February 27, 1869.

See also: Civil Rights Act of 1866; Douglass, Frederick; Fifteenth Amendment; Fourteenth Amendment; Freedmen's Bureau; Radical Republicans

Walter C. Rucker

Bibliography

Foner, Eric. *Reconstruction: America's Unfinished Revolution, 1863–1877.* New York: Harper & Row, 1988.

Franklin, John Hope. *Reconstruction: After the Civil War.* Chicago: University of Chicago Press, 1961.

Karenga, Maulana

Dr. Maulana Karenga (1941–), professor, activist-scholar, ethical philosopher, author, and leading Afrocentric cultural theorist, was born in Parsonsburg, Maryland. The youngest of 14 children, he migrated to California in the late 1950s to attend the University of California at Los Angeles. He first attended Los Angeles City College before transferring to UCLA where he received a BA (cum laude) and a masters degree in political science and African studies. Dr. Karenga holds two PhD's; the first in political science from the United States International University, and the second in social ethics from the University of Southern California. He also holds an honorary doctorate of philosophy from the University of Durban-Westville, South Africa. Best known as the creator of *Kwanzaa,* Karenga has distinguished himself as one of the leading African-centered scholars and activist-intellectuals in the 20th and 21st centuries.

The framework for Karenga's intellectual and practical work is *Kawaida,* a philosophy of culture and struggle that he began to develop early in his career. As a student in the early 1960s, Karenga's meetings and discussions with Malcolm X had a tremendous impact on his developing social consciousness. Building on Malcolm's teaching, he defined the goals of the Black Power movement and his organization, US, as self-determination, self-respect, and self-defense. He also drew on the works of Sekou Toure, Marcus Garvey, Frantz Fanon, Julius Nyerere, and others to develop Kawaida, a Swahili term he defines as meaning a synthesis of tradition and reason. Central to Kawaida philosophy is the *Nguzo Saba,* the Seven Principles. They are *Umoja* (Unity), *Kujichagulia* (Self-Determination), *Ujima* (Collective Work and Responsibility), *Ujamaa* (Cooperative Economics), *Nia* (Purpose), *Kuumba* (Creativity), and, *Imani* (Faith). The *Nguzo Saba* is also the value system on which the pan-African holiday *Kwanzaa* is based. Created by Karenga and first celebrated by US in 1966, today Kwanzaa is widely celebrated by millions throughout the African community on every continent in the world. Moreover, the Seven Principles are used by thousands of organizations and institutions as value orientations for their projects.

During the height of the Black Power movement, Karenga interrupted his studies to become an active participant. After the Watts rebellion in 1965, he formed US in Los Angeles and began to establish himself as an activist-scholar and movement leader. Eventually, US would also become a leading cultural and social change organization.

Grounded in the philosophy of Kawaida and dedicated to the liberation and empowerment of black people, US and its supporters often found themselves at odds and/or competing with the Black Panther Party, who had also committed themselves to the right of self-defense, self-determination, and the liberation of African people. Both groups were targets under the FBI's COINTELPRO infiltration program, which consciously provoked conflict between them. Conflict between the two groups spilled over from the community to the UCLA campus where a personal confrontation between members of both groups led to a shootout in 1969 that resulted in the death of two members of the Black Panther Party, the wounding of an US member, and charges being brought against several members of US. Marred by attempts to discredit him and US, Karenga, still a target of law enforcement officials, endured a period of incarceration from 1971–1975 after he was convicted of felonious assault, a case he maintains was a political prosecution. This led to US's temporarily going underground, but strengthened Karenga's resolve to remain committed to the black liberation movement. He wrote extensively during his captivity. In his essays, he laid out the essential tenets of his philosophy, including developmental changes on issues of race, class, and gender. After his release, he returned to rebuild his organization and became active again in the movement.

For more than four decades, Karenga has played a key role in national united front efforts in the black community. In the late 1960s, he was a founding member of the executive committee of the Black Power conferences and later, in the 1980s and 1990s, assumed leadership roles in the National Black United Front, the National African American Leadership Summit, and the African American Leadership Family Retreat. In 1984, US held the first annual Ancient Egyptian Studies Conference in Los Angeles and Karenga invited the late scholar, Jacob Carruthers, to cohost it with him. Out of this conference grew the Association for the Study of Classical African Civilizations. Karenga also serves as Chairman of the National Association of Kawaida Organizations (NAKO), which was established in 1987, and as director of the Kawaida Institute of Pan-African Studies in Los Angeles. In 1995, he served on the national organizing committee of the Million Man March/Day of Absence and authored the *Mission Statement* for the project.

Dr. Karenga has had a profound and far-reaching effect on black intellectual and political culture. Through his organization US and his philosophy, *Kawaida*, he has played a vanguard role in shaping the Black Power movement, the black studies movement, the black arts movement, the black student union movement, and the black independent school movement. Moreover, he has been instrumental in the development of Afrocentricity, rites of passage programs, African life-cycle ceremonies and the Simba Wachanga Youth Movement.

Professor and former chairman of the Department of Black Studies at California State University, Long Beach, Karenga serves on the board of the National Council for Black Studies and the Cheikh Anta Diop International Conference. His publications are extensive. The recipient of numerous awards and honors, Karenga has gained national and international recognition. He has lectured on the life and struggle of African peoples on the major campuses in the United States, Africa, the Caribbean, the People's Republic of China, Britain, and Canada. He is credited with having a profound impact on the development of black cultural and political consciousness throughout the African world.

See also: Afrocentricity; Asante, Molefi Kete; Black Power; Kwanzaa; National Council for Black Studies; US Organization

Patricia Reid-Merritt

Bibliography

Brown, Scot. *Fighting for US: Maulana Karenga, the US Organization, and Black Cultural Nationalism.* New York: New York University Press, 2003.

Karenga, Maulana. *Kwanzaa: A Celebration of Family, Community, and Culture.* Los Angeles: University of Sankore Press, 1998.

Karenga, Maulana. *Kawaida and Questions of Life and Struggle: African American, Pan-African, and Global Issues.* Los Angeles: University of Sankore Press, 2007.

Kennedy, John Fitzgerald

John Fitzgerald "Jack" Kennedy (1917–1963), served as the 35th President of the United States from 1961 until his assassination in 1963. Kennedy was a tremendous figure in U.S. history as it related to the experience of African Americans during the crucial years of the Civil Rights movement. Indeed, the struggle over civil liberties was perhaps the most pressing domestic issues of the Kennedy administration. As a strong advocate of the movement, Kennedy helped push civil rights legislation through Congress, supported the integration of schools and universities throughout the South, and collaborated extensively with leaders of the Civil Rights movement.

In 1954, the U.S. Supreme Court ruled that racial segregation in public schools was unconstitutional in a federal court case called *Brown v. Board of Education*. However, this ruling was widely ignored throughout the South and schools as well as restaurants, theatres, bathrooms, and many other public facilities remained segregated. As a result, the struggle for civil rights and social justice became an issue that necessitated action. Led by individuals such as Dr. Martin Luther King Jr. and by organizations such as the Southern Christian Leadership Conference (SCLC), the Civil Rights movement began to take action in the form of a series of sit-ins and non-violent protests. As early as 1957, astute congressional leaders began to recognize that civil rights legislation would eventually become inevitability.

In 1956 and 1957, as the Junior Senator from Massachusetts, Kennedy designed a strategy for how to accommodate African Americans as well as a wide variety of Democrats in regards to civil liberties. However, this strategy was hardly the position of a stanch civil rights advocate. Instead, it was a political maneuver and calculated with thoughts of a campaign for the presidency in 1960. Kennedy engaged in debates on the Senate floor regarding Titles III and IV of a bill, which would give the U.S. Attorney General the power to intervene in school desegregations with military force. He was able to support this bill without upsetting northern liberals or southern conservatives, both constituencies that he would need in his bid for the presidency in 1960. Indeed, Kennedy walked a very thin line, which brought criticism from several stanch civil rights advocates.

This legislation culminated in the Civil Rights Act of 1957, which created a commission to monitor violations of civil liberties, especially as it applied to voting. It also upgraded the Civil Rights office to the Justice Department and gave that office the power to commence civil measures against states that discriminated based on race. Further, many saw Kennedy's support of a bill carrying an amendment guaranteeing the right of all Americans to serve on federal juries as a fake bill with no real substantive power to change the status quo. However, the Civil Rights Act of 1957 was the first time since Reconstruction that the United States Congress had acted in any way to protect the civil liberties of African Americans. Thus, Kennedy's journey down the path of civil rights began, and public sentiment held that he was trying to press forward with equal treatment of African Americans, but that he was most concerned with securing national unity through a legality course.

In Kennedy's bid for the White House in 1960, against Richard Nixon, he chose the tenuous position to advance civil rights. This position was politically expedient as it secured the African American vote as well as consolidated the votes of northern liberals whom were antisegregation. However, Kennedy was taking a political gamble in losing the support of southern Democrats such as A. Willis Robertson and Harry F. Byrd of Virginia who were pro-segregation. Kennedy began to add many leaders of the Civil Rights movement to his staff including Marjorie Lawson, William Dawson, and Frank Reeves who advised him on how to espouse an aggressive civil rights agenda. The Kennedy campaign also encouraged the creation of a national organization to create a nationwide voter registration drive within African American communities.

Throughout the campaign, Kennedy applauded the peaceful non-violent strategies of civil rights activists; he spoke at several engagements at predominantly African American conferences, and criticized the inaction of previous presidents whom failed to bring integration sooner. Further, he promised to support civil rights legislation including a pledge to see more African Americans hired in the highest levels of the federal government. Kennedy also cultivated favor amongst African Americans when he telephoned Coretta Scott King in regards to the jailing of her husband, Dr. Martin Luther King Jr. Indeed, not only did Kennedy sympathize with Mrs. King, but also his phone calls, as well as those of his brother Bobby, convinced Georgia's governor, Ernest Vandiver, to set Dr. King free. This multifaceted strategy landed Kennedy the support of African Americans in his bid for the presidency in 1960. Given the slim margin of victory (about 100,000 votes), African American voters played a significant role in sealing the victory for Kennedy. Richard Nixon's attempt to strengthen his support among southern voters, as well as his silence about issues surrounding civil liberties caused many African American voters to reconsider their old ties to the Republican Party, which went back to the party's pro-civil rights record during Reconstruction in the mid to late 1860's.

Upon winning the presidency, which was one of the closest elections in U.S. history, Kennedy grew increasingly concerned about the violence surrounding the Civil Rights movement, and particularly the Freedom Rides. His interests in civil liberties continued to display this concern as his policies addressed the prevention of further disorder and violence. Because of his stance during the election, Kennedy was in a fixed position amongst southern democrats.

However, it actually freed him to aid the Civil Rights movement in several ways. His first act as president towards support of the movement was the issuance of Executive Order Number 11063. This order obliged government agencies to discontinue discriminatory practices in federal housing. Kennedy also named Vice President Lyndon Johnson to be the chair of a newly appointed Committee on Equal Employment. Further, nominating African Americans to a number of posts including Thurgood Marshall to the Second Circuit Court of Appeals, Carl Rowan to Deputy Assistant of the Secretary of State, and George L. P. Weaver to Assistant Secretary of Labor further ingratiated Kennedy to African Americans.

One of the defining moments of the Kennedy Administration in regards to civil rights was on June 25, 1962. James Meredith had applied to the University of Mississippi, had been rejected based on his race, and thus filed a complaint for racial discrimination in the U.S. Circuit Court of Appeals. The Fifth circuit ruled that the University should admit Meredith, but the Governor of Mississippi (Ross Barnett) stated that he would physically stand in the way of integration. As a result, Kennedy sent 300 federal marshals to enforce the court's decision. There were riots on campus that yielded the deaths of 2 individuals, over 200 arrests, and many federal marshals sustained serious injuries. Kennedy then put the Mississippi National Guard under federal jurisdiction and made sure that Meredith was admitted. Indeed, Kennedy did not back down or succumb to the stubborn challenge from southern governors. Later, in June of 1963, Kennedy took the same action against George Wallace in the desegregation of the University of Alabama.

In August of 1963, Kennedy proposed to Congress the strongest civil rights bill yet seen in U.S. History. However, the strong bloc of southern voters in the House and Senate were able to keep the bill from passing. In support of Kennedy's bold new legislation a coalition was formed between several civil rights organizations including the SCLC, NAACP, CORE, and SNCC, which organized a massive march in Washington. Later that August, about 250,000 marchers gathered near the Lincoln Memorial in support of equality in the job market, freedom, and civil justice through the passage of Kennedy's legislation. This is the context for Dr. Martin Luther King Jr.'s famous "I Have a Dream" speech and the march was a visual and palpable representation of that dream. African Americans and whites, young and old, men and women gathered in the hopes that their children could one day live in a nation where they will not be "judged by the color of their skin but by the content of their character." Using television images, many Americans witnessed this important protest of racial discrimination and there was no doubt that the March on Washington helped pave the way towards the passage of the Civil Rights Act of 1964. However, in an act that became a double-edged sword for the Civil Rights movement, the assassination of John F. Kennedy in November of 1963 proved to be a tremendous loss, but also perhaps a tremendous gain for the movement.

The legacy of John F. Kennedy as it related to the Civil Rights movement was fully realized by the passage of the Civil Rights Act of 1964. After the death of Kennedy, Vice-President Lyndon B. Johnson was inaugurated the 36th president of the United States. Johnson, having only taken the oath of office four days prior, disclosed to the nation that he planned to support Kennedy's civil rights bill as a testament to Kennedy's work towards civil justice. A southerner from Texas, many leaders of the Civil Rights movement feared that Johnson would only buttress the southern voting bloc in the legislature that had kept such a bill from previous passage. However, with years of legislative experience at work, Johnson was able to push the bill through Congress despite massive resistance in the form of southern filibusters. It is safe to say that the Civil Rights Act of 1964 was the zenith of decades and even centuries of work on behalf of the African American in U.S. history. The act banned segregation and racial discrimination in public facilities such as restaurants, hotels, schools, libraries, and swimming pools.

The Civil Rights Act of 1964 also called for a ban of racial discrimination in the American workforce. No longer could employers discriminate based on race, religion, ethnicity, or sex when considering a hire, promotion, or termination. To enforce these positions, the federal government was granted the power to withhold federal funding to any organization that was discriminating in any way. Finally, the Civil Rights Act of 1964 lead to the desegregation of many public schools, it created the Employment Opportunity Commission to oversee practices of racial prejudice in employment, and it gave the attorney general the power to initiate prosecution on behalf of those who had been the victims of unfair injustice. This is perhaps one of the greatest legacies of the Kennedy administration as it related to the Civil Rights movement. Unfortunately, it was not until after Kennedy's premature death that the dream was fully realized.

In August of 1965, Congress passed another act that augmented the 1964 legislation. The Voting Rights Act of 1965, although signed into law by Lyndon Johnson was also a part of the Kennedy civil rights legacy. This act outlawed the educational requirements throughout many states in the South that called for the reciting of the constitution or for the "proper" interpretations of various sections of the constitution in order to vote. Many of these requirements had kept African Americans from voting and therefore had a tremendous affect on the racial bias of state and local elections. The Voting Rights Act of 1965 also gave the attorney general the power to assign federal voter registrars to record African American voters. This had a tremendous influence on the numbers of the African American electorate. For instance, in Mississippi alone, the number of enrolled African American voters grew from 28,000 in 1964 to over 250,000 in 1968.

Many have called John F. Kennedy a reluctant participant in the Civil Rights movement, but he was an essential participant nonetheless. To be sure, he was a politician with a calculated agenda. However, Kennedy had also accomplished more for the civil rights of African Americans than any other president in U.S. history, perhaps with the exception of Abraham Lincoln. Further, his extra-legislative support such as phone calls, meetings, and words of encouragement given to the leaders of the Civil Rights movement lent moral support from the highest office in the land. There have been very few Presidents in the U.S. history who risked so much for the freedoms and liberties of African Americans. Indeed, Kennedy was advocating a position that almost half of the country disagreed with. Indeed, he realized that the African American deserved equal rights, and that they lived in a country where all men were created equal and were endowed with certain inalienable rights. John F. Kennedy was the first American president to interpret that statement of the constitution quite literally.

See also: Castro, Fidel; Civil Rights Act of 1964; Hoover, J. Edgar; Johnson, Lyndon Baines; King, Martin Luther Jr.; March on Washington, 1963; Marshall, Thurgood; Voting Rights Act of 1965

Otis Westbrook Pickett

Bibliography

Dallek, Robert. *An Unfinished Life: John F. Kennedy, 1917–1963.* New York: Little, Brown, 2003.

O'Brien, Michael. *John F. Kennedy: A Biography.* New York: Thomas Dunne Books an imprint of St. Martin's Press, 2005.

Rorabaugh, W. J. *Kennedy and the Promise of the Sixties.* Cambridge, UK: Cambridge University Press, 2002.

Rosenberg, Johnathan, and Zachary Karabell. *Kennedy, Johnson, and the Quest for Justice: The Civil Rights Tapes.* New York: W. W. Norton, 2003.

Stern, Mark. *Calculating Visions: Kennedy, Johnson, and Civil Rights.* New Brunswick, NJ: Rutgers University Press, 1992.

Kennedy, Robert F.

Robert "Bobby" Francis Kennedy (1925–1968), or "RFK," was a leading and influential political figure during the struggles for racial and economic equality of the 1960s. Formally trained as a lawyer and experientially as a politician, RFK served as attorney general to the United States from 1961 to 1964, during some of the most pivotal years of the Civil Rights movement. From 1965 until his assassination in 1968, he served as the United States Senator from New York, using his position and his political expertise to champion for racial, social, and economic equality.

Born the seventh of nine children into the prominent, powerful, and wealthy Kennedy family, Robert Kennedy graduated from Harvard University in 1948 with a degree in government and earned a law degree from The University of Virginia Law School in 1951. Throughout the 1950s, RFK worked as a lawyer for the United States Department of Justice and for various Senate Committees. In 1952, he served as campaign manager for his brother, John Fitzgerald Kennedy Jr., vying to become the U.S. Senator from Massachusetts. And in 1959, he managed another JFK campaign: his bid to become the 35th President of the United States.

Elected to the presidency in 1960, JFK appointed Robert Kennedy as his attorney general. Robert Kennedy's job was to ensure the constitutional rights of the American people, and nowhere was he called to do so more than in the southern struggles for racial equality. Initially, Robert Kennedy believed that the most necessary gain in these struggles would be unhindered access to the ballot box. African American citizens in the South often faced harassment for exercising their right to vote, so RFK dispatched federal marshals into these southern states to investigate and begin prosecuting counties that condoned voter intimidation.

While RFK tried to contain the Justice Department's policies to legislation, students, and civil rights leaders opted for a different strategy. Lunch counter sit-ins, freedom rides, protest marches, school integration, and many other varieties of nonviolent direct action proliferated across the South. Robert Kennedy provided Justice Department support wherever possible. He dispatched federal marshals to pacify angry mobs during the first Freedom Rides of May 1961. He encouraged President Kennedy to provide armed protection for endangered persons, such as for James Meredith, who in September 1962 integrated the University of Mississippi in Oxford. And RFK negotiated with segregationist southern leaders—such as Alabama governor John Patterson, who opposed the integration of the University of Alabama at Tuscaloosa—to enforce federal law.

By this time, Robert Kennedy understood that although enfranchisement was certainly important, only a more comprehensive guarantee of civil liberties could ensure the rights of U.S. citizens. He urged his brother to draft a comprehensive civil rights bill to send to Congress, and he insisted that President Kennedy publicly address the civil rights issue. Thus, on June 11, 1963, President Kennedy became the first president to publicly declare the struggle for racial equality a moral issue. Immediately thereafter, civil rights leaders began planning a national March on Washington for Freedom, Jobs, and Justice to advocate for quick passage of this legislation. Robert Kennedy's Justice Department guaranteed the marchers federal protection.

The March on Washington took place on August 1963, but JFK did not live to see the passage of the civil rights legislation. He was assassinated on November 22, 1963. His vice president, Lyndon Baines Johnson, assumed the presidency and asked Robert Kennedy to remain attorney general. In July 1964, RFK witnessed the signing of his brother's civil rights bill into law as the Civil Rights Act of 1964. The next month, RFK resigned his post as attorney general in order to campaign in New York for an U.S. Senate seat.

As a U.S. senator, Robert Kennedy continued to fight for racial equality, as well as for economic and social equality. In the latter half of the 1960s, nonviolent protest gave way to more confrontational methods. Riots erupted in urban centers around the country, but rather than condemn the rioters, Robert Kennedy encouraged people to consider the conditions that might engender such actions. He called attention to inequities in education, housing, employment, and living wages. He took steps to mitigate against such injustices, supporting, for example, the United Farm Workers and forming the Senate Subcommittee on Indian Education. He visited the impoverished Mississippi Delta in 1967 and afterwards, actively pursued food assistance for the area.

Such community rehabilitation endeavors, the most famous of which revitalized the Bedford-Stuyvesant community in Brooklyn, occupied his Senate career. He implemented community development corporations, programs that combined residents' needs and energies with federal grants and private sector investment in community improvement.

In March 1968, Robert Kennedy announced that he would challenge Lyndon Johnson for the presidency. Over the next few months, RFK stormed the primary race, bolstered by the overwhelming support of those to whom he reached out most African Americans, Hispanics, student protestors, the poor, the dispossessed, and the suffering. On June 4, 1968, celebrating an important primary win in California, Robert Kennedy was shot at the Ambassador Hotel. He died two days later. Much like Dr. Martin Luther King Jr., assassinated only two months earlier, Robert Kennedy believed in the principles of equality and progress on which the United States was founded so deeply that he struggled and sacrificed to preserve them.

See also: Civil Rights Act of 1964; Freedom Rides; Hoover, J. Edgar; Kennedy, John Fitzgerald; King, Coretta Scott; King, Martin Luther Jr.; Meredith, James; Los Angeles, California, Riot of 1965

Aghigh Ebrahimi

Bibliography
Branch, Taylor. *Parting the Waters: America in the King Years, 1954–63.* New York: Touchstone, 1988.
Huevel, Vanden, and Milton Gwirtzman. *On His Own: Robert F. Kennedy.* New York: Doubleday, 1970.
Kennedy, Robert F. *To Seek A Newer World.* New York: Doubleday, 1967.
Palermo, Joseph A. *Robert F. Kennedy and the Death of American Idealism.* New York: Pearson Education, 2008.
Schlesinger, Arthur M. Jr. *Robert Kennedy and His Times.* Boston: Houghton Mifflin, 1978.
Thomas, Evan. *Robert Kennedy: His Life.* New York: Simon and Schuster, 2000.

Kenyatta, Jomo

Jomo Kenyatta (1889–1978) was the figurehead of the Kenyan independence movement and Kenya's first freely elected prime minister. Kenyatta was born a part of Kenya's largest cultural group, the Kikuyu, who were a sedentary, agricultural people inhabiting a stretch of land extending northeast from Nairobi, around the base of Mount Kenya and onward north. At the age of 10, Kenyatta wandered away from home and into a Scottish mission, which took him in and gave him a Christian education. Kenyatta eventually ran away to Nairobi, which was nearly a westernized, European city by the turn of the century, and he found employment there as a clerk. In Nairobi in the early 1920s, Kenyatta began participating in the Young Kikuyu Association (later the Kikuyu Central Association, KCA), a group of Kenyan youth with mission educations who spoke out against governmental inequities toward Kenyan workers and farmers. In 1925, Kenyatta took up full-time political work and published a monthly newspaper, *Mwigwithanla,* with the aim of uniting the Kikuyu to regain control of their land.

In 1929, Kenyatta traveled to London as a representative of the KCA to voice the Kikuyu grievances to the British government. The colonial office ignored Kenyatta's protestations, but he remained in Europe and spent nearly two years traveling and meeting with liberal politicians. In 1931, Kenyatta returned to London to argue for Kikuyu rights, and this time Kenyatta's platform in favor of returning seized land and ceding equal representation to Kenyans was entertained by various committees, although only marginally and unofficially. Kenyatta briefly moved to Birmingham and attended classes at a Quaker college called Woodbrooke, before returning to London. From 1933 to 1936, Kenyatta worked in the Department of African Phonetics at University College, as well as teaching Kikuyu at the School of Oriental and African Languages. In 1936, Kenyatta attended the London School of Economics and earned a degree in anthropology. Expanding the anthropological work he had done on the Kikuyu, Kenyatta published it in the form a book, *Facing Mount Kenya,* in 1938.

Kenyatta began lecturing in anthropology in 1939, but with the outbreak of World War II, he moved to Sussex where he farmed, spoke to local groups about Kenya, and lived a quiet country life. The trials of war and suppression of the KCA resulted in the governmental effective silencing of the situation in Kenya for more than five years. In 1945, Kenyatta assisted in the organization of a pan-African congress in Manchester on which he sat as the representative of the KCA. The congress resulted in the formation of the Pan-African Federation that aspired to coordinate the independence movements that were ripening in the colonies. Realizing that his own power to effect

change in London was limited and placing hope in a unified African petition for human rights, Kenyatta returned to Kenya in 1946.

On his return to Kenya, Kenyatta worked with the Kikuyu Independent Schools Association, and, in 1947, he was elected president of the Kenya African Union (KAU), a group that united the various splintering factions of contemporary Kenyan politics. The political climate had grown dark by the time Kenyatta arrived home, with multiple special interest organizations acting on their own and isolating themselves from a larger community. Accommodating the incongruous demands of these parties was impossible, and Kenyatta submitted to maintaining partiality while trying to encourage positive social protest. In the end, Kenyatta was able to do little to persuade the masses, whose backgrounds and beliefs differed greatly, to adopt unified, nonviolent, and democratic resistance.

As conditions worsened in Kenya, gangs resorted to vandalism, acts of terrorism against Europeans, and the murder of Africans who refused to take part or allegedly sympathized with the government. Kenyatta became an easy target for blame, as he was widely revered and still regarded as the leader of the Kikuyu. The rebellion came to a bloody climax in 1952 and on October 20, by decree of the governor, Kenyatta and close to 200 Kenyans were arrested under suspicion of their participation in the ongoing uprising known as Mau Mau. In 1953, Kenyatta was charged with organizing Mau Mau and, in a questionable trial, he and five Kikuyu leaders were sentenced to seven years in prison. Despite the arrests, Mau Mau continued in Kenya and the four years of conflict (1950–1954) resulted in more than 13,000 deaths, less than 1 percent of them European.

In 1961, Kenyatta was released from prison and quickly rose to the head of the Kenya African Nationalist Union (KANU). Kenya obtained official independence from Great Britain in 1963, at which time Kenyatta was elected prime minister in the country's first free general elections. Selecting ministers who would represent the multiple cultures couched within Kenya's borders, as well as the interests of the settlers who remained, Kenyatta focused on the unification of Kenya fractured populace in the first years of independence. He initially took many positive steps toward economic recovery and land reform, but he could not prevent the political dissidence that divided the KANU into two parties in 1966 and led to further divisions between people of different cultures. When violence broke out in

Jomo Kenyatta, newly elected prime minister of Kenya, waves to supporters on June 19, 1963. (Library of Congress)

1969 along party lines, Kenyatta banned the opposition party and imprisoned a number of its leaders, although this did not stop the feuding that would continue to shake the balance of Kenyan politics throughout Kenyatta's tenure. During the 1970s, Kenyatta promoted industrialization and foreign investments that led Kenya to rapidly expand and develop into a westernized nation. Kenyatta led Kenya until his death in 1978 and despite the turmoil that shrouded his term as prime minister, he is remembered as a great leader, a powerful orator, and an enduring voice for human rights. *See also:* African Imperialism; Du Bois, W. E. B.; Nkrumah, Kwame; Pan-Africanism

Matthew Evans Teti

Bibliography
Arnold, Guy. *Kenyatta and the Politics of Kenya.* London: Dent, 1974.
Kenyatta, Jomo. *Facing Mount Kenya: The Tribal Life of the Gi-kuyu.* New York: Vintage Books, 1965.
Kenyatta, Jomo. *Suffering Without Bitterness: The Founding of the Kenya Nation.* Nairobi: East African Publishing House, 1968.
Murray-Brown, Jeremy. *Kenyatta.* New York: E. P. Dutton, 1973.

Kerner Commission Report

In the aftermath of the so-called long hot summer of 1967, the nation was convulsed by major outbreaks of racial violence in Newark, Detroit, Cleveland, and numerous smaller cities. The official response to the riots was President Lyndon Baines Johnson's Executive Order 11365, issued on July 29, 1967, which established a National Advisory Commission on Civil Disorders. Two days earlier, Johnson appointed the

11-member commission during a presidential address to the country. In essence, the commission would investigate civil disorders and would make recommendations to the president, Congress, governors, and mayors for implementing measures to help contain race riots in the future. After seven months of investigation, the commission completed and submitted a report on February 29, 1968 named after its chairman, Illinois governor and later federal judge Otto Kerner Jr. Kerner was, in many ways, a prototypical member of the commission. Like New York Mayor John Lindsay, vice chair of the commission, Senator Edward Brooke of Massachusetts, and Roy Wilkins of the NAACP, Kerner was a political moderate.

The Kerner Commission Report was issued as a 426-page book, which, ironically, became a national bestseller, with more than 2 million copies in print. Charged by Johnson to investigate what happened, why it happened, and what could be done to prevent it from happening again, the commission issued findings that were surprisingly progressive given the embrace of moderate political ideology

of most the its 11 members. According to the commission white racism was the cause of race riots between 1965 and 1967, and the country was becoming "two societies, one black, one white—separate and unequal." The Kerner Commission Report dispelled a number of myths embraced by President Johnson and Federal Bureau of Investigation (FBI) Director J. Edgar Hoover. The principal misconception corrected by the Kerner Commission Report was that race riots were not the product of black extremists or white radicals. Instead, they were the result of a suffocating mix of high unemployment (and underemployment), chronic poverty, poor housing conditions, poor schools, lack of access to affordable health care, police brutality, and harassment faced by millions of African Americans living in inner cities. The formation of the racial ghetto, the Kerner Commission Report claimed, was the fault of white America and, as white America was a factor in its creation, whites were also responsible for the conditions that made race riots possible.

The Kerner Commission Report recommended fundamental changes in federal policy to ameliorate the oppressive

Meeting of the Special Advisory Commission on Civil Disorders (the Kerner Commission), at the White House on July 29, 1967. From left to right, Roy Wilkins, Governor Otto Kerner (Chairman), and President Lyndon B. Johnson. (Lyndon B. Johnson Museum and Library)

conditions faced by African Americans. Specifically, the Commission called for federal initiatives directed at improving public services, schools, employment opportunities, and housing in predominantly African American inner-city neighborhoods. In addition, it called for a complete restructuring of the welfare system and for a national system of income supplementation that would address underemployment and single-parent households. By 1968, the political winds had shifted considerably. With the election of President Richard M. Nixon, many of the Kerner Commission Report's recommendations would be ignored or greatly delayed.

See also: Johnson, Lyndon Baines; Long Hot Summer Riots, 1965–1967; Urban Ghetto; War on Poverty

Walter C. Rucker

Bibliography

Blaustein, Albert P., and Robert L. Zangrando. *Civil Rights and African Americans: A Documentary History.* Evanston, IL: Northwestern University Press, 1991.

Boger, John Charles, and Judith Welch Wegner. *Race, Poverty, and American Cities.* Chapel Hill: University of North Carolina Press, 1996.

Harris, Fred R. *Locked in the Poorhouse: Cities, Race, and Poverty in the United States.* Lanham, MD: Rowman & Littlefield, 1998.

Meranto, Philip J. *The Kerner Report Revisited.* Urbana: Institute of Government and Public Affairs, University of Illinois, 1970.

King, Coretta Scott

Coretta Scott King (1927–2006) was the wife of civil rights leader Martin Luther King Jr., an author, and a civil rights leader in her own right. Born on April 27, 1927, in Heiberger, Alabama, she was raised on a farm owned by her parents, Bernice McMurry Scott and Obadiah Scott. The second of three siblings, King's family was not wealthy despite her father's entrepreneurial spirit. Obadiah Scott owned a truck, ran a barbershop, owned a lumber mill, all while growing cotton on the family's own land. In the midst of the Great Depression, she and her siblings picked cotton to supplement the meager family income. As a school-age child, King walked five miles each day to attend the Crossroad School, a segregated, one-room school in neighboring Marion, Alabama. Owing to her parents' emphasis on education and King's own innate academic skills, she excelled in her studies, graduating from Lincoln High School

as class valedictorian in 1945. She entered Antioch College in Yellow Springs, Ohio the following autumn on an academic scholarship. During her time as an undergraduate, she joined the Antioch chapter of the NAACP and the Race Relations and Civil Liberties Committees. After receiving word that the Yellow Springs school board would not allow her to do required practice teaching, she continued her education at the New England Conservatory of Music in Boston with a scholarship to study concert singing.

Shortly after transferring to the New England Conservatory, King met Martin Luther King Jr. who, after his graduation from Morehouse College, was enrolled as a divinity student at Boston University. A year after their first meeting, the two were married on June 18, 1953. She completed her degree in voice and violin and moved with her husband in September 1954 to Montgomery, Alabama. Within a few short months of becoming pastor of the Dexter Avenue Baptist Church, King and his wife became involved in the Montgomery bus boycott. Between 1955 and 1968, King would often be with her husband at the front lines of various struggles against segregation and injustice. The couple would have four children: Yolanda (b. 1955), Martin Luther III (b. 1957), Dexter (b. 1961), and Bernice (b. 1963). After her husband's assassination on April 4, 1968, King was involved in organizing a commemorative service at Ebenezer Baptist Church in Atlanta every January 15 to mark his birth and honor his life. This commemoration was expanded to serve as the basis for calls for a national holiday. By Act of Congress, national observances of the holiday began in 1986. King also played a pivotal role in establishing the King Center for Nonviolent Social Change in Atlanta, which opened its doors to the public in 1981.

Between the 1970s and 1990s, King was actively involved in a number of movements seeking equality, justice, and civil rights. She had been an ardent opponent of the apartheid regimes of South Africa, working tirelessly with Winnie Mandela and the African National Congress (ANC) as well as politicians in the United States, including President Ronald Reagan, to combat the racist policies and denial of liberties to the black majority in the beleaguered nation. In addition to her opposition to apartheid, King was actively involved in addressing capital punishment; HIV/AIDS prevention; and lesbian, gay, bisexual, and transgender rights, and has been a staunch critic of the 2003 invasion of Iraq and various policies of President George W. Bush, including the push to propose a marriage amendment. In honor of her continuing role as a voice for justice, she was awarded the Gandhi Peace Prize in 2004 by the government of India. After a lifetime of struggle, King's health began to fail in 2005 when she suffered a stroke and a mild heart attack. On January 30, 2006, King died at the age of 78 in Rosarito Beach, Mexico of complications from ovarian cancer. On November 20, 2006, her remains were laid to rest next to her husband's at the King Center in Atlanta.

See also: Antiapartheid Movement; King, Martin Luther Jr.; Southern Christian Leadership Conference

Walter C. Rucker

Bibliography

"Coretta Scott King: The First Lady of the Civil Rights Movement, (1927–2006)." *The Journal of Blacks in Higher Education.* 50 (Winter, 2005/2006):60.

McCarty, Laura T. *Coretta Scott King: A Biography.* Santa Barbara, CA: ABC-CLIO, 2009.

Vivian, Octavia B. *Coretta: The Story of Coretta Scott King.* Minneapolis: Fortress Press, 2006.

King, Martin Luther Jr.

More than a civil rights leader, Martin Luther King Jr. (1929–1965) was the human symbol of the quest for racial integration in the United States. His emergence, notoriety, evolution, and demise paralleled that of the Civil Rights movement itself. He became the nation's preeminent spokesman for the strategy of nonviolent direct action, the dismantling of Jim Crow laws in the South, and the creation of a larger "beloved community." He negotiated between the push of political expediency and the pull of militant black activists, all the while combating enemies who perceived him as a dangerous radical. A complex man burdened by political responsibility and torn by personal temptation, he forged an evolving vision of social justice that transformed the American political landscape.

Born in Atlanta, Georgia, on January 15, 1929, King was raised in relative privilege. His father was pastor at the Ebenezer Baptist Church, which served a middle-class clientele. The second of three children, Martin enjoyed a comfortable home life, material security, and the attention of a loving family. Of course, he periodically endured the indignities of segregation. He mostly thrived, however, within the institutions of the black bourgeoisie, especially the church. A serious and moody child, Martin possessed erratic work habits but precocious intelligence. He graduated high school at 15 and attended Morehouse College, a training ground for Atlanta's young, elite African American men. Here he developed not only his mind, but also his taste for dandy clothes and pretty women. Before his senior year, less out of spiritual fire than professional resolve, he decided to follow his father's footsteps and enter the ministry.

King attended Crozer Theological Seminary in Chester, Pennsylvania from 1948 to 1951. At this tiny, liberal, predominantly white institution, he laid the deep and wide intellectual foundation that later informed his crusades for justice. He read the classics of Western philosophy, the key texts of Hinduism and Islam, and the writings of Mohandas Gandhi, whose campaign of nonviolent resistance fascinated King. He also questioned the liberal, optimistic belief in progress; influenced by Reinhold Neibuhr, he interpreted human nature as inherently sinful, and he believed that social change demanded not just reason but the stirring of passionate faith. From 1951 to 1953, King attended Boston University, from which he received his doctorate in theology in 1955. In Boston he met and romanced Coretta Scott, a student at the New England Conservatory of Music. They married in 1953. King also developed enthusiasm for Georg Hegel's notion of the dialectic, a theory of history that resonated with his capacity for absorbing and amalgamating opposing ideas into a useful whole. His intellectual talents, however, did not include original scholarship; his dissertation is rife with unattributed passages from other scholars' work.

In 1954, King took the pastorship at Dexter Avenue Baptist Church in Montgomery, Alabama, the site of his unlikely surge to national prominence. Dexter catered to a small congregation of black professionals, and King's early sermons had little political bent. But in December 1955, the Montgomery police arrested Rosa Parks, a dignified seamstress and National Association for the Advancement of Colored People (NAACP) secretary, for refusing to vacate her seat on the segregated city buses. The black leadership recognized the political opportunity, declared a bus boycott, and formed the Montgomery Improvement Association; they elected the 26-year-old King president only because he had avoided the rivalries among the older ministers. King soon displayed his oratorical gifts, stirring a mass meeting to a fever pitch with an impassioned fusion of American democracy and Christian righteousness. He urged nonviolent protest, which not only placed the protestors on higher moral ground, but also engendered support from white liberals. For more than a year, Montgomery's black citizens walked and established carpools, and King endured unjustified arrests and a bombing of his home. The national media paid King and the boycott significant attention. In November 1956, the Supreme Court ruled Montgomery's bus segregation unconstitutional, and the next month King and his aides triumphantly boarded a bus and sat in front.

In the public mind, King had become the preeminent African American leader. His appearances inspired crowds of joyous hope. He met with President Dwight Eisenhower, sidestepped attacks by an insane black woman and a hateful member of the American Nazi Party, traveled to Ghana for its 1957 independence celebration, and toured India for a month to further absorb Gandhi's lessons. He founded and

Dr. Martin Luther King Jr., president of the Southern Christian Leadership Conference and Mathew Ahmann, executive director of the National Catholic Conference for Interrracial Justice, in the Civil Rights March on Washington, D.C., on August 28, 1963. (National Archives)

led the Southern Christian Leadership Conference (SCLC), a political network for civil rights activism.

With Roy Wilkins and A. Philip Randolph he led a 1957 mass meeting in Washington, D.C., known as the prayer pilgrimage, but it failed to attract much attention from the media or the federal government. King was struggling to give direction to this nascent movement. In 1959, he resigned from Dexter and based himself at SCLC headquarters in Atlanta. He had so far failed to inspire widescale grass roots activism or a political victory on par with Montgomery.

The student sit-in campaigns of 1960, starting in Greensboro, North Carolina, and spreading through much of the South, energized the Civil Rights movement. These protests of segregated public facilities awakened a generation of young black activists. They both needed King, because he already reigned as the spokesman of racial justice, and resented him, for they regarded nonviolent direct action as a temporary tactic rather than a bedrock element of faith. In April 1960, King spoke at the organizing meeting of the Student Nonviolent Coordinating Committee (SNCC). During the next year's Freedom Rides, when activists from the Congress of Racial Equality (CORE) and SNCC encountered violence while desegregating bus terminals in the South, King again offered encouragement and political clout, but he declined to place himself on the dangerous frontlines of the Freedom Rides. "Where is your *body?*" asked the young activists. They wanted less moral support and more aggressive leadership.

King did face harassment, violence, and jail. In October 1960, he began a four-month sentence in an Atlanta prison on a trumped-up traffic violation. Here King's national stature proved critical. Republican Vice President Richard Nixon had been Dwight Eisenhower's point man on civil rights, and he had worked behind the scenes to get King released. But Democratic presidential candidate John F. Kennedy, distant from black protestors and quiet on King's arrest, placed a concerned telephone call to Coretta. The Kennedy campaign publicized the gesture in black newspapers and in pamphlets distributed to black churches, helping deliver a close election over Nixon.

Yet the Kennedy administration resisted any alliance with King. Kennedy feared King's capacity to stir up disorder, and he first invited to the White House more established black leaders such as the NAACP's Roy Wilkins. Attorney general Robert Kennedy also sanctioned FBI surveillance of King and his associates. FBI director J. Edgar Hoover, a Puritanical man with little sympathy for blacks, considered King a disloyal radical. King's trusted white adviser, Stanley Levison, moreover, once had financially supported the Communist Party. So Hoover's agents, who offered little protection to the civil rights demonstrators in the South, tapped the telephones of King and Levison. Hoover's obsessive hatred aside, the FBI tapes reveal nothing politically incriminating about King.

What the tapes (and other sources) do reveal is that King had his own flaws and weaknesses. He could be vain and pompous. In private, he offered the occasional crude comment. He enjoyed bawdy late-night drinking sessions and smoked cigarettes, although never in public. King also indulged in pleasures of the flesh. Sexual temptation followed him throughout his constant travels, and King did not resist. His sexual romps were not public knowledge, although friends warned him of the dangers to his image, and elements of the black community whispered rumors. J. Edgar Hoover regarded him a moral degenerate and maintained the FBI surveillance. Such behavior should reinforce that King was not a god but a human being. His transgressions, moreover, reinforced his own view of human nature. His private guilt over his sins may even have informed his public calls for self-discipline among African Americans by using nonviolent protest in the civil rights struggle.

In December 1961, King arrived in Albany, Georgia, at the behest of the Albany movement, a coalition of community civil rights groups. His involvement gradually escalated from a speech, to a protest march, to an arrest, and finally to a longer commitment for the city's desegregation. King brought media attention and SCLC resources to this civil rights campaign, but the Albany movement faltered. The NAACP fretted about militant SNCC tactics; local leaders resented the condescension of SCLC deputies; SNCC feared that King would leave Albany with a symbolic victory but little change to the substance of racial patterns. Police chief Laurie Pritchett also defused the demonstrators' tactics of moral theater by avoiding crude violence before television cameras and by arranging to jail demonstrators outside the city. King was arrested twice, but city leaders paid his fine and suspended his sentence, so that he could not become a media martyr. King left Albany in 1962 with his prestige bruised and with few public facilities desegregated.

The lessons of Albany, however, did inform the triumphant 1963 SCLC campaign in Birmingham, Alabama. The city's poisonous race relations were personified by the notorious commissioner of public safety, "Bull" Connor. Unlike in Albany, King and SCLC gave direction to the entire series of protests, and "Project C" began with specific targets: the desegregation of three downtown department stores, leading to broader desegregation, the hiring of blacks for city jobs, and the formation of a biracial council. They trained volunteers in nonviolent resistance and raised reserves of money. Through early April, SCLC held sit-ins, marches, and mass meetings. After a state court injunction barring further protests, King led another march and was arrested. His admirers noted that it was Good Friday.

While in prison, he read that liberal white clergymen had condemned his campaign for "extremism" from "outsiders." King's response, scribbled on scraps of paper with a smuggled-in pen and referred to as "Letter from Birmingham Jail," powerfully outlined King's basic philosophies. He defied state law, he wrote, because of a higher moral law. He rejected the plea that African Americans must be patient, arguing that freedom for the oppressed arrives only when the oppressed demand freedom. Nonviolent direct action, moreover, did not promote racial ill will so much as bring it to the surface. Finally, he cited history's great "extremists": exponents of Christian love such as Jesus Christ and Martin Luther, and symbols of American democracy such as Thomas Jefferson and Abraham Lincoln. His disquisition slowly filtered into the American consciousness, but when King emerged from jail on Easter Sunday, Project C was floundering.

In May, SCLC began using children for their protest marches. Thousands poured from the 16th Street Baptist Church, singing freedom songs and clapping their hands. This sublime street theater invigorated Project C. Now, too, Bull Connor responded with violence, unleashing policemen on black demonstrators with billy clubs, electric cattle prods, attack dogs, and high-pressure fire hoses— images that circulated throughout the nation. The protestors maintained the demonstrations, pressuring the city's business community and gaining a settlement that met SCLC's original demands. Birmingham's violence continued, but a corner had been turned. Civil rights protests again spread throughout the South, and national attention focused on the plight of black southerners. President Kennedy now proposed a civil rights bill desegregating public accommodations, calling it a "moral issue…as old as the Scriptures and as clear as the American Constitution." King had pricked the nation's conscience.

The momentum continued in late August with the March on Washington. An interracial throng of 250,000 congregated at the Lincoln Memorial to hear speeches from assorted civil rights, labor, and religious leaders on live television. King supplied the climax. He began his speech solemnly, with a measured pace, using the metaphor of a promissory note to recall the American government's unfulfilled commitment to protect the constitutional rights of its black citizens. Then he summoned the preaching rhythms of his sermons at mass meetings. "I have a dream," he declared, providing poetic examples of racial brotherhood. "Let freedom ring," he intoned, not just in the South but throughout the nation. Only upon transcending the barriers of race and religion and region could the nation achieve true freedom. The "I Have a Dream" speech, beamed into America's living rooms, proved an iconic moment in the nation's history.

After Birmingham and the March on Washington, the nation's racial fissure seemed to fill with a high tide of liberal goodwill, particularly washing over King. *Time* named him Man of the Year in 1963. In 1964, he won the Nobel Peace Prize. In June 1964, Congress also passed the Civil Rights Act, prohibiting the segregation of public facilities and backing it with significant enforcement mechanisms. Passage of the act depended not only on the political skills of new President Lyndon Johnson, but also on the climate of moral justice embodied by King.

Nevertheless, the barriers to racial peace stayed high, liberal optimism started to fizzle, and King could no longer embody any consensus of black political thought. SCLC's 1964 campaign in St. Augustine, Florida, featured white mobs so vicious that any progress was impossible; only a King oration kept the city's blacks from responding with violence in kind. For some activists, King had become too moderate. SNCC members mocked him as "De Lawd" for his preachy ego. When the interracial Mississippi Freedom Democratic Party tried to obtain delegate seats at the 1964 Democratic Convention, King urged acceptance of a compromise proposal, alienating him from militants. The ultimate converse to King, of course, was Malcolm X, both before and after his 1964 exile from the Nation of Islam. The fiery leader countered King's values of nonviolence and integration with calls for eye-for-an-eye justice and black nationalism.

In 1965, King and SCLC came to Selma, Alabama. The campaign illustrated the forces buffeting King. President Johnson urged patience as the Civil Rights Act went into effect. Not wishing to antagonize Johnson, King left for Atlanta in early March, before a planned march to the state capital of Montgomery. The march began without him, and television cameras captured the brutal violence on the Edmund Pettus Bridge, as the Selma police turned back the marchers with clubs and tear gas. King returned to Selma. By accepting Johnson's compromise to halt a second march upon reaching the bridge, he angered SNCC and other civil rights supporters.

The Selma campaign nevertheless succeeded. The violent police response led Johnson to propose a voting rights bill on national television, capped by the phrase "We shall overcome." The march to Montgomery was accomplished with the protection of federal marshals. And in August Congress passed the Voting Rights Act, eliminating the procedures that had long disfranchised most southern blacks. Along with the Civil Rights Act, the Voting Rights Act transformed the South, finally allowing African Americans access to the rights guaranteed by the Constitution.

As King realized, however, the road to racial equality only began with these basic rights. In ghetto neighborhoods outside the South, African Americans faced police harassment, possessed little political power, lived in substandard public housing, and suffered the economic and social dislocations of poverty. So King expanded his vision, visiting Chicago in 1965 and launching a campaign for open housing in 1966. Leading protest marches and lobbying city leaders for the elimination of de facto housing segregation, King faced resistance as stiff as that in the South. The ills of the ghetto also demanded more radical solutions than King could muster. He had developed a reputation as a black messiah, generating unfair expectations. When he failed, as in Chicago, his followers were disillusioned. Meanwhile, the political winds of African American protest drifted from King's core values of nonviolence and integration. During a June 1966 march from Memphis, Tennessee, to Jackson, Mississippi, King remained a folk hero, revered by the black masses. But when Stokely Carmichael of SNCC called for "black power," black activists cheered the messages of self-defense and rejection of white liberal support.

King's own call for social justice evolved and broadened. By 1967, he was an outspoken critic of the Vietnam War. He called for a "revolution of values" in the United

States that transcended the greed governing American involvement in Vietnam. His stance alienated many liberals and infuriated Lyndon Johnson, but King, sailing beyond the political mainstream, upheld his Christian principles. In 1967, King also announced an interracial crusade called the Poor People's Campaign. The movement would be highlighted by an encampment on the Washington Mall, designed to force the federal government to more deeply address the concerns of the American poor. Some of the SCLC staff doubted the political wisdom of such a radical call, but again King forged beyond the boundaries of liberal reform.

In March 1968, in the midst of planning the Poor People's Campaign and again guided by his swelling cry for economic justice, King arrived in Memphis to lend support to striking sanitation workers. During an April 3 speech, King predicted that he might not arrive at the "Promised Land" with everyone else. Typically, he suggested his own impending martyrdom. This time he was right. The next day, stepping onto his motel balcony, King was struck by an assassin's bullet and died. A political era seemed to perish with him. His death sparked 130 separate instances of racial violence, leading to the deaths of 46 people. That summer's Poor People's Campaign, led by King lieutenant Ralph Abernathy, suffered from disorganization and ended in failure. His vision of a beloved community seemed a distant memory.

Martin Luther King's spirit, however, still courses through the veins of the nation. Within his own time, King had become the public face for an entire movement, and he represented the ideals of racial brotherhood and Christian love. His leadership was integral to generating the federal legislation that reconfigured the South. His icon proved important for injecting African Americans into the larger national consciousness. His conscience prodded political complacency as the movement's goals changed. And his legacy continues to inform how we view the Civil Rights era, both its triumphs and its tragedies. In 1986, King's birthday became a federal holiday. That gesture recognizes not only the man, but the ideals that he embodied.

See also: Abernathy, Ralph David; Affirmative Action; Baker, Ella; COINTELPRO; King, Coretta Scott; March on Washington, 1963; Montgomery Bus Boycott; Poor People's Campaign; Southern Christian Leadership Conference

Aram Goudsouzian

Bibliography

Ansbro, John J. *Martin Luther King, Jr.: The Making of a Mind.* Maryknoll, NY: Orbis Books, 1982.

Branch, Taylor. *Parting the Waters: America in the King Years 1954–63.* New York: Simon and Schuster, 1988.

Branch, Taylor. *Pillar of Fire: America in the King Years 1963–65.* New York: Simon and Schuster, 1998.

Carson, Clayborne et al., eds. *The Papers of Martin Luther King, Jr.: Symbol of the Movement, January 1957-December 1958.* Berkeley: University of California Press, 2000.

Carson, Clayborne et al., eds. *The Papers of Martin Luther King, Jr: Threshold of a New Decade, January 1959-December 1960.* Berkeley: University of California Press, 2005.

Dyson, Michael Eric. *I May Not Get There With You: The True Martin Luther King, Jr.* New York: Free Press, 2000.

Garrow, David J. *Bearing the Cross: Martin Luther King, Jr. and the Southern Christian Leadership Conference.* New York: Vintage, 1986.

Garrow, David J. *The FBI and Martin Luther King, Jr.* New York: Penguin Books, 1981.

King, Martin Luther. *The Autobiography of Martin Luther King.* New York: Intellectual Properties Management in association with Warner Books, 1998.

King, Martin Luther. *A Testament of Hope: The Essential Writings and Speeches of Martin Luther King, Jr.* San Francisco: HarperSanFrancisco, 1990.

Oates, Stephen B. *Let the Trumpet Sound: The Life of Martin Luther King, Jr.* New York: Harper & Row, 1982.

Posner, Gerald L. *Killing the Dream: James Earl Ray and the Assassination of Martin Luther King, Jr.* New York: Random House, 1998.

Korean War (Black Participation in)

The Korean War was the catalyst for the racial integration of the United States Armed Forces. Whereas the African American community openly protested racism and pressed for civil rights during World War II, it was more reluctant to criticize American foreign policy and race politics during the Korean War.

On July 26, 1948, President Harry S Truman issued Executive Order 9981 with the intent to establish equal treatment and opportunity in the armed services for peoples of any race, color, religion, or national origin. The Committee on the Equality of Treatment and Opportunity in the Armed Forces, established by this order, reviewed the racial situation within the armed forces and pushed for the implementation of racial integration with the secretary of defense and the service secretaries. The upcoming presidential election, pressure from civil rights groups, and international attention compelled Truman to act. Truman hoped to gain the support of blacks, both in the election and in the struggle against communism. He also wanted the promise of equality in the military to improve America's international civil rights record, which played a vital role in the cold car conflict.

The navy and the air force were initially more open to integration than the army, which argued that integration threatened national security. The advent of the Korean War in June 1950, however, revealed the urgent necessity of racial integration of the military and accelerated its implementation. As a result of the growing need for combat troops, the military, in particular the army, soon realized that segregation endangered combat readiness and the war's ultimate success. It proved inefficient and ineffective to continue training and using soldiers in segregated units and on segregated posts. The numbers of African Americans entering the army increased rapidly, so that the all-black units could no longer absorb all black enlistees. The white units, however, especially on the front line, were in dire need of new recruits. The military eventually began to integrate African Americans on posts and in combat units. Military integration increased morale for black and white soldiers alike. Military performance improved and the troops became more effective.

During the three-year war, at least 600,000 African Americans served and about 3,200 died in action. The African American community welcomed the integration of the armed forces in the Korean War, observing its progress and criticizing its flaws. As in preceding wars, many African Americans believed that black military service and participation in the war would help improve the status of their race and propel them toward full equality. The majority of the black press celebrated the performance of African Americans in the war and showcased it as proof of the patriotic dedication of the black community and the untenability of the argument of white racial superiority.

In 1954, the military declared that the armed forces were officially desegregated. This was certainly not the case

Men from the 24th Infantry Regiment, the U.S. Army's first all-black unit, move up to the firing line in Korea on July 18, 1950. (National Archives)

on all levels. Furthermore, this assertion did not solve the problem of continuing racism within the military. Race still played an important role in assessing, sometimes unfairly, the performance of African Americans. Nevertheless, with military desegregation and the Korean War, a microcosm and rather conservative force of American society was fundamentally altered.

On the home front, the Korean War amplified the anticommunist hysteria and McCarthyism. Critics, whether affiliated with communism or not, were monitored, restricted, and chastised. The fear of McCarthyism and the pressure of Cold War conformity were omnipresent. These developments negatively affected the African American quest for civil rights by reducing Truman's civil rights activism and by stifling more radical forms of activism that had proved so powerful during the World War II. The Civil Rights movement felt pressured to limit its more radical mass movement activism and its affiliation to left-wing groups.

The majority of the African American Civil Rights movement backed the government's anticommunist quest and initially the Korean War effort. It often relied on Cold War rhetoric to solicit civil rights and assess the events in Southeast Asia. The integration of the armed forces furthered their support for the war. Many viewed the war as a necessary and appropriate tool against the spread of communism and, as such, believed that African Americans should participate.

The African American attitude toward the Korean War shifted between support for and criticism of the American "police action" because of its latent racist underpinnings. Only a minority of African Americans, however, dared openly oppose the seemingly pervasive anticommunist consensus. Black dissenters were enraged by being denied equal rights at home while being recruited to fight for democracy that did not exist for them in the United States. Those who dared to speak up were assigned the devastating label of "communist sympathizers" and were thereby discredited and silenced. Leading antiwar African American activists, like Paul Robeson and W. E. B. Du Bois, were chastised for their open protest of the war.

See also: Cold War and Civil Rights; Du Bois, W. E. B.; Jim Crow; Robeson, Paul

Christine Knauer

Bibliography

Bogart, Leo, ed. *Project Clear: Social Research and the Desegregation of the United States Army.* New Brunswick: Transaction Publishers, 1992.

Fousek, John. *To Lead the Free World: American Nationalism & the Cultural Roots of the Cold War.* Chapel Hill: The University of North Carolina Press, 2000.

Fried, Richard M. *Nightmare in Red: The McCarthy Era in Perspective.* New York: Oxford University Press, 1990.

Marable, Manning. *Race, Reform, and Rebellion: The Second Reconstruction in Black America, 1945–1990.* Jackson: University Press of Mississippi, 1991.

Mershon, Sherrie, and Steven Schlossman. *Foxholes & Color Lines: Desegregating the U.S. Armed Forces.* Baltimore: Johns Hopkins University Press, 1998.

Mullen, Robert W. *Blacks in America's Wars: The Shift in Attitudes from the Revolutionary War to Vietnam.* New York: Monad Press, 1973.

Nalty, Bernard C. *Strength of the Fight: A History of Black Americans in the Military.* New York: Free Press, 1986.

Ku Klux Klan

During Reconstruction (1866–1877), agents of the Democratic Party revived the tradition of pre-Civil War regulators and slave patrols to create paramilitary vigilante groups. These secretive ritual fraternities, quickly subsumed under the label Ku Klux Klan, endeavored to counter the Freedman's Bureau, destroy the Republican Party infrastructure, reestablish control over black labor, and restore racial subordination in all aspects of Southern political, economic, and social life. Klansmen murdered thousands and terrorized tens of thousands of prominent Republicans, merchants who bought from and sold to freedmen, landowners who rented land to freemen, independent black farmers and railway workers, and indeed, any black person who breached the code of social deference.

Conflating sexual fear and partisan politics, Klansmen posed as chivalrous avengers of victimized white womanhood, their chosen symbol of the white South. They asserted their own racial privileges by forcing Republicans to engage in sexual acts, raping black women, and sexually mutilating black men. Although localized and lacking synchronization, Klan violence, including uncounted whippings, beatings and rapes, murders, and massacres played a major role in disarming black militia and preventing black voting in at least eight states.

Republican parties were destroyed at the local level and in many cities, while Georgia and Louisiana succumbed to white supremacy. The Republican-controlled Congress responded with a series of Enforcement Acts that broke the Klan in 1872, but by that time the terrorists had served their purpose. After 1873, when Congress defeated the anti-Klan Enforcement Act and the Supreme Court ruled that the Fourteenth and Fifteenth Amendments did not protect violations of civil rights by private parties, remaining Reconstruction governments steadily collapsed before white paramilitaries and mob intimidation. Although other paramilitary groups such as Mississippi's "whitecappers" sprung up in the mid-1890s and mid-1900s, lynching and the legal system maintained a rigid caste system in the South for the next four decades.

During this period, American history textbooks lauded Klansmen as heroes who had redeemed the South from a corrupt regime. Thomas Dixon's 1905 novel *The Klansmen* popularized this view, portraying Klansmen as latter-day Galahads who had resorted to violence only under extreme provocation. Using revolutionary cinematic techniques, D. W. Griffith adapted the novel for his 1915 epic film *The Birth of a Nation*. The film portrayed freedmen as beasts who dragged Southern society into anarchy. In the climactic scene, mounted Klansmen rode in to save the white heroine from rape, to castrate and lynch her African American assailant, and to redeem the South by ending fratricide among white men and reuniting the nation.

The film inspired circuit-riding minister and fraternal organizer Col. William Simmons to revive the Klan and combat modern sexuality, slackers, and aliens. The Second Klan was confined to Georgia and Alabama until 1920,

Members of the Ku Klux Klan (KKK) burn a cross in Swainsboro, Georgia, on February 4, 1948. (Library of Congress)

when Simmons employed anti-Saloon League veteran and tenement activist Elizabeth Tyler and her companion in the Southern Publicity Association, Edward Clarke. The two agents used modern advertising and mass marketing techniques to study local communities, identify the political and social concerns of conservative Protestants, and employ recruiters to offer membership in the Knights of the Ku Klux Klan. Although strongest in the upper Midwest and West, the secret fraternal order quickly spread across the nation. By the mid-1920s, the Second Klan had become a predominantly urban, mainstream social movement of 4 million members that represented a cross section of white Protestant denominations and social classes. In the context of the time, these Klansmen were no more reactionary, racist, ethnocentric, religiously bigoted, or socially alienated than the general white Protestant population. Klansmen propounded anti-Catholic and anti-Semitic nativism, especially in the North and West, but black migration to urban areas also created small-business, employment, and housing competition, posing a direct challenge to conservative conceptions of America as an Anglo Saxon Protestant nation.

Racist ideology was central for the smaller Klan units that engaged in vigilante violence against blacks in the South. Here Klansmen also assaulted whites for a variety of moral offenses, but terrorized blacks for voting, owning property, or defending themselves against white violence. Armed supporters of Mary McLeod Bethune stood down a squad of Klansmen in Daytona, Florida during the 1920 election, but six blacks and two whites were killed in the central Florida town of Ocee during a mob attack on black voters. Three years later, Klansmen joined a mob of 250 whites that destroyed Rosewood, a mostly black town in Levy County and, according to survivors, killed 40 black residents. Sexual scandals and the failure to enforce Prohibition led to decline after 1925, but Klan activity never disappeared in parts of the South. Where racist rhetoric remained apocalyptic, Klansmen used extralegal coercion, lynching, flogging with rawhide straps, and other forms of vigilante violence to terrorize and murder African Americans. As economic destitution, unionization, and New Deal programs combined to undermine white supremacy during the 1930s, Klansmen fused racism with anticommunism to prevent black men from entering the skilled trades. In Alabama and Georgia, urban police, rural sheriffs, and Klansmen worked together to terrorize labor organizers in

the steel plants and cotton fields. In Florida, the Tampa seaman's union and the United Citrus workers were attacked. Klan vigilantes also flogged and murdered union organizers in cities such as Dallas and Atlanta.

World War II provided a new context, as black veterans spearheaded the Double Victory campaign. The largest Klan was concentrated in Georgia, but Klans also grew in Alabama, Florida, and North Carolina. Despite the tireless efforts of anti-Klan activists such as Stetson Kennedy to mobilize the Justice Department against them, Klan terrorists responded to African American activism with arson and dynamite, targeting black businesses, homes, and churches in the 1940s and early 1950s. Florida Klansmen dynamited integrated housing projects and murdered two black men in 1951. On Christmas Eve, Klansmen and police assassinated Florida NAACP activist Harry Moore and his wife, detonating a bomb they had planted in their bedsprings. Federal authorities managed to convict only three Klansmen on perjury counts, and Moore's murderers walked free. Klansmen terrorized Dade County landowner Mamie Clay and flogged a group of her friends whom police had arrested and turned over to them; however, federal authorities convicted a sheriff on civil rights violations. Federal and state prosecutions were also very successful in the Carolinas in 1953, where scores of Klansmen, including a police chief, had engaged in a two-year campaign of cross-border terror.

Implementation of the 1954 Supreme Court decision in *Brown v. Board of Education* in the border states led to the organization of Citizens' Councils by middle-class whites throughout the South. The ultimate failure of massive resistance, however, turned people toward the Klan. Alabama Klansmen bombed black homes and churches in Montgomery and abducted and castrated black handyman Edward Aaron near Birmingham. During a 15-month period in 1957–1958, 46 bombs exploded at black and Jewish institutions in Miami, Jacksonville, Nashville, and Atlanta. In the Deep South, the politics of massive resistance retreated in the face of accelerating direct action protests after 1960. The beginning of token school desegregation, combined with federal enforcement of the Civil Rights Act of 1964 and the Voting Rights Act, spurred tens of thousands of lower-middle class and working class whites to join Klans in the urban and Piedmont South. Vigilantes were often sponsored by local police: Birmingham police gave Klansmen full license to beat the Freedom Riders in 1961, a sheriff deputized the Klansmen who led violent counter-demonstrations in St. Augustine Florida during 1963–1964, and the city government sponsored the Bogalusa, Louisiana Klan, which harassed demonstrators in 1965.

Klan violence also grew more lethal in the 1960s. In September 1963, Klansmen planted a massive bomb beneath the 16th Street Baptist Church in Birmingham Alabama. It exploded during Sunday church services, killing three little girls. In 1964, Georgia Klansmen killed black serviceman Lemuel Penn. In Mississippi 35 shootings, 30 bombings, 35 church burnings, 80 beatings, and at least 6 racially motivated murders took place during the first eight months of 1964. Fourteen died in civil rights-related killings that year and four more murders were perpetrated in 1965. Victims included two black teenagers and three civil rights workers who were murdered by police and Klansmen near Meridian during Freedom Summer. In 1967, Mississippi Klansmen killed Vernon Dahmer with a firebomb, the same method that had been used against Frank Morris in Ferriday Louisiana three years earlier. In rural Louisiana, a black self-defense force called the Deacons for Defense and Justice protected civil rights workers from white mobs and engaged in gun battles on nightriders, but Louisiana Klansmen killed pioneer Sheriff's Deputy O'Neal Moore. During the Selma to Montgomery march, Alabama Klansmen shot and killed civil rights worker Viola Liuzzo as an FBI informant made mental notes. The Klansmen who killed Penn, Dahmer, Liuzzo, and the three civil rights workers near Meridian were all convicted in federal court during the 1960s. One Klansmen was convicted of murder in the Birmingham church bombing in 1977, and a handful of others have been convicted between the 1990s and the opening decade of the 21st century. Yet the killers of Morris, Moore, and a number of other victims may never see a court of law.

Between 1964 and 1971, media -exposure, selective enforcement of local law, tax audits, and a FBI covert action program finally neutralized Klan violence. Klan membership declined to a few thousand, as white supremacy slowly changed from being an integral part of Southern life into an extremist ideology. Klans revived in the rural South during the late 1970s and attacked civil rights activists with weapons on a number of occasions. On November 3, 1979, a group of Klansmen and neo-Nazis, led by a police informant, fired on an interracial group of anti-Klan protesters in North Carolina, killing five. Despite television footage of the methodical killings, all were acquitted. In 1987, the Southern Poverty Law Center won a multimillion-dollar suit on behalf of the mother of Michael Donald, murdered by members of the United Klans of America, destroying the largest Klan organization in the country. By then, racists were joining neo-Nazi, skinhead, or Christian Identity groupings, and the Klans had splintered into a myriad of tiny groups. In general, however, as society changed around it, white supremacists lost touch with the mainstream. Although racists continue to commit racist murders, such as the brutal lynching of James Byrd Jr., in Jasper Texas in 1998, they are prosecuted and convicted by outraged jurors. The overwhelming majority of Americans today roundly condemn both white supremacist ideology and racist violence.

See also: Fifteenth Amendment; Fourteenth Amendment; Lynching; *The Birth of a Nation;* White Citizens' Council; White Mob Violence; White Supremacy

John Drabble

Bibliography

Chalmers, David. *Hooded Americanism: A History of the KKK.* New York: Franklin Watts, 1981.

Feldman, Glenn. *Politics, Society and the Klan in Alabama, 1915–1949.* Tuscaloosa: University of Alabama Press, 1999.

Hill, Lance. *The Deacons of Defense: Armed Resistance and the Civil Rights Movement.* Chapel Hill: University of North Carolina Press, 2004.

Jackson, Kenneth T. *The Ku Klux Klan in the City, 1915–1930.* New York: Oxford University Press, 1967.

MacLean, Nancy. *Beyond the Mask of Chivalry: The Making of the Second Ku Klux Klan.* New York: Oxford University Press, 1994.

Nelson, Scott Reynolds. *Iron Confederacies: Southern Railways, Klan Violence and Reconstruction.* Chapel Hill: North Carolina University Press, 1999.

Newton, Michael. *The Invisible Empire: The Ku Klux Klan in Florida.* Gainesville: University Press of Florida, 2001.

Newton, Michael and Judy Ann. *The Ku Klux Klan: An Encyclopedia.* New York: Garland, 1991.

Trelease, Allen W. *White Terror: The Ku Klux Klan Conspiracy and Southern Reconstruction.* Baton Rouge: Louisiana University Press, 1999.

Wade, Wyn Craig. *The Fiery Cross: The Ku Klux Klan in America.* New York: Simon and Schuster, 1987.

Lawson, James

A founder of the Student Nonviolent Coordinating Committee (SNCC), James Morris Lawson Jr. (1921–) participated in many of the significant civil rights initiatives of the 1960s including the Nashville sit-ins, the Freedom Rides, and the Memphis sanitation strike. Born on September 22, 1928, in Uniontown, Pennsylvania to the Reverend James M. Lawson Sr. and Philane Cover, Lawson grew up in Massillon, Ohio, where his father was pastor of a Methodist church. After graduating high school, Lawson studied sociology at Baldwin Wallace College in Berea, Ohio. While at Baldwin Wallace, he received notice to report for military service. Because he was a committed pacifist, Lawson refused to serve. As a result he was convicted of draft evasion and sentenced to two years in prison. Lawson returned to Baldwin Wallace after serving 13 months of his sentence to finish his sociology degree.

After graduation, Lawson traveled to India as a missionary for the Methodist Church. While in India he was exposed to the nonviolent teachings of Mohandas K. Gandhi. As Lawson studied nonviolence, the philosophy was being applied in the American South by Martin Luther King Jr. in the Montgomery bus boycott. When he returned to the United States, Lawson met with King while he was a student at Oberlin College's school of theology. Profoundly moved by the struggle to dismantle segregation in the South, Lawson was determined to play a role in it. He was appointed southern regional director for the Fellowship of Reconciliation (FOR), an organization devoted to nonviolence.

After one year of study at Oberlin College, he enrolled in Nashville's Vanderbilt Divinity School. While in Nashville, Lawson married Dorothy Wood and they had three sons: John, Morris, and Seth. In addition to his position with the Fellowship of Reconciliation, Lawson was also appointed projects director for the Nashville chapter of Martin Luther King's Southern Christian Leadership Conference (SCLC). In these roles he conducted workshops on Christian nonviolence for students from Nashville's African American colleges: American Baptist, Fisk, Meharry Medical, and Tennessee A&I.

Several of Lawson's students, inspired by his commitment to nonviolence, launched sit-in demonstrations at several downtown Nashville lunch counters on February 13, 1960. The demonstrations continued until May 10, when government and businesses leaders agreed to desegregate downtown stores. Lawson's leadership during the Nashville sit-ins made him one of the leading civil rights figures in the American South. But there was a cost. Angered over Lawson's leadership of the sit-ins, Vanderbilt

Chancellor Harvie Branscomb expelled him in March 1960. Undeterred, Lawson completed his divinity degree at Boston University and continued to spread the gospel of Christian nonviolence.

As the Nashville sit-ins reached their climax, Lawson traveled to Raleigh, North Carolina's Shaw University in April 1960 to attend a gathering of students committed to the civil rights struggle. At this meeting SNCC was formed to expand civil disobedience throughout the South. In May 1961 the Congress of Racial Equality (CORE) adopted nonviolence with its Freedom Ride demonstrations. The rides were designed to pressure President John F. Kennedy and the Interstate Commerce Commission to enforce a 1960 Supreme Court declaring segregated bus terminals unconstitutional. When demonstrators were attacked by an angry white mob in Montgomery, Alabama, Lawson joined the effort. Boarding a bus at Montgomery, Lawson and several other Nashville sit-in veterans journeyed to Jackson, Mississippi where they were arrested and sentenced to 30 days in the state penitentiary at Parchman. When Lawson was released from prison, he returned to divinity school in Boston.

After graduation from Boston University, Lawson was appointed pastor of Scott Church in Shelbyville, Tennessee, and in 1962 he was assigned to Centenary Methodist in Memphis. Although the elimination of racism and segregation was Lawson's primary focus, he did look beyond the struggle in the South. The Memphis pastor also expanded his promotion of Christian nonviolence to include the controversial war in Vietnam. In 1965, he traveled to Southeast Asia as a representative of the Fellowship of Reconciliation's Clergymen's Emergency Committee on Vietnam. While in Southeast Asia the committee met with a cross section of people including students, U.S. and South Vietnamese government leaders, North Vietnamese soldiers, and labor leaders. Upon their return Lawson and the other committee members issued a report calling on the United Nations to intervene in the conflict to bring peace to the region. Although Lawson remained concerned about the war in Vietnam, events in Memphis led him to again confront American racism.

In February 1968, sanitation workers, poorly paid and forced to endure unsafe conditions, spontaneously walked off the job. When Memphis Mayor Henry Loeb refused to negotiate, the strike became much more than a labor dispute. Because workers were predominantly African

American and desperately poor, Lawson joined their struggle and emerged as the most eloquent civil rights leader in Memphis. Drawing on his involvement in SNCC, Lawson and other leaders formed the Committee on the Move to Equality (COME). Lawson extended an invitation to Dr. King to speak in Memphis, which led to King's death in April 1968. Lawson continued to agitate for social change in Memphis until he moved to Los Angeles in 1974 to pastor Holman United Methodist Church. In 1982, he chaired the Peace Sunday Movement, which staged a large demonstration at the Rose Bowl. Lawson retired from the pulpit in 1999 but remains one of America's most eloquent leaders in the ongoing struggle to achieve social progress by just and peaceful means.

See also: CORE; Freedom Rides; King, Martin Luther Jr.; Lewis, John; Nash, Diane; Sit-In Movement; Student Nonviolent Coordinating Committee; Southern Christian Leadership Conference

Gerald Wayne Dowdy

Bibliography

Beifuss, Joan Turner. *At the River I Stand: Memphis, the 1968 Strike, and Martin Luther King.* Memphis: B & W Books, 1985.

Branch, Taylor. *At Canaan's Edge: America in the King Years, 1965–68.* New York: Simon & Schuster, 2006.

Halberstam, David. *The Children.* New York: Random House, 1998.

League of Revolutionary Black Workers

The League of Revolutionary Black Workers was officially launched in Detroit, Michigan in October 1967 after the Detroit Rebellion of that same year. It was the final outcome of a combination of independent black industrial labor-related movements in the Detroit metropolitan area. The league grew as a result of the United Auto Workers (UAW) failure to address the racist and inhumane working conditions of black people employed in Detroit's manufacturing sector. It consisted of radical, prolific blue-collar black workers with strong organizational skills. Historic and heroic struggles of black people provided the movement's strengths, inspiration was garnered by the revolutionary struggles of the developing world, and their convictions were guided by a

Marxist-Leninist ideology. The league's goal was to unify black workers across Detroit.

In the 1960s, the UAW began to lose touch with minority members whose weekly organizational fees were deducted from their wages, although they had little representation on the organization's board of directors. Black workers held the view that the UAW was racist, oppressive, and not representative of their needs. The league developed out of the frustration of black workers who grew weary of the UAW's failure to meet their demands about improving their working conditions. Their demands were not unfounded, as the historical record reveals factory owner's productivity strategies that center on forced labor of black workers to work harder and faster in unsafe and unhealthy conditions. Throughout the late 1960s and early 1970s, conditions at the plants continued to deteriorate. Management hid these problems from outsiders, projecting plant life as harmonious and well paid. Unions were often loosely organized and too polarized to project to outsider a real picture of what was actually happening in the plants. The league arose in response to these conditions.

The League of Revolutionary Black Workers united radical black organizing activists in Detroit's factories, neighborhoods, high schools, and colleges and university campuses against the horrendous racially charged circumstances that dominated life for black workers in the 1960s and 1970s. Revolutionary Union Movements (RUMs), built by ordinary black workers from Detroit's auto factories were at the heart of the league. The RUMs effectively organized black workers to resist the racist and exploitive conditions in these factories and within the white-dominated UAW that officially represented the workers.

General Gordon Baker, John Watson, John Williams, Luke Tripp, Kenneth Cockrel, Mike Hamlin, and Chuck Wooten sat on the league's seven-man executive committee. Hamlin, Watson, and Cockrel held leadership positions and provided different but equal strengths to the mission of the organization. Hamlin embodied the stance that favored community building and student support, which enabled the league to carry out demonstrations when court injunctions stopped workers from protesting. Watson advocated the power of and need for an independent newspaper that would educate the public and challenge the ruling elite's power structure. In 1967, he actualized his vision through his editorial position on Wayne State University's student paper the *South End.* Watson used the paper as a political arm for all radical revolutionary groups throughout the Detroit metropolitan area. He supported the equal publication of all views, and the paper was widely distributed to segments outside the university, including automobile factories. Cockrel provided legal expertise; he served the league by filing for a nonprofit status and keeping league activities within the law to avoid convictions from criminal and civil actions. The league's awareness of the reality of this aspect of organizing is how they differed from the Black Panther Party.

In 1971, the league began to take a different form and merged with the Black Workers Congress whose manifesto centered on worker's rights, worker's demands, the elimination of racism, the liberation of women, and foreign policy questions. The Black Workers Congress had a strong beginning but petered out, as it was unable to put its ideology into practice and spent the majority of its time in meetings and setting up, but not applying, potential agendas. Eventually, the former members of the league dropped out and formed the Communist League, which advocated a multiracial communist party based on the writings of Lenin and Marx. It accepted whites and all people from the developing world and emphasized the role of industrial workers and professional revolutionaries.

The legacy of the League of Revolutionary Workers is extensive. Despite repression from the joined forces of Chrysler, Ford, General Motors, the UAW, and Detroit and suburban police departments, it distributed mass circulation newspapers and plant bulletins, organized pickets and rallies, formed community and student groups, ran opposition union candidates, and led wildcat strikes that successfully shut down production. In these ways the league is responsible for building the last sustained mass revolutionary unions in the United States.

See also: Detroit, Michigan, Riot of 1967

Jill E. Rowe-Adjibogoun

Bibliography

Boggs, James. *The American Revolution: Pages from a Negro Worker's Notebook.* New York: Monthly Review Press, 1963.

Boyd, Herb, and Robert Allen. *Brotherman: The Odyssey of Black Men in America.* New York: One World, 1995.

Georgakas, Dan, and Marvin Surkin. *Detroit: I Do Mind Dying.* New York: St. Martin's Press, 1975.

Geschwender, James A. *Class, Race and Worker Insurgency: The League of Revolutionary Black Workers.* New York: Cambridge University Press, 1977.

Gould, William. *Black Workers in White Unions.* Ithaca, NY: Cornell University Press, 1977.

Mast, Robert, ed., *Detroit Lives.* Philadelphia: Temple University Press, 1994.

Meier, August, and Elliot Rudwick. *Black Detroit and the Rise of the UAW.* New York: Oxford University Press, 1979.

Lee, Spike

Shelton Jackson Lee (1957–), or "Spike" Lee, is best known for his popular black films like *Do the Right Thing, Jungle Fever,* and *Mo' Better Blues.* Affectionately terming his films "Spike Lee Joints," much of Lee's work primarily consists of race films like his *Bamboozled* and *Get on the Bus* that have been produced by Lee's own company, 40 Acres & a Mule Filmworks. In addition to these, Lee's impressive filmography includes more than 45 film credits as director, and more than 70 film credits overall, serving as producer or writer in other films such as *Drop Squad* and *Tales from the 'Hood.* Moreover, in addition to his specifically black films, Lee's filmography also include mainstream motion pictures like *25th Hour* and *Inside Man* as well as a host of documentaries exploring sports figures like *Jim Brown: All American* and historical figures such as *A Huey P. Newton Story.*

As a director, Spike Lee is best known for his unique stylistic elements, which include signature close-up shots, repetition, and montage just to name a few. Spike Lee joints are typically identified by the number of scenes with the actor and camera both placed on a dolly, such as Pierre Delacroix's circular motion that introduces the plot of *Bamboozled* or his use of montage to advance the story of "Indigo" and "Clark" confronting a cheating "Bleak Gilliam" in *Mo' Better Blues.* Also, the small cadre of black actors including Denzel Washington, his sister Joie Lee, and Delroy Lindo help to distinguish a Spike Lee film when they are all cast together. And last, the regular practice of casting his own part in the film is another Spike Lee feature that began with his first film. Much of Lee's unique style and critical acclaim began with *She's Gotta Have It,* which was noted both for the film itself, as well as for Lee's part as "Mars Blackmon." Shot at one location in black and white, and edited in Lee's own apartment, *She's Gotta Have It* was made with only $175,000 and in 12 days but went on to gross over $7 million in box office receipts. Many of the elements first attempted in *She's Gotta Have It* have since

Film director Spike Lee. (Onestepbeyond70/Dreamstime)

been refined and now continue to punctuate Lee's larger body of work.

Over the course of Lee's career, the reception of his brand of filmmaking has oscillated between controversial and celebratory, garnering much debate for his depiction of women (in films like *Girl 6*) while also hailed for its ability to represent communities of African Americans through popular cinema. His heavy-handed artistic touch makes films like *Malcolm X* an important piece for scholars of black film because of its mixed reception—critiqued by some for its historical inaccuracy, but also applauded as an artistic endeavor heavily supported by black celebrities like Janet Jackson and Michael Jordan who funded its completion. Lee's style and politics almost force a commitment to his vision that not only congeals his films into a single body of work across film genres, but also compel his fervor to finance his own films.

Viewers of Lee's work will also find pieces of the director's own biography dispersed throughout the films, and across characters in a single film. So Spike Lee's life story beginning with his birth in Atlanta Georgia on March 20, 1957 to Bill Lee, a jazz musician, and Jacquelyn Lee, a schoolteacher, is signaled in the parents of "Bleek Gilliam" in *Mo' Better Blues*. And although Lee moved to Brooklyn, New York, during adolescence to complete his secondary education before returning to Atlanta for college, the

significance of Brooklyn as a backdrop is iterated across his entire body of work. Lee even found a fictional place for the actual loss of his mother on screen, by interspersing the story of migration between New York and Atlanta with the story of a family losing its matriarch in *Crooklyn*. Lee's filmic portrayal of the historically black college experience retold through *School Daze* also speaks to his own choice to follow in the footsteps of his father and grandfather and attend Morehouse College in Atlanta, Georgia.

Developing his film interests in college, Lee quickly gained recognition for his talent. Upon completing a bachelor degree, he went on to New York University film school where he made award-winning films "the Answer" to D. W. Griffith's *The Birth of a Nation* and *Joe's Bed-Stuy Barbershop: We Cut Heads* as a graduate student. Since then Lee has firmly established himself as a noted black filmmaker. Although he has yet to receive an Academy Award, he has been recognized with a nomination for best documentary for his film *Four Little Girls*, while his *When the Levees Broke: A Requiem in Four Acts* went on to win the Human Rights Film Award and the Venice Horizons Documentary Award at the 2006 Venice Film Festival.

See also: Bombingham; Million Man March; *The Birth of a Nation*; X, Malcolm

Jasmine Nichole Cobb

Bibliography

Arnold, David. *Pocket Essential: Spike Lee.* London: Herts, 2003.

Bogle, Donald. *Toms, Coons, Mulattoes, Mammies, and Bucks: An Interpretive History of Blacks in American Films,* 3rd ed. New York: Continuum, 1994.

Cobb, Jasmine Nichole, and John L. Jackson Jr. "They Hate Me: Spike Lee, Documentary Filmmaking, and Hollywood's 'Savage Slot.'" In *Fight the Power! The Spike Lee Reader,* Janice D. Hamlet and Robin Means Coleman, eds., 251–72. New York: Peter Lang Publishers, 2008.

Lewis, John

John Lewis (1940–) was a student leader in the Civil Rights movement, serving as chair of the Student Nonviolent Coordinating Committee (SNCC) from 1963 to 1966. Lewis was born on February 21, 1940, in rural Alabama, one of 10 children. His parents were poor sharecroppers who managed to buy their own small farm when Lewis was four. As a boy, he made his playmates listen to impromptu sermons he gave, and he imagined becoming a pastor. As he grew older, he heard Martin Luther King's radio preaching, and at 16, Lewis's pastor allowed him to give his first sermon. He was in high school when the Montgomery bus boycott started.

In 1957, he went to American Baptist Theology (ABT) Seminary in Nashville, Tennessee, a school that allowed students to work in exchange for tuition. He met James Bevel at ABT, another man who would emerge as a leader. The next year Lewis met James Lawson and began studying the principles of nonviolence with him. Nashville students began having regular workshops in preparation for nonviolent actions protesting segregation in the future, which included role-playing sessions in which some students would pretend to be segregationists while others acted as protestors.

On February 1, 1960, four African American students sat at a whites-only lunch counter in Greensboro, North Carolina. Lewis and his peers had been preparing for a moment like this, and the Nashville sit-ins began February 13. Within a couple of weeks, protestors were being attacked and arrested. This movement was eventually successful, and Nashville's lunch counters were integrated. Following the spread of the sit-in movement throughout the South, students formed SNCC in April, and Lewis was a major organizer. In the wake of the sit-ins, northern universities began inviting Lewis and other leaders to speak about the movement.

In 1961, Lewis took part in the Freedom Rides, designed to test a Supreme Court ruling banning segregation on interstate buses. The interracial group of riders planned to board buses in Washington, D.C. and ride them to New Orleans. Lewis had to leave the original group early because of an obligation, but he returned to Nashville to organize additional riders to keep the rides going in light of the violence the original riders endured. Lewis left with a group from Nashville and faced a violent mob at Birmingham's terminal. When Lewis disembarked in Montgomery, he faced a worse situation, and mobs beat Lewis and other riders severely. Police arrested riders in Jackson, Mississippi; they were eventually sent to Parchman Prison. Hundreds of other students, witnessing these events, began following Lewis's path on buses throughout the South.

Lewis and his peers next turned their efforts to discrimination against African Americans in employment.

The Nashville Student Movement (NSM) picketed and boycotted Nashville stores that took African Americans' money but would not employ them. In the fall, Lewis enrolled at Fisk University and became chair of the NSM.

In June 1963, Lewis was elected as SNCC's Chair, and he moved to Atlanta to fulfill his duties. He thus was one of the "Big Six" civil rights leaders at the August 1963 March on Washington. Lewis also gave one of the speeches at the March, although other leaders pressured him to revise his speech because they thought it too inflammatory. He and his SNCC colleagues did so moments before the speech was to begin.

Lewis continued working on a variety of civil rights projects. Major ones included the Mississippi Freedom Democratic Party (MFDP), which would run a slate of African American candidates in that state, and Freedom Summer in 1964, which would bring hundreds of white volunteers from the North into Mississippi, well known as the most dangerous southern state for civil rights workers. In fact, on June 21, the day the first wave of volunteers began their journey South, three civil rights workers were murdered, one African American and two whites. The results of Lewis's and his colleagues' efforts in Mississippi were mixed: many African Americans registered to vote, but the Democratic Party refused to seat the MFDP's delegation at its August convention.

After Freedom Summer, SNCC faced increasing organizational problems. Because of its growth, it was becoming difficult for committee members to continue making decisions by consensus. In addition, more and more SNCC workers were becoming less attached to nonviolence as a tactic, whereas others, like Lewis, remained deeply committed to it as a philosophy. SNCC had projects in operation all over the South, and although Lewis tried to keep abreast of all of them, in January 1965, he turned his attention to voter registration in Selma, Alabama. This action involved potential voters marching to the courthouse and attempting to register, where they were refused entrance and often arrested or beaten.

In the wake of a protestor's death—police shot him in the stomach as he tried to protect his mother from a beating—Lewis and others organized a march from Selma to Montgomery. The day the march was to begin, March 7, is now known as "Bloody Sunday" because mounted police severely beat, stomped, and tear gassed protestors as they attempted to cross the Edmund Pettus Bridge. Lewis led the marchers and was among the first to be beaten; he had to be hospitalized with a fractured skull.

After the Civil Rights Act of 1964 and Voting Rights Act of 1965 passed, the already-simmering issues of African American separation and the rejection of nonviolence came to the fore within SNCC. In May 1966, at the end of SNCC's annual meeting, in this case a long, contentious, and emotion-filled one, SNCC elected the fiery Stokely Carmichael as chair, replacing Lewis. He remained with SNCC for a short time, leaving in the wake of controversy over the June Meredith March in Mississippi and the emergence of the black power slogan.

Since leaving SNCC, Lewis has most recently served as the U.S. Representative from Georgia's 5th District, representing Atlanta since 1986. Before becoming a member of Congress, he worked on the Voter Education Project in the South and then in the Carter administration as associate director of ACTION, which oversaw volunteer programs. He also served on Atlanta's City Council, taking office in 1982.

See also: Black Power; Bloody Sunday; Freedom Rides; Lawson, James; March on Washington, 1963; Mississippi Freedom Summer, 1964; Selma March; Sit-In Movement; Student Nonviolent Coordinating Committee

Erin Boade

Bibliography

Arsenault, Raymond. *Freedom Riders: 1961 and the Struggle for Racial Justice.* New York: Oxford University Press, 2006.

Branch, Taylor. *At Canaan's Edge: America in the King Years 1965–68.* New York: Simon & Schuster, 2006.

Branch, Taylor. *Parting the Waters: America in the King Years 1954–63.* New York: Simon & Schuster, 1988.

Branch, Taylor. *Pillar of Fire: America in the King Years 1963–65.* New York: Simon & Schuster, 1998.

Carson, Clayborne. *In Struggle: SNCC and the Black Awakening of the 1960s.* Cambridge, MA: Harvard University Press, 1995.

Hogan, Wesley. *Many Minds, One Heart: SNCC's Dream for a New America.* Chapel Hill: University of North Carolina Press, 2007.

Lewis, John, and Michael D'Orso. *Walking with the Wind: A Memoir of the Movement.* New York: Simon & Schuster, 1998.

Little Rock Nine

In the battle for school integration, nine black students became heroes to civil rights supporters when they enrolled at Central High School in Little Rock, Arkansas, for the 1957 school year. The "Little Rock Nine," as the students were known, participated in one of the more famous integration conflicts, as white students and parents actively opposed their attempt to integrate the Little Rock school district. After the *Brown v. Board of Education* decision, in which the Supreme Court ruled segregation illegal in public schools, members of the Little Rock School Board began working on a plan for integration. After three years of deliberations and controversy, the board settled on a plan that would gradually integrate the district, beginning with high schools in the 1957–1958 school year. Initially, the board selected 17 black students to attend Central High, but by August, the number had dwindled to 9. A group of anti-integration Central High parents, called the Mother's League, sought a federal injunction to stop the school from integrating, but a judge refused their request. The students planned to enter the school for the first time on September 3, 1957.

Orval Faubus, the governor of Arkansas, had not been as militant in his opposition to integration as some of his southern counterparts, but he ultimately decided to oppose the integration of Central High. The night before the students were scheduled to attend school there, he addressed the state via television. Claiming to have received word that white supremacists were traveling to Little Rock to prevent the integration of Central High, he ordered troops from the Arkansas National Guard to prevent any black students from entering the school. The students did not attend class the first day of school, but Daisy Bates, an official with the National Association for the Advancement of Colored People (NAACP), decided that the students should attempt to enter Central on September 4. The group planned to arrive at school together with Bates. Eight of the students did meet before school, but one student, Elizabeth Eckford, did not have a phone and was not aware of the plan. When the eight students arrived, they were shouted at and threatened by an angry mob of white segregationists. Members of the National Guard denied the students entrance into the school. Because of the violence, NAACP leaders decided to postpone integration until they could expect better conditions for the students.

Determined to enforce the orders of the federal courts, President Dwight Eisenhower arranged a meeting with Faubus. At the meeting, Faubus agreed to order National Guard troops to protect the students, but he later reneged on that promise. On September 20, a federal judge ruled that Governor Faubus could not legally use the Arkansas

National Guard to deny the students entrance into Central High. Although he expressed disappointment with the decision, Faubus accepted it and agreed not to send troops to the school. On September 23, the students planned to attend school. Before they arrived, another angry mob of white parents and segregation supporters gathered outside the school. They harassed and physically harmed several black reporters who were in Little Rock to cover the event. When the students arrived, the mob attacked them, shouting insults and threats. Although the students made it safely inside the building, by late morning the city police who were patrolling the school felt the mob was uncontrollable. Worried for the physical safety of the children if the mob overcame police barricades, school officials sent the students home out the back entrance of the school.

To ensure that the children could attend the school without threat of physical injury, President Eisenhower ordered the 101st Airborne Division into Little Rock to protect the students. With the troops' assistance, the students were able to attend school safely. To make sure that the students were safe once inside the building, members of the 101st served as escorts for them. After several months, the 101st troops left, and the students had to fend for themselves. They faced consistent persecution from their fellow students, including threatening letters, harassing phone calls, and physical abuse. Despite the harassment, the black students continued to attend school. Eight of the nine students completed the school year. Minnijean Brown was suspended in December for responding to harassment by pouring her soup on two white boys. She was expelled during the spring semester for insulting white students. Ernest Green was the only senior of the group. In May, he became the first black graduate of Central High School. The following school year, Governor Faubus closed down Little Rock schools in an effort to avoid further integration. When courts ruled his act unconstitutional, the school district was forced to integrate for the 1959 school year. Jefferson Thomas and Carlotta Walls, two of the original "Little Rock Nine," were the only two black students assigned to Central High. The students' ordeal was another example of tenacious white resistance to integration. The actions of the "Little Rock Nine" ensured that, despite the resistance, Little Rock schools would eventually integrate.

See also: Bates, Daisy; *Brown v. Board of Education;* National Association for the Advancement of Colored People

Blake A. Ellis

Bibliography
Bates, Daisy. *The Long Shadow of Little Rock: A Memoir.* Fayetteville: University of Arkansas Press, 1986.
Beals, Melba Pattillo. *Warriors Don't Cry: A Searing Memoir of the Battle to Integrate Little Rock's Central High.* New York: Washington Square Press, 1994.
Huckaby, Elizabeth. *Crisis at Central High, Little Rock, 1957–1958.* Baton Rouge: Louisiana State University Press, 1980.
Jacoway, Elizabeth, and C. Fred Williams, eds. *Understanding the Little Rock Crisis: An Exercise in Remembrance and Reconciliation.* Fayetteville: University of Arkansas Press, 1999.
Record, Wilson, and Jane Cassels Record, eds. *Little Rock, U.S.A.: Materials for Analysis.* San Francisco: Chandler, 1960.

Long Hot Summer Riots, 1965–1967

The term "Long Hot Summer" is often applied to the riots occurring in the United States during the spring and summer months of 1965, 1966, and 1967. These violent disturbances often began in hot weather, often required the assistance of the National Guard, and caused much financial damage, many arrests, and many deaths. They helped to point out to the nation the discrimination still prevalent at the time, as well the reforms needed to heal a nation divided by race.

Part of understanding the Long Hot Summer Riots is understanding the effect of the Great Migration. From about 1890 until 1965, black Americans from the South migrated to northern cities. They were looking for opportunity and a better life. In the South, there was violence against blacks, lynchings, and Jim Crow laws (laws that limited the voting rights of black Americans). And the primarily agricultural-based economy of the South was in trouble: there was an attack of the boll weevil as well as a drought. The North offered opportunity, especially during World War I when European immigration declined and there was a growing need for laborers in northern factories and businesses.

Typical of other immigrants, these black Americans who migrated to the North congregated in neighborhoods—most often in the older, less desirable parts of inner cities. But unlike other immigrants, blacks were excluded from moving into better neighborhoods because of discriminatory practices. In fact, segregation by neighborhoods continued into the latter part of the 20th century. (The Fair Housing Act of 1968 legally put an end to these practices.)

Continued discrimination, overcrowding, high unemployment, and inadequate schools made these neighborhood potential powder kegs, especially if their populations were aware of news being reported by the media.

Although the media did report on continuing civil rights gains before to the period of 1965 through 1967, they also presented images of racism and violence. In 1955, 14-year-old Emmett Till was lynched in Money, Mississippi, and pictures of his battered body appeared in *Jet* magazine. This was also the year of the highly publicized stance by Rosa Parks in Alabama. In 1957, media images showed federal troops in Little Rock as they enforced the desegregation of Central High School. In 1963, there were violent outbreaks in Savannah, Cambridge, Maryland, Philadelphia, Chicago, and especially in Birmingham, Alabama, where racists bombed a church, killing four little girls. In 1964, there were a number of disturbances and racially motivated murders: three civil rights leaders were lynched in Mississippi and law enforcement was implicated; blacks started using Molotov cocktails; a number of cities, including the New York neighborhoods of Harlem and Bedford Stuyvesant, had violent altercations. All of these events were reported in the media. Things were heating up.

Then, on August 11, 1965, in the Watts neighborhood of Los Angeles in the middle of a summer heat wave, a simple incident ignited a major riot. A highway patrolman stopped a speeding black driver and arrested him for driving under the influence. A mob started to congregate and events escalated. Passing white motorists were dragged out of their cars and beaten; automobiles were overturned and set on fire. Eventually, the National Guard had to be called in to restore order. In all, 34 people were killed, nearly 4,000 people were arrested, and there was $35 million in damages.

In the spring of 1966, emotions again flared in Watts, although not to the extent they had the previous year. But in July, Chicago exploded with rock-throwing and fire-bombing. Again it required the National Guard to quell the violence. Three people were killed by stray bullets and there were 533 arrests. Within weeks, violence requiring the National Guard also broke out in the Hough neighborhood of Cleveland. Later the same month, the courts had to ban demonstrations by white extremists in Baltimore, Maryland. In all, 43 different cities had racially violent events in 1966.

In 1967, nearly 150 cities had racial disturbances. Those in Detroit and Newark were major. But it seemed that just as a violent situation in one city began to calm, violence broke out in another, from Nashville (April 7), to Jackson, Mississippi (May 10), to Houston (May 16) to Tampa (June 11), to Cincinnati (June 12), to Atlanta (June 17).

Then in July 1967, the two worst riots of the summer broke out, the first in Newark, New Jersey. Lasting from July 14 to July 17, the riots in Newark began in the Central Ward and spread into the downtown area. In the end, there was $10 million dollars in damage, 725 people injured, 1,500 arrested, and 23 people killed. The unemployment rate for black males between 16 and 19 was 37.8 percent, and there was a long history of perceived police brutality.

The Detroit riots began on July 23 and lasted for five days. The flash point for the violence was the arrests of 82 people who were at an after-hours bar celebrating the return of two Vietnam War veterans near the home of Danny Thomas, a Vietnam veteran who had been killed by a gang of white youths. The neighborhood became inflamed and the violence escalated. In the end, there was $22 million dollars in damage, 1,189 people injured, and 43 people killed—the youngest was 4 years old and the oldest, 68—and 7,000 people arrested.

As a result of all the violence, President Lyndon Johnson appointed a Commission on Civil Disorder on July 28, 1967 to be chaired by Governor Otto Kerner of Illinois. Their famous conclusion stated, "Our nation is moving toward two societies, one black, one white—separate and unequal" (*The Kerner Report*, p. 1).

See also: Detroit, Michigan, Riot of 1967; Johnson, Lyndon Baines; Kerner Commission Report; Los Angeles, California, Riot of 1965; Urban Ghetto; Urbanization

William P. Toth

Bibliography

Allen, Rodney F., and Charles H. Adair, ed. *Violence and Riots in Urban America*. Worthington, OH: Charles A. Jones Publishing, 1969.

Fuguitt, Glenn V., John A. Fulton, and Calvin L. Beale. *The Shifting Patterns of Black Migration from and into the Nonmetropolitan South, 1965–95*. Washington, DC: U.S. Department of Agriculture Rural Development Research Report No. 93, 2001.

The National Advisory Commission on Civil Disorders. *The Kerner Report*. New York: Pantheon, 1968.

Upton, James N. *A Social History of 20th Century Urban Riots*. Bristol, IN: Wyndham Hall Press, 1984.

Los Angeles, California, Riot 1965

The Los Angeles riot of 1965, also known as the Watts riot, or Watts rebellion, was one of the most explosive, racially charged civil disturbances of the 1960s. The riot began on August 11 when a white police officer, Lee W. Minikus, stopped Marquette Frye, a 21-year-old African American man, and Ronald Frye, his 22-year-old brother, for reckless driving. After Marquette, the driver, failed the standard Highway Patrol sobriety test, Minikus informed him that he was under arrest for drunk driving. Having arrived on a motorcycle with no way to take Marquette to jail, Minikus radioed for a police vehicle and a tow truck to remove the car from its location at 116th Street and Avalon Boulevard, a predominantly black neighborhood two blocks away from the Frye home in the Watts community.

After learning that Minikus would not release the car to him, Ronald went home to find his mother, hoping she could claim the vehicle and prevent impoundment. Mrs. Frye, Ronald, the tow truck, the patrol vehicle, and Minikus's motorcycle partner arrived simultaneously, as a growing number of residents and passers-by watched Marquette's arrest unfold. By this time, Minikus called in for more reinforcements as the number of onlookers quickly swelled from dozens to hundreds, intensifying tensions between the Frye family and the officers. These tensions erupted into violence within minutes when Mrs. Frye became enraged over the forcible arrest of Marquette. Witnesses grew increasingly more hostile, as Marquette, Ronald, and their mother fought with the arresting officers, leading to the subsequent arrest of the entire family. As the scene cleared, the crowd became irate, throwing bottles and rocks—even spitting—at officers, resulting in the arrests of two other African Americans who police alleged incited the crowd to violence.

Within hours of the arrests, rumors spread throughout the Watts community about police treatment of the Frye family, and those arrested from the crowd; chaos and rebellion ensued. A number of Watts community members engaged in violence and vandalism throughout the night and into the early hours of the morning. By the next day, police still failed to gain complete control over the pockets of disturbances erupting throughout Watts. Over the course of the next two days, local community activists, religious leaders, teachers, business owners, and the Los Angeles County Human Relations Committee worked to prevent further outbreaks of violence and destruction, but their efforts were largely unsuccessful. Violence, looting, and destruction permeated the Watts community and some adjacent areas for the next few days.

In an attempt to restore peace, then Governor Pat Brown sent the National Guard to quell the unrest. The arrival of National Guardsmen, however, only served to heighten tensions and spread the destruction into southeast Los Angeles. Guardsmen found it difficult to control each incidence of rebellion; they also found it difficult to distinguish African American victims of the riot from African American participants, prolonging the riot's end. Lasting six days, the riot left 34 people dead, more than 900 seriously injured, and 4,000 arrested, as well as more than $35 million in property damage and destruction.

To many white Americans, the rioting and destruction in Watts appeared to be a violent reaction to an isolated event. To others, the rioting was simply inexplicable, an unlawful and terrifying response to things of which they had no complete knowledge. Furthermore, media images and descriptions of African American rioters served to intensify already demonized perceptions of African Americans held by whites, who had little to no real contact with them. The Frye arrest symbolized much more for many of the residents of Watts, and rioting represented a dramatic solution to deeply rooted problems within the African American community that both the local and federal government ignored for decades.

When the rioting ended, Governor Brown enlisted the help of a government panel, the McCone Commission, to find reasons why the Watts community exploded as it had, and to provide details on what exactly occurred during the days of unrest. The McCone Commission, led by former CIA director John McCone, released a comprehensive report—*Violence in the City: An End or a Beginning?*—in December 1965 detailing their findings on the revolt, and pointing to several of its underlying determinants. The commission concluded that unemployment, underemployment, inadequate schooling, and a tense relationship between the Los Angeles Police Department and African American residents all contributed to the unfolding of the Watts riot. They also maintained that the presence and illegal activities of African American gangs and petty criminals were other important mitigating factors in the six-day rebellion.

Although the McCone Commission arrived at many accurate conclusions, in a sense, they were obvious, particularly to those living in African American communities in and around Los Angeles. Moreover, implicit and explicit prejudices about poor African Americans and Hispanic Americans informed the commission's conclusions. They overlooked and underestimated the persistence of conflicts within poor African American families caused by outside factors of unemployment, insufficient educational resources, and a lack of proper housing in Watts and other African American communities in Los Angeles. Furthermore, the report downplayed the ongoing problem of police brutality against African Americans by the Los Angeles Police Department, an issue which, by the 1960s, became more salient as its occurrences rose. Therefore, the assertion that the Los Angeles Police Department struggled to control African American criminal activity in Watts, without acknowledgement of its tendency to brutalize and terrorize African Americans—specifically young African American men—was a major failure in the McCone Commission report. This, however, was merely one of several instances within the report in which the McCone Commission overlooked or minimized the social and historical factors that led to the riot.

In the two decades before the Los Angeles riot, African Americans experienced extreme prejudice in the job and housing markets, and the same sources of discrimination largely excluded them from full participation in the American economy. Also, despite the gains of civil rights activists and organizations, such as Thurgood Marshall and the NAACP, forcing integration in the educational system through legislation, many schools throughout the United States remained segregated. White Americans fled into suburban communities to avoid sending their children to school with African American youths, allowing middle class African Americans to move into formerly white-occupied areas, and increasing the number of poor African American ghettoes throughout the nation. Despite the diligent efforts of civil rights activists to create greater African American inclusion in American society, African American communities continued to endure restrictive housing provisions limited to overcrowded urban areas, or underdeveloped suburban and rural areas. Likewise, employment opportunities for African Americans were often limited to positions of service to white Americans. In short, where African Americans did not create political, economic, educational, and social spaces in which they could participate

fully, few, if any, existed. The McCone Commission's failure, or inability, to recognize these overwhelming problems in the daily lives of many African Americans in Los Angeles reflects perhaps their greatest source of discontent, for it was an outgrowth of yet another point of frustration in African American life—invisibility.

High levels of segregation, poverty, and discrimination made African Americans, poor African Americans especially, in Los Angeles figuratively invisible to white and middle class Americans. At the very least, they were domestic, and public servants of varying sorts, those who lived on the other side of town. At most, they were agitators of racial integration and racial equality, or sources of racial conflict. Invisibility therefore, played a significant role in the actions of many African Americans during the Los Angeles riots. For some, it was an attempt at gaining national attention, a drastic move to expose the great inconsistencies within the professed American ideals of freedom and equality, and the praxis of those ideals. Indeed, a significant number of studies revealed that African American rioters did not randomly destroy property in Los Angeles, but that much of the property burned or looted belonged to business owners who discriminated against African American community members. Conversely, a significant number of rioters had no underlying political motives; the civil unrest provided an opportunity to commit crimes or provided access to things they would not have ordinarily afforded. Still others in the African American community did not participate in the riots; the extent of their involvement was through the media, or through voluntary aid to those seriously injured during the riots. Consequently, the commission's failure to address or acknowledge the issues vital to preventing further outbreaks of civil rebellion left many in the African American community disillusioned.

The feeling of disillusionment among African Americans was merely one of many impacts of the Los Angeles riot. Rioting in Watts, and its national media coverage, sparked rioting in hundreds of other cities around the United States throughout the 1960s. African American communities in New York City; Washington, D.C. Providence, Rhode Island; Hartford, Connecticut; Phoenix, Arizona; Chicago, Illinois; Cambridge, Massachusetts; Detroit, Michigan; and Jersey City, New Jersey all erupted into revolt. Each city had its own legacy of long-term social and political exclusion and discrimination. Watts and other African American communities in Los Angeles remained largely poor communities segregated from upper and middle class Los Angeles residents. The plight of poor African Americans in Los Angeles gained greater media coverage, and increased white Americans' awareness of their plight, but white American attitudes about African Americans shifted very little, if at all. White Americans now understood what happened in African American communities, but because of the riot, they were less inclined to sympathize, thus maintaining a strenuous relationship between white Americans and African Americans. Conversely, African American rioting in Los Angeles and other African American communities forced all Americans to rethink the nature and impact of race on all groups within the United States. For those who did riot with underlying political agendas, at least some part of their grievances was recognized. Still, gaining heightened recognition for the legion of problems plaguing inner-city black communities did not necessarily generate useful solutions. Yet another impact of the riot was the shift in African American leadership, from the older generation of African Americans who used legal strategies and nonviolent means of civil disobedience to address discrimination, to the younger generation who had lost faith in the previous strategies of political agitation and were not opposed to violent means of civil disobedience if necessary. This new leadership represented a shift in the African American Civil Rights movement that brought with it messages of cultural pride, nationalism, and empowerment, and gave rise to organizations such as the Black Panther Party and the black arts movement.

Perhaps the most discouraging impact of the riot in Los Angeles is the relative lack of change in the area. The lessons of the riot and its successors throughout the country have seemingly gone largely ignored. To a great extent, the problems that existed for many African American Los Angeles residents in the 1960s remain prevalent. The greatest example of this was the occurrence of the Los Angeles riots of 1992, which included residents of various economic, racial, and ethnic backgrounds. Nonetheless, there are many existing civil rights organizations within Los Angeles working to address the persisting problems of social injustice in Los Angeles.

See also: Kerner Commission Report; Johnson, Lyndon Baines; Long Hot Summer Riots, 1965–1967; Urban Ghetto; Urbanization

Lacey P. Hunter

Bibliography

Harding, Vincent, Robin D. G. Kelley, and Earl Lewis. "We Changed the World: 1945–1970." In *To Make Our World Anew: A History of African Americans.* Robin D. G. Kelley and Earl Lewis, eds., 445–542. New York: Oxford University Press, 2000.

Horne, Gerald. *The Fire This Time: The Watts Uprising and the 1960s.* Charlottesville: University Press of Virginia, 1995.

Johnson, Paula B., John B. McConahay, and David O. Sears. "Black Invisibility, the Press, and the Los Angeles Riot," *The American Journal of Sociology* 76, no. 4 (1971):698–721.

The McCone Commission. "Violence in the City: An End or a Beginning?" and Bullock, Paul [excerpts from] *Watts: The Aftermath.*" In *Taking it to the Streets: A Sixties Reader.* Alexander Bloom and Wini Breines, eds., 142–52. New York: Oxford University Press, 1995.

Los Angeles, California, Riot 1992

The ill-famed beating of a 25-year-old African American on March 3, 1991 and the equally notorious assault of a 33-year-old white truck driver on April 29, 1992, "bookended" 109 hours of violence and looting in Los Angeles, California, from April 29 through May 4, 1992. The toll of the Los Angeles Riot of 1992: 53 dead, 2,383 injured, 12,000 arrested, 7,000 fires, and 3,100 businesses damaged or destroyed, at a loss estimated at between $700 million and $1 billion, makes Los Angeles the site of the most deadly and costly riot in contemporary U.S. history.

The Los Angeles Riot of 1992 is a story of intersections. The intersection of Foothill Boulevard and Osborne Road in the middle-class Lake View Terrace neighborhood of Los Angeles is where George Holliday—an Argentinean-born plumbing supply salesman—videotaped the beating and arrest of Rodney G. King by four officers of the Los Angeles Police Department (LAPD) in the early morning hours of March 3, 1991, after King was pulled over for speeding. The intersection of West Florence and South Normandie Avenues in gritty South Central Los Angeles is where Reginald Denny was pulled from his truck, beaten and robbed by six young men in an expression of lawlessness, fueled ostensibly by rage at the April 29, 1992 acquittal of the four LAPD officers for the beating of King. Filmed from a helicopter hovering some 1,000 feet above Florence and Normandie, the Denny beating was broadcast live from coast to coast.

The video of two brutal beatings, at two starkly different intersections in America's second largest city, serves as an iconography of cause and effect. In the almost 20 years since the riot, scholarship has explored other intersections in attempts to explain why Los Angeles erupted in violence in 1992. For some scholars and students of urban America, the beating of King and the subsequent acquittal of Officers Laurence Powell, Timothy Wind, Theodore Briseno, and Sergeant Stacey Koon ignited decades of smoldering resentment against a police department at once praised and yet vilified for a "tough-on-crime" approach to policing that many saw as harboring a violent racism at its core. Such was the conclusion of an independent commission at the time of the Rodney King beating whose examination of the LAPD wrote of an alarming disregard for unwarranted force under the "color of law."

Other scholars point to economic disenfranchisement, paying particular attention to the decline of manufacturing in Los Angeles, and the concomitant growth of an increasingly suburban-centered service economy in the high-technology "knowledge-industries," as well as increasing competition for low-paying unskilled jobs among African Americans and Hispanics. A protracted economic recession in 1992 contributed to already high inner-city unemployment, which in turn contributed to an increase in the illegal drug trade, property crime, and assault. The impact of this recession on the chronically unemployed young men and women in the city of Los Angeles devastated an already distressed group at the margins. In 1992, unemployment approached 50 percent for inner-city youth. Rodney King was emblematic of the lives of the men and women of his generation. On March 3, 1991, King was an underemployed part-time usher at Dodger stadium who three months earlier was released from prison after serving time for an armed robbery.

In 1990, sociologist Theodore Caplow and his colleagues noted a 20-year decline in rioting and violent demonstration in the United States, which they attributed to the use of the courtroom and litigation as the primary mode of nonviolent struggle in the post-Civil Rights era. At first glance, the Los Angeles riot seems to belie this conclusion. Yet almost 48 hours after the verdict in the LAPD criminal trial, Rodney King broke his long silence to declare the he would have his day in court. King, perhaps more than anyone else, understood that the criminal prosecution of four police officers was not a final instance of justice denied. In a civil suit against the City of Los Angeles, King was awarded $3.8 million dollars in compensation for his brutal beating.

A 1993 federal civil rights trial against the four officers resulted in a guilty verdict against Powell and Koon for violating King's civil rights.

On April 29, 1992, acquittal mixed with hopelessness was the base for an alchemy of rage, not only for the beating of King, but for the violent death of 15-year-old Latasha Harlins, who was killed in Compton, California on March 16, 1991, just 10 days after the beating of Rodney King. Harlins was shot in the back of the head after an altercation with Soon Ja Du, a 49-year-old Korean-immigrant merchant who wrongly accused Harlins of stealing a container of orange juice. Convicted of voluntary manslaughter, Du was sentenced to five years probation, 400 hours of community service, and a $500.00 fine; the sentence was upheld on appeal. Harlins's brutal slaying was recorded by the store's security camera. Like the King videotape, the videotaped slaying of Latasha Harlins seemed to show that justice was yet again denied to an African American. The jury acquittal in the beating trial of the four LAPD officers *and* the sentence imposed on Du were the two events that caused the eruption of lawlessness and violence that began on the evening of April 29, 1992.

The Los Angeles riot began as a violent insurrection in response to a perception of the failure of the American system of justice. Anger and chaos during a period of economic decline quickly led to what witnesses described as a "party-like" atmosphere of gleeful looting by inner-city poor of all ages and races. Political pundits on the right attributed a "culture of poverty" to the looting; critics on the left viewed the riot as a response to nascent economic disenfranchisement resulting from globalization. Scholars of the "new media" place Holliday's videotape at the advent of "citizen-journalism," pointing out that Holliday's video led to sweeping reforms of the LAPD. Other analysts accuse the media of simplifying the King beating and particularly charge that the editing of the Holliday tape for broadcast left out important images of King that led the jury in the criminal trial to conclude that King was violently resisting arrest.

When Rodney King assured the public that he would have his day in court, he also pleaded, "Can we all get along?" This simple question goes to the heart of the agonizing history of conflict and social relations in the United States. It is the image of an unidentified young African American man, however, who, more than any other, captured the essence of the riot. Surrounded by antipolice graffiti, a photographer captured the young man just moments after he spray-painted the powerful message that emerged from Los Angeles in the Spring of 1992, *no justice, no peace.*

See also: Los Angeles, California, Riot of 1965; Urban Ghetto; Urbanization

David Alan Rego

Bibliography

Cannon, Lou. *Official Negligence: How Rodney King and the Riots Changed Los Angeles and the LAPD.* New York: Basic Books, 1999.

Gooding-Williams, Robert, ed. *Reading Rodney King, Reading Urban Uprising.* New York: Routledge, 1993.

Jacobs, Ronald F. *Race Media, and the Crisis of Civil Society: From the Watts Riots to Rodney King.* New York: Cambridge University Press, 2000.

Los Angeles Times. *Understanding the Riots: Los Angeles Before and after the Rodney King Case.* Los Angeles: Los Angeles Times, 1992.

Louima, Abner

In August 1997, Abner Louima (1966–) was beaten and sexually assaulted by New York Police Department (NYPD) officers at the 70th Precinct in Brooklyn. The Louima case, like the earlier Rodney King case in Los Angeles, exposed police brutality to the public. The abuse of Louima was also one of several instances of police violence against unarmed black men in New York City in the late 1990s and after. Ten years after the torture of Louima, the activist Reverend Al Sharpton stated, "Louima is to police-community relations what Selma was to the voter rights movement" ("One Man & One City Forever Changed").

Louima, then a security guard in his early thirties, had immigrated to the United States from Haiti in the early 1990s to escape political violence. On August 9, 1997, he was arrested for a crime he did not commit. Officer Justin Volpe, then 25 years old, arrested Louima after a fight broke out at Club Rendez-Vous in Flatbush, Brooklyn, falsely claiming Louima had hit him. The abuse began as Louima was transported to jail. Another man, Patrick Antoine, accused of being involved in the fight, was arrested and struck by police officers.

At the 70th Precinct station, Volpe, with the help of Officer Charles Schwarz, took Louima into a bathroom and beat him. Volpe sodomized him with a stick, the handle from a toilet plunger, tearing Louima's colon and bladder. Volpe then forced the stick into Louima's mouth and broke several teeth. The officers left Louima bleeding and half-naked on the dirty floor. Hours after the attack, an ambulance was summoned to bring Louima to a hospital. Police initially dismissed Louima's ruptured colon as the result of consensual sexual activity. A nurse doubted this explanation, and the case was reported to the NYPD Internal Affairs Bureau, which did not follow up on the call.

Louima's case came to public awareness when Mike McAlary of New York's *Daily News,* tipped off by NYPD officers, wrote a series of columns that eventually won the Pulitzer Prize for Commentary. Officer Eric Turetsky came forward soon after McAlary's series began, saying he saw Volpe and Schwarz go into the bathroom with Louima, and that Volpe proudly displayed the stick afterwards. (McAlary died of cancer in late 1998.)

In August 1997, thousands marched with members of Louima's family to City Hall to demand redress from Mayor Rudolph Giuliani. During Giuliani's term in office (1994–2001), the shooting deaths of two unarmed black men, Amadou Diallo in 1999 (an immigrant from West Africa), and Patrick Dorismond in 2000, kept police brutality a prominent issue. The city of New York paid more than $18 million in settlements in these cases and in police brutality cases that unfolded after Giuliani left office. Louima received a settlement of $8.75 million in 2001. (Patrick Antoine, who was also arrested and beaten that night, received a settlement of $250,000 in 2000.)

At trial, Volpe testified to sodomizing Louima and threatening his life if he ever came forward. Volpe was convicted of raping and beating Louima and sentenced to 30 years in federal prison, not to be released before 2025. Charles Schwarz was convicted of lying about participating in the attack. He served five years in federal prison and was released in May 2007.

Other officers accused of lying about Volpe and Schwarz's actions had varying fates. Thomas Bruder and Thomas Wiese were convicted in 2000 and had their convictions overturned in 2002. Both were fired. Each later sued, but failed to have his job restored. Rolando Aleman and Francisco Rosario received probation. Michael Bellomo was acquitted.

After the court settlement, Louima and his family moved to Florida. Louima has used the money to pay tuition for hundreds of students in Haiti. Fueled in part by his real estate work, the Abner Louima Foundation has worked to establish hospitals in Haiti. Since 1997, Louima has spoken out about his own and other cases of police brutality. He marched with Reverend Al Sharpton in a demonstration against the December 2006 police shooting of Sean Bell, an unarmed black man. Ten years after his abuse by police, Louima reported still feeling physical pain from his injuries. He stated that he forgave, but could not forget, the attack. In an editorial for New York's *Daily News,* he wrote he was lucky to have survived and stressed the importance of community involvement in curbing police brutality.

See also: Sharpton, Al

Denise S. Guidry

Bibliography

Chan, Sewell. "The Abner Louima Case, 10 Years Later." *New York Times,* City Room. http://cityroom.blogs.nytimes.com/2007/08/09/the-abner-louima-case-10-years-later/.

Delattre, Edwin J. *Character and Cops: Ethics in Policing.* Washington, D.C.: AEI Press, 2002.

Destafano, Anthony M. "Ten Years After a Brutal Assault by NYPD Officers, Abner Louima Says His Suffering Helped Expose Bad Cops." *Newsday (New York),* August 5, 2007, Nassau edition. Lexis-Nexis.

Louima, Abner. "I Fight So This Will Never Happen Again, Louima Says." *Daily News (New York),* August 5, 2007. http://www.nydailynews.com/news/ny_crime/2007/08/05/2007-08-05_i_fight_so_this_will_never_happen_again_.html.

Marzulli, John, and Brian Kates. "One Man & One City Forever Changed." *Daily News (New York),* August 5, 2007, sports final edition. Lexis-Nexis.

"NYPD's Costly Brutality Cases." *Daily News (New York),* November 29, 2006, sports final edition. Lexis-Nexis.

Pulitzer Prize Board. The Pulitzer Prize Winners: 1998—Commentary: Mike McAlary of the New York *Daily News.* http://www.pulitzer.org/year/1998/commentary/works/index.html.

Lowndes County Freedom Organization

The Lowndes County Freedom Organization (LCFO) was an effort initiated by the Student Nonviolent Coordinating Committee (SNCC) in 1966 to organize an independent political party in Lowndes County, Alabama. Black residents of rural Lowndes County were impoverished, and few if any blacks actually owned land. Although blacks made up the majority of the population in the county, they held no elected offices and were virtually excluded from participating in local politics. Lowndes County was often referred to as "Bloody Lowndes" because of its history of racial violence.

Before the passage of the 1965 Voting Rights Act, African Americans in Alabama who were registered to vote constituted less than 20 percent of those eligible to vote. Civil Rights organizations like the Southern Christian Leadership Conference (SCLC), SNCC, and Congress of Racial Equality (CORE); along with the Alabama Democratic Conference (ADC)—a political action group—worked to increase the number of black registered voters in the state. Increased voting registration activity in neighboring Selma in 1965 spurred some action in dormant Lowndes County.

Unlike the Mississippi Freedom Democratic Party (MFDP), an interracial political party created to empower rural southern blacks, LCFO was not an alternative to the Alabama Democratic Party, but rather, a third party. The goal of LCFO was not initially to form an all-black political party; the lack of participation by whites facilitated such circumstances. The goal of the organization, however, was to circumvent the existing political structures that prevented blacks from participating in the local political process. The LCFO, also known as the Black Panther Party, adopted the image of a black panther as the symbol for the political party. The panther symbol, when juxtaposed against the Alabama Democratic Party's symbol of a white rooster, was meant as a representation of strength. If the LCFO were successful, SNCC planned to organize political parties similar to the LCFO in other areas of Alabama.

Despite the dangers that African Americans faced when they attempted voter registration activity, local blacks met with members of SCLC on March 19, 1965 and formed the Lowndes County Christian Movement for Human Rights (LCCMHR). The LCCMHR was created to facilitate black voter registration, as well as to act as an intermediary between the black community and the local government. John Hulett, Lowndes County native and one of only two African Americans registered to vote in the county, was elected the first chairman. Although SCLC had initially helped to establish the LCCMHR, it failed to continue to support the organization. When no support staff was sent to Lowndes County to begin political organizing, Hulett reached out to SNCC for help.

The passing of the Voting Rights Act of 1965 outlawed disfranchisement tactics such as literacy tests and as a result Lowndes County saw an increase in black voter registration. The rise in black political activity strengthened white opposition. On August 20, 1965, civil rights worker Jonathan Daniels was killed when a deputy sheriff fired a shotgun at a group of protesters. SNCC cited the deaths of white civil rights sympathizers Jonathan Daniels and Viola Liuzzo as pivotal events that strengthened the resolve of the organization to raise black political consciousness in Lowndes County. SNCC took the lead in helping to form the Lowndes County Freedom Organization. John Hulett was also elected to head LCFO.

A specification in Alabama state law permitted the establishment of a political party at the county level. After the failed seating of the MFDP in Atlantic City in 1964, members of SNCC decided that an independent political party would better serve the black residents of Lowndes County. The independent party could gain recognition when nominated candidates of the independent party received 20 percent of the votes in the county election. The 1966 elections proved to be crucial for LCFO. Despite the defeat of LCFO candidates in the general election, scholars believe that the creation of LCFO proved to be an important step in the emergence of black power politics.

The LCFO represented a change from previous SNCC projects. Stokely Carmichael served as project director and brought a brash new militancy that counterbalanced the rural grassroots movement in Lowndes County. The Lowndes County project was the first project since the 1964 Mississippi Freedom Summer project that was not an interracial movement. In 1966, Huey P. Newton and Bobby Seale founded the Black Panther Party for Self-Defense in Oakland, California. Inspired so much by the Stokely Carmichael and the LCFO, Newton and Seale adopted the black panther symbol to represent their organization. In 1969, the LCFO merged with the National Democratic Party of Alabama.
See also: Black Panther Party; Black Power; Carmichael, Stokely (Kwame Ture); MFDP; Mississippi Freedom Summer, 1964; Student Nonviolent Coordinating Committee; Voting Rights Act of 1965

Shirletta J. Kinchen

Bibliography

Branch, Taylor, *At Canaan's Edge: America in the King Years, 1965–1968*. New York: Simon and Schuster, 2006.

Carmichael Stokley, and Michael Thelwell, *Ready for the Revolution: The Life and Struggle of Stokely Carmichael (Kwame Ture)*. New York: Scribner Publishing, 2003.

Carson, Clayborne. *In Struggle: SNCC and the Black Awakening of the 1960s.* Cambridge, MA: Harvard University Press, 1981.

Eagles, Charles W. *Outside Agitator: Jon Daniels and the Civil Rights Movement in Alabama.* Chapel Hill: University of North Carolina Press, 1993.

Jeffries, Hasan Kwame. *Bloody Lowndes: Civil Rights and Black Power in Alabama's Black Belt.* New York: New York University Press, 2009.

Joseph, Peniel. *Waiting 'Til the Midnight Hour: A Narrative History of the Black Power Movement in America.* New York: Henry Holt, 2006.

Walton, Hanes. *Black Political Parties: An Historical and Political Analysis.* New York: Free Press, 1972.

Lynching

Lynching is a form of extralegal violence that has been used as a means of enforcing white supremacy and social control in the United States. In its 1940 definition of lynching, the Tuskegee Institute stipulated that "there must be legal evidence that a person has been killed, and that he met his death illegally at the hands of a group acting under the pretext of service to justice, race, or tradition" (*Lynching in the New South,* p. 17). Lynching has taken multiple forms, including hanging, shooting, burning, and beating to death. In some cases it involved dismemberment and torture, and on some occasions was performed as a spectacle before large crowds.

The term lynching is derived from Colonel Charles Lynch, a patriot in frontier Bedford County, Virginia, during the American Revolution. Plagued by Tories and outlaws, Lynch and other community leaders decided to take matters into their own hands in order to control lawlessness and restore peace and security. Acting outside formally constituted law enforcement mechanisms, Lynch presided over an informal court and thus established "lynch law" in the region. Similar practices were used in other areas of Revolutionary Virginia and elsewhere.

The Revolutionary War furnished the ideological justification for the violent abuse of alleged enemies of the public good. The democratically inspired doctrine of popular sovereignty was cited by vigilantes who worked "out of doors" to protect and perpetuate established patterns of social and political order, especially when community members felt threatened. Vigilante groups, including lynch mobs, were frequently led by those with a vested interest in maintaining the status quo, including businessmen, professionals, planters, politicians, and law enforcement officers. Accordingly, vigilantism can be interpreted as a socially conservative phenomenon.

Lynching, along with other forms of vigilantism and social violence, was used in antebellum America to discipline those perceived to transgress social, political, and racial orthodoxies. Black and white abolitionists were frequently targeted, the most famous incident being the lynching of newspaper editor Elijah Lovejoy in 1837. Members of religious minority groups such as Catholics and Mormons were also victimized by lynching during this period. Lynching was applied as an alternative system of justice in the Old West; the San Francisco Vigilance Committee of 1856 was the iconic embodiment of organized frontier justice.

Although lynching did not disappear in other regions of the country—a 1920 lynching of three black men in Duluth, Minnesota, provided one noteworthy example—after the Civil War it became an increasingly southern and racial affair. Reconstruction-era violence in the South was particularly bloody, with the Ku Klux Klan and other parallel groups acting as the paramilitary arm of the white Democratic Party. Most violence in this period targeted African Americans who sought to challenge the white power structure through upward mobility in education, politics, or economics. Whites who were working in the South to secure African American rights or promote the Republican Party were also victimized. Lynching represented an effective means of suppressing African American assertiveness, maintaining a pliant and subservient black labor force, and smothering black political power. Federal troops were largely successful in breaking up the Klan in South Carolina after the passage of the 1871 Civil Rights Act, but white terrorism continued virtually unabated in other states, especially Mississippi, Louisiana, and Florida.

The height of the lynching era in the United States lasted from roughly 1880 to 1930. The Tuskegee Institute recorded the lynching of 3,437 African Americans and 1,293 whites from 1880 to 1951. Sociologists Stewart Tolnay and E. M. Beck counted 2,462 black victims in 2,018 separate incidents of lynching from 1882 to 1930. In addition, 1,977 blacks were legally executed in 10 southern states (as opposed to only 451 whites) during the same period, for a combined total of 4,291 blacks who were violently put to death in the South from 1882–1930—an average of about one African American killed every four days. Lynching statistics, kept in systematic fashion only from 1882 to 1968,

are understandably imprecise, as they were often based on incomplete information, and there were many additional lynchings that went unrecorded. Patterns of lynching varied from state to state and county to county: Virginia, for instance, had substantially fewer lynchings than Georgia, and approximately one-third of southern counties had no black lynchings from 1882–1930.

The most common rationale for southern lynching was that it was an exercise in popular justice. Southern whites believed there existed a kind of social contract between the races that defined the limits of acceptable behavior; lynching was one means of policing those boundaries and punishing transgressors. Legally constituted mechanisms for enforcing social order were considered too slow or feeble, and many Southerners expressed doubt in the criminal justice system's ability to carry out its responsibilities. Rather than seeing themselves engaged in illegal activity, lynchers believed they were serving the larger social good and a higher law, sidestepping the more precise and tedious process of establishing guilt through evidence and then meting out proportional punishment. Historian Michael Pfeifer has argued that 19th- and early 20th-century lynching existed as part of a conflict over the nature of criminal justice, pitting rural and working-class supporters of "rough justice" against middle-class and progressivist advocates of due process. In most cases, there was little proof that lynching victims actually committed the purported offenses they were killed for. Only a tiny number of white participants in lynch mobs were ever apprehended, and fewer still were convicted. Most lynchings therefore were performed with at least the tacit consent, if not approval, of the surrounding white community.

Scholars have offered a number of theories to explain the causes of black lynching, reflecting the complexity of the phenomenon. Early sociological views argued that mob violence was the result of weak educational, religious, and civic institutions; exploitative economic relationships; poverty; and ineffective law enforcement. Because lynching was associated with a premodern rural culture, the modernization of the southern economy would strike at the roots of the practice. A more recent historical treatment posited that lynching served to teach all southerners, black and white, male and female, precisely where in the social hierarchy they stood, with blacks as debased, white women as vulnerable, and white men as the protectors of womanhood and civilization. Another theory suggested that lynching was a reaction to the possibility of post-emancipation interracial relationships between black men and white women, and represented an effort by psychologically frustrated white men to maintain their own status as well as control over black female sexuality. Other historians have situated lynching within the context of the Southern culture of honor or white insecurities fueled by the combined force of race hatred, sexual fears, honor, moralism, and localistic republicanism. Yet another approach sees lynching as a form of human sacrifice connected to the peculiar version of Protestant Christianity practiced in the postbellum South. Some of the most recent interpreters of lynching have emphasized its role as a means of labor control, specifically in maintaining a large, inexpensive, and submissive labor force. They suggest that it served as a crucial mechanism for perpetuating a plantation economy in the postbellum South and was attached to the distinctiveness of southern politics and cotton culture.

Rather than viewing lynching as an outdated relic of premodern barbarity or primitivism, it is more useful to understand it as a modern phenomenon. The essentially modern character of lynching was particularly prominent in spectacle lynchings such as Henry Smith (Paris, Texas, 1893), Sam Hose (Newnan, Georgia, 1899), and Jesse Washington (Waco, Texas, 1916). The thousands of people, including women and children, who assembled to witness the lynchings drove cars or arrived on specially chartered trains, took photographs of the event and the victims, and spread the news via newspapers, telegraph, and radio. The mass production of lynching postcards, distributed nationally through the mail, made even more people virtual participants. "Trophies" acquired from the victim's body were displayed in the front window of Main Street stores. For many white southerners, spectacle lynchings were a grisly but popular form of mass entertainment.

African Americans mounted a sustained opposition to lynching, particularly in the late 19th and 20th centuries. One of the most prolific and vocal critics of lynching was Ida B. Wells. In contrast to the prevailing myth among whites that lynching was primarily used to discipline black rapists and murderers, Wells demonstrated that lynching victims were accused of rape in only about one-third of cases, and approximately two-thirds of all lynchings were for small offenses such as shoplifting and "insolence." Driven out of Memphis, Tennessee, because of her antilynching writings, Wells moved to New York and also traveled to Great Britain where she helped foster a transatlantic antilynching crusade.

Many other prominent African Americans also spoke out against lynching, including Mary Church Terrell, Mary McLeod Bethune, Walter Francis White, W. E. B. Du Bois, and Paul Robeson. The National Association for the Advancement of Colored People advocated laws to halt the practice and conducted an in-depth study that resulted in the publication *Thirty Years of Lynching in the United States, 1889–1918*. The American Communist Party and International Labor Defense made antilynching a cornerstone of their platform designed to attract African Americans as members. Black newspapers documented and condemned lynchings, and black playwrights wrote 14 antilynching plays from 1916–1935. Interracial groups formed to protest lynching, and southern white women sought to end the practice via the Association of Southern Women for the Prevention of Lynching.

For the most part, the federal government was timid in its response to lynching. In 1901, George Henry White, the last former slave to serve in Congress, introduced a bill that would make lynching a federal crime, but it was summarily defeated. President Theodore Roosevelt made public statements against lynching, engendering harsh feelings from white southerners, but he did little in terms of concrete action. The Dyer Anti-Lynching Bill, introduced in 1918, passed the House of Representatives before being killed by filibuster in the Senate. Yet another antilynching bill, the Costigan-Wagner Bill, was defeated in 1935. Despite pressure from his wife Eleanor, President Franklin D. Roosevelt refused to speak out in favor of the bill, fearing backlash from the core Democratic constituency of the white South. Some progress was made after World War II, and the Truman administration called for federal antilynching legislation in 1947, but the power of southern Democrats over Senate committees prevented any movement on the issue. In short, the federal government never passed an antilynching bill, a failure that the U.S. Senate formally apologized for in 2005.

Lynching was used against other minority groups in American history as well. An estimated 600 Mexicans were lynched between 1848 and 1930, with at least 163 lynched in California alone from 1848–1860. Native Americans and Chinese Americans were also lynched in the West. Italian Americans, particularly Sicilian immigrants, were lynched in numerous states in the late 19th and early 20th centuries.

Indeed, the largest mass lynching in American history occurred in New Orleans in 1891, when 11 Italians were lynched after being acquitted of murdering the city police chief. One of the most famous individual lynchings in the United States, which helped lead to the resurrection of the Ku Klux Klan in 1915, was of the Jewish factory owner Leo Frank in Atlanta.

Persistent opposition to lynching, combined with an increased commitment to law and order by southern state politicians, led to a significant decline in the practice, as the rate fell to about 10 blacks lynched per year in the South during the 1930s. Lynching continued to wane in the 1940s and 1950s until surging in reaction to civil rights activism in the 1960s. Mississippi was particularly violent, headlined by the Klan-orchestrated murder of James Chaney, Andrew Goodman, and Michael Schwerner in Philadelphia during the 1964 Freedom Summer. Lynching has fallen to negligible levels since the 1960s; when it has occurred, such as in Alabama in 1981 and Texas in 1998, the white perpetrators have been apprehended, convicted, and even executed by the state.

See also: Antilynching Campaign; Ku Klux Klan; National Association for the Advancement of Colored People; Wells-Barnett, Ida; White Mob Violence

Patrick Q. Mason

Bibliography

Allen, James et al. *Without Sanctuary: Lynching Photography in America,* 7th ed. Santa Fe, NM: Twin Palms Publishers, 2005.

Brundage, W. Fitzhugh. *Lynching in the New South: Georgia and Virginia, 1880–1930.* Urbana: University of Illinois Press, 1993.

Dray, Philip. *At the Hands of Persons Unknown: The Lynching of Black America.* New York: Random House, 2002.

Pfeifer, Michael J. *Rough Justice: Lynching and American Society, 1874–1947.* Urbana: University of Illinois Press, 2004.

Tolnay, Stewart E., and E. M. Beck. *A Festival of Violence: An Analysis of Southern Lynchings, 1882–1930.* Urbana: University of Illinois Press, 1992.

Waldrep, Christopher. *Lynching in America: A History in Documents.* New York: New York University Press, 2006.

Manchester Conference, 1945

Held in Manchester, England, from October 13–21, 1945, the Manchester Conference—often referred to as the Fifth Pan-African Congress—brought together more than 200 delegates from across Africa, the West Indies, and North America in its call for black self-determination. For many scholars, the Manchester Conference represents a turning point in the history of Pan-Africanism and nationalism in Africa. Previous Pan-African conferences, namely the series of congresses organized by W. E. B. Du Bois and the National Association for the Advancement of Colored Peoples (NAACP), never offered a direct challenge to the nature or future of European rule in Africa, but instead the conferences' organizers focused their attention on securing political, social, and economic reforms from the colonial powers. The Manchester Conference, however, dramatically altered the method and message of the Pan-African struggle, as its delegates demanded the immediate end to European rule in all of Africa and the West Indies. For the next two decades, the radical message of the Manchester Conference set the tone for the African struggle for independence as a new generation of nationalist figures—led by Kwame Nkrumah, Jomo Kenyatta, and I.T.A. Wallace-Johnson—invoked the lessons of Manchester as they guided their respective countries to independence in the 1950s and 1960s.

The ambition to hold a fifth Pan-African conference grew out of a desire on both sides of the Atlantic to resurrect the Du Boisian congresses of the 1910s and 1920s. These conferences, beginning in Paris in 1919, represented an important meeting ground for a growing diasporic concern for events in Africa. African American and West Indian delegates dominated the debates at these conferences as they called on the colonial powers and the international community to exercise greater responsibility in the governing of African affairs. In particular, they demanded reforms in the fields of land ownership, labor, and education. After the 1927 New York Pan-African Congress, Du Bois began to set his sights on holding the Fifth Pan-African Congress within Africa itself. This fifth conference was to take place in Tunis in 1929. Yet, it never got off the ground, as it encountered resistance from a French government nervous about allowing a potentially subversive and embarrassing meeting to convene in one of its colonies. Furthermore, the onset of the Great Depression further stymied Du Bois and others' efforts at organizing a fifth congress in 1929 or in the early 1930s.

By the mid-1940s, the political and social exigencies of World War II had led many to seek the renewal of the Du Boisian Pan-African movement with a Pan-African conference to be held on the continent itself. Through pressure from Amy Jacques Garvey, the first wife of the famed black nationalist Marcus Garvey, Du Bois began to explore the idea of holding a Pan-African conference in Liberia at the conclusion of the war. In his preparations, he contacted black leaders throughout the United States, the West Indies, and in Europe. Yet in Britain, he encountered resistance to his ambition for a Liberian conference as he learned of preparations for a fifth conference already being made by the little known and newly formed Pan-African Federation (PAF).

Led by prominent British-based activists George Padmore, Ras T. Makonnen, and I.T.A. Wallace-Johnson, the PAF represented a union of African and black student and activist organizations aimed at challenging the political and social structure of life within Britain and its empire. Issues of race, unequal distribution of wealth, labor, and education emerged as the most prominent interests of the PAF and its member organizations as they made preparations for a conference set to coincide with the second meeting of the World Trade Union Congress (WTUC) scheduled for September 1945 in Paris. This conference was not merely intended to renew the Pan-African tradition forged by Du Bois in the 1910s and 1920s. Rather, the PAF also looked to its envisioned conference as an opportunity to incorporate a more diverse and radical collection of black voices in shaping the future of Pan-African politics. For the leaders of the PAF, this included a greater emphasis on the involvement of black student organizations, as well as of African and West Indian labor leaders through the forthcoming Pan-African conference.

From the United States, Du Bois looked on the PAF's arrangements with both interest and concern. In his correspondence with Padmore and others, he cautioned against holding another conference in Europe, citing the need to extend the movement into Africa itself. He further expressed his dismay at the failure of the PAF to approach the NAACP for support in the conference's organization. For its part, the PAF did not refute Du Bois's suggestion at holding a conference in Africa. Instead, the organization even acquiesced to Du Bois's wish to classify the proposed Paris conference as an "exploratory conference" for a future meeting on the continent. In spite of this, Du Bois and the PAF were never able to clear the tensions between them. Padmore and the PAF continued with their preparations with only minimal input from Du Bois and the NAACP. For instance, Padmore, the PAF, and its affiliated organizations decided the conference's agenda, dates, and even the

ultimate venue change from Paris to Manchester, England, without Du Bois's or the NAACP's prior notice or approval. As a result, when the Manchester Conference convened in October 1945, it did so as a meeting of British-based black and African organizations primarily concerned with challenging the problems of race and colonialism within the scope of the British Empire. Yet in spite of the tensions between him and the organizers, Du Bois not only attended the conference, but also accepted the organizers' invitation to serve as the "International President of the Congress" in celebration of his pioneering role in shaping the 20th-century Pan-African movement.

The Manchester Conference's first panel opened on October 15 with a discussion of the "The Colour Problem in Britain." Introducing the topics to the delegates, Edwin Du Plan of the Gold Coast reminded them that, after World War I, Britain's black community faced large-scale unemployment with the return of white soldiers from the war. The need for soldiers and the creation of low-paid factory work during the World War II helped alleviate the country's problem with black unemployment, yet Du Plan noted it had little effect on countering the political and social barriers faced by Britain's black community. Even when black workers were employed, Du Plan emphasized that many of them faced the constant threat of deportation after the termination of their contracts. In addition to these labor problems, the panel discussed the government's failures in addressing issues of family, youth, and education in Britain's black and mixed-race communities. As a result of these racially driven oversights, the panel argued that the government had left these communities disproportionately poor and susceptible to violence and arrest by the country's predominately white police force.

The hallmark of the Manchester Conference, however, came in its discussion over the future of European rule in Africa. For most of the conference's delegates, imperialism had run its course. In panels on West, South, and East Africa, the Manchester delegates argued that imperialism had unequivocally failed to bring the widespread "progress" and "civilization" promised to the peoples of Africa through colonial rule. Instead, the delegates argued that, through colonial rule, African peoples suffered from violently enforced policies of forced labor, the systematic destruction of their precolonial political and social institutions, and widespread illiteracy and political repression. In addition to these debates, other panels focused on the continued imperial threats to the world's three independent black states—Ethiopia, Liberia, and Haiti—and on labor issues in the Caribbean. After a week of deliberations, the conference closed on October 21, 1945 with an assertion of the rights of all African peoples to the principle of self-determination and a demand for an immediate end to colonial rule on the continent.

The aftermath of the conference thus ushered in a new era in the history of African nationalism. No longer were discussions of colonial reform sufficient. Political and labor leaders, such as Kwame Nkrumah and I.T.A. Wallace-Johnson, invoked the lessons of Manchester as they sharpened their attacks on the colonial system in the postwar years. For Nkrumah, this included the publication of his first book *Towards Colonial Freedom* (1947) and, with Wallace-Johnson, the founding of the West African National Secretariat (WANS). The WANS attracted the interest of other Manchester delegates such as Bankole Awooner-Renner and G. Ashie-Nikoi with its aim to create a single, socialist state uniting West Africa. Nkrumah's 1947 return to the Gold Coast resulted in the breakdown of the WANS. Yet, in the Gold Coast, he, along with fellow Manchester alumni (Joe Appiah, Awooner-Renner, Du Plan, and Ako Adjei), adopted the conference's message of self-determination as they began their nine-year struggle for independence. In other African colonies, Jomo Kenyatta returned to Kenya in 1946 where he was imprisoned for 10 years before taking over as the country's first president in 1963. Hastings Banda and his Nyasaland African Congress led Malawi to its independence in 1964.

The legacy of the Manchester Conference and its effect on the future of Pan-African politics has long been debated among scholars. Unlike any previous conference, the Manchester Conference opened a space for young African leaders to assert themselves on an international stage. For many scholars in the 1960s and 1970s, however, the Manchester Conference also signaled the moment in which the international meaning of "Pan-Africanism" shifted from that of black solidarity to that of African continental unity. As a result, this scholarship, exemplified in the classic works of Colin Legum, Ali Mazrui, and Vincent Baktepu Thompson, understood post-Manchester Pan-Africanism in terms of the political and diplomatic processes leading to the formation of the Organization of African Unity (OAU) and the operations of this institution. More recently, diasporic scholars such as Penny von Eschen, James Meriwether,

and Kevin Gaines have begun to challenge this position by highlighting the roles of prominent African American and diasporic figures in postwar Africa. Even more important, these scholars have begun to explore the political, social, and cultural meanings that African achievements, such as the continent's struggle for independence, had in shaping the methods and discourse of the black freedom movement in the United States during the 1950s, 1960s, and 1970s.

In 1995, several events marked the 50th anniversary of the Manchester Conference. In October, three separate conferences met in Manchester with panels on the relationship between Pan-Africanism and labor, gender, immigration, and neocolonialism, as well as discussions on the legacy of Nkrumah and other historical figures. Furthermore, British historians Marika Sherwood and Hakim Adi used the conference's anniversary to mark the publication of their edited collection *The 1945 Manchester Pan-African Congress Revisited* (1995). Adi and Sherwood's work is unparalleled by any previous research on the conference. They not only meticulously documented the events leading to the conference, but also included previously unpublished accounts of the conference by two of its lesser-known delegates, as well as brief biographies of more than 120 individuals and organizations who took part in the conference. Even more important, this collection includes a complete reprint of George Padmore's 1947 conference report titled *Colonial and Coloured Unity*.

See also: African Imperialism; Du Bois, W. E. B.; Garvey, Marcus; Gold Coast; Kenyatta, Jomo; Nkrumah, Kwame; Organization of African Unity; Pan-African Congresses; Pan-Africanism

Jeffrey S. Ahlman

Bibliography

Adi, Hakim. *West Africans in Britain, 1900–1960: Nationalism, Pan-Africanism and Communism*. London: Lawrence & Wishart, 1998.

Adi, Hakim, and Marika Sherwood. *The 1945 Manchester Pan-African Congress Revisited*. London: New Beacon Books, 1995.

Du Bois, W. E. B. *The World and Africa: An Inquiry into the Part Which Africa Has Played in World History*. New York: International Publishers, 1965.

Langley, J. Ayodele. *Pan-Africanism and Nationalism in West Africa, 1900–1945: A Study of Ideology and Social Classes*. Oxford: Claredon Press, 1973.

Nkrumah, Kwame. *Towards Colonial Freedom: Africa in the Struggle against World Imperialism*. London: Farleigh Press, 1947.

Padmore, George. *Pan-Africanism or Communism?: The Coming Struggle for Africa*. London: Dennis Dobson, 1956.

Thompson, Vincent Bakttepu. *Africa and Unity: The Evolution of Pan-Africanism*. London: Longmans, Green, 1969.

Mandela, Nelson

Nelson Mandela (1918–) was the first democratically elected president of South Africa. From 1994 to 1999, Mandela led his country in its first five years of democracy and reconciliation. Before Mandela assumed this position, he was a staunch antiapartheid activist. Mandela actively participated as a card-carrying member and leader of the African National Congress (ANC). After joining the political body in 1942, he was one of the activists who advocated for the formation of an ANC Youth wing in 1944, which he, Walter Sisulu, and others succeeded in establishing. Besides working within a political organization, Mandela also challenged the state. In his quest to oppose white domination, Mandela earned the government's ire with his participation in several protest activities. Chief among them was the 1952 defiance campaign when participants burnt their passbooks. Mandela also spoke publicly. For his activism, Mandela became a government target and eventually operated underground. With the American CIA's help, the South African government arrested this trained lawyer in 1962. Mandela was ultimately convicted of high treason. Sentenced to life imprisonment on Robben Island, Mandela carried the struggle forward even within the prison system. There, he led protests to secure healthier food, longer trousers, and study privileges. Affectionately known as Madiba, this world-renowned leader has contributed immensely to solving problems on the African continent, to expanding South African borders to embrace other Africans, to fighting for children's causes and becoming a spokesperson on the confronting and fighting the crippling disease of AIDS. In leading the country in the forefront of struggle and global equality, Mandela has also championed human rights.

Before Mandela catapulted into international fame, he grew up in a tiny village in Umtata located in the former Transkei along South Africa's eastern coast. Born on June 18, 1918, his parents named him appropriately Rolihlahla, which "means to shake a tree" or "to stir up trouble." A Methodist teacher renamed him Nelson after the famed admiral Horatio Nelson because the pronunciation of his real name gave the educator difficulty. Mandela's father was the principal acting chief to a paramount in Thembuland. His father, according to his biographer Tom Lodge, viewed Mandela's mother as his favorite wife. On his father's death, Mandela assumed the position of a paramount chief's ward. Although this appeared to be his destiny, Mandela chose another career path. He became a lawyer. This Wesleyan mission-educated product ultimately attended the University of Fort Hare, where he earned a bachelor of arts degree. Mandela even participated in school politics by joining the Student Representative Council (SRC). His allegiance to his fellow students landed him in trouble when he participated in a protest boycott that resulted in his suspension from the college.

After his suspension, Mandela went to Johannesburg, the fabled city of gold. There, he met Walter Sisulu who took him on as a mentee. Sisulu was also Mandela's confidant. The two remained lifelong friends (Sisulu died in 2003). Mandela used his position in Johannesburg to further his education. He received a bachelors of arts degree at the University of South Africa (UNISA) by correspondence and immediately after this milestone, he began studying law at the University of the Witwatersrand (WITS). There, at WITS, Mandela met future struggle colleagues, Joe Slovo, Harry Schwarz, and Ruth First. Besides the academic community that he embraced, Mandela made his home in the northeastern township of Alexandra. As a black and colored township community, Alexandra was a stronghold and leader of resistance struggles such as bus boycotts, especially during the 1940s before the Nationalist Party entrenched segregation beginning in 1948. Swept up into this political current, Mandela joined the ANC and thus continued his crusade against tyranny and oppression. Mandela credits many people for his political education. Chief among them were the teachings of Mahatma Gandhi whose ideas of Satyagraha resonated with him. Mandela engaged in many peaceful protests, and for his actions he became one of the 156 people arrested on December 5, 1956 and charged with treason. At this trial, the government allowed defendants to speak. Mandela took the opportunity to explain what actions that the ANC proposed to take to end the system of inequality that defined South Africa at the time. The treason trial took place over five years, with all of the accused acquitted.

The success, or lack thereof, with nonviolence began to change Mandela's intellectual framework. Initially a

Nelson Mandela revisits the prison on Robben Island, South Africa, where he was incarcerated for more than two decades as a political prisoner, February 11, 1994. (Louise Gubb/The Image Works)

proponent of nonviolence, Mandela reconsidered this strategy after the Sharpeville Massacre. On March 21, 1960, the Pan-African Congress (PAC) called for a pass protest. Instead of the peaceful demonstration that the organizers had arranged, the police opened fire, killing 69 people, and injuring other fleeing parties. After this disturbance, the government banned the ANC and PAC, and made it unlawful for these organizations to operate. Mandela, already operating underground, and considered a government threat and dubbed the "Black Pimpernel," helped to create the Mandela or M-Plan. This strategy called for the creation of cell units having three to four people, but no more than five, who would engage in guerrilla warfare. This indoctrination included political education and military training in camouflage, reconnaissance, topography, photography, fire training, and communication.

As part of the Umkhonto weSizwe (MK or Spear of the Nation) an underground movement founded on December 16, 1961, Mandela renounced his stance on nonviolence. Besides his role as an activist, Mandela, a divorcee (his first wife was Evelyn Mase with whom he had four children), struggled with seeing a newlywed wife, Winnie Madikizela-Mandela, because soon after their nuptials he went underground for 17 months. The couple had two daughters, Zindzi and Zenani. While on the run, Mandela made speeches and recorded interviews. During one interview, a day after the Sharpeville massacre, Mandela donning an Afro, with a part centered in the middle, and a fully grown beard, spoke about South Africa's political situation and the state of Africans. In responding to the question what do Africans want, Mandela told a news correspondent that Africans need the right to vote and full political equality with whites. It took 52 years before Mandela and other South Africans realized this goal. Within that time frame, the MK strategized to destroy railway lines, government installations, electrical facilities, and other hard and soft targets.

To further MK's objectives, leaders often met at clandestine locations. One of these places was the Lilliesleaf Farm in Rivonia. There, insurgents met to discuss strategy in a place considered a refuge. Rivonia was a safe house until a tip by the American Central Intelligence Agency informed the South African government of Mandela's whereabouts and the disguises that he wore. On August 5, 1962, the police arrested Mandela. The state charged him with the crimes of leaving the country illegally and inciting workers to strike in 1961. The arrests continued. On July 11, 1963, while Mandela lay in prison, his colleagues such as Ahmed Kathrada, Walter Sisulu, and Govan Mbeki among others faced arrest. All of the accused were tried and convicted of charges of sabotage, which Mandela confessed he did, but denied a second charge of plotting a foreign invasion of South Africa. Mandela used the opportunity to convey his thoughts on the political situation under which black South Africans lived as second-class citizens. Once on the dock, Mandela recounted how he had fought against white domination and that he was prepared to die in his quest for democracy, freedom, and racial harmony. Even in the state's presence, Mandela spoke from the heart. He chose his words deliberately to convey his disdain for any forms of domination no matter what race or ethnicity.

In showing this balanced account, Mandela appealed to liberals while he also reinforced his position against apartheid. Mandela also offered his vision of a new South Africa. Similar to Martin Luther King Jr.'s "I have a Dream" speech, Mandela called for equality based on people's character rather than their skin color. In sharing this ideal with King, Mandela showed how he envisioned the ANC's policy of nonracialism. Despite his appeal, Mandela faced life imprisonment on Robben Island. He remained on the isle once reputed as a bird sanctuary, a leper colony, and World War II naval base for 18 years. He spent the other nine years at Pollsmoor Prison. Unlike PAC leader Robert Sobukwe who had a house all to himself on Robben Island, Mandela served his term mixed with the general population. Younger ANC adherents or political prisoners belonging to other organizations revered Mandela and often sought his counsel. Even with his senior authority, Mandela was not above the inhumane practice of *tauza,* when inmates jumped up and down and had their private cavities searched. During his tenure, the world's most well-known prisoner barely received visits and had his mail read and doctored before he received them.

With his privacy violated on many levels, Mandela helped to remake the prison environment in which he lived. Political prisoners taught each other and received study privileges to conduct correspondence courses as part of the reformation of the prison system. While Mandela and the others altered the political terrain within the prison by having hunger strikes and befriending the wardens, he kept up negotiations with the South African government. Former President P. W. Botha initially began talks with Mandela, but when Mandela refused to renounce violence, the white minority leader rescinded his offer. Still left to resolve this problem was the next South African President F. W. De Klerk who did decide to release Mandela on February 11, 1990. Mandela left prison donning a gray suit and holding his wife's hand and clenching his fist with the other. De Klerk not only signed for Mandela's release, he also repealed major cornerstones of apartheid such as the 1950 Group Areas Act (GAA), which required that all race groups live in their designated areas. For their efforts in ending apartheid, Mandela and De Klerk received the Nobel Peace Prize in 1993. Two years later in 1995, after the formation of an interim government, Mandela assumed the presidency and won 63 percent of the vote. He used his presidency to advocate for reconciliation, even dubbing the New South Africa as "the rainbow nation."

As president, Mandela was the consummate statesman. He traveled around the world on behalf of South Africa. Mandela also participated in negotiating affairs with other African nations. For example, Mandela helped to resolve the ongoing dispute between Muammar Gaddafi and the United States. With Mandela's urging, Gaddafi agreed to release the men responsible for the Lockerbie plane crash on December 21, 1988. Mandela arranged to have the trial in a third country, rather than the countries representing the plaintiffs such as the United States and Britain. He even spoke on the defendant's behalf. Mandela also stood up for his friends, such as Cuban ally Fidel Castro. Castro supported the ANC during apartheid and allowed South Africans to inhabit his country, something that, to the chagrin of the West, Mandela refused to overlook. The Xhosa leader has also shown his public admiration for Gaddafi's Libya.

Even with his high approval rating, some criticisms developed. His inability to direct more attention to the AIDS crisis earned him consternation from AIDS activist Edwin Cameron. Mandela, as well as successor Thabo Mbeki, failed to propose funding to develop AIDS research or to create some kind of plan to impede the disease's progress, which consumes hundreds of South Africans. Other criticisms are concerned with domestic policy. Some pundits believe that

Mandela's outreach globally hindered the country's development because he granted little attention to the plight of the homeless and the dire economic poverty that paralyzes portions of the nation's sector. The ANC promised homes and delivered; however, the contractors constructed them rapidly and they contained structural problems. Needless to say, Mandela was no saint, but he was a man of courage and conviction, and for that Madiba earns deep respect and reverence.

His political role continues as a retired statesman. Concerned with the problems besetting the world, his third wife Graca Machel, along with Desmond Tutu, called a special meeting with the world's leaders in Johannesburg. With projects such as these, Mandela, the retired South African president not only keeps physically busy but he also stimulates his mind. As a retiree, Mandela engages directly with the ongoing AIDS crisis. He experienced first hand the debilitating effect that the disease inflicts upon its host. His son Makgatho died of the disease on January 6, 2003. Unlike during his presidency, Mandela has given his verbal and financial support to AIDS research. He has supported an AIDS fundraising campaign. Mandela also served as a spokesperson in support of HIV/AIDS research at the XV International AIDS Conference in Bangkok, Thailand. Mandela leads by example. As a children's advocate, Mandela won the Global Friend's Award in 2005. His community outreach and support of national and international programs remains an inspiration to many leaders, the educated, and lay people.

Behind the public persona that has appeared national and international television screens is a humble and graceful man. Mandela still engages in a strict physical regime, which has him up at four in the morning for calisthenics. This former boxer has always stayed in shape even while in prison in a small prison cell, which not only confined him intellectually but also physically. His height is six feet and above. Several authors have written books about Mandela, some offering an authorized portrait, others a more critical analysis of Mandela's presidency, his role in the liberation struggle, his prison term, and his retirement. Mandela traces his life from his regal beginnings in Umtata to his imprisonment in *Long Walk to Freedom*, published in 1994. Readers learn about early South African history, especially the impact that Alexandra had on his political development. The work also deals with his relationship with Winnie Madikizela-Mandela. Through his prose, readers learn a lot about Mandela, the man, not the national and international hero that he became. Readers feel the frailty.

Besides written works penned by Mandela or scholars are cinematic reproductions. In the film *Mandela and De Klerk,* the director relayed the story of Mandela's release from prison. Sidney Poitier offered a riveting performance playing Mandela. Another cinematographic feat, *Goodbye Bafana,* a film that was screened at the Berlin Film Festival in 2007, portrays Dennis Haysbert as Mandela, and reconstructs Mandela's relationship with his prison guard James Gregory. His immortalization continues with public monuments in South Africa and abroad in such places as London. On March 31, 2004, the country witnessed the renaming of Sandton Square to Nelson Mandela Square. Three years later in 2007, in London, the city honored Mandela by unveiling a statue at Parliament Square. Mandela accepted the honor on behalf of all South Africans. This attitude attests to Mandela's humanity and graciousness. He is truly a modern hero.

See also: African Imperialism; African National Congress; Antiapartheid Movement; Biko, Steve; Castro, Fidel

Dawne Y. Curry

Bibliography

Limb, Peter. *Nelson Mandela: A Biography.* Westport, CT: Greenwood Press, 2008.

Lodge, Tom. *Mandela: A Critical Life.* Oxford: Oxford University Press, 2007.

Mandela, Nelson. *Long Walk to Freedom: The Autobiography of Nelson Mandela.* Boston: Little, Brown, 1994.

Sampson, Anthony. *Mandela: The Authorized Biography.* New York: Knopf, 1999.

Turnley, David C. *Mandela!: Struggle & Triumph.* New York: Abrams, 2008.

March on Washington Movement, 1941

In 1941, A. Philip Randolph pushed for an all-black march on Washington to demand equal rights in government positions in the defense industry and the military. The organizers canceled the march when President Franklin D. Roosevelt issued Executive Order 8802.

The onset of World War II in Europe and the subsequent enforced war preparation created millions of new jobs, especially in the defense industry. This seemed to offer new opportunities for African Americans to improve their status and finally reach full citizenship. Hoping to take part in the economic upswing, African Americans migrated from the South to the new jobs centers; however, blacks met with racism, exclusion, and often violence. The situation was not much different in the armed forces where African Americans served in segregated units and were mostly assigned to service units. The federal government tended to ignore the issue or even supported racial discrimination.

In contrast to World War I, African Americans were no longer willing to tolerate their underprivileged and oppressed status based on the separate-but-equal premise. They demanded federal and state officials, as well as the president, to intercede and force companies to hire on an equal basis. The NAACP and the National Urban League joined a number of groups that focused on equal rights in employment. They demanded the creation of a committee to scrutinize and investigate racial discrimination. Government officials, however, did not consider it necessary to establish a separate committee to cover race issues.

A. Philip Randolph, the president of the Brotherhood of Sleeping Car Porters, believed a mass demonstration in Washington would be the most effective way to address the employment inequities faced by African Americans at this time. His idea for the march was strongly influenced by Ghandian concepts of nonviolent civil disobedience and his labor experience in protest marches and in rallying. Putting massive pressure on the government to demand jobs and equal participation in national defense was the only promising strategy for change. Having petitioned relentlessly, he grew frustrated with the reluctance of companies, the government, and the American president to make changes.

In January 1941, Randolph founded the March on Washington movement (MOWM) and called for 10,000 African Americans to join this protest march in Washington, D.C. scheduled for July 1, 1941. Its specific aim was the issuance of an executive order by the president to abolish racial discrimination in the government, military, and national defense industry.

The African American community foremost hailed and supported Randolph's call for an African American mass march on Washington. The MOWM made extensive use of the African American press that acted as an important information link between the organizers and the

participants in the march. Randolph used his methods of communication and the following he established during his fight for the Brotherhood of Sleeping Car Porters. The leading Civil Rights movements, the NAACP and the National Urban League, among others, embraced Randolph's plan and joined forces with him. Their appeals to President Roosevelt demanding a reformation of the defense program had not been crowned with success.

Initially meeting with protest, Randolph planned to exclude white supporters from the march. In an effort to build black self-esteem and community, he wanted the march to be organized, financed, and carried out solely by blacks. Furthermore, he feared that white communists would infiltrate and co-opt the march, thereby discrediting the event.

The March on Washington Committee, responsible for rallying and organizing, was made up of people from various Civil Rights movements, churches, and black organizations and acted nationally and locally. They planned for the marchers to walk silently behind muffled drums through the city to the Lincoln Memorial. The numbers of people wanting to participate rose sharply above 10,000. By June 1941, the organizers expected 100,000 African Americans to participate.

The initial reaction of the government was a demand to call off the march, arguing it would only stir racial hatred. The unwillingness of the organizers to comply with the president's request and the rising numbers of African Americans willing to participate started to concern government officials and the president. Roosevelt sent his wife Eleanor Roosevelt and Fiorello LaGuardia, the mayor of New York, to talk with and appease Randolph and White on June 13. They were unsuccessful in convincing the organizers to call off their march.

On June 19, 1941, the president finally met with Randolph and White. They informed Roosevelt that 100,000 people were planning to march and that only the passage of an executive order to ban all racial discrimination in the war industries and armed forces could prevent the march and satisfy the African American community. Despite serious reservations within the government, Roosevelt acquiesced at least partially to the demands of the MOWM. On June 25, 1941, Roosevelt issued Executive Order 8802, which prohibited employment discrimination on the basis of race, creed, color, or national origin in federal agencies and war-related industries. The order established the Federal Employment Practices Committee (FEPC) to monitor employment in defense industries and government agencies. Roosevelt, however, was not willing to end segregation in the military. To the dismay of many of his followers, Randolph called off the March on Washington.

Cancellation of the march notwithstanding, Randolph continued his MOWM organizing local rallies and marches to protest race discrimination. Most established Civil Rights movements, however, no longer supported Randolph, but rather criticized him for his methods. Despite this fall from grace, his MOWM and Randolph's methods were the paragon for the March on Washington in 1963.

See also: Brotherhood of Sleeping Car Porters; March on Washington, 1963; National Association for the Advancement of Colored People; Randolph, A. Philip; Roosevelt, Eleanor; White, Walter

Christine Knauer

Bibliography

Barber, Lucy G. *Marching on Washington: The Forging of an American Political Tradition.* Berkeley: University of California Press, 2002.

Bracey, John H. Jr., and August Meier. "Allies or Adversaries? The NAACP, A. Philip Randolph and the 1941 March on Washington," *Georgia Historical Quarterly* 75 (1991):1–17.

Garfinkel, Herbert. *When Negroes March: The March on Washington Movement in the Organizational Politics for FEPC.* Glencoe, IL: Free Press, 1959.

Pfeffer, Paula F. *A Philip Randolph, Pioneer of the Civil Rights Movement.* Baton Rouge: Louisiana State University Press, 1990.

Sitkoff, Harvard. "Racial Militancy and Interracial Violence in the Second World War," *The Journal of American History* 58 (1971):661–81.

Wynn, Neil A. *The Afro-American and the Second World War.* New York: Holmes & Meier Publishers, 1976.

March on Washington, 1963

On August 28, 1963, more than 250,000 demonstrators from all across the country descended on the nation's capital to participate in a March on Washington focusing on Jobs and Freedom. Not only was it the largest demonstration for human rights in U.S. history, but it also showcased, for the first time, unity among the various civil rights organizations. The event began with a rally at the Washington Monument featuring several celebrities and musicians. Participants then marched across the mile-long National Mall to the Memorial. The three-hour long program at the Lincoln Memorial included speeches from prominent civil rights and religious leaders. The day ended with a meeting at the White House between the leaders and organizers of the march and President John F Kennedy.

The idea for the 1963 March on Washington was conceived by A. Philip Randolph, international president of the Brotherhood of Sleeping Car Porters, president of the Negro American Labor Council, and vice president of the AFL-CIO. Randolph, a long-time civil rights activist, was committed to improving the economic condition of black Americans.

In 1941, Randolph threatened to assemble 100,000 black Americans in the capital to help convince President Franklin D. Roosevelt to sign an executive order banning discrimination in the armed services and creating the Fair Employment Practices Committee. As a result of this meeting with Roosevelt, Randolph postponed his idea for more than two decades. In 1962, however, the 73-year-old elder statesman of the Civil Rights movement reprised his idea with renewed motivation. With black employment at double the rate of white employment, and with civil rights for black Americans still unrealized, Randolph proposed a new march for jobs and freedom. When he first proposed the march in late 1962, he received little response from other civil rights leaders. But he knew that cooperation would be difficult because each of the civil rights organizations had their own agenda for the Civil Rights movement, and the leaders competed for funding and press coverage. Nonetheless, success of the March on Washington would depend on the participation of the "Big Six" civil rights organizations. These organizations and their leaders were Roy Wilkins of the National Association of the Advancement of Colored People (NAACP); Whitney Young Jr., of the National Urban League (NUL); Dr. Martin Luther King Jr., of the Southern Christian Leadership Conference (SCLC); James Farmer of the Conference of Racial Equality (CORE); and John Lewis of the Student Nonviolent Coordinating Committee (SNCC).

By June 1963, Dr. King had agreed to cooperate with Randolph on the march. The older, more conservative NAACP and NUL were still ambivalent. But after winning Randolph's promise that the march would be a nonviolent as well as a nonconfrontational event, Roy Wilkins of the NAACP pledged his organization's support. The promise of a nonviolent and nonconfrontational demonstration disappointed the more militant CORE and SNCC leaders who had already joined with Randolph. In addition, white supporters such as labor leader Walter Reuther, as well as Jewish, Catholic, and Presbyterian officials offered their participation and help.

The organization and details of the march were handled by Bayard Rustin, a close associate of Randolph's. Rustin, an antiwar and civil rights activist, had extensive experience in organizing mass protests. Before the March on Washington, his most notable mass protest was organizing the first Freedom Ride in 1947. He had also participated in Randolph's plans for the 1941 march. With only two months to plan, Rustin established his headquarters in Harlem, with a smaller office in Washington. He and his core staff consisting of 200 volunteers quickly organized the largest peaceful demonstration in U.S. history. While Randolph and the NUL focused on jobs, the other civil rights groups centered on freedom. To finance the march, money was raised from the sale of buttons promoting the march at 25 cents per button. Thousands of people also sent in cash contributions.

A flyer produced by the National Office of the March on Washington for Jobs and Freedom articulated the six major goals of the march: meaningful civil rights laws, a massive federal works program, full and fair employment, decent housing, the right to vote, and adequate integrated education. More specifically, what was demanded in the March on Washington was passage of "meaningful" civil rights legislation at this session of Congress—no filibustering; immediate elimination of all racial segregation in public schools throughout the nation, a big program of public works to provide jobs for all the nation's unemployed including job training and a placement program, a federal law prohibiting racial discrimination in hiring workmen, either public or private, two dollars an hour minimum wage across the board nationwide; withholding of federal funds from programs that discriminate; enforcement of the Fourteenth Amendment, reducing congressional representation of states where citizens are disenfranchised, a broadened Fair Labor Standards Act to include currently

Civil rights leaders, including Roy Wilkins (bottom left) and A. Philip Randolph (bottom center), join hundreds of thousands of Americans in a march on Washington, D.C., in a multiracial demonstration for civil rights and equal opportunity in August 1963. (Lyndon Baines Johnson Library and Museum)

excluded employment areas, and authority for the attorney general to institute injunctive suits when any constitutional right is violated.

As plans progressed, however, the primary goal of the march turned toward passing federal civil rights legislation put forward by President Kennedy in the wake of the demonstrations in Birmingham, Alabama. The proposed march initially caused great concern within the Kennedy administration. From the administration's point of view, they had cause for concern. In May, massive black demonstrations in Birmingham had culminated with a night of rioting. Other parts of the country were ready to explode as well. Bob Moses, field secretary for SNCC, testifying before a House subcommittee on the president's civil rights bill to end discrimination in public places, education, and employment, warned congressmen they were facing a situation in Mississippi that had the potential to be far worse than Birmingham. With this information in hand, Kennedy believed that a mass gathering in Washington had the potential to undermine efforts being made to secure civil rights legislation and would damage the image of the United States globally. The president was also concerned that the event might intensify already heightened racial tensions across the country. Kennedy was also concern that the march might erode the public support for the Civil Rights movement at large. Kennedy called Dr. King and other civil rights leaders to the White House in late June 1962 to try to convince them to cancel the march, but he was unable to persuade them.

Various influential organizations and individuals also opposed the march. Besides the expected, such as southern segregationists and members of the Ku Klux Klan, the black separatist group, National of Islam, and its outspoken member, Malcolm X, also opposed the march. Malcolm X referred to it as the "farce on Washington," and any member of the Nation of Islam who attended the march was subjected to a 90-day suspension from the organization. The National Council of the AFL-CIO also chose not to support the march, adopting a position of neutrality. A number of international unions, however, independently declared their support and attended the march in substantial numbers. Hundreds of local unions also fully supported the march.

On August 28, the marchers arrived in chartered buses, trains, planes, and private cars. More than 200,000 had assembled by the Washington Monument on the National Mall, where the march was to begin. It was a very diverse crowd consisting of black and white, rich and poor, young and old, white collar, blue collar, unemployed, celebrities, and everyday people. The diversity of those in attendance was also reflected by the event's presenters and performers. Some of these included Marian Anderson, Daisy Lee Bates, Joan Baez, Bob Dylan, John Lewis, Odetta, Peter, Paul, and Mary, Rabbi Joachim Prinz, A. Philip Randolph, Walter Reuther, Bayard Rustin, Josh White, Roy Wilkins, and Whitney Young Jr.

Televised live to an audience of millions, the march provided numerous rhetorical moments in the form of speeches, songs, prayers, and actions (i.e., black and white people holding hands). Although the official march goals included an endorsement of Kennedy's civil rights bill—in part because the administration had officially cooperated with the march—some of the most passionate speeches criticized the bill as incomplete. John Lewis, the 23-year-old president of SNCC promised that without meaningful legislation, blacks would "march throughout the South." His speech prepared with other members of SNCC had originally suggested in the speech that they could not support the Kennedy legislation because it did not guarantee the right of black people to vote. In another part of the speech, SNCC had suggested that there was very little difference between the major political parties. They suggested that, as a movement, blacks could not wait on the president or the members of the Congress; they had to take matters into their own hands. Some people suggested that this portion of the speech was too inflammatory and that it might motivate people to riot. As a result, Lewis was forced to rewrite his original speech, which generally called the Kennedy legislative agenda for civil rights "too little, too late." Randolph and Wilkins also gave speeches. The most memorable speech of the day, however, came from Dr. King. The speech, reportedly delivered extemporaneously, would forever be known as the "I Have a Dream" speech. King's speech began with a powerful indictment of the nation's injustices against black Americans, then focused on a message of hope and determination, and a proclamation of what America could become, epitomizing the day's message of racial harmony, love, and a belief that blacks and whites could live together in peace. "I Have a Dream" is considered one of the greatest and most influential speeches in American history.

The march was an American landmark event for the early Civil Rights movement, and an overwhelming success owing to the organizers, leaders, participants, and extensive coverage by the media. The march is partly credited with winning passage of the federal Civil Rights Act of 1964. Although there was a presigned executive order authorizing 1,000 plus military intervention in case of rioting, there were no major disturbances. The behavior of the participants and onlookers proved that the presence of the military was unnecessary. Many Americans witnessed, for the first time, black and white people united, marching and celebrating together.

After the march, King and other civil rights leaders met with President Kennedy and Vice President Lyndon B. Johnson at the White House. Feeling the pressure of more than 200,000 Americans, Kennedy told them that he intended to throw his whole weight behind civil rights legislation. The march had not only achieved tangible goals, but it had also brought widespread attention to the struggle for civil rights. *See also:* Abernathy, Ralph David; Anderson, Marian; Bates, Daisy; Civil Rights Act of 1964; Kennedy, John Fitzgerald; King, Martin Luther Jr.; National Association for the Advancement of Colored People; Lewis, John; March on Washington Movement, 1941; Rustin, Bayard; Southern Christian Leadership Conference; Student Nonviolent Coordinating Committee; X, Malcolm

Janice D. Hamlet

Bibliography
Carson, Clayborne, ed. *The Autobiography of Martin Luther King, Jr.* New York: Warner Books, 1988.
Carson, Clayborne, David J. Garrow, Gerald Gill, Vincent Harding, and Darlene Clark Hine, ed. *The Eyes on the Prize Civil Rights Reader.* New York: Penguin Books, 1991.
Hampton, Henry, and Steve Fager, eds. *Voices of Freedom: An Oral History of the Civil Rights Movement from the 1950s through the 1980s.* New York: Bantam Books, 1990.
Williams, Juan. *Eyes on the Prize: America's Civil Rights Years, 1954–1965.* New York: Penguin Books, 1982.

Marshall, Thurgood

Thurgood Marshall (1908–1993) was born Thurgood Marshall (a name he later shortened legally) to Norma and William Marshall in the age of Jim Crow. Although Thurgood Marshall is perhaps best remembered for his historic position as the first black Supreme Court Justice and other men, such as Martin Luther King Jr., have garnered more fame for their leadership in the Civil Rights movement, Marshall's most direct and lasting contributions to the advancement of the race came in the years before the movement. Marshall, as an activist, laid the groundwork for the movement. As a direct result of Thurgood Marshall's and other civil rights leaders' efforts to uplift the race by overturning their subordinate legal status, blacks have earned political influence and arguably a stronger sense of community.

Throughout his life, Marshall was intimately and passionately involved with issues pertaining to equal rights for all men and women, regardless of race, ethnicity, or creed. Marshall's activism extended from his time at the NAACP (1932–1961) through his time as U.S. solicitor general (1965–1967). This can also be seen in the opinions and dissentions he wrote on the country's highest court (1967–1991). His NAACP tenure was a pivotal time for the organization when overturning racial segregation was one of its primary mandates. It was at the beginning of his career that Marshall began his work on his first segregation case, *Murray v. Pearson,* to open admission at the University of Maryland Law School to blacks—the same institution that denied him admittance only a few years earlier. By the time Marshall joined the bench of the Supreme Court, he had argued 32 cases before that body and won 29 of them, mostly in the name of racial desegregation and other civil rights causes.

The gains made by the *Murray* decision were small, for it only opened the law school; other graduate programs would be sued in the coming decade. Nevertheless, *Murray* was a significant step toward the larger educational accomplishments of Marshall and the NAACP. During the next two decades leading up to *Brown* (1954), which overturned *Plessey v. Ferguson* (1896), Marshall's cases challenged the foundation of American law itself. His goal was not merely to remind the nation to adhere to the Fourteenth Amendment—equal protection—but to demonstrate that the rules that he fought to overturn were wrong.

Marshall challenged segregation case after case. Although most of his cases dealt with educational equality, the future Justice also fought for blacks' right to vote in Texas primaries (*Smith v. Allwright,* 1944), the right to rent or buy any place of residence, and for equality of pay. In 1954, Marshall argued *Brown v. the Board of Education, Topeka, Kansas* in front of the U.S. Supreme Court. The *Brown* case encompassed five school segregation cases in Virginia, South Carolina, Delaware, Kansas, and Washington, D.C. After 17 years of success in opening postsecondary and graduate education through a series of court

Thurgood Marshall, the first African American appointed to the U.S. Supreme Court, built a remarkable legal career on the premise that all forms of racial segregation were unconstitutional. (Joseph Lavenburg, National Geographic Society, Collection of the Supreme Court of the United States)

cases, Marshall, the Legal Defense Fund, and the NAACP were ready to take on educational segregation on a primary school level. Separate was clearly unequal. This inequality was apparent in Clarendo County, South Carolina, for example; per capita spending for white students was $179 compared to spending for black students of $43, and the student-to-teacher ratio in the white schools was 28:1, but in the black school system it was nearly double, 47:1.

Topeka, Kansas was different. The facilities were equal. Marshall's argument in *Brown* had to go further than the need for equal facilities; otherwise the Court could uphold *Plessy* and again rule that school segregation was permissible as long as facilities were equal. Marshall wanted educational integration. He focused on testimony presented by experts about the terrible effects of state-sponsored segregation on black children. Marshall argued "that segregated schools, perhaps more than any other single factor, are of major concern to the individual of public school age and contribute greatly to the unwholesomeness and unhappy development of the personality of Negroes which the color

caste system in the United States has produced" (*Supreme Justices*, p. 52). The case was not easily won; it was almost a year-and-a-half after the Court began hearing the case that Chief Justice Warren finally read the Court's unanimous decision "Separate educational facilities are inherently unequal" (*Brown v. Board of Education* 347 U.S. 483).

The Supreme Court extended the *Brown* decision beyond education by expanding the principle to desegregate other public facilities. Through a series of signed and *per curiam* opinions, the Court ordered equal access to public parking lots, restaurants, cemeteries, hospitals, parks, golf courses, buses, beaches, and amphitheaters.

Marshall realized the impact of the *Brown* decision. He believed that *Brown* "probably did more than anything else to awaken the Negro from his apathy to demanding his right to equality" (*A Defiant Life*, p. 147). Therefore, the 1954 decision can be seen as the foundation for the Civil Rights movement; however, Marshall did not think *Brown* alone made the movement. When reflecting on the importance of his victories in *Smith* and *Brown*, Marshall once said, "I don't know whether the voting case or the school desegregation case was more important. Without the ballot, you've got no goddamned citizenship, no status, no power, in this country. But without the chance to get an education, you have no capacity to use the ballot effectively. Hell, I don't know which case I'm proudest of" (*Supreme Justices*, p. 75). *See also: Brown v. Board of Education;* Houston, Charles Hamilton; Johnson, Lyndon Baines; National Association for the Advancement of Colored People; Thomas, Clarence

Noah D. Drezner

Bibliography
Ball, Howard. *A Defiant Life: Thurgood Marshall and the Persistence of Racism in America.* New York: Three Rivers Press, 2001.
Drezner, Noah D. "Thurgood Marshall: A Study of Philanthropy Through Racial Uplift." In *Uplifting A People: Essays on African American Philanthropy in Education,* Marybeth Gasman and Katherine V. Sedwick, eds., 98–100. New York: Peter Lang, 2005.
Smith, J. Clay, ed. *Supreme Justices: Speeches and Writings.* Philadelphia: University of Pennsylvania Press, 2003.

Matthews, Victoria Earle

Social reformer, journalist, and settlement house founder, Victoria Earle Matthews (1861–1907) committed her life to service. Born May 27, 1861, as one of nine children to a Virginia-born slave in Georgia, Victoria was part of the urban migration after emancipation. First moving to Richmond and Norfolk, Virginia, Victoria and her family arrived in New York City in 1873. She gained some education through the public schools, but she had to leave and find employment as a domestic to help her family. At 18, she married William Matthews, a coachman, and began to write articles and short stories for the *Waverly* magazine under the pen name, Victoria Earle. Her writings appeared in children's magazines and in both black and white newspapers as a way to earn money and as an intellectual outlet. Soon widowed and following the death of her only son, Matthews devoted her time to social welfare activities.

An admirer of Ida B. Wells, journalist and leader of the antilynching movement, Matthews joined with other black women in the New York City-Brooklyn community to honor Wells at a testimonial dinner in Lyric Hall on October 5, 1892. This event led to the formation of two important women's clubs: the Woman's Loyal Union, organized by Matthews and Maritcha Lyons later that month, and the Woman's Era Club of Boston, founded by Josephine St. Pierre Ruffin in January 1893.

As founder and first president of the Woman's Loyal Union, Matthews assumed a leadership position in the emerging club movement. She attended the first conference of black women in the summer of 1895, delivering a speech, "The Value of Race Literature." She was party to the formation of the National Federation of Afro-American Women in 1895 and became a delegate to the Congress of Colored Women at the Atlanta Exposition in December 1895. Despite the racial segregation at the Exposition, Matthews attended, heard the speech of Booker T. Washington, and visited other southern cities to gather information about the condition of black women in cities. She brought back this information to the New York women. The next summer, Matthews joined these black women in Washington, D. C to merge two national organizations into the National Association of Colored Women, for which Matthews served as the national organizer.

On the trip back from the Atlanta Exposition and her tour of southern cities, she witnessed conditions for young, black women coming from the rural South to the northern cities in search of better wages, working conditions, and opportunities. Traveler's aid was unconcerned about black women being duped by unscrupulous men at the docks.

After her return to her Brooklyn home on Poplar Street, she gathered clubwomen together to develop a protective service for young working girls. The White Rose Home opened on February 11, 1897 to shelter and protect these young migrants and train them in practical self-help. Matthews and her helpers filled the need for travelers' aid by meeting the arrivals at the boats. The service expanded by providing agents at the Norfolk docks and became the White Rose Travelers' Aid Society in 1905. In addition to temporary lodging and training, services similar to employment agencies emerged to protect the women at work and obtain fair wages. Protecting and training black domestics received the support of white benefactors Mrs. C. P. Huntington, Grace Dodge, and Mary L. Stone, who contributed money and served as volunteers.

Matthews balanced training in practical skills (cooking, laundry, sewing, chair caning, and wood burnishing) with lectures on race history and leadership. Matthews turned over her personal collection of race literature to the settlement library and encouraged the young women to read the books to establish race pride. When race leaders visited New York City, Matthews invited them to speak to the women and encourage them to achieve.

Matthews and her sister clubwomen served as administrators, fundraisers, and teachers/volunteers. Alice Moore Dunbar taught in the kindergarten. Hallie Q. Brown served as assistant superintendent. When Matthews's health declined, Frances Reynolds Keyser assumed the leadership for the White Rose Home. Matthews died of tuberculosis on March 10, 1907. Services were held at her church, St. Philips Episcopal, followed by her burial in New York City's Maple Grove Cemetery.

Her legacy lived on through the White Rose Home, which became a model settlement house. The services provided impetus for the formation of the National League for the Protection of Colored Women in 1906. Urban multiservice centers grew out of these homes or missions for the protection of young black women. The centers filled the needs for lodging, job placement, night classes, industrial training, day nurseries, kindergartens, libraries, boys and girls clubs, savings clubs, choir and music programs, and social gatherings. They became the training ground for black visiting nurses and social workers graduating from emerging educational programs in social work. The centers cooperated with the National Urban League through affiliation and laid the foundation for major social services in black communities for generations.

See also: Antilynching Campaign; National Association of Colored Women; Wells-Barnett, Ida.

Dorothy Salem

Bibliography

Logan, Shirley W. *With Pen and Voice: A Critical Anthology of Nineteenth-Century African-American Women.* Carbondale: Southern Illinois University Press, 1995.

Salem, Dorothy. *To Better Our World: Black Women in Organized Reform, 1890–1920.* Brooklyn: Carlson Publishing, 1990.

White, Deborah Gray. *Too Heavy a Load: Black Women in Defense of Themselves, 1894–1994.* New York: W. W. Norton, 1999.

McKay, Claude

Poet, journalist, editor, and black radical, Claude McKay (1889–1948) is best known for the literary contributions he made to the period in African American history commonly known as the Harlem Renaissance (1920–1930). Claude McKay was born in the upper Clarendon Parish in Jamaica in 1889 to Thomas Francis McKay and Hanna Ann Elizabeth Edwards. The youngest of eight children, McKay lived a sheltered life of relative ease as a result of the hard work of his parents. The McKay family's economic circumstances situated them as members of a small elite group of black farmers, but their dark skin ensured a somewhat marginalized social status among the lighter complexioned people whose skin color granted social status. These earlier experiences greatly influenced McKay's writing.

Before leaving his homeland of Jamaica in 1912 at the age of 22, McKay wrote two volumes of poetry in dialect. These volumes established McKay as an important literary figure among his local constituency. His arrival at Tuskegee Institute in Alabama that same year marked the beginning of an important period of self-discovery. The harsh realities of southern racism in part prompted McKay to leave Tuskegee a few months later to attend Kansas State College, a decision that proved unsatisfactory socially, but was beneficial to his career and intellectual development. It was during his two year stay in Kansas that McKay first read W. E. B. Du Bois's work, *The Souls of Black Folk* (1903). For McKay, Du Bois clearly articulated the marginalized social, political, and economic position that blacks in America occupied. Arguments made by Du Bois resonated with McKay's own experiences, both in Jamaica and in America. His poetry and writing reflected a growing sense of racial and class consciousness that was further enhanced by his encounters with other writers, artists, and intellectuals whom he met during his years in New York.

By the summer of 1914, McKay found himself in Harlem, New York, married to Eulalie Imelda Lewars, a long-time friend from Jamaica. During his early years in New York, McKay found employment as a porter, waiter, and briefly as an unsuccessful restaurant owner. He continued honing his writing skills and incorporated bits and pieces of his employment experiences into his poetry and fiction.

New York offered ample opportunities to engage in social activities, and McKay often did so with abandon. It was also here that he began further exploring his own homosexuality, which no doubt played a role in the dissolution of his marriage after only six months. His wife returned to Jamaica where she bore McKay's only child, a daughter whom he never saw.

By 1918, New York was becoming a hot bed of social protest. McKay was able to surround himself by like-minded radicals such as black socialist, Hubert Harrison. McKay also established working relationships with prominent men and women able to advance his writing career, such as Frank Harris, publisher of *Pearson's Magazine,* and Crystal Eastman, sister of Max Eastman, chief editor of the radical magazine the *Liberator,* and scholar Arthur Schomburg. McKay's reputation as a notable writer of the Harlem Renaissance era is both national and international. During his lifetime he contributed poems, short stories, and critical essays to many of the most popular literary journals of his time. Notably, in the aftermath of the 1919 Chicago race riot, he published "If We Must Die"—a militant poem that, in many ways, was an immediate precursor to the Harlem Renaissance. Claude McKay died in 1948 of heart disease.

See also: Chicago Race Riot of 1919; Harlem Renaissance; "If We Must Die"; New Negro Movement; Red Summer Race Riots

Beverly A. Bunch-Lyons

Bibliography

Cooper, Wayne F. *Claude McKay: Rebel Sojourner in the Harlem Renaissance, A Biography.* Baton Rouge: Louisiana State University Press, 1987.

Holcomb, Gary Edward. *Claude McKay, Code Name Sasha.* Gainesville: University Press of Florida, 2007.

Ramesh, Kotti Sree, and Kandula Nirupa Rani. *Claude McKay: The Literary Identity from Jamaica to Harlem and Beyond.* Jefferson, NC: McFarland, 2006.

Tillery, Tyrone. *Claude McKay: A Black Poet's Struggle for Identity.* Amherst: University of Massachusetts Press, 1992.

Media Stereotypes

The stereotyping of African Americans within American media has been occurring since before the Civil War. Scholars have noted that the most prevalent forms are the slick Zip Coon, the savage Brute, the passive Uncle Tom, and the no-nonsense Mammy. Also present were images of the young black child as Pickaninny, the dim-witted yet noble Buck, and the tragically confused biracial Mulatto. Many of these images have appeared in print (posters, advertisements), heard on radio shows (the unseen banter of white men pretending to be Black on *Amos n' Andy* from 1928 to 1937), film (since before *The Birth of a Nation* in 1915 to contemporary "urban dramas"), and television programming of all genre. In each of these depictions, African Americans are reduced to caricatures of racial representations that often misinformed popular culture. A stereotype is defined as a standardized way of perceiving members of a group. Those who often seek to stereotype various groups (in this case, African Americans) reduce a complex, multifaceted people into homogeneous groups with only a subtle degree of variation.

Exposure of these media stereotypes began early in American history. During the days of minstrelsy, images appeared on billboards advertising upcoming stage shows. Many of these posters depicted the grinning Zip Coon wearing upscale garments that were mismatched and poorly fitted. This same pretentious character represented the free black's inability to fit into white society. The Brute, however, often appeared in the popular mainstream press as a reminder of how dangerous freed blacks could be. Misshapen and hideously unattractive, the Brute evoked fear in the hearts of white Americans. The editorial pages of many early newspapers reminded readers that these men (and women) would be set free to roam among them if abolitionists had their way. In advertising, images of the older, gray-haired Uncle Tom sitting placidly on a backwoods porch often appeared, seemingly content within his life of servitude. The Mammy was his female counterpart, often large and dark-skinned, cooking and cleaning for the master and missus, raising their children and occasionally working the fields when needed.

It has been argued by media scholars that these stereotypes are still with us today in newer, more modern guises. Many African American comedians still "skin and grin" as did Zip Coon; using comic routines that are buffoonish and self-deprecating. Young black men as brutish gang members threaten our streets while older, more conservative "Toms" supposedly support the slow, but gradual process of America society. Meanwhile, many sitcoms have featured large, mammy-like women doting after children and carrying out their expected duties.

During the 1960s and beyond, many media stereotypes of African Americans, previously coarse in their demeanor, were now transformed into articulate and highly intelligent people. For many black audiences, these countertypes attempted to send the message that they now had many of the same innate possibilities for success as did their white counterparts. For other audiences, black people had become assimilated into lifestyles that helped support the status quo of society, law, and order. Some movies and television shows featured black detectives and lawyers. Social responsibility was demonstrated by doctors and teachers working within the community, and social equality was shown through successful African American business owners. Each of these generalizations attempted to draw attention away from ongoing struggles against racial inequality and injustice.

Audiences often learn about other cultural groups from media, reinforcing cultural beliefs and subsequent values. Stereotypes have allowed writers and producers of programming and images to create shorthand versions of characters. These well-worn constructs often avoid explanations of motivations and instead use stereotypes to represent what these motivations *probably* are. Within an urban crime drama, it is not important to know the motivations of a young black man trapped within gang life. Through media stereotypes, audiences can make assumptions about criminal behavior and probable intent, allowing the hero/heroine to rescue society from the young man's criminality and chaos. These plots posit constructs and then move forward with a pretense, a problem, and the resolution. Stereotypes within narrative often take complex notions of the real world and make them easier to understand through oversimplification.

Media stereotypes have also affected the self-definition of African Americans. These "internalized media stereotypes" cause African American audiences to alter their self-image. Young black males may behave in a more aggressive fashion because of how *their* lives are depicted in videos. Assumptions about relationships are based on televised depictions of black marriages and romances. Traditionally black neighborhoods are considered undesirable based solely on how a television show (especially news coverage) frames them. Media stereotypes have been so pervasive that many other countries have seemingly come to "understand" African Americans through what they have seen in American media.

See also: BET; Jim Crow; *The Birth of a Nation*

Darrell Newton

Bibliography

Anderson, Lisa M. *Mammies No More: The Changing Image of Black Women on Stage and Screen.* Lanham, MD: Rowman & Littlefield, 1997.

Bogle, Donald. *Toms, Coons, Mulattoes, Mammies, and Bucks: An Interpretive History of Blacks in American Films.* New York: Continuum, 2001

Cripps, Thomas. *Making Movies Black: The Hollywood Message Movie from World War II to the Civil Rights Era.* New York: Oxford University Press, 1993.

Martinez, Gerald *What It Is—What It Was!: The Black Film Explosion of the '70s in Words and Pictures.* New York: Hyperion, 1998.

Watkins, S. Craig. *Representing: Hip Hop Culture and the Production of Black Cinema.* Chicago: University of Chicago Press, 1998.

Meredith, James

James Meredith (1933–) is a civil rights activist who is best known for becoming the first African American student to attend the University of Mississippi in October 1962. Meredith's entry into the school served as a major turning point for the Civil Rights movement. James Howard Meredith was born June 25, 1933, in Kosciusko, Mississippi to farmers, Moses and Roxie Meredith. Moses Meredith was one of few African Americans in Mississippi who not only owned his own farm, but was also registered to vote, and he made a strong effort to make sure that James and his nine brothers and sisters were sheltered from the racism of the surrounding community. After graduating high school, James Meredith immediately joined the U.S. Air Force, which he served in from 1951 to 1960. In 1956, he married Mary June Wiggins, and the pair had three sons. After his discharge from the military, Meredith enrolled at Jackson State College for two years before applying for a transfer to the University of Mississippi at Oxford. Despite his excellent grades, he was denied admission twice before finally gaining acceptance in 1962. Then-governor Ross Barnett adamantly opposed Meredith's admission to the University, and personally traveled there to prevent Meredith from registering for classes. Meredith finally gained entrance to the school on October 1, 1962, where his presence sparked riots all over the campus. In all, 5,000 federal troops and 500 U.S. marshals were needed to quell the violence, which left two people dead and hundreds injured.

Many students treated Meredith poorly during his two semesters at the university. Although some apparently accepted his presence and he made friends, some students living in his dorm would bounce basketballs on the floor directly above Meredith's room at all hours of the night to disturb him. When Meredith would go to the cafeteria, people turned their backs to him, and if he sat at a table with other students, those students, who were all white, would immediately get up and move to another table. Despite this poor treatment, Meredith graduated with a degree in political science on August 18, 1963.

Following his time at the University of Mississippi, Meredith continued his education at the University of Ibadan in Nigeria before receiving a law degree from Columbia University in 1968. In addition to continuing his studies, Meredith remained a pivotal figure in the Civil Rights movement throughout the 1960s. Most notably, he led a civil rights march from Memphis, Tennessee to Jackson, Mississippi in the summer of 1966. Calling his march the "Walk Against Fear," he hoped that his example would encourage the nearly half-million disenfranchised in Mississippi to overcome their fear of white retaliation and they would register to vote. Meredith did not invite any national civil rights groups to join him, instead choosing to march alone. On June 6, the day after the march started, Meredith was shot by sniper Aubrey James Norvell after walking only 28 miles. Although wounded, Meredith healed enough to finish the march two weeks later, this time joined by Dr. Martin Luther King and other nationally recognized

James Meredith (photo taken in 1966) is a civil rights activist who is best known for becoming the first African American student to attend the University of Mississippi in October 1962. (Library of Congress)

civil rights activists. A photograph of Meredith after he was wounded won a Pulitzer Prize in photography in 1967.

Meredith ceased his civil rights activism in the late 1960s and authored a memoir about his time at the University of Mississippi entitled *Three Years in Mississippi*, published in 1966. He then settled into a career as a stockbroker before running unsuccessfully for a congressional seat in 1972, and then serving as a domestic advisor on the staff of U.S. Senator Jesse Helms, a one-time segregationist, beginning in 1989. Although he received a barrage of criticism from the civil rights community, Meredith, a staunch Republican, defended his decision to work for Helms, stating that he had written letters to every member of the House of Representatives and Senate offering his services and only Helms had replied. Meredith's most recent publication a historical work, *Mississippi: A Volume of Eleven Books,* was published in 1995. He presented his papers to his alma mater, the University of Mississippi, on March 21, 1997.

In 2002, Meredith's son Joseph graduated from the University of Mississippi with a doctorate in business administration. Joseph Meredith also received honors for being the most outstanding student in the school of business administration.

Today, Meredith distances himself from the Civil Rights movement of which he was such an instrumental part, referring to himself instead as a citizen who fought to protect the rights extended to all Americans. He currently lives in Jackson, Mississippi with his second wife, journalist Judy Alsobrooks, and runs a small used-car dealership.

See also: Black Conservatives; Kennedy, John Fitzgerald; Republican Party; White Mob Violence

Sara K. Eskridge

Bibliography
Barrett, Russell H. *Integration at Ole Miss.* Chicago: Quadrangle Books, 1965.
Doyle, William. *An American Insurrection: The Battle of Oxford, Mississippi, 1962.* New York: Doubleday, 2001.
Lord Walter. *The Past That Would Not Die.* New York: Harper and Row, 1965.
Meredith, James. *Three Years in Mississippi.* Bloomington: Indiana University Press, 1966.

MFDP

The Mississippi Freedom Democratic Party (MFDP), founded on April 26, 1964 in Jackson Mississippi, was organized as an alternative to the regular Mississippi Democratic Party that denied African Americans in the state their voting rights. Spurred on by the Student Nonviolent Coordinating Committee (SNCC) and the Council of Federated Organizations (COFO), the MFDP had two objectives from the outset: to affirm black self-determination and to challenge northern-based white allies to take a stronger stance in support of the southern-based Civil Rights movement.

Building on SNCC's years of organizing around voter registration in the state, the MFDP was inspired by the 1963 "Freedom Ballot," a mock gubernatorial election in which nearly 80,000 black Mississippians cast votes. It envisioned itself as the catalyst to organizing black political participation in the state while serving as a nonexclusionary party open to both blacks and whites and running an integrated slate of candidates. Further, unlike mainstream political parties, women occupied leadership roles in the MFDP. Two of the most noticeable women were Fannie Lou Hamer and Victoria Gray, who ran for the House and Senate, respectively, in the state primary races for Congress. Noting the danger of bucking the establishment of the racist political structure in Mississippi, Hamer, who had received many death threats for her participation in civil rights activities, stated, "But if I fall, I'll fall five feet four inches forward in the fight for freedom" (*Freedom's Daughters*, p. 315).

In addition to the central roles Hamer and Gray played, Ella Baker acted as a voluntary director of the MFDP's Washington, D.C. office and keynoted the party's convention. Displaying a keen understanding of the long-term effect of the MFDP's ability to politicize poor African Americans in the state and develop a new grassroots leadership Baker noted, "It is important that you go to the [Democratic National] convention whether you are seated or not. It is even more important that you develop a political machinery in this state. The MFDP will not end at the convention. This is only the beginning" (*Freedom's Daughters*, p. 317).

On August 21, 1964, the 68 MFDP delegates arrived in Atlantic City, New Jersey and began to lobby for support to be seated as Mississippi's official delegation for the Democratic National Convention. President Lyndon Johnson was so worried that a high-profile fight over seating the MFDP would cost him reelection by losing southern votes that he attempted to undercut support for the party. In a well-known show of insecurity and power politics, as Fannie Lou Hamer was addressing 110 members of the convention's Credentials Committee, Johnson called a press conference so that media attention would be drawn away from Hamer's compelling testimony about what it meant to be black and poor in Mississippi, which was being broadcast nationwide.

Seeing that the MFDP would not be deterred, President Johnson made an effort to placate the upstart delegation. Johnson offered a compromise; he would allow two of the party's delegates that he hand-picked to be seated as nonvoting delegates-at-large, and the rest of the MFDP's delegates would be accepted as guests of the convention. Although some MFDP delegates were initially in favor of the compromise and some heavyweight civil rights leaders such as Roy Wilkins and Martin Luther King urged the MFDP to accept the deal, the party rejected it.

Johnson was incensed by the party's refusal and had their phones tapped. Further, at Johnson's request, FBI agents posed as NBC correspondents to try to extract information from party delegates. The most underhanded incident occurred when Hubert Humphrey and Walter Mondale brought the rejected compromise to the Credentials Committee as if the MFDP had accepted it. Based on the assumption that the MFDP was in favor of the compromise, both the Credentials Committee and full Democratic Convention approved the compromise without the knowledge of the MFDP. With that, the MFDP was locked out of participating in the convention the same way as Mississippi residents were barred from voting.

Although 20 MFDP delegates managed to enter the convention hall and stage a protest that was nationally televised, with credentials passes given to them by other sympathetic delegates, in the end the MFDP was unable to unseat the regular Mississippi Democratic delegation. The mainstream Democrats viewed the MFDP as a threat to business as usual and, as journalist Carl Braden noted, "They [the MFDP] were really serving notice that if [they] are going to be involved in politics, it's going to be an entirely different kind of politics and different people are going to run things.... I mean this is a threat.... If you're somewhere in power you don't want that happening (*Freedom's Daughters*, pp. 323–24).

The Mississippi Freedom Democratic Party may not have been seated at the Democratic National Convention, but it brought the struggle and injustice that African Americans in Mississippi faced to a national spotlight, helped pass the 1965 Voting Rights Act, and led to an overhaul of the Democratic Party, opening it up to groups that previously had little or no representation in its councils before the MFDP's challenge. Thinking back on the MFDP, civil rights activist Bob Moses noted, "The MFDP was raising an important question with this country, and with the Democratic Party, as one of its major political institutions: Generations of Black people had been denied access to the political process; could they get it now?... We were challenging them [the Democratic Party] to recognize the existence of a whole group of people—white and Black and disenfranchised—who form the underclass of this country" (*Radical Equations*, pp. 82–83).

Although the answer to Moses's question was a resounding "NO," according to civil rights scholar Leslie McLemore, the MFDP represented, "the coming of political age of Black people in Mississippi in a way that had not been seen since Reconstruction" (Olsen, 2001, 324).

Further, John Lewis, a SNCC chairman during the 1960s, indicates that the MFDP's challenge was the turning point of the Civil Rights movement, noting that until the Democratic Convention failed to seat the MFDP, most civil rights activists held on to the belief that the democratic system would eventually work. After the Atlantic City debacle, however, such faith in the system was lost and people now saw that if change was going to happen, they were going to have to make it happen.

See also: Baker, Ella; Disfranchisement; Hamer, Fannie Lou; Lowndes County Freedom Organization; Johnson, Lyndon Baines; Mississippi Freedom Summer, 1964; Moses, Robert; Student Nonviolent Coordinating Committee; Voting Rights Act of 1965

Paul T. Miller

Bibliography

Carson, Clayborne. *In Struggle: SNCC and the Black Awakening of the 1960s.* Cambridge, MA: Harvard University Press, 1981.

Lewis, John. *Walking with the Wind.* New York: Simon & Schuster, 1998.

Moses, Robert. *Radical Equations: Math Literacy and Civil Rights.* Boston: Beacon, 2001.

Olsen, Lynn. *Freedom's Daughters: The Unsung Heroines of the Civil Rights Movement from 1830 to 1970.* New York: Scribner, 2001.

Ransby, Barbara. *Ella Baker & the Black Freedom Movement: A Radical Democratic Vision.* Chapel Hill: The University of North Carolina Press, 2003.

Million Man March

On October 16, 1995, an estimated 850,000 African American men gathered on Washington, D.C.'s National Mall for one of the largest political rallies in U.S. history. By comparison, 250,000 people of all ethnic and racial backgrounds gathered for the 1963 March on Washington for Jobs and Freedom to hear Martin Luther King's "I Have a Dream" speech. The so-called Million Man March was organized principally by the controversial leader of the Nation of Islam, Minister Louis Farrakhan, and was meant to generate discussions about self-help and to engage African American men to commit to their families and to help stop drug use, violence, and other vices in their communities. These themes were repeated in the speeches delivered by more than 60 African American and diasporic African dignitaries including Maya Angelou, Reverend Jeremiah

Wright, Martin Luther King III, Rosa Parks, Reverend Jesse Jackson, Reverend Benjamin Chavis, Minister Rasul Muhammad, Dick Gregory, and Senator Aldebert Bryan of the Virgin Islands. Concentrated on the themes of atonement, reconciliation, and responsibility, the Million Man March was not—as projected in the media—another frustrated attempt to uncover racism and the hands of white America in the plight of African Americans.

The march was organized in the context of troubling political trends showing that African American concerns were being pushed to the periphery of the political landscape. In 1994, sweeping Republican Party victories in congressional elections—based in part on the positive reception of the Contact with America—led to Republicans becoming the majority party in the U.S. House of Representatives for the first time in 40 years. Republicans, like Minority Whip Newt Gingrich and Tom DeLay, played active roles in setting political agendas for President Bill Clinton, particularly on issues like law enforcement and welfare reform, which concerned African Americans. In many ways, the Million Man March can be seen as a direct reaction to two Republican-led initiatives in mid- to late-1995—the Taking Back Our Streets Act (which called for the building of new prisons and tougher sentencing) and the Personal Responsibility Act (which called for significant reforms in welfare programs).

On the same day as the Million Man March, female leaders associated with the march organizers called for the National Day of Absence, which would be observed by those who could not be in attendance in Washington, D.C. On the National Day of Absence, African Americans were encouraged to be absent from school and work and to attend either teach-ins or worship services, which would facilitate discussions and contemplation on the livelihood and self-sufficiency of African American communities across the country. Organizers of both the march and the Day of Absence hoped to move the movements beyond political discourse and sought to engage the issues plaguing African American communities on a spiritual level. Given the role played by ministers of the Nation of Islam and Christian religious leaders in both movements, the fact that they emphasized spiritual healing as the foundation for solutions to various social ills makes sense.

The various themes of spiritual healing, atonement, reconciliation, and responsibility were highlighted in the Million Man March Pledge. After the speech delivered by

Minister Louis Farrakhan, he asked all men in attendance to raise their right hand and to repeat the following:

I _____ pledge that from this day forward, I will strive to love my brother as I love myself.

I _____ from this day forward will strive to improve myself spiritually, morally, mentally, socially, politically and economically for the benefit of myself, my family and my people.

I _____ pledge that I will strive to build business, build houses, build hospitals, build factories and enter into international trade for the good of myself, my family and my people.

I _____ pledge that from this day forward I will never raise my hand with a knife or a gun to beat, cut or shoot any member of my family or any human being except in self defense.

I _____ pledge from this day forward, I will never abuse my wife by striking her, disrespecting her, for she is the mother of my children and the producer of my future.

I _____ pledge that from this day forward, I will never engage in the abuse of children, little boys or little girls, for sexual gratification. But I will let them grow in peace to be strong men and women for the future of our people.

I _____ will never again use the "b" word to describe any female, but particularly my own Black sister.

I _____ pledge that from this day forward that I will not poison my body with drugs or that which is destructive to my health and my well-being.

I _____ pledge from this day forward that I will support Black newspapers, Black radio, Black television. I will support Black artists who clean up their acts and show respect for themselves and respect for their people and respect for the heirs of the human family.

I _____ will do all of this, so help me God.

After the pledge, each man in the crowd was asked to hug another. Although controversies about the lack of involvement and support by President Clinton and the actual size of the crowd during the Million Man March would shape some of the public discourse surrounding the events on October 16, 1995, the march helped initiate internal discussions and reassessments within African American communities. Moreover, it spawned a number of similar movements, including the Million Woman March (1997), the Million Youth March (1998), and the Million Family March (2000). The energy and discussions created by the movement were highlighted in Spike Lee's 1996 movie *Get on the Bus*.

See also: Clinton, William Jefferson; Farrakhan, Louis; March on Washington, 1963; Nation of Islam

Walter C. Rucker

Bibliography

Cottman, Michael H., and Deborah Willis. *Million Man March*. New York: Crown Trade Paperbacks, 1995.

Hull, Mary. *Struggle and Love, 1972–1997: From the Gary Convention to the Aftermath of the Million Man March*. Philadelphia: Chelsea House, 1997.

Moore, Lenard D., and Eugene Redmond. *Gathering at the Crossroads: The Million Man March*. Winchester, VA: Red Moon Press, 2003.

Reid, Frank Madison, Jeremiah A. Wright, and Colleen Birchett. *When Black Men Stand Up for God: Reflections on the Million Man March*. Chicago: African American Images, 1996.

Sadler, Kim Martin. *Atonement: The Million Man March*. Cleveland, OH: Pilgrim Press, 1996.

Mississippi Freedom Summer, 1964

During the summer of 1964, hundreds of black and white students volunteered to enter the Deep South to work on a program called Freedom Summer. The impetus behind Freedom Summer was to work on voter registration, establish freedom schools, and get the black community involved in local politics. Most of the volunteers were members of the Student Nonviolent Coordinating Committee (SNCC), Congress of Racial Equality (CORE), and The National Association for the Advancement of Colored People (NAACP). These groups together combined to make the Mississippi Council of Federated Organization for the sole purpose of politically organizing black communities, in Mississippi

Mississippi was an important place for civil rights work for several reasons. First, perhaps out of the entire South, blacks in Mississippi had horrible political and economic conditions, especially in the Mississippi Delta. In 1962, Mississippi only had 6.7 precent of the black population registered to vote. Despite the constitutional right for all citizens to be able to vote, black Mississippians were constantly in fear of losing their home, jobs, and lives from white retaliation. Furthermore, the white political machine continually disfranchised the black community through enforcement of poll taxes and literacy test.

The second reason Mississippi was important was the continued economic oppression facing the black community. The Mississippi Delta was severely impoverished. Mechanization caused a lot of workers to lose their jobs, and those who still had jobs were in fear of losing them because they fought to be able to vote. Black Mississippians and SNCC organizers believed the key to a brighter economic future rested in the hands of those who ran the government. Many communities in Mississippi had a black majority, so they should not only be able to vote but also hold political office.

One of the local individuals that helped organize and galvanize a nation for political and economic improvement in Mississippi was Mrs. Fannie Lou Hamer. Born in Montgomery County, Mississippi, Hamer was raised by sharecroppers and continued working as a sharecropper in the Mississippi Delta. Once SNCC became active in Mississippi during the summer of 1962, Hamer worked with them to educate and register to vote thousands of poor blacks living in the area. Hamer was also not intimidated by the white community. When the owner of the plantation she worked for asked her not to register to vote, she did so anyway, despite the threats of being removed from the land she had worked so hard on.

Although she was Hamer continued to work for voter rights in Mississippi. One of the events that placed her into the national spotlight was her arrest in Winona, Mississippi after returning from a citizenship class in Charleston, South Carolina. She was arrested on trumped-up charges and severely beaten while in jail. There was a highly publicized court case, in which the defendants were found not guilty. After all the publicity from Hamer's beating and subsequent trial, however, her name began garnering national attention both for her personally and for the state of Mississippi.

Hamer was also a founder and organizer of the Mississippi Freedom Democratic Party (MFDP) in the spring of 1964. The creation and sustaining of the MFDP became one of the primary goals of Freedom Summer. Volunteers

Volunteer worker urges Southern African Americans to register to vote in 1964. (National Archives)

traveled from house to house in the black community urging individuals to vote and become active in the political process. The creation of the MFDP was especially important because of the upcoming presidential election. They wanted to make President Johnson realize that the needs of the black community had to be met and the Democratic Party, as it currently was, did not represent black America. The main goal of the MFDP was to unseat the all-white Mississippi Democratic regulars at the Democratic Convention in Atlantic City, New Jersey, and be recognized as the true representatives of Mississippi.

On August 20, 1964, MFDP delegates arrived, including Hamer. Upon their arrival, the convention had to decide who would represent Mississippi on the convention floor. The Credential Committee held a hearing that was broadcast live across the nation. Hamer spoke on the injustices going on in Mississippi and the political climate of the South. Just as her speech was starting to get impassioned, President Johnson interrupted the broadcast with an impromptu press conference.

Despite President Johnson's attempt to cut Hamer off, the nation had already seen enough to give national support to the MFDP. President Johnson was afraid that if he issued his support for the MFDP, he would lose the southern Democratic vote and ultimately the presidency. A compromise had to be reached. The convention decided to offer the MFDP two seats at large and bar any delegation guilty of discrimination. All but four of the regular Democrat delegates from Mississippi walked off the floor, and the MFDP tried to obtain those seats but were not allowed on the floor. Ultimately, the MFDP turned down the two seats. The MFDP did not get seated at the convention, but the creation and support of the party helped to achieve a major goal of Freedom Summer—getting the local community interested and active in local politics and garnering the nation's attention toward black voting rights in the South.

Beyond the local community, hundreds of white volunteers from the North helped spread the word and educate the black community about their voting rights. Community centers were created where children could have not only "traditional" educational classes, but also organize for political change in their communities. Before these northern volunteers went to Mississippi, they received training in Oxford, Ohio, led by Jim Forman and other SNCC members, including Fannie Lou Hammer. The purpose of training was to introduce them to nonviolence tactics and give them an understanding of what mob violence might be like. If past events, like the Freedom Rides, were any indication of how white mobs acted on both black and white bodies, the volunteers knew that violence, if not death, was likely.

Nothing illustrated that threat better than the disappearance of a black volunteer, James Chaney, and two white volunteers, Andrew Goodman and Michael Schwerner. These three men set out on June 21 for Philadelphia, Mississippi to investigate the bombing of a black church. The men were arrested and then released that same evening, never to be seen again. Press conferences were held and the families of all three men begged the public for any information about their whereabouts. President Johnson even launched an FBI investigation into their disappearance. The wife of Michael Schwerner, Rita, publicly addressed the fact that if all the men had been black, there would be no national attention over their disappearance and that it was a shame that white men had to die before the violence in Mississippi, and the South in general, would be noticed by the American public. Eventually, the scorched remains of their car were found, leading everyone to fear they were dead. Their suspicions were confirmed on April 4 when their bodies were found buried together in a shallow grave. The FBI had offered $30,000 to a Ku Klux Klan member for the information on where they were buried. All three were killed by gunshots to the head, and Chaney was also severely beaten. The families of the three men wanted them all to be buried together, but because of continued segregation in cemeteries, their wish could not be fulfilled.

The disappearance of the three men did have a positive impact on the events of that summer. It placed more media attention on the volunteers and perhaps resulted in less violence than normal toward the workers. Despite the media, approximately 80 volunteers were beaten and 1,000 were jailed over the course of the summer. In addition, houses, Freedom Schools, churches, and other centers of volunteer activity were burned or firebombed. Despite the fear of violence, students were eager to work in Mississippi. Although cooperation between black and white workers showed the nation how all people could work together to effect change in Mississippi, however, people began to question whether the presence of whites was actually a positive for accomplishing the goals of Freedom Summer.

For instance, local blacks could expect more harassment from local whites for just talking with the volunteers.

Immediately, white youth started driving through the black communities where white volunteers were staying and would break windows, start fires, or make other threats against the black community. The black community was inviting violence by talking to the volunteers, and this was obviously a very dangerous situation. Some white volunteers would become frustrated because any black person who was outspoken or supported the efforts of the volunteers would loose their jobs or worse. It was not uncommon for the local police or local whites to follow the volunteers into the black community and report their findings back to their employers or other members of the community.

Another issue that was debated was the role of white women. Southern attitudes about what "white womanhood" meant and how it was threatened by going into the black community did not go over very well with the southern white men. In an effort to protect volunteers and black citizens, a majority of white women were given jobs that involved the Freedom Schools instead of canvassing the black communities. Their presence became a mixed blessing because the volunteers were able to open up more schools than they originally planned. Many more students wanted to attend the schools than previously thought. Some students were so eager to learn they showed up for school as early as 6 A.M.

The schools went beyond the scope of a regular classroom. The children learned not only American and world history, but also about their culture and American politics. Children were taught why it was important to be active in their community politics and how to be activist throughout their life. This lesson was an essential goal of Freedom Summer, as the organizers wanted the black community to learn to be a social force to recognize not only in Mississippi, but also the country.

In all, Freedom Summer left behind a strong legacy. First, black disfranchisement was brought to the forefront with the passage of the Voting Rights Act of 1965. The passage of the Voting Rights Act would allow federal examiners to take over voting registration in places where there was a history of discrimination and banned literacy tests as a requirement for registering to vote. The impact on voter registration in Mississippi was tremendous. The percent of blacks registered to vote rose from 6.7 percent to nearly 60 percent. There was also a substantial increase in voter registration across the country. Second, the MFDP had opened up the world of politics to black Mississippians. Black

Americans realized that they could and should have a place in American politics.

Lastly, Freedom Summer opened up Mississippi to the rest of the country. As a result, more Americans were aware of the various civil rights issues plaguing Mississippi and it was not just black Americans saying that change had to occur. White Americans were becoming just as vocal as black Americans, and this made the rest of the country stand up and take notice.

See also: Carmichael, Stokely (Kwame Ture); CORE; Freedom Schools; Hamer, Fannie Lou; MFDP; Moses, Robert; National Association for the Advancement of Colored People; Student Nonviolent Coordinating Committee; Voting Rights Act of 1965

Cristy Casado Tondeur

Bibliography
Carmichael, Stokely. *Ready for Revolution: The Life and Struggles of Stokely Carmichael.* New York: Scribner, 2003.

Carson, Clayborne et al., eds. *The Eyes on the Prize: Civil Rights Reader: Documents, Speeches, and Firsthand Accounts from the Black Freedom Struggle, 1954–1990.* New York: Penguin Books, 1991.

Mills, Hay. *This Little Light of Mine: The Life of Fannie Lou Hamer.* New York: Penguin Group, 1993.

Payne, Charles. *I've Got the Light of Freedom: The Organizing Tradition and the Mississippi Freedom Struggle.* Berkeley: University of California Press, 1995.

Montgomery Bus Boycott

The Montgomery Bus Boycott is often heralded as the beginning of the modern Civil Rights movement. Sparked by Rosa Parks's refusal to give up her seat for a white passenger, the bus boycott engaged all of Montgomery's African American community in a nonviolent, mass protest of Jim Crow segregation that spanned 381 days, financially crippling the Montgomery City Lines. After the U.S. Supreme Court affirmed a lower court ruling that Alabama's segregated bus law was unconstitutional, the community boycott and segregated buses in Montgomery ended. Yet the Montgomery bus boycott by the city's black community ushered in an era of direct action by African Americans across the South against the inequities of Jim Crow.

The social, political, and economic structure of the South rested on a bifurcated racial hierarchy and institutionalized racial segregation that permeated virtually every aspect of southern life. This Jim Crow system consistently deprived African Americans of equal opportunity, access to public spaces and facilities, and their constitutional rights. Southern white society controlled African Americans with time-worn customs and inequitable Jim Crow laws, as well as the use of intimidation and terror. Overt threats and merely the intimation of lynching kept many African Americans from challenging the status quo.

In Montgomery, as in many cities throughout the segregated South, African Americans rode in the rear of the bus. The front was reserved for white passengers. Blacks paid at the front, just as white passengers, but they then had to exit the bus and walk to the rear to board through the back door. As part of the degradation inherent in Jim Crow, bus drivers—this often depended on the capriciousness or the viciousness of the individual bus driver—sometimes drove away before they could board at the rear, leaving them stranded and out their bus fare. Although the black section was always in the rear, the color line was not static. When whites were not on the bus, blacks could sit nearer to the front. As more whites boarded, and the seats filled, the color line moved farther back. Black passengers, at that point, were expected to give their seats to the white passengers, gender notwithstanding.

The Women's Political Council (WPC), headed by Jo Ann Robinson, an English professor at Alabama State College, had been entertaining for some years the idea of a boycott of the bus system and looking for a test case to challenge Montgomery's segregation ordinances. The case of Claudette Colvin initially seemed to be the most promising. On March 2, 1955, the 15-year-old Colvin had been arrested for not giving up her seat after the bus driver ordered her to move. Colvin had been seated in a row not normally reserved for whites, which Montgomery's segregation ordinance did not specifically cover. Robinson and others in the WPC consulted with E. D. Nixon, president of the Montgomery NAACP, and Clifford Durr, a former Roosevelt New Dealer and local white attorney. In the end, they decided against using Colvin's arrest as either a test case or to rally support for a boycott. Colvin's standing in the community—she was young, unwed, and pregnant—did not bode well for its success. In all, they rejected three possible test cases before Rosa Parks's arrest.

As Rosa Parks rode home from work on the evening of December 1, 1955, she sat in the first row of seats reserved

for African Americans. When more passengers boarded bus No. 2857, and the white rows filled, the bus driver, James F. Blake, ordered Parks and three others to give their seats to the white passengers. Although the other three complied, Parks refused. Dispelling the myth that she refused to move because her feet hurt, Parks later said, "the only tired I was, was tired of giving in" (*Rosa Parks,* p. 116). Blake called the police and police officers Fletcher B. Day and Dempsey W. Mixon arrested Parks in front of the Empire Theater for violating the city's segregation ordinance. Parks had problems with Blake previously, in 1943, when he forced her off the bus for not exiting the front door after paying her fare and entering the bus from the rear. After that incident, Parks avoided Blake's bus for more than 12 years.

Nixon and Durr arranged for Parks's release on bond, and she agreed to allow her arrest to be used as a test case. Parks had a sterling reputation in the community: she was married, articulate, and held a stable job at the Montgomery fair, a popular department store. When contacted by black attorney Fred Gray (who had been contacted by Nixon) about Parks's arrest, Robinson and the WPC began circulating thousands of leaflets calling for a boycott of the city's buses. Nixon organized a meeting of black leaders for the night of December 2 at Dexter Avenue Baptist Church where he challenged them to lead such an effort.

The first day of the boycott, December 5, was highly successful. More than 90 percent of the black community boycotted the buses. That same day, a Montgomery court convicted Parks and fined her $10.00, plus $4.00 in court costs. In an afternoon meeting at the Mount Zion African Methodist Episcopal (AME) church, community leaders created an organization to run the boycott, the Montgomery Improvement Association (MIA), the name suggested by Reverend Ralph D. Abernathy of the black First Baptist Church of Montgomery. At this meeting, the MIA's first president, 26-year-old Martin Luther King Jr., the pastor of Dexter Avenue Baptist Church, had been unanimously elected, not because of his "potential of leadership" but because of the rivalries between other black leaders in Montgomery and the fact that King had only been in the city a short time and had not yet made enemies in the community. Mount Zion AME hosted a mass meeting that night, but the boycott's initial success and Parks's conviction clearly meant that the boycott would continue until the bus line changed their policies. The African American churches played a large role in disseminating information and providing a source of strength and support for the black community during the boycott.

The MIA demanded three things from the Montgomery City Lines: courtesy from bus drivers; the hiring of four black bus drivers; and more equitable seating on the buses, although they did not demand integrated seating. The MIA's plan called for blacks to be seated from the rear to the front and whites from the front to the rear, without any seats being reserved for a specific race. According to Jo Ann Robinson, the reason that they did not demand integration openly was that "no one was brazen enough to announce publicly that black people might boycott city buses for the specific purpose of integrating those buses. Just to say that minorities wanted 'better seating arrangements' was bad enough.... To admit that black Americans were seeking to integrate would have been too much; there probably would have been much bloodshed and arrests of those who dared to disclose such an idea!" (*The Montgomery Bus Boycott and the Women Who Started It,* p. 23). The bus company refused to meet any demands.

For the next 381 days, African Americans refused to ride the buses in Montgomery. They walked and they organized carpools. Those who owned their own automobiles volunteered their vehicles or drove people themselves. Black cab drivers charged only a fraction of their fares to black riders. The MIA purchased station wagons to transport people back and forth from work or the store. Donations poured in from outside the state as churches, both black and white, raised money and sent gifts such as shoes.

The bus boycott also had white support, but it was extremely limited in scope. White liberals such as Clifford and Virginia Durr and Reverend Robert Graetz, the white minister of Trinity Lutheran Church, openly supported the boycott. Others, such as Juliette Hampton Morgan, wrote letters to the newspaper praising the effort. In many cases, white employers picked up and dropped off their maids and housekeepers or paid their cab fare. In response, Montgomery police ticketed white women for transporting their maids and newly organized White Citizens' Councils used pressure and threats to stop the practice. The Montgomery City Lines, which depended heavily on black riders, suffered tremendous financial hardship without them.

During the course of the boycott, King and other black leaders became the targets of white discontent. The Montgomery police arrested King for speeding, and both his and Nixon's homes were bombed. Such harassment created greater solidarity among the black community at large and reinforced their commitment to resist injustice and maltreatment. Other supporters of the boycott faced white violence as well. Even after the boycott ended, white extremists bombed Abernathy and Graetz's homes, as well as Bell Street Baptist Church, Hutchinson Street Baptist Church, Abernathy's First Baptist Church, and Mount Olive Baptist Church.

Montgomery's city government also tried to stop the boycott, but without such overt violence. The Alabama legislature had passed an antiboycott law in 1921 that Montgomery city officials used in an attempt to end the boycott. A Montgomery grand jury indicted 89 black leaders, 24 of them ministers, for conspiring to boycott the Montgomery City Lines. King, of all of the 89 conspirators, was the only one tried. He was found guilty and levied a $500 fine. King's trial, far from quashing the boycott, attracted national attention and helped establish him as a national figure. In the aftermath of the trial, *Jet* magazine described King as "Alabama's Modern Moses."

Although the MIA initially wanted to use Parks's case to challenge bus segregation, it also decided to challenge segregation directly in federal court. On February 1, 1956, Attorneys Fred Gray and Charles D. Langford filed suit on behalf of four African American women, Aurelia S. Browder, Susie McDonald, Mary Louise Smith, and Claudette Colvin, who had been mistreated on Montgomery city buses. As Gray made clear, "I wanted the court to have only one issue to decide—the constitutionality of the laws requiring segregation on the buses in the city of Montgomery" (*Bus Ride to Justice,* p. 69). Gray feared that having Parks's prosecution associated with the petition might distract from that issue.

Browder v. Gayle (Montgomery Mayor William A. Gayle) came before the three-judge U.S. Court of Appeals for the Fifth Circuit. On June 5, 1956, the panel, in a two-to-one decision, ruled Alabama's segregation bus laws unconstitutional. Judges Frank M. Johnson Jr. and Richard T. Rives, both white Montgomerians, courageously found for the plaintiffs at great personal cost, citing *Brown v. Board of Education* as a precedent for their decision. On November 13, 1956, the U.S. Supreme Court affirmed the judgment of the 5th Circuit, upholding the lower court decision. It rejected the city and state's appeals on December 17. The Supreme Court order to desegregate the buses arrived in Montgomery on December 20, 1956, prompting the MIA to end the bus boycott.

The Montgomery bus boycott demonstrated the power and influence of a committed African American community. Unlike subsequent civil rights campaigns, the press played a relatively minor role in the boycott's success, the credit for which should be attributed largely to Montgomery's black leadership. As historian J. Mills Thornton notes, "the participants in the demonstrations by and large derived their enthusiasm and dedication from the prospect of effecting specific changes in their own municipalities" rather than a devotion to larger, national civil rights strategies (*The Walking City*, p. xxi). In this way, the Montgomery Bus Boycott foreshadowed future civil rights campaigns.

See also: *Brown v. Board of Education;* Jim Crow; King, Coretta Scott; King, Martin Luther Jr.; Parks, Rosa; Rustin, Bayard; White Citizens' Councils

Dan J. Puckett

Bibliography

Branch, Taylor. *Parting the Waters: America in the King Years, 1954–63.* New York: Simon & Schuster, 1988.

Garrow, David J., ed. *The Walking City: The Montgomery Bus Boycott, 1955–1956.* Brooklyn, NY: Carlson Publishing, 1989.

Gray, Fred D. *Bus Ride to Justice: Changing the System by the System: The Life and Works of Fred Gray.* Montgomery, AL: The Black Belt Press, 1995.

King, Martin Luther Jr. *Stride Toward Freedom: The Montgomery Story.* New York: Harper and Brothers, 1958.

Parks, Rosa (with James Haskins). *Rosa Parks: My Story.* New York: Dial Books, 1992.

Robinson, Jo Ann. *The Montgomery Bus Boycott and the Women Who Started It: The Memoir of Jo Ann Gibson Robinson,* ed. David J. Garrow. Knoxville: University of Tennessee Press 1987.

Thornton, J. Mills III. *Dividing Lines: Municipal Politics and the Struggle for Civil Rights in Montgomery, Birmingham, and Selma.* Tuscaloosa and London: The University of Alabama Press, 2002.

Moore, Queen Mother Audley

Queen Mother Audley Moore (1898–1996) was a prominent civil rights activist, an advocate of Pan-Africanism, and an active participant in a number of movements, causes, and organizations for more then eight decades. She was born in New Iberia, Louisiana in 1898, the oldest of three daughters born to Henry and St. Cyr Moore. Her father had served as a sheriff in New Iberia, and her mother died when Moore

was five years old. Having witnessed the lynching of her mother's father and her grandmother's husband, Moore gained an early understanding of racism and racial violence in the early-20th-century South. After the untimely death of Moore's mother, her father sent Moore and her two siblings to live with her maternal grandmother in New Iberia while her father moved to New Orleans. Reunited with her father a few years later, Moore and her sisters moved to New Orleans and lived with him until his death when Moore was in the fourth grade. Forced to drop out of school to care for her sisters, Moore used some of her father's assets to rent a house and earned income as a hairdresser in order to support her family.

Experiencing the sheer brutality of racism and lynch law in the South, as well as the daily injustices experienced by people of color in New Orleans, Moore was perhaps predisposed to radical political expressions later in life. In 1919, Marcus Garvey came to New Orleans to give a speech at a meeting hall and to establish a branch of his newly formed United Negro Improvement Association (UNIA). Although local police initially prevented Garvey from speaking, a group of armed African Americans ensured he would not be interrupted the following night. Moore, in attendance at both rallies, brought two pistols with her during the second attempt by Garvey to delivery an address. When police attempted to interrupt the rally, she was among those who waved their guns and turned away the white police in an unprecedented display of defiance. Moore immediately became a member of the UNIA and served in the organization for much of her subsequent life.

Moore and her family left the South during the Great Migration, making temporary stops in California and Chicago before settling permanently in Harlem in 1922. While in Harlem, Moore was a dedicated follower of Garvey and she began to expand her activism. Concerned with the working conditions of African American domestic workers, Moore organized the Harriet Tubman Association as a mechanism to address their particular plight. Her active interests in working class and subaltern peoples led her to become affiliated with the Communist Party by 1930. Given her dedication to Garvey, the UNIA, and—by extension—African American capitalism, this embrace of communism may seem difficult to comprehend. Although Garvey was imagining African repatriation for the African American masses, Moore understood that something had to be done to ameliorate the exploitative conditions faced by African

Americans throughout the country. This transition in her organizing activities might also be linked to the deportation of Marcus Garvey by 1925 and the resulting marginalization of the UNIA.

Initially joining the International Labor Defense (ILD), she officially joined the Communist Party in 1933. Both the ILD and the Communist Party had taken active roles in the Scottsboro case and, in the midst of the Great Depression, communism seemed to offer real answers for the exploitation of workers, white supremacy, and racism. In addition to fighting racial discrimination and the rights of African American working women, Moore also played a role in the integration of major league baseball and the Coast Guard. In the 1940s, she served as the campaign manager for Benjamin E. Davis Jr., an African American communist politician in New York who made two successful bids for the New York City Council. In the midst of the McCarthy era, Moore renounced the Communist Party and resigned her membership. In the period between the 1950s and the 1970s, she gravitated toward more mainstream political expressions and movements, including involvement with—or membership in—the National Council of Negro Women and the NAACP. Moore also greatly expanded the scope of her activism, including participation in the Pan-African Congresses and the Organization of African Unity. To this end, she founded, or was a founding member of, the University Association of Ethiopian Women, the World Federation of African People, the Congress of African People, and the Republic of New Africa. As a direct result of her international activities, in 1972 Moore received the title of "Queen Mother" of Asante in recognition of her efforts to bring about Pan-African unity. Over the last two decades of her life, Moore became increasingly involved in the reparations movement. Shortly before her death, she made her last public appearance at the Million Man March in October 1995. Queen Mother Moore died of natural causes in a Brooklyn nursing home on May 2, 1997.

See also: Black Nationalism; Garvey, Marcus; Million Man March; Universal Negro Improvement Association

Walter C. Rucker

Bibliography

Moore, Audley, and Cheryl Gilkes. *Interview with Audley (Queen Mother) Moore: June 6 and 8, 1978.* Cambridge, UK: Schlesinger Library, Radcliffe College, 1986.

Rediger, Pat. *Great African Americans in Civil Rights. Outstanding African Americans.* New York: Crabtree Publishing, 1996.

Smith, Jessie Carney. *Epic Lives: One Hundred Black Women Who Made a Difference.* Detroit: Visible Ink Press, 1993.

Moorish Science Temple

The Moorish Science Temple was a quasi-Islamic black nationalist movement established in Newark, New Jersey, in 1913 as the Canaanite Temple. Although explicitly unorthodox, it was the first broad-based movement in America espousing any form of Islamic ideology or beliefs. The founder and initial leader of the group, Timothy Drew (1886–1929), was known by the appellation Prophet Noble Drew Ali. The group's supposed connection to Moorish culture arose from Ali's fundamental teaching that African Americans were Muslims of Moroccan heritage descended from the Old Testament Moabitic line of Canaanites. In this vein, the group adopted as their symbol the red banner of Morocco with its green five-pointed star, the points representing love, truth, peace, freedom, and justice. Within 10 years, the group's membership soared to between 20,000 and 30,000 followers, claiming members in most of the leading cities of the Northeast and Midwest, as well as a handful in the South. The birth of the movement and its rapid expansion directly correlated with the Great Migration of African Americans from the South to the urban centers in the North.

Factionalism split the movement several times, and, in 1925, Ali removed himself and many of his followers to Chicago, where three years later the group officially became known as The Moorish Science Temple of America. Shortly thereafter, Ali wrote the *Seven Circle Quran,* which, despite its name, bore no resemblance to the Quran of orthodox Islam. It consisted of a broad range of doctrines, beliefs, and teachings, fusing Masonic symbolism, Christian mysticism, and Rosicrucianism, with Islamic terminology and preexisting Moorish Science beliefs. Many of the book's passages were adopted wholesale from contemporaneous works of the religious fringe. The *Seven Circle Quran* played a major role in Moorish rites and religious gatherings; it was reverently recited in whispered tones at most events.

Several hallmarks of the movement distinguished its members. They appended their names with the surname El or Bey, wore turbans or fezzes, greeted each other with their right hand raised while saying "Peace" or "Islam," and owing to their original beliefs, referred to black people as Asiatics. They prohibited the consumption of pork, alcohol, and tobacco, as well as dancing and attending the theater. Prayers were held three times a day, at sunrise, midday, and sunset; and they met in congregation on Fridays, strictly upholding gender separation. Furthermore, a fundamental aspect of Moorish belief was loyalty and respect for America and its laws, as well as participation in the electoral process. Ali also promoted peace and love between Asiatics, who in their totality included virtually all people of color. On the other hand, he taught that Europe and people of European descent were from the pagan, uncivilized regions of the world and therefore the mixing of Asiatic blood with Europeans was despised.

The group had many influences, including Marcus Garvey's Universal Negro Improvement Association, Freemasonry in the form of the Mystic Shrine, Theosophy, and several others. In fact, Drew Ali's name, Noble, is a clear claim to membership as a Shriner, and Garvey's calls for economic self-reliance can be seen in the founding of the Moorish Science Corporation. The business ventures of the corporation included selling various herbal remedies, and the establishment of restaurants and stores. Very few of the beliefs in Moorish Science derived from orthodox Islam; nonetheless, orthodox Muslims took a dim view of Ali and the Moorish Science Temple. In 1929 and 1930, the movement was condemned in three fatwas (Islamic rulings) in Egypt and Sudan, including one from the venerable Al-Azhar Mosque in Cairo.

By the late 1920s, Ali's hold on the community was failing as further factionalism, financial impropriety, and an increasing hostility between some members and white law enforcement reached a violent crescendo. Ali was jailed under the accusation of ordering the death of a political rival, and he died a few months later on July 20, 1929, while out on bond and awaiting trial. Whether his death was caused by revenge or natural causes is unclear. Dissension within the movement increased as a battle for leadership furthered the series of violence and arrests. Kirkman Bey was eventually elected leader of the movement and held the position until his death in 1959. The group's growth continued unabated during the 1940s, when it was estimated that at least 50 temples were active across America. The movement came under intense scrutiny by the FBI, which was convinced that the Moorish-American espousal

of Asiatic unity equaled complicity with the Japanese during World War II.

The FBI continued to monitor and actively pursue the destruction of the movement until the 1970s. The Moorish Science movement has remained intact to the present, albeit smaller and further factionalized, and has successfully extended its activities to the U.S. prison system, where it has a strong following.

See also: Ali, Noble Drew; Black Nationalism; Garvey, Marcus; Great Migration; Universal Negro Improvement Association

Brent D. Singleton

Bibliography

Allen, Ernest Jr. "Identity and Destiny: The Formative Years of the Moorish Science Temple and the Nation of Islam." In *Muslims on the Americanization Path?* Yvonne Yazbeck Haddad and John L. Esposito, eds., 163–214. Oxford: Oxford University Press, 2000.

Curtis, Edward E., IV. *Islam in Black America: Identity, Liberation, and Difference in African-American Islamic Thought.* Albany: SUNY Press, 2002.

Dannin, Robert. *Black Pilgrimage to Islam.* Oxford: Oxford University Press, 2002.

Gomez, Michael A. *Black Crescent: The Experience and Legacy of African Muslims in the Americas.* New York: Cambridge University Press, 2005.

Turner, Richard B. *Islam in the African-American Experience,* 2nd ed. Bloomington: Indiana University Press, 2003.

Morrison, Toni

Toni Morrison (Chloe Anthony Wofford) (1931–), a noted novelist, was born on February 18, 1931, in Lorain, Ohio, the second of four children. Her parents, George Wofford and Ramah Willis Wofford were sharecroppers and had moved to the North to escape the rampant racism in the South. Morrison's father worked three jobs for 17 years to provide for his family. Beginning at a young age Morrison developed an interest in reading. She was an extremely avid reader, reading authors like Jane Austin and Tolstoy among many others.

Both Morrison's parents instilled in their children a great sense of pride in their Southern and African American heritage and let their children know that hard work and determination were the keys to success. This advice held true for Morrison who graduated high school with honors in 1949. Morrison later went on to obtain a bachelor's degree in English with a minor in the classics from Howard University in 1953, and in 1955 Morrison obtained her master's degree from Cornell University. It was also at Howard University where Morrison started referring to herself as "Toni," a shortened version of her middle name.

Upon graduating from Howard, Morrison began teaching introductory English at Texas Southern University in Houston, returning later in 1957 to Howard as a member of the faculty. While back at Howard, Morrison fell in love with Jamaican-born architect Harold Morrison. They eventually married in 1961 and had two boys. The marriage proved to be an unhappy one ending in divorce after Morrison was pregnant with their second child. To escape the unhappiness of her union, Morrison joined a small writer's group, where she started writing a story about a girl who prayed to God for blue eyes, a girl from Morrison's childhood. After a trip to Europe, Morrison returned to Lorain, Ohio with her sons in tow to live with her parents.

In 1964, she was hired by a textbook subsidiary of Random House in Syracuse, New York, as an associate editor. In 1967, she was transferred to New York City and became a senior editor at Random House, a job where she would stay for the next 20 years. While editing books for some of the most prominent African Americans in the country, such as Angela Davis, Muhammad Ali, and Alex Haley, Morrison was still attempting to turn her small story into a novel. While working as an editor for Random House by day, Morrison began writing at night, bringing more imagination and detail to the story, and in 1970 *The Bluest Eye* was published. Although it was not a huge commercial success right away, it has continued to garner critical acclaim.

Morrison's second novel, *Sula,* was published in 1973. Excerpts of the book were later republished in *Redbook*

American writer Toni Morrison receives the Nobel Prize in literature from King Carl XVI Gustaf of Sweden in the Concert Hall in Stockholm, Sweden, December 10, 1993. Morrison is the first black woman to receive this prize. (AP Photo)

magazine, and in 1975, the novel was nominated for the National Book Award in Fiction. As Morrison watched her sons grow up, she began to write a novel that focused more on the lived experiences of African American males. With the publication of *Song of Solomon* in 1977, Morrison's third novel, Morrison gained national and international acclaim. The book won the National Book Critic's Circle Award and the American Academy and Institute of Arts and Letters Award. *Tar Baby,* Morrison's fourth novel was published in 1981, and Morrison's picture appeared on the cover of *Newsweek* magazine in March of that same year. Also from 1976 to 1977, Morrison worked as a visiting lecturer at Yale University in New Haven, Connecticut.

In 1983, Morrison left Random House as senior editor and in 1984 was named the Albert Schweitzer Professor of the Humanities at the State University of New York in Albany. Her fifth novel, *Beloved,* was published in 1987 and was based on the true story of the enslaved woman, Margaret Garner, who escaped a plantation in Kentucky with her husband Robert. When the enslavers eventually catch Garner, Garner attempted to kill her children hoping that they would make it to heaven and not be forced to endure a life of servitude as enslaved, but she was successful in killing only one. Morrison writes the novel from Garner's point of view, making her the benevolent protagonist who is haunted by her murdered daughter. The novel gained worldwide acclaim, earning Morrison the 1998 Pulitzer Prize for fiction, and was made into a film in 1998 with the aid of Oprah Winfrey. In 1987, Morrison was named the Robert F. Goheen Professor in the Council of Humanities at Princeton University, where she was the only African American woman to hold a named chair at an Ivy League University.

Her sixth novel, *Jazz,* which was about how murder is shaped by love and relationships, was published in 1992, and Morrison became the eighth woman and first African American to win the Nobel Prize in Literature in 1993. In 1999, Morrison published *Paradise;* her eighth novel, *Love,* was published in 2003. *A Mercy* was published in 2008, and Morrison continues to publish a plethora of short stories and plays. In June 2005, Toni Morrison received a Doctor of Letters from Barnard College.

Toni Morrison is one of America's most critically acclaimed novelist and writers of our time. Her style of writing, original in its conceptual and rhetorical patterning, has proved to be the reason why she is so beloved by many. In her interview with Nellie McKay, Morrison described how she began the writing process with an idea and how the characters for her novels were outgrowths of such ideas. Throughout her writing career, Toni Morrison has always stressed how important African American history and African American culture are to the history of America and how her work reflects and attempts to maintain this sentiment.

See also: Davis, Angela; Ebo Landing; Haley, Alex; Transmigration

Kaila A. Story

Bibliography

Beaulieu, Elizabeth Ann. *The Toni Morrison Encyclopedia.* Westport, CT: Greenwood Press, 2003.

McKay, Nellie. *An Interview with Toni Morrison. Conversations with Toni Morrison.* Jackson: University Press of Mississippi, 1994.

Rigney, Barbara. *The Voices of Toni Morrison.* Columbus: Ohio State University Press, 1991.

Taylor-Guthrie, Danielle. *Conversations with Toni Morrison.* Jackson: University Press of Mississippi, 1994.

Moses, Robert

Robert Paris Moses (1935–), a noted civil rights activist, was born on January 23, 1935, in Harlem, New York. Moses's family was not well-off and he grew up in a Harlem housing project. His intellectual prowess was evident early on and, after passing a city-wide exam, he gained entrance to an elite public school, Stuyvesant High School. After graduating from high school in 1952, Moses earned a scholarship to Hamilton College in New York and later earned a master's degree from Harvard University in 1957. Although Moses specialized in mathematical logic, he studied philosophy and was greatly influenced by the work of French philosopher Albert Camus. Through reading Camus and in his travel abroad during college, Moses was exposed to the ideals of pacifism, ideals that would remain at the core of his value system for the rest of his life. In 1959, while teaching high school math at Horace Mann in Manhattan, Moses helped civil rights activist Bayard Rustin organize the second Youth March for Integrated Schools. The next spring, Moses took part in a demonstration in Newport News while visiting his uncle in Virginia. From that point forward, Bob Moses would dedicate himself to the Civil Rights movement.

Bob Moses placed a great deal of emphasis on developing local black leadership in Mississippi because these local residents not only had a vital stake in the successful outcome of civil rights projects, they could also identify with each other and help each other along. Local blacks thought about their work with the Student Nonviolent Coordinating Committee (SNCC) in terms of making some sense out of living in Mississippi. In addition, Moses encouraged young people to enter the civil rights struggle because he felt that young blacks would not be limited as much by the economic responsibilities that faced their elders and would be free to act more assertively. Moses was also keenly aware of the necessity to face and minimize black fears while conducting the Voter Registration Project in Mississippi. In 1963 Moses stated that "You dig into yourself and the community to wage psychological warfare; you combat your own fears about beatings, shootings and possible mob violence; you stymie, by your mere physical presence, anxious fear of the Negro community (*In Struggle,* p. 78). Moses lived this philosophy, leading the way by example, quelling the fear of anxious Mississippi residents by putting himself squarely in front of danger and often beating it back. So often did he do this that one local resident once noted of Moses, "Poor Bob took a lot of beatings....Sometimes I think he was Moses in the Bible. He pioneered the way for black people in McComb...He had more guts than any one man I've ever known" (*In Struggle,* p. 78).

In 1960, after seeing the resolute and courageous faces of southern blacks taking part in the sit-in movement, Moses went to work in the Atlanta office of the Southern Christian Leadership Conference (SCLC). There was little there for him to do but stuff SCLC fund-raising packages, however, and when Jane Stembridge, a member of SNCC who worked in the same office suggested that he assist that organization by recruiting black leaders in the South, Moses readily agreed. From Atlanta Moses traveled through Mississippi in the summer of 1960, a trip on which he met Amzie Moore, the head of the Cleveland, Mississippi NAACP. Moses recalls that "Amzie was the first one to really speak to me about the potential in Mississippi of the students' energy to blow open the issues of racial discrimination and white supremacy" (*Radical Equations,* p. 41). In the summer of 1961, Moses headed a voting registration project in McComb, Mississippi, where he, Reginald Robinson, and John Hardy opened a school to train black residents to take Mississippi's literacy test for voters. Moses

experienced his first confrontation with the state's authorities on August 15 of that year when, after escorting three black residents to the courthouse in Liberty, Mississippi to register to vote, he was arrested and charged with interfering with the discharge of the arresting officers' duties. The arresting officer, who knew exactly who Moses was and how important the voter registration project was in changing the balance of power in the state, asked, "You the nigger that came down from New York to stir up a lot of trouble?" (*Radical Equations,* p. 48). Following his own code of ethics that mandated the struggle begin with the individual, Moses stood up to the officer and subsequently spent two days in jail before allowing the NAACP to post his bond.

Almost two weeks later Moses experienced a more violent encounter after attempting to register more local blacks. Billy Jack Caston, cousin of the local sheriff, and two other white residents beat Moses nearly unconscious, a crime for which Caston was acquitted. Violence was no stranger to the South; but on September 25, 1961, an event occurred that would bring the voting rights project to a standstill for the remainder of that year. On that day, E. H. Hurst, a white state legislator, shot and killed Herbert Lee, a founding member of the Amite County NAACP. Hurst, who claimed Lee attacked him with a tire iron, was never charged with Lee's murder. Moses recollects, "Lee's killing paralyzed the voter registration movement, stopped it cold, with no Black person in all of rural southwest Mississippi willing to make an attempt at registering" (*Radical Equations,* p. 50). Although Moses and practically all of the local blacks who had worked closely with him had been jailed and the McComb experience acted as a temporary setback for SNCC, Moses remained determined to make progress.

In the summer of 1962, Moses went to work expanding his young SNCC staff and by spring of 1963, 6 SNCC offices and 20 black field secretaries were operating in Mississippi. In an effort to minimize conflict between the various civil rights organizations, SNCC field secretaries worked under the auspices of the Council of Federated Organizations (COFO) where Moses was named director of voter registration. Moses continued his efforts to the western part of the state, this time edging away from his earlier policy of relying on entirely local black leadership. SNCC organized a food drive for residents of Leflore County that involved a number of the organization's northern branches and thus made the problems of poor rural Mississippians visible to a wider rage of people. Not only did this food drive feed people but, as Moses explained, "Whenever we were able to get a little something to give to a hungry family, we also talked about how they ought to register" (*In Struggle*, p. 80). In this way Moses and SNCC linked receiving assistance to taking personal responsibility for achieving freedom by registering to vote.

Signaling a dramatic shift in the voting rights project, in an April 1963 meeting before the SNCC general conference, Moses argued that Mississippi's blacks were unlikely to gain the franchise quickly enough to win electoral victories before they lost their jobs to industrial automation and lack of education. He insisted that because illiterate whites were allowed to vote, and because blacks in the state were denied equal educational opportunities, blacks were owed either the right to vote irrespective of being literate or the opportunity to immediately learn to read and write. As such, Moses's position initiated the "one man, one vote" campaign, a movement that would encourage all blacks in the state to participate in the political process.

The 1964 Mississippi Summer Project, designed specifically to expose the intolerance of racist whites to a national audience while creating the environment for a confrontation between state and federal authorities whereby federal agents would be forced to protect civil rights activists, was another turning point in the evolution of SNCC. By this time, although local blacks had worked hard and sacrificed greatly to achieve voting rights, Moses was convinced that only outside intervention and greater national publicity about the deplorable conditions in rural Mississippi would bring about the kind of large-scale change he was trying to create. This would require bringing in hundreds of whites from around the country to help with the voter registration project, a marked departure from the almost exclusive used of local blacks thus far in the voting rights campaign. The first step was for Moses and Allard Lowenstein, a white activist and friend of Moses, to organize a "Freedom Vote." This campaign would allow local blacks to vote for their own set of candidates in their own communities, as many blacks were barred from voting in the 1963 November general election. In what was deemed as an encouraging sign, more than 80,000 local blacks voted in this symbolic election, setting the stage for the next challenge.

Building on the success of the Freedom Vote, Moses and COFO set about creating a nonracist political organization that would lay legitimate claim to the Democratic Party delegation at the Democratic National Convention in 1964. To that end, on April 26, 1964, the Mississippi Freedom Democratic Party was formed at a rally in Jackson, Mississippi. In addition to creating a political party, COFO members established Freedom Schools to teach traditional academic subjects, as well as contemporary issues, leadership development, and political skills. Although the MFDP was unable to unseat the regular Democratic delegation at the Democratic National Convention in Atlantic City, New Jersey, it brought the issues of white supremacy and voting rights for the state's blacks front-and-center on a national stage and forced long-term changes in the Democratic Party. As Moses recalls, "The MFDP was raising an important point with this country, and with the Democratic Party, as one of its major political institutions: Generations of Black people had been denied access to the political process; could they get it now?.... We were challenging the [Democratic Party] to recognize the existence of a whole group of people—white and Black and disenfranchised— who form the underclass of this country" (*Radical Equations*, pp. 82–83). The MFDP's challenge served notice to the nation that being black and poor was no longer going to act as a barrier in the way of the residents of Mississippi as they laid claim to their rights as U.S. citizens.

Shortly after the Summer Project concluded, SNCC arrived at a crossroads, as an ideological split between James Foreman and Bob Moses pointed in two different directions. Foreman, who viewed SNCC as a permanent organization, believed that it also needed a more centralized leadership to carry out its mission. Moses, on the other hand, was committed to SNCC's emphasis on informal leadership and consensus building, where a broad range of voices had equal opportunities to be heard. As a result of his unwillingness to push his own agenda and his sense that large segments of SNCC and COFO had grown dependent on his leadership, Moses grew ever reluctant to express his views, and his influence on policy decisions waned through the mid-1960s.

Moses, who was conflicted by Camus's dilemma of maintaining a balance between moral purity and political effectiveness, resigned as director of COFO in late 1964. He was discouraged with the hard-line approach SNCC had taken under the leadership of Stokely Carmichael, an approach that attempted to centralize control of the organization under a small group of people who wanted to dictate what local branches should be doing. In 1965, Moses took a leave of absence from SNCC to focus on antiwar activities. He challenged the argument made by many black leaders that civil rights activists should devote their energy to black community organizing and not risk previous gains by involving themselves in the antiwar or other movements. He noted, "Certainly one of the most basic rights we have been seeking is the right to participate fully in the life of this country. Now if by participating—that is; taking part in the discussions of the great issues that face the country—we threaten the right to participate, we have to begin to wonder whether the right is real" (*In Struggle*, p. 185). Moses quit SNCC in 1966 and moved to Canada to avoid the Vietnam War draft.

After living in Canada and then teaching in Tanzania from 1969–1975, Moses returned the United States where he completed a doctorate and taught high school math. In 1982, he received a McArthur Foundation "Genius Grant" and started the Algebra Project, a program that teaches math literacy as a key that opens the door both higher education and thus employment opportunities for poor and minority students. According to Moses, algebra is a gatekeeper, a subject that students must master or they are effectively shut out of higher level math-based subjects such as physics, calculus, and engineering. As he sees it, math literacy is a contemporary civil rights issue much the way the right to vote was in the 1960s because proficiency in these subjects is critical for being successful in the technology-driven 21st century. The Algebra project runs in more than 25 cities and serves more than 40,000 students.

See also: Carmichael, Stokely (Kwame Ture); MFDP; Mississippi Freedom Summer, 1964; National Association for the Advancement of Colored People; Rustin, Bayard; Southern Christian Leadership Conference; Student Nonviolent Coordinating Committee

Paul T. Miller

Bibliography

Branch, Taylor. *At Canaan's Edge: America in the King Years, 1965–68*. New York: Simon & Schuster, 2006.

Carson, Clayborne. *In Struggle: SNCC and the Black Awakening of the 1960s*. Cambridge, MA: Harvard University Press, 1981.

Hogan, Wesley C. *Many Minds, One Heart: SNCC's Dream for a New America*. Chapel Hill: University of North Carolina Press, 2007.

Moses, Robert. *Radical Equations: Math Literacy and Civil Rights*. Boston: Beacon Press, 2001.

MOVE Bombing

The MOVE bombing of May 13, 1985 was one of the most controversial episodes in Philadelphia's history. MOVE emerged around 1972 in Philadelphia as a small but radical group of African Americans led by John Africa. His commune first settled at North 33rd Street near Pearl Street in the Powelton Village area of Philadelphia. There they lived according to the self-styled teachings of John Africa. He promoted a communal "back to nature" lifestyle, vegetarianism, reverence for all animal life, and scorn for "The Establishment." From their house, MOVE members often gave public speeches denouncing Philadelphia's mayor and police department. In addition, the presence of open garbage, insects, rats, and other animals on the MOVE premises posed public health hazards for Osage Avenue residents.

Neighborhood complaints about the lifestyle of MOVE brought the radical organization into confrontation with the city of Philadelphia throughout the 1970s. On March 28, 1976, Philadelphia police confronted several MOVE members at the 33rd Street house. MOVE later claimed that Janine Africa and her baby were thrown to the floor by police and that the baby later died. Angry MOVE members stepped up criticism of Philadelphia mayor Frank Rizzo, and Rizzo reacted with a court order to demolish the MOVE compound. On August 6, 1978, a gun battle between police and MOVE erupted during which MOVE member Delbert Africa was beaten by Philadelphia police officers and one policeman was killed. Delbert Africa and eight other MOVE members were arrested and brought to trial; nine MOVE members were sentenced. In 1981, however, the three police officers accused of beating Delbert Africa were acquitted.

After the 1978 incident, MOVE went underground. It reemerged in 1982, settling in the house of John Africa's sister, Louise James, in a Philadelphia neighborhood known as Cobbs Creek. During this time, MOVE members who were frustrated about not winning the release of their jailed members stepped up their public harangues against the neighborhood and the police. On Memorial Day 1984, W. Wilson Goode, Philadelphia's first African American mayor, met with Osage Avenue residents who asserted that MOVE was infringing on their rights. Goode was advised by the FBI and other law enforcement officials that there were no grounds for action against MOVE. The neighbors of MOVE, however, formally organized themselves in February 1985 into a group called "United Residents of the 6200 Block of Osage Avenue." On May 1, 1985, the United Residents said in a press conference that the MOVE house had become a military bunker. The next day the United Residents informed Mayor Goode that a five-gallon gasoline can was hoisted to the roof of 6221 Osage Avenue. It was then that the mayor and Philadelphia police knew that a violent confrontation between the city and MOVE was imminent. Arrest warrants for four MOVE members were approved by a city judge.

On May 13, 1985, Mayor Goode authorized Philadelphia police to surround the house at 6221 Osage Avenue, which now had a bunker constructed on its roof as well as a gasoline can. Using a bullhorn, police asked that the four MOVE members for whom they had arrest warrants to come out and surrender. None did. Then the mayor gave permission for a pilot in a police helicopter to drop a bomb in order to dislodge the bunker. The bomb missed its target and instead hit the gasoline can, igniting the entire house. City officials decided not to put out the fire immediately but to "let the bunker burn." Eleven MOVE members burned to death including five children. Among the dead was MOVE founder John Africa. A woman, Ramona Africa, and a boy, Birdie Africa, escaped from the house alive. Ramona Africa was arrested and taken into custody by police. In 1986, Ramona Africa was put on trial and was found guilty of riot and conspiracy charges and was given a seven-year sentence. She was released from prison in 1992.

The MOVE bombing of May 13, 1985, in Philadelphia made international headlines. Some applauded the city of Philadelphia's handling of the crisis, but others, such as MOVE supporters, condemned it. Philadelphia African Americans in particular were critical of Mayor Goode who in response formed an investigatory commission. The Philadelphia Special Investigation Commission issued its report in 1986. The commission found the city of Philadelphia negligent in the death of the 11 people and careless in its handling of conflict resolution. It found that Mayor Goode did not negotiate with MOVE earlier and that he allowed the confrontation on May 13, 1985 to spin out of control.

But the MOVE bombing story does not end there. More than 60 houses on Osage Avenue and Pine Street also burned down, leaving 250 people homeless. Between 1985 and 1996, the city of Philadelphia rebuilt the Osage Avenue homes, but many residents were unhappy, citing various defects. Milton Street, elected mayor of Philadelphia in 1999, sympathized with their plight and offered each family $150,000 for a new house and moving expenses. In all, 37 families on Osage Avenue and part of Pine Street took the buy-out offer, but 24 families refused. So in 2003, they went back to court. In April 2005, a United States District Court

jury awarded each homeowner a sum of $530,000 for punitive damages against city officials, breach of contract, and damages for emotional distress. Today MOVE members are still active in Philadelphia but keep a low profile.

See also: Black Power

Eric Ledell Smith

Bibliography

Anderson, John, and Hevenor, Hilary. *Burning Down the House: MOVE and the Tragedy of Philadelphia.* New York and London: W. W. Norton, 1987.

Bracey, LaVon Wright. *Making Them Whole: A Philadelphia Neighborhood and the City's Recovery from the MOVE Tragedy.* Philadelphia: Affie Enterprises, 1990.

Goode, W. Wilson, and Stevens, Joann. *In Goode Faith.* Valley Forge, PA: Judson Press, 1992.

Philadelphia Special Investigation Commission. *The Findings, Conclusions, and Recommendations of the Philadelphia Special Investigation Commission, March 6, 1986.* Philadelphia: The Commission, 1986.

Muhammad, Elijah

Elijah Muhammad (Elijah Poole) (1897–1975), leader of the Lost-Found Nation of Islam in the Wilderness of North America, was born in Sandersville, Georgia in October 1897 to William and Mariah Poole. His father was a pastor at Bold Spring and Union Baptist churches while sharecropping and working in sawmills to provide for a quickly growing family. Mariah Poole worked as a domestic for white families and, instead of earning wages, she was often paid in parts from slaughtered animals. Young Elijah Poole, like his six siblings, grew up in the black church and frequently listened to his father's fiery sermons. In fact, Elijah became so enamored by the Bible, he began to preach and evangelize at a young age—even, at times, correcting errors in his father's sermons. A close student of biblical scripture, Elijah joined the church at age 14, at his father's behest, yet he struggled with what he considered inconsistencies in the Bible and Christian doctrine.

Elijah had a brief stint in school, leaving between the fourth and eighth grades, because the Poole children needed to help generate income for the family. He began working at age 10, providing firewood and other services after the family relocated from Sandersville to Cordele, Georgia. Although denied formal education, Elijah had practical and transformative experiences with white supremacy and racial oppression during his early years, claiming later in life to have witnessed the aftermath of three lynchings in Georgia. On once occasion, a white man proudly showed him the severed ear of a lynched African American. On another occasion, in the winter of 1907, Elijah witnessed an 18-year-old African American youth hanged and his body riddled with bullets after being accused of raping a white woman. Both the mob murder and the lack of reaction by the African American community enraged the then 10-year-old Elijah and this anger would later fuel his antipathy for all whites.

In 1919, Poole married Clara Evans of Cordele and by 1922 the couple had their first two children—Emmanuel (1921) and Ethel (1922). With a growing family, Poole—an employee of the Southern Railroad Company as a gang laborer—experienced mounting levels of stress in trying to provide sufficient support for Clara and their children.

Between 1920 and 1921, Poole and one of his brothers were witnesses to the lynching of another black man, and this may have played some role in his decision to relocate his family to Detroit, Michigan in April 1923. As part of a flood of black southern migrants in the 1920s, the Poole family struggled to establish an economic foothold in Detroit. As Poole went from job to job, the family grew even larger with the addition of three more children—Lottie (1925), Nathaniel (1926), and Herbert (1929).

By the late 1920s and early 1930s, Poole was frequently unemployed, as the Great Depression ravished the labor market. In the midst of his despair, Clara Poole found the family's salvation in the most unlikely of places—in the guise of Wallace Dean (W. D.) Fard Muhammad. Influenced by the Moorish Science Temple of America and Marcus Garvey's UNIA, Fard Muhammad was preaching a fiery, black nationalists brand of Islam in Detroit in his self-proclaimed quest to wake the "dead" nation of Islam in the

Elijah Muhammad, as spiritual leader of the Nation of Islam in the United States, established a religious organization that gave poor urban African Americans a sense of racial pride and economic and political self-sufficiency. (Library of Congress)

West. At the insistence of Clara, Elijah Poole made a visit to one of Fard Muhammad's sermons in the fall of 1931. Later that same year, Poole met Fard Muhammad after a particular speech and was so inspired by his message that Poole asked Fard if he were the "one we read in the Bible that…would come in the last day under the name Jesus" (*An Original Man,* p. 22). To this suggestion, Fard Muhammad answered in the affirmative. Unbeknownst to either man at the time, this brief exchange would change both their lives and would lead to the creation and growth of one of the most powerful black organizations in U.S. history.

At the age of 33, Elijah Poole became a disciple of a man he variably knew as Fard (pronounced Far-ad) Muhammad, the Mahdi, Jesus, and "Allah in the Flesh." After joining Fard Muhammad's movement, Poole received a new surname—Karriem—and became the "supreme minister" of Allah's Temple of Islam as Fard Muhammad's second in command. The normally soft-spoken Karriem was not an extraordinarily effective or gifted public speaker, and this was painfully apparent during his first talks given at Detroit's Temple of Islam. Despite this seeming limitation, Karriem had a peculiar kind of charm and charisma that swayed audiences to favor and pay attention to his word.

Between 1932 and 1934, the movement began to take further shape as Fard Muhammad and his supreme minister created a fully functional organizational apparatus. Fard Muhammad changed the name of the organization from the Allah Temple of Islam to the Nation of Islam. In addition, he developed the Fruit of Islam, a security force under the command of Supreme Captain Kalot Muhammad (Elijah's younger brother), as well as the Muslim Girl's Training and General Civilization Class, which emphasized the instruction of women in the domestic realm. Finally, for the benefit of children in the movement, Fard Muhammad created the University of Islam to serve as a grade school providing instruction in history, Arabic, mathematics, and the sciences. This forward momentum was halted when a man allegedly associated with Nation of Islam committed a ritualized murder of another man named James Smith. Fard Muhammad was arrested and released on the condition that he permanently leave Detroit.

Fard Muhammad went to Chicago were he founded Temple No. 2 of the Nation of Islam. Karriem, who changed his name to Elijah Muhammad in 1933, assumed the role of leader of the Detroit Temple (No. 1). The next year, in 1934, Fard Muhammad mysteriously disappeared and Elijah

Muhammad became the "minister of Islam" and the new leader of the movement. In attempting to quell factional disputes within the Nation of Islam in the wake of Fard Muhammad's disappearance, Elijah Muhammad fought an uphill battle for several years. By 1935, he left Detroit and settled his family in Chicago, thereby establishing Chicago Mosque No. 2 as the official headquarters of the Nation of Islam. As part of a recruitment effort to generate more loyal converts, Muhammad started a newspaper called *The Final Call to Islam.* The newspaper floundered, however, and, within a year, it ceased publication. In the meantime, Muhammad was still in the midst of quelling factional disputes within the organization and received a number of personal death threats. As a result, he moved to Milwaukee to establish Temple No. 3 and, then, Washington, D.C. (Temple No. 4) where he lived, separated from his family, for the next few years.

In 1942, Muhammad was arrested for resisting the military draft. He left Washington, D.C. and relocated in Chicago to rejoin his family. In 1943, Muhammad was arrested again on eight counts of sedition for instructing members of the Nation of Islam to not register with Selective Service or serve in the U.S. Army. On those charges, he was found guilty and served three-and-a-half years of a five-year sentence in a federal prison at Milan, Michigan. Although the temples he helped to establish remained in operation, membership in the Nation of Islam fell to about 1,000 by the time of his release from prison in 1946. After his release, the Nation of Islam went through an unprecedented period of growth. Between 1946 and 1955 alone, it constructed 12 new Muslim temples in various parts of the country. By 1959, the Nation of Islam could boast 50 temples in 22 states, including the District of Columbia.

Embracing the notion of the "double-duty dollar," Muhammad encouraged the growth of black-owned businesses, particularly those owned by loyal members of the Nation of Islam. Members, barred from buying anything on credit, opened grocery stores, book stores, restaurants, barber shops, bakeries, cleaners, and other businesses across the country. With the influence of popular and charismatic figures like Malcolm X, Muhammad Ali, and Louis (X) Farrakhan, membership in the organization swelled to as many as 20,000 by the mid-1960s. The sizable membership was matched by the financial resources of the Nation of Islam, which were estimated at more than $75 million by 1972.

The meteoric rise of Muhammad's version of the Nation of Islam was not without significant controversy. Despite the popularity of the charismatic Malcolm X, he and Elijah Muhammad became increasingly distant for a variety of reasons. As far back as 1955, Malcolm X had heard of rumors of Muhammad's alleged adultery. A succession of six of Muhammad's personal secretaries had become pregnant and, because of the prohibition against premarital sex in the Nation of Islam, each woman received sentences of 1 to 5 years of isolation from the Muslim community. In all, Muhammad has been accused of taking nine "wives," getting six pregnant, and fathering at least eight children out of wedlock. When two of these women filed paternity suits charging that Muhammad fathered their combined four children, they revealed that they both had sexual relations with Muhammad beginning when they were teenagers. Both women eventually approached Malcolm X who was shocked and alarmed about the allegations.

Tensions between Muhammad and Malcolm X grew between April 1963 and January 1964. In April 1963, Malcolm went to Phoenix, Arizona to confront Muhammad about his alleged adultery. Thinking of a way to explain this inconsistency in his mentor, Malcolm had already developed an excuse by referring to biblical prophecy; David had coveted another man's wife, Lot committed incest with a daughter, and Moses fornicated with Ethiopian women. Thus, many prophets had erred and committed sin before and Muhammad was no different. According to Malcolm X, Muhammad admitted to the allegations and praised him for his insight into biblical prophecy. When Malcolm X set out to inform other Muslim officials in an attempt to quash the rumors, however, many of them, including Louis X (Farrakhan), turned on him and reported to Muhammad that Malcolm was trying to undermine him.

The tensions became increasingly awkward as Malcolm's stature in the media grew and Muhammad's was consequently eclipsed. When Malcolm's picture was placed on the front cover of Louis Lomax's 1963 work *When the Word Is Given,* officials at Chicago Temple No. 2 were outraged. By 1964, Malcolm was the second most sought after speaker at American universities. He was asked to sit for magazine interviews (*Life, Newsweek,* and *Playboy*) and TV talk shows ("Meet the Press"), many of which he refused to avoid jealousies generated at the Chicago headquarters. The final insult for members loyal to Muhammad was the $20,000 advance and contract from Doubleday for an autobiography of Malcolm X. The jealousies emanating from Chicago's Temple No. 2, although not necessarily from Elijah Muhammad himself, provide the context for the series of punishments Malcolm X faced after his inflammatory comments regarding the November 22, 1963 assassination of President John F. Kennedy. In many regards, Malcolm's suspension and eventual assassination were due to the fear that he would completely eclipse Muhammad—not to statements attributed to him regarding a white president.

On February 24, 1975, Elijah Muhammad died of congestive heart failure in Chicago. At the time of his death, the Nation of Islam had 79 temples in 70 cities, but membership had been in decline since Malcolm's murder. Muhammad was succeeded by his son Wallace Dean Muhammad who changed the organization's name to the World Community of Islam in the West and altered its theology to be in accord with more orthodox interpretations of Islam. By 1978, Louis Farrakhan led a splinter group to reestablish the Lost-Found Nation of Islam based on the original teachings of Fard Muhammad and Elijah Muhammad. In 1985, the World Community of Islam in the West was disbanded, leaving Farrakhan's group as Elijah Muhammad's sole organizational legacy.

See also: Ali, Muhammad; Black Nationalism; Destination, Detroit, Michigan; Farrakhan, Louis; Nation of Islam; X, Malcolm

Walter C. Rucker

Bibliography

Berg, Herbert. *Elijah Muhammad and Islam.* New York: New York University Press, 2009.

Clegg, Claude Andrew III. *An Original Man: The Life and Times of Elijah Muhammad.* New York: St. Martin's Press, 1997.

Evanzz, Karl. *The Messenger: The Rise and Fall of Elijah Muhammad.* New York: Pantheon, 1999.

Muhammad, Elijah. *Message to the Blackman in America.* Chicago: Muhammad Mosque of Islam No. 2, 1965.

Walker, Dennis. *Islam and the Search for African-American Nationhood: Elijah Muhammad, Louis Farrakhan, and the Nation Of Islam.* Atlanta, GA: Clarity Press, 2005.

Nash, Diane

Diane Judith Nash (1938–) is a pacifist and outspoken advocate of civil rights for African Americans, women, veterans, and young people. She became the leader of the Nashville sit-in movement in 1960 at the age of 22. Nash continued to exercise nonviolent protest for civil rights in the South during the 1960s and is one of the most iconic and well-known female leaders to emerge from the era commonly known as the Civil Rights movement.

Diane Judith Nash was born in Chicago's South Side on May 15, 1938. Nash's father, Leon Nash, migrated north from Mississippi and held a clerical job in the military during World War II. Dorothy Bolton Nash, Diane's mother, also migrated north from her Tennessee birthplace. Raised by her grandmother, Carrie Bolton, until she was seven, Nash was taught to turn a blind eye toward racial injustice and strive to be a polite and accepting girl. Growing up, she attended the Sisters of the Blessed Sacrament parochial school, which was operated by nuns who taught only minority students. Later she would attend public high school and go on to Washington, D.C. to begin her college career at Howard University. Soon after, in 1959, Nash decided to transfer to Fisk University in Nashville Tennessee.

Although the racial climate in Chicago was by no means harmonious, Nash was still shocked by the severity of segregation in Nashville and throughout the South. Years later, in an interview published in the renowned Civil Rights documentary *Eyes on the Prize,* Nash stated that she understood the facts and stories surrounding segregation, but had no emotional relationship with the policy. It was only after she moved to the South and saw the signs that said "white" and "colored" and actually could not drink out of the water fountain or go to the ladies room that Nash said she had a real emotional reaction.

After a degrading encounter at the Tennessee State Fair, Nash vowed to seek out people and organizations intent on putting an end to segregation. Nash soon found that a man attending Vanderbilt Divinity School named Reverend James M. Lawson Jr. was organizing a series of workshops that added the methods of nonviolent protest to the arsenal of tactics used by young persons in their quest for equal rights.

At first, Nash was skeptical of the nonviolent approach and she later confessed that it was years before she was convinced. After taking part in the workshops held under the auspices of the Nashville Christian Leadership Conference (NCLC), Nash was elected chair of the Student Central Committee. Although the workshops involved role playing that often got rough, it was not until she and the other Nashville students staged sit-ins at the lunch counters of two of the city's department stores during November and December

1959, that she was given a chance to test the effectiveness of nonviolent protest. Nash, along with John Lewis, James Bevel, Marion Berry, and several others repeatedly bought items and attempted to sit at lunch counters. Unfortunately, the actions did not achieve the goal of desegregation. But Nash and her fellow protestors did not give in easily.

It was not until the sit-in staged in Greensboro, North Carolina, by four students from North Carolina Agricultural and Technical College on February 1, 1960 that the movement was launched into the national spotlight. The Nashville student group attempted to desegregate Nashville's lunch counters once again, and this time they were successful. From February 13 to May 10, 1960, the Nashville sit-in movement directed protest at Kress, Woolworths, McClellans, Walgreens, and city bus terminals. At first, there was little resistance, but after two weeks, the 81 protestors were jailed for disorderly conduct. Although the NCLC and its allies raised enough bail money to release the students, they chose to stay in jail on principal.

After escalation of white violence, the students marched to City Hall and upon reaching the steps of the building, Nash confronted Mayor Ben West asking: "Do you feel it is wrong to discriminate against a person solely on the basis of their race or color?" Mayor West confessed that he did. Nash and the student group she led had initiated desegregation of public places in Nashville, the first southern city to begin the departure from Jim Crow laws.

It was also during this time that Diane Nash had the opportunity to become active with the Student Nonviolent Coordinating Committee (SNCC) as it was beginning to take shape. From April 1960, Nash, along with James Bevel and Marion Barry, traveled to Raleigh, North Carolina to attend a conference at Shaw University that would serve to solidify goals and unite all participants of the movement. It was here that Nash, who was one of the few young women leading the student movement, met Ella Baker who became a much needed female role model and source of confidence for Nash.

Instead of returning to Fisk to resume her traditional education, Nash devoted her time and energy to keeping the momentum of nonviolent protest going. Taking the helm of the Direct Action Committee of SNCC, Nash, along with Charles Sherrod, J. Charles Jones, and Ruby Doris Smith, traveled to Rock Hill, South Carolina in early February 1961. While rallying for support of nine students from Friendship College who had been convicted of trespassing and sentenced to 30 days hard labor after participating in lunch counter sit-ins, Nash along with her companions were immediately arrested as well. She was sent to the York County Jail where she penned a poignant letter-to-the-editor of the Rock Hill Herald stating the intentions of the protestors who were only trying to help focus attention on a moral problem.

Nash also became involved with another sort of protest in the form of Freedom Rides. The first of the Freedom Rides began in Washington, D.C. in May 1961. Discouraged by the levels of aggression, some Freedom Riders wanted to abandon the endeavor, but Nash stepped in arguing that if they let them stop protesters with violence, then the movement would die. After this Nash coordinated Freedom Rides from Birmingham, Alabama to Jackson, Mississippi. In the end, Attorney General of the Unites States Robert Kennedy successfully urged the Interstate Commerce Commission to enforce total desegregation of all interstate terminals.

After a second victory, Nash moved on from fighting for desegregation to advocating voting rights for blacks in the South. In 1962, Nash was sentenced to serve two years in prison for teaching lessons of nonviolent protest to children in Jackson, Mississippi where she and her husband, James Bevel, were living. This time, Nash was four months pregnant. She was released on appeal and did not serve the full term.

For her work with the Voting Rights Committee of SNCC, Nash was asked by President John F. Kennedy to serve on the committee that led to the passing of the Civil Rights Act of 1964. She also joined the staff of the Southern Christian Leadership Conference and worked closely with Dr. Martin Luther King as an organizer, strategist, field-staff person, race-relations staff person, and workshop instructor. In 1965, she and Bevel were awarded the Southern Christian Leadership Council's Rosa Parks Award for planning and carrying out the campaign for voter registration in Selma, Alabama.

Nash's lifework is to empower young people to feel that they can bring awareness to any injustice they may be experiencing in their lives through nonviolent means. She has spoken at countless college and universities, youth organizations, and human rights conferences and currently resides in Chicago where she has worked for several decades in tenant organizing, housing advocacy, and real estate.

In 2003, Nash received the "Distinguished American Award" presented by the John F. Kennedy Library Foundation. A year later, the LBJ Award for Leadership in Civil Rights was bestowed on Nash by the Lyndon Baines Johnson Library and Museum. Her most recent honor was the bestowal of the National Civil Rights Museum's Freedom Award in 2008.

See also: Baker, Ella; Freedom Rides; Lawson, James; Lewis, John; Sit-In Movement; Southern Christian Leadership Conference; Student Nonviolent Coordinating Committee

Mary Jo Fairchild

Bibliography

Halberstam, David. *The Children.* New York: Random House, 1998.

Mullins, Lisa. *Diane Nash: The Fire of the Civil Rights Movement.* Miami, FL: Barnhardt & Ashe Publishing, 2007.

Williams, Juan. *Eyes on the Prize: America's Civil Rights Years, 1954–1965.* New York: Penguin, 1988.

Wynne, Linda T. "The Dawning of a New Day: The Nashville Sit-Ins, February 13–May 10, 1960." *Tennessee Historical Quarterly* 50 (1991):42–54.

Nation of Islam

The Nation of Islam had its beginnings in Detroit during the 1930s. In the context of both the Great Migration and the Great Depression emerged a mysterious man who called himself Wallace Dean (W. D.) Fard Muhammad. Influenced by Noble Drew Ali's Moorish Science Temple, Marcus Garvey, and the African American church, Fard Muhammad spread his unique interpretation of Islam among African Americans in Detroit. Based on police and FBI records, he was born in either New Zealand or Portland, Oregon, on February 25, 1891 to Hawaiian or British and Polynesian parents. Using a variety of aliases, Fard Muhammad had married and fathered a son before abandoning his family to move to Los Angeles by the 1920s. Between 1918 and 1929, he was in and out of jail and prison until leaving Los Angeles permanently in June 1929. Fard Muhammad relocated to Detroit, with a brief stop in Chicago, where he became a retail salesman and, in the lore of the Nation of Islam, he was a "silk peddler." While displaying and selling his wares, Fard Muhammad would discuss African American history, racial oppression, and Islam with his potential customers. By 1931, he rented public halls in order to deliver lengthy speeches, and these meetings became the actual genesis of the Lost-Found Nation of Islam in the Wilderness of North America.

According to Fard Muhammad—who would famously claim to be Allah in the flesh—he was sent on a mission to wake the "dead" and lost nation in the West, to teach them the truth about whites, and to prepare them for the coming Battle of Armageddon. In his unique rendition of Armageddon, when the forces of good and evil would prepare for battle at the mountain of Megiddo in the Great Plain of Esdraelon in Asia Minor, the combatants would really be black "Asiatics" and white "Devils," and the location of the battle would be North America. For the next three years, Farad Muhammad spread his teachings until his mysterious disappearance in 1934. In the meantime, he encountered a very impressionable Elijah Poole (late Elijah Karriem and, eventually, Elijah Muhammad). During their first encounter, Fard Muhammad revealed to Poole that he was the returned redeemer—Jesus—although he would later claim to all of his followers that he was, in reality, Allah himself.

After Fard Muhammad's disappearance in 1934, Elijah Muhammad became the "messenger" and leader of the Nation of Islam. The movement grew steadily until World War II when Muhammad and his followers refused to bear arms for the United States. In 1943, Muhammad was convicted of encouraging resistance to the draft and served 3.5 years of a 5-year sentence in a federal prison. When he was released in 1946, the Nation of Islam's membership dropped from a high of 8,000 in the last year of Fard Muhammad's leadership to just under 1,000 by the end of World War II. In the two decades between 1946 and 1966, however, Elijah Muhammad was to turn this situation around and make the Nation of Islam one of the strongest black organizations in North America.

Upon his release from prison in 1946, Muhammad relocated to Chicago in order to establish a foothold in the city. In 1954, Temple No. 2 on Chicago's South Side was established and became the headquarters of the Nation of Islam. Between 1946 and 1955, a total of 12 new Muslim temples were constructed in various parts of the country. By 1959, the Nation of Islam had 50 temples in 22 states and the District of Columbia and an estimated 3,000 registered and paying Muslim members, 15,000 believers, and about 50,000 sympathizes (or people who did not attend services at a temple and who were likely Christians, but who supported the ultimate goal of the Nation). The influence of this movement spread more widely that can be readily measured. Through their newspaper, *Muhammad Speaks,* founded by Malcolm X in 1957, hundreds of thousands of African Americans read and were inspired by the words of Elijah Muhammad. In July 1959, a TV documentary entitled "The Hate That Hate Produced" was aired, which introduced the Nation of Islam to white America and put Malcolm X on a national stage as the most articulate and passionate spokesman of black anger and rage. Liberal whites and moderate civil rights leaders joined in their condemnation of what they considered a black hate group that advocated black supremacy.

With charismatic and transcendent leaders and members like Malcolm X, Muhammad Ali, Khalid Muhammad, and Louis Farrakhan, the Nation of Islam perfected a formula for remaining relevant to black urban communities across the United States. Oddly enough, the Nation of Islam is a politically conservative organization, influenced heavily by both Booker T. Washington and Marcus Garvey. Beginning with Elijah Muhammad, leaders of the organization lecture about self-reliance, hard work, and moral uplift. Members of the Nation of Islam have strictly regimented lives. They cannot drink alcohol, engage in public cursing, use drugs, fornicate or have premarital sex, carry concealed weapons, buy anything on credit, or purchase pornography. Men in the Nation of Islam are encouraged to attend Monday night training sessions Fruit of Islam, the organization's security force. Women have specialized classes on some Wednesday and Thursday nights.

Theologically, the brand of Islam embraced by members of the Nation differs radically with what can be considered more orthodox variations of the religion. With a blend of black nationalism, a strong antipathy for whites, and some basic tenants of Islam, the "true knowledge" as members refer to it has both intriguing and problematic aspects. According to Nation of Islam doctrine, 66 trillion years ago, there were 13 black tribes of humanity (the original man) until one was destroyed in an incident that led to the creation of the moon. From that time and until 6,000 years ago, the Nation of Islam claims that 12 black tribes ruled the planet uncontested until a "big-headed" scientist named Yacub sought to create his own tribe. A master of genetics and the principles of magnetism, Yacub realized that like repels, but unlike attracts. Thus, if he could create a race so different from others, they would attract—and therefore dominate—all others. On the island of Patmos, Yacub grafted germs (genes) from the original black Asiatics to make brown people, then red people, yellow people, and finally whites. With each successive generation of lighter peoples, the races of Yacub became more and more susceptible to wickedness and evil. Thus, whites were "grafted Devils" and, with the use of "tricknology" they conquered the world and continue to control it.

The concept of black nationalism with the Nation of Islam is wrapped around the unique theology of the organization. According to their teachings, Allah would allow the grafted white Devils to rule the world for 6,000 years before destroying these abominations. The time of the grafted Devils was to end in 1914 (the onset of World War I), but Allah issued a reprieve, for destroying the Devils in North America would also lead to the destruction of his chosen people—the lost-found Nation. Fard Muhammad was sent to awaken the lost-found Nation—the black Asiatic people—and convince them to separate from white America. Apparently, their teachings claim that the Book of Revelations includes the prediction that 1970 would be the year that Allah was to destroy the grafted Devils once and for all. If African Americans had not managed to separate from whites by then, they too would be destroyed by Allah's wrath.

Of course 1970 came and went and neither a black nation was created nor were whites destroyed. In the last iteration of this story, Allah had issued another reprieve—this time until the year 2000. At that time, Allah would send a mothership to transport his chosen people away from North America before destroying whites. After the year 2000, the Nation of Islam has moved away from making predictions about Armageddon and the end of the reign of whites.

In terms of the more practical side of the Nation of Islam's teachings, the organization has been key in reforming and transforming ex-convicts, with Malcolm X serving as the epitome of this phenomenon. In 1985, it began the "Dopebusters" antidrug program in Washington, D.C.'s Mayfair Mansions. In the course of a handful of months, Fruit of Islam task forces cleaned drugs and drug dealers out of an African American government project. Likewise, Louis Farrakhan and the Nation of Islam provided the organizational apparatus for the 1995 Million Man March, the 1997 Million Woman March, and the 2000 Million Family March. Finally, Nation of Islam temples and mosques engage in community outreach and employment programs. Many of these endeavors explain why so many African Americans—fully aware of the contradictions in the Nation of Islam's history, actions, and ideology—tend to be loyal to the organization and its leaders when the

Nation is critiqued by white liberals, politicians, or media pundits.

See also: Black Nationalism; Farrakhan, Louis; Million Man March; Muhammad, Ali; Muhammad, Elijah; X, Malcolm

Walter C. Rucker

Bibliography

Curtis, Edward E. *Black Muslim Religion in the Nation of Islam, 1960–1975.* Chapel Hill: University of North Carolina Press, 2006.

Gardell, Mattias. *In the Name of Elijah Muhammad: Louis Farrakhan and the Nation of Islam.* Durham, NC: Duke University Press, 1996.

Muhammad, Elijah. *Message to the Blackman in America.* Phoenix: Secretarius MEMPS Ministries, 1973.

Ogbar, Jeffrey Ogbonna Green. *Black Power: Radical Politics and African American Identity.* Baltimore: Johns Hopkins University Press, 2004.

White, Vibert L. *Inside the Nation of Islam: A Historical and Personal Testimony by a Black Muslim.* Gainesville: University Press of Florida, 2001.

National Association for the Advancement of Colored People

Currently headquartered in Baltimore, Maryland, the National Association for the Advancement of Colored People (NAACP) is an advocacy and civil rights organization that has fought to ensure equality, justice, and inclusion for African Americans throughout its long and distinguished history. With approximately 400,000 members as of 2007, the NAACP is the largest civil rights organization in the United States, with regional offices in California, New York, Michigan, Missouri, Georgia, and Texas, as well as local, youth, and college chapters in practically every state in the United States.

The origins of the NAACP can be found within two separate historical trajectories, both linked directly or indirectly to lynching and racial violence. First, the savage 1899 lynching of Sam Hose, in Newnan, Georgia, set into motion a series of events that would lead to the founding of the Niagara Movement. On April 23, 1899, Hose—an African American migrant farm worker who had previously killed his white employer—was tortured, dismembered, and burned alive in front of 2,000 whites. W. E. B. Du Bois, having heard about the arrest of Hose and fearing the potential of his lynching, prepared a letter to be delivered to Joel Chandler Harris, editor of the Atlanta *Constitution,* which sought to provide a reasoned description of the evident facts. Before Du Bois arrived at the editorial office, news had reached him that Hose had already been lynched and that his knuckles were on display at a grocery store in downtown Atlanta. As Du Bois would later recount in his autobiography, the Hose lynching served as a "red ray," which disrupted his goal of becoming a "scientist" who would seek to resolve issues regarding equality and justice through scholarship and his work as a professor at Atlanta University. In many ways, the Hose lynching was the genesis of Du Bois's transformation into a scholar-activist.

In the decade leading up to Hose's lynching, 115 black Georgians had been murdered by white mobs. Du Bois and others demanded that Governor Allen Candler actively protect the state's black population from these frequent acts of murderous violence. This appeal fell on deaf ears and the Hose incident was linked to the tumult that surrounded the issue of black suffrage by white supremacist politicians. This was the height of the black nadir, and the white South was seemingly determined to ignore the Fourteenth and Fifteenth Amendments, using any justification available. The myth of the black murderer and rapist represented a sufficient rationalization for the continued subjugation of African Americans throughout the South. The emotion of the Hose case and the continued frustrations created by white opposition to the human rights of African Americans coalesced in the form of a political statement by Du Bois— *The Souls of Black Folk* (1903).

In attacking the problematic leadership of Booker T. Washington, Du Bois created a platform for future black activism in *The Souls of Black Folk.* He called for suffrage rights, civil rights, and the education of black youth. Although he had earlier been a strong supporter of Washington's economic program, Du Bois grew to realize that Washington's accommodationist doctrine had shifted the burden of resolving the racial divide squarely on the shoulders of African Americans—the victims of suffocating levels of oppression. As a direct result of Washington's efforts to accommodate white supremacy, white southerners not only placed the blame on the victims of their deleterious policies, they also began to steadily erode the few remaining rights of African Americans. In Du Bois's diatribe against Washington in *The Souls of Black Folk,* he rightly points out that during the years of Washington's leadership,

the movement to disfranchise black men in the South had widened, the Supreme Court had moved to officially sanction racial segregation, and monetary aid was being steadily withdrawn from black liberal arts colleges. The specter of Sam Hose denied any attempt to blame the victims of white supremacy and, in Du Bois's evolving world view, made necessary resistance, constant pressure, and activism.

The Souls of Black Folk produced a significant amount of political momentum and led to the founding of the Niagara Movement in Fort Erie, Ontario, in July 1905. A total of 32 prominent African Americans, including Du Bois, William Monroe Trotter, and John Hope, met to discuss the means by which civil rights and an end to racial discrimination could be achieved. Expanding on the platform Du Bois outlined in *The Souls of Black Folk,* this organization listed a number of major objectives: voting rights, an end to discrimination in public accommodations, social integration, judicial equality, and the education of black youth. Despite Du Bois's attempt to credit William Monroe Trotter with creating the organization's political platform, the Niagara Movement's goals were largely based on concepts articulated by Du Bois two years earlier. At the next meeting, scheduled for August 15, 1906, in Harper's Ferry, West Virginia, the estimable Ida B. Wells-Barnett joined the Niagara Movement and the group incorporated her antilynching campaign into its platform. By the end of 1906, the Niagara Movement had established 30 branches and, although underfunded and understaffed, the organization had managed a handful of victories for civil rights at the local level.

The second historical trajectory that led to the founding of the NAACP was the 1908 Springfield, Illinois race riot. In a city preparing to celebrate the centennial of its most famous son in 1909, Abraham Lincoln, a race riot began on August 14, 1908, which led to seven deaths—including one lynching—and the destruction of dozens of homes and businesses. White progressives in Springfield and across the country were appalled by the details of the riot and the fact that it occurred in, of all places, the birth city of Lincoln. In response to the race riot, socialist William English Walling wrote an article entitled "Race War in the North" for the *Independent* that described, in graphic detail, the Springfield riot and called on progressive whites to come to the aid of their fellow black citizens. Among those influenced by the article was Mary White Ovington, a New York socialist and social worker. Ovington sought out Walling and, along with Jewish social worker Dr. Henry Moskowitz, the three white progressives launched a call for a national conference on the plight of African Americans during the commemoration of Lincoln's centennial birthday on February 12, 1909. Among the 60 people attending the conference were a number of notable African American activists and intellectuals: Du Bois, Wells-Barnett, Mary Church Terell, Mary McLeod Bethune, and Arthur Spingarn, among others.

During the February 12, 1909 conference, the National Negro Committee was formed to serve as the organizational apparatus that would articulate a platform for African American civil rights. In May 1910, the National Negro Committee organized a permanent body to be known as the National Association for the Advancement of Colored People, and Ovington was appointed as the executive secretary. Other members of the NAACP's executive committee included Moorfield Stoery (national president), William English Walling (chair of the executive committee), John Milholland (treasurer), and Du Bois (director of publicity and research); Du Bois was the only African American in the NAACP's early leadership core. The platform and goals set forth by the NAACP were adopted from the Niagara Movement. In this way, the two historical trajectories— the Niagara Movement and progressive/radical whites— merged together to create one of the most powerful and effective civil rights organizations in U.S. history.

Notable early activities of the NAACP include the 1913 protest against segregation in the federal government sanctioned by Woodrow Wilson, the boycott of the 1915 film *The Birth of a Nation,* and the 1917 Silent March against lynching and racial violence in New York City. As a result of its early emphasis on local organizing and rigorous recruitment, the NAACP's membership grew dramatically. In addition, the number of branches increased from just 50 offices and 6,000 members in 1914 to more than 300 branch offices and 90,000 members reported by 1919. With the publication of *Thirty Years of Lynching in the United States: 1889–1918,* the NAACP launched a more concerted effort to record and investigate lynchings, with the goal of encouraging legislative action to bring an end to this evil practice. Although the NAACP never successfully forced antilynching legislation at the federal or state level, the organization's commitment and efforts in this regard led to the gradual decline in the annual number of lynchings in the United States. One effective mechanism used by the NAACP to highlight lynchings was the distribution of flags to all branches the denote each time "'A Black Man Was Lynched Today.'"

In the midst of its ever-expanding fight against lynching and racial violence, the NAACP began to address other areas of African American life that needed dire attention. By the 1930s, the NAACP began to look at education, housing, health care, public transportation, employment, and other issues that limited the life chances of African Americas. It was also during this era that the organization's hesitance to engage in mass direct action became apparent. Instead of staging mass marches, pickets, or boycotts, the organization engaged in court room battles and political lobbying as means to fight for enforcement of the Fourteenth and Fifteenth Amendments. In the three decades after 1936, the NAACP won or significantly contributed to a number of courtroom and legislative battles, including *Murray v. Maryland* (1936), *Gaines v. Canada* (1938), *Smith v. Allwright* (1944), *Morgan v. Virginia* (1946), *Shelley v. Kraemer* (1948), *Sipuel v. University of Oklahoma* (1948), *Sweatt v. Painter* (1950), *McLaurin v. Oklahoma State Regents* (1950), *Brown v. Board of Education* (1954), the Civil Rights Act of 1957, the Civil Rights Act of 1964, and the Voting Rights Act (1965). The work of Charles Hamilton Houston, Thurgood Marshall, Walter White, and Roy Wilkins were significant in these victories.

By the 1960s, the NAACP began to expand its activism beyond the court room and state and federal law-making bodies and began to engage in direct action. In 1960, the NAACP's Youth Council began a series of lunch-counter sit-ins around the South, resulting in the desegregation of more than 60 department store lunch counters. In addition to sit-ins, NAACP organizers engaged in other forms of nonviolent social protest including marches and civil rights rallies. As a result the successes of direct action as a tactic, the NAACP named its first field director to oversee the legal and safety concerns of nonviolent protesters. Ironically, field director and highly successful organizer Medgar Evers was fatally shot outside his home in 1963.

In keeping with the constant changes occurring with the Civil Rights movement, the NAACP went through various transformations as well. By the 1970s and 1980s, the organization became a strong advocate for black political participation and actively engaged in voter registration drives, the creation of voting sites in high schools, and extending the Voting Rights Act. In addition to emphasizing political engagement and participation in the African American community, the NAACP helped increase the mounting global pressure against apartheid in South Africa by encouraging a boycott of the nation. By 1993, the antiapartheid movement was successful owing, in part, to the concerted activities of the NAACP and allied organizations.

See also: Antiapartheid Movement; Antilynching Campaign; Du Bois, W. E. B.; Houston, Charles Hamilton; Jim Crow; Marshall, Thurgood; Niagara Movement; Springfield Race Riot of 1908; Terrell, Mary Church; Wells-Barnett, Ida; White, Walter; Wilkins, Roy

Walter C. Rucker

Bibliography

Berg, Manfred. *The Ticket to Freedom: The NAACP and the Struggle for Black Political Integration.* Gainesville: University Press of Florida, 2005.

Bernstein, Patricia. *The First Waco Horror: The Lynching of Jesse Washington and the Rise of the NAACP.* College Station: Texas A&M University Press, 2005.

Hughes, Langston. *Fight for Freedom: The Story of the NAACP.* New York: Norton, 1962.

Jonas, Gilbert. *Freedom's Sword: The NAACP and the Struggle against Racism in America, 1909–1969.* New York: Routledge, 2005.

Kellogg, Charles Flint, ed. *NAACP: A History of the National Association for the Advancement of Colored People, Volume I, 1909–1920.* Baltimore: Johns Hopkins University Press, 1973.

Sullivan, Patricia. *Lift Every Voice: The NAACP and the Making of the Civil Rights Movement.* New York: New Press, 2009.

Tushnet, Mark V. *The NAACP's Legal Strategy against Segregated Education, 1925–1950.* Chapel Hill: University of North Carolina Press, 1987.

Wedin, Carolyn. *Inheritors of the Spirit: Mary White Ovington and the Founding of the NAACP.* New York: Wiley, 1998.

Zangrando, Robert L. *The NAACP Crusade against Lynching, 1909–1950.* Philadelphia: Temple University Press, 1980.

National Association of Colored Women

The National Association of Colored Women (NACW) was the preeminent association of African American women from its founding in 1896 through the first decades of the 20th century. The NACW grew rapidly and, within 20 years of its founding, had 50,000 members in more than 1,000 clubs around the nation. African American women organized themselves around the need to uplift the race, better their communities, defend the morality of black women, and improve the lives of poor black women and children. Whereas other women's organizations in the late 1930s began to erode its dominance, the NACW has continued

to provide fellowship for black women and social welfare benefits to African Americans around the country.

African American women have a long tradition of self-help, benevolent associations, and social clubs. In the post–Civil War period, many women joined church women's auxiliaries, the Woman's Christian Temperance Union, the King's Daughters, and other associations that dispensed charity to needy blacks in their community and fought for temperance, suffrage, education, and civil rights for African Americans.

By the 1890s, women flocked to new secular women's clubs organized around social welfare and race uplift. In the summer of 1892, elite clubwomen came together in Washington, D.C. to form the Colored Woman's League of Washington, D.C. Led in part by Mary Church Terrell, a wealthy school principal, in 1894 the league began to affiliate with other women's leagues to become a national organization. The next year, Josephine Ruffin, a clubwoman from Boston and editor of the *Woman's Era* monthly journal, founded the National Federation of Afro-American Women. In 1896, to avoid competition and factionalism, the two organizations merged into the National Association of Colored Women, with Terrell as the first president. This new organization listed as its goals promoting education for African American women, raising home standards, aid to women and children, especially working women and children, political rights for African Americans, and interracial understanding.

Leaders of the NACW argued that women had to uplift the race by helping African Americans gain respectability through improved morals, especially for women. Clubwomen's emphasis on morality stemmed from the lack of respect accorded black women. Ruffin had founded the National Federation of Afro-American women partly in response to a slanderous letter sent by John Jacks, a Missouri editor, to Florence Balgarnie, a British suffragist and reformer. Jacks accused African American women of sexual immorality, as well as thievery and deceit. Clubwomen focused on proving the morality of black women; promoting middle class norms for homes, children, education; cleanliness; and improving social and economic conditions that would protect women from sexual abuse. Clubwomen sometimes caused resentment among the poor whom they were trying to aid, because their emphasis on respectability inevitably placed the burden of improvement on blacks themselves, who were often innocent victims of sexual abuse and institutional racism. The NACW motto, "Lifting as We Climb," expresses this classism. When women in the NACW worked to aid African American women, they believed that they worked to benefit the entire race because they believed that the perceived immorality of black women held back all African Americans. Furthermore, they argued that because men had lost power through disfranchisement, women had to take the lead. Such a dominant role for women in race uplift occasionally caused tensions with black men who wanted women to yield such leadership to black men.

The NACW first convened in 1897 in Nashville, where, in addition to emphasizing women, children, and the home, they discussed the convict lease system, Jim Crow conditions, especially in railroad travel, and lynching. Many projects spearheaded by local clubs were related to education and children's issues. The kindergarten department was one of the first departments established in 1901 under president Josephine Silone-Yates. The Charleston (South Carolina) Free Kindergarten Associations, established in 1902, sold copes of a speech written by Mary Church Terrell to raise the funds needed to open two kindergartens. Clubwomen were also particularly interested in opening homes for delinquent girls in the South and for migrant girls in the North. One of the earliest efforts was the White Rose Mission in New York, founded by Victoria Mathews, which took in southern girls arriving in New York City. It aided 5,000 girls in the first 15 years. Southern state federations of women's clubs also opened homes for delinquent girls and schools offering an industrial education, often because their states refused to allocate public funding for such projects. Clubwomen also turned their attention to health care; the Neighborhood Union in Atlanta established a health clinic for children, and the Phyllis Wheatley Woman's League of Chicago sponsored talks on health and sanitation.

In addition to social welfare, the NACW also promoted black history and literature, evident in the inclusion of black literature on the program of one of the earliest conventions, in Buffalo in 1901. They made a significant contribution to public history when, in 1916, the Frederick Douglass Memorial and Historical Association (FDMHA) requested the aid of the NACW in raising funds to save the former home of civil rights leader Douglass. The NACW raised enough to burn the mortgage at the 1918 meeting in Denver, and NACW members worked through the FDMHA and the NACW to continue to raise money for the home's upkeep.

In the 1920s, NACW leadership increasingly focused on internationalism and interracial cooperation. Prominent NACW women became involved in pan-African issues and global women's organizations. Anna Julia Cooper attended the first Pan-African Conference in 1900, and Mary Church Terrell attended three international meetings, including the International Conference of Women in Paris in 1919. The most well-known clubwomen in the nation formed the International Council of Women of the Darker Races, an organization that studied conditions of women of color around the world and established correspondence with women's groups in Liberia, South Africa, Haiti, and Brazil. Clubwomen also became active in the Women's Division of the Commission on Interracial Cooperation (CIC), a regional group begun after Atlanta clubwoman Lugenia Burns Hope invited two white women to the 1920 meeting of the NACW. The CIC focused on issues such as improved working conditions for domestic servants and antilynching law. Such cooperation in the CIC followed an earlier decision of the General Federation of Women's Clubs not to seat Josephine St. Pierre Ruffin in 1900 and to exclude black women from their organization.

The NACW began to lose authority in the 1920s as the explicitly masculine UNIA and male-dominated Harlem Renaissance moved the spotlight back on men as the leaders of the race. Furthermore, the changing sexual mores of the 1920s departed from the NACW's strict emphasis on chastity. In 1928, the association started a Better Homes drive to improve dress, manners, and hygiene for black children; and two years later the NACW eliminated all other departments in order to focus exclusively on the mother, the home, and the child, as well as women in industry. African American women more interested in the political fight for civil rights increasingly turned to the National Council of Negro Women, established by former NACW president Mary McLeod Bethune. The NACW continued to organize women's clubs that focused more narrowly on their local community needs. In so doing, it has helped thousands of communities around the country, in particular in areas concerning education, children, and social welfare.

See also: Antilynching Campaign; Bethune, Mary McLeod; Matthews, Victoria Earle; Pan-Africanism; Terrell, Mary Church; Tubman, Harriet; Universal Negro Improvement Association; Wells-Barnett, Ida.

Joan Marie Johnson

Bibliography

Davis, Elizabeth. *Lifting as They Climb.* Washington, D.C.: National Association of Colored Women, 1933.

Giddings, Paula. *When and Where I Enter: The Impact of Black Women on Race and Sex in America.* New York: William Morrow, 1984.

Johnson, Joan Marie. *Southern Ladies, New Women: Race, Region, and Clubwomen in South Carolina, 1890–1930.* Gainesville: University Press of Florida, 2004.

Salem, Dorothy. *To Better Our World: Black Women in Organized Reform.* Brooklyn, NY: Carlson, 1990.

Shaw, Stephanie. "Black Club Women and the Creation of the National Association of Colored Women." *Journal of Women's History* 3 (Fall 1991):10–25.

Wesley, Charles H. *The History of the National Association of Colored Women's Clubs: A Legacy of Service.* Washington, D.C.: The Association, 1984.

White, Deborah Gray. *Too Heavy a Load: Black Women in Defense of Themselves, 1894–1994.* New York: W. W. Norton, 1999.

National Council for Black Studies

Founded in 1975 by a group of academics from various disciplines concerned about the future of the emerging field of black studies, The National Council for Black Studies, Inc. (NCBS) is the premier organization for professionals committed to the development of the discipline. In its brief 30-year history, it has successfully established itself as a leader of the black studies movement in both the national and international community, and has steadfastly held to committing itself to academic excellence and social responsibility.

The birth of the black studies movement was a natural extension of the social turbulence of the Civil Rights and Black Power movements that rocked the nation in the 1960s. As noted by Karenga (2002) in *Introduction to Black Studies,* black student demand on college campuses led to the creation of academic and community-based programs that were a reflection of the history and culture of people of African descent. As college and universities struggled to fulfill student demands for a meaningful and relevant education, a cadre of black scholars and intellectuals emerged as leaders in the field.

The many ambiguities surrounding the content, structure, purpose, and nature of the discipline led Bertha Maxwell Roddey to convene and assume leadership of a new organization dedicated to strengthening and promoting academic and community programs in the area. Under Roddey's leadership (1975–1978) and those that followed, (William King, William "Nick" Nelson, Carlene Young, Delores P. Aldridge, Charles Henry, Selase Williams, William Little, James Stewart, Shirley Weber, and Charles Jones) NCBS successfully influenced the development of a core curriculum for the discipline, provided a base for activist scholars; challenged institutional attacks on black studies programs and faculty members who supported them; and played a vanguard role in the development and institutionalization of black studies programs on college and university campuses throughout the United States.

Among its many achievements, NCBS assumed a leadership role in the development of curriculum standards. The 1981 publication of the *Black Studies Core Curriculum,* developed by a committee chaired by Perry Hall, was a major step in this direction. The organization's ability to focus its attention on the continued development of uniform standards for the discipline was strengthened by a three-year, $300,000 grant awarded by the Ford Foundation in 1988. In 1990, the release of the *Holistic Afrocentric Curriculum Model* report, which resulted from a collaborative effort among board members William Little, Carolyn Leonard, and Edward Cosby, was hailed as a breakthrough in the conceptualization of black studies from an Afrocentric rather than a Eurocentric worldview. In addition, the Ford Foundation grant allowed the organization to focus on professional development for new scholars and administrators entering the field. NCBS established summer institutes that allowed new scholars to study with some of the preeminent scholars in the field, and offered new administrators the opportunity to explore the challenges of leadership for chairs and program coordinators of Africana/black studies. The success of these initiatives resulted in a three-year extension and an additional $300,000 grant from the Ford Foundation.

A recent collaboration between NCBS and the National Black United Fund Federation Charities has provided the organization with funding to support community outreach programs. This initiative, led by board member Patricia Reid-Merritt, allows federal employers to contribute to NCBS through the combined federal campaign. Affiliated institutions receive grants to support educational and service programs in the black community.

The NCBS annual conferences have consistently offered scholars the opportunity to present their research and to partake in scholarly discourse with others in the field. Scholars from a cross section of traditional and nontraditional disciplines engage in ongoing debates about their positioning and linkages to the field of black studies. In addition, new emerging young scholars offer insights from the first generation of trained scholars with terminal degrees in the field of black studies. The growth of degree-granting programs in black studies led to the creation of the first national honor society to recognize outstanding achievement for majors and minors in Africana/black studies. Ankh Maat Wedjau was established by NCBS in 2004. Senior scholars in the field served as charter members and, in March 2005, the first class of student achievers was inducted.

Coupled with its many successes, the organization has also experienced numerous challenges from both internal and external forces. Steeped in a radical belief that promotes the primacy of African culture to African-ascendant people, NCBS has often been forced to defend its own philosophy, beliefs, and practices as it fought, publicly, against those who attacked black studies scholars, the legitimacy of the discipline, and the organization founded to define, promote, and strengthen its presence in the academy and the community. The interdisciplinary nature of black studies has often led to conflict and confusion among those who experienced difficulty in separating themselves from traditional disciplines. More specifically, NCBS has fought diligently to demonstrate the need for a collective, organized, independent body of scholars, academics, and intellectuals whose primary commitment is to the development of the field of black studies.

With a strong membership base and institutional affiliates from across the country, NCBS continues its mission to develop and promote black studies and black scholars, to engage in effective community outreach strategies, and to participate, fully, in all actions leading to the empowerment of African people.

See also: Afrocentricity; Asante, Molefi Kete

Patricia Reid-Merritt

Bibliography

Asante, Molefi K., and Ama Mazama, eds. *Encyclopedia of Black Studies.* Thousand Oaks, CA: Sage Publications, 2005.

Fenderson, Jonathan. 2009. "Toward Organizational Dialogue in Black Studies." *Journal of Black Studies.* 39, no. 4 (2009): 497–507.

Karenga, Maulana. *Introduction to Black Studies.* Los Angeles: University of Sankore Press, 1993.

Marable, Manning. *Dispatches from the Ebony Tower: Intellectuals Confront the African American Experience.* New York: Columbia University Press, 2000.

National Council of Negro Women

The National Council of Negro Women (NCNW), founded on December 5, 1935, became the first umbrella organization to consolidate the power of all black women's groups to more effectively gain action from the national government. NCNW founder, Mary McLeod Bethune, as past president of the National Association of Colored Women (NACW), saw women's potential for organizing and fundraising. In 1929, she invited organizations to meet and form a national council dedicated to African American women's issues as white women had earlier done through the National Council of Women. In all, 29 women representing 14 organizations attended the founding meeting at the 137th Street Branch of the YWCA in Harlem. Debate ensued, leaving the NACW leadership split on the value of the new organization. Supporters, including Mary Church Terrell, Dr. Dorothy Ferebee, and Charlotte Hawkins Brown, selected Bethune as the first president.

Bethune used her friendship with Eleanor Roosevelt to gain assistance from the federal government on race issues. As the head of the Division of Negro Affairs at the National Youth Administration (1936–1943), Bethune viewed racial inclusion as a means to influence policy. She helped organize the Federal Council on Negro Affairs (informally called the black cabinet), which brought more managers and administrators into Washington, D.C. She used this power base to advance the rights of black women. By 1937, the NCNW gained public attention from the "National Conference on the Problems of the Negro and Negro Youth" held at the Labor Department. In 1938, more recognition came with the "Conference on Governmental Cooperation in the Approach to the Problems of Negro Women and Children" held at the Department of the Interior. These conferences created public recognition of the NCNW and brought its leaders into direct discussions with government officials.

Under Bethune, the NCNW grew in members, structure, and recognition; developed a full-time paid staff; and purchased a national headquarters building in 1943. The

Mary McLeod Bethune addresses an annual meeting of the National Council of Negro Women, established in 1935. (National Park Service-Mary McLeod Bethune Council House NHS, Washington, D.C.)

NCNW became the clearinghouse for information related to black women and race issues and disseminated this information through its publication, *Aframerican Woman's Journal.* During World War II, the NCNW campaigned for integration of the military and for admission of black women into the Women's Army Corps (WACS). NCNW sponsorship resulted in the *S. S. Harriet Tubman,* the first ship to honor a black woman. Bethune represented the NCNW as an advisor to the U.S. delegation at the founding conference of the United Nations in 1945. By 1949, the NCNW represented 22 national organizations including sororities, professional associations, occupational societies, women's auxiliaries, denominational groups, and clubs.

Well-qualified and dedicated women followed Bethune. Dorothy Boulding Ferebee (1949–1953) and Vivian Carter Mason (1953–1957) continued the direction of

the NCNW. Dorothy Irene Height (1957–1998) created a professional staff capable of program delivery and won tax-exempt status in 1966, enabling the NCNW to gain grants and contributions for its programs addressing youth, health, employment, hunger, civil rights, international relations, and family life. Growth in membership through affiliation progressed through the years from 500,000 in the 1930s to 4 million by the 1980s. Government agencies recognized the NCNW as the predominant national organization, hence, reinforcing the organization's representative power.

Collaboration and coalition building remain. Dorothy Height continues as president emerita and chair following her retirement in 1998. The NCNW belief in commitment, unity, and self-reliance appears in their current promotion of financial security, health issues, achievement, and recognition of African American women leaders.

See also: Bethune, Mary McLeod; Black Cabinet; National Association of Colored Women; Roosevelt, Eleanor; Terrell, Mary Church

Dorothy Salem

Bibliography

Collier-Thomas, Bettye. *N.C.N.W., 1935–1980.* Washington, D.C.: National Council of Negro Women, 1981.

Height, Dorothy I. *Open Wide the Freedom Gates: A Memoir.* New York: Public Affairs, 2003.

Negro League Baseball

Andrew "Rube" Foster formed the Negro National League in 1920, thereby establishing the most organized and stable league for black players throughout the years of segregated baseball. Earlier leagues had existed. Black men participated in the National Colored League as early as the mid-1840s, and there had been integrated teams and all-black clubs during the Civil War era, particularly in the Northern states.

In 1867, the Brooklyn Uniques challenged the Philadelphia Excelsiors to the "championship of colored clubs," the earliest game in which scores are available for all-black teams; Philadelphia won, 37–24. That same year, the Philadelphia Pythians attempted to join the newly formed National Association of Base Ball Players, the first organized baseball league in the country, but they—along with any other team with black players—were not permitted to join this all-white league.

Nevertheless, black players did occasionally participate on teams consisting of white players. In 1878, John "Bud" Fowler pitched for the International League, breaking the minor league color barrier. In 1883, a Toledo team in the Northwestern League signed catcher Moses Fleetwood "Fleet" Walker, a black man who had played integrated baseball for Oberlin College. The next year, Walker's team merged with the American Association, thereby making Walker the first black player on a major league ball club roster, several decades before Jackie Robinson's sensational signing.

Actually, Robinson was far from the first African American to play professional ball. During the 1880s, 13 black players participated on minor leagues teams populated by white players, with 1887 being their peak year. Difficulties were significant for these players, with fans threatening them, and white teammates refusing to pose for team photos if they appeared in them. Moreover, if a black man pitched, some teammates would deliberately make errors to prevent the pitcher from winning his game.

On July 14, 1887, National League star Cap Anson refused to play against George Stovey for racial reasons; the next day, the International League agreed to ban all future contracts with players of color. Frank Grant and Bob Higgins continued to play on integrated teams through 1888, and Fleet Walker through 1889, but the ban was in full effect by then.

In 1885, Frank Thompson formed the first all-black professional team, the Cuban Giants. Other important professional teams followed, including the Philadelphia Orions, the Boston Resolutes, the Lord Baltimores, the St. Louis Black Stockings, the New York Gothams and Cuban X Giants, and the Michigan Page Fence Giants.

Challenges abounded for black players and the owners of these teams. Owners generally lacked sufficient funding, so players' wages were uncertain. Some teams followed predetermined schedules, which assisted them in collecting greater gate fees; but they also barnstormed, traveling across parts of the country and challenging local teams to matches. The teams divided gate receipts in ways that were determined before the game.

In 1901, Baltimore Orioles manager John McGraw attempted to pass light-skinned Charlie Grant as a Native American, in hopes of circumventing the ban on black players. His ruse was uncovered, and the talented second baseman was prohibited from play.

Initially, Rube Foster's National Negro League was formed by eight teams located in Chicago, Illinois; Dayton, Ohio; Detroit, Michigan; Indianapolis, Indiana; Kansas City, Kansas; and St. Louis, Missouri; this was named the Western League. Shortly thereafter, six more teams formed the Eastern Colored League, and the two divisions met in their own version of the World Series.

Foster became ill in 1926; the Eastern League collapsed in 1928, and the Western League folded after the 1930 season. Two leagues—the Negro Southern League and the East-West League—appeared in 1932, and then the Negro National League name was revived. With six to eight teams each year, this organization lasted through 1936. Starting in 1937, two divisions re-formed, and the league flourished until 1947, when Brooklyn Dodgers manager Branch Rickey signed Jackie Robinson to a contract. This began the integration of modern-day baseball in the National League, and that year, Robinson won the Rookie of the Year Award. Also that year, Bill Veeck of the Cleveland Indians signed Larry Doby, thereby breaking the color barrier in the American League. Doby participated in All-Star games from 1949–1954.

Other players who made a successful transition from the Negro leagues to major league baseball include Leroy "Satchel" Paige who, after pitching for black teams for 22 years, joined the Cleveland Indians in 1948 and pitched well into his fifties. Another was catcher Roy Campanella, who also played for Branch Rickey's Dodgers. Perhaps the most sensational player to cross the color line was the last to do so, Hank Aaron, who signed with the Milwaukee Braves in 1954 and went on to break the major league home run record (755) and the record for runs batted in (2,297).

Other men who played their entire careers in the Negro leagues, but who clearly had the skill to play in the all-white major leagues, include "Smokey" Joe Williams, Josh Gibson, "Buck" O'Neil, "Mule" Settles, Oscar Charleston, "Bullet" Joe Rogan, and "Cool Papa" Bell. Starting in 1971, a Negro League Committee selected nine players for Baseball National Hall of Fame and Museum induction; in the years since, the Veterans Committee has continued honoring talented men from these leagues.

See also: Black Athletes; Jim Crow; Robinson, Jackie

Kelly Boyer Sagert

Bibliography
Cottrell, Robert C. *Blackball, the Black Sox and the Babe: Baseball's Crucial 1920 Season.* Jefferson, NC: McFarland, 2002.
Hauser, Christopher. *The Negro Leagues Chronology: Events in Organized Black Baseball, 1920–1948.* Jefferson, NC: McFarland, 2006.
James, Bill. *The New Bill James Historical Baseball Abstract.* New York: The Free Press, 2001.
Lanctot, Neil. *Negro League Baseball: The Rise and Ruin of a Black Institution.* Philadelphia: University of Pennsylvania Press, 2004.
Loverro, Thom, ed. *The Encyclopedia of Negro League Baseball.* New York: Facts of File, 2003.

Negro Seamen Acts

The Negro Seamen Acts were a series of laws passed in Southern coastal states during the antebellum period intended to prevent seditious communication between slaves and foreign or Northern free blacks. Although South Carolina's Negro Seamen Acts were the most controversial and have received the most scholarly attention, similar laws were also passed in Georgia (1829), North Carolina (1830–1831), Florida (1832), Alabama (1839, 1841), and Louisiana (1842). These acts prompted innumerable protests from Great Britain and intensified the rising sectional tensions between Northern critics of slavery and Southern defenders of states' rights that eventually culminated in the American Civil War.

The first Negro Seamen Acts were passed in South Carolina on December 21, 1822, five months after the discovery of an apparent slave revolt led by a Charleston free black man named Denmark Vesey. Suspicions that visiting free black seamen had encouraged and assisted Vesey in planning the rebellion prompted calls to forestall the consequences of free black seamen influencing the state's slaves. Under the provisions of the acts, free blacks employed on board vessels docking at a South Carolina port from any other state or foreign nation were to be seized and placed in jail until the vessel was ready to depart the state. Furthermore, the captains of these vessels were required to pay for the expenses of these confinements, and if they failed either to remove the free black seamen from the port or refused to pay for their detentions, the captains could be fined at least $1,000 or imprisoned for two months, and the free black seamen could be sold as slaves.

Almost immediately the acts were greeted with widespread opposition and nearly endless controversy. In February 1823, captains of American vessels argued that the acts subjected their ships to considerable expense, inconvenience, and delay. And members of Charleston's Chamber of Commerce complained in 1826 and 1830 that the laws not only drove away commerce and thus impoverished the city, but also that the acts were regularly evaded and failed to prevent interactions between free black seamen and slaves. But the most steady and fervent salvos were launched from representatives of the British government, who decried the treatment of free British subjects and argued that the acts violated the free trade provisions of the 1815 Commercial Convention between the United States and Great Britain.

Not confining their discontent to petitions and protests, however, opponents of the Negro Seamen Acts also questioned and challenged their constitutionality. Only weeks after the acts' passage, a lower court in South Carolina upheld their constitutionality. Then in August 1823, the U.S. Circuit Court ruled that the laws violated the exclusive right of the federal government to regulate commerce and was therefore unconstitutional. Defenders of the Negro Seamen Acts responded that South Carolina had a right to protect its citizens from "moral pestilence," and compared the laws to maritime quarantine regulations enacted to prevent the importation of deadly infectious diseases. But proponents more generally argued that the court's decision violated the state's sovereignty and independence, thus placing the emerging doctrine of states' rights at the heart of the defense of the Negro Seamen Acts.

Officials in South Carolina accordingly disregarded the ruling and continued to imprison free black seamen, igniting what some historians consider the first nullification crisis between the state and federal governments. Despite this consistent and fervent defense of the Negro Seamen Acts and the principle of states' rights, the acts did undergo several alterations. The South Carolina legislature passed the first modifications to the acts in December 1823, repealing the enslavement provision and exempting free black sailors on naval vessels contingent on their remaining on board their ships while in port. But at the urging of the South Carolina Association—a group of prominent Charlestonians formed after the Vesey conspiracy to preserve order and implement stricter controls over the city's black population—the 1823 law also enacted more severe penalties for free black offenders, and, in 1835, the enslavement provision was reinstated. In 1856, the Negro Seamen Acts were again amended, allowing free black seamen to remain on board their vessels rather than being removed to the jail after captains provided bonds to ensure that their colored mariners would not go ashore. Like previous versions of the law, however, this provision produced unintended consequences. One ship captain petitioned the Charleston City Council in March 1858 asking to be relieved from a fine, claiming that his free black crewmen had been lured ashore by persons desiring to collect the portion of the fine given to informants.

Protests and legal battles over the Negro Seamen Acts persisted throughout the remainder of the antebellum period, and champions of the acts and the principle of states' rights consistently came to their defense, sometimes using violent or extralegal means. For instance, when Massachusetts agent Samuel Hoar arrived in Charleston in late 1844 to initiate legal suits again challenging the arrest of free black citizens of the Bay State, the South Carolina legislature condemned him as a seditious danger to public safety, and Hoar was compelled to flee under the threat of mob violence. Similarly, South Carolina authorities derided the Massachusetts legislature in 1845 for its increasing hostility toward the institution of slavery. White Southerners were thus increasingly suspicious of any action that challenged their peculiar institution or the laws enacted to police the South's considerable slave population. Before long this sectional rift would boil over into a Civil War that would abolish slavery and the Negro Seamen Acts.

See also: Vesey, Denmark

Michael D. Thompson

Bibliography

Hamer, Philip M. "British Consuls and the Negro Seamen Acts, 1850–1860." *Journal of Southern History* 1 (May 1935):138–68.

Hamer, Philip M. "Great Britain, the United States, and the Negro Seamen Acts, 1822–1848." *Journal of Southern History* 1 (February 1935):3–28.

Pearson, Edward A. *Designs against Charleston: The Trial Record of the Denmark Vesey Slave Conspiracy of 1822.* Chapel Hill: University of North Carolina Press, 1999.

New Negro Movement

The New Negro movement was a bold effort to transform American images of African Americans through art and literature, while instilling race pride within the black community itself. Pursuing racial renewal through cultural diplomacy, the new Negro movement gave birth to the Harlem Renaissance (1919–1934), a period of black artistic efflorescence. A golden age of black cultural nationalism, the Harlem Renaissance was a grand response to the call of W. E. B. Du Bois, who, in November 1920, wrote that an age of black literature was due. The literati of the Harlem Renaissance—Alain Locke, James Weldon Johnson, Jean Toomer, Zora Neale Hurston, Jessie Redmon Fauset, Wallace Thurman, Langston Hughes, Countee Cullen, Claude McKay, and others—were the vanguard of the new Negro movement, fulfilling their roles as part of what W. E. B. Du Bois called "the talented tenth." Graphic artists, such as Aaron Douglas, William H. Johnson, and Miguel Covarrubias, complemented their verbal genius with visual forms. Collectively, the writers, artists, intellectuals, and performers were known as the "new Negroes," and their era would be called the Harlem Renaissance. For the first time in American history, African Americans could rightfully claim to have produced a distinctive culture and to have contributed significantly to the American experience.

The term "new Negro" actually predates the "new Negro movement" itself. Henry Louis Gates has traced the use of this metaphor back to its origins. The term "new Negro" had been variously used to refer to transplanted Africans as slaves in the New World, then to newly emancipated slaves, and then to politically activist African Americans. In 1900, Booker T. Washington wrote *A New Negro for A New Century*. From 1905 to 1910, the Niagara Movement, an organization founded by W. E. B. Du Bois, became the forerunner of the National Association for the Advancement of Colored People (NAACP), an interracial organization founded in Springfield, Illinois in 1909. The New Negro movement should be distinguished from Hubert Harrison's radicalist "new Negro manhood" movement. From August–October 1919, Harrison (d. 1927) edited the ephemeral *New Negro* magazine, but stood outside the mainstream new Negro movement. Although it championed many of the political ideals of black activists of the time, the new Negro movement itself was not political.

The term "new Negro" was already a social reality, and the new Negro movement simply solidified the emergent and robust self-consciousness of that new reality. The "new Negro" was really the product of the Great Migration (1915–1920) of more than a million blacks who moved from the rural South to the urban North in search of prosperity. In Harlem, a black middle class emerged, and a convergence of social forces made Harlem the cultural capital of African Americans from the 1920s to the mid-1930s. The new Negro movement stood in tense counterpoise with separatist Jim Crow laws—America's apartheid.

Meanwhile, in December 1924, *Vanity Fair* heralded the advent of the "new Negro" in a two-page feature, "Enter, The New Negro, a Distinctive Type Recently Created by the Coloured Cabaret Belt in New York." Mexican caricaturist Miguel Covarrubias drew striking images of African Americans that radically departed from the old stereotypes, and African American writer Eric Walrond, future author of *Tropic Death* (1926), wrote the captions. In the *Vanity Fair* feature, Walrond proclaimed the demise of artistic stereotypes of the "old Negro". At a time when African Americans had virtually no political recourse, their voice could best be heard through their distinctive music, poetry and art—a creative and humanistic effort to achieve the goal of civil rights by producing positive images of African Americans and promoting activism through art.

In its heyday, the effective leader of the new Negro movement was philosopher Alain Locke (1885–1954), whose roles as both race leader and cultural pluralist proved a rare combination. As the first African American Rhodes Scholar, his exquisite education abroad in Oxford and Germany—culminating in his Harvard doctorate in philosophy—prepared Locke to become the most important African American intellectual between the great W. E. B. Du Bois and Martin Luther King Jr. As the spokesman and chief strategist of the new Negro movement during the Harlem Renaissance period and beyond, Locke resolved to sweep away the pejorative stereotypes of the "old Negro" through the transformative ideas and visual rhetoric of art, music, drama, and literature.

The most spectacular cultural product of the new Negro movement was the Harlem Renaissance. The ideology of the new Negro movement expressed itself through the Harlem Renaissance, which sparked a new pride in everything African American, and presented, to both white and black audiences, the artistic and literary gifts of the "talented tenth"—the vanguard of that African American elite who could best represent the new image of African Americans to America at large. This was a watershed period in African American history for psychological revalorization and race vindication. Although blacks were being objectified as icons of exotic, African-rooted primitivism, the Harlem Renaissance achieved a major objective of the new Negro movement, which was to instill a race pride in blacks and a corresponding respect for blacks by mainstream America.

Locke's cultural pluralism was a novel strategy: Launch a cultural movement that would enrich America and gain the respect of the white majority, and the masks of black stereotypes (which were nonthreatening because they reinforced black inferiority in the eyes of whites) would disappear, revealing the true humanity of African Americans beneath the façade. Although its success was short-lived, the new Negro movement was brilliantly conceived and masterfully promoted.

The Harlem Renaissance presented itself as a microcosm or "self-portraiture" of black culture to America and to the world. For Locke, art ought to contribute to the improvement of life—a pragmatist aesthetic principle that may be characterized as "meliorism." The new Negro movement transfused black consciousness by shaping a new self-image through powerful literary and artistic images. Although the movement is frozen in history, Locke's ideology is very much alive. In 2004, philosopher José Medina transposed Locke's "new Negro" ideology and applied it to the concept of the "new Hispanic." As for reliving the experience of the Harlem Renaissance, which is the legacy of the new Negro movement, this can be experienced in a new way today, thanks to the Virtual Harlem Project, developed by the Electronic Visualization Laboratory of the Department of Computer Science at the University of Illinois at Chicago.

The new Negro movement also had a transformative effect on America at large. The writers of the new Negro movement fundamentally altered the way in which America views itself, although that change has been slow in coming. The changes in race relations today are partly the delayed impact of the new Negro movement, which advocated what Alain Locke would later call, "a new Americanism."

See also: Du Bois, W. E. B.; Harlem Renaissance; Hughes, Langston; Locke, Alain; McKay, Claude; Negritude

Christopher George Buck

Bibliography

Baker, Houston A., Jr. *Modernism and the Harlem Renaissance.* Chicago: The University of Chicago Press, 1987.

Buck, Christopher. *Alain Locke: Faith and Philosophy.* Los Angeles: Kalimat Press, 2005.

Holmes, Eugene C. "Alain Locke and the New Negro Movement." *Negro American Literature Forum* 2, no. 3 (Fall 1968):60–68.

Locke, Alain, ed., *The New Negro: An Interpretation.* New York: Albert and Charles Boni, 1925, 1927.

Long, Richard A: "The Genesis of Locke's *The New Negro.*" *Black World* 25, no. 4 (1976):14–20.

Medina, José. "Pragmatism and Ethnicity: Critique, Reconstruction, and the New Hispanic." *Metaphilosophy* 35, nos. 1/2 (2004):115–46.

Nadell, Martha Jane. *Enter the New Negroes: Images of Race in American Culture* Cambridge, MA: Harvard University Press, 2004.

Scholz, Sally J. "Individual and Community: Artistic Representation in Alain L. Locke's Politics." *Transactions of the Charles S. Peirce Society: A Quarterly Journal in American Philosophy* 39, no. 3 (Summer 2003):491–502.

Watts, Eric King. "African American Ethos and Hermeneutical Rhetoric: An Exploration of Alain Locke's *The New Negro.*" *Quarterly Journal of Speech* 88, no. 1 (2002):19–32.

New Orleans Riot of 1900

The week of July 23, 1900, proved to be one of the bloodiest weeks in the Crescent City's history. Police went on a manhunt for Robert Charles (1865–1900), a biracial man who shot 24 whites including seven police officers, even as a mob composed primarily of white men and boys thronged the streets inflicting random acts of violence on blacks who were routinely chased, beaten, and shot.

The events began in New Orleans on Monday evening, while the 34-year-old Charles and his 19-year-old roommate, Lenard Pierce, sat quietly on the doorsteps of a white family's house at 2815 Dryades Street. According to historian William Ivy Hair, the two men were awaiting the return of Charles' girlfriend, Virginia Banks, who lived nearby in a back room of 2849 Dryades Street when three New Orleans policemen, Sergeant Jules C. Aucoin, Patrolman August T. Mora, and Officer Joseph D. Cantrelle, approached the two men claiming that they looked suspicious. When the officers approached Robert Charles, he did not have a previous criminal record in New Orleans, although he had once been arrested in Mississippi in 1894 for peddling alcohol in a dry county. Charles moved to New Orleans shortly after his brush with the law, but voluntarily returned to Mississippi in October 1896 to stand trial for the charge, and received a verdict of not guilty.

The exchange between Charles, Pierce, and the three officers is sketchy, with conflicting accounts of the ensuing gunfire that erupted between Officer Mora and Robert Charles. Reverend D. A. Graham of the A.M.E. Church in New Orleans reported to the Indianapolis newspaper, *The Freeman,* that when the policemen began clubbing Charles, he drew the Colt revolver he was carrying in an inside coat pocket. Afterwards, Officer Mora admitted to using his billet and drawing his gun before Charles drew his pistol. Both men were shot in the exchange, although Charles escaped with a bullet wound in his leg.

Seven white police officers and a civilian arrived at Charles's one-room home at 2023 Fourth Street sometime during the early morning hours of July 24, precisely the location where Charles had fled to dress his wound. The officers intended to kill him on sight. Instead, another gun battle ensued with Charles killing Captain John T. Day and Patrolman Peter J. Lamb. Charles fled and took refuge at the home of acquaintances Silas and Martha Jackson. He remained hidden in the Jackson's home located at 1208 Saratoga Street for the week, even as violence raged on in a city boiling with racial conflict.

By Wednesday, July 25, a white mob estimated in the thousands began a tragic reign of lawlessness in which numerous black men and women were assaulted and killed, including a newsboy who was knifed, a man who was dragged from a car and beaten to death, and a 75-year-old man on his way to work in the French Market. On Friday, July 27, a black informant led police to Saratoga Street where Charles was cornered inside an upstairs bedroom. The mob remained outside the two-story house during the standoff in which Charles refused to surrender.

Eventually Charles, armed with a Winchester rifle and home-made bullets, was shot multiple times while exiting the house after a mattress was set ablaze and thrown inside the house producing a cloud of black smoke. Charles continued to fire his weapon as his body was riddled with bullets. A Tulane medical student on the scene, Charles A. Noiret, fired the bullet that killed Charles. After his death, the mob dragged Charles's body into the street where it was repeatedly shot, punched, kicked, and mutilated. That night the rioting continued, and an African American public school named for philanthropist Thomy Lafon was burned.

In her pamphlet "Mob Rule in New Orleans," civil rights activist Ida B. Wells-Barnett described the mob that roamed the streets throughout the week as completely lawless. She went on to say that the mob was in the streets daily, beating, shooting, and killing African Americans at will.

Robert Charles (also known as Curtis Robertson or Robinson) migrated to New Orleans from Copiah County, Mississippi, only six years before the fateful drama. Charles maintained a membership in the International Migration Society, an organization promoting a Back-to-Africa Movement, and sold Bishop Henry M. Turner's publication, *Voices of Missions,* which advocated African American rights to fight in self-defense. He worked as a laborer and was described by those who knew him as an intelligent man who dressed well. He also wrote prolifically, having filled scores of composition books with unknown content that were removed from his home after his death and subsequently lost. Charles owned several "well-worn text-books" that were removed by police and souvenir seekers. Notwithstanding the murders that Charles unquestionably committed and journalist labels such as "fiend" and "Negro desperado," evidence suggests that Charles was a thinker and a writer who lacked formal education, yet possessed an interest in the complexity of race relations and a predilection toward intellectual improvement.

A month after the rioting had quieted, Reverend Graham noted in a letter to *The Freeman* that never before had African Americans been as victimized and terrorized by whites in the South. Still, numerous people who knew or were in the vicinity where Charles hid on Saratoga Street were arrested and incarcerated for at least a year. Charles was buried in an unmarked grave in Holt's Cemetery in New Orleans.

See also: Jim Crow; Lynching; Turner, Henry McNeal; Wells-Barnett, Ida; White Mob Violence

Jayetta Slawson

Bibliography

Hair, William Ivy. *Carnival of Fury: Robert Charles and the New Orleans Race Riot of 1900.* Baton Rouge: Louisiana State University Press, 1976.

Wells-Barnett, Ida B. "Mob Rule in New Orleans." *On Lynchings.* New York: Arno Press, 1969.

New York Silent March of 1917

The New York "Silent March" of 1917 is considered one of the first mass demonstrations by African Americans in the 20th century. On July 28, 1917, an estimated 10,000 African American men, women, and children marched silently down Fifth Avenue in New York City to the sound only of muffled drums. The demonstration served as a response to an eruption of racially motivated violent attacks on the black community. James Weldon Johnson, at that time field secretary for the NAACP, served as the principal organizer of the New York "Silent March," also known as "The Negro Silent Protest Parade." The East St. Louis riots of 1917 emerged as the central motivating factor for the protest.

The racial tension in East St. Louis, Illinois increased during the early months of 1917, as a result of African Americans replacing white workers in the city's industrial factories. The tension began to boil over on July 1, 1917, when members of the white community drove into a black residential area and began firing guns. Moments later, two white out-of-uniform police officers drove into the area and were subsequently shot and killed. On July 2, 1917, East St. Louis's white residents retaliated against the African American community and began shooting at black men, women, and children. They also burned their houses, lynched men from streetlamps, destroyed their businesses, and beat people to death. The East St. Louis massacre left 39 African Americans dead and 8 white fatalities. The rioters destroyed more than $400,000 worth of property and nearly 6,000 African Americans were driven from their homes and forced to seek refuge.

At a meeting of the NAACP's Harlem branch, the East St. Louis riot served as its primary topic. The executive committee initially planned to organize a mass meeting at Carnegie Hall to discuss the massacre and voice their concerns. James Weldon Johnson recalled a conversation he had with Oswald Garrison Villiard, journalist and NAACP treasurer, and suggested a silent protest parade. He called for the participation of all classes of African Americans in the Greater New York area to join this effort. A planning committee of pastors from leading churches and other influential African American men and women made preparations for the march.

Although the East St. Louis riots served as the primary motivator for the march, the memories of numerous lynchings, most notable the lynchings of Ell Persons in Memphis, Tennessee, and Jesse Washington in Waco Texas, also inspired the black community to organize and demonstrate their frustrations to the nation. Members of the African American community assembled at 59th Street and Fifth Avenue in New York and marched into the center of Manhattan on July 28, 1917. The procession was headed by children, some as young as six years old, wearing white. They were followed by the women also dressed in white and men in the rear dressed in dark clothes. W. E. B. Du Bois was among the many prominent marchers. A banner that stretched half the width of the street read, "Your Hands Are Full of Blood," immediately followed by a marcher carrying an American flag.

As planned, no one in the demonstration spoke a word. An apathetic crowd of approximately 20,000 spectators

Silent March in New York City on July 28, 1917. The parade was organized by the National Association for the Advancement of Colored People and religious leaders in Harlem to protest violence against African Americans throughout the United States. (Library of Congress)

consisting of blacks, as well as whites, lined the streets as they, too, abided by the code of silence. There were no bands, cheering, or hand clapping to break the monotony. Although no one spoke a word, the demonstrators conveyed their messages to the nation through numerous signs that read: "Mother, Do Lynchers Go To Heaven?"; "Mr. President, Why Not Make America Safe for Democracy"; "Maligned As Lazy, Murdered When We Work"; "Race Prejudice Is the Offspring of Ignorance, and the Mother is Lynching."

The New York "Silent March" of 1917 created a model for future public demonstrations. The event succeeded as a result of the efforts from nearly 100 churches, fraternal lodges, and civil rights organizations. The NAACP held the most prominent role in the protest and launched its crusade against lynching and other forms of racial injustice.

See also: Antilynching Campaign; Du Bois, W. E. B.; East St. Louis, Illinois, Riot of 1917; Lynching; National Association for the Advancement of Colored People

Darius Young

Bibliography

Bernstein, Patricia. *The First Waco Horror: The Lynching of Jesse Washington and the Rise of the NAACP.* College Station: Texas A&M University Press, 2005.

Dray, Philip. *At the Hands of Persons Unknown: The Lynching of Black America.* New York: The Modern Library, 2002.

Johnson, James Weldon. *Along This Way: The Autobiography of James Weldon Johnson.* New York: Penguin Books, 1933.

Zangrando, Robert L. *The NAACP Crusade Against Lynching, 1909–1950.* Philadelphia: Temple University Press, 1980.

Newton, Huey P.

Huey Pierce Newton (1942–1989) was a leader and co-founder of the Black Panther Party for Self-Defense. Named after Louisiana senator Huey Long, Newton was the seventh child of Armelia and Walter Newton in Monroe, Louisiana. At age three, Huey Newton migrated to Oakland, California, with his family, searching for economic opportunity and a better quality of life. During the years following World War II, Oakland boasted a burgeoning African American population and a busy port that promised more possibilities than Louisiana ever could. For the Newton family and other black families like them, however, Oakland was not the Promised Land: schools were substandard,

living accommodations were meager, at best, and jobs were ephemeral.

Melvin Newton and Walter "Sonny Man" Newton Jr., Newton's two older brothers, and Walter Newton Sr., Newton's father, were most influential in Newton's childhood development. Melvin epitomized the potential of pursuing a life of ideas. He attended San Jose State College and taught his brother Huey the value of learning. "Sonny Man," leaving home as a teenager, thrived in the illegal economy and showed Newton the allure of street life. Huey Newton would later recall that while Sonny Man appeared to live freely, this freedom was only an illusion. Despite the illusion, Walter provided Huey Newton with lessons to negotiate life on Oakland's streets. To Huey, Newton Sr. was the glue that held their family together. Holding multiple jobs and performing the duties of a Christian minister, Walter Newton Sr. combined spirituality with pragmatism and taught his sons the necessity of opposing white racism.

Never feeling at home in structured classrooms, Newton received his education during his formative years on the streets of Oakland. There he and his friends experimented with, acted out, and constantly engaged the politics of masculinity and found the hustler's life appealing. In the 10th grade at Oakland Technical High School, Newton was expelled for his behavior and he transferred to Berkeley High School in Berkeley, California. Newton's experience at Berkeley High School was only a little better. In fact, it was at Berkeley High School that Newton's trouble with the law began, forcing him to go to juvenile hall. Unable to attend Berkeley High School upon leaving juvenile hall, Newton returned to Oakland Technical High School and graduated in 1959.

Social promotion and the politics of bureaucratic public high schools allowed Newton to graduate without possessing requisite scholastic aptitude. After a period of self-directed study under the tutelage of his brother Melvin, however, Newton entered Oakland City College in the autumn of 1959. It was at Oakland City College from 1959 to 1966 that Newton began actively seeking answers to the problems plaguing African American communities nationwide. Reading radical theorists like Che Guevara, Malcolm X, Franz Fanon, Karl Marx, and Mao Zedong, and participating in black cultural and political organizations, Newton began to develop his own theoretical framework. The first organizations he joined were the Afro-American Association and the Soul Students Advisory Council, student groups devoted to studying African American history, political thought, and cultural production, and creating a black studies curriculum on campus. Disappointed with the presence of political consciousness but lack of political activity in the two organizations, especially the two groups' dismissal of black working poor men, Huey Newton and Bobby Seale, a friend and student at Oakland City College, created the Black Panther Party for Self-Defense.

The Black Panthers were initially organized in 1966 as an armed police patrol to protect black community residents from brutal police violence. By 1969, with Bobby Seale as its chairman and Huey P. Newton as its minister of self-defense, the organization went nationwide, with more than 40 chapters devoted to the daily concerns of black urban communities.

In autumn 1967, Newton's life took a dramatic turn when a police traffic stop turned deadly. Newton had been a victim of police harassment since his days of police patrols in 1967. After being pulled over for unknown circumstances in the early morning hours of October 28, 1967, an altercation with the police left Patrolman John Frey dead, Patrolman Herbert Heanes wounded, and Newton near death with a bullet in his stomach. Treated for his bullet wounds at Kaiser Hospital, Newton was interrogated, brutalized, and chained to a gurney by police. Newton retained the services of Charles Garry, a prominent lawyer known for working with leftist causes. Accused of murder, felonious assault, and kidnapping, Newton awaited trial in San Quentin Prison and the Oakland County Jail. After months on trial, on September 8, 1968, Newton was found guilty of manslaughter and sentenced to a 2- to–15-year sentence at the California Men's Colony, East Facility, in San Luis Obispo, California. Most of Newton's 22 months at the penal colony were spent in isolation. While Newton was imprisoned, Charles Garry feverishly worked to obtain an appeal. On May 29, 1970, the California Appellate Court announced that Newton's conviction was reversed and determined that, because the jury had been denied critical information in determining Newton's fate, a new trial was ordered. In August 1970, Newton was released on bail. In the early 1970s, Newton's defense team participated in two more trials to save him from imprisonment. Both ended in a mistrial. Cleared of all charges, Newton set out to rebuild the party.

The Federal Bureau of Investigation's Counter-Intelligence Program (COINTELPRO) from 1970–1974, however, made bolstering the party difficult. Also, Newton's move to possess absolute authority in the party, going by names like the supreme commander, the servant of the people, and the supreme servant of the people, made strengthening the party difficult. Furthermore, Newton's stardom among the country's celebrities, who provided him with luxury items, drugs, and alcohol, compromised his position among those individuals the party purported to serve.

Newton's drug abuse and alcoholism may have contributed to his fleeing the country in 1974 and further estranged the Black Panther Party from black communities. In late 1973, Newton allegedly shot a prostitute, Kathleen Smith, and brutalized a tailor, Preston Callins, for calling him "baby." Shortly after being arrested and posting bail for assaulting Callins, Newton fled the United States and obtained asylum in Cuba where he remained until 1977, relinquishing control of the declining Black Panther Party to Elaine Brown. Upon his return to the United States, Newton was imprisoned, released on bail, and eventually acquitted for the murder of Smith. Callin's case was dropped after he declared that he could not remember his assaulter. Newton also resumed control of the party after Elaine Brown resigned her post, citing irreconcilable differences with Newton.

After the Black Panther Party officially disbanded in 1982, Newton's wife, Fredericka, left him, and his drug and alcohol abuse, as well his problems with law enforcement, continued. In 1985, he was suspected but never indicted for burglary. In 1986, he was cleared of possessing illegal firearms. In 1988, Newton served time in prison for parole violation. On August 22, 1989, Newton was fatally wounded after being shot three times in what seems to have been a drug deal gone awry.

Despite COINTELPRO initiatives created by the Federal Bureau of investigation to discredit Huey Newton, Newton's involvement with the criminal justice system, his authoritarianism within the party, and his drug problems, especially during the last decade of his life, Huey P. Newton was a scholar and the Black Panther Party's chief theoretician. In 1966, after six years of study, Newton received his associate's degree, was awarded a bachelor's degree in education and politics from the University of California at Santa Cruz in 1974, and won his doctorate from the History of Consciousness Program at the University of Santa Cruz in 1980 by successfully defending his dissertation "War Against the Panthers: A Study of Repression in America."

Interestingly, although graduating high school with substandard educational skills, Newton was a prolific writer who (co)authored five books and scores of articles, essays, and position papers. These writings are indicative of Newton's openness to ideas, his ability to synthesize political theories, and a willingness to develop his own understanding of the oppressive forces and strategies to eliminate structural inequalities that jeopardized African American's social, political, and economic well-being.

In 1966, when the party was initially organized, Newton was a black nationalist and posited that only black people's control of capitalists' institutions in their community could bring about African American empowerment. In 1969, Newton's understanding of marxism led him to embrace revolutionary socialism as an ideology necessary to seize economic and political power from the elite ruling class and end the exploitation of the poor and working classes. By 1970, Newton hypothesized that only an internationalist struggle linking radical and progressive forces in different countries could bring about fundamental change. In 1971, Newton's intercommunalism combined ideas of empire and imperialism to articulate an understanding of social movements that transcended the confines of national boundaries.

Newton's political growth and demise was symptomatic of the shifts in the U.S. post-Civil Rights era political economy. In the 1970s, the most ostensible constraints on African Americans' well-being were apparently removed with 1960s civil rights legislation, the end of white mob rule, and the ascendance of neoconservative ideologists who coopted notions of equal protection. Heterogeneous black working class communities that had been created only decades before were floundering under burdens of northern racism, capitalist exploitation, and black people's search for cultural and political identity. Newton's ideological and political development and ultimate ruin is indicative of the hope, potential, and reality of progressive factions in American society who challenged systems of oppression and exploitation. Huey P. Newton may not fit the American fantasy of a spotless, pure hero, but he does epitomize the complex nature of the radical liberation movements in a global age.

See also: Black Panther Party; Black Power; Brown, Elaine; Cleaver, Eldridge; COINTELPRO; Seale, Bobby

Jamie J. Wilson

Bibliography

Brown, Elaine. *A Taste of Power: A Black Woman's Story.* New York: Pantheon Books, 1992.

Churchill, Ward. *Agents of Repression: the FBI's Secret War Against the Black Panther Party and the American Indian Movement.* Boston: South End Press, 1988.

Churchill, Ward. "'To Disrupt, Discredit, and Destroy': The FBI's Secret War Against the Black Panther Party." In *Liberation, Imagination, and the Black Panther Party.* Kathleen Cleaver and George Katsiaficas, eds., 79–117. New York: Routledge, 2001.

Clemons Michael and Jones, Charles E. "Global Solidarity: The Black Panther Party in the International Arena." In *Liberation, Imagination, and the Black Panther Party.* Kathleen Cleaver and George Katsiaficas, eds., 20–39. New York: Routledge, 2001.

Foner, Philip S. *The Black Panthers Speak.* New York: Da Capo Press, 1995.

Grady-Willis, Winston A. "The Black Panther Party: State Repression and Political Prisoners." In *The Black Panther Party Reconsidered.* Charles E. Jones, ed., 363–90. Baltimore: Black Classic Press, 1998.

Jeffries, Judson. *Huey P. Newton: The Radical Theorist.* Jackson: University Press of Mississippi, 2002.

Johnson, III, Ollie A. "Explaining the Demise of the Black Panther Party: The Role of Internal Factors." In *The Black Panther Party Reconsidered.* Charles E. Jones, ed., 391–414. Baltimore: Black Classic Press, 1998.

Jones, Charles E. and Jeffries, Judson. "Don't Believe the Hype": Debunking the Panther Mythology." In *The Black Panther Party Reconsidered.* Charles E. Jones, ed., 25–55. Baltimore: Black Classic Press, 1998.

Lockwood, Lee. *Conversations with Eldridge Cleaver, Algiers.* New York: Dell Publishing, 1970.

Newton, Huey P. *To Die for the People: The Writings of Huey P. Newton.* New York: Vintage Books, 1972.

Newton, Huey P. *Revolutionary Suicide.* New York: Harcourt Brace Jovanovich, 1973.

Newton, Huey P. *War Against the Panthers: A Study of Repression in America.* New York: Harlem River Press, 1996.

Pearson, Hugh. *The Shadow of the Panthers: Huey Newton and the Price of Black Power in America.* Reading, MA: Addison Wesley Publishing, 1994.

Seale, Bobby, *Seize the Time: The Story of the Black Panther Party and Huey P. Newton.* New York: Random House, 1970.

Umoja, Akinyele O. "Repression Breeds Resistance." In *Liberation, Imagination, and the Black Panther Party.* Kathleen Cleaver and George Katsiaficas, eds., 3–19. New York: Routledge, 2001.

Niagara Movement

In response to Booker T. Washington's cautious approach to social justice, W. E. B. Du Bois, Frederick McGhee, and Monroe Trotter agreed that something had to be done. Du Bois suggested that they convene a meeting of the talented tenth who were interested in creating an organization dedicated to the freedom and growth of the Negro. The name, Niagara Movement, was derived from their vision and because Niagara Falls was where the meeting took place.

Du Bois sent invitations to 60 African American leaders who were secure in their profession and principles to resist any backlash from Booker T. Washington to meet in Buffalo, New York, to organize an organization dedicated to the freedom and growth of the Negro and for racial equality. On July 9, 1905, 29 black intellectuals and professionals and 1teenager, met in Buffalo. Because of racial prejudice at the hotel in Buffalo, the meeting moved to the Eric Beach Hotel, Fort Erie, Ontario, July 10. Those in attendance included Du Bois, Trotter, Fred L. McGhee, Reverdy Ransom, Charles B. Purvis, Lafayette Hershew, Freeman H. M. Murray, J. Max Barber, Edwin Jourdain, Rev. Bryron Gunner, Alonzo F. Herndon, Henry L. Bailey, W. H. H. Hart, George Jackson, and William H. Richards, who were known as the Niagarites.

The structure of the movement reflected what Du Bois had suggested to Washington during the meetings for the Committee of Twelve. The structure included an executive committee, several committees, and a chairman for each Niagara state chapter, which were to be organized immediately after the meeting. Membership dues were $5 annually. Du Bois was elected as secretary; Jackson was elected treasurer; Trotter served as chair of the Press and Public Opinion committee, which Du Bois also served on; and the Constitution and By-Laws of the Niagara Movement was voted on. The Niagara Movement was officially formed and incorporated in January 1906.

The Declaration of Principles, drafted by Du Bois and Trotter, was signed by all those who were in attendance. The declaration recognized the progress within the African American communities—buying of property, uplift in home life, the advance in education, literature and art, crime prevention, and the constructive and executive ability of religious, economic, and educational institutions. The principles called for suffrage for men and women, civil liberty, economic opportunities, quality education, equal justice within the court system, better health care, permanent employment and membership into labor unions, removal "Jim Crow" cars, and rewarding soldiers for their service with promotions and the opportunity to be admitted to the military academy. Finally, the principles stated duties that every person should adhere to. More important,

the Niagaraites called on the government to enforce the Thirteenth, Fourteenth, and Fifteenth Amendments to the Constitution.

The second meeting, held August 15, 1906, at Storer College, Harper's Ferry, West Virginia, occurred during the 100th anniversary of John Brown's birth and the 50th anniversary of the battle of Osawatomie. More than 150 people, representing 34 state chapters, including the Massachusetts Niagara Women's Auxiliary, were in attendance. Speeches by Reverdy Ransom and Du Bois spoke straight to the heart of the Niagara movement. Ransom addressed the significance of John Brown's anniversary, calling him a man true to the slave. Ransom also spoke of the two classes of African Americans and their opposing perspectives. In his speech "Address to the Country," Du Bois presented a five-point resolution calling for quality education, enforcement of the Fourteenth Amendment and the reduction of congressional seats for states where African Americans could not vote, justice, and jobs. He ended his speech by urging young people to stand up for their rights, to prove themselves worthy of their heritage, to treat men as men, and to have courage.

Unlike the first meeting, a number of women traveled to Harper's Ferry with their husbands and fathers. Mrs. Gertrude Wright Morgan, Mss. O. M. Walker, Mrs. H. F. M. Murray, Mrs. Mollie Lewis Kelan, Ms. Ida D. Bailey, Miss Sadie Shorter, and Mrs. Charlotte Hershaw were only a few of the women who attended the meeting in 1906. Even though they could not attend any of the sessions, they participated in the program, attended the opening and closing sessions, had a women's meeting, and attended the celebration for John Brown. Mrs. Mary Ovington, a reporter for the New York Evening Post, also attended the meeting and, later in 1908, became the first white member of the Niagara movement.

The 1907 Niagara movement meeting was held at Boston's Faneuil Hall, with 800 people in attendance. At this meeting that Trotter resigned as chairmen of the press and public opinion committee and a disagreement between Trotter and Clement Morgan had a major impact on the meeting. By 1908, strife and conflict, lack of funding and central leadership, and the pressure from the Tuskegee machine began to take its toll on the organization. Thus attendance at both the1908 and 1909 annual meeting, which was held in Oberlin, Ohio and Sea Isle City, respectively, was low. The 1910 meeting was cancelled.

Du Bois let it be known that African Americans would not cease protesting for their rights, but it would be by voting, persistent hammering at the truth, sacrifice, and work that they would get their rights as freeborn Americans. This was the mission and purpose of the Niagara movement.

See also: Du Bois, W. E. B.; Jim Crow; National Association for the Advancement of Colored People; Springfield Race Riot of 1908; Trotter, William Monroe

LaVerne Gyant

Bibliography

Aptheker, H. *A Documentary History of the Negro People in the United States,* Vol. 2. New York: Citadel Press Book, 1992.

Drinkard-Hawkshawe, D. "Prelude to the Niagara Movement and the NAACP," *Crisis* 84, no. 2 (1977):53–57.

Du Bois, W. E. B., *The Autobiography of W. E. B. Du Bois: A Soliloquy on Viewing My Life from the Last Decade of the First Century.* New York: International Publishers, 1968.

Lewis, D. L. *W. E. B. Du Bois: Biography of a Race.* New York: Henry Holt, 1993.

Nicodemus, Kansas

Nicodemus, Kansas, was a town settled by and for African Americans from Kentucky and Tennessee who were seeking a better life in the American West in 1877. It derived its name from an enslaved African who was believed to be the first to purchase his own freedom in America. Many of the settlers of Nicodemus were enslaved before the American Civil War. They were seeking a new life in Kansas in response to escalating racism in the American South by white politicians and their constituencies, angered over what they perceived as unfair gains by blacks during Reconstruction.

The town itself was a planned community devised by a small committee of seven known as the Nicodemus Town Company. Simon P. Roundtree, a black preacher, and W. R. Hill, a white planner, led the group's efforts. The wide circulation of a document created by Roundtree spurred the growth of the settlement. This flier warmly invited African Americans to settle in the new community. The Nicodemus Town Company created a supporting flier repeating the invitation. An early resident of the town, Benjamin "Pap" Singleton, was instrumental in spreading the word through his own personal distribution of these invitations to black communities outside the state of Kansas.

The first winter in the settlement was difficult for its new arrivals. There had not been enough time to plant and harvest crops before the weather grew bitterly cold. Food and supplies were scarce. The new settlers were greatly aided by their Native American neighbors in the Osage Nation who supplied them with food and other necessities. The next year settlers saw success in farming and in finding employment with the local railroads.

By 1879, the population of Nicodemus was close to 600 residents. As the town continued to grow, several of its inhabitants became successful. Anderson Boles was the owner of a hotel and also a prominent local farmer. Z. T. Fletcher was the town's first postmaster and also owned a hotel. A. T. Hall and E. P. McCabe made their fortunes in real estate. The latter became the first African American politician elected to statewide office in Kansas when he became state auditor.

The residents of Nicodemus believed that the presence of a railway line through the town would attract new businesses and more residents to the growing community. In 1887, town residents voted in favor of issuing $16,000 in bonds to persuade the Missouri Pacific Railroad to offer service through the town. The community also courted another rail company, the Union Pacific. The promise of a rail line excited residents, creating a great deal of optimism about the future of the settlement; however, neither of the railroad companies pursued by the town decided to lay tracks in Nicodemus. The Union Pacific Railroad determined that a location to the south of the settlement was the best place for their operation.

Nicodemus-based business owners, seeing the location of a rail line as the lifeblood of a new settlement, followed the railroad to the nearby area that later came to be known as the city of Bogue, Kansas. This loss of business was gradual but irreversible, leading to rapid population decline in the early half of the 20th century. Only 16 people were listed as residents of the town by 1950, rebounding slightly to about 80 in the 1980s.

In 1976, the town was selected as a National Historic Landmark and in 1996 a National Site. The last designation provided funds for preservation of various town landmarks and the creation of public programs detailing the history of the settlement.

See also: Black Nationalism; Exoduster Movement; Singleton, Benjamin "Pap"

Christopher Keith Johnson

Bibliography

Frazier, Ian. *Great Plains.* New York: Penguin Books, 1990.

Painter, Nell Irvin. *Exodusters: Black Migration to Kansas after Reconstruction.* New York: Knopf, 1977.

Schwendemann, Glen. "Nicodemus: Negro Haven on the Solomon." *Kansas Historical Quarterly* 34 (1968):10–31.

Nkrumah, Kwame

Kwame Nkrumah (1909–1972) was an African activist, intellectual, and statesman, and the first prime minister and later president of Ghana, the first sub-Saharan African country to gain independence. He played a pivotal role in developing the concept of Pan-Africanism.

Kwame Nkrumah was born on September 18, 1909, and baptized as "Francis" a few days later in the local Roman Catholic Church in Nkroful, a village located in what was then called the British-ruled Gold Coast Colony and today called Ghana. His father, a goldsmith, gave him the name Nwia Kofi Ngonloma, but Nkrumah often used this as well as his day-name Kwame (for Saturday) on many instances throughout his life. Nkrumah, a gifted student, was schooled in Africa, America, and England where he would subsequently earn several degrees in various subjects. He attended the Roman Catholic elementary school in his father's town Half Assini where he became a pupil teacher by the age of 14. From there, he would attend a government training college in Accra that was eventually merged with the Prince of Wales College at Achimota. Upon graduation, Nkrumah became employed as a teacher at the Roman Catholic junior school at Elmina but eventually received a position as headmaster of a Catholic junior school at Axim within a year. While also considering a career as a priest, two years after teaching at Axim, Nkrumah accepted a teaching post at the Catholic seminary in Amissano.

Kwame Nkrumah was influenced by Kwegyir Aggrey, African vice principal of Achimota, who was educated in America to study abroad. He was accepted and attended Lincoln University in Pennsylvania, a university for black men supported by the Presbyterian Church, on a modest scholarship between 1935 and 1939. He earned a BA degree in economics and sociology from Lincoln in 1939 and also secured a degree in sacred theology. Nkrumah earned a master of science in education in 1942 from the University of Pennsylvania while teaching at his alma mater.

As a student, Nkrumah became increasingly interested in issues related to African and African American liberation. At this time that he began to associate with black student organizations and radical ideologies. Kwame Nkrumah became radicalized in Jim Crow America while reading Karl Marx, Marcus Garvey, and W. E. B. Du Bois and associating with radical black student organizations. He pledged the all-black fraternity Phi Beta Sigma Fraternity, Inc., and began to write essays detailing his anticolonial ideas. Nkrumah was elected president of the African Students Organization of America and Canada while teaching at Lincoln. His first major publication, *Towards Colonial Freedom,* published in 1947, was written between 1942 and 1945. It was also during this time that Nkrumah met the Trinidadian Marxist C.L.R. James in 1943. He left America for England in 1945 where he registered to study at the London School of Economics in the doctoral program in anthropology and a degree in philosophy at University College, London where he worked with A. J. Ayer. While in England, he also met and assisted the West Indian activist George Padmore in organizing the Fifth Pan-African Congress in Manchester in 1945. He also created the West African National Secretariat to support the end of colonialism in Africa and became vice president of the West African Student Union (WASU) while in England.

In 1947, he returned to Ghana to serve as general secretary of the newly created African nationalist party the United Gold Coast Convention (UGCC). As a consummate organizer, Nkrumah was able to transform the UGCC into a mass movement by linking it with numerous local affiliate groups disenchanted with colonial rule. In February 1948, a series of riots took place in Accra and other towns involving disgruntled veterans and workers (the veterans having been initially fired upon). The British jailed several members of the UGCC, including Nkrumah, suspecting that they instigated the riots. The members of the UGCC were eventually released and Nkrumah was subsequently catapulted to national leadership as he traveled throughout the country calling for "self-government." The Watson Commission of Enquiry was set up to investigate the riots. This commission would ultimately recommend a greater role for Africans in the governance of the country, echoing the pattern set by the Burns Constitution (1946) that granted Africans a greater role in the legislative council. The commission would go further in that a new Constitution was established by an all-African Committee and open elections were to be held. Nkrumah was disenchanted with the gradualist approach adopted by the British and would proactively continue to support self-governance for Africans.

The UGCC included a network of associations with youth groups, organized labor, and host of local interest cliques. Nkrumah used his personal contacts within the larger framework of the UGCC to establish a base of support within a vanguard party that eventually broke away from the UGCC. As a result of this split with the UGCC,

Nkrumah formed the Convention People's Party (CPP) in 1949. Nkrumah, having gained popular support at the grassroots level, began his "self-government NOW" campaign that included a general strike. Kwame Nkrumah was jailed for his activities in 1950 but after the CPP captured nearly all of the elective seats in the legislative assembly (22, 780 of 23, 122 votes) in the elections of 1951, he was released. Nkrumah was able to develop a working relationship with the British Governor Sir Charles Arden Clarke between 1951 and 1954 that developed from a diarchy of leadership between Africans and the British to internal self-government under the leadership of Kwame Nkrumah as prime minister of Ghana by 1952. The CPP was able to gain 72 of 104 available seats in the legislature by 1954 and nearly 70 percent of the seats by 1956. Ghana became an independent republic after 1957 under the leadership of Kwame Nkrumah. Ghana was the first sub-Saharan African

Kwame Nkrumah was the first prime minister and later president of Ghana, the first sub-Saharan African country to gain independence in 1957. (Library of Congress)

state to achieve independence. Nkrumah married an Egyptian, Fathia Halen Ritz, in 1957, with whom he had three children. Nkrumah would come to play an integral role in the development of Pan-Africanism after 1957 as the leader of the first independent sub-Saharan African country and come to influence other African leaders in the region. In April 1958, Nkrumah came to host the All African People's Convention, and this organization was the precursor to the creation of the Organization of African Unity. Kwame Nkrumah was declared the first president of an independent Ghana in 1960.

Kwame Nkrumah made a series of attempts to improve Ghana while serving as president. These activities included attempts to industrialize Ghana's economy, the development of an Africanized civil service, and the Volta River project created to use hydroelectric power resources. He also developed a modern military by implementing conscription and the acquisition of ships and aircraft. As a result of increased revenue from Ghana's major export crop, cocoa (world price of cocoa increased dramatically in 1954), Nkrumah moved to improve education and health services. This consisted of the building of a new university and a deep water port. Domestic tensions in Ghana did not dissipate with the leadership of Nkrumah. He introduced restrictions on civil liberties and all political opposition was severely curtailed. He used the profits from the rising cocoa prices, not to benefit the farmers, but to build up the country's infrastructure. This fostered hostilities among his former constituents. Strikes were outlawed and political opponents were jailed under the Nkrumah regime. The internal improvement projects orchestrated by Nkrumah were partially financed through foreign loans catapulting the country into great debt. Despite these internal problems, Nkrumah remained largely popular on the world stage among African people worldwide that eventually led to the creation of the Organization of African Unity in 1963. He remained committed to the idea of a united Africa throughout much of his life, as evidenced with the 16 books he wrote on the subject of African liberation.

Kwame Nkrumah played a fundamental role in shaping the independence of Ghana, West African independence movements, and in the development of Pan-African ideologies worldwide. He was not only a symbol to Africans but to African Americans as well struggling for freedom in the United States through the 1950s and 1960s. Nkrumah had significant intellectual exchanges with people of African descent interested in black liberation throughout his life across the African Diaspora from the Americas to Africa including C. L. R. James, George Padmore, and W. E. B. Du Bois. Du Bois was invited to Ghana to complete a comprehensive volume of peoples of African descent before his death in 1963. Nkrumah's reading of Marx made him a committed socialist as reflected with such works written by him as *Neo-Colonialism: The Last Stage of Imperialism* (1965) and *African Socialism Revisited* (1967). Nkrumah occupies a place in world history as an important proponent of both Pan-Africanism and African socialism. The people of West Africa were galvanized by the activism of Nkrumah, and this inspired a proliferation of liberation movements throughout Africa. In 1960s America, civil rights activists such as Stokely Carmichael were also inspired by Nkrumah as well. Carmichael changed his name to Kwame Ture (combining the name Kwame with that of Sekou Toure, president of Guinea at the time). Upon Nkrumah's overthrow in 1966, it was Sekou Toure who gave him sanctuary.

As Kwame Nkrumah adopted increasingly restrictive measures of governance; he engendered many internal and external enemies. These enemies, when apprehended, were often detained without trials. During Nkrumah's presidency, trade unions lost their autonomy, political parties organized around regional or ethnic identities were outlawed, and laws such as the Preventive Detention Act made it possible to arrest political opponents on the charge of treason without trial. The Nkrumah administration became rife with nepotism and corruption as the country fell into heavy debt. In 1964, Nkrumah declared himself life president as all political opposition was suppressed. Although the Volta Dam project opened to much fanfare in January 1966, while on a visit to Vietnam a month later, Nkrumah was overthrown in a military coup. He was exiled in Conakry, Guinea as the guest of President Sekou Toure. Toure honored Nkrumah with the title of co-president during his stay. Nkrumah continued to write while in exile completing such works as *Voice from Conakry* (1967) and *Handbook of Revolutionary Warfare* (1968). When London-based publishers refused to print his works, Nkrumah created Panaf Books in 1968. Kwame Nkrumah died of cancer on April 27, 1972 in Bucharest, Romania. Several works written by Nkrumah were published posthumously including *The Struggle Continues* (1973), *I Speak of Freedom* (1973), and *Revolutionary Path* (1973).

The idea of African liberation as fostered by Kwame Nkrumah has had a profound impact on the development of black-nationalist ideologies worldwide. Nkrumah was both statesman and intellectual in terms of his enduring political and intellectual contributions. His writings are seminal when considering the intellectual history of modern African resistance movements and the impact of these movements on black freedom struggles in the African Diaspora. The connections he fostered with black intellectuals were a part of a long history of exchanges across the African Diaspora in reaction to a common historicocultural experience of oppression. While the methods he used as president of Ghana will remain in great debate, his importance in the history of black liberation is not in great dispute. Several sub-Saharan African nations moved swiftly toward independence on the liberation of Ghana after 1957.

See also: African Imperialism; Du Bois, W. E. B.; Garvey, Marcus; Manchester Conference, 1945; Pan-African Congresses; Pan-Africanism

Hettie V. Williams

Bibliography

Aldo, Ebenezer O. *Kwame Nkrumah: A Case Study of Religion and Politics in Ghana.* Lanham, MD: University Press of America, 1997.

Arhin, Kwame., ed. *The Life and Work of Kwame Nkrumah.* Trenton, NJ: Africa World Press, 1993.

Birmingham, David. *Kwame Nkrumah: The Father of African Nationalism.* Athens: Ohio University Press, 1998.

Milne, June. *Kwame Nkrumah, A Biography.* London: Panaf Books, 2007.

Nkrumah, Kwame. *The Autobiography of Kwame Nkrumah.* New York: Brill Academic Publishers, 1973.

Poe, Daryl Z. *Kwame Nkrumah's Contribution to Pan-African Agency: An Afrocentric Analysis.* New York: Taylor & Francis, 2003.

Norton, Eleanor Holmes

Eleanor Holmes Norton (1937–), civil rights activist, lawyer, and U.S. Congresswoman, was born into an industrious educated family who instilled in her a drive for self-reliance and success. Her father, Coleman Sterling Holmes, was a member of the first graduating class of the Washington's Cardozo Business High School, the first of its kind for African Americans. His father was a firefighter and his grandfather was a fugitive slave who escaped from Virginia. Vela Lynch, her mother, was from a hard working family in North Carolina. She received a BA from Howard University in 1947 and became an educator, teaching in the D.C. public school system. Eleanor Holmes, named for first lady Eleanor Roosevelt, was born in June 13, 1937, in segregated Washington, D.C.

In 1942, Norton entered kindergarten at Bruce Monroe Elementary then attended Banneker Junior High School (now senior high school) before entering Paul Laurence Dunbar High School in 1952, the first public high school for African Americans in the country. Her leadership skills, praised throughout her adult career, were predetermined at an early age. In elementary school, she was president of the school glee club and treasurer of the student council. She was president of her class at Banneker, graduating in 1952 with honors, and with the Danforth Foundation Award, given to a junior high school graduating student with outstanding qualities. One year after the *Brown v. Board of Education* decision that ended separate educational facilities, Norton graduated from Dunbar's last segregated class in 1955 with a Ford Foundation scholarship.

She entered Antioch College in 1957, with plans to become a doctor. Although medical school proved difficult, it was her participation in socially conscious school organizations and an observation of mounting racial protests around the country that determined a switch from pre-med to a pre-law and history academic program. As president of the college's NAACP chapter, she organized the trip to Washington, D.C. for the Pilgrimage of Prayer and spent a summer at the Encampment for Citizenship in New York. In February 1960, the year she graduated from Antioch, the Greensboro, North Carolina sit-in at the Woolworth lunch counter by four North Carolina A&T university students prompted her participation in the picketing of segregated Geyer's restaurant and the bowling alley in nearby Xenia.

She continued to be socially active after entering law school at Yale University during the social intensity of the 1960s. While studying law and history, and teaching English and Speech at New Haven College, she helped to start a student chapter of Congress on Racial Equality (CORE). During the summer of 1963, while a member of Student Nonviolent Coordinating Committee (SNCC), she negotiated the release of Fannie Lou Hamer and Lawrence Guyot who had been beaten and jailed in Winona, Mississippi.

While at Yale, she established lifelong relationships with other activists including feminist lawyer Pauli Murray. Norton received her law degree in 1964 and later that year, a friend introduced her to Edward Worthington Norton, who would later become her husband.

Having no interest in electoral politics at this point in her career, Norton's social activism of her college years carried over into her professional career. She lobbied for a black voice in the traditionally all-white Mississippi Freedom Democratic Party (MFDP) state delegation national convention. In October of 1964, she was a clerk for Judge A. Leon Higginbotham Jr., the first black district court job in Philadelphia. During the spring of 1965, she was reacquainted with Edward Norton and they married in October of that year. At the time of their marriage, he was in his final year at Columbia University Law School, so the couple made their home in New York City where she worked as a lawyer for the American Civil Liberties Union (ACLU). In the beginning, her cases dealt with antiwar and civil rights, but as the scope of civil liberties broadened with the unrest of the 1960s, her defense of First Amendment violations increased. One of her most controversial cases was the successful representation of segregationist George Wallace in his bid to speak at New York City's Shea Stadium during his run for president in 1968. Ot was her successful argument before the Supreme Court in 1966, which overturned a judgment that prevented the National States Rights Party from organizing a protest in Princess Ann County, Maryland, however, that brought her national attention.

In the 1970s, Norton's personal and professional life underwent several changes. On July 8, 1970, she gave birth to a daughter Katherine Felicia and to her son John Holmes on March 17, 1972. She added another specialty to her legal expertise when she began teaching one of the first women-and-the-law courses at New York University's law school. She also argued an ACLU discrimination class action suit filed by women researchers at *Newsweek* magazine, which broke new ground in the area of women's rights. She also coauthored with 30 other women lawyers *Sex, Discrimination and the Law: Causes and Remedies* (1975), the first case book on women. President Jimmy Carter appointed her the first female chair of the Equal Employment Opportunity Commission (EEOC) in 1977, which brought her back to a very changed Washington, D.C.

Rotating directors and a critical backlog of cases had labeled the EEOC as ineffective. For the next 10 years, Norton worked to turn its reputation around by first reorganizing staff and then attacking the case backlog. Civil rights issues were no longer at the forefront. In a transitional era of stiff competition for jobs by blacks and women, Norton focused her legal skills on Affirmative Action. By the time she resigned in 1981, after Carter's defeat by Ronald Reagan, she was considered one of the most influential women in America.

Norton remained busy as a lecturer and visiting professor at Berkeley and the Boalt Law School. She was later appointed professor at Georgetown University Law Center where she taught labor law, employment law, and negations and set up a fellowship program on women's law and public policy. She also became the voice of the Free South African Movement, participating in the sit-in at the South African Embassy. Friends encouraged her to run for the district's lone congressional seat following Walter Fauntroy's decision not to run another term. In 1990, Norton was elected along with Sharon Pratt Kelly as mayor. Her many accomplishments include the restructuring of the financial

Eleanor Holmes Norton has served five terms in the House of Representatives as the elected delegate from Washington, D.C. (U.S. House of Representatives)

relationship between Washington and Congress, the first vote on DC statehood, and negotiating the continued residency of major government employers such as the Department of Transportation. She currently is in her eighth term as Congresswoman and continues to be awarded for her contributions to the field of law and politics.

See also: Congressional Black Caucus; MFDP; Student Nonviolent Coordinating Committee

Donna M. Wells

Bibliography

Lester, Joan Steinau. *Eleanor Holmes Norton: Fire in My Soul.* New York: Atria Books, 2003.

Obama, Barack

Barack Hussein Obama is the first African American to hold the highest office in the government and was elected 44th president of the United States of America on November 4, 2008. He was born on August 4, 1961, in Honolulu, Hawaii, to his white mother, Stanley Ann Dunham from Wichita, Kansas, and his black father Barack Obama Sr. of Luo ethnicity from the Nyanza province of Kenya. They met at the University of Hawaii where they were both students and married in 1961 at a time when miscegenation was still considered illegal in many states. They divorced in 1964 after Obama Sr. left to attend Harvard. Upon graduation, he went back to Kenya and came back to visit again only once in 1971. Barack Obama Sr. died in a car accident in 1982 in Kenya.

In 1966, his mother remarried Indonesian Lolo Soetoro, whom she met as a student in Hawaii, and the family moved to Jakarta, Indonesia. After the birth of their daughter, Maya Kassandra Soetoro on August 15, 1970, Ann and Lolo separated. They divorced in 1980. In 1971, at age 10, Barack Obama returned to Hawaii and stayed with his maternal grandparents, Madelyn and Stanley Armour Dunham. His mother also moved to Hawaii from 1972 to 1975, earned her PhD, and returned to Indonesia to undertake fieldwork. She later become a program officer at the Ford Foundation. Obama decided to stay in Hawaii, where he lived with his grandparents and entered Punahou Academy from which he graduated in 1979. His mother came back to the United States in 1994, but died one year later, on November 7, 1995, at 52 from ovarian cancer.

In 1979, Barack Obama attended Occidental College in Los Angeles and after two years, transferred to Columbia University in New York where he received a BA in political science in 1983. After working at the Business International Corporation and the New York Public Interest Research Group, he moved to Chicago where he became a community organizer and worked for a church-based organization for three years with low-income residents in Roseland community and the Altgeld Gardens public housing development on the city's South Side.

Although he did not receive a religious education, in 1988 Barack Obama joined Trinity United Church of Christ and was an active member for two decades until a controversy broke out during the 2008 presidential campaign over Reverend Jeremiah Wright's sermons and comments. In 1986, he met two of his Kenyan siblings, his sister Auma, who was visiting, and later his brother Roy, who lived in the United States. In 1988, Obama went to Kenya to meet the rest of his paternal relatives in Alego, north-western Kenya.

After this trip he entered Harvard Law School and became an editor of the *Harvard Law Review*. He was the first African American to become president of the journal two years later, which got him a contract to write a book on race relations, published in 1995 under the title *Dreams from My Father: A Story of Race and Inheritance.* The audio version earned him the Grammy Award for Best Spoken Word Album in 2006. He graduated with a JD magna cum laude from Harvard in 1991. He met his wife, Michelle Robinson, in June 1989 as they were both working for the same law firm. They married on October, 3, 1992. Their first daughter, Malia Ann, was born in 1998 and the second daughter, Natasha, in 2001. He then returned to Chicago where he worked as a civil rights lawyer. In 1992, under his leadership Project Vote helped register 150,000 of 400,000 unregistered African Americans during Bill Clinton's presidential campaign. From 1992 to 2004, he taught Constitutional Law at the University of Chicago. During the same period he also worked as an attorney for a law firm specializing in civil rights litigations and neighborhood development.

He ran for the Illinois State Senate as a Democrat and was elected in 1996 from the south side neighborhood of Hyde Park and served for eight years. He served as chairman of the Public Health and Welfare Committee. He worked on a bipartisan platform to draft legislation on ethics, health care, and childhood education for the poor. He

Barack Obama speaks at a town hall meeting in Texas during his campaign for president in 2008. Obama, the first black man to serve as president, was sworn in as the 44th president of the United States in January 2009. (Star Image/Dreamstime)

also worked on creating a state earned-income tax credit for the working poor.

In 1999, after three years in the Illinois State Senate, he tried to run for the First Congressional District of Illinois, challenging Bobby Rush, cofounder of the Illinois Black Panther Party and longtime congressional representative, but lost 30 percent to 61 percent in the Democratic primary in 2000. He won the Democratic primary for the U.S. Senate in 2004 with 52 percent of the vote. On July 26, 2004, he delivered the keynote at the Democratic National Convention in Boston. In November he was elected to the U.S. Senate with a landslide vote of 70 percent against 27 percent for Alan Keyes, an African American candidate. Barack Obama was the fifth African American senator and the third to be popularly elected. He sat on the Foreign Relations, Environment and Veteran Committees

and opposed the war in Iraq as early as 2002. He resigned from his Senate seat on November 13, 2008.

On February 10, 2007, he announced his candidacy to the election of President of the United States of America in Springfield, Illinois, where Abraham Lincoln had delivered his "House Divided" speech in 1858. After a long race against Hillary Rodham Clinton—who endorsed him on June 7—he was the designated candidate of the Democratic party for the election of President of the United States, with Delaware Senator, Joseph Biden, as his running mate. He then started campaigning against John McCain, the Republican nominee. He was the first major candidate to turn down public financing since the creation of the system in 1976. Barack Obama won the presidency against John McCain, with 52.9 percent of the popular vote against 45.7 percent and 365 electoral votes to 173.

In 2004, he signed a contract to write three books. The first, *The Audacity of Hope*, published in 2006, has been at the top of the *New York Times* Best Seller list ever since. The second will be a children's book to be coauthored with his wife Michelle and their two daughters.

See also: Clinton, William Jefferson; Congressional Black Caucus

Veronique Helenon

Bibliography

Kennedy-Schaffer, Alan. *The Obama Revolution.* New York: Phoenix Books, 2009.

Mendell, David. *Obama: From Promise to Power.* New York: Harper Collins, 2008.

Obama, Barack. *Dreams from My Father: A Story of Race and Inheritance.* New York: Three Rivers, 1995.

Obama, Barack. *The Audacity of Hope: Thoughts on Reclaiming the American Dream.* New York: Three Rivers, 2006.

Operation PUSH

Operation PUSH (People United to Serve Humanity) was founded in 1971 by Reverend Jesse Jackson to serve as a vehicle for the promotion of progressive civil rights and political activism. The organization specifically arose out of an internal dispute within the Southern Christian Leadership Council (SCLC) between Jackson and Reverend Ralph David Abernathy. Under the auspices of SCLC, Operation Breadbasket—the predecessor to Operation Push—was founded in 1962 to address the economic struggles within African American communities. Jackson had been selected by Dr. Martin Luther King Jr. to head the Chicago chapter of SCLC's Operation Breadbasket in 1966. Within Chicago's South Side, Operation Breadbasket—under Jackson's leadership—worked to boycott white-owned businesses in order to secure jobs for African Americans and to facilitate the purchase of goods and services for African American contractors. The underlining operating principle within Operation Breadbasket and, later, Operation PUSH was black self-sufficiency and community self-determination—two seemingly black nationalists themes.

After King's assassination in 1968, Abernathy succeeded him as head of the national SCLC. Almost immediately, Abernathy and Jackson began to clash, culminating in the December 1971 suspension of Jackson from his administrative duties. Shortly after the suspension, Jackson officially broke away from SCLC—and thus Operation Breadbasket—and started Operation PUSH. Despite early financial struggles, Operation PUSH outlasted and exceeded Operation Breadbasket. By 1976, the organization launched PUSH-Excel, which was a program aimed at urban minority teenagers, emphasizing education and job placement as measures against youth violence and criminality. In addition, the organization engaged in direct-action campaigns, encouraging minority youth reading, and job creation and placement programs throughout the 1970s. Perhaps the organization's most successful campaign was encouraging major corporations in Chicago to adopt affirmative action programs that would focus on hiring more black executives and would purchase from minority businesses. By the 1980s, several highly publicized boycotts against corporations like Coca Cola, CBS, Nike, Kentucky Fried Chicken, Budweiser, and Anheuser Busch were organized in order to secure affirmative action hires and patronage for minority businesses. Operation PUSH began a slow decline, largely in connection to Jackson's bids for the Democratic Presidential nomination in 1984 and 1988.

Directly after his stint as shadow senator from 1991 to 1996, Jackson moved to merge Operation PUSH with the National Rainbow Coalition and the resulting entity—Rainbow/PUSH—combined the goals of the two organizations he previously founded. Whereas Operation PUSH focused on education, economic uplift, self-sufficiency, and job placement, the National Rainbow Coalition was a purely political organization that grew initially out of Jackson's presidential bid in 1984. During the campaign, Jackson called for a "Rainbow Coalition" of various disadvantaged peoples from a wide array of racial and ethnic backgrounds to advocate for voting rights, affirmative action, and the Great Society-type social engineering that had largely been relegated to the periphery during the Reagan years.

From 1998 to 2009, Rainbow/PUSH has been involved in a number of endeavors, from trying to increase minority involvement in NASCAR to forcing Freddie Mac to earmark more than $1 billion in mortgage loans specifically for minority home buyers. Perhaps the most significant and successful work by Rainbow/PUSH was the organization's investigations of hate crimes and its outcry and relief efforts during Hurricane Katrina and the widespread devastation it caused along the Gulf Coast.

See also: Abernathy, Ralph David; Jackson, Jesse; Southern Christian Leadership Conference

Walter C. Rucker

Bibliography

Bruns, Roger. *Jesse Jackson: A Biography.* Westport, CT: Greenwood Press, 2005.

House, Ernest R. *Jesse Jackson & the Politics of Charisma: The Rise and Fall of the PUSH/Excel Program.* Boulder, CO: Westview Press, 1988.

Jackson, Jesse. *A Time to Speak: The Autobiography of Reverend Jesse Jackson.* New York: Simon & Schuster, 1987.

Organization of African Unity

Founded on May 25, 1963, the Organization of African Unity (OAU) ushered in a new way of addressing problems besetting the African continent. Member states, which numbered 54 until Morocco renounced its allegiance in 1984, pledged to honor each country's sovereignty and to fight for Zimbabwe's and other countries' liberation, still under colonialist rule at the time of the OAU's founding. Besides being dedicated to eradicating colonialism, the OAU's paramount objective was to obtain unity among Africa's ethnically and linguistically diverse nations. The problem was that African leaders had different strategies for obtaining this goal. Three opposing groups formed: the Casablanca group, the Monrovian group, and the Brazzaville group. Led by Ghana's Kwame Nkrumah, the Casablanca Bloc, which consisted of Ghana, Algeria, Guinea, Morocco, Egypt, Mali and Libya, called for a federation of African states; the Monrovian Bloc led by Senegal's Leopold Senghor, which comprised Nigeria, Liberia, and Ethiopia, advocated for unity through economic cooperation. Lacking the power to challenge these dominating groups, the Brazzaville bloc of former French colonies, such as Senegal, Tunisia, and Algeria, acquiesced. Even with this concession, a debate still raged regarding the best strategy for obtaining African unity. To resolve the quandary, Emperor Haile Selassie I, who became the OAU's first chairperson, invited the factions to Addis Ababa, where the OAU ultimately established its headquarters and celebrated the diplomatic unification of 32 of Africa's 54 states. Despite its lack of authority, its inability to enforce decisions, plus create an armed military unit, the OAU represented a major symbolic force on Africa's vast continent.

Not withstanding its shortcomings, the OAU had laudable goals. OAU members wanted to ensure that all African nations received equal treatment. The body wanted all of its citizens to have proper representation before the OAU. Human rights were another issue that the OAU addressed. Violations of human rights was an issue that developed because of the myriad ways that colonial powers or the apartheid regime had infringed on the liberties of African citizens. Torture, police brutality, and draconian legislation represent some of the human rights violations that Africans endured while under the yoke of colonialism or apartheid. By resolving the human rights issues, Africans faced the possibility of lessening the economic and diplomatic stranglehold that colonial authorities or African dictatorships had over Africa's heterogeneous population. To ensure a better quality of life by obliterating poverty, the OAU wanted to raise the living standards of African nations. This included better sewage facilities, education, infrastructure improvements, food sustainability, and development. In the diplomatic arena, the OAU sought to provide its member states with a forum to settle disputes. The problem was that its members vowed not to interfere in the policymaking decisions of its sister states, creating further discord especially when civil wars erupted or ethnic genocide occurred.

Lack of enforcement coupled with a noninterference policy left Africa's contestations in the hands of outsiders, such as the United Nations (UN), which tried to resolve the refugee problem in 1964 when it established a commission on refugees. It was only four years later in 1968 that the UN achieved success, when OAU members signed an agreement to help refugees. Members also agreed to limit interstate conflicts by containing problems stemming from the refugee issue within the borders of origination. This system worked for a while. Africa's refugee problems continued to flourish as a result of ethnic wars in the Sudan and Rwanda among other places. Other problems also existed. Nigeria's Ogoni people faced neocolonialism as foreign companies, such as Shell, drilled for oil, causing environmental damage with pipes above ground and flames burning 24 hours. As leader of the Movement for the Survival of the Ogoni People (MOSOP), Ken Saro-Wiwa pleaded before his death in 1995 for OAU and UN intervention. Adherence to noninterference crippled the OAU by rendering it ineffective in resolving this ongoing dispute and extreme violation of human rights.

Throughout its 39 years of existence, the OAU also achieved some successes. It stood at the forefront of ending colonial and white minority rule. By supplying liberation movements such as South Africa's African National Congress (ANC) and Zimbabwe's African Union (ZANU) with weaponry and military training, the OAU took an active role in fulfilling one of its goals, the liberation of countries under systems of racism and oppression. As an antiapartheid activist, the OAU prevented South African planes from flying over the rest of the continent. That was not all. At the OAU's behest, South Africa was prevented from using African harbors and was expelled from the United Nations. Furthermore, in an attempt to foster economic growth and a sustainable future, the OAU established the African Development Bank in 1964. Despite these achievements, the OAU came under fierce scrutiny and criticism. OAU critics asserted that the body represented a dictator's club and that it did little to ensure the rights and liberties of its citizens. This presented a problem for a lot of reasons, namely that the OAU failed to fulfill its predetermined objectives, the unity of the continent. Seeing the inherent problems within the OAU, its last chairperson South African President Thabo Mbeki disbanded the body on July 9, 2002 and replaced it with the African Union (AU). Unlike the OAU, the AU has the authorization to engage indirect interventions into member states to help resolve conflicts and to eventually create a peacekeeping force to regulate ethnogenocide, modern slavery, and other problems that Africa faces.

See also: African Imperialism; African National Congress; Antiapartheid Movement; Nkrumah, Kwame; Pan-Africanism

Dawne Y. Curry

Bibliography

El-Ayouty, Yassin. *The Organization of African Unity After Thirty Years.* Westport, CT: Praeger, 1994.

Gilbert, Erik, and Jonathan T. Reynolds. *Africa in World History: From Prehistory to the Present.* Princeton, NJ: Prentice Hall, 2004.

Harris, Gordon. *Organization of African Unity.* New Brunswick, NJ: Transaction Publishers, 1994.

Naldi, Gino. *The Organization of African Unity: An Analysis of Its Role.* London: Mansell, 2000.

Saro-Wiwa, Ken, and William Boyd. *A Month and a Day: Detention Diary.* New York: Penguin, 1996.

Organization of Afro-American Unity

The Organization of Afro-American Unity (OAAU) was founded by Malcolm X on June 28, 1964, in Harlem, New York. It was a black nationalist organization that hoped to unite African Americans to defend their civil and human rights. The OAAU advocated self-determination, self-defense, and a number of political, economic, and educational initiatives aimed at empowering African Americans. Inspired by the Organization of African Unity (which sought unity among recently decolonized African nations), the OAAU promoted Pan-African unity and viewed the U.S. black freedom struggle in a global context.

In March 1964, Malcolm X officially broke with the Nation of Islam (NOI). Personal tensions with the NOI contributed to the split, but Malcolm also wanted to take bolder action on civil rights issues. Although he started his own separate religious organization, the Muslim Mosque Inc., the formation of the OAAU represented his decisive shift toward secular political organizing. Malcolm's 1964 travels in Africa and the Middle East also shaped the OAAU. He was exposed firsthand to the anticolonial struggle and to nationalist ideology and practice. He came to view recently decolonized nations and their leaders as potential allies, and he began perceiving the African American struggle in an international framework.

The OAAU was a "nonsectarian" and "nonreligious" organization that sought unity among all African Americans fighting for civil rights. It supported the self-determination and cultural uplift of black urban communities and advocated self-defense, education, and the mobilization of African Americans' internal resources. It sponsored or planned to sponsor a wide range of activities. These included the formation of "defense units" and "rifle clubs," and political initiatives such as voter registration and the formation of political clubs. Malcolm X advocated such tactics as rent strikes and called for community control of black schools. The OAAU stressed the need for education and established a Liberation School that offered classes on history and politics, as well as consumer education, child care, and other spheres of private life. Malcolm X proposed a number of OAAU activities, including a drug rehabilitation program, a "Guardian system" for youth, and community anticrime initiatives.

The OAAU viewed the African American struggle in global terms. It saw black people in the United States as part of a global majority rather than a domestic minority, and it viewed African governments and the African Diaspora as allies. This "internationalizing" of the Civil Rights movement presented new strategic openings for the OAAU. Malcolm X began referring to "human rights" instead of "civil rights" as a goal, and he announced plans to bring the United States before the United Nations on charges of racism. He also became more critical of capitalism and began calling for a new political, economic, and social system.

During its brief existence, the OAAU held rallies in Harlem, with attendance typically between 250 and 800 when Malcolm spoke. It had a headquarters in Harlem and started a short-run newsletter, *The Blacklash,* with an average circulation between 200 and 300. Its membership was never more than several hundred, with a few dozen dedicated people at its core. Dues were $1, with a $2 initiation fee to join. The OAAU also established international branches in London, Paris, Ghana, Kenya, and Egypt, and it founded an Information Bureau in Ghana to exchange news on African and African American struggles.

Malcolm X was the indispensable leader of the OAAU, but he had a circle of intellectuals and professionals around him who played secondary leadership roles. Malcolm was not able to fully devote himself to the OAAU while he was alive, and his assassination undercut his plan to spend more time building the group. The OAAU was an all-black organization, although Malcolm X's views on white alliances had shifted since his NOI days. Although still skeptical of whites and still insistent on an all-black organization that could achieve independent black power, he was more open to forming alliances with anyone who shared the OAAU's goals.

Throughout its existence, the OAAU faced obstacles. It was under constant surveillance by the FBI and other intelligence organizations, and a leading member turned out to be a police infiltrator. Malcolm X wanted the group to be a collectively run organization, but this desire clashed with the OAAU's dependence on Malcolm's prestige, charisma, and leadership. Furthermore, traditional black Muslims were skeptical of the OAAU's secular orientation, whereas some members thought Malcolm was becoming "soft" on white racism with his increased openness to working with whites. Malcolm consciously included women in leadership roles, but they still struggled with male chauvinism within the OAAU.

Malcolm X's sister, Ella Collins, assumed control of the OAAU shortly after Malcolm's assassination on February 21, 1965. Without Malcolm's leadership, however, the organization quickly withered away. Still, the legacy of the OAAU as an embodiment of Malcolm X's political and organizational thinking persisted. The OAAU offered the seeds of a radical black urban political program and international vision that African American activists in the following years would draw from.

See also: Black Nationalism; Organization of African Unity; Pan-Africanism; X, Malcolm

Derek Wolf Seidman

Bibliography

Breitman, George. *The Last Year of Malcolm X.* New York: Merit Publishers, 1967

Sales, William W. *From Civil Rights to Black Liberation: Malcolm X and the Organization of Afro-American Unity.* Boston: South End Press, 1994.

Owens, Jesse

James Cleveland "Jesse" Owens (1913–1980) was the first American track-and-field athlete to win four gold medals in a single Olympic competition. In three events, he also set records. Yet, he is best remembered as the black athlete who triumphed in Berlin in 1936, while Nazi Chancellor Adolf Hitler, who believed in the irrefutable superiority of the Aryan nation, looked on.

Owens was born on September 12, 1913, in Oakville, Alabama, the youngest child of Henry Cleveland Owens, a sharecropper, and Mary Emma (née Fitzpatrick). The family moved to Cleveland, Ohio, most likely in 1922; one story says that, when Owens started school there, he introduced himself as J. C. (James Cleveland). His teacher, though, heard those sounds as "Jesse."

After Charles Riley, his gym teacher at Fairmount Junior High, watched Owens run, he invited him to train with the track team; Owens quickly began breaking records. As a senior at Cleveland East Technical High School, he tied the 100-yard dash world record (9.4 seconds) at the Interscholastic Championships in Chicago. He set other records there, including in the 220-yard dash (20.7 seconds), and the long jump (24 feet, 9-5/8 inches). Reports of his success nearly always mentioned his race; he was called, among other descriptors, "saddle-colored," or the "streak of ebony."

Owens was recruited by several colleges, but he chose Ohio State University. Because scholarships were not available, he worked part-time jobs to pay for his tuition. Because of the segregated nature of American society, he stayed in housing apart from white teammates and ate in different places. They also traveled separately.

On May 25, 1935, Owens broke three world records and tied another, all within the span of one hour: 220-yard sprint (20.3 seconds), long jump (26 feet, 8-1/4 inches), 220-yard low hurdles (22.6 seconds), and the 100-yard dash (9.4 seconds). On July 5, 1935, he married Minnie Ruth Solomon, the mother of his three-year-old daughter, Gloria. They later had two more daughters: Beverly and Marlene. A year later, Owens qualified for the Olympic team, but because Hitler had revoked the citizenship of German Jews, the American Olympic Committee considered boycotting the 1936 Olympiad XI. Meanwhile, the Negro press was comparing Hitler's treatment of Jews to how blacks were treated in the United States; these journalists debated whether a black person should refuse to compete, regardless of official decisions.

The Olympic boycott, however, did not happen, and Owens did compete, tying the world record in the 100-meter dash (10.3 seconds), setting an Olympic record in the long jump (26 feet 5-1/4 inches) and in the 200-meter sprint (20.7 seconds), and participating in the world record-setting 400-meter relay (39.8 seconds). All of these records remained unbroken until the late 1940s; the long jump record was held until 1960.

Hitler did not shake Owens's hand after his victories; it was later described as a snub, but German officials claimed that a decision was made to stop congratulating athletes, for fear of missing someone. Hitler had particular reason to despise Owens; the runner scored 40 points, about two-thirds of the score of the entire male track team from Germany.

After the games, Owens decided not to return to Ohio State. He wanted to race professionally and make public appearances. After opportunities became less available, though, he could not return to amateur racing status, being suspended after choosing professional venues. He therefore participated in more moneymaking ventures, one of which

Jesse Owens at the start of his record-breaking 200 meter race at the 1936 Olympic Games in Berlin. The grandson of a slave, Owens won four gold medals in track and field at the summer games. (Library of Congress)

led him to bankruptcy court. He also raced against horses before Negro League baseball games.

In 1953, Owens was appointed secretary of the Illinois State Athletic Commission. He formed his own public relations agency and presented lectures to schools and other groups. He toured India, Singapore, Malaysia, and the Philippines for the U.S. Department of State; and, in 1956, President Dwight Eisenhower asked him to serve as one of the country's representatives at the Olympic Games in Australia. During the 1960s, he endorsed products and worked as running coach for the New York Mets.

Ohio State awarded Owens an honorary Doctorate of Athletic Arts degree in 1972. In 1976, President Gerald Ford honored him with the Medal of Freedom, the highest honor an American civilian can receive. In 1979, Jimmy Carter decorated him with the Living Legend Award. Carter also offered a tribute when Jesse Owens died from cancer on March 31, 1980, at the age of 66: "Perhaps," Carter said, "no athlete better symbolized the human struggle against tyranny, poverty and racial bigotry. His personal triumphs as a world-class athlete and record holder were the prelude to a career devoted to helping others. His work with young athletes, as an unofficial ambassador overseas, and a spokesman for freedom are a rich legacy to his fellow Americans."

After his death, his widow continued to operate the Jesse Owens Foundation, which provides financial assistance to youth. In 1982, the road leading to the Berlin stadium where Owens ran was renamed "Jesse Owens Allee;" members of his family attended the ceremony. In 1990, George Bush presented Ruth Owens with the Congressional Gold Medal in honor of her husband's accomplishments; in 2001, Ohio State University completed the Jesse Owens Memorial Stadium.

See also: 1936 Summer Olympics, Berlin; Black Athletes

Kelly Boyer Sagert

Bibliography
Baker, William J. *Jesse Owens: An American Life.* New York: The Free Press, 1986.
Owens, Jesse. *The Jesse Owens Story.* New York: G. P. Putnam's Sons, 1970.
Owens, Jesse, with Paul G. Neimark. *Blackthink: My Life as Black Man and White Man.* New York: William Morrow, 1970.

Pan-African Congresses

The Pan-African Congresses were a series of five international conferences that took place between 1919 and 1945. These meetings contributed to the articulation of Pan-African ideas and represented an important part of the Pan-African movement. The congresses offered a forum for the discussion of Pan-Africanism. Their objectives were to foster unity among peoples of African descent and to encourage the creation of an institutional framework that could support the development of a strong Pan-African movement. Despite many attempts to establish a stable organizational apparatus, the different congresses reflect a failure to coordinate the goals and ideals of a diverse group of peoples. Lacking an institutionalized tradition, many of the shortcomings and achievements of the congresses were dependent on individual figures. The most important was W. E. B. Du Bois who provided intellectual continuity and

logistical support to the first four congresses, and contributed to the establishment of a tradition that would serve as a model for the fifth Pan-African Congress.

During the 19th century, African peoples faced the threat of the growing colonial ambitions of European nations, and black peoples in the United States and the West Indies had to deal with discrimination and economic exploitation. These circumstances contributed to the growth of Pan-African ideas. These generally stated that peoples of African descent throughout the world shared a common cultural heritage and the historical experience of exploitation and inequality. Pan-Africanism developed as a body of ideas and movements that advocated for solidarity among peoples of African descent and asserted their rights for social, political, and economic equality.

Before 1919, there were meetings that already announced the emergence of different Pan-African ideologies. In 1893, there was a Congress on Africa in Chicago. At this meeting representatives from Africa and the Americas discussed issues related to the political rights of black peoples. In 1900, the recently created African Association sponsored the organization of a Pan-African Conference in London. Thirty-two delegates from Africa, the United States, and the West Indies attended this event. The Conference produced a document called "To the Nations of the World" that condemned racism and the exploitation of peoples of African descent. As a result of the conference, the African Association became the first Pan-African Association. The association planned to organize a meeting every two years; its purpose was to provide continuity to the movement and promote its growth. The association, however, was short-lived. Plagued with internal conflicts and financial instability, it would soon disappear. Despite these shortcomings, this first Pan-African Conference and the Pan-African Association were important on a symbolic level. They contributed to the articulation of a notion of Pan-Africanism that would influence future generations of activists and intellectuals.

Between 1900 and 1919, social and political changes affected the development of the Pan-African movement. The ideals of democracy and equality started to become popular among peoples throughout the globe, and the educated elements of societies that lived under oppressive conditions started to achieve economic and political strength. These changes were evident in the emergence of nationalist ideas in parts of West Africa and South Africa, and in the tensions that developed in the United States that would later result in the Civil Rights movement. An important result of these changes was the emergence of W. E. B. Du Bois, one of the most important ideologues of the Pan-African movement.

Among many other things, W. E. B. Du Bois was a pioneer in the study of the history and sociology of African Americans in the United States, and one of the most articulate critics of racial inequality. Although the origins of Pan-African ideas go back to the 18th and 19th century, Du Bois has been credited with the articulation of the notion of Pan-Africanism as the belief that all peoples of African descent share a common heritage and should unite to fight against discrimination and racial injustice. He contributed to the creation of the National Association for the Advancement of Colored People (NAACP), a group that supported the organization of the first two Pan-African Congresses.

It was the NAACP that sent Du Bois to Paris in 1919. He was sent to investigate allegations of mistreatment of black soldiers in the U.S. Army who were stationed in France. He was also charged with representing African interests in the peace conference that was about to take place. While in Paris, Du Bois organized the first Pan-African Congress with the objective of voicing the needs of African peoples on the eve of the Paris Peace Conference.

A total of 57 delegates representing 15 countries attended the Congress. Du Bois outlined an agenda that included an assessment of the conditions that affected black peoples and the articulation of their demands. Among the requests of the Congress were the administration by the Allies of the former German colonies in Africa as a condominium, the improvement of living conditions (abolition of slavery, corporal punishment and forced labor, general access to education), the inclusion of Africans in the government of their own countries as soon as their level of development allowed for it, and the granting of self-rule to Africa at some point in the future.

When compared with the demands of the 1900 London Congress, the requests of the Paris Congress were relatively moderate. From an organizational point of view, the achievements of the Paris Conference were also modest compared with those of London, as no permanent organization was created as a result of the Congress.

The second Pan-African Congress took place at different sessions in London, Paris, and Brussels in 1921. In total, 110 delegates attended the Congress and more than 1,000 visitors were present at the event. There were 41 delegates from the United States, 7 from the West Indies, and 24 from Africa and Afro-Americans living in Europe. The resolutions passed at this congress were more radical than those approved in Paris. The congress produced a document entitled "Declaration to the World," which is also known as the London Manifesto. The final resolutions fully supported the principles of racial equality and self-government, without taking into consideration differences in the level of development of various societies. In this regard, the 1921 congress returned to the tradition initiated in 1900. More specifically, the manifesto was divided in four parts. The first one was a general critique of the relations between black and white peoples. The second part focused primarily on condemning the policies of the major colonial powers. The third section demanded that the sovereignty of the governments of Abyssinia, Liberia, and Haiti was respected. Finally, the congress issued a general challenge to the rest of the world.

During the second congress, differences started to emerge among various groups that represented diverse approaches to Pan-African ideas. Some delegates from the French-speaking African territories disagreed with the hard criticism levied against French and Belgian colonial policy. Blaise Diagne, who had been instrumental in the organization of the first Pan-African Congress, was among those who thought that the language of the resolutions was too radical. Even though he was African, he was in effect a French politician as a representative of Senegal in the French Chamber of Deputies. He found the declaration too extreme and abandoned the movement.

Another conflict emerged between the followers of Marcus Garvey and Du Bois. Garvey was a Jamaican activist who traveled in South America and Europe and was in contact with important African American activists such as Booker T. Washington. Washington himself had been in conflict with Du Bois over their different views about education for African Americans. Garvey founded the Universal Negro Improvement and Conservation Association and African Communities League, better known as the Universal Negro Improvement Association (UNIA) in 1914. The objectives of this association included the creation of a confraternity among black peoples, the promotion of race pride, and the development of independent Negro nations. Garvey traveled to the United States in 1916, when Harlem was in the process of becoming an important African

American area. There he found fertile ground for his ideas. In New York, Garvey started a New York branch of the UNIA and founded a number of short-lived publications of which the *Negro World* became the most important vehicle for spreading his ideas.

Garvey created a number of subordinate organizations geared at putting in practice his Pan-African ideas. UNIA organized annual conventions that were celebrated in Harlem. These meetings were well attended and rivaled the congresses organized by Du Bois. They openly demanded the liberation of African peoples. This direct approach conflicted with the more gradualist attitude that characterized the Pan-African congresses, and became the main reason for the strong clash between Garvey and Du Bois.

Du Bois agreed with the aims of Garvey; however, he did not approve of his methods. Garvey's approach, together with his slogan "Africa for the Africans" was condemned in Brussels and Paris. After bitter discussion it was decided that Garvey would not be invited to the next congress.

Despite the problems that plagued the second congress, delegates agreed to create a second Pan-African Association. The presidency was given to Gratien Candace, a Guadeloupe-born intellectual and politician, and the general secretary was Isaac Béton, a young schoolmaster from Martinique. In practice, the association was in the hands of the individual figures of Du Bois and Béton, which undermined its capacity to achieve institutional strength. It was poorly financed and the tensions between the Anglophone and Francophone sections of the organization were a continuous obstacle. Despite the many disputes that plagued the association, a third Pan-African Congress was organized, mostly as a result of the efforts of Du Bois.

The third Pan-African Congress met in 1923 in London and Lisbon. It was badly organized and poorly attended. Only 11 countries were represented and the majority of the delegates were from the United States. As a consequence, the activities of the congress were more modest than the previous ones. Delegates decided to promote the creation of Pan-African committees, and they issued a statement in which they identified some fundamental needs of peoples of African descent. Among the things discussed were the right of Africans to participate in their own government, the need to make education available at all levels, access to land and other economic resources, and the abolition of slave trade. The resolutions also mentioned more specific demands such as home rule and responsible government

for West Africa and British West Indies; the abolition of white minority rule in Kenya, Rhodesia, and South Africa; and the elimination of lynching and mob laws in the United States.

The limitations of the Pan-African Association prevented it from organizing a Pan-African meeting in 1925. Despite the many difficulties, Du Bois continued to work for the growth and development of the Pan-African movement. His efforts resulted in the organization of the fourth Pan-African Congress in New York in 1927. The congress took place from August 21–24. It was attended by 208 delegates from 11 countries. The American contingent was the largest; Africans were scarcely represented, with a few delegates from Liberia, Sierra Leone, and the Gold Coast. Other countries represented were Haiti, the Virgin Islands, the Bahamas, Barbados, and South America. There were also some non-African attendees, including the renowned anthropologist Melville Herskovits. The resolutions of this congress echoed the ones agreed on at the previous congress.

After the fourth congress, Du Bois decided that it was time to take the Pan-African congress to the African continent. Given the logistical problems of the movement and the economic crisis that surged in 1929, however, these plans were thwarted. The economic and political problems that affected most of the world during the 1930s interrupted the development of the Pan-African congresses. The movement, however, continued to evolve.

The congresses that took place between 1919 and 1927 were unsuccessful in achieving the goals of African liberation and racial equality. They also failed to provide a strong organizational framework for the development of the Pan-African movement. Du Bois had provided the intellectual foundations to the movement and much of the logistical work. Despite these limitations, these congresses were important in sowing the seeds of Pan-Africanism. They introduced Pan-African ideas to an international audience and fostered both debate and unity among peoples of African descent on both sides of the Atlantic Ocean. In doing this they provided direction and guidance to those who revitalized the Pan-African movement after World War II.

The Abyssinian crisis of 1935 and the end of World War II contributed to the reemergence of the Pan-African movement. Numerous organizations were created to condemn the Italian invasion of Ethiopia and to offer support to the Ethiopian peoples and royal family. The crisis raised serious questions about the ability of the League of Nations to safeguard the rights of African peoples. Moreover, it cast serious doubts on the commitment of European states to protect African interests.

The end of World War II brought to the front difficult questions for European colonial powers. Having fought in the name of freedom and equality, Allies would face growing discontent in their colonies and increasing demands for political participation and social and economic development. The Atlantic Charter signed in 1941 stated the right to self-determination and gave legitimacy to the aspirations of millions of peoples throughout the world who lived under colonial control. European powers, however, were unwilling to extend these rights to their colonial subjects, at least not before they had been properly prepared. This was an unacceptable state of affairs for people who had contributed heavily to the cause of the Allies during the war and whose ambitions for independence had become quite evident in the growth of mass nationalist movements in many parts of Africa.

The hypocritical attitude of colonial governments strengthened the conviction of many organizations that had emerged in Europe and Africa, and the quest for the political liberation of Africa became the galvanizing force behind the creation of the Pan-African Federation (PAF) in 1944. This organization was composed of numerous political and labor groups. It served to canalize their demands and helped articulate their objectives. Their goals were to promote the well-being and unity of African peoples and to foster collaboration with peoples who share the aspirations of peoples of African descent. The organization was located in Manchester. It planned to fulfill its mission by creating centers devoted to the study of African history and culture, by sponsoring the publication of materials about Africa, and by organizing international conferences to promote the ideals of African freedom. The PAF proved to be an effective platform for the opposition to colonial rule in that it allowed member organizations to communicate more effectively with other groups and organize demonstrations, approve resolutions, and collect financial aid more efficiently.

The PAF was behind the organization of the fifth Pan-African congress that took place in Manchester in 1945. It had been originally proposed by in a meeting of the World Federation of Trade Unions that met in London earlier that year. The interest shown by various organizations allowed the PAF to make quick arrangements. Some of the organizers were Peter Milliard, George Padmore, Kwame Nkrumah, Jomo Kenyatta, and Peter Abrahams. The Congress opened on October 15. For the first time Africa was adequately represented. Many of those who attended went on to become important figures in their countries such as Obafemi Awolowo, Dr. Hastings Banda, and Joe Appiah. All the organizations that formed the PAF were represented, as well as numerous political and cultural organizations and trade unions. Other groups represented were the Federation of Indian Organizations and the Independent Labor Party of Britain. Despite the large attendance there were significant absences. There were no representatives from Haiti, the French Caribbean, Francophone Africa, Ethiopia, Portuguese Africa, the Belgian Congo, and Muslim North Africa.

The Manchester congress issued an unequivocal condemnation of colonialism and racial discrimination. Among the specific demands were immediate independence for African colonies, removal of British armed forces from Egypt, support for the struggle of African peoples in South Africa, full citizenship for peoples of African descent in the United States, and equal access to social and economic opportunity to all African peoples. The Manchester congress represented a comprehensive challenge to colonial ideology and racist practices founded in the principles presented in the Atlantic Charter.

This fifth Congress also marked a significant shift in the focus and direction of the Pan-African movement. Although it followed the intellectual tradition instituted by previous congresses, this meeting was clearly dominated by the issue of African political liberation. For the first time, Africans took center stage and adopted positions of leadership. Most important, the congress became a true vehicle for political pressure, as it incorporated trade unions and other popular organizations that provided added strength to their demands. In the end the congress combined the intellectual traditions of the past with the force of the masses.

The congress was instrumental in bringing together the ideas of Pan-Africanism and the strength of African nationalisms. It set the foundations for further cooperation among African states. The independence of Ghana helped pave the way for this collaboration. After the congress the PAF set up a committee presided by Du Bois and Kwame Nkrumah and it was decided that the headquarters of the Pan-African Congress would stay in London.

Although the values and ideas of Pan-Africanism continued to be important in the postindependence period, no more congresses were organized. The Pan-African movement became more focused on the issue of political and economic unity between African states, and the emphasis on solidarity with peoples of African descent became secondary.

See also: African Imperialism; Du Bois, W. E. B.; Garvey, Marcus; Kenyatta, Jomo; Manchester Conference, 1945; Nkrumah, Kwame; Pan-Africanism

Esperanza Brizuela-Garcia

Bibliography

Du Bois, W. E. B. *The World and Africa; An Inquiry into the Part Which Africa Has Played in World History.* New York: International Publishers, 1965.

Esedebe, P. Olisanwuche. *Pan-Africanism. The Idea and Movement, 1776–1963.* Washington, D.C.: Howard University Press, 1982.

Geiss, Imanuel. *The Pan African Movement. A History of Pan Africanism in America, Europe and Africa.* New York: Africana Publishing, 1974.

Muchie, M. *The Making of Africa-nation: Pan Africanism and the African Renaissance,* London: Adonis and Abbey Publishers, 2003.

Padmore, George. *Pan Africanism or Communism.* New York: Doubleday, 1971.

Pan-Africanism

Pan-Africanism is an ideology that states that peoples of African descent share a common cultural and historical heritage. Pan-African ideas have been the foundation of political and intellectual movements that historically have advocated for one or more of the following principles: Africa as the homeland of all peoples of African descent, the existence of a distinct African personality, the assertion of Africa's pride in its past as well as its culture, the right of all peoples of African descent to self-determination and economic advancement, political and economic unity.

Pan-African ideas first originated among African Americans in North America and the West Indies. The lack of political freedoms and economic opportunities that characterized the life of blacks in much of the Americas contributed to the emergence of ideas of unity, solidarity, and resistance among African American peoples.

During the 18th and 19th centuries people of African descent took different actions to assert their rights and improve their quality of life. These responses were important factors that influenced the emergence of Pan-African movements. Among the most important were movements that promoted the return of free blacks to Africa. The best example of this was the emigration schemes organized by the American Colonization Society that relocated 13,000 Africans in Liberia between 1817 and 1857.

During the 19th century the contacts between Europeans and Africans increased. Debates over the abolition of the slave trade and slavery revealed a widely held racist attitude toward people of African descent. This became the justification of European nations for their growing intervention in African affairs, as well as for the mistreatment of blacks in the Americas. Faced with these situations, African, African American, and West Indian intellectuals started to formulate ideas that asserted the value of African cultures and societies. Among those who produced early writings were J. A. B. Horton, Edward W. Blyden, and the Reverend James Johnson.

In 1897, Sylvester Williams, a barrister from Trinidad, created the African Association. The objectives of the organization were to lobby the British parliament and government and to inform the public about the issues that affected the lives of African peoples. The headquarters for the association were in London, and membership was restricted to Africans and African Americans. From its inception, Williams hoped the association would sponsor international conferences where delegates from different areas of the world could discuss the issues that affected black peoples.

The first Pan-African Conference took place in 1900. In all 32 delegates from the United States, the West Indies, and Africa attended it. During the conference the delegates petitioned for the improvement of the political and social conditions that affected the lives of Africans living under colonial regimes. They also produced a document called "To the Nations of the World" in which they condemned the use of racist ideas to justify the exploitation of African people.

The first Pan-African Conference provided a formal forum for the discussion of Pan-African ideas and marked the beginning of a more distinct, if yet diverse, Pan-African movement. An example of this was the transformation of the African Association into the Pan-African Association.

The original plans were to organize a meeting every two years to provide continuity and growth to the Pan-African movement. The first meetings were to take place in the United States in 1902 and in Haiti in 1904. The association also published a newspaper, *Pan-African*. This was edited by Sylvester Williams and was published monthly.

The association was short-lived because of internal conflicts and financial instability. The next Pan-African Conference took place in 1919. The years that led to it were marked by social, political, and economic changes that had a significant impact on the ideology and movement of Pan-Africanism. The spread of democratic ideas had started to reach people who lived under all kinds of oppressive conditions, and the educated elites in many of these societies were becoming economically and sometimes even politically powerful. These changes can be appreciated in the emergence of nationalist ideas in areas of West Africa and South Africa. This period also saw the emergence of tensions in the United States that would give way to the Civil Rights movement years later. From these emerged one of the most important ideologues of the Pan-African movement, W. E. B. Du Bois.

Among many other things, W. E. B. Du Bois was a pioneer in the study of history and sociology of African Americans in the United States, and one of the most articulate critics of racial inequality. He had attended the 1900 London Conference and has been credited as the first to articulate some of the fundamental principles of Pan-Africanism.

Before 1919, Pan-African ideas continued to be discussed in different forums. For example, in 1911 there was a Universal Races Congress that was aimed at improving relationships among people of different races. The congress was organized by the International Union of Ethical Societies and attracted a significant number of participants from different areas of the world. In 1912, the ideological rival of Du Bois, Booker T. Washington, organized the International Conference on the Negro. This conference was aimed at examining the education methods that were being used in the United States to improve the lives of black people and to explore the possibility of applying such methods in Africa and the West Indies.

These meetings helped promote Pan-African ideas and influenced individuals who made significant contributions to the growth of the movement. A good example of this was Mohamed Ali Duse, an Egyptian man who lived in England

and attended the Universal Races Congress. He launched the *African Times and Orient Review*, a publication aimed at providing accurate information about Africans and peoples of African descent. This journal contributed to the dissemination of Pan-African ideas that would become important in the definition of the Pan-African movement after World War I.

The Pan-African movement was reinvigorated after World War I when Du Bois called for a meeting in Paris in 1919. The objectives of this Pan-African Congress were to examine the situation of black people; identify their social, political, and economic needs; and articulate their demands of development and equality. A total of 57 delegates representing 15 countries attended the Congress. The resolutions passed demanded that the recently created League of Nations looked after the welfare of African peoples and requested that Africans be allowed to participate in their own government.

The Second Pan-African Congress was celebrated in London, Paris, and Brussels in 1921. A total of 110 delegates attended. The resolutions passed at this congress may be found in the document "Declaration to the World," which came to be known as the "London Manifesto." The resolutions called for racial equality and self-government. The radical tone of the document caused debates among the delegates, some of whom were in favor of a less confrontational approach to the issue of decolonization.

The congress also succeeded in creating a new Pan-African Association. The leaders of this organization were Du Bois and Isaac Béton, a schoolmaster from Martinique. The association was poorly financed and deeply divided, however, and it failed to provide continuity to the Pan-African movement.

A third Pan-African Congress was organized despite the problems of the Pan-African Association and thanks to the indefatigable work of Du Bois. It met in 1923 in Lisbon and London; however, the organization and the attendance were poor. Only 11 countries were represented and, as usual, African Americans dominated the congress.

The activities of this congress were more modest than previous ones. Delegates issued a statement in which they identified some fundamental needs of African peoples such as political participation, access to land and other economic resources, and education at all levels. They also demanded home rule and responsible government for West Africa and British West India; the abolition of white minority rule in

Kenya, Rhodesia, and South Africa; and the suppression of lynching and mob laws in the United States.

Because of the failure of the Pan-African Association to resolve its internal conflicts and establish a strong organizational structure, no congress was held in 1925. Despite these difficulties Du Bois continued to push for the growth of the Pan-African movement. He managed to organize a fourth Pan-African congress in New York, in 1927. A total of 208 delegates from 11 countries participated in this meeting. African Americans continued to dominate the event. Africans were scarcely represented, with a few delegates from Liberia, Sierra Leone, and the Gold Coast. The resolutions of this congress echoed those formulated in the previous meeting.

After the fourth congress, Du Bois decided to hold the next congress on African soil. Given the organizational weakness of the movement and the economic crisis that developed in 1929, however, it became impossible to organize this event. The next Pan-African Congress would have to wait until the end of World War II.

While Du Bois promoted his views on Pan-Africanism through these congresses, other important movements were also influenced by Pan-African ideas. Marcus Aurelius Garvey, a Jamaican-born activist, developed an alternative approach to Pan-Africanism. Garvey traveled in South America and Europe, was in contact with Mohammed Ali Duse, and was influenced by the writings of authors such as Booker T. Washington. In 1914, he created the Universal Negro Improvement and Conservation Association and African Communities League, generally known as the Universal Negro Improvement Association (UNIA). The objectives of this association included the creation of a confraternity among black peoples, the promotion of race pride, and the development of independent Negro nations. Garvey traveled to the United States in 1916 when Harlem was in the process of becoming an important African American area. There he found fertile ground for his ideas. In New York Garvey started a branch of the UNIA and founded a number of short-lived publications, of which the *Negro World* became the most important vehicle for spreading his ideas.

Garvey created a number of subordinate organizations geared at putting in practice his Pan-African ideas. UNIA organized annual conventions that were celebrated in Harlem. These meetings were well attended and rivaled the congresses organized by Du Bois. They openly demanded the liberation of African peoples. This direct approach conflicted with the more gradualist attitude that characterized the Pan-African congresses and became the main reason for the strong clash between Garvey and Du Bois.

Garvey's quest for the liberation of Africa encouraged him to establish concrete connections to the continent. In 1920, he sent a delegation to Liberia to explore the possibilities of settling Afro-Americans in that country. The plan seemed to be well received at first, but soon conflicts with the local Liberian authorities and the opposition of colonial powers, as well as the United States, prevented Garvey from settling in Liberia.

Garvey also faced a crisis back in the United States where he was accused of mismanagement and fraud. Garvey was arrested and later sent to prison. His wife continued with the organization of UNIA as much as she could and the conventions continued to be held. In 1927, Garvey was pardoned and expelled from the United States after which he returned to Jamaica and tried to reorganize his movement. He traveled to the West Indies and Europe where he had mixed receptions. In 1930, the section of UNIA in the United States finally collapsed. The *Negro World* continued to be published until 1933. He died in 1940 after multiple and failed attempts to reorganize his movement and clear his name.

Garvey represented a radical approach to Pan-Africanism. His unequivocal demands for African liberation injected his views on racial equality and pride with new energy and made them more appealing to a large number of black people.

Between the two wars, there were other organizations that promoted Pan-African ideas. Among the most important were the National Congress of British West Africa (NCBWA) and the West African Students Union (WASU), both based in London. Some pressure groups were also formed by exiles in France. Some were the *Ligue Universelle pour la défence de la race noire,* the *Comité de la defense de la Race Negre,* and the *Ligue de la défense de la Race Negre.* Most of these advocated for the rights of black people to education and economic development and challenged the notions of inferiority of the black race.

Between 1934 and 1945, several Pan-African groups in England started to move closer together and become better defined and organized. Two wings became dominant: a "conservative Pan-Africanism represented by the Jamaican Harold Moody and his organization, the League of Colored

Peoples (LCP), and a more radical Pan-Africanism represented by George Padmore.

The LCP was created in 1931. Moody arrived in Britain in 1904 and developed an ideology of Pan-Africanism that was mitigated by his strong Christian beliefs. Moody believed in the importance of working with Europeans to improve the lives of Africans and West Indians. He worked mainly with religious groups. At first the LCP was not a political organization; however, the Abyssinian invasion and German aspirations to regain control of their lost colonies turned the meetings of the LCP into forums for the discussion of such issues.

At the other end of the spectrum was George Padmore, whose real name was Malcolm Ivan Nurse. He was born in Trinidad to a middle class family and claimed to be the nephew of Sylvester Williams. He had studied in the United States and had been a member of the Communist Party. His approach to the issue of African liberation was more radical than that of Moody. He actively participated in the creation and running of several organizations that advocated for the political rights of African peoples and helped reinvigorate and redefine the postwar Pan-African movement.

The Abyssinian crisis (1935) was a galvanizing moment for the Pan-African movement. It called into question the ability of the League of Nations and the commitment of European powers to safeguard the interests of African peoples. The end of World War II and the signing of the Atlantic Charter in 1941 marked the beginning of a new understanding of the right to freedom and self-determination. African people were aware of the significance of this moment and increased their demands for independence. This culminated in the creation, in 1944, of the Pan-African Federation (PAF) under the initiative of a number of African organizations.

The PAF, with its headquarters in Manchester, served to articulate the demands of the various groups that composed it. It advocated for the welfare and unity of African people and people of African descent. It planned to fulfill its mission by promoting the study of Africa and organizing conferences. The PAF proved to be an effective platform for the opposition to colonial rule, as it enabled member organizations to operate more efficiently.

The PAF organized the fifth Pan-African Congress, which took place in Manchester in 1945. For the first time Africa was adequately represented, and many of those who

attended became political leaders in their own soon-to-be-independent nations. All the organizations that formed PAF were represented, as well as numerous political and cultural organizations and trade unions.

Delegates at the Manchester Congress unequivocally condemned colonialism and racial discrimination. Among other things they demanded immediate independence for African territories, removal of British armed forces from Egypt, support for the struggle of African people in South Africa, and full citizenship for the people of African descent in the Americas. The congress successfully articulated the political aspirations of African people and served as a catalyst for the growth of the nationalist movements that achieved independence for many African states.

African nationalist leaders took center stage at the Manchester Congress. They reinforced the Pan-African movement by combining the influence of elites and intellectuals with the strength of the masses. In doing so they produced a shift in the focus and nature of the Pan-African movement.

The focus of the Pan-African movement after the Manchester Congress gave great importance to the issue of African unity. In 1958, Kwame Nkrumah, the leader of Ghana, organized a meeting of independent African states in the Ghanaian capital of Accra. The countries represented were Egypt, Ethiopia, Ghana, Liberia, Libya, Morocco, Sudan, and Tunisia. This was the first step in a process toward African unity that would be plagued with problems and controversy. Some nations favored immediate political unity, but others advocated for a more gradual approach. This resulted in the creation of two camps, the Casablanca group and the Monrovia Group.

After numerous meetings where the differences between the two groups were further debated, the Pan-African ideals took the form of the Organization of African Unity(OAU), in May 1963 in Addis Ababa. The organization was originally formed by 32 governments. Gradually, 21 more states joined this group. South Africa became the 53rd member in 1994. The objectives of the OAU were to promote solidarity and unity among African people; coordinate cooperation; improve the lives of common people; defend sovereignty, territorial integrity, and independence; eradicate colonialism; and promote international cooperation. The OAU has faced the numerous political and economic crises that have affected the African continent in the postcolonial era. After many failures to pursue the objectives for which it was created, it was agreed that a new organization was needed.

In a meeting in 1999 called to amend the OAU charter, the delegates in attendance decided to establish the African Union. Among the objectives of the new organization are to accelerate the political and socioeconomic integration of the continent; promote peace, security, and stability; promote democratic principles and institutions; and foster sustainable development in all areas of human endeavor. The objectives of the African Union reflect the social and political changes experienced by African people in the postcolonial period. To that extent, this new organization reflects the evolving values of modern Pan-Africanism.

See also: Du Bois, W. E. B.; Garvey, Marcus; Manchester Conference, 1945; Nkrumah, Kwame; Organization of African Unity; Pan-African Congresses

Esperanza Brizuela-Garcia

Bibliography

Bandele, Ramla M. *Black Star: African American Activism in the International Political Economy.* Urbana: University of Illinois Press, 2008.

Esedebe, P. Olisanwuche. *Pan-Africanism. The Idea and Movement, 1776–1963.* Washington, D.C.: Howard University Press, 1982.

Geiss, Imanuel. *The Pan African Movement. A History of Pan Africanism in America, Europe and Africa.* New York: Africana Publishing, 1974.

Moses, Wilson Jeremiah. *Classical Black Nationalism: From the American Revolution to Marcus Garvey.* New York: New York University Press, 1996.

Muchie, M. *The Making of Africa-nation: Pan Africanism and the African Renaissance.* London: Adonis and Abbey Publishers, 2003.

Padmore, George. *Pan Africanism or Communism.* New York: Doubleday, 1971.

Parks, Rosa

On December 1, 1955, Rosa Louise Parks (1913–2005) refused to give up her seat on a Montgomery, Alabama, bus for a white passenger. This act of defiance against Jim Crow segregation sparked the Montgomery bus boycott—often heralded as the beginning of the modern Civil Rights movement—a nonviolent economic boycott of Montgomery's bus system by the black community that successfully ended racial segregation on the city's public transit. For her courage and actions, Parks is widely considered the mother of the Civil Rights movement.

Rosa Louise McCauley was born on February 4, 1913, in Tuskegee, Alabama, to James and Leona McCauley. After James and Leona separated, Leona moved with her children, Rosa and Sylvester, to Pine Level, Alabama, a town on the outskirts of Montgomery where they lived with Leona's parents. By the age of 11, Rosa attended the Montgomery Industrial School for Girls, and a few years later, she attended the laboratory school at Alabama State Teacher's College for Negroes in Montgomery. Family illnesses forced Rosa to abandon her education to support her family.

While living in Montgomery, 18-year-old Rosa met Raymond Parks, a barber. The self-educated Parks had been one of the charter members of Montgomery's NAACP and had been actively involved in supporting the Scottsboro Boys' defense in the early 1930s. Parks's courage, at a time when black activism was extremely dangerous, deeply impressed Rosa. They were married on December 18, 1932, in Pine Level. Historian and Parks's biographer Douglas Brinkley has noted that her husband was a significant factor in her radicalization during the Great Depression, as he would discuss the NAACP an its strategies for encouraging African American suffrage and integration with Parks. Encouraged by her husband, Rosa Parks returned to school and earned her high school diploma in 1933.

Until World War II, Parks had not been involved in the black civil rights struggle. This changed after she took a job at Maxwell Field in Montgomery in 1941. By 1943, all military bases, Maxwell Field included, had been desegregated. Unlike Montgomery's city buses, she rode integrated trolleys on base and her experience at desegregated Maxwell prompted her to join the Montgomery NAACP. At her first meeting, Parks was elected secretary of the organization. In this capacity, she helped lead a voter registration drive, although white registrars worked diligently to keep African Americans off the voter rolls. It took until April 1945 for Parks to finally be registered to vote.

After the war, Parks continued as secretary of the Montgomery NAACP, but she also worked as a housekeeper and seamstress, most notably for the liberal white activists Clifford and Virginia Durr. In July 1955, Virginia Durr arranged for Parks to attend a two-week session on racial desegregation at the Highlander Folk School in Monteagle, Tennessee. The experience at Highlander, and her exposure to individuals such as civil rights pioneer Septima Clark, strengthened her desire to work for civil rights.

Just months after her return from Highlander, on the evening of December 1, 1955, Parks violated segregation laws by refusing to give her seat to a white passenger on a city bus. Parks initially had been seated in the first row of the black section, but as more whites boarded the bus, the color line moved farther back. When this occurred, African Americans were expected to relinquish their seats to make room for the white passengers. Parks refused. The bus driver, James F. Blake, called the police and had Parks arrested. As she recounted in her autobiography, she was not physically tired. A few days later, Parks was found guilty of

disorderly conduct and violating a Montgomery ordinance and fined $10, plus $4 in court costs.

In response to Parks's arrest, E. D. Nixon and Jo Ann Robinson, a professor at Alabama State College, met to discuss a boycott of the bus system by Montgomery's African Americans. At a subsequent mass meeting, Martin Luther King Jr., the pastor of Dexter Avenue Baptist Church, was chosen to lead the effort. The entire African American community supported the Montgomery bus boycott, refusing to ride the city's buses for 381 days, placing a tremendous financial strain on the bus company. On May 11, 1956, a federal court decision in *Browder v. Gayle* ruled Alabama's bus segregation laws unconstitutional, upheld by the United States Supreme Court on November 13, 1956. The boycott came to an end on December 20, 1956, after the city passed

Rosa Parks, whose refusal to give up her bus seat to a white passenger sparked the Montgomery Bus Boycott and fueled the Civil Rights movement, sits in the front of a bus on December 21, 1956. (Library of Congress)

a desegregation ordinance for the city's buses. Whereas the boycott propelled King into national prominence as the leader of the Civil Rights movement, Rosa Parks's courageous refusal to give in to the inequities of the Jim Crow system made her a symbolic figure whose inspiration reached well beyond the borders of the United States.

Hounded by death threats and at odds with the local leaders of the Civil Rights movement, Rosa and Raymond Parks, along with Leona McCauley, moved to Detroit, Michigan, in July 1957, to live with family members. In Detroit, Parks worked as a seamstress but continued to be involved in the Civil Rights movement, lecturing widely to diverse groups. Her interest in politics led to a job with U.S. Representative John Conyers in 1965, for whom she work until she retired in 1988. In honor of her husband Raymond, who died in 1977, she founded the Rosa and Raymond Parks Institute for Self-Development in February 1987, to mentor youths to achieve their full potential.

Although Parks was a symbol of the Civil Rights movement and an inspiration to millions because of her courage and quiet dignity, official recognition of her contributions to American history came late in her life. On September 9, 1996, President William J. Clinton presented her with a Presidential Medal of Freedom, the highest award given to a civilian. A few years later, on May 3, 1999, she received a Congressional Gold Medal. *Time* magazine also recognized her as one of the 100 most influential people of the 20th century. Rosa Parks died on October 24, 2005, in Detroit at the age of 92. In striking contrast to her notoriety as one of the most detested figures in the United States after the boycott, Rosa Park became the first woman in American history to lie in state in the United States Capitol. It is estimated that 50,000 people paid their respects to the "Mother of the Civil Rights Movement."

See also: King, Coretta Scott; King, Martin Luther Jr.; Montgomery Bus Boycott; Robinson, Jo Ann

Dan J. Puckett

Bibliography

Branch, Taylor. *Parting the Waters: America in the King Years, 1954–63.* New York: Simon & Schuster, 1988.

Brinkley, Douglas. *Rosa Parks.* New York: Viking Penguin, 2000.

Parks, Rosa, with Gregory J. Reed. *Quiet Strength: The Faith, the Hope, and the Heart of a Woman Who Changed the Nation.* Grand Rapids, MI: Zondervan Publishing House, 1994.

Parks, Rosa, with Jim Haskins. *Rosa Parks: My Story.* New York: Dial Books, 1992.

Plan de San Diego

The 1915 Plan de San Diego was intended to be a multi-racial militant coalition involving Latinos, African Americans, and Native Americans against whites in South Texas. A number of forces led to the planning of this rebellion, but more than two decades of abject racial violence in the form of lynchings and beatings were perhaps most important. In January 1896, Aureliano Castelon was shot eight times and his body was burned in San Antonio by a white mob. In response, 25 Mexicans drafted a notice entitled "Slaughter the Gringo," which called for the death of all *gringos* and Germans, excluding African Americans, Italians, and Cubans. The "Slaughter the Gringo" notice served as an important precursor to events occurring in southern Texas between 1915 and 1917.

South Texas became the cite of a massive shift to commercialized farming after 1900 that had social and economic reverberations for decades thereafter. Before this period, this region was primarily a ranch society and the economy revolved around livestock raising. By 1904, technological advances such as dry farming techniques, irrigation systems, and refrigerated railcars made intensive farming possible in this semiarid region. As a result, land prices sky-rocketed and many struggling Mexican ranchers sold their lands to primarily white farmers. Before this agricultural revolution, Mexican workers were employed as *vaqueros,* or cowboys. After 1904, the only work for Mexican laborers in South Texas was as migrant farm workers, tenant farmers, or sharecroppers.

The growth of commercial agriculture in South Texas had other implications for Mexican workers. Many Mexicans coming to Texas after 1910 were from northern Mexico, a region primarily dominated by mining and ranching interests. The mines paid relatively high wages because of their remote location, the various dangers involved with mining, and the fact that North Mexico was sparsely populated. The Mexican Revolution, however, led to the physical destruction of many of the mines, forcing mine workers to find work elsewhere. The mine workers were soon followed by *vaqueros* in their exodus to Texas because the entire ranching economy was symbiotically linked to mining; essentially, the ranches of North Mexico provided food and leather goods for the mining operations. Both the miners and *vaqueros* could have chosen to go south, but then they would have likely become debt peons on the numerous *haciendas,* or landed estates, which predominated in Central and South Mexico. This was a fate that many Mexican workers had sought to avoid in the first place by relocating to North Mexico. Their only other option was to cross the northern border where they thought a thriving ranching society was to be found. Instead they were to become a landless peasantry in a system far worse than the Mexican *hacienda.*

Haciendas in South Mexico and Mexican-owned ranches in North Mexico and South Texas had one thing in common—paternalistic work arrangements that somewhat mitigated the conditions faced by peons and *vaqueros.* The agricultural revolution beginning in Texas created a decided shift away from paternalistic relations. The introduction of transplanted farm societies from the Midwest and North led to massive dislocations, and Mexican laborers in Texas effectively transformed into a proletariat. Paternalism would no longer be a mitigating factor in their lives; instead the cold and calculating science of capitalism would dictate their existence. In addition, this massive transformation had a racial character that inevitably drove an even deeper social wedge between Mexicans and whites.

It is in this context that the events occurring in Texas between 1915 and 1917 can be best understood. During this time period, the valley and border regions of southern Texas became a virtual combat zone. In January 1915, Basilio Ramos Jr. was captured and subsequently charged with conspiracy to levy war against the United States. On his person was found a document that is now known as the "Plan de San Diego." Similar in language to the "Slaughter the Gringo" notice, this plan called for the death of all white males over the age of 16 and the creation of the "Liberating Army for Races and Peoples," which was to be composed of Latinos, African Americans, and Japanese. The plan is considered irredentist by many historians because it called for the independence of Texas, New Mexico, Arizona, Colorado, and Upper California, the same regions that the drafters of the plan stated were robbed during the 1836 Texas Revolution and the 1846–1848 Mexican War.

This movement was far beyond simple irredentism, however, because another provision of the plan called for the distribution of land to Native Americans and African Americans upon successful completion of the revolution. These lands would be set up as independent republics that would be annexed by Mexico only if it was expedient. The plan was to begin on February 20, 1915, but nothing of note happened until July. Between July and October 1915, the entire Lower Rio Grande Valley region was disrupted by a serious of raids and attacks. The attackers burned bridges, derailed trains, cut telegraph and phone lines, sabotaged irrigation pumping plants, and attacked Texas Rangers and U.S. Army personnel stationed throughout the region. By August 1915, this primarily rural struggle was beginning to gain support among Mexicans in urban areas. In San Antonio, for example, 28 Mexicans were arrested after showing sympathy for the rebellion.

White backlash to the plan resulted in even more racial violence in 1915. Mexicans suspected of engaging in raids were executed without due process and lynchings became an everyday occurrence. In July 1915, two Mexicans were shot to death by law enforcement agents in Mercedes. In August, a Mexican man was lynched near San Benito. In September, 14 Mexicans were shot and their bodies were publicly displayed as a warning to sympathizers of the "Plan de San Diego." This backlash resulted in the exodus of thousands of Mexicans from the border area. Many were forced to leave because Texas Rangers and white vigilante groups confiscated their weapons and ordered them to move to towns were they could be better controlled. It is estimated that well over a hundred Mexicans were killed in 1915 alone. As a result of the white backlash, the hostilities intensified again by May 1916, as sympathizers of the plan engaged in more disruptive and destructive activities. In response to the 1916 raids, the U.S. government ordered virtually all armed forces ready for combat duty to be stationed along the Lower Rio Grande. This act brought an end to the raids, but similar hostilities persisted in southern Texas throughout much of the 20th century.

See also: Lynching; Mexican War; White Mob Violence

Walter C. Rucker

Bibliography

Acuna, Rodolfo. *Occupied America: A History of Chicanos.* New York: Harper Collins Publishers, 1988.

Barr, Alwyn. *Black Texans: A History of Negroes in Texas, 1528–1971.* Austin, TX: The Pemberton Press, 1973.

Montejano, David. *Anglos and Mexicans in the Making of Texas, 1836–1986.* Austin: University of Texas Press, 1987.

Rosenbaum, Robert J. *Mexicano Resistance in the Southwest: The Sacred Right of Self-Preservation.* Austin: University of Texas Press, 1981.

Plessy v. Ferguson

In *The Souls of Black Folk* (1903), W. E. B. Du Bois wrote that the principle problem of the 20th century will be that of the color line. Being black was "strange" largely because of the estrangement between the races in America. The "color line" was drawn in bold by *Plessy v. Ferguson*, 163 U.S. 537 (1896). By keeping the Jim Crow status quo, *Plessy* deepened the racial divide. This is the notorious "separate but equal" case. Although not part of the decision *verbatim*, these three words, which accurately express the legal fiction of the Supreme Court's ruling, gave legal sanction to Jim Crow segregation. Thus "separate but equal" equals "Jim Crow affirmed."

This opinion is couched in legal language that requires an understanding of constitutional law to decode. The high court held that the separation of the races within states does not violate the Fourteenth Amendment, which had previously granted African Americans equal protection under the laws. The technical terms notwithstanding, the Court's purport was patent. In black and white, Justice Henry Billings Brown kept blacks from whites. This bad result was "good law" for nearly six decades. It would take *Brown v. the Board of Education*, 347 U.S. 483 (1954) to overrule Justice Brown. If, except for the *Dred Scott* case, *Plessy* was the worst Supreme Court ruling ever handed down, as Justice Harlan indicated in his dissent, then the *Brown* decision may rank as the greatest Supreme Court decision. To appreciate the greatness of *Brown v. Board of Education*, it is necessary to understand *Plessy* first.

Democracy is a process of progressive equalizing. It is a matter of degree. Mollified by democratic language and reasoning, nevertheless *Plessy* is a harsh and fundamentally undemocratic decision. More than undemocratic, it was antidemocratic because *Plessy* may be characterized as an antidemocratic reaction to the then-recent democratic reforms of Reconstruction (1865–1877).

Reconstruction was the nation's first experiment in economic emancipation and interracial democracy. The three Reconstruction Amendments—the Thirteenth, Fourteenth, and Fifteenth Amendments (1865, 1868, and 1870, respectively) established (legally but not factually) civil rights for all Americans. But the experiment failed; or rather, America failed the experiment. The reforms introduced by Reconstruction were being systematically

dismantled in the South. For instance, the promise of "forty acres and a mule" was proclaimed by General William T. Sherman but never delivered by Congress. Reconstruction was progressive; *Plessy* was regressive. *Plessy*, in fact, was the ultimate deconstruction of Reconstruction—the final judicial nail in its historical coffin. Far worse were its social and historical consequences, for the decision legitimized legal segregation. *Plessy* was a pact with the devil of Jim Crow, and it legitimatized the American apartheid of systemic segregation. *Plessy*'s "separate but equal" doctrine was an oxymoron. Yet, as the supreme law of the law, it held sway for well over a half-century. It would take the *Brown* decision to successfully overturn it. *Brown v. Board of Education* exposed the *Plessy* decision as a contradiction, ruling that "separate but equal" is inherently unequal.

The 1890 Louisiana Separate Car Act provided that railway companies in Louisiana would have equal but separate accommodations and facilities for whites and nonwhites. Violation of this act triggered a fine and imprisonment. The local, activist *Comité des Citoyens* (Citizens' Committee) decided to challenge the constitutionality of this law. On June 7, 1892, Homer Adolph Plessy (1863–1925), a "Creole of Color," bought a first-class ticket at the Press Street Depot in New Orleans. This shoemaker, a man in his late twenties, was about to board a train on the East Louisiana Railroad for passage to the city of Covington, which was in St. Tammany Parish (county) in Louisiana. His ticket was for a seat in the first-class carriage, on a train scheduled to depart at 4:15 P.M. The trip was to have taken around two hours in its traverse to Covington, which was 30 miles to the north, on the other side of Lake Pontchartrain, near the Mississippi border. Plessy never reached his physical destination because he had a legal destination in mind. A dignified gentleman donning suit and hat, he quietly took his seat in a compartment reserved for whites only. Upon collecting his ticket, the conductor asked if Plessy were a "colored man." To this query, Plessy answered in the affirmative and the conductor instructed him to go to the coach reserved for nonwhites.

This unruffled admission was not inevitable; it was planned in advance, for Plessy could easily have passed as white. Thus the conductor would probably have believed Plessy had he answered in the negative. Was Plessy white or black? To use the inartful slang of the day, Plessy was an "octoroon" (a person of one-eighth black blood), an accident of "hypodescent" (a peculiar American doctrine that classifies anyone with the least trace of African ancestry as "colored," with all of the legal and social stigmas that would attach to that pejorative classification). Phenotypically, Plessy exhibited none of the physical features associated with his race. There are no extant photographs of Homer Plessy, but the record is clear: he was identifiably a "bi- multi-racial" man, as the Supreme Court acknowledged in its decision. Facially, Plessy was white; racially he was black by the standards of that day. He was the perfect man to challenge the constitutionality of the Louisiana Separate Car Act.

Needless to say, both the conductor and passengers were taken aback. Pursuant to Louisiana law, Conductor J. J. Dowling informed Plessy that he had to move to the "colored car." Reeking of soot and smoke, this Jim Crow car was typically hitched right behind the locomotive. Its seats were wooden, while the first-class seats were cushioned. With adamantine equipoise, Plessy refused. Law enforcement was summoned, and "Detective" Chris C. Cain appeared on the scene. Identifying himself as a private detective, he evidently was deputized and held police rank. In any event, Plessy did not question "Captain" Cain's authority. When directed to leave with Cain, Plessy did so, without incident. Plessy complied with the officer of the law in order to challenge the law itself.

Captain Cain took Plessy to the Fifth Precinct police station on Elysian Fields Avenue. There he was booked for violating the Separate Car Act. His hearing took place on the morning of June 8. Waiving his right to a hearing, Plessy was released on $500 bail, a tidy sum in those days, paid by Paul Bonseigneur, treasurer of the *Comité des Citoyens*. Plessy returned to his home on brick-paved 244 1/2 North Clairborne Avenue in the integrated, middle-class Faubourg Tremé district, where his wife Louise was waiting for him. Plessy resumed his respectable trade of making leather shoes and boots to order in Patricio Brito's shoemaking business in the French Quarter.

The arraignment was set for October 13, nearly five months later. Plessy was to appear before John H. Ferguson, judge of Section "A" of the Criminal District Court, Parish of Orleans. In the case filed as *19117 The State of Louisiana v. Homer Adolph Plessy,* Judge Ferguson heard arguments by 55-year-old James Campbell Walker, a local Creole attorney, and Assistant District Attorney Lionel Adams, who was reputed to be a "crack trial lawyer." Walker had agreed to defend Plessy and took the case for $1,000. Ironically, Homer Plessy and Judge Ferguson had the very same skin

color. After failing in his motion to have the case dismissed, Walker filed a motion to stay the proceedings so that arguments on the constitutionality of the Separate Car Act could be heard. Judge Ferguson then set a date for October 28.

Meanwhile, in his October 14 brief, Walker had argued that the Louisiana statute violated the Thirteenth and Fourteenth Amendments. By requiring him to sit in a Jim Crow car, the state was branding Plessy with a "badge of slavery," although proscribed by the Thirteenth Amendment (1865). The Separate Car Act also offended the Fourteenth Amendment (1868), which forbade any state's abridging the rights of U.S. citizens. The judge then congratulated Walker for the work that was evident in his brief. Judge Ferguson rendered his decision on November 18, finding that there was no evidence that Plessy was not to be provided with equal accommodations and that he was simply denied the freedom of violating a state law. On November 22, Plessy appealed to the Louisiana Supreme Court, which was docketed as case number 11134.

Albion Winegar Tourgée (1838–1905) took over as lead attorney for Plessy, although Walker remained as part of Plessy's legal team. Tourgée argued as before, and with the same result. The brief challenging the constitutionality of the Separate Car Act (collaboratively written by Tourgée and Walker) had 14 paragraphs. After reviewing the statutory language of the Separate Car Act, the Louisiana high court noted a recent decision regarding the act's constitutionality in which they held that the act would be unconstitutional because it ceded too much power and authority to Congress in its duties to regulate commerce and travel between the states. Because Plessy's destination was intrastate, however, the Commerce Clause was not implicated. The court then cited a Supreme Court case known as *Civil Rights Cases,* 109 U.S. 3, in order to dismiss Plessy's Thirteenth Amendment claim.

His Thirteenth Amendment claim having failed, the court then addressed Plessy's alternative pleading—his challenge of the Separate Car Act as a violation of the Fourteenth Amendment. Having cited a number of precedents on which it relied, the court held that the accommodations were, indeed, equal and thus a violation of the Fourteenth Amendment did not occur. Then, in a prescient, almost prophetic pronouncement, the court went on to say that to hold that the requirement of separate, though equal, accommodations in public conveyances violated the Fourteenth Amendment would nullify the statutes establishing separate schools or those prohibiting interracial marriage. All are laws based on difference of race, and if such difference cannot furnish a basis for such legislation in one of these cases it can not in any case. Clearly, had *Plessy* gone the other way, school segregation might have been struck down as unconstitutional far in advance of *Brown v. Board of Education.*

Needless to day, Homer Plessy did not prevail before the Louisiana high court. But that was as it should have been. That way, the case could be appealed all the way to the Supreme Court, which was Plessy's real goal in challenging the constitutionality of the Separate Car Act in the first place. Although the necessary court documents were filed by the end of February 1893, it took more than three years until the matter came before the Court. The case was argued on April 13, 1896, and the Court handed down its decision on May 18, 1896. Albion Winegar Tourgée represented Homer Plessy, with former Solicitor General Samuel F. Phillips serving as co-counsel. (James C. Walker's health prevented him from making the trip to Washington.) Tourgée and Walker had filed one of the two briefs on Plessy's behalf (argued in 23 numbered paragraphs), and Phillips submitted the other. Alexander Porter Morse defended Judge Ferguson against a charge of judicial error, and M. J. Cunningham, attorney general of the State of Louisiana, and Lionel Adams prepared the legal brief on Ferguson's behalf.

"The gist of our case," Tourgée declared in his opening statement, "is the unconstitutionality of the assortment [racial discrimination]; *not* the question of equal accommodation." Space does not permit a detailed analysis of Tourgée's and Walker's constitutional arguments as laid out in their brief, which Charles A. Lofgren analyzes as (1) the Restrictive Rights Argument, and (2) the Affirmative Rights Argument (*The Plessy Case,* pp. 152–64). Nor does space allow for an epitome of Samuel Phillips's three-page brief, which focused solely on the Fourteenth Amendment issue. These briefs, however persuasive, were not determinative.

Justice Henry Billings Brown delivered the opinion of the Court. In *Plessy v. Ferguson,* 163 U.S. 537 (1896), Justice Brown dismissed Plessy's Thirteenth Amendment argument in short order by noting that legal equality and social equality are two distinct issues. The role of the Court was to rule on the former and decline from deciding on the latter, as the question of social equality was clearly outside its purview. The Fourteenth Amendment implicated a different,

albeit related, set of issues. Justice Brown assessed that the main objective of the Fourteenth Amendment was to enforce the absolute equality of the two races before the law. In his view, however, it could not have been intended to abolish distinctions based on color, or to enforce social, as distinguished from political equality, or a commingling of the two races on terms unsatisfactory to either. Thus Brown contended that laws permitting or requiring, their separation in places where they are liable to be brought into contact do not necessarily imply the inferiority of either race to the other, and have been generally, if not universally, recognized as within the competency of the state legislatures in the exercise of their police power.

The Court concluded that the enforced separation of the races, as applied to the internal commerce of the Louisiana, neither abridges the privileges or immunities of African Americans and other people of color, deprives them of their property without due process of law, nor denies them the equal protection of the laws, within the meaning of the Fourteenth Amendment. Nothing could be further from the truth, of course. The Deep South, for all practical purposes, became a dual society. Like oil and water, black and white were not supposed to mix. Yet the metaphor falls short in its symbolic power, for oil and water do not combust, but racial tensions do. The *Plessy* decision could only exacerbate those social tensions. Legal questions aside, social issues had to be addressed. The Court perforce had to speak to the issue of racial prejudice and the role of the law in promoting social equality beyond legal equality (or the fiction of such equality).

Here, besides discounting the Thirteenth Amendment challenge entirely (finding that forced segregation is not a vestige or "badge of servitude"), the Supreme Court completely disavows any social responsibility for the public's general welfare in terms of race relations. By giving legal sanction to Jim Crow laws, the high court was on low moral grounds. Even on purely legal grounds, the decision applies a mere test of reasonableness to the Separate Car Act. Constitutional scholars call the reasonableness standard the "rational basis test" or "rational scrutiny." This is the way that the Supreme Court has typically deferred to "states' rights" in constitutional controversies. Yet this same legal tradition has produced powerful dissenting opinions. Such was the case in *Plessy.*

Justice Harlan's Sidelined: In one of the most celebrated dissents in Supreme Court history, Justice Harlan eloquently took his fellow justices to task for a fundamentally flawed decision. His dissent is all the more remarkable considering the fact that Justice John Marshall Harlan (1833–1911) was "a former slaveholder" from Kentucky (Lofgren 3). Harlan's "color-blind" rhetoric echoes in court chambers, classrooms, and in civic spheres to this very day. But there was simply no jurisprudential framework at that time for asserting an individual's "fundamental rights" over "states' rights."

By modern legal standards, the *Plessy* case should have triggered "strict scrutiny," but, historically, that would be a gross anachronism. Under current equal protection theory, the Supreme Court holds all racial classifications to be constitutionally suspect and subject to strict scrutiny, which is the most stringent form of judicial review. Under strict scrutiny, a race-based law cannot pass constitutional muster absent a compelling state interest that cannot be protected by any less drastic means. But the idea that gave rise to strict scrutiny did not appear until 1938 in *U.S. v. Carolene Products Co.*, 304 U.S. 144, 153 n.4 (1938), where the Supreme Court called for a "more exacting judicial scrutiny" in certain circumstances or cases. Four years later, in *Skinner v. Oklahoma*, 316 U.S. 535 (1942), the Supreme Court coined the term "strict scrutiny" for the first time, to define the new judicial standard that the Court would apply to laws that deprive individuals of their civil rights.

Hardening of the Color Line: On January 11, 1897, more than four-and-a-half years after his arrest, Homer Adolph Plessy found himself before Orleans Parish Criminal District Court once more. On the charge of having violated Section 2 of Act 111 of the Separate Car Act, Plessy pled guilty. He duly paid his fine of $25. Nationally, his case was met with apathy; privately, Plessy faded into obscurity. On Sunday, March 1, 1925 at 5:10 A.M., Plessy died. A local paper reported a two-line notice of his death. But Homer Adolph Plessy is immortal as a symbol of the struggle for equality and racial justice.

W. E. B. Du Bois was right. The color line would be the central problem of the 20th century. *Plessy v. Ferguson* reinforced that color line in stark black and white, even though Homer Plessy and Judge Ferguson each had the same skin color—light brown. In causing racial and legal status to converge, *Plessy*'s "separate but equal" was a "bright line" rule. First, the rule of hypodescent sustains a binary opposition between black and white and defines anyone with a perceptible trace of African ancestry as black. Based on this simple classification scheme, all blacks must be segregated from whites where Jim Crow laws demand it. Homer Plessy was thus the perfect man to put the Separate Car Act to test, for he exposed the absurdity of hypodescent and its legal consequences. Although he was, by legal fiat, black, his skin color was as white as Judge Ferguson, who sat in initial judgment of him. Added to this irony is the fact that, as a gentleman who comported himself with the utmost dignity by aristocratic Southern standards, Homer Plessy exploded the negative stereotype of the "Negro" that the Jim Crow laws were meant to protect against.

Although the Louisiana courts differentiated between racial segregation and racial discrimination, the bottom line remains the same: race segregation is race subordination. History proves this to be true. In a certain sense, historian David Brion Davis was right: the Confederacy won the Civil War ideologically, at least insofar as civil rights were concerned. *Plessy* calcified entrenched Jim Crow laws and gave them Supreme Court sanction. "Rather, whatever the realities of the hardening color line in America," Lofgren concludes, "the formula associated with *Plessy* [separate but equal] could be invoked against the worst deprivations" (*The Plessy Case*, p. 201). Like cracks in glass, the "separate but equal doctrine" spread throughout the Jim Crow states, as transportation segregation reinforced education segregation. Thus it took 58 years before the *Brown* decision overruled Justice Brown's 1896 ruling to erase the color line legally, although not socially. *Plessy v. Ferguson* did not justly resolve the America dilemma of racism, but it did focus legal attention on it. In that sense, *Plessy* was as much of a milestone as it was a setback.

See also: Brown v. Board of Education; Fourteenth Amendment; Jim Crow

Christopher George Buck

Bibliography

Anderson, Wayne. *Plessy v. Ferguson: Legalizing Segregation.* New York: Rosen Publication Group, 2004.

Boxill, Bernard R. "Washington, Du Bois, and *Plessy v. Ferguson.*" *Law and Philosophy* 16, no. 3 (May 1997):299–330.

Elliot, Mark. *Color Blind Justice: Albion Tourgee and the Quest for Racial Equality from the Civil War to Plessy v. Ferguson.* New York: Oxford University Press, 2009.

Fireside, Harvey, and Marc H. Morial. *Separate and Unequal: Homer Plessy and the Supreme Court Decision That Legalized Racism.* New York: Carroll & Graf, 2004.

Lofgren, Charles A. *The Plessy Case: A Legal-Historical Interpretation.* New York: Oxford University Press, 1987.

Medley, Keith Weldon. *We As Freedmen: Plessy v. Ferguson.* Gretna, LA: Pelican Publishers, 2003.

Roback, Jennifer. "The Political Economy of Segregation: The Case of Segregated Streetcars." *Journal of Economic History* 46 (1986):893–917.

Thomas, Brook, ed. *Plessy v. Ferguson: A Brief History with Documents.* Boston: Bedford Books, 1997.

Poitier, Sidney

Sidney Poitier (1927–) was born prematurely in Miami, Florida. His parents, Reginald James and Evelyn Outten Poitier, were impoverished Bahamian tomato farmers. Three months after his birth, Poitier and his family moved to Cat Island in the Bahamas. Because of the family's poverty, Poitier's formal education did not begin until he was 11. By age 12, he had finished his education to help his father work on the fruit farm. Hoping Poitier would have more opportunities, his father sent him to Miami to live with his brother Cyril in 1943. He worked several jobs until the Ku Klux Klan threatened him for failing to deliver a package to the rear door. In fear, he fled to New York and worked as a dishwasher. Unable to pay for housing, Poitier was jailed for vagrancy and eventually found shelter at an orphanage. Looking for a change, he joined the army at age 16 and pretended to be the required age of 18.

A year later, Poitier was discharged and found a job as a dishwasher and janitor in New York. Upon seeing an advertisement for black actors in Harlem's *Amsterdam News,* he auditioned for a role. Because of his thick West Indian accent and poor reading skills, Poitier was rejected. After learning how to read and working on his accent, Poitier reauditioned and was accepted into the American Negro Theater. In 1945, he earned his first role with the American Negro Theater as the understudy of Harry Belafonte in the *Days of Our Youth.* A year later, he made his first starring appearance on Broadway in *Lysistrata.* Poitier stumbled though his lines, but the critics found his foibles humorous. This performance then led to a role in *Anna Lucasta* in 1947 and a tour of the play in 1948.

Poitier took his success on the stage to acting in films in 1949. He started with an appearance in an army documentary called *From Whom Cometh My Help.* A year later, Poitier starred in his first Hollywood production titled *No Way Out.* He expanded his acting credits to include the films *Red Ball Express* (1952), *Go, Man, Go* (1954), and *Blackboard Jungle* (1955). Critics took notice of Poitier and praised his emotional range, especially in his performance of *Cry, the Beloved Country* in 1955. Poitier's acting accomplishments then led to a host of laudable performances in *Goodbye, My Lady* (1956), *Band of Angels* (1957), *Something of Value* (1957), *Edge of the City* (1957), *The Defiant Ones* (1958), *Mark of the Hawk* (1958), *Virgin Island* (1958), and *Porgy and Bess* (1959).

In-between acting, Poitier found time to marry Juanita Marie Hardy, a dancer, in 1950. After having four children, they divorced in 1965. In 1976, Poitier married Joanna Shimkus, an actress, and they later had two daughters. Poitier returned to the theater in 1959 and played the lead role in Lorraine Hansberry's *A Raisin in the Sun.* In 1960, he appeared in the acclaimed film version. Poitier continued his notable roles in *All the Young Men* (1960), *Paris Blues* (1961), and *Pressure Point* (1962). In 1963, he won an Academy Award for his performance in *Lilies of the Field* and became the first African American actor to win in the category of leading actor. He followed this performance with impressive work in *The Long Ships* (1964), *The Greatest Story Ever Told* (1965), *A Patch of Blue* (1965), and *To Sir, With Love* (1967). Poitier's most significant roles came with his next two films *Guess Who's Coming to Dinner* (1967) and *In the Heat of the Night* (1967). Both roles promoted equal treatment of blacks and social integration. He later turned to television movies and played Supreme Court Justice Thurgood Marshall in *Separate but Equal* in 1991 and Nelson Mandela in *Mandela and de Klerk* in 1997.

After finding success in acting, Poitier turned his attention to directing. His debut came with *Buck and the Preacher* in 1972. This western movie showed the significance of African Americans in the West's development and featured black heroes. Poitier's second directorial film, *A Warm December* (1973), had nominal success. He rebounded in 1974 with *Uptown Saturday Night.* The popular film showcased the talents of Bill Cosby, Harry Belafonte, Flip Wilson, and Richard Pryor. He later reteamed with Bill Cosby in *A Piece of Action* (1977) and *Ghost Dad* (1990). In 1980, he directed Richard Pryor in the hit *Stir Crazy.* His later directing projects, *Shoot to Kill* (1998) and *Little Nikita* (1988), also received some praise.

Poitier reflected on his successful career in his 1980 autobiography *This Life.* He wrote another memoir in 2000 titled *The Measure of a Man: A Spiritual Autobiography* and won a Grammy Award for the text's reading in 2001. Poitier has also been the recipient of several other accolades, including the Kennedy Center Honors Lifetime Achievement Award in 1995, the NAACP's Hall of Fame Award in 2001, and the Academy of Motion Pictures Honorary Award in 2002. He continues to be a revered figure in the acting community and participant in the NAACP and the Martin Luther King Jr. Center for Nonviolent Social Change.

See also: Belafonte, Harry; Cosby; Bill; King, Martin Luther Jr.; Marshall, Thurgood; National Association for the Advancement of Colored People; Pryor; Richard

Dorsia Smith Silva

Bibliography
Goudsouzian, Aram. *Sidney Poitier: Man, Actor, Icon.* Chapel Hill: University of North Carolina Press, 2004.
Keyser, Lester J. *The Cinema of Sidney Poitier: The Black Man's Changing Role on the American Screen.* San Diego: A. S. Barnes, 1980.

Poor People's Campaign

The Poor People's Campaign was a movement organized and led by the Southern Christian Leadership Conference (SCLC) and its director, Dr. Martin Luther King Jr. It was intended to dramatize the plight of the nation's poor and address economic injustice. The plan was to bring thousands of poor people of all races to Washington, D.C., where they would engage in radical nonviolent direct action in order to convince Congress and President Lyndon B. Johnson to make eliminating poverty the number one goal of the nation.

The masses of African Americans appeared to be untouched by the most sweeping legislation guaranteeing civil rights since Reconstruction. In 1965, almost one-third of African Americans lived below the poverty line, and half of all black households lived in substandard dwellings. Indeed, the percentage of poor blacks had actually increased between 1959 and 1965. The unemployment rate for blacks was almost double that of whites; for black teenagers, it was more than twice that for white teens. The crumbling infrastructure of inner-city neighborhoods was further eroded by so-called urban renewal; the employment situation was exacerbated by the movement of jobs

to the suburbs. The high school dropout rate soared, drug abuse became rampant, and fragile families were further strained.

Northern urban communities with thousands of poor, black residents were also fertile ground for the nascent Black Power movement. The nonviolent direct action that had been so successful in the past held no appeal for the hundreds of thousands of blacks who were trapped there with little to no opportunity for improvement. Nor had the War on Poverty, developed by the administration of President Lyndon B. Johnson to eradicate poverty in America, been much help. Although noble, its efforts were too little, and it was opposed by powerful politicians at the local level and whites who felt Johnson was giving handouts to the undeserving poor. The poor, their hopes raised by community action programs and maximum feasible participation, again found their hopes unanswered. As such, the cities became simmering cauldrons of frustration, alienation, and hopelessness that exploded in 1965.

Every summer from 1965 through 1969, northern cities were visited by urban rebellions, sometimes referred to as race riots. The Los Angeles neighborhood of Watts was the first of these on August 11, 1965. Six days of rioting reduced Watts to rubble, claimed 34 lives, and recorded property damage of $35 million. Urban rebellions also occurred in 1966, but arguably the worst year of the phenomenon was 1967. A total of 59 riots occurred, the deadliest being in Newark, New Jersey and Detroit, Michigan. The Newark rebellion left 27 dead, including children, a police officer, and a fire fighter, and caused millions of dollars in damage. Conditions in Detroit were so bad that 43 blacks were killed. Not even 800 state and city police and the National Guard could restore order. President Lyndon Johnson was forced to send in the 82nd and 101st Airborne to restore order.

After the Newark and Detroit riots, Johnson established the National Advisory Commission on Civil Disorders, commonly known as the Kerner Commission after its leader, Governor Otto Kerner of Illinois. Johnson recognized that the only way to end the despair of the masses of blacks was a sustained government program designed to end joblessness, substandard housing, poverty, and disease. The Kerner Commission report surprisingly blamed white racism as the chief cause of the riots and warned that America was once again becoming a dual society, one black and one white.

Poor People's March in Washington, D.C., on June 18, 1968. (Library of Congress)

King and the SCLC were keenly aware that the times called for bold measures. He recognized that the campaign would be different from those implemented during the Civil Rights movement; it was demanding nothing less than a wholesale transformation of American capitalism. Moreover, King intended to force the nation to choose between eliminating poverty, which he saw as a moral issue, and continuing an increasingly unpopular war in Vietnam, against which he had become a vocal critic. To him the two were inextricably linked.

The Poor People's Campaign had three stages. First, it would crisscross the nation putting together a group of several thousand black, Latino, Native American, and white Appalachian poor people who would travel to Washington to live in a shanty town much like that erected by the Bonus Army of the early 20th century. They would participate in daily demonstrations in the capital and be joined by parallel demonstrations in cities across the country. These would be crowned by a mass march echoing the 1963 March on Washington. Second, the demonstrations would engender mass arrests as they had in the South, further dramatizing the plight of the poor. Finally, there would be an economic boycott of the most powerful businesses in America. The Poor People's Campaign would show that all the gains of the Civil Rights movement were hollow without economic parity and opportunity. It would either be a brilliant success or a humiliating failure.

King and the SCLC were instantly attacked by the media, the political Left, and white Americans who were weary of the struggle for equality. Leaders of the other civil rights organizations also criticized King, not only for the campaign, but for his stinging and public rebuke of the Vietnam War. Most of organized labor refused to support the effort. Finally, President Lyndon Johnson turned against King, too, and he lost the warm working relationship they had developed. But King pressed on.

His empathy for and support of the poor took him to Memphis, Tennessee, where he marched in solidarity with city garbage collectors who were seeking a living wage and better working conditions. On April 4, he was assassinated.

Coretta Scott King, his widow, and the SCLC decided to continue the Poor People's Campaign under the leadership of the Reverend Ralph Abernathy, the close friend and confidant of King. From May 14 to June 24, more than 2,500 poor people lived in a shanty town they had erected and named Resurrection City. The camp boasted a city hall, cultural capital, a medical facility, dining hall, psychiatrist, a university, and zip code. It fanned out across the Reflecting Pool to the base of the Lincoln Memorial. Residents policed themselves and provided a model for interracial cooperation. Thousands of them fanned out daily across locations in the capital to shame the U.S. government into significant action against poverty.

Unfortunately, conditions in the camp quickly turned miserable. Washington was unusually cool that year in May and June, and it rained 28 of the 42 days of the operation. Residents were soon knee deep in mud, trash, and rotting food. On June 4, Senator Robert F. Kennedy, who had become a champion of the poor and was running for the Democratic nomination for president, was assassinated. Finally, it was clear that the leadership of Dr. King was sorely missed; Reverend Ralph Abernathy lacked the charisma and contacts of Dr. King. and he spent little time at the camp, appearing to prefer the comfort of the black-owned Pitts Hotel to the muddy squalor of Resurrection City. By the middle of June, fewer than 300 people remained in the camp.

Fighting and near-riots broke out in the camp on June 22. Police were called in, but police dogs and more than a thousand tear gas grenades failed to stem the trouble. On June 24, about 1,000 police closed Resurrection City, arresting Reverend Abernathy and 175 people. Charges of assault against police officers, disorderly conduct, curfew violations, and public drunkenness were levied against those arrested. The Poor People's Campaign failed to persuade public officials to pour more resources into eliminating poverty, and it was deemed a failure and the end of the Civil Rights movement.

Recent scholarship, however, has reevaluated the campaign and somewhat redeemed its reputation. The Poor People's Campaign ignited the third wave of the Civil Rights movement: economic empowerment. The interracial structure of the effort showed that a strong alliance based on class was not only important but necessary. Indeed, the Reverend Jesse Jackson would bring this alliance to fruition with his emphasis on a Rainbow Coalition during his 1988 presidential campaign. The Poor People's Campaign highlighted the weaknesses of runaway capitalism and consumerism in a manner not seen since the Great Depression.

See also: Abernathy, Ralph David; Jackson, Jesse; Johnson, Lyndon Baines; King, Martin Luther Jr.; Southern Christian Leadership Conference; War on Poverty

Marilyn K. Howard

Bibliography
Freeman, Roland L. *Mule Train: A Journey of Hope Remembered.* Nashville, TN: Thomas Nelson. 1998.
Honey, Michael. *Going Down Jericho Road: The Memphis Strike, Martin Luther King's Last Campaign.* New York: W. W. Norton, 2007.
McKnight, Gerald. *The Last Crusade: Martin Luther King, Jr., the FBI and the Poor People's Campaign.* New York: Westview Press. 1998.

Populist Party

The populist movement was a revolt by farmers in the South and Midwest against the Democrats and Republicans for ignoring their interests and difficulties. In the 1880s, a drought had caused the farmers to experience crop failures, falling prices, debt, and lack of credit facilities. The farmers organized the National Farmers' Alliance and the Colored Farmers' Alliance in an attempt to remedy their problems. They achieved regional victories but were of little influence nationally. In the 1890s, the agrarian interests refocused their energies and reorganized their efforts by forming the Populist Party. The Populist Party, also known as the People's Party, evolved from the Grange, Greenback Party, and Farmers' Alliances and campaigned to have the federal government buffer economic depressions, regulate banking and corporations, and provide assistance to the suffering farmers.

In 1892, the Populist Party held its first national convention. Delegates met in Omaha, Nebraska and nominated James B. Weaver as its presidential candidate and James G. Field as its vice presidential candidate. The Omaha Platform endorsed free coinage of silver, a graduated income tax, the secret (Australian) ballot, direct election of senators, a single term for the president and vice president, government ownership and operation of railroads, and an eight-hour working day. Weaver, a former Union army general and Iowa congressman, and Field, a Virginia ex-Confederate general, collected more than 1 million popular votes. The voters also elected several Populist Party congressmen,

three governors, and hundreds of minor officials and legislators. Most of the party's strength came from the agrarian
areas of the Midwest, but poor Southerners also showed a
strong support for the party.

Poverty was a common denominator among blacks
and whites, and the party leaders envisioned a program
that would benefit both races and be injurious to neither.
The party's success had depended on black cooperation,
and party leaders made concessions to gain the support it
needed. In some ways the party broke down racial barriers.
In the South, the populist movement approached the blacks
for support and forged a common cause between poor
whites and blacks. In Georgia, Tom Watson led the Populist Party revolt against the Democrats by promising black
voters that the party would respect their civil and political
rights. Blacks participated in the party, not just as figurehead appointments but at the innermost levels. They were
elected to local and national party committees and served
as delegates to the national conventions. They campaigned
to mixed audiences and spoke from the same platforms
as white campaigners. Populist Party sheriffs made sure
blacks were represented on jury duty and populist newspapers praised the achievements of black citizens. In Texas,
the party tried to build a coalition of black and white voters but was unable to persuade the majority of Texas blacks
to abandon the Republican Party. Throughout the South,
conservatives dominated politics and feared Negro domination. The conservatives began making efforts to defeat
the populists by buying black votes and intimidating black
voters. Eventually the Black Populists became apathetic and
factionalized.

In 1896, the Populist Party fused with the Democrats
after William Jennings Bryan, a free-silver candidate, was
defeated in his bid for the presidency. The Populist Party
gradually disappeared as a political force. By 1900, the
party was no longer politically effective, and by 1908, it had
ceased to exist.

See also: Colored Farmers Alliance

Nancy A. McCaslin

Bibliography
Brexel, Bernadette. *The Populist Party: A Voice for the Farmers
in the Industrialized Society.* New York: Rosen Publishing
Group, 2003.
Goodwyn, Lawrence. *The Populist Moment: A Short History of the
Agrarian Revolt in America.* Oxford, UK: Oxford University
Press, 1978.

Powell, Adam Clayton Jr.

Adam Clayton Powell Jr. (1908–1972) was born in New
Haven, Connecticut, on November 29, 1908. He rose to
prominence in the early 1930s and 1940s as a preacher,
civil rights activist, and national politician. Powell's family
moved to New York City, where his father, Adam Clayton
Powell Sr., served as the 17th pastor of Abyssinian Baptist
Church in Harlem. As a child, Adam Clayton Powell Jr.,
attended New York City public schools. He earned a BA
in 1930 from Colgate University, and in 1932 he received
an MA in religious education from Columbia University
Teachers College. The next year Powell married Harlem's
Cotton Club chorus line dancer, Isabel Washington.

Shortly after graduating from Columbia, Powell served
as an associate pastor at his father's church, where he developed a charismatic preaching style. He assisted his father in
alleviating the economic strain of the Great Depression on
the black community in Harlem by organizing soup kitchens, distributing clothing to the poor, and finding jobs for
the unemployed. On November 1, 1937, Powell succeeded
his father as pastor of Abyssinian. During his early tenure
as pastor, Powell substantially increased the size of the
congregation through community outreach and inspired
preaching.

During the New Deal, Powell used his status to improve
the employment situation of African Americans in New
York City. In the late 1930s, he cofounded the Greater New
York Coordinating Committee for Fair Employment. This
organization consisted of various professional groups, including black fraternities and sororities, black nationalists,
and Communists. Powell's organization protested against
antiblack hiring practices throughout the city in public utilities, such as the electric and telephone companies.

In the 1930s, Powell also helped organize rent strikes
and public boycotts led to the hiring and promotion of African American employees in restaurants and department
stores in Harlem, the New York City bus company, the
public utilities, Harlem Hospital, and officials at the 1939
World's Fair. Along with his community activism, from
1936 to 1944, Powell cofounded and published the radical
weekly newspaper, *The People's Voice.* The paper served as a
platform for Powell to inform the African American community about his crusade for better housing, schools, and
employment opportunities.

In the early 1940s, Powell became a professional politician and represented Harlem by winning a seat in 1941 on the New York City Council. While serving on the council, Powell continued his campaign against racial discrimination, bringing attention to employment discrimination at the telephone company and city colleges. Between 1942 and 1944, he also served as a member of the New York State, Consumer Division, Office of Price Administration. From 1942–1945, he was a member of the Manhattan Civilian Defense. He used his growing political clout to speak at rallies, in support of World War II and use those speaking opportunities to denounce racial segregation in the military.

In 1945, Powell was elected on the Democratic ticket to serve in the House of Representatives, representing Harlem's 22nd Congressional district. Powell became the first black congressman from New York. In the same year, he divorced Isabel and married popular pianist and actress, Hazel Scott, who gave birth to his first child, Adam Clayton Powell III, in 1946.

A prominent civil rights spokesman, Adam Clayton Powell Jr. was elected to the U.S. House of Representatives from New York in 1945 and became chair of the Education and Labor Committee in 1961. (Library of Congress)

On his arrival in Washington, Powell continued his civil rights campaign. Although Powell was only one of two African American congressional representatives, he successfully challenged de facto segregation on Capitol Hill. Black representatives were then prohibited from using Capitol dining areas, which were reserved only for the white Congressional leaders. Powell, however, would bring Harlem residents to eat with him in these restaurants. Powell also confronted the racial bigotry of staunch segregationists like John E. Rankin of Mississippi on the floor of the House of Representatives.

In the House, Powell would attach an antidiscrimination clause to significant pieces of legislation. His clause eventually became referred to as the Powell Amendment. In 1955, he attended the historic Bandung Conference of Asian and African nations in Bandung, Indonesia. These formerly colonized countries met to discuss ways in which to promote cultural and economic cooperation and to oppose U.S. and European colonialism. On Powell's return to the United States, he urged President Dwight D. Eisenhower to support the emerging, but less developed, countries. During the same decade, Powell began to experience legal problems and in the mid-1950s, he stood trial for tax evasion and fraud. After a hung jury, the Department of Justice decided not to retry the case.

In 1960, Powell divorced and married for the final time. This time he wed Yvette Diago, and she bore him a second son, Adam Clayton Diago Powell. In addition to a new marriage, Powell became chairman of the prestigious and powerful Labor and Education Committee in 1961. During that decade, as a supporter of President Lyndon B. Johnson's Great Society program, Powell's committee passed dozens of measures that authorized federal programs to improve education and training for the deaf, provide college student loans and public school lunches, and increase the minimum wage, thus expanding opportunities for all Americans, including African Americans.

Powell's legal and professional troubles continued into the 1960s. Colleagues accused him of misappropriating his committee's budget, taking trips overseas at tax payers' expense, and missing congressional sessions and committee meetings. He was also criticized for refusing to pay a slander judgment to a Harlem constituent, Ester James. In 1967, the House Democratic Caucus removed Powell as committee chairman. The House also declined to return him to his seat until the federal government investigated the allegations against him.

In June 1969, the Supreme Court ruled that the House had unconstitutionally excluded Powell from Congress, and he returned to his seat in the 90th Congress, but without any seniority or back pay. In the summer of 1970, Charles B. Rangel defeated Powell in the Democratic primary in Powell's district in New York City. Powell then tried and failed to make the November ballot as an independent candidate. In 1971, he resigned as pastor of Abyssinian Baptist and permanently retired to the Bahamian island of Bimini. On April 4, 1972, he died at the age of 63 of complications from prostate cancer at Jackson Memorial Hospital in Miami, Florida. His body was cremated and his ashes scattered over the Caribbean around Bimini.

See also: Johnson, Lyndon Baines; Kennedy, John Fitzgerald; Rustin, Bayard

Dwayne A. Mack

Bibliography

Hamilton, Charles V. *Adam Clayton Powell, Jr.: The Political Biography of an American Dilemma.* New York: Atheneum, 1991.

Haygood, Will. *King of the Cats: The Life and Times of Adam Clayton Powell, Jr.* New York: Houghton Mifflin, 1993.

Powell, Adam Clayton, Jr. *Adam by Adam: The Autobiography of Adam Clayton Powell, Jr.* New York: Dial Press, 1971.

Powell, Adam Clayton, Jr. *Marching Blacks: An Interpretive History of the Rise of the Black Common Man.* New York: Dial Press, 1945.

Powell, Colin

Colin Powell (1937–) is a distinguished black military and political luminary and a prominent Republican, whose commitment to help his community and to serve his country make him one of the most respected public figures in the annals of American and African American history. Powell was born in South Bronx, New York City. His parents, Luther and Maud Powell, migrated from Jamaica and worked in the Manhattan garment industry. Growing up in a multicultural social environment, Powell attended local public schools and the City College of New York.

Powell joined the army in 1959 as a second lieutenant. After his training at second infantry school, he commanded a platoon at Fulda Gap, West Germany. At Fort Devens, Alabama, Powell met Alma Johnson, whom he married in 1962. In the same year he went to South Vietnam for his first tour as a military adviser and earned his first Purple Heart and a Bronze Star for his distinguished service.

As a young black captain in Georgia, Powell was insulted because of his race and for being a serviceman in Vietnam. He was refused services at a hotdog stand. He had a similar experience at a restaurant in Birmingham, Alabama. He had to go to the back door where African Americans came to place their order. In 1966, Powell went for his second tour in South Vietnam. He was stationed at Chu Lui and then assigned as a military planner under General Charles M. Gettys. In this tour he was injured in a helicopter crash. Despite his broken ankle, Powell saved the entire crew from the wreckage. For this heroic act in a noncombat situation, he received the second Purple Heart and the Soldier's Medal for bravery.

After he returned from Vietnam, he earned his masters degree in business administration in 1971 from George Washington University. The next year he worked for the Office of Management and Budget at the White House. In the 1980s, Ronald Reagan appointed him to his cabinet as the national security adviser. His biggest moment came when he was appointed the chairman of the Joint Chiefs-of-Staff in 1989, the very year in which he conducted an invasion of Panama. Two years later, Powell was given a second term as the Joint Chiefs-of-Staff. During this time he directed Operation Desert Storm in 1991. Powell split openly with the Congressional Black Caucus over the use of force during the Persian Gulf War.

Along the lines of these black representatives in Congress, Reverend Jesse Jackson believed that Powell was guilty of associating with the Reagan and Bush administration even though he was aware that their policies impeded African Americans' social and economic progress. Because of Powell's association with the Republican Party, Joseph Lowery, the president of the Southern Christian Leadership Conference (SCLC) protested against Powell's presence at the King Week parade in Atlanta that celebrated the birthday of Martin Luther King Jr.

In 1993, Powell retired from army after 35 years of distinguished service. Remembering his segregated past in the army, two years before his retirement, in his address to the Twentieth Annual Convention of the Tuskegee Airmen in Detroit, he expressed his gratitude to those black men and women who served under the racially separated system.

Powell's failure to criticize Washington's policy of putting disproportionate numbers of black men and women in harm's way and his reconciliation in the Los Angles Riots in 1992, after the beating of Rodney King, infuriated the NAACP and civil rights leaders. They blamed him for siding with the white community. Even though he was not forthcoming in criticizing the racial atmosphere in the army, Powell, in his capacity as a military leader, demonstrated his commitment to help young black men and women succeed in the armed forces.

Powell was well respected in the black community for his philanthropic activities as the chairman of the nonprofit America's Promise foundation and for his fight for active government involvement in protecting the Civil Rights Act of 1964, ensuring constitutional protection for all Americans. On December 16, 2001, the Bush administration nominated Powell secretary of state. He was the first African American to hold the highest position in the state department and the highest-ranking black official in any U.S. administration. He was regarded as a moderate voice on several issues in the Bush administration, notably on Iraq. Powell urged caution and at times seemed at odds with his cabinet colleagues. His views in favor of involving the UN and giving Iraq a last chance to disarm eventually prevailed.

Even though a loyal Republican, Powell was extremely critical of the party's record on racism, and he advised Republicans to get rid of its southern strategy of pandering to certain constituencies at the expense of black voters. In the 2000 Republican Convention, he challenged the party to live up to the language of reconciliation, to adopt policies that lead to inclusiveness, and to provide minorities the opportunity to rise up the social ladder. In 2008, Powell openly supported and voted for Democratic presidential candidate Barack Obama, and, for this decision, he has been criticized by conservatives like Rush Limbaugh and Dick Cheney. Powell's passionate beliefs in family and his heartfelt love for the country made him a shining star in the galaxy of prominent Americans. Whether it was the humiliation inflicted on him as a black serviceman traveling in the Deep South or as an African American in the dangerous thickets of Vietnam, Powell survived the challenges. He stands as an inspiring example for future generations of Americans and more importantly for African Americans and immigrants.

See also: Clinton, William Jefferson; Congressional Black Caucus; Obama, Barack

Sivananda Mantri

Bibliography

Harari, Oren. *The Leadership Secrets of Colin Powell.* New York: R. R. Donnelleys Sons, 2002.

Means, Howard. *Colin Powell: Soldier/ Statesman-Statesman/ Soldier.* New York: Donald I. Fine, 1992.

Powell, Colin L., and Joseph E. Persico. *My American Journey.* New York: Random House, 1995.

Roth, David. *Sacred Honor: Colin Powell: The Inside Account of His Life and Triumphs.* Grand Rapids, MI: Zondervan Publishing House, 2003.

Wukowits, John F. *The People in News.* San Diego, CA: Lucent Books, 2000.

Pratt, Geronimo Ji Jaga

Geronimo Ji Jaga Pratt, former deputy minister of the Los Angeles branch of the Black Panther Party, spent 27 years in jail for the alleged murder of Caroline Olsen and the shooting of her husband, Kenneth, in 1968. Two black men allegedly attacked Caroline and Kenneth Oslen on a tennis court in December 1968. Three years later, Kenneth Oslen positively identified Geroniomo Pratt as one of the assailants, from a photo given to him by the Los Angeles Police Department. Pratt was the fourth black man whom Oslen had identified.

Ji Jaga maintained his innocence throughout his incarceration. He always proclaimed that he was 400 miles away at a Black Panther Party meeting in Oakland at the time of the murder. Ji Jaga was apprehended in 1970 and charged with kidnapping and murder.

Ji Jaga was raised in Louisiana where he claimed to have witnessed lynchings and intimidation by groups such as the Ku Klux Klan. He later joined the army and was a highly decorated Vietnam veteran who served two combat tours in Vietnam. In total he earned 18 medals including two Purple Hearts.

On leaving the army he moved to Los Angeles and enrolled at UCLA. Within months of his arrival, Ji Jaga met Alprentice "Bunchy" Carter who was the founder of the local Black Panther Party (BPP) branch. In 1969, Carter and fellow BPP member John Huggins were murdered at Campbell Hall at UCLA in a dispute with US Organization members. George and Ali Stiner along with Claude Hubert of the US Organization were arrested, convicted, and sent to San Quentin prison for their involvement.

After Carter's death, BPP members found a tape Carter had previously recorded that instructed the Los Angeles

BPP to make Ji Jaga minister of defense. This made Ji Jaga a key member of the organization. Ji Jaga's combat experience and skills also became crucial as federal agencies led by the FBI targeted the BPP.

In the 1960s, the BPP and other revolutionary, leftist, and progressive organizations and individuals were targeted by the FBI's COINTELRPO (Counter Intelligence Program). Operations against the Panthers included continuing harassment by police agencies, misinformation supplied to Panthers to encourage tension among the ranks, and also deadly assaults like the 1969 December 4 raid in Chicago that killed Fred Hampton and Mark Clark. Four days later, the LAPD SWAT squad invaded the Los Angeles Panthers headquarters; however, the building had been fortified under the instructions of Ji Jaga, which prevented the police from gaining full access to the building.

As the Panthers held out inside the building, masses gathered around the police line, forcing the police to retreat. Six Panthers were wounded, 13 were arrested, but because of their successful self-defense, no Panthers were killed that night. The arrested Panthers were charged with assaulting the police and Ji Jaga spent two months in jail. All charges against the Panthers were later dropped.

When news of this event broke out, the FBI set out to "neutralize" Ji Jaga. On a nationwide tour, Ji Jaga was hounded by police surveillance and COINTELPRO disinformation designed to foster distrust against him within the BPP. In June 1970, the FBI sent out a memorandum on Ji Jaga along with his picture to FBI offices in New York, New Haven, Atlanta, Chicago, Sacramento, San Diego, and San Francisco.

This plot would result in his conviction for the robbery and murder of Caroline Olsen. The murder case was based on three primary contingencies. First was the ability of the key prosecution witness (Julius Butler) to convince the jury that he had heard Ji Jaga confess to the crime despite being a paid informant for the FBI and the LAPD. The district attorney convinced the jury that he was not simply a "snitch" or a paid informant. Second was the ability of the key prosecutor to conceal facts from the jury proved pivotal. On this note, the jury was never informed about the facts that Butler was a paid informant and that Kenneth Olsen had identified someone else as his wife's killer in a lineup. Third was the ability of the FBI to suppress any evidence in its possession that would support Ji Jaga's alibi that he was in Oakland at the time of the murder. All of this combined led to Ji Jag spending 27 years in jail.

Elmer "Geronimo" Pratt (photo taken in 1971) was a member of the Black Panther Party in Los Angeles. (AP Photo)

Ji Jaga was designated a prisoner of conscience by Amnesty International. Amnesty International first called for a full federal inquiry into Pratt's case in a report published in October 1981. The organization also called on the governor of California to conduct an inquiry into the case in 1988. Over the years Ji Jaga and his defense team led by Johnnie Cochran filed a series of unsuccessful appeals against his conviction. In 1996, the defense was eventually allowed an evidentiary hearing based on new evidence that included information showing that Julius Butler was listed as a confidential informant in the state prosecutor's files at the time of Ji Jaga's initial trial.

Even after revelations about the FBI's COINTELPRO program in the late 1970s confirmed that Butler had been a police spy, Los Angeles authorities continued to oppose any retrial of Ji Jaga. According to the memoirs of former FBI agent Wesley Swearingen, the FBI also had a wiretap of the BPP headquarters in Los Angeles during the period that Caroline Olsen was killed. These wiretap logs showed that Ji Jaga was in San Francisco at the time of the murder, not in Los Angeles where the murder occurred.

Ji Jaga's alibi for the initial conviction was further undermined because the COINTELPRO operation had also succeeded in driving a wedge between different factions of the Panthers, and leading Panthers were discouraged from testifying in Ji Jaga's defense. At the initial trial, only Kathleen Cleaver testified in Ji Jaga's behalf. In 1996, however, six former BPP members testified that Ji Jaga was in San Francisco at the time of the murder.

In 1997, Orange County Court Judge Evertt Dickey, a conservative Republican, ruled that that Ji Jaga's 1972 conviction on murder and kidnapping charges should be overturned because of misconduct by the Los Angeles district attorney's office. In June 1997, Geronimo Ji Jaga Pratt was released from prison after spending 27 years in jail. In 1999, the Los Angeles district attorney's office noted that they would not seek a retrial. In 1997, the key witness against Ji Jaga, Julius Butler, resigned from the board of the First African Methodist Episcopal Church.

Ji Jaga considers himself to have been a political prisoner and still fights for the freedom of other inmates who he says have been repressed because of their political views, including Leonard Peltier, the American Indian advocate, and Mumia Abu Jamal, another ex-Black Panther. In April 2005, Ji Jaag also spoke at the funeral of his late lawyer, Johnnie Cochran.

See also: Black Panther Party; BPP, Los Angeles Branch; Cleaver, Kathleen Neal; COINTELPRO; Abu Jamal, Mumia

James Thomas Jones III

Bibliography

Cochran, Johnnie, *A Lawyers Life*. Los Angeles: Thomas Dunne Books, 2002.

Jones, Charles E., ed. *The Black Panther Party: (Reconsidered)*. Baltimore: Black Classic Press, 1998.

Olsen, Jack. *Last Man Standing: The Tragedy and Triumph of Geronimo Pratt*. New York: Anchor Books, 2001.

Swearingen, W. *FBI Secrets: An Agent's Expose*. Boston: South End Books, 1994.

Racial Profiling

In spite of the significant legacy of the civil rights and due process movements on American public institutions, African Americans still face persisting problems of racial prejudice. Along with discrimination in education, employment, or housing, the salience of race in American contemporary society is particularly exemplified through racial profiling. Most commonly known as "Driving While Black" or "Driving While Brown" (D.W.B.), this highly controversial law enforcement practice refers to police-initiated stops that appear to target disproportionately African American and Hispanic drivers compared to their number on the highways. Minor traffic violations are used as a pretext to stop and interrogate motorists and look for drugs or weapons. For the African American collective memory, these much debated practices are reminiscent of the former slave patrols apprehending runaways in the antebellum South or of the traffic stops designed to arrest black political activists in the 1960s. Part of the American criminal justice history, they perpetuate the lasting mistrust between police and minorities and contribute to the widespread feeling among black citizens that they are excluded from the public space and alienated from their national citizenship.

These law enforcement procedures have increasingly been deployed since the War on Drugs, which was launched under the Nixon Administration. Created in 1973, the Drug Enforcement Agency (DEA) elaborated in the 1970s a "drug courier profile" in order to identify narcotics smugglers in the airports. Along with various behavioral predictive characteristics (e.g., cash payment of airline tickets, evidence of nervousness, use of an alias), the ethnic factor was an important component of these new criminal identification techniques. The law and order agenda that surfaced in the 1980s and festered in the 1990s paved the way for new coercive social control frameworks that led to a major political shift in state power conception. In a context of moral panic about violence and lawlessness, stringent law enforcement and massive penal containment were voiced by opinion-formers and policymakers as the only efficient solutions for the expansion of crack markets and for the rise of the youth gun violence. Under the "Operation Pipeline," a training program set off by the DEA, police officers multiplied from the mid-1980s on pretextual traffic stops on the highways of all 50 states.

With the support of civil rights advocates and organizations, African Americans have criticized the legitimacy of these proactive devices, which undermine their confidence in the police at the local and national levels. Even if law enforcement agencies have long denied the use of racial profiling, several statistical analyses have firmly established, as a result of court actions, the ordinary and arbitrary nature of these police practices. As part of the settlement of *Wilkins v. Maryland State Police* (1993), a civil lawsuit filed by a black Harvard Law School graduate, data analyzed by expert John Lamberth from Temple University showed that if African Americans represented 72 percent of the traffic stops initiated by the Maryland State Police, they only committed 17 percent of the traffic violations. In *State of New Jersey v. Soto* (1996), the same expert called by the defense in this criminal case found out that if blacks constituted 13 percent of the driving population, 73 percent of the arrested motorists by the New Jersey State Troopers were black. In 1999, the New Jersey Attorney General's Office acknowledged in an official report that African Americans were twice as likely to be the target of police stops.

Exacerbated by prevalent stereotypes of a violent and criminal black lower class, the high rates of homicide suffered by African Americans and their overrepresentation in the official arrest statistics enabled police organizations to give tacit support to racial profiling. Building on a "statistical discrimination" theory, economists have actually argued that these law enforcement procedures were not an accurate testimony of intentional racial discrimination but an effective method for maximizing "hit rates," namely the successful arrests of drug traffickers and seizures of narcotics contraband. Conversely, legal scholars, as well as social scientists, have pointed out that those investigation techniques had a fateful consequence on the racial demographics of the prison population, which saw for the last two decades a dramatic increase in the incarceration rate of young black males. By disproportionately scrutinizing minorities, racial profiling mechanically contributes to the racialization of criminal justice.

In spite of multiple legal challenges to those police procedures, American judicial institutions have supported these investigation techniques, which have been extensively deployed since the 1980s by law enforcement agents. On the one hand, plaintiffs in civil cases have met tremendous difficulties to prove that police officers were motivated by an intentional racial discrimination and violated the equal protection guarantee of the Fourteenth Amendment. On the other hand, the United States Supreme Court has given over the years increasing power to law enforcement agents in order to effect search and seizure. As early as 1968, the Supreme Court articulated in *Terry v. Ohio* the first legal principle according to which investigative stops were not

a constitutional violation of the unreasonable search and seizure clause of the Fourth Amendment. In 1996, this ruling was notably reinforced in *Whren v. United States*. Dismissing the racial argument, the Court asserted that the traffic violation can be considered by itself a probable cause or a reasonable suspicion for a police-initiated stop even if this offense rationale is only an excuse for a drug investigation. In 1997, the Supreme Court went even further; in *Maryland v. Wilson* it stated that police officers may command the driver or any passenger out of the vehicle during a lawful stop and search. These successive decisions were deeply criticized by legal scholars and civil liberties organizations, as law enforcement agents were given significant latitude in making searches and seizures that could lead to police misconduct and brutality against law-abiding and minority citizens.

As racial profiling is strongly embedded in social practices and legal mechanisms, it deeply influences African Americans' perceptions of the legitimacy of democratic institutions. These investigation devices broaden the racial cleavage, as they are considered very differently by blacks and whites. According to a December 1999 Gallup Poll, if 77 percent of blacks and 56 percent of whites believed that racial profiling was widespread, 42 percent of blacks compared to only 6 percent of whites felt that police-initiated stops were motivated by their racial or ethnic background. The survey also underlined the unequal confidence in the criminal justice system fairness, as 58 percent of blacks compared to 85 percent of whites had a favorable opinion of their local police. Regardless of their law obedience and social status, black motorists driving on the highway and black pedestrians walking in white neighborhoods feel particularly humiliated to be stopped, interrogated, and searched disproportionately by police officers. African Americans have to adjust their daily behaviors to these law enforcement practices by avoiding lavish cars and certain racially identified places and also by training their children to react properly to police-initiated stops. In this respect, these investigation devices contribute objectively to the perpetuation of residential segregation, as African Americans may prefer to live in a black neighborhood where they feel they will be less subject to police stops. Enacted primarily for criminal purposes, profiling techniques not only perpetuates the persistent beliefs about inequality within minority communities but also maintain racial hierarchy in American society.

Political leaders took stock in the late 1990s of the impact of racial profiling on civil liberties and race relations. In 1997, Representative John Conyers of Michigan introduced the Traffic Stops Statistics Act, which passed in March 1998 by a unanimous vote the House of Representatives, but not the Senate. Its purpose was to enhance the accountability and strengthen the control of these investigation techniques. The bill required that data on each police-initiated traffic stops should be collected on a nationwide basis and analyzed by the attorney general. It addresses the need for consistency in reporting data such as the date and location of the stop, the ethnicity and age of the motorist, the alleged traffic offense, as well the rationale for the search. Supporting this legislative initiative, the American Civil Liberties Union (ACLU) launched a campaign in 1999 to end to the use of pretext stops and to pass the Traffic Stops Statistics Act. It also called on the U.S. Justice Department to ensure that racial profiling was not used in federally funded drug interdiction programs. With other civil rights organizations such as the National Association for the Advancement of Colored People (NAACP), the ACLU also filed lawsuits against several states such as Colorado, Illinois, Maryland, Michigan, Oklahoma, and Pennsylvania. Even though this bill has not since become a federal law, some states have passed legislation and adopted written guidelines on traffic stops. During the 2000 presidential debates, the two candidates asserted that racial profiling was damaging for minority communities.

The September 11 terrorist attacks brought to an end the uneasy consensus that was emerging across the national political spectrum in the late 1990s on the inappropriateness of racial profiling. The U.S. Patriot Act of 2001 authorized police to search for any property and seize any material pursuant to a search warrant that represents evidence of a criminal offence in violation of the laws of the United States. Arab Americans, Middle Easterners, South Asians, and Muslims have since been the prime target of these provisions. Recalling the detainment of Japanese Americans during World War II, which was authorized in 1942 by President Roosevelt and endorsed in 1944 by the U.S. Supreme Court (*Korematsu v. United States*), the ACLU, the Congressional Black Caucus, and the NAACP questioned, among other organizations, the legitimacy of the antiterrorist laws regarding the protection of civil liberties. They also pointed out how these provisions might roll back the minor improvements realized in matters of racial

profiling for an African American population that has increasingly been embracing Islam. Revealing how much the debate is far from closed, a bipartisan group of lawmakers in the House of Representatives and Senate introduced the End Racial Profiling Act in 2004.

Part of African American history, the changing racial profiling patterns demonstrate the flexibility of a social control technique that can be deployed by law enforcement agencies to address tragic historical situations but also maneuvered to a large extent by policymakers and opinion-formers to answer moral panic that they themselves helped to create.

See also: Fourteenth Amendment

Jean-Philippe Dedieu

Bibliography

Bass, Sandra. "Policing Space, Policing Race: Social Control Imperatives and Police Discretionary Decisions." *Social Justice* 28 (2001):156–76.

Domke, David, Philip Garland, Andre Billeaudeaux, and John Hutcheson. "Insights into U.S. Racial Hierarchy: Racial Profiling, News Sources, and September 11." *Journal of Communication* 53 (2003):606–23.

Harcourt, Bernard E. "Rethinking Racial Profiling: A Critique of the Economics, Civil Liberties, and Constitutional Literature, and of Criminal Profiling More Generally." *The University of Chicago Law Review* 71 (2004):1275–381.

Harris, David. "'Driving While Black and All Other Traffic Offenses: The Supreme Court and Pretextual Traffic Stops." *The Journal of Criminal Law and Criminology* 87 (1997):544–82.

Harris, David. *Profiles in Injustice: Why Racial Profiling Cannot Work.* New York: New Press, 2002.

Heumann, Milton, and Lance Cassak. *Good Cop, Bad Cop: Racial Profiling and Competing Views of Justice.* New York: Peter Lang, 2003.

Kennedy, Randall. *Race, Crime, and the Law.* New York: Pantheon, 1997.

Miller, Jerome. *Search and Destroy: African American Males in the Criminal Justice System.* New York: Cambridge University Press, 1996.

Weitzer, Ronald, and Steven A. Tuch. "Perceptions of Racial Profiling: Race, Class, and Personal Experience." *Criminology* 40 (2002):435–56.

Radical Republicans

The Radical Republicans were a faction of the Republican Party during Reconstruction who wanted to punish the South and completely uproot its feudal race-based society and replace it with an egalitarian and democratic system.

During the Civil War, the radicals opposed President Abraham Lincoln's call for a quick and lenient readmission of Southern states into the Union. They wanted tougher restrictions against former Confederates and greater civil rights protections for the freedmen, as well as ratification of the Thirteenth Amendment and repudiation of the Confederate war debt. Lincoln used a pocket veto to prevent the radical Wade-Davis bill from becoming law in 1864. Congress retaliated by refusing to seat delegations from three Southern states who met Lincoln's less stringent qualifications.

After Lincoln's assassination, President Andrew Johnson adopted a reconstruction policy that greatly restricted the rights of the former slaves, and he freely pardoned former Confederate officers. These policies outraged the radical Republicans who had after the war become an alliance of the prewar abolition movement and the newly freed slaves. To undo Johnson, the radicals in Congress passed the Civil Rights Bill of 1866, a Southern Homestead Act, the Fourteenth Amendment, and extension of the Freedmen's Bureau. Johnson vetoed all of these bills, but Congress easily overrode the president. In 1867, the conflict between Johnson and the radicals led Congress to a failed attempt to remove the president from office.

The Radical Republican agenda reached its zenith with the Reconstruction Acts of 1867. These acts divided the South into five military districts. Congress entrusted the army to guarantee that African Americans had the ability to exercise their civil and suffrage rights. The acts further stipulated that Southern states must ratify the Fourteenth Amendment (and later the Fifteenth Amendment) in order to be readmitted to the Union.

The alliance between black and white Republicans in the South was often contentious. African Americans were concerned that they did not get their due share of patronage and offices, considering that they made up the overwhelming majority of Republican voters in the South. Increasingly, however, they became more assertive in their demands as they gained political power and experience. During Reconstruction, 16 Radical black Republicans served in Congress, including two United States senators. Blacks held one governorship and many other higher state offices throughout the South. More than 600 African Americans served in Southern state legislatures.

The Southern state governments established by the Radical Republicans after 1867 had to carry most of the burden of Reconstruction without financial assistance from Congress or the moral support of the Northern electorate. Radical state governments throughout the South supported a program of wide sweeping reforms as revolutionary as those of 1776. These reforms bettered the interests not only of the freedmen, but also the poor whites. Reforms included subsidization of railway construction, which provided both jobs and access to markets for the poorer agricultural areas; a system of free public education; regulations curbing abuses in the tenant farming system; purchase of land for redistribution; a liberalized penal code; and bans on discriminatory election laws.

By 1870, the influence of Radical Republicans in Washington was in sharp decline. The Ku Klux Klan Act of 1870 and a watered down Civil Rights Act in 1875 were the last dying gasp of radicalism. In a series of important decisions handed down in the 1870s and 1880s, the United States Supreme Court weakened the provisions of the Fourteenth and Fifteenth Amendments, undermining the efforts of the radicals to gain African American equality. The death of Representative Thaddeus Stevens in 1868 and Senator Charles Sumner in 1874 deprived the radicals of their strongest leaders. Economic issues arising from industrial society and mass immigration attracted the attention of the Northern voters, as they deemed conditions in the South inconsequential to their interests.

At the state level, following readmission of the Southern states, conservative white Democrats used violence and intimidation to frighten African Americans from the polls. The Achilles heel of the radical program had been the necessity to borrow heavily and raise taxes in order to finance their reforms. As conservative whites used race as a wedge issue to divide poor and middle class whites from the Radical African American Republicans, they leveled a series of volatile accusations against the radicals, including financial mismanagement, corruption, and race baiting. Although examples of corruption abound, they were neither more numerous, nor more egregious than they were at contemporary Northern state or the national legislatures. Moreover, native Southern whites showed no scruples when it came to overcharging the radical state governments for services such as bond sales.

One by one as conservative white Democrats captured state governments, they implemented grandfather clauses, literacy tests, and other means to restrict black suffrage. When President Rutherford B. Hayes withdrew the last of the federal troops from the South in 1877, Radical Republicanism ceased to exist. Gains made by African Americans in civil and political rights during Radical Reconstruction were lost by the end of the 19th century.

See also: Civil Rights Act of 1866; Civil Rights Act of 1875; Fifteenth Amendment; Fourteenth Amendment; Hayes, Rutherford B.; Johnson, Andrew; Joint Committee of Fifteen; Lincoln, Abraham; Reconstruction Era Black Politicians; Republican Party; Stevens, Thaddeus; Sumner, Charles

Gregory J. Dehler

Bibliography

Foner, Eric. *Reconstruction: America's Unfinished Revolution, 1863–1877.* New York: Harper and Row, 1988.

Hahn, Steven. *A Nation Under Our Feet: Black Political Struggles in the Rural South, From Slavery to the Great Migration.* Cambridge, MA: Harvard University Press, 2003.

Hyman, Harold M. *The Radical Republicans and Reconstruction, 1861–1870.* Indianapolis: Bobbs-Merrill, 1967.

Summers, Mark Wahlgren. *Railroads, Reconstruction, and the Gospel of Prosperity: Aid Under the Radical Republicans, 1865–1877.* Princeton, NJ: Princeton University Press, 1984.

Trefouse, Hans. *The Radical Republicans: Lincoln's Vanguard for Racial Justice.* New York: Knopf, 1969.

Randolph, A. Philip

Asa Philip Randolph (1889–1979) was an African American trade union and civil rights leader who advocated the use of labor movements as a promising tool in the African American struggle for civil rights. He founded the Brotherhood of the Sleeping Car Porters and organized mass protests to end segregation and discrimination in employment and the army.

Randolph was born to an African Methodist Episcopal minister and a seamstress in Crescent, Florida. Although Randolph grew up in a very religious environment, he later became an atheist, but always maintained his strong belief in nonviolence. In 1891, his family moved to Jacksonville, Florida, a city with a thriving African American community. His parents wanted to provide a good education to Randolph and his brother and sent them to Cookman Institute, a superior black school. Randolph was an excellent student and was the valedictorian of his class. After high school, he experienced employment discrimination and segregation firsthand, in that he could find only low-paying manual labor jobs. During this time, he gained his first experience in organizing black workers to protest against their bad situation.

Part of the first wave of African American migration from the Deep South to Northern cities in search for a better future, Randolph moved to New York City and settled down in Harlem with plans to become an actor. Working again in menial jobs during the day, he took classes at the City College of New York and New York University at night. He soon realized that the employment opportunities and conditions of blacks in the North were not as different from the Deep South as he had hoped. After his parents forbid him to pursue an acting career, he switched majors from drama to politics and economics, but never graduated.

In 1914, he married Lucille Green, a widow six years his senior, who operated a beauty shop and was able to finance them both. Through his wife, Randolph met Chandler Owen, a Columbia University student, who shared his ideas and socialist convictions. They both joined the Socialist Party and dispersed their ideas as soapbox orators in Harlem. Both men considered socialism the remedy for the social and political problems of America and the route to promote social justice and political equality for African Americans.

As the majority of African Americans were part of the labor force, Randolph believed organizing and mobilizing black workers in labor movements was the way to eventually achieve civil rights. He fused labor rights with civil rights. Although never opposing racial integration, Randolph oscillated between all-black activism and interracial cooperation. Throughout his life, Randolph was convinced that change had to come from within the black community. Blacks should no longer beg for improvement. Randolph believed that only the pressure of black mass movement and nonviolent civil disobedience could change politics and public opinion and improve the position of African Americans.

In November 1917, Randolph and Owen began publishing *The Messenger*, a socialist monthly magazine that gained an excellent reputation in the African American community As an intellectual voice for the Harlem community, *The Messenger* advocated socialism and unionism among blacks. Through the magazine, Randolph opposed World War I and African American participation in it and protested racism and racial violence in the United States.

Although treasuring racial pride, Randolph rejected racial separatism and became one of Marcus Garvey's most forthright opponents. For Randolph, racial pride and racial integration were compatible. With the help of George Schuyler, the two managed to continue publishing the financially variable magazine.

Between 1917 and 1923, Randolph and Owen independently founded numerous labor unions to include blacks in the labor movement. Randolph continuously fought unions and the American Federation of Labor (AFL) and the Congress of Industrial Organizations (CIO) for their racism and exclusion of black workers. Although Randolph was initially a staunch advocate of socialism, he was to remain an fervent anticommunist throughout his life.

In 1925, knowing Randolph's support of black workers' rights, the Pullman porters, an all-black service staff of the Pullman sleeping cars, asked him to help them found and

A. Philip Randolph won respect for his quiet dignity and his firmness in a life-long commitment to racial justice. A union organizer and socialist early in life, he became the country's best-known African American trade unionist and a nationally prominent leader in the struggle for civil rights during the early to mid-20th century. (Library of Congress)

lead a trade union to fight for their rights. Underpaid and exploited, they wanted better employment and working conditions. Randolph met with the porters and on August 25, 1925, they founded the Brotherhood of Sleeping Car Porters (BSCP). For the next 10 years, under Randolph's leadership and using *The Messenger* and later his magazine *Black Worker* as a medium, the union struggled to reach their goals. The Pullman company defamed Randolph and continuously refused to negotiate with the union. In 1935, the union finally forced the company to negotiate. After two years of bargaining, the company agreed to a contract that included wage increases and work-hour reduction. With the signing of the contract, the Brotherhood became the officially accepted representative of the Pullman porters. It was the first victory of an all-black union over an American company. Randolph remained the president of the BSCP until 1968. In 1978, the union dissolved and its remaining members merged with the Brotherhood of Railway and Airline Clerks.

Through his efforts for economic improvement combined with civil rights, Randolph gained a respected status in the African American community. In 1936, during his struggle for the BSCP, Randolph became president of the newly founded National Negro Congress (NNC). The NNC was a loose association of African American groups and white supporters. It was especially committed to the labor movement and cooperated closely with trade unions to create a blacks mass movement. Randolph left the NNC when he thought it to be increasingly influenced by Communists and white labor movements.

With the rising number of job opportunities in the defense industry in the late 1930s and early 1940s, the second wave of black migration from South to North took place. African Americans, however, often met with racial discrimination when searching for work in the defense industry. Despite serious efforts and pleas, the White House did not help improve the situation of African Americans who became increasingly frustrated and angry. Basing his activism on this anger, Randolph called for a march of 100,000 African Americans on Washington to protest discrimination in defense industry and the armed forces. He launched the March on Washington Movement (MOWM), demanding an executive order to abolish discrimination in the defense industry and the military. With his plan for mass mobilization, Randolph became the advocate of a new approach in the Civil Rights movement. The date for the all-black march was set for July 1, 1941. Initially hesitant to submit to the pressure, Roosevelt gave in due to the mere threat of a protest march of tens of thousands of African American in Washington. On June 25, 1941, President Roosevelt issued Executive Order 8802 that forbade government contractors to practice employment discrimination based on race, creed, color, or national origin and included the creation of a Fair Employment Practices Committee (FEPC) to enforce the order. Randolph canceled the march. After the political success of the planned march, he continued the MOWM. The all-black mass movement that stood for nonviolent civil disobedience acted locally and organized rallies against discrimination.

After the war, Randolph turned his attention to an issue that he had failed to attain with his March on Washington in 1941—the integration of the armed forces. In 1947, the Congress and the American public discussed a Selective Service Act and Universal Military Training without considering the abolishment of segregation. To fight military segregation, Randolph and Grant Reynolds founded the Committee against Jim Crow in the Military Service and later the League of Nonviolent Civil Disobedience Against Military Service. Initially, the committee used traditional means of communication and publishing, but soon it stepped up pressure by threatening that African Americans would no longer bear arms for the United States if the armed forces did not integrate and ban discrimination. It urged black youth to resist induction and military service. In a meeting with President Truman and a speech before the Senate Armed Service Committee, Randolph laid out his position and could not be dissuaded from his militant plans to launch as mass movement boycotting the military. Needing the black vote in the upcoming presidential election and fearing Randolph's civil unrest, President Truman issued Executive Order 9981 on July 26, 1948. It ordered the equal treatment and opportunity for all and the formation of an advisory committee. Randolph was pleased and called off the civil disobedience campaign in August 1948.

After the end of the League of Nonviolent Civil Disobedience Against Military Service in 1948 and of the Committee Against Jim Crow in the Military Service with the beginning of the Korean War, Randolph worked again more powerfully for an end to labor discrimination and trade union segregation. In 1955, he was elected vice president of the newly merged AFL-CIO's Executive Council.

To pressure trade unions and the AFL-CIO to improve the position of African Americans in unions, Randolph founded the Negro American Labor Council (NALC) over which he presided from 1960 to 1966.

Randolph cooperated more closely with the NAACP and other civil rights groups and gave up his idea of establishing his own Civil Rights movement. With his trade union activism, he also supported the fight and organized protest marches for the integration of American schools. He continued to organize marches, pressuring the administration for change. In cooperation with the NAACP and Martin Luther King Jr., he organized, for example, The Prayer Pilgrimage on May 17, 1957, where about 50,000 people protested and prayed for freedom in front of the Lincoln Memorial. Randolph's belief in the effectiveness of mass movements influenced the development of the new generation of Civil Rights movements and their strategies to attain full civil rights.

In March 1962, Randolph conceived a plan for a new march on Washington protesting the slow economic progress, especially of black youth. Randolph worked with Martin Luther King Jr., and his planned Jobs Rights March and Mobilization became the March on Washington for Jobs and Opportunities. The movement was an interracial project that, in contrast to Randolph's initial plans, was a protest for new civil rights acts rather than only economic improvement. Randolph became the director of the march and cooperated closely with Bayard Rustin whom he considered the best organizer and logistician. On August 28, 1963, a march on Washington conceived by Randolph finally materialized. Though broadened in its aims and modernized, it was based on his earlier March on Washington Movement and the fulfillment of his long-held dream. After the 1963 March on Washington, black protest radicalized and often rebutted nonviolent civil disobedience. Randolph rejected these developments and stood for more traditional and less militant methods of activism. The new movements often castigated him for his opinion.

In 1964, Randolph received the Presidential Medal of Freedom from President Lyndon B. Johnson. In 1968, he retired as the President of the BSCP and became president of the A. Philip Randolph Institute, a national organization of black trade unionists, founded by Randolph and Bayard Rustin in 1965. Supported by the AFL-CIO, the institute pledged to bridge the gap between the African American community and the trade unions. In 1979, A. Philip

Randolph died at the age of 90. He is well remembered in the African American community for his struggle for black workers and civil rights.

See also: Brotherhood of Sleeping Car Porters; Jim Crow; March on Washington Movement, 1941; March on Washington, 1963; National Association for the Advancement of Colored People

Christine Knauer

Bibliography

Anderson, Jervis. *A. Philip Randolph: A Biographical Portrait.* New York: Harcourt Brace Jovanovich, 1973.

Barber, Lucy G. *Marching on Washington: The Forging of an American Political Tradition.* Berkeley: University of California Press, 2002.

Bates, Beth Tompkins. *Pullman Porters and the Rise of Protest Politics in Black America, 1925–1945.* Chapel Hill: University of North Carolina Press, 2001.

Davis, Daniel S. *Mr. Black Labor: The Story of A. Philip Randolph, Father of the Civil Rights Movement.* New York: E. P. Dutton, 1972.

Garfinkel, Herbert. *When Negroes March: The March on Washington Movement in the Organizational Politics for FEPC.* Glencoe, IL: Free Press, 1959.

Harris, William H. *Keeping the Faith: A. Philip Randolph, Milton P. Webster, and the Brotherhood of Sleeping Car Porters 1925–37.* Urbana: University of Illinois, 1977.

Pfeffer, Paula F. *A Philip Randolph, Pioneer of the Civil Rights Movement.* Baton Rouge: Louisiana State University Press, 1990.

Wright, Sarah E. *A. Philip Randolph. Integration in the Workplace.* Englewood Cliffs, NJ: Silver Burdett Press, 1990.

Ray, James Earl

James Earl Ray (1928–1998) was a career criminal who confessed to the slaying of Dr. Martin Luther King Jr. in Memphis, Tennessee, on April 4, 1968. Despite his admission of guilt in open court the next year, Ray's ambiguous statements before, during, and after his trial raised serious questions about what had motivated him and whether or not he had acted alone. The entire truth about the assassination may never be known.

Born in Alton, Illinois, on March 10, 1928, Ray was the oldest of the nine children of George (Speedy) and Lucille Maher Ray. Raised in extreme poverty in the country town of Ewing, Missouri, Ray dropped out of school and left home at the age of 16. After enlisting in the U.S. Army just before his 18th birthday, he served in Germany for almost three years until December 1948, when he was given a general discharge for ineptness and lack of adaptability for military service.

Within a year of his dismissal from the army, Ray began a life of crime and punishment. He committed a number of armed robberies, and from October 1949 until his escape from the Missouri State Penitentiary in April 1967, Ray spent more than 14 years behind bars. While a fugitive, he traveled extensively using money most likely accumulated from dealing contraband in prison. After visiting New Orleans in December 1967, he apparently began to stalk Dr. King for the purpose of killing him. Ray's racism had been obvious to many people who came in contact with him, and his intolerance of African Americans had festered for years.

Ray purchased a high-powered rifle, scope, and ammunition in Alabama at the end of March and drove to Memphis a few days later. He checked into a rooming house across the street from the Lorraine Motel where King and other members of the Southern Christian Leadership Conference were staying. They had come to support black sanitation workers in their strike against the city and planned to lead a march downtown on the following day. As the group prepared to leave the motel for dinner at about 6:00 P.M., a single gunshot rang out, fatally wounding King.

Ray left the scene immediately, narrowly avoiding a police dragnet. Investigators recovered a rifle with Ray's fingerprints on it almost immediately. The assassin drove to Atlanta, got on a northbound bus, and slipped across the border to Canada less than 40 hours after the murder. Two months later, immigration officers at Heathrow Airport in London apprehended Ray when he attempted to board a plane for Brussels. The British government quickly extradited him to the United States.

After Ray fired his first lawyer, Judge Preston Battle reset the legal proceedings for April 7, 1969. Instead of standing trial, Ray took his attorney's advice and pled guilty to murder in exchange for a 99 year sentence. Within days, he changed his mind, dismissed his counsel, and petitioned the judge for a reversal of his sentence. From that time until his death from liver disease in 1998, Ray proclaimed his innocence and insisted that an elaborate conspiracy lay behind the assassination of King. Despite his constant agitation, the state of Tennessee never granted him a new trial.

See also: King, Martin Luther Jr.; Southern Christian Leadership Conference

Michael Thomas Gavin

Bibliography

McMillan, George. *The Making of an Assassin: The Life of James Earl Ray.* Boston: Little, Brown, 1976.

Posner, Gerald. *Killing the Dream: James Earl Ray and the Assassination of Martin Luther King, Jr.* New York: Random House, 1998.

Seigenthaler, John. *A Search for Justice.* Nashville, TN: Aurora Publishers, 1971.

Reagon, Bernice Johnson

Bernice Johnson Reagon (1942–), a musician, writer, activist, educator, cultural historian, and curator, devoted her entire career to weaving her life experiences into the study of African American history. She was born on October 4, 1942 in Albany, Georgia to Beatrice Wise and Reverend Jessie Johnson. The third of eight children, she was exposed at an early age to the challenges facing blacks living in the South and learned the value of struggle and protest in facing those challenges.

Reagon grew up with music as the cornerstone of her professional career. From her father, also a singer, she learned the basics and began singing in his Baptist church at the age of five. In the fall of 1959, she entered Albany State College in Albany, Georgia where she majored in music and also studied German lieder and Italian arias.

While at Albany, she was secretary of the local Youth Chapter of the NAACP but found she preferred the more confrontational style of the Student Nonviolent Coordinating Committee (SNCC) and participated in a march in her hometown protesting the arrest of two students in 1961. She was arrested along with other members of SNCC and was suspended from school for her involvement. It was her attraction to the protest songs sung by the marchers and the songs sung by fellow incarcerated women that moved her to join SNCC's Freedom Singers in 1962, and to enter Spelman College in Atlanta that same year as a history major. She left within a year, however, to join SNCC's Freedom Singers, performing at mass meetings, fundraisers, and voter registration drives. During this time, she met and married Cordell Reagon, a SNCC field worker and Freedom Singer from Tennessee. She left the Freedom Singers to give birth to her first child, Toshi, in 1964; she later gave birth to a son, Kwan Tauna, in 1965. She was the founder of the a capella group, the Harambee Singers in 1966 and recorded her first solo album, Songs of the South in 1966 followed by Sound

of Thunder in 1967. For several years, following her divorce from Cordell also in 1967, Reagon pursued her study of traditional African American music.

Reagon left Atlanta in 1968 to perform during the Poor People's Campaign on the Washington Mall where she was first exposed to the Smithsonian Institution's Festival of American Folklife, an annual event that presents American culture in a festival-type setting. After completing her studies at Spelman in 1970, she moved to Washington, D.C. permanently to work as a field researcher for the Folklife Festival. She began working full-time at the Smithsonian Institution in 1974 as the founder and cultural historian in the African Diaspora Project of the Division of Performing Arts where she conducted extensive research on the relationship between black cultural expression throughout Africa, the Caribbean, and South America. The project later evolved into the Program in African American Culture.

In 1973, she founded Sweet Honey in the Rock, an internationally renowned a capella group of women that performs a broad repertoire of music ranging from traditional blues and spiritual music to modern folk and protest songs. Sweet Honey evolved from Reagon's continued interest in merging education and music with social and political issues. Sweet Honey has performed all over the world, not only in festivals and concerts, but in significant political and cultural venues such as the United Nations Decade for Women Conference in Nairobi, Kenya in 1985.

While working at the Smithsonian and performing with Sweet Honey during its infancy, Reagon pursued a doctorate degree in history at Howard University, which she was awarded in 1975. Her dissertation, *Songs of the Civil Rights Movement, 1955–1965: A Study in Culture History,* explores oral traditions and examines both freedom protests songs of the 1960s and popular commercial protests songs as oral history sources for reconstructing historical periods. When Smithsonian's Performing Arts Division was dismantled, Reagon was transferred to the Public Programs Division of the National Museum of American History in 1983 where she continued to direct the Program in African American Culture until she was promoted to curator of the Division of Community Life in 1988.

While at the Smithsonian, Reagon was instrumental as a contributor and consultant to the award-winning *Voices of the Civil Rights Movement: Black American Freedom Songs 1960–1966,* a collection of freedom songs documented within the context of African American musical culture. In

1993, she retired from the Smithsonian and was made Curator Emeritus of the National Museum of American History. Also that year, she was appointed Distinguished Professor of history at American University where she taught until 2002.

Throughout retirement, Reagon has remained active, serving as scholar, producer, and host of the groundbreaking radio series *Wade in the Water: African American Sacred Music Traditions,* a collaborative production of National Public Radio and the Smithsonian Institution, which began broadcasting in 1994, for which she received the Peabody Award for Significant and Meritorious Achievement in Broadcasting in 1994. She was a contributor author and editor of *We'll Understand it Better By and By: Pioneering African American Gospel Composers* (1992) and *We Who Believe in Freedom: Sweet Honey in the Rock Still on the Journey* (1993). In 1998 she served as composer and compiler of the sound score for the award-winning documentary film *Africans in America: America's Journey Through Slavery.* Reagon composed and produced much of Sweet Honey's repertoire, but in 1996, she retired as artistic director, participating instead as part of a collective artistic directorship. After more than 30 years of performing with the group, she fully retired from Sweet Honey in 2004.

Throughout her career, Reagon has been recognized for her artistry and scholarship in African American history and culture. She was awarded the genius award from the John D. and Catherine T. MacArthur Foundation Fellowship in 1989 and received the Presidential Medal for her contributions to public understanding of the humanities in 1995. In 2003, she received the Heinz Award for the Arts and Humanities. She returned to Spelman as the William and Camille Cosby Endowed Professor in the Fine Arts for the 2002-2003 academic year. For more than 40 years, Reagon has contributed to the study of African American culture and history as a scholar, educator, artist, and activist. She continues to lecture on the evolution of cultural history.

See also: Albany, Georgia Movement; National Association for the Advancement of Colored People; Poor People's Campaign; Student Nonviolent Coordinating Committee

Donna M. Wells

Bibliography
Harding, Vincent, and Rosemarie Freeney Harding. *Bernice Johnson Reagon: The Singing Warrior.* Denver, CO: Veterans of Hope Project, 2000.

Stuckey, Sterling. *Going Through the Storm: The Influence of African American Art in History.* New York: Oxford University Press, 1994.

Reconstruction Era Black Politicians

After the American Civil War and the implementation of the Reconstruction Acts, African Americans for the first time in U.S. history had the opportunity to take part in the political process. Among those who tried to implement social, political, and economic reform during Reconstruction were a small percentage of African American politicians.

Approximately 2,000 African Americans held political office at the local, state, and national level during Reconstruction (1865–1877). These individuals who had been disenfranchised now stood at the center of power. They came from diverse backgrounds. Nearly half had been free before the Civil War while the other half had experienced the horrors of slavery and acquired their freedom through manumission, running away, or simply purchasing themselves. Approximately 100 of the nearly 2,000 African American politicians during Reconstruction in the South were Northern blacks who migrated to the South after the war to assist in securing the rights of millions of former slaves.

The professional training that African American politicians possessed varied as much as their origins. Individuals who held local political office—sheriffs, tax collectors, town councilmen, etc.—generally had limited education and some were illiterate. They depended on others for help in conducting business. African American politicians who held state and national office were usually educated and many had extensive formal education. For example, Hiram Revels, who was elected to the U.S. Senate from Mississippi in 1870, was an ordained minister of the African Methodist Episcopal Church and received formal training at a Quaker seminary in Indiana and at Illinois's Knox College. The first major foray for many African Americans into politics after the Civil War was in the state constitutional conventions held throughout the former Confederate states. Although each state had constitutional conventions with African American members, the number and influence of those members varied from state to state. For example, South Carolina's 1868 state constitutional convention was composed of a majority of African Americans. By contrast, Alabama's constitutional convention was composed of only a small minority of African Americans and therefore they wielded less influence.

The states where African Americans had a major presence in the state constitutional conventions usually translated into a major presence in a state's legislature. In the first South Carolina legislature, there were a total of 127 members; 87 were African Americans. Where they had a majority in state legislatures, African Americans were able to bring about major changes to protect the rights of the newly freed people. African American politicians were also concerned with providing education and a way for all African Americans to pursue the American dream of land ownership.

Despite the tenacity of many African American politicians at the state level, they faced constant opposition. In Georgia in September 1868, for example, the white members of the state legislature refused to seat all of the African American members. The white legislators simply declared that the African American members were ineligible. One year later Georgia's Supreme Court ruled that African Americans were eligible to serve in the Georgia legislature and were allowed to assume their seats; however, they continued to face opposition to any legislation they proposed.

The first African American congressmembers of the United States (from left to right): Senator Hiram Revels of Mississippi, Representatives Benjamin Turner of Alabama, Robert C. De Large of South Carolina, Josiah Walls of Florida, Jefferson Long of Georgia, Joseph Rainy of South Carolina, and R. Brown Elliott of South Carolina. (Library of Congress)

African American politicians confronted animosity not only from their counterparts in state assemblies, but from hate groups as well, most notably the Ku Klux Klan. Between 1867 and 1868 approximately 10 percent of African Americans who served as delegates at constitutional conventions had become victims of Klan violence.

Regardless of the animosity exhibited toward many African American politicians at the state level, some were able to build a strong base of support and enact reform, at least on the local level, in favor of African Americans. For example, Blanche K. Bruce (who would become the first African American to win a full six-year term in the U.S. Senate) created a strong political machine in Bolivar County, Mississippi. At one point during Reconstruction he held three offices—sheriff, tax collector, and superintendent of education.

Even though many African American politicians were able to have some influence locally in voting rights and education, their influence was limited because at no time during Reconstruction was there a complete African American rule in the South. The only African American who came closest to controlling the governorship in any former Confederate state was Pickney B. S. Pinchback, the lieutenant governor of Louisiana. After the impeachment of the state's governor, Henry Wormoth, in December 1872, Pinchback served as governor for 41 days. There would not be another African American governor in the United States until 1990.

A handful of African American politicians at the state level used their positions for personal gain. For example, Thomas W. Cardozo, who served as Mississippi's superintendent of education, was convicted of embezzling funds marked for Tugaloo College.

At the national level African American politicians held seats in the U.S. House of Representatives and U.S. Senate. Although small in number—only 18 African Americans served in the U.S. Congress from 1868–1877, they fought not only for the rights of African Americans, but pushed for improvements to local infrastructure, protective tariffs, and relief for Native Americans.

Despite the presence of African American politicians at the national, state, and local level, the steps they had taken toward true equality were thwarted by the mid-1870s as whites and former Confederate officials began to "redeem" their governments and implement repressive measures that excluded African Americans from the political process. Although African American politicians may not have accomplished all they had hoped, they proved that they were as worthy of political office as much as any white politician. Furthermore, it gave many African Americans hope that one day they would be treated as equals in all levels of society.

See also: Bruce, Blanche K.; Disfranchisement; Fifteenth Amendment; Ku Klux Klan; Republican Party; Revels, Hiram; White Supremacy

Jonathan A. Noyalas

Bibliography

Drago, Edmund L. *Black Politicians and Reconstruction in Georgia: A Splendid Failure*. Athens: University of Georgia Press, 1992.

Holt, Thomas. *Black over White: Negro Political Leadership in South Carolina during Reconstruction*. Urbana: University of Illinois Press, 1977.

Rabinowitz, Howard N., ed. *Southern Black Leaders of the Reconstruction Era*. Urbana: University of Illinois Press, 1982.

Red Summer Race Riots

The year 1919 marked a turbulent era in American history. The country experienced economic instability, labor strife, and a xenophobic tide of hatred under the banner of the "Red Scare" in the wake of World War I. Entwined in this postwar turmoil, clashes between the races intensified. James Weldon Johnson dubbed this period the "Red Summer" for the blood that flowed in the streets as a result of white-on-black violence. Between the tumultuous months of April and October, at least 26 race riots erupted across the country. Although these acts of brutality had occurred before and would endure for some years to come, the Red Summer of 1919 represents a particularly dismal chapter in race relations in the United States.

Overarching structural factors—demographic, economic, and political conditions—stirred racial animosities during the Red Summer. Beginning in the 1890s, African Americans left the rural South for better prospects in southern cities, the North, and the West. This "Great Migration" saw an exodus of 500,000 black southerners between 1916 and 1919. World War I particularly prompted this migration, as people of color found more opportunities outside of the South as foreign immigration dwindled and the military draft created labor shortages on the home front. The influx of people, especially in northern cities, often resulted in strains on housing, food, and public transportation, contributing to already tense race relations. Economic conditions and labor strife also fed into the violence. Adding to this racial resentment, businesses also used blacks as strikebreakers. Furthermore, authorities often ignored or displayed open hostility toward people of color. Some policemen and militia members turned a blind eye toward rioters or even actively participated in the violence themselves.

These structural concerns reinforced the cultural mindset that flourished after World War I. The radical ideology that emerged in the late 19th century, which incorporated Social Darwinism and scientific racism, continued to feed whites' views of supremacy, and these beliefs led to a paranoid fear of sexual attacks on the sanctity of white women. White newspapers fed this cultural consensus that allowed white-on-black riots to thrive during the Red Summer. They not only provided the fuel before race riots—running stories and rumors of alleged black crimes and atrocities while downplaying white infractions—but also generated the "official" version of events afterward.

Although structural factors and cultural attitudes set the scene for violence, precipitating events—alleged or real attacks, murders, or other infractions—created the immediate spark that prompted whites to act. Moreover, as people of color continued to assert their rights as citizens, whites strove to hold them back. World War I only heightened these tendencies. As the black population increased, and when whites believed that blacks encroached into their spheres of work, neighborhoods, and recreation, violence often resulted.

Not solely centered in one geographical locale, race riots appeared across the United States in 1919. Places as varied as Bisbee, Arizona; New, London, Connecticut; New Orleans; Omaha, Nebraska; New York City; and Longview, Texas experienced white-on-black riots during the Red Summer. Riots in Washington, D.C., Chicago, and Phillips County, Arkansas, stand out as particularly brutal. After weeks of lurid and sensationalized news stories in Washington, D.C.'s newspapers about white women allegedly suffering attacks by black men, white soldiers, sailors, and marines invaded streetcars and African American neighborhoods for three days starting on July 19, after a white woman contended that two black men attacked her.

Although newspapers reported that 15 people died in the violence, actual numbers may have been two to three times that many. In Chicago, white and black gangs squared off for 13 days beginning July 27, after a black youth accidentally swam across the "color line" in Lake Michigan and drowned after being met with rocks from the white beachgoers. African Americans identified the white culprits, but authorities instead focused on one of the black accusers. When the violence subsided, 23 blacks and 15 whites had died, more than 500 people suffered injuries, and 1,000 black families had no homes. In Phillips County, Arkansas, hundreds of whites from surrounding counties and states arrived after a shootout occurred on September 30 between two white law enforcement officials and a group of African Americans meeting to organize a sharecroppers and tenant farmers union. By October 3, the violence had subsided after nearby federal troops patrolled the area. At least 25 blacks and 5 whites died, but many observers believed that as many as 200 people of color perished during the riot.

People of color responded to violence and ideology by creating newspapers, organizations, and literature to assert that they would not assume a subordinate position in society. The NAACP, for example, focused its efforts on exposing and putting a stop to white brutality. Through its newspaper, *The Crisis,* it provided detailed statistics, and in 1919, it published the book *Thirty Years of Lynching in the United States* to highlight the causes and atrocities of this type of violence. Black newspapers, especially the *Chicago Defender,* also became outspoken critics of black America's plight. Moreover, this era proved a rich and powerful time for African American inspiration, producing the new Negro movement and the Harlem Renaissance, which stressed a sense of worth and boldness.

Out of these forces emerged the horrors of the Red Summer. National conditions and local circumstances built an environment that allowed race riots to flourish throughout the country. These months marked both the apex of white violence against African Americans and the beginning of a heightened black response.

See also: Chicago Race Riot of 1919; Elaine, Arkansas, Riot of 1919; Great Migration; "If We Must Die"; Jim Crow; Lynching; McKay, Claude; National Association for the Advancement of Colored People; New Negro Movement; White Mob Violence

Ann V. Collins

Bibliography

Stockley, Grif. *Blood in Their Eyes: The Elaine Race Massacres of 1919*. Fayetteville: University of Arkansas Press, 2001.

Tuttle, William. *Race Riot: Chicago in the Red Summer of 1919*. Urbana: University of Illinois Press, 1996.

Williamson, Joel. *The Crucible of Race: Black-White Relations in the American South Since Emancipation*. New York: Oxford University Press, 1984.

Redlining

Redlining is a practice whereby companies or institutions deny goods and services to certain groups on the basis of race or where they live. Mortgage and car insurance industries are widely known to engage in the practice. Key stakeholders in redlining are borrowers, lenders, government regulators, realtors, and fair housing advocates. African Americans living in highly populated urban areas tend to experience the worst impacts of redlining. Redlining was historically supported by a combination of government policies and private-sector practices.

In the 1930s, Federal Housing Administration (FHA) lending guidelines provided a critical policy basis for redlining in the housing industry. When deciding to grant or deny mortgages and mortgage insurance, FHA regulators relied on underwriting guidelines. One reason the FHA put forth to justify its redlining policy was to prevent inharmonious racial groups from mixing. The FHA also argued that separating homeowners by race would prevent property values from declining. These policies resulted in limited housing opportunities for African Americans who increasingly lived in racially segregated neighborhoods. The housing available to African Americans had lower assessed property value, was substandard in quality, and was more overcrowded than housing available to whites.

The federal government created the Home Owners Loan Corporation (HOLC) in 1933. The HOLC introduced the practice of amortizing, or paying off mortgage loans over time at agreed upon interest rates, as well as a color-coded rating system to appraise property values. Amortizing made loans widely available and affordable. The color-coded rating system mostly benefited white buyers entering the housing market after the Great Depression. It included a red-colored designation for undesirable properties and is credited as the basis for the term "redlining."

Areas with significant African American populations tended to fall into this category.

Realtors used restrictive covenants to carry out redlining. A restrictive covenant is language included in housing-related legal documents, usually deeds, to prevent homes from being sold to, or purchased by, certain racial groups. The existence of restrictive covenants helped to perpetuate the segregated neighborhoods caused by redlining and provided a convenient rationale for denying loans to African Americans. It was not until the U.S. Supreme Court struck down the power to enforce restrictive covenants in the *Shelly v. Kraemer* case of 1948, that African Americans gained some relief from the most adverse effects of redlining. One drawback to the decision is that, although it became illegal for the government to enforce restrictive covenants, the decision did not outlaw the housing industry practice.

The laws and public policies supporting redlining have changed in recent decades. The most significant government legislation enacted to expand housing access, and limit exclusionary practices like redlining, was the Fair Housing Act of 1968. Lenders could no longer use race as a factor to determine credit worthiness. Over the next several years, government regulators were lax in enforcing the law. Fair housing advocates engaged in various protests to resist bank redlining and bring to light the injury caused to African Americans by banks and lenders who practiced redlining. Their actions successfully brought attention to the practice and influenced Congress to pass further antiredlining legislation.

When Congress passed the Home Mortgage Disclosure Act (HMDA) in 1975 and the Community Reinvestment Act (CRA) in 1977, fair housing advocates tackled redlining head-on through protests, lawsuits, and consumer education in the community reinvestment movement. Throughout the 1980s, government regulators enforced HMDA by requiring banks to collect data about where they made housing loans and to document efforts to make loans in previously underserved communities. Despite these advances, lenders continued to deny loans to African Americans into the 1990s at rates that were about twice that of white borrowers.

A turning point in the fight against redlining occurred in the 1990s with more aggressive government support for programs to expand African American homeownership. Lenders in the private sector simultaneously developed loan products that made it easier for African Americans to qualify for home mortgages. The drawback to these increased opportunities was high interest rates and confusing repayment terms. Fair housing advocates soon after introduced a new term, "reverse redlining," to explain troubling new lending practices.

Reverse redlining is a process in modern credit markets that makes it easier for lenders to exploit African American borrowers. Predatory lending and subprime loans are key components to the new approach. Lenders target African Americans to purchase or refinance mortgages at high interest rates in the subprime market, rather than qualify them for low interest rates in the prime market. Reverse redlining practices contributed to record home ownership levels among African Americans in the early 2000s, but gave way to unprecedented default and foreclosure rates near the end of the decade. Fair housing advocates urge the government and private companies to combat reverse redlining by using objective criteria and fair terms when lending to African American borrowers.

See also: Urban Ghetto; Urbanization

Lezlee J. Hinesmon-Matthews

Bibliography

Bullard, Robert D., J. Eugene Grisby, III, and Charles Lee, eds. *Residential Apartheid: The American Legacy.* Los Angeles: CAAS Publications, 1994.

Immergluck, Dan. *Credit to the Community: Community Reinvestment and Fair Lending Policy in the United States.* Armonk, NY: M. E. Sharpe, 2004.

Squires, Gregory D., ed. *From Redlining to Reinvestment: Community Responses to Urban Disinvestment.* Philadelphia: Temple University Press, 1992.

Thomas, June Manning and Ritzdorf, Marsha, eds. *Urban Planning and the African American Community: In the Shadows.* Thousand Oaks, CA: Sage Publications, 1997.

Reparations

The idea that African Americans are owed reparations for their ancestors' labor as slaves has captured public attention at many times since the Civil War and is now in a period of resurgence. That resurgence is a result of several factors. First, some other groups have received limited reparations. Most notably, 82,000 Japanese Americans interned during World War II received $20,000 each in 1988. And there have been limited cases where Native Americans received compensation, such as the 1972 Native Alaska Claims Settlement Act, which provided nearly $1 billion to settle Native American claims to land in Alaska. Second, there is increasing concern that the Civil Rights movement's agenda of bringing about equality is unfulfilled and the affirmative action movement is declining.

Much of the modern reparations movement traces its origins to 1969, when James Forman interrupted Sunday morning services a the Riverside Church in Harlem and delivered the black manifesto. But reparations are also highly controversial. According to a recent poll by the *Mobile* [Alabama] *Register,* 5 percent of whites support reparations, whereas 66 percent of blacks support them. The controversy results from vastly different ways of viewing our history and its impact on the present.

Reparations proponents (who are often called reparationists) begin their case with talk about centuries of injustice—the violence of beatings, torture, psychological brutalization that lay at the heart of slavery. Slavery began with trafficking in human beings, kidnapping people from Africa, unspeakable conditions on transatlantic ships to the Americas, and then generations of slavery in North America. Slavery in North America entailed the destruction of families, statutes prohibiting education or marriage, random beatings, lack of opportunity to advance economically, and generations of forced labor that made their owners wealthy.

There was some opportunity when slavery ended in 1865 to give the recently freed slaves the opportunity to realize the promise of America that whites held. There was much talk about 40 acres and a mule, a phrase taken from General William Sherman's Field Order No. 15, which promised to use property confiscated from Confederate supporters to provide land to newly freed slaves. But those promises were not fulfilled. A primary role of the federal government after the war was to oust newly freed slaves from their land and return it to the prior white owners. Instead of assistance, newly freed slaves were greeted with harsh Black Codes and long-term labor contracts.

The problems continued during the era of Jim Crow—the period of segregation and legalized discrimination, including limited voting, schooling, housing, and employment rights, that ran from the end of Reconstruction in 1877 until the modern Civil Rights era. It was not until the civil rights revolution of the 1950s that there was anything approaching equal treatment of African Americans by law.

The Civil Rights Act of 1964 prohibited private discrimination in employment.

According to reparationists, the problems of slavery and Jim Crow are continuing. According to recent census data, nearly one in four (25%) African Americans live in poverty, compared with 8 percent of non-Hispanic, white Americans; 30 percent of African American children live in poverty, compared with 9 percent of non-Hispanic white children. Median income for African American families is less than $31,000 and for white non-Hispanic families it is nearly $46,000. The case for reparations is built on such inequalities. If there were no inequalities in income today, there would be little reason to talk about reparations. We might then conclude that slavery and the Jim Crow era had little continuing effect.

Reparationists seek to make the lives of African Americans better and to make opportunities more available. Thus, they propose a series of actions for reparations. Those actions begin with relatively modest proposals, like a national truth commission, to study the effects of slavery and Jim Crow and its effects on the present. Representative John Conyers has lobbied since 1989 for a national commission to study the history and legacy of slavery. A study might also include a national slavery museum and a national apology. Reparationists see those kinds of actions as a way of changing how we think about our history of racism. They optimistically think that it might be possible to educate about the multiple connections between past harm and present inequality and in that way remake social policy. They seek more talk of what President George Bush said in 2003 while visiting Goree Island, that the slave trade was "one of the greatest crimes of history."

Reparationists also seek local action, such as truth commissions, to investigate individual localized crimes such as the Tulsa Race Riot of 1921, the Rosewood Massacre, the Tuskegee syphilis experiment, the sterilization of welfare recipients in North Carolina, the Wilmington, North Carolina, riot of 1898, and the Greensboro, North Carolina, massacre of 1979. Institutions are also investigating their culpability in slavery. In 2000, the Aetna Insurance Company apologized for writing life insurance policies on slaves and the *Hartford Courant* apologized for printing ads for runaway slaves. Many schools that date back to the era of slavery, like the University of Alabama and Brown and Yale Universities, are also investigating their past.

Most reparationists want much more than truth commissions and apologies. They want money in some form. They typically ask for funding for community-building programs, which will fund primary education, health care, and business development. Reparationists commonly propose the use of trust funds to administer the programs. Some of the most radical reparationists even propose payments to individuals, but those are rare. And in a few extreme cases, reparationists draw on black nationalist thinking, and they request a separate black state.

Central and as yet unanswered question, is how would one measure reparations payments and how much would they likely cost? There are two basic ways of measuring the amount owed. The more modest measure is known as the unjust enrichment measure. It measures the amount that African Americans have contributed through their labor, which they have not been paid for. That involves estimating the value of African American contributions. The second, larger measure is known as the tort measure. It measures the harm to slaves (in terms of stolen labor, physical and emotional abuse, loss to families) and to their descendants (in terms of lost educational and business opportunities). Here the harm is enormous, for slavery's crimes continue to replicate victims for generations. Reparations is aimed at changing all this—redistributing property and correcting for generations of violence and lack of opportunity.

There are two primary means by which reparations are sought. One is through lawsuits. That method is difficult, because lawsuits are not well suited to deal with large-scale societal problems. They are best able to handle discrete disputes between individuals and corporations. And the few lawsuits filed for reparations have proven relatively unsuccessful. A series of lawsuits filed in 2002 against corporations that benefited from slavery were consolidated under the titled, *In re African American Slave Descendants Litigation,* and were dismissed in January 2004. A major lawsuit for victims of the Tulsa, Oklahoma race riot of 1921 was dismissed in March 2004. It was filed by the Reparations Coordinating Committee (RCC), a group of lawyers, social scientists, and activists dedicated to pursing the cause of reparations. The RCC is led by Adjoa Aiyetoro, Charles Ogletree, and Randall Robinson.

There have been a few successful lawsuits. One, *Pigford v. Glickman,* settled claims by African American farmers denied loans by the Department of Agriculture in the 1980s.

By late 2004, farmers had received approximately $660 million in settlement. Another case settled for $20 million is a class action lawsuit against New York Life Insurance Company for life insurance policies for people who were killed by the Turkish government during the Armenian genocide in 1915. Individual lawsuits might be the basis for limited reparations; they might also raise public consciousness. But for the great crimes in American history, reparations are going to have to come through legislation in Congress and in state legislatures.

Reparationists face a significant uphill struggle. Opponents advance a series of arguments. Some deny any liability for slavery. They say that the evils of slavery and Jim Crow were committed by others and that current taxpayers should not have to pay. Although the innocence argument is powerful, many taxpayers are beneficiaries of a system in which some people have an easier time advancing economically than others; many of those taxpayers are beneficiaries of a system that involved oppression of African Americans. But many are innocent (and probably have little or no benefit). The nature of social legislation, however, is that taxpayers are often asked to pay to improve the lives of people who have been injured. The sad fact, of course, is that it takes generations to eradicate the effects of slavery and Jim Crow. And the sad fact is that slavery and Jim Crow produced more harm than the benefits they conferred. Thus, there are probably people who will be asked to pay—taxpayers—who are in some sense innocent. That is the unfortunate part of being part of American society. We have obligations that must be paid independent of fault. That is particularly clear after 9/11, when the Airline Stabilization Act provided millions of dollars to the families of 9/11 victims, even though no one thought the United States was at fault for the attacks.

A second objection states that slavery is the cause of current problems. The income differential between blacks and whites is often attributed to factors such as single parenthood. There is room for additional research on the role of slavery and Jim Crow, as well as black culture in determining the current chasm between black and white wealth. Reparationists attribute single parenthood to welfare policy, which is in some ways yet another consequence of slavery.

A third objection is that reparations does not make sense as social policy. They are too backward-looking, too divisive between blacks and whites, and are not the best way to redistribute property. One should ask whether there are other programs that are better suited to closing the income gap. Reparations talk is, indeed, divisive, for it uses a sordid history to challenge the distribution of wealth in the present. Reparations holds out the promise, when used in conjunction with other programs, of resolving conflict and overcoming the past.

A fourth objection is that the debt has already been paid through the people who died during the Civil War and through welfare programs like the Great Society. Finally, some say, with indignant nobility, that we cannot put a price on the legacy of slavery. But we miss the chance to revisit our history. And the way to repair damage is to pay for some of it. Of course we cannot repair all the past damage to everyone. Reparations skeptics often ask about Egypt paying the Jews or the Babylonians paying people they oppressed. But reparations for slavery and Jim Crow present a different kind of claim for harms that are very alive and leading to differential impacts right now.

Despite recent setbacks in the courts, reparations action continues. Recently, the Chicago City Council has required that companies that do business with the city disclose any connections they have to slavery. The California legislature required insurance companies to disclose any insurance policies they wrote on slaves' lives. As the collection of information grows and as people see the many ways that slavery contributed to economic growth and continues to affect Americans today, it is likely that reparations talk will continue.

See also: Field Order No. 15; Forty Acres and a Mule; Jim Crow; King, Martin Luther Jr.; Muhammad, Elijah; Nation of Islam; Rosewood, Florida, Riot of 1923; Stevens, Thaddeus; Tulsa, Oklahoma, Race Riot of 1921; Tuskegee Experiment; X, Malcolm

Alfred L. Brophy

Bibliography

Barkan, Elazar. *The Guilt of Nations: Restitution and Negotiating Historical Injustice.* Baltimore: Johns Hopkins University Press, 2000.

Brooks, Roy L. *Atonement and Forgiveness: A New Model for Black Reparations.* Berkeley: University of California Press, 2004.

Brophy, Alfred L. *Reconstructing the Dreamland: The Tulsa Race Riot of 1921–Race, Reparations, Reconciliation.* New York: Oxford University Press, 2002.

Robinson, Randall. *The Debt: What America Owes to Blacks.* New York: Dutton, 2001.

Winbush, Raymond. *Should America Pay?: Slavery and The Raging Debate on Reparations.* New York: Amistad, 2003.

Yamamoto, Eric. *Interracial Justice: Conflict and Reconciliation in Post-Civil Rights America.* New York: New York University Press, 2000.

Republic of New Afrika

The Republic of New Afrika (RNA) is the name given to the proposed independent African American nation within the borders of the United States that consist of the southern states of Louisiana, Mississippi, Alabama, Georgia, and South Carolina. These "Black Belt" states were chosen because of their large black populations and their historical significance as states where African Americans worked, tilled, and lived on the land—first as slaves, then as freedpersons—for centuries. The Provisional Government of the Republic of New Afrika (PG-RNA), a black nationalist organization created during a conference held in Detroit, Michigan, in 1968, proposed the independent nation as an example of black self-determination, believing that African Americans will never enjoy full freedom, justice, and equality under the U.S. government and constituted a "nation within a nation," that laid rightful claim to the proposed territory as just compensation for centuries of oppression. The PG-RNA also supports reparations for African Americans as compensation for forced enslavement, Jim Crow segregation, racial violence, and continued forms of racism.

On March 31, 1968, the Malcolm X Society and the Group on Advance Leadership (GOAL), two Detroit-based organizations involving the Obadele brothers, Gaidi (Milton Henry, 1920–2006) and Imari Obadele (Richard Henry, 1930–), close associates of Malcolm X, called together 500 black nationalists in Detroit, Michigan to discuss the political situation of African Americans. Building on Malcolm's call for black self-determination and his admonition that land is the basis of independence, the 500 nationalists called for the formation of the independent Republic of New Afrika. The original demands of the PG-RNA called for a negotiated cessation by the United States of the five southern states based on the results of a national plebiscite of black folks; the establishment of a sovereign and independent government to be eligible for membership in the United Nations; and for reparations as compensation for injustices perpetuated against African Americans by the United States government for the past 300 years. Finally, the conferees produced a Black Declaration of Independence drafted and signed by 100 delegates, a constitution, and the framework of a provisional government.

Robert F. Williams, a human rights advocate most famously known for his stand against Klan terrorism in Monroe, North Carolina, in the late 1950s, and subsequent flight from the United States on false charges of kidnapping, was elected president while living in China; Gaidi Obadele was elected first vice president; Betty Shabazz, widow of Malcolm X, was elected second vice president; Imari Obadele I served as minister of information; and Obaboa Olono, was treasurer. The governing body of the PG-RNA is the People's Center Council, which combined legislative and judicial power and supervised industries and land, and the president served as chair of the council. The PG-RNA based its political philosophy on the principles of Ujamaa—cooperative economics and community self-sufficiency—promoted by Tanzanian President Julius Nyerere.

For the next several years, the PG-RNA set about achieving several goals, including negotiating with the U.S. Congress over reparations and land; building consulates in cities such as New York, Chicago, Washington, D.C., Baltimore, Los Angeles, Cleveland, and San Francisco; calling for the formation of local "People's Militias" and developing a standing army to defend the territory; and meeting with representatives from countries such as China, Vietnam, the USSR, Sudan, and Tanzania to gain international recognition for the proposed Republic. By 1970, the organization would concentrate much of its activities in Mississippi, specifically the capital of Jackson, where the PG-RNA established its headquarters and began the work of organizing the plebiscite and garnering the support of black Mississippians, particularly black college students at Tougaloo College. Also in 1970, Imari Obadele was elected president. Robert F. Williams had resigned the presidency after returning to the United States, prompting an interim government administered by the Obadele brothers. A Ujamaa Committee headed by Hekima Ana (Thomas Norman) replaced it before electing Obadele. A new constitution, the Code of Umoja, was also adopted. In 1971, the RNA began efforts to acquire land in Mississippi to establish El Malik as the capital of the nation.

Because of its political philosophy and black nationalist orientation, the RNA has had several confrontations with local, state, and federal police, prompting the Federal

Bureau of Investigation (FBI) to designate it as a subversive organization. This made the RNA a target of the FBI's Counter Intelligence Program (COINTELPRO) and subjected to numerous raids and arrests. The most well-known confrontation came on August 28, 1971, when 11 members (RNA-11), including Obadele, were arrested in Jackson, Mississippi, and charged with various crimes including murder and waging war on the state. All were eventually acquitted.

The PG-RNA still exists and is headquartered in Washington, D.C. The official slogan is "Free the Land." It is a leading organization within the National Coalition of Blacks for Reparations in America (NCOBRA) along with other progressive organizations.

See also: Black Nationalism; Black Power; COINTELPRO; Shabazz, Beatty X; Williams, Robert F.

Tony Gass

Bibliography

Cunnigen, Donald. "The Republic of New Africa in Mississippi." In *Black Power in Belly of the Beast,* Judson L. Jeffries, ed. 93–115. Chicago: University of Illinois Press, 2006.

Davenport, Christian. "Understanding Covert Repressive Action: The Case of the U.S. Government Against the Republic of New Africa." *Journal of Conflict Resolution* 49 (February 2005):120–40.

Obadele I, Imari Abubakari. "The Struggle Is for Land." *Black Scholar* 3 (February 1972):24–36.

Obadele I, Imari Abubakari. "The Struggle of the Republic of New Africa." *Black Scholar* 5 (June 1974):32–41.

Revels, Hiram

Hiram Revels (1822–1901) was the first African American to serve in the legislative branch after the Civil War. He was a prominent civil rights activist who struggled in the aftermath of Reconstruction. Born in 1822 in Fayetteville, North Carolina, Hiram Revels was the free son of a mixed marriage between African and Croatan/Indian parents. Details of his early life are sketchy. At the age of 16, Hiram became apprenticed to his brother, Elias P. Revels, as a barber in Lincolnton, North Carolina. In 1841, his brother died in an unfortunate accident, leaving Hiram to manage the barbershop. Over the next three years, he managed the barbershop with minimal results. In 1844, clamoring to expand his education, Hiram became a student at an abolitionist

Quaker School in Liberty, Indiana, which was the center of abolitionist activism in the state. Revels continued his education when he attended school in Ohio and eventually attended Knox College in Illinois. Revels's matriculation at the school was a logical choice for the aspiring young abolitionist African American.

After his brief stint as a student at Knox College, Revels started a career as an evangelist. He became an ordained minister in the African Methodist Church. As a young minister, he traveled throughout the Midwest, specifically to African American congregations in Ohio, Illinois, Indiana, Tennessee, Kentucky, Missouri, and Kansas. After his career as an itinerant preacher, Revels settled in Baltimore, Maryland. While there he became the principal of a school geared for African American students. He also became the pastor of a local church. He continued in this capacity until the outbreak of the Civil War in 1861.

In 1861, South Carolina, along with six other Southern states, seceded from the Union. The disgruntled states protested the victory of Republican Abraham Lincoln in the election of 1860. In the first year of the conflict, the state of Maryland, despite the presence of slavery within its borders, remained loyal to the Union.

The status of Maryland as a border Union state provided Revels with an opportunity to prove his status as a patriotic American. Revels was a firm believer in the necessity to maintain the Union, at whatever costs. To a certain degree, Revels had a personal stake in the Civil War. If the Union was dismantled, Revels, as an African American, was in danger of losing his personal liberties. He decided to become actively involved in the war. In 1861, Revels organized two regiments of African American troops to fight against the Confederates. Over the next year, he traveled extensively, ending up in St. Louis, Missouri. St. Louis, with a population of 115,000 slaves, afforded Revels the opportunity to form a sizable regimental group. In 1863, Revels was able to recruit enough men to create one African American regiment. In addition to his recruiting talents, Revels also joined in active service. In 1863, he became Union chaplain with a Mississippi regiment of free blacks. He also became the provost marshal of Vicksburg, Mississippi, the site of one of the bloodiest battles of the Civil War. As provost in Vicksburg, Revels handled the affairs of ex-slaves living in the city. After the war, Revels returned to the ministry. He settled in Natchez, Mississippi, where he participated in the local chapter of the African Methodist Episcopal Church.

Hiram Revels was the first African American to serve as a U.S. senator. In January 1870, he was elected to the U.S. Senate seat once occupied by Confederate president Jefferson Davis. (Library of Congress)

In his years at Natchez, Revels assumed a position of leadership among the newly freed African American population. He specifically had to handle the relations between the Reconstruction Act of 1867 and the newly created state government. In late 1868, the military governor of Mississippi, Adelbert Ames, appointed Revels to the Natchez City Board of Aldermen where he gained valuable experience in municipal politics. In 1869, John Lynch, a prominent local African American leader in Natchez, encouraged Revels to become a candidate for the state legislature. Over the next few months, Revels introduced numerous local bills in the legislature. In December 1869, the Mississippi Republican caucus, wishing to push the civil rights of African Americans in the South, nominated Revels to become a U.S. Senator from Mississippi, essentially filling a void left when Jefferson Davis vacated his seat to become president of the Confederacy in 1861. After a delay from many Southern Senators, on February 23, 1870, Hiram Rhodes Revels was accepted into the Senate by a vote of 48 to 8. Two days later, Revels was seated in the Senate, becoming

the first African American to gain admission as a senator and congressman.

Over the course of his brief stint, Revels dealt with significant issues. Among the most important issues were the debate over the readmission of Georgia into the Union without civil rights protections for African American. In 1870, Revels was the first African American to give an official speech on the floor of the Senate over the issue of Georgia. On March 4, 1871, he vacated his seat. In the years after his congressional career, Revels acted as president of Alcorn College. He died on January 16, 1901 and was the first African American to serve in the U.S. Senate.

See also: African Methodist Episcopal Church; Lincoln, Abraham; Reconstruction Era Black Politicians; Southern Free Blacks; Union Army

Jaime Ramón Olivares

Bibliography
Lawson, Elizabeth. *The Gentleman from Mississippi, Our First Negro Congressman, Hiram R. Revels.* New York: J. S. Oglivie, 1960.
Thompson, Julius. *Hiram R. Revels, 1827–1901: A Biography.* New York: Arno Press, 1983.

Revolutionary Action Movement

The Revolutionary Action Movement (RAM) founded in 1962 was one of the first revolutionary nationalist formations of the 1960s created in response to the oppression of people of African descent living in America. Blacks were being oppressed politically, economically, socially, and physically, and this became the impetus for the creation of a number of groups to respond and counter these actions. These individuals and groups who desired to be self-determined and free from the hegemonic actions widely practiced throughout the United States became participants in what became known as the Black Power movement. Although there were many perspectives on how to gain liberation from oppression, simplistically put, there were two major ideological camps involved in the Black Power movement. There were those who advocated for integration and a demand for the American government to live up to the promises of citizenship and equality and those who believed chances were slim that America would recognize blacks as equal and therefore advocated for black separatism. RAM's ideology favored the latter and consisted of ideals around blacks constituting a separate nation within America, although not all of their members agreed with this. Their ideals of black separatism influenced many of the other black power groups in the 1960s who were advocating for radical change in relation to the treatment of blacks.

This organization existed primarily underground, resulting in details about them being more limited than other black revolutionary nationalist groups. Those included in the formation of this group were college students, the working class, and some intellectuals who identified themselves as New Afrikan nationalists. New Afrikan nationalists adhere to the idea that people of African descent are a distinct nation within the United States and should have sovereignty. Students played a large role in the formation of RAM. During the 1960s, many groups fighting race-based oppression were either started or comprised mainly of students on college campuses throughout the United States, and RAM was no exception.

This organization was composed of individuals commonly defined as black revolutionary nationalists and they used a motto of "One Purpose, One Aim, One Destiny," with theoretical underpinnings much like that of Marcus Garvey. The organization produced two publications, the bimonthly *Black America* and the weekly *RAM Speaks*. In addition to educating black communities using this literature, this grassroots organization had "street meetings" consisting of informal gatherings targeting inner-city youth to inform them about the ideals RAM espoused and as a means of recruitment.

Max Stanford, aka Akbar Muhammad Ahmad, the first field chairman, articulated a number of objectives for the organization including giving black people a sense of racial pride, solidarity, dignity, unity, and commitment to the struggle for independence. Another of RAM's objectives was for people of African descent everywhere to be free of colonial and imperialist rule. Also, those of African descent in America should demand sovereign nationhood and reparations and take the U.S. government to the World Court and the United Nations for human rights violations and genocidal treatment of this group. To reach these objectives, members of RAM believed they must engage in guerilla warfare. Because of their decision to operate underground, members of this group often conducted their work through other established groups such as Malcolm X's Organization for African American Unity (OAAU),

Afro-American Association, Student Nonviolent Coordinating Committee (SNCC), Conference of Racial Equality (CORE), National Association for the Advancement of Colored People (NAACP), Dodge Revolutionary Union Movement (DRUM), and the League of Revolutionary Black Workers (LRBW) in Detroit, Michigan. Their primary objective was to make these groups more militant, often resulting in a revolutionary faction within the respective groups. RAM was also successful at organizing black youth into a paramilitary force called the Black Guards in 1967.

RAM's ideals of separatism did not stop with blacks in America but encompassed a Pan-African stance, with some members identifying as black internationalists. RAM's internationalist ideals aligned with beliefs that non-European people throughout the world should seek to free themselves from imperialist domination through revolution. Because no black person is free until all black people are free. organizing for the liberation of people of African descent globally became an important aspect of their platform.

The organization's life was relatively short, ending in 1968 as a result of the FBI counterinsurgency program COINTELPRO, as well as internal issues. RAM, among other black nationalist groups, was identified and targeted as a threat to America by then FBI Director J. Edgar Hoover and consequently came under attack. Although the individuals who made up the various black nationalist groups were under constant assault and scrutiny, as one group disbanded another was in its formative stages. For instance, former RAM members created the Black Liberation Party, the Black Panther Party for Self-Defense, and the Provisional Government of the Republic of New Afrika.

See also: Black Panther Party; Black Power; COINTELPRO; Republic of New Afrika; Student Nonviolent Coordinating Committee; Williams, Robert F.; X, Malcolm

Efua S. Akoma

Bibliography

Kelley, Robin. "Stormy Weather: Reconstructing Black (Inter)Nationalism in the Cold War Era." In *Is It Nation Time? Contemporary Essays on Black Power and Black Nationalism*. Eddie S. Glaude Jr., ed., 67–90. Chicago: University of Chicago Press, 2002.

Robinson, Dean. *Black Nationalism in American Politics and Thought*. Cambridge, UK: Cambridge University Press, 2001.

Umoja, Akinyele O. "Repression Breeds Resistance: The Black Liberation Army and the Radical Legacy of the Black Panther Party." *New Political Science* 21, no. 2 (1999):131–55.

Van Deburg, William, ed. *Modern Black Nationalism: From Marcus Garvey to Louis Farrakhan.* New York: New York University Press, 1997.

Robeson, Paul

Paul LeRoy Bustill Robeson (1898–1976), a truly multi-talented genius, was a singer, actor, linguist, amateur and professional athlete, and an ardent advocate of African American civil rights and anti-imperialism. He was born on April 9, 1898, in Princeton, New Jersey, to Reverend William Drew Robeson and Maria Louisa Bustill Robeson. In 1860, Paul's father—likely a descendant of Igbo-speaking people from the Niger River Delta—had escaped from a North Carolina plantation at age 15, graduated from Lincoln University in Pennsylvania, and eventually became a pastor of Witherspoon Street Presbyterian Church. Robeson's mother was a school teacher who came from an abolitionist Quaker family. Although his mother died in a fire by the time Robeson turned six, both his parents instilled in him the importance of education and sharpening his considerable mental abilities.

During his senior year at Somerville High School, Robeson won a statewide scholarship competition and entered Rutgers College in 1915. He was only the third African American to be admitted to Rutgers and was the only student of color on campus during his four years there. During freshmen tryouts for the Rutgers football team, Robeson was savagely beaten by several white players, leaving him with a broken nose and a dislocated shoulder. After recovering from his injuries, Robeson made a second attempt at tryouts in which a future teammate stepped on his hand with a cleated foot, ripping away several of Robeson's fingernails. After Robeson literally lifted the player over his head, in an attempt to injure him, the coaches of the football team informed him that he had made the varsity squad. An imposing 6'2", 210-pound player at defensive end, Robeson's athletic prowess was certainly a factor in Rutgers's average margin of victory of 41 points during the 1915 season. His freshman campaign was followed by two consecutive seasons as a first-team football All-American. In addition to football, Robeson also played varsity basketball and baseball and ran track. In total, he accumulated 15 varsity letters before his graduation.

Robeson's athletic prowess was matched, or surpassed, by his abilities in the classroom. After maintaining a 3.8 GPA during his freshman year, Robeson was only one of three students at Rutgers accepted into Phi Beta Kappa and was one of four students selected in 1919 to Cap and Skull, the honors society at Rutgers. That same year he delivered the valedictory speech in which he predicted that he would be governor of New Jersey by 1940 and a prominent African American leader. After graduation, Robeson entered Columbia Law School in 1920 and moved to Harlem. While a full-time law student, he began playing professional football for the Akron Pros and the Milwaukee Badgers in the American Professional Football Association, which later became the National Football League. In addition to his professional football career, Robeson also began performing as a singer and stage actor to pay his way through Columbia.

While maintaining a busy career, Robeson married Eslanda Cardozo Goode, head of the pathology laboratory at Columbia Presbyterian Medical Center and daughter of a prominent mixed-race family in New York, in August 1921. Despite Paul's extramarital affairs, the two stayed married until Eslanda's death in 1965. In 1923, Robeson graduated from Columbia Law School and accepted a job at Stotesbury and Miner in New York City while singing part-time at Harlem's world-famous Cotton Club. His interest in law soon faded after a white secretary refused to dictate from him. Robeson soon quit the firm and became a full-time performer and part-time student at the School of Oriental Languages at the University of London. In 1924, he played two leading roles in *All God's Chillun Got Wings* and Eugene O'Neill's *The Emperor Jones*. By 1925, Robeson's professional singing career reached a new height as he began to sing Negro spirituals at concert halls throughout the United States and Europe.

At the age of 29, Robeson was already considered one of the most famous and recognizable Americans in the world. He was voted into the "All Time All-American College Eleven," the first college football Hall of Fame, in 1927. His deep bass voice, chiseled face, and imposing physique were iconic hallmarks. In 1928, he sang "Ol' Man River" for the first time while playing Joe in the London production of *Show Boat*. In many ways, this song became his personal signature. Not only is his rendition of "Ol' Man River"

Paul Robeson as Othello in the Theatre Guild Production of Othello, *Broadway, 1943–1944. (Library of Congress)*

considered definitive, but Robeson would consciously change the lyrics over time, rendering the once southern lament into a song of social change and revolution. If "Ol' Man River" was the song that became his signature, then his 1930 role as *Othello* in England held a similar stature. Although no U.S. production company would employ Robeson to play Othello, given his close physical interactions, on stage, with a white Desdemona, he reprised the role in New York in 1943 and toured the United States until 1945. Robeson was a 1945 winner of the NAACP's Spingarn for his role as Othello, and his Broadway run of the play was the longest of any Shakespeare play in history.

In 1933, Robeson starred in the movie version of Emperor Jones and began intensive language training at the School of Oriental Languages. Over the course of several years of formal and self-study, he learned to read and sing in Spanish, Russian, Chinese, Arabic, French, German, Swahili, and several other African languages. In sum, Robeson mastered as many as 20 languages. In the 1930s alone,

Robeson starred in four movies, three plays, and sang internationally all while taking language courses in London.

Although Robeson was one of the most famous Americans in the 1930s and early 1940s, from the late-1940s until his death in 1976, he almost completely disappeared from public view, and specific efforts were made to erase him from history and public record. Robeson was retroactively removed from the 1918 All-American first team. Likewise, Rutgers University systematically removed his name from sports records, a move that was not reversed until 1995. As a result of his political affiliations and public pronouncements, the U.S. government moved to undercut his influence abroad and his ability to earn income at home. Robeson was essentially blacklisted. Prevented from movie and stage roles, singing in concert halls, or appearing on radio or TV, his income went from more than $100,000 per year in the 1930s to less than $6,000 year in the late 1940s and throughout the 1950s.

With his facility for the languages of the world community and his fame as a performer, Robeson used his stage to combat Jim Crow in the United States, fascism and Nazism in Europe, and imperialism in Africa and Asia. Moreover, at the height of the Cold War, McCarthyism, and red baiting in the United States, Robeson embraced communism and the Soviet Union. This culminated in the 1949 Peekskill, New York riot in which anticommunist (and largely antiblack and anti-Semitic) protesters violently disrupted a Robeson concert in the weeks after a controversial statement he made at the World Peace Conference in Paris about African Americans not wanting war against the Soviets. In 1950, the Sate Department revoked his passport and, during an appeals hearing in February 1952, the State Department issued a brief citing Robeson's political activity on behalf of the colonial peoples of Africa as a reason why he should be denied the right to travel beyond the borders of the United States.

Investigated by the House Un-American Activities Committee (HUAC) and publicly criticized by Eleanor Roosevelt, Jackie Robinson, Roy Wilkins of the NAACP, and just about every other African American leader, with the exception of W. E. B. Du Bois, Robeson was increasingly isolated as a result of his unwavering political stances. In 1958, he published his only book entitled *Here I Stand,* which was a detailed articulation of his political ideology. Later that same year, his passport was restored and Robeson returned to the international stage as a performer and political activist. His last two decades were fraught with poor health, exhaustion, and rumors of CIA and MI5 surveillance. After retiring from the public eye to live a relatively quiet life in Philadelphia, Robeson died on January 23, 1976. Since 1995, Robeson has been the posthumous recipient of a number of awards and honors in an attempt to rewrite his important legacy back into history and public memory.

See also: African Imperialism; Black Athletes; Black Folk Culture; Cold War and Civil Rights; Du Bois, W. E. B.; Harlem Renaissance; Robinson, Jackie

Walter C. Rucker

Bibliography

Boyle, Sheila Tully and Andrew Bunie. *Paul Robeson: The Years of Promise and Achievement.* Amherst: University of Massachusetts Press, 2001.

Brown, Lloyd L. *The Young Paul Robeson: On My Journey Now.* Boulder, CO: Westview Press, 1997.

Foner, Philip Sheldon, ed. *Paul Robeson Speaks: Writings, Speeches, Interviews, 1918–1974.* New York: Brunner/Mazel, 1978.

Ford, Carin T. *Paul Robeson: "I Want to Make Freedom Ring."* Berkeley Heights, NJ: Enslow, 2008.

Robeson, Paul. *Here I Stand.* Boston: Beacon Press, 1988.

Robinson, Jackie

The Negro Leagues showcased some of the greatest players in the history of baseball. Although perhaps not the greatest player in Negro League baseball history, Jackie Robinson (1919–1972) is certainly the most famous. Robinson is well known for breaking the color barrier in white professional baseball. Born January 31, 1919, in Cairo, Georgia to sharecroppers Millie and Jerry Robinson, Jackie Roosevelt Robinson grew up in Pasadena, California. Of the five Robinson children, Jackie was the youngest. His mother taught him at a young age to combat racism by using his talents. Jackie's means of showcasing his talents became sports.

After a stint at Pasadena Community College, Robinson attended UCLA in 1939. While there he excelled in the classroom and in football, track, and baseball. He earned varsity letters in all four sports, the first to do so at UCLA. After college, Robinson played semiprofessional football in Hawaii. He also worked for a few months as an athletic director in the National Youth Administration. He was drafted by the United States Army in 1942 to fight in World War II. He was sent to Fort Riley, Kansas, where he became an officer and was part of a segregated unit there.

In 1943 in Fort Hood, Texas, he was involved in a racial incident when a bus driver tried to make him go to the back of a bus. His refusal to give up his seat led to his being charged with conduct unbecoming an officer and willful disobedience. This experience sharpened his sense of racial injustice, so he spoke assertively about the unjust conditions that African Americans were subjected to. With the help of the black press, fellow service men, and the NAACP, the court martial was dropped and he was later acquitted and honorably discharged in 1944. Thus, his spirit of activism became evident before he embarked on the famous "experiment."

By 1945, Robinson joined the famous Kansas City Monarchs where he played with the great Satchel Paige. In 1946, Branch Rickey signed Robinson to play with the Brooklyn Dodgers. Robinson became the player to end segregation in Major League baseball. While stoically enduring incredible racial abuse such as name calling and foul play during games from players on both sides, fans, and umpires, he led his team to the league title, won Major League Rookie of the Year, and finished with a .297 batting average and a league-leading 29 stolen bases.

After three years of silence, he began to speak up when pitchers narrowly missed his head, fans shouted epithets, or obscene mail came to his home. He fought the denial of equal service in eating and sleeping quarters, or wherever he faced discrimination. Finally, the curative effects of time and recognition of Robinson's value to the team caused the majority of players to settle into the spirit of cooperation.

Before the Dodgers came calling, Robinson coached a basketball team in Austin, Texas. He later signed to play second base with the famous Kansas City Monarchs in 1945, where he performed admirably on a team of talented veterans like Satchel Paige. A primary reason Branch Rickey chose Robinson instead of one of the more talented, established Negro League Stars was Robinson's stamina and tolerance, extreme patience, and forbearance.

Jackie Robinson's performance made the world recognize that black people and especially, Negro League players, could perform exceptionally well. In fact, with Robinson on the roster, the Dodgers won National League pennants in 1947, 1949, 1952, 1953, 1955, and 1956. In

Jackie Robinson was the first African American to play Major League Baseball. (Library of Congress)

1955 they defeated the New York Yankees in the World Series. Robinson is remembered not just for his enormous talents on the field, but for his inner resolve and human character that allowed him to restrain himself from retaliating to severe racist abuses with so much at stake. Throughout Robinson's career, he was able to persevere and achieve at high levels despite the overt racism in American sports and society. In his later years Robinson was attacked for being conservative, particularly as a result of his well-publicized criticisms of Paul Robeson and other African American leaders. During the McCarthy era, Robinson was called before the House Un-American Affairs Committee (HUAC) to denounce Robeson as a communist sympathizer. Despite the criticism regarding Robinson's political stances, none can deny the radical statement his integration of major league baseball made in 1947.

See also: Black Athletes; Negro League Baseball; Robeson, Paul; World War II (Black Participation in)

Thabiti Lewis

Bibliography

Lewis, Thabiti. *Ballers of the New School Race and Sports in America.* Chicago: Third World Press, 2009.

Rampersad, Arnold. *Jackie Robinson: A Biography.* New York: Knopf, 1997.

Robinson, Jo Ann

Jo Ann Gibson Robinson (1912–1992) was born April 17, 1912 in rural Georgia, the youngest of 12 children. She played an instrumental, although often overlooked, role in the events leading up to the Montgomery bus boycott, as well as in the boycott itself. An educator throughout her life, she acquired a master's degree in English from Atlanta University, which led her to accept a professorship at Alabama State College in 1949.

There she joined the Women's Political Council (WPC). After Robinson experienced a humiliating experience on a bus at the hands of a racist driver who objected to her sitting in the fifth row on a nearly empty bus, she decided to convince the other WPC women to focus on segregation in public transportation.

Segregation on the Montgomery City Lines was similar to that in public transportation in most southern cities and towns. The first five rows of seats were reserved for white patrons, and African Americans were to use the back four rows, which meant that African Americans had to stand beside empty whites-only seats if the rest of the seats were full. In addition, if the first five rows were full and a white rider boarded and all other seats were occupied, four African American riders would be forced to give up their seats so the white rider could sit, as African Americans were barred from sitting in the same row as a white. These rules resulted in situations such as Robinson experienced, when she was asked to vacate a seat regardless of the lack of other passengers, and that Rosa Parks experienced, when she refused to give up her seat on a full bus.

For the next six years, the WPC, along with other groups, complained to Montgomery's city commissioners about how badly bus drivers and white riders treated African American bus patrons, and they prepared for a boycott. Contrary to the narrative many learn about the Montgomery movement, it did not spontaneously erupt in the wake of Rosa Parks's arrest. In fact, Robinson wrote a letter to Montgomery's mayor in which she spoke of a potential bus boycott by African Americans, making it clear that they comprised the majority of the bus system's patrons and thus could take away its profits. She wrote this letter shortly after the *Brown v. Board of Education of Topeka* (1954) decision declared school segregation unconstitutional.

Following Rosa Parks's arrest on December 1, 1955, Robinson and other African American leaders decided that the perfect time had come to execute their one-day boycott plans. Others had been arrested that year as well, but Robinson and others felt that their cases would not be as sympathetic; one of those arrested was a teenage girl who was a few months pregnant. Parks, on the other hand, was well respected, and she was an officer of the NAACP. Robinson, two fellow faculty members, and two students stayed up all that night copying and bundling notices announcing the boycott, set to begin December 5, the day of Parks's trial. Members of the WPC distributed tens of thousands of flyers the next day, and by the end of that Friday, almost all Montgomery African Americans knew of the plans.

The boycott proved so successful that boycotters decided to continue it. Robinson and others organized the Montgomery Improvement Association (MIA), and Robinson served on its executive board and edited its newsletter, which eventually expanded to four pages. The MIA handled donations, organized car pools and taxis to transport boycotters to work, and served as a liaison between the mass movement and white bus and city officials. Robinson was selected to be a member of this latter delegation.

The MIA delegation's initial proposals included the following: bus drivers should be courteous to African American passengers; African Americans would take seats from the back to the front of the bus and whites from front to back, and once the bus was full, no one would have to give up a seat; and African American drivers should be hired on predominantly African American routes. In a series of meetings, white officials continued to reject these proposals, so the boycott continued. In late January, white officials announced they would no longer meet with the African American contingent to discuss options, and police harassed boycotters; Robinson herself got 17 unjustified traffic tickets. By February, pro-boycott attorneys filed suit against the city, and this suit eventually made its way to the Supreme Court, which struck down segregation. Meanwhile, a grand jury in Montgomery declared the boycott illegal and ordered the arrest of leaders, including Robinson. On December 20, 1956, however, the marshals served the Supreme Court order on Montgomery's city officials; the next day, African Americans again rode the buses, this time integrated ones.

Several years after the boycott was over, Robinson and other teachers left Alabama State in the wake of investigations by a state committee into those faculty members it suspected of organizing the boycotts. These investigations intensified because of a 1960 sit-in some of the college's students organized. Robinson resigned after the spring semester in 1960. She took a position at Grambling College in Louisiana but left the next year, leaving the South to teach high school in Los Angeles until retiring in 1976. Her memoir about her Montgomery years was published in 1987, and the Southern Association for Women Historians gave it a publication prize. Robinson died in 1992.

See also: Jim Crow; King, Martin Luther Jr.; Montgomery Bus Boycott; Parks, Rosa

Erin Boade

Bibliography

Branch, Taylor. *Parting the Waters: America in the King Years 1954–63.* New York: Simon & Schuster, 1998.

Crawford, Vicki L., Jacqueline Anne Rouse, and Barbara Woods, eds. *Women in the Civil Rights Movement: Trailblazers and Torchbearers, 1941–1965.* New York: Carlson Publishing, 1990.

Garrow, David J. *Bearing the Cross: Martin Luther King, Jr., and the Southern Christian Leadership Conference.* New York: William Morris, 1986.

Robinson, Jo Ann Gibson. *The Montgomery Bus Boycott and the Women Who Started It.* Knoxville: University of Tennessee Press, 1987.

Robnett, Belinda. *How Long? How Long?: African-American Women in the Struggle for Civil Rights.* New York: Oxford University Press, 1997.

Robinson, Ruby Doris Smith

Ruby Doris Smith Robinson (1942–1967) was a civil rights activist, a member of the Student Nonviolent Coordinating Committee (SNCC), and one of the organization's most important leaders and organizers before her untimely death at the age of 25. Born in Atlanta, Georgia, on April 25, 1942, Ruby Doris Smith was the second oldest of seven children. From their family home, both her mother and father ran separate business enterprises. Her mother, Alice Smith, was a beautician operating a beauty shop out of rooms attached to the house. Her father, J. T. Smith, owned and operated a store and also drove a cab and operated a local restaurant. After Robinson entered high school, her father founded a Baptists church and became its principal pastor. The social elevation experienced through her parents' hard work meant that Robinson was among the burgeoning African American middle class in Atlanta. She was a debutante as a high school senior and, after high school, in the fall of 1959, she entered Spelman College, a prestigious historically African American college for women.

Although Spelman, Morehouse, and other Atlanta University Center (AUC) schools were symbols of the African American elite, these institutions were also known for the progressive administrators, faculty, and students of their past and present including W. E. B. Du Bois, Benjamin E. Mays, Martin Luther King Jr., Howard Zinn, Gwen Robinson, and Julian Bond, among many others. Given someone of Robinson's social standing, background, and skin color, Spelman seemed to be a perfect fit for her. With the activist tradition of the AUC and recent events in the United States and the world—Ghana's independent in 1957, simultaneous calls by Malcolm X and Robert F. Williams for armed self-defense in 1959, and the early successes of the Civil Rights movement—Robinson's matriculation at Spelman served as a catalyst to her radicalization. By 1960, Robinson joined the Atlanta Committee on Appeal for Human Rights, which held a demonstration at the State Capitol.

As an actively involved member of the Atlanta Student Movement, Robinson worked with others to help desegregate Grady Memorial Hospital and, in 1961, she heeded Ella Baker's call to attend an organizing conference at Shaw University in Raleigh, North Carolina. This conference, which led to the launching of SNCC as a student-oriented civil rights organization, is where Robinson began to expand her activism. She joined the May 1961 Freedom Rides. After serving a 60-day jail sentence, Robinson became involved in voter registration in McComb, Mississippi. During this phase of her involvement in SNCC, many took note of her leadership and organizing abilities. Known for a sharp mind, a quick wit, and a steady determination, Robinson quickly gained the respect of her colleagues in SNCC—male and female, white and black alike. She often volunteered for some of the most dangerous assignments in SNCC, and her courage, assertiveness, and bold action were a source of inspiration for her peers.

By late 1962, Robinson was less active in the field and began to focus more of her energies on organizational administration and leadership. Indeed, she was one of the key members of a small cadre of leaders within SNCC and perhaps the most respected female in the entire organization. After her marriage to Clifford Robinson in 1963 and the birth of their son, Robinson found it difficult to juggle the demands of commitment to SNC and her new family. As the stress mounted, Robinson's health began to falter as early as 1964. In spring 1965, she earned her BA in physical education from Spelman College and became a member of SNCC's Personnel Committee after her election as executive secretary. After the organization moved to open calls for black power the next year, Robinson embraced the change and even gravitated more toward black nationalism and Pan-Africanism. She provided critical logistical support for initiatives in both the North and South during the early months of SNCC's black power phase. Despite her continued radicalization, Robinson likely voted against or abstained form voting on the measure that led to the ouster of whites from SNCC. Soon after the December 1, 1966 vote, Robinson fell ill and, by April 1967, she was diagnosed with terminal cancer. On October 7, 1967, Ruby Doris Smith Robinson died at the age of 25.

See also: Black Power; Freedom Rides; Student Nonviolent Coordinating Committee

Walter C. Rucker

Bibliography

Collier-Thomas, Bettye, and V. P. Franklin. *Sisters in the Struggle: African American Women in the Civil Rights-Black Power Movement.* New York: New York University Press, 2001.

Fleming, Cynthia Griggs. *Soon We Will Not Cry: The Liberation of Ruby Doris Smith Robinson.* New York: Rowman & Littlefield Publishers, 1998.

Fleming, Cynthia Griggs. "Black Women Activists and the Student Nonviolent Coordinating Committee: The Case of Ruby Doris Smith Robinson." In *"We Specialize in the Wholly Impossible:" A Reader in Black Women's History.* Darlene Clark Hine, Wilma King, and Linda Reed, eds. 561–77. Brooklyn, NY: Carlson Publishing, 1995.

Ross, Rosetta E. *Witnessing and Testifying: Black Women, Religion, and Civil Rights.* Minneapolis: Fortress Press, 2003.

Roosevelt, Eleanor

Eleanor Roosevelt (1884–1962), human rights activist, was born Anna Eleanor Roosevelt into a prominent New York City family. A niece of U.S. President Theodore Roosevelt and the wife of President Franklin Delano Roosevelt, Roosevelt became a force for social change in American society. An influential First Lady, she integrated the White House and advised the president on the country's economic and social problems, including civil rights of African Americans. Roosevelt served as a United States Delegate to the United Nations (1945–1952; 1961–1962) and as a chairperson of the UN Commission on Human Rights (1947–1948). The Universal Declaration of Human Rights was established under her leadership.

Eleanor Roosevelt was the daughter of Elliott Roosevelt and Anna Hall. Roosevelt's father was the godfather of Franklin Delano Roosevelt (who was Eleanor's fifth cousin). Despite her family's wealth, Roosevelt had an unhappy childhood. Her father was an alcoholic and her mother was aloof; both died before Eleanor's 10th birthday. While at a boarding school in England, Roosevelt was mentored by the schoolmistress who recognized her student's desire to help the oppressed. After returning to New York City (1902), Roosevelt taught dancing to immigrants and investigated laborer conditions. Eleanor Roosevelt and Franklin Delano Roosevelt married in New York City where President Theodore Roosevelt gave his niece away (1905). Six children were born thereafter: a daughter and five sons. Busy with her growing family, Roosevelt dealt with an interfering mother-in-law while her husband became active in politics. After love letters between her husband and social secretary were discovered in 1918, Eleanor Roosevelt left Franklin Roosevelt and offered him a divorce, which he refused. After he promised fidelity, they reconciled. Thereafter, Eleanor Roosevelt pursued her own interests with the suffrage movement and the League of Women Voters. She taught history and government at Todhunter School in New York City. After Franklin Roosevelt nearly died from polio (1921), Eleanor Roosevelt persuaded her husband to continue with his life and political career, despite his disability.

Eleanor Roosevelt immersed herself with African American issues. She befriended Mary McLeod Bethune, president of Bethune-Cookson College. The FBI started a file on Roosevelt in 1924. After Franklin Roosevelt's election as president (1933), the First Lady encouraged Americans to contact her for concerns. A popular First Lady, she received many letters, traveled to investigate concerns locally, and reported back to the president. She advised her husband to establish the National Youth Administration (NYA), where Mary McLeod Bethune was later appointed as chief of NYA's Division of Negro Affairs. Roosevelt prompted her husband to start discussions with African American leaders on antilynching legislation and desegregation of the armed forces. She agreed with the NAACP's opposition to wage differences based on race.

The president sometimes listened to his wife: he halted the firing of African American women in the Census Bureau, but he would not support the Senate antilynching bill (1937). Sharecroppers were invited to the White House to meet with the President and First Lady, who later visited their homes in the South. The First Lady defied Alabama's segregation laws by joining her African American colleagues at the Southern Conference for Human Welfare (1938). She resigned from the Daughters of the American Revolution (DAR) when it refused to allow an African American singer, Marian Anderson, to perform at Constitution Hall (1939). In 1942, Roosevelt gave the Tuskegee Airmen her support in their request to join the United States Air Force pilots in the war against Nazi Germany. She also pushed for the Army Nurses Corps to admit African American nurses. She joined the NAACP board of directors and the National Council of Negro Women. White southerners who opposed the First Lady's human rights agenda complained to the president, but Franklin Roosevelt quietly supported his wife, as he preserved her letters.

Eleanor Roosevelt's activism continued after her husband's death (1945). She hosted events to honor her husband's memory and legacy while serving as U.S. Delegate to the United Nations and later as goodwill ambassador. After supporting the integration of the public schools, Roosevelt received death threats and the Ku Klux Klan placed a bounty on her head. She persevered by traveling worldwide, giving speeches, and hosting a radio program. Roosevelt's "My Day" columns were popular, appearing in newspapers across America (1935–1962). Her columns reflected her varied interests on human rights, children issues, parenting, and politics. Despite failing health, she was on the President's Commission on the Status of Women in her final year. She died on Nov. 7, 1962, in New York City. Anna Eleanor Roosevelt was buried beside her husband in the Rose Garden of the Franklin D. Roosevelt Presidential Library in Hyde Park, New York.

See also: Anderson, Marian; Bethune, Mary McLeod; Kennedy, John Fitzgerald; Ku Klux Klan; National Association for the Advancement of Colored People; National Council of Negro Women; Tuskegee Airmen

Margaret Prentice Hecker

Bibliography

Anthony, Carl S. "Skirting the Issue: First Ladies and African Americans." *American Visions* 7, no. 5 (1992):28–32.

Bickerstaff, Joyce, and Wilbur C. Rich. "Mrs. Roosevelt and Mrs. Bethune: Collaborators for Racial Justice." *Social Education* 48, no. (1984):532–35.

Black, Allida M. "Championing a Champion: Eleanor Roosevelt and the Marian Anderson 'Freedom Concert.'" *Presidential Studies Quarterly* 20, no. 4 (1990):719–36.

Freeman, Elsie T., Walter Bodie, and Wynell Burroughs. "Document of the Month: Eleanor Roosevelt Resigns from the DAR: A Study in Conscience." *Social Education* 48, no. 7 (1984):536–41.

Gerber, Robin. *Leadership the Eleanor Roosevelt Way: Timeless Strategies from the First Lady of Courage.* New York: Portfolio; Penguin Group, 2003.

Nolde, O. Frederick. "Freedom's Charter: the Universal Declaration of Human Rights." *Headline Series* 76 (1949):3–62.

Roosevelt, Eleanor. *You Learn by Living.* Louisville, KY: Westminster John Knox Press, 1960.

Tyler, Pamela. "'Blood on Your Hands': White Southerners' Criticism of Eleanor Roosevelt during World War II." In *Before Brown: Civil Rights and White Backlash in the Modern South.* Glenn Feldman, ed., 96–115. Tuscaloosa: University of Alabama Press, 2004.

Van Thoor, Mieke. "The Missing Civil Rights in Eleanor's Roosevelt's Autobiographies." *European Contributions to American Studies* 39 (1998):216–26.

Rosewood, Florida, Riot of 1923

Beginning on New Year's Day 1923 and lasting for a week, a series of white attacks on the black residents of Rosewood, an unincorporated community in Levy County inside Florida's Panhandle, resulted in the documented deaths of six blacks and two whites and the complete destruction of the mostly black populated village. The events of the Rosewood riot or massacre were forgotten by history until Gary Moore, a Florida journalist, rediscovered and reported on them in the 1980s. In 1994, Florida legislators, after a state investigation and report, passed a claims bill that provided compensation for survivors and descendants of the victims. Rosewood remains one of the worst episodes of racial violence in Florida and one of many violent clashes between whites and blacks in the United States during the early 20th century.

Rosewood's nightmare began on the morning of January 1, 1923, when Fannie Taylor, a white woman in nearby Sumner, claimed that an unidentified black man had assaulted her. Some Rosewood survivors reported that

Taylor's assailant was not a black man, but her white lover, who was in her home while her husband was away at work. On that January morning, however, most of Sumner's white residents accepted her story and formed a posse to begin the manhunt. The posse believed that the assailant was Jessie Hunter, a black convict who had recently escaped from a local work crew. Hunter was supposedly hiding out around Rosewood after securing help from Sam Carter, a black man who lived between Sumner and Rosewood. The posse captured Carter, who confessed to hiding and taking Hunter away by wagon. Now a vengeful mob, the posse tortured and killed Cater and then moved on to Rosewood. There it confronted another black man, Aaron Carrier, whom the whites believed had also aided Hunter's escape. Before the mob could lynch Carrier, Edward Pillsbury, a sympathetic white man, managed to hide Carrier and remove him to safety.

Unfortunately, Sylvester Carrier, another member of the Carrier clan, was not so lucky. Two days after Carter's murder, a reduced white posse was still in search of Jessie Hunter (he was never found) when they heard news of a gathering of blacks at Sylvester Carrier's house in Rosewood. Sylvester Carrier had a reputation for standing up to whites and had made it known that he would not allow whites to bully him or members of his family. The white posse returned to Rosewood to investigate the reported black meeting at Carrier's house. Because of the recent violence, about two dozen members of Carrier's extended family had sought refuge inside Carrier's house, where they prepared to defend themselves.

When the posse arrived on the evening of January 4, Sylvester Carrier refused to allow any of the white men to enter his home. When two posse members, Harry Andrews and C. P. Wilkerson, attempted to force their way into the house, the blacks opened fire, killing Andrews and Wilkerson and wounding several other posse members, who returned fire against the house. Reports of the fight spread rapidly through Levy and neighboring Alachua County, where a white posse formed and moved on to Rosewood to reinforce the white men besieging Carrier's house.

Fighting at the house raged into the early morning of January 5. By then, several whites and blacks had been wounded and Sylvester Carrier and his mother, Sarah Carrier, lay dead inside the house; the rest of Carrier's family managed to escape during a lull in the shooting before dawn. News of the battle soon reached the other black residents of

An African American home in flames, the work of a white mob during the burning of Rosewood in 1923. (UPI-Bettmann/Corbis)

Rosewood. Many of them fled into the nearby woods and swamps, where they joined the Carrier refugees in hiding. After the fight, the enraged white posse burned down the Carrier house and a dozen other black homes in Rosewood. The whites also killed 50-year-old Lexie Gordon, a black woman, while she was trying to flee her burning home.

The violence at Rosewood continued for two more days. During that time, the white mob killed two more blacks, Mingo Williams and James Carrier, Sylvester's brother, who had been among the family members that escaped the Carrier house on January 5. On Sunday, January 7, the white mob celebrated the Sabbath by burning down the rest of the black homes and buildings in Rosewood. After a week of killings, two whites and at least six blacks were dead (undocumented reports claim many more blacks died), and the Rosewood community lay in ruins. The surviving black residents never returned. Rosewood disappeared from history.

Almost 60 years passed before Rosewood reclaimed public attention. In 1982, Gary Moore, a reporter for the *St. Petersburg Times*, published an article on Rosewood based on his reading of contemporary newspaper accounts and interviews with white and black witnesses. Moore continued to report on Rosewood but despite substantial initial public interest and a highly acclaimed segment on Rosewood on CBS News's *60 Minutes* in 1983, national awareness of the massacre largely receded.

Ten years later, however, Rosewood regained state and national attention when the Florida legislature brought up a claims bill to compensate Rosewood survivors and descendants who claimed that the State of Florida had failed to protect the black residents of Rosewood because of their race. After a tough legislative battle, the Florida House and Senate passed the Rosewood bill, which Governor Lawton Chiles signed into law in 1994. The bill provided proven survivors $150,000 each in compensation, created a $500,000 fund to reimburse the Rosewood families who had lost property during the riot, funded 25 annual college scholarships for minority students (the scholarships gave preference to descendants of Rosewood survivors), and allowed the state to begin a criminal investigation of the violence. Renewed interest in Rosewood led to Director John Singleton's 1997 film, *Rosewood,* which dramatized the 1923 massacre.

See also: Jim Crow; Lynching; White Mob Violence; White Supremacy

Ridgeway Boyd Murphree

Bibliography

D'Orso, Michael. *Like Judgment Day: The Ruin and Redemption of a Town Called Rosewood.* New York: G. P. Putnam's Sons, 1996.

Jones, Maxine Deloris, and Kevin McCarthy. *African Americans in Florida.* Sarasota, FL: Pineapple Press, 1993.

Ortiz, Paul. *Emancipation Betrayed: The Hidden History of Black Organizing and White Violence in Florida from Reconstruction to the Bloody Election of 1920.* Berkeley: University of California Press, 2005.

Rustin, Bayard

Bayard Rustin (1912–1987) was born on March 17, 1912, in West Chester, Pennsylvania, the illegitimate son of Florence Rustin. Florence's parents, Janifer and Julia, raised Bayard in West Chester. Julia Rustin was raised as a member of the Society of Friends or Quakers. Her belief in the Quaker doctrine of pacifism and her social activism in organizations like the National Association for the Advancement of Colored People (NAACP) helped Rustin become a social activist.

While in high school, Rustin began to protest racism. He refused to leave a West Chester restaurant that denied him service. He defiantly sat in the all-white section of the local theater. When traveling as a member of the West Chester High School track team, Rustin threatened not to run unless he and his black teammates were given integrated housing. After high school graduation in 1932, Rustin studied at Wilberforce University and Cheyney State University, but did not graduate. Bored with school, Rustin went to New York City to live with a relative in 1937. He

found temporary employment in New York through the Works Progress Administration (WPA). In 1938, he enrolled at the City College of New York but again did not graduate because he was performing with the folk group Josh White Singers and folk singer Huddie Ledbetter. Furthermore, Rustin had become a youth organizer for the Young Communist League (YCL). In June 1941, however, after the YCL declared that the fight against fascism was more important than fighting racism, Rustin resigned. He had met the socialist labor union leader A. Philip Randolph while with the YCL, and, when he left the YCL, Rustin went to work for him. Randolph planned a "March on Washington" by thousands of African Americans if President Franklin Roosevelt did not end Jim Crow in the defense industries. Roosevelt gave in to Randolph's demand, issuing an executive order banning discrimination practices by federal defense contractors. Randolph cancelled the march, but Rustin disagreed. It was the first of several rifts between Randolph and Rustin.

In the late summer of 1941, Rustin was hired as race relations secretary for the Fellowship of Reconciliation (FOR), a religious pacifist organization. In FOR, Rustin came under the mentorship of the pacifist A. J. Muste. Muste introduced him to the teachings of Mahatma Gandhi and taught him how to weld Gandhi's philosophy, the organizational skills of the Communist Party, and the pacifism of his Quaker religion into his future life work: civil rights. In 1942, Rustin and others cofounded the Congress for Racial Equality (CORE). Unlike FOR, which emphasized pacifism, CORE focused on race relations. While still at FOR, Rustin took an additional job as a CORE field secretary. On a bus trip to Nashville, Tennessee, in 1942, Rustin defied the law by sitting in the "whites only" section. He was arrested but later released. He faced a longer period of incarceration, however, for being a pacifist during World War II. In 1944, Rustin registered as a conscientious objector but refused to report for a physical examination for assignment to a camp for conscientious objectors. As a result, Rustin served 28 months in a federal penitentiary for draft evasion.

After his release from prison in 1946, Rustin worked again with A. Philip Randolph, this time with his Committee against Discrimination in the Armed Forces. Randolph opposed a new federal law requiring universal military training because it sanctioned racial segregation. He put pressure on President Harry Truman to issue an executive order revising the law. Facing reelection in 1948 and desiring to keep the black vote, Truman succumbed to Randolph's demand. He issued Executive Order 9981 outlawing discrimination on the basis of race, color, religion, or national origin in the American military. Having succeeded, Randolph wished to disband the committee; however, Rustin and others expressed dissent with Randolph in a national press conference, an action Rustin later regretted.

In 1947, Rustin was part of a group of 16 CORE and FOR activists participating in what may be the earliest known "freedom ride" in the South. The bus trip was officially known as the "Journey of Reconciliation." The purpose of the journey was to test enforcement of the 1946 U.S. Supreme Court decision *Morgan v. Virginia* outlawing discrimination in interstate travel. CORE and FOR riders deliberately sat in segregated sections of buses and trains while traveling through the South. In Chapel Hill, North Carolina, Rustin and three others were arrested and charged with violation of the state's segregation laws. Rustin was sentenced to 30 days of hard labor on a chain gang, but he was released because of good behavior after 22 days. Afterwards Rustin lectured and wrote about his chain gang experience. Several years later the state of North Carolina abolished chain gangs.

Rustin's work with FOR took on an international dimension in 1951 when he helped organize the Committee to Support South African Resistance, which later became the American Committee on Africa. In 1952, FOR sent Rustin to Africa to meet with two of the leaders of the African independence movement: Kwame Nkrumah of Ghana and Nnamdi Azikiwe of Nigeria. Back in the United States, Rustin was touring to raise money for another African trip when disaster struck. Openly gay, Rustin was arrested on a "moral charge" in Pasadena, California, in 1953 and was sentenced to 60 days in jail. His arrest made national news. In disgrace, Rustin resigned from FOR. He soon found a job with a secular pacifist group: the War Resisters League (WRL). During Rustin's 12 years at WRL, he served as executive director, co-editor of the magazine *Liberation,* and spokesperson for the WRL at international pacifist meetings.

A. Philip Randolph helped Rustin obtain a leave of absence from WRL to assist the Reverend Dr. Martin Luther King Jr. during the Montgomery bus boycott in 1956. Dr. King knew of Gandhi's writings but was unclear about how a nonviolent protest should be carried out. Rustin's involvement in the Montgomery bus boycott ended when other boycott leaders asked Rustin to leave town for fear that publicity about his past would harm the boycott. Yet Dr. King continued to call on Rustin. In 1957, he asked Rustin to help organize the Southern Christian Leadership Conference (SCLC)'s Prayer Pilgrimage to the Lincoln Memorial in Washington, D.C. Rustin also organized the National Youth Marches of 1958 and 1959. He was set to organize a SCLC demonstration at the 1960 Democratic Convention until Congressman Adam Clayton Powell threatened to expose him as gay unless he quit the project.

When a March on Washington was proposed in 1963, Rustin and A. Philip Randolph saw an opportunity to do what they dreamed of. Because he originated the idea of a march back in 1942, A. Philip Randolph was selected by the major civil rights leader to be executive director of the march. Randolph, in turn, selected as his deputy director, Bayard Rustin, and it was Rustin who actually coordinated the planning of the event. Planning was going smoothly until South Carolina Senator Strom Thumond took the floor of the U.S. Senate and denounced Rustin as a Communist, a draft dodger, and a homosexual. Although Thurmond's tirade triggered a call by some civil rights leaders for Rustin's resignation, Randolph and Dr. King continued to back Rustin as the march strategist. Rustin's job was anticipating the marchers' needs for housing and transportation, reconciling differences between civil rights and labor groups, lining up speakers and performers, and working with law enforcement officials to ensure a peaceful march. More than 200,000 whites and blacks attended the historic event on August 28, 1963. At the end of the day, the major civil rights leaders met with President John F. Kennedy at the White House. But Rustin was not among them because the other leaders said his presence would embarrass them. Nevertheless, Rustin's accomplishment as strategist of the 1963 March on Washington was the high point of his life.

Rustin and Randolph believed that the 1963 march owed its success to an alliance between organized labor and civil rights groups. Therefore Rustin and Randolph cofounded the A. Philip Randolph Institute, an organization funded by the American Federation of Labor and the Congress of Industrial Organizations (AFL-CIO). The Randolph Institute gave Rustin a formal leadership role in the Civil Rights movement and an organization promoting the coalition politics Rustin believed in. The Randolph Institute promoted the Recruitment and Training Program designed to increase minority participation in the building and construction trades. It also fostered voter registration and lobbied for labor interests in Congress. Rustin was president of the Institute from 1966 to 1979, and co-chairman from 1979 until his death. When he began working at the Randolph Institute, Rustin resigned from his job at the WRL and left the pacifist group, the Committee for Nonviolent Action.

With no time available for the peace movement, Rustin refused to participate in antiwar demonstrations during the 1960s and 1970s. He ridiculed civil rights leaders such as Dr. Martin Luther King Jr., who condemned the Vietnam War, arguing that civil rights and pacifism do not mix. Rustin held this position despite the fact that early in his career he himself was part of both movements. During this period, Rustin adopted opinions that were controversial in the black community. He opposed black studies and black power because he thought coalition building rather than separatism was the way to gain racial justice. Rustin promoted the tactics of nonviolence while there were riots in many American cities. He urged African Americans to support Israel rather than the Palestinians. Rustin's alienation from other civil rights leaders, the Black Power movement, and the antiwar movement caused one publication to call Rustin "the lone wolf of civil rights." After the 1940s, Rustin wrote many essays, speeches, and editorials that were published in newspapers and magazines. In 1971, Rustin published a number of these writings in a book entitled *Down the Line.* A second book followed in 1976: *Strategies for Freedom: The Changing Patterns of Black Protest.*

During the final decades of his life, Rustin worked with the A. Philip Randolph Institute as well as two international organizations. He was active in the International Rescue Committee (IRC), a group devoted to dealing with refugee problems around the world. With IRC, Rustin traveled to places like Southeast Asia espousing refugee relief in Cambodia, for instance. He was also a representative for Freedom House, traveling to places like Chile, El Salvador, Grenada, Dominican Republic, Pakistan, Zimbabwe, South Africa, and Haiti to monitor elections, protest dictatorships, and promote human rights.

Rustin was in Haiti assisting in setting up democratic elections in 1987 when he suddenly became ill and was rushed back to the United States. He died in New York City on August 24, 1987. His legacy grew after his death and books on his life and work appeared. On January 20, 2003, a documentary entitled *Brother Outsider: The Life of*

Bayard Rustin was first broadcasted on educational television. Formerly relegated to the background of the civil rights struggle by his peers and historians, Bayard Rustin is now being recognized as an important figure in the Civil Rights movement.

See also: CORE; King, Martin Luther Jr.; March on Washington, 1963; Montgomery Bus Boycott; Randolph, A. Philip; Southern Christian Leadership Conference; Scottsboro, Alabama Case

Eric Ledell Smith

Bibliography
Anderson, Jervis. *Bayard Rustin: Troubles I've Seen—A Biography.* New York: HarperCollins Books, 1997.
Carbide, Devon W., and Donald Weise, eds. *Time on Two Crosses: The Collected Writings of Bayard Rustin.* San Francisco: Cleis Press, 2003.
D'Emilio, John. *Lost Prophet: The Life and Times of Bayard Rustin.* New York: Free Press, 2003.
Haughton, Buzz. "Bayard Rustin: An Annotated Bio-Bibliography." *Afro-Americans in New York Life and History* 24, no. 2 (2000):7–56.
Levin, Daniel. *Bayard Rustin and the Civil Rights Movement.* New Brunswick, NJ: Rutgers University Press, 2000.
Rustin, Bayard. *Down the Line: The Collected Writings of Bayard Rustin.* Chicago: Quadrangle Books, 1971.
Rustin, Bayard. *Strategies for Freedom: The Changing Patterns of Black Protest.* New York: Columbia University Press, 1976.

Scottsboro, Alabama Case

On March 25, 1931, nine young African Americans boarded a Southern Railroad freight train traveling from Chattanooga to Memphis, Tennessee. After an altercation between the nine African Americans and a group of white youths, and the subsequent ejection of the white youths from the train, authorities stopped the train in Paint Rock, Alabama, and arrested the nine African Americans. On the train, the authorities also found two white women, Victoria Price and Ruby Bates, both disguised as boys. After being arrested and taken to jail in nearby Scottsboro, Alabama, Victoria Price claimed she had been raped by several of the African Americans. To ward off possible lynch mobs, Alabama Governor Benjamin Meek Miller ordered the Alabama National Guard to protect the jail and promised a speedy trial for the accused black men. The nine African Americans—Haywood Patterson, Clarence Norris, Willie Robertson, Andy Wright, Eugene Williams, Ozie Powell,

Roy Wright, Charles Weems, and Olen Montgomery—collectively became known as the Scottsboro Boys.

The trials of the Scottsboro Boys, which began 12 days after their arrest, prompted one of the most infamous examples of racial injustice in Alabama's history. As was the custom in the Jim Crow South, an all-white jury heard the case, presided over by Judge A. E. Hawkins. The Scottsboro Boys' attorneys, Stephen Roddy and Milo Moody, provided an incompetent defense. When the trials ended, eight of the nine defendants had been found guilty of rape and sentenced to death. A mistrial was declared in the case against Roy Wright, who was only 12 years old. The prosecution had sought a life sentence because of Wright's age, but 11 of 12 jurors held out for the death penalty.

After their initial convictions, the International Labor Defense (ILD), the legal arm of the American Communist Party, assumed the Boys' defense and brought national attention to the case. The Communist Party campaigned to defend the Scottsboro Boys, not only as a way to fight blatant injustice, but also because the publicity surrounding the case offered a tremendous recruiting opportunity among northern liberals and African Americans. Upon appeal, the Alabama Supreme Court upheld all but one of the convictions, when it ruled that Eugene Williams should not

have been tried as an adult because he was only 13 years old. On November 7, 1932, however, the United States Supreme Court, in *Powell v. Alabama,* overturned the Scottsboro Boys' convictions. The Court determined that the defendants' right to competent legal council under the Fourteenth Amendment's due process clause had been violated by the state and remanded the case to the lower court.

The Scottsboro Boys' new legal team consisted of Samuel S. Leibowitz, a defense lawyer from New York, and Joseph Brodsky, the lead attorney for the ILD. The ILD brought in the flamboyant and highly successful Leibowitz, a non-Communist, to head the defense team, but the combination of Leibowitz, a New York Jew, and the communist ILD defending accused black rapists outraged southern whites and helped the Scottsboro case to become a *cause célèbre,* unleashing a torrent of suspicion, racism, and anti-Semitism in Alabama and throughout the South. It also galvanized the northern critics of Jim Crow society.

The second round of trials began on March 30, 1933, in Decatur, Alabama, presided over by Judge James E. Horton Jr. After Leibowitz unsuccessfully challenged Alabama's practice of excluding African Americans from its jury rolls, Haywood Patterson's trail began, as each of the Scottsboro Boys had to be tried separately. The trial was tension-filled

These nine African American youths, known as the Scottsboro Boys, were imprisoned in Scottsboro, Alabama, after being falsely accused of raping two white women in a freight car. Here, the young men are pictured conferring with civil rights activist Juanita Jackson Mitchell in 1937. (Library of Congress)

as Leibowitz and prosecutor Thomas G. Knight Jr., attempted to discredit the other's witnesses. Leibowitz had a measure of success poking holes in the testimony of the prosecution's main witness, Victoria Price. He also secured the surprise appearance of Ruby Bates, who recanted her earlier statement that she had been raped, but Bates's evasions on the witness stand made the prosecution's charge that she had been bribed by the defense more believable. Dr. Marvin H. Lynch, one of the doctors who initially examined Price and Bates, spoke with Judge Horton behind closed doors and told him that he was convinced the girls had not been raped, but he refused to testify because he feared his practiced in Scottsboro would be ruined.

In the closing remarks, Wade Wright, the Morgan County solicitor, emphasized both Leibowitz and the communists' participation in the trial and charged the jury to show them that justice in Alabama could not be bought by "Jew money" from New York. Wright's inflammatory speech had the desired effect. On April 9, 1933, the jury, which had deliberated for only five minutes, found Patterson guilty of rape and sentenced him to death. Disappointed with the jury's verdict and convinced of the Scottsboro Boys' innocence, Judge Horton, on June 22, courageously set aside the jury verdict and ordered a new trial. His decision to overturn the verdict cost Horton his political career. In the 1934 Democratic primary election—*the* election in the South—Horton was defeated and returned to private practice. In a clear rebuke of Horton's decision, Alabamians overwhelmingly elected Thomas Knight as lieutenant governor.

Despite Horton's belief in the Scottsboro Boys' innocence, Knight pressed ahead with another round of trials in late November 1933. A new judge, William W. Callahan, ruthlessly favored the prosecution, going as far as to instruct the jury that a white woman would not voluntarily have sex with a black man. Juries found both Haywood Patterson and Clarence Norris guilty of rape and sentenced them to death. Leibowitz wasted no time in filing their appeals. Judge Callahan postponed the remaining trials until the appeals process was completed.

As before, the Alabama Supreme Court refused to overturn the verdicts. And as before, the Scottsboro Case went to the United States Supreme Court, which heard arguments on February 15, 1935, on both the Patterson and Norris cases. Leibowitz argued that the verdicts should be overturned because the state excluded blacks from juries,

in violation of the due process clause of the Fourteenth Amendment. Forged jury rolls during the Patterson and Norris trials showed African Americans on the rolls, and this attempt at subterfuge outraged the justices. On April 1, 1935, the Court, in *Norris v. Alabama,* unanimously held Alabama's system of jury selection to exclude African Americans unconstitutional and overturned the convictions of Norris and Patterson.

Because public opinion in Alabama remained steadfastly in favor of prosecuting the accused Scottsboro Boys, the state went forward with another round of trials. Haywood Patterson's fourth trial opened on January 6, 1936, with Judge Callahan presiding once again. With this round of trials, the ILD withdrew from the case, and Leibowitz, profoundly unpopular in Alabama, allowed Clarence Watts, a Huntsville attorney, to take the lead. Although Leibowitz stayed in the background, he remained thoroughly involved in Patterson's defense. Lieutenant Governor Knight returned as the lead prosecutor. Patterson's conviction by another all white jury came as no surprise, but instead of giving him death as expected, the jury sentenced him to only 75 years.

Between Patterson's conviction in January 1936 and the Norris trial that opened on July 15, 1937, prosecutor and Lieutenant Governor Thomas Knight died, leaving the prosecution in the hands of Thomas Lawson, the assistant attorney general. Judge Callahan, determined to move quickly and bring the Scottsboro Case to an end, scheduled subsequent trials one after the other. In a trial that lasted only two days, another all white jury found Norris guilty of rape and sentenced him to death. After this conviction, Clarence Watts withdrew from the Scottsboro Boys' cases, leaving Leibowitz again to lead their defense. Lawson waived the death penalty in the following trials. In rapid succession, other all-white juries quickly convicted Andy Wright and sentenced him to 99 years, and Charley Weems received 75 years. Ozie Powell pleaded guilty to assaulting a deputy, but the state dropped rape charges against him. All charges were dropped against the remaining four Scottsboro Boys, Robertson, Montgomery, Williams, and Roy Wright.

In October 1937, the United States Supreme Court refused to review Patterson's conviction. Alabama Governor Bibb Graves commuted Norris's death sentence to life imprisonment after the Alabama Supreme Court affirmed the death sentence of Norris and the prison sentences of

Wright and Weems. By this time, the Scottsboro Case had severely tarnished Alabama's image worldwide and Alabamians grew weary of the drawn-out spectacle. A number of prominent Alabama attorneys and newspapermen lobbied Graves to parole the imprisoned Scottsboro Boys, and Graves personally interviewed the remaining five. Whether incensed by their malevolence toward him or as a result of political cowardice, Graves refused to grant any pardons before he left office in 1939. He even refused to meet with President Franklin D. Roosevelt to discuss the matter.

It took until November 17, 1943, for the Alabama's Pardons and Parole Board to release Charlie Weems. In January 1944, it paroled both Norris and Wright. They both broke parole and were imprisoned once again. In late 1946, the board released Powell and paroled Norris once again. Norris broke his parole and left Alabama never to return. He lived as a fugitive until Governor George C. Wallace granted him a full and unconditional pardon in October 1976. As for Haywood Patterson, the board would not grant a parole, as they considered him the most dangerous and incorrigible of all the Scottsboro Boys. Nevertheless, Patterson managed to escape prison in the summer of 1948 and, after avoiding a large police manhunt, eventually reached his sister's home in Detroit. Patterson hid there for two years until his arrest by the Federal Bureau of Investigation, but Michigan Governor G. Mennen Williams refused his extradition to Alabama. Alabama officials let the matter die. While Patterson hid from authorities in Detroit, he wrote an account of his experiences, *Scottsboro Boy*, which appeared in 1950. Although he was not returned to Alabama, he remained troubled. After stabbing a man in a barroom fight on December 18, 1950, a jury in Detroit convicted Patterson of manslaughter and sentenced him to 15 to 20 years in prison. He died of cancer only two years later.

On June 9,1950, Andy Wright left Kilby prison, the last of the Scottsboro Boys to be set free. The other Scottsboro Boys, as well as most of the other figures associated with the Scottsboro Case, remained out of the public eye. Only Samuel Leibowitz achieved notable success. After the Scottsboro Case ended, he returned to his highly successful law practice in New York City and later became a justice of the New York Supreme Court in 1962.

See also: Jim Crow; National Association for the Advancement of Colored People

Dan J. Puckett

Bibliography
Carter, Dan T. *Scottsboro: A Tragedy of the American South.* Revised Edition. Baton Rouge and London: Louisiana State University Press, 1979.
Gilmore, Glenda Elizabeth. *Defying Dixie: The Radical Roots of Civil Rights, 1919–1950.* New York and London: W. W. Norton, 2008.
Goodman, James E. *Stories of Scottsboro.* New York: Knopf, 1994.
Howard, Walter T., ed. *Black Communists Speak on Scottsboro: A Documentary History.* Philadelphia: Temple University Press, 2008.
Kinshasa, Kwando Mbiassi. *The Man From Scottsboro: Clarence Norris and the Infamous 1931 Alabama Rape Trial, in His Own Words.* Jefferson, NC and London: McFarland Publishers, 1997.
Norris, Clarence, and Sybil D. Washington. *The Last of the Scottsboro Boys: An Autobiography.* New York: G. P. Putnam's Sons, 1979.
Patterson, Haywood, and Earl Conrad. *Scottsboro Boy.* New York: Doubleday, 1950.

Seale, Bobby

Bobby Seale (1936–) is a prominent civil rights advocate and cofounder of the Black Panther Party. Seale and the Black Panthers advocated a militant approach to civil rights. The organization in general and Seale, in particular, strongly opposed the nonviolent and integrationist stances of Martin Luther King and other moderate civil rights leaders. Seale and the Panthers, furthermore, advocated militancy when necessary in order to acquire black liberation.

Robert George Seale was born October 22, 1936, in Dallas, Texas. Bobby and his family resided in Texas until World War II, and then moved to Oakland, California. Seale attended Berkeley High School until his senior year. Right before graduation Seale was informed that he would not graduate owing to poor grades in the last term. In anger he tried to enter both the Army and Air Force. Seale was turned down by both organizations because of an injury he received years earlier when a car ran over his foot. Angered by his failure, Seale returned to the Air Force recruitment center and tried to plead his case. After convincing doctors and recruiters that his foot injury would not inhibit his ability to perform, the Air Force inducted him into their program. After completing basic training, Seale went to Amarillo, Texas, to train as an aircraft sheet metal mechanic. After six months in Texas, Seale chose to go to

Rapid City, South Dakota. Seale's specialties were needed at the Ellsworth Air Force Base in Rapid City. After almost four years in the Air Force, Seale was discharged for disorderly conduct.

Seale's discharge came after a battle between him and his commander. When the commander ordered Seale to hand in his drums, Seale refused, and was discharged. Seale's discharge was only one example of many when his temper and rage overcame him. Seale was known for having an uncontrollable temper and built up rage. While in the Air Force he beat a fellow troop member with a bedadaptor.

After his discharge, Seale returned to Oakland to work as a sheet metal mechanic at various plants. He simultaneously worked to earn his high school diploma while attending night school. He finally received his diploma and, in 1962, began school at Merritt College, the city college of Oakland. At Merritt, Seale took classes in engineering and drafting. To make money on the side he was a bartender and stand-up comedian. While attending Merritt, Seale joined the Afro-American Association. Through this organization Seale met

Bobby Seale (left) and Huey Newton cofounded the Black Panther Party, which advocated black power and black opposition to the Vietnam War. (AP/Wide World Photos)

Huey Newton. Within a few years, Newton and Seale became frustrated with the Afro-American Association. To Newton and Seale the association was not going far enough. Both men believed strongly in Malcolm X and the black power that he professed. In place of the Afro-American Association, Newton and Seale created the Soul Students Advisory Counsel.

Around this time, Seale married and on July 9, 1965, he and his wife Artie had a son, Malik Nkrumah Stagolee Seale. While Seale had started a family, he continued his fight for black liberation. In October 1966, Seale and Newton organized the Black Panther Party for Self-Defense. Fellow classmate and friend, Bobby Hutton was enlisted as the first member and became the treasurer of the party. The goal of the Black Panther Party (BPP) was set forth in their famous ten point program. The program advocated self-defense and militancy to bring black liberation. The Black Panthers, however, did not necessarily advocate separatism. The organization frequently worked with whites, if they too wished to advance the black race. The Panthers also set up a number of community programs, such as their infamous free breakfast program.

Although the BPP started out as an Oakland organization, it quickly gained national attention. The BPP adopted uniforms that contained black berets, black pants, black leather jackets, black shoes, and powder blue shirts. By 1968, BPP offices were opening up nationwide. The militancy of the Black Panthers quickly gained the attention of the national government. The Black Panthers often carried guns, which furthered concerned and drew the attention of the government. In 1968, J. Edgar Hoover, head of the Federal Bureau of Investigation (FBI), ordered an investigation into the BPP.

Seale and many other Black Panthers gained additional national attention after protesting at the Democratic Convention in Chicago in 1968. Seale's involvement in Chicago, however, landed him in significant trouble with the government. In September 1969, Seale and seven white radicals were indicted under the antiriot provision of the Civil Rights Act of 1968. The provision forbids anyone from crossing state lines to riot.

When Seale came to trial, the judge of the case declared him bound and gagged after numerous outbursts in court. Seale consequently was sentenced to four years in jail for contempt of court. While in jail, Seale was charged for ordering the execution of Alex Rackley, a former Black

Panther who was suspected of being a government informer. In May 1971, Seale was cleared of all charges when a hung jury could not reach a decision. The following year Seale was released from prison and the contempt charges were dropped.

When Seale returned to Oakland, he found a decimated Black Panther Party from the one he had left. The violence and militancy that the BPP advocated had left many members dead. Internal strife also had led to a decrease in popularity and membership. In 1973, Seale ran for mayor of Oakland but came in second out of nine candidates. He left the Black Panthers in 1974 but continued to fight against social and political injustices. Today, Seale continues to support various organizations that fight injustices in the world. His own organization, REACH, is dedicated to youth education and advancement.

See also: Black Panther Party; Civil Rights Act of 1968; Cleaver, Eldridge; COINTELPRO; Newton, Huey P.

Mindy R. Weidman

Bibliography

Jones, Charles E., ed. *The Black Panther Party Reconsidered.* Baltimore, MD: Black Classic Press, 1998.

Seale, Bobby. *A Lonely Rage: The Autobiography of Bobby Seale.* New York: New York Times Books, 1978.

Seale, Bobby. *Seize the Time: The Story of the Black Panther Party and Huey P. Newton.* Baltimore, MD: Black Classic Press, 1991.

Selassie, Haile

Born Lij Tafari Makonnen in the village of Ejersa Goro (then Abyssinia), Haile Selassie (1892–1975) was the emperor of Ethiopia (1930–1936; 1941–1974) and became a powerful Pan-African figure and religious symbol for the Rastafarian movement. As the son of a prominent governor and grandnephew of Emperor Menelik II, the young Tafari excelled in school and soon caught the attention of his great uncle, who appointed him governor over portions of Sidamo province at the tender age of 14. After the death of Menelik four years later, Tafari took the same post his father had held and became governor of Harar. In April 1911, he formally entered the city and took the name Ras Tafari. (*Ras* is an Amharic term meaning *Duke*) On August 3, 1911, Tafari married Menen Asfaw, niece of Empress Lij Iyasu, whom he helped depose in September 1916. As a Coptic Christian,

Tafari opposed Menelik's Muslim grandson and successor, Lij Yasu. Menelik's daughter Zauditu became empress in 1916, with Tafari named as regent to the throne. Upon Zauditu's death on April 2, 1930, Tafari became Emperor Haile Selassie I (meaning "Holy Trinity") and claimed that his imperial lineage ran deep into Ethiopia's past. Selassie maintained that he was a direct descendent of Makeda (the Queen of Sheba) and King Solomon of Israel, and at his coronation in Addis Ababa on November 21, 1930, he took the full title His Imperial Majesty, Emperor Haile Selassie I, King of Kings and Lord of Lords, Conquering Lion of the Tribe of Judah, Elect of God.

Selassie had played a crucial role in outlining Menelik's modernizing reforms throughout the 1920s, including the formal abolishment of slavery in 1924 and calling for Ethiopia's admission to the League of Nations in 1923. As emperor, he continued to stress internal reforms, introducing the country's first written constitution in 1931. The new constitution established a bicameral legislature and helped facilitate a degree of popular political representation unknown in the region's history. It was Italy's invasion of Ethiopia in 1935, however, that introduced Selassie to most of the world. On June 30, 1936, he traveled to Geneva and delivered an impassioned speech to the League of Nations asking for global support against fascist aggression. Selassie's contention—that World War II would be imminent if the League of Nations did not collectively come to the aid of nations like Ethiopia—would prove to be prophetic, and his stirring delivery helped solidify his place in the world's spotlight. After the League failed to take action, Italy invaded Ethiopia during the Second Italo-Abyssinian War and occupied the country for six years. Selassie fled to Europe in exile during this period until Italy's defeat at the hands of United Kingdom, and Ethiopian forces liberated the country in 1941.

Upon his return to power, Selassie continued to stress internal reform and the importance of Ethiopia's role in the emerging global community. Ethiopia became a charter member of the United Nations (UN), and Selassie introduced a revised constitution in 1955 that further extended political representation through the establishment of a lower house of parliament. In addition, he helped the country embark on a plan of massive educational reform and initiated a number of large-scale development projects aimed at modernizing Ethiopia's infrastructure. During the 1960s, Selassie began to champion Pan-Africanism while simultaneously aligning Ethiopia with the West. In 1963, he presided over the formation of the Organization of African Unity (OAU), headquartered in Addis Ababa, and traveled internationally throughout the decade and into the 1970s. As the head of state with the longest tenure in office, the emperor continued to garner respect and accolades at international events around the world. He was given precedence over all other leaders at the state funerals of President John F. Kennedy and Charles de Gaulle.

In 1972, severe drought caused a famine to spread in the Wollo province while Selassie celebrated his 80th birthday. The Imperial government kept many of the facts surrounding the scope of the famine from both Selassie and the rest of the world. When news of its existence finally reached the international community, Selassie suffered a serious drop in popularity, both within and outside Ethiopia. Wracked by his ill health and fledgling popularity, he was further weakened by economic disruption and a military coup deposed him on September 12, 1974. On August 28, 1975, state media reported that Selassie had died of complications following prostate surgery. Many, including his doctor, denied the government's version of events and charged that the ex-emperor had been murdered while under house arrest following his removal from power. Others believed that Selassie never passed away at all, including many within the Rastafari movement.

Beginning in the 1930s on the island of Jamaica, a growing movement based on Marcus Mosiah Garvey's "Back to Africa" campaign began to take hold among the more impoverished descendents of slaves imported to the island from West Africa. Based on a syncretic blend of Christianity and West African ritual, the Rastafarian movement was a particular form of Ethiopianism—a theology that posits the black race as the original Israelites of the Old Testament and interprets that the returned Messiah of the New Testament will be a redeemer for all African people. For many followers of the Rastafari movement, Garvey's writings and comments were prophecies fulfilled by the reign of Selassie and embodied in the emperor himself. Most within the movement see Selassie as God incarnate, a black Messiah who will unite the African Diaspora and lead the black race to freedom.

Selassie did not claim to be a deity, although he never denounced the Rastafari movement and its contention that he was the Redeemer prophesized in the New Testament Book of Revelation. In addition, his claim to the line of King Solomon and the titles he took on becoming emperor were direct references to the Book of Revelation and the Messiah. Selassie's defiance and eloquence before the League of Nations—and later, the United Nations—solidified his popularity throughout the African Diaspora. In addition, Ethiopia's defeat of Italy in 1941 and Selassie's subsequent return to power further enhanced the Rastafari contention that Ethiopia was a spiritually significant land, a pure and unfettered Africa that had remained free from colonial oppression. Selassie's call for Pan-African solidarity also indicated to many followers his status as a redemptive figure for the black race and helped fuel the growing messianic cult surrounding him.

On April 21, 1966, more than 100,000 Rastafarians gathered in Kingston when Selassie paid his first visit to Jamaica. Many came to view the man whom they believed to be God, and Selassie appeared frightened and surprised by the crowd. Nevertheless, Selassie left the airport at the behest of prominent Rasta leader Mortimer Planner and successfully toured Kingston amidst a throng of followers. It was here that Rita Marley, wife of musician Bob Marley, first viewed Selassie and converted to Rastafarianism. Her influence would later draw Marley himself into the faith, and the growing globalization of roots reggae music became a powerful conduit for Rastafarian ideals beginning in the late 1960s. One of Marley's most popular songs, titled "War," included lyrics drawn directly from Selassie's influential antiracism speech before the United Nations in 1963. Marley also wrote the prominent Rasta-infused song "Jah Live" as a reaction to Selassie's purported death in 1975.

Early influential Rastas, like Leonard Percival Howell, faced a fierce backlash from the Jamaican state. The government charged Howell with sedition after the leader refused to declare himself a loyal subject of King George V of England, instead pledging himself to Emperor Selassie. The earliest Rastas most likely considered Selassie a king for all African people and a symbol of black pride and unity; however, his status as a spiritual figure developed quite quickly. In 1963, Jamaica achieved its independence from England. Coupled with the growing popularity of roots reggae and Rasta culture, the faith began to spread and flourish worldwide. Fueled by emigration from the West Indies, a growing number of religious Rastas appeared in the United States and flourished in small communities, most commonly in urban areas. In addition, cultural Rastafarianism flourished to a greater degree as the popularity of Jamaican music continued to rise throughout the 1970s.

Rastafarian words and symbols directly reference Selassie as a prophet of the black race. Rastas pronounce the Roman numeral in "Haile Selassie I" as the first person pronoun "I" and commonly repeat the refrain "I-in-I" to signify their individual attachment to Selassie and the greater African race. Rastas also speak of Selassie as "Jah Rastafari Selassie," and believe that marijuana (*ganja*) helps facilitate a deeper spiritual connection with both Selassie and each other. Some Rastafarians believe that Selassie is still alive; others insist that he will return to earth one day to facilitate a judgment of all peoples, calling the faithful to reside forever in Holy Mount Zion, a mythical place in Africa.

Selassie did not publicly denounce the Rastafari, but he did become more conservative in his rhetoric later in life and tried at times to redirect the movement. Despite his goal of Pan-African unity, he called on Planner, Howell, and other early Rasta leaders to encourage liberation and racial uplift in Jamaica itself, instead of outright emigration to Ethiopia. He also remained committed to the Ethiopian Orthodox Church and is said to have confided in Orthodox leaders his frustration with the course of the Rastafari movement in Jamaica. In the face of Italian aggression, his impassioned request for support from the League of Nations actually drew criticism from some black nationalists, including Marcus Garvey. In a 1967 interview, Selassie appeared to rebuff his status as a supernatural figure and denied being a divinity. Nevertheless, Selassie sympathized with the movement and its followers, donating a piece of land south of Addis Ababa for use by Jamaican Rastafarians in 1948. Called *Shashamane,* a small Jamaican community with a number of devout Rastas still inhabits the colony to this day.

See also: African Diaspora; African Imperialism; Ethiopian Peace Movement; Garvey, Marcus; Organization of African Unity; Pan-Africanism

Lane Demas

Bibliography
Chevannes, Barry. *Rastafari: Roots and Ideology.* Syracuse, NY: Syracuse University Press, 1994.

Chevannes, Barry, ed. *Rastafari and Other African-Caribbean Worldviews.* New Brunswick, NJ: Rutgers University Press, 1995.

Getachew, Indrias. *Beyond the Throne: The Enduring Legacy of Emperor Haile Selassie I.* Addis Ababa, Ethiopia: Shama Books, 2001.

Lockot, Hans Wilhelm. *The Mission: The Life, Reign, and Character of Haile Selassie I.* New York: St. Martin's Press, 1989.

Marcus, Harold. *Haile Sellassie I: The Formative Years.* Los Angeles: University of California Press, 1987.

Schwab, Peter. *Haile Selassie I: Ethiopia's Lion of Judah.* Chicago: Nelson-Hall, 1979.

Self-Segregation

Self-segregation, a concept rearticulated in the late 20th century as "community-control black nationalism," was embraced by a number of African American intellectuals and activists at the turn of the 20th century. In particular, this concept was given voice in the literary work of Sutton Griggs (*Imperium in Imperio*) and in the polemical writings of W. E. B. Du Bois. By the late 1960s, the term "black power" captured much of the essence of self-segregation as articulated by Griggs and Du Bois. In essence, self-segregation was a call to create autonomous and self-sufficient black communities in Jim Crow America.

As one of the principal advocates of self-segregation, Du Bois witnessed a remarkable ideological transformation between the publication of *The Souls of Black Folk* in 1903 and his resignation as the editor of *Crisis* and his first resignation from the NAACP on June, 26 1934. In the months leading up to his eventual resignation, Du Bois—apparently disenchanted with the prospects of defeating Jim Crow segregation—began to advocate for independence from white communities and reliance on black institutions and organizations. In a series editorials published in *Crisis,* the national organ of the NAACP, Du Bois began to articulate and give shape to his plan for self-segregation. In the April 1934 edition, he wrote that blacks should organize their strength as consumers, learn to cooperate and become producers, and create and run their own institutions. When Walter White, executive secretary of the NAACP, criticized Du Bois for this controversial stance, he responded by reminding readers that the light-complexioned spokesperson of the organization could pass for white and did not have to suffer the daily indignities of blackness and Jim Crow segregation. This war of words between editor and executive secretary would leave Du Bois no other choice but to tender his resignation from the newsletter he founded a quarter-century earlier.

After he left the editorial office of the *Crisis,* Du Bois gave a number of speeches that fleshed out, more fully, his idea of self-segregation. These efforts culminated in the publication of "A Negro Nation within the Nation" in June 1935. This article would be the most sustained treatment on the issue offered by Du Bois to date. He began the article with a discussion of the social, economic, and political problems facing blacks in the Depression-era South and North. Evoking concepts once championed by his arch rival, Booker T. Washington, Du Bois noted that African Americans had not successfully created a sound economic foundation in the aftermath of emancipation. The failure of Radical Reconstruction was the failure to provide freed people with land on which they could base an independent existence in America. Because he saw few available allies and no forthcoming changes in American society, Du Bois concluded the article by stating that the only plausible solution was racial separation and black community autonomy.

This call for "self-segregation" closely mirrors community-control black nationalism espoused by black power advocates. Stokely Carmichael (Kwame Ture) and Huey P. Newton would have found a great degree of resonance with Du Bois's suggestion that African Americans could be self-sufficient through the creation of consumer cooperatives in which farmers sold their produce to black-owned grocers and technicians trained at Hampton and Tuskegee could guide black industry. What is startling about this change in Du Bois's worldview is not only that it embraced Washington's ideas about the utility of vocational training but it also incorporated some of the structural concepts operationalized by another one of his chief rivals—Marcus Garvey.

See also: A Negro Nation Within the Nation; Black Nationalism; Black Power; Du Bois, W. E. B.; Garvey, Marcus; Griggs, Sutton

Walter C. Rucker

Bibliography

Bracey, John, August Meier, and Elliott Rudwick, eds. *Black Nationalism in America.* Indianapolis: Bobbs-Merrill, 1970.

Du Bois, W. E. B. "A Negro Nation with A Nation," *Current History and Forum* 42 (1935):265–70.

Du Bois, W. E. B. "Segregation in the North," *The Crisis* 41 (1934): 115–17.

Griggs, Sutton E. *Imperium in Imperio.* New York: Arno Press, 1969.

Moses, Wilson Jeremiah. *The Golden Age of Black Nationalism, 1850–1925.* New York: Oxford University Press, 1978.

Selma March

The Selma march was a five-day event in 1965 during which an interracial group of protestors traveled more than 50 miles on foot from Selma, Alabama, to the state capital of Montgomery. It culminated in a mass rally on the steps of Alabama's capitol building where a crowd of 25,000 people, including civil rights activists, religious leaders, and everyday people from across the United States, heard one of Martin Luther King Jr.'s most remembered speeches. The Selma march focused national attention on the exclusion of African Americans from the electoral process and galvanized public sentiment in support of the Voting Rights Act of 1965. The event was one of the last large-scale protest demonstrations of the Civil Rights movement's "classic" phase during which a series of public protests drew national attention to the impact of racial segregation and helped bring an end to the legal structures of the system of racial discrimination known as Jim Crow.

The march that eventually made it to Montgomery began on Sunday, March 21, 1965, when approximately 3,000 people left Brown Chapel AME Church in Selma, Alabama, and crossed the Edmund Pettus Bridge on the eastern edge of the city. The procession continued along both highways and rural county roads, enduring rain and cold weather, as well as threats of violence, along the way. By court order, only 300 of the marchers were permitted to walk the entire distance from Selma to Montgomery, but as the march made its official entry into Montgomery on Thursday, March 25, its ranks swelled once again.

The march that reached Montgomery actually represented the third attempt to do so. On Sunday, March 7, in an event known as "Bloody Sunday," a group of marchers made its way from Brown Chapel Church as far as the Pettus Bridge only to be set upon by state troopers and other law enforcement officers. With many of them attacking from atop horses, the officers pursued the marchers all the way back to Brown Chapel and continued their assault until no African Americans could be found on Selma's streets. John Lewis of the Student Nonviolent Coordinating Committee (SNCC) was among the most seriously injured, suffering a fractured skull, and numerous others were treated for cuts, broken bones, and exposure to tear gas. In a development that was unusually swift for the time, film footage of the attack aired that same evening on ABC, interrupting the network's broadcast of the film *Judgment at Nuremberg.*

Two days later, Martin Luther King Jr. fronted a second march, but once again it only went as far as the Pettus Bridge. Per an advance agreement designed to comply with a federal court's injunction against proceeding all the way to Montgomery, King did not attempt to lead the group across the bridge. Instead, the group knelt in prayer and returned to Brown Chapel. That evening, attacks by local whites resulted in the death of James Reeb, a white seminary student who had traveled to Selma from Boston to participate. Reeb's death and the violence of Bloody Sunday prompted an address by President Lyndon Johnson before a joint session of Congress in which he called for passage of the Voting Rights Act and invoked the civil rights anthem "We Shall Overcome." Six days after Johnson's speech, the court lifted its injunction, and the third and final march commenced.

The full story of the march, however, stretched back further even than Bloody Sunday. For several years before 1965, a cadre of SNCC fieldworkers had been working with local black leaders and organizations in an effort to challenge racial discrimination in Selma and develop indigenous black leaders. These activists built their efforts around the issue of voter registration and coordinated regular processions of would-be black registrants to Selma's downtown courthouse. Their efforts prompted sustained and often violent reactions from local whites including state, county, and city officials who jealously guarded the political hold they maintained across Alabama's Black Belt.

The ability to count on such stubborn resistance was one of the reasons that, in 1964, Martin Luther King Jr. and the Southern Christian Leadership Conference (SCLC) accepted an invitation to come to Selma and lend King's national recognition to the continuing demonstrations. Although his arrival amplified existing tensions between

Flag-bearing demonstrators march from Selma to Montgomery, Alabama, in the historic March 1965 voting rights protest. The march led directly to the 1965 Voting Rights Act, which outlawed Southern states' attempts to prevent African Americans from voting. (Library of Congress)

SNCC and the SCLC, King brought additional resources and exposure to the Selma campaign. Racial tensions increased after King's arrival as Dallas County Sheriff Jim Clark met the protestors with violence and mass arrests. Clark jailed at least 4,000 demonstrators between January and March 1965. Events in Selma even prompted a visit from Malcolm X. In February, Jimmie Lee Jackson, a black resident of Marion, Alabama, was murdered during one of the numerous marches taking place simultaneously in the rural areas surrounding Selma. A proposal to carry Jackson's coffin to Alabama's state capital made his death the genesis of what became the Selma march.

In the years and decades that followed the Selma march, the city continued to be the site of civil rights activity as African Americans met resistance in their efforts to translate their newfound voting rights into tangible political power. Although the persistence of racial tensions revealed the Selma march to have been less than a panacea for many local concerns related to race, its contributions to the national Civil Rights movement are undeniable.

See also: Bloody Sunday; Johnson, Lyndon Baines; King, Martin Luther Jr.; Lewis, John; Southern Christian Leadership Conference; Student Nonviolent Coordinating Committee; Voting Rights Act, 1965; Williams, Hosea

Robert Warner Widell Jr.

Bibliography
Ashmore, Susan Youngblood. *Carry it On: The War on Poverty and the Civil Rights Movement in Alabama, 1964–1972*. Athens: University of Georgia Press, 2008.
Branch, Taylor. *At Canaan's Edge: America in the King Years, 1965–1968*. New York: Simon & Schuster, 2006.
Chestnut, J. L. *Black in Selma: The Uncommon Life of J. L. Chestnut, Jr.* Tuscaloosa: University of Alabama Press, 2007.
Thornton, J. Mills. *Dividing Lines: Municipal Politics and the Struggle for Civil Rights in Montgomery, Birmingham, and Selma*. Tuscaloosa: University of Alabama Press, 2002.

Shabazz, Betty X

Betty X Shabazz (1934–1997), also known as Betty Dean Sanders and Betty X, was a former member of the Nation of Islam, wife of Malcolm X, and a longstanding professor and administrator at Medgar Evers College in New York. Born in either Detroit, Michigan or Pinehurst, Georgia in 1934, Shabazz was likely abused by her biological mother,

prompting her adoption at age 11 by Lorenzo and Helen Malloy, a prominent entrepreneur in Detroit and his activist wife. After high school, Shabazz attended Tuskegee Institute in Alabama where she encountered frequent examples of overt racism. Finding southern racism incomprehensible, Shabazz moved to New York City in the mid-1950s where she attended the Brooklyn State Hospital School of Nursing. On one Friday night, a friend working at the hospital invited her to dinner and to attend a lecture by a minister of the Nation of Islam at Harlem Temple No. 7. Although Shabazz was not initially moved to join the organization, she did meet Malcolm X who later talked to her about her experiences with overt racism in Alabama.

By the time Shabazz graduated from nursing school in 1958, she was already a dedicated member of the Nation of Islam and, on January 14 of the same year, she and Malcolm X were married in Lansing, Michigan. Within seven years of their marriage, the couple had six daughters. Shabazz was, in fact, pregnant with twins on February 21, 1965, the day her husband was assassinated at New York's Audubon Ballroom. After Malcolm's death, Shabazz went back to school, earning a master's degree in public health education from Jersey City College in 1970 and a doctorate in education administration from the University of Massachusetts in 1975. In 1976, she began her work at Medgar Evers College in New York as an associate professor of health administration and, eventually, director of the school's Department of Communications and Public Relations.

Shabazz also played a significant role in elevating the Black Panther Party for Self-Defense to the national stage. Early in 1967, she was invited to appear at the Malcolm X Memorial Day Conference, the offices of *Ramparts Magazine*, and at the Black House—a cultural center in San Francisco—where she was escorted and guarded by several Black Panthers during her stay. Among those in Shabazz's armed guard detail were Huey P. Newton and Bobby Seale, two of the three founders of the Black Panther Party. In fact, the series of events that led to Shabazz's visit to the Bay area in 1967 also prompted Eldridge Cleaver's first meeting with Newton and Seale and his eventual decision to join the Black Panthers. Newton and Cleaver needed someone to draft an invitation letter to Shabazz and the person they enlisted was Cleaver, a follower of the teachings of Malcolm X while he was in prison.

In the 1990s, Shabazz engaged in a number of activities, from serving as a consultant for Spike Lee's film *Malcolm X* to publicly linking Louis Farrakhan to the assassination of her husband. Shabazz and Farrakhan reconciled after Qubilah Shabazz—her second daughter with Malcolm—was accused of trying to hire an assassin to kill Farrakhan. Farrakhan later participated actively in fundraisers for Qubilah's defense and invited Shabazz to give a speech at the October 1995 Million Man March. Tragically, Shabazz died on June 23, 1997 three weeks after suffering extensive burns in a fire set by her 12-year-old grandson who was, ironically, named after her husband. Her death was met with an international outpouring of grief by those touched by her perseverance and strength.

See also: Black Nationalism; Muhammad, Elijah; Nation of Islam; X, Malcolm

Walter C. Rucker

Bibliography
Clarke, John Henrik, A. Peter Bailey, and Earl Grant, eds. *Malcolm X: The Man and His Times.* New York: Macmillan, 1969.
Rickford, Russell John. *Betty Shabazz: A Remarkable Story of Survival and Faith before and after Malcolm X.* Naperville, IL: Sourcebooks, 2003.
Shabazz, Ilyasah, and Kim McLarin. *Growing Up X: A Memoir by the Daughter of Malcolm X.* New York: One World/Ballantine Books, 2003.
X, Malcolm, and Alex Haley. *The Autobiography of Malcolm X.* New York: One World/Ballantine Books, 1992.

Shakur, Assata

Assata Shakur (1947–), former member of the Black Panther Party, is currently living in exile in Cuba. While activists and artists in the United State and around the world hail Assata Shakur as a revolutionary thinker, the Federal Bureau of Investigation is offering $1 million for her capture. Assata Shakur was born in Jamaica Queens, New York as Joanne Deborah Byron. She was later known as Joanne Chesimard. Her birth date is believed to be July 16, 1947, but in her autobiography *Assata,* Shakur states with pride that the FBI has had difficulties gaining information about her origins. During her early life, Shakur lived with her grandparents in Wilmington, North Carolina. When her grandparents died she moved back to New York where she later enrolled in Manhattan Community College, intending to major in business administration.

While enrolled at the community college and later at City College in the 1960s, Shakur discovered the literature of the black arts movement and was involved in many political activities. After she graduated she became involved in the Black Panther Party for Self-Defense and owing to charges that she assisted in an attempted bank robbery, she was forced to go underground as a member of the Black Liberation Army, the underground wing of the Black Panther Party. From this point on, she was on the run from law enforcement. It was later discovered that the bank she was accused of robbing did not even exist at the time. On this note, the alleged bank robbery may have been the result of a COINTELPRO operation.

Between 1971 and 1972, Shakur was accused of three different banks robberies and in late 1972 and early 1973, she was accused of kidnapping and murdering a heroin dealer and attempting to murder policemen. None of these cases resulted in conviction. In 1972, the FBI used Assata Shakur as the face of a "manhunt" that they were engaged in against the Black Liberation Army, characterizing her as the "revolutionary mother hen" who nurtured the violence of the organization.

On May 2, 1973, Assata Shakur, along with Sundiata Acoli and Zayd Malik Shakur, were stopped allegedly for a defective taillight. As defense attorney Lennox Hinds explains, however, pulling over these three activists was consistent with the COINTELPRO guidelines of the FBI, which used the arrests of activists for minor violations as part of a larger strategy to disrupt the work of progressive and radical organizations. This incident resulted in a shootout in which Zayd Malik Shakur and State Trooper Werner Foerster were killed and Assata Shakur was shot and wounded. Although doctors testified that Shakur was too severely injured by the multiple gunshot wounds that she received to have resisted or fought back, she was charged as an accomplice to the murders of both Zayd Malik Shakur and Foerster and of assault on Trooper James Harper with intent to kill.

Police reportedly tortured Shakur while she was hospitalized. Officers held guns to her head in unsuccessful attempts to force her to confess to crimes and to provide information about Sundiata Acoli. Shakur's first lawyer, her aunt Evelyn Williams, was forced to strip naked to be searched before she visited Shakur, who was hospitalized, partially paralyzed, and handcuffed to a bed. She was the first female prisoner to be placed in the all-male prison on Riker's island and was subjected to inhumane treatment by prison guards because of her "dangerous" political beliefs. It was during this period of brutal incarceration that

Assata Shakur became a mother and suffered the trauma of not being able to spend more than a few minutes with her daughter after giving birth.

Defense attorneys including Evelyn Williams, Lennox Hinds, Florence Kennedy, Bob Bloom, William Kunstler, and Ray Brown supported Assata Shakur's innocence, but she was eventually convicted as an accomplice in the murders of Zayd Shakur and Foerster by an all-white jury.

On November 2, 1979, Assata Shakur escaped from prison. No one was harmed in her prison break. Shakur lived as a fugitive for the next few years until she relocated, by unrevealed means, to Cuba in 1984, where she was granted political asylum by the Cuban government. The head of the FBI said that its attempt to find Shakur were hampered by the fact that residents of the neighborhoods they searched were not willing to help. In 1985, Shakur was reunited with her daughter, Kakuya. Assata Shakur remains a cultural worker and international icon living in Cuba today.

In 1987, Assata Shakur's autobiography *Assata* was published. Activists often cite reading *Assata* as a turning point, with an impact comparable to that of *The Autobiography of Malcolm X*. Personal and poetic, *Assata* is accessible to a wide range of readers. Assata Shakur's example has mobilized elders in the black freedom struggle, prison abolitionists, and members of the hip-hop generation. Known popularly as Tupac Shakur's godmother, Assata Shakur is praised in songs by hip-hop artists including Common, Cee-lo, and Mos Def who are, themselves, active players in the campaign against her continued criminalization.

The continuing story of Assata Shakur's life is a testament to the persistent struggle for freedom within the context of black captivity and imprisonment. Her solidarity with the Cuban Revolution and Cuba's support of her status as an unjustly convicted political prisoner has encouraged many to be critical of the United States' antagonistic relationship with Cuba. Along with Angela Davis and Kathleen Cleaver, Assata Shakur is one the living former members of the Black Panther Party who remains an icon and a catalyst for action in the contemporary movement for human rights and social justice.

See also: Black Panther Party; COINTELPRO; Destination, Cuba

Walter C. Rucker

Bibliography

James, Joy. *Imprisoned Intellectuals: Political Prisoners Write on Life Liberation and Rebellion.* Lanham, MD: Rowman & Littlefield, 2003.

Perkins, Margo V. *Autobiography as Activism: Three Black Women of the Sixties.* Jackson: University Press of Mississippi, 2000.

Shakur, Assata. *Assata: An Autobiography.* Chicago: Lawrence Hill Press, 1987.

William, Evelyn. *Inadmissible Evidence: The Story of the African-American Trial Lawyer who Defended the Black Liberation Army.* Brooklyn NY: Lawrence Hill Books, 1993.

Sharecroppers Union

The Sharecroppers Union (SCU) was a communist-led labor union of mostly African American farmers and farm workers in Alabama and Louisiana during the 1930s. Inspired by a local uprising of rural poor people in Arkansas, Angelo Herndon, a black Communist, organized the Croppers' and Farm Workers' Union in Tallapoosa County, Alabama in the summer of 1931. Ralph Gray, a local black tenant farmer and one-time small landowner, led the first local. Initially, the union demanded that tenant farmers be allowed to grow subsistence foods, to market their own crops, and to pick cotton for a minimum wage. Attacks by local police and vigilantes nearly crushed this nascent group.

In August remaining union members re-formed as the Sharecroppers Union. Al Murphy, a black ex-sharecropper and communist organizer, took control of the union in May 1932 and focused its efforts on the struggle for African American self-determination in the plantation region of the South. He likened the union effort to past slave revolts. Murphy delegated powers to local union "captains," who directed day-to-day organizing. He also encouraged the captains to defend their communities against further white violence, with arms if necessary. Union meetings, advertised as Bible classes, often bristled with guns of all sorts. Women joined these locals through auxiliary units called "Sewing Clubs." Organizers did not approach poor whites in these years because they did not trust them. After members clashed again with police in early 1933, the union became widely known for its militant stance and people joined in droves. The union had 73 locals by June.

In the mid-1930s, the union launched a series of strikes to protest planter abuse of New Deal legislation. Although cotton strikes in 1933 and 1934 failed to make significant gains, they reinforced the union's militant reputation. By the spring of 1935, the union claimed more than 10,000 members. At this high point, Communist Party USA abandoned confrontational tactics for participation in the Popular Front. The Central Committee replaced Murphy with Clyde Johnson, a white Communist from Minnesota.

During the Popular Front era, Johnson tried to transform the SCU from a secretive, armed movement into a public trade union. To do this, he sought to ally the union with other agrarian organizations. Although early efforts failed, black sharecroppers in Louisiana joined the union in late 1935. By May 1936, the union claimed more than 1,000 members in Louisiana. Later that year, the union merged with the Alabama Farmers Union (AFU), the state wing of the left-leaning National Farmers Union. The Louisiana locals were chartered as the Louisiana Farmers Union (LFU). This enlarged union called for New Deal legislation to help tenants achieve farm ownership, mortgage relief, and crop loans, and to establish price controls. Shifts in cotton production, however, had demoted most black members into wage labor by 1937. Seeking better representation, wage workers left the AFU and LFU that year and formed District 9 of the CIO-affiliated United Canning and Packing Workers of America (UCAPAWA). Tenants remained in the LFU. Economic and bureaucratic changes weakened both unions. Led by Hosea Hudson, a black Communist from Alabama, District 9 claimed only 2,000 members in 14 locals in late 1938; the LFU, meanwhile, had only 900 members. By 1940, District 9 had collapsed. The LFU grew to as many as 3,000 members by 1940, but suffered because of its communist ties. It disappeared during World War II.

See also: Colored Farmers Alliance

Jarod H. Roll

Bibliography

de Jong, Greta. *A Different Day: African American Struggles for Justice in Rural Louisiana, 1900–1970.* Chapel Hill: University of North Carolina Press, 2002.

Kelley, Robin D. G. *Hammer and Hoe: Alabama Communists During the Great Depression.* Chapel Hill: University of North Carolina, 1990.

Rosengarten, Theodore. *All God's Dangers: The Life of Nate Shaw.* New York: Knopf, 1974.

Sharecropping

Sharecropping was a labor system that grew in the wake of the Civil War and passage of the Thirteenth Amendment. Penniless and landless, former enslaved African Americans became "croppers," working on the same lands owned by their former owners. Because most landowners lacked cash and had to borrow money to produce crops, they employed croppers without paying them wages in most cases. Croppers would receive a portion of the crop yield on land designated from them, in exchange for a one-half or one-third share of the crop, farming tools, seed, and the use of mules and other beasts of burden (e.g., horses and oxen). With their share of the crop, African Americans could sell it to the merchant who extended credit to the land owner, or they could buy things like food and clothing on credit, normally at exorbitant rates, from a furnishing merchant, who, in some cases, was also the landowner.

In many ways, this labor system was akin to slavery or, at the minimum, debt peonage, in that croppers generated 100 percent of the labor in exchange for food, clothing, and shelter. With that said, there were a handful of significant differences for African American croppers. Although they earned no wages, croppers worked the land allotted to them as families, not as work gangs, and they typically did not work under direct white supervision. Without the ability to read or write, many African American sharecroppers were cheated out of their fair share of the crop, did not received the correct value for their crop when purchasing items on credit, and were stuck in a constant cycle of debt. Sharecropping was perhaps singular proof that the key failure of Reconstruction was the failure to redistribute confiscated and abandoned land to ex-slaves. Until the Great Migration, the lives of the majority of African Americans would be bound to crop cultivation on the lands of former slave owners well into the 20th century.

See also: Black Nadir; Forty Acres and a Mule; Sharecroppers Union; Thirteenth Amendment; Washington, Booker T.

Walter C. Rucker

Bibliography

Davis, Ronald L. F. *Good and Faithful Labor: From Slavery to Sharecropping in the Natchez District, 1860–1890.* Westport, CT: Greenwood Press, 1982.

Jaynes, Gerald David. *Branches Without Roots: Genesis of the Black Working Class in the American South, 1862–1882.* New York: Oxford University Press, 1986.

Nieman, Donald G. *From Slavery to Sharecropping: White Land and Black Labor in the Rural South, 1865–1900.* New York: Garland, 1994.

Royce, Edward Cary. *The Origins of Southern Sharecropping.* Philadelphia: Temple University Press, 1993.

Sharpton, Al

Alfred Charles Sharpton Jr. (1954–), a black Pentecostal minister and a civil rights activist known for his inflammatory speeches on racial injustice, led a series of protest marches and sit-ins during the 1970s and 1980s in New York City. This controversial public figure represented the extreme wing of black activism.

Sharpton was born in a middle-class neighborhood in Brooklyn, New York, until a domestic tragedy forced his move to a housing project in the Brownsville area of the borough. This firsthand experience of the living conditions in this poor neighborhood, along with his profound admiration to the developing new black conscious and protests in the decades after World War II, directed Sharpton to the Civil Rights movement.

Dropping out of Brooklyn College, New York, he became the first youth director of Operation Breadbasket, an organization that boycotted and picketed corporations and supermarkets that conducted unfair business. In his biggest confrontation with the grocery chain store A&P, he was arrested along with Reverend Jesse Jackson.

In 1971, Sharpton became the youngest director of National Youth Movement (NYM), which aimed at combating police brutality and fighting drug abuse. Associating with James Brown, an American music legendary, Sharpton organized Hit Brown, a black concert promotion strategy and made concerted efforts to change the racial composition of the music business. But his endeavor in this direction did not bear fruit because he was suspected of having links with organized crime. This jeopardized his image and that of his movement in the community.

Sharpton protested against the New York City administration on several occasions. During the 1970 sit-in at New York City Hall, he demanded more summer jobs for blacks and for fair hiring and proper treatment of African Americans. A few months later, he led a group of black leaders to the New York deputy mayor's office meeting to protest the death of a 14-year-old black youth. In both instances he was arrested for his role in instigating racial tensions.

During the series of killings in the 1980s, Sharpton was a vibrant voice in his community. He stood in the front line of protest marches and sit-ins. The first instance that ignited racial violence was during the shooting death of four black unarmed teens. Bernard Goetz, a white man, was charged

for this crime, but was later acquitted of murder charges. Sharpton and a group of his followers held a protest vigil at the steps of the New York City courthouse condemning the all-white grand jury for this decision. He led protest marches and sit-ins strikes on transit rail tracks after a white mob assaulted three black men at Howard Beach in Brooklyn, New York.

In this atmosphere of racial polarity, Sharpton organized another strike at the Grand Central Station rail tracks during morning rush hour to protest the hiring policy of the Metropolitan Transit Authority (MTA). His public debate with New York Governor George Pataki forced the highest official in the state to appoint the first black MTA board member, Laura Blackburn. This incident was a stepping stone for his rise to prominence in the national media as a civil rights leader.

In 1987, Tawana Brawley, an African American teen from Wappinger's Falls, New York, was found inside a garbage bag with racial epithets and dog feces smeared on her face. A gang of white men did the same to another black woman in Newton, New Jersey. In both these cases justice was not served. Sharpton held rallies at the steps of the New York City courthouse and brought national media attention to these injustices in the judicial system.

Two years later, a white mob killed a 16-year-old African American teen, Yusuf Hawkins, in Bensonhurst, New York. While leading a march to protest this crime, Michael Riccardi, a 27-year-old white man stabbed the minister in his chest. After this incident, Sharpton changed his strategy in fighting racial injustice. Even though he adopted a conciliatory approach to race relations and tried to establish ground in the white community, he came under FBI investigation of his past income tax returns.

He attempted to run twice for the U.S. Senate, garnering only a small percentage of the vote in the election primaries. Despite this failure, he was one of the few African Americans who won a place as a power broker in the New York political scene, who led a campaign during Decision 2000 in favor of Albert Gore Jr., the Democratic presidential candidate, and the only African American in the 2004 Democratic presidential primaries.

Sharpton stands as a committed advocate of the rights of the African Americans. He, along with Reverend Jesse Jackson and other civil rights leaders, continues the fight against racism, urban poverty, and racial violence in the nation.

Reverend Al Sharpton leads a protest to stop the execution of Troy Davis, a Georgia death row inmate, October 2008. (Katherine Welles)

See also: Bensonhurst, New York, Incident of 1989; Brown, James; Diallo, Amadou; Howard Beach Incident, 1986; Jackson, Jesse

Sivananda Mantri

Bibliography

Sharpton, Al, and Anthony Watkins. *Go and Tell Pharaoh: The Autobiography of The Reverend Al Sharpton.* New York: Doubleday Dell Publishing Group, 1996.

Sharpton, Al, and Karen Hunter. *Al on America.* New York: Dafina Books, 2002.

Shuttlesworth, Fred

Reverend Fred Lee Shuttlesworth (1922–), a minister and human rights activist, was one of the staunchest and most courageous opponents of racial discrimination and segregation during the Civil Rights movement of the 1950s and 1960s. Shuttlesworth and the organization he led, the Alabama Christian Movement for Human Rights (ACMHR), were instrumental in desegregating Birmingham, Alabama, one of the most segregated cities in the South and the home of Eugene "Bull" Connor, the notorious segregationist who used violence to maintain racial discrimination. The civil rights demonstrations in Birmingham during the spring of 1963, where police dogs and fire hoses were used to assault peaceful civil rights activists, some of them children, were broadcast on television to the United States and the world, prompting widespread support for desegregation. More important, the violence compelled President John Kennedy to enact legislation that would eventually become the Civil Rights Act of 1964, which outlawed segregation in public accommodations. Although Dr. Martin Luther King Jr. and his organization, the Southern Christian Leadership Conference (SCLC) led the protests in conjunction with the ACMHR, King and the SCLC have received most of the credit for the success of the Birmingham demonstrations. Activists and scholars agree, however, that it was the work of Shuttlesworth and the ACMHR that ultimately made the demonstrations successful.

Fred Shuttlesworth was born Freddie Lee Robinson on March 18, 1922, in Mt. Meigs, Alabama to Alberta Robinson and Vedder Greene. The unmarried couple also produced a daughter, Cleola. It was from his mother that Shuttlesworth would get his combative personality, earthy spirituality, and indomitable will, traits that would prove invaluable when challenging the authority of Bull Connor and the rigid code of race relations in Birmingham and the South as a whole. In 1925, Ms. Robinson and the children moved to Oxmoor, Alabama, where she would later marry William Nathan Shuttlesworth, a farmer and former miner. Both Fred and his sister would take his last name. Seven siblings would follow soon after. Although Shuttlesworth and his family grew up in poverty, they were able to maintain some stability. His childhood would cement identification with poor and working-class folk, and it was this segment of the African American population that proved to be Shuttlesworth's staunchest supporters.

Birmingham was known as a rigidly segregated city that would not hesitate to violently keep African Americans in their "place." In fact, African Americans referred to the city as "Bombingham," and one black community was known as "Dynamite Hill," for the number of bombings that took place there. Any African American who protested against discriminatory treatment could be attacked or even killed. It was while attending high school in Birmingham that Shuttlesworth would come face-to-face with racial discrimination, growing resentful of the rundown conditions of buses used to transport black children to equally dilapidated schools while white children enjoyed newer facilities and more reliable transportation. He was also subjected to the discriminatory behavior of the Birmingham police force. Shuttlesworth would distinguish himself as a student and athlete at Rosedale High School, graduating as class valedictorian in May 1940. Within a year of graduating, Shuttlesworth would marry the former Ruby Keeler, a union that produced four children: Patricia, Ruby Fredericka (Ricky), Fred Jr., and Carolyn.

Now with a growing family, Shuttlesworth would gradually embark on a career as a minister, a vocation he began to think about after graduating high school. Moving the family to Mobile, Alabama, to work as a truck driver on an air base, Shuttlesworth would study the Bible. Initially an African Methodist, Shuttlesworth would become a Baptist, and began occasional preaching at the invitation of Pastor E. A. Palmer of Corinthian Baptist Church. Talented as a preacher, Shuttlesworth would receive invitations to preach before other congregations and would further his theological education at Cedar Grove Academy in Prichard, Alabama. In September 1947, after completing the Academy, Shuttlesworth enrolled at Selma University. The next year, he was ordained as a Baptist minister on August 10, 1948, at Corinthian Baptist Church.

In 1949, the family moved to Montgomery and Shuttlesworth enrolled at Alabama State College, later serving as pastor of First (African) Baptist Church in Selma in 1950. It was at First Baptist that Shuttlesworth would encounter some of the class conflicts within the black community that would later plague his relationship with some churches in Birmingham. Shuttlesworth's class orientation, folksy preaching style, and blunt, direct manner caused problems with the more middle-class sensibilities of the church congregation, and Shuttlesworth left after two years. The next year Shuttlesworth accepted the pastorate of Bethel Baptist Church in an African American section of North Birmingham known as Collegeville. It was here that Shuttlesworth and his followers would begin a veritable crusade against the evils of Jim Crow segregation and other forms of racial discrimination in the city known unofficially as the "Johannesburg of the South."

Shuttlesworth began his crusade in earnest after the Supreme Court ruled in favor of the National Association for the Advancement of Colored People (NAACP) in the *Brown v. Board of Education* case in May 1954, which ruled school segregation unconstitutional. Determined to make the ruling a reality, Shuttlesworth joined the local branch of the NAACP. Headed by some members of the African American middle-class, the leadership was slow to respond to Shuttlesworth's suggestions and demands, which included petitioning the city for more black police officers and complying with the *Brown* decision. The local leadership and the city both rejected the requests.

In reaction to increasing demands of African Americans to dismantle segregation and extend freedom and democracy to all American citizens in the aftermath of the *Brown* decision, white state authorities in Alabama in 1956 were successful in banning the Alabama NAACP, preventing the organization from operating within the state. Shuttlesworth and members of his congregation then formed the Alabama Christian Movement for Human Rights on June 5, 1956, to carry on the fight, basing the organization on Christian and patriotic principles while calling for desegregation and expanded employment opportunities. Its membership consisted of mostly working-class African Americans, with the majority being black women, and they used direct action protests such as marches and sit-ins to highlight grievances. The ACMHR also believed strongly that God supported their efforts and their religious fervor spread rapidly to other African Americans. It would soon be the only organization in Birmingham to stand up to Bull Connor and other segregationists.

Shuttlesworth's courage knew no bounds, and his actions suggested that he and his family were willing to make sacrifices to bring about equality. After bus segregation was declared unconstitutional on December 20, 1956, Shuttlesworth announced that African Americans would ride the buses on a nondiscriminatory basis, despite resistance from the City Commission to a petition submitted by the ACMHR. On Christmas Day, Shuttlesworth's home next to the church was bombed when dynamite exploded under his bed. Although Bethel Baptist and the home were severely damaged, miraculously, Shuttlesworth received only scratches. Shuttlesworth and his followers took this as a sign that God was protecting him to lead the movement. Shuttlesworth would have other opportunities to put himself in harm's way. Demanding school desegregation,

Shuttlesworth attempted to enroll his daughters at all-white Phillips High School; that same day, President Dwight Eisenhower signed the Civil Rights Act of 1957. A white mob beat Shuttlesworth severely with chains and baseball bats while his wife was stabbed and children suffered injuries. Again, Shuttlesworth survived. In 1958, the *Birmingham World* named Shuttlesworth "Newsmaker of the Year," for 1957.

Between 1958 and 1961, Bull Connor increased his harassment of Shuttlesworth and the ACMHR as they continued to demand that the city commission hire black policemen and desegregate schools and parks. When black students began a sit-in at segregated stores and restaurants in 1960, Shuttlesworth encouraged them. Shuttlesworth was arrested several times during this period, and Bethel Baptist Church was also bombed for a second time. The activism would extend to Shuttlesworth's children, as Pat, Ricky (Fredericka) and Fred Jr. were arrested in Gadsden, Alabama, for allegedly causing a disturbance on a Greyhound bus on August 16, 1960. Shuttlesworth would experience personal problems, however, as he and Ruby disagreed over money, his civil rights activities, and church responsibilities. Shuttlesworth also experienced problems in Bethel Baptist, causing him to agree to the pastorate of Revelation Baptist Church in Cincinnati, Ohio in 1961, although he continued to be heavily involved in Birmingham.

Shuttlesworth immersed himself in the Civil Rights movement in other parts of Alabama and throughout the South. He attended meetings of, and pledged financial support to, the Montgomery Improvement Association, the organization created after Rosa Parks refused to give up her seat on a segregated city bus on December 1, 1955, prompting the Montgomery bus boycott that brought Martin Luther King Jr. to national prominence. He was a founding member of the Southern Christian Leadership Conference in 1957, a major civil rights organization created for Dr. King to support local civil rights struggles throughout the South. And during the Freedom Rides of 1961, Shuttlesworth served as the point person for the Congress of Racial Equality (CORE), taking care of riders who were attacked in Birmingham.

In 1962, SCLC looked for a situation that would garner more national and international support for the Civil Rights movement. Shuttlesworth continuously urged Dr. King and the SCLC board to conduct demonstrations in Birmingham, feeling that if segregation could be broken there, it would cause desegregation in other parts of the South. At the same time, Dr. King and the SCLC needed something to push a reluctant federal government to end segregation. They hoped to do that by demonstrating to the public, through marches and sit-ins, how far segregationists would go to continue to deprive African Americans of their citizenship rights.

In spring 1963, King and the SCLC agreed to work with the ACMHR to carry out Project "C" (for confrontation) to advance the local and national movements, demanding total desegregation of schools and public facilities and the removal of obstacles to voter registration while forcing the Kennedy administration to act. Shuttlesworth led mass marches on city hall and helped organize other demonstrations and support. He later suffered injuries from a fire hose while demonstrating downtown. Although Shuttlesworth would disagree with some of King and the SCLC's decisions regarding negotiations with the city, it was he who declared the demonstrations ended in May 1963 when the SCLC and the city reached a limited agreement on gradual desegregation of public facilities and gradual upgrading of black employees. The demonstrations directly resulted in the Civil Rights Act of 1964, outlawing segregation in public accommodations among other provisions.

Shuttlesworth would continue his activism in the succeeding years, remaining involved in the local movement in Birmingham while also demonstrating against unfair conditions in and around Cincinnati. In March 1989, he established the Shuttlesworth Housing Foundation to provide low-cost housing to poor families. He experienced continued strained relationships in his personal life, divorcing his wife Ruby in 1970 after 29 years of marriage and resigning from Revelation Baptist Church in 1966 to form another congregation. Shuttlesworth has received several accolades for his activism, the city of Birmingham renaming Huntsville Road in his honor in September 1978 and having a statue of his likeness erected in front of the Birmingham Civil Rights Institute and Museum in November 1992. In 2008, the Birmingham International Airport was renamed Birmingham-Shuttlesworth International Airport in his honor. He currently resides in Birmingham after retiring from the ministry in 2006.

See also: Bombingham; Jim Crow; National Association for the Advancement of Colored People; Southern Christian Leadership Conference; Sixteenth Street Baptist Church

Tony Gass

Bibliography

Branch, Taylor. *Parting the Waters: America in the King Years, 1954–1963.* New York: Simon & Schuster, 1988.

Branch, Taylor. *Pillar of Fire: America in the King Years, 1963–1965.* New York: Simon & Schuster, 1998.

Eskew, Glenn T. *But for Birmingham: The Local and National Movements in the Civil Rights Struggle.* Chapel Hill: University of North Carolina Press, 1997.

Manis, Andrew. *A Fire You Can't Put Out: The Civil Rights of Birmingham's Reverend Fred Shuttlesworth.* Tuscaloosa: University of Alabama Press, 1999.

White, Marjorie, and Andrew Manis, eds. *Birmingham Revolutionaries: The Reverend Fred Shuttlesworth and the Alabama Christian Movement for Human Rights.* Macon, GA: Mercer University Press, 2000.

Simpson, O. J.

The life of Orenthal James ("O. J.") Simpson (1947–) was forever changed on July 8, 1994. On that day Simpson, who was once one of the most beloved American sports icons, was charged with the double murder of his ex-wife Nicole Brown Simpson and her friend Ronald Goldman. Before his tragic fall from grace, Simpson was a model of meritocracy for African Americans and was well respected by whites as an acceptable black who made the transition to the mainstream. He was an adored TV pitchman and sports commentator for NBC, and he had a somewhat successful stint as an actor. Simpson was even welcomed in country clubs during the 1980s, freely interacting in the segregated world of wealthy whites, and because of his huge popularity, he was the first African American crossover athlete to receive major corporate endorsements. Simpson paved the way for the lucrative advertising contracts that Michael Jordan, Tiger Woods, and LeBron James now enjoy.

Using sports as a means to escape the pitfalls of Potrero Hill, the San Francisco neighborhood in which he grew up, Simpson emerged as an All-American football hero in the late 1960s. He came from a humble background, as his father left when Simpson was a child, forcing Simpson's mother to bear the burden of supporting four children. Although he often got into trouble as a teen, Simpson graduated from Galileo High School in 1965 and enrolled at City College in San Francisco. He not only did well on the field but also in the classroom, as he was able to pull his grades up to qualify to play at a Division I-A school. In 1967, Simpson transferred to the University of Southern California (USC) and married his first wife, Marguerite L. Whitley. He helped lead USC to the Rose Bowl and a national championship that year and earned All-American honors. In 1968, Simpson won the Heisman trophy and the next year was chosen as the first pick of the Buffalo Bills in the American Football League (AFL) draft. Simpson struggled to live up to his college reputation on the gridiron during his first three seasons, averaging a little over 600 yards. By his fourth year, after the AFL merged with the National Football League (NFL), Simpson was an offensive juggernaut and became the first NFL player to gain over 2,000 yards in one season. Simpson wowed Bills fans with his explosive running style, which catapulted him to celebrity status both on and off the field. In 1969, he got his first product endorsement with Chevrolet, and when Hertz hired him in 1975, Simpson became the first black celebrity spokesman for a major corporation. The Hertz commercials led to other contracts with companies such as Tree Sweet Orange Juice, Foster Grant Sunglasses, RC Cola, and Nabisco.

Five years after he signed the Hertz deal, Simpson's 11-year marriage to Marguerite ended. A knee injury forced him to retire from football in 1979, the year after he was traded to the San Francisco 49ers. Facing life for the first time without football at the relatively young age of 32, Simpson used his fame for big payoffs in the business world. He hired lawyers who invested his football fortunes in food franchises such as Pioneer Chicken and Honey-Baked Ham stores, and he was also the main attraction at celebrity golf tournaments and convention banquets.

Simpson was inducted into the Football Hall of Fame in 1985, the same year he married Nicole Brown. Their marriage was very unstable, and in 1989 Nicole filed assault charges against Simpson, but he was given a light sentence—a $470 fine, 120 hours of community service, and mandated counseling twice a week. Unable to reconcile their differences, Nicole filed for divorce in 1992. Simpson not only lost his wife, but also was starting to lose his celebrity image as his popularity declined in the 1990s.

When Simpson was charged with the murders of his ex-wife Nicole and Ronald Goldman, race became a dominating factor in how the trial was covered and perceived. Having been a favorite son of America, many whites were disturbed and even felt betrayed by Simpson, who they thought played by all the rules to achieve the American dream. Thus, in many ways, the Simpson tragedy was a bitter reminder to the nation that a colorblind society did not exist.

Newsweek and *Time* magazines had some of the most controversial pretrial coverage of Simpson's disgraced image. In an article titled "Day and Night," *Newsweek* reporter Evan Thomas described Simpson as a man who eventually went wrong because he tried to go white. Using the theme of "two-ness"—a term W. E. B. Du Bois coined that relates to the struggle of being American as well as black—Thomas depicted Simpson as a black man who deliberately played the race card to get ahead. Thomas likened Nicole to a trophy wife and criticized Simpson for aspiring to be a successful actor, a goal Thomas said was based more on hope than reason. Although Simpson's company, Orenthal Productions, made four successful TV movies for NBC, Thomas does not credit him for being a smart business owner. Although he concedes that whites did not perceive Simpson as a threat, Thomas's constant referrals to Simpson as a face man in the business world and Simpson's attraction to white women conveyed the image of the black male white America fears.

Time's June 27, 1994 story, "End of the Run," was somewhat objective in its reporting, but stereotypical in its presentation of Simpson's mug shot on the cover. *Time* used a computer to darken Simpson's appearance, making him appear more blurred and heavily bearded, which brought charges of racism from prominent African Americans. In an editorial for *The Chicago Defender,* Earl Ofari Hutchinson claimed that *Time* darkened Simpson's photo to make him look more menacing and that the magazine's treatment of Jeffrey Dahmer, a confessed serial killer, was more favorable than its coverage of Simpson. Hutchinson pointed out that *Time* did not tamper with the photographs of Dahmer but presented him as a contrite young man. He also explained that *Time* did not scrutinize Dahmer's personality or make judgments about his character, but highlighted speculation about Simpson and called his relationship with Nicole dysfunctional and characterized by physical abuse.

As *Newsweek* and *Time* chose to examine controversial traits of Simpson's life, the black press was divided in its coverage because Simpson was not considered the usual black victim, and some African American reporters expressed no sympathy for him. Black newspapers did point out the disparity in terms of how white men had been portrayed in the media who committed similar crimes. Yet, owing to Simpson's crossover appeal, black publications such as *The New Pittsburgh Courier* reprimanded him for abandoning his community and claimed he had reneged on his obligation to black America. Most black newspapers did not indicate a presumption of guilt as *Newsweek* and *Time* had done, but rather asserted that Simpson had allowed himself to become too deeply entrenched into the mainstream.

After Simpson was arraigned for the murders of Nicole and Goldman, he stated that he was "absolutely, one hundred percent not guilty" during his second court appearance on July 23, 1994. He assembled a defense of high profile lawyers, whom the press nicknamed the Dream Team, which included Johnnie Cochran, Alan Dershowitz, Barry Scheck, Robert Kardashian, F. Lee Bailey, and Robert Shapiro. The trial lasted eight months and was covered daily by Court TV and a plethora of other media outlets. The prosecution argued that Simpson killed his wife and Goldman out of envious rage and attempted to use DNA evidence to convince the jury of Simpson's guilt. DNA experts testified that blood found in Simpson's home and truck matched Nicole and Goldman's. The defense, however, argued that Simpson was a victim of a setup by the police, claiming that evidence had been planted and blood samples were contaminated. One of the major turning points in the trial occurred when the defense exposed tapes of LAPD detective Mark Fuhrman using the word "nigger" in reference to African Americans. This contradicted Fuhrman's earlier testimony that he had not used derogatory terms to describe blacks, and it cast reasonable doubt on his claim to having found a black leather glove stained with Nicole and Goldman's blood, as well as blood in the driveway of Simpson's home. Another gaffe of the prosecution was their request for Simpson to try on the bloody glove, which had undergone extensive examination in the crime lab. The glove was apparently too small for Simpson's hand and Cochran, in perhaps one of the most famous quotes from the trial, urged the jury that "if it doesn't fit you must acquit."

Of the 12 jurors, 9 were black, and when Simpson was acquitted of the murders on October 3, 1995, race became a prevalent polarizing factor in how many Americans believed the jury reached its verdict. A *Newsweek* poll taken 13 days after the jury's decision revealed that 54 percent of whites disagreed with the "Not Guilty" verdict, but 85 percent of blacks believed it was the right ruling; 66 percent of blacks thought Simpson probably did not commit the slayings, but 74 percent of whites thought he probably did. Simpson immediately became a social outcast, as most whites believed he had escaped conviction. He endured constant scorn on golf courses and sneers in restaurants, as many accused him of craving the attention he received before his legal troubles began.

The Goldman and Brown families filed a civil suit against Simpson after the criminal trial and won $8.5 million on February 4, 1997. Punitive damages were later brought against Simpson for $25 million to be shared between Fred Goldman and Nicole's children. Simpson appealed the verdict, but the civil judgment was upheld in court. Since the civil trial, Simpson has become a constant tabloid figure, appearing on various cable shows still trying to tell his side of the story and proclaim his innocence. Eleven years after the criminal trial, he made what many considered one of his most arrogant moves with the release of the book *If I Did It*. *If I Did It* was not a confession but as Simpson claimed, an account of how he would have committed the murders of Nicole and Goldman. Ron Goldman's father was awarded the rights to the book to help pay the damages ordered by the civil suit judgment, but most bookstores refused to promote or sell it. Simpson received approximately $630,000 after *If I Did It* was completed, but the book was cancelled as a result of the public's extreme opposition.

Late in 2007, Simpson infamously made the headlines again when he and two associates were accused of robbing and kidnapping sports memorabilia dealers at gunpoint in a Las Vegas hotel-casino. Simpson maintained that he was trying to retrieve items that belonged to him and pleaded not guilty to all charges. The armed robbery case was not the cultural and racial spectacle that the media fueled in 1995, but the factor of race was again questioned, as no African Americans were on the jury. Thirteen years to the exact date that Simpson was acquitted of double murder, the jury found him, along with co-defendant Clarence (C. J.) Stewart, guilty of first-degree kidnapping, armed robbery, and 10 other charges in connection with the Las Vegas holdup. Simpson's attorneys plan to appeal, arguing that Simpson was a victim of racial prejudice associated with the 1995 homicide ruling. Both Simpson and Stewart face up to life in prison.

The armed robbery case brought attention to the national division in terms of how African Americans and whites feel regarding Simpson. Less than 30 percent of whites today believe that Simpson is not guilty of murder, but almost 90 percent of blacks still think he is innocent. Many African Americans also question the criminal proceedings and the nature of the Las Vegas case, as they did the 1995 trial. Those who absolutely loathe Simpson,

however, consider his current status as a convicted felon an indirect way of bringing him to justice.

See also: Black Athletes

Jessica A. Johnson

Bibliography

Edwards, Harry. "We Must Let O. J. Go: Separating Fact from Image." *Sport* (February 1995):80.

Gibbs, Jewelle. *Race and Justice: Rodney King and O. J. Simpson in a House Divided.* San Francisco: Jossey-Bass Publishers, 1996.

Gibbs, Nancy. "End of the Run." *Time Magazine* (June 27, 1994): 28–35.

Hoversten, Paul. "Time Criticized over O. J. Cover." *USA Today* (June 22, 1994):D1.

Hutchinson, Earl Ofari. "The O. J. Case and Hidden Racism." *The Chicago Defender* (September 6, 1994):12.

Thomas, Evan. "Day and Night: He Lived Two Lives. An Inside Look at O. J. Simpson's World." *Newsweek* (August 29, 1994): 42–49.

Singleton, Benjamin "Pap"

Benjamin Singleton (1809–1892) pioneered the large-scale black emigration movement from the South to the Midwest during the last quarter of the 19th century. The self-proclaimed "Moses of the Colored Exodus" inspired thousands of African Americans, known as the Exodusters, to permanently relocate to Kansas and other states in the 1870s and 1880s.

Details of Singleton's early life are sketchy. Born a slave in Nashville, Tennessee, he learned the carpenter and cabinetmaker trades as he grew up. Although his owner sold him to Gulf Coast slaveholders numerous times, he always escaped and made his way back. Eventually, he fled briefly to Canada, but soon after took up residence in Detroit, where he surreptitiously aided other fugitives until the end of the Civil War. Singleton then returned home to Middle Tennessee in 1865 and began his public career in Edgefield as an advocate for the newly freed slaves. Mild-mannered, compassionate, and friendly, he became known universally as "Pap."

Asserting that the ownership of land offered the greatest opportunity for advancement and security, Singleton encouraged freed people to save their money to purchase small plots, rather than rent them. He and his associates organized the Tennessee Real Estate and Homestead

Association (1869), which attempted to locate available tracts on the outskirts of Nashville. Although some white people aided and encouraged Singleton, the endeavor failed. Most landowners either refused to sell to black people at all or demanded high prices for worn-out cropland.

Singleton's lack of success in this effort led him to conclude that freed people needed to separate entirely from their former masters and establish new lives outside the South. He looked at Kansas, the former home of abolitionist John Brown, as a possible refuge. Beginning in 1869, small parties of African Americans had ventured to the fertile prairies and began sending back encouraging reports of the conditions there. Singleton himself journeyed to Kansas in 1873 and, favorably impressed, returned with a group of pioneers to the southeastern part of the state, where he founded Singleton's Colony on 1,000 acres near Baxter Springs.

After coming back to Nashville the following year, "Pap" immediately made plans to take additional colonists west. Aided by like-minded colleagues in Tennessee, such as Columbus Johnson and A. D. DeFrantz, Singleton's revitalized Tennessee Real Estate and Homestead Association recruited and prepared likely emigrants; located suitable public lands for settlement (such as the communities of Dunlap and Nicodemus); and arranged special rates with steamboat companies for transportation to Topeka.

Wary of educated people and distrustful of politicians, Singleton acted, he believed, in the interests of the common people. In most of the South, sharecropping was proving to be little better than slavery, political promises had borne scarce fruit, and legal protection had steadily deteriorated. Many contemporary black leaders with statewide or national reputations opposed large-scale migrations out of the South as undermining black political strength. Singleton, however, disputed this rationale and insisted that the social and economic benefits of the exodus outweighed the political costs.

In the spring of 1880, an investigative committee of the United States Senate called Singleton to Washington to explain the agenda and goals of the Exoduster movement. He dramatized the impoverished position of African Americans in the South and asserted that only a mass emigration could provide the impetus for positive change. He claimed full responsibility for putting the undertaking into motion and dismissed those who ascribed more mundane causes for the exodus as unwilling to give him the proper credit that he deserved.

By 1880, years of black immigration to Kansas had severely taxed that state's resources. The later arrivals tended to be poorer than those who came earlier and almost no employment opportunities existed. After urging prospective homesteaders not to come to Kansas, Singleton and his allies searched for a new destination outside the United States for those leaving the South. After considering Canada but ultimately rejecting it as too cold, they settled on Liberia, where African Americans could have a government of their own. Few people, however, immigrated to Africa at that time.

By the mid-1880s, Singleton was more than 75 years old and was growing feebler, but he still devoted his energy to the cause. After years of promoting black nationalism, "Pap" had accumulated little to see him through old age. As his personal honesty and sincerity remained apparent to all who came in contact with him, and in recognition of a lifetime of service, the black community of the Midwest embraced "Pap" until the end of his life. Each year on his birthday, hundreds of African American supporters gathered at a suitable outdoor venue in either Topeka or St. Louis for a party that honored Singleton and served as a fundraiser for his support in the coming year. These annual celebrations continued until 1892, when Singleton died in Topeka at the age of 83.

See also: Exoduster Movement; Nicodemus, Kansas

Michael Thomas Gavin

Bibliography

Athearn, Robert. *In Search of Canaan: Black Migration to Kansas, 1879–1880.* Lawrence: Regents Press of Kansas, 1978.

Bontemps, Arna, and Jack Conroy. *Anyplace But Here.* New York: Hill and Wang, 1966.

Entz, Gary R. "Image and Reality on the Kansas Prairie: 'Pap' Singleton's Cherokee County Colony." *Kansas History* 19 (1996):124–39.

Higgins, Billy D. "Negro Thought and the Exodus of 1879." *Phylon* 32 (1971):39–52.

Painter, Nell Irvin. *Exodusters: Black Migration to Kansas after Reconstruction.* New York: Alfred A. Knopf, 1977.

Sit-In Movement

The sit-in movement was just one of a number of techniques used by civil rights supporters in their campaign to end racial segregation. They appealed to the courts, the legislature, and sometimes the President of the United States for relief.

From time to time they depended on the actions of the federal government to sweep away discrimination in the military or in education. But the sit-in movement, which was not mandated by a Presidential Executive Order or driven by a Supreme Court decision, was just as important. It helped sweep away legal and cultural barriers that had blocked African Americans from equal access to food service, and enabled the Civil Rights movement to take greater advantage of an untapped resource: young African Americans.

The idea of the sit-in as a way to end food service segregation was not new. It had been tried in Chicago and St. Louis in the 1940s and in Baltimore in 1953. But little attention was paid to the attempts or the reasons for them. The idea gained new energy in the wake of the Montgomery bus boycott in 1955, where African Americans, using nonviolent methods, effectively ended the practice of segregated bus seating in Montgomery, Alabama. Montgomery's civic leaders expected African Americans to tolerate the humiliation of riding in the back of city busses to and from their downtown shopping trips. If the local economy could be crippled by a bus boycott, and whites required to treat African Americans with respect, could not the same be done by a sit-in?

In 1958, civil rights leaders began sponsoring a series of workshops throughout the South to train people in the ways of nonviolent protest. Many African American college students in and around the Nashville, Tennessee area attended those workshops. Their ultimate goal was to desegregate the lunch counters in Nashville's department stores. It did not make sense to them that although the stores would sell them clothes and school supplies, they would refuse them service when they wanted something to eat. The students' training was designed to prepare themselves for the day when they would break the color barrier at Nashville's lunch counters.

But four African American students from North Carolina's College of Agriculture and Technology beat them to the punch. On February 1, 1960, Joseph McNeil, Franklin McCain, David Richmond, and Ezell Blair Jr. strolled into the Woolworth's department store in downtown Greensboro. They bought toothpaste and school supplies, and then settled into seats at the lunch counter and ordered coffee. First, they were ignored. Then they were told they would not be served. Finally, the store manager called the police to complain. The police did nothing because the protesters were doing nothing. Four well-dressed young African American college students were sitting quietly at the lunch counter, waiting for service and doing their homework while

they waited. Exasperated, the manager closed early. The four young men left, only to return. But this time there were six of them. By the end of the week there were more than 300 African American students seeking service at lunch counters at Woolworth's and at S. H. Kress and Company, another department store in Greensboro. They tried to order food. They were denied service, but remained at the counter, waiting quietly. Joining the sit-in were white students. Newspaper reporters and photographers were also on hand to record the events. When businesses considered the potential impact of the protest on their bottom line, many of them, including Woolworth's, rethought their policies, and by August, 1960, desegregated their lunch counters.

But the lunch counter sit-ins had repercussions that went far beyond Greensboro's city limits. Soon black and white students were staging sit-ins at restaurants, play-ins at segregated parks, and read-ins at segregated libraries across the United States. A few weeks after the events in Greensboro, students in Nashville began sitting in at lunch counters in their city. There was violence, as white students attacked the demonstrators, and later arrests, as the police moved into to take them to jail. But every time an African American student was removed from a lunch counter, there was another student waiting to take his/her place. The nonviolent protests, and the sometimes violent reaction, continued until May, when Nashville changed its policies and began serving African Americans at department store lunch counters.

The sit-ins also caused the leadership of the Civil Rights movement to think about how best to capitalize on this infusion of youthful energy. The answer materialized in late 1960 when the Southern Christian Leadership Conference (SCLC) underwrote the creation of the Student Nonviolent Coordinating Committee (SNCC). "Snick," as it was called, was originally composed of black and white university students who would enter the Civil Rights movement armed with energy and enthusiasm, determined to achieve equality wherever inequality might be found. In 1961, veterans of the sit-ins were participating in Freedom Rides, venturing into the Deep South on commercial busses to test compliance with federal laws guaranteeing equal treatment in interstate bus terminals. Later those same students would be in Mississippi, helping to register voters for the 1964 presidential election. The lunch counter sit-ins energized the Civil Rights movement by adding youth to the campaign to end inequality and adding national attention to the cause.

On February 1, 1960, four young African American college students walked into the Woolworth's in Greensboro, North Carolina, sat down at a whites-only lunch counter and triggered the Civil Rights movement that spread across the nation. Shown here on February 2, 1960, are (left to right) Joseph McNeil, Franklin McCain, Billy Smith, and Clarence Henderson. (Library of Congress)

See also: Baker, Ella; Freedom Rides; Lewis, John; Nash, Diane; Southern Christian Leadership Conference; Student Nonviolent Coordinating Committee

John Morello

Bibliography

Boyer, Paul. *Promises to Keep: The United States since World War II*, 2nd ed. Boston: Houghton Mifflin, 1999.

Garrow, David J. *Atlanta, Georgia, 1960–1961: Sit-Ins and Student Activism*. Brooklyn, NY: Carlson Publications, 1989.

Moss, George Donelson. *America in the Twentieth Century*. Upper Saddle River, NJ: Prentice Hall, 2004.

Oppenheimer, Martin. *The Sit-in Movement of 1960*. Brooklyn, NY: Carlson Publications, 1989.

Torres, Sasha. *Black, White, and in Color: Television and Black Civil Rights*. Princeton, NJ: Princeton University Press, 2003.

Williams, Juan. *Eyes on the Prize: America's Civil Rights Years, 1954–1965*. New York: Viking Press, 1987.

Sixteenth Street Baptist Church

Sixteenth Street Baptist Church in Birmingham, Alabama is an important historic site of the Civil Rights movement.

The home of Birmingham's first African American congregation, the church became a center of civil rights activity and the location of a tragic racially motivated bombing.

Birmingham, Alabama's first African American church was established in 1873, less than two years after the city was incorporated. Founded by migrants from rural Alabama who had come to work in the new industrial city's mines and mills, The First Colored Baptist Church of Birmingham met in a tinner's shop. The growing congregation later moved into its own downtown building. In July 1882, the congregation purchased a lot on the corner of Sixth Avenue North and Sixteenth Street, where the church now stands, and took the name Sixteenth Street Baptist Church. By 1887, the congregation constructed an impressive gothic revival building on the site, with several members of the church mortgaging their homes to help complete the project. This building was demolished in 1909 and replaced in 1911 with the present structure, designed by African American architect Wallace A. Rayfield. Largely Romanesque in design, the brick church features a central entrance porch flanked by two towers and stained-glass windows.

By the early 20th century, Sixteenth Street Baptist Church had grown to more than 1,000 members and was a major church of Birmingham's African American elite and middle class. Many members held professional positions, such as educators, and many were successful business people and community leaders. Located in Birmingham's downtown black business district, and with a seating capacity of 1,600, the church hosted concerts and other cultural events and political meetings.

From the late 19th century to the 1960s, the City of Birmingham strictly enforced an extensive system of racial segregation. African Americans and whites were separated by law in many public facilities including street cars and busses, theaters, hospitals, and restaurants. Separate schools, libraries, and parks were maintained for blacks and whites, and facilities for African Americans were always inferior to those provided whites. Almost all Africans Americans in the city were prevented from voting, and before the late 1960s, Birmingham had no black elected officials, police officers, or fire fighters.

Ambulance attendants load the body of an African American girl, one of four killed in the bombing of the Sixteenth Street Baptist Church in Birmingham, Alabama, on September 15, 1963. (AP Photo)

African Americans protested segregation and racial discrimination through legal actions in the courts, boycotts, sit-ins, and street demonstrations. In the spring of 1963, the Southern Christian Leadership Conference, led by Martin Luther King Jr., worked with the Birmingham-based Alabama Christian Movement for Human Rights (ACMHR) led by Fred L. Shuttlesworth to organize large-scale demonstrations. Sixteenth Street Baptist Church hosted some of the weekly mass meetings sponsored by ACMHR. Because of its size and central location, Sixteenth Street Baptist Church was used as a site to organize and launch daily demonstrations. These demonstrations generated worldwide publicity, as more than 3,000 demonstrators, including children, were jailed, and Birmingham authorities used police dogs and fire hoses against the demonstrators. Nationwide public reaction to the Birmingham protests encouraged the United States Congress to pass the 1964 Civil Rights Act.

Birmingham's public schools were desegregated during the second week of September 1963. Five African American students were placed in formerly all white schools, and violent protests occurred around the schools. In retaliation for the school desegregation, members of the Ku Klux Klan placed a bomb outside Sixteenth Street Baptist Church sometime during the night of Saturday, September 14. The bomb exploded the next morning at approximately 10:20 A.M., just as Sunday school classes were ending and before the start of the service. The explosion tore a large hole in the side of the church, blew out windows, and damaged the interior of the building. Four girls, Denise McNair (age 11), Addie Mae Collins (age 14), Cynthia Wesley (age 14), and Carole Robertson (age 14) were killed inside the basement women's rest room; they were crushed by falling debris. Several other members of the congregation were injured.

White supremacists had committed dozens of racially motivated bombings in the Birmingham area since the late 1940s, but the Sixteenth Street Baptist Church bombing was the first in which people were killed. The bombing and the deaths of the four girls were reported worldwide, and the incident generated both sympathy and outrage. Birmingham mayor Albert Boutwell, a segregationist, wept when told of the deaths. The City of Birmingham established a reward fund to encourage witnesses to come forward with information.

Carole Robertson's funeral was held Tuesday, September 17 at St. John AME Church, as Sixteenth Street Baptist Church was too badly damaged, and nearly 2,000 people attended. The next day a mass funeral for the other three girls was held at Sixth Avenue Baptist Church. Martin Luther King Jr. preached the sermon at this service and a crowd estimated at 7,000 people filled the church and the street outside.

The Birmingham Police Department, the Alabama Department of Public Safety, and dozens of agents from the Federal Bureau of Investigation investigated the bombing. On September 30, the State of Alabama arrested three known Klansmen, Robert Chambliss, John Wesley Hall, and Charles Cagle. But the suspects were charged only with illegal possession of dynamite and were fined.

The church received contributions from throughout the world totaling more than $200,000 to repair the damage done by the bombing. Sixteenth Street Baptist Church reopened in June 1964. In 1965, parishioners installed a large stained glass window over the front door of the sanctuary. Known as the Wales Window, it was donated by the people of Wales and depicts a black figure of Christ crucified and bears the inscription "You do it to me."

No other arrests were made until Alabama Attorney General Bill Baxley reopened the investigation in 1971 and won a conviction of Robert Chambliss in 1977. Chambliss, whose nickname was "Dynamite Bob," was a long-time Klansmen suspected in other racial bombings. He was sentenced to life in prison and died in 1985.

Public and media attention to the bombing was sporadic for more than a decade after the Chambliss conviction. Neither state nor federal law enforcement agencies made any serious efforts to investigate the case further or indict more suspects. But the church became a symbol of civil rights activism and sacrifice and was added to the National Register of Historic Places in 1980. In 1992, the Birmingham Civil Rights Institute, a museum and research center, opened across the street from Sixteenth Street Baptist Church. Nearby Kelly Ingram Park was renovated and several pieces of sculpture honoring Martin Luther King Jr. and the Birmingham civil rights demonstrators were placed in the park. More than 200,000 people visit the area, now designated the Civil Rights District, each year.

By 1995, a change of leadership in the Birmingham office of the Federal Bureau of Investigation led to a reopening of the case. The FBI did not announce the reopening until 1997, and that same year filmmaker Spike Lee released *Four Little Girls,* his documentary about the bombing. The film was nominated for the Academy Award

and focused new international attention on the case. Also in 1997, President Bill Clinton appointed Doug Jones as U.S. attorney for the northern district of Alabama. Jones worked closely with the FBI and, in 2000, secured murder indictments against the two suspects still alive, Tommy Blanton and Bobby Frank Cherry. The two were tried separately. Blanton was convicted in 2001 and Cherry in 2002. Both were sentenced to life in prison.

In the 21st century the membership of Sixteenth Street Baptist Church has declined to about 200, but the church is a popular tourist and pilgrimage site. Because of the large number of visitors, weekly attendance at Sunday services averages 2,000. In 2007, the church completed the first phase of a major restoration, and fundraising continued to complete the restoration of the structure.

See also: Black Churches; Bombingham; King, Martin Luther Jr.; Shuttlesworth, Fred

James L. Baggett

Bibliography
Cobbs, Elizabeth H., and Petric J. Smith. *Long Time Coming: An Insider's Story of the Birmingham Church Bombing that Rocked the World.* Birmingham, AL: Crane Hill Publishing, 1994.

Fallin, Wilson Jr. *The African American Church in Birmingham, Alabama, 181501963: A Shelter in the Storm.* New York: Garland Publishing, 1997.

Feldman, Lynne B. *A Sense of Place: Birmingham's Black Middle-Class Community, 1890–1930.* Tuscaloosa: University of Alabama Press, 1999.

Hamlin, Christopher M. *Behind the Stained Glass: A History of Sixteenth Street Baptist Church.* Birmingham, AL: Crane Hill Publishers, 1998.

Romano, Renee C. "Narratives of Redemption: The Birmingham Church Bombing Trials and the Construction of Civil Rights Memory." In *The Civil Rights Movement in American Memory.* Renee C. Romano and Leigh Raiford, eds., 96–133. Athens: University of Georgia Press, 2006.

Schnorrenberg, John M. *Aspiration: Birmingham's Historic Houses of Worship.* Birmingham, AL: Birmingham Historical Society, 2000.

Sikora, Frank. *Until Justice Rolls Down: The Birmingham Church Bombing Case.* Tuscaloosa: University of Alabama Press, 2005.

Soledad Brothers

Despite its contemporary revolutionary connotations, the origin of the term "Soledad Brother" is far removed from progressive politics and revolutionary struggle. The term originally denoted an African American incarcerated in California's Soledad Prison. During the early 1970s, the term became integral to a political lexicon that divided Americans along New Left, Liberal, Moderate, and Conservative lines. For black power advocates, the "Soledad Brothers" were an example of the spirit needed to overthrow American racial apartheid.

The "Soledad Brothers" legend centers on George Jackson (1941–1971). Although Jackson was born in Chicago, it would be on the West Coast, where the family migrated in the mid-1950s, that the legend of George Jackson would be established. Shortly after his arrival, Jackson fell into a pattern of juvenile delinquency, which landed him in the Paso Robles Youth Authority Corrections facility. Confinement proved to be no deterrent, as George continued his criminal behavior upon release. Jackson's petty crimes led to a charge of stealing $71 from a local gas station. Considering Jackson's prior criminal activities, the judge sentenced the 18-year-old to a term of one year to life at Soledad Prison.

Once incarcerated, Jackson made several life-altering observations. Inspired by the revolutionary polemics of the Black Panther Party's (BPP) Huey P. Newton, Jackson began the process of becoming politicized. During his relatively frequent stays in solitary confinement, Jackson used his time wisely and voraciously devoured the works of Karl Marx, W. I. Lenin, Leon Trotsky, and Mao Tse-tung (Zedong). Informed by such thinkers, Jackson emerged from solitary confinement with radical ideas. Before accepting a field marshall position with the BPP, a politicized Jackson formed the Black Guerilla Family (BGF) with fellow inmate W. L. Nolen. The BGF was initially intended to be a vehicle that politicized black and Hispanic inmates and organized in efforts to secure prison reforms. Despite Jackson's intentions, correction officers labeled the group a prison gang. Ironically, Black Panther Party cofounder Huey P. Newton would be murdered by a street-level drug dealing BGF member on August 22, 1989. The BGF wrought an immediate reaction from correction officers. Toward dismantling the BGF, corrections officers struck a lethal blow. On January 13, 1970, BGF cofounder W. L. Nolen, along with two other inmates, was murdered. When contextualized with other mid-1960s law enforcement attacks on black radicals, Nolen's demise was predictable.

Despite the natural desire to exact some form of retribution for Nolen's death, Panther politics forbid it; such behavior was considered counterrevolutionary. BPP Field

Marshall George Jackson was mired in a peculiar dilemma; his personal desire for revenge, which BPP Chairman Huey P. Newton denounced as "reactionary suicide," was supported, if not mandated, by Soledad's prison culture. Toward countering such tendencies within the BPP, Newton invalidated reactionary violence in two position papers: "*In Defense of Self-Defense*" and "*The Correct Handling of a Revolution*." Newton had taught his cadre that it was a similar pursuit of retribution after Martin Luther King's assassination that led to the death of Lil' Bobby Hutton; Hutton had been the first to join the BPP. Jackson was torn between revolutionary edicts and prison culture. The matter was largely settled, however, after a grand jury ruled the murders justifiable homicide. In direct violation of existing revolutionary policies, George Jackson, Fleeta Drumgo, and John Clutchette murdered correction officer John Mills on January 13, 1970.

Within a late-1960s/early-1970s period of radicalism, the murder of a white correction officer by black inmates made sensational copy. Similar to Huey P. Newton's October 28, 1967 shootout, the "Soledad Brothers" became the cause célèbre for black revolutionaries and white radicals. Jackson's popularity would only increase with his legendary tomes: *Soledad Brother* and *Blood in My Eye*. Unbelievably, George Jackson's legend was extended by events that occurred absent his presence.

On August 7, 1970, Jonathan Jackson, George's younger brother, bodyguard for University of California, San Diego, Professor Angela Davis, stormed the Marin County Courthouse; the teenage Jackson executed the plan alone because the BPP deserted him moments before the attack was to commence. Jackson intended to send an unforgettable message via an unprecedented display of revolutionary actions. Jackson burst into the Marin County Courthouse brandishing a machine gun and carrying armaments for the three San Quentin prisoners—James McClain, William Christmas, and Ruchell Magee—involved in the day's court proceedings. Jackson instructed the others to take the judge, prosecutor, and three jurors' hostage. The teen-age Jackson planned to use the hostages as human shields while commandeering a local radio station. Jonathan intended to issue a national plea for the immediate end of the intolerable conditions present in the California penal system. Most important, Jackson sought to propagate the "Soledad Brothers" case and order their immediate release.

Unbeknownst to Jackson, officers had mobilized in the parking lot where a van awaited his return; as Jackson attempted to exit, officers opened fire on the vehicle. When the firing ceased, Jonathan Jackson, inmates William Christmas and James McClain, and Judge Harold Haley were mortally wounded. The district attorney was paralyzed by gunfire. Inmate Ruchell Magee was struck, yet survived. The kidnapped jurors were unharmed. As a result of what came to be commonly referred to as "The August 7th Rebellion," Magee would be charged with murder, kidnapping, and conspiracy.

Incredibly, the blame for Jackson's attack was also laid at the doorstep of University of California, San Diego, Professor Angela Davis. Davis had already achieved prominence via her public battle with California Governor Ronald Reagan over academic freedom and free-speech issues; both concepts proved anathema to California's highest elected public official throughout his public career. Despite his demise, Jackson had succeeded in bringing attention to the Soledad Brothers; however, tragedy loomed on the horizon.

In preparation for George Jackson's trial, authorities transferred him to San Quentin Prison. Three days before the trial, August 21, 1971, BPP Field Marshall George Jackson was gunned down by prison guards while standing in San Quentin's prison yard. Corrections officers alleged that Jackson was in the midst of an escape attempt that had commenced earlier that day via a prison riot that left two guards and three inmates dead. Officers bolstered their charges by alleging Jackson had a 9-mm automatic pistol in his possession during the escape attempt. The alluded to weapon was allegedly smuggled in by Jackson's legal counsel Stephen Bingham; Bingham would eventually be acquitted of the charges. Eyewitnesses to Jackson's horrific demise testified that Jackson was neither attempting an escape nor did he have a weapon in his possession when officers mortally struck Jackson with gunfire. Those present maintain that Jackson was murdered by officers seeking retribution for their two fallen colleagues. When pressed to support their theory that Jackson was armed, prison officials were unable to produce either the weapon or records showing its destruction. George Jackson was 29 when slain by San Quentin Prison correction officers.

See also: Black Panther Party; Black Power; Davis, Angela; Newton, Huey P.

Bibliography

Brown, Elaine. *A Taste of Power: A Black Woman's Story.* New York: Doubleday, 1992.

Churchill, Ward. *Agents of Repression: The FBI's Secret Wars Against the Black Panther Party and the Indian Movement.* Boston: South End Press, 1988.

Cleaver, Kathleen. *Liberation, Imagination and the Black Panther Party: A New Look at the Black Panthers and their Legacy.* New York: Routledge, 2001.

Collier, Peter. *Destructive Generation: Second Thoughts About the 60's.* New York: Free Press Paperbacks, 1989.

Durden-Smith, Jo. *Who Killed George Jackson?* New York: Knopf, 1976.

Jackson, George. *Blood in My Eye.* Baltimore, MD: Black Classic Press, 1990.

Jackson, George. *Soledad Brother: The Prison Letters of George Jackson.* New York: Coward-McCann, 1970.

Jackson, George. "A Talk with George Jackson." Interview with Jessica Mitford. *New York Times* (June 13, 1971):30.

James, Joy, ed. *The Angela Y. Davis Reader.* Malden, MA: Blackwell Publishers, 1998.

Jones, Charles, ed. *The Black Panther Party Reconsidered.* Baltimore, MD: Black Classic Press, 1998.

Mann, Eric. *Comrade George; An Investigation into the Life, Political Thought, and Assassination of George Jackson.* New York: Harper & Row, 1974.

Newton, Fredericka, *The Huey P. Newton Reader.* New York: Seven Stories Press, 2002.

James Thomas Jones III

Southern Christian Leadership Conference

The Southern Christian Leadership Conference (SCLC) is a civil rights organization formed in January 1957 that played a key role in administering direct-action, nonviolent campaigns against legalized segregation in the United States. The chief founder, and first president of SCLC, the Reverend Martin Luther King Jr., successfully collected a partial payment on that "unpaid check" he had spoken of in his "I Have a Dream" speech in Washington, D.C. in August 1963, by overseeing the implementation of new laws and desegregating many aspects of public life in the South.

SCLC is located in the "Sweet Auburn" historic district, in the center of downtown Atlanta, Georgia. Originally housed at 208 Auburn Avenue, the SCLC offices were moved into the Prince Hall Masonic Temple building located at 334 Auburn. Today, the SCLC staff resides in their new headquarters on Edgewood Avenue, in the historic district of Atlanta.

Civil rights demonstrators from the Student Nonviolent Coordinating Committee (SNCC) and the Congress of Racial Equality (CORE) chained to a federal courthouse in New York City in protest of civil rights abuses in Jackson, Mississippi, 1965. (Library of Congress)

The significance of Auburn Avenue and the history of SCLC dates back to January 15, 1929, when King was born in the upstairs bedroom of a modest Victorian style home located at 501 Auburn. From 1955 to 1960, the Reverend Martin Luther King Sr. was pastor of the Ebenezer Baptist Church located on the same avenue, just two blocks west of their home on Auburn. Young Martin would often deliver guest sermons at Ebenezer, and eventually, in 1960 officially began serving as co-pastor.

It was at Ebenezer, within walls that reverberated with King's fiery speeches and sermons, that various African American leaders gathered in the first weeks of 1957 to discuss the formation of a southern organization grounded in Christian principles and committed to nonviolent social change. For civil rights leaders such as Bayard Rustin, Stanley Levison, Ella J. Baker, C. K. Steele, and many involved

in the victorious Montgomery, Alabama bus boycott from December 1, 1955 to November 13, 1956, King represented a distinctive approach to social reform.

In retrospect, it seems clear that King's move to Montgomery in May 1954 to become pastor the Dexter Avenue Baptist Church began a new era in the African American liberation movement in the United States. Soon after his arrival, he joined the local NAACP and other advocacy organizations and encouraged participation by members of his church. King's personality played a decisive role in the bus boycott and the establishment of the first genuine grassroots movement directed pointedly against segregation in the South. King appeared as a vigorous and determined leader who bridged church and society as no one had in the long southern struggle for racial equality.

The founders of SCLC seized the grassroots momentum created in Montgomery and carried it into Atlanta. Ebenezer church served as more than SCLC's founding location; in subsequent years, the church building provided accommodations for various meetings, rallies, and their 1967 annual convention. King, the church membership, and SCLC participants were molded into an inseparable, united movement.

The first SCLC convention was held in Montgomery in August 1957. During this meeting, members adopted their official name and selected King as their first president, with C. K. Steele as the first vice president. The key to understanding the effectiveness of SCLC lies in viewing the composition of the organization as a loose connection of church groups capable of uniting in a mobilized campaign under the auspices of their leadership.

Under the guidance of King and Steele, SCLC participants made the decade of the 1960s a pivotal period in the history of the American Civil Rights movement. In less than five years, successful SCLC campaigns prompted African Americans to find and enjoy a new freedom, as segregation, Jim Crow customs, and lynching became part of the South's past. Notably, the Albany, Georgia campaign of 1961–1962 was pivotal in shaping the approach of SCLC to direct-action campaigns. In July 1962, while in an Albany jail, King became convinced that a "four-pronged approach" was the best means of unifying society. This approach consisted of legal action, direct action, selective buying, and voter registration.

During the Birmingham campaign of 1963, SCLC and King propelled the Civil Rights movement to national attention in an effort to gain leverage in negotiation and apply pressure to the United States government. In his "letter from a Birmingham Jail," King outlined four stages of a nonviolent campaign: investigation to determine whether injustice existed, negotiation with local officials, self-purification, and direct action. Subsequently, the St. Augustine, Florida campaign of 1964 would test every stage of the nonviolence campaign. The following year brought the successful Selma, Alabama campaign. The famous Selma to Montgomery march prompted Congress to pass the 1965 Voting Rights Act.

By 1965, King had led SCLC to three cardinal gains. First, it had psychologically raised the hopes of African Americans by giving them a sense of pride, dignity, and confidence in themselves as a people. Second, SCLC and its allies had gathered and consolidated a tremendous amount of political leverage in gaining desegregation of facilities and polling booths. Last, the SCLC campaigns had laid important groundwork and precedent for future generations who were now armed with the right to vote, eat, sit, study, and live as they wished.

SCLC Presidents:

Martin Luther King Jr. (1957–1968)

Ralph D. Abernathy (1968–1977)

Joseph E. Lowery (1977–1997)

Martin Luther King, III (1997–2004)

Fred Shuttlesworth (February 2004–November 2004)

Charles Steele Jr. (November, 2004–)

See also: Abernathy, Ralph David; Albany, Georgia, Movement; King, Martin Luther Jr.; March on Washington, 1963; Montgomery Bus Boycott; Selma March; Shuttlesworth, Fred; Williams, Hosea

Bobby R. Holt

Bibliography

Abernathy, Ralph David. *And the Walls Came Tumbling Down: An Autobiography.* New York: Harpercollins, 1991.

Branch, Taylor. *Parting the Waters: America in the King Years, 1954–1963.* New York: Simon & Schuster, 1989.

Branch, Taylor. *Pillar of Fire: America in the King Years, 1963–1965.* New York: Simon & Schuster, 1989.

Fairclough, Adam. *To Redeem the Soul of America: The Southern Christian Leadership Conference and Martin Luther King, Jr.* Athens: University of Georgia Press, 2001.

Garrow, David J. *Bearing the Cross: Martin Luther King, Jr., and the Southern Christian Leadership Conference.* New York: William Morrow, 1986.

King, Jr., Martin Luther. *Autobiography,* ed. Clayborne Carson. New York: Warner Books, 1998.

Peake, Thomas R. *Keeping the Dream Alive: A History of the Southern Christian Leadership Conference from King to the Nineteen Eighties.* New York: Peter Lang, 1987.

Springfield Race Riot of 1908

For two days in August 1908, a race riot ravaged the streets of Springfield, Illinois. Two African Americans were brutally murdered, four whites were killed by gunfire, more than 100 people were hospitalized, 40 African American homes were burned, and two dozen businesses were damaged or destroyed.

Two local events helped spark the riot. First, on July 4, 1908, Earl Ballard, a white man, was stabbed and killed by Joe Johnson, an African American. Second, on August 13, 1908, Mabel Hallam, a married white woman, reported that an African American man broke into her home during the night, choked her, and dragged her into her backyard, and proceeded to assault her. Neighbors came to her aid, but the assailant was already gone. Mrs. Hallam, bruised and badly shaken, told police that a young African American male, wearing a colored shirt and work clothes, was responsible. Police arrested George Richardson, an African American, who despite being misidentified twice by Hallam, was booked into the county jail.

On August 14, a white mob arrived at the jail to lynch Ballard and Richardson. Sensing trouble, local officials had transported the suspects 60 miles north to Bloomington, Illinois to avoid retribution. Rumors circulated that a local restaurant owner, Harry Loper, had allowed police to use his automobile to transport the prisoners. The mob turned its rage on Loper's restaurant, first throwing a brick through the window, and then by firing shots into the establishment. Louis Johnson, a white man, was hit by the gunfire and died on the scene. Still unsatisfied, the mob made its way to the African American neighborhood, known as the Levee, where they destroyed homes and businesses. When they came across Scott Burton, an African American barber, they hanged him from a tree, shot him, and burned his body. An estimated 3,700 militiamen arrived in the town, dispersed the crowd, and opened the state armory to the homeless and badly shaken African Americans. Hundreds more African Americans fled the town.

On August 15, the mob re-formed and proceeded to the home of 80-year-old William Donnegan, a wealthy African American who had been married to a white woman for 32 years. Claiming he fired at them, the mob slashed Donnegan's throat, hanged him from a nearby tree, and proceeded to burn his home.

Two weeks after the riot, Hallam recanted her story. She claimed that Richardson was not the man who attacked her. She gave the description of another African American male. Later, she told a special grand jury that she was not attacked by an African American man after all. Her assailant was a white man, with whom she was having an affair. Hallam and her family moved from Springfield a few months after the riot. Richardson was released from jail and continued to live in Springfield, and James was tried for the murder of Clergy Ballard and found guilty and hanged.

The scene in Springfield was eerily reminiscent of a lynching in Georgia just four years earlier. In 1904, in Statesboro, Georgia, a mob burned alive two African American men who were each accused of murder and destroyed the property of several other African Americans. By 1908, lynchings were a southern phenomenon. Between 1884 and 1900, 2,000 African Americans were lynched in the South. Springfield was among the first northern cities to witness the racial violence that would later sweep cities like East St. Louis, Illinois in 1917 and Chicago in 1919.

The two-day riot in Springfield, Abraham Lincoln's adopted home town, startled many Americans. As a result, the National Association for the Advancement of Colored People (NAACP) was organized on Lincoln's birthday six months after the Springfield race riot. On August 13, 1994, a Springfield nonprofit group called Monument 1908 put headstones on four previously unidentified graves believed to belong to two African American and two white victims of the Springfield race riot of 1908.

See also: Lynching; National Association for the Advancement of Colored People; White Mob Violence

Samuel Paul Wheeler

Bibliography

Krobe, James, *Summer of Rage: The Springfield Race Riot of 1908.* Springfield, IL: Sangamon County Historical Society, 1973.

Pokorski, Doug. "Springfield Prepares to Honor Victims of Race Riot," *The State Journal-Register.* (August 11, 1994):11.

Senechal de la Roche, Roberta. *In Lincoln's Shadow: The 1908 Race Riot in Springfield, Illinois.* Carbondale: Southern Illinois University Press, 2008.

Senechal de la Roche, Roberta. *The Sociogenesis of a Race Riot: Springfield, Illinois in 1908.* Urbana: University of Illinois Press, 1990.

Stevens, Thaddeus

Thaddeus Stevens (1792–1868) was a lawyer and, as a Republican representative from Pennsylvania from 1858 to 1868, a leading radical voice in Congress. He consistently agitated for emancipation and later for the full legal equality of former slaves. Controversial throughout his life, Stevens never achieved the entire program he desired, but he helped shape some of the most important legislation of the Civil War and Reconstruction.

The second of four sons, Stevens was born on April 4, 1792, in Danville, Vermont, to shoemaker and surveyor

Joshua Stevens and Sarah Morrill. His father deserted the family when Stevens was 12. Stevens learned the shoemaking trade, but his mother moved the family to Peacham, Vermont in 1807 so that her children could attend the Caledonia Grammar School, also called the Peacham Academy. In 1811, Stevens entered Dartmouth College in Hanover, New Hampshire and graduated in 1814. He then relocated to Danville and began studying law with Judge John Mattocks.

On the recommendation of a Dartmouth classmate, Stevens moved to York, Pennsylvania in February 1815, where he became a teacher at the York Academy and studied with lawyer David Cassat. After passing the bar exam in 1816, Stevens moved to Gettysburg and established his own law office. He soon became one of the most prominent lawyers in southern Pennsylvania and served on the Gettysburg Council from 1822 to 1831. He demonstrated his commitment to the abolition of slavery early in his career, taking on the defense of fugitive slaves by the mid-1820s. In addition to his legal work, Stevens established the Mifflin Forge and Maria Furnace around 1826 and later an ironworks he named the Caledonia Forge.

Stevens became active in local and state politics, particularly the campaign against Masonry's secrecy and exclusion. His increasing political profile won him election to the state legislature in 1833. While serving in the Pennsylvania House of Representatives from 1833 to 1836 and again in 1839 and 1841, Stevens successfully argued for public education and the recharter of the Bank of the United States in Pennsylvania. Stevens left the legislature as anti-Mason political clout waned, and financial troubles with his ironworks following the Panic of 1837 prompted Stevens to set up a new law practice in Lancaster, Pennsylvania in 1842. While in Lancaster, Stevens participated in the Underground Railroad and continued to defend fugitive slaves against capture. In 1843, he also hired a biracial woman named Lydia Hamilton Smith as his housekeeper. Stevens never married and lived with her until his death, and the nature of their relationship inspired endless conjecture. Most historians agree that there is insufficient evidence to prove that Stevens and Smith had a romantic relationship.

In 1848, Stevens entered national politics, winning a seat in the House of Representatives as a Whig and serving until 1852. There, he gained renown for his impassioned speeches against the expansion of slavery into newly acquired territories. After the Whig party fractured in 1854, Stevens was integral to the organization of Pennsylvania's Republican Party. He returned to the House of

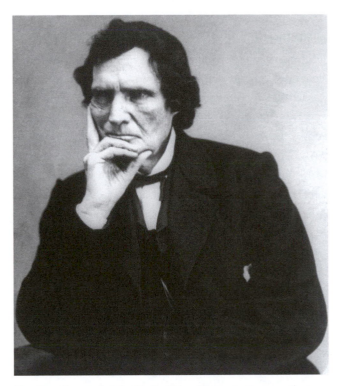

Thaddeus Stevens led the Radical Republicans in Congress during the Reconstruction period and was the primary instigator in the impeachment of President Andrew Johnson. (Library of Congress)

Representatives in 1858. With the advent of the secession crisis in 1860 and 1861, Stevens, who was by now chairman of the powerful Ways and Means Committee, emerged as a vehement foe of any compromise with the rebellious South. Stevens believed that national reunification required the abolition of slavery, and throughout the Civil War, he urged President Abraham Lincoln to do so. Although Stevens was often frustrated with Lincoln's progress toward declaring emancipation, he also became one of the administration's most important congressional allies in other respects. Stevens guided such legislation through the House as higher protective tariffs and the first income tax, which expanded the economic authority of the federal government. He also supported the passage of the Confiscation Acts and the first military draft in 1863. He was an early advocate of the enlistment of African American soldiers and late in 1863 successfully proposed legislation to give black soldiers equal pay and repeal the Fugitive Slave Law. Stevens also supported the Thirteenth Amendment abolishing slavery, which passed in 1865.

Some of Stevens's most radical suggestions involved the fate of the South after the Civil War. He unsuccessfully pushed for the seizure of the estates of rebellious planters for redistribution among former slaves. Stevens set himself firmly against the Reconstruction plan of President Andrew Johnson, which permitted the reorganization of Southern state governments and required only an oath of loyalty to pardon ex-Confederates. Especially as the new Southern governments began to adopt restrictive Black Codes, Stevens worked to galvanize opposition to Johnson. Congress passed the Civil Right Act of 1866 over Johnson's veto and in 1867 wrested control of Reconstruction from the President with the passage of the Reconstruction Act. This measure imposed military rule on the South and required its states to remove racial restrictions on voting in their new constitutions. In a final blow to Johnson, Stevens helped bring impeachment charges against him in February 1868 after Johnson attempted to replace Secretary of War Edwin Stanton without congressional approval. By this time, however, Stevens was too ill with dropsy and stomach ailments to lead the charge, which some historians blame for the impeachment effort's failure in May.

Stevens died at midnight at his Washington, D.C., home on August 11, 1868. After lying in state at the Capitol, he was buried at Schreiner's Cemetery in Lancaster, a site selected by Stevens because it was racially integrated.
See also: Civil Rights Act of 1866; Fourteenth Amendment; Johnson, Andrew; Lincoln, Abraham; Radical Republicans; Republican Party; Sumner, Charles; Thirteenth Amendment; Underground Railroad

Francesca Gamber

Bibliography

Brodie, Fawn. *Thaddeus Stevens: Scourge of the South.* New York: W. W. Norton, 1959.
Foner, Eric. *Free Soil, Free Labor, Free Men: The Ideology of the Republican Party Before the Civil War.* New York: Oxford University Press, 1970.
Foner, Eric. *Reconstruction: America's Unfinished Revolution, 1863–1877.* New York: Harper & Row, 1988.
Trefousse, Hans L. *Thaddeus Stevens: Nineteenth-Century Egalitarian.* Chapel Hill: University of North Carolina Press, 1997.

"Strange Fruit"

In 1935, Abel Meeropol saw a photograph of the lynching of Thomas Shipp and Abram Smith, which had taken place in Marion, Indiana, on August 7, 1930. The image haunted Meeropol for days and in response he wrote a three verse poem, "Strange Fruit." The poem depicted the memory of trauma in the landscape, echoing the trope of the haunted tree in Hannah Crafts's *The Bondwoman's Narrative* (1859), Charles Chesnutt's story "Po Sandy" (1888), Paul Dunbar's poem "The Haunted Oak" (1903), and Angelina Weld Grimke's poem "Tenebris" (1927). Here Meeropol reminded readers that some trees were used for multiple lynchings and also evoked numerous tales of encounter with lynching's aftermath (scenes of shoes, bones, teeth, and the strange fruit of the victim's dismembered corpse). His poem spoke of a cultural haunting.

A union activist and a member of the American Communist Party, as well a Jewish schoolteacher, Meeropol published the poem under the pseudonym Lewis Allan in the *New York Teacher* in 1937 and in *New Masses* in 1939. After he set the poem to music, it was regularly performed at leftist gatherings, including once at a fundraiser for antifascists during the Spanish Civil War. But he is virtually forgotten as the original author of the lyrics to "Strange Fruit." In January 1939, he took his song to the newly opened Café Society in Greenwich Village—Manhattan's only integrated nightclub and the venue where Billie Holiday performed. He asked Holiday to listen and played his song at the piano. Meeropol remembered that afterwards Holiday asked only one question: what did "pastoral" mean?

Holiday was only 23 years old and had not yet recorded a political song. Before 1939 much of her material consisted of upbeat swing numbers, and she had sung with Count Basie and Artie Shaw's bands before landing a solo engagement at Café Society in December 1938. Meeropol's song would now mark a turning point in her career. She first performed her own version of "Strange Fruit" later in January 1939, at Café Society. "There wasn't even a patter of applause when I finished," Holiday recalled. "Then a lone person began to clap nervously. Then suddenly everyone was clapping" (*Lady Sings the Blues,* p. 85). Meeropol later added of her rendition: "She gave a startling, most dramatic and effective interpretation . . . which could jolt the audience out of its complacency anywhere. . . . Billie Holiday's styling of the song was incomparable and fulfilled the bitterness and shocking quality I had hoped the song would have" (Greene, 59).

After that first performance, audience responses to the song continued to be extreme. For a long time it was rarely played on the radio and was almost impossible to find in record stores. Holiday's label had refused to record it and so she released it with the obscure label Commodore. She performed her own version around the country throughout the 1940s, sometimes encountering such violent audience responses that she was forced to stop singing or leave town. The South African government banned the song during apartheid. Yet others could not get enough. This was the first time anyone had sung so explicitly about lynching and many listeners were gripped. In October 1939, one journalist for the *New York Post* wrote that a record had obsessed him for two days. Even after 10 hearings "Strange Fruit" would "make you blink and hold to your chair," he explained. "Even now, as I think of it, the short hair on the back of my neck tightens and I want to hit somebody" (*Billie Holiday: A Biography*, p. 62).

Still others recognized the song as a call to arms in a year when three lynchings took place, a survey revealed that 60 percent of southerners thought lynching was justifiable, and audiences flocked to see *Gone With the Wind*. The film, later criticized for its romanticized "moonlight and magnolias" approach to American history, was sweeping the nation; but in "Strange Fruit" a smell of burning flesh accompanies the "scent of magnolias," as the lyrics put it. It is rare that a protest movement does not have a great protest song at its heart, and "Strange Fruit" was the anthem of the antilynching movement from 1939 onwards. It became one of the most influential protest songs ever written—often compared to Bob Dylan's "The Death of Emmett Till" (1963) and Nina Simone's "Mississippi Goddam" (1963).

It has been re-recorded by more than 100 musical artists to date, including Abbey Lincoln, Nina Simone, Sting, and Tori Amos. Black singer Josh White began singing "Strange Fruit" a few years after Holiday, and in 1941 he released it on his album *Southern Exposure* with a liner note by Richard Wright. Jazz writer Leonard Feather described it as the first unmuted cry against racism, and record producer Ahmet Ertegun called it a declaration of war and the beginning of the Civil Rights movement. Although *Time Magazine* initially dismissed it as propaganda for the National Association for the Advancement of Colored People, by 1999 the magazine had hailed the song as the best of the century. Four years later the British magazine *Q* ranked it sixth in a list of 100 songs that have changed the world.

The song's presence also extended to a controversial exhibition of lynching photographs. In 2002, the exhibition *Without Sanctuary* opened in Atlanta. It featured the photograph that had haunted and inspired Meeropol in 1935, along with Meeropol's lyrics on one of the foyer walls. And as visitors looked at the photographs, the sound of "Strange Fruit" filled the gallery.

See also: Antilynching Campaign; Black Folk Culture; Lynching; White Mob Violence

Zoe Trodd

Bibliography

Davis, Angela. *Blues Legacies and Black Feminism.* New York: Pantheon Books, 1998.

Greene, Meg. *Billie Holiday: A Biography.* Westport, CT: Greenwood Press, 2006

Holiday, Billie. *Lady Sings the Blues.* New York: Penguin, 1986.

Margolick, David. *Strange Fruit: Billie Holiday, Cafe Society, and an Early Cry for Civil Rights.* Philadelphia: Running Press, 2000.

Nicholson, Stuart. *Billie Holiday.* Boston: Northeastern University Press, 1995.

O'Meally, Robert. *Lady Day: The Many Faces of Billie Holiday.* New York: Arcade Press, 1991.

Student Nonviolent Coordinating Committee

The Student Nonviolent Coordinating Committee (SNCC) was one of the most important organizations to participate in the 1960s African American Civil Rights movement. Often referred to as the "shock troops" of the movement, SNCC remained on the cutting edge of the southern black freedom struggle. The organization differed from other groups such as the Southern Christian Leadership Conference (SCLC) in its organizational style and leadership. Unlike the SCLC, SNCC believed in creating and developing leadership. In accordance with SNCC founder Ella Baker's famous stance that "strong people do not need strong leaders," SNCC based most of its actions on creating grassroots leadership in African American communities. This leadership style facilitated the emergence of different types of leaders who would have most likely been marginalized by other organizations in the movement. Northern blacks, women, whites, and especially local people held prevalent positions in SNCC and were essential to its development. Creating leaders among these groups enabled the organization to maintain a great deal of diversity and promoted community-based activism. The dynamics of the grass-roots leadership style encouraged by SNCC brought local communities into the forefront of the modern Civil Rights movement and helped pave the way for future generations of leaders among black southerners.

On the afternoon of February 1, 1960, four black students at North Carolina A & T entered a Woolworth's department store in Greensboro. Franklin McCain, Joseph McNeil, Ezell Blair, and David Richmond spent several dollars in the department store and then took seats at the store's segregated lunch counter where they were refused service. The four young men remained seated and refused to leave until served. They stayed at the lunch counter for nearly one hour before the store closed and they were forced to leave. The young students returned the next day with 20 of their classmates and took seats at the segregated counter. The four young men came back to the lunch counter for several consecutive days, bringing more classmates each time. By February 5, hundreds of young people, including some whites, joined the sit-in protest only to be denied service each time.

Within days of the initial protest, African American students in nearby Winston-Salem, Durham, and Raleigh, began conducting their own sit-ins at segregated lunch counters throughout the state. News of the sit-ins continued to spread, and eventually African Americans outside of North Carolina joined the movement. By mid-February, there were sit-ins in Norfolk, Virginia; Rock Hill, South Carolina; Baltimore, Maryland, and Nashville, Tennessee. By late March, students in Nashville and Atlanta, Georgia had begun massive sit-in demonstrations that commanded the attention of the American media.

Many people across the country were extremely impressed by this burgeoning movement that was being led by college-blacks. Included among these sit-in supporters was 56-year-old Ella Baker who was a veteran activist and current executive secretary for the SCLC. Ms. Baker realized the potential of these students if they could coordinate their protests through a national organization. She lobbied SCLC for an $800 grant to be used to construct such an organization, and SNCC was born at an April conference in Raleigh, North Carolina, which was attended by sit-in leaders from across the South.

SNCC's first major campaign began on the eve of the one-year anniversary of the original Greensboro sit-ins. On January 31, 1961, 10 young African Americans were arrested for sitting at a segregated lunch counter in Rock Hill, South Carolina. Upon their arrest, SNCC arrived in the city and began a campaign that would be known as "jail-ins." SNCC leaders knew that they would be arrested for sitting at the segregated lunch counters in Rock Hill, but did so anyway in order to fill the city's jails. This would apply pressure on city officials who would have to use a vast amount of resources to arrest and detain large numbers of protesters. The "jail-in" strategy that SNCC used in Rock Hill would become one of the most important tactics used during the Civil Rights movement.

Later that year, SNCC joined forces with the Congress of Racial Equality (CORE) to test a 1961 Supreme Court decision that banned segregation on interstate busses. In *Boynton v. Virginia,* the United States Supreme Court ruled that segregation on interstate busses and terminals was unconstitutional. Like every other victory for integration, however, the court decision would have to be tested to ensure that the United States government would back the rights of African Americans. Freedom Rides were designed to test *Boynton v. Virginia.* Members of CORE and SNCC planned to travel on buses through the South, desegregating bus terminals as they went. The original group included seven blacks and six whites who left Washington, D.C. for New Orleans on May 4, 1961. The trip was relatively uneventful at first, but the Freedom Riders met violence upon reaching the Deep South. On May 9, two of the protesters were attacked at the bus terminal in Rock Hill. A few days later, white segregationists slashed the bus tires outside of Anniston, Alabama and the group had to switch buses to proceed even deeper into the Jim Crow South. The violence reached a pinnacle outside of Birmingham, Alabama when white supremacists, aided by the absence of policemen, entered the bus and attacked all of the Freedom Riders and bombed their vehicle. Volunteer James Peck was beaten so badly that it took 53 stitches to close the wound he received from a blow to the head. The next day, pictures of the attack appeared on the front page of most of the nation's newspapers. This coverage of the violence that Freedom Riders faced forced the Kennedy administration to provide protection for future Freedom Riders.

SNCC experienced its first major internal conflict during the months after the Freedom Rides. Two factions emerged within the organization. One faction encouraged direct action protests such as sit-ins and marches. Another favored voter registration. Ms. Baker suggested that both sides pursue their objectives by their chosen means, and SNCC grew into two separate entities that worked together but chose to conduct different forms of activism.

The first major voter registration project took place in McComb, Mississippi and was led by Bob Moses who had been stirred into action after learning of the nationwide sit-in movement that began in February 1960 at the Greensboro Woolworth's. Moses was a 26-year-old high school teacher in Harlem, New York when he first heard of the sit-in movement. It immediately propelled him into action and he joined SNCC in 1960. By 1961, Moses had become SNCC's field secretary in Mississippi after entering the nation's most segregated state with nothing more than a list of contacts gathered by Ms. Baker during her decades of prior activism. In Mississippi, Moses was able to connect into underground networks of activists who had been fighting for black freedom in the state for decades. These activists were able to connect Moses to local people. By 1961, Moses had created a beachhead in Mississippi. True to SNCC's founding philosophy of grassroots organizing, most of the leaders in Mississippi were locals. Many outsiders entered the state to join Moses, but the majority of groundwork was done by local people who were mired in one of the nation's worst forms of poverty in 1961. The median income of local blacks was less than half the poverty level for a four-person household. This poverty extended into the state's racist educational system as well. Mississippi blacks were extremely undereducated. The state took aims to ensure that its black students did not achieve any form of academic freedom. Many local blacks did not even know that they had a constitutional right to vote. If they did pursue this right, Mississippi blacks were subject to violence. Because of the incredibly dangerous characteristics of white supremacists in the state, SNCC was severely limited in its ability to recruit organizers and incorporated anyone willing to risk their lives into the organization. Women, older black men, black youths, and some whites played key parts in the state as SNCC's presence in Mississippi grew in 1961.

Voter registration campaigns were key to the struggle for black freedom in Mississippi for two reasons. First, only a very small percentage of African Americans had been allowed to register over the previous decades. Counties like McComb, where only 5 percent of age-eligible citizens were registered to vote, were typical. Second, the state was characterized by an culture of extreme racial violence. The Mississippi Justice Department simply refused to prosecute whites who committed violence against African Americans. White supremacists in Mississippi knew fully well that any violence inflicted on African Americans would go unchecked. A black civil rights activist could be killed at any time. Direct-action campaigns in Mississippi were more dangerous to conduct than anywhere else.

In August, 1961, with the help of funds from the federal government's Voter Education Project (VEP), Moses began a voter registration project in McComb. SNCC workers traveled door-to-door in an attempt to convince potential black voters to register. Initially, the organization experienced some success as members began to venture out into other black communities to canvass potential voters and recruit new SNCC volunteers. Voter registration was often slow, however, owing to the prevalence of fear among black Mississippians. This fear was confirmed by the 1961 murder of Herbert Lee who was a native Mississippian who had been transporting SNCC workers throughout black communities. Lee was shot in broad daylight by a member of the Mississippi House of Representatives who was quickly acquitted. This confirmed to most black Mississippians that voter registration was impossible, and the murder greatly slowed SNCC's progress throughout the state. The organization kept fighting, however, and continued to spread into other regions of Mississippi including the rural Mississippi Delta where the majority of citizens were black. SNCC encountered the most impoverished and disenfranchised group in the state when it entered the delta, but it also incorporated an incredibly driven and able group of local black activists into the organization. Included among these local people was Fannie Lou Hamer of Ruleville, Mississippi who did not know that she should be allowed to vote until she attended a SNCC-sponsored meeting that took place in her local church in 1962. She was 44 years old and became one of the most important local leaders in Mississippi and symbols of the potential of grassroots organizing.

The direct-action division of SNCC also experienced several setbacks in 1961. Led by former Freedom Riders Charles Sherrod and Cordell Reagon, SNCC entered Albany, Georgia in October 1961 to lead protest activities in the city. The organization was effectively able to recruit local people to join movement activities, but it also encountered an obstacle that clashed with SNCC's basic philosophies. Initially, SNCC led marches and demonstrations in the city that were designed to protest segregation, discriminatory hiring practices, and the systematic disenfranchisement of black voters. Just weeks into their campaign, however, a local leader asked Martin Luther King Jr. to join black Albanians' fight for equality and freedom. King's leadership style was contradictory to the SNCC leadership tradition that promoted grassroots organizing.

Upon his arrival, King immediately assumed the leadership of peaceful marches through downtown Albany. He was arrested soon after, and building on SNCC's "jail-in" philosophy, King vowed to spend Christmas in prison if necessary. King arrived in Albany in December and brought the attention of the media with him. SNCC always welcomed media attention that would expose the plight of African Americans, but the newsmen focused almost exclusively on King. He became the face and symbol of the Albany movement. This would have drastic repercussions for local people who were pushed from leadership positions. Albany leaders, fearful of the media frenzy that the incarceration of the most famous black preacher in the United States could create, negotiated a deal with King without involving local leaders or SNCC. Upon King's release from prison, he declared victory and left the city. After King left Albany, local officials denied an accord had ever been reached. They reneged on their agreement with King and Albany's racial caste system continued as usual. SNCC leaders then had a hard time remobilizing local people who had become so dependent on King's leadership and prestige. Over the next several months, SNCC struggled against white officials to achieve nothing more than a stalemate that hardly threatened the status quo before the organization's involvement in the city.

By July 1962, SNCC had begun to reestablish leadership in Albany. King and his SCLC followers returned to the city that same month to assume leadership of the local people that SNCC had spent months mobilizing. As he had the previous year, King began leading demonstrations in the city; however, King's absence over the previous seven months had left many local people wary of his leadership position and he had trouble invoking large-scale protests. King was arrested twice more in Albany, but he could not fill the jails. SNCC was powerless to do so as well because King undermined the organization's leadership. Eventually, King left the city without any further concessions made by white officials. Leadership had been split, and both King and SNCC had been rendered ineffective as a result of the changing characteristics of Albany leadership. The

developments in Albany reinforced to SNCC that it had to remain largely autonomous from national movement figures, especially King, in order to be effective. It also motivated the student-led organization to recruit even more local people into leadership positions as it conducted localized campaigns throughout the South.

The year 1963 was a turbulent one in the Civil Rights movement and a definitive one for SNCC. In May, King-led protests in Birmingham captured the world's attention as policemen and firefighters used German shepherds and fire hoses to break-up peaceful demonstrations on the Alabama city's streets. This protest inspired demonstrations across the country. In all, approximately 930 protests occurred in 115 U.S. cities. More than 20,000 people were arrested for demonstrating against Jim Crow and discrimination. Later that year, the SCLC, NAACP, CORE, and SNCC led a massive March on Washington, during which more than 250,000 protestors gathered on the mall in D.C. to protest segregation. King gave his famous "I Have a Dream" speech during that protest and cemented the moral righteousness of the Civil Rights movement. SNCC conducted various direct-action campaigns across the South with the help of an influx of volunteers, including many whites. White individuals such as Bob Zellner, Sam Shirah, Jane Stembridge, and Sandra Hayden either joined the fight against Jim Crow or became more prevalent leaders in the organization. By the fall of 1963, 20 percent of SNCC members were white. Voter registration activities spread throughout the South's Black Belt, and SNCC began to experience breakthroughs in Mississippi.

In November 1963, SNCC conducted a mock election called the Freedom Vote in Mississippi. This campaign was designed to allow Mississippi African Americans an opportunity to participate in their first election, as well as to show the federal government that black Mississippians truly desired a stake in national and state politics. To illustrate the political potential of African Americans in the state, SNCC conducted an independent election. Because African Americans had been systematically excluded from Mississippi's regular Democratic Party, SNCC created an alternative Democratic organization named the Mississippi Freedom Democratic Party (MFDP). SNCC, which now included a large number of white volunteers fanned the state. Black candidates ran on the MFDP ticket and were elected to mock offices, including the governorship. More than 80,000 black Mississippians participated in the Freedom

Vote. This clearly showed that many more blacks desired a vote in Mississippi than the average of approximately 5,000 blacks who regularly voted in statewide elections. The Freedom Vote also helped lay the ground for a statewide voter registration campaign.

By the end of 1963, SNCC had come of age. The organization claimed large amounts of members from diverse racial and socioeconomic backgrounds. The Civil Rights movement was at its height, and the nation saw nearly 1,000 protests during the course of one year. SNCC leaders attempted to build on this momentum when planning for 1964. The organization knew that it could register black Mississippians if allowed. The Freedom Vote had showed that the disenfranchised African Americans in the state could and would be called into political action if SNCC took the proper measures. The other lesson that SNCC had learned over the previous years was that it could recruit a highly diverse and capable group of organizers from across the nation. Young people, including northern whites, cared about the SNCC cause and had shown in the years before 1964 that they were willing to risk injury and death in order to fight Jim Crow. These factors would all play a major influence on SNCC's planning for 1964.

In 1964, SNCC conducted the most ambitious and audacious civil rights campaign in the history of the United States when it launched an all-out campaign to crack Mississippi. Although the organization had achieved some previous successes in Mississippi, most of these, such as the Freedom Vote, were largely symbolic. The biggest deterrent in the state was the large-scale amount of unchecked violence that constantly threatened civil rights activists. SNCC could not get the federal government to help its cause even though Mississippi segregationists were blatantly violating the rights of black citizens. In 1964, SNCC decided that it needed a force large enough to effectively mobilize black Mississippians and prestigious enough to force the federal government to protect civil rights workers in the state. Based on SNCC's recent influx of white volunteers and sympathetic groups throughout the nation, the organization believed that it could recruit a large force of white college students to join the black freedom struggle in Mississippi during the summer of 1964. SNCC also believed that such a large group of white volunteers would force the federal government to protect civil rights workers in Mississippi. In the winter of 1963, SNCC representatives began appearing on northern college campuses to recruit young white students to participate in its 1964 Freedom Summer campaign.

Perhaps the most important goal of Freedom Summer was drawing attention to Mississippi and forcing federal intervention. The volunteers who would arrive in the state during the summer of 1964 were well positioned to do so. During the winter of 1963–1964, SNCC had recruited the children of American privilege. The organization believed that the more affluent its summer workers were, the greater chance of federal intervention. In all, 40 percent of the project's applicants came from Stanford, Harvard, Yale, and Princeton. Their parents included esteemed historian Arthur Schlesinger Jr., Congressman Don Edwards, and U.N. Ambassador Sidney Yates. As nearly 1,000 of these students poured into the state in late June, the nation took notice. Unfortunately, SNCC's greatest success in drawing federal intervention came at the expense of three lives. On June 21, SNCC workers Michael Schwerner, James Chaney, and Andrew Goodman were arrested in Philadelphia, Mississippi. Local police officers then held the three young men until dark before delivering them into the hands of Klansmen from Meridian and Neshoba County. The Klansmen, who had been tracking SNCC veteran Schwerner's moves for months, then executed the three young men and buried them under an earthen dam just outside of Philadelphia. The disappearance of the three workers, two of whom were white, drew the nation's interest and forced the federal government to build a presence in the state. It took the deaths of three young men for the federal government to launch a campaign against the KKK in the state, but their deaths probably saved dozens of lives during Freedom Summer.

Another important aspect of Freedom Summer was a program designed to create an active leadership class among Mississippi's black youths. Freedom Schools were taught mainly by white volunteers and provided training in the basic remedial skills absent from regular black schools in the state. The schools were also explicitly designed to incorporate young African Americans into the freedom struggle. Freedom Schools educated young blacks about the rich traditions of African American protest. They also encouraged high levels of student participation and let the black youths dictate the subject matter. Finally, the schools included training in civil rights protest activities such as sit-ins, letter-writing campaigns, and various forms of organizing. By the end of Freedom Summer, the students at

Freedom Schools showed encouraging signs of leadership potential.

The final, and perhaps most practical, goal of Freedom Summer was to register black voters. Hundreds of volunteers canvassed black communities to convince local people to attempt to register. The volunteers often met various forms of violent resistance and reluctance from the black community, but did successfully convince approximately 17,000 age-eligible voters to attempt to register. The canvassers solicited votes as part of the MFDP, which was planning its own ambitious civil rights demonstration to take place later that year.

In 1960, the regular Mississippi Democratic Party split from the National Democratic Party in the presidential election. Rather than voting for John F. Kennedy, who rhetorically promoted civil rights, the Mississippi Democrats supported another Democratic candidate. In 1964, it looked like the regular Mississippi Democrats would again refuse the national Democratic nominee, incumbent President Lyndon B. Johnson, because of his strong civil rights platform. Based on this, and the exclusion of African Americans from the regular Mississippi Democratic Party, the MFDP concluded that it could successfully lobby to replace the traitorous Mississippi regulars at the 1964 National Democratic Convention to be held in Atlantic City in August. During the Freedom Summer, the MFDP successfully lobbied support from Democrats across the nation who promised to vote for the MFDP if the issue should hit the convention floor. By August, the MFDP believed it had enough support to unseat the Mississippi Democratic Party on the convention floor, thereby winning a major victory in front of a national audience. The challenge, however, would not go as planned.

Although the MFDP had support from a large faction of the National Democratic Party, it did not have the support of the party's leader, Lyndon B. Johnson. Johnson knew that the Mississippi Democrats would probably support Republican Barry Goldwater in the election and that the MFDP enjoyed a lot of support among national Democrats, but the president was afraid that if the MFDP was allowed to replace the Mississippi regulars, then important border states such as Kentucky, Tennessee, and Maryland could fall to the Republicans as well. The president also desired an orderly convention so as not to upset what he and his advisors perceived to be an enormous landslide in the oncoming election. To ensure that the convention went smoothly, Johnson used the power of the White House to suppress the challenge. He called a press conference during an emotionally charged and nationally televised press conference in which Fannie Lou Hamer described the horrors in Mississippi. He also threatened MFDP supporters with demotions and blacklisting should they support the civil rights group. Finally, he promised Hubert Humphrey the vice presidency if Humphrey could suppress the challenge. Johnson's tactics worked and the MFDP was offered a token compromise of seats. Enraged that they had been betrayed by the national Democratic Party, many MFDP leaders stormed out and became extremely alienated with the party and Johnson. The MFDP challenge severely discouraged many SNCC volunteers. As the summer wound down, and the summer workers left the state to return to their northern universities, SNCC experienced a great deal of displeasure and frustration. SNCC peaked during the Freedom Summer of 1964, but the disappointment from the MFDP challenge led many to leave the organization. Although it would conduct several meaningful protests after the MFDP challenge, SNCC would never be the same.

Over the next several years, SNCC led protests across the Southern Black Belt and did achieve meaningful successes. The level of activity after 1964, however, must be seen as disappointing in comparison to the massive campaigns before Freedom Summer. Overall, however, SNCC remained at the forefront of the movement and black intellectual thought. Black power, a term coined by SNCC staffer Stokely Carmichael, emerged in the late 1960s as an answer to the critics of the Civil Rights movement who were often frustrated by the limitations of working with the Democratic Party. SNCC also facilitated the growth of many of the major movements that characterized late 1960s protest including the antiwar movement, the feminist movement, and Latino movements in the southwestern United States. Many of the leaders of such movements came of age and experienced their first taste of leadership while in SNCC. Despite the frustrations that arose toward the end of SNCC, the organization played a major role in mobilizing African American communities, enforcing various aspects of civil rights legislation, and providing a model for grassroots leadership.

See also: Baker, Ella; Black Power; Lowndes County Freedom Organization; Lewis, John; Nash, Diane; Robinson, Ruby Doris Smith, Sit-In Movement; Southern Christian Leadership Conference

William Mychael Sturkey

Bibliography

Carson, Clayborne. *In Struggle: SNCC and the Black Awakening of the 1960s.* Cambridge, MA: Harvard University Press, 1995.

Greenberg, Cheryl Lynn. *A Circle of Trust: Remembering SNCC.* New Brunswick, NJ: Rutgers University Press, 1997.

Hogan, Wesley C. *Many Minds, One Heart: SNCC's Dream for a New America.* Chapel Hill: University of North Carolina Press, 2007.

Mullins, Lisa. *Diane Nash: The Fire of the Civil Rights Movement: A Biography.* Miami, FL: Barnhardt & Ashe, 2007.

Murphree, Vanessa. *The Selling of Civil Rights: The Student Nonviolent Coordinating Committee and the Use of Public Relations.* New York: Routledge, 2006.

Zinn, Howard. *SNCC: The New Abolitionists.* Cambridge, MA: South End Press, 2002.

Students for a Democratic Society

Students for a Democratic Society (SDS) was a radical student group that was very active in the 1960s. It evolved from the Student League for Industrial Democracy, which was the young people's branch of an organization developed in 1905 called the Intercollegiate Socialist Society. The group changed its name in the 1960s so as not to seem totally focused on labor issues, thereby appealing to a broader group of young people.

The organization held its first meeting in 1960 in Ann Arbor, Michigan. There an SDS staffer named Tom Hayden introduced his political manifesto, the *Port Huron Statement.* Hayden criticized the political system in general and the United States government specifically for its failure to realize world peace, the Cold War, the nuclear arms race, racial discrimination, economic inequality, and big business. He advocated reforming the two dominant political parties and developing a governmental system that would encourage, support, and sustain participatory democracy. Hayden also called for corporations to encourage more participation by their employees and an expansion of the welfare state to include a concerted effort to eliminate poverty. Finally, Hayden supported nonviolence as a tactic in the struggle for a more democratic, humane, and inclusive society.

The Port Huron Statement was unique among leftist groups for several reasons. First was the recognition that every organization needed a clear vision about its reasons for being. Second, the statement recognized that the problems in society were linked to one another, meaning that a more holistic approach to their resolution was needed.

Third, SDS made a commitment to work with any interested group regardless of its position in the political spectrum. Finally, unlike most left-leaning organizations, it rejected the militant anticommunism so prevalent in those organizations.

SDS grew slowly in part because of its policy of decentralization, a position it adopted from the Student Nonviolent Coordinating Committee (SNCC). Rhe group had a national office with a president, vice president, and secretary, but it had few resources and was mostly a loose collection of campus-based chapters. During its early years, it mainly assisted SNCC in its civil rights work. Its 1964 summer convention revealed the fissures already developing between those who embraced traditional campus-based activism and those who wanted to branch out into other activities. Another outcome of the convention was the development of a more stable organization that included centralized administrative functions and increased attention to recruiting new chapters.

The year 1964 was a propitious one for SDS. On October 1 at the Berkeley campus of the University of Southern California, the free speech movement was born. Led by the charismatic Mario Savio among others, students protested against the administration, demanded that it cancel the ban on political activities, and give students more academic freedom. Hundreds of students demonstrated, held meetings, and engaged in strikes, virtually shutting down the university. SDS had truly become a national force with which to be reckoned.

The next year the administration of President Lyndon B. Johnson escalated the war in Vietnam by bombing the North Vietnamese and introducing ground troops into South Vietnam. The military draft was reactivated, and college students realized that there was more at stake than an esoteric exercise. SDS shifted its focus from civil rights to antiwar activities, and held its first teach-in against the war at the University of Michigan. It also organized a march against the war, which was held in Washington D.C. on April 17, 1965. Approximately 25,000 demonstrators converged on the city. Moreover, the organization expanded its antidraft activities to include protests against colleges and universities that had begun to supply the names and grade point averages of its male students, thereby assisting the military in deciding who would be drafted.

As the Black Power movement developed and white students became unwelcome in SNCC, SDS increasingly focused its attention on the development of campus-based activism through local chapters. It also stepped up its demonstrations against the Vietnam War and the draft, organizing several highly successful student strikes around the country. Like SNCC, it also became more militant. The organization demonstrated against businesses it deemed as profiting from the war, drawing the attention and increased criticism of the U.S. government. These activities drew the attention of the Federal Bureau of Investigation (FBI), who had for some time had been working against SDS through a secret operation known as COINTELPRO.

In the autumn of 1967, SDS sponsored a well-attended demonstration at the Madison campus of the University of Wisconsin. Madison police attacked the demonstrators and a number of students were injured and arrested. Their action signaled to SDS that the nonviolent tactics it had borrowed from the Civil Rights movement were no longer effective, and thereafter its demonstrations became more like guerilla warfare as they engaged in raids on draft offices and the like.

Local SDS chapters organized a nationwide effort known as Ten Days of Resistance, which consisted of sit-ins, marches, and rallies against the war. In a show of interracial cooperation, SDS and Student Afro Society activists shutdown Columbia University, and it was estimated that about 1 million students skipped class on April 26, 1968, the largest student strike ever reported. Flush with power, the organization saw a huge increase in membership that year.

Solidarity was difficult to maintain, however. At the 1969 national convention, various factions of SDS faced off. A manifesto that said, in part, "You don't need a Weatherman to know which way the wind blows" was distributed to each conventioneer. Among the 11 members who contributed to the work, Bernardine Dohrn and Mark Rudd became the leaders of the so-called Revolutionary Youth Movement with SDS. Supporters of Dohrn and Rudd split off into yet another faction, which came to be known as the Weathermen or Weather Underground Organization. Its stated intention was the overthrow of the capitalist system, and its tactics were much more aggressive than any other campus-based organization. SDS never held another national convention, and by 1970 the Weather Underground had issued a declaration of war, committing bombings, arson, robbery, and murder in support of its goals. Several of its member went underground eluding authorities for decades, but by the 1980s most had turned themselves in.

Eventually they became involved in the very establishment they had fought so hard against.

See also: Black Panther Party; Black Power; COINTELPRO; Johnson, Lyndon Baines

Marilyn K. Howard

Bibliography
Barber, David. *A Hard Rain Fell: SDS and Why It Failed.* Jackson: University Press of Mississippi, 2008.
Hayden, Tom. *The Port Huron Statement.* New York: Perseus Publishing, 2005.
Pekar, Harvey, Gary Dumm, and Paul Buhle. *Students for a Democratic Society: A Graphic History.* New York: Hill and Wang, 2008.
Rudd, Mark. *Underground: My Life with SDS and the Weathermen.* New York: William Morrow, 2009.

Suffrage Movement, Women's

Throughout the long and painful struggle to secure the franchise for Americans of both genders and all races, many suffrage activists tended to frame the battle for the vote, quite literally, in black and white terms. Both before and after the Civil War, abolitionists and suffragists fiercely debated whether it would be more expedient to seek full political rights for white women or African American men first. Although the very terms of this debate inevitably pushed African American women to the margins of the discussion, African American suffragists consistently and fiercely resisted being thus marginalized. From the beginnings of the suffrage movement in 1848, to the enfranchisement of women in 1920, and beyond, black female activists insisted on African American women's right, not only to the vote, but also to full, equal access to political empowerment and authority.

During the 1820s and 1830s, the first radical abolitionist movement took shape in America. From the very beginnings of abolitionism, African American antislavery activists insisted that if America was to be a truly egalitarian republic, abolitionists needed to fight, not only for the end of slavery, but also for the civic and political empowerment of free African Americans. During the rise of political abolitionism during the 1840s and 1850s, many African American abolitionists called for the franchise to be extended to African American men. All too often treated as second-class citizens within white-led antislavery organizations, black male abolitionists insisted that they needed the vote if they were to be treated as equals both within antislavery circles and within American society as a whole.

The 1840s witnessed not only an increasing emphasis on politics within the abolitionist community, but also the birth of an organized woman's rights movement, which, among other demands, called for female suffrage. In July 1848, in Seneca Falls, New York, a group of women (and a few men) assembled to hold the first woman's rights convention in the United States. At this convention, organizers called for full voting rights for women, a radical move that was widely ridiculed by the popular press of the day. Despite the powerful hostility that woman's rights advocates faced in the decades leading up to the Civil War, they persisted in holding conventions, and boldly insisting on women's right to the franchise, throughout the 1850s. Although the formal woman's rights movement was dominated by both white women and African American women, the needs of African American women and concerns were all too often marginalized within woman's rights circles. Nonetheless, African American female activists were among the most powerful and persuasive voices in early struggles for female suffrage.

Much like white suffragists, many African American suffragists came to the woman's rights movement through their involvement in abolitionism. Antislavery activists Margaretta Forten, Frances E. Watkins Harper, and Harriet Forten Purvis, for example, were all deeply involved in female antislavery societies and abolitionist activism before the Civil War and ardent supporters of female suffrage after it. Pioneering educator, author, and newspaper editor Mary Ann Shadd Cary consistently blended abolitionist, civil rights, and prosuffrage rhetoric in her newspaper the *Provincial Freeman* during the 1850s. Shadd Cary joined the National Woman's Suffrage Association after the Civil War, advocating female suffrage both in the United States and Canada. Perhaps the most famous abolitionist and suffragist of the pre-Civil War era was Sojourner Truth, the formerly enslaved orator and activist who electrified the North with her eloquent speeches during the 1840s and 1850s. In a world in which white suffragists all too often ignored the claims of African American women, and African American men all too often prioritized the political empowerment of men over the needs of African American women, Truth insisted that securing full political rights for African American women would be a vital part of achieving the free and egalitarian America that all abolitionists and suffragists ostensibly longed for.

In 1865, America's long and bloody Civil War came to an end, leaving the shattered and bleeding nation to rebuild its society anew. In the 1860s and 1870s, Americans fiercely debated what this "brave new world," in which slavery had been abolished and millions of formerly enslaved Americans were suddenly free, ought to look like. One of the bitterest and most divisive of these discussions centered on questions of suffrage. It seemed plausible to many former abolitionists that widespread respect for African American men's valiant military service in the Union army during the war might make the white public receptive, for the first time in American history, to giving black men the right to vote. Abolitionists such as Frederick Douglass passionately insisted that it was the "Negro's hour": a rare and precious chance for black men to seize the political rights that had been denied to them for so long. Although Douglass was himself a staunch supporter of woman's suffrage, he was firmly convinced that the enfranchisement of black men would be a vital part of rebuilding the postwar South, and securing newly liberated slaves' rights in the American government.

Some female suffragists agreed with Douglass's line of reasoning. Although devoted to securing votes for women in the future, female suffragists such as Frances E. Watkins Harper felt that enfranchising African American men first would best serve the interests of the African American community as a whole. Facing a violent, tumultuous South, inhabited by former slaveowners eager to preserve their dominance in southern society, suffragists such as Harper called for immediately granting African American men the franchise, so that African American men could vote for policies and elect officials who would protect their interests and preserve their rights. Other female suffragists, however, insisted that it was of vital importance that activists push for the simultaneous enfranchisement of African American men and all women, lest they never again be presented with such a remarkable opportunity. Sojourner Truth was a powerful voice in favor of universal suffrage in the years immediately after the Civil War, insisting that to give black men, but not black women, the vote, would establish dangerous inequalities within the African American community. "There is a great deal of stir about colored men getting their rights," Truth affirmed in one speech, "but not a word about the colored women; and if colored men get their rights, and colored women not theirs, the colored men will be masters over the women, and it will be just as bad as before."

In 1869, two national suffrage movements were founded, each organization taking a different side on the question of African American male suffrage. The National Woman's Suffrage Association (NWSA) (led by white suffragists Susan B. Anthony and Elizabeth Cady Stanton) focused on the enfranchisement of women, and the American Woman's Suffrage Association (AWSA) (led by white abolitionists Lucy Stone and Henry Blackwell) called for the enfranchisement of African American men first, and all women second. African American female suffragists joined both organizations, although slightly more activists became part of AWSA than they did NWSA. One year after the founding of NWSA and AWSA, the Fifteenth Amendment was passed, giving African American men the right to vote. So bitter was the spilt between NWSA and AWSA that the two organizations did not reunite in the wake of the Fifteenth Amendment's passage, despite their common goal of securing voting rights for all American women. Although neither organization prioritized the needs of African American women, NWSA especially distanced itself from its roots in the abolitionist movement and struggles for African American civil rights. Stanton and Anthony accepted money from George Francis Train, a wealthy businessmen prone to airing his racist views, in order to fund their suffrage newspaper, the *Revolution*. Stanton and Anthony themselves increasingly incorporated nativist and anti-African American rhetoric into their suffrage speeches and writings, lamenting that "ignorant" men should have been given the vote before white, middle- and upper-class women.

Frustrated by their persistent marginalization within mainstream, white-led suffrage institutions, African American feminists often pursued their suffrage goals through independent, African American led organizations in the decades after the Civil War. One important site of African American women's suffrage activism during the 1880s and 1890s were women's clubs. In these clubs, middle-class African American women met to pursue intellectual self-improvement, to organize on behalf of less fortunate members of their communities, and to agitate for causes such as female suffrage and temperance. In 1896, representatives from African American women's clubs across the country

came together to form the National Association of Colored Women, under the leadership of prominent activists including Anna Julia Cooper, Charlotte Forten Grimké, Frances E. Watkins Harper, and Mary Church Terrell. Throughout the late 19th century and early 20th centuries, the NACW was a powerful force for African American women's suffrage in American society.

In 1890, the formerly feuding NWSA and AWSA reunited to become the National American Woman's Suffrage Association (NAWSA). African American female suffragists continued to work within and alongside the predominantly white NAWSA, but they faced persistent marginalization and discrimination within the organization. Between 1890 and 1920, NAWSA increased its efforts to draw white southern women into the suffrage cause. These white southern suffragists often used racist rhetoric in making their arguments for votes for women, insisting that if white southern women were granted the franchise, they could counteract the "pernicious" effect that African American male voters had allegedly had on southern society. (What would become of black southern female voters in this scenario was left deliberately vague.) African American women faced similar difficulties in seeking to become fully involved in other white-dominated, prosuffrage organizations such as the Women's Christian Temperance Union (WCTU). Although some white WCTU leaders, such as Amelia Bloomer, advocated the full integration of African American women into the WCTU's efforts to secure the vote for women and combat alcohol abuse, most WCTU chapters remained decidedly segregated along racial lines.

In the 1910s, a younger, more radical contingent arose within the suffrage movement, which argued that American suffragists ought to follow the example of their British counterparts and use dramatic, and even violent, means to secure their suffrage goals. Lead by two white suffragists, Alice Paul and Lucy Burns, in 1913, this faction of the movement organized a huge suffrage parade, the same day as Woodrow Wilson's inauguration as president. Eager not to offend white southern suffragists, Paul and Burns informed African American suffragists that, although they might participate in the parade, they would need to march in a segregated group at the back of the procession. Some African American suffragists, including Mary Church Terrell, agreed to this restriction; but others, including suffragist and antilynching advocate Ida B. Wells-Barnett, refused to comply with the order. On the day of the parade,

Wells-Barnett and several of her African American female suffragist colleagues waited in the crowd, and then marched out into the middle of the designated "whites only" part of the parade, where they remained for the duration of the event. In part because of the dramatic theatrics, violent protests, and sustained hunger strikes of militant suffragists during the 1910s, female suffrage was finally granted when the Nineteenth Amendment was passed on August 26, 1920.

Although the Nineteenth Amendment made the enfranchisement of all American women the law of the land, much like the Fifteenth Amendment before it, for many decades, the Nineteenth Amendment did not truly benefit African Americans. In the decades after 1920, African American women and men who sought to exercise their voting rights, especially in the South, were barred from casting their ballots by a brutal, systematic campaign of violence and intimidation waged by white supremacists. One of the central goals of the Civil Rights movement of the 1950s and 1960s was to make the promises of the Fifteenth Amendment and the Nineteenth Amendment a reality for African Americans across the United States. Female civil rights activists such as Ella Baker, Fannie Lou Hamer, and Ann Moody fearlessly denounced the bigotry and violence of whites who forcibly sought to prevent African Americans from voting, and, in the face of sustained, violent attacks, they went to the South to register new African American voters. Although America's contemporary political scene is far from ideal, with voters of color (particularly economically disadvantaged voters of color) facing significant obstacles to the full exercise of the franchise, the tireless efforts and courageous sacrifices of generations of African American suffragists has nonetheless helped to move American government and society closer to realizing their promise of being truly free, democratic, and representative.

See also: Cary, Mary Ann Shadd; Cooper, Anna Julia; Douglass, Frederick; Fifteenth Amendment; Liberty Party; National Association of Colored Women; Smith, Gerrit; Terrell, Mary Church; Truth, Sojourner; Wells-Barnett, Ida

Holly M. Kent

Bibliography

Gilmore, Glenda Elizabeth. *Gender and Jim Crow: Women and the Politics of White Supremacy in North Carolina, 1896–1920.* Chapel Hill: University of North Carolina Press, 1996.

Gordon, Ann, and Bettye Collier-Thomas, eds. *African-American Women and the Vote, 1835–1965.* Amherst: University of Massachusetts Press, 1997.

Terborg-Penn, Rosalyn. *African-American Women in the Struggle for the Vote, 1850–1920.* Bloomington: Indiana University Press, 1998.

Talented Tenth

The term "talented tenth" was coined in 1896 by the Reverend Henry L. Morehouse, who envisioned a class of erudite and upright African Americans emerging as a vanguard for the black community. But it was W. E. B. Du Bois (1868–1963) who gave this theory prominence. In 1903, Du Bois published his classic manifesto, "The Talented Tenth." The theory was simple yet profound: Cultivate the talents of the best and brightest African Americans and they will advance the interests of all black Americans. Du Bois proposed: "Men of America . . . The Talented Tenth of the Negro race must be made leaders of thought and missionaries of culture among their people. No others can do this work and the Negro colleges must train men for it. The Negro race, like all other races, is going to be saved by its exceptional men" (156–57). These remarkable men held promise. But would they fulfill it? Du Bois reflected on this question for 45 years before he substantially modified his theory.

His theory was the product of his own experience. In 1900, Du Bois was struck by the plight of his people: "American Negroes were an inferior caste, were frequently lynched and robbed, widely disfranchised, and usually segregated in the main areas of life." Then came his vision: "I looked upon them and saw salvation through intelligent leadership; as I said, through a Talented Tenth. And for this intelligence I argued we needed college-trained men" ("The Talented Tenth: Memorial Address"). As part of this process of mutual, social "salvation," Du Bois was the talented tenth's living exemplar, embodying all of its ideals. As a strategy for racial advancement, a critical mass of highly educated blacks could theoretically produce a sea change in the collective destiny of all African Americans. At the other end of the social spectrum was the "submerged tenth," an underclass of "criminals, prostitutes and loafers" (*The Philadelphia Negro*, p. 311).

Critics tasked Du Bois for placing too great an emphasis on the educated elite—those who today are occasionally nicknamed "blackademics." Pilloried by black radical Hubert Harrison as the "Subsidized Sixth," the talented tenth theory was supported in principle by no less than Alain Locke—W. E. B. Du Bois's intellectual equal and sometimes rival—who later became the first African American president of the American Association for Adult Education in 1945. This is a prime instance of a member of the talented tenth effecting a change in the fortunes of African Americans. In this case, Locke touched the lives of all Americans receiving adult education under the institutional auspices of the American Association for Adult Education.

Speaking of the talented tenth, Du Bois wrote: "Can the masses of the Negro people be in any possible way more quickly raised than by the effort and example of this aristocracy of talent and character?…There can be but one answer: the best and most capable of their youth must be schooled in the colleges and universities of the land" (*The Autobiography of W. E. B. Du Bois*, pp. 139–40). This implied some opposition to Booker T. Washington's emphasis on industrial training for racial economic independence and his policy of quiescent accommodation as well. Eschewing "industrialism drunk with its vision of success" (*The Autobiography of W. E. B. Du Bois*, p. 149), Du Bois was careful to say that "these two theories of Negro progress were not absolutely contradictory" (*The Autobiography of W. E. B. Du Bois*, p. 236).

Later in life, Du Bois refined his theory. In August 1948, Du Bois delivered his "The Talented Tenth Memorial Address" at Wilberforce University to an audience of distinguished African Americans (representing the talented tenth), to whom he said: "My Talented Tenth must be more than talented, and work not simply as individuals. Its passport to leadership…would be its willingness to sacrifice and plan for such economic revolution in industry and just distribution of wealth, as would make the rise of our group possible" (*The Autobiography of W. E. B. Du Bois*, p. 163). Then, transcending this Marxist agenda, Du Bois spoke of the "Guiding Hundredth" (*The Autobiography of W. E. B. Du Bois*, pp. 177), which was his "new idea for a Talented Tenth" (*The Autobiography of W. E. B. Du Bois*, p. 168).

The "guiding hundredth" was to be a "group-leadership, not simply educated and self-sacrificing, but with a clear vision of present world conditions and dangers, and conducting American Negroes to alliance with culture groups in Europe, America, Asia and Africa, and looking toward a new world culture" (*The Autobiography of W. E. B.*

Du Bois, p. 168). The "guiding hundredth" would be open-ended, capable of forming alliances with other groups and races, including whites. This doctrine democratizes and internationalizes Du Bois's strategy for racial advancement by placing it in a global context. Numerically narrower yet strategically broader, the "guiding hundredth" represents the evolution of Du Bois's original theory of the "talented tenth." In 1996, Henry Louis Gates Jr. and Cornel West reflected on the significance of Du Bois's theory of the talented tenth in *The Future of the Race*.

See also: Du Bois, W. E. B.; Historically Black Colleges and Universities; Locke, Alain; Washington, Booker T.

Christopher George Buck

Bibliography

Battle, Juan, and Earl Wright II. "W. E. B. Du Bois' Talented Tenth: A Quantitative Assessment." *Journal of Black Studies* 32, no. 6 (2002):654–72.

Du Bois, W. E. B. *The Autobiography of W. E. B. Du Bois: A Soliloquy on Viewing My Life from the Last Decade of Its First Century.* New York: International, 1968.

Du Bois, W. E. B. *The Philadelphia Negro.* New York: Schocken Books, 1967.

Gates, Henry Louis Jr. Appendix: "W. E. B. Du Bois and 'The Talented Tenth.'" In *The Future of the Race,* eds. Idem and Cornel West. 115–32. New York: Knopf, 1996.

Green, D. S. "W. E. B. Du Bois' Talented Tenth: A Strategy for Racial Advancement." *Journal of Negro Education* 46, no. 3 (1977):358–66.

Locke, Alain. "The Role of the Talented Tenth." *Howard University Record* 12, no. 7 (1918):15–18.

Morehouse, Henry L. "The Talented Tenth." *Independent* (April 23, 1896):1.

Rabaka, Reiland. "W. E. B. Du Bois's Evolving Africana Philosophy of Education." *Journal of Black Studies* 33, no. 4 (2003):399–449.

Terrell, Mary Church

Mary Church Terrell (1863–1954) was a social and political activist and a champion of the women's suffrage movement. Born Mary Eliza Church on September 23, 1863, in Memphis, Tennessee, Terrell was the product of formerly enslaved parents. Her father, Robert Reed Church, was the son of a Mississippi planter and one of his female servants. Terrell's mother, Louisa Ayres, was a bondswoman who gained literacy while in the clutches of slavery. Once legally emancipated, Ayres opened a store specializing in hair products. Ayres's establishment served as a major attraction for affluent women of Memphis and allowed her to generate enough wealth to purchase a home for her family.

Mary Church, often referred to as "Mollie" by members of her family, was protected from the vices of poverty and hopelessness that plagued a large segment of the newly freed black populace of Memphis. Nonetheless, her maternal grandmother, Eliza Ayres, shared her recollections of the traumatic incidences of slavery with "Mollie." Because of her parents' divorce and her mother's subsequent relocation to New York City in 1870, Terrell was sent to Yellow Springs, Ohio to attend the integrated Model School on the campus of Antioch College. She was one of the few African American children enrolled at the school. At age 12, Terrell moved to Oberlin, Ohio to complete her high school education, and later enrolled at Oberlin College.

During the late 1800s, very few women, and even fewer African American women, were afforded a college education. Terrell was one of the first African American women to attain a college degree in the United States. One year after her graduation from Oberlin College in 1884, she began teaching courses in grammar, mineralogy, and French at Wilberforce University. In 1886, Terrell moved to Washington, D.C. to teach at the premiere Colored High School. In 1888, acting on the advice of her father, Terrell commenced teaching and moved to Europe to study. Her experiences abroad allowed her to briefly escape American racism and segregation. In Europe Terrell began to crystallize her personal mission toward liberating the *darker race* and women.

In 1891, after her return to the United States, the then Mary Eliza Church married Robert Terrell, a colleague from the Colored High School and the first African American to graduate from Harvard University. Afterward, in compliance with the social customs of the era for women, she permanently withdrew from teaching. During the late 19th and early 20th centuries, women were not considered to possess the aptitude or intellectual capacity for higher education. Consequently, many women were relegated to perform domestic duties. Terrell, thereby, receded to domestic work.

In 1892, Terrell shed the chrysalis of domesticity to engage in a myriad of social and political activities centered on elevating the status of African Americans and women in the United States. During this same year, she began participating in the antilynching campaign. She joined forces with abolitionist Frederick Douglass to petition president Benjamin Harrison to publicly denounce lynching in a congressional address. Her involvement in the women's suffrage movement during the last decade of the 19th century, however, far exceeded her involvement in the protest of lynching, the southern convict lease system, alongside a number of other social ills.

In 1895, Terrell became the first African American and the second woman to serve on the Board of Education in Washington, D.C. Her position on the board allowed her to challenge unjust decisions proposed by the predominately white committee. In 1896, she became president of the National Association of Colored Women (NACW), which represented a merger of the independent clubs that existed among black women. Although Terrell used an integrated approach to resolving the issue of women's disenfranchisement, she scorned the discriminatory practices of the General Federation of Women's Clubs (GFWC), the national

Mary Church Terrell, an African American suffragist, was president of the National Association of Colored Women and a charter member of the National Association for the Advancement of Colored People. (Library of Congress)

organization established by white women to improve the "situation" of women in America. Although the GFWC and the NACW sought to fulfill similar objectives to ensure the betterment of life for women, the NACW was also committed to improving the situation of African Americans. Terrell, being thoroughly engaged in the struggle to ensure equal rights for women, as well as racial equality for black Americans, was one of the movement's most critical agents.

Remaining dedicated to the struggle for racial equality, in 1909 Terrell helped organize the National Association for the Advancement of Colored People and became a charter member. Although her husband, who was a political ally of Booker T. Washington, discouraged Terrell's decision, she abided with the organization and in 1919 became vice president of the Washington, D.C. local branch. Throughout the course of her life, Terrell made groundbreaking achievements and overcame great odds that many African Americans and women alike could not surpass. She is most remembered for her commitment to justice and equality for America's 19th-century pariahs—African Americans and women.

See also: Antilynching Campaign; National Association for the Advancement of Colored People; National Association of Colored Women; Washington, Booker T.; Wells-Barnett, Ida

Talitha L. LeFlouria

Bibliography
Giddings, Paula. *When and Where I Enter: The Impact of Black Women on Race and Sex in America.* New York: William Morrow, 1984.
Jones, Beverly Washington. *Quest for Equality: The Life and Writings of Mary Eliza Church Terrell, 1863–1954.* Brooklyn: Carlson Publishing, 1990, from Darlene Clark Hine, ed., *Black Women in United States History,* vol. 13.
Sterling, Dorothy. *Black Foremothers: Three Lives.* New York: The City University of New York, 1988.
Terrell, Mary Church. *A Colored Woman in a White World.* New York: Ransdell, 1940.

The Birth of a Nation

The Birth of a Nation, released in 1915, heralded a revolution in American film-making, but its laudatory portrayal of the Ku Klux Klan and its thoroughly racist depiction of African Americans have subjected it to extensive criticism. Thomas Dixon Jr.'s novel and play *The Clansman* provided

the inspiration for director D. W. Griffith's three-hour epic, which drew enormous crowds despite an exorbitant $2 ticket price and nationwide protests by the NAACP. Fans included Woodrow Wilson, who screened the film in the White House and commented "it is like history written with lightning." *The Birth of a Nation* takes as its subject matter the Civil War, Reconstruction, and "redemption" by the Ku Klux Klan. The film's main conclusion—that Reconstruction was the most horrific experiment in the nation's history because it elevated a naturally inferior race to equality—both reflected and helped shape the pro-Southern view of 19th century history that would dominate popular and scholarly thought in the first half of the 20th century.

The film begins when Phil Stoneman, the son of the "great parliamentary leader" Austin Stoneman (who is undoubtedly based on Thaddeus Stevens, a Pennsylvania Congressman and Radical Republican), visits Piedmont, South Carolina to stay with his friend Ben Cameron. News of Lincoln's election, however, sends Stoneman back home to Pennsylvania to enlist in the Union Army. After the war, Col. Ben Cameron, wounded in battle, is nursed back to health by Elsie Stoneman, the Congressman's oldest daughter. The pair fall in love and move to the Cameron home in South Carolina.

The onset of Radical Reconstruction, however, allows Northerners like Representative Austin Stoneman to seize power and institute a plan to "crush the white South under the heel of the black South." African American enfranchisement gives the vote to a people entirely unprepared to handle it, like the freedman who proclaims that "ef I doan' get 'nuf franchise to fill mah bucket, I doan' want it nohow!" Griffith portrays a Reconstruction government made up almost entirely of African Americans, who eat chicken, drink whiskey, and take their shoes off while the state Congress is in session, and pass a series of bills designed to ensure black dominance over Southern whites. Silas Lynch, Austin Stoneman's protégé, a mulatto "drunk with wine and power," comes to epitomize the danger of empowering African Americans when he is elected lieutenant governor.

In despair over the chaos, destruction, and perversion of the social order wrought by Reconstruction, Ben Cameron founds the Ku Klux Klan in an effort to reestablish white control. The film's damaging racial stereotypes are especially apparent in the scene in which Gus, a black Union soldier, whose bulging eyes and foaming mouth make him look more like a beast than a man, seeks to "marry" (or rape) Flora Cameron, Ben's youngest sister. The final montage of the film depicts an epic battle between the forces of good and evil, as the Klan, led by Ben Cameron, swoops into the city, restores order to the streets, rescues Elsie Stoneman from the clutches of the villainous Silas Lynch, saves the residents of a small cabin from an attack by crazed African Americans, and finally puts an end to Reconstruction by keeping blacks from voting in the next election. The film ends with a double honeymoon, as Ben Cameron and Elsie Stoneman get married, along with their younger siblings Margaret and Phil. The weddings represent a reunion of North and South under a banner of white supremacy.

The portrayal of African Americans in *The Birth of a Nation* is one of the most egregious examples of overt racism in cinematic history. Reflecting and enlarging prevailing Southern stereotypes around the turn of the century, the film's black characters (all of whom are played by white actors in black face) are portrayed either as hopelessly childlike and naïve, or as violent, criminal, lustful brutes with uncontrollable passions and unspeakable desires. Griffith's racism had a political and historical purpose, however. African Americans are not portrayed as innately depraved; it is the addition of political equality and social power during Reconstruction that accounts for their dangerous and destructive behavior, and it is this power and equality that the Klan seeks to end. Early in the film, the Cameron's slaves are happy and faithful to their masters. It is Lynch, who has been elected to office, and Gus, who has served in the Union army, who come to represent the dark side of black equality. The film's portrayal of rioting and violent African Americans, therefore, attests to the dangers of a society in which the proper racial hierarchy has been inverted and seeks to justify the segregated and oppressed status of African Americans in the 1915 South.

Perhaps the most interesting historical contribution of *The Birth of a Nation* is its visual encapsulation of the racial worldview of white Southerners in the late 19th and early 20th century. The film's idealization of antebellum Southern society, its antipathy toward Reconstruction, and its disturbing obsession with black sexuality and white female purity reflect the lines of thought that allowed black disfranchisement, lynching, and the rise of a Jim Crow South between 1890 and 1910. While it is of little use as a history of Reconstruction, *The Birth of a Nation* remains a fascinating primary source, which speaks to the nature of racism in the early 20th century and the manner in which history may be mobilized to justify oppression in the present.

See also: Ku Klux Klan; Lynching; White Supremacy

K. Stephen Prince Jr.

Bibliography

Blight, David. *Race and Reunion: The Civil War in American Memory.* Cambridge, MA: Harvard University Press, 2001.

Chadwick, Bruce. *The Reel Civil War: Mythmaking in American Film.* New York: Alfred A. Knopf, 2001.

Dixon, Thomas Jr. *The Clansman: An Historical Romance of the Ku Klux Klan.* Lexington: The University Press of Kentucky, 1970.

Lang, Robert. *The Birth of a Nation* (Rutgers Films in Print). New Brunswick, NJ: Rutgers University Press, 1994.

The Elevator

Founded by Philip Alexander Bell in 1865, *The Elevator* became one of the longest published African American newspapers of the 19th century. This "weekly journal of progress" reported on current events, American politics, science, and the arts for more than 40 years. Prominently displayed on the masthead, the motto of the newspaper expressed its chief concern: "Equality before the Law." Bell planned to use the newspaper in the pursuit of social and political equality for African Americans. Under his leadership, *The Elevator* became one of the most widely read and influential black newspapers in California.

Bell, along with Peter Anderson, founded *The Pacific Appeal* in 1862, but a disagreement between the two over editorial policy prompted Bell to create *The Elevator* as a rival newspaper in 1865. Bell envisioned that *The Elevator* would serve as a venue for blacks to publicly enter the political debate over enfranchisement. Five influential black Californians who served on the Executive Committee of the California State Convention of Colored Citizens supported Bell's plans. These five made up *The Elevator*'s Publishing Committee: William H. Yates, James R. Starkey, R. A. Hall, James P. Dyer, and Frederick G. Barbadoes. The paper's prospectus stated that it was the organ of the executive committee, and will advocate political and civil equality to all American citizens. Bell and the committee wanted African Americans to be treated as Americans, not as a separate group.

Although the paper was based in San Francisco, it attracted a national readership, with published reports from communities across the country. *The Elevator* used well-known contributors and subscription agents. James J. Spelman, editor of *The Baptist Messenger,* was a regular correspondent using the pseudonym Private L. Overture. John J. Moore, the founder of San Francisco's first black church, regularly contributed editorials about the need for equality and self-development. William J. Powell served as *The Elevator's* corresponding editor. Robert Hamilton, the son of *Abolition Times* journalist Robert Hamilton, also served on the staff. David Ruggles, publisher of *The Mirror of Liberty* and *The Genius of Freedom,* served as the newspaper's treasurer.

Bell and the contributors hoped to persuade readers that blacks should be given the right to vote because of their patriotism and loyalty to the country that had granted them their freedom. When the mainstream papers were suggesting that blacks may take up arms against whites, *The Elevator's* writers tried to dispel such fears and downplay any militancy images. They argued that the country's underlying principles supported nothing less than universal suffrage. Indeed, hopes were high in October 1865 that an official petition to the California legislature for the black vote would be favorably received. The California State Convention of Colored Citizens met to discuss matters and *The Elevator* printed the proceedings. Unfortunately, the legislature refused to debate the issue. The national political scene also showed signs of increased disinterest. These discouraging developments were reflected in the newspaper's reduction in editorials on the enfranchisement topic.

Despite these disappointments, *The Elevator* continued to comment on political issues, and the Chinese labor question was no exception. Chinese immigration was rapidly increasing and Bell often spoke against it, claiming that the Chinese were taking job opportunities from blacks and lowering wages. *The Elevator* also continued to closely follow the California elections. In 1867, the newspaper endorsed the Union Party candidates and Bell discussed the various issues of the election. Bell had always been a supporter of the Republican Party, and this stance was clearly reflected in his comments. He was disappointed, however, that the Union Party did not directly address black suffrage in this

election. When the Union Party lost the 1867 elections, Bell was concerned that equal rights would disappear from the political agenda.

Hope for the resurrection of the enfranchisement issue was raised anew with the election of President Grant. In the spring of 1869, Congress approved the Fifteenth Amendment, prohibiting the states or the federal government from using a citizen's race, color, or previous status as a slave as a voting qualification. Two-thirds of the states needed to approve the amendment, and Bell wanted California to be one of them. Once again, the topic of black enfranchisement dominated *The Elevator,* persuading voters to approve it. Updates on the ratification process across the country were regularly reported. Although California voters rejected the amendment, *The Elevator* was finally able to celebrate victory when the necessary amount of states did approve the amendment in 1870.

The Elevator had seen its major goal, black enfranchisement, achieved. The paper continued its mission to educate blacks about American politics, as well as commenting on specific reforms such as the need for equality in the educational system. Bell remained involved with *The Elevator* until his retirement in 1885. Although the exact date that the paper ceased publication is unclear, it was at least produced until 1898.

See also: Abolition, Slavery; Bell, Phillip A.; Colored Convention Movement; Republican Party

Donna Smith

Bibliography

Dann, Martin E., ed. *The Black Press: 1827—1890: The Quest for National Identity.* New York: Capricorn Books, 1972.

Goodyear, Frank H. "Beneath the Shadow of her Flag: Philip A. Bell's *The Elevator* and the Struggle for Enfranchisement, 1865—1870." *California History* 78 (Spring 1999):26–39.

Penn, I. Garland. *The Afro-American Press and its Editors.* Springfield, MA: Willey, 1891.

Thomas, Clarence

Clarence Thomas (1948–) is the second black Supreme Court Justice in the United States. The second of three children, Clarence Thomas was born in Pin Point, Georgia, a small poor community outside Savannah that was given to freed slaves after the Civil War. He was born on June 23,

1948, to Leola and M. C. Thomas. His father abandoned the family shortly after Clarence was born.

After years of living in poverty with no indoor plumbing, Thomas moved to Savannah, Georgia, to live with his maternal grandfather, Myers Anderson, a religious man and self-taught entrepreneur. According to Thomas, this move proved to be a turning point in his life. For the first time, Thomas and his brother had an adult male figure and a comfortable home, with indoor plumbing and adult supervision. His grandfather enrolled Thomas in St. Benedict the Moor, a Catholic grade school that was started to educate poor African American children. Although Thomas had difficulty adjusting, this school pushed Thomas to excel and made him believe he could achieve great things as long as he worked hard. The stern hand of his grandfather proved influential in his life, teaching him discipline, the importance of an education, and hard work.

Because Anderson wanted Thomas to be a priest, he enrolled his grandson in St. John Vianney Minor Seminary, a Catholic boarding school, where he experienced bigotry for the first time. After graduating the seminary, in 1967, Thomas entered Immaculate Conception Seminary in Missouri to prepare for the priesthood; however, the prejudices there almost cost Thomas his faith. He was faced with southern bigotry from young men who were to be ordained as Catholic priests, something that troubled him. Ultimately, Thomas would enroll in Holy Cross College in Massachusetts. While at Holy Cross, Thomas worked part-time, participated in community service programs, and help establish the Black Student Union. In 1971, he graduated with an honors degree in English and soon thereafter married Kathy Grace Ambush who had his only child.

Thomas attended law school at Yale, where he had been accepted as part of an affirmative action program. To avoid being identified as the black student, Thomas often sat in the back of the class and avoided taking any civil rights courses. Instead he took business classes and studied tax and property law because he did not want to be labeled a civil rights attorney. This was his first experience, as he recalls, having the "monkey on his back," being at Yale to satisfy some social goal, not because of his credentials but because of his race. It was at Yale that Thomas formulated his opinion against affirmative action programs because they helped more middle-class blacks and he was poor. After graduation from Yale in 1974, he accepted a position in Missouri to work in the Office of the State Attorney General John

Danforth, a position that allowed him to work in the tax division. When Danforth won a seat in the U.S. Senate, Thomas became a corporate lawyer for the Monsanto Company and later went back to work as a legislative assistant for Danforth, who was now a senator.

In 1980, President Ronald Reagan gained an interest in Thomas when he attended the Fairmont Conference for black conservatives, and the *Washington Post* wrote an article about him. He was offered a job as the assistant secretary for civil rights in the U.S. Department of Education. Soon after, Reagan promoted him to chairman of the U.S. Equal Opportunity Employment Commission (EEOC) where he changed the environment of the agency. Under Thomas's leadership the EEOC stopped the use of timetables, numeric goals, and the use of trials that relied on statistical evidence of discrimination, a move that angered many civil rights groups.

President George Bush then appointed Thomas in 1990 to the U.S. Court of Appeals in Washington, D.C. In 1991, he

Clarence Thomas was seated on the U.S. Supreme Court in 1991. (U.S. Supreme Court)

was picked by President Bush to be the successor to Justice Thurgood Marshall, who had retired. There was widespread outcry by civil rights groups, particularly the National Association for the Advancement of Colored People (NAACP) and the Congressional Black Caucus, against his nomination as an associate justice because of Thomas's opposition to affirmative action. Women's rights groups also opposed his nomination because of charges of sexual harassment from Anita Hill. During Senate confirmation hearings, which were broadcast nationally, Thomas denied all allegations. The Senate Judiciary Committee recommended him to the full Senate for confirmation and Thomas was confirmed by a 52 to 48 vote in the Senate, the closest confirmation vote in history. He took the oath of office October 23, 1991 and is the youngest member of the Court.

Thomas is considered a conservative justice who attracts much debate. As a black Republican, Thomas is strongly supported by conservatives and despised by black intellectuals. Yet, Thomas argues that America should not expect blacks to speak in a monolithic voice.

See also: Black Conservatives; Congressional Black Caucus; Hill, Anita; Marshall, Thurgood; National Association for the Advancement of Colored People

Angela K. Lewis

Bibliography

Foskett, Ken. *Judging Thomas: The Life and Times of Clarence Thomas.* New York: HarperCollins, 2004.

Greenya, John. *Silent Justice: The Clarence Thomas Story.* Fort Lee, NJ: Barricade Books, 1997.

Mayer, Jane. *Strange Justice: The Selling of Clarence Thomas.* Boston: Houghton Mifflin, 1994.

Thomas, Andrew Peyton. *Clarence Thomas: A Biography.* San Francisco: Encounter Books, 2001.

Till, Emmett

Emmett Louis Till (1941–55), was a young Chicago native whose lynching in Mississippi helped galvanize the modern Civil Rights movement. He was born on July 25, 1941, to Mamie and Louis Till. The latter died serving in Europe during World War II leaving only a ring with the initials L. T. At the age of five, Emmett was stricken with polio, which left him with a slight stutter.

In the summer of 1955, 14-year-old Till traveled to Money, Mississippi, to visit his great-uncle Moses Wright.

Because of the Supreme Court's *Brown v. the Board of Education* decision several months before, which mandated integrated schools, racial tensions in the area were volatile. Not long after his arrival, Till and some other teenagers visited Bryant's Grocery and Meat Market. Accounts of what happened have varied. Some say that Till whistled at store owner Carolyn Brant, which could have been misinterpreted because of Till's stutter. Others say Till said "bye baby" as he left the store. Four days later, Carolyn Bryant's husband Roy and his brother J. W. Milam threatened Moses Wright and kidnapped Till. Bryant and Milam were arrested for kidnapping Till and three days later, Till's body was found in the Tallahatchie River tied to a cotton gin fan. The body could be identified only through the L. T. initial ring. Bryant and Milam were later charged with murder.

Emmett Till's body was brought back to Chicago and newspaper photographers captured pictures of Mamie Till fainting. Till's mother decided to hold an open casket funeral and invited the press so that everyone could see Till's body. Tens of thousands of people gathered at the funeral. *Jet* magazine and the *Chicago Defender* published pictures, and local television stations aired funeral footage. Although black communities throughout the South had experienced lynching before, this was one of the first times that the aftermath was widely publicized. In addition to mobilizing the black community around civil rights, Till's lynching also had an effect on white northern journalists: it cemented the fact that the South was "worthy" of national news coverage.

Roy Bryant and J. W. Milam's trial began in Sumner, Mississippi on September 19. No black men or women of any ethnic background were allowed to serve on the jury. Although Moses Wright stood in open court and identified Bryant and Miliam as the kidnappers, after 67 minutes of deliberation, the jury acquitted both men on the murder charges. A juror was later quoted as saying the deliberations would have taken less time if they had not taken a break. Outrage surrounding the verdict was published in newspapers all over the world including Belgium, France, and Germany. Moses Wright and Willie Reed, a black sharecropper who also testified against the men, fled to Chicago. Several months later Wright and Reed returned to Mississippi to testify on the kidnapping charges; however, the grand jury refused to indict.

In January 1956, *Look* magazine offered Bryant and Milam $4,000 for an interview with journalist William Bradford Huie. Milam went on the record and admitted to kidnapping Till and stated that they only intended to beat

Emmett Till and his mother, Mamie Till Mobley. The 14-year-old Till was murdered by vigilantes in Mississippi in 1955. (Library of Congress)

him. Because Till remained defiant, however, Milam forced him to strip and shot him at close range in the head. Huie later wrote a follow-up article that stated Bryant and Milam were ostracized by both the black and white communities, which put their stores out of business.

J. W. Milam died in 1980 and Roy Bryant died in 1990, both of cancer. Mamie Till Mobley died in 2003 a few weeks before PBS aired a documentary chronicling Emmett's lynching. In 2004, Senator Charles Schumer and Representative Charles Rangel urged the Justice Department to reopen the investigation into Till's murder because of new evidence that suggested Bryant and Milam did not act alone. On May 10, 2004, the Justice Department and the Mississippi District Attorney's Office officially reopened the case.

See also: Jet Magazine; Lynching; White Supremacy

Lisa Doris Alexander

Bibliography

Houck, Davis W., and Matthew A. Grindy. *Emmett Till and the Mississippi Press.* Jackson: University Press of Mississippi, 2008.

Metress, Christopher. *The Lynching of Emmett Till: A Documentary Narrative.* Charlottesville: University of Virginia Press, 2002.

Till-Mobley, Mamie, and Christopher Benson. *Death of Innocence: The Story of the Hate Crime that Changed America.* New York: One World, 2004.

Whitfield, Stephen J. *A Death in the Delta: The Story of Emmett Till.* New York: Free Press, 1988.

"To Secure These Rights"

"To Secure these Rights" was a landmark report on civil rights issued by Harry S. Truman's President's Committee on Civil Rights on October 29, 1947. It provided information on the contemporary status of civil rights and made recommendations for appropriate legislation and measures.

Despite certain economic and social improvements during World War II, segregation and racism still dominated America's societal and political structures. In the light of the growing African American quest for racial equality, the South, in particular, wanted to reinstate the strict system of segregation and white dominance. Racial tensions and violence against blacks were increasing.

Initially President Truman was hesitant to actively enforce civil rights, fearing the exasperation of the South and an increased split of the Democratic Party. But appalled by the increasing racial violence, he personally intervened, and on December 5, 1946, established the President's Committee on Civil Rights.

The committee consisted of 15 members representing industry, labor, the legal profession, the South, and the African American community, as well as various religious denominations. Its task was to investigate the current status of civil rights of minorities in the United States and the ways in which current laws and federal, state, and local authorities could enhance and protect civil rights for all. The executive order mandated that all executive departments and agencies of the federal government cooperate. The committee held public hearings, sought evidence, and corresponded with private organizations, individuals, cooperating government agencies and local public agencies.

On October 29, 1947, the committee issued its revolutionary report "To Secure These Rights," which set out the general situation of civil rights in the United States, emphasizing the special position of African Americans. The report was divided into four parts. Part One, entitled "The American Heritage: The Promise of Freedom and Equality," laid out the American ideal of equality and freedom consisting of four essential rights: The Right to Safety and Security of the Person, The Right to Citizenship and its Privileges, The Right to Freedom of Conscience and Expression, and The Right to Equality of Opportunity.

Part Two, "The Record: Short of the Goal," outlined the existing shameful inadequacies of civil rights, highlighting the defective condition of the four essential rights including lynching, police brutality, the inequality of the system of justice, and the continuance of involuntary servitude. The disfranchisement of African Americans in the South in particular and the segregation in the Armed Forces were also listed as signs of the infringement of citizenship rights and privileges. The inequalities with respect to employment opportunities, on-the-job discrimination, education,

housing, health services, public services, and accommodations were also noted. The report condemned segregation and the separate-but-equal premise as unfair and essentially contradicting the concept of American citizenship. Segregation had not only created unequal facilities and opportunities, but also hostility between the races. Only by ending segregation could the American society attain equal rights and racial accord.

Part Three, "Government Responsibility: Securing these Rights," pointed to the special role of government in safeguarding civil rights. It argued that the federal government could not evade its responsibilities and should take immediate action to guarantee civil rights for all. For moral and economic reasons, the United States was obliged to abolish the existing inequalities and segregation. It furthermore argued that the abominable status of civil rights would continue to adversely affect foreign policy interests and the image of the United States, specifically Washington, D.C. and its symbolic position.

Part Four, "A Program of Action: The Committee's Recommendations," suggested a broad range of measures to guard and expand civil rights and to end segregation. African American voting rights were to be protected. The report demanded the establishment of a permanent Fair Employment Practices Committee (FEPC). It recommended the reorganization, empowerment, and enlargement of the Civil Rights Section of the Department of Justice. In addition, it urged the government to establish a special section focusing on civil rights in the FBI, law enforcement agencies in the states, and a permanent commission on civil rights in the Office of the President, the Congress, and the states. The government was encouraged to enact legislation banning all segregation and discrimination on all levels and in all aspects of American society, including abolishing poll taxes, police brutality, forbidding lynching, and ending forced servitude. It demanded the end of segregation and discrimination in the Armed Forces and in all departments of the government.

The metropolitan newspapers praised the report, but the South mainly condemned it as inflaming racial hatred. The African American community welcomed the report, but most were skeptical about what real impact the report would have on African Americans.

Truman considered the report a landmark, but did not initially address its implementation. He used the report as the basis for a civil rights message to Congress in February

1948. It also led him to issue executive orders integrating of the Armed Forces and ending of discrimination in the civil services.

See also: Cold War and Civil Rights; National Association for the Advancement of Colored People; White, Walter

Christine Knauer

Bibliography

Berman, William C. *The Politics of Civil Rights in the Truman Administration.* Columbus: The Ohio State University Press, 1970.

Billington, Monroe. "Civil Rights, President Truman and the South," *The Journal of Negro History* 58 (1973):127–39.

Gardner, Michael R. *Truman and Civil Rights: Moral Courage and Political Risks.* Carbondale: Southern Illinois University Press, 2002.

McCoy, Donald R., and Richard T. Ruetten. *Quest and Response: Minority Rights in the Truman Administration.* Lawrence: University Press of Kansas, 1973.

United States. President's Committee on Civil Rights, *To Secure these Rights: The Report of the Civil Rights Committee on Civil Rights.* New York: Simon and Schuster, 1947.

Trotter, William Monroe

William Monroe Trotter (1872–1934) was a newspaper publisher, a radical civil rights activist, and a critic of Booker T. Washington and his accommodationist approach to white racism. He was born in Springfield Township, Ohio, on April 7, 1872, the son of James Monroe and Virginia Isaacs Trotter. His father, who was recorder of deeds for Washington, D.C. under President Grover Cleveland, was also the author of an 1878 book and a former Union soldier who had enlisted in the famous 55th Massachusetts Regiment under the command Colonel Thomas Wentworth Higginson. William Monroe Trotter was a child of privilege, as he grew up in a mostly white neighborhood in Boston. In 1890, he graduated from the Hyde Park High School as class president and valedictorian of his class. In 1891, Trotter entered Harvard and, because of his academic acumen, he received the coveted Prize Deturs and was elected to Phi Beta Kappa in his junior year—the first African American student to do so in the history of the school. He graduated magna cum laude from Harvard University in 1895 and continued his education, earning his MA in 1896 before returning to Boston. He became a real estate broker, engaged in political activities for the Republican Party, and was married on June 27, 1899, to Geraldine Louise Pindell.

In 1901, Trotter and George Forbes, an assistant librarian at the West End Branch of the Boston Public Library, founded the *Boston Guardian,* a weekly publication that gave voice to Trotter's opposition to the powerful sway of Booker T. Washington and that advocated, in radical and aggressive fashion, the full inclusion of African Americans into the American mainstream. Trotter and Forbes modeled their paper after William Lloyd Garrison's the *Liberator,* publishing the *Guardian* from the same building and even on the same floor as the *Liberator.* Even before W. E. B. Du Bois launched his infamous attack against Washington in the 1903 publication of *The Souls of Black Folk,* Trotter was publishing acerbic diatribes against Washington and accommodationist approaches to white supremacy in the pages of the *Boston Guardian.* In one particularly sharp editorial published on December 20, 1902, Trotter alludes to Washington's "cowardice" and labels him a race traitor for making conciliatory remarks about southern state constitutions that had ignored the Fifteenth Amendment by actively evoking fears of "Negro Domination" as a rationale for denying African American suffrage. Through his bitter and even satirical editorials, Trotter successfully conveyed the notion that Washington was, in effect, the voice of the African American collective who blindly agreed with everything the so-called Wizard of Tuskegee wanted.

On July 30, 1903, Trotter and a group of his supporters disrupted a speech that Washington delivered at the Columbus Avenue African Methodist Episcopal Zion Church in Boston. By constantly heckling the speaker and shouting questions that challenged Washington's ideological stances, Trotter and the actions of his associates created a tremendous amount of chaos, which later came to be known as the Boston Riot. As a result of his actions, and at the insistence of Washington's supporters, Trotter and two others were arrested. Trotter and Granville Martin were fined $50 and spent a month each in the Charles Street Jail when they lost their appeal in the superior court. This incident solidified the mutual disdain and animus Washington and Trotter would have for each other. Moreover, the so-called Boston Riot catapulted Trotter to the national stage.

In 1905, Trotter, W. E. B. Du Bois, and other prominent African American intellectuals and activists concerned with the various aspects of the black nadir—the brutal combination of disfranchisement, segregation, sharecropping, and racial violence—founded the Niagara movement. Although Trotter helped push Du Bois toward a greater militancy in his approach to civil rights, the two quarreled over tactics, with Trotter insisting that any national civil rights organization be led and financed entirely by African Americans. To this end, Trotter founded the National Equal Rights League in 1908. Despite his philosophical and tactical disputes with Du Bois, Trotter participated in the 1909 merger of the Niagara movement with the group of white progressives from Springfield, Illinois who founded the National Association for the Advancement of Colored People (NAACP), although he continued to vehemently oppose white involvement in the organization.

A political independent, Trotter initially supported Georgia Democrat Woodrow Wilson for president in 1912. When Wilson's policies began to illustrate his unfaltering commitment to segregation and disfranchisement, however, Trotter turned against the president and personally confronted Wilson with his concerns in the White House in November 1914. After a heated exchange, Wilson ordered Trotter to leave his office after stating that segregation was actually to the benefit of African Americans.

In 1915, Trotter organized boycotts and demonstrations against D. W. Griffith's racist film, *The Birth of a Nation,* a film President Wilson had shown in the White House. Trotter led more than 1,000 people in a march on the Massachusetts State House in opposition to the film and its glorified depiction of the rise of the Ku Klux Klan. In 1919, to Wilson's great annoyance, Trotter announced his intention to attend the Versailles Peace Conference to push for inclusion of a racial equality clause in the peace treaty ending World War I. When the U.S. government denied him a visa, Trotter took a job as ship's cook and so secured passage to France. Although he failed to obtain a hearing at the Versailles Peace Conference, his trip and continued editorials in the *Guardian* won international publicity for the cause against segregation and white supremacy.

In the decade between 1920 and 1930, Trotter became increasingly radicalized and was actively involved in the Scottsboro, Alabama case, and petitioned for the release of the soldiers involved in the 1917 Houston mutiny. Although a lifelong political independent, Trotter became a staunch supporter of the policies of President Franklin Delano Roosevelt, seeing in him a humanitarian and someone who could potentially embrace civil rights as a means of strengthening the entire nation. Hit hard by the Great Depression, Trotter lost control of the *Guardian* in 1934. He died at the age of 62 on his birthday, April 7, 1934, when he fell from the roof of a three-story Boston building.

See also: Du Bois, W. E. B.; Houston, Texas, Mutiny, 1917; Niagara Movement; Washington, Booker T.

Walter C. Rucker

Bibliography

Fox, Stephen R. *The Guardian of Boston: William Monroe Trotter.* New York: Atheneum, 1970.

Harrison, William. "Phylon Profile IX: William Monroe Trotter-Fighter." *Phylon* (1940–1956), 7, no. 3 (1946):237–45.

Lunardini, Christine A. "Standing Firm: William Monroe Trotter's Meetings with Woodrow Wilson, 1913–1914." *The Journal of Negro History,* 64, no. 3 (Summer, 1979):244–64.

Puttkammer, Charles W., and Ruth Worthy. "William Monroe Trotter, 1872–1934." *The Journal of Negro History,* 43, no. 4 (1958):298–316.

Schneider, Mark R. *Boston Confronts Jim Crow, 1890–1920.* Boston: Northeastern University Press, 1997.

William, Jeremiah Moses. *The Golden Age of Black Nationalism, 1850–1925.* New York: Archon Books, 1978.

Tulsa, Oklahoma, Race Riot of 1921

On the morning of May 30, 1921, the Greenwood section of Tulsa was one of the most prosperous African American communities in the country. It had more than 6,000 residents, numerous businesses, lawyers, physicians, a hospital, a school, two newspapers, and two movie theaters. Two days later, on the afternoon of June 1, the community had been destroyed. More than 35 blocks had been burned to the ground; virtually every black person in the city was being held in custody.

The origins of the riot can be found in several places. First, the Greenwood community was becoming more self-confident and prosperous. Tulsa's African American community grew rapidly in the decade before the riot. Migrants came from the Deep South and from other parts of Oklahoma. They were drawn by Greenwood's prosperity and job opportunities. The weekly newspaper, the *Tulsa Star,* edited by A. J. Smitherman, fostered the community's independence. Each week Smitherman's stories and editorials emphasized racial uplift, pride, and the need to protect against violence. When a young black man was taken from a jail in Oklahoma City in 1920, for instance, Smitherman chastised the Oklahoma City community for failing to take more aggressive action to protect him. He wrote that citizens had the right to use force—including taking life—to prevent a lynching.

Smitherman and other leaders of the Greenwood renaissance met frequently to discuss the news of racial inequality and violence and to take action. For example, J. B. Stradford filed a lawsuit in 1910 to challenge his arrest for violating a railroad segregation statute. J. D. Spears, a lawyer, was heard to remark that every time he heard of a lynching, it made him want to get some more ammunition. Still other Greenwood leaders were veterans of World War I, who had fought in France and had seen how the world might be organized differently from the segregation and deference demanded by white Tulsans.

But as aspirations and expectations in Greenwood soared, whites expected a return to prewar patterns of deference and subordination. Moreover, white Tulsans feared the freedom of the Greenwood community, where in music halls blacks and whites danced and drank together. Thus when a sensational newspaper story appeared in the May 31, 1921 edition of the *Tulsa Tribune*, Tulsa was primed for a racial showdown. The article told of a young white orphan, Sarah Page, who was attacked in an elevator by 19-year-old Dick Rowland. By late afternoon, there was talk of lynching and Tulsa's black citizens were becoming alarmed.

A group of veterans decided to go to the courthouse and protect Rowland around 7 P.M. Once at the Courthouse, they saw an angry white mob. They also received assurances that the sheriff would protect Rowland. Throughout the night, groups made periodic trips to the courthouse to check on the progress of the mob.

By 10 P.M., when the white mob had not dispersed, several dozen veterans appeared at the courthouse. The leader was a man of whom it was said after the riot that he had come back from France with outlandish ideas about equality. Someone, perhaps a police officer, tried to disarm the veterans and when they refused, riot erupted.

Smoke billows over the African American community of Greenwood during the Tulsa Race Riot of 1921, which left nearly 300 people dead. (Library of Congress)

The police department deputized perhaps 250 men. One white man present that evening recalled that he was instructed to "get a gun and get busy and try and get a nigger." (*Reconstructing the Dreamland,* p. 40) Back in Greenwood, people also got out their rifles and prepared for the attack. The police formulated a plan to disarm everyone in Greenwood and take them into custody. Most surrendered peacefully, but there were some pitched battles, and some who refused to give up their guns were killed. After the arrests were made, the mobs followed with looting, then burning. Civilization broke down in Tulsa on June 1. There were reports of cold-blooded killing of unarmed men and women; a man was dragged behind a car. There are many unconfirmed reports of airplanes dropping turpentine balls on Greenwood to speed the destruction.

The arrests were completed by about 10 A.M., and the burning and looting were completed shortly afterwards. Then units of the National Guard arrived from Oklahoma City and restored order. Over the next several days, Greenwood residents were released from custody, but only when white employers came and vouched for them. Many left town immediately for places like Chicago, Los Angeles, and Kansas City. Those who stayed on lived in tents for months until they rebuilt homes.

The city refused to accept responsibility for the riot or for reconstruction. The all-white grand jury that investigated blamed the riot on Greenwood residents. The city attempted to prevent rebuilding in Greenwood by passing a building ordinance that required use of fireproof material. That ordinance was struck down as an interference with residents' property rights. Moreover, insurance companies refused to pay on fire insurance policies, citing "riot exclusion" clauses, and the city was immune from suit.

The riot was brought back into public discussion in 1997 when the Oklahoma legislature established a commission to investigate it. In 2001, the commission recommended paying reparations, which the legislature declined to do. Then in 2003, a legal team led by Charles Ogletree and Johnnie Cochran filed a lawsuit on behalf of the riot victims. The city argued that it was filed too late. The plaintiffs argued, however, that the Oklahoma courts were effectively closed at the time of the riot and for decades afterwards. As the riot illustrated, when Greenwood residents tried to assert their rights, they were subject to extreme violence. Moreover, in 1923, Oklahoma's governor declared martial law to reclaim control of the state from the Ku Klux Klan. In March 2003, the lawsuit was dismissed. In dismissing the suit, the federal court acknowledged that the courts were unavailable, but it said that the plaintiffs should have filed their case when the courts became available again. Riot victims were left, once again, waiting for justice.

See also: Franklin, John Hope; Ku Klux Klan; White Mob Violence; White Supremacy

Alfred L. Brophy

Bibliography

Brophy, Alfred L. *Reconstructing the Dreamland: The Tulsa Race Riot of 1921—Race, Reparations, Reconciliation.* New York: Oxford University Press 2002.

Ellsworth, Scott. *Death in a Promised Land: The Tulsa Race Riot of 1921.* Baton Rogue: Louisiana State University, 1982.

Turner, Henry McNeal

Henry McNeal Turner (1834–1915) was a bishop of the African Methodist Episcopal (AME) Church and one of the most influential and outspoken African Americans in the late 19th-century South. Turner used his position and pulpit as a means of actively promoting economic, social, and political reform. He is particularly known for his contributions to the AME Church, Reconstruction politics, black nationalism, pan-Africanism, and black theology.

Turner was born free in Newbury Courthouse, South Carolina, in 1834. His paternal grandmother was a white plantation owner, and his maternal grandfather was reported to be an African prince. He grew up in Abbeville, South Carolina, working alongside field slaves on a local cotton plantation. As a teenager, he learned to read and write while working as a janitor in an Abbeville law firm.

After converting to Christianity in his late teenage years, Turner decided to become a preacher. He was licensed by the Methodist Episcopal Church in 1853 and served as an itinerant, traveling and preaching all over the South. Turner married Eliza Ann Preacher, daughter of a wealthy free black family in Columbia, in 1856. Together they had 14 children, although only four survived into adulthood and only two outlived their father. Following

Eliza's death in 1889, Turner married three more times, the last of which, at the age of 73 to his secretary, evoked considerable controversy.

Turner joined the AME Church in 1858 and studied Latin, Greek, Hebrew, and theology at Trinity College in Baltimore. In 1860, he moved his family to Washington, D.C., where he became pastor of Union Bethel Church. In Washington he became exposed to politics, and he developed friendships with leading Republicans such as Thaddeus Stevens, Charles Sumner, and Benjamin Wade. Turner was part of a group that lobbied President Lincoln to allow freedmen to enlist in the Union Army, and when the first black regiment was created in 1863, he served as its chaplain. He was with the regiment as it fought numerous battles in Virginia during the closing years of the Civil War.

After the war ended, Turner was appointed by President Johnson to a post with the Freedmen's Bureau. He moved to Georgia, where he split time working with the bureau in providing education, relief, and suffrage for blacks and organizing AME churches around the state. Encouraged by emancipation and the Radical Republican commitment to black civil rights, Turner was hopeful for racial reconciliation and equality.

Turner was very active in politics during the late 1860s and early 1870s. He was instrumental in organizing the Republican Party in Georgia, acted as the leader of black Republicans in the state during the Reconstruction era, and was a delegate to the state constitutional convention. In 1868, Turner was elected to the state legislature from Macon, but, along with the other black representatives elected that year, he was barred illegally by whites from taking his seat. Eventually seated in 1870 at the behest of the U.S. Congress, Turner lost his reelection bid the next year, in part as a result of white political fraud and intimidation. Afterward he blamed moderate white Republicans for not more actively speaking up on his behalf and for betraying black political and civil rights more broadly.

Because of his role as an active preacher-politician in the Reconstruction South, Turner's life was threatened by whites on numerous occasions. He avoided armed mobs by hiding in houses, woods, and a hollow log at one point. On one occasion he narrowly escaped the Ku Klux Klan, who assassinated his speaking partner in Columbus, Georgia, and sought to kill him as well. In Macon, the homes of Turner and Jefferson Long, Georgia's only black congressman during Reconstruction, were once protected by 150 armed blacks who sought to prevent white vigilantes from doing harm to their political leaders.

As Reconstruction ended and white terrorist violence continued unabated, fewer black ministers believed in the efficacy of politics, and the black church gradually slid into a phase of relative conservatism. Turner proved to be the exception to this trend, as he vocally denounced the leadership of both national political parties. He became particularly disenchanted with the prospect of African Americans in the United States after the 1883 Supreme Court decision invalidating the Civil Rights Act of 1875; a few years later, in a private letter he referred to the Court as "an organized mob against the negro" (*Respect Black,* p. 78).

By the mid-1880s, Turner was generally embittered by the nation's betrayal of the progress and promises of Reconstruction. He taught that it was providential that Africans were brought to America, which, despite the horrors of slavery, allowed them to embrace Christianity and learn the principles of self-reliance and the rule of law. In the context of political rejection and the tightening grip of Jim Crow, however, it became evident that blacks in America could never gain their full manhood, a subject that Turner often dwelt on in sermons and speeches. He even suggested that unless something drastic changed, racial extermination was inevitable.

Disillusioned by the loss of black civil rights and by the increased quantity and brutality of lynching in the South, Turner concluded that there was no future for blacks in America, and embraced African emigration as the only remaining strategy for African Americans. He was elected an officer of the American Colonization Society in 1876, and later helped organize the International Migration Society. During the 1890s, he was one of the most prominent black nationalists in the United States and the most vocal advocate of recolonizing American blacks in West Africa. He traveled to Africa four times in the decade, surveying emigration opportunities and building the AME Church on the continent. Although he made few converts to the cause of emigration, partly as a result of negative reactions of returned emigrants to Liberia, Turner's pan-African vision and support for colonization provided an important precedent for the more popular movement led by Marcus Garvey two decades later.

Turner was well aware that by the 1890s he was on the radical edge of southern black leadership. It was a position he relished. As opposed to Booker T. Washington and other southern blacks who were tied into the white power structure, Turner's independence allowed him to launch fiery diatribes at whites, to be publicly offensive in condemning Jim Crow, and to deride hypocrisy of both whites and blacks wherever he saw it. His endorsement of emigration can be seen as a black nationalist alternative to the accommodationist posture of Washington during this period, although the latter was ultimately more successful in achieving his aims. Turner urged blacks to arm themselves to defend their homes, their leaders, and their manhood. He criticized black participation in the Spanish-American War, saying that fighting to liberate oppressed colored peoples abroad was for naught, given the intensity of race-baiting and lynching back home in the United States. In 1896, he called on blacks to register a protest vote, and although he supported William Jennings Bryan's bid for the presidency in 1900, he came to consider himself a Prohibitionist rather a supporter of either major political party.

Throughout his period of political activism, Turner remained an energetic and effective missionary and institution builder for the AME Church. His efforts were rewarded in 1880 when he became the first southern bishop elected in the denomination. He was the first AME bishop to ordain a woman, Sarah Ann Hughes, as a deacon in the church. In 1885, he published *The Genius and Theory of Methodist Polity,* demonstrating his theological and ecclesiastical acumen. An active writer and editor, he also founded three church-related periodicals (although he often devoted their pages to political and social issues): *The Southern Christian Recorder* (founded 1889), *The Voice of Missions* (1892), and *The Voice of the People* (1901).

Turner believed strongly that the black church should play a prominent role in improving the embattled black psyche and self-image. In a way that offended whites and some blacks who were more committed to separate roles for church and state, he combined religion and politics, believing that both were ultimately concerned with freedom from bondage and that they could and should work together for the uplift of the race.

His belief in religion's function as an agent of social and political change was perhaps best revealed in one of his most controversial and memorable statements. In 1895, at a conference in Atlanta that helped lead to the creation of the black National Baptist Convention, Turner famously proclaimed that "God is a Negro." The assertion reflected a culmination of his previous teachings rather than a departure or radically new idea. In the 1880s, he spoke of black angels in heaven and forcibly denounced the notion that God was white and the devil was black. In proclaiming God's blackness, which he asserted as an ontological rather than strictly physical fact, Turner became the first prominent African American leader to directly confront the issue of God's racial identity rather than simply reflecting on his divine commiseration with blacks as an oppressed people, an idea that had existed since slavery.

Rather than merely protesting against the dominant culture of whiteness, Turner's rhetoric of God's blackness was a conscious and proactive strategy to uplift the race through the affirmation of a more positive self-image. Turner considered his discussion of God's color, which whites criticized as heresy, as a means to the end of racial progress and a testimonial to the dignity and even sacredness of blackness. He has thus appropriately been seen by some scholars and churchmen as an important predecessor to the black theology movement of the 1960s.

The last of the group of preacher-politicians with roots in slavery and emancipation who played a substantial role in the expansion of black freedom during Reconstruction, Turner was one of the most popular black leaders of the late 19th century, particularly among the black lower class that he came from and ministered to. Old age, an increasingly oppressive racial climate, and the growing conservatism of the black church all combined to marginalize him as a public figure after the turn of the 20th century. In his final years he traveled to Canada, helping to establish the AME Church there and ministering to blacks who had fled north of the border in the pursuit of greater freedoms. He died in 1915 in Windsor, Canada. Turner Theological Seminary in Atlanta is named in his honor, as well as numerous churches throughout the United States and Canada.

See also: African Methodist Episcopal Church; American Colonization Society; Jim Crow; Ku Klux Klan; Lincoln, Abraham; Pan-Africanism; Republican Party

Patrick Q. Mason

Bibliography

Angell, Stephen Ward. *Bishop Henry McNeal Turner and African-American Religion in the South.* Knoxville: University of Tennessee Press, 1992.

Cone, James H. *For My People: Black Theology and the Black Church.* Maryknoll, NY: Orbis Books, 1984.

Redkey, Edwin S., ed. *Respect Black: The Writings and Speeches of Henry McNeal Turner.* New York: Arno Press, 1971.

Tuskegee Airmen

The Tuskegee Airmen were a group of black pilots who flew missions and escorted heavy bombers over Italy and Germany during World War II and set out to prove that African Americans could fly combat aircraft. Despite early setbacks, the experiment proved successful and, by the end of the war, they had earned 150 Distinguished Flying Crosses and Legions of Merit, lost 66 pilots killed in action, and did not lose a single bomber to German fighters during escort duties over Italy and deep in the industrial heart of Germany.

Since 1607, both free and enslaved African Americans have served America traditionally in the infantry or cavalry. Once their service was completed, African Americans were marginalized back to the fringes of society as second-class citizens. Yet, more than 400, 000 African Americans served in the Civil War and each of the two world wars. Moreover, black soldiers who served in the infantry and cavalry were at an economic disadvantage because of a lack of technical training. The pace of technology changed rapidly during World War I. By 1918, the use of aircraft in support of infantry was an integral part of military strategy.

More pilots were needed. Institutional racism and quotas prevented African Americans from entering the Army Air Corps. A 1925 Army War College report suggested that African Americans were incapable of operating aircraft, undisciplined, unskilled, and did not desire to fly as whites did, especially in war. The report lacked evidence, but its findings were accepted by the American military. Nevertheless, American black pilots such as Bessie Coleman, Willa Brown, William Powell, Cornelius Coffey, John C. Robinson, and ace Eugene Bullard distinguished themselves in World War I while attached to the French Air Force. Despite the report, Walter White, secretary of the NAACP, pressured the War Department to allow African Americans to fly in the military.

Subsequently, black aviation clubs sprang up in the cities of Chicago and Los Angeles. William Powell started the Bessie Coleman Flying Schools. Black leaders and politicians pushed for all-black airports and airlines; however, the movement died because of insufficient funding, the lack of political support, and the Great Depression.

Everyone was hit hard by the depression, as 25 percent of Americans were out of work. Poor whites suffered but African Americans were hit harder because many were already living well below the poverty line and tried to join the military as a way out. But the military would only take a limited number of African Americans in unskilled positions.

As war winds swept across Europe and Asia, however, the time was right to effect changes in military policy at home. Two key events changed the fortunes of black pilots wanting to serve their country. First, in 1939, Wyoming senator Harry H. Schwartz pushed for Public Law 18, which allowed black civilian pilots to train under the Civil Aeronautics Authority. The passage of this law opened the door for black pilots in the army.

Second, the chairman of the Civilian Committee on Participation of Negroes in the National Defense, Howard University Professor Rayford W. Logan, pushed for raised quotas in the armed forces. Logan's efforts were successful, as the Selective Service Act of 1940 raised the numbers for existing black quotas in the military.

Combined with pressure from other black leaders, these acts of legislation led to the creation of an experimental black pilot program at the Tuskegee Institute in Alabama. By January 1940, and under direction of George L. Washington, chief of aeronautics at the institute, training was underway at Montgomery, Alabama about 40 miles from Tuskegee. The long roundtrip from Montgomery to Tuskegee prompted the building of a new airfield only 12 miles from the school. A closer airfield made for less weary pilots and increased training time.

In May 1940, the first pilots were awarded their private pilot's license and two years later five of these pilots were commissioned into the Army Air Force and were the first members of the 99th Fighter Squadron; Captain Benjamin O. Davis Jr. was placed in command. The newly formed unit was only five pilots strong and too weak to ship out and could not fly with white units owing to segregation. The 99th Squadron could only sit and await the graduation of more black pilots.

Pilot training was a five-week course and army brass wanted the best crop of black pilots they could get. Entrance requirements were strict and the first few classes had a 70 to 80 percent washout rate. For example, the second class

The Tuskegee Airmen at Tuskegee Army Air Field. The Tuskegee Airmen were the only African American Air Corps officers during World War II. (Library of Congress)

of pilots entered with 10 men, but only 3 graduated. Typically, the average soldier in the first few classes held a bachelor's degree; some even had master's degrees. As wartime attrition drained human resources, however, entrance requirements became less stringent. As a result, by the end of 1942, enough pilots completed training to form four fighter squadrons collectively known as the 332nd Fighter Group and assigned to the 15th Army Air Force.

In 1943, however, just before the invasion of Sicily, the 99th Fighter Group became the first of the 332nd to leave for war and was sent to Casablanca. While there, the 99th received their new P-40 fighters and were visited by several noted dignitaries, Hollywood stars, and war veterans. A critical visitor was Lieutenant Colonel Philip Cochran of the famed Flying Tigers. Cochran lived and trained with

the 99th in Casablanca, imparting invaluable lessons from his combat experience in China. He treated the black pilots with respect and as fellow Americans. Phil Cochran was highly respected and regarded by veterans of the Tuskegee Airmen until his death in 1980.

Leaving Casablanca in May 1943, the 99th moved to an old German air base in Algeria and placed in the 33rd Fighter Group under the command of Colonel William "Spike" Momyer who virtually ignored their existence at first. Shorthanded, the 33rd pressed the 99th into action against the island of Pantellaria as the invasion of Sicily loomed. The 99th scored early successes against German fighters and ground targets. The island soon fell, however, and the 99th turned to escorting bombers over the Italian mainland.

During these escorts, it was soon discovered that the P-40 was slower and less maneuverable than the German aircraft, but it could take more enemy fire and turn tighter than the FW-190s or the ME-109s. Despite the P-40s' disadvantages, the 99th successfully escorted several bombing raids and did not lose a single bomber to German aircraft.

With Sicily secured and a foothold established in southern Italy, the 99th moved to the air base at Foggia, Italy. Assigned to bomb in support of the assault against the virtually impregnable Monte Cassino, the 99th did not engage many enemy aircraft. Shooting down fewer planes than their white counterparts, the black pilots were perceived as ineffective in combat. According to journalist Ernie Pyle, however, the actions of the 99th at Monte Cassino were extremely successful.

Consequently, prewar ghosts returned to haunt the 99th as Army Air Force leaders claimed that black pilots lacked the guts, discipline, organization, stamina, and aggressiveness to be good combat pilots. The Tuskegee experiment was in danger as Momyer and Hap Arnold threatened to dissolve the 99th and have the men reassigned to a rear area.

In the midst of this controversy, Davis was sent home. While there, he went to the Pentagon to argue on behalf the Tuskegee Airmen. He suggested that improper training, fewer pilots, more missions resulted in the 99th requesting more leave than their white counterparts. Davis also took responsibility as a unit leader, claiming he had been too conservative in order to protect the Tuskegee experiment. As a result, Arnold changed his mind and convinced Army Chief of Staff George C. Marshall to keep the black pilot program in operation.

In the meantime, the 99th was reassigned to the 79th Fighter Group and sent to the Allied airbase at Madna. The 79th was an independent unit that did not have specific combat duties. The 99th was in limbo and its future was uncertain. However, the 79th was led by Colonel Earl Bates and, like Cochran at Casablanca, Bates treated the black pilots with respect. Bates was a no-nonsense commander that expected the 99th to perform at its best at all times. While there, the 99th flew more than 500 missions in support of the British Eighth Army where their morale, stamina, combat aggressiveness, and confidence all increased.

Soon after, the fortunes of the Tuskegee Airmen would change forever. In January 1944, the 99th was given the full responsibility of supporting the American landings at Anzio. A fierce five-minute dogfight over the beachhead erased five months of disappointment as 12 fighters of the 99th engaged 15 German fighters, shooting down eight of them. These pilots knew this was the last chance they had to impress their detractors and they made the most of it. A few months earlier an article in *Time Magazine* criticized the 99th as an ineffective and incapable unit. After the Anzio landings, the magazine ran another story giving the Tuskegee Airmen their full support.

By May 1944, the other three units of the 332nd Fighter Group had joined the 99th in Italy. The 332nd was moved northward to Ramitelli airbase to escort Allied bombers over Germany. Striking at the industrial heart of Germany, these missions were dangerous but crucial to the war effort, especially after the D-Day landings in June 1944.

By this time the cumbersome P-40s were replaced by the sleek and powerful P-51 Mustang. Army regulations allowed pilots and units to paint nose art on their planes to personalize it. A supply problem resulted in a surplus of red paint at Italian airfields. Black ground crews painted the tail assemblies of the 332nd P-51s solid red. Thereafter the Tuskegee Airmen became known as the Red Tail Angels in the skies over Germany. And by the time of the German surrender in May 1945, the 332nd did not lose a single bomber to German planes.

After the German surrender, the 332nd Fighter Group and the inactive 477th Bomber Group formed the 477th Composite Group, which was deactivated in 1946. The 332nd was re-formed and remained an active unit until 1949 after President Harry S. Truman desegregated the armed forces. The Tuskegee Airmen proved successful. The combat success of the 332nd proved false any report that African Americans could not, or lacked the desire to, fly. And by 1946, the training program at Tuskegee Army Air Field under the command of General Noel F. Parish produced almost 1,000 black pilots.

See also: National Association for the Advancement of Colored People; Roosevelt, Eleanor; Tuskegee Institute; White, Walter; World War II (Black Participation in)

Jeffery Othele Mahan

Bibliography

Buchanan, Russell A. *Black Americans in World War II.* Santa Barbara: ABC-CLIO Books, 1997.

Francis, Charles E. *The Tuskegee Airmen: The Men Who Changed A Nation.* Boston: Branden Publishing, 1955.

Holway, John M. *Red Tails Black Wings: The Men of America's Black Air Force.* Las Cruces, NM: Yucca Tree Press, 1997.

Homan, Lynn M., and Thomas Reilly. *Black Knights: The Story of the Tuskegee Airmen*. Gretna: Pelican Publishing, 2001.

Lee, Ulysses. *The United States Army in World War II: The Employment of Negro Troops*. Washington D.C.: Center for Military History, 1963.

McKissack, Patricia and Frederick. *Red Tail Angels: The Story of the Tuskegee Airmen of World War II*. New York: Walker, 1995.

Pyle, Ernie. *Brave Men*. New York: Henry Holt, 1944.

Sandler, Stanley. *Segregated Skies: All-Black Combat Squadrons of World War II*. Washington D.C.: Smithsonian Institution Press, 1992.

Wynn, Neil A. *The Afro-American and the Second World War*. New York: Holmes & Meier, 1976.

Tuskegee Experiment

The *Tuskegee Study of Syphilis in the Negro Male*, better known as the Tuskegee Syphilis Study, was one of the most reprehensible and controversial scientific studies involving human subjects to take place in the United States. The study was conducted from 1932–1972 in Macon County, Alabama. The blistering racial climate that characterized much of the Deep South during this period accounted for the exploitation of the 399 black men selected to participate in the study of untreated tertiary syphilis in black men. Because blacks were believed to be unkempt, unsanitary, and libidinous, the high incidences of syphilis among African Americans in Macon County was believed to have extended from these variables. The high rate of poverty and illiteracy made Macon County residents vulnerable to the exploits of the U.S. Public Health Service who provided long-term funding for the project.

Entrenched in scientific racism, the impetus behind the Tuskegee Syphilis Study was a desire to prove that syphilis had different effects on African Americans than on whites. Whites were believed to suffer more from the neurological complications of the disease in its latent phase, whereas blacks were believed to suffer from its cardiovascular effects. Late 19th- and early 20th-century scientific curiosities about certain physiological aspects of African Americans (cranial size as a measurement of intellect), in addition to blacks presumed susceptibility and/or resistant to certain diseases (pellagra, malaria) aided in the justification of the experiment. Thus when the syphilis epidemic struck in the mid 1920s, as a result of the prominence of the disease among African Americans, it was immediately coined a "black disease." By 1932, when the study properly began as an offspring of the former syphilis demonstrations throughout the South, the medical community was wedded to the belief that certain diseases were racially specific in regard to their effects.

The Tuskegee Study, in particular, was a continuation of the Oslo Study conducted by Dr. E. Bruusgaard, chief of the Venereal Disease Clinic in Oslo, Norway between 1891 and 1910. The Oslo Study was designed to show the effects of untreated syphilis in whites. The primary justification for the experiment was to observe the effects of untreated syphilis in African Americans in an effort to juxtapose scientific findings with the former Oslo Study.

Macon County, Alabama was a *gold mine* for researchers who wanted to learn more about syphilis. In the 1920s, the U.S. Public Health Service (PHS), with help from the Rosenwald Fund, set out to perform syphilis demonstrations throughout the South. The demonstrations were intended to test individuals for the disease to get an estimated number of infected carriers. When the Great Depression struck in the 1930s, however, there was no funding to treat the subjects. Researchers did not want to completely abort their efforts, and alternatively sought to apply their efforts toward the examination of the effects of untreated syphilis on black males.

When the study initially began in the early 1930s, there was no reliable cure for syphilis. The syphilitic subjects in the Tuskegee Study were provided some minor treatment that consisted of mercury and salvarsan that was highly toxic and ineffective. The toxicity and unreliability of the early treatments were the basis for Public Health Service officials denying treatment altogether. Even with the introduction of penicillin during the 1940s, the study subjects were still denied treatment. As a compensation for their cooperation, the men were offered incentives such as free physical exams, transportation to and from the clinic, meals after examinations, free medical treatment for nonsyphilis-related illnesses, and the promise that burial stipends would be provided to patients' families. Many of the men were unaware of the severity of their medical condition and were merely told that they had "bad blood," a term that the population applied to virtually every ailment. Nurse Eunice Rivers served as the nurse in the experiment from its inception to its collapse in 1972, when Jean Heller of the *Washington Star* published the story.

Nurse Rivers was employed by the PHS to monitor the study participants. She was in many was a cultural mediator, "bridging the many barriers that stemmed from the educational and cultural gap between the physicians and the subjects" (*Bad Blood*, p. 6). The study participants trusted Rivers and were unaware that she was partially responsible for their detainment. Rivers never openly contested the experiment and, to secure employment, conceded with the PHS and doctors' orders.

Because of the Tuskegee Syphilis Study, the medical community has tightened up restrictions on experiments involving human subjects. Internal review boards have been established on college campuses and elsewhere to monitor the efficacy and legitimacy of such experiments. The enforcement of certain mandates and restrictions to regulate human experimentation has proved beneficial in preventing studies similar to the Tuskegee experiment.

See also: Clinton, William Jefferson; Tuskegee Institute

Talitha L. LeFlouria

Bibliography
Gray, Fred D. *The Tuskegee Syphilis Study: The Real Story and Beyond.* Montgomery, AL: Black Belt Press, 1998.
Jones, James H. *Bad Blood: The Tuskegee Syphilis Experiment.* New York: Free Press, 1993.
Reverby, Susan M., ed. *Tuskegee's Truths: Rethinking the Tuskegee Syphilis Study.* Chapel Hill: University of North Carolina Press, 2000.
United States Commission on Civil Rights; Alabama Advisory Committee. *The Tuskegee Study: A Report of the Alabama Committee to the United States Commission on Civil Rights.* Washington, D.C.: United States Public Health Service, 1973.
United States. *Tuskegee Syphilis Study Ad Hoc Advisory Panel, Final Report.* Washington, D.C.: United States Public Health Service, 1973.

Tuskegee Institute

The Tuskegee Institute is an African American school that opened in the Black Belt of Alabama in 1881. Through the years, Tuskegee played a critical role in the education of African Americans. Today the Institute remains a prominent school for multiple disciplines in Tuskegee, Alabama.

On July 4, 1881, the Tuskegee Normal and Industrial Institute opened its doors. Originally created to train teachers, the school developed over time into an institution to train the masses of African Americans. The education African Americans received at the Tuskegee Institute was

different from that of most schools. Booker T. Washington, the first president of Tuskegee, promoted the school as an industrial, or hands on, education. At Tuskegee, African American students participated in practical training in homemaking, agriculture, mechanics, and other industrial trades. The skills and trades practiced at Tuskegee were those in which African Americans were commonly engaged throughout the South.

Tuskegee's style of education received a lot of positive feedback from many whites, but some African Americans took were offended by it. While white students at other schools were gaining a literary education, African Americans at Tuskegee were concentrating largely on industrial skills and trades. African Americans at Tuskegee did study some academic coursework; however, the large majority of their education was based on practical training. Washington argued that the education gained at Tuskegee helped African Americans make a life and living for themselves. This consequently would allow African Americans to advance economically. Washington believed economic advancement would result in eventual social advancement as well. Washington's opponents, however, claimed that Tuskegee's form of education did not help to advance African Americans but instead further estranged them from their white counterparts. Southern whites who had previously fought against the education of African Americans came to accept the Tuskegee Institute because they believed the school taught and encouraged African Americans to accept their inferior economic and social status. The school was so highly praised by many whites that prominent white businessmen such as Andrew Carnegie and Seth Low donated large sums of money to Tuskegee.

Tuskegee was the product of a political negotiation made in 1881. Lewis Adams, a former slave, and W. F. Foster, an Alabama senator, negotiated a deal that resulted in the founding of Tuskegee. Adam had never received any formal education, but he was able to read and write, as well as succeed in various trades. Adams was a prominent African American in Macon County, Alabama. In 1880, when Foster, a state senator, was up for reelection, he sought the help and support of Adams. In turn for Adams securing the African American vote for Foster, Foster agreed to help Adams establish a school for African Americans in Alabama.

When Foster was reelected, he along with fellow legislature Arthur Brooks succeeded in passing House Bill

Laboratory at Tuskegee Institute in Alabama, about 1902. (National Archives)

165, which granted $2,000 to the creation of Tuskegee. The money was only enough to employ staff for the school. Consequently, the first year of classes, which began on July 4, 1881, was held in a church building. When Washington received money from the Hampton Agricultural Institute, he purchased an abandoned plantation and used it to build up a campus for his school. The students at Tuskegee worked over the next few years to construct the school themselves on the recently purchased plantation. Over the years Tuskegee continued to grow and flourish. The initial academic course work was on an elementary level, but it quickly expanded to the secondary level, and in 1923 added postsecondary study.

Tuskegee gained national attention thanks to its president, Booker T. Washington. Washington was president of the Institute until his death in 1915, at which time Robert Moton became president. Moton helped create the Veteran's Administration Hospital. Dr. Frederick Patterson followed Moton in 1935. Patterson created the Tuskegee Airmen flight training program. The all-black airmen were highly decorated World War II veterans. The group also is credited with advocating for civil rights and bringing the movement to the forefront.

In 1985, Tuskegee received university status. With more than 40 majors, the school is attended by thousands of African Americans every year. Thus the brain child of Lewis Adams and the project of Booker T. Washington has remained standing and has continued to prosper for more than 100 years. The school played an integral role in educating African Americans at a time when many whites did not support the idea. For this Tuskegee will remain an important part of African American history.

See also: Historically Black Colleges and Universities; Tuskegee Airmen; Washington, Booker T.

Mindy R. Weidman

Bibliography
Harlan, Louis R. *Booker T. Washington: The Wizard of Tuskegee, 1901–1915.* New York: Oxford University Press, 1983.
Thrasher, Max Bennett. *Tuskegee: Its Story and Its Work.* New York: Negro Universities Press, 1969.

Universal Negro Improvement Association

The goal of the Universal Negro Improvement Association (UNIA), an international organization, was the liberation of all peoples of African descent by developing economic self-sufficiency, cultural pride, political independence, and newfound levels of race consciousness, thus creating an international brotherhood among black people.

During his international travels, Marcus Garvey interacted with scholars, writers, philosophers, and religious leaders who helped shape his worldview, which was ultimately introduced to the world through his creation of the Universal Negro Improvement and Conservation Association and African Communities League (UNIA-ACL). The UNIA-ACL was created by Garvey while he was living in his native home of Jamaica in 1914. Shortly after his arrival to Harlem, the UNIA-ACL gave way to what would be known around the world as simply, the UNIA.

Unlike any other organization at the time, the UNIA championed a black nationalist approach against religious deceit contrived by colonial Christians to validate slavery, enduring psychosocial effects of European imperialism, economic deprivation, political disenfranchisement, and cultural suppression among Africans and African Americans around the world.

By July 1918, an original constitution and book of laws was developed as an instrument of governance and to maintain consistency among chapters. Within the core belief system of the UNIA, a comprehensive list of affirmations served as the critical framework for building racial solidarity. On a daily basis, members' actions were an outward manifestation of the belief system, which posited that rights of all men are to be respected, all races must work to preserve their pure lineage. God shall be the guiding force, interracial marriage will lead to the annihilation of the Negro race, development of an almighty Negro nation in Africa must be promoted, those of African heritage should always be proud, dominion of Negro women by whites is unacceptable, and racial separation serves as the optimal means to maintain cultural ideals.

From its inception in 1914 until the 1940s, the UNIA in the United States held active chapter membership in Ohio, Michigan, New York, Pennsylvania, and Illinois. Focused on fighting racial injustice and violence aimed at African Americans in the United States, the UNIA established networks throughout the country that focused on uplifting the race. Through partnerships with clergy from black churches, businesses, political leaders, and intellectuals who shared the UNIA vision, programs were instituted to provide social services, religious motivation, cultural integrity, political awareness, education, and gainful employment.

To resolve economic hardships endured by deprived and often uneducated poor and working class African Americans, the UNIA initiated collaborative efforts with labor unions that yielded financial benefits to the economically disadvantaged by balancing wages in skilled labor markets throughout the United States and Canada. Business owners unwilling to extend opportunities for employment to African Americans found the UNIA to be a formidable force through mass protests that encouraged people to stop spending money in businesses that contribute to oppressing the race. Auxiliary groups within the UNIA, such as the Black Cross Nurses and African Legionnaires, existed to further ensure that the overall needs of members were being met.

As representatives from more than 1,000 chapters convened from August 1, 1920 through August 31, 1920, the First International UNIA Convention was successfully hosted in New York City, which later became home to the organization's first Liberty Hall. With attendees coming from more than 40 countries, nearly 2,000 members were present, including regional delegates who shared updates regarding local membership drives, fundraising efforts, propaganda aimed at destroying the reputation of the organization, and community issues to be addressed.

Economic developments and effective strategies to alleviate rights infringements were important, but the most significant accomplishment of the 1920 Convention was the adoption of the Declaration of the Rights of the Negro

Peoples of the World, as presented by the organization's Supreme Executive Council or international leadership. Published in the September 11, 1920 edition of *The Negro World,* the declaration gave life to the organization's motto, *"One God! One Aim! One Destiny!"* In the declaration active members found solace and strength that not only guided but reaffirmed their shared belief in global racial allegiance.

After the success of the first convention, subsequent conventions and celebratory parades were hosted at Liberty Hall during August of 1921 and 1922. Along with the Constitution, Declaration of Rights, and core belief systems, the UNIA developed its own pledge of allegiance to be recited in the presence of the definitive red, black, and green flag. Within the pledge, members committed to lifelong service that would further the goal of liberation, unity, and knowledge among African descendants around the world.

International leadership of the organization believed that the race could one day shape international politics once a unified vision was established, disseminated, and adopted by all chapters. Worldwide strategic goals were set throughout international regions to best meet the needs left void by corresponding governments. UNIA chapters in Africa and the Caribbean focused on developing political participation among natives to overcome cultural inequalities established during European colonization.

In March 1920, efforts of UNIA leaders began to make the infamous "Africans for Africans" slogan ring true. Research and preliminary planning for colonization of Liberia, including provisions for economic, political, and social growth independent of European influence, was initiated. Consistent with steps taken in American cities, the UNIA planned to create an environment in Liberia that fostered a sense of empowerment among Africans and African Americans by building schools that incorporated an Afrocentric viewpoint into education, sustainable employment opportunities, social enrichment through cultural activities, and long-term health through universal health care initiatives. Enthusiasm toward the growing project was echoed by members in Africa and the United States. Carrying enlightened African Americans to Liberia, the S. S. Phyllis Wheatly was purchased as the ship to fully complete the "Africa for Africans" charge of the UNIA, but it was unable to do so.

To their dismay, UNIA organizers who tirelessly worked until June 1924 to develop and negotiate what would be one of the largest ventures for the organization were told that progress would come to a screeching halt in Liberia because of conflicts of interest. The Fourth International UNIA Convention in 1924 marked a shift within the organization as the Black Star Line was reestablished as the Black Star Steamship Company. In addition to reclaiming their most notable business venture, members of the UNIA regrouped from the disappointing news of the Liberia project by focusing on avenues to create political power. Establishment of the Negro Political Union was the organization's strongest effort to directly challenge the political disenfranchisement of the race on a large scale.

During the Fifth International UNIA Convention, the organization worked to continue its mission while maintaining a dwindling membership. Although resistance to the UNIA grew in some African countries, the organization achieved success in other parts of the world including Central America. Substantial efforts were exerted in the region to mitigate deplorable working conditions, substandard living accommodations, and political inactivity among inhabitants of African descent. Between August 1, 1929 and August 31, 1929, the Sixth International UNIA Convention was hosted in Kingston, Jamaica, which was the final formal convention. Beyond participation in their own conventions, representatives of the UNIA participated in international conventions hosted by organizations with similar goals including the International Convention of the Negro Peoples of the World.

By January 1918, Harlem was not only the headquarters of the UNIA but it also set the stage for the first printing of the weekly newspaper. Subsequent editions were printed and distributed to all members around the world in multiple languages. Through the publication and distribution of *The Negro World,* members of the UNIA were unified on a global scale as the messages often reinforced the organization's mission and goals. To increase awareness of the mission, local chapters relied on independent black-owned newspapers in Chicago, Egypt, London, New York, and other key cities where UNIA chapters were forming.

Within each edition, UNIA members published updated committee reports on membership development, fundraising efforts, business enterprises, and social programs. In addition to committee reports, the newspaper announced special events and world news that affected the development of the organization, and recounted details of regional and national conventions for those unable to attend. As the newspaper was the thread that weaved together the organization's international membership, opponents of the UNIA sought to destroy the unprecedented circulation of *The Negro World* by banning circulation and imposing severe penalties on those caught distributing the newspaper.

Weekly advertisements encouraging members and supporters to patronize African American-owned businesses were placed in each edition of *The Negro World*. The UNIA was responsible for developing its own economic independence through the development of grocery stores, laundries, restaurants, insurance companies, tailoring company, record companies, newspaper subscriptions, and sales of stock in the Black Star Line, all of which were advertised in *The Negro World*.

Differing opinions among members as to the future actions of the organization began to create factions within the group. At the same time, civil rights organizations whose focus embraced integrationist approaches to resolving racial issues gained national notoriety, which further added to the UNIA's membership crisis.

In response to increasing violence against African Americans in the South, Marcus Garvey believed that by reiterating the UNIA's goal of racial separation would deter violence inflicted by members of the Ku Klux Klan (KKK). Representing UNIA leadership, Garvey visited KKK headquarters in Atlanta during June 1922 but was unsuccessful in his attempt to find a solution to the racial hostility felt among KKK members. Coincidentally, as violence against African Americans continued in the South, the Atlanta meeting caused greater alienation among members who felt the organization was taking the wrong approach toward civil rights violations.

The Black Star Line was officially started on June 27, 1919 with the purchase of the UNIA's first ship named Yarmouth. In its second purchase, the UNIA's Black Star Line was expanded to include the S. S. Shadyside. Following the success of the first two ships, the S. S. Antonio Maceo was purchased as sales of the Black Star Line stocks began to increase. Subsequent ships were named after world-renowned scholars who held differing ideological perspectives from UNIA leaders, but were nonetheless influential in the early stages of the organizations development—the S.S. *Frederick Douglass* and S.S. *Booker T. Washington*.

Revenue generated by sales of Black Star Line stocks initially supported activities of the UNIA, but income did not sustain the organization for long. Criminal charges filed against Marcus Garvey suggesting long-term use of the mail system to defraud investors in the Black Star Line cast the UNIA in a negative light among members and critics. Skeptics of the UNIA used the charges against Garvey as impetus to publicly diminish the organization's image by painting it as a racist cult whose national leadership contradicted its own goals of racial unity and empowerment.

Marcus Garvey's formal sentence to five years imprisonment caused UNIA members already disappointed with the direction of the organization to denounce their membership publicly. In December 1927, remaining members of the UNIA traveled to New Orleans to send off the organization's first leader as he was being deported to Panama.

See also: Black Nationalism; Black Star Line; Garvey, Marcus; Ku Klux Klan; Moore, Queen Mother Audley; Pan-Africanism

Caroline M. Harper

Bibliography

Akpan, M. B. "Liberia and the Universal Negro Improvement Association: The Background to the Abortion of Garvey's Scheme for African Colonization." *The Journal of African History* 14 (1973):105–27.

Christian, Mark. "Marcus Garvey and African Unity: Lessons for the Future from the Past." *Journal of Black Studies* 39 (2008):316–31.

Cronon, Edmond D. *Black Moses: The story of Marcus Garvey and the Universal Negro Improvement Association.* Madison: University of Wisconsin Press, 1969.

Garvey, Amy J. *The Philosophy & Opinions of Marcus Garvey or Africa for the Africans.* Dover, MA: The Majority Press, 1986

Rolinson, Mary G. *Grassroots Garveyism: The Universal Negro Improvement Association in the Rural South, 1920–1927.* Chapel Hill: University of North Carolina Press, 2007.

Shelby, Tommy. *We Who Are Dark.* London: The Belknap Press of Harvard University Press, 2005.

Smith-Irvin, Jeannette. *Footsoldiers of the Universal Negro Improvement Association: Their Own Words.* Trenton, NJ: Africa World Press, 1989.

Stephens, Ronald J. "Garveyism in Idlewild, 1927 to 1936." *Journal of Black Studies* 34 (2004):462–88.

Vincent, Theodore G. *Black Power and the Garvey Movement.* Baltimore: Black Classic Press, 2006.

Urban Ghetto

The term "ghetto" is an Italian word originally used to refer to those sections of the European city set aside for Jews. In the Middle Ages, Jews were heavily discriminated against, denied access to employment, and deprived of access to quality housing. The result was extreme spatial congregation and segregation into what ultimately became known as urban "ghettos."

In the U.S. the rise of the urban ghetto is a recent occurrence. It describes the geographically isolated, run-down, and impoverished residential districts of the inner city where mostly black and Latino people are crowded together. Like their European predecessors, America's urban ghettos are clearly demarcated spaces easily recognizable by vacant lots, abandoned buildings, and physical deterioration.

Almost all European immigrants to the United States spent some time in an urban ghetto, benefiting from the social networks, cultural comforts (e.g., language, food, religion), and protection against hostilities. Although outsiders saw the ghetto as a squalid, unclean, foul, tenement-ridden environment, for insiders, these were communities that provided much of what they needed to achieve the American dream and make the transition into the American middle class.

A number of factors converged to transform these early ghettos to the sites of high unemployment, social pathologies, and poverty they are today. One was the large-scale black migration north during the early 20th century. Segregation, discrimination, and racial hostilities were notable in the cities that experienced high levels of African American migration. Blacks, faced with restricted housing markets and job ceilings that blocked economic progress, experienced a similar spatial segregation as that experienced by Jews in Europe. As was the case with Jews and other early immigrants to the United States, often it was easier (and safer) to live among one's own kind. Another factor contributing to the transformation of the American ghetto was the out-migration of the white population. Whites were willing to pay to live in areas with few, or no blacks. Once they became acculturated into American society and acquired the language skills and higher incomes, they were well positioned to take advantage of the opportunities offered them by the federal government and consequently fled the inner cities in massive numbers and moved to other places. This has not been the case with African Americans and Latinos who now occupy the areas abandoned by earlier immigrant groups. Although economically African American ghettos started out well owing to the high wages paid in manufacturing, continued high rates of black migration north combined with white flight to the suburbs resulted in an increasingly isolated black inner city population. Thus

racism, discrimination in the form of institutionalized racial preferences, and exclusionary practices all converged to produce today's American urban ghetto.

Like the ghettos occupied by their European predecessors, the early African American ghettos were safe havens where people worked together, played together, worshipped together, and were educated together. Unlike their European predecessors, however, African Americans and Latinos did not experience comparable opportunities for upward—and outward—mobility. When they did, they left behind a place with little or no moral and social leadership. The urban ghetto today is a site where conditions have worsened.

There are three explanations for urban ghettos: social, economic, and structural. The social explanation suggests that ghettos form in places where there are high concentrations of people who exhibit "pathological" behaviors. In the minds of most Americans, urban ghettos are synonymous with public housing and thus are viewed as receptacles for "problem" families. In this sense, ghettos are lifestyle choices made by individuals. The individuals and the areas they inhabit are characterized by high rates of unemployment, illegitimacy, family dissolution, welfare dependency, violence, school dropout, teenage pregnancies, alcohol, and drug abuse and crime. Accordingly, they are a product of social institutions and cultural values resulting from poverty and social isolation. Ghetto dwellers have few job prospects and for males in particular, participating in illegal activities (e.g., drug trafficking) becomes an attractive option.

An alternative explanation for urban ghettos is the economic explanation. It suggests that ghettos are the result of closed alternatives. It is discrimination in access or the inability to fully participate in the job market that ultimately produces urban ghettos. African Americans and Hispanics are in ghettos because their limited access to job markets restricts their access to housing markets. They cannot afford (or are not allowed) to purchase better housing elsewhere.

The structural explanation maintains that urban ghettos are areas that have experienced significant losses of jobs, businesses, and population. Although they are located near busy central business districts of most major cities, culturally, intellectually, and economically they are highly isolated, which in turn impedes opportunities for financial, employment, business, and cultural contacts with the larger community.

See also: Great Migration; Kerner Commission Report; Urbanization; War on Poverty

Rickie Sanders

Bibliography

Anderson, Elijah. *Code of the Streets*. New York: W. W. Norton, 1999.

Anderson, Elijah. *Streetwise: Race, Class and Change in an Urban Community*. Chicago: University of Chicago Press, 1990.

Du Bois, W. E. B. *The Philadelphia Negro*. New York: Schocken Press, 1967.

Frazier, John, F. Margay, and E. Tettey-Fio. *Race and Place: Equity Issues in Urban America*. Boulder, CO: Westview Press, 2003.

Jencks, Christopher, and P. Peterson, eds. *The Urban Underclass*. Washington, D.C.: Brookings Institution, 1991.

Kusmer, Kenneth. *A Ghetto Takes Shape: Black Cleveland 1870–1930*. Urbana: University of Illinois Press, 1978.

LeGory, Mark, and J. Pipkin. *Urban Social Space*. Belmont, CA: Wadsworth Publishing, 1992.

Spear, Allan. *Black Chicago: The Making of a Negro Ghetto, 1980–1920*. Chicago: University of Chicago Press, 1967.

Wilson, Julius. *The Truly Disadvantaged*. Chicago: University of Chicago Press, 1987.

Wilson, Julius. *When Work Disappears*. New York: Knopf, 1996.

Urbanization

Urbanization is a two-pronged process. For a society, it is the transformation from being rural and agricultural to being urban and industrial. For individuals, the urbanization process is behavioral and spatial. It involves individuals making the spatial move from the rural countryside to the city and once there, adopting new behaviors, attitudes and ways of seeing the world. As a geographical concept, urbanization is visible on the landscape in the form of large, dense agglomerations of socially heterogeneous populations, high concentrations of settlements and/or businesses, and a wide range of other specialized services and activities. In addition to its being a process that represents itself on the landscape, urbanization is also a social process resulting in cultural and behavioral changes (e.g., changing attitudes toward work, family structure, role of women, identity, and economic status). It brings about changes in lifestyle and psychology; and social, cultural, economic, and political thinking. To be fully realized, the urbanization process requires both the move across space and the adoption of new ways of viewing the world.

Over time, the United States has become an urbanized society. In 1800, only 6.1 percent of the population lived in urban areas. By 1990, that number had increased to 75.2 percent. The two explanations commonly given for this exponential increase are increases in technological know-how and industrialization. As new more efficient technologies were applied to the agricultural sector, more and more people became redundant; their work was no longer needed. The jobs they had done were taken over by machines. Thus they were "released" from farm work. Left without a means of income, they were pushed off the farm and pulled to other, larger areas that offered more opportunities for employment. At the same time that labor was being released from farms, demand for machine produced goods was increasing. Urban areas with their ideal locations, greater economic and social capital, and large populations were perfect sites for planting the seeds of America's industrial revolution. People came in droves from rural areas and abroad in search of a life that offered more.

African Americans were a part of this. The migration of blacks from the rural south to the cities of the Northeast, Midwest, and West during the early 20th century has been described as the largest internal movement of people in the history of the United States. Between 1900 and 1940, more than 1 million African Americans participated in this mass movement. Early on blacks had begun to move away from the South. During the 1870s, large numbers of blacks left the South, seeking their fortunes in places that were familiar—rural areas in Texas, Kansas, and Oklahoma. By 1910, new destinations were sought and in what came to be known as the Great Migration more than a quarter of a million blacks converged in the cities of the Northeast, the Midwest, and the West.

The Great Migration created the first large, concentrated urban black communities in cities such as Chicago, Detroit, New York, Los Angeles, and Cleveland. During the 1910s and 1920s, Chicago's black population grew 148 percent, Cleveland's by 307 percent, Detroit's by 611 percent. Although the migration slowed during the Depression, nearly one-fourth of all blacks lived in cities of the North or West by 1940. The move to the cities continued during and after World War II. By 1960, 40 percent of all blacks lived outside the South and 75 percent lived in cities. Between 1910 and 1970, the country's African American population was transformed from a predominately southern, rural group to a northern, urban one. By shedding their rural, southern backgrounds, and embracing their new life in cities, African Americans created a new black culture, complete with music, language, dress, and art.

The movement out of the South and to the cities of the North was the result of push and pull factors. Push factors are negative attributes of the place of origin. They included lack of opportunities, poverty, and overt racism. Pull factors are positive attributes at the destination. They included the prospect of jobs, schooling, and socioeconomic mobility. The war years witnessed the greatest influx of southern blacks to the cities of the North and Midwest. Northern-based industries were experiencing loss of labor owing to military enlistments. Foreign immigration was slowed owing to restrictions placed on immigration, but demand for industrial goods was increasing. The result was a severe labor shortage in most northern and western cities. Blacks were available to provide the cheap, plentiful labor that was needed for the emerging factories.

African Americans' encounters with city skyscrapers, new technologies, streetlights, automobiles, and masses of people profoundly affected their behavior, attitudes, and goals. A few were energized by the new environment and were lucky enough to turn it into a new home with satisfying jobs, homes, and communities. Another small number never succeeded and either returned to their rural origins or resorted to a life of repeated disappointments. For all, however, it was clear that the city contained new kinds of segregation and that their hopes were not to be fully realized. The notion that one could climb from rags to riches was one of America's greatest myths.

For a time, the initial encounter with the city embodied all the promises of urbanization progress, economic security, culture, and hope. Despite its promise, however, the rural urban migration of African Americans failed to deliver the dream. Today the city has a different set of associations that have less to do with progress and light than with decay, crime, and poverty. African American urban life today is characterized by a host of adverse economic and social conditions—anonymity, institutional racism, disrupted family structures, low socioeconomic standing, underachievement, underemployment, teen pregnancy, divorce, and a host of other problems.

The African American urban experience has been impacted by a number of social, economic, political and technological issues. Early on, access to housing and jobs became a major source of friction between blacks and whites. To maintain residential segregation, many cities adopted residential segregation ordinances and restrictive covenants. These were formal, institutionalized restrictions forbidding white property owners from selling their property to blacks. For whites who violated these agreements, the punishment was harsh. Thus African Americans were confined to all-black neighborhoods, in what eventually became known as urban ghettos. Although jobs were plentiful owing to the war effort, African Americans experienced significant job discrimination. Discrimination was so pronounced that in 1911, a concerned group of social workers, white philanthropists, and black leaders, founded the National Urban League. The National Urban League is the nation's oldest community-based organization devoted to empowering African Americans and facilitating their entry into the economic and social mainstream. At its inception, the mission of the Urban League was to dismantle the systems of institutionalized racism that prevented African Americans in cities from obtaining jobs.

More recently, one of the major issues facing African Americans in cities is gentrification. Gentrification may be defined as the process by which deteriorating, blighted properties in declining neighborhoods are purchased by middle class residents, renovated, beautified, and subsequently occupied by more affluent tenants. It tends to occur in neighborhoods with particular qualities (i.e., convenient to downtown, cheap but distinctive housing stock, and vibrant, lively communities). Gentrification is a general term for several simultaneous changes—an increase in median income, a decline in the proportion of racial minorities, a reduction in household size, changes in neighborhood character and culture (e.g., ideas about what is attractive, codes of public behavior, noise, and nuisance). It often results in the displacement of older residents who are forced to sell their property and move away if they cannot afford the rent and tax increases. It has been the cause of deep racial and class conflicts and has been described as a miscarriage of social justice in which wealthier, usually white, newcomers are used to carry out the wishes of urban developers and planners desiring to displace poor, minority residents so that the area they occupy can be put to a more profitable use.

On the other hand, the gentrification process has the potential for producing desirable results, reducing crime, spawning new investments in infrastructure, and increasing economic activity in neighborhoods. Unfortunately, older residents who manage to stay are often left on the sidelines—socially, culturally, and economically marginalized.

Another issue facing African Americans in cities is suburbanization or urban sprawl. Traditionally, urbanization has been associated with thriving central business districts in the downtown core. Post-World War II, however, has seen residential areas shift outward giving rise to suburbs. The beginnings of suburbanization can be marked by the proliferation of the automobile owing to Henry Ford's mass production assembly line, the desire of returning veterans for more living space, the growing middle class, and the desire for racial homogeneity. Levittown was the first planned suburban development. It was built in the early 1950s. It fit all of the criteria; space (all of the homes had a yard and garage), new appliances (which offered convenience to their owners), mortgages guaranteed by the federal government (small down payments), and racial exclusion (returning black veterans could not purchase homes in Levittown).

The trend to move farther and farther away from the downtown core continues today, leading to what many describe as urban/metropolitan sprawl. Sprawl may be defined as large scale, low-density urban expansion that extends beyond the urban fringe. Sprawl has led to an increase in traffic congestion, pollution, and infrastructure costs as American drive longer distances to and from work. For African Americans and other minorities in particular, the steady decentralization of entry level jobs away from the city core has resulted in a spatial mismatch or a diseconomy in travel time and service provision. Thus, low-skilled minorities residing in inner cities face adverse labor market outcomes in the form of higher rates of unemployment, lower average wages, and increased time spent commuting. Urban sprawl has also led to suburbanites' feelings of detachment from inner city problems.

The spatial mismatch hypothesis argues that sprawl exacerbates certain dimensions of racial inequality in America. It has also raised concerns about social polarization because of suburbanites' physical and psychological remoteness from inner city problems.

Neither of these issues can be separated from the economic climate in which they occur. The new service economy and the rise of the creative class have taken center stage and has become the engine driving 21st-century American urbanization. This has changed the city's economic core. Old retailers who resided in the urban core and who supplied goods to the working class population have been undermined by upscale boutiques, specialty shops, and restaurants catering to the new creative class. During the past 25 years, employment in manufacturing as a share of total employment in America's inner cities has fallen dramatically. Between 1967 and 2001, the United States lost 9 percent of its manufacturing jobs. In the cities of the industrial heartland, the loss reached more than 40 percent. There are two explanations for the declining employment in manufacturing. First, the phenomenal increases in worker productivity have given rise to dramatic increases in manufacturing output. Just as in the early days of urbanization/industrialization when increased agricultural productivity produced redundancy and prompted rural urban migration; today, in the manufacturing sector technological advances are again contributing to a situation where fewer workers are needed.

A second explanation for the decline in manufacturing employment is globalization. Lowering restrictions on trade has put the American worker in competition with overseas workers who are paid less, not represented by unions, and enjoy few of the benefits associated with work in the United States. Because manufacturers seek to reduce their labor costs, it is economically rational to move production to places where labor costs are lower.

In both instances, a steadily decreasing proportion of the American workforce is employed in manufacturing. Typically, industrial plants are closed down and not replaced. This phenomenon, known as deindustrialization, has had a significant impact on the social lives of African Americans and has been identified as a key determinant in urban and African American poverty. It has contributed to widening income inequality and high unemployment in America's cities. It has also been associated with a cycle of urban decay that seems immune to most policy recommendations and well-intentioned government interventions. Social conditions in the old industrial core have deteriorated fueling abandonment and decay. The culture of poverty that results has generated a system of ruthless, exploitative relationships for those confined to urban ghettos.

African American migration to urban areas was preceded by waves of immigrants from Europe. Roughly 10 million European immigrants came to the United States between 1860 and 1890. Nearly all of them settled in the great cities of the Northeast and the Midwest. Immigrants from other places (e.g., Asia) were few. They settled primarily in the West, attracted by the possibility of working on the expanding railroad system. Most immigrants were poor, lived in crowded tenements, and worked in factories. During the decade between 1900 and 1910, nearly 9 million immigrants entered the United States and more than 90 percent were from Europe. By 1950, the number of immigrants had dropped to slightly more than 1 million but significantly, only half were from Europe. In the 1980s, the number of immigrants increased to approximately 8 million, but 84 percent of these immigrants were from Latin America and Asia. Immigrants from Europe were less than 15 percent of the total immigration stream.

Similar to previous immigrants, most of the new immigrants move directly into cities in search of employment. Because they are willing to work for low wages and work under less than desirable conditions, they add to the already well-stocked, unskilled labor pool in urban areas. They also compete directly with inner city African Americans for low-paying jobs. As tensions rise between newer immigrant groups and established African American communities, conflict has erupted.

Cities were the Land of Opportunity for African Americans coming from the rural south and for many past and present immigrants. For most, however, they came to realize that it was also a far-off dream. The city had the opportunities, but they were not as available in the quantity as they had first hoped. In recent years, the long-term out-migration of African Americans from the south to the great cities of the Northeast, West, and Midwest has been reversed. Southern metropolitan areas, particularly Atlanta have led the way in attracting black migrants. Detroit, Chicago, New York, Philadelphia, and San Francisco experienced the greatest out-migration of African Americans.

See also: Great Migration; Kerner Commission Report; Redlining; Urban Ghetto

Rickie Sanders

Bibliography

Baldwin, Davarian L. *Chicago's New Negroes: Modernity, the Great Migration, & Black Urban Life.* Chapel Hill: University of North Carolina Press, 2007.

Goings, Kenneth, and Raymond Mohl, eds. *The New African American Urban History.* Thousand Oaks, CA: Sage Publications, 1996

Harrison, Alferdteen. *Black Exodus: The Great Migration from the American South.* Jackson: University Press of Mississippi, 1991.

Hartman, Chester, and Sarah Carnochan. *City for Sale: The Transformation of San Francisco.* Berkeley: University of California Press, 2002.

Horne, Gerald. *Fire This Time: The Watts Uprising and the 1960s.* Charlottesville: University Press of Virginia, 1995.

Kusmer, Kenneth L., and Joe William Trotter. *African American Urban History Since World War II.* Chicago: The University of Chicago Press, 2009.

Lemann, Nicholas. *The Promised Land: The Great Black Migration and How It Changed America.* New York: A. A. Knopf, 1991.

Self, Robert O. *American Babylon: Race and the Struggle for Postwar Oakland.* Princeton, NJ: Princeton University Press, 2003.

Tate, Gayle T., and Lewis A. Randolph. *The Black Urban Community: From Dusk Till Dawn.* New York: Palgrave Macmillan, 2006.

US Organization

In the months after the 1965 Watts Riot, Maulana (Ron) Karenga, Hakim Jamal, Dorothy Jamal, Tommy Jacquette-Mfikiri, Karl Key-Hekima, Ken Seaton-Msemaji, Samuel Carr-Damu, Sanamu Nyeusi, and Brenda Haiba Karenga founded a new black power organization called "US." Despite claims later made by a number of Black Panthers, US never meant "united slaves" and this continued reference is part of the legacy of the conflict between the two groups. Instead, US was an allusion to the group's mission to serve "us" blacks as opposed to "them" whites. In addition, the dispute that drove a permanent wedge between the Black Panthers and US was over whether cultural nationalism or political/revolutionary nationalism was the best solution for African American communities. Initially, the US Organization was founded on the ideological principles forwarded by Malcolm X after his break with the Nation Islam and through his assassination on February 21, 1965. Malcolm X's shift from religious nationalism to political and secular nationalism, which coalesced in the creation of the Organization of Afro-American Unity (OAAU), proved to be powerfully influential for Karenga and the other founders of US. Malcolm X's vision of the OAAU as a vanguard that would launch a cultural revolution was embraced by US who collectively understood that a cultural revolution was necessary before a violent revolution could take place.

According to the US Organization's first newspaper, Hakim Jamal was the official founder and Karenga was designated as the chairman of US. By the summer of 1966, however, Jamal split with US leaving Karenga to become the undisputed leader of the organization. Jamal's departure was likely due to ideological differences and his strong preference for following the teachings of his former associate, Malcolm X, while Karenga was pushing the organization more toward cultural nationalism. This ideological transformation was reflected in the symbolism of the US Organization as members shifted from wearing T-shirts bearing Malcolm X's face to ones with Karenga's likeness. Almost immediately after Jamal's departure, US and Karenga began the mission of fulfilling Malcolm X's goal of creating a cultural revolution by first building a "new" black culture that would be based on a number of African concepts, value systems, and traditions.

Since Karenga previously taught Kiswahili, and even met a number of the first members of US within the context of his language classes, he emphasized the use of African languages in order to express the goals, the organizational structure, and the cultural conceptualizations that served as foundations for US. *Simba Wachanga* (young lions) was the youth movement in US and served as its paramilitary wing; the Circle of *Isihlangu* (circle of the shield) were the organization's highest title holders, including Karenga's own title as *Maulana* or Master Teacher; *Kawaida* was the group's cultural nationalist philosophical, moral, and spiritual orientation; and two of the lasting legacies of US—*Nguzo Saba* (the seven principles of blackness) and the holiday *Kwanzaa* became popular beyond the US Organization and continue to be shaping influences throughout African American communities in the 20th and 21st centuries.

The particular brand of cultural nationalism espoused by Karenga and US is a blend of Kiswahili, Zulu, Kemetic (Egyptian), Gikuyu, and other African influences. *Kawaida*, Karenga's personal philosophy and theory of cultural nationalism, was borrowed from Zulu religious precepts and shaped by his antipathy for Christianity and other organized religions. According to Karenga, Kawaidists are part of the spiritual and theoretical legacy of Marcus Garvey and Malcolm X and the philosophy itself is meant to promote self-awareness and consciousness through the seven principles of blackness embodied by *Nguzo Saba: Umoja* (unity), *Kujichagulia* (self-determination), *Ujima* (collective work and responsibility), *Ujamaa* (cooperative economics), *Nia* (purpose), *Kuumba* (creativity), and *Imani* (faith). In this way, *Kawaida* undergirds and embodies the US Organization.

As a reflection of their change in consciousness and acceptance of *Kawaida,* US members—who often called themselves "advocates"—typically wore afros or shaved heads, donned Afrocentric clothing and jewelry, punctuated greetings with African phrases, adopted African names, and embraced other elements of an African aesthetic. US was an all encompassing organization for its advocates and became, in essence, a total way of life that permeated seven main facets: the family, the community, revolutionary schooling, the temple, the congregation, the revolutionary party, and nation building. This primarily inward focus, however, became a point of criticism by the group's detractors—including the Black Panther Party—who would label the cultural nationalism advocated by US as "pork-chop" or apolitical, reactionary, and nonrevolutionary nationalism.

Even so, in its early years, the US organization gained support nationally and abroad. By 1967, US advocates formed a chapter in San Diego and a group of black marines had even formed an affiliate chapter in Vietnam. In addition, the organization began to engage in coalition building as part of its strategy to create the united front of black nationalist organizations that Malcolm X envisioned when he formed the OAAU. Between 1967 and 1969, US formed coalitions with, and connections to, SNCC and the Black Panther Party for Self-Defense. Efforts to establish a coalition among these organizations is best epitomized by the August 11, 1967 *Uhuru* Day rally, an event designed to commemorate the 1965 Watts Uprising. The rally not only attracted US members, but also the likes of H. Rap Brown of SNCC and Huey P. Newton of the newly formed Black Panther Party, both of whom delivered guest speeches. At least in 1967, the idea of a united front seemed viable and before internal conflicts—fueled by FBI instigation—disrupted this momentum, umbrella movements like the Free Huey campaign, the Black Congress, the Black Federation, and the Congress of African People were created and US advocates were actively involved.

By early 1968, the roots of the infamous US/Black Panther conflict began when the two organizations had a dispute over security arrangements for a "Free Huey" rally scheduled at the Los Angeles Sports Arena on February 18, 1968. From that point forward, real and imagined differences between US and the Black Panthers were augmented by the FBI's COINTELPRO, as well as the egos of Karenga, Eldridge Cleaver, Newton, and members of the LA Branch of the Black Panther Party. By September 1969, the FBI stepped up its program to destabilize the creation of a united front and the Black Congress by actively stoking the fires of the US-Panther divide. In a series of contrived letters that threatened the assassination of Karenga by Panther Party members, the tensions between the two groups escalated to the point that violence was almost certain and clearly imminent. On January 17, 1969, a shootout between US and Panther members led to the deaths of two LA Panther leaders—John Huggins and Alprentice "Bunchy" Carter. This shootout proved the undoing of the Black Congress, which was effectively defunct by spring 1969, and the US-Panther divide continued.

As a result of the protracted conflict between the two organizations, the Panthers and the FBI generated a number of myths about Karenga and US. Among these myths was the notion that Karenga was a paid agent or informant of the United States government and that he was a diagnosed paranoid schizophrenic. Karenga and US were not without blame as a number of their actions between 1969 and 1971 discredited the organization and its leader. Karenga's meeting with LA Police Chief Thomas Reddin soon after the assassination of Dr. Martin Luther King Jr. to apparently head off and prevent black rioting, demonstrated a willingness to work with the white power structure in ways that may not have matched his rhetoric. Moreover, Karenga agreed to meet with then Governor Ronald Reagan that only added to the claims that he and his organization were willingly working with the agents of repression and reaction.

By late 1969, internal FBI memos point to a 50 percent decline in membership in the US Organization and the San Diego branch completely broke away as a direct result of COINTELPRO operations. Then, in 1971, Karenga and two others were convicted for felony assault and false imprisonment in the brutal torture of two female US members—Deborah Jones and Gail Davis. The group went into hiatus until Karenga was released from prison on parole in 1975. From 1975 until the present, US has begun to slowly rebuild alliances and develop Afrocentric educational programs and institutions. Currently, US maintains the African American Cultural Center, the Kawaida School of African American Culture, an independent cultural school for children, the Kawaida Institute of Pan-African Studies, and the University of Sankore Press. After earning a PhD from USC, Karenga's activism and influence has helped popularize Black Studies while he taught at a variety of universities across southern California, including a recent stint as department chair of Black Studies at California State University-Long Beach. In addition to *Kwanzaa* and *Nguzo Saba,* the movements to create Black Student Unions and Black Studies departments can be seen as legacies, in part, of the US Organization and its cultural nationalist agenda.

See also: Afrocentricity; Black Panther Party; Black Power; COINTELPRO; Karenga, Maulana; Kwanzaa

Walter C. Rucker

Bibliography

Brown, Scot. *Fighting for US: Maulana Karenga, The US Organization, and Black Cultural Nationalism.* New York: New York University Press, 2003.

Brown, Scot. "The US Organization, Black Power Vanguard Politics, and the United Front Ideal: Los Angeles and Beyond." *Black Scholar* 31 (2001):21–30.

Brown, Scot. "The US Organization, Maulana Karenga, and Conflict with the Panther Party: A Critique of Sectarian Influences on Historical Discourse." *Journal of Black Studies* 28 (1997):157–70.

Hayes III, Floyd W., and Judson L. Jeffries. "Us Does Not Stand for United Slaves!" In *Black Power in the Belly of the Beast,* Judson L. Jeffries, ed., 67–92. Chicago: University of Illinois Press, 2006.

Karenga, Maulana. "Kawaida and Its Critics: A Sociohistorical Analysis." *Journal of Black Studies* 8 (1977):125–48.

Warren, Nagueyalti. "Pan-African Cultural Movements: From Baraka to Karenga." *Journal of Negro History* 75 (Winter/Spring 1990):16–27.

Vietnam War (Black Participation in)

The Vietnam War, in which the United States was involved from 1945 to 1975, was the first American war to be fought with a completely desegregated military. Throughout the course of the war, African American attitudes would shift from viewing the military as a valuable path to respectability and prosperity to viewing it as a racist institution complicit with the oppression of blacks in America. Although the military was officially desegregated, racism among white officers and troops and institutionalized discrimination against African Americans combined with changes in black consciousness on the home front to produce an unprecedented level of racial conflict between black and white service members. During the course of the war in Vietnam, the military would also see the rise of radical black organizations composed of African Americans in the armed forces. These organizations played an important role in the GI movement against the war, itself a key element in the United States' withdrawal of combat troops.

American involvement in Vietnam began in 1945, when American naval ships aided the French in their reconquest of the country; however, significant numbers of combat troops did not reach Vietnam until 1964. At this time, large numbers of African Americans had a positive view of the military, stemming from several factors. First, drawing on a long tradition in black political thought, many argued that service in the armed forces was incontestable proof of black loyalty and entitlement to equal rights. Second, the military offered steady work at pay rates, which were often hard for African Americans to find in the civilian sector. The bonuses accruing to combat troops also help explain the high rates of black reenlistment and volunteering for combat duty during the war's early years. Finally, many African Americans joined the military out of a sense of patriotic duty to the United States.

Despite this goodwill, there were signs even during this early phase of the war that the military reproduced the racism of the larger U.S. society. Until the late 1960s, African Americans faced casualty rates disproportionate to their numbers in the armed services as a whole. Part of this disproportion is attributable to African Americans volunteering for combat duty as described previously, but a significant portion is traceable to racism in the military. African Americans often found it harder to win conscientious objector status (which exempted the recipient from combat duty) than whites. The widespread stereotype of African Americans as criminals led many draft boards to deny black draftee's profession of pacifism, and members of the Nation of Islam found that draft boards simply refused to treat their faith as a real religion. These draft boards were locally controlled, and typically composed white businessmen; in some cases, open Ku Klux Klan members headed local boards. African Americans also found themselves drafted in disproportionate numbers, as lower average incomes meant far fewer black families could afford to send their children to college and earn a student deferment.

The draft had a far different impact in black communities than in white ones. Children from white families with means and a good chance of success in civilian life generally escaped the draft. By contrast, the racism of the draft boards combined with widespread poverty in the black community meant that those drafted were much more likely to be upwardly mobile than their white counterparts. Many civil rights workers, for example, found themselves at the unfriendly attention of a local draft board, prompting Whitney Young and other black leaders to characterize the draft as a weapon against civil rights struggle.

Once inside the military, African Americans faced further discrimination. The test by which various branches of the military assigned service members to their positions, the Armed Forces Qualification Test (AFQT), was heavily biased toward whites. Because African American serving in Vietnam had often attended underfunded or segregated schools, they faced a marked disadvantage on the AFQT when compared with whites. Also, black sociologists argued that the AFQT was culturally biased toward European Americans (when the AFQT was replaced by a more culturally neutral test in 1973, black scores rose dramatically while white scores remained unchanged). As a result of their lower test scores, African Americans were often assigned to combat rather than positions like engineering or communications.

U.S. Army soldiers fire at a suspected Viet Cong position during a search-and-destroy mission. (National Archives)

Although black support for the military generally remained high during the war's early years, there were a few visible exceptions. The most important was Muhammad Ali's 1966 refusal to be drafted. Ali had caught the attention of his draft board in 1964, but he failed the reading and writing portion of the induction test. In 1966, however, the military revised its standards, and Ali became eligible to serve. Informed of the news, he made his now famous declaration that no Viet Cong had ever called him "nigger." Ali was stripped of his boxing title and charged with a felony for his refusal (the Supreme Court reversed his conviction in 1971). His linkage of the war with American racism, although isolated at the time, would become a touchstone for young African Americans opposing the war.

Part of the reason Ali's voice would prove to be prophetic was black soldiers' experiences in Vietnam. Black GIs found that in addition to disproportionate casualty rates, they also had to deal with racial friction with white service members. Although combat could be a situation in which racial tensions from back home were overcome, the situation outside the field was far different. On base, black soldiers faced the hostility of white officer corps, whose discretion in matters of military justice often weighed heavily against African Americans. Off base, local entertainment facilities such as bars or brothels were frequently segregated as rigorously as public facilities in the deep South.

Some of the worst instances of racial conflict took place between black and white enlisted personnel. The complete desegregation of the military, by allowing far greater contact between black and white soldiers, vastly increased the potential for racial conflict. The sources of tension were many. One of the most commonly cited was music programming. Whereas black soldiers wanted soul music on armed forces radio and in base recreational clubs, older white soldiers fought to keep country and western instead. Another source of friction was "dapping," the intricate handshakes that were developed primarily by black soldiers. The term originated in the Vietnamese word *dep,* meaning beautiful. Daps became a creative means by which black soldiers could express solidarity in the armed forces. The gestures involved could be quite complex and time consuming, and dapping in the chow line became a frequent source of tension between black and white soldiers. More generally, many whites resented the cliquishness they perceived in the practice.

Black soldiers also had to deal with the enemy in a different manner than whites. The National Liberation Front and the Democratic Republic of Vietnam were highly adept at using American racism as a weapon in the propaganda war. The Vietnamese left pamphlets informing black soldiers that they would not be hurt if they did not attack the Vietnamese. Numerous soldiers recounted stories of being found by Vietnamese forces and left uninjured. Even more devastating to black soldiers' morale were the leaflets the Vietnamese dropped that asked black soldiers why they fought for a country that lynched them. The greatest blow came when the military withheld news of Dr. Martin Luther King Jr.'s assassination out of fear of its effects on black soldiers. Instead, they were left to learn of the murder from Vietnamese.

King's death marked the moment when black support for Vietnam began dropping precipitously. In 1966, two-thirds of black soldiers reenlisted. By 1970, less than 13 percent would. The experience of racism in the armed forces, the revolution in black consciousness at home, King's assassination, and the Tet Offensive's exposure of American military vulnerability all combined to drastically change black perceptions of the military.

One sign that black soldiers were not as pleased with the military as they had been in the past was the sharp increase in racial violence. From 1968 onwards, the armed services were plagued with violence between white and black soldiers. Dr. King's assassination was one of the earliest sparks for this violence. Some white soldiers openly celebrated King's murder. At the Naval Headquarters Building in Cam Ranh Bay, whites hoisted a confederate flag over the base when they heard the news. Black grief and anger over the assassination often translated into a refusal to accept further racist treatment in the military. Violence between black and white soldiers spread throughout the military, and soon reports of incidents were coming in from all over the world, from Vietnam to bases in Germany to training camps in the United States.

The growing manifestations of black anger were intimately linked with the rise in black political militancy inside the armed forces. As the civilian antiwar movement grew in size after 1968, it found a counterpart inside the military. Black soldiers played a key role in this movement. Several large antiwar GI groups, the Movement for a Democratic Military, GIs United Against the War, and the American Servicemen's Union, had significant black membership. Other groups, like the Black Berets and the Malcolm X Society, were entirely black. Even largely white groups like

Vietnam Veterans Against the War, the largest GI antiwar group, paid special attention to racism in the military as a result of the organizing done by black soldiers.

The rise of a politically radical black antiwar movement in the military contributed to the larger breakdown of the American military in Vietnam. Given the disproportionate presence of black soldiers in combat units, their radicalization had a relatively larger effect on combat units than that of white GIs. In the I Corps (the army corps stationed at the northern edge of South Vietnam, where the fighting was the most intense), racial conflict and demonstrations by black soldiers were nearly constant after a fight between black and white soldiers in 1970. Military police found that large numbers of soldiers were carrying illegal weapons to defend themselves against attacks by other GIs. Black GIs' refusal to accept racist treatment meant that the American military could not continue functioning as it had.

Military officials reacted with panic to the rise of black radicalism inside the ranks. In 1970, Commander George L. Jackson published his article "Constraints of the Negro Civil Rights Movement on American Military Effectiveness." Jackson argued that Dr. King's stand against the war in 1967 and increasing use of the American military in peacekeeping operations at home threatened the morale of black soldiers and reduced American military effectiveness. In response, he advocated increased sensitivity to black grievances.

Department of Defense officials implemented a whole host of reforms in response to the rise of black militancy. In 1970, the Defense Department instituted an aggressive affirmative action program. In 1971, they opened the Defense Race Relations Institute in Florida to monitor racial tension in the military and encourage equal treatment by officers. As mentioned earlier, the culturally biased Armed Forces Qualification test was removed in favor of the Army Classification Battery. In addition to these ameliorative programs, the military began quietly moving black troops away from the front in hopes of restoring military effectiveness. By 1972, African Americans accounted for only 7.6 percent of annual American casualties.

The shifting of black soldiers away from the front occurred simultaneously with the larger American troop withdrawal from Vietnam. Once back in the United States, black veterans found themselves with an entirely new set of problems. Their unemployment rate was about 1 in 3, whereas white veterans had a rate of 1 in 20. Black veterans also found themselves incarcerated at disproportionate rates. A 1976 Veterans Administration study found that veterans made up a quarter of the prison population, and half of all imprisoned veterans were black.

Thirty years after the end of the Vietnam War, its effects are still being felt in black America. The epidemic of black veteran homelessness and poverty continues. The shift to an all-volunteer military, partially in response to the troop rebellion in Vietnam, has meant increased attention by recruiters to low-income minority communities. In turn, the armed services have used black soldiers as a signifier of the progressive, diverse nature of the American military. Far from heralding the end of the tangle of race and the military, Vietnam signaled an era in which the two would be more visibly linked than ever.

See also: Ali, Muhammad; Black Power; King, Martin Luther Jr.; Student Nonviolent Coordinating Committee; Students for a Democratic Society; X, Malcolm

Paul M. Heideman

Bibliography

Allen, Joe. *Vietnam: The (Last) War the U.S. Lost.* Chicago: Haymarket Books, 2008.

Cortright, David. *Soldiers in Revolt: GI Resistance During the Vietnam War.* Chicago: Haymarket Books, 2005.

Gettleman, Marvin E. et al., eds. *Vietnam and America: A Documented History.* New York: Grove Press, 1995.

Terry, Wallace. *Bloods: An Oral History of the Vietnam War.* New York: Random House, 1984.

Westheider, James E. *Fighting on Two Fronts: African Americans and the Vietnam War.* New York: New York University Press, 1997.

Voting Rights Act of 1965

In July 1964, President Lyndon Johnson signed in the Civil Rights Act, which contained some voting-related provisions. Title I condemned state discrimination in voter registration. The bill prompted outrage from conservative white southerners, who were only slightly mollified that it was signed by a Texan. Yet many in the African American community criticized the act as well, feeling that it had not gone far enough. Just as the Fourteenth Amendment of 1868 had failed to secure full legal rights for freed slaves, so the 1964 Civil Rights Act did not ensure the voting rights of African Americans. Recognizing this, Johnson followed the Civil Rights Act with a bill on voting rights, in an echo of Congress's actions in ratifying the Fifteenth Amendment in 1870 to prevent restriction of the ballot on the basis of race.

Existing federal antidiscrimination laws had not been sufficient to overcome state officials' resistance to the Fifteenth Amendment. Even after passage of the Enforcement Act of 1870 and the Force Act of 1871, black citizens encountered strong resistance to their enfranchisement. White supremacist groups practiced violent intimidation and election districts were gerrymandered. In the 1890s, some states enacted disenfranchising laws: poll taxes, literacy tests, and disqualification for "crimes of moral turpitude." By 1910, nearly all black citizens in the former Confederate states were disenfranchised, and in 1965 only a third of eligible African Americans (compared to two-thirds of eligible whites) were registered in these states. Literacy tests and poll taxes kept black voting registration low, especially in Mississippi, Alabama, and Louisiana. Only 6 percent of eligible black citizens were registered in Mississippi.

Johnson began work on the new bill in the fall of 1964, right after "Freedom Summer," which saw three voter registration volunteers murdered in Mississippi. The FBI declared that local law enforcement officials were involved in the murders. He announced the bill in his State of the Union address of January 1965, and on March 15, 1965, he gave a speech to Congress on voting rights. The speech, titled "The American Promise," pointed to the unkept promises of the Declaration of Independence and the Emancipation Proclamation, then heralded the civil rights protest as the driving force behind the new legislation. There would have been no progress, Johnson said, were it not for the faith and bravery of black campaigners. He quoted the anthem of the Civil Rights movement, a freedom song titled "We shall overcome."

On August 5, Congress passed Johnson's bill, which was the most comprehensive voting rights legislation to date. Section 2 followed the language of the Fifteenth Amendment: "No voting qualification or prerequisite to voting, or standard, practice, or procedure shall be imposed or applied

President Lyndon B. Johnson moves to shake hands with Dr. Martin Luther King Jr. in the Capitol rotunda following the signing of the Voting Rights Act on August 6, 1965. The law was the first national legislation to guarantee all Americans the right to vote. (Yoichi R. Okamoto/Lyndon B. Johnson Library)

by any State or political subdivision to deny or abridge the right of any citizen of the United States to vote on account of race or color." Section 4 ended the use of literacy requirements for voting in Alabama, Georgia, Louisiana, Mississippi, South Carolina, and Virginia, and many North Carolina counties. The bill also provided for unprecedented federal intervention. It authorized the attorney general to appoint federal voting examiners and decreed that the Justice Department would take control of the registration process if any county failed to register 50 percent of eligible black voters. It did not prohibit the poll tax, instead directing the attorney general to challenge its use, but in 1966 the Supreme Court found Virginia's poll tax to be unconstitutional under the Fourteenth Amendment.

After his voting rights speech, Johnson went on to express support for equal outcomes policies. On June 4, 1965, he gave an address at Howard University titled "To Fulfill These Rights." In language that would later be used by affirmative action advocates, he told the graduating students: "You do not take a person who, for years, has been hobbled by chains and liberate him, bring him up to the starting line of a race and then say, 'you are free to compete with all the others,' and still justly believe that you have been completely fair" (*Freedom Is Not Enough*, p. 16). It was not enough, Johnson explained, just to open the gates of opportunity. Citizens needed the ability to walk *through*.

Nonetheless, the act did have an impact. Most southern states opened voter registration lists to black citizens and control passed to the Justice Department in the 62 counties that remained resistant. In Mississippi, black voting enrollment went from 6 percent to 44 percent by 1968. Johnson's bill was extended in 1970, again in 1975 (when it was amended to protect language minority citizens from voting discrimination), and again in 1982. On January 20, 2001, ahead of the Shadow Inauguration, some 2000 people marched to the Supreme Court and took a vow to uphold Johnson's Voting Rights Act.

See also: Disfranchisement; Grandfather Clause; Johnson, Lyndon Baines; Literacy Tests; National Association for the Advancement of Colored People; Selma March; Student Nonviolent Coordinating Committee

Zoe Trodd

Bibliography
Branch, Taylor. *Pillar of Fire: America in the King Years, 1963–65.* New York: Simon & Schuster, 1998.

Garrow, David J. *Protest at Selma: Martin Luther King, Jr. and the Voting Rights Act of 1965.* New Haven, CT: Yale University Press, 1978.
Kotz, Nick. *Judgment Days: Lyndon Baines Johnson, Martin Luther King Jr., and the Laws That Changed America.* New York: Houghton Mifflin, 2005.
Walters, Ronald W. *Freedom Is Not Enough: Black Voters, Black Candidates, and American Presidential Politics.* Lanham, MD: Rowman and Littlefield, 2007.

Walker, Alice

Alice Walker (1944–), an African American writer, is most famous for the novel *The Color Purple*. Walker was born in the small town of Eatonton, Georgia to sharecroppers, Willie Lee Walker and Minnie Tallulah Grant Walker. The youngest child of eight, she had five brothers and two sisters. In 1952, she was accidentally shot in the right eye with a BB gun by her older brother during a game of Cowboys and Indians. She never fully recovered and was left partially blind in that eye. With her loss of sight in her eye, she lost confidence. Walker grew depressed and as she frequently contemplated suicide, she used writing as an outlet for her emotional pain.

After reconstructive surgery to her eye, at 14, she eventually gained back some confidence, becoming prom queen and graduating valedictorian from high school, before going on to college via scholarships. She attended Spelman College in Atlanta, Georgia from 1961–1963 and graduated from Sarah Lawrence College in Yonkers, New York, in 1965. Before leaving Spelman College, she was an activist in the Civil Rights movement. In 1964, as a senior at Sarah Lawrence College, she wrote her first book, *Once*, a collection of essays. Also during 1964, Walker discovered she was pregnant. Before terminating her pregnancy, she grew more depressed. Considering suicide, she continued to turn to writing to channel her emotions, and with the help of her teacher, Muriel Ruykeyser, she published, in 1965, *To Hell with Dying*.

After college, she moved to New York, to work for the welfare system. She soon after returned to the South to continue participating in the Civil Rights movement. In 1966, she taught black studies and writing in many universities throughout Mississippi. In 1968, *Once* was eventually published.

In 1966, while in Mississippi, she met Melvyn Rosenman Leventhal, an attorney, who was also an activist in civil rights. The pair married in March 1967, but there was much controversy over the interracial match, which was the only one in Mississippi, at that time. Soon after she became writer-in-residence at Tougaloo College, and in 1972 taught at Wellesley College, where she began one of the first "Gender Studies" courses in the country. While looking for course material, she was greatly influenced by the work of Zora Neale Hurston. In 1974, Walker became a fiction editor of *Ms.* magazine, and, in 1975, she published an article that brought restored awareness to Zora Neal Hurston's work.

In 1976, after nine years of marriage, Leventhal and Walker divorced. They had a daughter, Rebecca Walker, who is a feminist like her mother. Soon after her divorce from Leventhal, she fell in love Robert Allen, a colleague and editor of *Black Scholar.* Four years later, in 1978, Walker moved to San Francisco's Japantown, where she still lives today.

Walker's work includes poems, stories, essays, criticism, and novels, but she is most widely known for her third novel, *The Color Purple,* published in 1982. This novel won the National Book Award in 1983, and in the same year she became the first African American woman to win a Pulitzer Prize for fiction. In 1988, it was made into a Steven Spielberg motion picture, casting Oprah Winfrey and Whoopi Goldberg. *The Color Purple* depicts discrimination against African American woman in a sexist and racist society. The novel caused some controversy because of Walker's negative portrayals of men as sexist, abusers, and rapists through its depiction of socially oppressed, African American women who rise above discrimination through their female relationships. The major theme in the novel is womanhood, focusing on African American women, their interactions with men who abuse them, and how these women relate to one another. The novel's subordinate themes include self-discovery and growth, which is developed in letters exchanged between Celie and Nettie, two sisters, and in letters Celie addresses to God tell the story. In the spring of 1982, because of *The Color Purple's* success, Walker was offered a position as a professor at the University of California at Berkeley. She also went on to work at Brandeis University the following fall.

Her other works include novels *The Third Life of Grange Copeland* (1970), *Meridian* (1976), *By the Light of My Father's Smile* (1994), and *Now Is the Time to Open Your Heart* (2004). *The Temple of My Familiar* (1989) and *Possessing the Secret of Joy* (1992) are novels about female circumcision in Africa. Volumes of her poetry include *Once* (1968),

Alice Walker, celebrated author, womanist, and social activist. (AP/ Wide World Photos)

Revolutionary Petunias and Other Poems (1973), and *Goodnight, Willie Lee, I'll See You in the Morning* (1979). Walker's nonfiction essay collection includes *In Search of Our Mothers' Gardens: Womanist Prose* (1983) and *Living by the Word* (1988), where Walker defines "womanist" a term she uses for the black feminist, and *Anything We Love Can Be Saved* (1997). Her short-story collection includes *In Love & Trouble: Stories of Black Women* (1973), *You Can't Keep a Good Woman Down* (1981), and the partially autobiographical *Her Blue Body Everything We Know: Earthling Poems 1965–1990* (1991), *The Way Forward Is with a Broken Heart* (2000), and *Absolute Trust in the Goodness of the Earth* (2003). Her most recent work, *Sent by Earth: A Message from the Grandmother Spirit After the Bombing of the World Trade Center and the Pentagon,* was written in response to New York City's World Trade Center tragedy. *See also:* Hurston, Zora Neale; King, Martin Luther Jr.

Nicole Joy DeCarlo

Bibliography

Banks, Erma Davis, and Keith Byerman. *Alice Walker: An Annotated Bibliography, 1968–1986.* New York: Garland, 1989.

Butler-Evans, Elliott. *Race, Gender, and Desire: Narrative Strategies in the Fiction of Tini Cade Bambara, Toni Morrison, and Alice Walker.* Philadelphia: Temple University Press, 1989.

Gates, Henry L., ed. *Alice Walker: Critical Perspectives, Past and Present.* New York: Amistad, 1993.

Howard, Lillie P., ed. *Alice Walker and Zora Neale Hurston: The Common Bond.* Westport, CT: Greenwood Press, 1993.

Lauret, Maria. *Alice Walker.* New York: Palgrave Macmillan, 2000.

White, Evelyn C. *Alice Walker: A Life.* New York: W. W. Norton, 2004.

War on Poverty

The War on Poverty was declared by Lyndon Johnson in his State of the Union address in 1964. It was a critical component of his larger vision of a Great Society and was intended to expand the reach of government to improve life for all Americans. At the time, approximately 35 million Americans lived in poverty. Moreover, the Civil Rights movement and events such as the *Brown v. Board of Education* decision, the Montgomery bus boycott, the decision to send federal troops to enforce desegregation at Central High School in Little Rock, and the Birmingham, Harlem, and Watts "riots" all highlighted previously unacknowledged links between race, poverty, and opportunity.

Ideologically, the War on Poverty was a progressive campaign drawn from the belief that the causes of poverty were a systemic lack of opportunity. Only government leadership directed toward changing the structures of opportunity that kept people impoverished could defeat the problem. In this way, Johnson's ideas aligned themselves with the liberal tradition of Franklin Delano Roosevelt and his New Deal.

For the War on Poverty to be fully implemented, all branches of government had to work together. For Johnson, this commitment was the only way to solve America's problems. Thus, the Economic Opportunity Act (EOA) required federal, state, and local participation and was designed to mobilize the resources of the country to address the numerous challenges it faced. The aim was not merely to expand old programs or improve what is already being done, but to chart a new course and address the cause of poverty, thereby eliminating it. The EOA was committed to lowering barriers to political participation, employment, housing, and education for African Americans. It also proposed economic development programs for America's cities and towns. Johnson subsequently established the Office of Economic Opportunity (OEO) as the legislative site with responsibility for administering War on Poverty programs. Some of the programs were Head Start, the Community Action Program, the Job Corps, food stamps, work study, Medicare/Medicaid, Volunteers in Service to America (VISTA), Upward Bound, comprehensive health services, family planning, emergency food and medical services, Senior Opportunity Services, and legal services. The OEO reported directly to the president. It existed from 1964 to 1973. Between the time of its inception in 1964 and its demise in 1973, social welfare spending increased from $75 billion to $185 billion. In terms of percent, spending increased ~4.6 percent between 1950 and 1965 and ~7.2 percent between 1965 and 1976.

OEO was officially disbanded in 1973 by President Richard Nixon. Responsibility for its many social welfare programs was transferred to the newly established Community Services Administration (CSA) in the Department of Health and Human Services. CSA received little support from President Carter and was finally dismantled by the Reagan administration in 1981. Between 1964 and 1973, however, the impact of the War on Poverty was such that it was impossible for government to embrace any new initiative without being asked, "How does it help the poor?"

Looking back, the results of the Great Society and its War on Poverty were less than hoped for. There are several explanations for its limited effectiveness. The first was funding. As military engagement in the Vietnam War escalated and thoughts of how to extricate U.S. troops occupied more of the nation's attention, the OEO received less of the funding it needed to carry out the programs it proposed. Local areas that had responsibility for many medical, emergency food, and legal services found themselves with little money to continue. Programs funded at the federal level (e.g., Head Start) remained intact but suffered under the weight of diminishing resources.

A second explanation was ideological. Four concerns have been cited. First, there was the split between those who viewed welfare as social insurance and those who saw it as public assistance. Second, there were those who claimed that the War on Poverty was unwilling to attribute the cause of poverty to the American economic system. Accordingly, the result was superficial, Band-aid solutions. Although opportunities were created, structural inequalities were untouched. Third, many claim that the attention given to black America created a racial backlash. The white middle class felt that it was footing the bill for ever-increasing services to the poor and as the economy declined during the 1970s, many whites lost sympathy for Great Society programs. Finally, women also felt they had been ignored. Despite the fact that the majority of positions (e.g., community aide, community worker, and parent aide) were filled by women, the OEO held the traditional view that women's work was voluntary, unpaid labor. Strategies for preventing poverty focused on expanding employment opportunities for poor men and neglected the actual contributions of women as staff members and administrators.

Today, of the many Great Society programs, most support remains for Medicare, which serves the elderly, and for Head Start, which serves the youngest of the poor. The basic assumption of the Great Society—that government must take the leadership in reducing poverty—has been replaced by the 1990s belief that government support for the poor leads to dependency and undermines the work ethic. Whereas the Great Society emphasized the institutional and structural roots of poverty, contemporary poverty policy focuses on the individual behaviors and choices of people who are poor.

See also: Johnson, Lyndon Baines; Kerner Commission Report; Long Hot Summer Riots, 1965–1967; Urban Ghetto

Rickie Sanders

Bibliography

Clark, Robert. *The War on Poverty: History, Selected Programs, and On-going Impact.* Lanham, MD: University Press of America, 2002.

Harrington, Michael. *The Other America, Poverty in the United States.* New York: Touchstone, 1962.

Haveman, Robert. *A Decade of Federal Antipoverty Programs: Achievements, Failures, and Lessons.* New York: Academic Press, 1977.

Katz, Michael. *In the Shadow of the Poorhouse: A Social History of Welfare in America.* New York: Basic Books, 1996.

Ware, Bill

William "Bill" Ware (1935–) was born in Cannonsburg, Mississippi. At the age of six, he and his family moved to the small rural town of Stanton, Mississippi, 12 miles outside of Natchez. There Ware received his grade school education, first in a dilapidated one-room schoolhouse where two teachers, but most often one teacher, provided instruction for eight grades of students and later at a local Catholic school named Holy Garden, which he attended for high school. As a young child raised during the height of the Great Depression, Ware's parents and paternal grandparents stressed the importance of education. Although both had little formal education, they understood its value and instilled its importance into their children. Named after his paternal grandfather who labored as a sharecropper, Ware adopted many of his esteemed characteristics and saw education as a tool to improve not only his personal lot but also his community's condition. As a result, he developed a fondness for learning and, as time went on, excelled academically.

In 1950, Ware entered high school at Holy Garden where he gradually became known for his outstanding academic achievements. His hard work would eventually earn him a citizenship award and, most important, a scholarship to attend St. John's University, an all-male, predominantly white, Catholic school in Minnesota. In the fall of 1954, Ware left the humid confines of the Magnolia state for the cold terrain of Minnesota. Although Ware had a full tuition scholarship, he did not have much money to cover living expenses; in fact, he arrived to campus with only $35. Because of his financial straits, he quickly found work at the school cafeteria as a dishwasher and enrolled in St. John's ROTC program to cover his living expenses. Although lack of money at times proved challenging, Ware also had to confront the North's racism. Ware was no stranger to racial bigotry, having been fed a steady diet from Mississippi's white supremacist menu, but it still proved challenging. As time went on, however, he developed several amicable relationships with his white counterparts.

Once Ware became settled, he pursued a degree in English and became involved in various extracurricular activities such as the Young Christian Students Organization in addition to writing for the school newspaper. His involvement in these endeavors proved to be critical to his development as a person and as a student, but they would pale in comparison to something that occurred during his junior year. In 1957, Ware witnessed a transformative event in the form of Ghana's declaration of independence in March of the same year. Not only did Ghana provide people of African descent with a tangible model for liberation, it gave many African people great hope and enormous psychological upliftment. Moreover, Ghana's independence countered the myriad racist images of Africa and her descendants, and the notions of buffoonery and anti-intellectualism that whites commonly associated with African-descended people throughout the world. Ghana's independence quickly resonated with Ware, as it did with countless people of African descent, and it piqued his interest in one day visiting the coastal West African country. This sojourn would have to wait almost five years. In the meantime, Ware graduated with a bachelors of arts in English in the spring of 1958, and, in October 1960, his obligation to the military ended. In January 1961, he embarked on a brief term as a history teacher at a local high school in Minneapolis.

After his stint as a history teacher ended, Ware joined the Peace Corps in 1962. Admittedly, he notes that he primarily joined the organization after he learned that members had the option to travel to Ghana. After joining the Peace Corps, he became enamored with the teachings of black sociologist St. Clair Drake, who developed one of the first African studies programs in the United States and helped train Peace Corps volunteers. While in Ghana, Ware quickly absorbed Ghana's first Prime Minister Kwame Nkrumah's teachings of black nation-building and Pan-Africanism. He soon embraced the idea of uniting African people worldwide, as well as certain elements of cultural nationalism such as wearing African garb and adopting African names. In June1963, he returned to the United States to work with the Student Nonviolent Coordinating Committee (SNCC) in Mississippi shortly after white supremacist Byron De La Beckwith assassinated NAACP field secretary Medgar Evers. In 1964, after a brief stint in Minnesota on a SNCC fundraising trip, he returned to the South to become a full-time worker within the organization.

In the fall of 1965 en route to a civil rights workshop in Frogmore, South Carolina at the behest of civil rights activist Septima Clark, Ware became aware of the Georgia State Legislature's refusal to seat former SNCC member and legislator-elect Julian Bond because of his unwavering support of SNCC's statement against the Vietnam War. The news immediately created great shock and anger within the black community. As such, Ware did not see the value of attending a civil rights workshop in South Carolina if Bond could not take his seat in Atlanta. He immediately decided to go to Atlanta, where he and a small number of SNCC members urged James Forman, SNCC's executive secretary, to organize a group that would galvanize the residents of Bond's Vine City district in support of him. Thus, in February 1966, SNCC established the Atlanta Vine City Project under the direction of Bill Ware and Gwendolyn Robinson in which both served as co-directors.

Although the Atlanta Project engaged in numerous grassroots organizing activities, it is most commonly known for the release of the black power position paper. In March 1966, project members Michael Simmons, Ronald Snellings, and Ware wrote and released a position paper that called for, among other things, the outright expulsion of whites from the organization. The paper immediately generated tremendous controversy, and, although both black and white SNCC members believed the paper to be anti-white and counterproductive, its black nationalist and Pan-Africanist threads resonated with many within SNCC. The release of the position paper came at a critical time when SNCC members constantly debated the role of whites and the organization's ideological and tactical direction. Before the position paper's release, SNCC organizers discussed white participation only in small circles. The position paper created space for the open discussion of this question, led to the outright expulsion of whites from SNCC in December of 1966, and in turn pushed the organization towards black nationalism and black power. Thus the Atlanta Project's position paper played a critical role in the emergence of the Black Power movement.

Ultimately ideological and tactical conflicts plagued the relationship between the Atlanta Project and SNCC's national leadership throughout most of the branch's one-year existence. At the beginning of 1967, SNCC's national leadership effectively disbanded the Atlanta Project as a result of a dispute over a SNCC-owned vehicle. This marked the end of the Atlanta Project and left a tremendous grassroots organizing void that SNCC never filled.

Bill Ware currently resides in Baton Rouge, Louisiana, where he continues to be of great service to the black community. He mentors Southern University students as well as young people in the surrounding community through his work with Bob Moses's Algebra Project and he also teaches young adults how to play chess.

See also: Black Nationalism; Black Power; Nkrumah, Kwame; Student Nonviolent Coordinating Committee

Jason M. Perkins

Bibliography

Carson, Clayborne. *In Struggle: SNCC and the Black Awakening of the 1960s.* Cambridge, MA: Harvard University Press, 1981.

Forman, James. *The Making of Black Revolutionaries.* New York: Macmillan, 1972.

Grady-Willis, Winston A. *Challenging U.S. Apartheid: Atlanta and Black Struggles for Human Rights, 1960–1977.* Durham, NC: Duke University Press, 2006.

Harmon, David Andrew. *Beneath the Image of the Civil Rights Movement and Race Relations: Atlanta, Georgia, 1946–1981.* New York: Garland Publishing, 1996.

Jeffries, Hasan, Kwame. "SNCC, Black Power, and Independent Political Party Organizing in Alabama, 1964–1966." *Journal of African American History.* 92, no. 2 (Spring 2006):171–206.

King, Mary. *Freedom Song: A Personal Story of the 1960s Civil Rights Movement.* New York: William Morrow, 1987.

Lewis, John, and Michael D'Orso. *Walking with the Wind: A Memoir of the Movement.* New York: Harcourt Brace, 1998.

Ogbar, Jeffrey O. G. *Black Power: Radical Politics and African American Identity.* Baltimore: The John Hopkins University Press, 2004.

Perkins, Jason, M. "The Atlanta Vine City Project, SNCC, and Black Power, 1965–1967." Unpublished Thesis, The Ohio State University, 2008.

Sellers, Cleveland. *The River of No Return: The Autobiography of a Black Militant and the Life and Death of SNCC.* New York: William Morrow, 1973.

Washington, Booker T.

As a former slave, coal miner, and educator, Booker Taliaferro Washington (1856–1915) lifted himself up out of the lowest levels of poverty and oppression to represent and advocate a distinctive approach to improving race relations in the U.S. South. He insisted that African Americans must begin forging their own pathway to equality through work, determination, skills development, and education. For Washington, self-sufficiency was the key attribute that would facilitate legal and social reform. He led by example, creating and building the preeminent center for educating African Americans following emancipation—the Tuskegee Institute. Located in the heart of the former Confederacy, in Tuskegee, Alabama, many African Americans such as George Washington Carver and the "Tuskegee Airmen" benefited from Washington's work.

Washington possessed the gift of tenacity, a virtue that helped lift him out of the ignorant, oppressive condition of slavery and into the respected role as a professor and founder of Tuskegee Institute. The opportunity for an education and social advancement for African Americans during Reconstruction in the South was limited at best; poverty and oppression, however, failed to deter his overwhelming desire to obtain an education and help improve the conditions of his race.

Washington believed that regardless of race, if an individual performed with a high degree of skill in his or her profession, whatever it may be, then that individual would eventually become recognized and given an equal place in society. He publicly elaborated this creed in an address delivered at the 1895 Cotton States International Exposition in Atlanta, Georgia. In what would become known as the "Atlanta Compromise," Washington told African Americans to "cast down your bucket where you are," as he urged them to learn useful skills and perform them so well that they would become invaluable partners with their white neighbors. The address greatly increased his popularity among white southerners; however, he received considerable opposition from many of his African American colleagues, most notably W. E. B. Du Bois.

Washington's life and struggle was testimony to the benefits of hard work and determination. Born into slavery near Hale's Ford, in Franklin County, Virginia on April 5, 1856, he lived the earliest part of his life toiling in slave labor. Just as he was unable to control the conditions into which he was born, he was also unable to control the conditions of his freedom, a life that included: poverty, white supremacists, and lack of opportunity for educational and social improvement. This precarious condition failed to ignite resentment or ill feelings. He knew that many people have had to struggle for freedom and prosperity, and his race would be no exception.

As a young man he recalled only two siblings and his mother. He never met his father. At a very early age he developed an appetite for knowledge. His mother helped him the only way she could by giving him a "blue-back" speller; he used the book to teach himself the alphabet. His family later moved to West Virginia, where he worked in the coal mine to earn a meager living for his family. Whenever possible, although not very often, he attended the segregated and newly formed school for blacks. The majority of his time, however, was spent in the deep, dark, coal-rich mine shafts of West Virginia.

One day while working in the mines, he overheard two of his co-workers talking about an educational facility for African Americans called Hampton Normal and Agricultural Institute located near the Tidewater area of Eastern

Booker T. Washington was the founder of the Tuskegee Institute, a leading center of African American education. (Library of Congress)

Virginia. He immediately made up his mind to attend. Upon completing the 500-mile journey to Hampton, he was given an admissions test that consisted of sweeping a room. He was aware his future depended on how well he performed the task assigned to him. He set out to make the room spotless; upon finishing, the room was inspected, and he was promptly admitted to the school.

Hampton Institute was founded in 1868 by General Samuel C. A. Armstrong, who quickly became a mentor and moral inspiration to Washington. After completing his training at Hampton, Washington devoted his time to teaching, eventually returning to Hampton to teach Indians. It was during this time that Armstrong recommended him to oversee the development of a normal school for blacks in the small southern town of Tuskegee. In June 1881 he arrived in the heart of the "Black Belt" with no place to hold classes, as he noted in *Up From Slavery,* except an old horse stable and a hen house.

Washington's autobiographical account, first published in 1901, quickly became an important and influential piece of American nonfiction literature. In clear and concise prose, he recounts episodes from his early life through his ascendance into historical prominence. In the book, Washington skillfully recalls how his character and political philosophy were shaped by his experiences and firsthand observations. He offers considerable commentary on building the school and curriculum at Tuskegee, as well as his 1895 speech in Atlanta. In print for more than a century, *Up From Slavery* continues to introduce new generations to the rewards of self-help.

Soon after his arrival in Tuskegee, Washington set out to observe the culture of the local community. After careful evaluation, he realized the enormity of his task. With this in mind Washington set an educational agenda for Tuskegee that included the basic practice of personal hygiene, the development of social manors, farming, and craftsmanship skills. The permanent site of Tuskegee Institute would be located on an abandoned plantation, about a mile outside the town. The lot was purchased for $500. Washington was innovative when it came to the construction of the buildings—the students built them. They made bricks, dug the holes, laid the foundations, all while attending classes in make-shift buildings.

In his writing, Washington reported an agreeable perception of his white neighbors. He found the citizens of Tuskegee as helpful and enthusiastic as any he had met throughout the South. He realized the importance of making the best of a difficult situation. The two races had no choice except to live together in the South, so every effort should be made to live in harmony. In fact, Washington often cited the advantages of making every effort to respectfully acquaint one's self with his or her white neighbors rather than resting their hopes on white integrationists who lived hundreds of miles to the North.

Washington, however, did not overlook the help that northerners could provide; he spent a considerable amount of time there fundraising for the school, as he traveled extensively throughout northern states in an effort to secure funds from philanthropist. During this time he was often invited to speak at engagements, an area he greatly excelled in. Although he was often very nervous, he had the ability to bring crowds to their feet. It was his gift of oratory, coupled with his conservative approach to integration, that prompted the invitation from the directors of the Atlanta

Exposition. He humbly accepted, noting in his autobiography that with the invitation to speak came much responsibility and opportunity.

As Washington rose to the platform to begin his speech in Atlanta, he stood before an overflowing and segregated crowd of onlookers. His audience was attentive as he focused on the task before him. He was completely unmoved by an insult the previous speaker launched at him. In his speech, he noted that African Americans accounted for one-third of the southern population, and that it would be unwise to ignore such a dominant constituency. He also recognized the importance of the Exposition in bridging the social gap between the races. Only three decades had passed since ratification of the Thirteenth Amendment that ended slavery. Washington believed that following the bitter American Civil War, not only did the Southern white men need time to adapt to the newly reconstructed South, but, the former slaves needed time to adapt to free life.

Washington largely ignored the social and legal oppression African Americans had suffered since 1865. He viewed the Atlanta Exposition as the beginning of a lasting friendship between the races for two reasons. First, the event planners had dedicated an entire section of the Exposition to showcase African American achievement. Second, his invitation to address a white audience on the same platform with white members was evidence that the times had drastically changed. Less than 30 years earlier, he could have been their legal property. He viewed that day as the beginning of the future as he urged members of his race to look forward instead of dwelling on the past.

Washington recalls in his autobiography that during some of his travels, he observed a church congregation consisting of a membership of just over 200 but with 18 ministers. Also, he met a family who owned a grandfather clock that they were making payments on, but no one in the family could tell time. Washington's point is that the majority of the population must make their living by working with their hands, and in the South there was much opportunity for skilled work. Frivolous ornamentation such as grandfather clocks, he felt, was a mere distraction from the important necessities of everyday life.

In his Atlanta speech, Washington made a resounding case for the white citizens of the South to accept and embrace the education of African Americans. By working together, either they can advance the nation as a whole, or, alternatively, one-third of the South's citizens can contribute

to ignorance and crime. He was not urging members of his race to accept an inferior position. He knew that the opportunity to earn a dollar must precede the opportunity to spend the dollar.

Washington's popularity greatly increased after his speech, and he became a major, but controversial, figure of history. His legacy has centered on his "Atlanta Compromise" speech, while critics largely overlook his personal achievements or his work at Tuskegee. Many viewed the compromise as accommodating. His life was testimony to the difficulties of the period. It was a transitory stage in American history. The transition, however, would evolve over many years, culminating with the Civil Rights movement in the 1960s. Washington's compromise was an initial step in that evolution. He firmly believed his race deserved full social and political equality. His insistence on individual self-improvement through education would help equip the next generation with the background they would need for direct-action, nonviolent confrontation.

Washington died in 1915 at age 59. He was buried on the grounds of the school he founded; today it is called Tuskegee University.

See also: Accommodationism; Cotton States Exposition; Du Bois, W. E. B.; Tuskegee Airmen; Tuskegee Institute

Bobby R. Holt

Bibliography

Harlan, Louis R. *Booker T. Washington: The Making of a Black Leader, 1856–1901.* New York: Oxford University Press, 1975.

Harlan, Louis R. *Booker T. Washington: The Wizard of Tuskegee, 1901–1915.* New York: Oxford University Press, 1986.

Meier, August. *Negro Thought in America, 1880–1915: Racial Ideologies in the Age of Booker T. Washington.* Ann Arbor: University of Michigan Press, 1963.

Norrell, Robert J. *Reaping the Whirlwind: The Civil Rights Movement in Tuskegee.* Chapel Hill: University of North Carolina Press, 1998.

Washington, Booker T. *Up From Slavery.* New York: Dodd, Mead, 1965.

Washington, Harold

Harold Washington (1922–1987) was an articulate and astute lawyer and elected official who served his city and constituency in numerous capacities. He deserves attention for being the first black mayor of Chicago, Illinois. Washington used his rich professional and political career to address civil liberties, civil rights, and political equity. In this way he permanently changed the political landscape of Chicago.

During the 1960s and 1970s, the Chicago Democratic Party machine controlled 35,000 jobs in the public sector and 10,000 jobs in the private sector. These jobs and control of the city's government contracts were only a small part of the patronage system in Chicago. The machine and its operatives controlled the electoral apparatus, that is, the counting and casting of ballots, determining the validity of all nominating petitions, certifying election outcome, validating the legality of voter status, and deciding when voter fraud has taken place. The influence and clout of machine politics allowed a white minority of citizens to maintain political power and privilege at the expense of black citizens and other ethnic groups.

Washington helped form a reformist coalition of all ethnic groups outside the political mainstream created by Mayor Richard J. Daley who was one of the last of the big city machine bosses. As mayor, Harold Washington set a progressive agenda for reform, which included equal treatment of all Chicago's citizens in regard to housing, jobs, and reducing the city's budget deficit. Much of his energy during his first term as mayor was spent on dealing with the resistance of the white political alliance. Before Washington could serve his second term and implement more of his progressive plans, he died on November 25, 1987, the day before Thanksgiving.

Washington was the fourth child born to Bertha and Roy Lee Washington on April 15, 1922, in Cook County Hospital, in Chicago's segregated South Side. His father was from a small town in Kentucky. He moved to Chicago and worked in a meat packing company during the day and attended law school during the night. He later became an ordained African Methodist Episcopal minister and a Democratic precinct captain concerned with recruiting voters for the Democratic Party.

He graduated from Chicago Kent College of Law two months after Washington's birth. During this same year, Roy Lee Washington Sr. passed the Illinois bar examination and opened his own law practice. Several years later, he became an assistant prosecutor for the city. His mother was a comely and vigorous lady who was aspiring to attain a career in the theater. Consequently, she left Roy Washington Sr. and their children in the summer of 1926; they were

divorced four years later. Roy was granted legal custody of their children.

Washington and his brother Edward were sent to St. Benedict The Moor, a Catholic boarding school in Milwaukee, Wisconsin. The Moor was considered perfect for the children of African American professionals; Washington remembers having sound judgment and a free spirit that was never broken by The Moor's institutionalized regimentation. Within the next 34 months, the brother ran away from school 14 times. Washington grew up around the black political elite, and by the age of 12 he was helping his father in the precinct and running errands for the Democratic Party. While attending Du Sable High School, he was known as an avid reader and a talented athlete.

In 1939, Washington dropped out of school and joined the Civilian Conservation Corps (CCC), one of Franklin Delano Roosevelt's New Deal programs that provided employment for young men in forests and fields. The CCC sent him to Michigan to do limestone quarrying and to plant evergreen trees. He was drafted into the Army Air Force when the Japanese attacked Pearl Harbor. Washington earned his high school equivalency diploma between army missions. He became a soil technician and a first sergeant while in the South Pacific.

In 1941, Washington and his girl friend, Nancy, whom he called Peaches, obtained parental permission to get married; the marriage ceremony was performed by his father in his living room. After leaving the army in 1945, Washington used his GI Bill benefits to pay for matriculation in Roosevelt University and later Northwestern University Law School. Roosevelt was one of the few racially integrated institutions of higher education. His major was political science and economics; he was a serious student who was appointed a part-time lecturer during his junior year. His classmates, 95 percent of whom were white, also elected him senior class president in 1949.

After graduation from Northwestern University Law School, Washington worked in his father's law firm. Their office was across the hall from alderman Ralph Metcalfe, a popular African American figure in the city. After his father died in 1954, Washington served as an assistant city prosecutor from 1954 to 1958. For the next six years, he was the only African American arbitrator for the Illinois Industrial Commission. He then opened a successful law practice until he decided to engage himself on a fulltime basis in Illinois politics. Washington served in the Illinois

House from 1965–1976. During this time he began to show his independence by voting against machine-supported bills and helping to organize the first black caucus for the state. Washington was concerned with attaining recognition of Martin Luther King's birthday as a statewide holiday. He also helped establish the Fair Employment Practices Commission.

After Daley died in 1976, Washington ran for mayor but garnered only 11 percent of the vote, losing even among African American voters. He then vowed to continuously challenge Chicago's Democratic Party machine. While serving in the State Senate from 1977–1980, he was nominated 11 times as one of the 10 best state legislators by his colleagues. From 1981–1983, Harold Washington was a member of the U.S. Congress. His constituency was so pleased with him that they reelected him with 92 percent of the vote. In 1983, Harold Washington became Chicago's first African American mayor. He was reelected to serve as mayor of Chicago in 1987, but tragically Washington died in office on November 25, 1987.

See also: World War II (Black Participation in)

Marva Strickland-Hill

Bibliography

Clavel, Pierre, and Wim Wiewel. *Harold Washington and the Neighborhoods: Progressive City Government in Chicago, 1983–1987.* New Brunswick, NJ: Rutgers University Press, 1991.

Kleppner, Paul. *Chicago Divided: The Making of a Black Mayor.* Dekalb: Northern Illinois University Press, 1985.

Rivlin, Gary. *Fire on the Prairie: Chicago's Harold Washington and the Politics of Race.* New York: H. Holt, 1992.

Travis, Dempsey. *"Harold": The People's Mayor: An Authorized Biography of Mayor Harold Washington.* Chicago: Urban Research Press, 1989.

Wells-Barnett, Ida

Ida B. Wells-Barnett (1862–1931) was an African American journalist, civil rights activist, and most important, an active critic of lynching in the South. She was also instrumental in aiding in women's suffrage, which ultimately ended in the passage of the Nineteenth Amendment in 1920.

In the early 1860s, the United States was embroiled in a violent Civil War. In the small town of Holly Springs, Mississippi, a slave carpenter witnessed the birth of his daughter, Ida Wells. On July 16, 1862, Ida Wells was born in Holly Spring, Mississippi. Because she was born in the slave state of Mississippi, the young Ida was born into a life of slavery. Her parents, Jim and Elizabeth Wells, were slaves and she became the property of the respective plantation owner. With the conclusion of the Civil War in 1865, the life of the Wells family did not improve dramatically. The father decided to continue working for the slave owner. Unfortunately, Ida's life assumed a tragic tone in 1878 when her parents became victims of a yellow fever epidemic that ravaged Holly Springs. This left the 16-year-old Ida in charge of her seven brothers and sisters. She decided to get her certificate in teaching and gain employment in one of the local schools. In 1881, Ida took two of her younger siblings and went to Memphis, Tennessee in search of better economic and financial opportunities. While in Memphis, she continued to teach to support her siblings. At the same time, Ida decided that a college education was a necessity for an African American woman. As a result, in 1880, the 18-year-old Ida entered Fisk (Rust) University.

One of the issues that most concerned Ida Wells was the issue of racial equality. In the South, law was still governed by the Jim Crow. That is, a state of legal segregation continued to be the rule throughout much of the South. In the 1880s, Wells decided to challenge a particular aspect of the Jim Crow South. In 1884, she started a campaign against segregation on local railroads. In the summer of 1884, she was forcibly removed from a white only carriage. Ida Wells believed this to be a moral injustice. She sued the Chesapeake, Ohio, and Southwestern Railroad. The lawsuit was instigated to try to weaken the Jim Crow laws in regard to segregation. The local courts judged in favor of Ida Wells. The Court of Appeals repeatedly overturned the lower court decisions. She recounted her story of the lawsuit in the black church weekly called *The Living Way.* Despite the setbacks, the resistance initiated by Wells became a symbol of African American resistance to the Jim Crow laws of the South.

In the late 1880s, Wells also became involved in journalism. In the summer of 1887, she was appointed as the secretary of the Afro-American Press Association. She also became part-owner of the *Memphis Free Speech* and was in charge of the editorial operations.

As Wells recovered from the challenges of the segregationist laws of the South, she engaged in another campaign, which became the centerpiece of Wells's career as an activist. In the late 1880s, lynching was a severe problem in the

Ida B. Wells was a civil rights activist, journalist, and crusader against lynching. (Library of Congress)

South. The local governments tolerated the actions while the national government looked the other way. In 1889, 728 African American men and women were lynched. The lynchings were mostly unprovoked. Of the 728 lynching, 66 percent were over small differences and issues. As an African American intellectual, Wells could not tolerate this behavior. In addition, her activism in regards to lynching stemmed from a personal experience. On March 9, 1891, three African American proprietors, who were also Wells's personal friends, Thomas Moss, Calving McDowell, and Wil Stewart of the People's Grocery Store, were lynched. Allegedly, an interracial dispute in front of the store led to the violent lynching. Wells wrote and a scathing editorial indictment of lynching called "Eight Men Lynched" in the *Free Speech* on May 21, 1892. This led to the destruction of the newspaper and her exile from the South. She then began writing for the *New York Age* and adjusted to her new life in the North. This event was significant in Wells's life. She immediately started a public campaign to publicize the atrocities of lynching. She became part-owner of the newspaper,

The Free Speech and Head Light. Wells, under the pseudonym of Iola, would write editorial pieces and eyewitness accounts of lynchings in the South. Despite the repeated threats on her life, she continued to publicize lynching in the North, as well as internationally.

Her public life in essence started in 1892. On October 5, 1892, Wells gave a speech in New York City in front of 250 African American women about her difficult experiences dealing with the Southern lynch codes. She subsequently published "Southern Horrors: Lynch Law in All its Phases," a pamphlet describing the realities of African Americans in the reconstructed South. In *Southern Horrors,* Wells traced a pervasive belief that African American men are natural "rapists." She also reminded her readers that during the Civil War, Southern men left their plantations and families in the hands of black men. She concluded by noting that "lynching was an institutionalized practice supported and encouraged by established leaders of the community and the press they influenced." Wells had brought the atrocities of lynching to the fore in the public mind.

In 1893, Wells decided (or was forced) to move to Chicago, Illinois to continue her career in journalistic writing. The Chicago newspaper, the *Chicago Inter-Ocean,* hired Wells as editor to write exposé articles against lynching in the South. In a particular exposé, the paper proposed that Wells secretly pose as a widower to examine the lynching of C. J. Miller in the small town of Bardwell, Kentucky. By the time she arrived in Bardwell, the lynchers publicly acknowledged that they had killed the wrong man. After investigating the case, Wells concluded that the victim, Miller, was used as a scapegoat. Although thousands were involved in the lynching, no one was punished. Wells decided to depart for Chicago when she realized that there was not a resolution to the problem. Her reporting and the risks she was willing to take earned Wells an international reputation. She received an invitation from the "Brotherhood of Man" to visit Great Britain for a lecture tour. She cheerfully accepted the offer as a way to spread her opposition to lynching. While on her lecture tour, Wells shared her antilynching message with several groups. At the same time, she sent articles to the *Chicago Inter-Ocean* newspaper. While still in England, the American press began writing insipid articles about Wells. She also lectured at the British Anti-Lynching Commission, as well as other prominent antilynching societies in England. While in England, she received assurance that the issue of lynching was indeed an issue with international repercussions. She also lectured throughout towns of England with the purpose of drumming up international support for antilynching. Unfortunately for Wells, the threats against her life in the South had become more vicious. In addition, opponents of her vision firebombed her newspaper headquarters. She thus had to move to Chicago, Illinois to escape the threats and violence.

In 1895, after her marriage to the prominent African American lawyer from Chicago, Ferdinand Barnett, Wells-Barnett continued to be a vocal and outspoken critic against lynching in the South. She published numerous articles and books, which offered statistical analysis of this chronic social problem. Her most important book was entitled, *The Red Record*, in which she offered the first statistical report on lynching in the South. The book was hailed as a masterpiece, as well as symbolic of the state of race relations in the late 19th century. As a nationally prominent figure in the crusade against lynching, Wells-Barnett visited President McKinley in 1898, demanding government action in the case against a black postmaster who was lynched in South Carolina. A few years later, in 1901, she wrote *Lynching and the Excuse for It*. She offered a sociological examination of the reasons southerners engaged in this violent behavior. Wells-Barnett noted that white southerners engaged in lynching as a way to intimidate blacks from getting involved in politics. The end result of this alienation was that power would continue to reside in the White South. The impact of *Lynching* was national. As Progressives and Theodore Roosevelt read the works of Ida Wells-Barnett, they became more disgusted by the state of race relations in the nation. The political system in the South was repressive to the extent that any challenge to that system would be viewed as a radical challenge. In 1896, Wells-Barnett formed a collective organization called the *National Association of Colored Women*. Even though she helped form the organization, she asked Mary Tyrell to serve as its first president while Wells-Barnett raised her children. The creation of this organization acted as a starting point for Wells-Barnett's political activism. As Booker T. Washington dined with President Roosevelt, other "radical" leaders like Wells-Barnett and W. E. B. Du Bois sought alternative forms of equality.

While becoming active on the issue of racial equality and lynching, Wells-Barnett also became entangled with the local chapter of the progressive movement. In August 1889, two women in Chicago, Jane Addams and Ellen Gates Starr, founded a settlement home in Chicago. At Hull House,

college-educated women would settle in local immigrant enclaves and teach the immigrants the ideals of American life. The ideal was to create a sense of civic pride in the recently arrived immigrants, thus creating productive citizens.

Wells-Barnett, who was a friend of Jane Addams, decided that the "settlement house" concept could be tried among the African American community. Sensing that there existed a need for the same type of social relief, Wells-Barnett opened a settlement house in Chicago, geared primarily for African Americans. She founded the Woman's Era Club, which was the first civic organization for African American women. The name of the club was later changed in honor of the founder of the club. The club aided African American women in occupations and culture. It was an efficient organization that in the long run proved to be successful in aiding the community. In addition to the settlement houses, Wells-Barnett and Addams also became involved in a campaign to block the continued segregation of public schools in Chicago. Wells-Barnett also served as secretary for the National African American Council and the Negro Fellowship League. Wells-Barnett's national fame as a promoter of civil rights was reaching an apex.

In addition to the Woman's Era Club, Wells-Barnett also became involved in national politics. The leadership of Booker T. Washington, who she viewed as accommodationist, particularly angered Ida Wells-Barnett. She believed that Washington's accomodationist stance was too lenient and did not offer African Americans any semblance of identity. Other African Americans, including W. E. B. Du Bois, agreed with Wells-Barnett's beliefs. In June 1905, W. E. B. Du Bois led a delegation of 29 blacks to Niagara Falls, New York, demanding equality and political rights. Ida Wells-Barnett was one of two African American women who supported the National Association for the Advancement of Colored People (NAACP) and their quest for political and social equality. In the short term, Wells-Barnett had a falling out with Du Bois over her seeming radicalism, and the NAACP developed without her strong leadership qualities. When the first edition of *The Crisis* was published, Wells-Barnett's name was not even mentioned as a founding member of the organization.

With the NAACP appearing on the national scene, Wells-Barnett turned her attention to other issues, specifically women's suffrage. In the early 20th century, women had struggled for suffrage; Carrie Chapman Catt and her National American Woman Suffrage Association (NAWA) clamored for a suffrage amendment. Nationally, the progressives were ill prepared to offer women the right to vote. Ida Wells-Barnett became involved in the local suffrage movement in Chicago. In 1909, she became the first black woman suffrage associate at the Alpha Suffrage Club of Chicago, which had been a predominantly white organization. She was instrumental in women gaining the right to vote as she gained national acclaim for her struggles with civil rights and lynchings. She now became a standard bearer for the Nineteenth Amendment. As the NAWSA marched in Washington, D.C. in 1916, she also led the way to gain suffrage for all women.

In 1917, the United States became militarily involved in World War I. During the war, African Americans performed a variety of functions in numerous capacities. Many served on the domestic front as cooks and sanitation workers. There was a substantial amount of African Americans who fought in Europe, the most significant being the 369th Regiment out of Brooklyn. Thus, African Americans served in a variety of areas during the war.

The issue that bothered Wells-Barnett during World War I was a contradiction. Many Africa Americans sacrificed their lives in Europe to protect the freedoms of Americans. Yet, in the United States, African Americans were not given political and social rights, despite their sacrifices. She became especially concerned over the events in Houston in 1917 involving African American soldiers.

In August 1917, black soldiers reacting to segregation and abuse by the local police attacked white citizens; 16 whites and black 4 soldiers died. The U.S. Army indicted 118 soldiers, 110 of whom court martialed. Nineteen blacks were executed by hanging. This event, along with an increase in discrimination and violence, angered Wells-Barnett. She publicized the event on the national stage as another form of lynching.

In the years after the war, Ida Wells-Barnett focused on rearing her four children. This new caretaker role did not diminish her continued activities toward racial and social activity. During the 1920s, she worked with the national government to legally end the practice of lynching. Her last work was the publication of her autobiography, *Crusade for Justice*. A few months before her death, legislation was signed making lynching a federal crime. This was the highpoint of her active political career. In 1931, Ida Wells-Barnett, mother, civil rights leader, journalist, and activist died of uremia in Chicago.

See also: Antilynching Campaign; Black Self-Defense; Exoduster Movement; Great Migration; Lynching; National Association for the Advancement of Colored People; Niagara Movement; Suffrage Movement, Women's; Washington, Booker T.; White Mob Violence

Jaime Ramón Olivares

Bibliography

Barnett, Ida. *Crusade for Justice: The Autobiography of Ida Wells*. Chicago: University of Chicago Press, 1970.

Davis, Simone W. "The 'Weak Race' and the Winchester: Political Voices in the Pamphlets of Ida B. Wells-Barnett." *Legacy: A Journal of American Women Writers* 12, no. 2 (1995):77–97.

Fradia, Dennis. *Ida B. Wells: Mother of the Civil Rights Movement*. New York: Clarion Books, 2000.

Ida B. Wells: A Passion for Justice. Videotape. William Greaves Productions, 1990. 58 min.

Logan, Shirley W. "Rhetorical Strategies in Ida B. Wells's 'Southern Horrors': Lynch Law in All Its Phases." *SAGE: A Scholarly Journal on Black Women* 8, no. 1 (1991):3–9.

McMurry, Linda O. *To Keep the Water Troubled: The Life of Ida B. Wells*. New York: Oxford University Press, 1998.

Ochiai, Akiko. "Ida B. Wells and Her Crusade for Justice: An African American Woman's Testimonial Autobiography." *Soundings* 75 (1992):365–81.

Schecter, Patricia. *Ida B. Wells Barnett and American Reforms, 1880–1930*. Chapel Hill: North Carolina Press, 2001.

Thompson, Mildred I. *Ida B. Wells-Barnett: An Exploratory Study of an American Black Woman, 1893–1930*. Brooklyn, NY: Carlson, 1990.

White, Walter

Born in Atlanta, Georgia, Walter Francis White (1893–1955) led the National Association for the Advancement of Colored People (NAACP) from 1929 to 1955. The White family was part of the black social elite of the early 20th century, some of whom had light skin, demonstrating their biracial backgrounds. Walter White had blond hair and blue eyes, features that allowed him secretly to attend whites-only affairs to get information for his black allies. The fact that White did not look physically black, yet chose to identify with the group of his birth, confounded those people who at the time could not realize any value in African American cultural life. Walter White, in contrast, knew that he was a black man and believed that the violence perpetrated against blacks by southern whites was reason enough to validate his championing of the race.

The Atlanta Race Riot of 1906 served as a catalyst for the race consciousness of Walter White. Thirteen-year-old White had accompanied his father, a federal postal carrier, in the mail carriage. For weeks, two competing city newspapers published sensationalized articles describing the brutal assaults of white women by black men. Although most of these stories had little truth to them, white Atlantans became incensed over the supposed attacks. On September 22, 1906, after both papers printed multiple stories of the alleged attacks of white women in both morning and evening editions, mobs of whites attacked blacks in streets, in businesses, and in homes. Walter White and his father escaped the downtown mobs because attackers assumed they were white. Along the way home, the father rescued a black woman chased by whites, demonstrating to his son that despite the seeming advantage in their light complexions, they still had an obligation to help other blacks no matter the consequences. Later that night a mob attempted to burn down the White family home, turning back only when harassed by gunshots from a neighboring store. Later in life, White would express both gratitude toward the neighbors who helped him avoid becoming a killer at 13, and dismay toward the whites who almost forced him to kill at such a young age to protect his home.

Certain of his racial obligations, White attended historically black Atlanta University, graduating in 1916, and going to work for Standard Life Insurance Company. He also helped found the Atlanta branch of the NAACP in 1916, serving as its executive secretary. Early in 1918, he relocated to New York at the urging of national secretary James Weldon Johnson to assist in antilynching reform. For 10 years, White would serve as assistant secretary, using his skin complexion as a cover to witness antiblack disturbances across the nation. In some instances, White became the target of would-be lynchers when someone revealed his racial identity. White sent wire reports to the NAACP in New York that became part of a series printed in the *Crisis*, the national journal edited by W. E. B. Du Bois.

White also published *Rope and Faggot* in 1929, a book detailing more than 30 lynchings and race riots. The book created renewed calls for antilynching legislation in Congress and eventually forced southern officials to do better at protecting blacks alleged with crimes against whites. One finding White made that agreed with the investigations done by reformer Ida B. Wells was that most lynchings did not have a direct connection to real black criminal activity. Instead, angry whites attacked blacks perceived as economic competitors who refused to submit to the racial status quo in the nation.

Living in New York, White participated in the artistic period known as the Harlem Renaissance. During these years, he published *Fire in the Flint* in 1924, a fictional book based on his travels for the NAACP. Two years later came *Flight,* a story about the black migration from the rural South to the North during the Great Migration. White also involved himself socially in New York, working with other prominent leaders to secure philanthropic funding for Harlem Renaissance artists.

As head of the NAACP, White provided the needed leadership that produced the 1954 *Brown v. Board of Education* decision by the United States Supreme Court, ending the legal sanctioning of racial segregation that had existed since *Plessy v. Ferguson* in 1896. White hired Charles Hamilton Houston and Thurgood Marshall, both from Howard University Law School in Washington, D.C., to plan a strategy to attack legalized segregation in the South. After years of court victories that chipped away at segregation, the NAACP won *Brown,* the case that finally called for overturning the precedent set in *Plessy.* Walter White died the next year, survived by his second wife, Poppy Canon.

See also: Atlanta, Georgia, Riot of 1906; Du Bois, W. E. B.; Houston, Charles Hamilton; Lynching; Marshall, Thurgood; National Association for the Advancement of Colored People

David Kenneth Pye

Bibliography
Cannon, Poppy. *A Gentle Knight: My Husband, Walter White.* New York: Rinehart, 1956.
Janken, Kenneth R. "Civil Rights and Socializing in the Harlem Renaissance: Walter White and the Fictionalization of the New Negro in Georgia," *Georgia Historical Quarterly* 80 (1996):817–34.
Janken, Kenneth R. *White: The Biography of Walter White, Mr. NAACP.* New York: New Press, 2003.
White, Walter. *A Man Called White: The Autobiography of Walter White.* New York: Viking Press, 1948.
White, Walter. *Rope and Faggot: A Biography of Judge Lynch* New York: A. A. Knopf, 1929.

White Citizens' Council

The White Citizens' Council was the Southern white reaction to the Supreme Court's landmark 1954 *Brown v. Board of*

Education decision, which mandated the end of racially segregated public schools, varied widely. Groups such as the Ku Klux Klan sought to resist integration through ritual violence and terror, and "high-minded" southern politicians hoped to forestall the demise of Jim Crow with a revival of archaic constitutional theories, such as nullification and interposition. The White Citizens' Council, a segregationist organization that would eventually draw in thousands of anxious members across the South, appealed to the more "respectable" elements of society in its quest to undermine *Brown* and sustain the racial caste. Eschewing the predatory tactics of the Klan, the Councils instead relied on political pressure, economic intimidation, and legal maneuvering to achieve its goals. Before petering out in the 1960s, the Citizens' Council became one of the most powerful and effective instruments in rallying white public opinion against desegregation.

Residents of Indianola, Mississippi organized the first chapter of the White Citizens' Council in July 1954. Within a matter of months, the council movement had spilled over into Alabama, Georgia, Virginia, and eventually all the former states of the Confederacy. Events such as the Montgomery bus boycott and the integration of the University of Alabama by Autherine Lucy, along with efforts by the NAACP to desegregate local school districts in the wake of *Brown,* propelled thousands of whites into the group. By 1956, arguably the council's peak year, organizers claimed more than 250,000 dues-paying members, making it, in the vaunted words of one official, one of the greatest mass movements of public opinion in American history. To better facilitate action and policy between the scattered chapters, council officials created the Citizens' Councils of America (CCA) in April 1956 and established headquarters in the Delta town of Greenwood, Mississippi. Leadership of the national organization fell to Robert Patterson, cofounder of the original Citizens' Council in Indianola, and William J. Simmons, who became the editor of the group's widely distributed newsletter, the *Citizens' Council.*

The council movement found its most fertile ground in the Black Belt regions of the South, where African Americans composed a substantial portion of the population and, for the most part, continued to earn their livings as sharecroppers and tenant farmers. The ranks of the early councils were filled with the middle and upper classes of southern white society—planters, lawyers, bankers, doctors, businessmen, and politicians—who foresaw an erosion of their political hegemony with the implementation of

Brown and who shuddered at the thoughts of their children attending class alongside the offspring of their employees and clients. To counter such a threat, thousands of prominent lowland whites readily adopted the council philosophy, which demanded a rigorous defense of the social order, strict conformity to the ideals of white supremacy, and a veritable holy war against the evils of "miscegenation" and "mongrelization."

In its crusade to stamp out proponents of integration, the Citizens' Councils used numerous legal and economic tactics. Members were encouraged to fire black workers who supported desegregation or who attempted to register to vote. Tenants and sharecroppers were ordered to vacate farms if they were suspected of "radical" or otherwise questionable activity. And the council routinely published the names of NAACP members to discourage their continued activism.

African Americans were not the sole targets of the council's wrath. White racial moderates and others who appeared "soft" on integration also found themselves at the mercy of the expanding movement. Council leaders conducted scurrilous campaigns to destroy the political careers of such "neo-Populists" as Jim Folsom of Alabama and Earl Long of Louisiana, men who refused to trumpet the rhetoric of white supremacy and racism. As a result, both men lost sway with the electorate. In Arkansas, the Capital Citizens' Council led the opposition to the 1957 integration of Central High School in Little Rock. Members flooded Governor Orval Faubus's office with letters, urging him to use emergency powers to prevent integration; harangued local school board members for "betraying" the white race with plans for desegregation; and took out newspapers ads to expose the plot between the NAACP and school officials. Largely because of such efforts, the integration of Central High flared into a constitutional crisis. In Mississippi, council officials, led by William J. Simmons, enjoyed a veritable stranglehold on state government and routinely flexed their political muscle to ensure strict adherence to the organization's racial orthodoxy. Councilors there pressured lawmakers into passing favorable segregationist legislation, scoured libraries and schools for pro-integration materials, and waged a brutal campaign to subvert the freedom of the press. As a result, the Magnolia State, according to one observer, became a "closed society," where moderation was tantamount to treason.

By the early 1960s, after enjoying years of unbridled political and social influence, the Citizens' Council movement began to decline. Random acts of violence by council members, petty infighting, and, most important, its failure to uphold segregation destroyed the organization. After passage of the Civil Rights Act of 1964 and the Voting Rights Act of 1965, all that remained were the diehards and "bitter-enders" who refused to accept the inevitable tide of history. *See also:* Ku Klux Klan; National Association for the Advancement of Colored People; White Supremacy

Gary S. Sprayberry

Bibliography

Bartley, Numan V. *Rise of Massive Resistance: Race and Politics in the South during 1950's.* Baton Rouge: Louisiana State University Press, 1969.

Cook, James Graham. *The Segregationists.* New York: Appleton-Century-Crofts, 1962.

Martin, John Bartlow. *The Deep South Says Never.* New York: Ballantine Books, 1957.

McMillen, Neil R. *The Citizens' Council: Organized Resistance to the Second Reconstruction, 1954–64.* Chicago: University of Illinois Press, 1971.

White Mob Violence

White mob violence toward African Americans in the late 19th and early 20th centuries was both frequent and brutal. White mobs killed around 3,000 African Americans in the South between 1882 and 1930, although the exact figures will never be known because many of these crimes went unrecorded. African American men, however, were not the only victims of white supremacist brutality. White mobs attacked Jews, Catholics, Mexicans, and other minority groups all over the United States in this period, including some women and children. Nonetheless, African American men bore the brunt of white racism from the Civil War until the mid-20th century; and most of these attacks took place in the Jim Crow South.

Before the Civil War, deviant white men, such as thieves or abolitionists, who threatened Southern values were most likely to suffer at the hands of mob violence, or "lynch law." Punishments tended to be much milder than later in the century, as mobs flogged their victims or banished them from the area rather than put them to death. Slaves were rarely the targets of white mob violence in the antebellum period because they were valuable property and thus protected by their masters. Only in extreme circumstances like

insurrection scares were slaves subjected to lynch law. During Reconstruction, however, African Americans became the main focus of white supremacist violence. Southern lynch mobs, some ephemeral and reactionary, but others longstanding and organized (such as the Ku Klux Klan), victimized and intimidated African Americans on a daily basis, with the full support of their community.

Definitions of what constitutes a "mob" vary, but the usually involve a group of more than three or four people, acting in concert. Early work on collective violence, such as that of Gustave LeBon, seemed to justify the actions of mobs, arguing that people in a crowd lose their individual morals and character and form a collective mentality. Although this theory has been criticized for absolving the members of lynch mobs of their crimes, it is important to note that the perpetrators of mob violence against African Americans were ordinary people of all ranks of society and were not deviant members of the community. It is therefore necessary to try to understand why they committed such terrible atrocities.

Mob violence was an expression of collective values; it unified the white community by reaffirming white supremacy, and thus the perpetrators of such violence did not risk punishment. This was particularly the case with the highly ritualized, spectacle lynchings that attracted audiences in the thousands, including women and children. Mob violence toward African Americans took place when whites thought that the black population was threatening the social order. Whites believed that they needed to keep African Americans "in their place," as after the Civil War the boundary that divided black and white along caste lines (which had been less crucial under slavery because of the legal subjugation of African Americans) became increasingly blurred.

This perceived threat from the black population came in a variety of forms. Whites maintained that they were merely protecting white women from the sexual aggression of black men, but in 1892 antilynching campaigner Ida B. Wells dispelled this myth; her investigations found that only one third of lynchings of African Americans were for raping a white woman. Historians have instead pointed to political and economic factors to explain the virulence of white mob violence. Whites used lynching to intimidate African Americans in order to prevent them from voting or seeking employment coveted by whites. White mobs also targeted those African Americans who they perceived as having achieved too much economic success, as they thought they were attempting to cross the caste boundary. This is why mob violence tended to increase during times of economic depression.

Whites often used African Americans as scapegoats for their feelings of inadequacy, as they both psychologically and physically emasculated black men in order to reassert their supremacy. White mobs hanged or shot most of their victims, but they reserved the most brutal punishments for those African Americans who had committed the most serious "crimes" and sometimes burned them alive or tortured them to death. This process was often highly ritualized, involving mutilation of the body, including castration, both before and after death.

African Americans did not just passively accept lynching, however. Individuals such as W. E. B. Du Bois and Ida B. Wells, and later the National Association for the Advancement of Colored People (NAACP), campaigned tirelessly on a national level against white supremacist violence, and in doing so risked their lives. Many African Americans also pushed the boundaries of caste in their own communities, challenging white supremacy on all levels despite the possibility of retaliation. After World War II the tide had turned against lynching, and in 1946 President Truman hosted the National Emergency Committee Against Mob Violence, which condemned the actions of the Ku Klux Klan and the lynching of African Americans, and eventually led to the establishment of a permanent civil rights commission and the desegregation of the military. Although white mob violence did not disappear with civil rights, and still sometimes takes place today, by mid century-the majority of the white population no longer considered it acceptable.

See also: Jim Crow; Ku Klux Klan; Lynching; Plan de San Diego; Wells-Barnett, Ida

Lydia Plath

Bibliography
Brundage, William Fitzhugh. *Under Sentence of Death: Lynching in the South.* Chapel Hill: University of North Carolina Press, 1997.
Royster, Jacqueline Jones, ed. *Southern Horrors and Other Writings: The Anti-Lynching Campaign of Ida B. Wells, 1892–1900.* Boston: Bedford Books, 1997.
Shapiro, Herbert. *White Violence and Black Response: From Reconstruction to Montgomery.* Amherst: The University of Massachusetts Press, 1988.
Waldrep, Christopher, ed. *Lynching in America: A History in Documents.* New York: New York University Press, 2006.
White, Walter. *Rope and Faggot: A Biography of Judge Lynch.* New York: A. A. Knopf, 1929.
Williamson, Joel. *The Crucible of Race: Black/White Relations in the American South since Emancipation.* New York: Oxford University Press, 1984.

White Primaries

During the early-20th century all southern states except Florida, North Carolina, and Tennessee barred African Americans from voting in Democratic Party primary elections. Established to nominate candidates for political office, primaries are an integral part of the electoral process. This was especially true in the American South where, in the years after Reconstruction, government was dominated by the Democratic Party. Because there was no effective opposition, the South was virtually a one-party state. Like the poll tax, literacy test, and grandfather clause, the whites-only primary was designed to restrict African American's constitutional right to vote.

In establishing white primaries, southern Democrats were motivated by two major assumptions. First they desired to prevent African Americans from achieving social and political equality, and second, white southerners mistakenly believed that African Americans would forever remain loyal to the Republican Party. Despite white resistance, southern blacks challenged their exclusion from the American political process.

In 1923, the Texas legislature passed a law declaring all African Americans ineligible to vote in a Democratic primary election. The next year Dr. Lawrence A. Nixon, an El Paso physician and member of the National Association for the Advancement of Colored People (NAACP), attempted to vote in the Democratic primary election. When he was prevented from casting a ballot, Nixon filed suit arguing the new law violated his Fourteenth Amendment right to equal protection and his right to vote guaranteed by the Fifteenth Amendment. The case made its way to the U.S. Supreme Court, which upheld Nixon's argument that his right to equal protection under the law was violated; however, the court did not rule on the question of voting rights.

Undaunted by the Supreme Court's action, the Texas legislature granted political parties the authority to decide who could vote in party elections. Soon afterwards, the state Democratic Executive Committee adopted a resolution that stated only white citizens were allowed to vote in primaries. Nixon, refusing to accept these discriminatory actions, tried to vote and was again rebuffed. Filing a second lawsuit, Nixon's case was again heard by the U.S. Supreme Court. The equal protection clause was again used by the court to strike down the Texas primary law. But this did not settle the matter.

In 1932, the Texas Democratic Party convention adopted the policy that only white Texans were eligible to vote in party primaries. The NAACP declined to challenge the suit, but Houston barber Richard R. Grovey did. For the third time in a decade the U.S. Supreme Court heard a case regarding the constitutionality of white primaries. Grovey argued along the same lines as Nixon, but the court did not accept that the actions of the Texas Democratic Party violated his Fourteenth Amendment rights. Instead, the court held that the white primary was created by a private association rather than the state and thus was not bound by the equal protection clause.

Despite this setback, African Americans continued to challenge white primaries. In 1940, Houston dentist Lonnie E. Smith was prevented from voting in the Texas Democratic primary by election official S. S. Allwright. Like Nixon and Grovey, Smith filed suit and arguments were heard by the U.S. Supreme Court. Reversing itself, the court ruled that the white primary violated Smith's, and by extension all African Americans, Fifteenth Amendment right to vote. As a result, black voting across the south increased dramatically. In Texas, for example, voter registration increased from 30,000 in 1940 to 100,000 in 1947. Although it did not eliminate all voting restrictions, the *Smith* decision was an important step in achieving lasting civil rights for African Americans in the United States.

See also: Disfranchisement; MFDP; National Association for the Advancement of Colored People; Voting Rights Act 1965

Gerald Wayne Dowdy

Bibliography
Key, V. O. Jr. *Southern Politics in State and Nation.* New York: Alfred A. Knopf, 1949.
Klarman, Michael J. *From Jim Crow to Civil Rights.* Oxford, UK: Oxford University Press, 2004.

White Supremacy

White supremacy is a racist ideology that has existed for hundreds of years. When Bartolomé de las Casas argued in the 16th century that Spaniards were cruel and barbaric in enslaving the Taino of Hispaniola, his critics responded that Native Americans were more like monkeys than humans and the indigenous people were mere children.

White supremacy shaped every aspect of antebellum society and undergirded a paternalistic society built on the superiority of slaveholders over their property, enslaved Africans. Slaveholders gained immense benefits from supremacist ideology. The inferiority of African Americans confirmed the benevolence and necessity of the institution of slavery. Furthermore, racist ideologies encouraged poor whites to identify with slaveholders and discriminate against African Americans.

With the destruction of the institution of slavery after the Civil War and the passage of the Thirteen Amendment in 1865, white supremacy thrived during and after Reconstruction in the South. After 4 million African Americans gained their freedom, Southerners and other Americans looked for ways to control them and to justify white economic, political, and social dominance. After the Civil War, African Americans endeavored to join the middle class in order to counter white supremacy. They graduated from colleges and universities and black men won elections at the state and local levels.

The rise of the Ku Klux Klan was one attempt to undo the gains of African Americans and enforce white supremacy. The Mississippi Plan was a bold effort by the Democrats to use force to win elections and uphold white supremacy in the South. The rise of Jim Crow politics systematized disfranchisement, and the Democratic Party promoted black disfranchisement and white supremacy.

The forced separation of races became the foundation for white racial identity, but black homes, businesses, churches, and bodies threatened to buttress black autonomy and provide a challenge to white supremacy. Lynchings, however, denied the existence of black space, and even the bodies of African Americans could be invaded at any time by whites.

See also: Jim Crow; Ku Klux Klan; Lynching; White Citizens' Council; White Mob Violence

Nathan Herrod

Bibliography

Berlin, Ira. *Many Thousands Gone: The First Two Generations of Slavery in North America.* Cambridge, MA: Harvard University Press, 1998.

Blight, David. *Race and Reunion: The Civil War in the American Memory.* Cambridge, MA: The Belknap Press, 2001.

Gilmore, Glenda Elizabeth. *Gender and Jim Crow: Women and the Politics of White Supremacy in North Carolina, 1896–1920.* Chapel Hill: University of North Carolina Press, 1996.

Grace Elizabeth Hale, *Making Whiteness: The Culture of Segregation in the South, 1890–1940.* New York: Vintage Books, 1998.

Wilkins, Roy

Roy Wilkins (1901–1981) was a prominent member and leader of the National Association for the Advancement of Colored People (NAACP). During his tenure with the organization, Wilkins and the NAACP helped to usher in the popular Civil Rights movement of the 1960s and push for popular legislation such as the Civil Rights Act of 1964 and the Voting Rights Act of 1965.

Roy Ottoway Wilkins was born August 30, 1901, in St. Louis, Missouri. Wilkins remained in Missouri with his mother, father, sister Armeda, and brother Earl until the death of his mother. Then Armeda, Earl, and Roy moved to St. Paul, Minnesota to live with their deceased mother's sister Elizabeth and her husband Sam. Although Roy's father was still alive, in many ways he respected and viewed his Uncle Sam as his stand-in father.

Wilkins began school at the Whittier Grammar School at the age of six. He graduated salutatorian of his class in June 1919 and then went to the University of Minnesota. Wilkins grew up with a benign look at race. Although he was the only African American at Whittier, he was always treated fairly and never viewed race as an issue. When Wilkins began studying at the University of Minnesota, however, this view changed. In the summer of 1920, three African Americans in Duluth, Minnesota, were unfairly lynched for the rape of a white woman. While all the evidence supported the innocence of the African American boys, they nonetheless were found guilty. This incident in Duluth forever altered Wilkins's view of race.

In 1922, Wilkins became the editor of the St. Paul Appeal—the voice of African Americans at the University of Minnesota and in the St. Paul community at large. The next year Wilkins graduated from the University with a degree in sociology and a minor in journalism. After graduation in October 1923, Wilkins moved to Kansas City to take a job with the *Kansas City Call.* Once in Kansas City, Wilkins became entrenched in the Jim Crow South. As he saw members of his race being treated unfairly and he himself was treated unfairly, he turned more and more active in the promotion of black equality. While at *The Call,* Wilkins fought southern racism in his articles and editorials.

In the late 1920s, Wilkins lost his Aunt Elizabeth, Uncle Sam, and sister Armeda within one week's time. Roy's brother Earl moved to Kansas City to be with him. In September 1929, Wilkins then married Minnie Badeau. The two never had any children, but stayed together until Wilkins's death. Wilkins's outspoken editorials at *The Call* gained national attention from the NAACP. The organization offered Wilkins a position with their newspaper, *The Crisis,* but Wilkins turned it down. A few years later, in 1931, the NAACP again offered Wilkins a position as assistant secretary, which he accepted. The position at *The Crisis* was merely a business position to Wilkins. As assistant secretary, however, Wilkins would be able to work side by side with some of the most prominent civil rights advocates in the country. In August, Roy moved to New York and began work with the NAACP. In 1934, when W. E. B. Du Bois left the organization, Roy took over as editor of *The Crisis.*

In 1949, Executive Secretary Walter White requested a leave of absence from the NAACP. Wilkins temporarily took over the position. In 1951 White returned. Four years later, in 1955, White died and Wilkins became the executive secretary of the NAACP. Although many African Americans in the 1950s were promoting a gradual or slow pace for civil rights, Wilkins pushed for more progress. He felt blacks had been treated unfairly long enough. As executive secretary, Wilkins not only promoted, but participated in, civil rights events such as the March on Washington in 1963 and the Selma marches in 1966.

In the 1960s, the Civil Rights movement exploded. The NAACP had ushered in the Civil Rights movement, but many other organizations were on the scene by 1965. Many of these new groups supported black power and separation of the races. Wilkins fought hard for black equality, but he would never support separatism as advocated by black power supporters. To Wilkins separatism was a reinstatement of *Plessy v. Ferguson* and the case's separate but equal doctrine.

Roy Wilkins, Executive Secretary of the NAACP, holds a hangman's noose mailed to his organization's headquarters, undated photo. (Library of Congress)

Throughout Wilkins's time with the NAACP, he met with Presidents Roosevelt, Truman, Eisenhower, Kennedy, Johnson, Nixon, Ford, and Carter. Through these meetings Wilkins helped to promote black equality. He encouraged Kennedy and Johnson to pass the famed Civil Rights Act of 1964 and the Voting Rights Act of 1965. Wilkins always advocated civil rights through legislative means. He protested to the legislative, executive, and judicial branches of the government. He felt it was through these organizations that African Americans would receive their long-awaited equality.

In July 1977, Wilkins retired from the NAACP. Although this was not the end of the relationship between Wilkins and the NAACP, it was the end of his active role in the organization's leadership. Until his death in 1981, Wilkins continued to advocate for the NAACP and civil rights.

See also: Cold War and Civil Rights; Du Bois, W. E. B.; March on Washington, 1963; National Association for the Advancement of Colored People; Robeson, Paul; White, Walter

Mindy R. Weidman

Bibliography

Wilkins, Roy with Tom Mathews. *Standing Fast: The Autobiography of Roy Wilkins.* New York: DeCapo Press, 1982.

Williams, Hosea

Hosea Lorenzo Williams (1926–2000) was a pastor and civil rights activist known for his boundless energy. Born January 5, 1926, in Attapulgus, Georgia, to blind parents, Williams was raised by his grandparents after his mother died while giving birth to his younger sister Teresa. His mother's untimely death left them in the care of her parents, Turner and Lela Williams, with whom he stayed until he was 13 years old. While growing up under his grandparents' guidance in Decatur County, a poor area in southwest Georgia, Williams's affection and concern for the poor and underprivileged began as he became aware that many whites limited the life chances of African Americans in order to prevent them from accumulating wealth and property.

In 1939, Williams had a more intense introduction to the racial tension of the segregated South. A group of racist whites from Decatur County accused him of having an "affair" with a white girl from the area and sought to lynch him for his alleged inappropriate behavior. This mob approached his grandparents' home seeking Williams, but as he described later, his grandfather held them at bay with a gun until a friendly white neighbor interceded to prevent further violence.

Williams would later move to Tallahassee, Florida, and then back to Decatur County finding work on farms, cleaning homes, serving as a caretaker, and working at a bus station between Decatur County, Georgia and Tallahassee Florida. Williams enlisted in the United States Army in 1942, serving a weapons carrier, as well as time as a staff sergeant under General George S. Patton, and fought in the Battle of the Bulge, one of the most significant battles in France during World War II.

After returning to the United States, Williams was awarded the Purple Heart for wounds received in service. Life after military service for Williams was not the happiest of times. At a segregated Greyhound bus station in Americus, Georgia, he drank from a "Whites Only" water fountain and a mob of whites nearly beat him to death for his actions. Williams later enrolled at Morris Brown College in Atlanta, Georgia, receiving a BS in chemistry in 1951, and later an MA in chemistry from Atlanta University.

Williams moved to Savannah, Georgia, and was employed by the U.S. Department of Agriculture Bureau of Entomology, becoming one of the first African American research chemists in the South. In Savannah, he began working with W. W. Law, who was the Savannah National Association for the Advancement of Colored People (NAACP) president. Under Law's direction, Williams became vice president of the Savannah NAACP branch, and they would lead the first sit-ins and night marches in Savannah in the early 1960s. He would also help desegregate the DeSoto Hotel. Williams gained statewide attention with this local movement and later became vice president of the Georgia NAACP.

In 1962, Williams left Savannah for Atlanta to become part of the national Civil Rights movement as head of the national board of the NAACP. Faced with discrimination within the organization, in 1963 he was brought into the Southern Christian Leadership Conference (SCLC) by Dr. Martin Luther King Jr., who saw Williams as someone who could be beneficial to the movement. At this time, the SCLC began to implement marches as a tactic to combat the injustices adhered to through segregation.

Williams's role in the SCLC is first remembered as he and John Lewis, the national leader of the Student Nonviolent Coordinating Committee (SNCC), led a march from Selma, Alabama, to Montgomery, Alabama, on March 7, 1965. This march became known as "Bloody Sunday." The objective of the march was to give then Governor George C. Wallace a petition demanding the voting rights of blacks in Alabama as guaranteed by the Fifteenth Amendment to the United States Constitution. In the aftermath of Bloody Sunday, many marchers endured injuries; Williams suffered a concussion and fractured skull. Within days, President Lyndon B. Johnson passed legislation guaranteeing voting rights for blacks in America. On August 6, 1965, this legislation was put into law, as it disposed of the literacy tests and other policies that were designed to disfranchise blacks in the South from voting.

Despite the rifts within leadership, Hosea Williams was of great use to Dr. Martin Luther King Jr. and SCLC. Many people did not agree with Williams's ideology but still had respect for him. Aside from his role in "Bloody Sunday," Williams served numerous roles after the Civil Rights movement. In 1968, he was director of Dr. King's Poor People's Campaign, a movement whose mission was to end poverty in the United States. Much of the aspirations for the Poor People's Campaign dwindled with the assassination of Martin Luther King Jr. at the Lorraine Motel in Memphis, Tennessee, on April 4, 1968. Williams was present with King at this unfortunate time.

The numerous arrests of Hosea Williams's demonstrated his dedication to African Americans gaining civil rights. Williams also founded the Hosea Williams Feed the Hungry and Homeless Foundation in 1970. In 1973, he led a boycott against the department store Rich's Incorporated, and later took Richard H. Rich, the founder of Rich's, to court on a civil action suit against the corporation's practices.

While serving in the Georgia General Assembly, which he was elected to in 1974, Williams, as head of the Atlanta chapter of the SCLC, led a demonstration outside of an Atlanta hotel where President Gerald Ford was in attendance. Williams and 50 other demonstrators demanded to see the president to ask for jobs for the poor. After refusing to listen to the pleas of one of the aides to President Ford, Williams and three others were arrested and charged with trespassing and disorderly conduct. In 1987, Williams led 20,000 people into Forsyth County, Georgia, just north of Atlanta, to protest the racial tensions in the area that were elevated by the Ku Klux Klan.

Throughout his life, Williams showed determination to accomplish what he had his heart set on—changing the social, political, and economic status of blacks in America. Williams died in 2000 after a three-year battle with cancer. *See also:* King, Martin Luther Jr.; National Association for the Advancement of Colored People; Southern Christian Leadership Conference

Robert A. Bennett III

Bibliography

Branch, Taylor. *Parting the Waters: America in the King Years 1954–63.* New York: Simon & Schuster, 1989.

Fayer, Steve with Sarah Flynn. *Voices of Freedom: An Oral History of the Civil Rights Movement from the 1950s through the 1980s.* New York: Bantam Books, 1990.

Friedly, Michael with David Gallen. *Martin Luther King, Jr.: The FBI File.* New York: Carroll and Graf Publishers, 1993, 720.

Garrow, David J. *Bearing the Cross: Martin Luther King, Jr., and the Southern Christian Leadership Conference.* New York: Vintage Books, 1988.

Hannah, John A., chairman. *Hearing before the United States Commission on Civil Rights.* Washington, D.C.: U.S. Government Printing Office, 1969.

Hornsby, Jr., Alton. *Chronology of African American History: From 1492 to the Present.* Detroit, MI: Gale Research, 1997.

Hornsby, Jr., Alton. *Milestones in 20th-Century African American History.* Detroit, MI: Visible Ink Press, 1993, 529

Hornsby, Jr., Alton. *A Short History of Black Atlanta, 1847–1990.* Atlanta, GA: Apex Museum, 2003.

Marable, Manning. *Race, Reform, and Rebellion: The Second Reconstruction in Black America, 1945–1990.* Jackson: University Press of Mississippi, 1991, 283.

Raines, Howell. *My Soul is Rested: Movement Days in the Deep South Remembered.* New York: G. P. Putnam's Sons, 1977.

Shapiro, Herbert. "After Montgomery". *Freedomways,* First Quarter 1966, 89.

Washington, James Melvin, ed. *A Testament of Hope: The Essential Writings of Martin Luther King, Jr.* San Francisco: Harper & Row, Publishers, 1986.

Williams, Robert F.

Robert F. Williams (1925–1996) was born on February 26, 1925, in Monroe, North Carolina. In the 1950s, he became a militant civil rights activist whose radicalism would have a tremendous influence on the Black Power movement. As early as 1941, his resistance to racial discrimination during a federal job-training program prompted the Federal Bureau of Investigation (FBI) to launch an investigation into his ties with Communists. Racial clashes in American cities during World War II, coupled with his 18-month military service, further politicized Williams, who was discharged in 1946. Between 1947, when he married Mabel Ola Robinson, and 1953, Williams worked in the auto industry in Detroit before returning to the South, where he honed his skills as a writer at several all-black colleges. In 1954, after working in Harlem and California, financial problems prompted Williams to join the U.S. Marines, but his defiance toward racist discrimination in the military led to an early discharge in 1955.

Back in Monroe, Williams revived the town's defunct chapter of the National Association for the Advancement of Colored People (NAACP). As the chapter's president, he attracted many working-class members and, in 1957, launched a nonviolent protest campaign against Monroe's segregated swimming pool. Faced with a wave of violent intimidation from the Ku Klux Klan, Williams organized a black self-defense organization that successfully protected the local movement against white aggression. A year later, Williams widely publicized the controversial case of two black boys, who had been sentenced to reform school for kissing a white girl. Skillfully exploiting the ideological Cold War struggle between the United States and the Soviet Union, the NAACP activist eventually secured the release of the two children.

In 1959, Williams's public statement that blacks would have to meet violence with violence when confronted with racist terrorism cemented his radical reputation and prompted the national NAACP to dismiss him as president of the Monroe chapter. Undaunted, Williams continued his civil rights activism, publishing the newsletter *Crusader* to disseminate his militant ideas on self-defense, black pride, economic nationalism, and anticolonial internationalism. Williams counted among his friends white socialists, black nationalists such as Malcolm X, and revolutionaries such as Fidel Castro, but his uncompromising militancy prevented his acceptance into the mainstream of the Civil Rights movement.

In 1961, Williams and his family were forced into Cuban exile. That year, a nonviolent protest by student activists in Monroe escalated into racial violence. Williams fled to avert bloodshed and to elude the FBI, which sought to prosecute him for allegedly kidnapping a white couple during the race riot. In Havana, Williams produced his own radio program, Radio Free Dixie, and continued to publish the *Crusader* to spread his ideas, which became increasingly radical. Going beyond his original call for black self-defense to protect the struggle for racial integration, he now advocated revolutionary guerilla warfare and favored black separatism. During the second half of the 1960s, Williams's militant program had a tremendous impact on black power groups such as the Black Panther Party, the Revolutionary Action Movement, and the Republic of New Africa.

By 1965, Williams's relations with the Cuban government had soured, prompting him to move to China. Residing in Beijing, he became an ardent opponent of the escalating Vietnam War and sought to influence its outcome by producing antiwar propaganda. In 1969, Williams finally returned to the United States, where he briefly worked at the University of Michigan's Center for Chinese Studies before withdrawing from the national limelight to settle for a secluded life in Baldwin, Michigan. In 1976, the state of North Carolina dropped the remaining criminal charges against him. Robert Williams died of Hodgkin's disease on October 15, 1996.

See also: Black Nationalism; Black Power; Black Self-Defense; Castro, Fidel; Destination, Cuba; Ku Klux Klan; National Association for the Advancement of Colored People; Republic of New Afrika; Revolutionary Action Movement; X, Malcolm

Simon Wendt

Bibliography

Cohen, Robert Carl. *Black Crusader: A Biography of Robert Franklin Williams.* Secaucus, NJ: Lyle Stuart, 1972.

Rucker, Walter. "'Crusader in Exile': Robert F. Williams and the Internationalized Struggle for Black Freedom in America." *Black Scholar.* 36 (2006):19–34.

Tyson, Timothy B. *Radio Free Dixie: Robert F. Williams and the Roots of Black Power.* Chapel Hill: University of North Carolina Press, 1999.

Williams, Robert F. *Negroes with Guns.* New York: Marzani and Munsell, 1962.

Wills, Frank

Frank Wills (1948–2000) is best known as the man who revealed the Watergate conspiracy; an event that forever transformed American politics and the American presidency. Born in North Augusta, South Carolina, on February 4, 1948, Frank Wills was a high school dropout who earned his GED through the Georgia Job Corps. Wills traveled to Detroit and Fort Custer, Michigan, in search of employment before eventually settling in Washington D.C. in 1971. In 1972, Wills was 24 years old when he was hired by General Security Services, a private security firm in Washington, D.C. Wills earned $80 a week working as a night security guard in an office building in the Watergate complex.

While Wills was making his rounds on June 17, 1972, he discovered a conspiracy that led to the resignation of the highest elected official in the United States. Shortly after midnight Wills noticed a door taped so that it would not latch properly. He removed the tape, thinking the building's maintenance staff responsible and continued his rounds. Several hours later, just before 2 A.M., he checked the door again and found someone had replaced the tape. Wills immediately phoned the police. Three plainclothes policemen arrived within minutes and he showed them the taped door. Wills was told to stay in the lobby in case anyone tried to escape while the police went upstairs to investigate. The police arrested five men in the process of placing surveillance equipment in the Democratic National Committee headquarters. Wills's diligence sparked a chain of events that became known as "Watergate." The scandal eventually led to the resignation of, among others, President Richard Nixon, who had approved the break-in plan.

The immediate aftermath of Watergate treated Frank Wills well. Soon Wills took a new security job that afforded him a $5 a week raise. He was paid for interviews and photographs, he hired an attorney to manage his business affairs, and he was given a lifetime membership by the NAACP. A little over a year later, however, Wills was unemployed and claimed that fear of the Nixon administration, which was still in power, kept potential employers from hiring him. Wills's lawyer, Dorsey Evans, claimed that it was Wills's race that kept him from being a national hero and gaining the recognition he deserved.

In August 1974, while still unemployed, Wills was given the Southern Christian Leadership Conference's highest honor, the Martin Luther King award. In 1976, Wills appeared as himself in the opening scenes of Woodward and Bernstein's tale of Watergate, the film *All the President's Men*. As the years passed Wills tried to write a book about his life and participation in Watergate, but publishers were not interested. Wills became increasingly bitter about his role and lack of recognition. In 1982, Wills was arrested for shoplifting a pair of $12 tennis shoes from a store in Augusta, Georgia. The shoes were allegedly a present for his son. Several New Jersey politicians raised money to post Wills's bond and he did not serve his one-year sentence for the theft.

In 1990, Wills moved back to his hometown of North Augusta, South Carolina to care for his ill mother. She died several years later, but Wills remained in his hometown. On September 27, 2000, Frank Wills died while at the University Hospital in Augusta Georgia from complications relating to a brain tumor; he was only 52 years old.

See also: National Association for the Advancement of Colored People

Kara M. Kvaran

Bibliography
Olsen, Keith W. *Watergate: The Presidential Scandal that Shook America.* Lawrence: University Press of Kansas, 2003.

Winfrey, Oprah

Oprah Winfrey (1954–) is most famous for rising to prominence as a talk show host in the late 20th century, but she has also garnered attention as an actress, film and television producer, magazine publisher, and philanthropist. Winfrey was born in rural Mississippi and spent a number of her early years with her grandparents. Her relationship with both of her parents and half-siblings was troubled, and by her own account, she had a difficult childhood. She was sexually abused as a child and became pregnant at the age of 14. Her son, born prematurely, died shortly after birth.

Oprah Winfrey won the Miss Black Tennessee pageant in 1971, and soon began her media career on the radio in Nashville. She attended Tennessee State University, but did not complete her degree until 1987. Her work on the radio led to opportunities on television, and Winfrey became the first African American woman and the youngest person to anchor the news at Nashville's WTVG-TV. She worked in Baltimore as a co-anchor on the 6:00 News and as co-host of a local talk show, and then moved to Chicago in 1983 to host a show that would become *The Oprah Winfrey Show.*

In the midst of starting her broadcasting career, Winfrey also began a film career, playing roles in adaptations of prominent African American novels such as Richard Wright's *Native Son* (1986) and Alice Walker's *The Color Purple* (1985). Winfrey received an Academy Award nomination for her role as Sofia in *The Color Purple,* a film adaptation directed by Steven Spielberg that was very controversial. Both the novel and the film were accused of presenting coonish or demonizing representations of African American men. Winfrey would later star in *The Women of Brewster Place* (1989), *There Are No Children Here* (1993), and *Before Women Had Wings.* Her most high-profile leading role was in the adaptation (1998) of Toni Morrison's Pulitzer Prize winning novel *Beloved* (1988), a story inspired by escaped slave Margaret Garner's decision to kill her child rather than allow all of her family to be taken back into slavery. Winfrey played the lead, Sethe, to mixed reviews.

Winfrey's most prominent success, however, has been through her talk show. Winfrey's show became nationally syndicated in 1986 and she is credited—and disparaged—for revolutionizing the industry. The talk show host broke down the boundary between host and guest with her confessional style of show. She brought her history with sexual abuse, pregnancy, drug use, and ongoing struggles with weight loss into the show, thereby forging a bond with audiences. Winfrey's success inspired a new term—"Oprahfication"—connoting intimate, confessional forms of public interaction.

Another innovation of Winfrey's talk show format was the successful inclusion of a book club that encouraged a national audience to read selected texts and tune in for the discussion on the show. Like many of Winfrey's projects, the book club has garnered both praise and denigration, but it was embraced by many in the publishing industry and inspired a number of scholarly discussions of Winfrey's importance to a culture of reading in the waning days of print culture's influence. Winfrey's love of reading and literature is well documented, and she has not only starred in but produced a number of adaptations of her favorite books.

In 2003, Oprah Winfrey became the first black woman billionaire, and one of the few black billionaires in the

Oprah Winfrey on the cover of her O magazine. (PRNewsFoto/ Oxmoor House)

during his campaign for president. Winfrey's high-profile support for a political candidate was unprecedented for her. Winfrey champions many causes, but she has explicitly stated that she is not a political person.

See also: Obama, Barack

Rebecca Wanzo

Bibliography

Illousz, Eva. *Oprah Winfrey and the Glamour of Misery.* New York: Columbia University Press, 2003.

Konchar, Cecilia Farr. *Reading Oprah: How Oprah's Book Club Changed the Way America Reads.* Albany: State University of New York Press, 2005.

Mosk, Matthew. "The Magic Touch? Winfrey Lends Her Brand and Her Empire in Support of Obama's Presidential Bid." *The Washington Post,* September 5, 2007, p. A06.

Otis, Ginger Adams. "Oprah's Painful Years." *The New York Post,* May 27, 2007, p. 18.

Ridgeway, Karen. "Winfrey Says She Had Baby at 14." *USA Today,* May 4, 1990, 1D.

Samuels, Allison. "Oprah Goes to School." *Newsweek,* January 8, 2007:46–49.

Shattuc, Jane. *The Talking Cure.* New York: Routledge, 1997.

world. Her wealth was not only a result of her lucrative talk show but also of her other business interests. Her talk show is produced by Harpo Productions, a company behind a variety of other successful film and television productions. In 2000, Winfrey launched *O, The Oprah Magazine,* a successful monthly woman's magazine with a self-help thrust. She was also one of the founders of the Oxygen television network.

Winfrey is a well-known philanthropist. She formed The Oprah's Angel Network (1997), which has given money to projects in the United States and around the world. Such projects include education, housing, and youth development. Her most high-profile philanthropic project was the creation of a $40-million school for girls in South Africa in 2007. A luxurious boarding school designed to meet the educational and psychological needs of the girls and prepare them for leadership, the school was met with a number of criticisms and was troubled by controversy about its management shortly after opening.

Because of Winfrey's wealth and popularity, people have periodically suggested that she run for public office. In the early 21st century, the closest Winfrey has come to state or presidential politics is her support of Barack Obama

Woodson, Carter Godwin

Dr. Carter Godwin Woodson (1875–1950), one of the most prominent African American historians and social analysts of the 20th century, earned his much deserved notoriety as the innovator of "Negro History Week" celebrations (now Black History Month). He never married, spending much of his time, energy, money, and resources launching the foundations for the inclusion of black studies as a legitimate intellectual inquiry in American schools. Woodson wanted to reestablish dignity to people of African descent so that the world would no longer have to wonder what the Negro was good for.

Woodson was born on December 19, 1875, in New Canton, Buckingham County, Virginia, to proud parents and former slaves Anne Eliza Riddle and James Henry Woodson. Woodson was born 18 years after the infamous Dred Scott decision and 1 year before the 1876 presidential election between Democrat Samuel Tilden and Republican Rutherford B. Hayes.

The United States Supreme Court speaking through Chief Justice Roger Taney proclaimed in the Dred Scott case that no African free or slave could be a citizen; whites were not bound to respect any rights proclaimed by African Americans. The 1876 presidential election brought an end to the Reconstruction era and enabled the Southern states to reduce African Americans to near slave status. The social and political system placed little value on the lives of African Americans; between 1890 and 1926, an African American was lynched every two-and-a-half days. Many people of African decent were so humiliated, dehumanized, and afflicted with low self-esteem that they did not attempt to know their past.

The Social Darwinism era, whereby much of America unashamedly condoned slavery and segregation, the academic community that justified racial subjugation and discrimination, and Dr. Woodson's proud parents inspired Woodson to search for the truth, refuting the misrepresentations of the African contributions to world civilization. He used education in black history as a primary conduit for political empowerment of African Americans. Carter Goodson was the first and only African American of slave parentage to earn a PhD in history. This child of former slaves nurtured a desire for learning that culminated in a rich and extraordinary career spanning 40 years.

Woodson was undaunted by the prejudice, challenges, and difficulties of his life. His father was an impoverished carpenter who had to supplement his income by sharecropping. Woodson was the eldest of nine children; two of his siblings died in infancy. He was required to work long, arduous hours to help his family. Because the local schools in Virginia operated on an agricultural calendar, opening only four months of the year owing to the rigors of farming, Woodson was primarily self-taught until age 19.

After working long hours during the day, he would often read aloud newspapers to his father, thereby learning about national and international events and places. During this time period, he would listen to accounts of slavery shared by the adults around him. Although his parents could not read or write, Woodson gave his father credit for influencing the course of his life. He later wrote that his father insisted that one could lose one's soul if one betrayed one's people, misled one's fellow human being, compromise on principle, and accept insult.

His knowledge about black history expanded when his family moved to West Virginia where they worked in the coalmines. During off-duty times, black laborers would rest and eat at the establishment of Oliver Jones, a black civil war veteran who was interested in black history. Woodson

would read the newspaper to these workers and, in exchange, listen to their accounts of life in antebellum days. He acquired appreciation for African folk culture and the African American masses.

Woodson went to school full time when he turned 20 and earned enough money to support himself. In 1895, he enrolled in Douglas High School in Huntington, West Virginia, where he finished the four-year curriculum and earned his diploma in less than two years in 1896. From 1896 through 1898, he continued his education by attending Berea College, which was racially integrated in all aspects of institutional life: dormitories, classrooms, dining hall, entertainment, and extracurricular activities.

While matriculating at Berea, Woodson experienced interpersonal contact with William Frost, the president of the college. From Frost, the faculty, and his colleagues, he acquired a commitment to teaching and an abiding respect for the value of a combination of vocational and classical education to transform the lower income classes of society, believing this would build character and prepare them for life. The next three years, 1897–1900, Woodson began teaching in a one-room school established by black miners for their children in Winona Fayette County, West Virginia. He returned to his high school alma mater, Douglass High School, in 1900–1903 to teach history and serve as acting principal, replacing his cousin Carter Harrison Barnett. Finally, in 1903, he graduated from Berea College with a bachelor of literature degree.

Carter taught English, health, and agriculture in the Philippines from 1903 through 1909 and became the general superintendent of education with the U.S. Bureau of Insular Affairs. He took correspondence courses in French and English from the University of Chicago so that he could effectively communicate with his students at the school in San Isidro. Having become fluent in French and Spanish, he traveled in Europe and Asia and studied history for a semester at the Sorbonne in Paris, France. He went to a myriad of museums and libraries, learning basic principles of locating primary materials for research and strategies for incorporating this material into his scholarly works.

On his return to the United States, Woodson decided to begin graduate studies at the University of Chicago. Just as Berea did not accept all of his credits from Douglas High School, the University of Chicago did not give him full credit for his course work at Berea. Woodson was not disheartened; he simultaneously worked on his master's degree and another bachelor's degree. His major was history and his thesis examined French diplomatic relations with Germany in the 18th century. After completing his BA in 1907 and his MS in history, romance and literature, one year later, Woodson enrolled in Harvard University and finished his coursework by 1909.

He accepted a teaching position with the Washington, D.C. public schools system. While working full-time at M Street High School, he inspired many students to study Negro history, prepared for his PhD comprehensive examinations, and worked on his dissertation on the secession of Virginia at the Library of Congress. In 1912, he became the second African American in the United States to receive a doctorate in history. Du Bois, who came from a free Northern background, was the first African American to earn a PhD in history in 1895. The third African American to receive a doctorate in history was Charles H. Wesley, whose parents were born free in Kentucky. Although James Henry Woodson's other children and their relatives had professional careers as teachers, doctors, and businessmen, only Carter Godwin Woodson became widely known as an intellectual.

Woodson sought the support of his dissertation committee to publish his dissertation. This was an exercise in futility in that Frederick Jackson Turner, the most positive member of the committee, declined to provide assistance to acquire publication. He wrote in a letter two months after Woodson's request stating that the dissertation was too similar to Charles Henry Ambler's, Sectionalism in Virginia from 1776 to 1861, which was published in 1910. Ambler's book was a revision of his 1908 University of Wisconsin doctoral dissertation. Turner explained that he doubted that the Harvard history department would include Woodson's dissertation in its series of published dissertations or the Harvard University Press would publish it. Turner also warned Woodson that he might have to pay a subvention to have the dissertation published, as the book would probably not have a market and would not make money.

Woodson encountered similar difficulty with his first book, which was completed while he made revisions to his dissertation. He ended up submitting a subvention and *The Education of the Negro Prior to 1861* to G. P. Putnam's Sons; they agreed to publish it in 1915. The book was favorably and widely reviewed in historical journals, as well as the white popular press. Mary Church Terrell, a civil rights advocate and African American suffragist, indicated that she was pleased with the book as "a work of profound historical research." Even Turner praised the book as a "substantial contribution to the subject."

All the while, publishers who refused to publish Woodson's dissertation, did so for white historians writing on the same subject. Four authors prevented Charles Henry Ambler from having the final say on the succession movement in Western Virginia. Only Richard Orr Curry's *House Divided: A Study of Statehood, Politics and the Copperhead Movement in West Virginia* cited Woodson's 1912 dissertation. This book is still cited by contemporary historians.

Despite these achievements and struggles, Woodson did not begin his life's mission until he and George Cleveland Hall, personal physician to Booker T. Washington and a surgeon at Chicago's Provident Hospital; Alexander L. Jackson, then executive secretary of the YMCA; and James E. Stamps, a Yale University graduate student founded the Association for the Study of Negro Life and History on September 9, 1915. This was the first historical society devoted exclusively to researching the life and history of African Americans in America, Africa, and throughout the world. Also in 1915, D. W. Griffith released the racist movie *The Birth of a Nation*, which was vehemently protested by blacks and some white liberals. From the establishment of the association until his death on April 4, 1950, Woodson made the association and its work his life's mission. He never wavered in maintaining his independence from outside control.

The annual meetings of the association provided black scholars an opportunity to present papers before their peers. The next year the association launched its scientific quarterly the *Journal of Negro History*. Woodson included substantial portions of his never published dissertation into articles that appeared in the *Journal*. The *Journal* documented information that was previously ignored by mainstream historians. It was innovative in its methods of research used to collect data and in its interpretation of history. Woodson covered a wide range of subjects and emphasized a shift in the focus of historical analysis to the perspective of slave, away from that of the master's.

Journal contributors used oral histories, birth and death certificates, marriage registers, letters, diaries, and census data to research black history. Today many historians have adopted these methods. Benjamin E. Mays wrote in his "I Knew Carter G. Goodson," that the *Journal* documented black life so well that any research on the Negro by perforce had to refer to it.

Woodson published the first issue of the *Journal of Negro History* at his own expense. Although the association had an executive council, Woodson did much of the work directing, organizing, producing, writing, and providing most of the funding. Obtaining adequate funding was a constant challenge; Woodson exerted much of his energy to keeping the organization afloat. He had to secure further employment in order for him and the association to survive.

From 1918 to 1919, he was principal of Armstrong Manual Training School in Washington, D.C. He then worked for one year at Howard University as professor of history, head of the graduate faculty, and dean of the School of Liberal Arts. He developed the graduate program but only one of his five students, Arnett J. Lindsay, completed the Howard graduate program under his tutelage. Later, Woodson published part of Lindsay's thesis in the *Journal*. He left Howard because of disputes with University President J. Stanley Durkee over academic freedom.

The next year Woodson became dean of West Virginia Collegiate Institute (now State College) in 1920. During this time, he established the Associated Publishers and wrote several books: *The History of the Negro Church* in 1921, *The Negro in Our History* in 1922, *and The Mind of the Negro As Reflected in Letters Written During the Crisis, 1800–1860* in 1926. After his second position as dean, he retired from the teaching profession in 1922 to concentrate on the association. Although he obtained small contributions from rich white supporters such as Julius Rosenwald and grants from the Carnegie and Rockefeller Foundations, Woodson and his association stayed afloat mainly on his teaching salary, book royalties, the black masses, and the contributions of African American organizations. The foundation funding dried up as a result of concerns of power broker Thomas Jesse Jones who wanted Woodson to relinquish control and affiliate the association with a university. The problem of funding became acute because Woodson was forced to rely more on the black masses and organizations at the zenith of the Great Depression.

Through the difficult times, Woodson was able to accomplish much. He was interested in the black nationalist movement led by Marcus Garvey. He became a frequent contributor for Garvey's weekly publication, the *Negro World*. He wrote more than 100 articles and 125 book reviews in his capacity as a contributor to the *Journal*. Woodson was also editor and founder of the *Negro History Bulletin* and author of more than 30 books. His most popular book is *The Mis-Education of the Negro*, originally issued by Associated Publisher in 1933. In this book, he criticized any educational enterprise that did not serve the needs of the students.

In 1926, Woodson launched Negro History Week, which became Black History month in 1976. This pioneering educator, historian, and social analyst died in Washington, D.C. on April 3, 1950 at the age of 74. His mission and message provided an opportunity for America to acknowledge and understand the heritage of African Americans. *See also:* Association for the Study of African American Life and History; Du Bois, W. E. B.; Franklin, John Hope.

Marva Strickland-Hill

Bibliography

Conyers, James L. *Carter G. Woodson: A Historical Reader.* New York: Garland Publishers, 2000.

Goggin, Jacqueline. *Carter G. Woodson: A Life in Black History.* Baton Rouge: Louisiana State University Press, 1993.

Scally, M. Anthony. *Carter G. Woodson: A Bio-Bibliography.* Westport, CT: Greenwood Press, 1985.

Woodson, Carter Godwin. *The Mis-Education of the Negro.* Trenton, NJ: Africa World Press, 1990.

World War I (Black Participation in)

African Americans have participated in every American war from colonial times to Iraqi Freedom, and their contributions to American military history have been severely underappreciated and virtually ignored. The United States entered World War I in 1917, and the all-black 92nd and 93rd Infantry divisions were sent to France and served bravely until the Armistice in 1918 and play a vital role in the defeat of Germany.

As African Americans were asked to sacrifice for their country, a wave of violence was perpetrated against them in 1916–1917, with about 120 lynchings, mostly in the South. Race riots occurred in New York, St. Louis, and Houston as a result of the combination of African American troops demanding their basic rights as citizens and American soldiers in a largely Jim Crow city. These waves of violence prompted the United States Army to rely on National Guard and conscripts rather than regular African American enlistees. Famous units such as the 9th and 10th Cavalries, the Buffalo Soldiers, were not sent to France; however, these units provided much needed border security in Arizona and California and were spared the carnage of European battlefields.

The first American troops arrived in France in 1917 as the American Expeditionary Force (AEF) led by General John Pershing and included units of the 93rd Infantry division. The 93rd, the last of which arrived in April, under American leadership guarded German prisoners of war and directed supplies to the other units.

President Woodrow Wilson's Secretary of War Newton D. Baker ordered Pershing to keep the AEF under American command while in Europe. The all-black 93rd, under the command of white officers, was seen as undesirable and detrimental to the American war effort and was quickly transferred to French command where they had to turn in all American equipment except for their uniforms. This included the Springfield 30.06 rifles, which were far superior to the French Lebel rifle. The Springfield was better suited for open warfare, rather than trench warfare, for which the U.S. soldiers had trained, and many were expert marksmen with the Springfield.

The 93rd consisted of three National Guard units and one drafted unit and was organized into four regiments: the 369th, 370th, 371st, and 372nd. The 369th set an American World War I record for 191 days of unbroken combat with

Some of the men of the 369th Infantry, also known as the Harlem Hellfighters, who received the Croix de Guerre for gallantry in action during World War I. (National Archives)

French black colonial troops in the French sector of the Argonne Forest where they repelled massive German assaults at Chateau-Thierry and Belleau Wood.

Known as the Blue Helmet soldiers, they came to be respected by the French and feared by the Germans for their fierce determination and bravery under fire. Approximately 3,500 Blue Helmet soldiers were killed in action. Moreover, they distinguished themselves by earning 42 American Distinguished Service Crosses, 4 Medaille Militaire (the highest French military honor), 325 Croix de Guerre, and 1 Congressional Medal of Honor. President George Herbert Walker Bush posthumously awarded the Medal of Honor to Corporal Freddie Stowers who was killed in action in 1918.

The all-Black 92nd Infantry Division did not enjoy the same success. Made up of all draftees, the 92nd was organized into four infantry regiments and, like their brothers-in-arms, received insufficient training, poor equipment, and white officers. General Charles C. Ballou was the first commander. Despite his prejudices, Ballou sought to give a square deal to his troops and treat them fairly. Once they arrived in Europe in June 1918, however, command of the division was given to General Robert Bullard who shared the typical racial views of the era.

In August 1918, the 92nd was assigned to the St. Dié sector close to the German border and was supposed to train with French units until their withdrawal and subsequently take over the sector; however, the friction of war caused both French and American delays. The division arrived in the midst of German counterattacks and was quickly introduced to trench and chemical warfare. By the time they were pulled out of the sector in September 1918, the 92nd had repelled 11 German patrols and secured the French villages at Frapelle and Ormont.

Less than a week later, the 92nd was reassigned to the American sector of the Argonne Forest in preparation for the large American assault. Pershing's plan called for a simultaneous push with French units on the left and American units on the right. His plan had one fatal flaw that created an 800-meter gap between the French and American lines. Reserve French units and the largely inexperienced 92nd were to fill the chasm. In the fog of battle, inexperience, lapses in communications, and poor planning resulted in the 92nd's failure to hold the line. Subsequently the 92nd was ordered out of the Argonne and relegated to patrol duty until the Armistice in November and was largely regarded as ineffective in combat.

See also: Buffalo Soldiers; Houston, Texas, Mutiny, 1917; "If We Must Die"; Red Summer Race Riots

Jeffery Othele Mahan

Bibliography

Barbeau, Arthur E., and Florette Henri. *The Unknown Soldiers: Black American Troops in World War I.* Philadelphia: Temple University Press, 1974.

Ellis, Mark. *Race, War, and Surveillance: African Americans and the United States Government during World War I.* Bloomington: Indiana University Press, 2001.

Jamieson, J. A. et al. *Complete History of the Colored Soldiers.* New York: Bennett and Churchill, 1919.

Roberts, Frank E. *The American Foreign Legion: Black Soldiers of the 93rd in World War I.* Annapolis, MD: Naval Institute Press, 2004.

World War II (Black Participation in)

Since colonial times the African American has served this nation in war and peace. The first all-black unit in American history was the 54th Massachusetts Infantry that fought bravely in the Civil War. The 10th cavalry, the famed Buffalo Soldiers, won acclaim fighting Native Americans and at San Juan Hill with future U.S. President Theodore Roosevelt. African Americans served in World War I in the 93rd Infantry Division, a segregated unit, and won countless medals. World War II was a unique era, as African Americans fought a war on two fronts against a tough and deadly enemy abroad and against strong, often violent, racial attitudes at home. Yet this period created more opportunities for black participation in the military, produced meaningful victories against discrimination, and planted the seeds for the Civil Rights movement of the mid-20th century.

After World War I, the National Urban League (1907), the National Association for the Advancement of Colored People (1910), and the Universal Negro Improvement Association challenged social norms. Moreover, almost half of all southern African Americans moved north or from rural areas to the city during the Great Migration. In New York during the 1920s, this migration ignited the Harlem Renaissance movement, which was a celebration of black artistry, culture, and an increased recognition of the black struggle for racial equality.

In black history, World War II represented a gap between the Harlem Renaissance and the landmark *Brown v. the Board of Education* that legally ended segregation. In this period, approximately 12.8 million African Americans resided in the United States. Membership in the NAACP grew and the organization gained momentum politically. Moreover, some institutions within the federal government took a more active role in protecting civil rights. For example, U.S. Attorney General Frank Murphy created the Civil Liberties Unit within the Department of Justice and Wisconsin Governor Robert La Follette started the Civil Liberties Committee.

Before Pearl Harbor, President Franklin D. Roosevelt and many political leaders realized that America would be in the war as Nazi armies swept across Europe and amid ever increasing tensions with Japan. Both human and material resources would be at a premium for the war effort. Discussions were well underway how to best use the black population in the war effort.

Black leaders and politicians directed their efforts at war industries that were still hiring African Americans in nonessential jobs. In an investigation, the National Urban League uncovered discriminatory hiring practices that prevented African Americans from receiving the proper training for top jobs. Acting on these findings, A. Philip Randolph, Walter White, Mary McLeod Bethune, Dr. Channing H. Tobias, George E. Haynes, and Lester B. Grange organized and threatened to march on Washington, D.C.

Eleanor Roosevelt and New York Governor Fiorello La Guardia feared this march would alienate southern voters and convinced organizers to cancel the march and meet with President Roosevelt. The eventual meeting produced Executive Order 8802 and the Committee of Fair Employment Practice, which were among the first efforts to ensure fair hiring practices in industry and coupled with good timing more opportunities were created for black women and men not in the military.

At the same time, World War I veteran Rayford W. Logan with the support of the NAACP and the all-black newspaper the *Pittsburgh Courier* established the Committee for the Participation of Negroes and National Defense and pushed for larger black quotas in the military. Successful in their efforts, an amendment to the Selective Service Bill of 1940 increased black enlistments but did not end segregation in the military.

At the end of World War I, there were more than 400,000 African Americans in uniform including about 1,300 commissioned officers. By 1939, however, less than 3,500 black soldiers and five commissioned officers, mostly chaplains, were in the army. Few African Americans served in the navy as support and kitchen personnel. African Americans were denied entry into the Marine Corps and the Army Corps. By 1942, however, Colonel Benjamin O. Davis was made the first African American general and enlistments were above 460,000 and entrance into the Army Air Corps and Marines had been gained.

Despite the new quotas, African Americans were rejected for military service at a higher rate than whites for several reasons. Segregation retarded African American education and caused poor performance on entrance exams. With many African Americans already impoverished, the deprivations of the Great Depression left many in poor physical condition. Statistically, 12 percent of African Americans were rejected as a result of poor health, 15.8 percent for reasons unrelated to physical, and 35.6 percent were rejected because of their educational background. The units that did serve ultimately, however, opened the door for President Harry S. Truman to desegregate America's Armed Forces in 1948.

The first African American unit to see action was the 99th Pursuit Squadron of the 332nd Fighter Group, collectively known as the Tuskegee Airmen because of their flight training at the Tuskegee Institute in Alabama. The first 40 pilots were rushed into service because of manpower needs in the North African campaign. Rather than opting for top recruits, only pilots that had already completed civilian courses through the Civil Aeronautics Board were chosen. Basic training was shortened by several weeks.

Nevertheless, the 99th was shipped to Africa in early 1943 and produced disappointing early results. Inexperienced and not as aggressive as their white counterparts, the 99th was assigned to the rear for more training and to await less hastily trained African American pilots who had arrived from the United States. While there, the 99th flew missions with the 79th Fighter Group, an independent air wing. Experiencing fair treatment from the 79th, the Tuskegee Airmen gained invaluable experience and confidence that would serve them well in the skies over Italy and Europe. By the end of the war, the famed "Red Tails" of the 332nd escorted heavy bombers, raided oil refineries, and targeted key installations in Italy, the Balkans, and key components of the Nazi infrastructure deep in the heart of Germany. The 332nd became a hardened, battle-tested unit in the final months of World War II.

Another unit of the Tuskegee Airmen was the 447th Bombardier Group. Frustration, conflict, and a well-disciplined, nonviolent strategy against the institutional racism of the army marked their wartime efforts. Black leaders and politicians realized that flying the huge bombers would better serve African Americans in the postwar world. Although gallant in their efforts, the 332nd fighter experience would be virtually useless in commercial aviation. Bomber experience could open doors for better jobs for African Americans as commercial pilots.

Racism and insufficient numbers prevented this unit from seeing active combat. Less than 20,000 African Americans served in the air corps, far below the necessary numbers required to supply replacement pilots for the 332nd or flight and maintenance crews for bombers. Throughout their training, however, they challenged army reluctance to press the unit into service at their installations and they were a forerunner of the Civil Rights movement of the 1950s.

Subsequently, the 93rd Infantry Division of World War I fame was reactivated in May 1942. Unlike other segregated units, the 93rd trained at one military post and was not truncated. In 1944, the 93rd was sent to the Pacific theater as an occupation force. They arrived on Guadalcanal after the majority of the Japanese resistance had ended. Only the 24th Infantry of the 93rd saw any appreciable action on Bougainville in March 1944. Inexperienced, they were overrun by the Japanese. For the remainder of the war, the 93rd was relegated to patrol and guard duty.

Unlike the 93rd, the 92nd Infantry Division saw extensive combat action in Italy and trained at four separate installations across the nation: Fort McClellan, Alabama, Camp Atterbury, Indiana, Camp Breckenridge, Kentucky, and Camp Robinson, Arkansas. Part of Mark Clark's Fifth Army, poorly trained, and equipped, with an average fourth grade education because of educational discrimination, the 92nd fought against a deadly veteran German Army and suffered a high casualty rate. Several incidents of self-sacrifice and bravery, however, were noted during the war and recognized more than 50 years later by President William Jefferson Clinton, who awarded two of its members the Congressional Medal of Honor.

First Lieutenant John Robert Fox was a forward observer for the 598th Field Artillery Battalion, undertaking training maneuvers near Sommocolonia, Italy on Christmas Day 1944. Stopping to rest for the night in the village, Fox and his platoon awoke to discover that Germans disguised as partisans had encircled their positions during the night. Rapidly under assault, Fox's platoon was nearly overwhelmed and outnumbered.

Many rescue attempts could not breech the German lines, which prompted Fox to call for artillery fire only 60 yards from his platoon. Desperate, Fox called for artillery to fire directly on his own position killing Fox and most of his platoon; however, about 100 Germans were killed, and several hours later an Allied counterattack reclaimed the village. Fox was awarded the Purple Heart and Bronze Star at the time of the incident. Years later he was awarded the Distinguished Cross and the Medal of Honor.

Lieutenant Vernon J. Baker was a member of the 360th Regimental Combat Team of the 92nd Infantry Division. Ordered to assault Hill X and Castle Aghilnofi behind German Gothic Line on 5 April 1945, Baker lost nearly two-thirds of his platoon. Intense German artillery fire prevented Baker from obeying orders to withdraw his decimated unit. Baker destroyed one machine gun nest and a German observation tower virtually single handedly. Accompanied by a fellow platoon member, Baker demolished more gun emplacements and drew enemy fire away from rescue efforts.

The next day Baker led the counterattack through mine fields to eventually take the original objectives of the mission, earning him the Purple Heart, Bronze Star, and Distinguished Service Cross and, like Fox, the Medal of Honor. Only five other black Americans, all posthumously, received the nation's highest honor from World War II: Private George Watson, Sergeant Edward A. Carter Jr., Private Willy F. James Jr., Sergeant Ruben Rivers, and First Lieutenant Charles L. Thomas. *See also:* Double-V Campaign; Evers, Medgar; National Association for the Advancement of Colored People; Randolph, A. Philip; Robinson, Jackie; Tuskegee Airmen; World War I (Black Participation in)

Jeffery Othele Mahan

Bibliography

Baker, Vernon J., and Ken Olson. *Lasting Valor.* New York: Bantam Books, 1997.

Buchanan, Russell A. *Black Americans in World War II.* Santa Barbara, CA: ABC-CLIO, 1997.

Hine, Darlene Clark. *Black Women in White: Racial Conflict and Cooperation in the Nursing Profession, 1890–1950.* Bloomington: Indiana University Press, 1989.

Honey, Maureen, ed. *Bitter Fruit: African American Women in World War II.* Columbia: University of Missouri Press, 1999.

Lee, Ulysses. *The United States Army in World War II: The Employment of Negro Troops.* Washington D.C.: Center for Military History, 1963.

Motley, Mary Penick. *The Invisible Soldier: The Experience of the Black Soldier, World War II.* Detroit, MI: Wayne State University Press, 1975.

Sandler, Stanley. *Segregated Skies: All-Black Combat Squadrons of World War II.* Washington, D.C.: Smithsonian Institution Press, 1992.

Wynn, Neil A. *The Afro-American and the Second World War.* New York: Holmes & Meier, 1976.

X, Malcolm

Malcolm X (1925–1965) was an author, activist, and minister of the Nation of Islam who has become the most enduring contemporary symbol of African American militant protest. Given the name Malcolm Little at birth, he became Malcolm X after entering the Nation of Islam and finally changed his name to el-Hajj Malik el-Shabazz while on pilgrimage to Mecca in 1964. Malcolm X's public career lasted only six years and ended abruptly with his assassination. Nonetheless, his influence on recent African American history is enormous. He left behind no lasting organization or movement, no record of changed legislation, no institutional legacy, no accomplishment of improved conditions for black people in America, and no developed political philosophy. His achievements were cultural. His most important and long-lasting contribution was *The Autobiography of Malcolm X,* written with Alex Haley. Beyond that, as a media figure between 1959 and 1964, he introduced the black community to a new model of black leadership, an unprecedented public display of black rage, and a new mode of aggressive black masculinity that continues to have a profound effect on popular culture today.

Born May 19, 1925, in Omaha, Nebraska, Malcolm was his father's seventh child. Reverend Earl (Early) Little, a freelance Baptist minister and a part-time organizer for Marcus Garvey's Universal Negro Improvement Association (UNIA), already had three children from a previous marriage and three children with his second wife, Louise (Louisa), Malcolm's mother. According to Malcolm, Louise was so fair that she looked white while his father was very dark-skinned. Malcolm begins his autobiography with an account of his mother, pregnant with him, confronting armed Ku Klux Klan riders who surrounded the family house in Omaha while his father was away; however, Louise Little has denied that this incident ever occurred.

Malcolm was more light-skinned than any of his brothers and sisters, with reddish-brown hair. He was apparently his father's favorite child. His relationship with his mother was more troubled. There was considerable violence within the home. Earl beat Louise and also beat his children almost savagely, except for Malcolm. All of Malcolm's beatings came from his mother. In 1931, when Malcolm was six years old, his father was killed. Malcolm would later insist that he was murdered by white supremacists, but all contemporary evidence indicates that he died in a street car accident. With seven children to care for and overwhelmed by poverty during the Depression, Louise Little tried to maintain her family intact, but without success. Malcolm was placed in the care of a white family by the welfare authorities. He admitted to being glad when it happened. In 1939, after giving birth to an eighth child and being abandoned by the new baby's father, Louise was judged insane and was formally committed to a state mental hospital. She remained there for 25 years. Malcolm visited her occasionally, but she did not recognize him. In his autobiography, he blames social workers for driving his mother insane.

In 1941, at the age of 15, Malcolm moved to Boston to live with his half-sister, a daughter of his father's first marriage, Ella Collins. Despite her efforts to introduce him to her respectable friends and to keep him in school, Malcolm was almost immediately attracted to the criminal underworld of the city. His first part-time job as a shoeshine boy in the Roseland State Ballroom men's room was a thin disguise for a number of illegal activities, such as selling marijuana or putting his customers in touch with prostitutes. He also began a long-term relationship, over Ella's furious objections, with an older white woman he called "Sophia" in his autobiography (Beatrice Caragulian, later Beatrice Bazarian). Drafted into the army during World War II, he managed to avoid service by feigning insanity. He pursued a career of petty criminality that included a short stay in Harlem before he returned to Boston. There he was arrested for burglaries he had carried out with the help of his white girlfriend, her sister, and his male cohorts. In February 1946, at the age of 20, he was sentenced to three concurrent 8- to 10-year sentences at hard labor. Malcolm attributed the harsh punishment to the judge's anger over his sexual relationship with a white woman.

During his early days in prison, Malcolm earned the nickname "Satan" because of his outspoken atheism and his hostility toward religion. As he relates in his autobiography, his efforts to educate himself in prison began long before his conversion to the National of Islam. He enrolled in correspondence courses, studied the dictionary, and voraciously read books from the prison library. While serving time in prison, Malcolm was introduced to the teachings of the Nation of Islam by his brother Reginald, who had joined the group. Initially showing no interest, Malcolm was a deeply committed convert by the time he was released from prison in August 1952.

Ella had arranged for Malcolm to move to Detroit, where his brothers Wilfred, Philbert, and Wesley and his sister Hilda lived, after his release from prison. All of his siblings were now active members of the Nation of Islam there. Malcolm soon visited the leader of the movement, Elijah Muhammad, in Chicago, where he was given special recognition. Like most members of the Nation of Islam, he changed his last name to X, to symbolize his rejection of white oppression. He explained in his book: "The Muslim's 'X' symbolized the true African family name that he never could know. For me, my 'X' replaced the white slavemaster name of 'Little' which some blue-eyed devil named Little had imposed upon my paternal forebears. . . . Mr. Muhammad taught that we would keep this 'X' until God Himself returned and gave us a Holy Name from His own mouth." (*The Autobiography of Malcolm X*, p. 199.)

He actively recruited new converts for the Nation of Islam and was an effective proselytizer. The Federal Bureau of Investigation opened a file on Malcolm in 1953, after learning that he had referred to himself as a communist. He remained under FBI surveillance for the rest of his life. He expanded the Nation of Islam in Detroit, established the Nation's first Temple in Boston, and found new recruits in Philadelphia. In 1954, he was chosen to head Temple No. 7 in Harlem, and he rapidly expanded its membership there also.

In 1958, after receiving permission from Elijah Muhammad, Malcolm married Betty X (neé Sanders, later Betty Shabazz) in Lansing, Michigan. The couple eventually had six daughters: Attallah (b. 1958), Qubilah (b. 1960), Ilyasah (b. 1962), Gamilah Lumumba (b. 1964); and twin girls, Malaak and Malikah, born in 1965 after their father's death. During the marriage, Malcolm was often away from the home traveling, speaking, or attending to the business of the Nation of Islam.

Malcolm X during a press conference for Dr. Martin Luther King Jr. in 1964. (Library of Congress)

Malcolm X first became a public media figure in 1959, when he appeared in a television documentary broadcast in New York City, entitled "The Hate That Hate Produced." On that program he explained that, according to the teaching of the Nation of Islam, black people were a divine race; he frankly denounced the white race as evil, incapable of good. The audience saw footage of the University of Islam, where Muslim children were taught that whites were devils. This message appeared in such sharp contrast to the theme of brotherhood being put forward by the Civil Rights movement that the Nation of Islam, and Malcolm in particular, immediately became the objects of national media attention. Although Malcolm would later complain about the negative publicity, it was his almost demonic media image that brought the National of Islam into the fore. He did everything he could to cultivate that image in media interviews.

At this time, Malcolm's public statements adhered strictly to the teachings of the Nation of Islam as given by Elijah Muhammad. Malcolm unabashedly spoke of a self-righteous hatred of whites. In his autobiography, begun in 1963, Malcolm repeated the Nation of Islam's official teaching that white people were an artificial race of mutant people who had been created in prehistory, through genetic experimentation, by an evil black scientist named Yacub.

Elijah Muhammad imposed a strict rule against political activity and protest on the Nation of Islam, including banning social involvement that might improve conditions for blacks. His teaching was that God would soon liberate his people without effort on their part, and that the followers of the Nation of Islam should simply wait for this inevitable divine event. All of these teachings would eventually become a problem for Malcolm X and lead to his break with the movement.

Malcolm X became the national representative, the chief spokesman, for the Nation of Islam. He was in much demand as a public speaker on college campuses and other venues and was sought after for television appearances. He was also interviewed as a spokesman for black Americans by journalists from other countries. He established the Nation of Islam's first national newspaper, *Muhammad Speaks.* From these platforms he sharply criticized the leaders of the Civil Rights movement for advocating that blacks should integrate into white society, rather than build separate black institutions. He rejected their stance that black people should respond with nonviolence when faced with attacks from the white community.

Malcolm's popularity with the media and his obvious position as the second most important leader of the Nation of Islam, after Elijah Muhammad himself, caused tensions to develop within the movement. A book about the Nation of Islam, *When the Word Is Given,* published in 1963, featured Malcolm X on its cover and included transcripts of five of his speeches, but only one of Elijah Muhammad's, much to the chagrin of the latter. Publishers asked for the rights to Malcolm's autobiography, not for Elijah Muhammad's. Members of Elijah Muhammad's family and other high-ranking Muslim leaders in Chicago began to maneuver against Malcolm's position within the Nation.

Tensions developed between Malcolm and his leader, Elijah Muhammad, over the Nation of Islam's general noninvolvement policy, with Malcolm moving toward more action and engagement in the black social struggle taking place around them in the early 1960s. For example, when Ronald Stokes, member of the Nation, was killed and six other Muslims were wounded in a police raid on the Muslim Temple in Los Angeles in April 1962, a furious Malcolm

X sought to organize the black community around the issue and bring a legal case against the police for brutality. Elijah Muhammad, however, eventually ordered him to discontinue his efforts in Los Angeles and return to New York. In the summer of 1963, Malcolm (without authorization from Elijah Muhammad) announced that Temple No. 7, in Harlem, would begin a voter registration drive. Against standing policy, he publicly advocated that the Nation of Islam should form a "united black front" with civil rights organizations. Malcolm was also deeply shaken by his knowledge of financial corruption at the Nation's headquarters in Chicago and the increasing confirmation he received of Elijah Muhammad's adulterous affairs and illegitimate children with former secretaries. He began discussing these issues with a few other Muslims.

These conflicts came to a head with the assassination of President John Kennedy. In keeping with his policy of caution and noninvolvement, Elijah Muhammad had strictly instructed all Muslim ministers to make no comment on the assassination. Malcolm complied for a few days, but then after one of his talks in New York, someone asked about Kennedy. Comparing the assassination to that of Patrice Lumumba and other deaths that he said the president had been responsible for, Malcolm remarked: "Chickens coming home to roost never did make me sad; they've always made me glad." (*The Autobiography of Malcolm X,* pp. 300–301). This statement was widely reported and criticized in the press.

The next day, Elijah Muhammad suspended Malcolm from making any public statements for 90 days in order to distance the Nation of Islam from his remarks. A few weeks later, Malcolm was relieved of his positions as the national representative of the Nation and as the Minister of Temple No. 7. Loyal Muslims were quietly told to shun him and perhaps even to kill him. The ban on his public speaking was extended indefinitely. Realizing that his disputes with the Nation of Islam were now irreconcilable, Malcolm announced his break with the movement on March 8, 1964. He formed the Muslim Mosque, Inc., in Harlem, to continue his work to liberate and uplift African American people. He would later also found the Organization of Afro-American Unity (OAAU), a secular organization devoted to the same ends. Both organizations were a direct challenge to the Nation of Islam.

Almost immediately after leaving the Nation of Islam, Malcolm decided to make a pilgrimage to Mecca. The trip was financed by his sister, Ella. He was received with hospitality by the Saudi royal family, who made him a guest of the state. The deputy chief of protocol for Prince Faisal accompanied him on his pilgrimage. Malcolm claimed that his pilgrimage amounted to a conversion experience that allowed him to reject the idea that white men were devils and embrace the racial brotherhood taught by orthodox Islam. While in Mecca he changed his name to el-Hajj Malik el-Shabazz. In any case, the pilgrimage provided Malcolm with an opportunity to reformulate his message to his followers and to the public. From Saudi Arabia, he conducted a campaign of writing letters, postcards, and public statements to proclaim his conversion to orthodox Islam and his newfound belief in the unity of the human race.

After his return from pilgrimage, Malcolm X remained a popular media figure. He spoke regularly at the Muslim Mosque, Inc., and at meetings of the Organization of African Unity. Tensions with the Nation of Islam escalated, and there were a number of threats and attempts on his life. On February 21, 1965, while addressing a meeting of the OAAU at the Audubon Ballroom in New York, and before an audience of 400 supporters, who included his wife and children, Malcolm was shot 16 times, with a shotgun and with pistols, by at least three assassins. He died at the podium. The gunmen were seized by the crowd and by Malcolm's bodyguards. Three men, all affiliated with the Nation of Islam, were eventually convicted of the murder and served prison sentences. They have since been released.

Malcolm X certainly had a greater impact on the African American community after his death than he did while he was alive. His autobiography was published posthumously and became a best seller. His militant stance was echoed by subsequent black activists such as the Black Power movement and the Black Panthers, for which his book was a standard inspiration. During the late 1980s and early 1990s, Malcolm's face and the symbol "X" were marketed on T-shirts, baseball caps, and other casual attire. The clutter of "X" products and paraphernalia eventually lost touch with any political message. In 1992, Spike Lee released a major motion picture based on Malcolm's life that was successful at the box office. While this commercial popularity has since waned, Malcolm X remains an iconic figure for an entire generation of African American youth.

See also: Black Nationalism; Black Power; Haley, Alex; Muhammad, Elijah; Nation of Islam; Organization of Afro-American Unity; Pan-Africanism; Shabazz, Beatty X; Universal Negro Improvement Association

Anthony A. Lee

Bibliography

Carson, Clayborne. *Malcolm X: The FBI File.* New York: Carroll & Graf, 1991.

Clegg III, Claude Andrew. *An Original Man: The Life and Times of Elijah Muhammad.* New York: St. Martin's Press, 1997.

Collins, Rodney P., and A. Peter Bailey. *The Seventh Child: A Family Memoir of Malcolm X.* London: Turnaround, 2002.

Dyson, Michael Eric. *Making Malcolm: The Myth and Meaning of Malcolm X.* New York: Oxford University Press, 1996.

Jenkins, Robert L., ed. *The Malcolm X Encyclopedia.* Westport, CT: Greenwood Press, 2002.

Perry, Bruce. *Malcolm: The Life of a Man Who Changed Black America.* Barrytown, NY: Station Hill Press, 1991.

Shabazz, Ilyasah with Kim McLarin. *Growing Up X.* New York: One World, 2002.

X, Malcolm with the assistance of Alex Haley. *The Autobiography of Malcolm X.* New York: Ballantine Books, 1965.

Categorical Index

Culture, Identity, and Community: From Slavery to the Present

Political Activity and Resistance to Oppression: From the American Revolution to the Civil War

Forten, Charlotte, **407–408**. *See also* Abolition, slavery; Forten, James

Forten, James, 378, 413, 461, 506, 573

Free African Society (FAS), 281, 298, 301, 325, **410–411**, 457. *See also* Benevolent societies

Free Soil Party, 349, **411–412**, 412 (illustration), 484. *See also* Abolition, slavery; Brown, John; Fugitive Slave Act of 1850; Republican Party

Freedom's Journal, 280–281, 295, 318, 347, 356–357, **413–414**, 516–518, 569, 580. *See also* American Colonization Society; Cornish, Samuel; Crummell, Boston; Liberia; Russwurm, John

Fugitive Slave Act of 1793, **415–416**, 521. *See also* Compromise of 1850; Fugitive Slave Act of 1850; Fugitive slaves

Fugitive Slave Act of 1850, 282, 324, 340, 350, 359, 393, **416–417**, 418 (illustration), 423, 508, 521, 535, 538, 562, 758. *See also* Destination, Canada; Fugitive Slave Act of 1793; Fugitive slaves; *Uncle Tom's Cabin*; Underground Railroad

Fugitive slaves, **417–420**. *See also* Destination, Canada; Fugitive Slave Act of 1793; Fugitive Slave Act of 1850; Underground Railroad

Gabriel (Prosser), **420–421**, 475, 534. *See also* Slave resistance

Gang system, **422**. *See also* Slave plantations; Task system

Garner, Margaret, **422–424**, 423 (illustration). *See also* Fugitive slaves; Slave resistance; Underground Railroad

Garnet, Henry Highland, 293, 296, 307, 317, 318, 346, 363, 377, 393, **424–427**, 425 (illustration), 479, 509–510, 537, 539, 569. *See also* African Civilization Society; Colored Convention Movement; Liberty Party

Garrison, William Lloyd, 281, 303–304, 305, 324, 326, 343, 345, 388, 394, 397, 417, **427–430**, 428 (photo), 435, 448, 461–462, 464, 488, 506, 508, 512, 513, 525, 549, 553, 573, 580. *See also* American and Foreign Anti-Slavery Society; American Anti-Slavery Society; Douglass, Frederick; Immediatism; the *Liberator*; Lincoln, Abraham; Tappan, Arthur; Tappan, Lewis

Gradual emancipation, **430–431**. *See also* Abolition, slavery; Garrison, William Lloyd; Jefferson, Thomas;

Lincoln, Abraham; Northern slavery

Great Awakening, **431–433**, 481. *See also* Abolition, slavery; Evangelism

Grimke, Angelina and Sarah, 289, 304, 408, **433–436**, 434 (illustration), 1046. *See also* Abolition, slavery; Garrison, William Lloyd

Haitian Revolution, 375, **436–441**, 469, 470–474, 475, 510, 520, 567, 569; foreign invasion, **438–439**; Leclerc-Rochambeau expedition, **440–441**; Louverture's reign, 438 (illustration), **439–440**; road to revolution, **436–437**; slave uprising, **437–438**. *See also* Louverture, Toussaint

Hall, Prince, **441–442**. *See also* Abolition, slavery; American Revolution; Continental Army; Prince Hall Masonry

Hamilton, William, **442–444**. *See also* Abolition, slave trade; Black Nationalism; Colored Convention Movement; *Freedom's Journal*; Pan-Africanism; Williams, Peter, Sr.

Hammon, Jupiter, **444–445**. *See also* Abolition, slave trade; Abolition, slavery; Moral uplift

Hemings, Sally, **445–446**. *See also* Jefferson, Thomas; Miscegenation

House servants, **446–447**. *See also* Field hands; Hemings, Sally; Jacobs, Harriet; Newsom, Celia; Slave plantations

Immediatism, **447–448**. *See also* Abolition, slavery; Garrison, William Lloyd; the *Liberator*; Liberty Party

Jacobs, Harriet, **449–450**. *See also* Douglass, Frederick; Fugitive Slave Act of 1850; Fugitive slaves; House servants; Slave resistance

Jay, John, 296, **450–452**, 451 (illustration), 550. *See also* Abolition, slavery; American Revolution; Gradual emancipation

Jefferson, Thomas, 132, 276, 280, 288, 332, 370–372, 420, 431, 445–446, 452, **452–453**, 462, 469, 571, 849. *See also* American Revolution; Banneker, Benjamin; Declaration of Independence; Gabriel (Prosser); Haitian Revolution; Hemings, Sally; Louisiana Purchase

Jennings, Elizabeth, **454–455**. *See also* Douglass, Frederick;

Garnet, Henry Highland; Jennings, Thomas L.; New York Draft Riots; Pennington, James William Charles

Jennings, Thomas L., 344, 394, **455–456**, 577. *See also* Abolition, slavery; Colored Convention Movement; Destination, Haiti; Jennings, Elizabeth; Williams, Peter, Jr.

Jones, Absalom, 298, 301, 318, 325, 410, **457–458**, 523. *See also* African Methodist Episcopal Church; Allen, Richard; Benevolent societies

Kansas-Nebraska Act, 1854, 290–291, 331, 412, **458–459**, 465, 469. *See also* Brown, John; Louisiana Purchase; Missouri Compromise

Langston, John Mercer, 316, **459–461**, 459 (photo). *See also* Abolition, slavery; Destination, Canada; Reconstruction Era Black Politicians; Republican Party; Underground Railroad

The *Liberator*, 428–429, 431, 435, 448, **461–462**, 488, 511, 525, 542, 580. *See also* Abolition, slavery; Garrison, William Lloyd; Thirteenth Amendment

Liberia, 14, 30, 288, 294, 299, 307–308, 358, 362–363, **462–463**, 510, 518, 822, 948, 954. *See also* Abolition, slavery; American Colonization Society; Crummell, Alexander; Crummell, Boston; Destination, Sierra Leone

Liberty Party, 426, 448, **463–464**, 508, 536, 539. *See also* Abolition, slavery; American Anti-Slavery Society; Birney, James; Free Soil Party; Garrison, William Lloyd; Smith, Gerrit; Tappan, Lewis

Lincoln, Abraham, 351, 354, 369, 372, 373, 390, 429, 458, **464–467**, 489, 545–546, 554, 621, 652, 719, 756 (photo), 762, 763, 830, 849, 941, 975, 1035. *See also* Abolition, slavery; American Colonization Society; Civil War (U.S.); Clay, Henry; Compromise of 1850; Emancipation Proclamation; Kansas-Nebraska Act, 1854; Missouri Compromise; Union Army

Lord Dunmore, 33, 311–312, 355, **468–469**. *See also* American Revolution; Fugitive slaves; Slave resistance

Louisiana Purchase, 109, **469**, 470 (illustration), 527. *See also* Haitian

Index

Aaron, Hank, 647
Abbott, Thomas, 692–693
Abdul-Jabbar, Kareem, 646
Abelman v. Booth, **282–284**. *See also Dred Scott v. Sandford*; Fugitive Slave Act of 1793; Fugitive Slave Act of 1850; Fugitive slaves
Abernathy, Ralph David, **594,** 851, 898, 966. *See also* Albany, Georgia, Movement; King, Martin Luther, Jr.; Montgomery Bus Boycott; Southern Christian Leadership Conference
Abolition, slave trade, 26, 29, 33, 72, 283, **284–287**. *See also* Atlantic slave trade; Cugoano, Quobna Ottobah; Equiano, Olaudah; Wilberforce, William
   in England, **284–286**
   in the U.S., **286–287**
Abolition, slavery, **287–291**, 453. *See also* American and Foreign Anti-Slavery Society; American Anti-Slavery Society; Birney, James; Brown, John; Douglass, Frederick; Emancipation Proclamation; Fugitive Slave Act of 1850; Fugitive slaves; Garrison, William Lloyd; Gradual emancipation; Immediatism; Kansas-Nebraska Act, 1854; Liberia; Smith, Gerrit; Tappan, Arthur; Tappan, Lewis; Thirteenth Amendment; Truth, Sojourner; Tubman, Harriet
Abolition of Slavery Bill (1834), 320

Abu Jamal, Mumia, **594–596,** 595 (photo). *See also* Black Power; COINTELPRO
Accomodationism, **596–597**. *See also* Black Nadir; Cotton States Exposition; Jim Crow; Washington, Booker T.
Acculturation, **9–10**. *See also* Amalgamation; Atlantic Creoles; Double consciousness; Salt-water negroes
Adams, Henry, 762
Adams, John Quincy, **292–293**, 292 (photo), 328, 337, 340, 372, 411, 453, 484. *See also* Abolition, slavery; *Amistad* (schooner)
Affirmative action, **597–599**. *See also* Fourteenth Amendment; Johnson, Lyndon Baines; Kennedy, John Fitzgerald
Afonso (King of Kongo), 8
Afric-American Literary Society, 542
Africa and Africans in the Making of the Atlantic World (Thornton), 7, 127
African American Civil Rights movement, 712–713
African American English (AAE), **149–150**
African American Vernacular English (AAVE), **149–150**
African Blood Brotherhood (ABB), **599–600**. *See also* Black Nationalism; Harlem Renaissance
African Burial Ground, New York City, **10–12,** 11 (photo), 130. *See also* Africanisms; Grave decorations

African Civilization Society, **293–294,** 307, 393, 426, 539. *See also* Delany, Martin; Douglass, Frederick; Garnet, Henry Highland; Nell, William Cooper; Pennington, James William Charles; Remond, Charles L.; Smith, James McCune
African Diaspora, **12–13,** 117, 127, 128, 145, 202, 223, 234, 247, 248, 251, 268, 269, 362–363, 443, 691, 759, 945, 980, 1010. *See also* Atlantic slave trade; Black Atlantic; Pan-Africanism; Ring shout; Trans-Saharan slave trade
African Dorcas Association, **295–296,** 357. *See also* African free schools; Jennings, Elizabeth
African Free Schools, **296–297,** 365, 424, 456, 509, 510, 578. *See also* African Dorcas Association; Crummell, Alexander; Garnet, Henry Highland; Smith, James McCune; Williams, Peter, Jr.
African Grove Theater, **297**. *See also* Black Folk Culture
African imperialism, **600–601**. *See also* Berlin Conference, 1884–1885; Fanon, Frantz; Pan-Africanism
African Methodist Episcopal Church (AME), 145, 148, 193, 281, **298–300,** 300–303, 341, 499–500, 502, 990, 1012, 1060–1062. *See also* Allen, Richard; Black churches; Jones, Absalom